TRUST TAXATION

Planning After the
Finance Act 2006

AUSTRALIA
Law Book Co.
Sydney

CANADA and USA
Carswell Toronto

HONG KONG
Sweet & Maxwell Asia

NEW ZEALAND
Brookers
Wellington

SINGAPORE and MALAYSIA
Sweet & Maxwell Asia
Singapore and Kuala Lumpur

TRUST TAXATION

EMMA CHAMBERLAIN and
CHRIS WHITEHOUSE

Planning After the
Finance Act 2006

LONDON
SWEET & MAXWELL
2007

Published in 2007 by
Sweet & Maxwell Limited of
100 Avenue Road, London NW3 3PF
(http://www.sweetandmaxwell.co.uk)
Typeset by Servis Filmsetting Ltd, Manchester
Printed in England by
T.J. International, Padstow, Cornwall

A CIP catalogue record for this book
is available from the British Library

ISBN-10 0421 965304
ISBN-13 9780421965300

All rights reserved. Crown Copyright material is reproduced with the permission of the Controller of HMSO and the Queen's Printer for Scotland.

No part of this publication may be reproduced or transmitted, in any form or by any means, or stored in any retrieval system of any nature, without prior written permission, except for permitted fair dealing under the Copyright, Designs and Patents Act 1988, or in accordance with the terms of a licence issued by the Copyright Licensing Agency in respect of photocopying and/or reprographic reproduction. Precedent material included in this publication may be used as a guide for drafting of legal documents specifically for particular clients, though no liability is accepted by the publishers or authors in relation to their use. Such documents may be provided to clients for their own use and to the solicitors acting for other parties to the transaction subject to acknowledgement of the course of the precedent. Precedents may not otherwise be distributed to other parties. Application for permission for other use of copyright material including permission to reproduce extracts in other published works shall be made to the publishers. Full acknowledgement of author, publisher and source must be given. The authors assert their moral rights.

©
Sweet & Maxwell
2007

PREFACE

The Paymaster General[1] explained the new rules for the IHT treatment of settlements in the following terms:

> "Because trusts do not die, there is no natural occasion on which inheritance tax might be paid, so it disappears into a labyrinth . . . on discretionary trusts, the tax regime already recognises (that) reality . . . The two types of trust that have, until now, been exempt from the charges are accumulation and maintenance and interest in possession trusts. There is no clear rationale for privileging those trusts in that way, and it has become clear that some wealthy individuals have taken advantage of that special treatment as a convenient way of sheltering their wealth from inheritance tax . . . The measure that was announced goes to the heart of the difference between money put into trusts and outright gifts . . . It is somewhat simplistic to think that the two activities are identical just because they received the same inheritance tax treatment in the past. The recipient of a gift can do whatever they want with it . . . Things are quite different for the beneficiary of a trust . . . In short, someone making a gift relinquishes control of whatever they are giving. Someone setting up a trust does the opposite. By leaving instructions for trustees, the control of those who set up trusts can linger long after they have died."[2]

As a justification for the introduction of the changes in Schedule 20 these comments illustrate how the Government saw this change as one which would reduce tax avoidance. This is something barely mentioned in BN 25[3] which is couched in language intended to convey the message that here is a technical adjustment to the rather arcane rules taxing settlements (an "alignment").

The Minister also defended the decision that privileged trusts for young people (the so-called accumulation and maintenance trust) should be abolished with the only replacement being a bereaved minor trust requiring capital to vest at 18. Her suggestion that this age had been agreed by professional bodies during the so-called "trust modernisation" exercise was misleading and her introduction of the 18–25 trust (something of a "U turn") was explained on the basis that "the amendments tabled by the Government make sure that the

---

[1] The Rt. Hon. Dawn Primarolo, MP.
[2] Standing Committee Debates, June 13, 2006 at col. 569 *et seq*.
[3] BN 25 is reproduced in Appendix III.

legislation for trust for bereaved minors operates in line with our intentions". Nothing like blaming civil servants and the poor old Parliamentary draftsman!

Schedule 20, therefore, rather like the pre-owned assets legislation in FA 2004, has ended up as something of a "bodge job" not underpinned by any coherent policy and enacted against widespread opposition. The Minister referred to modernisation and simplification but there is precious little sign of either and the trust modernisation consultation produced little of real benefit whilst adding to the prolixity of the legislation. The Government's claims rarely match its achievements. For example it was claimed that "the Government took the opportunity to bring the rules [on the IHT treatment of disabled trusts] into line with the equivalent parts of the income tax and capital gains tax rules". Anyone reading ss.89–89B of IHTA 1984 would conclude that drafting a settlement to attract relief from all taxes is a task of some magnitude with success by no means guaranteed.

The weary practitioner might feel that with all the changes of recent years a period of stasis must surely be at hand. Such thoughts would appear misplaced, however, given the ever present threat posed by the Tax Rewrite Committee which is now promising to turn its attention to capital gains tax. To date its activities surely only confirm that, as so often in life, more is less and that brevity is a virtue. O for the old fashioned legislative draftsman and for a Prime Minister to comment, as Palmerston did, ". . . there is really nothing to be done. We cannot go on adding to the Statute Book ad infinitum. Perhaps we may have a little law reform: but we cannot go on legislating for ever. . .".[4]

One result of the changes must be a growing reluctance to accept the burdensome job which is trusteeship. "A trust is an office necessary in the concerns between man and man and . . . if faithfully discharged attended with no small degree of trouble and anxiety . . . it is an act of great kindness in any one to accept it."[5] Who in their right mind would wish to undertake an office involving (a) the submission of IHT 100 returns to comply with the (in parts) impenetrable Part III Chapter III of IHTA 1984[6]; or (b) determining whether it is appropriate, or indeed possible, to make a CGT sub-fund election[7] or (c) if the beneficiary is disabled determining whether trust attracts relief from all (or indeed any) of income tax, CGT and IHT.[8] And this is just a sample of problems that the changes in taxation in the last six months have thrown up!

We are indebted to Robert Jamieson for the calculations in Appendix IV (aficionados of 50s and 60s popular music will appreciate his examples). Thanks are also due to Christine Morgan and Ann Geddes at 5 Stone Buildings for wrestling with the manuscript and to Andrew Strivens who dared to read it. We would also thank Sweet & Maxwell and especially Steve Warriner for encouragement and, above all, forbearance.

The law is stated at November 1, 2006.

E.M.C.
C.J.W.

---

[4] Quoted in Southgate, *The Most English Manor* (1966, Macmillan at p.528).
[5] *Knight v Earl of Plymouth* (1747) Dick. 120 at 126 *per* Lord Hardwicke LC.
[6] Try, for instance, the accumulated income calculation: see para.20.13.
[7] See para.7.72.
[8] See Ch 26.

CONTENTS

Preface	v
Table of Cases	xi
Table of Statutes	xix
Table of Statutory Instruments	xxxv

PART I: GENERAL

1. The trust	3
2. Residence and domicile	10
3. Overview of the taxation of trusts	35
4. Income Tax	51

PART II: CAPITAL GAINS TAX

5. CGT definitions	83
6. CGT on creation of a settlement	100
7. Actual and deemed disposals by trustees of UK resident settlements	105
8. The disposal of a beneficial interest	137
9. CGT hold-over relief	147
10. Offshore trusts	173
11. UK settlor interested trusts	197
12. Loss relief	207

PART III: INHERITANCE TAX

13. IHT, reservation of benefit and pre-owned assets income tax	219
14. The new IHT rules: an overview	239
15. IHT definitions and classifications	256
16. Creation of settlements: IHT position	276
17. Qualifying interest in possession trusts	283
18. When IHT is charged on qualifying interest in possession trusts (including transitional relief)	298

19. Immediate post-death interests and other qualifying interests in possession after FA 2006	313
20. Taxation of relevant property settlements	322
21. Accumulation and maintenance (A+M) trusts	343
22. Excluded property	357
23. Liabilities	389
24. Gifts with reservation and the pre-owned assets income tax regime	404

PART IV: SPECIALIST TOPICS

25. Trusts for minors and for older children	427
26. Trusts for vulnerable and disabled beneficiaries	459
27. Reverter to settlor trusts	476
28. Tax efficient will drafting	493
29. Planning after death	515
30. Bare trusts	545
31. The family home and chattels	550
32. Businesses and farms (BPR and APR)	604
33. Insurance-based arrangements	626
34. Trusts and divorce	635
35. Stamp Duty Land Tax and Stamp Duty	648
36. Compliance and disclosure	654

APPENDIX I

LEGISLATION

Inheritance Act 1984	668
Finance Act 1986	688
Taxation of Chargeable Gains Act 1992	695

APPENDIX II

PRECEDENTS

Bare trust	702
Disabled person's trust	703
Bereaved minor trust	709
18-25 trust	710
Specimen Will clauses	710
IPDI trust of residue for (minor) children	715
Debt/charge documents	716
Deed of variation	718
Disclaimer of a life interest	721
Appointment of IPDI trust out of a two-year discretionary trust	722

APPENDIX III

MISCELLANEOUS MATERIAL
BN 25 Budget 2006	726
SDLT and NRBDT: HMRC statement	728
POA Guidance Notes	730
POA COP 10 Letter	760
Schedule 20: Questions and Answers	783
Tax Bulletin 83: HMRC statement on *Hastings-Bass*	802
POA correspondence with HMRC on elections: October 2006	805

APPENDIX IV

Examples of the IHT charging provisions for relevant property settlements	807
Index	819

TABLE OF CASES

A–F and ATC Trustees (Cayman) Ltd v Rothschild Trust (Cayman) Ltd, July 27, 2005 ....1.19
Abacus Trust Co (Isle of Man) Ltd v Barr; sub nom. Barr's Settlement Trusts, Re [2003]
 EWHC 114; [2003] Ch. 409; [2003] 2 W.L.R. 1362, Ch. D 1.18, 1.20, A3.146
Abacus Trust Co (Isle of Man) Ltd v NSPCC; sub nom. Abacus Trust Co (Isle of Man)
 Ltd v National Society for the Prevention of Cruelty to Children [2001] S.T.C. 1344;
 [2002] B.T.C. 178, Ch. D A3.146
Adam & Co. International Trustees Ltd v Theodore Goddard (A Firm) [2000] W.T.L.R.
 349; (1999–2000) 2 I.T.E.L.R. 634, Ch. D 2.49
Agulian v Cyganik. *See* Cyganik v Agulian
Alexander v Inland Revenue Commissioners [1991] S.T.C. 112; (1991) 23 H.L.R. 236, CA
 (Civ Div) 23.06
Allen v Revenue and Customs Commissioners [2005] S.T.C. (S.C.D.) 614; 8 I.T.L. Rep. 108,
 Sp Comm 2.31
Allen-Meyrick's Will Trusts, Re; sub nom. Mangnall v Allen-Meyrick [1966] 1 W.L.R. 499;
 [1966] 1 All E.R. 740, Ch. D 20.13
Amott v Groom (1846) 9 D.62 ....2.34
Andrews v Partington (1791) 3 Bro. C.C. 401 ....21.14
Arkwright (Williams Personal Representative) v Inland Revenue Commissioners; sub
 nom. Inland Revenue Commissioners v Arkwright [2004] EWHC 1720; [2005] 1 W.L.R.
 1411; [2004] S.T.C. 1323, Ch. D; reversing [2004] S.T.C. (S.C.D.) 89; [2004] W.T.L.R. 181,
 Sp Comm 13.05, 28.03, 28.08, 31.42, 33.16
Arnander and Others (Executors of McKenna Deceased) v Revenue and Customs
 Commissioners (2006) Sp 565 Comm 32.16A–E
Attorney General v Boden [1912] 1 K.B. 539, KBD 32.28
B v B [1982] F.L.R. 298, CA 34.08
Baker (Inspector of Taxes) v Archer Shee; sub nom. Archer Shee v Baker (Inspector of
 Taxes) [1927] A.C. 844, HL 4.21
Barclays Mercantile Business Finance Ltd v Mawson (Inspector of Taxes); sub nom. ABC
 Ltd v M (Inspector of Taxes) [2004] UKHL 51; [2005] 1 A.C. 684; [2004] 3 W.L.R. 1383,
 HL 3.30, 3.31
Barnes (Deceased), Re [1939] 1 K.B. 316, CA; affirming [1938] 2 K.B. 684, KBD 17.06,
 23.14
Batey v Wakefield [1982] 1 All E.R. 61; [1981] S.T.C. 521, CA (Civ Div) 31.04, 31.06
Bennett v Inland Revenue Commissioners [1995] S.T.C. 54 ....13.01, 31.31
Berry v Warnett (Inspector of Taxes) [1982] 1 W.L.R. 698; [1982] 2 All E.R. 630; [1982]
 S.T.C. 396, HL 6–01
Boardman v Phipps; Phipps v Boardman [1967] 2 A.C. 46; [1966] 3 W.L.R. 1009, HL 1.04
Bond (Inspector of Taxes) v Pickford [1983] S.T.C. 517, CA (Civ Div) 5.39, 7.55, 7.57,
 7.58A3.111
Booth v Ellard [1980] 1 W.L.R. 1443; [1980] 3 All E.R. 569; [1980] S.T.C. 555; 53 T.C. 393;
 [1980] T.R. 203; 124 S.J. 465, CA (Civ Div) 5.06
Bouch, Re; sub nom. Sproule v Bouch (1887) L.R. 12 App. Cas. 385, HL 4.07
Breadner v Granville-Grossman [2001] Ch. 523; [2001] 2 W.L.R. 593, Ch. D A3.146
Bricom Holdings Ltd v Inland Revenue Commissioners [1997] S.T.C. 1179; 70 T.C. 272,
 CA (Civ Div) 2.58

Brockbank, Re; sub nom. Ward v Bates [1948] Ch. 206; [1948] 1 All E.R. 287 ....5.08
Brodie's Trustees v Inland Revenue Commissioners 17 T.C. 432 ....4.26
Brooks v Brooks; sub nom. B v B (Post Nuptial Settlements) (Pension Fund), Re [1996]
  A.C. 375; [1995] 3 W.L.R. 141; [1995] 3 All E.R. 257, HL 34.03, 34.04
Browne v Browne [1989] 1 F.L.R. 291; [1989] Fam. Law 147, CA (Civ Div) 34.08
Bulmer v Inland Revenue Commissioners; Kennedy v Inland Revenue Commissioners;
  Oates v Inland Revenue Commissioners; Macaulay v Inland Revenue Commissioners
  [1967] Ch. 145; [1966] 3 W.L.R. 672; [1966] 3 All E.R. 801, Ch. D 4.32
Burrell v Burrell [2005] EWHC 245; [2005] S.T.C. 569, Ch. D 1.20, 14.04, 14.28,
                                                                                                            32.34, A3.146
Buswell v Inland Revenue Commissioners [1974] 1 W.L.R. 1631; [1974] 2 All E.R. 520, CA
  (Civ Div) 2.30
Butler (Inspector of Taxes) v Wildin [1989] S.T.C. 22; 62 T.C. 666, Ch. D 4.30
Cameron v M&W Mack (ESOP) Trustee Ltd [2002] W.T.L.R. 647, Ch. D 7.39
Campbell v Inland Revenue Commissioners [2004] S.T.C. (S.C.D.) 396; 7 I.T.L. Rep. 211;
  [2004] S.T.I. 1831, Sp Comm 3.30
Carreras Group Ltd v Stamp Commissioner; sub nom. Stamp Commissioner v Carreras
  Group Ltd [2004] UKPC 16; [2004] S.T.C. 1377; [2004] B.T.C. 8077, PC (Jam) 3.29, 3.30
Carver v Duncan (Inspector of Taxes); Bosanquet v Allen [1985] A.C. 1082; [1985] 2
  W.L.R. 1010; [1985] S.T.C. 356, HL 4.15, 15.24
Charalambous v Charalambous [2004] EWCA Civ 1030 ....34.05
Charman v Charman [2006] EWHC 1879, Fam Div 34.09
Chinn v Hochstrasser (Inspector of Taxes); sub nom Chinn v Collins (Inspector of Taxes)
  [1981] A.C. 533; [1981] 2 W.L.R. 14; [1981] 1 All E.R. 189, HL 5.26
Churston Settled Estates, Re [1954] Ch. 334; [1954] 2 W.L.R. 386; [1954] 1 All E.R. 725;
  98 S.J. 178, Ch. D 22.37, 22.38
Clark v Inland Revenue Commissioners [2005] S.T.C. (S.C.D.) 823 ....32.06
Clore (Deceased) (No.2), Re; sub nom. Official Solicitor v Clore [1984] S.T.C. 609, Ch. D ...2.29
Cochrane, Re [1906] 2 I.R. 200 ....27.09
Cochrane v Inland Revenue Commissioners [1974] S.T.C. 335 ....16.08
Collector of Stamp Revenue v Arrowtown Assets Ltd [2003] HKCFA 46; [2004] I.T.L.
  Rep. 454 ....3.31
Commissioners of Stamp Duties v Hope [1891] A.C. 476 ....23.09
Cook (Inspector of Taxes) v Medway Housing Society Ltd. *See* Medway Housing Society
  Ltd v Cook (Inspector of Taxes)
Cooper v Billingham (Inspector of Taxes); Fisher v Edwards (Inspector of Taxes); sub
  nom. Edwards (Inspector of Taxes) v Fisher; Billingham (Inspector of Taxes) v Cooper
  [2001] EWCA Civ 1041; [2001] S.T.C. 1177; 74 T.C. 139, CA (Civ Div); affirming [2000]
  S.T.C. 122; [2000] B.T.C. 28, Ch. D 10.29, 28.10
Countess Fitzwilliam v Inland Revenue Commissioners [1993] 1 W.L.R. 1189; [1993] 3 All
  E.R. 184; [1993] S.T.C. 502, HL 27.07, 29.58
Craven (Inspector of Taxes) v White; Baylis (Inspector of Taxes) v Gregory; Inland
  Revenue Commissioners v Bowater Property Developments Ltd; Craven (Inspector of
  Taxes) v White [1989] A.C. 398; [1988] 3 W.L.R. 423; [1988] S.T.C. 476, HL 3.28
Crawford Settlement Trustees v Revenue and Customs Commissioners; sub nom. Trustees
  of the Crawford Settlement v Revenue and Customs Commissioners [2005] S.T.C.
  (S.C.D.) 457; [2005] W.T.L.R. 797, Sp Comm 21.10
Crossland (Inspector of Taxes) v Hawkins [1961] Ch. 537; [1961] 3 W.L.R. 202; 39 T.C.
  493, CA 4.32
Crowe v Appleby. *See* Pexton v Bell
Cunard's Trustees v Inland Revenue Commissioners [1946] 1 All E.R. 159, CA 4.26, 4.28
Cyganik v Agulian; sub nom. Agulian v Cyganik [2006] EWCA Civ 129; [2006] 1 F.C.R.
  406; [2006] W.T.L.R. 565, CA (Civ Div) 2.26, 2.30
Davies v Hicks. *See* Hicks v Davies
Dawson v Inland Revenue Commissioners [1990] 1 A.C. 1; [1989] 2 W.L.R. 858; [1989]
  S.T.C. 473, HL 2.42
De Lasteyrie du Saillant v Ministere de l'Economie, des Finances et de l'Industrie (C9/02)
  [2005] S.T.C. 1722; [2004] E.C.R. I-2409; 6 I.T.L. Rep. 666, ECJ (5th Chamber) 2.61, 9.28
De Vigier v Inland Revenue Commissioners [1964] 1 W.L.R. 1073; [1964] 2 All E.R. 907, HL ... 4.45
Dewar v Inland Revenue Commissioners [1935] 2 K.B. 351, CA 29.44
Dilke, Re; Verey v Dilke; sub nom. Dilke's Settlement Trusts, Re [1921] 1 Ch. 34, CA 22.37,
                                                                                                                       22.38

Dixon v Inland Revenue Commissioners [2002] S.T.C. (S.C.D.) 53; [2002] W.T.L.R. 175, Sp Comm 32.13
Dunmore v McGowan (Inspector of Taxes) [1978] 1 W.L.R. 617; [1978] 2 All E.R. 85; 52 T.C. 307, CA (Civ Div) 28.19
E v E (Financial Provision) [1990] 2 F.L.R. 233; [1989] F.C.R. 591 ....34.03, 34.07
Earl of Coventry's Indentures, Re; sub nom.Smith v Earl of Coventry; Smith v Coventry [1974] Ch. 77; [1973] 3 W.L.R. 122, Ch. D 22.38
Edge v Pensions Ombudsman [2000] Ch. 602; [2000] 3 W.L.R. 79, CA (Civ Div) A3.146
Estill v Cowling Swift & Kitchin Bean v Cowling Swift & Kitchin [2000] Lloyd's Rep. P.N. 378; [2000] W.T.L.R. 417, Ch. D 16.01
Farmer (Exors of Farmer dec'd) v Inland Revenue [1999] S.T.C. (S.C.D.) 321 ....28.27, 32.03, 32.06, 32.08
Faulkner v Inland Revenue Commissioners [2001] S.T.C. (S.C.D.) 112; [2001] W.T.L.R. 1295; [2001] S.T.I. 943, Sp Comm 15.02
Fetherstonaugh (formerly Finch) v Inland Revenue Commissioners; sub nom. Finch v Inland Revenue Commissioners [1985] Ch. 1; [1984] 3 W.L.R. 212; [1984] S.T.C. 261, CA (Civ Div) 32.23, 33.16
Frankland v Inland Revenue Commissioners [1997] S.T.C. 1450; [1997] B.T.C. 8045, CA (Civ Div); affirming [1996] S.T.C. 735, Ch. D 1.20, 20.33, 29.52
Fry (Surveyor of Taxes) v Shiels Trustees; sub nom. Inland Revenue Commissioners v Shiels's Trustees, 1915 S.C. 159; 1914 2 S.L.T. 364, IH (1 Div) 4.22
Fuld (Deceased) (No.3), In the Estate of; sub nom. Hartley v Fuld (Conflict of Laws) [1968] P. 675; [1966] 2 W.L.R. 717, PDAD 2.29, 2.30
Furness v Inland Revenue Commissioners [1999] S.T.C. (S.C.D.) 232 ....32.06
Furse (Deceased), Re; sub nom. Furse v Inland Revenue Commissioners [1980] 3 All E.R. 838; [1980] S.T.C. 596, Ch. D 2.30
G v G (Financial Provision: Equal Division) [2002] EWHC 1339; [2002] 2 F.L.R. 1143; [2003] Fam. Law 14, Fam. Div 34.15
Gartside v Inland Revenue Commissioners; sub nom. Gartside's Will Trusts, Re [1968] A.C. 553; [1968] 2 W.L.R. 277; [1968] 1 All E.R. 121, HL 16.08
Goodwin v Curtis (Inspector of Taxes) [1998] S.T.C. 475; 70 T.C. 478, CA (Civ Div) 31.02
Green v Cobham [2002] S.T.C. 820; [2002] B.T.C. 170; [2000] W.T.L.R. 1101; (2001–02) 4 I.T.E.L.R. 785 ....2.67
Green v Inland Revenue Commissioners [1982] S.T.C. 485; 1982 S.C. 155, IH (1 Div) 31.14
Griffin (Inspector of Taxes) v Craig-Harvey [1994] S.T.C. 54; 66 T.C. 396, Ch. D 31.08
Grimwood Taylor v Inland Revenue Commissioners [2006] S.T.C. (S.C.D.) 39 ....32.03
Guthrie v Walrond (1883) L.R. 22 Ch. D. 573, Ch. D 29.44
Hall (Executors of Hall) v Inland Revenue Commissioners [1997] S.T.C. (S.C.D.) 126 ....32.06
Halstead's Will Trusts, Re [1937] 2 All E.R. 570, Ch. D 7.59
Hampden's Settlement Trusts, Re [1977] T.R. 177; [2001] W.T.L.R. 195, Ch. D 7.59, 21.09
Hardcastle v Inland Revenue Commissioners [2000] S.T.C. (S.C.D.) 532; [2001] W.T.L.R. 91, Sp Comm 23.25
Hargreaves v Hargreaves [1926] P. 42, PDAD 34.04, 34.06
Hastings-Bass (Deceased), Re; sub nom. Hastings-Bass Trustees v Inland Revenue Commissioners [1975] Ch. 25; [1974] 2 W.L.R. 904, CA (Civ Div) 1.20, 3.23, A3.146
Hatton v Inland Revenue Commissioners [1992] S.T.C. 140; 67 T.C. 759, Ch. D 15.11, 15.12, 18.11
Heatherington's Trustees v Lord Advocate; sub nom. Sneddon v Lord Advocate; Sneddon v Inland Revenue Commissioners; Heatherington's Trustees v Inland Revenue Commissioners [1954] A.C. 257; [1954] 2 W.L.R. 211, HL 31.75
Henke v HMRC [2006] S.T.C. 28 ....31.15, 31.18
Hicks v Davies (Inspector of Taxes); sub nom. Davies (Inspector of Taxes) v Hicks [2005] EWHC 847; [2005] S.T.C. 850; [2005] B.T.C. 331, Ch. D 2.57, 2.60
Higginson's Executors v Inland Revenue Commissioners [2002] S.T.C. (S.C.D.) 483; [2002] W.T.L.R. 1413, Sp Comm 32.13
Hill v Permanent Trustee Co of New South Wales [1930] A.C. 720, PC (Aus) 4.07
Hoare Trustees v Gardner (Inspector of Taxes) [1979] Ch. 10; [1978] 2 W.L.R. 839; [1978] S.T.C. 89, Ch. D 5.15, 7.55
Honour (Inspector of Taxes) v Norris [1992] S.T.C. 304; 64 T.C. 599, Ch. D 31.06
Horton, Re (1979) 88 DLR (3d)264 (Brit. Columbia) A2.25
Howard v Howard [1945] P. 1; [1945] 1 All E.R. 91, CA 34.08

Howell v Trippier (Inspector of Taxes); sub nom. Red Discretionary Trustees v Inspector of Taxes [2004] EWCA Civ 885; [2004] S.T.C. 1245; 76 T.C. 415, CA (Civ Div) 4.07
Ingram v Inland Revenue Commissioners [2000] 1 A.C. 293; [1999] 2 W.L.R. 90; [1999] S.T.C. 37, HL; reversing [1997] 4 All E.R. 395; [1997] S.T.C. 1234, CA (Civ Div); reversing [1995] 4 All E.R. 334; [1995] S.T.C. 564, Ch. D 13.16, 13.16, 16.08, 24.44, 31.32, 31.35, 31.52
Inland Revenue Commissioners v Berrill [1981] 1 W.L.R. 1449; [1982] 1 All E.R. 867; [1981] S.T.C. 784, DC 4.01, 4.12
Inland Revenue Commissioners v Botnar [1999] S.T.C. 711; 72 T.C. 205; [1999] B.T.C. 267 ... 11.07
Inland Revenue Commissioners v Bullock [1976] 1 W.L.R. 1178; [1976] 3 All E.R. 353, CA (Civ Div) 2.30
Inland Revenue Commissioners v Chubb's Settlement Trustee; sub nom. Inland Revenue Commissioners v Chubb's Trustee 1971 S.C. 247; 1972 S.L.T. 81; 47 T.C. 353; [1971] T.R. 197, IH (1 Div) 12.05
Inland Revenue Commissioners v Crossman; Inland Revenue Commissioners v Mann; sub nom. Crossman, Re; Paulin, Re, [1937] A.C. 26, HL 23.06
Inland Revenue Commissioners v Duchess of Portland [1982] Ch. 314; [1982] 2 W.L.R. 367, Ch. D 2.33
Inland Revenue Commissioners v Eversden; sub nom. Essex (Somerset's Executors) v Inland Revenue Commissioners; Inland Revenue Commissioners v Greenstock's Executors [2003] EWCA Civ 668; [2003] S.T.C. 822; 75 T.C. 340, CA (Civ Div); affirming [2002] EWHC 1360; [2002] S.T.C. 1109; [2002] B.T.C. 8035, Ch. D 13.10, 13.14, 13.16, 13.16, 13.34, 13.43, 15.02, 16.08, 16.09, 22.68, 24.05, 24.09, 24.37, 27.09, 28.08
Inland Revenue Commissioners v George; sub nom. Stedman's Executors v Inland Revenue Commissioners; George v Inland Revenue Commissioners [2003] EWCA Civ 1763; [2004] S.T.C. 147; 75 T.C. 735, CA (Civ Div); [2003] EWHC 318; [2003] S.T.C. 468; [2003] B.T.C. 8037, Ch. D 32.03, 32.06, 32.08
Inland Revenue Commissioners v Hawley [1928] 1 K.B. 578, KBD A3.114
Inland Revenue Commissioners v Holmden; Holmden's Settlement Trusts, Re; sub nom. Holmden's Settlement, Re [1968] A.C. 685; [1968] 2 W.L.R. 300; [1968] 1 All E.R. 148, HL 7.61
Inland Revenue Commissioners v Lloyds Private Banking Ltd [1998] S.T.C. 559; [1999] 1 F.L.R. 147, Ch. D 15.02, 15.26, 15.29
Inland Revenue Commissioners v McGuckian; McGuckian v Inland Revenue Commissioners [1997] 1 W.L.R. 991; [1997] 3 All E.R. 817; HL (NI) 3.27, 3.28
Inland Revenue Commissioners v Macpherson [1989] A.C. 159; [1988] 2 W.L.R. 1261; [1988] 2 All E.R. 753, HL 17.16
Inland Revenue Commissioners v Mills (Hayley); sub nom. Mills (Hayley) v Inland Revenue Commissioners [1975] A.C. 38; [1974] 2 W.L.R. 325; [1974] S.T.C. 130, HL 4.32
Inland Revenue Commissioners v Plummer [1980] A.C. 896; [1979] 3 W.L.R. 689; [1979] 3 All E.R. 775; S.T.C. 793, HL 4.32, 15.01
Inland Revenue Commissioners v Regent Trust Co. Ltd [1980] 1 W.L.R. 688; [1980] S.T.C. 140, Ch. D 4.09
J v M [2002] J.L.R. 330 03
Jackson's Trustees v Inland Revenue Commissioners 25 T.C. 13 ....4.28
Jenkins (Inspector of Taxes) v Brown; sub nom. Warrington (Inspector of Taxes) v Brown [1989] 1 W.L.R. 1163; [1989] S.T.C. 577, Ch. D 5.06
Joel's Will Trusts, Re; sub nom. Rogerson v Brudenell-Bruce [1967] Ch. 14; [1966] 3 W.L.R. 209; [1966] 2 All E.R. 482; 110 S.J. 570, Ch. D 25.17
Joicey, Re (1932) 76 Sol. Jo. 459 ....22.38
Jones v Garnett (Inspector of Taxes) [2005] EWCA Civ 1553; [2006] 1 W.L.R. 1123; [2006] 2 All E.R. 381; [2006] S.T.C. 283, CA (Civ Div) 4.30, 4.44
Judge and Other (representatives of Walden Dec'd) v Revenue and Customs Commissioners [2005] S.T.C. (S.C.D.) 863 ....15.25, 15.28, 15.29, 15.30, 28.10, 28.12
Kidson (Inspector of Taxes) v MacDonald; sub nom Kidson (Inspector of Taxes) v Mawle's Executors [1974] Ch. 339; [1974] 2 W.L.R. 566; [1974] 1 All E.R. 849; [1974] S.T.C. 54, Ch. D 5.06, 35.04
Kirby (Inspector of Taxes) v Thorn EMI Plc [1988] 1 W.L.R. 445; [1988] 2 All E.R. 947; [1987] S.T.C. 621, CA (Civ Div) 5.39
Lee (Deceased), Re. *See* Sinclair v Lee
Lewis v Lady Rook [1992] S.T.C. 171 ....31.02, 31.06

Lloyds Bank Plc v Duker [1987] 1 W.L.R. 1324; [1987] 3 All E.R. 193, Ch. D 5.09
Lloyds TSB Bank Plc (Personal Representative of Antrobus (Deceased)) v Inland Revenue
    Commissioners [2002] S.T.C. (S.C.D.) 468; [2002] W.T.L.R. 1435, Sp Comm 32.13, 32.15
Locker's Settlement, Re; sub nom. Meachem v Sachs [1977] 1 W.L.R. 1323; [1978] 1 All
    E.R. 216, Ch. D 20.13
Longson v Baker (Inspector of Taxes) [2001] S.T.C. 6; 73 T.C. 415, Ch. D 31.14
Lord Advocate v Jaffrey; sub nom. Mackinnon's Trustees v Lord Advocate; Mackinnon's
    Trustees v Inland Revenue Commissioners [1921] 1 A.C. 146; 1920 S.C. (H.L.) 171,
    HL 2.33
Lord Inglewood v Inland Revenue Commissioners; sub nom. Baron Inglewood v Inland
    Revenue Commissioners [1983] 1 W.L.R. 366; [1983] S.T.C. 133; (CA (Civ. Div.) 14.15,
                                                                                                                21.08, 21.09, 21.10
Macfarlane v Inland Revenue Commissioners 1929 S.C. 453; 1929 S.L.T. 395, IH (1 Div) 4.21
MacKenzie, Re [1941] Ch. 69, Ch. D 2.30
MacNiven (Inspector of Taxes) v Westmoreland Investments Ltd; sub nom.
    Westmoreland Investments Ltd v MacNiven (Inspector of Taxes) [2001] UKHL 6;
    [2003] 1 A.C. 311; [2001] 2 W.L.R. 377; [2001] S.T.C. 237, HL 3.27, 3.28, 3.30, 3.31, 5.40
Makins v Elson [1977] 1 W.L.R. 221; [1977] 1 All E.R. 572; [1977] S.T.C. 46, Ch. D 31.02
Mark v Mark; sub nom. Marks v Marks (Divorce: Jurisdiction) [2005] UKHL 42; [2006]
    1 A.C. 98; [2005] 3 W.L.R. 111; [2005] 3 All E.R. 912, HL 2.32
Markey (Inspector of Taxes) v Sanders [1987] 1 W.L.R. 864; [1987] S.T.C. 256, Ch. D 31.05
Marshall (Inspector of Taxes) v Kerr [1995] 1 A.C. 148; [1994] 3 W.L.R. 299; [1994] 3 All
    E.R. 106, HL 5.26, 29.34
Martin v Nicholson [2004] EWHC 2135; [2005] W.T.L.R. 175, Ch. D 29.22
Medway Housing Society Ltd v Cook (Inspector of Taxes); sub nom. Cook (Inspector of
    Taxes) v Medway Housing Society Ltd [1997] S.T.C. 90; 69 T.C. 319, Ch. D 32.03
Melville v Inland Revenue Commissioners [2001] EWCA Civ 1247; [2002] 1 W.L.R. 407;
    [2001] S.T.C. 1271, CA (Civ. Div.); affirming [2000] S.T.C. 628; [2000] B.T.C. 8025,
    Ch. D 3.16, 8.09, 9.43, 22.40
Mesher v Mesher [1980] 1 All E.R. 126 (Note); *The Times*, February 13, 1973, CA (Civ.
    Div.) 34.16
Mettoy Pension Trustees Ltd v Evans [1990] 1 W.L.R. 1587; [1991] 2 All E.R. 513,
    Ch. D 1.17, A3.146
Miller v Inland Revenue Commissioners [1987] S.T.C. 108, CS 15.24
Miller v Miller; McFarlane v McFarlane; sub nom. M v M (Short Marriage: Clean Break)
    [2006] UKHL 24; [2006] 2 W.L.R. 1283; [2006] 3 All E.R. 1, HL 34.08, 34.10
Minden Trust (Cayman) v Inland Revenue Commissioners [1985] S.T.C. 758; (1985)
    82 L.S.G. 2824, CA (Civ Div); affirming [1984] S.T.C. 434; (1984) 81 L.S.G. 2224,
    Ch. D 15.07, 22.10
Minwalla v Minwalla [2004] EWHC 2823; [2005] 1 F.L.R. 771, Fam Div 34.08
Moore v Thompson (Inspector of Taxes) [1986] S.T.C. 170; 60 T.C. 15; (1986) 83 L.S.G.
    1559, Ch. D 31.02
Morgan v Cilento; sub nom. Morgan (Attorney of Shaffer) v Cilento [2004] EWHC 188;
    [2004] W.T.L.R. 457, Ch. D 2.30
Muir v Muir [1942] A.C. 468 ....7.59
New South Wales Stamp Duties Commissioner v Perpetual Trustee Co. Ltd [1943] A.C.
    425; [1943] 1 All E.R. 525, PC (Aus) 13–16, 16.08
New York Life Insurance Co v Public Trustee [1924] 2 Ch. 101, CA 22.45
Newhill Compulsory Purchase Order, Re [1938] All E.R. 163 ....32.18
Nichols (Deceased), Re; Nichols v Inland Revenue Commissioners [1975] 1 W.L.R. 534;
    [1975] 2 All E.R. 120; [1975] S.T.C. 278; [1974] T.R. 411; (1974) 119 S.J. 257, CA (Civ
    Div) 31.35
Norton v Frecker (1737) 1 Atk. 524 ....23.02
Oakes v Commissioner of Stamp Duties of New South Wales [1954] A.C. 57; [1953] 3
    W.L.R. 1127; [1953] 2 All E.R. 1563, PC (Aus) 16.07, 32.78
Oakley v Inland Revenue Commissioners [2005] S.T.C. (S.C.D.) 343; [2005] W.T.L.R. 181 .... 15.02
Parkside Leasing Ltd v Smith (Inspector of Taxes) [1985] 1 W.L.R. 310; [1985] S.T.C. 63;
    58 T.C. 282, Ch. D 28.19
Pearson v Inland Revenue Commissioners; sub nom. Pilkington Trustees v Inland
    Revenue Commissioners [1981] A.C. 753; [1980] 2 W.L.R. 872; [1980] 2 All E.R. 479;
    [1980] S.T.C. 318, HL 4.13, 15.19, 15.20, 15.21,
                                                                                                        15.23, 15.24, 15.26, 20.01

Pettifor's Will Trusts, Re; sub nom. Roberts v Roberts [1966] Ch. 257; [1966] 2 W.L.R. 778, Ch. D 29.07
Pexton v Bell; Crowe v Appleby; sub nom. Pexton v Colbourne's Will Trusts [1976] 1 W.L.R. 885; [1976] 2 All E.R. 914, CA (Civ Div); [1975] 1 W.L.R. 707; [1975] 1 All E.R. 498; 51 TC 457,Ch. D 5.09, 5.12, 5.13, 5.14, 5.15, 7.36, 7.41, 7.42, 9.38, A3.137
Phillips and Others (Exors of Phillips Deceased) v Inland Revenue Commissioners [2006] S.T.C. (S.C.D.) 639 ....32.04
Phillips, Re; Lawrence v Huxtable [1931] 1 Ch. 347, Ch. D 22.37, 22.38
Pilkington v Inland Revenue Commissioners; sub nom. Pilkington's Will Trusts, Re; Pilkington v Pilkington [1964] A.C. 612; [1962] 3 W.L.R. 1051; [1962] 3 All E.R. 622, HL 7.59, 21.09
Playfair (Deceased), Re; sub nom. Palmer v Playfair; Hickman (Henry Thomas)'s Will Trusts, Re [1951] Ch. 4; [1950] 2 All E.R. 285, Ch. D 5.35
Potter v Lord Advocate; sub nom. Potter v Inland Revenue Commissioners 1958 S.C. 213; 1958 S.L.T. 198, IH (2 Div) 31.75
Power's Settlement Trusts, Re; sub nom. Power v Power [1951] Ch. 1074; [1951] 2 All E.R. 513; [1951] 2 T.L.R. 355; 95 S.J. 467, CA 31.25
Prescott (otherwise Fellowes) v Fellowes [1958] P. 260; [1958] 3 W.L.R. 288; [1958] 3 All E.R. 55, CA 34.04
Prinsep v Prinsep (No.1) [1930] P. 35, CA; reversing [1929] P. 225, PDAD 34.03
Public Trustee v Aspinall. *See* Smith, Re
R. v Dimsey; R. v Allen [2001] UKHL 46; [2002] 1 A.C. 509; [2001] 3 W.L.R. 843; [2001] S.T.C. 1520, HL 31.90
R. v Inland Revenue Commissioners Ex p. Fulford-Dobson [1987] Q.B. 978; [1987] 3 W.L.R. 277; [1987] S.T.C. 344, QBD 2.25
Reynaud v Inland Revenue Commissioners [1999] S.T.C. (S.C.D.) 185 ....23.21
Roome v Edwards [1982] A.C. 279; [1981] 2 W.L.R. 268; [1981] 1 All E.R. 736; [1981] S.T.C. 96 ....5.15, 5.29, 5.32, 5.38, 7.55, 7.56
Rosser v Inland Revenue Commissioners [2003] S.T.C. (S.C.D.) 311; [2003] W.T.L.R. 1057 ....31.31, 32.10, 32.11, 32.12
Russell v Inland Revenue Commissioners [1988] 1 W.L.R. 834; [1988] 2 All E.R. 405; [1988] S.T.C. 195, Ch. D 29.02, 29.21
Rysaffe Trustee Co (CI) Ltd v Inland Revenue Commissioners; sub nom. Rysaffe Trustee Co (CI) Ltd v Customs and Excise Commissioners; Customs and Excise Commissioners v Rysaffe Trustee Co (CI) Ltd [2003] EWCA Civ 356; [2003] S.T.C. 536; [2003] B.T.C. 8021, CA (Civ Div); affirming [2002] EWHC 1114; [2002] S.T.C. 872; [2002] B.T.C. 8019, Ch. D 15.07, 15.14, 20.15, 22.23, 22.25, 22.26, 23.21, 29.59, 33.09
St Barbe Green v Inland Revenue Commissioners; sub nom. Green v Inland Revenue Commissioners [2005] EWHC 14; [2005] 1 W.L.R. 1772; [2005] S.T.C. 288, Ch. D 13.05, 13.06, 17.06, 23.12, 31.47, 31.94
Sansom v Peay (Inspector of Taxes) [1976] 1 W.L.R. 1073; [1976] 3 All E.R. 375, Ch. D 7.06, 28.16, 31.20, 31.21
Saunders v Vautier 41 E.R. 482; (1841) 4 Beav. 115 ....1.05, 5.06
Schär (Deceased), Re; sub nom. Midland Bank Executor & Trustee Co Ltd v Damer [1951] Ch. 280; [1950] 2 All E.R. 1069; 94 S.J. 804, Ch. D 29.44
Scottish Provident Institution v Inland Revenue Commissioners; sub nom. Inland Revenue Commissioners v Scottish Provident Institution [2004] UKHL 52; [2004] 1 W.L.R. 3172; [2005] 1 All E.R. 325, HL 3.30, 3.31
Secretan v Hart [1969] 1 W.L.R. 1599; [1969] 3 All E.R. 1196; 45 T.C. 701; [1969] T.R. 313 ....23.03
Secretary of State for Trade and Industry v Deverell [2001] Ch. 340; [2000] 2 W.L.R. 907, CA (Civ Div) 31.90
Shepherd v Revenue and Customs Commissioners [2005] S.T.C. (S.C.D.) 644, Sp Comm; [2006] S.T.C. 1821 ....2.06
Sieff v Fox; sub nom. Bedford Estates, Re [2005] EWHC 1312; [2005] 1 W.L.R. 3811; [2005] 3 All E.R. 693; [2005] W.T.L.R. 891, Ch. D 1.17, 1.19, 1.20, A3.146
Sinclair v Lee; sub nom. Lee (Deceased), Re [1993] Ch. 497; [1993] 3 W.L.R. 498; [1993] 3 All E.R. 926, Ch. D 4.07
Skerritts of Nottingham Ltd v Secretary of State for the Environment, Transport and the Regions (No.1); sub nom. Secretary of State for the Environment, Transport and the Regions v Skerritts of Nottingham Ltd [2001] Q.B. 59; [2000] 3 W.L.R. 511, CA (Civ Div) 31.07

Smith, Re; sub nom. Public Trustee v Aspinall [1928] Ch. 915, Ch. D 1.05
Smith v Smith (Disclaimer of Interest under Will); sub nom. Smith (Deceased), Re [2001] 1
　W.L.R. 1937; [2001] 3 All E.R. 552; [2001] W.T.L.R. 1205; (2001) 98(28) L.S.G. 43 D 29.44
Smyth, Re; Leach v Leach (1808) 22.45
Sneddon v Lord Advocate. *See* Heatherington's Trustees v Lord Advocate
Soutter's Executry v Inland Revenue Commissioners [2002] S.T.C. (S.C.D.) 385; [2002]
　W.T.L.R. 1207, Sp Comm 29.27, 29.28
Stanley v Inland Revenue Commissioners [1944] K.B. 255; [1944] 1 All E.R. 230, CA 4.29
Starke v Inland Revenue Commissioners [1995] 1 W.L.R. 1439, CA (Civ Div); affirming
　[1994] 1 W.L.R. 888; [1994] S.T.C. 295, Ch. D 32.10, 32.11
Stenhouse's Trustees v Lord Advocate; sub nom. Stenhouse's Trustees v Inland Revenue
　Commissioners [1984] S.T.C. 195; 1984 S.C. 12, OH 5.09
Stephenson (Inspector of Taxes) v Barclays Bank Trust Co Ltd [1975] 1 W.L.R. 882; [1975]
　1 All E.R. 625; [1997] S.T.C. 151, Ch. D 5.06, 5.07, 5.11, 7.40
Stevenson (Inspector of Taxes) v Wishart [1987] 1 W.L.R. 1204; [1987] 2 All E.R. 428, CA
　(Civ Div) 4.27
Sugden v Kent (Inspector of Taxes) [2001] S.T.C. (S.C.D.) 158; [2001] S.T.I. 1143, Sp
　Comm 33.15
Swales v Inland Revenue Commissioners [1984] 3 All E.R. 16; [1984] S.T.C. 413,
　Ch. D 15.31
Swires (Inspector of Taxes) v Renton [1991] S.T.C. 490; 64 T.C. 315, Ch. D 1.13, 7.55, 7.58
T Settlement, Re [2002] W.T.L.R. 1529; (2001–02) 4 I.T.E.L.R. 820, Royal Ct (Jer) 10.19
Thomas v Inland Revenue Commissioners [1981] S.T.C. 382, Ch. D 15.11
Thomas v Marshall (Inspector of Taxes); sub nom. Marshall (Inspector of Taxes) v
　Thomas [1953] A.C. 543; [1953] 2 W.L.R. 944; [1953] 1 All E.R. 1102, HL 4.39
Thomas v Thomas [1995] 2 F.L.R. 668; [1996] 2 F.C.R. 544, CA (Civ Div) 34.08
Tomlinson (Inspector of Taxes) v Glyn's Executor & Trustee Co; sub nom. Glyn's
　Executor & Trustee Co v Tomlinson [1970] Ch. 112; [1969] 3 W.L.R. 310, CA (Civ
　Div) 5.05
Trafford's Settlement, Re; sub nom. Moore v Inland Revenue Commissioners [1985] Ch.
　32; [1984] 3 W.L.R. 341; [1984] 1 All E.R. 1108, Ch. D 15.33
Trennery v West (Inspector of Taxes). *See* West (Inspector of Taxes) v Trennery
Triffitt's Settlement, Re; sub nom. Hall v Hyde [1958] Ch. 852; [1958] 2 W.L.R. 927; [1958]
　2 All E.R. 299; 102 S.J. 382, Ch. D 22.38
Turner v Follett [1973] S.T.C. 148; 48 T.C. 614, CA (Civ Div) 6.01
Udny v Udny (1866–69) L.R. 1 Sc. 441; (1869) 7 M. (H.L.) 89, HL 2.29
Unmarried Settlor v Inland Revenue Commissioners [2003] S.T.C. (S.C.D.) 274; [2003]
　W.T.L.R. 915 ....11.05
Van Hilten-Van der Heijden's Heirs v Inspecteur van de Belastingdienst/Particulieren/
　Ondernemingen Buitenland te Heerlen (C513/03) [2006] W.T.L.R. 919; [2006] S.T.I. 535,
　ECJ (3rd Chamber) 9.28
Varty (Inspector of Taxes) v Lynes [1976] 1 W.L.R. 1091; [1976] 3 All E.R. 447; [1976]
　S.T.C. 508, Ch. D 31.15
WT Ramsay Ltd v Inland Revenue Commissioners; Eilbeck (Inspector of Taxes) v
　Rawling [1982] A.C. 300; [1981] 2 W.L.R. 449; [1981] 1 All E.R. 865; [1981] S.T.C. 174;
　54 T.C. 101; [1982] T.R. 123; (1981) 11 A.T.R. 752; 125 S.J. 220, HL 15.07
Wallach (Deceased), Re; sub nom. Weinschenk v Treasury Solicitor [1950] 1 All E.R. 199;
　66 T.L.R. (Pt. 1) 132, PDAD 2.33
Walsh v Queen, The [1894] A.C. 144, PC (Aus) 23.09
Warrington v Sterland [1989] S.T.C. 577 ....5.06
Watts, Re; sub nom. Coffey v Watts [1931] 2 Ch. 302, Ch. D 22.37, 22.38
Welbeck Securities Ltd v Powlson (Inspector of Taxes); sub nom. Powlson v Welbeck
　Securities Ltd [1987] S.T.C. 468; [1987] 2 F.T.L.R. 298, CA (Civ Div) 5.39, 8.09
West (Inspector of Taxes) v Trennery; sub nom. Tee v Inspector of Taxes; Trennery v
　West (Inspector of Taxes) [2005] UKHL 5; [2005] 1 All E.R. 827; [2005] S.T.C. 214,
　HL; reversing [2003] EWCA Civ 1792; [2004] S.T.C. 170; [2004] B.T.C. 3, CA (Civ
　Div) 3.11, 5.25, 7.04, 7.64, 11.02, 11.06, 11.07
White v White and King (1972) 116 Sol. Jo. 219, CA 34.07
Whitehead's Will Trusts, Re; sub nom. Burke v Burke [1971] 1 W.L.R. 833; [1971] 2 All
　E.R. 1334, Ch. D 2.49
Williams & Humbert Ltd v W&H Trade Marks (Jersey) Ltd; Rumasa SA v Multinvest
　(UK) [1986] A.C. 368; [1986] 2 W.L.R. 24, HL 10.18

Williams (Inspector of Taxes) v Merrylees [1987] 1 W.L.R. 1511; [1987] S.T.C. 445, Ch. D 31.04
Winans v Attorney General (No.1) [1904] A.C. 287, HL 2.30
Woodhall v Inland Revenue Commissioners [2000] S.T.C. (S.C.D.) 558; [2001] W.T.L.R. 475, Sp Comm 15.02, 17.07, 28.12
X v A [2000] 1 All E.R. 490; [2000] Env. L.R. 104, Ch. D 7.36, 30.02
Young (Inspector of Taxes) v Pearce; Young (Inspector of Taxes) v Scrutton [1996] S.T.C. 743; 70 T.C. 331, Ch. D 4.37
Youngman v The Queen [1991] 90 DTC 6322 .... 31.103

TABLE OF STATUTES

1837 Wills Act (7 Will.4 & 1 Vict. c.26)
    s.33 .... A2.25
1915 Finance (No.2) Act (5 & 6 Geo.5 c.89)
    s.47 .... 22.09
1925 Trustee Act (15 & 16 Geo.5 c.19) 30.02
    s.31 .... 1.10, 1.11, 4.29, 7.52, 14.23,
              15.03, 17.14, 18.17, 18.21,
              21.01, 21.07, 21.11, 25.04,
              25.06, 25.15, 25.19, 25.24,
              25.30, 25.39, 25.43, 28.40,
              30.05, 30.10, A2.07, A2.15,
              A2.16, A2.25, A3.109,
              A3.134, A3.135, A3.136
        (1)(ii) 4.29
        (2) 4.24, A3.135
            (i) 30.04
    s.32 .... 8.07, 1.11, 1.13, 25.19,
              30.13, A2.07, A2.25, A3.109
        (1)(a) 14.15, 25.42, A2.25
            (c) 25.18
    s.33 .... 4.40, 25.18
    s.36(1) 2.49
    s.37(1)(b) 7.59
            (c) 2.49
1925 Law of Property Act (15 & 16 Geo.5 c.20)
    s.34 .... 5.06, 15.01, 28.03
    s.35 .... 28.03
    s.36 .... 5.06, 15.01
    s.149(3) 31.51
          (6) 15.02
    s.164 .... 21.11
        (1)(a) 26.21
    s.165 .... 21.11
    s.188 .... 31.107
        (1) 31.107
1925 Administration of Estates Act (15 & 16 Geo.5 c.23) 26.08
    s.46 .... 25.15
        (1)(i) 19.06
    s.47(1) 25.15
1931 Finance Act (21 & 22 Geo.5 c.28)
    s.22 .... 22.09

1957 Finance Act (5 & 6 Eliz. c.49)
    s.38 .... 24.17
1958 Variation of Trusts Act (6 & 7 Eliz.2 c.53) 7.61
1965 Finance Act (c.25)
    s.42 .... 10.04
1969 Family Law Reform Act (c.46)
    s.1(3) 4.24, 4.29, 17.14,
                          21.01, 21.07
    Sch.1 Pt 1 .... 4.24, 4.29, 17.14,
                          21.01, 21.07
1970 Taxes Management Act (c.9)
    s.33 .... A3.85
    s.43 .... 9.09
    s.71 .... 4.01
    s.76 .... 4.02
1973 Matrimonial Causes Act (c.18) ... 34.11, 34.15
    s.24 .... 34.03, 34.04
        (1)(c) 34.05
            (d) 34.07
1973 Domicile and Matrimonial Proceedings Act (c.45) 2.33
    s.1(1) 2.33
        (2) 2.33
    s.3(1) 2.34
    s.4 .... 2.34
        (2) 2.34
1975 Finance Act (c.7)
    Sch.5 para.9 .... 22.23
1975 Inheritance (Provision for Family and Dependants) Act (c.63) .. 2.26, 2.30, 15.27, 28.39
1976 Finance Act (c.40) 21.12
1979 Capital Gains Tax Act (c.14)
    s.126 .... 9.01
1980 Finance Act (c.48)
    s.79 .... 9.01
1980 Limitation Act (c.58)
    s.8 .... 23.02
    s.29(5) 23.02
1981 Finance Act (c.35)
    s.80 .... 10.05
1982 Finance Act (c.39)
    s.82(1) 9.01

1983	Mental Health Act (c.20) 26.03	1984	Inheritance Tax Act (c.51)—*contd*
	Pt VII A2.13		s.9 .... 20.18
1984	Capital Transfer Tax Act A1.04,		s.10 .... 10.19, 13.35, 14.32,
	A1.05, A1.06, A1.07, A1.08,		17.11, 17.12, 17.15, 25.31,
	A1.10, A1.11, A1.12, A1.13,		31.87, 34.13, 34.14, 34.15,
	A1.14, A1.15, A1.16, A1.17,		34.17, A3.126
	A1.19, A1.20		(1) 17.05
1984	Inheritance Tax Act (c.51) ... 3.17, 9.33,		s.11 .... 13.01, 17.21, 24.25,
	24.33, A1.04, A1.05, A1.06,		34.14, 34.18, A3.23
	A1.07, A1.08, A1.10, A1.11,		(6) 34.14
	A1.12, A1.13, A1.14, A1.15,		s.16 .... 25.31, A3.126
	A1.16, A1.17, A1.19, A1.20,		s.17 .... 29.41, A3.23
	A3.23, A3.79		s.18 .... 13.01, 13.02, 13.23,
	Pt II Ch.I 23.01		13.34, 14.05, 14.11, 14.16,
	Pt II Ch.II 15.09, 23.01		14.20, 14.25, 18.02, 20.01,
	Pt III Ch.III A3.05, A3.125		25.12, 28.32, 29.52, 34.13
	Pt III Ch.III 14.03, 14.08, 15.08,		s.19 .... 13.01, 24.25, 24.26, A3.23
	15.14, 17.01, 17.16, 20.01,		s.20 .... 13.01, 24.25, 24.26, A3.23
	21.21, 24.05, A3.04		s.21 .... 13.01, 31.31, 33.09, 3602
	Pt V Ch.I 14.11, 32.01		s.23 .... 17.22, 18.02, 18.06
	Pt V Ch.II 14.11		s.24 .... 20.33
	Pt VI Ch.I 23.23		ss.36–42 .... 29.24
	s.2(3) 9.33		s.39A 28.28
	s.3 .... 22.42		s.42(1) 24.05
	(1) 22.29, 22.35, 22.42		s.43 .... 1.16, 5.04, 15.14,
	(1A)(c)(iii) 14.17, 14.22, 25.12		22.23, 30.10, A3.136
	(2) 22.01, 22.04, 22.35,		(2) 14.10, 15.01, 15.07,
	22.66, 23.21		15.14, 22.23, A3.22
	(3) 22.41		(a) 15.01, 15.02, 30.10
	s.3A 14.09, 18.05, A1.01		(b) 15.01, 15.03, A3.135
	s.3A(1)(c) 15.17, 16.01, 21.05		(3) 15.04, 22.46,
	(1A) 14.09, 18.14,		31.51, 31.88
	19.07, 19.15		s.44 .... 5.17, 22.24
	(a)(iii) 25.37		(1) 15.12, 22.52
	(c) 19.15		(2) 5.20, 5.31, 9.34,
	(i) 9.45, 18.14, 19.07		15.11, 20.05
	(ii) 9.45, 19.07, 19.15,		s.45 .... 15.01, 15.16
	26.32		s.46 .... 22.46
	(iii) 19.07, 25.16		s.46A 33.05, 33.06
	(iii) 25.25, 26.32		(4) A3.139
	(2) 14.31, 25.05		s.46B 33.06
	(6) 17.17		(5) A3.139
	(3A) 19.07, 19.15		s.46A–B 18.20
	(3B) 19.07, 25.25, 25.37, 26.32		s.47 .... 14.09, 17.04, 22.44
	s.4 .... 13.21, 21.13, 25.30		s.47A 3.16, 8.09, 22.40, 22.41
	(1) 13.05, 17.10, 32.20		s.48 .... 3.23, 8.02, 13.06,
	s.5 .... 13.06, 14.09, 21.13,		13.21, 14.09, 17.27, 22.33
	23.01, A1.02		(1) 22.47, 22.46, 22.48,
	(1) 13.05, 13.06, 13.21,		22.49, 22.50, 31.47
	17.20, 22.01, 22.04, 22.66,		(a) 17.15
	23.13, 23.14		(b) 3.17, 27.09
	(a) 22.44		(c) 22.46
	(ii) 16.02		(3) 13.22, 22.06, 22.22,
	(ii) 17.05		22.30, 22.32, 22.34, 22.47,
	(2) 3.16, 22.41, 32.17		22.49, 22.53, 22.65, A3.34,
	(3) 17.06, 23.02, 23.10,		A3.59
	23.12, 23.13, 23.14		(3)(a) 22.49, 22.50
	(3)–(5) 28.19		(b) 22.49
	(5) 13.06, 23.03		(3A) 22.12, 22.53, A3.23
	s.6 .... 13.21, 22.01		(4) 22.09
	(1) 22.48, 22.49		s.49 .... 14.28, 14.31, 14.32,
	s.8 .... 20.18		19.02, 22.30, 22.71, A1.03

1984 Inheritance Tax Act (c.51)—*contd*
   s.49(1) 3.19, 7.48, 9.45,
          13.02, 13.03, 13.05, 13.16,
          13.16, 13.17, 14.02, 14.09,
          14.13, 14.31, 15.15, 15.27,
          16.02, 17.03, 17.05, 17.06,
          17.07, 17.08, 17.10, 18.01,
          18.13, 18.18, 19.01, 20.01,
          21.13, 21.17, 22.29, 22.32,
          22.52, 22.65, 23.10, 23.14,
          23.18, 24.07, 24.32, 24.33,
          25.05, 25.09, 25.19, 25.30,
          25.45, 26.22, 26.30, 27.31,
          31.70, 32.20, 32.24
     (1A) 9.45, 15.15, 21.17,
          26.30, 27.20
       (iii) 14.16
       (b) 14.13
       (c) 18.13, 18.14
     (1B) 25.15, 25.45
     (2)(b) 18.18
   s.49A 17.01, 19.04, 19.05,
          19.09, 25.24, 25.25,
          25.40, 29.13, 29.15,
          A1.04, A3.114,
          A3.120
     (2) 33.05
     (3) 29.53
     (4) 33.06
     (5) 25.25
   s.49B 7.52, A1.05
     (2) 33.05
     (5) 33.06
     (5)(a) 25.16
   s.49B–D 14.31
   s.49B–E 17.01, 18.13, 18.14
   s.49C 14.31, 18.16, 18.19,
          A1.06, A3.107
     (1) 18.16
     (3) 18.15, 18.16, A3.108,
          A3.112
   s.49D 14.31, 18.19, 33.07,
          33.08, A1.07
     (3) A3.112
     (4) 14.31, 18.19
   s.49E 18.20, 33.04, 33.07,
          33.08, A1.08
     (4) 18.20
   s.50(1) 17.07, 18.22
     (2) A3.141
     (5) 17.07, 18.22
     (6) 17.09
   s.51 .... 17.05, 17.10, 24.07,
          27.08, 34.17
     (1) 17.12, 18.16, A3.112,
          A3.142
       (a) 34.17
     (1B) A3.142
     (2) 17.21
   s.52 .... 17.10, 18.16, 23.10,
          24.07, 31.41,
          32.24, 34.17

1984 Inheritance Tax Act (c.51)—*contd*
   s.52(1) 17.11, 17.12, 26.22,
          28.34, 32.20, 34.17
     (2) 17.11, 17.12
     (2A) 18.04
     (3) 17.16, 23.04, 25.31
   s.53 .... A3.60
     (1) 17.20
     (1A) 25.15
     (2) 21.13, 25.30, 27.07
     (3) 27.03, 27.04, 27.14, 27.19
     (3)–(5) 17.17
     (4) 27.03, 27.04, 27.19
     (5) 27.07
     (6) 27.07
   s.54 .... A3.60
     (1) 17.17, 27.03, 27.19
       (b) A3.143
     (2) 17.17, 27.03, 27.19
     (2A) 27.25
     (3) 27.07
   s.54A 18.09, 18.12, 18.13,
          18.15, A3.143
     (1)(a) 18.15
     (1A) 18.12, 18.13, A3.143
     (2A) 18.15
   s.54B 18.09
   s.55(1) 17.15
   s.57 .... 17.18, 36.03
   s.58 .... 14.08, 20.01, 20.02,
          20.34, 21.05
     (1) 14.03, 19.01
       (a) 20.34
     (4)(f) 22.04
   ss.58–63 .... 20.34
   s.59 .... 14.03, 14.09, 19.01, 20.01
     (1) 14.09
       (a)(i) 19.02
     (2) 17.01
       (c) 19.07
     (2)–(4) 19.02
   s.60 .... 15.14, 22.24
   s.61(1) 20.03
     (2) 15.09
   s.62 .... 15.07, 15.09, 28.40,
          33.09, 36.05
   s.64 .... 20.13, 21.05, 36.05
   s.65 .... 20.30, 29.52, 36.05, A3.125
     (1) 20.07
       (a) 9.33, 20.24
       (b) 23.04, 25.31
     (2) A4.02
     (4) 9.37, 20.12, 29.52
     (5) 20.07, 25.31
     (6) 25.31
   s.66 .... A4.04
     (2) 20.21, 20.22, A4.09
     (3) A4.04
     (4)(a) A4.04
       (c) 28.40
     (5)(a) A4.04
       (b) A4.04

1984 Inheritance Tax Act (c.51)—*contd*
s.66(6) 20.16
s.67 .... 15.14, 20.26, 33.10, A4.07
  (1) 20.26
  (4) 20.31, 22.07
  (3)(b)(i) 33.09
s.68 .... A3.125
  (2) 20.28, 25.32, 29.52, A4.03
  (3) 20.24
  (4) 20.28
    (b) 20.09, A4.02
  (5) 20.08, 20.28
    (a) 32.25, A4.02
    (b) 28.40
    (c) A4.07
  (6) 20.30
s.69 .... 20.18, A4.05, A4.08
  (1) 32.25
  (2) 20.23, 20.24
  (3) 20.23
  (4) 20.23, 20.24
s.70 .... 20.34
  (1) 20.34
  (3)–(8) 25.35
  (6) 21.15, 25.35
  (10) 25.35
s.71 .... 9.36, 14.03, 14.14,
              14.29, 14.30, 20.03, 21.01,
              21.02, 21.03, 21.04, 21.06,
              21.11, 21.16, 21.17, 21.18,
              21.19, 25.01, 25.02, 25.04,
              25.14, 25.17, 25.18, 25.21,
              25.35, 25.44, 27.07, 29.19,
          A1.09, A3.05, A3.129, A3.130
  (1)(a) 14.15, 14.30,
              21.01, 21.02, 21.07, 21.10
    (b) 21.11, 25.17
  (1A) 21.02
  (1B) 21.22
  (2) 21.12
  (3) 21.17
    (b) 21.15
  (4) 9.36, 21.05, 32.24
    (a) 21.17
    (b) 21.14
    (a) 7.41
  (5) 21.15, 25.21, 25.35
  (8) 25.14
s.71A 14.14, 18.14, 19.05,
              19.07, 19.08, 19.13, 21.22,
              25.13, 25.15, 25.16, 25.24,
              25.25, 25.30, 25.31, 25.36,
              25.41, 28.39, 29.53, 29.54,
              29.56, 29.61, A1.10, A3.121,
             A3.126, A3.128, A3.142
  (1) 25.15
  (2) 25.15
  (3) 21.08
    (a) 14.15
    (b) 25.17
    (c) 25.17
    (iii) 25.17

1984 Inheritance Tax Act (c.51)—*contd*
s.71A(4) 14.14, 14.23, 25.18
ss.71A–D 25.38
s.71B 25.13, 25.14, 25.20,
              25.31, A1.11, A3.126
s.72B(1) 25.20
s.71B(2) 25.20, 25.21
  (2)(a) 25.19
    (b) 7.52, 25.19
    (c) 14.14, 14.23, 25.15,
              25.18, 25.19, 25.31, 25.38
  (3) 25.21, 25.35
  (4) 25.21
s.71C 25.14, A1.12
s.71D 7.41, 7.52, 9.37, 9.41,
              14.15, 14.18, 14.21, 14.22,
              14.23, 14.24, 14.29, 14.30,
              17.16, 19.07, 19.08, 20.01,
              20.03, 21.01, 21.18, 21.20,
              21.21, 21.22, 21.23, 25.10,
              25.11, 25.12, 25.12, 25.13,
              25.15, 25.16, 25.19, 25.21,
              25.24, 25.29, 25.30, 25.31,
              25.32, 25.34, 25.35, 25.36,
              25.37, 25.38, 25.39, 25.40,
              25.41, 25.42, 25.43, 25.44,
              25.45, 25.49, 28.39, 28.40,
              29.53, 29.54, 29.56, 29.61,
             A1.13, A2.26, A3.121,
             A3.125, A3.127, A3.128,
             A3.130, A3.132, A3.142,
             A4.09
  (1) 25.44, A3.130
  (2) 25.30, 25.44, A3.130
  (3) 25.44, A3.127, A3.130
  (3)–(4) 14.29, 21.17, 21.20
  (4) 21.22, A3.127, A3.130
  (5) 25.30, A3.142
    (a) 25.30, 25.37
      (ii) 25.30
    (c) 25.16
      (i) 25.45
      (ii) 25.25, 25.40
  (6) 21.08, 21.17,
              21.20, 25.44
    (a) 25.43, A3.127
    (b) 14.15
  (7) 21.20
s.71D–G 14.15, 21.20, 25.29
s.71E 9.37, A1.14, A3.125, A4.10
  (1) 25.31
    (c) 25.37
  (2)(a) 25.31
    (b) 7.52, 25.31
    (c) 25.31
    (d) 25.31
  (3) 25.31, A3.126
  (4) A3.126
s.71F 7.52, 14.15, 19.07, 21.23,
              25.31, 25.32, 25.33, 25.34,
              25.36, 25.42, A1.15,
             A3.125, A4.10

1984 Inheritance Tax Act (c.51)—*contd*
s.71F(2) 7.52
    (3) 14.15
    (4) 25.32
    (5) 25.32
    (8) 25.32
        (c) 25.32
s.71F–G 25.31
s.71G 25.31, 25.35, 25.35, A1.16
    (3) 25.38
s.71H 25.14, A1.17
s.72(1B) 26.32
s.73 .... 17.23, 19.04
s.74 .... 26.18
s.75 .... 20.33
s.76 .... 20.34
    (1)(a) 20.33
       (b) 20.33
       (c) 20.33
s.77 .... 20.33, 20.34
s.80 .... 9.07, 15.09, 15.10,
                             19.07, 22.15
    (1) 28.34
    (4) 20.05, 28.40
       (a) 15.10
       (b) 15.10
ss.80–82 .... 22.03, 22.15
s.81 .... 7.19, 9.33, 15.08,
                        15.14, 20.25, 22.17
    (1) 15.07
s.82 .... 22.17, 22.18, 22.19
s.83 .... 20.03, 28.40
s.86 .... 22.31
    (3) 20.34
s.87 .... 20.34, 22.31
s.88 .... 14.15, 17.23, 19.04,
                             20.34, 25.18
    (3)–(6) 19.04
    (5) 19.04
s.89 .... 14.13, 14.13, 18.13,
             19.07, 19.14, 19.15, 25.30,
             25.30, 26.01, 26.13, 26.18,
             26.19, 26.22, 26.23, 26.24,
             26.25, 26.26, 26.28, 26.29,
             26.31, 26.32, A2.09, A2.12,
                       A2.23, A1.18
    (4) 26.03, 26.24, A3.06
s.89A 14.13, 19.14, 26.24,
                26.25, 26.26, 26.27, 26.28,
                26.29, 26.30, 26.31,
                      26.32, A1.19
    (1) 26.32
       (a) 26.25
       (b) 26.25
       (c) 26.25
         (i) 26.26
    (2) A3.138
    (3) A3.138
s.89A–B 26.01
s.89B 9.45, 14.13, 14.18,
              15.10, 16.02, 19.07, 19.14,
             20.12, 21.03, 25.01, 25.30,

1984 Inheritance Tax Act (c.51)—*contd*
s.89B 26.23, 26.29, 28.39, 30.13,
                          33.02, A1.20
    (c) 9.45, 18.13, 26.32
    (1)(a) 26.26, 26.31
       (c) 7.51, 14.11, 17.01,
                18.12, 19.12, 19.14,
                26.26, 26.31
       (d) 7.51, 14.11, 17.01
s.90 .... 16.07
s.91 .... 19.03, A3.113
s.92 .... A2.53
s.93 .... 17.24, 29.05, 29.30,
                          29.47, 29.48
s.101(1) 19.03
s.102(3) 22.06
s.103 .... 36.03, A2.57, A2.59
    (1) 32.21, A3.125
       (a) 32.21
       (b) 32.21
    (4) 36.03
ss.103–114 .... 17.26, 20.13
s.104(1) 32.19
s.105 .... 32.23
    (1)(a) 32.09, 32.22,
                         32.23, 32.26
       (b) 32, 22, 32.26
       (bb) 32.25
       (cc) 32,22, 32.26
       (d) 32.26
       (e) 32.22
    (3) 32.03, 32.04, 32.06
s.106 .... 32.09, 32.30, 32.24
s.107 .... 32.24
s.108 .... 32.24
s.110 .... 13.06, 23.23, 23.25
s.114(1) 32.01, 32.02
s.115 .... 32.21
    (1) A3.125
    (2) 32.15, 32.16
    (3) 32.14, 32.15, 32.16
ss.115–124C 17.26, 20.13
s.116(1) 32.19
    (2)(a) 32.22
       (b) 32.22
s.117 .... 32.09
s.141 .... 17.04, 17.25
s.142 .... 13.34, 14.16, 17.24, 17.25,
             29.02, 29.04, 29.05, 29.10,
             29.17, 29.21, 29.23, 29.28,
             29.30, 29.41, 29.48, A1.21,
            A3.120, A3.143, A3.144,
                            A3.145
    (1) 19.09, 25.16, 29.02, 29.05,
             29.12, 29.21, 29.23, 29.31,
             29.41, A2.61, A3.23, A3.58
    (2A) 29.04
    (4) 29.25
    (5) 29.05, 29.30
s.144 .... 1.20, 14.21, 14.28, 19.09,
             19.09, 19.11, 20.33, 25.16,
             25.28, 25.30, 25.41, 28.02,

1984 Inheritance Tax Act (c.51)—*contd*
  s.144 .... 28.04, 28.08, 28.25, 28.26,
      28.31, 28.40, 29.01, 29.21,
      29.23, 29.49, 29.50, 29.52,
      29.53, 29.54, 29.55, 29.57,
      29.59, 29.60, 29.61, 29.62,
      31.25, A2.64, A1.22, A3.116
    (1) 29.49, 29.51
      (a) 29.52
      (b) 29.54
    (1A) 25.16, 29.49
    (2) 20.12, 29.51
    (3) 29.53
      (a) 29.55
    (3)–(6) 15.29, 19.09
    (4) 29.53
      (c)(ii) 25.16
    (5) 25.16, 29.56
    (6) 29.56
      (b) 25.16
  s.151 .... 20.34
  s.151A–C 36.08
  s.157(4) 22.13
  s.160 .... 13.06, 31.37, A3.24, A3.43
  s.161 .... 31.42
    (4) 31.42
  s.162 .... 23.01, 31.92
    (1) 23.04
    (2) 23.05
    (4) 13.06, 23.06, 23.08, 23.12,
      23.23, 23.25, 31.31, 32.17
    (5) 23.06, 23.08
  s.165 .... 9.53
  s.167 .... 33.09
  s.170 .... 17.09
  s.171 .... 13.06, 33.16
  s.199 .... 36.03
    (1)(b) 13.06
    (2) 13.06
  s.200(1)(b) 25.06
    (c) 13.26
  s.201 .... 17.03
    (1) 16.05
  s.203 .... 36.03
  s.204(8) 13.06
    (9) 13.26
  s.211(3) 13.06, 13.26, 36.09
  s.216 .... 16.04, 36.01, 36.03, 36.12
    (1) 3606
    (b) 36.03
    (c) 36.03
  s.218 .... 16.04, 36.10, 36.12
    (1) 36.10
    (2) 36.10
  s.218A 29.04
  s.219 .... 36.10
  s.219A 36.10
  s.227 .... 16.04, 20.13
  ss.227–229 .... 36.09
  s.245A 36.12
  s.267 .... 2.36, 13.22, 22.02, A3.34
    (3)(a) 15.14

1984 Inheritance Tax Act (c.51)—*contd*
  s.268 .... 15.07, 15.12, 24.36,
      31.74, A3.23
    (1)(b) 15.12
  s.269(2) 32.26
    (3) 32.26
  s.272 .... 3.16, 15.11, 22.40
  s.273 .... 17.19
  Sch.2 para.3 .... 20.18
  Sch.3 .... 20.33
  Sch.4 .... 20.33
    para.1 .... 20.34
    para.3(1) A3.23
    para.8 .... 20.34
  Sch.6 para.2 .... 17.19, 27.10
1986 Finance Act (c.41) 3.14, 13.34,
      18.05, 29.12, 31.73, A3.23,
      A3.56, A3.78
  Pt 5 .... A3.29
  s.100(1) A1.02, A1.04, A1.05,
      A1.06, A1.07, A1.08, A1.10,
      A1.11, A1.12, A1.13, A1.14,
      A1.15, A1.16, A1.17, A1.19,
      A1.20
    (2) A1.02
  s.101 .... 15.17, 16.01, 18.05,
      21.05, 25.05
    (1) 17.24, 20.09, 20.26,
      20.30, 20.31
    (3) 17.24, 20.09, 20.26,
      20.30, 20.31
  s.102 .... 13.16, 13.17, 24.05,
      24.08, 24.10, A1.23, A3.99
    (1) 13.08, 13.10, 13.13,
      13.24, 22.30, 24.03,
      24.06, 31.74, 31.87
      (a) 24.03
      (b) 24.03, 32.31
    (2) 24.03
    (3) 13.18, 13.18, 13.20,
      13.21, 13.23, 16.02, 22.30,
      22.32, 22.35, 23.09, 23.22,
      24.22, 27.10, 27.17, 28.37,
      31.39, 31.66, 31.67, 32.30,
      A3.29, A3.35, A3.55, A3.78,
      A3.79, A3.104, A3.147
    (4) 13.19, 13.24, 22.33,
      22.35, 22.43, 23.22, 24.11,
      24.22, 24.41, 24.42, 27.10,
      27.17, 27.24, 31.66, 32.30,
      A3.29, A3.55, A3.78, A3.104,
      A3.147
    (5) 13.10, 13.16, 24.05,
      24.09, 31.41
      (a) 13.17, 13.34
      (d)(i) 13.34
      (d)–(i) A3.23
      (h) A3.23
    (5A) 13.17, 13.34, 24.09,
      A3.50, A3.51
    (5A)–(5C) 13.17
    (5B) 3.15, 13.17, 24.10

1986 Finance Act (c.41)—contd
  s.102(5C) 13.17
    (6) A3.69
    (8) A3.78
  s.102ZA 7.24, 7.53, 13.09,
    13.17, 14.17, 14.22, 19.07,
    24.08, 27.24, 28.37, 29.16,
    29.18, 29.20, 31.41, 31.55,
    31.70, A1.24, A3.58
  s.102A 13.13, 13.34, 16.03,
    31.36, 31.87, A1.25, A3.48,
    A3.49, A3.52
    (1) 31.87
    (3) 31.53, 31.55
    (5) 24.20, 31.53, 31.54
  ss.102A–C 3.15, 13.15
  s.102B 24.38, s.27.05, 31.59,
    31.70, A1.26
    (2) 31.59
    (3)(a) 31.66
    (4) 13.34, 24.38, 27.10,
    31.59, 31.60, 31.61, 31.62,
    31.63, 31.64, 31.65, 31.66,
    31.69, 31.70, 31.71, 31.83,
    31.106, 32.29, A3.23, A3.35,
    A3.45
  s.102C A1.27
    (3) 24.38, A3.23
  s.103 .... 11.07, 13.06, 23.01, 23.09,
    23.16, 23.17, 23.18, 23.19,
    23.20, 23.21, 23.22, 28.02,
    28.19, 28.22, 28.23, 28.24,
    31.32, 31.39, A1.28, A3.53
    (1) 23.16, 28.22
    (2) 23.16, 23.17
      (b) 23.17
    (3) 23.21
    (4) 23.16, 23.17, 23.21
      (a) 23.21
      (b) 23.21
    (5) 23.16
  s.105(1)(b) 14.02
  s.105(A)–(C) 24.10
  Sch.8 para.8 .... 13.25
  Sch.19 para.1 ..... 15.17, 16.01, 18.05,
    21.05, 25.05
    para.17 .... 20.26, 20.31
    para.18 .... 20.09, 20.30
    para.24 .... 17.24
  Sch.20 .... 13.38, 24.05, 31.73,
    A3.78, A3.96
    para.2 ..... 24.12, 31.74, A3.35
    para.2(b) 16.09
    para.2(1) 31.65
    para.2(2)(a) 31.74
    para.2(2)(b) 31.65, 31.74,
    31.88, A3.23, A3.35
    para.2(4) 24.07
    para.2(5) 24.07
    para.3 .... 24.15, 24.16
    para.4(2) 31.79
    para.4A ... 14.22, 28.37, A1.29

1986 Finance Act (c.41)—contd
  Sch.20 para.5 .... 24.13, 24.17,
    31.74, A1.30
    para.5(1) 24.16
    para.5(2) 24.13, 24.15,
    24.16
    para.5(3) 24.16
    para.5(4) 24.16, 24.17
    para.5(4)(b) 33.12
    para.5(5) 24.13
    para.6 ..... 13.34, 24.38, 31.39,
    31.67, 31.99, 31.101, 32.28,
    A3.23, A3.78, A3.99
    para.6(1)(a) 13.11, 24.20,
    31.99, 32.31, A3.37,
    A3.44, A3.45
    para.6(1)(c) 13.08, 31.74,
    31.76, 31.104
    para.6(2)(b) 31.101
    para.7 .... 13.13
    para.8 .... 32.30
    para.8(1) 32.30
    para.8(1A)(a) 32.30
    para.8(1A)(b) 32.30
    para.8(2) 32.30
    para.8(2)(a) 32.30
    para.8(5) 32.30
1986 Insolvency Act (c.45)
  s.335A 28.03
1987 Finance Act (c.16)
  s.58 .... 17.15
  Sch.8 para.1 .... 17.14
1987 Family Law Reform Act (c.42)
  s.33(1) 4.41
  Sch.2 para.2 .... 4.41
1987 Finance (No.2) Act (c.51) 18.05
  s.96(1) 18.09, 25.05
    (1)–(3) 18.05
    (6) 18.09
    (2) 18.09, 25.05
  s.98(4) 20.34
  s.104 .... 25.05
    (4) 18.05
  Sch.7 para.1 .... 18.09
  Sch.9 Pt III 18.05, 25.05
1988 Income and Corporation Taxes
  Act (c.1)
  s.1A 4.21
  s.65 .... 2.12
  s.334 .... 2.02
  s.336 .... 2.02
  s.338 .... 3.27
  s.348 .... 4.23
  s.547 .... A3.27
  s.615(3) 20.34
  s.624 .... 20.34
  s.660A A3.27, A3.29,
    A3.81, A3.104
    (1) 4.49, A3.81
    (6) 4.47, 4.49, 4.51
  ss.660A–G 4.31
  s.660B 3.10, 30.05

1988 Income and Corporation Taxes
    Act (c.1)—*contd*
    s.660B(1)(b) 30.05
    s.660G(1) 4.47
    ss.677–682A 4.31
    s.685A 4.01
    ss.685B–D 4.01, 4.32
    s.685D 29.39
    s.685E 4.01, 4.05
        (1) 4.01
    s.685G 4.01
    s.686 .... 4.01, 4.05, 4.06, 4.08,
                  4.11, 4.12, 4.14, 4.16, 4.18,
                  4.25, 4.29, 21.01
        (2)(a) 4.11, 4.12
           (b) 4.11, 4.14, 4.33
           (c) 4.11
           (d) 4.15
        (2AA) 4.11, 4.18
           (b) 4.15
    s.686A 4.06
        (2) 4.06
           (d) 4.06
           (j) 4.06
    s.686D 4.05
    ss.686–687 .... 14.11, 25.07
    s.687 .... 4.19, 4.20, 4.24, 21.01
        (3) 4.20
    s.689B 4.11
    s.691(2) 9.45
    ss.710–728 .... 4.06
    s.739 .... 4.10, 22.71, A3.27
    ss.739–740 .... 2.47, 4.10
    s.740 .... 4.10, 10.34
    s.776 .... 4.06
    s.832(5) 4.39
    s.844 .... 20.34
    Sch.9 para.32 .... 20.34
1988 Finance Act (c.39)
    s.55(3) 4.11
1989 Finance Act (c.26)
    s.110 .... 2.42
    s.151(2)(a) 4.01
    s.171(5) 13.34
        (6) 13.34
1991 Finance Act (c.31)
    s.72 .... 12.01
1992 Social Security Contributions and
    Benefits Act (c.4)
    s.64 .... 26.05
    s.71 .... 26.05
1992 Taxation of Chargeable Gains
    Act (c.12) 9.26, 3.02
    Ch.2 .... 12.01
    s.2 .... 2.18
        (2) 12.04
        (5) 12.02
    s.2A(1) 12.01
    s.2(A)(3) 9.25
    s.2A(8)(b) 8.24
    s.3 .... 26.01
    s.4 .... 7.01

1992 Taxation of Chargeable Gains
    Act (c.12)—*contd*
    s.10 .... 8.25, 2.11
    s.10A 2.19, 2.22, 2.23, 2.25, 12.10
        (3) 2.21
        (9C) 2.17
        (10) 2.21, 2.22
    s.12 .... 2.15
        (2) 2.12
    s.13 .... 2.19, 2.23, 12.11
        (8) 12.11
        (10) 10.27
    s.16(2A) 12.01
        (4) 2.13, 12.01
    s.18(3) 6.02
    s.21(1)(c) 8.09
    s.22 .... 5.39, 5.40, 8.09
    s.24 .... 8.09
    s.29 .... 8.09
        (5) 8.09
    s.30 .... 8.09
    s.31 .... 7.52
    s.38 .... 7.68
        (4) 12.05
    s.51(1)(a) 8.25
    s.58 .... 25.04, 31.32, 34.12
    s.60 .... 4.01, 5.02, 5.06, 25.08, 30.06
        (1) 5.04, 5.05, 5.06, 7.36
        (2) 5.07, 5.08, 7.36
    s.62 .... 13.26, 29.34
        (1) 29.34
        (4) 31.28
        (6) 29.34, A2.61
           (a) 29.31, 29.34
           (b) 29.31, 29.34
        (6)–(10) 29.12
        (7) 29.33
    s.63(3) 7.59
    s.65(1) 5.38
    s.68 .... 4.01, 5.02
        (6) 11.10
    s.68A 5.16, 11.10
        (2)(a) **5.17**
        (6)(a) 5.19
    ss.68A–C 4.01
    s.68B 2.45, 5.16, 5.23, 5.25
        (3) 5.23
    s.68C 5.16, 5.26, 29.35
    s.69 .... 5.37
        (1) 2.38, 2.39, 2.52,
                       2.66, 7.01, 35.04
        (2C) 2.45
        (3) 4.01, 5.38
        (4) 7.03, 7.45
    s.70 .... 6.01
    s.71 .... 5.04, 5.11, 5.14, 5.40,
                7.37, 7.52, 7.53, 7.60, 9.07,
              12.05, 15.07, 18.18, 21.01,
                                A1.31
        (1) 7.33, 7.34, 7.46, 7.50,
                   7.52, 7.55, 8.04, 12.06
        (2) 3.10, 7.43

1992 Taxation of Chargeable Gains
   Act (c.12)—contd
   s.71(2A) 3.10, 7.43, 12.05, 12.07
   s.72 .... 3.13, 7.33, 7.48, 7.51,
         25.19, 27.13, 28.40, 29.15,
         A1.32, A3.14, A3.137
      (1) 7.41, 7.48, 19.04, 34.19,
         A3.137
         (a) 7.48
         (b) 7.41
      (1A) 14.14, 19.04
         (b) 7.52, 25.39
      (1B) 7.52, 19.04
         (b) 25.24
      (2) 7.49
      (3) 7.48
      (4) 7.48
   s.73 .... 3.13, 7.33, 7.46, 7.48,
         7.51, 25.19, 27.13, 28.40,
         A1.33, A3.14
      (1)(b) 17.17, 27.13
      (2) 7.47
      (2A)(a) 25.24
         (b) 25.39
   s.74 .... 7.46, 9.09, 9.46, A1.34
   s.76 .... 8.02, 8.09, 8.18, 8.24,
         8.26, 22.54
      (1) 8.01, 8.05, 8.18, 17.04,
         17.05, 27.07, 31.47
      (1A) 3.09, 8.14
      (1B) 8.14
      (2) 8.04, 8.05
      (3) 8.14
   s.76A 3.11
   s.76B 3.11, 7.62, 10.20
   s.77 .... 2.58, 2.59, 4.33, 5.19, 7.01,
         7.30, 7.65, 7.74, 8.16, 8.21,
         10.09, 10.20, 10.21, 11.01,
         11.07, 11.10, 11.11, 12.02,
         12.04, 12.09, 12.10, 26.15,
         27.12, 27.14, 29.37, A3.27
      (2) 8.17
         (b) 7.04
         (A) 11.03
      (2A) 6.04, 7.04, 11.03
      (3A) 26.06
      (3B) 11.05
      (5) 11.05
      (8) 11.06, 11.07
   ss.77–79 .... 7.04, 4.30
   s.78 .... 7.04, 11.01
   s.79 .... 5.21, 11.10
      (1) 11.10
   s.79A 3.03, 3.11, 7.44, 8.18,
         12.06, 12.07
   s.80 .... 2.53, 2.54, 2.60, 2.61,
         2.67, 5.40, 9.24, 9.25,
         15.09, 15.10
      (1) 2.52
      (2) 2.51
      (3) 2.55
   s.81 .... 2.66

1992 Taxation of Chargeable Gains
   Act (c.12)—contd
   s.81(5)–(7) 2.67
   s.82 .... 2.54
   s.83A 2.59, 2.62
   s.85 .... 2.64, 3.11, 8.09, 8.10,
         8.11, 8.13, 8.14
      (1) 8.05, 8.12
      (3) 8.10, 8.12, 8.13
      (10) 2.64, 8.13
   s.85A 10.27
   s.86 .... 2.58, 3.09, 4.30, 5.38, 7.31,
         7.62, 7.65, 8.10, 8.14, 2.15,
         2.19, 2.21, 9.40, 10.07, 10.08,
         10.09, 10.10, 10.11, 10.13,
         10.15, 10.16, 10.17, 10.19,
         10.19, 10.20, 10.23, 10.24,
         10.25, 10.26, 10.33, 10.37,
         10.41, 10.42, 11.05, 12.02,
         12.08, 12.09, 12.10, 12.11,
         29.37, A3.27
   s.86A 10.37
   ss.86–87 .... 2.23, 2.58, 5.19, 10.22
   s.87 .... 2.64, 3.09, 3.12, 7.31, 7.65,
         8.10, 8.14, 2.15, 2.19, 2.21,
         9.39, 10.07, 10.09, 10.10,
         10.19, 10.20, 10.21, 10.23,
         10.24, 10.25, 10.26, 10.27,
         10.31, 10.33, 10.34, 10.37,
         10.40, 10.41, 10.42, 10.43,
         12.08, 12.09, 12.10, 12.11,
         24.11, 29.34
      (2) 10.32
      (4) 10.32
      (5) 10.32
      (7) 10.35
      (9) 10.26
   ss.87–97 .... 5.29
   s.90 .... 10.19, 10.31, 10.43
      (5)(a) 10.42, 10.42
   ss.91–95 .... 10.38
   s.97 .... 10.31
      (1) 10.28, 10.29
      (2) 10.28, 10.29, 10.31
      (5)(b) 10.31
      (7) 5.02, 5.30
   s.98A 10.44
   s.102(5) 34.19
   s.105 .... 2.60
   s.106A 2.57, 2.60
      (5) 2.57
   s.152 .... 2.11
   ss.152–162 .... 7.11
   s.162 .... 9.22
   s.164 .... 3.09
   s.165 .... 3.11, 3.17, 6.03, 6.04, 6.06,
         7.19, 7.48, 8.18, 9.03, 9.05,
         9.07, 9.09, 9.10, 9.19, 9.33,
         9.38, 9.38, 9.42, 9.44, 9.45,
         14.06, 15.07, 15.08, 25.28,
         25.30, 29.37
      (1)(b) 9.09

1992 Taxation of Chargeable Gains Act (c.12)—*contd*
s.165(2) 9.11
   (8)(a) 9.11
   (10) 9.53
s.166 .... 9.22
s.168 .... 7.03
   (1) 9.23
   (3) 9.29
   (5) 9.27
   (7) 9.23
   (8) 9.23
   (10) 9.29
s.169 .... 9.22
s.169B 9.45, 25.04
s.169B–G 3.17, 9.33
s.169C 9.44, 9.45, 14.11
   (2) 11.10
   (6) 9.44
s.169D 9.45, 26.14
   (1) 9.45
   (3) 9.45
   (5) 9.45
   (7) 9.45
s.169F 25.04
   (3A) 14.08, 14.11
   (4A) 14.11
   (4B) 14.11
s.185 .... 2.51
s.222 .... 31.11
   (2) 31.14
   (5) 31.08, 31.60
   (8) 31.12
ss.222–224 .... 31.01
s.223 .... 31.11
   (2)(a) 9.47
s.225 .... 3.19, 7.06, 9.07, 14.21,
        15.28, 15.30, 27.13, 27.14,
        27.34, 28.03, 28.16, 29.15,
        31.01, 31.19, 31.20, 31.22,
        31.23, 31.25, 31.26, 31.41,
        34.16
s.225A 31.27
s.226A 9.47
s.239 .... 6.01, 9.06
s.251(1) 28.19, 34.16
s.260 .... 3.17, 6.04, 7.04, 7.19, 7.41,
        7.46, 7.49, 7.52, 7.53, 8.18,
        9.05, 9.07, 9.09, 9.33, 9.35,
        9.36, 9.37, 9.38, 9.39, 9.42,
        9.44, 9.45, 9.46, 9.54, 14.06,
        14.15, 15.08, 20.24, 25.04,
        25.04, 28.39, 29.37, 29.60,
        31.47, A3.137
   (1) 9.33, 9.36
      (c) 9.09
   (2) 9.35
      (a) 3.17, 6.03, 7.48, 9.37,
        9.54, 14.11, 25.30, 25.31,
        25.39, 31.71, 31.100, A3.14
      (d) 9.36, 21.01, A3.14
      (da) 9.37, 14.14, 25.19

1992 Taxation of Chargeable Gains Act (c.12)—*contd*
s.260(2)(db) 9.37
   (7) 9.53
s.262(1) 31.100
   (4) 31.100
s.274 .... 7.46, 13.06
s.279 .... 2.09
s.281 .... 6.07
s.286 .... 34.12
Sch.1 para.1 .... 26.01
   (1) 26.14
   (6) 26.14
  para.2 .... 7.07
   (4) 7.07
   (7) 7.07
Sch.2 .... 7.33
Sch.4 para.4 .... 9.30
Sch.4A 3.11, 5.40, 7.33, 8.16, 8.18,
        8.21, 8.23, 11.01
  para.8(1) 8.20
  para.11 .... 8.21
  para.13 .... 8.22
Sch.4B 3.11, 5.40, 7.33, 7.62,
        7.65, 7.68, 7.71, 10.41, 10.42,
        10.43, 11.01, 11.07, 23.15
  para.3(4) 2.65, 7.65
Sch.4C 2.64, 3.12, 5.40, 7.33,
        7.65, 10.20, 10.27, 10.41,
        10.42, 14.43, 10.43
Sch.4ZA 4.01, 7.72
  para.2(1) 7.74
  para.9(2) 7.74
  paras 10–13 .... 7.74
Sch.5 .... 10.08
  para.1(2) 12.10
  para.6 .... 10.09
  para.7 .... 5.21
  para.9 .... 10.14
   (3) A3.139
   (7) 10.10
   (10A) 10.15
Sch.5A 10.44
Sch.5B 7.11
Sch.7 .... 9.09
  para.1 .... 9.31
  para.2 .... 9.17
   (a)(ii) 9.17
  para.2–3 .... 9.17
  para.3 .... 9.16
  para.4(2)(c) 9.17
  para.5 .... 9.15, 9.17
  para.6 .... 9.15
  para.7(1)(a) 9.18
   (b) 9.18
Sch.A1 .... 7.72
  para.6(1)(b) 7.25
   (2)(b) 7.25
  para.9 .... 31.13
  para.17 .... 7.32
1993 Finance Act (c.34)
s.83 .... 26.01

1993 Finance Act (c.34)—*contd*
   s.87 .... 9.11
   Sch.7 para.1(1) 9.11
1994 Finance Act (c.9) 10.44
1995 Finance Act (c.4) 7.11
   s.74 .... 7.01
   Sch.17 para.27
1995 Disability Discrimination Act
   (c.50) 26.03
1996 Finance Act (c.8) 7.33
   s.73 .... 4.21
   s.154(7) 17.27
      (9) 17.27
   s.201 .... 17.17
   Sch.13 .... 28.19
      para.2 .... 3.30
   Sch.28 para.8 .... 17.27
   Sch.39 para.5 .... 7.48
      (2) 7.48
      para.6 .... 7.46
      (2) 17.17
      (4) 17.17
      (5) 17.17
1996 Trusts of Land and Appointment
   of Trustees Act (c.47) 15.19,
                                 31.25, A3.116
   s.1(2)(a) 30.02
   s.5 .... 5.06, 15.01
   s.6(1) 30.02
   s.11(1) A2.22
   s.12 .... 14.02, 15.31, 28.10,
                                    28.11, 28.12,
                                     31.25
   ss.12–15 .... 15.30
   s.13 .... 15.31, 17.07
      (3) 28.14
   s.14 .... 28.11
   ss.14–15 .... 28.03, 28.14
   s.25(2) 5.06
   s.140(2) 3.09
   Sch.2 .... 15.01
      para.3 .... 5.06
      para.4 .... 5.06
   Sch.4 .... 5.06
   Sch.277 .... 3.09
1997 Finance Act (c.16)
   Sch.7 para.12 .... 4.11
1997 Finance (No.2 Act) (c.58)
   s.32(6) 4.11
1998 Finance Act (c.36) 2.17, 3.09,
                              10.07, 10.13, 10.26,
                              10.37, 12.09, 22.03
   s.128 .... 17.04
      (1)(a) 8.01, 8.18
   s.129(2) 5.02
   s.132 .... 10.13
   s.140(4) 3.11, 9.11
   s.143(4)(a) 20.34
   s.161 .... 22.09
   s.165 .... 9.35, 20.34
   Sch.21 para.6(1) 7.01
   Sch.27 Pt IV 9.35, 20.34

1999 Finance Act (c.16) 3.10, 30.05,
                              31.36, 31.98
   s.64 .... 30.05
   s.75 .... 3.10
      (1) A1.31
   s.104 .... 3.15, A1.26, A1.27
   s.198 .... 36.12
2000 Finance Act (c.17) 3.09, 3.11, 3.12,
                              7.26, 7.62, 9.19,
                              10.17, 10.20, 10.41,
                              11.07
   s.90(2) 9.33
      (3) 9.11, 9.17
   s.91(1) 3.11
   s.92(1) 7.62
      (2) 7.62
   s.93 .... 3.11
   s.95 .... 3.11, 8.13
      (5) 8.13
   s.119 .... 3.11
   Sch.24 .... 3.11, 8.16
   Sch.25 .... 7.62
   Sch.26 Pt II para.4 .... 5.02
2000 Trustee Act (c.29) 30.02
   s.40(1) 4.24, 4.29, 17.14,
                              21.01, 21.07
   Sch.2 para.25 .... 4.24, 4.29, 17.14,
                              21.01, 21.07
2001 Finance Act (c.9)
   s.78 .... 7.16
2002 Finance Act (c.23) 3.09, 3.16, 3.17,
                              12.02, 29.04
   s.120(1) 17.24
      (2) 29.04
      (4) 29.04
      (7) 29.04
   Sch.11 .... 3.09, 12.02
2003 Income Tax (Earnings and Pensions)
   Act (c.1) 3.02, A3.87
   Pt 3 .... A3.28
   ss.97–113 .... 31.90
   s.181 .... A3.26, A3.27
2003 Finance Act (c.14) 3.04, 3.09, 3.12,
                            7.25, 10.17, 10.20, 10.26,
                            10.32, 10.35, 10.40, 10.43,
                            22.12, 35.06
   Pt 4 .... 35.04
   s.43(4) 35.04
   s.47 .... 35.03
   s.49 .... 35.04
   s.50 .... 35.04
   s.79 .... 35.04
      (1) 35.02
      (3)(b) 35.02
   s.120(1) A1.21
   s.125 .... 35.06
   s.163 .... 10.43
   s.185 .... 3.15, 13.17
   s.186 .... 17.27
   s.296 .... 35.06
   s.539A A3.67
   Sch.3 para.1 .... 35.04

2003 Finance Act (c.14)—contd
Sch.3 para.3A(2)–(4) 35.03
    para.4 .... 29.43, A3.20
Sch.4 para.1(1) 35.04
    para.6 .... 35.03, 35.04
    para.8 .... 35.03
      (1A) 35.04
      (1B) 35.04
Sch.11 .... 35.02, 35.04
Sch.16 .... 35.01, 36.01
    para.3(1) 35.04
      (3) 35.04
    para.4 .... 35.04
    para.5(3) 35.02
    para.8 .... 35.04
Sch.39 .... 35.06

2004 Finance Act (c.12) 3.13, 3.17, 3.22,
        4.01, 31.29, 33.17
s.84 .... 24.18, A3.21
s.116 .... 9.17, 9.33, 9.42
s.117 .... 3.13, 7.06, 9.47
s.163 .... 3.12
s.203 .... 21.05
    (1) 20.34
    (4) 20.34
s.300(1) 35.03
s.301 .... 35.03
ss.306–319 .... 36.14
ss.307–318 .... 3.27
s.308(4) 36.16
s.314 .... 36.16
s.326 .... 20.34, 21.05, 35.03
s.393B 20.34
s.395 .... 20.34
Sch.15 .... 24.18, 24.23, 24.30,
      31.30, 31.39, 31.42, 32.32,
      A3.21, A3.22, A3.23, A3.24,
      A3.34, A3.35, A3.47, A3.56,
      A3.59, A3.60, A3.76, A3.78,
      A3.97, A3.99, A3.101, A3.147
    para.3 .... 27.16, 31.38,
      31.63, A3.23, A3.34,
      A3.39, A3.64, A3.102
      (1) A3.57
      (2) A3.38, A3.44,
      A3.45, A3.48, A3.50,
      A3.52, A3.53, A3.92
        (a) 13.34
        (ii) A3.36
        (A)(ii) A3.36
      (3) 13.34, A3.22,
      A3.35, A3.36, A3.53,
      A3.57, A3.92, A3.96
        (a) A3.92
        (b) A3.92
    paras 3–5 .... 13.35
    para.4 .... 13.12, 13.39,
      31.55, A3.25, A3.62,
      A3.64, A3.90,
      A3.99, A3.102
      (1) 31.39, 31.49,
      A3.90, A3.99

2004 Finance Act (c.12)—contd
Sch.15 para.4(2) A3.48, A3.50,
      A3.52, A3.102
    (c) A3.22
    (4) A3.25, A3.38,
      A3.102
    (5) A3.24, A3.61
  para.5 .... 13.12, 13.39,
      31.38, A3.25
    (1)(b) A3.87
  para.6 .... 13.35, 24.28,
      A3.23, A3.34
    (2) A3.49
      (a) 13.34
      (ii) A3.36
  para.6(3) 13.34, A3.36,
      A3.92, A3.96
  para.7 .... 13.35, 31.103, A3.26
    (2) A3.49
  para.8 .... 13.35, 24.27,
      24.28, 24.30, 24.37,
      24.39, 27.15, 27.16,
      A3.22, A3.34,
      A3.42, A3.51,
      A3.56, A3.64,
      A3.69, A3.104
    (2) 13.34
  paras 8–9 .... 24.27
  para.9 ..... 13.35, 24.28, 24.29,
      A3.27, A3.42, A3.51,
      A3.56, A3.95
    (1) A3.23
  para.10 .... 13.35, 24.24,
      24.25, A3.92
    (1) 24.24, 27.18,
      A3.45
      (a) 31.83, 31.86,
      31.89, 31.104,
      A3.44, A3.88,
      A3.89
      (ii) 31.87
      (b) 13.34, 27.35,
      31.32, A3.100
      (c) 13.34, 24.28,
      27.31, A3.50,
      A3.51, A3.100
    (2) 24.24, A3.35
      (a) 13.34, A3.53,
      A3.100
      (b) 13.34, 31.81,
      A3.100
      (c) 13.34, 24.19,
      31.80, 31.81, 31.105,
      A3.57, A3.96
      (e) 31.81, A3.96
    (3) 24.25, 31.81,
      A3.35, A3.50,
      A3.100
  para.11 .... 22.56, 22.69,
      22.70, 24.31,
      A3.23, A3.35,
      A3.56, A3.59,

2004 Finance Act (c.12)—*contd*
Sch.15 para.11 .... A3.75, A3.76,
A3.92, A3.103
(1) 13.42, 22.64,
22.65, 22.66, 22.69,
22.70, 24.31, 24.32,
24.33, 24.34, 24.39,
27.16, 27.17, 31.44,
31.47, 31.93,
A3.23, A3.25,
A3.54, A3.56,
A3.62, A3.63,
A3.74, A3.75,
A3.80, A3.94
(a) 22.65
(b) 22.66, A3.94
(ii) A3.94
(2) 24.34, 24.36
(3) 13.34, 13.07,
22.64, 24.38, 24.39,
27.16, 31.102, A3.96,
A3.102
(3)(a) 22.67, 22.68
(b) 22.68, A3.94
(5) 13.34, 22.71,
24.39, 31.103, A3.25
(a) 13.07, 22.67,
24.38, 31.63, 31.66,
A3.37, A3.45
(b)–(d) 24.20,
A3.35
(c) 13.34, 24.38,
31.63, 31.65, 31.83,
A3.35, A3.45
(d) 13.07, 13.34,
13.40, 24.38, 31.39,
31.67, 31.101, 31.102,
31.103, 32.32, A3.35,
A3.44, A3.45
(6) 22.59, 31.47,
31.94, 31.95, A3.54,
A3.62, A3.63, A3.73,
A3.74, A3.76
(6)–(7) 13.42
(7) 3.21, 22.59,
31.43, A3.54, A3.75,
A3.76
(8) 24.38, 31.65,
A3.35
(9)(a)(ii) A3.92
(11) 27.30
(12) 24.33, 27.30
para.12 .... 22.56, 22.69,
22.70, 24.39
(1) 22.56, 24.39
(2) 22.61, 22.62,
24.39, 31.93
(3) 22.63, 22.65,
22.69, 24.39, A3.34,
A3.59, A3.103
para.13 .... 31.47, A3.23,
A3.45, A3.56

2004 Finance Act (c.12)—*contd*
para.15 .... A3.24, A3.42,
A3.43
para.16 .... 13.34, 29.41
para.21 .... 24.40, 31.42,
A3.29, A3.77, A3.78,
A3.80
(1) A3.147
(a) A3.83
(2)(a) A3.80
(b)(i) A3.78
(ii) A3.78
(3) A3.79, A3.82
Sch.15 paras 21–23 .... 13.34
para.22 .... 24.40, A3.29,
A3.80
(1) A3.147
(2) A3.104
(a) A3.80
(b)(ii) A3.104
(3) A3.104
(b) A3.104
Sch.20 para.3 .... 16.02
para.8 .... 16.02
Sch.21 .... 3.13, 7.23, 9.42
para.4 .... 9.33
para.5(1) 9.33
(2) 9.33
para.9 .... 9.17
para.10 .... 9.42
(4) 9.33
Sch.22 .... 3.13, 7.06, 31.27
para.6 .... 9.47
para.8 .... 9.47, 9.48
Sch.36 para.56 .... 20.34
Sch.42 .... 20.34, 20.34
Pt 3 .... 21.05
Pt 4(2) 35.03
2004 Civil Partnership Act (c.33) 28.01
s.261(1) 21.01, 21.07
Sch.27 para.5 .... 21.01, 21.07
2005 Income Tax (Trading and
Other Income) Act
(c.5) 3.02, 4.01
Pt 3 .... 13.12
Pt 4 Ch.8 .... 28.19
Pt 5 Ch.5 .... 4.01, 4.31
Pt 6 Ch.8 .... 26.13
s.8 .... 4.01
s.34(3) 25.18
s.39 .... 25.14
s.258 .... 4.01
s.277 .... 4.06
s.361 .... 4.01
s.370 .... 28.18
s.619 .... 4.30
s.620 .... 1.16, 4.01, 4.30, 4.32,
4.33, 5.16, 5.17,
5.30
(1) 4.31, 4.47, 5.30
s.622 .... 4.14
s.623 .... 4.33

2005 Income Tax (Trading and Other Income) Act (c.5)—*contd*
   s.624 .... 4.33, 11.06, 13.41, 24.27, 24.28, 24.29, 27.12, 27.16, A3.22, A3.27, A3.29, A3.81, A3.104
     (1) 4.14
     (2) A3.22
   s.625 .... 4.34, 11.08, A3.104
     (1) 4.35
     (2)(a) 4.34
        (b) 4.34
        (d) 4.34
        (e) 4.34
     (3) 4.34
     (4) 4.33
   s.626 .... 4.37, 4.47, 4.51, 11.08
   s.628 .... 4.30
   s.629 .... 4.38, 4.39, 9.43, 29.40, 30.04, 30.05
     (1)(b) 25.08
     (3) 4.38
     (7)(a) 4.39
   s.633(3)–(5) 4.42
     (4) 4.42
   ss.633–643 .... 4.41
   s.634(1) 4.41
     (5) 4.41
   s.637(8) 4.43
   s.638(3)–(4) 4.42
   s.641 .... 4.43
   s.646 .... 4.34
     (8) 4.14
   s.648(2) 4.33
     (3) 4.33
   s.685A 4.33
   s.727 .... 31.39, 31.49
   s.733 .... 26.13
   ss.833–834 .... 2.12
2005 Finance Act (c.7) 2.23, 4.01, 7.03, 4.08, 4.18, 26.01, 26.15
   Pt 2 Ch.4 .... 26.01
   s.14 .... 4.02, 4.05
   ss.23–37 .... 26.15
   ss.23–45 .... 4.08, 26.01
   s.25 .... 4.39
   ss.25–29 .... 26.10
   s.28(5) 26.10
   s.30 .... 26.15
   s.30(1A) 26.12
   s.34 .... 26.07
     (2) 9.45
   s.35 .... 26.08
     (3)–(4) 26.09
   s.37 .... 26.11
   s.38(1) 26.05
     (2) 26.05
   s.39 .... 26.06
   Sch.1 .... 4.08
2005 Mental Capacity Act (c.9) 26.03
2005 Finance (No.2) Act (c.22) 10.17
   s.32(6) 2.22

2005 Finance (No.2) Act (c.22)—*contd*
   s.33 .... 2.59
   s.49 .... 35.04
   Sch.10 para.1 .... 35.04
     para.11 .... 35.04
2006 Finance Act (c.25) 1.10, 2.38, 2.60, 3.13, 4.01, 4.05, 4.06, 4.11, 4.25, 4.33, 5.01, 5.16, 5.23, 6.01, 7.01, 7.04, 7.24, 7.41, 7.53, 7.56, 9.33, 9.37, 10.02, 11.02, 13.09, 13.16, 14.17, 14.21, 14.22, 15.14, 15.23, 17.01, 17.02, 18.03, 18.04, 18.05, 18.12, 19.01, 19.06, 19.07, 20.01, 20.22, 21.01, 21.08, 21.17, 22.09, 22.16, 22.44, 23.03, 24.06, 24.31, 25.01, 25.04, 25.12, 25.13, 25.15, 25.16, 26.19, 27.09, 27.19, 27.24, 28.03, 28.05, 28.08, 28.15, 28.16, 28.25, 28.26, 28.34, 29.13, 29.14, 29.16, 29.35, 29.49, 30.13, 31.29, 31.42, 31.47, 31.70, 32.23, 32.24, 33.01, 34.01, 34.15, 36.13, A3.137, A4.09
   s.74 .... 2.60
   s.80 .... 3.23, 13.42, 22.60, 22.65, 22.66, 22.69, 22.70, 22.71, 22.72, 24.18, 24.33, 27.29, 27.31, 27.33, 27.35, 31.50
   s.89 .... 4.06
   s.156 .... 14.01, 24.08
   s.157 .... 3.23, 8.02, 22.53, 22.55
   s.158 .... 22.55
   s.165 .... 35.04
   Sch.12 .... 2.43, 3.13, 5.01, 5.02, 5.37, 5.40, 7.23, 10.19, 29.35, 34.19
     para.4 .... 14.11
     para.6 .... 7.72
     para.13 .... 11.06
     para.42 .... A1.33
     para.44 .... 7.72
   Sch.13 .... 3.13, 4.32
     para.3 .... 4.06
   Sch.20 .... 3.06, 3.21, 3.22, 7.17, 10.30, 14.01, 24.43, 24.44, 31.30, 31.50, 31.51, 31.70, 34.15, 34.16, A3.105, A3.139
     para.1 ...... 14.23, 25.14, 25.29
       (1) 21.20, A1.10, A1.11, A1.12, A1.13, A1.14, A1.15, A1.16, A1.17
     para.2(3) A1.09
     para.3 .... 14.29, 26.06
       (3) 21.19, A1.09, A3.130
     para.4 .... 18.14
       (1) A1.03
     para.5 .... 17.01, 18.13, 18.14, 28.37, 29.18, 29.20

2006 Finance Act (c.25)—*contd*
    Sch.20 para.5(1) A1.04, A1.05,
        A1.06, A1.07, A1.08
        para.6 ..... 17.01, 19.14, 21.03,
        24.42, 25.01, 26.01
        (1) 26.24, A1.19,
        A1.20
        (2) A1.18
        (3) 26.24
        para.9 ...... 14.22, 19.07, 19.15
        (6) A1.01
        para.10 .... 17.05
        (3) A1.02
        para.11 .... 18.20
        para.16 .... 18.15

2006 Finance Act (c.25)—*contd*
    Sch.20 para.20 .... 17.01, 19.01
        para.23 .... 15.10, 28.40
        para.24 .... 19.04
        para.27 ..... 14.21, 15.29, 19.09
        (5) A1.22
        para.30 .... 25.24
        (3) A1.32
        para.32 .... 9.37, 25.19
        para.33 .... 14.22
        (1) 24.08
        (2) 24.08, A1.24
        (3) A1.29
        (4) 24.08, 28.38

TABLE OF STATUTORY INSTRUMENTS

1980 Capital Transfer Tax (Settled Property Income Yield) Order (SI 1980/1000) 17.08
1987 Stamp Duty (Exempt Instruments) Regulations (SI 1987/516) ... 29.42, 35.06
1987 Inheritance Tax (Double Charges) Regulations (SI 1987/1130) .. 23.17
    reg.4 .... 31.47, A3.73
    reg.6 .... 23.17
1996 Land Registration Rules (SI 1996/2975) 26.01
2002 Inheritance Tax (Delivery of Accounts) (Excepted Transfers and Excepted Terminations) Regulations (SI 2002/1731) 36.04, 36.12
2002 Inheritance Tax (Delivery of Accounts) (Excepted Settlements) Regulations (SI 2002/1732) 36.05
2002 Inheritance Tax (Delivery of Accounts) (Excepted Estates) Regulations (SI 2002/1733) .. 36.07
2003 Inheritance Tax (Delivery of Accounts) (Excepted Estates) (Amendment) Regulations (SI 2003/1658) 36.07
2004 Tax Avoidance Schemes (Promoters and Prescribed Circumstances) Regulations (SI 2004/1065) .. 36.14
2004 Stamp Duty Land Tax (Amendment of Part 4 of the Finance Act 2003) Regulations (SI 2004/1069) 35.03
2004 Tax Avoidance Schemes (Prescribed Descriptions of Arrangements) Regulations (SI 2004/1863) ... 3.24, 36.14
2004 Tax Avoidance Schemes (Information) Regulations (SI 2004/1864) 3.24
2004 Tax Avoidance Schemes (Promoters and Prescribed Circumstances) Regulations (SI 2004/1865) ... 3.24, 36.14
2004 Tax Avoidance Schemes (Prescribed Descriptions of Arrangements) (Amendment) Regulations (SI 2004/2429) 36.14
2004 Tax Avoidance Schemes (Information) Regulations (SI 2004/2613) 36.14
2005 Charge to Income Tax by Reference to Enjoyment of Property Previously Owned Regulations (SI 2005/724) 13.39, 24.18, 24.25, A3.41, A3.45
    reg.4 .... A3.63, A3.64
    reg.5 .... A3.46
        (b) A3.86
        (2) A3.87
    reg.6 .... A3.71, A3.72
        (a)(ii) A3.72
2005 Civil Partnerships Regulations (SI 2005/3229) 11.03, 21.01, 21.06, 21.12, A1.23, A1.25
2005 Inheritance Tax (Double Charges Relief) Regulations (SI 2005/3441) 24.18, 24.43, A3.41
2006 Tax Avoidance Schemes (Prescribed Descriptions of Arrangements) (Amendment) Regulations (SI 2006/1543) 36.14

PART I: GENERAL

This introductory section provides an overview of a number of background matters before looking at the capital gains tax and inheritance tax treatment of trusts in detail (see Parts II and III respectively). Part IV covers specialist areas.

Chapter 1 considers the nature of a trust and the *Hastings-Bass* rule. Chapter 2 deals with the residence and domicile of individuals and trustees. Chapter 3 provides an overview of changes in the taxation of trusts since 1998 and summarises the provisions in the individual Finance Acts. It can be used as a cross-reference to other chapters and also considers in detail schemes such as *Melville* and "home loan arrangements" and looks at changes in judicial and HMRC attitudes to tax avoidance. Chapter 4 provides a brief summary of the income tax provisions affecting trusts.

Chapter 1

THE TRUST

- Anatomy of a trust **(1.01)**
- Trustees' powers **(1.09)**
- The settlor **(1.14)**
- Taxation issues **(1.15)**
- The principle of *Hastings-Bass* **(1.17)**

ANATOMY OF A TRUST

Much ink has been spilt in an attempt to define a trust. Rather like the elephant,[1] however, it is easier to describe than define and the following (derived from Professor Keeton's "*Law of Trusts*") is suggested as expressing the main ingredients: **1.01**

> "an equitable obligation binding the trustee to deal with property over which he has control either for the benefit of the beneficiaries (of whom he may be one) or for a charitable purpose or, exceptionally, for non-charitable purposes".

A number of the elements in this definition are worthy of further comment.

"**An equitable obligation**": this points to the origin of the trust which was developed by courts of Chancery.[2] **1.02**

"**Property**": a trust is a legal relationship involving property which can be of any type, real or personal, tangible or intangible and, if the earliest trusts largely involved land, today the majority exist to hold intangibles such as stocks and shares. Note that until the trustee is the owner of some item of property the trust has not been constituted. It is common practice— **1.03**

---

[1] Or a farmhouse, see *Taxation* June 15, 2000 at p. 277 (Twiddy).
[2] Some date the earliest trusts to Crusaders who before departing for the Holy Land would transfer their lands to a third party to hold for their benefit until they returned, otherwise for their heir.

(i) to establish the trust in "pilot" form (ie the settlement deed will commonly refer to the trust fund as comprising a nominal sum, typically £10, together with such other property as may later be added).[3]

(ii) then to add further property using the appropriate mode of transfer.[4]

1.04 **Trustee**: this is the person who holds the property (but is best described as the nominal rather than legal owner since the property may be equitable, such as an undivided interest in land) on trust for the benefit of the equitable owners (the beneficiaries). He is a fiduciary and as such subject to the duties of good faith laid down over the years by the courts of Chancery. Some would describe his obligations as "wholly burdensome": he is not entitled to remuneration unless this is expressly provided for in the trust instrument and generally may not profit from his trust.[5]

1.05 **Beneficiaries**: these comprise the equitable owners of the property so that if land is transferred to A to hold on trust for B for life remainder to C absolutely, B and C comprise the beneficiaries who are together absolutely entitled to the land in the eyes of equity. Accordingly they can if they so wish bring the trust to an end.[6]

Trusts may be set up for charitable purposes or, exceptionally, for non charitable purposes.

1.06 **"Dramatis personae"**: as can be seen from the above any trust will involve three characters: the settlor, the trustee and the beneficiaries. Commonly in family trusts the same individual will perform a multiplicity of roles: it is, for instance, common for the settlor to be one of the trustees (in this way he can retain a measure of control over the property) and it may be that he is also one of the beneficiaries.

EXAMPLE 1.1

Sid transfers shares into the names of himself and his son to be held on trust for Sid for life with remainder to his son and daughter in equal shares.

(i) Sid is settlor, trustee and life tenant (interest in possession beneficiary);

(ii) his son is a trustee and also entitled in remainder.

1.07 **The Protector**[7]: a protector is largely unknown in UK trusts but common in offshore trusts. His role is to consent to the "big" decisions affecting the

---

[3] The Chancery lawyer would consider there to be a single settlement made up of the original property and the additions (whether or not these were added by the original settlor or another). Additions can, however, create problems in the tax arena: see, for instance, 15.13 and 20.26.

[4] Note, however, that the settlor can declare that he holds specified property on trust: in this case he is his own trustee and no transfer of property is required.

[5] See, for instance, *Boardman v Phipps* [1967] 2 A.C. 46.

[6] *Saunders v Vautier* (1814) 4 Beav. 115; *Re Smith, Public Trustee v Aspinall* [1928] Ch. 915.

[7] He is thought to occupy a fiduciary role but will not normally be thought of as a trustee.

trusts: e.g. who should be given the capital. Usually he will also have power to replace trustees.

Establishing the Trust: there may be attractions for a settlor in establishing trusts in flexible form.   **1.08**

EXAMPLE 1.2

(1) A sets up a trust under which his daughter is entitled to a life interest with remainder to her two children in equal shares. This is commonly called a *fixed* trust: the daughter is entitled to income (but not to capital) and her children to capital on her death; *contrast*

(ii) B sets up a trust under which the trustees are given a discretion to pay income to such of C,D,E,F and G as they think fit with power during the accumulation period to accumulate the balance and with a power to appoint capital amongst those beneficiaries in their discretion. They also have power to add persons as beneficiaries. The trust is a *flexible discretionary trust*.

Whereas in (i) the interests are fixed so that if the daughter has a need for capital the trustees have no power to give it to her; in (ii) the trustees' powers are sufficiently wide to cater for any eventuality. It is desirable for the settlor to provide guidance for the trustees of a flexible trust in the form of a non-binding letter of wishes. This can, and should, be revised by the settlor during his lifetime in the light of changed circumstances.

TRUSTEES' POWERS

Commonly these are divided into administrative (concerned with the running of the trust fund, e.g. powers to invest the capital) and dispositive (powers to distribute income and divide capital amongst the beneficiaries). This division is not, however, wholly satisfactory with some powers being of a hybrid nature (the power for trustees to be remunerated; the power to make appropriations etc).   **1.09**

It is dispositive powers which are usually of most concern in the sphere of taxation. For instance: **1.10**

(i) if a beneficiary is entitled to the income as it arises (i.e. has an interest in possession) then for income tax purposes whilst the trustees are accountable for basic rate tax, any higher rate liability is that of the beneficiary. The IHT treatment of trusts has historically distinguished between trusts with and without an interest in possession. FA 2006 has largely eroded that distinction but there is still a category of trust with a "qualifying" interest in possession;

(ii) the statutory power of maintenance in the Trustee Act 1925, s.31 has both a vesting and a divesting effect. For instance, a trust "for A contingent on attaining 21 absolutely" will result in A becoming entitled to the income at 18 (albeit that capital entitlement depends on his becoming 21). By contrast a trust which gives a minor beneficiary a right to income ("to A for life" when he is aged two) is converted into a contingent interest and until he becomes 18 the trustees have power to apply income for his maintenance and accumulate any balance.

1.11 The statutory power of advancement in Trustee Act 1925, s.32 is equally important. Normally this is extended to permit the advancement of 100 per cent of the presumptive share of a beneficiary. A major use of the power in practice is not, however, to give the beneficiary his capital interest in the settlement before he is entitled to it, but to apply that capital for his "benefit". This word has been given the widest meaning by the courts and enables trustees to postpone the beneficiary's entitlement to capital if that is considered to be for his benefit. Normally this will be by the making of a "settled advance".

EXAMPLE 1.3

Under the Bloggs Family Trust, Sid is entitled to a substantial slice of the capital at age 30. He is currently aged 28 and, as a result of the operation of the Trustee Act 1925, s.31 in receipt of income. The trustees have a widened power of advancement which enables them to apply Sid's share of the capital for his benefit. Sid is currently a hopeless case and will fritter away the capital if it is paid out to him at 30. The trustees accordingly exercise their modified s.32 power to give Sid a right to income for life with a reserved power to give him capital at any time in their discretion and, subject to that, declare trusts for Sid's wife and young children.[8]

1.12 The exercise of both the power of advancement and of trustee powers of appointment is circumscribed by the terms of the power (e.g. it cannot be used to benefit non-objects[9]) and by the rule that for the purposes of accumulation of income and perpetuities any trusts which are created are governed by the periods prescribed in the settlement. In effect the exercise of the power is "read-back".

1.13 A distinction can be drawn (which is especially important for CGT purposes) between powers "in the wider" and "in the narrower" form. The former enable the trust property to be held on new trusts (in effect wholly removed from the old trusts) whereas the latter is a power to modify the existing trusts. A s.32 power is a wider-form power[10] whereas the normal power of appointment is a

---

[8] The exercise of the power in circumstances such as this has important tax implications. For instance, had Sid taken capital at 30, a CGT charge might have arisen on the deemed disposal provided for in TCGA 1992, s.71: by contrast if the trust has been "modified" by the making of a settled advance (rather than a new settlement created) this charge will have been avoided. See generally Ch. 6 and note that there are also significant IHT implications in extending the life of a settlement.

[9] Note, however, that non-objects may incidentally benefit if, in the case of the power of advancement, such an exercise is for the benefit of the object of the power.

[10] Many modern settlements give the trustees an express power to transfer property to the trustees of another settlement under which the same persons (or at least some of the same persons) can benefit.

modifying narrower form power. This, however, is merely the broadest generalisation and the precise terms of the particular power should be considered.[11]

THE SETTLOR

As has already been mentioned, the settlor may be a trustee and may also be a beneficiary of his trust. It is relatively common for him to be one of the trustees: many settlors wish to have a say in the running of their trust and wish to continue to manage the property. It is, of course, important to appreciate that once he becomes a trustee the settlor is a fiduciary and that the property is no longer his to do what he wants with. A failure to appreciate this can lead to actions for breach of trust! For a settlor to be a beneficiary of his trust has significant tax implications: for instance he will normally then be taxed on both the income and gains of the trust.[12] He may also find that he is caught by either the IHT reservation of benefit rules or by the pre-owned assets income tax charge. There is, however, no general rule of transparency and each tax has to be considered separately.[13]

1.14

TAXATION

Generally speaking the trust is a separate taxable entity distinct from both the settlor and the beneficiaries. Hence trustees are responsible for the making of tax returns and payment of tax due. This has resulted in avoidance opportunities in times when the rates of tax applicable to trusts have been less than those which apply to individuals. The present Government has generally raised tax rates for trusts so that they equate to the highest rates that apply to an individual in order to prevent advantages arising when property is held in trust. Recent years have also witnessed an extension of rules taxing the settlor, instead of the trustees, on income and gains of the trust.

1.15

The ill-starred trust modernisation programme sought to develop common definitions of basic trust concepts in the realm of income tax and CGT (although not IHT!). For the tax lawyer a "settlement",[14] especially in the realm of income tax, has a far wider meaning than the normal usage of that word (wider, for instance, than it would be understood by a chancery lawyer). It can include an outright transfer of assets (as where a father opens a bank account for his minor child) as well as an "arrangement". By contrast, the IHT definition is narrower[15] and corresponds more to the traditional chancery idea of a settlement.

1.16

---

[11] Even if there is a wider form power, it can be exercised narrowly: i.e. to modify an existing settlement rather than to create a new one. See, for instance, *Swires v Renton* [1993] S.T.C. 490 and *Example 1.3*, above.
[12] The capital gains tax implications of settlor interested trusts are considered in Ch. 11.
[13] There are cases where the settlor retains such a close connection with his trust that it may be thought to be a "sham". Curiously there are few reported cases in this area albeit much discussion in the textbooks and periodicals.
[14] See ITTOIA 2005, s.620.
[15] See IHTA 1984, s.43 and Ch. 15.

HASTINGS-BASS

1.17 The complexity of the UK tax law has led to trustees making mistakes. They may however be able to undo the mistake if they can successfully invoke what is known as the *Hastings-Bass* rule. This has recently been formulated in the following terms:

> "Where a trustee acts under a discretion given to him by the terms of the trust, but the effect of the exercise is different from that which he intended, the court will interfere with his action if it is clear that he would not have acted as he did had he not failed to take into account considerations which he ought to have taken into account, or taken into account considerations which he ought not to have taken into account."[16]

1.18 The most controversial areas have been:

1. whether the effect of a successful application makes the disposition void or voidable;
2. whether it is enough that the trustees *might* have acted differently if they had taken account of the tax relevant factors or whether it has to be shown that they *would* have done so; *and*
3. whether it also has to be shown that the trustees were at fault as suggested in *Abacus v Barr*.[17]

1.19 Jersey and the Cayman Islands (among other jurisdictions) have applied the *Hastings-Bass* principles in a number of tax cases. (See for example *A–F and ATC Trustees (Cayman) Ltd v Rothschild Trust (Cayman) Ltd* (July 27, 2005) where the principles set out in *Sieff v Fox* (the latest of a long line of UK cases on the point) were applied).[18]

1.20 It had been questioned whether the principle could come into play at all if the trustees were mistaken as to the fiscal effects of their decision rather than its substantive legal effect. In *Seiff* Lloyd L.J. did not accept this distinction. He held that the fiscal treatment of trust property is a proper and relevant consideration for trustees albeit that the trustees do not need to know "every detail" of the tax consequences of their acting or not acting so that being unaware of "some subtle and perhaps unforeseeable detail of tax consequences" may not be sufficient to lead to the rule in Re *Hastings-Bass* applying. What is required is a "material difference between the intended and actual

---

[16] *Seiff v Fox* [2005] 1 W.L.R. 3811 *per* Lloyd L.J. (sitting as a Judge of the High Court) at para.49 based on the formulation of Warner J. in *Mettoy Pension Trustees Ltd v Evans* [1990] 1 W.L.R. 1587 at 1621. It is important to appreciate that the courts set aside the act of the trustees (e.g. the exercise of the power of appointment but they are not competent to replace that act with the action which the trustees wish they had undertaken but did not! The doctrine is quite different from rectification in which an instrument is amended to reflect the true intention of the parties.

[17] [2003] EWHC 114.

[18] See for example *Abacus v NSPCC* [2001] S.T.C. 1 244. In *Burrell v Burrell* [2005] EWHC 245 (Ch.) the appointment was set aside because it resulted in unforeseen inheritance tax liabilities on the trustees.

fiscal consequences of any act". Hence the court would insist on a stringent application of the test as laid down, taking a reasonable view of what it is the trustees ought to have taken into account. One cannot say that every relevant but relatively trivial point they did not consider should mean that the action can be set aside.

EXAMPLE 1.4

> Susan died in September 2005 leaving her substantial estate on discretionary trusts. Her executor/trustees mindful of the IHT bill decide to appoint everything to her surviving spouse in accordance with IHTA 1984, s.144[19] so as to take advantage of the spouse exemption on Susan's death. Seeing no reason to delay and with a view to obtaining the grant of probate without the need to pay any IHT they make the appointment at the end of November 2005. Unfortunately that appointment will not have the fiscal effects which the trustees intended.[20] This is a classic situation where an application to court seeking to set aside the appointment might be made. On the current state of the authorities note that:
> (i) the fact that the trustee had received professional advice that the appointment would wipe out the IHT bill on Susan's death is irrelevant;
> (ii) if the appointment is set aside, the discretionary trusts continue with the consequent IHT charge on Susan's death. The court has no authority to deem the trustees to have made an appointment within the period prescribed for reading back in s.144.

Lloyd L.J. made no determination on the statement in *Abacus v Barr* that the act in question was voidable rather than void. However, he suggested that the court should adopt a critical approach to contentions that trustees would have acted differently had they realised the true position. In a case where it is a voluntary act of the trustees rather than a duty to act in any event the trustees may need to show that they "*would*" not merely "*might*" have acted differently.

On the third controversial point noted above, Lloyd L.J. in *Sieff* concluded (albeit obiter) that, despite the observations of Lightman J. in *Abacus v Barr*, *Hastings-Bass* is not limited to situations where there has been breach of duty by the trustees, their advisers or agents. i.e. the trustees do not have to be at fault for the principle to be applied.

Approach of HMRC: the *Tax Bulletin* has recently carried an article indicating how future cases will be approached and this is reproduced in Appendix III.

1.21

---

[19] S.144 is considered in Ch. 29.
[20] See *Frankland v IRC* [1977] S.T.C. 1450. Had the trustees waited three months (and then made the appointment within two years of Susan's death) all would have been well.

CHAPTER 2

RESIDENCE AND DOMICILE

- Residence **(2.02)**
- Income Tax **(2.07)**
- Capital Gains Tax **(2.09)**
- Domicile **(2.26)**
- Trust Residence **(2.38)**

2.01 Residence and domicile are both relevant in determining a settlor, trustee or beneficiary's tax liability in respect of settled property. In the 2002 Budget the Chancellor, Gordon Brown, announced a review of the rules of residence and domicile. This is still ongoing.

This chapter discusses:

(i) the rules governing the residence of an individual for income tax and CGT purposes. The tax consequences of non-UK residence are also briefly considered;

(ii) the meaning of domicile. The tax consequences of an individual having a foreign domicile are covered briefly;

(iii) the present and future rules governing the residence of a trust for income tax and CGT purposes;

(iv) the emigration of a UK resident trust and consequent tax charges. Other tax consequences of a non-UK resident trust are covered in more detail in Ch. 10.

RESIDENCE

Residence of an individual

2.02 An individual's "residence" and "domicile" is important in determining his exposure to UK income tax and CGT. (Domicile rather than residence is generally the critical issue for IHT purposes although a person's residence can be relevant in relation to the deemed domicile rules.[1])

[1] See Ch. 22.

HMRC's view of residence can be found in their booklet IR20 *Residents and non-residents: liability to tax in the United Kingdom*. Whether someone is resident in the UK is the subject of limited statutory provisions[2] but otherwise the question is governed by case law and practice. There is no certain statutory test in the same way as in other countries such as the USA. The following summarises the basic rules as stated in IR20.

An individual is regarded as UK tax resident for a tax year if he meets one of the following conditions: 2.03

(i) he is physically present in the UK for 183 days or more;

(ii) he visits the UK regularly on average 91 days or more in each tax year. The average is taken over a period of up to four years;

(iii) he comes to the UK permanently or for at least three years, in which case he will be resident (and ordinarily resident) in the UK from the date when he arrives;

(iv) he comes to the UK for a purpose (e.g. to take up employment) that will mean he remains in the UK for at least two years. In this scenario he will also be resident in the UK from the date he arrives;

(v) he intends from the start to make regular visits of the type described in (ii), in which case he will be resident and ordinarily resident from 6 April of the first tax year;

(vi) he decides, before the fifth year, that he is going to make such visits, in which case he will be resident and ordinarily resident from the beginning of the tax year in which he makes that decision;

(vii) he is a Commonwealth citizen, normally UK resident, who has left the UK only for occasional residence.

Ordinary residence

Ordinary residence is akin to habitual residence; if a person is resident in the UK year after year, he will be regarded as UK ordinarily resident. (It is possible to be UK-resident, but not ordinarily resident, for instance, if the person is here for more than 183 days in one tax year only, or conversely not resident, but ordinarily resident eg. if he normally lives in the UK, but spends an entire tax year abroad, e.g. on a holiday.) 2.04

If a person is coming to the UK for the first time, he will be treated as resident and ordinarily resident from the date of arrival if he intends to stay for at least three years. Owning or long-leasing accommodation in the UK will normally mean that he is regarded as ordinarily resident.

---

[2] See ss.334 and 336 of TA 1988.

Leaving the UK

2.05 An individual leaving the UK is regarded as non-resident if he satisfies the 183 and 91 day[3] rules and falls into one of the following categories:

(i) he emigrates permanently;

(ii) he or his spouse leave the UK to work full time abroad under a contract of employment or on a self-employed basis for a period which includes at least one complete tax year;

(iii) he goes abroad for some other settled purpose which lasts for at least one complete tax year.

An individual who departs without satisfying any of the above is treated as remaining UK resident. However, if in fact he satisfies the 183 and 91 day rules for three complete tax years his status is reviewed.

Case law

2.06 The above suggests that residence is generally a question of counting days and given that days of arrival and departure do not normally count as days in the UK, in theory it would be possible for an individual living abroad to work for four days each week in the UK for 45 weeks in the year and still be non-resident.

In *Tax Bulletin 52* (April 2001) HMRC state that when mobile workers retain a home and settled domestic life in the UK but work abroad in the week to such an extent that they are under the 90 day limit, they nevertheless remain UK resident.

Consider *Shepherd v HMRC*[4] in which an airline pilot's claim to have been non-resident was examined in detail and rejected by the Special Commissioner. Although Mr Shepherd satisfied the conditions of IR20 in terms of a strict day count, HMRC contended that this was not enough to establish non-residence. Subsequently, the High Court confirmed that the Special Commissioner had not misdirected herself in law but had accurately set out the legal test that she was required to apply. In *Shepherd* the taxpayer spent half the year outside the UK flying. He rented a flat in Cyprus and was in the UK for less than 90 days from 1999 to 2000 (excluding days of arrival and departure). However he continued to live mostly in the matrimonial home when returning to the UK (despite being separated from his wife) and he was not granted an immigration permit in Cyprus until February 2000. He had to be in the UK before and after each flight. The Special Commissioner concluded that he had never left the UK—there was no distinct break in the pattern of his life and even if he was resident in Cyprus during that year this was not sufficient to lose UK residence. The case repays careful study for the

---

[3] I.e. is not physically present in the UK for 183 days or more and does not spend an average of 91 days or more in each tax year over four years in the UK.

[4] [2005] S.T.C.(SCD) 644; [2006] S.T.C. 1821.

person going abroad who is not in full time employment and retains a house, spouse and children in the UK.

INCOME TAX

UK resident and domiciled individuals are liable to tax on their worldwide income, irrespective of whether that income is received in the UK. By contrast, where individuals are UK resident, but not UK domiciled, tax liability is normally limited to: **2.07**

(i) UK and Irish source investment income;
(ii) offshore investment income, to the extent that this income is remitted to the UK.

Non-UK domiciled individuals will, therefore, be best advised to hold investments offshore, to minimise the impact of UK income tax.

Non-UK residents are liable to UK tax on investment income arising in the UK only. The tax payable is normally limited to the amount of tax deducted at source. The exception to this is UK income from land, which is fully subject to UK tax, subject to relief for the usual expenses (e.g. agents' fees) and interest on a loan to purchase the property and with a credit for any tax collected at source from the tenants or agents of the property. **2.08**

CAPITAL GAINS TAX

An individual who is resident or ordinarily resident in the UK during any part of the year of assessment is taxed on his worldwide chargeable gains made during that year: the meaning of residence for CGT purposes is discussed further below.[5] There are two qualifications to this general proposition. **2.09**

First, where the gain is on overseas assets and cannot be remitted to the UK because of local legal restrictions, executive action by the foreign Government or the unavailability of the local currency, CGT will only be charged when those difficulties cease.[6] Secondly, an individual who is resident, but not domiciled, in the UK is liable to CGT only on such gains on overseas assets as are remitted to the UK.[7]

CGT consequences for an individual with a non-UK residence

By contrast, a person who is neither resident nor ordinarily resident in the UK is generally not liable to CGT on gains even if resulting from a disposal of **2.10**

---

[5] See 2.18, below.
[6] TCGA 1992, s.279.
[7] This is discussed further at 2.12, below.

assets situated in the UK. His domicile is irrelevant. Hence non-UK-resident trusts do not generally suffer CGT. In order to prevent UK residents avoiding tax by transferring all their assets into offshore trusts which then realise gains, a series of provisions have been introduced to catch gains realised by offshore trusts where the settlor/beneficiary is UK-resident and domiciled. These provisions, which are of great complexity, are discussed in Ch. 10.

Trading

2.11   A non-UK resident trust or individual will be subject to CGT if trading in the UK through a branch or agency. In this event the branch or agency assets are subject to tax.[8] The charge cannot be avoided by removing assets from the UK or by ceasing to trade in the UK. In both cases a deemed disposal at market value will occur (compare the deemed disposal which results from the emigration of a UK resident company).

EXAMPLE 2.1

The Salvia Trust is a non-UK resident trust which owns a portfolio of UK let properties in London plus UK farmland which it farms through a manager. The Trust sells all of its UK land. No tax is payable by the trustees[9] on gains in respect of the let properties but the trustees are subject to CGT in respect of gains on the UK farmland.[10]

Remittance of gains by a non-UK domiciliary[11]

2.12   An individual who is resident or ordinarily resident, but not domiciled, in the UK is chargeable to CGT only on the remitted gains from overseas assets, with no relief for any overseas losses. The definition of remittance is wide and catches a sum resulting from the gain which is paid, used or enjoyed in the UK or brought or sent to the UK in any form and a transfer to the UK of the proceeds of sale of assets purchased from the gain.[12] Anti-avoidance provisions[13] designed to catch disguised remittances are extended to CGT. The provisions apply, for example, where a loan (whether or not made in the UK so long as the moneys are remitted to the UK) is repaid out of the overseas gain.

---

[8] TCGA 1992, s.10.
[9] Depending on the domicile or residence of the settlor CGT may be assessed on him in the case of a settlor interested trust and there may be CGT charges on beneficiaries who are UK-resident and domiciled—see Ch. 10.
[10] It would be possible to make a roll-over claim if desired. See TCGA 1992, ss.152–159.
[11] See HMRC Manual CG 25350 ff.
[12] TCGA 1992, s.12(2).
[13] ITTOIA 2005, ss.833–834 (formerly TA 1988, s.65).

2.13 Foreign domiciliaries are not entitled to loss relief in respect of the disposal of assets situated outside the UK. Hence their offshore gains cannot be reduced by offshore losses.[14]

2.14 It is not possible to separate out the gain from the original capital and remit only the capital. The position is different in the case of a separation of income and capital.

EXAMPLE 2.2

> Ethel is resident but not UK-domiciled. She owns a second home in Cornwall that shows a large capital gain, which she wishes to sell. She has realised substantial losses from the disposal of her foreign investments managed by a broker in Switzerland. She cannot set those losses against the gains on the Cornish home. Nor can she set the losses against the gains from any other foreign or UK investments. If Ethel remits some of the gains from her foreign investments she will pay tax on the gains at the rates prevailing at the time of remittance.

EXAMPLE 2.3

> Pauline invested £1m in shares in a German bio-tech company, BTI Limited. These produce £20,000 dividends each year which are paid into her overseas income account. She eventually sells the BTI shares for £2m She remits £1m to the UK. She cannot successfully argue that the £1m represents the original capital and that the gain has not been remitted even if the sale proceeds have been split up. HMRC will tax her on half the remittance on the basis that remittances are treated as taxable gain in the proportion that the gains bear to the total amount in the account.[15] However, the dividend income that has been paid into the overseas income account is not taxable unless remitted.

2.15 A foreign domiciled taxpayer who is UK-resident would be better holding all foreign assets which are likely to show a gain through a trust in order to by-pass the remittance rules and indeed to avoid CGT even on UK-situated assets.

EXAMPLE 2.4

> Freda, who is non-UK domiciled, buys £1m worth of shares in the German company Z Limited. She settles the shares in an offshore trust from which she can benefit. There is no deemed remittance and the trust acquires the shares at market value of £1m. The trustees sell the shares

---

[14] TCGA 1992, s.16(4).
[15] See CG Manual 25401.

two years later realising a gain of £500,000. The trustees then pay capital to Freda in the UK. There is no taxable remittance by Freda since neither ss.86 or 87 apply[16] and s.12 is not applicable. (Note that in certain circumstances if the trust has accumulated income which has not been physically segregated there may be an income tax charge on Freda.) Even if the shares settled were UK-situated and the trustees sold the shares at a gain and distributed the proceeds to her in the UK, there would still be no tax charged on Freda, the remittance basis does not apply.

2.16 Many foreign domiciliaries will therefore hold their assets through trusts. Gains realised by the trustees of an offshore trust are not subject to CGT in the UK even if the assets are UK situated (unless trading assets) and even if the gains are remitted to the non-UK domiciled individual who is resident in the UK.

EXAMPLE 2.5

Anthony—non-UK domiciled but resident—owns a picture pregnant with gain which he may in due course wish to sell. It is situated in the UK. In order to avoid a possible CGT charge he takes it to the Isle of Man and gives it to an offshore trust.[17] The trustees acquire it at current market value but there is no remittable gain by Anthony. The trustees later sell the picture when it is back in the UK by which time it has again increased in value. No tax is payable even if the capital is distributed to Anthony in the UK.

The temporary non-resident individual[18]

2.17 As CGT is generally only charged on individuals either resident or ordinarily resident in the UK it could be avoided by the simple expedient of becoming resident and ordinarily resident outside the UK and then disposing of the asset. FA 1998 (as amended by F (No. 2) A 2005)[19] therefore introduced the concept of temporary non-residence for CGT purposes. An individual who is "temporarily non-resident" (as defined) is taxed on certain gains realised whilst non resident but only on his return to the UK. These rules came into effect from March 17, 1998.

2.18 CGT position before March 17, 1998: "residence" and "ordinary residence" are interpreted for CGT purposes in the same way as for income tax purposes.[20] As a taxpayer's residence was determined for a complete tax year, an individual resident in the UK at any time during that year was taxed on gains realised at any time during the year (TCGA 1992, s.2). It was only

---

[16] See Ch. 10.
[17] He cannot make the gift when it is situated in the UK otherwise the gain is immediately chargeable. Moreover a gift of a UK asset into trust would be chargeable for IHT purposes.
[18] TCGA 1992, s.10A.
[19] Inserting s.10A (9C).
[20] See 2.03 *et seq.*

by concession that the year could be split into periods of residence and non-residence (see ESC D2).[21]

TCGA 1992, s.10A—position on or after March 17, 1998: the basic rules on whether an individual is resident in the UK have not been altered for CGT purposes although from March 17, 1998 ESC D2 was amended to limit the circumstances when the year may be split. 2.19

However, an entry charge has been introduced so that if the following conditions are satisfied an individual who becomes non-resident is taxed on his return to the UK on gains realised during the period of non-residence:

(i) the individual was UK resident or ordinarily resident for at least some part of four of the seven tax years preceding the year of departure;

(ii) the individual becomes non-UK resident for less than five complete consecutive tax years;

(iii) during his period of absence he disposes of assets which he had owned when he left the UK, or he receives capital payments from an offshore trust,[22] or a trust of which he was the settlor realises a gain in circumstances where he would be taxed on those gains on an arising basis if he were UK resident and domiciled[23]; or gains from an offshore company are attributed to him.[24]

In these situations, the individual is taxed as if the gains accrued to him in the year of return to the UK. Because no distinction is made between one intervening year and another it follows that the CGT annual exempt amount is only available for the year of return (that being the year in which the gains are deemed to accrue) and that losses realised in later intervening years may be offset against gains from earlier years deemed to accrue in the year of return. 2.20

It is noteworthy that the Government chose not to impose an exit charge on individuals becoming non-resident. Instead it simply extended the length of period it was necessary for the individual to stay abroad before any CGT advantages could be achieved. It is thought this was partly due to EU constraints on the imposition of an exit charge. See *de Lasteyrie du Saillant v Ministère de L'Economie des Finances et de L'Industrie* [2005] S.T.C. 1722, where the ECJ seemed to accept that gains realised during brief absences can be taxed. See further 9.28, below.

A number of further points should be noted about this provision: 2.21

(i) it applies to losses as well as gains;

(ii) it does not (with certain exceptions) apply to disposals of assets which the taxpayer acquired at a time when he was non resident (s.10A(3)) ("the after-acquired assets rule");

(iii) the normal limitation period for CGT assessments is extended to two years after January 31, next following the year of return in order to catch gains made in the year of departure;

---

[21] See 2.26, below.
[22] TCGA 1992, s.87.
[23] TCGA 1992, s.86.
[24] TCGA 1992, s.13.

(iv) gains (and losses) are calculated in the normal way at the time when the asset is disposed of, as if the taxpayer were then UK resident. Tax will, however, be charged at rates current in the year of return;

(v) there are special rules to prevent a possible double charge under TCGA 1992, ss.86 and 87;

(vi) until the Budget 2005 it was thought that the charge could be neutralised by relief under a double tax treaty (see s.10A(10)).[25] HMRC have now indicated that they do not accept this view;

(vii) taper relief is given by reference to the period of ownership of the asset until sale not the period up to the date of return to the UK.

2.22 **Treaty relief:** s.10A is stated to be "without prejudice to any right to claim relief in accordance with any double taxation relief arrangements" (s.10A(10)). Hence it had been assumed that a capital gains article in a standard double tax treaty (such as between Belgium and the UK) which gave sole taxing rights on disposals of most assets to the country where the alienator was resident at the time of disposal, would apply to prevent a charge under s.10A in the year of return. This also appeared to be HMRC's stated view.[26]

However, while HMRC originally accepted the view that a Treaty can override a charge under s.10A this is no longer the case. F (No 2) A 2005, s.32(6) simply deletes s.10A(10). The change has effect in any case in which the year of departure is 2005/06 onwards. The explanatory notes state:

> "the reason it is being removed is that it is considered unnecessary: its continuing presence in s.10A might cause doubt to be cast on the effects of other tax provisions which do not contain a corresponding statement."

HMRC suggest that the only double taxation relief even in respect of emigrations before 2005/06 is that the individual is allowed to obtain a credit for the foreign tax he has paid (if any)! The country of residence does not have sole taxing rights over gains.

The HMRC view also leaves taxpayers who have already come back to the UK having relied on a double tax treaty and not spent the full five years out of the UK since March 1998 in a position of some uncertainty.

2.23 FA 2005 also introduced changes for taxpayers who became dual resident: i.e. those treated under the tie-breaker provisions as resident in the foreign state, (so treaty non-resident) but who never ceased to be resident or ordinarily non-resident in the UK. They did not need to rely on a five-year absence provided they maintained residence in both states and under the tie-breaker provisions would be treated as resident in the foreign state. However, whenever a person becomes treaty non-resident in or after 2005/06 they will in future be treated as non-resident for the purposes of s.10A. Hence they will need to do their full five years abroad in order to avoid a CGT charge on disposals of

---

[25] See 2.22, below.
[26] See CG Manual 26290: "although section 10A requires gains accruing in the intervening years between UK departure and return to be assessed to tax there is no intention that this charging provision should override the terms of any double taxation agreement. This will mean any exemption agreement specifically given under an agreement between the UK and another taxing state should be taken into account in arriving at any UK liability."

assets. As with non-residents generally, assets acquired and disposed of while treaty non-resident will not be subject to the five-year rule.

Although a treaty non-resident taxpayer will now be treated as non-resident for the purposes of s.10A, gains attributed to him under the ss.86 to 87 offshore settlement regime and TCGA 1992, s.13 will not be postponed until the tax year of arrival back in the UK. In effect gains attributed under such provisions will continue to be taxed as at present: ie on the basis that the taxpayer is treated as resident in the UK throughout the time.

If HMRC's view is correct, prior to March 16, 2005, persons who were not-UK resident under general UK law and lived for less than five years in a jurisdiction where there was a double tax treaty protecting them from gains are worse off than persons who remained UK-resident under general law who were merely treaty non-resident! On HMRC's view, the former have had to stay out for five years throughout the period since March 1998. The latter have not had to unless their departure is on or after March 16, 2005. **2.24**

ESC D2

As already discussed, CGT is charged on individuals resident or ordinarily resident at any time during a tax year on gains made during the course of that year. Heavily amended ESC D2 enables the year to be split so that gains arising after a person ceases to be resident are untaxed whilst gains arising before he becomes UK resident are similarly outside the tax net. Observe the following restrictions, however: **2.25**

(i) the concession does not apply to trustees;

(ii) like any concession it will not apply "if any attempt is made to use it for tax avoidance" (see *R v IRC Ex p. Fulford-Dobson*[27]);

(iii) in the case of an individual who becomes UK resident on or after April 6, 1998, split-year treatment will only apply if he has satisfied the s.10A five-year test. An individual leaving the UK on or after March 17, 1998 will only benefit from split-year treatment if he was not resident in the four out of seven years of assessment preceding that of his departure.

DOMICILE

Domicile is a concept of private international law.[28] It also affects the ability to bring a claim under the Inheritance (Provision for Family and Dependants) **2.26**

---

[27] [1987] S.T.C. 344.
[28] For a full discussion see *Dicey and Morris Conflict of Laws* (13th edn, 2000). In 1987 the Law Commission published recommendations for reforms of the general law of domicile but these proposals were formally abandoned in 1996 on the basis that the practical benefits did not "outweigh the risks of proceeding with them and ... justify disturbing the present long established body of case law on this subject." The 1988 Consultative Document suggested that the remittance basis would be abolished and those resident here for more than seven out of 14 years would be subject to an intermediate basis of taxation. These were abandoned. In 2003 the

Act 1975.[29] Persons who are not UK-domiciled may benefit from a more favourable tax regime.

General points

2.27 The domicile of a person is in general the place or country where he permanently resides or has his home or which is determined to be his permanent home by a rule of law. His home is that place or country in which he resides with the intention of remaining permanently or with regard to which he retains that intention though no longer in fact resident. A person cannot be without a domicile or have more than one domicile at a time.

The domicile may be a *domicile of origin*, a *domicile of choice* or a *domicile of dependence*. These three concepts are discussed briefly below. There is also a concept of *deemed domicile*, which is discussed in Chapter 22 in relation to IHT.

Domicile of origin

2.28 This is the domicile of an individual at his birth. At common law this is his father's domicile, unless he is illegitimate or born posthumously, in which case he takes his mother's domicile. This domicile is retained until the person (not being a minor) acquires another by choice or until, during his minority, the parent acquires another domicile of choice, when the child acquires a domicile of dependence.

A domicile of choice

2.29 This is acquired when a person fixes voluntarily his sole or chief *residence* in a particular place with an *intention* of continuing to reside there for an unlimited time: *In the Estate of Fuld (No. 3)*.[30] He must intend to abandon his previous domicile. In a sense therefore the acquisition of a domicile of choice involves an *actus reus* (physical presence in the territory) accompanied by the requisite mental state (*mens rea*).

Government published a background paper *Reviewing the Residence and Domicile Rules as they affect Taxation*. However, no concrete proposals were suggested: the paper merely summarised the current rules and looked at the jurisdictions of other countries such as Switzerland to determine how they taxed foreigners resident there.

In both the 2005 and 2006 Budgets the Government has stated it is continuing to review the residence and domicile rules as they affect the taxation of individuals and will "proceed on the basis of evidence and in keeping with its principles". Nothing concrete has emerged. It may be that politically a Labour Government needs to be seen to look at this area but in practice there will be no major change. Having said that, changes made elsewhere not directly targeted at foreign domiciliaries have had an adverse impact on their tax affairs. In a sense then their current tax breaks are being reduced by a less public battle of attrition.

[29] See the *Agulian* case at 2.30, below.
[30] [1966] 2 W.L.R. 717.

A domicile of origin will not be lost, even though a person has left that country with no intention of returning, if he has not decided definitely in which other country he will live. The domicile of a person born in England of parents domiciled here is ipso facto English, but if, for example, on attaining his majority he emigrates to Australia he will not lose his domicile of origin and acquire a domicile of choice until he settles in a particular Australian State with an *intention* of living permanently or indefinitely in that State. Residence alone is not enough.[31]

If he afterwards decided to leave that State without intending to return or settle anywhere else permanently, his domicile of origin would revive[32] and if he died before acquiring a new domicile of choice his domicile at death would accordingly be English.[33]

2.30 The residence must be freely chosen and not prescribed by necessity, such as the duties of office, the demands of creditors, or relief from illness,[34] and must be general and indefinite in its future contemplation. The tendency of many decisions has been to emphasise the adherence of the domicile of origin, and to attach less significance to residence, however long, as an indication of a change of domicile.[35] The recent case of *Agulian & Anr v Cyganik*[36] bears this out.[37]

In *Fuld's (No. 3)*,[38] Scarman J. said:

> "If a man intends to return to the land of his birth upon a clearly foreseen and reasonably anticipated contingency, e.g. the end of his job, the intention required is lacking; but if he has in mind only a vague possibility, such as making a fortune . . . such a state of mind is consistent with the intention required by law."

---

[31] A person cannot be domiciled in Canada, Australia or USA (or indeed the UK!) which are federal states: domicile requires connection to a particular territory subject to a single system of law. Hence each state is a separate territory for the purposes of domicile and one must be domiciled in a particular state or province. Difficulties can arise where a person moves from one state to another and he has a domicile of choice rather than origin in that state and a domicile of origin in the UK. If he ceases to reside in one state so that he has lost his domicile there then unless he immediately takes up residence in another state his domicile of origin revives.

[32] See *Udny v Udny* (1869) LR 1 Sc. & Div. 441.

[33] *Re Clore (No. 2)* [1984] S.T.C. 609.

[34] See *Re Mackenzie (No. 2)* [1941] Ch. 69, relating to a domiciled Australian who for the last 54 years of her life had lived in mental homes in England.

[35] *Winans v A-G* [1904] A.C. 287; *IRC v Bullock* [1976] 1 W.L.R. 1178.

[36] [2006] EWCA Civ 129.

[37] The deceased had been born in Cyprus in 1939. He had fled for safety reasons to London in 1957 but retained family in Cyprus. He bought land there and in 1972 returned to his home village intending to live there permanently. In 1974 Turkey invaded and occupied Northern Cyprus and he returned to London with his daughter. His daughter later returned to Cyprus but by his death he had lived in London for 43 years. He retained a Cypriot ID Card and lived the life of a Greek Cypriot in the UK, talking Greek and watching Cypriot TV. He got engaged to Renata Cyganik in 1999 and married her in 2003. He died unexpectedly shortly thereafter and apart from leaving £50k to Renata the rest of his estate went to family members. She made a claim under the Inheritance (Provision for Family and Dependants) Act 1975. For her claim to be successful she needed to demonstrate that the deceased had died UK-domiciled under general law. HMRC accepted that he was not domiciled here under general law (albeit deemed domiciled here for inheritance tax purposes). The judge at the High Court held that the deceased had acquired an English domicile of choice but the Court of Appeal overturned this decision. The High Court judge had over-emphasised the importance of the marriage and that the evidence was not sufficiently convincing to establish the change of domicile.

[38] [1996] 3 All E.R. 776.

This passage was approved by the Court of Appeal in *Buswell v IRC*[39] and *IRC v Bullock*[40] where Buckley L.J. said[41]:

> "I do not think it is necessary to show that the intention to make a home in the new country is irrevocable or that the person whose intention is under consideration believes that for reasons of health or otherwise he will have no opportunity to change his mind. In my judgment the true test is whether he intends to make his home in the new country until the end of his days unless and until something happens to make him change his mind."

In the *Bullock* case the taxpayer's domicile of origin was in Canada. His matrimonial home was in England, but he intended to return to Canada if he survived his wife. The Court held that this contingent intention prevented him from acquiring an English domicile. In the words of Buckley L.J.:

> "The question can perhaps be formulated in this way where the contingency is not itself of a doubtful or indefinite character: is there a sufficiently substantial possibility of the contingency happening to justify regarding the intention to return as a real determination to do so upon the contingency occurring rather than a vague hope or aspiration?"

These principles were applied with a different result in the Estate Duty case of *Re Furse, Furse v IRC*,[42] where an American citizen with a domicile of origin in Rhode Island had lived in Sussex for the last 39 years of his life, making annual visits to the United States. His intention was to return permanently to the United States when he became incapable of living an active physical life on his wife's farm in Sussex. It was held that he died domiciled in England, because the contingency of returning was too vague and indefinite and permitted of almost infinite adjustment to meet his wishes.

In *Re Shaffer, Morgan v Cilento & Others*[43] the question was whether the playwright Anthony Shaffer, who died aged 75 in London on November 6, 2001, had abandoned his English domicile of origin. The judge held that he had established a domicile of choice in Queensland and his English domicile of origin had not revived before his death, i.e. he had not abandoned his domicile of choice. His intention to return to Queensland may have been withering but it had not actually changed by November 2001.

2.31 A domicile of choice, unlike a domicile of origin, can be abandoned without acquiring any new domicile; but it is still necessary to show both a change of residence and a change of intention. It appears therefore that where a person loses mental capacity, having acquired a domicile of choice outside the UK, even if he becomes resident in England he will not lose his domicile of choice because he did not have the necessary intention to cease residing in the country of that domicile.

---

[39] [1974] 1 W.L.R. 1631.
[40] [1976] 1 W.L.R. 1178.
[41] At p. 1185.
[42] [1980] S.T.C. 596.
[43] [2004] W.T.L.R. 457.

In *Allen v Revenue and Customs Commissioners*[44] the Special Commissioner decided that an elderly deceased woman had not lost her domicile of choice in Spain (despite her UK domicile of origin and the fact that she had lived with relatives in the UK in the last few years of life) because she maintained a foreign home ready at all times for her occupation and it was clear that she would have returned to Spain if she could have persuaded relatives to look after her there. She had purchased a house in the UK shortly before death so this decision is somewhat surprising but the Special Commissioner was influenced by the fact that though she had an English domicile of origin she had spent very little of her adult life in the UK.

2.32 It has now been held by the House of Lords that a person in the UK illegally may acquire a UK domicile. While the illegality of the residence is a factor in deciding whether such a person has a genuine intention to remain in the UK, nevertheless it will not in itself mean they cannot acquire a UK domicile of choice.[45]

Domicile of dependence

2.33 At common law, the domicile of a married woman was the same as that of her husband[46] and her domicile of origin was not revived by reason only of her becoming a widow.[47]

This "dependent domicile" was abolished, with effect from January 1, 1974, by the Domicile and Matrimonial Proceedings Act 1973. Under s.1(1), which extends to the whole of the United Kingdom, the domicile of a married woman as at any time after December 31, 1973, instead of being the same as her husband's by virtue only of marriage, is to be ascertained by reference to the same factors as in the case of any other individual capable of having an independent domicile. This is qualified by s.1(2) under which, where immediately before January 1, 1974 a woman was married and then had her husband's domicile by dependence, she is to be treated as retaining that domicile (as a domicile of choice, if it is not also her domicile of origin) unless and until it is changed by acquisition or revival of another domicile either on or after January 1, 1974. Such a change is unlikely to come about except as the result of divorce or separation, since it is not open to a wife (any more than to a husband) to choose a domicile of choice in a different country unless it is supported both by the fact of residence there and by the necessary intention of permanent or indefinite residence there. It is not enough that the wife has a house in another country and lives there for 10 weeks in the year.[48]

2.34 As regards minors and pupils, under s.3(1), which extends to England and Wales and Northern Ireland (but not to Scotland), the time at which a person first becomes capable of having an independent domicile is to be when he attains the age of 16 or validly marries under that age. In Scotland a child can

---

[44] [2005] S.T.C. (SCD) 614.
[45] See *Mark v Mark* [2005] 3 All E.R. 912.
[46] *Lord Advocate v Jaffrey* [1921] 1 A.C. 146.
[47] *Re Wallach, Weinschenk v Treasury-Solicitor* [1950] 1 All E.R. 199.
[48] *IRC v Duchess of Portland* [1982] 2 W.L.R. 367.

acquire an independent domicile when out of pupillarity (ie, at the age of fourteen for a boy or twelve for a girl).[49]

Section 4, which extends to England and Wales, Scotland and Northern Ireland, relates to the dependent domicile of a child as at any time after December 31, 1973, when his father and mother are alive but living apart Under s.4(2) the child's domicile as at that time is to be that of his mother if (a) he then has his home with her and has no home with his father; or (b) he has at any time had her domicile by virtue of paragraph (a) and has not since had a home with his father.

Obtaining a domicile ruling from HMRC

2.35 HMRC will not comment on a person's domicile unless it is relevant to the determination of a current tax liability. Their practice for income tax and CGT purposes is set out in *Tax Bulletin 29*. If the individual has not yet submitted a tax return, HMRC will continue to give a written ruling for that tax year if a DOM1 form or P86 is submitted before the return is due. Otherwise the individual should self-assess by ticking the boxes on the non-residence pages etc of a return, claiming foreign domiciled status and HMRC may then choose to investigate as part of an enquiry.

2.36 An alternative strategy, particularly if the person has been UK-resident for some years but is not yet deemed domiciled (for IHT purposes) and wants a ruling quickly, is for him to settle foreign situate property of (say) £300,000 onto a discretionary trust. The trust is then reported to HMRC requesting confirmation that the person is not UK-domiciled. If he is held not UK-domiciled no IHT is due. If, however, he is UK-domiciled the transfer is chargeable. The authors' experience is that HMRC Capital Taxes will scrutinise a person's domicile with some rigour if this route is used. Indeed they may refuse to give a ruling at all if there is insufficient tax at stake. Their approach is to argue the person is domiciled here but not collect the tax which leaves the taxpayer in a position of some uncertainty. If a ruling can be obtained though, this route is also useful where a person with a UK domicile of origin leaves the UK permanently and he wants the comfort of knowing HMRC accept he has lost his UK domicile. Before asking for a ruling such a person has to wait until he loses his deemed domicile: i.e. he must wait at least three tax years after acquiring a foreign domicile of choice before setting up the trust otherwise there is IHT to pay.[50]

2.37 Any domicile ruling is only relevant and valid for the year in which it is given but if the person's personal circumstances do not change it is unlikely that HMRC will take a different view in later years. Of course continued residence in the UK beyond what was originally anticipated can in itself be evidence of change of intention and therefore a relevant circumstance which might give rise to a different domicile ruling.

---

[49] *Arnott v Groom* (1846) 9 D. 62.
[50] See s.267 of IHTA 1984 and Ch. 22, below.

TRUST RESIDENCE

CGT rules until April 5, 2007

2.38 The rules have been changed by FA 2006 with effect from April 6, 2007.[51] Prior to that date, a trust is non-UK resident for CGT purposes when:

(i) all or a majority of the trustees are neither resident nor ordinarily resident in the UK; and
(ii) the general administration of that trust is ordinarily carried on outside the UK.[52]

2.39 There is, however, a proviso to TCGA 1992, s.69(1) which is relevant for professional trustees. Where a person who is resident in the UK carries on a business consisting of or including the management of trusts and is acting as a trustee in the course of that business, he is treated in relation to the trust (for CGT purposes only) as non resident if the whole of the settled property consists of or derives from property that was provided by someone not at the time of making that provision domiciled, resident or ordinarily resident in the UK. The following points should be noted:

(i) it would appear that the trustee must act for remuneration otherwise he is not acting in the course of his business;
(ii) this let-out does not apply for income tax purposes and therefore is of limited use;
(iii) if, as a result of this rule, all or a majority of the trustees are non-resident, the general administration of the trust is deemed to be carried on abroad as well;
(iv) the aim is to encourage trust companies and professional trustees to attract foreign trust business to the UK;
(v) the trustee must himself carry on the business. HMRC[53] state that one cannot rely on the exception if the trustee is an employee of the firm carrying on the management of trusts or if the partner trustee retires. Watch the position where a UK resident partner retires;
(vi) the rule is compulsory: if a UK resident trust is required, a non-professional trustee should be appointed.

EXAMPLE 2.6

> Henry died leaving all his estate on qualifying interest in possession trusts for his nephew Jason. He was not UK-domiciled or resident when he died. Since Jason is UK resident and domiciled and he is entitled to

---

[51] See 2.43.
[52] TCGA 1992, s.69(1).
[53] TS&E Manual para.1460.

the income there is no income tax disadvantage in having the trust resident in the UK for income tax purposes since he is taxed on the income anyway. Jason acts as trustee along with his solicitor whose business includes the management of trusts and a friend resident in Jersey. The trust is non-resident for CGT purposes. If, however, the solicitor retires or dies, the trust at that point becomes UK resident.[54]

2.40 If the trustees are a corporate body, the central management and control test has to be watched.[55]

2.41 The meaning of the requirement that the general administration of the trust must be carried on abroad is not clear. HMRC say that:

> "this is treated as being carried on at the place where the trustees carry out their general duties as trustees, though we take account of all the circumstances of the trust when determining the location of its place of effective management. General administration is not the same as the concept of place of effective management used in Double Taxation Agreements."

Decision making, trustee meetings, trust bank accounts etc should all be abroad. HMRC comment:

> "The activities of an agent appointed by the trustees to manage the day to day affairs of the trust, for example, to look after the investments, should not normally be taken into account in determining where the general administration of the trust is carried on."[56]

Hence accounts could be prepared by an accountant in the UK but the actual financial records should be maintained outside the UK. Similarly UK investment managers could be appointed to manage trust investments but the trustees should be responsible for the ultimate decisions.

Residence for income tax purposes

2.42 A trust is resident in the UK if there is a sole trustee who is UK resident or if there is more than one trustee and all are resident in the UK. Mixed residence trusts are more problematic. Following the case of *Dawson v IRC*[57] the law was changed and FA 1989 s.110 now provides that where one or more trustees is resident in the UK and one or more is not, a trust is UK resident if the settlor was resident and domiciled in the UK when he made the settlement or at any time when he provided funds for the settlement whether directly or indirectly. If the settlement has more than one settlor this test is applied to each of them and the trust is UK resident if any of them was resident or domiciled in the UK when he made the settlement or provided funds.

---

[54] Although note the provisions in 2.66 in respect of death. See also *Green v Cobham* [2002] S.T.C. 820.
[55] On central management and control of companies, see SP 1/90 and *Wood v Holden* [2006] 443.
[56] See CG Manual 33380 onwards.
[57] 1989 S.T.C. 473.

EXAMPLE 2.7

> Mr A was not UK resident or domiciled when he settled assets into trust. The trustees comprise two friends resident in the UK and one non-resident. The trust is non-resident for income tax purposes but currently resident for CGT purposes unless one of the UK residents is a professional. The fact that Mr A subsequently became UK-resident does not matter provided he does not then add funds to the settlement. Note that if someone else, e.g. Mrs A, adds funds to the trust at a time when she is UK-resident then the trust becomes UK resident.

Trust Residence from April 6, 2007

2.43 FA 2006, Sch.12 amends s.69 so that from April 6, 2007 the test for residence of trustees will be the same for income tax and CGT purposes. The rules have broadly been aligned to the existing income tax rules.

2.44 From April 6, 2007, where a trust is created by a settlor who is resident, ordinarily resident and domiciled in the UK, all the trustees must be resident outside the UK if the trust is to be non-resident. If the settlor is non-resident and not domiciled in the UK it is only necessary that there is one non-resident trustee for the trust to be treated as non-resident for both income tax and CGT purposes. If the settlor is not UK domiciled but is UK resident at the date of setting up or funding the trust, all trustees must be non-resident. Note that the place where the administration of the trust is carried out will no longer be relevant for CGT purposes. Despite representations from the various professional bodies, the exemption for professional trustees will be abolished on the basis that it constitutes "state aid".

2.45 If the trust property is transferred from one trust to another, the residence of the settlor has to be tested both at the time the original trust was set up at the time of the transfer.[58]

A non-resident trustee will be treated as UK resident if he acts "in the course of a business which he carries on in the UK through a branch agency or permanent establishment there". See TA 1988, s.685 (E) (6) and TGCA 1992, s.69 (2D). This will require foreign corporate trustees to review their arrangements when they have UK offices of any substance.

EXAMPLE 2.8

> Mr A was not UK-resident or domiciled when he died leaving assets in trust. The trustees are two friends resident in the UK and one non-resident. The trust is non-resident for income tax purposes but currently resident for CGT purposes unless one of the UK residents is a professional. From April 6, 2007 it will no longer be UK-resident here for CGT purposes.

---

[58] See TA 1988, s.685E and s.68B and s.69(2C) of TCGA 1992.

Contrast:

EXAMPLE 2.9

>Mr A was resident but not domiciled here when he died leaving assets in trust. The trustees comprise one UK resident and two non-UK residents and the general administration is carried on abroad. The trust is currently UK resident for income tax purposes but non-resident for CGT purposes. From April 6, 2007 it will become UK resident for both CGT purposes and income tax purposes.

ESC D2[59] does not apply to trustees and hence the tax year is not split so that the UK-resident trustees may be taxed on gains realised later in the tax year after foreign-resident trustees have been appointed.

Protectors

2.46 Concern is sometimes expressed that appointing a UK resident protector might make the trust UK resident. Generally protectors have powers to appoint and possibly remove trustees and sometimes their consent is required to the exercise of appointments over capital. They may also need to consent to the exclusion or addition of beneficiaries. If the protector's powers are limited in this way it would seem that he is not a trustee[60]: no trust property is vested in him; he does not initiate action or decision over the trust property but is in effect merely vetoing the trustee decisions. It is desirable that he does not control income or the management of investments, not least to avoid any suggestion that he is a trustee.

Exporting a UK trust

2.47 Moving a trust offshore has usually been undertaken in order to obtain all or some of the following benefits: protection from a reintroduction of exchange control; deferment or even avoidance of CGT altogether; and deferment of income tax. So long as the settlor and any spouse are excluded from benefit, UK income tax will be avoided unless beneficiaries ordinarily resident in the UK receive a benefit and the trust produces "relevant income".[61]

For CGT purposes there are unlikely to be significant benefits in having the trust non-UK resident unless the settlor is not UK-domiciled and/or the beneficiaries are not UK-domiciled. If there are benefits in exporting the trust, the impact of the CGT exit charge needs to be considered.[62]

---

[59] See above at 2.25.
[60] See Underhill and Hayton, *The Law Relating to Trusts and Trustees* (16th edn) at p. 29.
[61] TA 1988, ss.739–740.
[62] See 2.51 and 9.27, below.

Can UK trusts be exported?: many trusts start off outside the UK but where a trust is to be moved abroad, what is the position if all the beneficiaries are UK-resident? Most modern trust deeds contain an express power to appoint non-residents as trustees even where the beneficiaries are UK-resident. **2.48**

Where there is no express power, it used to be said that: **2.49**

> "apart from exceptional circumstances, it is not proper to make such an appointment, that is to say, the court would not, apart from exceptional circumstances, make such an appointment; nor would it be right for the donees of such a power to make an appointment out of court. If they did, presumably the court would be likely to interfere at the instance of beneficiaries. There do, however, exist exceptional circumstances in which such an appointment can properly be made. The most obvious are those in which the beneficiaries have settled permanently in some country outside the UK and what is proposed to be done is to appoint new trustees in that country."[63]

This dictum suggested that appointing non-resident trustees is acceptable but usually "improper". The Trustee Act 1925, s.36(1) might imply that residence outside the UK for more than 12 months is unacceptable for a trustee whilst s.37(1)(c) may create difficulties for emigrations pre-January 1, 1997 given that a non-UK corporate trustee cannot be a "trust corporation".[64,65] However, since *Re Whitehead's Will Trusts* judicial attitudes have changed so that provided the export can be shown to be for the beneficiaries' advantage (e.g. in saving tax) the courts are not likely to interfere.[66]

HMRC will not be able to object to the appointment since they do not have *locus standi* but any UK trustee should consider taking indemnities from the new overseas trustees in case beneficiaries at some future date allege that breaches of trust have been committed and seek to set aside the appointment. It is also sensible to include in any trust instrument an express power for the existing trustees to retire in favour of non-resident trustees. **2.50**

Effects of emigration—the CGT export charge[67]

When trustees of a UK settlement become neither UK resident nor ordinarily resident, they are deemed to have disposed of assets in the settlement at market value and immediately to have reacquired those same assets. This deemed disposal is closely modelled on that which applies when a person becomes absolutely entitled to settled property and on the exit charge which is levied when a non-UK incorporated company ceases to be UK resident.[68,69] **2.51**

---

[63] Pennycuick V.C. in *Re Whitehead's Will Trusts* (1971).
[64] See *Adam & Co International Trustees Ltd v Theodore Goddard* [2000] W.T.L.R. 349.
[65] UK resident trustees do not get a good discharge on retirement unless there are at least two persons acting as trustee after retirement unless s.37(1)(c) has been excluded. Prior to January 1, 1997 it was necessary for the non-resident trustees to be two individuals.
[66] See Adam & Co above.
[67] TCGA 1992, s.80(2).
[68] TCGA 1992, ss.185.
[69] See Ch. 17 and 9.27.

Any gains accruing on disposals after migration but in the same tax year of migration are fully chargeable on the trustees although in practice such gains will not arise unless the assets appreciate significantly after the date of migration (when they are rebased) and the date of sale.

2.52 Imposing the exit charge gives rise to a number of problems. When, for instance, does the charge come into effect? Section 80(1) defines the phrase *"relevant time"* as meaning any occasion when trustees become non-UK-resident provided that the relevant time falls on or after March 19, 1991.

A second problem is when do trustees become non-UK-resident? A simple view would be that this will occur whenever UK trustees (A and B) are replaced by, say, two Jersey trustees (C and D). Certainly, if s.80 stood alone, such a simple change in the trusteeship would be "the relevant time". However, the section must be read in the light of the rest of the CGT legislation and under s.69(1) it is provided that:

> "The trustees of the settlement shall for the purposes of this Act be treated as being a single and continuing body of persons . . . and that body shall be treated as being resident and ordinarily resident in the United Kingdom unless the general administration of the trusts is ordinarily carried on outside the United Kingdom and the trustees or a majority of them for the time being are not resident or not ordinarily resident in the United Kingdom."

Replacing A and B with C and D will satisfy part of s.69(1) but the administration of the trust must also be conducted outside the UK. Until that occurs, the trustees C and D remain UK-resident.

2.53 So far as timing is concerned, the deemed disposal is said to take place "immediately before" the relevant time: accordingly the disponors are (assuming that the administration is moved abroad at the same time as the non-resident trustees are appointed) the retiring UK trustees who, given that the CGT year cannot generally be split, also remain liable for gains realised by the new trustees in the tax year in which they are appointed and the administration moved abroad.[70]

EXAMPLE 2.10

> Trustees of the Cloud Trust hold valuable UK land. The settlor is dead. The land shows a substantial gain. They decide that they wish to sell the land. If they sell the land they will realise a gain taxed at 40% They, therefore, decide instead to retire in favour of Jersey trustees in February 2005 when the general administration is moved to Jersey. In May 2005 (the following tax year) the Jersey trustees sell the land.
>
> The effect of s.80 is that there is a deemed disposal of the land in February 2005 and therefore the original trustees of the Cloud Trust realise a gain at that point. They pay tax at 40% and will need to ask the Jersey trustees for funds if the UK trustees have not made a sufficient retention to pay this tax.

---

[70] SP 5/92 para.2.

2.54 Who is liable to pay the export charge? As illustrated in the above example, because the deemed disposal is by the retiring UK trustees they are primarily responsible. It is therefore important that they retain sufficient assets to cover this liability. TCGA 1992, s.82 further provides that if tax is not paid by those trustees within six months of the due date, any former trustees of that settlement who held office during the "relevant period" can be made accountable.[71] The relevant period (broadly) means the 12-month period that ends with the emigration (although not back dated before March 19, 1991). Assume, for instance, that A and B, two professional trustees, retire on January 1, 1999 in favour of two family members. Those family trustees subsequently (on July 1, 1999) retire in favour of two non-UK-resident trustees, C and D, such retirement being without the prior knowledge of A and B. On these facts, the appointment of C and D constitutes the "relevant time" for s.80 purposes and any gain arising as a result of the deemed disposal will therefore be payable on January 31, in the following tax year (ie on January 31, 2001). If not paid within six months of that date HMRC may demand that tax from all or any of A, B and the family trustees.

2.55 However, a former trustee can escape liability if he retired more than 12 months before the migration or he can show that "when he ceased to be a trustee of the settlement there was no proposal that the trustees might become neither resident nor ordinarily resident in the UK" (s.82(3) and SP 5/92 para.5). It is advisable to put a clause in deeds of retirement to demonstrate that emigration was not in mind at the date the trustee stepped down.

2.56 The deemed disposal is of "defined assets" which (predictably) includes all the assets that constitute the settled property at the relevant time. The term does not include UK assets used for the purpose of a trade carried on by the trustees through a UK branch or agency. This is because such assets remain within the UK tax net even after the trustees become non-resident: hence there is no need to subject them to the deemed disposal.

2.57 **Bed and Breakfasting:** *Davies v Hicks*[72] related to the interaction of the bed and breakfast rules with the exit charge on the export of a settlement. It enabled UK-resident trusts to be exported without a tax charge through use of the identification provisions. The bed and breakfast provisions are designed to prevent the establishment of a capital loss (or gain) by the sale and subsequent repurchase of the same assets. TCGA 1992, s.106A provides that where securities are sold they must be identified with securities of the same class acquired by the same person in the period of 30 days. This eliminates any loss assuming that the values remain similar. The argument successfully run in *Hicks* at the Special Commissioners and then the High Court was that when UK trustees sold shares and then retired in favour of non-UK trustees who reacquired the shares within 30 days, s.106A required the share disposed of to be identified with the shares reacquired, thereby eliminating any gain or loss which would otherwise have arisen under general principles (unless in that short period the shares had increased in value). Did s.106A(5)(a) deem the shares to remain in trustee ownership throughout as HMRC maintained or

---

[71] This is presumably also to cover the possibility of any argument that the general administration of the trust remained in the UK after the appointment of non-resident trustees and therefore that they are liable for the tax when it is eventually moved abroad.
[72] [2005] S.T.C. 850.

did the trust emigrate with cash? Park J. held that there was nothing in s.106A that deemed the trustees still to hold shares at the date of export.

> "I cannot accept in this case that a provision which was intended to identify which shares acquired by a particular taxpayer should be matched with shares sold by the same taxpayer can be deemed to have had effects going far beyond that and requiring it to be imagined, for a quite different statutory purpose, that the assets held by the taxpayer at a different time did not consist of the actual assets then held by him, but rather consisted of different assets altogether."[73]

A bed and breakfast arrangement of this type was often combined with what was commonly known as "a round the world" scheme.

2.58 **Sheltering gains using a double tax treaty:** this involved trustees resident in, say, Jersey retiring in favour of trustees resident in a foreign jurisdiction with a suitable Double Tax Treaty. While in that country (e.g. New Zealand) the new non-resident trustees sold assets and before the end of the same tax year, UK-resident trustees were appointed. The aim was to avoid the ss.86–87 charge ensuring that at no time was there a single and continuing body of trustees with dual-resident status. The analysis was that ss.86–87 was inapplicable because of the trustees being resident in the UK at some time in the year of assessment albeit at a different time from the disposal. Further s.77 would not apply because the treaty would protect the gain.

There is, however, an argument that a treaty cannot protect against either a s.77 or 86 charge.[74] If the gains realised by the trustees are not what is taxed on the settlor but a *notional sum* equal to such gains is taxed on the settlor, then no relief is due. Alternatively it is said that a double tax treaty can protect against s.77 but not s.86 gains since under s.86 there has to be determined the gains that would accrue to the trustees if the trustees were resident in the UK throughout the year. By contrast s.77, uses a different wording and requires a calculation first of what gains the trustees would actually be taxable upon in the UK in the absence of s.77 before then attributing such gains to the settlor. The trustees arguably would not be taxable upon any gains that are protected by a treaty.[75]

2.59 In 2003 the Government amended the Mauritius and Canada treaties to stop trusts emigrating to those countries. In 2005 the New Zealand treaty was amended. And in F (No 2) A 2005, s.33 radical action was taken and the whole scheme stopped.

TCGA 1992, s.83A now provides that nothing in any double tax treaty precludes a charge to CGT arising when:

(a) the trustees are, at some time in the year of claim, resident in the UK; and

(b) are not resident in the UK at the time of disposal.

---

[73] There is some analysis of how far deeming provisions should be taken generally in para.26 of the judgment. Arguably the same analysis could apply to avoid CGT on export of a trust where there is no actual sale and reacquisition but merely a deemed disposal and reacquisition of securities by virtue of s.80 itself!

[74] See *Bricom Holdings v IRC* [1979] S.T.C. 1179, CA.

[75] The scheme was also used in respect of non-settlor interested trusts.

This new measure applies to disposals of settled property on or after March 16, 2005. The intention is to ensure that either the settlor is chargeable if the trust is settlor interested within s.77 or that the trustees are chargeable if the trust is not settlor interested.

The demise of *Davis v Hicks*: however, until FA 2006, TCGA 1992, ss.105 and 106A could still be used to nullify the effect of s.80 on shares if the UK trust emigrated. Although it could not be combined with a round the world scheme it was helpful if the settlor was also likely to become non-UK resident for five years and wanted to export his trust. **2.60**

FA 2006, s.74 however amended s.106A TCGA 1992 in respect of acquisitions of shares made on or after March 22, 2006 irrespective of when the disposal was made. The bed and breakfasting rules are disapplied where the person making the disposal of securities acquires them at a time when he is non-resident or treaty non-resident. Hence trustees can no longer avoid an exit charge on the export of their trust by buying and selling shares.

An EU uncertainty: in the light of the decision of the European Court of Justice in *de Lasteyrie du Saillant v Ministère*[76] there is an issue as to whether the s.80 exit charge is compatible with European law. This may have been why the Government has not introduced an exit charge for individuals. As already noted, in *de Lasteyrie* the ECJ indicated that taxing individuals on return after a brief stay abroad may be acceptable. **2.61**

Other implications of emigration

Disposals in year of migration: gains accruing on disposals after the emigration of a trust but in the same tax year remain fully chargeable. The trustees cannot rely on split year treatment because ESC D2 does not apply to trusts. Note that s.83A of TCGA 1992 provides with effect from March 17, 2005 that gains are chargeable if realised in the year of departure even if the new trustees are resident in a treaty country where the other non-UK company has sole taxing rights over capital gains. **2.62**

Capital payments: the gains in a s.87 pool of a non-resident trust are attributed to beneficiaries who receive capital payments in the same year as the gains accrue or who have received capital payments in earlier years where the gains are unallocated. A capital payment is brought into account for these purposes if the capital payment was received when the trust was resident and was made in anticipation of a disposal by the trustees when non-resident. **2.63**

Beneficial interests: a disposal of a beneficial interest under an offshore settlement is generally chargeable to CGT.[77] Of course, there is then the possibility of a double tax charge—once on the disposal of the beneficial interest and again when the beneficiary receives capital by virtue of s.87. Some measure of relief is given under s.85: if the settlement was formerly UK resident and has **2.64**

---

[76] [2004] 6 I.T.L.R. 666; [2005] S.T.C. 1722 and see 2.20.
[77] TCGA 1992, s.85.

migrated, any beneficiary whose interest was created or acquired before the date of migration has some relief. Any gain arising on a subsequent disposal of the beneficial interest is computed on the basis that the beneficiary acquired the interest at its market value at the relevant time. The relief does not apply if prior to being resident in the UK the trust was previously non-resident and at the relevant time it has unallocated trust gains within a s.87 or Sch.4C pool.[78]

2.65 **Trustee borrowing:** any trustee borrowing should be paid off before emigration if it is not within the let outs in Sch.4B. Outstanding trust borrowing under Sch.4B will become relevant once the trust is non-resident (unless the trust was settlor interested in which case it was already relevant): see 10.43.

Inadvertent emigrations

2.66 TCGA 1992, s.81 deals with involuntary exports and imports. Assume that the trustees of a settlement are Adam (UK resident) and Cedric (a Jersey-resident accountant), who does all the paperwork and performs the administrative tasks for the trustees. Adam dies with the result that the trust ceases to be UK resident.[79] On these facts, there was no intention to export the trust and imposing an exit charge in such a case would be unjust. Section 1 enables the charge to be avoided provided that within six months of Adam's death the trustees of the settlement become again UK resident. Not surprisingly, the exit charge remains in force for those defined assets that are disposed of during the period of non-UK residency (i.e. between the death and the resumption of residence).

2.67 The converse situation (a non-resident settlement becoming UK resident because of the death of a trustee) is dealt with in sub-ss.(5)–(7). Reverting to non resident status within six months of the death will not generally trigger the s.80 exit charge subject only to an exception where the period of UK residence has been used to add assets to the settlement and hold-over relief has been claimed on that transfer. Resuming non-resident status will result in a deemed disposal at market value of such assets.[80]

---

[78] TCGA 1992, s.85(10) See Ch. 8.
[79] See TCGA 1992, s.69(1).
[80] See *Green v Cobham* [2002] S.T.C. 820 for the difficulties that can arise where a trustee who was a professional retires hence ceasing to be a professional, and the trust inadvertently becomes UK resident as a result of CGT purposes.

CHAPTER 3

OVERVIEW OF THE TAXATION OF TRUSTS

- Introduction **(3.01)**
- Capital gains tax changes since 1997 **(3.09)**
- Main inheritance tax changes since 1997 **(3.14)**
- Controlling tax avoidance **(3.24)**

INTRODUCTION

When the Labour Government came to power in May 1997 the tax regime for trusts was, in retrospect, relatively benign. Capital gains of non-settlor-interested UK resident interest in possession trusts were only taxed at 23 per cent.[1] Hold over relief was available into and out of discretionary trusts whether or not they were settlor-interested. Trustees of a pre-1991 offshore trust could still realise gains tax free even if settlor-interested. Offshore trusts set up by foreign domiciled settlors could distribute capital to UK domiciled and resident beneficiaries free of capital gains tax. PETS were commonplace whether into or out of trusts. The reservation of benefit rules were easily circumvented through the use of *Ingram* or *Eversden* arrangements or by the making of cash gifts.[2] Pre-owned assets income tax was not even a speck in the Chancellor's eye. An individual could emigrate for three years or even (in some circumstances) for only one tax year and avoid paying capital gains tax. Stamp Duty was limited to written instruments. Stamp Duty Land Tax had not been heard of. **3.01**

This happy state of affairs now seems a distant memory. The pace of change since 1997 has been accelerating. The tax legislation is now found not in three but in five volumes. Whatever the Government's lip service to simplification or stability in the tax system, in the case of clients this is a mirage. The Tax Rewrite Committee is adding to the problem: consider the gigantic ITEPA 2003 running to 725 sections and eight schedules; ITTOIA 2005, which contains 885 sections and four schedules; and the so-called trust modernisation programme which has only added to the confusion by inserting new definitions without removing old ones. Much of the new legislation in so-called plain English does not aid comprehension but it certainly increases **3.02**

---

[1] Subsequently, all trust gains were taxed at 34 per cent (from 1998/99) and at 40 per cent (from 2004/5).
[2] For further detail see 13.15 and 13.16, below.

length! There are plans that the capital gains tax legislation is to be similarly "rewritten".

3.03 Above all else complexity has been caused by the Government's determination to stamp out what it deems unacceptable tax avoidance. Unfortunately, the weapons used to do this often have unintended side effects and may harm the innocent bystander as well as the guilty tax avoider. None of the anti-avoidance legislation is ever repealed even if later events make it superfluous. For example, the restrictions on hold over relief on transfers into settlor-interested trusts surely makes s.79A of TCGA 1992 redundant. Yet the section remains on the statute book.[3]

Retrospection and retroaction

3.04 There has been a further worrying development over the past few years. Prior to 2003 tax legislation was rarely retrospective. FA 2003 broke with this tradition in the area of offshore trusts. The Paymaster General was bullish in her defence in the Committee Stage Debates:

> "What could be clearer than the Finance Act 1981, which stated that there should be a charge? If taxpayers have found a way of not paying that charge when the legislation clearly states that they should, they are playing with fire and can expect any Government to act . . . those who play with fire must expect to have their fingers burnt when the Government restore the legislation."

One may doubt whether the legislation in 1981 was as clear as the Paymaster General suggested.

3.05 The move to retrospective or "retroactive" legislation continued apace with the announcement in December 2003 that there would be an income tax charge (pre-owned assets income tax) on those who had carried out "unacceptable" inheritance tax schemes *since 1986*. Any inheritance tax savings remained undisturbed but the penalty was an income tax "fine" from April 6, 2005. Hence the preferred term used by the Ministers was "retroactive" rather than retrospective.

3.06 The final straw for many private client practitioners came with the introduction of Sch.20 of the Finance Act 2006, presented as an "alignment" in the IHT taxation of trusts. It affects both "new" and "old" trusts.

3.07 Some may have some sympathy for the Government clampdown on tax avoidance schemes even if not for the way in which the legislation is expressed. After all the climate for tax planning may still be regarded as relatively benign compared with 1986 if "straightforward" arrangements are used. In 2006, it is still possible to give away unlimited amounts free of inheritance tax provided the donor makes outright gifts, survives seven years and does not reserve a benefit. This was not possible before 1986. Business and agricultural property can qualify for 100 per cent relief from inheritance tax even if disposed of immediately after the relevant death. The top rate of inheritance tax remains

---

[3] See 12.06.

40 per cent. Inheritance tax has now got onto the political agenda of all parties. It seems unlikely that it will remain in its present state in years to come whichever party is in power. Obvious targets for a Labour Government would seem to be the removal or further restriction of the PET regime and making business property relief and agricultural property relief conditional, or imposing further restrictions.[4]

3.08 This chapter summarises the main capital gains tax and inheritance tax changes to the taxation of trusts that have occurred since 1997 and cross-refers the reader to the relevant chapter where the position is considered in detail. There is then a very brief discussion of judicial and other developments.

CAPITAL GAINS TAX CHANGES TO TRUSTS SINCE 1997

Finance Act 1998

3.09 Major changes to the taxation of trusts were introduced which included the following:

(i) Indexation relief was abolished for periods of ownership by trustees and individuals after April 1998 and instead a completely different relief applicable only to individuals and trusts—taper relief—was introduced. The conditions governing business assets taper relief were modified substantially in FA 2000 and again in FA 2002 and FA 2003.[5]

(ii) Initially personal losses of the settlor could not be set against trust gains of a settlor-interested trust. This was modified in FA 2002, Sch.11 so that they could in some circumstances be set against settlor-interested trustee gains.[6]

(iii) Retirement relief was phased out and had disappeared by 6 April 2003.[7]

(iv) Offshore trusts underwent a major overhaul with effect from March 17, 1998.[8] There was an extension of the settlor charge under s.86 of TCGA 1992 to settlements created before 1991. The definition of "settlor-interested" in respect of future offshore trusts was extended to include grandchildren.

(v) With effect from March 6, (not 17) 1998, FA 1998 introduced a charge on disposals of a beneficial interest if the settlement had at any time been non-resident or if it had received property from a non-resident settlement.[9] The aim was to stop schemes intended to avoid a charge on gains which had accrued in foreign trusts by repatriating the trusts and the beneficiary then disposing of his beneficial interest.

---

[4] See Ch. 32.
[5] See 7.13 onwards.
[6] See 12.03 onwards.
[7] See FA 1998, s.140(2) and Sch.27, repealing s.164 of TCGA 1992.
[8] See Ch. 10.
[9] See 8.14, below and s.76(1A) of TCGA 1992. See *Example 8.6*.

(vi) UK resident and domiciled beneficiaries of an offshore trust set up by a foreign domiciled settlor for the first time became subject to capital gains tax under s.87 on any capital payments made to them if the trust realised gains on or after March 17, 1998.

(vii) With effect from March 17, 1998 an individual had to be non-UK resident for at least five complete tax years to avoid capital gains tax on assets disposed of while non-resident and owned before departure. Further restrictions were imposed in 2005 and 2006 to limit treaty relief and bed and breakfasting schemes.[10]

Finance Act 1999

3.10   Prior to 16 June 1999, if a beneficiary became absolutely entitled to trust property, any capital loss which had accrued to the trustees in respect of that property (including a carried forward loss) and which could not be offset against trustee gains for that year occurring prior to the beneficiary becoming so entitled, was transferred to that beneficiary.

From June 16, 1999 the availability of losses for the beneficiary became restricted to losses realised on the deemed disposal made by the trustees when a beneficiary becomes absolutely entitled to trust assets.[11] FA 1999 also modified the income tax advantages in using bare trusts for infants with effect from March 9, 1999.[12] Prior to that date the settlor could settle assets upon trust for his infant child absolutely and take advantage of their personal allowances without triggering what was then s.660B of TA 1988 (parental settlement provisions). Income arising from bare trusts set up by parents for minor children since then or additions to existing trusts for minor children is now taxed on the parent settlor.

Finance Act 2000

3.11   (i) Section 91(1) inserted provisions (now TCGA 1992, s.76B and Sch.4B) aimed at flip flop arrangements which had been widely employed in non-UK resident trusts. The legislation was widely drafted to catch UK trusts despite the fact that by 2000 the only benefit of the scheme was a 6 per cent saving (being the difference between the trust rate of 34 per cent and the settlor rate of 40 per cent). In any event the flip flop scheme was found not to work for UK-resident trusts.[13]

(ii) Section 95 amended s.85 (which imposes a charge on a disposal of an interest in a non-resident trust) to prevent the "in and out scheme".[14]

---

[10] See Ch. 2.
[11] See s.71(2)(2A) of TCGA 1992 as inserted by FA 1999, s.75 and see *Example 12.3*.
[12] See Ch. 30.
[13] See *West v Trennery* [2005] S.T.C. 214 and 11.06 *et seq*. For a discussion of the anti flip-flop legislation, see 7.62 *et seq* for UK trusts and 10.20 *et seq* for offshore trusts.
[14] With effect from March 21, 2000: see 8.13, below.

(iii) Schedule 24 inserted s.76A and Sch.4A into TCGA 1992. With effect from March 21, 2000 UK-resident trustees are treated as making a deemed disposal of all trust assets if there is a disposal of any beneficial interest by *any beneficiary* and if the trust is settlor-interested or has been so in the previous two years.[15]

(iv) Hold over relief under s.165 was restricted from November 9, 1999 on gifts to companies[16] and from April 6, 2003 (with a change in the definition of what is a trading company).[17]

(v) Section 79A of TCGA 1992 was inserted by FA 2000, s.93 to restrict the use of trustee losses where a transferor has added assets to the settlement claiming hold over relief and he or someone connected with him purchases an interest in the settlement.[18] The loss relief regime generally for trusts has become increasingly complex and arbitrary. See Chapter 12.

(vi) Section 119 FA 2000 introduced a stamp duty charge on a transfer of an interest in land to a connected company whether or not consideration was paid. This has been carried through to the SDLT legislation.

Finance Act 2003

Section 163 amended TCGA 1992 Sch.4C to close a loophole in the anti-flip flop legislation. Schedule 4C was a way of avoiding a s.87 charge on stockpiled gains. These "s.90 schemes" were widely used in an attempt to get rid of the stockpiled gains which could not easily be washed out in cases where all the beneficiaries were UK resident. The Government's response to the s.90 schemes was aggressive and "retroactive".[19] The resulting compliance complexity where trustees inadvertently combine transfers of value with "unauthorised borrowing" is a nightmare for trustees and beneficiaries.

3.12

Finance Acts 2004 and 2006

(i) Schedule 21 FA 2004 limited hold over relief on transfers into settlor-interested trusts in the case of disposals on or after December 10, 2003.[20] This finally put an end to *Melville* schemes.

(ii) FA 2004 s.117 and Sch.22 amended the rules on principal private residence relief: essentially principal private residence relief is denied on a disposal of an asset which has been subject to a hold over relief claim in the past although there are limited transitional provisions. It is

3.13

---

[15] See 8.16 *et seq*.
[16] See FA 2000 and 9.19.
[17] See FA 1998, s.140(4) and fn 21 at 9.11, below.
[18] See 12.05 *et seq*.
[19] See 10.43 *et seq*.
[20] See Chs 9 and 11 and in particular 9.42 *et seq*.

not merely the held over gain which is denied relief but the entire gain accruing during the period of ownership.[21]

(iii) The CGT definition of settlor-interested trusts in the case of UK resident trusts was extended with effect from April 6, 2006[22] so that a trust which can benefit living dependent children of the settlor, the settlor or the spouse (or civil partner) of the settlor is settlor-interested. The change affects all gains realised on or after April 6, 2006 by existing as well as new trusts. The provisions restricting hold over relief are draconian. A clawback charge on the original settlor can be triggered simply because a beneficiary has added property to the trust and it has become settlor-interested in relation to that beneficiary. Moreover it is possible now to have both inheritance tax and capital gains tax payable on the transfer of assets into a settlement without relief being given for one tax against the other.[23]

(iv) FA 2006 introduced the sub-fund elections for capital gains tax purposes.[24]

(v) Sections 72 of 73 of TCGA 1992 have been amended by FA 2006 so that if the interest in possession arises on or after March 22, there is generally no deemed disposal or base cost uplift to market value on the death of the life tenant.[25]

(vi) Schedules 12 and 13 of FA 2006 changes the rules governing the residence of trustees with effect from April 6, 2007.

MAIN INHERITANCE TAX CHANGES SINCE 1997

Background

3.14 Inheritance tax is an increasing mess. Capital transfer tax was introduced (without prior consultation!) in the 1974 Budget by the then Labour Chancellor, Dennis Healey. Its purpose was intended to achieve a major redistribution of wealth. All gifts of property whether made inter vivos or on death were cumulated with earlier gifts and progressive rates of tax applied to that cumulative total. The idea of a fully comprehensive cradle to the grave tax was abandoned in 1982 by the Conservatives in favour of 10-year cumulation. In FA 1986, 10 year cumulation was reduced to seven years and most lifetime gifts made more than seven years before death were removed from charge altogether (they became PETs). The rules taxing gifts with a reservation of benefit were reintroduced from the estate duty legislation. The tax was rechristened inheritance tax.

3.15 For the next 20 years those practitioners who engaged in inheritance tax planning operated under a relatively peaceful regime. There was the usual cat and

---

[21] See 9.46 *et seq.*
[22] See FA 2006, Sch.12.
[23] See 9.52 and *Example 9.22*. IHTA 1984, s.165 affords only limited relief if the donee pays CGT on the gift: see TGCA 1992, s.282.
[24] Discussed at 7.72 *et seq.*
[25] This follows from the restrictions on creating qualifying interests in possession after March 21, 2006.

mouse game between practitioners and HMRC to stop the taxpayer circumventing the reservation of benefit rules. Hence in 1999 targeted legislation to stop *Ingram* schemes was introduced.[26] In 2003 *Eversden* schemes were stopped in relation to disposals made on or after June 20, 2003.[27] The legislation did not attempt to go further and stop inheritance tax schemes more generally.

Melville schemes: The *Melville* scheme took two attempts to close down! Section 5(2) of IHTA 1984 provides that

3.16

> "a person who has a general power which enables him, or would if he were sui juris enable him, to dispose of any property other than settled property . . . shall be treated as beneficially entitled to the property or money. . ."

Hence if a person makes a revocable gift of property into settlement, s.5(2) does not apply and he is not treated as beneficially entitled to the settled property. Although he in fact has the power to revoke the gift, the property ceases to be part of his estate and prima facie there is a PET or an immediately chargeable transfer by him.

If the settlor were then to revoke the gift, the property would again form part of, and augment the value of, his estate; and if he made a further gift of it, it would be taxable as such, or if he died possessed of it, the property, would be part of his taxable estate on his death. In this situation the question arises: what is the value transferred by the revocable gift into settlement? In *Melville v IRC*[28] the settlor transferred property into a discretionary settlement under which he was a potential beneficiary, and reserved a power by which he could direct the trustees to transfer the fund back to him. The Revenue argued that the value transferred was the whole settled fund, no part of which remained in the settlor's estate; but Lightman J. decided otherwise. Under s.272 "property" includes rights and interests of any description, and he had no doubt that the power reserved by the settlor constituted a proprietary right or interest which he could at any time realise either by selling a release or by exercising the power in his own favour. He held that the *power itself* was property that formed part of the settlor's estate even though the settled property was excluded from the settlor's estate under s.5(2).[29] Its value would be approximately equal to that of the settled fund, so that the value transferred by the gift was insignificant and would fall within the settlor's available nil rate band. Agreeing with him, the Court of Appeal described as "a truly remarkable proposition" the Revenue's argument that although the holder of a general power has effective dominion over the settled property, nevertheless it is to be left out of account on his death.

The *Melville* decision was reversed, with effect from April 17, 2002, by FA 2002 which provided that a "settlement power" is not "property" for IHT purposes (see IHTA 1984, s.47A for the definition of "settlement power" and note the amended definition of "property" in s.272 of that Act). Further, in the case of deaths occurring before that date this change is deemed always to have had

---

[26] FA 1999, s.104 inserting new s.102A–C into FA 1986 and see 13.15.
[27] See FA 2003, s.185 inserting s.102(5B) into FA 1986 and see 13.16 and Ch. 24.
[28] [2000] S.T.C. 628; [2001] S.T.C. 1271.
[29] Subject to the reservation of benefit rules.

effect for the purpose of determining the value of a person's estate immediately before death. Consequently in those cases where a taxpayer died without having exercised a settlement power tax was not payable on any value attributable to that power.

This legislation was closely targeted to deal with the problems posed by "settlement powers" but did not prevent the same principle—namely that the settlor was taxed on the loss to his estate not the value of what he gave away—being adapted and used in further schemes ("*Melville Mark II Schemes*").

3.17 Assume that Mr A owned a substantial portfolio of investment properties and wished to put them into an accumulation and maintenance trust. The portfolio was pregnant with unrealised capital gains. Were Mr A directly to gift the properties into the desired trust then whilst there would have been no immediate IHT charge (since he would make a potentially exempt transfer) the disposal would have triggered a capital gains tax charge. It was the aim of "*Melville* arrangements" to enable Mr A to achieve his goal (of putting the properties into an A&M trust) without triggering any charge to the capital taxes. The first stage in the arrangement involved the creation of a discretionary trust. Provided that this involves a chargeable transfer by Mr A, any gains arising on the disposal of assets to the trust could be held over under s.260(2)(a) of TCGA 1992. Prior to April 17, 2002 Mr A retained a "settlement power" (such as a power to revoke the settlement). The fall in value of Mr A's estate would then be the difference between the value of the property settled (£1m) and the value of the settlement power retained (close to £1m). From April 2002 the alternative (rendered necessary by FA 2002) was to draft the discretionary settlement so that the settlor retained a valuable trust interest such as a remainder or reversionary interest. Although "reversionary interests" are generally excluded property this is not the case if it is one to which the settlor is beneficially entitled.[30] The fall in value of Mr A's estate would then be the difference between the value of the property settled and the value of the interest retained by him.

Taking the above factors into account a typical discretionary trust would exhibit the following features:

(i) the trustees would be given a power to distribute income during the "Trust Period" and would have power to accumulate any surplus;

(ii) at the end of the "Trust Period" (usually between three and six months) capital and income would revert to the settlor absolutely provided that he was then alive (this being the retained reversionary interest).

In simple terms A was entitled to the trust fund if he was still alive in (say) 100 days. He therefore lost the use of—and any income from—the trust property for that period whilst there was of course the risk that he would die during the 100-day period. In many cases the fall in value of the estate was minimal. The trustees' powers to distribute capital during this period were limited.

The objective of Mr A was eventually to put the properties into an A&M trust. Before the end of the Trust Period Mr A assigned his reversionary interest into an A&M trust: this was a potentially exempt transfer. At the end of that period the property then passed from the discretionary trust into the A&M with

---

[30] See IHTA 1984, s.48(1)(b) and 22.46.

hold-over relief). Alternatively the discretionary trustees were given a power of appointment exercisable during the Trust Period and which could be used to create the desired A&M trust. This power would require either the express consent of Mr A or his tacit acquiescence. If the power was duly exercised the effect was to render the value of Mr A's retained reversionary interest nominal.

In the Autumn Statement of December 10, 2003 the Chancellor announced that in the case of disposals of property on or after December 10, 2003 capital gains tax hold over relief under either s.165 of TCGA 1992 or s.260 on disposals to discretionary trusts would not be available if the disposal was to a settlor-interested truist.[31] This effectively put an end to *Melville* planning.

Home loan schemes

The home loan (or as it is sometimes called the "double trust") scheme was widely employed until December 2003. Curiously unlike *Ingram* and *Eversden* schemes no specific inheritance tax legislation has yet been passed to stop the home loan scheme which can still be done in modified form without the use of trusts[32] although HMRC have indicated that in their view some versions of the scheme fall within the reservation of benefit net.[33] **3.18**

Although a "guesstimate", it has been suggested that as many as 30,000 of these schemes were implemented. There was no "single" home loan scheme: rather there were a number of variants. The demand for the scheme was generated by the significant rise in house prices in the 1990s which was not accompanied by a corresponding increase in the IHT nil rate band. The result was that many individuals found that simply by virtue of owning a house, IHT would be payable on their death and so their wish (to pass the property to their children) would be thwarted.

The structure of a typical home loan scheme

Step 1: S set up a life interest trust ("Trust 1") under the terms of which he is a life tenant with the right to enjoy the income of the trust or to enjoy the use of trust property. The trustees are given the usual modern flexible powers: e.g. to advance capital to S or to terminate his life interest. The remainder beneficiaries of this trust are S's family. **3.19**

Step 2: S set up a second (generally) interest in possession trust ("Trust 2") for the benefit of his children. S was wholly excluded from benefit under this trust.

Step 3: S sold his house to the trustees of Trust 1 and S made them a loan to enable the transaction to proceed. In effect, the purchase price was left outstanding as a debt owned by Trust 1 to S.

---

[31] See FA 2004 which inserts s.169B–G into TCGA 1992 and Ch. 9.
[32] See Ch. 31.
[33] See revised HMRC POA guidance notes issued in May 2006. See Appendix III A3.61 and 31.43.

Step 4: the debt (i.e. the right to repayment) was gifted by S into Trust 2 (a PET by S).

Diagrammatically the position is as follows:

TRUST 1	TRUST 2
Owns property worth £450k and owes Trust 2 £450k	*Is owed £450k by Trust 1*
↓	↓
S is life tenant and hence can continue to live in the property PPR relief will be available to the Trustees under TCGA 1992, s.225.	S is excluded from all benefit—the beneficiaries are S's children.

The sale to the Trustees of Trust 1 will now attract SDLT: prior to December 1, 2003 (i.e. in the (good old) days of Stamp Duty) duty could be postponed by resting in contract.

On S's death the position was as follows:

(i) he enjoyed a life interest in Trust 1 and so was subject to IHT on the house (see IHTA 1984, s.49(1)). On these facts and if we assume no movement in the value of the property, because the debt reduced the value of the house to nil, the result was that the net value of the property subject to IHT was nil (value of house exactly offset by debt owing);

(ii) provided S survived by seven years, the PET of the debt was left out of account (*i.e.* it was an exempt transfer); and even if he did not, there was often a substantial discount if the debt was not repayable until the death of S.

3.20 It was in the precise terms of the loan that the schemes varied significantly:

(i) in some cases it was an interest-free demand loan;

(ii) in others it was interest-free but repayable on the death of S;

(iii) sometimes interest was payable and rolled up with the principal; in other cases the debt was indexed (e.g. by reference to RPI or to a property index);

(iv) in some cases the loan was structured as a relevant discounted security but repayable on demand and in other cases as a relevant discounted security repayable only on the death of S and

(v) one arrangement involved the use of a tripartite loan agreement between S and the two sets of trustees, thereby avoiding the necessity for a separate assignment of the debt by S. This might avoid capital gains tax problems on repayment of the debt to Trust 2 (given that the trustees of Trust 2 would not otherwise be the original creditor).

In some cases the trustees of Trust 1 incurred no personal liability for the debt. It could only be satisfied out of the assets of the Trust Fund and the trustees were not permitted to make distributions until the loan had been discharged. In other cases the trustees of Trust 1 incurred personal liability (albeit they probably did not realise this).

HMRC's approach to Home Loan Schemes: HMRC were aware of the existence of such schemes for a number of years and for some time indicated that they would challenge their effectiveness. In the event HMRC have indicated that they intend to challenge those home loan schemes where the debt is made repayable on demand even if interest bearing with interest rolled up and compounded. This is on the basis that by failing to call in the loan before the death of the donor he has reserved a benefit in the debt by associated operations. The result (if this argument is correct) would be that the debt was taxed as part of the settlor's estate on his death and the inheritance tax savings nullified. No case has yet reached the courts on this point.

3.21

In any event many home loan schemes have been wound up because of the POA charge that came into operation from April 6, 2005. There were various arguments against the POA Regime applying[34] but most people concluded that the double trust version of the home loan scheme was and is caught by POA on the basis that the debt is an "excluded liability" within para.11(7) Sch.15 of FA 2004. The options open to those who carried out home loan schemes have become increasingly limited following the Sch.20 changes.

The POA Legislation

FA 2004 introduced pre-owned assets income tax charge. The intention was to deter taxpayers from carrying out aggressive inheritance tax planning by imposing an (annual) income tax "fine" on them.

3.22

FA 2006: Sch.20 introduced major changes to the IHT taxation of trusts and s.80 stopped reverter to settlor trusts being used to circumvent the POA charge. Section 157 amended s.48 of IHTA 1984 to prevent death-bed schemes involving the acquisition of an interest under an excluded property settlement[35] and Sch.20 extends the reservation of benefit rules to deal with termination of interests in possession.[36]

3.23

The complexity of all this tax law had led to trustees making mistakes. They have a useful friend in the form of the *Hastings-Bass* rule. In *Tax Bulletin 83* HMRC have issued their own view of the case law on *Hastings-Bass*. (The statement is set out in Appendix III A3.147). *Hasting-Bass* is discussed further in Chapter 1, above.

CONTROLLING TAX AVOIDANCE

So far HMRC have dealt with tax avoidance by a combination of specific legislation to cover the particular scheme (sometimes with retroactive effect) combined with the introduction of a requirement to disclose tax schemes

3.24

---

[34] See *Pre-owned Assets Income Tax and Tax Planning Strategies* by Chamberlain and Whitehouse (2nd edn, 2005), Ch. 17 and 31.43, below.
[35] See Ch. 22.
[36] See 24.08.

involving avoidance of income tax, capital gains tax, corporation tax, SDLT and VAT.[37]

Inheritance tax schemes are still not subject to disclosure requirements although schemes to avoid pre-owned assets income tax generally are. The disclosure rules enable HMRC to act rapidly in closing down a particular loophole. The rules on the direct taxes came into effect from August 1, 2004 and from August 1, 2006 were widened to catch a greater variety of schemes.

3.25 No general anti-avoidance provision has so far been introduced.[38]

3.26 **Judicial approach:** HMRC have also in recent years been successful in the courts—judicial attitudes are, at present, not in favour of aggressive avoidance schemes in a line of cases reinterpreting the *Ramsay* principle. This chapter can do no more than briefly mention the cases.

3.27 In *Macniven v Westmoreland Investments Ltd*[39] the dispute between HMRC and the taxpayer was whether interest paid by a company ("WIL") was "paid" within the meaning of s.338 of the Taxes Act 1988. It arose because WIL paid the interest out of money lent by the creditor for the specific purpose of enabling it to be paid. The liability for interest was replaced by a liability for an additional capital sum. The transaction was circular: WIL borrowed capital and paid it back as interest. The only purpose of the transaction was to produce an allowable deduction for corporation tax.

The Special Commissioners found that the accrued interest was real, that it had been paid within the meaning of s.338, and that it gave rise to an allowable deduction. Their decision was reversed by Carnwath J, but restored by the Court of Appeal whose decision was upheld in the House of Lords.

Lord Nicholls of Birkenhead said that a genuine discharge of a genuine debt could not cease to qualify as a payment for the purpose of s.338 by reason only that it was made solely to secure a tax advantage. Nothing in the language or context of s.338 suggested that the purpose for which a payment of interest is made is material. Parliament could not have intended that "payment" in s.338 should bear some special meaning which would exclude cases where the interest debt was satisfied with money borrowed from the creditor.

Lord Hoffmann emphasised that:

> "Lord Brightman's formulation in the *Furniss* case, like Lord Diplock's formulation in the *Burmah* case, is not a principle of construction. It is a statement of the consequences of giving a commercial construction to

---

[37] See FA 2004, ss.307–318 and the Tax Avoidance Schemes (Promoters and Prescribed Circumstances) Regs 2004, the Tax Avoidance Schemes (Prescribed Descriptions of Arrangements) Regs 2004 and the Tax Avoidance Schemes (Information) Regs 2004. The rules were extended in SI 2006/1544. On disclosure, see Ch. 36.

[38] *C.f.* Australia and New Zealand which have a GAAP and see IFS Tax Law Review Committee's Proposal 1997 which suggested that a general anti-avoidance rule with proper safeguards might be preferable to the present uncertain state of case law. In 1998 the Revenue published a consultation paper on the proposed general anti-avoidance rule which was to apply to direct corporate taxes only. The TLRC then announced that it would be unable to support a GAAR of the type suggested by the Revenue in the paper.

[39] [2001] 2 W.L.R. 377.

a fiscal concept. Before one can apply Lord Brightman's words, it is first necessary to construe the statutory language and decide that it refers to a concept which Parliament intended to be given a commercial meaning capable of transcending the juristic individuality of its component parts. But there are many terms in tax legislation which cannot be construed in this way. They refer to purely legal concepts which have no broader commercial meaning. In such cases, the Ramsay principle can have no application."

Lord Hutton said that *Macniven* was not a case like *McGuckian*, where a taxpayer was on the point of incurring a tax liability and took an artificial step to avoid that liability. In *Westmoreland* the company had incurred a genuine loss for tax purposes and then took a step to enable it to claim the tax allowance for that loss.

3.28 Before *Macniven* the essentials of the *Ramsay* doctrine had been summarised in *Craven* v *White*[40] as follows:

(i) a series of transactions which at the time when the intermediate transaction was entered into were pre-ordained;

(ii) the transaction had no main purpose other than tax saving;

(iii) there was at that time no practical likelihood that the pre-planned events would not take place in the order ordained; and

(iv) the pre-ordained events did take place.

It was noteworthy that a distinction was drawn in *Craven* between "reforming transactions" and "ascertaining their reality". Lord Oliver commented: "in the latter case to link the end to the beginning involves no more than recognising the reality of what is effectively a single operation *ab initio*": i.e. recognising the facts as they actually were.

In *Macniven* Lord Hoffmann noted Lord Cooke's comment in *IRC v McGuckian* : "always one must go back to the discernible intent of the taxing Act". He suggested one did not look first to ascertain whether there was a composite transaction or pre-ordained series of events. One concentrated first on the proper interpretation of the statutory provision: what did the statute mean? One then considered whether the transaction in question was the sort of transaction which the statute had in mind. The Court thus seemed to be reducing the relevance of pre-ordination as a test in its own right, removing the difference between avoidance and mitigation and looking at "the intendment of the statute". A lecture by Lord Walker to the Chancery Bar Association in March 2004 rejected as over-simplistic the distinction between tax avoidance and tax mitigation.[41]

Although *Macniven* seemed to focus on the distinction between commercial concepts and juristic or legal concepts, Lord Hoffmann subsequently said in a 2003 lecture to the International Fiscal Association that this part of his judgment in *Macniven* had been misinterpreted. He indicated that one should not examine the particular words in a statute to ascertain whether they were

---

[40] [1988] S.T.C. 476, HL.
[41] The lecture is published in (2004) PCB at p. 249.

juristic or commercial but rather the whole transaction in its entirety. So the purposive approach was applied not just to the construction of a statute but also to the characterisation of the facts. Hence the same word (for example "*payment*") could be subject to a different analysis depending on the particular facts. Lord Walker's lecture appeared to support this approach. He suggested that the *Ramsay* principle is no more and no less than a new and more realistic approach to the construction of taxing statutes and as an associated issue the analysis of the facts to which the statutory provisions have to be applied.

3.29 The key questions to ask now appear to be:

(i) What does the statute mean?

(ii) Is this the sort of transaction that the legislation has in mind?

(iii) What is the transaction to which the statute should be applied?

Carreras Group Ltd v *The Stamp Commissioner*[42] was a Jamaican case heard by the Privy Council. On April 27, 1999 Carreras Group entered into a written agreement to transfer all the issued ordinary share capital (in Jamaica Biscuit) in exchange for a debenture issued by the purchasing company. It was not secured or transferable. The principal debt carried no interest and it was redeemable less than two weeks later. The debenture was redeemed on May 11, 1999. The question was whether the transfer of shares in exchange for the debenture was chargeable to transfer tax. Could the relevant transaction properly be regarded as a reorganisation (in which case there would be no tax) or should it really be regarded as a sale for cash?

Lord Hoffmann noted:

> "if the relevant transaction is confined to what happened on April 27, by virtue of the agreement executed on that date, there can be no doubt that it fell within [the description of a reoragnisation]. On the other hand if one is allowed to take a wider view into the terms of the debenture and its redemption two weeks later as part of the relevant transaction, it looks very different. From this perspective the debenture is only a formal step having no apparent commercial purpose or significance in the transaction by which the shares in Jamaica Biscuit were exchanged for money."

The transaction taken as a whole could not appropriately be categorised as an exchange of shares for debentures:

> "The *Ramsay* approach does not deny the existence or legality of the individual steps but may deprive them of significance for the purposes of the re-characterisation required by statute. This has been said so often that citation of authorities since *Ramsay* is unnecessary."

3.30 The courts must construe not just the legislation but also the facts: the courts held in *Carreras* that it was always intended the vendors would receive cash. Thus a relevant matter for analysis was the whole process of payment in

---

[42] [2004] S.T.C. 1377; PC.

Carreras not (unlike *Macniven*) just the act of loan and repayment. Hence one identifies the first step in the avoidance and applies *Ramsay* from that event onwards.

In *Campbell* v *IRC*[43] the Special Commissioners allowed an appeal by a taxpayer against the refusal of loss relief on the transfer to his wife of a relevant discounted security. Although the sole purpose of the taxpayer on the gift to his wife was to produce a tax loss, the taxpayer had a commercial purpose in subscribing for the loan notes in the first place. The circumstances in which a person sustained a loss on a relevant discounted security and the amount of such loss were specifically set out in FA 1996, Sch.13 para.2. The taxpayer sustained a loss under the express terms of the statute and one could not read in a condition that *the gift must not be made for the sole purpose of producing the loss*. The Special Commissioners appeared to rely on the distinction between commercial and legal concepts and held that the term "loss" in the context of para.2 was far removed from any "commercial" sense of the term. Presumably, if the original subscription for the loan notes had been done purely for tax avoidance reasons rather than as an investment, the decision might have been different. Whether this approach is correct in the light of the *Barclays Mercantile* and *Scottish Provident* decisions may be doubted.

Barclays Mercantile v Mawson[44] and *IRC v Scottish Provident Institution*[45]

In *Barclays Mercantile*, the House of Lords found in favour of the taxpayer and in the second case in favour of HMRC. The *Barclays* case might be regarded as similar in substance to the *Westmoreland* case in using a relief given by statute albeit with some circularity of finance. 3.31

Unusually both judgements were relatively short and were published as a joint decision of the Appellate Committee. In this format the Law Lords speak as one voice and presumably the intention was to prevent advisers looking for difference nuances in the judgments.

Barclays concerned a claim for capital allowances by the bank's leasing subsidiary on the purchase of a gas pipeline. The pipeline had been purchased from an Irish corporation to which it was subsequently leased back. What HMRC had found unacceptable was that the transaction was part of a series in which very little money actually passed between Barclays and the Irish corporation. The question was whether the circular nature of the financing negated Barclays' entitlement to capital allowances.

The House of Lords reviewed the authorities and noted the need for definitive guidance while commenting that:

> "it is no doubt too much that any exposition will remove all difficulties in the application of the principles because it is in the nature of questions of construction that there will be borderline cases about which people will have different views."

---

[43] (2004) Sp. C. 421; [2004] S.T.C. (SCD) 1831.
[44] [2004] UKHL 51.
[45] [2004] UKHL 52.

However, they noted that it should be "possible to achieve some clarity about basic principles".

The paramount question is always one of interpretation of the particular statutory provision and its application to the facts of the case but the Lords held that it was not necessarily the case that all elements of a transaction that have no commercial purpose must necessarily be disregarded. They referred to Ribeiro P.J.'s speech in *Arrowtown*[46] where he noted that the "ultimate question is whether the relevant statutory provisions construed purposively were intended to apply to the transaction viewed realistically." Although the financing of the transaction was circular it was not a necessary element in creating the entitlement to capital allowances and therefore this did not prevent the statutory conditions for capital allowances from being satisfied.

In *Scottish Provident*, the scheme involved taking advantage of the change in the rules on the taxation of gilts which was first announced in May 1995 but did not take effect until the following April. Scottish Provident and its financial advisers Citibank granted each other options over a number of gilts. The pricing of the cross options was structured to ensure that a tax loss but not a commercial loss would be generated. The Lords held that the use of cross options was an artificial device "chosen not for any commercial reason but solely to enable SPI to claim that there was no composite transaction". Importantly they held that the deliberate inclusion of a commercially irrelevant contingency could not be allowed to destroy the value of the *Ramsay* principle. So trying to insert some real commercial risk in order to prevent the application of *Ramsay* will not work. They said that to accept the company's proposition would mean a reversion to "the world of artificial tax schemes now equipped with anti-*Ramsay* devices".

It therefore appears that the *Ramsay* principle requires the legislation to be construed purposively to determine precisely what transaction falls within the statutory description and then establish whether the particular transaction in question actually does so. There is no ready made formula that can be applied to every case to decide the right answer and no effective anti-Ramsay device that can be inserted into an artificial tax scheme. The *Ramsay* line of authorities is based on ordinary principles of statutory construction.

---

[46] *Collector of Stamp Revenue v Arrowtown Assets Ltd* [2003] HKCFA 46; (2004) 6 I.T.L.R. 454.

CHAPTER 4

INCOME TAX

- Liability of trustees to income tax **(4.01)**
- Taxation of beneficiaries **(4.21)**
- The anti-avoidance provisions—taxing the settlor **(4.30)**
- Implications of the *Arctic Systems* case **(4.44)**

LIABILITY OF TRUSTEES TO INCOME TAX[1]

After various consultation and discussion papers, issued between December 2003 and March 2005, provisions were included in the Finance Acts of 2004, 2005 and 2006 aimed at "trust modernisation" in the taxation of trusts. The stated aim was to simplify the tax regime and to make the tax system "neutral" so that the amount of income tax or capital gains tax paid by trustees was neither greater nor less than that paid by an individual. It is doubtful whether either objective has been achieved.[2] This chapter briefly summarises the income tax rules applicable to UK resident trusts.[3] **4.01**

Trustees[4] are subject to basic rate income tax under the relevant income tax legislation on all the income produced by the trust fund.[5] They are not allowed

---

[1] The residence rules for trustees are considered in Ch. 2. Domicile is irrelevant. Trustees are now defined in TA 1988, s.685E(1) as a single person.
[2] Note that not all the proposals in the original consultation documents have been adopted. E.g. Income streaming has not been taken forward.
[3] Note that FA 2006 retains the definition of settlement in the anti-avoidance provision of ITTOIA s.620 but s.685A of TA 1988 inserts a definition of settled property. This is the same as that applicable to capital gains tax found in ss.60/68 of TCGA 1992. Thus settled property is any property held by trustees which is not nominee property. New ss.685B–685D define the term settlor—in the same way as ss.68A–C of TCGA 1992. However, the anti-avoidance definition of settlor continues to apply to ITTOIA 2005 Part 5, Ch. 5 so the practical impact seems limited to determining who is settlor when it comes to applying the residency rules in new s.685E to mixed-residence trusts. This is seriously called "simplification"!
[4] New TA 1988, s.685E(1) enacts that the trustees of a settlement are to be treated as a single person, distinct from the persons who may from time to time in fact be trustees. Previously there was no express statutory rule deeming trustees to be a single person for income tax purposes although case law achieved much the same result. See for example *IRC v Berrill* [1981] S.T.C. 784. Section 685E imports TCGA 1992, s.69(3) into income tax. This provides that the trustees of a settlement are a single person even if some are trustees of one fund and others are trustees of another fund. It should be read subject to the ability to make a sub-fund election which is discussed further below.
[5] See for instance ITTOIA 2005, s.8 under which the trustees are the persons liable because they

to deduct their personal allowances (the trust income is, after all, not their property) nor those of any beneficiary. Expenses incurred in administering the fund may not be deducted and are, therefore, paid out of taxed income.[6] Assessment to income tax at the basic rate may either be made on the trustees directly (e.g. where they are letting land) or they may receive investment income where tax has been deducted at source (e.g. bank interest). The tax deducted will satisfy the trustees' liability to pay tax at the basic rate. Assessments can be made in the name of any one or more of the relevant trustees. Relevant trustees in relation to income means the trustees to whom the income arises and any subsequent trustees.[7] Note that where a sub-fund election has been made for capital gains tax purposes under schedule 4ZA TCGA 1992[8] section 685G applies the sub-fund legislation for income tax purposes. A sub-fund election cannot be made earlier than April 6, 2006 but if made, the trustees of the sub-fund are treated as separate from the trustees of the principal settlement.

EXAMPLE 4.1

The trustees run a business. The profits of that business are calculated in accordance with the normal rules under ITTOIA 2005 and are subject to basic rate income tax in the trustees' hands. A change of trustees does not result in the discontinuance rules applying.[9] If a sub-fund election is made over part of the fund which is producing say investment income then the trustees of that sub-fund are not relevant trustees in respect of income tax due on the business income (and vice versa).

4.02 **Submitting a return:** In exceptional cases trustees of interest in possession trusts do not have to complete a return. If there are professional trustees acting, there is no untaxed income arising or any such income is mandated directly to a beneficiary and no capital gains tax will arise, the trustees are not required to submit a return but have to undertake to notify HMRC of any change in their circumstances. HMRC will also generally allow trustees not to submit a return where the only asset of the trust is a residential property which is occupied rent free by a beneficiary under the terms of the settlement. The beneficiary will be directly assessed on any income the trustees must notify HMRC of the name and address of the beneficiary.[10]

---

are the persons receiving or entitled to the profits and see TMA 1970, s.71. For the position when the income is taxed on the settlor under the anti-avoidance rules, see 4.14.

[6] For the deduction of trust management expenses in arriving at the charge under TA 1988, s.686, see 4.15.

[7] FA 1989, s.151(2)(a).

[8] Discussed in Ch. 7.

[9] ITTOIA 2005, ss.258, 361. See also Trust Management Expenses Guidance HMRC January 2006. Of course the expenses do not reduce the liability of trustees of a non-settlor interested trust to basic rate tax but reduce the liability of the beneficiary to any higher rate tax since he is effectively only taxed on the income he receives.

[10] See TSEM 3040 s.76 TMA 1970.

Further to FA 2005, s.14, trustees whose income not exceed £1,000 for 2006/7 is made up of net interest and UK dividends may need to make a return only periodically.[11]

Bare trusts: in general trustees are not required to make returns/pay tax in respect of bare trusts. Thus if they receive income, such income should be paid to the beneficiary who is responsible for tax on it.[12] However, with the agreement of the beneficiary the bare trusts may voluntarily return income (but not capital gains) and account for income tax at the appropriate rate (which will be the basic rate, lower rate or Schedule F rate: see 4.04).[13] **4.03**

Rates of tax

Trustees of an interest in possession trust (i.e. one in which a beneficiary has a right to income) suffer income tax at the following rates: **4.04**

 (i) income subject to tax at the dividend ordinary rate: 10 per cent[14];
 (ii) income subject to tax at the savings rate (e.g. interest which may be received either gross or net of 20 per cent tax): 20 per cent[15];
 (iii) income subject to tax at the basic rate: 22 per cent.[16]

Trustees of a discretionary or accumulation trust (i.e. one without an interest in possession) suffer tax under s.686 as follows[17]: **4.05**

 (i) tax at the trustees' rate (RAT): 40 per cent[18];
 (ii) on dividends: 32.5 per cent.[19]

Note, however, that for 2006/7 and subsequent years the first £1,000 of income taxable at the RAT for discretionary or accumulation trusts will, depending upon the source of the income, instead be taxed at either the basic, lower or dividend ordinary rate[20] ("the standard rate band"). The standard rate band applies after deduction of allowable trust management expenses. The total saving is in the region of £200.[21] It will be appreciated less tax is credited to

---

[11] See *Tax Bulletin*, August 2005.
[12] See generally, *Tax Bulletin*, February 27, 1997.
[13] Bare trusts are considered in Ch. 30.
[14] Dividend taxation is considered further at 4.20 and 4.25.
[15] If tax has been deducted at source there is no liability on the trustees.
[16] This will include income from trading; land and property; partnership income and foreign income.
[17] For a consideration of s.686, see 4.11.
[18] Until 2004/5 the rate stood at 34 per cent on all income with the exception of dividends. From 2004/5 onwards the rate was increased to 40 per cent to "align" it with the higher rate of tax for individuals.
[19] See 4.20 and 4.25. As with other income the rate was increased from 2004/5. Before that date the rate applicable to trusts in respect of dividends was 25 per cent.
[20] S.686D TA, 1988 as inserted by FA 2005, s.14 and amended in FA 2006 to raise the limit from £500 to £1000.
[21] TA 1988, s.686D as inserted by FA 2005, s.14. The rules for determining what income is subject

the tax pool which may be a factor in determining the size of distributions.[22] Of course if there is a sizeable tax pool or income is being accumulated then this will not matter and tax is then saved.

Section 686E inserts a new anti-fragmentation rule. Where the settlor has made more than one settlement the £1,000 exempt slice must be divided equally between the trusts or if greater, restricted to £200. Should a settlement have multiple settlors, s.685E is applied to it on the basis of the settlor who has made most settlements. Section 685E operates no matter how long ago any given settlement was made[23] and whether or not the settlements are inter vivos or testamentary, produce income, are settlor interested or interest in possession. Unlike the capital gains tax rules, non-resident trusts have to be counted. If a sub-fund election is made then the sub-fund is treated as a separate settlement for the purpose of dividing the £1,000.[24]

Capital receipts taxed as income

4.06 All trustees suffer CGT at a rate of 40 per cent.[25] In certain circumstances capital receipts are *deemed* to be income and taxed accordingly. They can benefit from the standard rate band if appropriate. FA 2006 introduced a new s.686A to gather together the various cases where capital receipts of trustees are taxed at income. Notice that this section can apply to interest in possession trusts and is not limited to trusts falling under s.686. It is the trustees not the life tenant who are liable for the tax since the receipts form part of the capital not the income of the trust fund. The capital receipts include:

    (i) *share buy-backs:* when trustees sell shares back to the company (a "share buy-back") the proceeds are generally taxed as income.[26] Unfortunately the buy-back provision was defectively drafted.[27] The previous s.686A TA 1988 provided that what was taxable was only the distribution element and excluded the original subscription price received by the company which issued the shares. The new s.686A introduces a common mechanism for the various types of capital receipt which are assessable to income tax in the hands of trustees receiving them to be charged at the special trust rates. However the new wording of s.686A means that on a buy-back of shares the whole of the payment by the company to

---

to this reduced rate are set out in s.14. As usual, dividends are treated as the highest slice of trust income. There are deeming provisions under which certain income is deemed to be one type (such as income subject to tax at the lower rate) rather than another for the purposes of working out how it is taxed. None of this can be described as a simplification: there is already a "dividend trust rate" and a "rate applicable to trusts".

[22] See 4.25 for distributions out of a discretionary or accumulation trust.
[23] Compare the capital gains tax position on annual exemptions—see Ch. 7.
[24] Whether all this complexity is seriously worth the paper it is written on is debateable. The relief given is not worth the additional complexity produced. Few people would set up trusts to take advantage of the £1000 allowance!
[25] For the CGT position of trustees, see Ch. 7.
[26] TA 1986, s.686A(2) inserted by FA 2006, s.89 Sch.13 para.3 in respect of payments made from April 6, 2006.
[27] See Ministerial Statement issued on October 9, 2006 by the Paymaster General.

the trustees is taxable including the original subscription price, not just the element representing the distribution.

HMRC have agreed that these changes were not intended and that amending legislation will be introduced in FA 2007 backdated to April 6, 2006 to restore the previous position;

(ii) *s.776 charges:* TA 1988 s.776 provides that capital receipts on a sale of land can be taxed as income if the land was acquired or developed with a view to realising a gain[28];

(iii) *Lease premium payments*: The grant of a lease for a period which does not exceed 50 years in consideration for the payment of a premium results in part of the premium being taxed as income[29];

(iv) *Offshore income gains*;

(v) *Gains from contracts of life insurance.*

Accrued income scheme and stock dividends

The accrued income scheme applies to trustees[30] (and, unlike personal representatives, trustees do not benefit from the *de minimis* £5,000 exemption). **4.07**

EXAMPLE 4.2

Assume that trustees purchase £10,000 of 5% Treasury Stock *cum div* i.e. with accrued interest of £175. When the interest of (say) £250 is paid the trustees get relief for the accrued interest (£175) leaving income (for tax purposes) of £75. The vendor is treated as entitled to extra interest of £175.

Where the assets of a trust include shares in a company and the trustees receive shares either as a stock dividend or on the demerger of the company, it can be uncertain whether in terms of trust law the shares received are an addition to income or capital. The courts have generally taken the view that the presumed intention of the settlor should be carried out. So if there is an express provision in the trust deed which covers the receipt of stock dividends, this is relevant in deciding whether the shares received belong to the income beneficiary or to the capital of the trust.

The position can be complex but the rules are summarised briefly as follows:

(i) the distribution of shares by way of simple bonus issue to trustees will be treated as capital of the trust.[31]

(ii) In the absence of a discretion for the trustees to determine whether demerged shares are to be treated as income or capital, on an indirect

---

[28] TA 1988, s.686A(2)(j).
[29] ITTOIA 2005, s.277, TA 1988 s.686A(2)(d).
[30] TA 1988, ss.710–728.
[31] *Bouch v Sproule* (1887) 12 App Cas 385.

demerger the trustees can treat the receipt of shares under the demerger as capital of the trust.[32]

(iii) On a direct demerger the demerged shares are generally received by the trustees as income of the trust, being a dividend out of accumulated profits under company law.[33]

The Inland Revenue Tax Bulletin October 1994 Issue 13 sets out the way in which the Revenue tax the receipt of such shares.

(iv) Stock dividends. The effect of the Court of Appeal decision in *Howell v Trippier*[34] is that stock dividends received by a discretionary trust are taxable at the dividend trust rate with a credit for tax at the dividend ordinary rate.[35]

4.08 There are two special rules—both introduced by FA 2005—which apply to accumulation and discretionary trusts (*viz* trusts which suffer 40 per cent taxation under s.686[36]) namely:

(i) a standard rate band which, for 2006–7, is £1,000. This has been discussed at 4.05 above.

(ii) a stated aim was "*to ensure that trusts established to protect the vulnerable are not disadvantaged by the tax system*". This resulted in the introduction from April 6, 2004 of a new tax regime for trusts for vulnerable beneficiaries.[37]

Non resident trustees[38]

4.09 The trustees are liable to income tax only on UK source income, e.g.

(i) profit from the business of renting UK land;

(ii) dividends from UK companies (with a 10 per cent non repayable tax credit);

(iii) interest e.g. on a UK bank account which may have suffered a 20 per cent withholding tax at source.

If the trust is accumulation or discretionary non resident trustees are subject to the normal 40 per cent RAT charge.[39]

4.10 **TA 1988 s.739–740:** these are the complex anti-avoidance rules that apply to the transfer of assets abroad by a transferor. Under s.739 a transferor who is ordinarily resident here is subject to income tax on the income arising within

---

[32] See *Re Lee (deceased)* [1993] 3 All E.R. 926.
[33] See *Hill v Permanent Trustee Company of New South Wales Ltd* [1930] AC 720.
[34] [2004] S.T.C. 1245.
[35] See Simon's Weekly Tax Intelligence 2005, p.276.
[36] See 4.11.
[37] FA 2005, ss.23–45, Sch.1. Note that this legislation was backdated to 2004/05. See Ch. 26.
[38] For when trustees are non-UK resident, see Ch. 2.
[39] *IRC v Regent Trust Company* [1980] S.T.C. 140. Note the potential collection problems for HMRC and see ESC B18.

the offshore structure (including the income of underlying companies owned by the trust) if he has "the power to enjoy" (defined widely) the income of the non resident person (including a trust), or can or does receive a capital sum (including a loan) from the trust. When this section applies the income is treated as that of the transferor.

Under s.740, a beneficiary who is ordinarily resident in the UK (and who receives a benefit from an offshore trust) is taxed to the extent of the "relevant income" in the trust.

In both cases if the transferor/beneficiary (as the case may be) is non UK domiciled the remittance basis applies in respect of foreign source income so that income tax is only charged on such income if remitted to the UK. Further neither section will apply if it can be shown that tax avoidance was not a purpose of the transfer *or* that the transfer was a bona fide commercial transaction not designed to avoid a tax liability.[40]

What trusts are subject to the RAT (rate applicable to trusts) imposed by TA 1988 s.686?

As noted previously, trustees are not liable to income tax at the higher rate because they are not individuals. However, the RAT (rate applicable to trusts) as well as the £1,000 standard rate band) applies to discretionary or accumulation trusts. The trusts in question are those where there is income arising to trustees in any year of assessment so far as it: **4.11**

(i) is income which is to be accumulated or which is payable at the discretion of the trustees or any other person (whether or not the trustees have power to accumulate it)[41];

(ii) is not income from service charges held in trust by a relevant housing body;

(iii) is not, before being distributed the income of any person other than the trustees[42];

(iv) is not income arising under a trust established for charitable purposes only[43]; and

(iv) exceeds the income applied in defraying the expenses of the trustees in that year which are properly chargeable to income (or would be so chargeable but for any express provisions of the trust).[44]

---

[40] This purpose test has been amended from December 5, 2005 so that the taxpayer has to satisfy either Condition A or Condition B to avoid the s.739/740 net. Condition A is that it would not be reasonable to conclude that avoiding tax was the purpose or one of the purposes for which the relevant transaction or any of them were effected. Condition B is that all the relevant transactions were genuine commercial transactions and it would not be reasonable to conclude that any one or more of those transactions was more than incidentally designed to avoid tax.

[41] TA 1988, s.686(2)(a).

[42] TA 1988, s.686(2)(b) as amended by FA 2006. This will exclude the situation where it belongs to an interest in possession beneficiary. For the position when the income is taxed on the settlor, see 4.14.

[43] TA 1988, s.686(2)(c) as substituted by the FA 1988, s.55(3) and as amended. Income produced by pension funds is likewise outside the charge.

[44] TA 1988, s.686(2AA) as inserted by the FA 1997, Sch.7 para.12 and as amended by the F(No. 2)A 1997, s.32(6), and see s.689B.

4.12 Broadly, trusts which contain a power for trustees to accumulate income, and trusts which give the trustees a discretion over the distribution of the income, are caught.

In *IRC v Berrill* the settlor's son was entitled to the income from the fund unless the trustees exercised a power to accumulate it. Vinelott J. held that TA 1988, s.686 applied because the income was "*income . . . which is payable at the discretion of the trustees*". "Discretion" is wide enough to cover a discretion or power to withhold income.

The phrase "*income which is to be accumulated*" in TA 1988, s.686(2)(a) presumably refers to income which the trustees are under a duty to accumulate. A mere power to accumulate is not sufficient, although it usually means that the income "is payable at the discretion of the trustees" within Section 686(2)(a).

4.13 The section does not apply to income which is treated as that of a person other than the trustees, for instance, where a beneficiary has a vested interest in the income (eg a life tenant). Presumably the type of settlement considered in *Pearson v IRC*,[45] in which the income of a life tenant could be taken from him after it had arisen by the exercise of a power to accumulate it, would be subject to the special rate as the income still belongs to the trustees.

4.14 **Position of trustees when the income is taxed as that of the settlor**[46]: the legislation is far from straightforward but note the following:

- ITTOIA 2005, s.624(1) treats the income as that of the settlor "and of the settlor alone". In a similar vein, s.622 states that the person liable for tax is the settlor;

- ITTOIA 2005, s.646(8) provides, however, that "nothing in s.624 . . . is to be read as excluding a charge to tax on the trustees as persons by whom any income is received". This means that there is an overlapping charge between the settlor and his trustees of basic rate (or equivalent tax). Further, HMRC appear to consider that changes made in the wording of s.686 by FA 2006 mean that when the trust is discretionary or accumulation the charge under s.686 (at either 40 per cent or 32.5 per cent as appropriate) can apply to trustees. This is presumably on the basis that the words "income of a person other than the trustees" do not include income deemed to be the income of the settlor but only income which actually belongs to someone else, e.g the life tenant.

Hence HMRC consider that the trustees are liable for tax at the rate applicable to trusts with the settlor taking credit.[47] There is no specific mechanism for the settlor to take the credit and there is some disagreement as to whether this is the correct reading of amended s.686(2)(b) and therefore whether the RAT is applicable at all where the trust is settlor interested.[48] It has also been confirmed that in appropriate cases when the settlor is not a higher rate taxpayer any excess tax paid by the trustees will be available for repayment (presumably to the settlor even though the trustees have paid it!). There is no

---

[45] See *Pearson v IRC* [1981] AC 753, [1980] 2 All E.R. 479, HL; and 15.21.
[46] See 4.00 for when a settlor is taxed on the income of his trust.
[47] See HMRC *Tax Bulletin 83*, p. 1306.
[48] See HMRC/CIOT correspondence published on CIOT website in October 2006.

formal notification procedure between the trustees and settlor to give details of income received or tax paid.[49]

Trust Management Expenses ("TMEs"): TMEs are not deductible in calculating the trustees' liability to tax at the basic rate but may be deducted in arriving at the amount of income chargeable at the rate applicable to trusts. (Note though that if the trust is settlor interested they are not deductible against the settlor's liability.) In *Carver v Duncan*[50] trustees paid premiums on policies of life assurance out of the income of the fund as they were permitted to do under the trust deed. The House of Lords held that the payments did not fall to be deducted under s.686(2)(d) (see now s.686 (2AA)(b)) which was limited to expenses properly chargeable to income under the general law. As the life assurance premiums were for the benefit of capital they should be borne by capital and accordingly the express authority in the instrument did not bring the sums within the section. 4.15

In recent years HMRC have sought to disallow general trust management expenses as an income expense and this approach is reflected in the final version of their guidance paper issued on February 2, 2006. Note in particular: 4.16

(i) *the relevance of TMEs:* they may reduce income which is subject to the rate applicable to trusts under s.686 and in arriving at the net amount of income to which an interest in possession beneficiary is entitled (and on which he may therefore suffer higher rate income tax or claim a repayment, as the case may be);

(ii) *why TMEs are unique:* they are different in kind from expenses of a trade or letting which are deducted in arriving at the taxable profit. They comprise the running costs of the trust and their treatment depends on whether *as a matter of trust* law they are capital or income;

(iii) *income expenses:* these are incurred *solely* for the benefit of the income beneficiary (e.g. in the collection/calculation of his income). By contrast expenses incurred for the benefit of the trust fund as a whole are payable out of capital: this will include the majority of trust expenses. In general the cost of having trust accounts prepared and audited and of preparing tax returns should be apportioned (on a just and reasonable basis) but HMRC consider that trustee remuneration is a capital expense. It seems likely that some at least of the views expressed in this document will be challenged before the Special Commissioners.[51]

Order of set off: TMEs allowable against income are to be set off against the following types of income in the following order 4.17

(a) income carrying a notional dividend tax credit of 10 per cent;
(b) income taxed at lower rate (e.g. savings income);
(c) income taxed at basic rate (e.g. rental income).

---

[49] Form R185 is used for payment to beneficiaries and is inappropriate in this case. For the right of a settlor to reimbursement for any tax that he has paid, see 4.30.
[50] [1985] A.C. 1082.
[51] For the trust law position, see Thomas and Hudson, *The Law of Trusts* (OUP 2004) at 10.52 *et seq.*

4.18 This order favours the beneficiary since the offset is first against income with the non repayable tax credit; then 20 per cent income and only finally 22 per cent.
Expenses should be grossed up at the appropriate rate. So, if TME's are £1,000, which have been paid out of net income, the gross equivalent is

(a) £1,110 if paid out of dividends;
(b) £1,250 if paid out of savings income;
(c) £1,282 if paid out of rental income.

In the case of trusts in which part of the fund is held on an interest in possession trust and part on discretionary trusts IR 392 expects the trustees to make a just and reasonable apportionment of TME's between the income of the trustees and the income of the beneficiaries who are entitled to it. In reality it is likely that more expenses will be attributed to the portion of the fund held on discretionary trusts where there is additional tax and accounting work.

EXAMPLE 4.3

Trustees of a discretionary trust have (non-dividend) investment income of £10,000 and incur administrative expenses of £1,000. Their income tax liability (using 2006–07 rates) is:

	£	£
Gross income	10,000	
Tax due at 20% (from which TMEs cannot be deducted)		2,000
Deduct allowable TME's		
$1,000 \times \frac{100}{80}$	1,250	
	8,750	
Less:		
Standard rate band	1,000	
	7,750	
Tax at s.686 Rate (40%)		3,100
Less tax deducted at source at 20% on £7,750		1,550
		£1,550

Total tax liability £2,000 + £1,550 = £3,550

Note: (i) the investment income of trustees commonly suffers the deduction of lower rate tax at source. The special rules for dividend income are considered at 4.20 below. (ii) the special trust rate charged under s.686 only applies to trust income after deducting expenses properly charged out of income (see TA Act

1988, s.686(2AA)) and likewise the reduced rate introduced by the FA 2005 applies to the first £1,000 of income not used to defray management expenses. Hence in the example the "basic rate band" is, in effect, £2,250.

Charge imposed by ICTA 1988 Section 687

If trustees distribute income in the exercise of their discretion and it becomes as a result the income of the payee for income tax purposes the payment is treated as a net amount after deduction of income tax at the relevant rate. 4.19

The recipient (or settlor), if liable at a lower rate, can claim repayment of income tax. The trustees must account for the income tax deemed to be so deducted, but are credited with the tax they have suffered. Trustees have a running total of income tax suffered, less income tax treated as deducted from payments.[52]

EXAMPLE 4.4

> On April 6, 2006 a discretionary trust had a tax pool brought forward of £498. In 2006–07 the trust receives non-dividend income of £2,000 on which it pays tax at 40% = £800. During that year, the trustees exercise their discretion to distribute income of £1,600. This is treated as a gross sum of £1,600 x 100/60 = £2,666 from which income tax at 40% = £1,066 has been deducted. The trustees must account to HMRC for £1,066, but have a credit of £498 plus £800 = £1,298 so that no further tax is payable and this leaves £232 tax carried forward in the "tax pool".

Dividend income

When dividend income is received and then distributed by discretionary trustees the position is more complex: 4.20

(i) that income is taxed at the "dividend trust rate" of 32.5 per cent;

(ii) only tax actually paid by the trustees is credited to the trust tax pool: therefore for a cash dividend of £90 the tax pool is credited with £22.50 tax (effectively 25 per cent of the net dividend): see TA 1988 s.687(3);

(iii) if the net income remaining is then distributed the rules of S.687 apply so that the trustees are accountable for tax at 40 per cent on the grossed up distribution in the normal way.

---

[52] This running total started on April 5, 1973 for a trust which then had income available for distribution. It is commonly referred to as the trust "tax pool".

EXAMPLE 4.5

This example illustrates the treatment of dividend income received by discretionary trustees.

	£
Dividend received	900.00
Tax credit (1/9th)	100.00
Gross income	1,000.00
Deduct: Tax @ 32.5%	325.00
Income after tax	£675.00
Tax due from trustees	325.00
Deduct: Tax credit	100.00
Additional tax due	225.00
Amount credited to tax pool	225.00

If the trustees accumulate the net income there is no further income tax to pay and £675 becomes capital. But if the trustees distribute that income the position is as follows:

(1) the non-repayable tax credit cannot be added to the tax pool, and so

(2) if the trustees distribute to a beneficiary the whole of the income after tax, the position is:

	£
Net income distribution to beneficiary	675.00
Addition for tax @ 40%	450.00
Gross income of beneficiary	£1,125.00
Tax due under TA 1988 s.687	450.00
Deduct: Tax credited to tax pool	225.00
Shortfall	£225.00

In this situation, unless there is a balance in the tax pool brought forward in order to "frank" the whole amount of the tax of £450.00, the shortfall has to be funded from other sources. In such cases the trustees may therefore have to adopt an alternative strategy. For instance, they may take the view that the distribution to the beneficiary and the tax payable under Section 687 must be wholly met from the net of tax income received, £675 in the above example. To achieve this, the distribution to the beneficiary must be limited to 60% of the cash dividend received. Continuing the example above, the result would be:

	£
Distribution to beneficiary £900 x 60%	540.00
Addition for tax @ 40%	360.00
Gross income of beneficiary	900.00
Tax due under TA 1988 s.687	360.00
Deduct: Tax credited to tax pool	225.00
Balance paid by trustees	135.00

This is met out of the cash balance held by the trustees of £675 less the net payment to the beneficiary of £540.

TAXATION OF BENEFICIARIES

4.21 A beneficiary who is entitled to the income of a trust as it arises (or is entitled to have it applied for his benefit) is subject to income tax for the year of assessment in which that income arises, even if none of the money is paid to him during that year.[53] The sum to which the beneficiary is entitled is that which is left in the trustees' hands after they have paid deductible administration expenses (TMEs) and discharged their income tax liability. The beneficiary is, as a result, entitled to a net sum which must be grossed up in order to find the sum which enters his total income computation and to a credit for some of the income tax paid by the trustees; not, however, for the full amount in cases where management expenses have been deducted.[54]

4.22 Depending on his other income and allowances, a beneficiary may be entitled to reclaim all or some of the tax paid by the trustees. Alternatively, he may be liable for tax at the higher rate. The income that he receives from the trust is not earned income even if it arises from a trade run by the trustees.[55]

EXAMPLE 4.6

Z is entitled to the income produced by a trust fund. In 2006–07 rental income of £6,000 is produced and the trustees incur deductible administrative expenses of £1,000. The trustees are subject to tax at 22% on the income of £6,000. The balance of the income available for Z is:

		£	£
Gross income			6,000
Deduct	Tax	1,320	
	Expenses	1,000	2,320
			£3,680

Z is, therefore, taxed on £3,680 grossed up by tax at 22% ie:

$$\frac{£3,680 \times 100}{78} = £4,717.95$$

Z is given a credit for that portion of the basic rate tax paid by the trustees which is attributable to £4,717.95: ie £1,037.95 but does not receive a credit for the rest of the tax paid by the trustees (£1,320 − £1,037.95 =

---

[53] *Baker v Archer-Shee* [1927] A.C. 844, HL.
[54] *Macfarlane v IRC* [1929] S.C. 453. When a beneficiary is entitled to savings income, the value of the credit passed on to him by the trustees is at the lower rate of 20 per cent by virtue of TA 1988, s.1A as inserted by FA 1996, s.73 and as amended.
[55] See *Fry v Shiel's Trustees* 1915 S.C. 159, Ct of Sess. However, in *Baker v Archer-Shee* [1927] A.C. 844, HL it appears that if a beneficiary is entitled to the income as it arises he is taxed according to the rules appropriate to that source of income.

£282.05) and the result is that management expenses have been paid out of taxed income so that the total cost of those expenses is £1,282.05.

"*Income*" for these purposes does not include items which are capital under general trust law although income tax may have been charged on them in the hands of the trustees.[56]

4.23 **Taxing an annuitant:** an annuitant under a trust is not entitled to income of the trust as it arises; instead he is taxed on the income that he receives. The trustees deduct income tax from the annuity under TA 1988, s.348 and the beneficiary is given credit for the basic rate tax deducted at source in the usual way.

4.24 **Taxing a discretionary beneficiary:** a discretionary beneficiary has no right to income but is merely the subject of the trustees' discretion. Any payments that he receives are charged as his income (they are annual payments because they may recur) and he receives a credit for the tax paid by the trustees and attributable to that payment.[57] As the trust is discretionary, that tax is at the rate applicable to trusts (40 per cent from April 6, 2004).

Once an irrevocable decision has been taken by the trustees to retain income as a part of the capital of the fund, the sum accumulated loses its character as income and is treated in the same way as the original fund, ie as capital. It follows, therefore, that the income tax suffered on that income (at 40 per cent) is irrecoverable and that no further income tax will be charged on the accumulations when they are eventually paid out to the beneficiaries as capital (although such distributions have capital gains tax and inheritance tax consequences). In deciding whether it is more advantageous to accumulate income or to pay it out to beneficiaries as income under their discretionary powers, trustees need to consider, inter alia, the tax position of the individual beneficiaries.[58]

EXAMPLE 4.7

In 2006/07 trustees receive non-dividend income of £10,000. A, B and C are three discretionary beneficiaries. A has no other income and has an unused personal allowance; B is a basic rate taxpayer; and C is subject to tax at a marginal rate of 40%. The trustees are deciding whether to pay income to any one or more of the beneficiaries or whether to accumulate it. The following tax consequences would ensue:

(1) The trustees are subject to tax at 40% on the trust income (ie £4,000 tax).

---

[56] See 4.06 above.
[57] TA 1988, s.687.
[58] Under the Trustee Act 1925, s.31(2) as amended by the Family Law Reform Act 1969, s.1(3), Sch.1 Pt I and by the Trustee Act 2000, s.40(1), Sch.2, para.25 the trustees may apply accumulations of income in the maintenance of the relevant beneficiary: the tax treatment of these payments is obscure. The better view is that they are capital payments.

(2) If the trustees decide to pay all the net income of £6,000 (ignoring expenses) to A (who has no other income) he is entitled to a repayment of tax as follows:

	£
Income (£6,000 x 100/60)	10,000
Deduct: personal allowance	5,035
Income chargeable to tax	£4,965

	£
Income tax:	
£2,150 at 10%	215.00
£2,815 at 22%	619.30
	834.30
Deduct: Tax treated as paid	4,000.00
Tax refund	£3,165.70

(3) If the trustees pay the income to B (the basic rate taxpayer), he is not entitled to a refund of any tax at the basic rate, but, depending on the amount of his other income, may obtain a refund of the extra 18% tax paid by the trustees.

(4) If the trustees pay the income to C (the higher rate taxpayer), no further tax is due.

(5) If the trustees accumulate the income, the £4,000 tax paid is irrecoverable and the net income of £6,000 is converted into capital.

From a tax viewpoint, the trustees should avoid payments to C, consider paying all or part of the income to A and B, and accumulate any balance.

Dividends: inevitably the position is more complex when the income distributed is dividends. The rules, which came into effect on April 6, 1999, have resulted in a basic or higher rate beneficiary being in a worse position if he receives such income via a discretionary trust (i.e. a trust subject to tax under s.686) than if he had personally owned the shares and hence directly received the dividend.[59] **4.25**

EXAMPLE 4.8

(i) *Position when individual owns shares/is an interest in possession beneficiary in a trust*
B, a higher rate taxpayer, receives a net dividend of £900 from the shares which he owns in Family Co. Ltd.

---

[59] The life tenant under a fixed interest trust is in no worse position than the outright owner of the shares, given that the tax treatment is essentially "transparent". As a result of the FA 2006 changes in the IHT treatment of trusts the problem may be solved by appointing the beneficiary an interest in possession in the shares before the dividend is declared.

		£
Gross dividend £1,000		
Tax at 32.5%		325
Deduct: Tax credit (10%)		100
Tax payable		£225

Net cash in hand £900 − £225 = £675.

If B had been a basic rate taxpayer he would have been left with cash in hand of £900.

(ii) *Position if dividends channelled through a discretionary trust*

But consider the position if the dividends had reached B via a discretionary trust under which the trustees (because of the lack of any tax pool) had adopted the alternative strategy of Example 4.5 above.

(1) If B is a higher rate taxpayer he receives a net distribution of £540 with a credit of £360 (representing the s.687 tax at 40%).

	£
Gross income	900
Deduct: Tax credit at 40%	360
Net cash in hand	£540

(b) If B is a basic rate taxpayer:

	£
Gross income	£900
Tax at 22%	198
Deduct: Tax credit	360
Repayment due	£162

Net cash in hand £540 + £162 = £702.

By contrast the non-taxpayer is no worse off than if he had received the dividend direct: in both cases (using the above figures) he ends up with £900 cash in hand.

4.26 **Dangers of supplementing income out of capital:** capital payments are not generally subject to income tax. If, however, a beneficiary is entitled to a fixed amount of income each year which is to be made up out of capital should the trust fail to produce the requisite amount of income, such topping up payments are taxed as income in his hands.[60] In other words to determine whether a sum forms part of a beneficiary's total income, it is necessary to ascertain, not whether the sum arises from capital or income of the trust, but whether it is received by the beneficiary "in the quality of income".

---

[60] See *Brodie's Will Trustees v IRC* (1933) 17 TC 432; *Cunard's Trustees v IRC* [1946] 1 All E.R. 159, CA.

EXAMPLE 4.9

(1) The testator's widow has been left an annuity of £4,000 a year; the trustees are required to pay it out of the capital of the trust fund if the income is insufficient. The widow is liable to income tax on the payments that she receives whether paid out of income or capital because they are annual payments.

(2) The settlor's widow is given an annuity of £4,000 a year and, in addition, the trustees have the power "*to apply capital for the benefit of the widow in such manner as they shall in their absolute discretion think fit*". Any supplements out of capital will escape income tax because the widow has an interest in both income and capital, and payments out of capital are treated as advances of capital rather than as income payments.

4.27 HMRC has in the past considered that payments made out of trust capital can be taxed as income in the hands of a recipient beneficiary even when the payments are not paid in augmentation of an income entitlement: the income nature of the payment in the hands of the recipient can be discovered by looking at its size, recurrence, and purpose. In *Stevenson v Wishart*[61] discretionary trust income was paid out in full each year to a charity and capital sums were then paid to one of the beneficiaries who had suffered a heart attack. The purpose of the payments was to cover medical expenses and the cost of living in a nursing home. HMRC's argument that these sums were paid out for an income purpose and were therefore subject to income tax was rejected both at first instance and by the Court of Appeal. Fox L.J. stated:

> ". . . there is nothing in the present case which indicates that the payments were of an income nature except their recurrence. I do not think that is sufficient. The trustees were disposing of capital in exercise of a power over capital. They did not create a recurring interest in property. If, in exercise of a power over capital, they chose to make at their discretion regular payments of capital to deal with the special problems of [the beneficiary's] last years rather than release a single sum to her of a large amount, that does not seem to me to create an income interest. Their power was to appoint capital. What they appointed remained capital."

4.28 The Court of Appeal stressed the exceptional nature of nursing-home payments. Fox L.J., for instance, stated that such expenditure, although involving day-to-day maintenance, was emergency expenditure of very substantial amounts which would usually fall outside normal income resources. It may be, therefore, that if the expenditure was not of an emergency nature the court would consider the payments to be income.

It is understood that HMRC currently treat advances or appointments out of trust capital as capital in the hands of the recipient beneficiary unless:

---

[61] [1987] 2 All E.R. 428, [1987] 1 W.L.R. 1204, CA.

(i) the payments in question are designed to augment income[62];

(ii) the payments in question really amount to an annuity[63]; or

(iii) the trust instrument contains a provision authorising the use of capital to maintain a beneficiary in the same degree of comfort as had been the case in the past.

4.29 **The effects of the Trustee Act 1925, s.31**[64]: the effects of s.31 (which may be excluded or modified by the trust instrument) may be stated in the following propositions:

(i) If a minor is absolutely entitled to the capital even though the income is retained by the trustees, it belongs to the minor. Therefore, s.686 is inapplicable because the income is that of a person other than the trustee; were the minor to die, both capital and income accumulations would belong to his estate and pass on his intestacy.

(ii) If a minor has a vested interest in income only (for example if the trust is to Z for life when Z is seven years old), the trustees may accumulate that income. Were the minor to die the accumulations would not pass to his estate. In this case s.31 has had a divesting effect and for income tax purposes the accumulating income is subject to the rate applicable to trusts because it does not belong to any particular beneficiary as it arises. In *Stanley v IRC*[65] it was stated that

> "s.31 has effected a radical change in the law. [The beneficiary] is, in fact, for all practical purposes in precisely the same position as if his interest in surplus income were contingent".

(iii) If a beneficiary is contingently entitled to trust capital on attaining an age in excess of 18, s.31 vests the income of that contingent interest in the beneficiary from the age of 18.[66] In this case the section has a "vesting effect." This provision was significant in the context of accumulation and maintenance trusts in which capital entitlement was deferred until age 25 (or later). The beneficiary normally becomes entitled to income at 18 as a result of the operation of s.31 unless specifically excluded. Where the age of capital vesting was over 25 s.31 of the Trustee Act could save a trust from falling outside the accumulation and maintenance trust rules.

---

[62] See *Jackson's Trustees v IRC* (1942) 25 TC 13.
[63] See *Cunard's Trustees v IRC* [1946] 1 All E.R. 159, CA.
[64] I.e. the Trustee Act 1925, s.31 as amended by the Family Law Reform Act 1969, s.1(3), Sch.1, Pt I and by the Trustee Act 2000, s.40(1), Sch.2, para.25.
[65] *Stanley v IRC* [1944] K.B. 255, [1944] 1 All E.R. 230, CA.
[66] Trustee Act 1925, s.31(1)(ii) as amended by the Family Law Reform Act 1969, s.1(3), Sch.1 Pt I.

THE ANTI-AVOIDANCE PROVISIONS—SETTLOR INTERESTED TRUSTS AND TRUSTS FOR MINOR CHILDREN OF THE SETTLOR

The arrangements discussed here are: **4.30**

(i) a settlement where the settlor retains an interest

(ii) a settlement on unmarried minor children of the settlor

(iii) capital payments including loans to the settlor.

When the anti-avoidance rules operate, they deem the income of a settlement to be that of the settlor, but (with the exception of (iii) above) they also enable him to recover from the trustees any tax that he suffers on that income.[67] The ultimate effect of the provisions, therefore, is that the trust income is charged with tax at the rates which it would bear if it formed the top part of the settlor's total income and this liability is borne by the trustees or beneficiaries. There are similar, although not identical rules

(i) *in CGT:* see TCGA 1992, ss.77–9 and note the widened scope of the settlor interested provisions in the case of offshore trusts (see s.86)[68];

(ii) *in IHT* with the reservation of benefit rules which are, however, significantly narrower in scope being limited to settlements in which the settlor himself either can or does benefit (there is no extension to spouses or minor children).[69]

The income tax provisions were enacted piecemeal during the twentieth century and finally rationalised (to some extent!) in 1995 becoming s.660A–G and s.677–682A of TA 1988. They were recently re-enacted into plain English(!) by ITTOIA 2005 in Chapter 5 of Part V. **4.31**

Definitions of settlements and settlor: The rules apply to a "settlement" which is widely defined as follows— **4.32**

> "includes any disposition, trust, covenant, agreement, arrangement or transfer of assets . . .".[70]

HMRC do not regard the rule as applicable only to spouses and minor children. It will apply to any arrangement for income to be payable to a person

---

[67] ITTOIA 2005, s.619. Note that a "settlement" is widely defined for these purposes: see ITTOIA 2005, s.620. On "arrangements" see *Butler v Wildin* [1989] S.T.C. 22, 61 TC 666 and see the consideration of the *Artic Systems* case at 4.44 *et seq*. The charge on the settlor does not apply to any qualifying income which arises under a trust, the trustees of which are resident in the UK, if given by the trustees to a charity in the year of assessment in which it arises, or if it is income to which a charity is entitled under the trust: ITTOIA 2005, s.628.

[68] See Chs 10 and 11.

[69] The POA income tax charge is similarly limited: see Ch. 24.

[70] ITTOIA 2005, s.620(1) on the scope of this provision, see the *Artic Systems* case at 4.44 *et seq*.

other than the settlor provided that the settlor has an interest in the settlement where the arrangements are:

- (i) bounteous or
- (ii) not commercial or
- (iii) not at arms length or
- (iv) in the case of an outright gift between spouses, wholly or substantially a right to income.[71]

Note therefore that an important limitation is that a settlement requires the settlor to give bounty: commercial arrangements are not therefore caught.[72] In general "spouse" includes a civil partner but not a separated or future spouse nor a widow or widower. Hence a settlement which enables the settlor's widow (but not the settlor nor his wife) to benefit after his death is not caught by these provisions. Covenanted payments are within the definition of a settlement and (apart from a covenanted payment to charity) not allowed as a deduction in calculating the total income of the settlor.[73]

As discussed at 4.01 in the context of the anti-avoidance provisions, **settlor** is defined as any person by whom the settlement was made although see also FA 2006, Sch.13 inserting s.685B–D, which defines settlor for general purposes without repealing s.620 of ITTOIA.[74] A person who:

- (i) has made or entered into the settlement directly or indirectly,
- (ii) has provided or undertaken to provide funds directly or indirectly for the purposes of the settlement, or
- (iii) has made with any other person a reciprocal arrangement for that other person to make or enter into a settlement.[75]

is deemed a settlor.[76] Where a settlement has more than one settlor, each settlor is to be treated as the only settlor of a deemed separate settlement, with rules as to the property and income which is to be treated as belonging to that separate settlement.[77]

Settlements in which the settlor retains an interest

4.33   Income arising under a settlement during the settlor's lifetime is taxed as his for all income tax purposes unless the income arises from property in which

---

[71] See HMRC TSEM 4200.
[72] *IRC v Plummer* [1979] S.T.C. 793; *Bulmer v IRC* [1966] 3 All E.R. 801: by contrast the IHT definition is not so limited, see 15.01.
[73] A covenanted payment to charity made after April 5, 2000 is not treated as a settlement and relief is allowable under the gift aid scheme.
[74] S.620 of ITTOIA 2005.
[75] Compare the definition of settlor for capital gains tax purposes at 5.16 and for inheritance tax purposes at 15.11.
[76] See *Crosland v Hawkins* (1961) 39 TC 493 CA and *Mills v IRC* [1974] SYC 130 HL.
[77] Compare inheritance tax provisions on multiple settlors—see Ch. 15, especially 15.12.

he has no interest. The income does not have to be paid to him: the settlor merely pays tax on this income at his highest marginal rate and can then reclaim that tax from the trustees. See 4.14 for further details on the effect of s.686(2)(b) TA 1988 on settlor interested trusts and whether it is the trustees or the settlor who should account for tax. Note that new section 685A ITTOIA (not TA 1988) provides that where trust income is taxed as that of the settlor a subsequent income distribution to a beneficiary is not taxed. This came into effect on April 6, 2006 although HMRC have said it reflects previous practice. S.623 ITTOIA has also been amended in FA 2006 to confirm that when income is deemed to be that of the settlor under ITTOIA s.620 he is entitled to the same deductions and reliefs as if the income were in fact his.

A settlor has an interest in property if it is or will or may become payable to or applicable for his benefit or that of his spouse[78] in any circumstances, including where the fund reverts to the settlor under a revocable settlement, or the settlor is a discretionary beneficiary or could be added.[79] However, there is an exception for a tax year in which the settlor is not domiciled or not resident or ordinarily resident in the UK. Income arising in that tax year is not treated as income taxable on the settlor if it would have been exempt from UK tax by virtue of the settlor's domicile or residence status. For example non-UK source income of an offshore trust.[80] Where income is excluded under this rule it may be treated as arising in a subsequent year in which it is remitted to the UK and is then taxable on the settlor if at that time on the assumption that the settlor was entitled to the income he would be chargeable to UK tax on it by reason of his residence in the UK.

When does the settlor retain an interest in a settlement? ITTOIA 2005, s.625 provides that the settlor shall *not* be deemed to have an interest in property if and so long as none of that property, and no derived property, could become payable to or applicable for the benefit of the settlor or the spouse or civil partner of the settlor, except in the event of: **4.34**

(i) the bankruptcy of some person who is or may become beneficially entitled to the property or any derived property[81];

(ii) an assignment of or charge on the property or any derived property being made or given by some such person[82];

(iii) in the case of a marriage settlement, the death of both parties to the marriage and of all or any of the children of the marriage[83]; or

(iv) the death of a child of the settlor who had become beneficially entitled to the property or any derived property at an age not exceeding 25.[84]

---

[78] Spouse includes since December 5, 2005 a registered civil partner.
[79] ITTOIA 2005, s.624). Compare the similar capital gains tax rules in the TCGA 1992, s.77 as amended. For the definition of a "spouse" for these purposes see ITTOIA 2005, s.625(4): note especially the exclusion of a separated spouse.
[80] S648(2)(3) ITTOIA 2005.
[81] ITTOIA 2005, s.625(2)(a).
[82] ITTOIA 2005, s.625(2)(b).
[83] ITTOIA 2005, s.625(2)(d).
[84] ITTOIA 2005, s.625(2)(e). See ITTOIA 2005, s.625(3) preventing any charge if a person is alive and under 25 years and during whose life the property cannot become applicable for the benefit of the settlor (or his spouse) save in the event of bankruptcy, assignment or charge. A typical

In addition a settlor will not be regarded as having an interest while there is a living beneficiary under the age of 25 during whose life the property or income can only be paid to or applied for the benefit of the settlor or his spouse/civil partner if the beneficiary becomes bankrupt or assigns or charges his interest in the property.

The settlor's spouse or civil partner does not include:

(i) a spouse/civil partner from whom the settlor is separated under a court order or a separation agreement;

(ii) a spouse from whom the settlor is separated where the separation is likely to be permanent (normally HMRC accept that a separation of 12 months is likely to be permanent);

(iii) the widow or widower of the settlor;

(iv) or a person to whom the settlor is not married or in a civil partnership but whom the settlor may later marry or enter into a civil partnership.

The settlor can recover any tax paid, either from the trustees or from any person to whom the income is payable.[85]

4.35 Accordingly, if there is a power to revoke the trusts (whoever possesses that power) and as a result the fund may revert to the settlor or his spouse, the income of the fund is treated as belonging to the settlor because the property "will or may" become payable to or applicable for the benefit of the settlor or his spouse.[86] If, under the terms of a discretionary settlement, any person has, or may have, the power to pay that income or property to the settlor or his spouse, then the income arising under the settlement is treated as belonging to the settlor.[87]

EXAMPLE 4.10

A creates a settlement in favour of his two adult daughters C and D, as concurrent life tenants. Because he has not disposed of the remainder interest, A has retained an interest in the fund with the result that the income is taxed as his.

4.36 The nature of the interest which the settlor must retain has given rise to some discussion. A power to participate in the management of the trust is not a sufficient interest; likewise, the possibility that a beneficiary might make a gift back to the settlor is to be ignored; and HMRC accept that if the trustees agree to pay the inheritance tax that arises on the creation of the settlement, this does not amount to the retention of an interest.[88] It is thought that the

---

accumulation and maintenance trust with a long-stop provision for the settlor or his spouse was thus covered.
[85] ITTOIA 2005, s.646.
[86] ITTOIA 2005, s.625(1).
[87] ITTOIA 2005, s.625(1).
[88] See HMRC SP 1/82.

possibility of acquiring an interest on the intestacy of a beneficiary does not give the settlor any interest in the settled property unless and until the possibility has become a reality.

4.37 If a settlement is made on the spouse of the settlor, income remains taxed as the settlor's unless the spouse is given an absolute interest in the property. Contrast the position where Mr A holds shares for Mrs A absolutely (income taxed as Mrs A's), with Mr A holding the shares for Mrs A for life, remainder to their son (income taxed as Mr A's).[89]

Payments to minor unmarried children of settlor

4.38 Income produced by a settlement which is paid during the settlor's lifetime to or for the benefit of the settlor's own minor unmarried child is normally treated as the income of the settlor. He can claim reimbursement of any tax suffered from the trustees. If income is accumulated under an irrevocable settlement of capital, however, the income is not treated as that of the settlor, but payments out of the fund are treated as the settlor's income up to the amount of the accumulations.[90]

EXAMPLE 4.11

> D settles shares for the benefit of his three children A, B and C in equal shares contingent on attaining the age of 21 years. They are all minors and unmarried. If the income of the fund is £10,000 a year the income tax position (for the tax year 2006/07) is as follows:
>
> (1) The trustees are liable for income tax at a rate of 40% (assuming that no dividend income is involved).
> (2) If the balance of the income (after the payment of tax) is accumulated, it is not treated as the income of the settlor. Therefore, so long as the income is retained in the trust no further income tax is payable.
> (3) If any of the income is paid to a child, it is treated as income of D. Say, for instance, that £1,200 is paid to, or for the benefit of, A. The result is that D's income is increased by £2,000 (£1,200 grossed up at 40%). He is given credit for the £800 tax paid by the trustees. Since the trust rate is now the same as the top rate of income tax he will not be subject to any further income tax charge.

---

[89] Contrast the capital gains tax provisions where a trust is treated as settlor interested if it can benefit a living dependent child of the settlor whether or not any trust gains or property is distributed to the child. See chapter 11. See also ITTOIA 2005, s.626: *Young v Pearce; Young v Scrutton* [1996] S.T.C. 743. For the application of the settlement rules in the context of shares in family companies owned by spouses, see the *Arctic Systems* case considered at 4.44 et seq.

[90] ITTOIA 2005, s.629. Note that there is *de minimis* provision whereby income paid to a child in a year of assessment is not taxed on the settlor provided that it does not exceed £100: ITTOIA 2005, s.629(3).

(4) If all the net income (£6,000) is distributed amongst the three beneficiaries (and, therefore, treated as D's income), any further distributions to the beneficiaries will be capital advancements.

4.39 Four other general matters should be noted, namely that:

(i) "child" is widely defined to include a stepchild,[91] an illegitimate child, and an adopted child,[92] but does not, presumably, include a foster child; and

(ii) the definition of settlement for these purposes includes a transfer of assets and an arrangement.[93]

(iii) if the settlor is not the parent of the child beneficiary, the above provisions do not apply; hence settlements funded by grandparents can, therefore, be advantageous from an income tax point of view.

(iv) discretionary income payments made on or after April 6, 2006 to unmarried minor children of a settlor, where that child is a vulnerable person for the purposes of FA 2005 and the trustees have made a claim under s.25 of FA 2005 for special income tax treatment, do not give rise to a charge to tax on the settlor under ITTOIA 2005, s.629.

4.40 **Other points on settlements for children:** there must be no power to terminate the trust in circumstances where the fund could revert to the settlor since otherwise he will be taxed on the income under s.624 (as a settlement in which he has retained an interest). It is of no import whether the power to terminate is given to the settlor or to a stranger. The settlement must be irrevocable. Furthermore, the income or assets from the fund must not be payable, according to the terms of the settlement, to or for the benefit of the settlor or his spouse except for payments made after the death of the child beneficiary or on the bankruptcy of the child, or on a purported charge or assignment of assets by the child. Therefore a settlement is irrevocable if the child is given a protected life interest under the standard trusts,[94] and if the settlement is to revert to the settlor on the death of the child beneficiary. Finally, a settlement is not irrevocable if it can be determined by act or default of any person. For example, a settlement that will terminate if the settlor ceases to be employed in a specified employment is not irrevocable.

Receipt of capital benefits

4.41 ITTOIA 2005, ss.633–643 contain provisions aimed at preventing the settlor obtaining any benefit from a settlement in which the income may be taxed at a lower rate than that which would have applied had the settlor retained it.[95]

---

[91] ITTOIA 2005, s.629(7)(a).
[92] TA 1988, s.832(5).
[93] *Thomas v Marshall* [1953] AC 543, [1953] 1 All E.R. 1102, HL. Parents may therefore create a settlement if they waive their entitlement to dividends in the family company as a result of which their minor children benefit.
[94] See TA 1925, s.33 as amended by the Family Law Reform Act 1987 s.33(1), Sch.2, para.2.
[95] With the increase in the trust rate to 40 per cent query whether these provisions are necessary.

In effect, capital payments to the settlor (or to his spouse) from the fund are matched with undistributed income of the fund and taxed as the settlor's income. The sum is grossed up at the 40 per cent rate; the settlor is entitled to credit for tax paid by the trustees, but not to any repayment.

A "capital sum" covers any sum paid by way of loan (whether or not on commercial terms) or a repayment of a loan and any sum paid otherwise than as income and which is not paid for full consideration in money or money's worth.[96] A capital sum is treated as paid to the settlor if it is paid to a third party at his direction or as a result of his assignment.[97]

4.42 A capital sum is only caught to the extent that it is less than, or equals, the income available in the settlement; this means the undistributed income of the trust fund from any year of assessment. Any excess is not charged in the year of receipt, but it may be charged later if income arises in the settlement in any of the next 10 years following the year in which it is paid[98] until the whole of the capital sum has been treated as income of the settlor. Any part of the capital sum which has not been matched with available income at the end of ten years following the year in which it is paid cannot be treated as income of the settlor.[99]

EXAMPLE 4.12

The undistributed net income of a settlement is as follows:

	£
Year 1	10,000
Year 2	nil
Year 3	12,000
Year 4	nil
Year 5	7,000

In Year 3, the trustees lend the settlor £45,000. That loan is a capital sum and, therefore, the settlor is charged to income tax in Year 3 on that sum to the extent that it represents available income. As the available income is £22,000 (Years 1–3) he is taxed on £22,000 grossed up at 40%; ie on £36,666. If he is liable to higher rate tax at 40% there is no further tax to pay. The remaining £23,000 is carried forward and taxed in succeeding years when income becomes available; in Year 5, for instance, £7,000 is available. If the loan is repaid, there is no further charge on income in subsequent years, but any tax paid during the loan period cannot be recovered.[1] Notably any tax payable by the settlor under these provisions cannot be recovered from the trustees.

Capital sums paid by a company connected with the settlement: The charge **4.43** also applies to a capital sum received by the settlor from a body corporate

---

[96] ITTOIA 2005, s.634(1).
[97] ITTOIA 2005, s.634(5).
[98] ITTOIA 2005, s.633(4).
[99] ITTOIA 2005, s.633(3)–(5).
[1] ITTOIA 2005, s.638(3)–(4).

connected with the settlement where the trustees have made an associated payment to the company. The payment by the company is deemed to have been made by the trustees. An associated payment in relation to a capital sum paid to a settlor means any capital sum paid to a company by the trustees and any other sum so paid or asset transferred, for less than full consideration, provided that it is made within five years before or five years after the date on which the sum is paid to the settlor. Generally, a company is connected with a settlement if it is a close company and the participators include the trustees of the settlement.[2] The width of the provision and its somewhat capricious nature[3] means that settlements often contain a clause prohibiting the payment of capital sums to the settlor or his spouse.

IMPLICATIONS OF THE ARCTIC SYSTEMS CASE[4]

4.44 It was the publicity surrounding the tax affairs of the married couple in *Jones v Garnett* (the *Arctic Systems* case)[5] which kick-started the recent concern shown by the tax profession over HMRC's views on the scope of the settlement legislation.

The facts of the case are reasonably straightforward. Mr Jones was an IT specialist and he had worked as an employee for several years. However, in 1992, he was made redundant and, following discussions with his wife, he decided to set up his own IT consultancy business. At an early stage, it became clear to Mr Jones that he would have to form a limited company because the IT agencies and their clients who would only deal with companies. As a result, on the advice of his accountants, Mr Jones and his wife acquired two shares in an off-the-shelf company called Arctic Systems Ltd, for which they each paid £1. Mr Jones was the sole director. As is customary with many small companies, he did not have a written service contract. Mrs Jones was the company secretary and she also undertook all the administrative work such as bookkeeping, invoicing and liaising with clients—she spent, on average, five hours per week on company business. The company paid them both a modest salary which was intended to meet their "basic needs", with the balance of the profits (after deduction of tax) being distributed as dividends. In his capacity as director, it was Mr Jones' decision as to when and in what sum dividends should be declared.

4.45 HMRC challenged the structure of Mr Jones' business and argued that the settlement provisions applied to the dividends received by Mrs Jones so that they should be taxed as the income of her husband. The case was heard in 2004 by two Special Commissioners who, very unusually, could not agree on the outcome.[6] Accordingly, the presiding Special Commissioner (Dr Brice) was entitled to exercise a casting vote. She was the one who had agreed with HMRC on the issues under consideration—the other Special Commissioner

---

[2] ITTOIA 2005, ss.637(8), 641.
[3] See, for example, *De Vigier v IRC* [1964] 2 All E.R. 907, [1964] 1 W.L.R. 1073, HL. As a result a settlor should not lend money to his settlement without first checking whether a repayment will be caught by these provisions.
[4] The authors are grateful to Robert Jamieson for the following analysis of this case.
[5] [2006] S.T.C. 283, CA.
[6] [2005] S.T.C. (SCD) 9.

(Miss Powell) had sided with Mr Jones—and so she gave her casting vote for the dismissal of Mr Jones' appeal against HMRC's 1999/00 assessment (which was the tax year under consideration). Mr Jones then appealed to the High Court.

4.46 In the High Court,[7] Park J found in favour of HMRC and dismissed Mr Jones' appeal. However, despite this reverse, Mr Jones decided to proceed to the Court of Appeal. The hearing took place at the end of November 2005 and a unanimous judgment in favour of the taxpayer was given on 15 December 2005.

4.47 *The Court of Appeal's decision and its consequences*: there were two substantive issues on which the Court of Appeal had to make a determination:

(i) whether there was a settlement within the statutory definition found in s.660G(1) of ICTA 1988 (see now s.620(1) of ITTOIA 2005); and

(ii) if so, whether it could be taken out of the charge to income tax by the let-out in s.660A(6) of ICTA 1988 (see now s.626 of ITTOIA 2005) for outright gifts to a spouse.

In the words of Sir Andrew Morritt:

> "The answer to the first question depends on the proper construction and application of the long-standing provisions to be found in ss.660A–660G ICTA 1988 in the light of the guidance afforded by a number of reported cases decided since 1939 (this is a reference to Copeman v Coleman (1939)). The answer to the second question depends on the true construction and application of s.660A(6) ICTA 1988."

4.48 After discussing in detail the case law which had been cited by both sides, Sir Andrew Morritt made a number of important points. He began by giving an indication of how his judgment would go when he said:

> "Counsel for Mr Jones submits that the only arrangement in this case was the acquisition of the share in the company by Mrs Jones in 1992. He contends that, on the findings of the Special Commissioners, that transaction involved no element of bounty because Mrs Jones gave full value for the share and the acquisition was made in the context of a decision by both Mr and Mrs Jones to set up a joint family enterprise for the purpose of which Mrs Jones provided services of substantial value.
>
> He submits that it is not legitimate to extend the arrangement, as HMRC seek to do, by reference to opportunities to which it might, but would not necessarily, give rise in the future. He contends that the arrangement cannot be enlarged to include the decisions in later years as to whether to pay any and, if so, what dividends because any such arrangement would be open-ended and lack the requisite "unity". How, he asks rhetorically, can there be an arrangement which for five years is not a settlement because there is no element of bounty yet in the sixth year becomes a settlement because a dividend is declared which entitles

---

[7] [2005] S.T.C. 1667.

Mrs Jones to a sum in excess of any value she contributed to the enterprise in that year? And, if the necessary element of bounty is to be found in that excess, how is it to be measured?"

He then goes on:

"Before the de-aggregation for tax purposes of the income of a married woman from that of her husband effected in 1990, this case could not have arisen because the income of Mrs Jones would have been aggregated with that of Mr Jones whether or not there was a settlement. It is also somewhat remarkable that this case could not have arisen after 1990 if Mr and Mrs Jones had lived together without being married. The provisions of S660A(2) ICTA 1988 may appear anachronistic, but they were not amended in 1989 or subsequently and must be given full effect. But that consideration does not, I think, require the Court to ignore the increasing tendency for married couples to be involved in the business of each other on a commercial non-bounteous basis. Such involvement may take the form of a partnership or a company in which each own shares. Though one spouse may generate the income of the firm or company, the services of the other may be just as commercially important in providing the essential administrative, accounting, support and back-up services."

He added:

"In this case, there can be no doubt but that the arrangement was or included the acquisition by Mrs Jones of her share in the company. Equally, there can be no doubt that the acquisition on its own was for full value in the context of a joint business venture to which both parties made substantial and valuable contributions. If the arrangement is confined to such acquisition, then I would agree with counsel for Mr Jones that it cannot constitute a settlement for the purposes of S660G(1) ICTA 1988 . . .

The "bounty" on which HMRC necessarily rely is that provided subsequently and in fact by the combination of the demand and charge-out rate for the services of Mr Jones, the salary in fact paid to Mr Jones, the other commitments of the company and the dividend subsequently declared and paid by the company to Mrs Jones. All these additional elements depended on the will of Mr Jones or wholly extraneous factors. He did not commit himself to working for the company at any particular rate of salary or at all. His charge-out rate necessarily depended on the demand for his services and the going market rate. Whether any and, if so, what profits were made depended not only on the difference between Mr Jones' charge-out rate and salary but the level of the company's overheads and other commitments. If the company made profits, whether to declare any and, if so, what dividend was a matter for Mr Jones as the sole director and controlling shareholder.

For my part, I do not think that these elements can be included in the "arrangement". They did not form any part of a structure of things or combination of objects; their uncertainty and fluidity is the converse of an arrangement. It is not that they were not legally enforceable, they were not settled at all. No doubt Mr and Mrs Jones hoped for the best, but it cannot be said that they had arranged it. Without these elements, there was no element of bounty and no settlement within the statutory definition."

He therefore concluded that there was no settlement in this case and, in arriving at his decision, he gave emphasis to one final salient point:

"In the absence of any service agreement between the company and Mr Jones, I am unable to accept that the payment of modest salaries to Mr Jones was any part of the arrangement. Similarly, the declaration of the dividends was not arranged in advance; it was dependent on the trading fortunes of the company. Further, as counsel for Mr Jones submitted and as I accept, the fact that the structure being set up might lend itself in the future to some tax mitigation is irrelevant to the existence of an element of bounty."

On the question of the possible application of s.660A(6) of ICTA 1988, Sir Andrew Morritt said that, if there had been a settlement, s.660A(6) of ICTA 1988 would not have disapplied s.660A(1) of ICTA 1988 because: **4.49**

(i) there was no outright gift of a share from Mr Jones to his wife, but that if there had been;

(ii) an ordinary share is *not* substantially a right to income.

This latter point specifically contradicts HMRC's view as set out in Examples 11 and 12 at the back of "*A Guide To The Settlements Legislation For Small Business Advisers*" (published in November 2004).

The other two judges agreed with Sir Andrew Morritt's conclusions. Carnwath L.J. made an interesting additional observation: **4.50**

"The lack of a clearly ascertainable legislative purpose underlines the need for caution in extending the concept of settlement beyond the scope of existing jurisprudence. HMRC's position in this case seems to me a significant extension. For the first time, they seek to apply the concept to what has been found to be a normal commercial transaction between two adults, to which each is making a substantial commercial contribution, albeit not of the same economic value. Such a difference, by itself, is not enough to my mind to take the arrangement into the realm of "bounty" as it has been understood in the existing cases. If the legislation wishes such an arrangement to be brought within a special regime for tax purposes, clearer language is necessary to achieve it."

In summary, the main points to come out of this decision are: **4.51**

(i) The reason why the taxpayer succeeded in this case was because, unlike many of the earlier settlement disputes (which typically involved parents settling income from the benefit of their children), there was *no* contract or mechanism in place at the outset either:

- to agree the future income of the business; or
- to decide on what might be done with any such income (eg. the payment of salaries or dividends at a later date).

(ii) HMRC have always argued that the settlement provisions can bite at any time—they said that it was necessary to review a business year by year in order to determine whether or not the settlement rules applied. The three judges totally disagreed with this contention—see Sir Andrew Morritt's words quoted above.

(iii) HMRC's interpretation of the settlement legislation in terms of a commercial venture between spouses was what one commentator has called "an unjustified extension to the scope of the rules".

(iv) If ordinary shares are the subject of an outright gift between husband and wife, the s.660A(6) of ICTA 1988 let-out (see now s.626 of ITTOIA 2005) will apply, given that an ordinary share cannot be "substantially a right to income".

4.52 There may still be problems in cases:

(i) where there are contracts in place at the outset (eg. to take over existing business arrangements); or

(ii) where the non-fee earning spouse plays no part in the business.

However, in (ii), fee earners should initially subscribe for *all* the shares in the new company and then make a gift of some of the shares to their spouses.

4.53 Finally, it should be noted that, although the three judges refused to give leave to appeal to the House of Lords, HMRC issued a statement on January 13, 2006 confirming that they had petitioned the House of Lords directly. On March 24, 2006, it was announced that the House of Lords would hear the appeal. Judgement is expected before the end of January 2007.

PART II: CAPITAL GAINS TAX

The CGT treatment of settlements has been subject to significant amendments since March 1998. FA 1998 substantially altered the taxation of offshore trusts; FA 2004 restricted hold-over relief in the case of UK resident settlor-interested trusts and FA 2006 has enacted some "modernisation" proposals for the taxation of trusts and further extended the definition of settlor-interested trust.

In this section, Chapter 5 sets out the key CGT definitions in relation to the taxation of trusts. Chapter 6 considers CGT issues on the creation of a settlement. Chapter 7 looks at actual and deemed disposals by trustees of UK resident settlements. Chapter 8 considers the capital gains tax position on the disposal of beneficial interests by beneficiaries and Chapter 9 is concerned with the hold-over relief provisions on disposals into and out of trusts. Chapter 10 considers the capital gains tax regime for non-resident trusts. Chapter 11 discusses the capital gains tax position of UK resident trusts which are settlor-interested and Chapter 12 considers the loss relief provisions for trusts and trustees.

CHAPTER 5

CGT DEFINITIONS

- The meaning of settled property **(5.02)**
- The definition of settlor **(5.16)**
- Single or multiple settlements; additions to settlements **(5.28)**
- The definition of trustees **(5.36)**
- When disposals arise **(5.39)**

The capital gains tax provisions tax settled property and not (generally) the value of the interests of the individual beneficiaries. Actual disposals by the trustees and certain deemed disposals may therefore trigger a charge: in other words, the legislation is primarily concerned with the gain or loss arising on the disposal of an asset which is comprised in the trust fund. Hence disposals of beneficial interests are normally exempt.[1] The creation and termination of a settlement may trigger actual and deemed disposals of "the assets" or "settled property" and therefore lead to a capital gains tax charge. FA 2006 has effected some "modernisation" and alignment with income tax.[2] **5.01**

THE MEANING OF SETTLED PROPERTY

"Settlement" is not defined, but *settled property*[3] is "any property held in trust"[4] with the exception of certain trusts detailed in TCGA 1992, s.60. **5.02**

When is property not settled for capital gains tax purposes?

In the following situations, although there is a trust, the property is not settled property but is treated as belonging to the beneficiary. In addition, settled **5.03**

---

[1] See generally Ch. 8.
[2] See generally FA 2006, Sch.12.
[3] As amended by Sch.12 of FA 2006 although the amendment merely adds the words "and references however expressed to property comprised in a settlement are references to settled property".
[4] TCGA 1992, s.68. For the purpose of the capital payment rules (relevant for trusts which are or have been non-UK resident), the income tax definition of a settlement is adopted: see TCGA 1992, s.97(7) as amended by FA 1998, s.129(2) and by FA 2000, Sch.26 Pt II para.4.

property for capital gains tax purposes does not include property which is held by personal representatives in the course of the administration of an estate.[5]

5.04 **Assets held by person as nominee or as bare trustee:** property is not settled where assets are held by a person as nominee for another person or as trustee for another person absolutely entitled as against the trustee. The provision covers both nomineeships and bare or simple trusts.[6]

EXAMPLE 5.1

> A parent settles a house on bare trust for his adult son giving the trustees administrative powers over the property.[7] The property is not settled property for capital gains tax purposes. Instead, the house is treated as belonging to the son so that the son's unused annual capital gains tax exemption will be available in respect of any gains made on a disposal by the bare trustee. The son is absolutely entitled as against the trustees in that he has the exclusive right (subject only to satisfying any outstanding charge, lien or other right of the bare trustees to resort to the asset for payment of duty, taxes or other outgoings), to direct how that asset shall be dealt with. The fact that the trustees may be given administrative powers to deal with the property does not make it settled property. The acts of the trustees are treated as the acts of the beneficiary.[8] Hence disposals of the property between nominee or bare trustee and the beneficiary are disregarded for capital gains tax purposes.[9]

5.05 **Property held on trust for a minor or person under a disability:** Property is not settled where it is held on trust for any person who would be absolutely entitled to that property but for being a minor or other person under a disability.[10]

EXAMPLE 5.2

> (1) A and B hold property for C aged 11 years absolutely. Because of his age C cannot demand the property from the trustees. On these facts there will be a settlement for income tax purposes although not it is thought

---

[5] Of course a trust (and therefore settled property) may arise at the conclusion of the administration.
[6] Bare trusts likewise do not fall within the definition of "settlement" for IHT purposes: see IHTA 1984, s.43 and Ch. 30.
[7] For bare trusts, see Ch. 30 and see App II for a precedent.
[8] See s.60(1).
[9] For example if a person becomes absolutely entitled to settled property on attaining the relevant age e.g. 21, the trustee is deemed to have disposed of the assets for market value at that time and to have reacquired them as bare trustee at that value (see TCGA 1992, s.71). When the trustee in his capacity as a bare trustee transfers the asset to the beneficiary that transfer is disregarded.
[10] TCGA 1992, s.60(1).

for inheritance tax purposes.[11] For CGT purposes, however, C is a person who would be absolutely entitled but for his minority and therefore he is treated as owning the trust property. Hence in addition to his annual exemption being available on any disposal of the property when C reaches 18 there is no deemed disposal so that there is no capital gains tax charge at that time.

(2) A and B hold property on trust for D, aged 12 years, contingent upon his attaining the age of 18 years. As with (1) above the beneficiary would be absolutely entitled were it not for his minority. D, however, is not entitled to claim the fund from the trustees *because of the provisions of the settlement*. Unlike (1) above, D's entitlement is contingent upon living to a certain age, so that, were he to ask the trustees to give him the property, they would refuse because he has not satisfied the contingency.[12] This, therefore, is settled property for the purposes of CGT.

Trust for two or more persons jointly absolutely entitled: property is not settled where property is held on trust for two or more persons who are or would be jointly absolutely entitled. The word "jointly" is not limited to the interests of joint tenants, but applies to concurrent owners and so covers more than one beneficiary concurrently entitled "in the same interest".[13]   **5.06**

Joint ownership covers a number of different situations as follows.

EXAMPLE 5.3—STATUTORY TRUSTS FOR SALE

A and B purchase Blackacre as tenants in common. The land is held on a trust of land as a result of the Law of Property Act 1925, ss.34 and 36,[14] but for the purposes of CGT the property is not settled and is instead treated as belonging to A and B equally.[15]

---

[11] See 15.03.
[12] See *Tomlinson v Glyn's Executor and Trustee Co* [1970] Ch. 112; [1970] 1 All E.R. 381, CA. In this case a settlor conveyed investments to trustees to hold in trust for such of the beneficiaries as shall attain the age of 21 or marry under that age. It was held that the beneficiaries were not absolutely entitled as against the trustees but for being infants because infancy was not the only impediment preventing the absolute entitlement. Their interests were defeasible and contingent. Hence the property was settled for capital gains tax purposes.
[13] See *Kidson (Inspector of Taxes) v Macdonald* [1974] Ch. 339, [1974] 1 All E.R. 849, [1974] S.T.C. 54. It was argued that property was not nominee property if the co-owners were tenants in common since s.60(1) refers to persons who are *jointly* entitled. This argument was rejected: it was held that jointly meant concurrently or in common.
  In *Stephenson v Barclays' Bank* and in *Booth v Ellard* [1980] 3 All E.R. 569; [1980] 1 W.L.R. 1443, CA, the question was whether the holders of successive interests (e.g. life interest and vested remainder interest) could be regarded as absolutely entitled if they were *sui juris* and together entitled to terminate the trust under the rule in *Saunders v Vautier* 41 E.R. 482. Such beneficiaries are jointly absolutely entitled but it was held that their interests have to be concurrent rather than consecutive for the purposes of s.60.
[14] Law of Property Act 1925, ss.34, 36 as amended by the Trusts of Land and Appointment of Trustees Act 1996, ss.5, 25(2), Sch.2, paras 3, 4, Sch.4.
[15] *Kidson (Inspector of Taxes) v Macdonald* [1974] Ch. 339; [1974] 1 All E.R. 849, [1974] S.T.C. 54.

EXAMPLE 5.4—POOLING ARRANGEMENTS

> T and his family own 72% of the issued share capital in T Ltd (their family company). In 1989 they enter into a written agreement as a result of which the shares are transferred to trustees and detailed restrictions, akin to pre-emption provisions in private company articles, are imposed. The beneficial interests of T and his family are not, however, affected in the sense that each shareholder has a beneficial interest corresponding to the shares transferred. It is just that the disposal of the beneficial interests is restricted. Subsequently the shares are transferred out again to the various members of the family in the same proportions. In such a "pooling arrangement" the shares are treated as nominee property with the result that there is no disposal for capital gains tax purposes either on the creation of the trust or on its termination.[16]

Similar arrangements are often made when parcels of land are transferred to trustees to secure better management of the whole but the individual share of each transferor in the whole corresponds to the land he contributed. (This is not uncommon where the ownership of parcels of land are split between different owners and they receive offers for the whole from a developer—they will often fare better in negotiations where they pool the land and operate together.)

HMRC formerly considered[17] that on a partition of real property each co-owner disposed of his undivided interest in the whole in consideration of the separate parcel he received on partition and by concession gave a form of rollover relief. In the light of *Jenkins v Brown*[18] it would appear that a partition which mirrors the underlying beneficial interests is not a disposal anyway so that no concession was needed.

5.07 **Absolute entitlement: TCGA 1992, s.60(2) provides as follows:**

> "It is hereby declared that references in this Act to any asset held by a person as trustee for another person absolutely entitled as against the trustee are references to a case where that other person has the exclusive right, subject only to satisfying any outstanding charge, lien or other right of the trustees to resort to the asset for payment of duty, taxes, costs or other outgoings, to direct how that asset shall be dealt with."

EXAMPLE 5.5

> (1) J is entitled to an annuity of £1,000 a year payable out of a settled fund held in trust for X absolutely. The property is settled for capital gains tax purposes.[19]

---

[16] Cf. *Booth v Ellard* above; and see *Jenkins v Brown* [1989] 1 W.L.R. 1163; *Warrington v Sterland* [1989] S.T.C. 577 in which a similar result was arrived at in the case of a pooling of family farms.
[17] ESC D26.
[18] ibid.
[19] *Stephenson v Barclays Bank Trust Co Ltd* [1975] 1 All E.R. 625; [1975] S.T.C. 151. The annuity is not a charge or outgoing and so causes the property subject to the annuity to be settled property.

(2) *Contrast*: L surrenders his qualifying interest in possession in July 2006 whereupon the settled property is held for M absolutely. M is "absolutely entitled" for CGT purposes although the trustees may insist on retaining assets to cover the risk of an IHT charge were L to die within seven years.[20]

5.08 TCGA 1992, s.60(2) does not offer any guidance on the question of when a beneficiary has the exclusive right to direct how the asset in the settlement shall be dealt with. Under general trust law, beneficiaries are not able to issue such directions unless they have the right to end the trust by demanding their share of the property.[21] Difficulties may arise in a number of circumstances. For example, suppose a beneficiary is one of a class and he satisfies the age contingency but the class has not yet closed.

EXAMPLE 5.6

Property is held on trust for such of the settlor's children as attain 21 years. Suppose he has four children and then becomes incapable of having further children.[22] The property remains settled property even after the children attain 21 unless and until the trustees apply to Court which can then give authority to distribute the trust fund.[23]

5.09 **Crowe v Appleby and appropriations:** what happens when one of a number of beneficiaries is entitled to a portion of the fund but other beneficiaries have not yet satisfied the contingency?

EXAMPLE 5.7

A trust fund is held for the settlor's three daughters (A, B and C) contingent upon attaining 21 and, if more than one, in equal shares. A, the eldest, is 21 years old and is, therefore, entitled to one-third of the assets.

Whether she is absolutely entitled as against the trustees to that share for *capital gains tax purposes* may depend upon the type of property held by the trustees. The general principle is that she is entitled to claim her one-third share, but not, in exceptional cases, when the effect of distributing that portion of the fund would be to damage the interests of the other beneficiaries. When the settled assets comprise land, this will be the result

---

[20] The surrender is a potentially exempt transfer for IHT purposes. If L did not have a qualifying interest in possession e.g he had an interest in possession that had arisen after March 21, 2006 which was not an immediate post death interest, transitional serial interest or disabled person's interest then his surrender is not a PET because the property in the trust is not in his estate for inheritance tax purposes. There will be an inheritance tax exit charge given that a relevant property settlement has ended and CGT hold-over relief will be available.
[21] See e.g. *Re Brockbank, Ward v Bates* [1948] Ch. 206; [1948] 1 All E.R. 287.
[22] As in *Figg v Clarke* [1997] S.T.C. 247.
[23] It is assumed that the trust does not provide for the class to close when the first child attains 21.

because the asset would often have to be sold to raise the necessary money.[24]

Hence if the fund comprises land, A is not absolutely entitled when she reaches 21; therefore, for capital gains tax purposes the settlement continues over the entire settled property until the land is sold by the trustees (in which event A takes one-third of the cash); all three daughters satisfy the contingency or the other two die before 21 years. Only then will the fund cease to be settled because one or more persons will, at that point, become jointly absolutely entitled.[25]

By contrast if A is entitled to demand her share (as would be the case if it were an investment portfolio), that proportion of the fund ceases to be settled (even though A may leave her share in the hands of the trustees who will then hold those assets as bare trustee or nominee subject only to their lien). HMRC accept that the principle of *Crowe v Appleby* may apply to other indivisible assets such as an Old Master painting or valuable antique.

5.10 However, even in relation to assets such as an investment portfolio which are readily divisible into shares, HMRC do not regard the beneficiary as having become absolutely entitled if the trustees have an express power of appropriation and do not exercise it.[26] In such cases they will treat A as absolutely entitled only when the trustees exercise that power (and only in respect of the assets so appropriated).

If no appropriation is made HMRC consider that the settlement continues until all beneficiaries are together absolutely entitled or the asset in question is sold if earlier.[27] It is questionable whether this view is correct.

5.11 It can produce apparently bizarre results: for instance, assume that A becomes entitled at age 25 to half the trust fund: his brother B will become entitled to the other half in two years time. Assume that the fund comprises some assets pregnant with gain and others showing neither gain nor loss. The trustees might appropriate the latter to A so that no CGT will be payable. In this connection—

---

[24] See *Crowe v Appleby* [1976] 2 All E.R. 914, CA and in particular the decision of Goff J. at High Court level, 51 TC 457, which decided that if the settled property was land in England or Wales there was no occasion of absolute entitlement on the occurrence of any contingency other than the final one. The land as a whole remained settled property and so any disposal of it is a disposal by the trustees. The position is different in relation to Scottish law trusts (even if the land is situated in England) and to land in Northern Ireland or the Irish Republic where the beneficiary can call upon the trustees to convey to him an undivided share in the property (see *Stenhouse's Trustees v Lord Advocate* [1984] S.T.C. 195, Ct of Sess). See further HM Revenue and Customs Capital Gains Manual CG37540 et seq. See generally *Snell's Equity* (31st edn) at 27.25. HMRC comment at 37540 that land owned by an English law trust in England, Wales or Scotland is within the scope of *Crowe v Appleby*.

[25] For problems that can arise on a division of a controlling shareholding, see *Lloyds Bank Plc v Duker* [1987] 3 All E.R. 193; [1987] 1 W.L.R. 1324. A is, of course, entitled to one-third of the income. For IHT purposes he is treated as the owner of one-third of the trust property.

[26] See 37521. It is thought that a similar approach will be taken in cases where there is only an *implied* power to appropriate.

[27] At CGM 37531: "until this power [of appropriation] is exercised the beneficiary cannot claim any specific asset and therefore it cannot be said that he or she is absolutely entitled to a fractional share of everything".

(i) It might be said that in so doing they were acting unfairly viz á viz B since his share will be diminished by the CGT payable on the CGT deemed disposal when he becomes entitled.[28]

(ii) HMRC's practice on appropriations is at odds with the following statement of Walton J. in *Stephenson v Barclay's Bank*.

> "When the situation is that a single person who is sui juris has an absolute vested beneficial interest in a share of the trust fund, his rights are not, I think, quite as extensive as those of the beneficial interest holders as a body. In general, he is entitled to have transferred to him (subject, of course, always to the . . . rights of the trustees . . .) an aliquot share of each and every asset of the trust fund which presents no difficulty so far as division is concerned. This will apply to such items as cash, money at the bank or an unsecured loan, stock exchange securities and the like. However, as regards land, certainly, in all cases, as regards shares in a private company in very special circumstances (see *Re Weiner's Will Trusts*) and possibly (although the logic of the addition in fact escapes me) mortgage debts (see *Re Marshall* per Cozens-Hardy MR) the situation is not so simple, and even a person with a vested interest in possession in an aliquot share of the trust fund may have to wait until the land is sold, and so forth, before being able to call on the trustees as of right to account to him for his share of the assets."

5.12 The application of *Crowe v Appleby* can produce other uncertainties. For example, it apparently does not apply where the trustees merely hold an equitable share in land.

EXAMPLE 5.8

> W dies in 2007 leaving her beneficial half share in the family home on discretionary trusts for her four children. Her husband owns the other half share and is after her death the sole legal owner. The trustees advance one-quarter of their half share to the eldest child. He becomes absolutely entitled to that share for all tax purposes.

5.13 *Crowe v Appleby* clearly applies where trustees have been left land by the settlor from the outset but what happens if trustees subsequently acquire it during the course of the trust? Should the rule also apply then? Apparently it does with the result that the trustees could defer a beneficiary's absolute entitlement indefinitely.

EXAMPLE 5.9

> The testatrix, W, leaves her residuary estate on trust for her three children contingent on attaining the age of 25. On her death the estate is made up

---

[28] See TCGA 1992, s.71.

of cash and quoted shares. The children are all minors. Just before the eldest child is 25 the trustees invest in real estate so that by the time the eldest child, A, is 25 the entire trust fund is comprised of residential properties. The trustees do not exercise their powers of appropriation (for example by allocating one house to A's share and another house of equal value to B and C's share). Instead the entire trust fund continues to be held in undivided shares. A does not become absolutely entitled to settled property when reaching 25. If the trustees later sell a house, one-third of that value belongs to A absolutely but the rest remains in trust.[29]

5.14 Suppose there are more complex trusts over the land: e.g. in 2006 a brother and sister each have a life interest in half the trust fund following the death of their parent. This will be a qualifying interest in possession being an immediate post death interest. Because the sister has no children the brother's children will take absolutely on the termination of the life interests.

If the brother dies in 2008, his children become absolutely entitled to one-half of the trust fund (the moiety in which the brother had enjoyed a life interest). However, the children will not be absolutely entitled for capital gains tax purposes until the death of the sister or the sale of the land, if earlier. Suppose the land is not sold and the sister dies in 2010. At that point the brother's children become entitled to the whole trust fund and there is a deemed disposal of the land under TCGA 1992, s.71.[30] For capital gains tax purposes there is a base cost uplift to market value as to one-half on the sister's death in 2010 and as to the other half share on the death of the brother in 2008. However, any increase in value on the brother's half share between 2008 and 2010 is chargeable on the trustees but with the benefit of continued taper relief.[31]

5.15 [32]A person can become absolutely entitled to assets without being "beneficially" entitled.[33]

THE DEFINITION OF SETTLOR

5.16 As part of the so-called modernisation process a new definition of settlor was inserted into TCGA 1992.[34] Section 68A defines the meaning of settlor; s.68B

---

[29] Note that if A dies there was a base cost uplift for capital gains tax purposes but only as to his one-third share in the entire trust fund: see 7.41. But note the changes resulting from FA 2006: see App. III A3.105.

[30] See 7.46.

[31] See Ch. 12 for taper relief and other problems arising out of *Crowe v Appleby*. In particular, there is no hold over relief in 2010 on the brother's share. Presumably the uplift on the brother's death in 2008 would be less than half the market value of the property on the basis that he was not absolutely entitled to it. See also App. III A3.105.

[32] For inheritance tax purposes there is no *Crowe v Appleby* rule so on the death of the brother his share ceases to be settled property and since the life interests taken by the brother and sister qualify as IPDI's there is no relevant property charge if the sister is still alive at the ten year anniversary of the death of the parent even though the children are not absolutely entitled to the brother's share for capital gains tax purposes. The problems this can cause are discussed in Ch. 7.

[33] Hence property can pass out of the settlement into another settlement: the trustees of the latter have become absolutely entitled as against the trustees of the former: see 7.55. See *Hoare Trustees v Gardner* [1978] STC 89; *Roome v Edwards* [1981] S.T.C. 96.

[34] See TCGA 1992, s.68A inserted by FA 2006. The equivalent provision in the income tax legislation is in ITTOIA 2005, s.620.

considers the identity of the settlor in the case of transfers between settlements, and s.68C identifies the settlor when there is a variation of a will or intestacy.

Settlor means: **5.17**

> "the person who has made or is treated . . . as having made, the settlement and includes a person (a) who has made or entered into a settlement directly or indirectly or (b) the settled property or property from which the settlement is derived, is or includes property of which he was competent to dispose immediately before his death and the settlement arose on his death, whether by will on his intestacy or otherwise".[35]

This includes property which was already in trust but was then held on new trusts as the result of the exercise of a general power of appointment. This is similar to the definition of settlor in ITTOIA 2005, s.620 and IHTA 1984, s.44 which both refer to a person making a settlement.

Where A enters into a settlement in accordance with reciprocal arrangements with B, B not A is treated as having made the settlement. **5.18**

EXAMPLE 5.10

> B persuades his cousin A to set up a trust fund for B's children into which A transfers shares worth £100,000. B agrees to give A £100,000. B is treated as the settlor of the settlement.

It is clear that for inheritance tax and capital gains tax purposes a person who has made or entered into a settlement has always been within the definition of settlor because it is not considered necessary for bounty to have been provided for a person to make a trust.[36] Hence where a company has set up a trust for employees, it is the settlor even though it may be acting for purely commercial (not bounteous) reasons. However, it is clear that for ss.77 and 86, 87[37] purposes some element of bounty was required.[38] What is not clear is whether this new definition means that a trust can now be treated as settlor-interested even if there is no element of bounty; it is thought that the position has not changed. **5.19**

Where someone adds property to the trust but that property is subsequently distributed to a beneficiary he ceases to be the settlor.[39] Presumably it will be necessary to be able to identify property provided by different settlors.[40]

---

[35] TCGA 1992, s.68A(2)(a).
[36] See CG Manual 33240.
[37] i.e. UK and offshore settlor-interested trusts and in respect of the beneficiary charge on offshore trusts.
[38] See *Tax Bulletin* 16.
[39] TCGA 1992, s.68A(6)(a).
[40] For a discussion of when property provided by different settlors is comprised in a single settlement: see 5.28.

EXAMPLE 5.11

> Mr P transfers a house into a trust which had been set up by his father and already holds £1m cash. The house is sold for £500,000 and the proceeds distributed to Mr P at a later date. Apparently Mr P ceases to be settlor of the trust. The father remains the settlor of the remaining assets.

5.20 This definition also raises the question of whether when a person who is not the original settlor adds property to an existing settlement he has created a separate settlement or becomes a settlor of the existing settlement.[41] As a matter of trust law it is common for additions to be merged with the existing trust property and treated as one fund for all purposes and there is nothing in the CGT legislation to displace this treatment.

5.21 Was a new definition of settlor needed? There is a specific definition in the case of settlor-interested trusts: in TCGA 1992, s.79 (UK resident settlements) and in Sch.5, para.7 (non-resident settlements). In both, the definition of settlor is related specifically to the settled property comprised in the settlement rather than the making of the settlement.

> "A person is a settlor . . . [for the purposes of s 77/s 86] in relation to a settlement if the settled property consists of or includes property originating from him".

The new definition does not amend these provisions and the result is confusion. The explanatory notes to F(No 2)A 2006 shed no light as to what the draftsman hoped to achieve and when the point was raised in the Finance Bill Committee debates, HM Paymaster General was equally mystifying in her response.[42]

5.22 **Resettlements:** When property is transferred from one settlement or fund to another settlement or fund the following issues arise:

(i) Who is the settlor of the transferred funds?

(ii) What is the effect of such a transfer in capital gains tax terms—is there a new settlement and hence a deemed disposal or does the property remain comprised in the original settlement in which case there is no disposal? The latter question is discussed in 7.55.

5.23 **Who is the settlor?** TCGA 1992, s.68B (inserted by FA 2006) contains specific identification provisions. The settlor of the property disposed of by the trustees of settlement 1 is treated from the time of the transfer as having made settlement 2 and is treated as the settlor of settlement 2. If there is more than one settlor of the original settlement it is not clear how the property is apportioned between the settlors.

---

[41] See the discussion at 5.28 regarding single or multiple settlements. Compare IHTA 1984, s.44(2): in the case of multiple settlors when "the circumstances so require" the property is treated as comprised in separate settlements.

[42] One of the many examples where the so-called plain English re-write adds to the complications already inherent in the tax legislation.

Example 5.12

> A and B jointly fund a settlement. A settles a house and B shares. The shares are transferred to settlement 2 a year later. The shares are worth 25 per cent of the whole of settlement 1. Is B the sole settlor of settlement 2 or are both A and B the settlors of settlement 2 as to 75%/25% (and does B cease to be a settlor of settlement 1?)? On a literal reading of s.68B(3) both are settlors of a proportionate part of the transferred property.

5.24 This problem was raised in the Finance Committee debates. HM Paymaster General, Dawn Primarolo MP, assured the Committee that where the property being transferred came from B alone (as in the above example) only B would be the settlor of the new trust. If it was not possible to establish a clear identification of the assets then each settlor would be treated as settlor of a proportionate part equivalent to the value settled.[43] "In most cases it should be possible to attribute property that has not been turned into cash by the original settlors." It "would depend on the facts" as to whether a settlor ceased to be a settlor of a settlement.

5.25 Nevertheless s.68B (and its equivalent provision in the income tax legislation) leaves a state of uncertainty. When trustees exercise a power of appointment it is the person who provided the original settled property, not the trustees, who has always as a matter of trust and tax law been treated as the settlor, so one questions why these provisions were required at all. And as noted above, the legislation confuses the position in a case where two settlors have settled property on a single trust and the trustees advance only some of the property to a new trust.[44]

5.26 **Instruments of variation of wills or intestacy:** the basic rule is that where the variation creates a settlement that would not otherwise have existed, the deceased is not treated as the settlor for income tax and capital gains tax purposes.[45]

Example 5.13

> Frederick dies leaving his foreign property absolutely to his son. Frederick was not UK domiciled. His son is. The son therefore executes a deed of variation under which the property is settled on trust for himself and his children. Reading back for inheritance tax purposes

---

[43] See 12th sitting of Standing Committee A.
[44] See *West v Trennery* [2005] 1 All E.R. 827 did not cast doubt on the settlor rather than the trustees being the settlor of the transferee trust. The question in that case was whether the trust was settlor-interested and the point that the settlor might not be the person who originally settled the funds was not even raised. The case is discussed in detail in Ch. 16. Another question is whether the two funds should be treated as one settlement either as a matter of trust law or under tax law—see extended definition of settlement for capital gains tax purposes on offshore trusts and for income tax purposes *Chinn v Collins* [1981] 1 All E.R. 189.
[45] TCGA 1992, s.68C and for deeds of variation generally, see Ch. 29.

Frederick is treated as a settlor of an excluded property settlement.[46] For capital gains tax purposes the son is the settlor.[47]

5.27 Contrast the position where a variation ends an existing trust set up under the will and establishes a new trust. In these circumstances the deceased is treated as the settlor.[48]

EXAMPLE 5.14

> Frederick dies leaving his property on life interest trusts for his spouse and then to his children outright. Spouse and children execute a deed of variation setting up new trusts for the grandchildren. The settlor is the deceased.

SINGLE OR MULTIPLE SETTLEMENTS

5.28 The question of when a separate settlement arises as the result of the trustees exercising a power of appointment or advancement is discussed at 7.55. However, the problem of whether there are two trusts or one can arise in other contexts, for instance:

(i) The testator may in his will leave different property on separate trusts for different beneficiaries. Is there one trust or two?

(ii) A settlor may add property to a trust. Is this to be treated as a new settlement for capital gains tax purposes or merely an addition?

(iii) A different person may add property to an existing trust. Is this a separate trust?

5.29 There is no general definition of the term "*settlement*" in the capital gains tax legislation. However, there is a special definition that applies in relation to TCGA 1992, ss.87–97, which apply where the trustees of the settlement are neither resident nor ordinarily resident in the UK. Where the trustees are resident in the UK, however, statute is silent and the court approaches the meaning of the terms "settlement" and "settled property" in the manner explained by Lord Wilberforce in *Roome v Edwards* at pp.292–3.

> "There are a number of obvious indicia which may help to show whether a settlement, or a settlement separate from another settlement, exists. One might expect to find separate and defined property; separate trusts; and separate trustees. One might also expect to find a separate disposition bringing the separate settlement into existence. These indicia may be helpful, but they are not decisive. For example, a single disposition,

---

[46] See Ch. 29.
[47] See *Marshall v Kerr* [1994] 3 All E.R. 106, HL.
[48] See further Ch. 29.

e.g. a will with a single set of trustees, may create what are clearly separate settlements, relating to different properties, in favour of different beneficiaries, and conversely separate trusts may arise in what is clearly a single settlement, e.g. when the settled property is divided into shares. There are so many possible combinations of fact that even where these indicia or some of them are present, the answer may be doubtful, and may depend upon an appreciation of them as a whole.

Since "settlement" and "trusts" are legal terms, which are also used by business men or laymen in a business or practical sense, I think that the question whether a particular set of facts amount to a settlement should be approached by asking what a person, with knowledge of the legal context of the word under established doctrine and applying the knowledge in a practical and common-sense manner to the facts under examination, would conclude."[49]

Offshore trusts: TCGA 1992, s.97(7) provides that the definition of "settlement" and "settlor" in s.620, ITTOIA 2005 shall apply in relation to offshore trusts but so as to include a settlement arising under a will. Section 620(1) ITTOIA 2005 defines a "settlement" as including— 5.30

> "any disposition, *trust*, covenant, agreement, arrangement or transfer of assets . . . " (our emphasis).

This definition is not an exhaustive definition. Its object is to extend the term "*settlement*" beyond the ordinary meaning that would be ascribed to the term when considering its meaning in a business or common-sense way, (compare the comments of Lord Wilberforce above).

The inheritance tax legislation provides for the possibility of separate settlements, for example where there are different settlors.[50] 5.31

Why does it matter whether there is one trust or two? This can be important for a variety of reasons: for example 5.32

(i) Each trust has its own annual exemption. Trusts made by the same settlor will have to share this equally. If there are multiple settlors of one trust then one annual exemption is given for the whole trust. Where the settlors have set up a number of other settlements, the exemption given is calculated by reference to the settlor who set up the most number of settlements! So if a trust holds property settled by A who set up 10 other trusts, the annual capital gains tax exemption is the minimum.[51] It cannot be increased by B (who has not made any other trusts) adding £100 to the trust.

(ii) A loss realised by the trustees can be set against gains of the same settlement. If assets are comprised in different trusts then the loss in one cannot be set against the gain in the other.

(iii) If the trusts are offshore or have been offshore it will be important to know whether one is dealing with one trust or two for the purpose of determining s.87 gains and capital payments.

---

[49] [1981] 1 All E.R. 736; [1981] S.T.C. 96.
[50] IHTA 1984, s.44(2).
[51] See Ch. 7.

(iv) Trustees of one settlement are liable for the capital gains tax payable by virtue of the disposal of any asset comprised in the settlement, even if the assets are vested in different trustees who may be resident abroad.[52]

(v) If one settlor is non-resident and not UK domiciled at the date the trust was set up then from April 6, 2007 the trust will not be resident here if there is one non-UK resident trustee. However, if someone who is resident or domiciled here later adds funds to the trust (rather than sets up a new trust) then the trust becomes UK resident as to the entirety of the assets.[53]

5.33 **Single Instrument—Multiple Trusts?** HMRC have set out in their manual[54] their practice in deciding whether there are separate settlements arising under a single deed of settlement or will. In their view one instrument can create separate settlements if:

(i) there are from the outset two or more completely segregated funds, each held on completely separate trusts;

(ii) the funds continue to be held on separate trusts in all circumstances. However, if there is a default provision under which one fund will accrue to another if the trusts of that fund fail this is suggestive of a single settlement;

(iii) There are no assets held in common.

However, the above criteria are no more than indications of whether there is a single settlement although (i) is probably the most important. The question may be difficult to determine in the case of a will which might have the same trustees, trusts in a similar form but different beneficiaries and different assets.

After all it is not uncommon for trustees to hold assets in separate funds within the same settlement and surely how the fund has been administered *after* the trusts have been constituted cannot determine whether or not one has a single settlement. For example if a will sets up two trusts the fact that the trustees are confused and administer them as one trust does not change the legal position. In the end it is a matter of construction of the instrument.

5.34 In *Bond v Pickford*[55] the Court of Appeal had to decide whether an exercise by trustees of a special power of appointment had created a new settlement. Slade L.J. pointed out that in such a case one relevant test, following the exercise of the power, was to ask:

> "Do the trustees of the original settlement still have duties to perform in regard to the relevant assets in their capacity as trustees of that [original] settlement?"

This test may be relevant in deciding whether or not there is a separate settlement in relation to assets derived from dispositions of a will. If, once the

---

[52] See for example *Roome v Edwards* [1981] 1All E.R. 736 HL.
[53] See Ch. 2
[54] See CG 33296—CG33305.
[55] [1983] S.T.C. 517.

executors of the will have transferred assets to A and B as trustees of one disposition in that will, neither the executors nor C and D as the trustees of a second separate disposition in the will have any duties to perform in regard to those assets, then it is difficult to see how A and B, as trustees of the first disposition in the will, can be trustees of the same settlement as C and D, as trustees of the second disposition in the will.

Indeed it is clear from the judgment of Lord Wilberforce (see above extract)[56] that, in principle, a will may create two separate settlements. Where there is "separate and defined property; separate trusts; and separate trustees" the fact that there is an initial identity of the dispositive provisions applicable to the two funds (e.g. discretionary trusts) does not prevent there being two separate settlements. Even if the trustees are the same this would not be conclusive in determining a single settlement.

5.35 **Additions to trusts:** under the general law when further property is transferred to the trustees of an existing settlement by the original settlor and accepted by them as an addition to the funds subject to the trusts of that settlement, that further property is not regarded as being subject to a separate settlement.[57]

Where property is transferred to an existing settlement by someone other than the original settlor it may be more likely that a new trust has been created.[58] One should look at whether there are separate trusts governing beneficial entitlement, separate trustees and separate administration, although none of these factors is conclusive.

DEFINITION OF TRUSTEES[59]

5.36 The trust modernisation exercise has resulted in a common definition of residence for income tax and capital gains tax purposes. This is discussed further at 2.38. Note that unlike the other modernisation changes which take effect from April 6, 2006, the harmonised residence test will take effect from April 6, 2007.

5.37 It is clear that trustees of settled property are and continue to be treated as a distinct, single and continuing body for capital gains tax purposes. Hence the trustees make disposals for capital gains tax purposes in their capacity as trustees and the taxation affairs of the trust are entirely separate from the taxation affairs of the individuals who act from time to time as trustees. There is generally no capital gains tax "event" on a change of trustee[60] because they are treated as a single and continuing body. Schedule 12, FA 2006 amended s.69, TCGA 1992 to state that trustees are to be treated as a single person rather than as "a single body of persons". It is not clear what the practical effect of this change may be.

---

[56] See 5.29.
[57] See *Playfair Palmer v Playfair* [1951] Ch. 4: A father had created a settlement on the marriage of his child and subsequently left a legacy by will to the trustees to be held by them on the trusts of that settlement. It was held that the will did not create a separate settlement.
[58] See CGT Manual 33320.
[59] See Ch. 2 for trustee residence.
[60] Unless the trust becomes non-resident: see Ch. 2.

5.38   Section 69(3) provides that trustees are a single continuing body of persons even if some of the property comprised in a settlement is vested in one set of trustees and some in another. This would arise where identical property is appropriated to separate trustees without creating a new settlement[61] (unless a sub-fund election was made: see 7.72).

HMRC need only assess one member of the single and continuing body to recover capital gains tax.[62] For the liability of retired trustees when a trust subsequently goes non-resident, see Ch. 2. Non-UK resident trustees are not generally liable for capital gains tax (see Ch. 10) although tax on gains attributed to the settlor under s.86 may be recoverable from them. There are different rules governing the liability of UK resident trustees for capital gains tax where the trust is settlor interested: see Ch. 11.

DISPOSALS

5.39   A disposal must occur before a capital gain or loss can arise. In the context of settled property, relevant capital gains tax disposals can be actual or deemed but the term "disposal" is not itself defined and does not generally include a transaction where an asset is not acquired but is merely extinguished (although if a capital sum is derived from assets the assets are in any event deemed to be disposed of).[63] An actual disposal is generally taken to mean the transfer of ownership of an asset by one person to another.[64] A deemed disposal does not necessarily require this.

5.40   Disposals of assets comprised in a trust fund will arise in any of the circumstances set out below. Some of these are "deemed disposals" and some are actual disposals. Generally a deemed disposal by trustees is treated as taking place at market value with a deemed reacquisition of the property by the trustees at that value.

(i) When assets are transferred into a trust by the settlor, either on creation of the settlement or by subsequent additions.[65]

(ii) On the death of a beneficiary entitled to a qualifying interest in possession in the settled property.[66]

(iii) If a beneficiary becomes absolutely entitled to the settled assets as against the trustees.[67]

(iv) On actual disposals of assets by the trustees themselves during the course of administering the trust.

---

[61] See *Roome v Edwards*.
[62] TCGA 1992, s.65(1). Hence a trustee can be accountable for gains accruing in respect of any of the assets of the settlement even if he has never controlled them himself. e.g because they are held in a separate sub-fund by other trustees.
[63] TCGA 1992, s.22.
[64] See *Welbeck Securities Ltd v Powlson* [1987] S.T.C. 468 and *Kirby Thorn EMI* [1987] S.T.C. 621. In *MacNiven v Westmoreland Investments Ltd* [2001] UKHL; [2001] S.T.C. 237 it was held the term disposal is a commercial concept and not a term of art.
[65] TCGA 1992, s.22.
[66] See Ch. 7.
[67] TCGA 1992, s.71: see Ch. 7.

(v) On the occasion when the trustees of a trust become non-resident or are treated as such under a double tax treaty.[68]

(vi) On the disposal of an interest in a settlor: interested trust for consideration.[69]

(vii) On transfer of assets from one trust to a new settlement.

(viii) On certain occasions where trustees make a transfer of value linked with trustee borrowing.[70]

(ix) When sub-fund elections are made.[71]

In addition, beneficiaries disposing of their beneficial interests under the settlement are in limited circumstances taxed on the value of those interests.[72]

---

[68] TCGA 1992, s.80 and see Ch. 2.
[69] TCGA 1992, Sch.4A and see Ch. 11.
[70] TCGA 1992, Sch.4B, C and see Ch. 10.
[71] FA 2006, Sch.12 and see Ch. 7.
[72] See Ch. 8.

CHAPTER 6

CGT ON CREATION OF A SETTLEMENT

- Disposals to trustees—connected party provisions **(6.01)**
- Hold-over relief **(6.03)**
- Instalment option double charges **(6.07)**
- Rates of tax **(6.09)**

DISPOSALS TO TRUSTEES

6.01 The occasion on which an asset becomes settled property is a complete disposal of the asset settled.[1] The disposal by the settlor is treated as taking place at market value[2] whether the settlement is revocable or irrevocable, and whether or not the settlor or his spouse is a beneficiary.[3] If chargeable assets are settled, a chargeable gain or allowable loss may result calculated according to the usual capital gains tax rules and with taper relief if appropriate. The rules on hold over relief are discussed in detail in Chapter 14. Taper relief is considered in Chapter 12 and settlor-interested trusts in Chapter 16.

6.02 As the settlor and his trustees are connected persons,[4] any loss resulting from the disposal is only deductible from a gain on a subsequent disposal to *those trustees*.

[1] See s.70 TCGA 1992 and *Berry v Warnett* [1982] S.T.C. 496. The fact that the settlor retains a life interest or is a trustee does not mean that the disposal is not a complete disposal for capital gains tax purposes.

[2] *Turner v Follett* (1973) 48 T.C. 614. Note that gifts into a settlement are at no gain no loss if the settlement is an employee trust. See TCGA 1992, s.239.

[3] See TCGA 1992, s.70. Note that this contrasts with jurisdictions such as the USA where disposals to grantor trusts can be treated as non-events for capital gains tax purposes and the trust is fiscally transparent and taxed as if the assets were still owned by the settlor. This was considered in the consultation on modernisation of trusts and it would have been a considerable simplification of the tax system to make settlor-interested trusts fiscally transparent for capital gains tax purposes (and more in line with what was then the inheritance tax treatment of settlor-interested trusts where the settlor took an interest in possession: the settlor was not prior to March 22, 2006 treated as making a transfer of value because his estate was not diminished.) In the event the inheritance tax changes in FA 2006 have moved away from the idea of fiscal transparency in these circumstances and the capital gains tax changes have merely extended the definition of what is settlor-interested without making such a trust fiscally transparent. Hence a settlor is taxed on gains arising in respect of a settlor-interested trust yet the disposal of assets by him into such a trust is treated as taking place at market value and no hold-over relief is available.

[4] TCGA 1992, s.18(3). For a consideration of the connected person rule, see *Tax Bulletin*, Issue 6, February 1993, p.56.

EXAMPLE 6.1

> Ambitious wishes to sell his investment portfolio which is standing at substantial capital gain. He also owns farmland which has fallen in value (and which he wishes to retain). Consider the following—
> (i) Ambitious settles both the shares and the farmland on a trust under which he retains an interest in possession (the trustees also have a power to pay or transfer capital to him).
> (ii) The disposal to the trustees triggers the gain (on the shares) and loss (on the land). The loss can be used to reduce the chargeable gain realised by Ambitious. The trust acquires the shares and land at market value at the date when they are transferred to the trustees.
> (iii) The trustees may then sell the shares and subsequently transfer the cash and farmland back to Ambitious.
>
> Note that if Ambitious had transferred the shares to one trust and the land to another although both trusts are connected with him he cannot set the loss on the land against the gain on the shares—the disposals must be to the same connected party.

Beware of (a) any suggestion that the arrangement is a sham and (b) the IHT position on the creation of new settlements after March 21, 2006. Prior to March 22, 2006 such a transfer would have been neutral for inheritance tax purposes because the settlor was treated as continuing to own the property beneficially. No transfer of value arose. After March 21, 2006, however, such transfers will prima facie be chargeable transfers for inheritance tax purposes irrespective of any interest retained by the settlor.[5]

HOLD-OVER RELIEF

A gain arising on the disposal of assets into trust may be held over[6]: **6.03**

(i) under TCGA 1992, s.165 if the assets in question are "business assets";

(ii) under TCGA 1992, s.260(2)(a) "if the disposal is made otherwise than under a bargain at arm's length and is a chargeable transfer within the meaning of IHTA 1984 . . . and is not a potentially exempt transfer". As a result of the 2006 changes in the IHT treatment of settlements, in most cases the creation of a settlement will now involve a chargeable transfer.[7]

It is important to bear in mind that for disposals made on or after December 5, 2003 no hold-over relief is available under either s.165 nor s.260 if the trust is **6.04**

---

[5] There is a limited let out for self-settlements where the settlor has reason to believe that he may become disabled and for interest in possession trusts for a disabled person: see Ch. 26.
[6] See Ch. 14.
[7] These changes are considered in detail in Ch. 11 onwards.

"*settler-interested*".[8] For disposals made into trust prior to April 6, 2006, only if the settlor, his spouse or civil partner could benefit was the trust treated as settlor-interested. For disposals into trust from April 6, 2006,[9] however, any unmarried minor child or stepchild of the settlor is taken into consideration in deciding whether the trust is settlor-interested.[10]

EXAMPLE 6.2

> In July 2006 X sets up a life interest trust for his wife. Although a chargeable transfer for IHT purposes, no hold over relief is available because the trust is settlor-interested. In 2010 the trustees—exercising a power to pay or apply capital—advance the trust fund to Mrs X.
>
> On the termination of the trust there is an IHT "exit" charge and CGT hold-over relief is available. Note that the restriction on hold-over relief for settlor-interested trusts only applies on disposals *into* the trust not out of it.[11]

6.05 If the trust becomes settlor-interested within the prescribed period (six years after the end of the tax year in which the disposal takes place) there is a clawback of any hold-over relief. This is discussed further in Ch. 9.

EXAMPLE 6.3

> (1) On April 6, 2006 A sets up a UK resident trust for the benefit of his children. One of his children is under 18. Unless that child is excluded from benefit until he or she reaches 18 there is no hold-over relief on creation of the trust. Any future gains realised by the trust will be subject to capital gains tax on the settlor with a right of reimbursement from the trustees. Consider the exclusion of children while minors or provide that no income or capital can be distributed to children of the settlor while they are minors. If they are the only beneficiaries the trustees may be required to accumulate income during their minority so that no distributions can be made.
>
> (2) A sets up a UK resident trust for his children (all of whom are adult but the class is open) in June 2006. He and his wife are excluded from benefit. Hold-over relief is available even though unborn minor children could benefit. In 2009 A divorces and remarries and his wife has a child aged 8 who becomes his stepchild. Unless that stepchild is at that point excluded from benefit, at least until he reaches 18, the trust becomes

---

[8] There is a minor exception for a transfer of business assets into a disabled trust which is settlor-interested because it is in favour of a dependant child of the settlor: see Ch. 11.
[9] TCGA 1992, s.77(2A) as amended.
[10] The definition of a settlor-interested trust is considered in greater detail in Ch. 11. If the settlor has no minor children alive—albeit that any would benefit—this fact does not make the trust settlor-interested. Spouse for this purpose includes a registered civil partner but not a separated spouse.
[11] For the deemed disposal on the ending of the trust: see Ch. 7.

settlor-interested within the claw back period and there is a clawback of the held over gain.

Continued availability of hold-over relief for bare trusts even if a "settlor-interested" trust: hold-over relief may continue to be available if property is transferred to a bare trust for the settlor's minor unmarried child. In this situation the property is not settled for CGT nor, it is thought, for IHT purposes.[12] The result is that the disposal is considered to be an outright disposal to the child and hence hold-over relief may be available if the property is business property qualifying within TCGA 1992, s.165. Moreover, on later disposal by the bare trustee the annual capital gains tax exemption of the beneficiary is available to set against the chargeable gain even though he is the minor unmarried child of the settlor.[13] 6.06

INSTALMENT OPTION DOUBLE CHARGES

Instalment option: If hold-over relief is not available (or is clawed back), any tax due may be paid (by election in writing) by ten equal yearly instalments if the gifted asset consists of any of the following: 6.07

(i) an interest in land;
(ii) shares or securities of a company which immediately before the disposal gave the transferor control;
(iii) any other unlisted shares or securities whether or not giving control: Section 281 of TCGA 1992.

The first instalment is due on January 31 following the tax year of disposal and the unpaid tax will attract interest which will be payable with each instalment. The outstanding balance and accrued interest may be paid at any time by the donor. Any unpaid tax becomes immediately payable if the trust subsequently disposes of the asset for valuable consideration.

Double tax charges: where a settlor transfers assets into a trust is there a potential double inheritance tax/capital gains tax charge? HMRC have commented as follows: 6.08

> "BN25[14] was misleading on this point and [we] apologise for that. The first bullet of paragraph 14 says CGT roll over relief will be available to transfers into trusts, but that is not true for settlor interested trusts and following the changes announced in BN 35 settlor interested trusts for CGT purposes does now include certain trusts where the minor children of the settlor are beneficiaries of the trust.
>
> [we] agree that in theory there can be a double charge to IHT and CGT on a transfer into a settlor interested trust—assuming IHT

---
[12] See Ch. 30, but also see App. III A3.105 (Question 33).
[13] Contrast the income tax position: see Ch. 30.
[14] For BN 25, see App. III A3.16.

business property or agricultural relief does not apply and the transfer is over the £285,000 limit. However where the transfer is a chargeable transfer for IHT the IHT is allowed as a deduction in computing the chargeable gain on the disposal by the transferee (s.260(7)) TCGA. Also under s.165 IHTA if the donee pays the CGT on the transfer the tax reduces the value of the transfer for IHT. So in practice there is no double charge."

This point was reiterated by the Paymaster General in the Finance Committee debates.[15]

A settlor who has to pay both capital gains tax and inheritance tax on transferring assets to the trust may not agree with the analysis that there is no double tax charge!

RATES OF TAX

6.09 If CGT is payable by the settlor on a disposal into trust then subject to any reduction in the effective rate of tax as a result of taper relief, a higher rate tax payer will suffer tax at 40 per cent. Since April 6, 2004 trustees have also been subject to CGT at a rate of 40 per cent. In cases where a beneficiary would be taxed at a lesser rate (or has unused losses) it may be advantageous for the trustees to transfer the assets to the beneficiary in cases where it will be possible to claim hold-over relief so that the disposal and gain is made by the beneficiary.[16]

---

[15] See also Ch. 16.
[16] Accrued taper relief is lost if a hold-over claim is made. This is discussed in Ch. 14.

CHAPTER 7

ACTUAL AND DEEMED DISPOSALS BY TRUSTEES OF UK RESIDENT SETTLEMENTS

- Actual disposals: rate and payment of capital gains tax; annual exemption and other reliefs, taper relief **(7.02)**
- Deemed disposals: absolute entitlement; *Crowe v Appleby*; use of trust losses; death of a beneficiary; resettlements; variations of trusts; flip flops; sub-fund elections **(7.33)**

A charge to capital gains tax may arise as a result of either actual or deemed disposals of property by trustees. Notice, however, that where, on a change of trustees, trust property is transferred from the old to the new trustees, there is no charge to capital gains tax[1] because they are treated as a single person.[2] Trust gains are taxed at a rate of 40 per cent before taper relief unless the settlor has retained an interest, when tax is charged at his rate (i.e. either at 10 per cent, 20 per cent or, more likely, 40 per cent).[3] Settlor-interested trusts are discussed in chapter 11. Trustees are generally only entitled to one half of the full capital gains tax annual exemption although this is restricted where the settlor has established more than one trust.[4] **7.01**

ACTUAL DISPOSALS

When chargeable assets are sold by trustees, e.g. on a change of investments, normal CGT principles apply in calculating their gain (or loss). If the disposal generates a loss it may be set off against trustees' gains of the same year or of future years. However, if the loss is still unrelieved when the trust ends it cannot be transferred to a beneficiary who has become absolutely entitled to all or part of the trust fund (although such loss can be set against gains realised by the trustees on the deemed disposal).[5] **7.02**

---

[1] Unless the trust emigrates: see Ch. 2.
[2] TGCA 1992, s.69(1) as amended by FA 2006.
[3] For the tax year 2006/07: see TCGA 1992, s.4 as amended. As to when a settlor reserves an interest for these purposes, see TCGA 1992, s.77 as substituted by the FA 1995, s.74, Sch.17, para.27 and as amended by the FA 1998, Sch.21, para.6(1) and FA 2006. See further Ch. 11. Non resident trusts are subject to a different charging regime which is considered in Ch. 11.
[4] This is discussed at 7.07.
[5] See 7.43.

Only on the occasion where a beneficiary becomes absolutely entitled to trust assets so that the trustees make a deemed disposal *and that deemed disposal* produces a loss can that loss be passed on to the beneficiary and be used against future gains. Even then it is "ring fenced" in his hands so that it can only be offset against a future disposal of *those* trust assets.[6]

Rate and payment of capital gains tax

7.03 CGT attributable to both actual and deemed disposals of settled property is generally payable by the trustees. Trustees of non-settlor-interested trusts pay tax at 40 per cent on chargeable gains realised from disposals on or after April 6, 2004.[7] If the tax is not paid within six months of the due date for payment, it may be recovered from a beneficiary who has become absolutely entitled to the asset (or proceeds of sale from it) in respect of which the tax is chargeable. The beneficiary may be assessed in the trustees' name for a period of two years after the date when the tax became payable.[8] FA 2005 directed that the rate applicable to trusts is not to apply to the first slice of income (now £1,000). It presumably follows that if a trust has £1,000 of chargeable gain but no income the gain will be taxed at 20 per cent not 40 per cent.

In cases where on the ending of a trust hold-over relief is claimed,[9] the trustees are at risk of the postponed tax if the beneficiary subsequently emigrates before the asset has been sold within six years[10] after the end of the tax year during which they became entitled to the asset. Retaining assets, or taking a secured indemnity from the relevant beneficiary, is sensible where trustees have ended a trust and a hold-over claim has been made. (See chapter 9 on hold-over relief.)

7.04 CGT on settlor-interested trusts[11]: the trustees are not liable to pay capital gains tax when the trust is settlor-interested. Instead tax is assessed on the settlor as if the gains had been realised by him and not by the trustees.[12] Having paid the tax, the settlor is then entitled to be reimbursed out of the trust fund.[13]

A settlor has an interest in a settlement if one of two conditions is met:

(i) If any property which is or may at any time be comprised in the settlement (or any derived property) it will or may become payable to or applicable

---

[6] See 7.43 and Ch. 12 for a detailed discussion of the loss provisions.
[7] The rates of capital gains tax for non-settlor interested trusts have increased significantly. In 1996/97, interest in possession trusts paid tax at 24 per cent on trust gains; discretionary trusts were taxed at 34 per cent. In 1997/98 interest in possession trusts paid tax at 23 per cent on trust gains and discretionary trusts at 34 per cent. From 1998/99 to 2003/04 inclusive, all trusts paid capital gains tax at 34 per cent. From 2004/05 this rate was increased to 40 per cent for all trusts. These rates are charged on trust gains after calculating any available taper relief.
[8] TCGA 1992, s.69(4).
[9] See Ch. 9.
[10] See TCGA 1992, s.168.
[11] For greater detail see Ch. 11.
[12] TCGA 1992, ss.77–79. When there was a differential between the rate of capital gains tax payable by individuals and that payable by trustees (at one time it was 40 per cent as against 25 per cent) this provision was significant. Now that the trustee rate is also 40 per cent it is of limited significance.
[13] TCGA 1992, s.78.

for the benefit of the settlor, his spouse, his civil partner,[14] or (with effect from April 6, 2006) a dependent child in any circumstances whatsoever; or

(ii) Such persons enjoy a benefit deriving directly or indirectly from property which is comprised in the settlement or any derived property.[15]

These conditions are discussed further in chapter 9 but note:

a. If an unmarried minor child of the settlor can potentially benefit from the trust but there is no such person alive, then the trust is not treated as settlor-interested until such minor child is born.
b. The 2006 extension covers all disposals made by trustees of existing as well as new trusts from April 6, 2006. Hence pre-April 6, 2006 trusts are affected.

EXAMPLE 7.1

Eric set up a discretionary trust for his minor children in 2004. He and his wife are excluded from all benefit. He claimed hold-over relief on the transfer of land into the trust under s.260 TCGA 1992.[16]

In July 2007 the trustees wish to sell the land and they will realise a gain. Unless before tax year 2007/8 all living minor children are excluded from benefiting until they are adults, any gains will be taxed on the settlor. If, however, the terms of the trust are altered to provide that the minors can only benefit from the settlement once they reach 18 then the trust is not settlor-interested at the time when the gains accrue and the settlor is not subject to capital gains tax.

Exemptions and reliefs: a number of exemptions and reliefs should be noted in the context of settled property.   7.05

Main residence exemption: may be available for a residence settled on either discretionary or interest in possession trusts.[17]   7.06

Annual exemption

Trustees are generally entitled to half of the annual exemption appropriate to an individual.[18] However, if the settlement is one of two or more made by the   7.07

---

[14] With effect from December 5, 2005.
[15] TCGA 1992, s.77(2)(b) and (2A) as amended in FA 2006. For the meaning of "derived property" see *West v Trennery* [2005] UKHL 5, [2005] S.T.C. 214, HL and Ch. 16.
[16] Which he was able to do because the transfer into trust took place before April 6, 2006 and note that the 2006 change does not involve any clawback of hold-over relief in respect of an earlier transfer into trust.
[17] TCGA 1992, s.225 as amended by the FA 2004, s.117, Sch.22; and see *Sansom v Peay* [1976] 3 All E.R. 375, [1976] 1 W.L.R. 1073. In general it does not matter that the beneficiary pays a rent for use of the property. See Ch. 31.
[18] Sch.1 para.2, TCGA 1992.

same settlor after June 6, 1978 then the half annual exemption has to be divided by the number of settlements made by the settlor after June 6, 1978 and each then has an exempt amount equal to the greater of the figure resulting from that division and one-tenth of the individual exempt amount.[19] In carrying out the division, the number of settlements includes settlor-interested trusts[20] and trusts established by the will of the settlor on his death but charitable trusts, non-resident trusts and retirement benefits and compensation funds are ignored.[21] Until 1997/98 brought forward losses could be carried forward if the annual exempt amount would otherwise be wasted. From April 6, 1998 this has no longer been possible for current year losses: any allowable losses for the year are deducted even if this reduces the net gains below the annual exempt amount. Brought forward losses, however, are only deducted to the extent required to reduce the net gains before taper relief to the annual exempt amount.

An unused annual exemption cannot be carried forward.

EXAMPLE 7.2

Trustees of a settlement make the following gains and incur the following losses:

Tax Year	Gain (£)	Loss (£)
Year 1	5,000	10,000
Year 2	8,500	4,500
Year 3	10,000	–

In *Year 1* no CGT is payable and the trustees will carry forward a loss of £5,000: their annual exemption for the year is wasted. In *Year 2* the loss for the year reduces the gain to £4,000 which is covered by the trustees annual exemption (£4,400 for 2006-7). The carry forward loss of £5,000 is therefore carried forward again to Year 3. In *Year 3* that loss reduces the gain to £5,000 so that after deducting their annual exemption the trustees are taxed on £600 at 40 per cent = *£240*.

7.08 HMRC Manual at CG 18092 comments on when a settlement is "made" for the purposes of considering whether it was pre or post June 1978.

"You should construe the word 'made' as referring to the various means by which a separate settlement may come into existence. This includes straightforward new deeds of settlement, assignments, appointments and transfers to new settlements but NOT additions to the settled property of an existing settlement."

Contrast this with their views on additions and new settlements in the inheritance tax context![22]

---

[19] Sch.1, para.2(4), TCGA 1992.
[20] Although note that a trust annual exemption *cannot* reduce settlor interested trust gains—a settlor-interested trust results in the gains being chargeable on the settlor and it is only his annual exemption that can be used.
[21] Sch.1, para.2(7)
[22] See 15.13.

EXAMPLE 7.3

> Emma set up three trusts. Trust 1 was made in 1975 but she added most of the funds to it in 1977. Trust 2 was set up in 1981 and is non-UK resident and Trust 3 is UK resident and was made and funded in 1999.
>
> In these circumstances Trust 3 has a full trust annual exemption for 2006/07 of £4,400. However, if Trust 2 becomes UK resident then the trust annual exemption is divided between them from that tax year and they each receive £2,200. Note that if Trust 2 realises £2,500 of gains and Trust 3 realises no gains in 2006/07, the unused annual exemption of Trust 3 cannot be set against Trust 2 gains. Trust 1 will not have a restricted annual exemption and is not taken into account in determining the exemption available to the other two trusts.
>
> If Emma had set up 10 UK resident trusts in 2006, the 2006/07 exemption for each trust is not £440 but £880.

Death exemption: the tax-free uplift on death is available for trusts with a qualifying interest in possession, but not for relevant property settlements. This is discussed further at 7.46 *et seq*.   **7.09**

Roll-over relief: relief on replacement of business assets is available only if the trustees are carrying on an unincorporated business.[23]   **7.10**

Deferral relief: relief for re-investment under the enterprise investment scheme is available in respect of all trusts provided that all the beneficiaries are either individuals or charities.[24]   **7.11**

Trusts for vulnerable beneficiaries: these qualify for special income and capital gains tax treatment.[25]   **7.12**

Taper relief

Trustees qualify for taper relief in the same way as individuals, wherever they are resident. After full business taper relief, trustees are taxed at an effective rate of only 10 per cent on disposals of business assets (40×25 per cent). After ten years' ownership, trustees are taxed at an effective rate of only 24 per cent on non-business assets (40×60 per cent). Accrued taper relief is lost if a hold-over election or deemed disposal is made (for example, on the creation or ending of a trust). In considering whether an asset owned by a trust qualifies for business or non-business assets taper relief one must have regard not only to the trustees' position but also to the position of the beneficiaries (in relation to interest in possession trusts).[26]   **7.13**

---

[23] See TCGA 1992, ss.152–162 as amended.
[24] See TCGA 1992, Sch.5B as inserted by the FA 1995 and as amended.
[25] See Ch. 26, below.
[26] See 7.17.

7.14 Trusts can be used as an "umbrella", in that a change of beneficial entitlement in a continuing trust does not affect the trustees' ownership period in respect of the trust assets.

EXAMPLE 7.4

In 1998 Henry settled shares into trust for himself in order to crystallise his retirement relief.[27] The shares have always qualified for business assets taper relief. In 2000 he feels that he can give up all interest in the shares held in the trust. He has four children. They are given immediate interests in possession and he is excluded from all benefit under the trusts. This is a PET for inheritance tax purposes but there is no disposal for capital gains tax purposes.[28] Hence no new taper relief period is started. If the trustees sell the shares in 2008 they are treated as having owned them for 10 years not merely for 8 years.[29]

7.15 **Business assets taper relief on shares:** pre April 2000. Prior to April 6, 2000, business assets taper relief was in general only available on shares if the following conditions were satisfied. The individual shareholder or trustees must be able to exercise either:

(i) at least 25 per cent of the voting rights of the company, *or*

(ii) at least 5 per cent of the voting rights of the company and the shareholder (in the case of individuals) or the eligible beneficiary (in the case of trusts) was a full-time working officer or employee of the company.

Only trading companies or groups were covered. There was no distinction made between listed and unlisted companies.

7.16 **Post April 6, 2000:** the rules were significantly relaxed and a distinction was made between listed and unlisted shares (the latter including AIM companies). Shares qualify if one of the following conditions is satisfied:

(i) All trusts (and individuals) holding shares in unlisted trading companies will qualify for business assets taper relief whatever their level of holding and irrespective of the type of trust.

(ii) All individuals or trusts holding shares in listed trading companies will qualify if the individual shareholder or trust holds at least 5 per cent of the voting shares.

(iii) An individual shareholder or trusts holding shares in listed trading companies will qualify for business assets taper relief where the individual shareholder or an eligible beneficiary of the trust is an officer or employee of the company. There is no need for full time employment.

---

[27] Before March 22, 2006 this was a non-event for IHT purposes.
[28] Assuming the trustees do not exercise their powers in wider form. See 7.55 on resettlements.
[29] Note that if the shares did not qualify for business assets taper relief until April 2000 the trustees might have preferred to engineer a resettlement in order to wash out the tainted period prior to this date.

(iv) An individual shareholder or trustee of a *non-trading* company can qualify for business assets taper relief where the individual or eligible beneficiary is an officer or employee of the company and the individual or trust does not have a material interest in the company. "*Material interest*" is defined as more than 10 per cent of voting rights, right to receive dividends, issued shares of any class or right to assets in a winding up. Rights of connected persons must be taken into account.[30]

"Eligible beneficiary": an eligible beneficiary is one who has an interest in possession, not being an annuity or fixed term entitlement unless the beneficiary will become absolutely entitled to the property at the end of the fixed term. FA 2006, Sch.20 has amended the definition of qualifying interest in possession for inheritance tax purposes and made amendments to the capital gains tax legislation in relation to the deaths of interest in possession beneficiaries. However, no amendment has been made to the definition of relevant interest in possession for taper relief purposes. Hence it would appear that a beneficiary who is an employee and has an entitlement to income under the trust which arose post March 21, 2006 is still an eligible beneficiary for the purposes of the taper relief legislation even though his interest is not a qualifying interest in possession for inheritance tax purposes.   7.17

Tainted periods: the changes affecting periods of ownership after April 5, 2000 do not mean that a trust holding shares before this date can ignore the old rules: the old rules still govern the business assets taper relief position for periods of ownership prior to that date even if the disposal takes place afterwards. Hence the trap of a "tainted" period.   7.18

EXAMPLE 7.5

On March 16, 1998 the "White Discretionary Trust" was established by Jim to hold 20% of the shares in his gardening business Greenpack Ltd.

(a) Until April 6, 2000 the shares did not qualify as business assets. The 25 per cent threshold was not satisfied.

(b) From April 6, 2000 they became business assets.

(c) Assume that the trustees sell the shares in April 6, 2004. Their gain must be apportioned on a time basis:
  (i) the business asset period runs from April 6, 2000 to April 6, 2004 and is 48 months long;
  (ii) the non-business period runs from April 6, 1998 to April 6, 2000 and is 24 months long;
  (iii) the total period of ownership is 72 months or six years.

Hence one-third of the gains (24/72) receives non-business taper over the period April 6, 1998 to April 6, 2004 (six years ownership plus the bonus)

---

[30] FA 2001, s.78 retrospectively applied to periods after April 5, 2000.

so that 75% of one-third of the gain is taxed; two-thirds of the gain receives business assets taper over the same period (six years with no bonus) so that only 25% of two-thirds of the gain is taxed.

An apportionment will continue to be required if the disposal by the trustees occurs at any time before April 6, 2010: only after that date can the non-business period of ownership be ignored. The apportionment is done on the basis of months not complete years, so if the trustees had sold in June 2004 a further two months' business assets relief would have been available (50/74).

7.19 By contrast, if the shares had been settled in June 2000 then after only two years they would be eligible for full business assets taper relief. Obviously the overall effect of the tainted pre-April 6, 2000 period is declining. In *Example 7.5*, the trustees could have appointed the shares into a new discretionary trust in 2000 if they did not show a gain.[31] The new trust would have been treated as acquiring the shares at the date of appointment and the earlier tainted non-business period would have been "washed out". Business assets taper relief would then have been available after only two years.

7.20 **Connected persons:** the connected party provisions need careful consideration in relation to trustees holding shares in non-trading companies where an eligible beneficiary is an employee.

EXAMPLE 7.6

Henry set up a trust in 2000 which owns 5% of the company shares. His child John is a beneficiary. Henry still owns 20% of the shares in the company. It is an investment company and although John works in the company no business assets taper relief is available because the trust is connected with Henry and together they own more than 10%. However, in 2003 Henry dies leaving his shares to his son. The trust is no longer connected with the settlor or the beneficiaries and does not have a material interest in the company even though the son owns more than 10 per cent personally. It appears that the trust obtains business assets taper relief on its shares but the son will not do so in the future on shares he owns personally.

7.21 **Multiple settlors:** where there are multiple settlors of the same trust, the shares cannot be cumulated so as to create a single umbrella settlement that would then qualify for relief.

EXAMPLE 7.7

A, B and C each own 3% in ICA, a listed trading company. They cannot transfer their respective holdings into a single trust in order to get over the 5% threshold. Although the trust now owns 9% of the shares in ICA

---

[31] No hold-over relief would be available under s.260 given it is a transfer between two discretionary trusts (see IHTA 1984, s.81) although s.165 might have been in point—see Ch. 9.

for taper relief purposes it is as if the shares are held in three separate settlements.

Planning: it is worth examining a trust to see if the business assets taper relief position can be improved.

7.22

EXAMPLE 7.8

In February 1998 Chris sets up a trust for his two adult children Johnny and Daisy, each having an interest in possession in half the trust ("Daisy's Fund" and "Jonny's Fund"). He settles 10% shares in his unlisted company Pots Ltd along with some cash that is used to buy a house which is now rented out. Daisy works in Pots Ltd full time. Johnny has his own business mending old cars. The trustees do not appropriate the assets to any particular fund and therefore although Daisy is an eligible beneficiary for the entire period from April 1998 only part of the shares will qualify for BATR up to April 6, 2000 since Jonny is not an eligible beneficiary. The gain on a later disposal will therefore need to be apportioned.

After April 2000 the trustees qualify in their own right since the shares are unlisted and it is not necessary to have any minimum holding or work requirement. Business assets taper relief is available on all the shares. Note though that until 2010 full business assets taper relief will not be available because when looking at the last 10 years of ownership or the period of ownership since April 1998 if shorter, the shares did not qualify for business assets taper relief throughout that period. Hence an apportionment is required between the pre- and post-April 6, 2000 periods of ownership.

If instead Chris had settled the shares into Daisy's fund and the cash into Jonny's fund, all the shares would have qualified for full business assets taper relief for the entire period of ownership.

As noted in *Example 7.5* above it was sometimes possible to dilute the effect of the apportionment rules by the trustees appointing the shares out to a new trust (Trust 2) for Jonny and Daisy. Hold-over relief would be claimed[32] and a new period of ownership started in the hands of the new trust. That meant Trust 2 would qualify for full business assets taper relief after only two further years of ownership and the effect of the more restrictive rules for shares prior to April 6, 2000 was eradicated.

7.23

However, transfers between trusts need some care now whether shares or other assets are being transferred. The restrictions in FA 2004, Sch.21 and FA 2006, Sch.12 deny hold-over relief if the new trust is settlor-interested or becomes so within the clawback period (six years from the end of the tax year of the disposal). Therefore, Jonny and Daisy (assuming they are not minor children of the settlor) should not add to such a trust from which they can benefit within the clawback period. Even though the shares did not originate from them, hold-over relief can still be clawed back if the second trust becomes settlor-interested.[33]

---

[32] Assuming that the relevant conditions were satisfied.
[33] See Ch. 9.

7.24   Further, a transfer of assets from one trust to another trust may now cause inheritance tax problems. In the above example, Jonny and Daisy have qualifying interests in possession. If they have interests in possession under the new trust and the transfer to Trust 2 took place prior to March 22, 2006 this would be a non-event for inheritance tax purposes. However, if the transfer to the new trust takes place after March 21, 2006 then the interests in possession taken by Johnny and Daisy are not qualifying interests under the transitional serial interest provisions contained in IHTA s.49BA. Hence although there is no entry charge for inheritance tax purposes: the assets comprised in the new trust fall into the relevant property regime.[34] The position is even worse when one remembers that they will be treated as reserving a benefit in the assets at the date of their death if they can still benefit from them[35] and yet there is no base cost uplift for capital gains tax purposes on their deaths because they no longer have qualifying interests in possession under the new trusts. A disaster!

However, if shortly thereafter the assets were appointed out of Trust 2 to Jonny and Daisy outright hold-over relief under TGCA 1992, s.260 would be available and any IHT exit charge would be small.

7.25 **Business assets taper relief on other assets: relief is available in the following circumstances:**

(i) Where trustees trade on their own account or in partnership. (Note, however, that for trustees operating in partnership, business assets taper relief is (arguably) only available on the asset in question from April 6, 2000.[36]

(ii) Where trustees own assets used in a trade by an "eligible" beneficiary or by a partnership of which that beneficiary is a member or by a qualifying company (and note the change above in what is a qualifying company pre- and post-April 2000).

(iii) Where trustees own assets used for the purposes of an office or employment held by an eligible beneficiary with a person carrying on a trade. Until April 6, 2000 the employment had to be substantially full-time.

(iv) FA 2003 provides that all assets used for the purposes of a trade carried on by individuals, trustees, personal representatives, partnerships whose members include such persons or qualifying companies will qualify for business assets taper relief *irrespective of whether the owner is involved in the carrying on of the trade*. These provisions only took effect for periods of ownership from April 6, 2004 and the intention is that the landlord's letting decision should be neutral as between incorporated and unincorporated businesses.

EXAMPLE 7.9

George is a farmer say that he lets agricultural land (a) to a neighbouring farmer or (b) to an unquoted farming company. In the first situation

---

[34] See Ch. 14; IHTA 1984, s. 53(2) and App. III A3.105 (Questions 8 and 9).
[35] FA 1986, s.102ZA as inserted by FA 2006.
[36] See para.5(3)(a).

the land was a non-business asset in George's hands until April 2004 but in (b) because the company is a qualifying company[37] business assets taper has been available since April 2000.[38]

7.26 This was probably an accident of drafting resulting from the revised definition of qualifying company in FA 2000. However, as (iv) above illustrates the Government extended the relief so that from April 6, 2004 business assets taper relief is available on almost all disposals of land let for trading purposes.[39]

EXAMPLE 7.10

An interest in possession trust with one life tenant A, owns a business park divided into separate units and lets out five of the units. All lettings commenced after April 6, 1998 but before April 6, 2004. Unit 1 is let to individual B who uses it for her trade. Unit 2 is let to a partnership C whose membership consists of companies, one of which is an unlisted trading company. The partnership uses the unit for the purposes of its trade. Unit 3 is let to a listed trading company that uses it for the purposes of its trade. No eligible beneficiary is employed by this company and the trust does not own 5% of the shares in it. Unit 4 is let to a partnership D whose members are all individuals apart from the trustees but the premises are not used for the purposes of a trade. Unit 5 is let to an unlisted trading company that uses it for its trade and neither the trust nor any eligible beneficiary own shares in the company.

7.27 For periods of ownership *before April 6, 2004* while the units are let as described, the treatment of those units for taper relief purposes will be as follows:

- Unit 1—will not qualify as a business asset because, although it is being used for the purposes of a trade carried on by an individual, individual B is not an eligible beneficiary.
- Unit 2—will not qualify as a business asset as although the partnership uses the asset for the purposes of its trade, neither the trust nor an eligible beneficiary is a member of the partnership.

---

[37] See TCGA 1992, Sch.A1 para.6(1)(b).
[38] See TCGA 1992, Sch.A1 para.5(2)(b).
[39] It is only necessary that the property is used for trading purposes. If, for example, a piece of land is let to a solicitors' firm who then sublets the premises to another partnership which uses it for trading, business assets taper relief can still be obtained on the whole provided all the premises are used for trading purposes. What happens if there is a period, say, of fitting out the premises prior to starting the trade? HMRC appear to accept that this qualifies for BATR. What if some of the premises are not used for trading purposes and some are? Arguably para.9 providing for apportionment does not work adequately since an asset is a business asset *if it is used wholly or partly* for the qualifying purposes. There is no need then to look at the actual purposes for which the whole land is used and full relief is available! HMRC do not accept this interpretation. Note the difficulties that can arise when there is one building, part of which is used for trading purposes and part is not. See CG Manual 17959 and *Taxation* article, July 14, 2005, "*Flatly Incredible*" by Mike Truman.

- Unit 3—will not qualify as a business asset as the listed trading company is not a qualifying company by reference to the trust.
- Unit 4—will not qualify as a business asset because it is not being used for a trade even though the trust is a partner.
- Unit 5—will qualify for BATR from April 6, 2000 but not for the period of letting before April 6, 2000, as prior to this date, the unlisted trading company was not a qualifying company by reference to the trust for the purposes of its trade.

7.28 For periods of ownership from *April 6, 2004* while the units are let as described, the treatment of the units for taper relief purposes is as follows:

- Unit 1—will qualify as a business asset as it is being used by an individual for the purposes of her trade even though neither a beneficiary nor the trust is the trader.
- Unit 2—will qualify as a business asset as at least one member of the partnership (the unlisted trading company) is a qualifying company by reference to the trust and the partnership is using the premises for the purposes of its trade.
- Unit 3—will not qualify as a business asset as the listed trading company is not a qualifying company by reference to the trust.
- Unit 4—will not qualify as a business asset because the partnership does not use the unit for the purposes of a trade.
- Unit 5—will qualify as a business asset as it is being used by a company that is a qualifying company by reference to the trust for the purposes of its trade.

7.29 On balance it is preferable for trustees to let to partnerships or sole traders provided that they will use the asset for trading purposes because then they are not required to consider the qualifying status of the company and whether or not it is a trading company for business assets taper relief purposes. This also avoids the worry of the unlisted trading company becoming listed and then ceasing to be a qualifying company in relation to the trust (see Unit 3 in *Example 7.10* above).

7.30 If the beneficiary has an interest in part only of the trust, he is an eligible beneficiary in relation to an asset if the asset is included within the part of the trust fund in which he has the interest in possession.

EXAMPLE 7.11

> Hugh sets up a trust with £200,000 in 1998 for himself and his brother Jack and they each enjoy an interest in possession in 50% of the trust fund. The cash is used to buy a property which is let out to Jack's business at a commercial rent. The trustees sell it on April 6, 2002. In these circumstances only one of the eligible beneficiaries who has an interest in possession in the land works in the business using the land. Hence

Jack's share will qualify for business assets taper relief but not Hugh's share. Hugh retains an interest in the trust so it is settlor interested and s.77, TCGA 1992 applies. The whole of the gain after taper relief is attributed to Hugh. However, he has benefited from enhanced business assets taper relief by transferring the land into a trust and including his brother as an eligible beneficiary. Jack's interest in possession could be ended after the sale and the sale proceeds appointed outright to Hugh.[40]

Non-resident trusts can also qualify for taper relief. Although not themselves subject to capital gains tax, taper relief on disposals of assets can reduce the chargeable gain and therefore the capital gains tax charged on a settlor under s.86 or on beneficiaries under s.87.[41] No taper relief is available to any trust wherever resident, in respect of gains made by a non-resident close company, although the shares of that company can qualify for taper relief.

7.31

Business assets taper relief is not available to trustees if the settlor of the trust is a company and the settlor company or an associated company is an actual or potential beneficiary or enjoys a benefit.[42]

7.32

DEEMED DISPOSALS

Deemed disposals: can arise on the following occasions:

7.33

(i) When a beneficiary or another trust becomes absolutely entitled to assets comprised in the trust fund.[43]

(ii) On the death of a person with a qualifying interest in possession in the settled property.[44]

(iii) On the trustees becoming neither resident nor ordinarily resident in the UK.[45]

(iv) On the disposal of an interest in a settlor-interested trust for consideration.[46]

(v) Where trustees of certain trusts make a transfer of value linked with trustee borrowing.[47]

(vi) on a sub-fund election being made.[48]

---

[40] Assuming that the trustees had the necessary powers for IHT purposes reverter to settlor relief would apply: see Ch. 27.
[41] See Ch. 10.
[42] TCGA 1992, Sch.A1 para.17.
[43] TCGA 1992, Sch.71(1).
[44] TCGA 1992, ss.72 and 73.
[45] Discussed in Ch. 2.
[46] TCGA 1992, Sch.4A—discussed in Ch. 8.
[47] TCGA 1992, Sch.4B and C—see also Ch. 10.
[48] TCGA 1992, Sch.12; FA 1996.

Beneficiary becoming absolutely entitled[49]:

7.34 At the time when a beneficiary becomes absolutely entitled as against the trustees to any settled property, the trustees are deemed to dispose of the assets which comprise that settled property at their market value at that time and to re-acquire them at that value. Hence it is trustee rates of capital gains tax and taper relief which are relevant. After the deemed disposal the trustees are treated as holding the assets as bare trustees for the beneficiary and it does not matter whether or not the assets are actually transferred to that beneficiary or not.

7.35 The deemed reacquisition by the trustees is treated as being by the person who is absolutely entitled to the settled property. The various reliefs and exemptions available to trustees on an actual disposal are available on the deemed disposal e.g. principal private residence relief; taper relief etc.

EXAMPLE 7.12

> Shares in D Ltd are held by trustees for S absolutely, contingent upon attaining the age of 25 years. S has just reached 25 years and the shares are worth £100,000. The trustees' base cost is £25,000. Because S is now absolutely entitled to the settled property the trustees are deemed to sell the shares (for £100,000) and to reacquire them (for £100,000). On the sale they have realised a chargeable gain of £75,000 (£100,000 − £25,000). The shares are now deemed to be S's property so that if he directs their sale and, say, £107,000 is raised, he has a chargeable gain of £7,000 (£107,000 − £100,000). His own annual exemption is available against that gain. (For simplicity this example ignores the possible impact of taper relief, expenses of sale, etc.)

7.36 As already discussed,[50] absolute entitlement means that the beneficiary has the right to direct how the asset is to be dealt with. A person under the legal disability of minority or mental incapacity is still treated as being absolutely entitled if this is the only reason for his not being able to give an effective direction to the trustees.[51] A person can be absolutely entitled even where the property is subject to a charge or lien in favour of the trustees for taxes, costs or other outgoings.[52]

7.37 Absolute entitlement may occur under the terms of the settlement or it may result from the exercise of the trustees' fiduciary powers. Normally absolute entitlement means absolute beneficial entitlement. However, trustees of another trust can become absolutely entitled to assets for these purposes.[53]

---

[49] TCGA 1992, s.71(1).
[50] See Ch. 5.
[51] TCGA 1992, s.60(1).
[52] See earlier discussion in Ch. xx of *Crowe v Appleby*. TCGA 1992, s.60(2) and see *X v A* [2000] 1 All E.R. 490. Although the beneficiary who has attained an absolute and vested interest in the trust is entitled to have the trust property transferred to him this right is still subject to the trustees' lien and if there are reasonably foreseeable liabilities (albeit remote or contingent) which may affect the trust fund they can retain part or all of the property. However, this does not mean that the beneficiary is not absolutely entitled to the property for capital gains tax purposes.
[53] See 7.55, below on resettlements.

EXAMPLE 7.13

> The terms of the Hibiscus Trust (which holds cash and quoted shares) provide for beneficiaries to become entitled to income in equal shares at 18 and for them to take capital at 25. The beneficiaries are three children, A B and C, all over 18. A reaches 25 in 2006 and receives her one-third share.[54] The other two beneficiaries B and C are only 19 and 20 at present. The trustees decide to reorganise the trust. They advance B her share of the capital absolutely before she is 25. A and B have become absolutely and beneficially entitled to settled property. The trustees then advance C's share to another trust for her benefit. The trustees of the second trust are absolutely but not beneficially entitled to the property.[55]

When do beneficiaries become absolutely entitled? HMRC have been known to argue that where trustees resolve in their discretion to advance an asset such as land to a beneficiary but the resolution is not under deed, the beneficiary does not become absolutely entitled until title to the property is transferred to the beneficiary, on the basis that the trustees are not bound by the resolution and the beneficiary cannot enforce it without consideration unless it is under deed. This can make a fiscal difference if the tax legislation changes between the date of the resolution and the date of the transfer (e.g. if rates of tax rise) or if the property increases in value. 7.38

In the update to the seventeenth edition of *Lewin on Trusts*, the editors note:

> "It is a matter of construction of a resolution of the trustees, having regard to the objective meaning of the language used in the context in which the resolution was made and the surrounding circumstances, whether they have advanced assets to a beneficiary absolutely or merely facilitated a future advance to the beneficiary by entitling him to apply for a transfer of the assets to him in exercise of the trustees' powers of advancement."[56]

In *Cameron v M. & W. Mack (E.S.O.P.) Trustees Ltd*,[57] which concerned an employee benefit trust, the trustees resolved in the following terms: 7.39

> "IT WAS RESOLVED to earmark the following numbers of shares for the undermentioned individuals with a view to such shares being advanced to such individuals for their own absolute use and benefit freed from the Trusts of the Settlement as and when requested by each of them."

The claimant was one of the "undermentioned individuals". Upon being dismissed from his employment, he applied for the transfer of his "earmarked" shares. The trustees refused. The court held that the term was used to describe

---

[54] The transfers to A and B are a non-event for IHT purposes since they have qualifying interests in possession. The transfer to a separate trust for C would not produce an IHT entry charge if C had an interest in possession in that trust (IHTA 1984, s.53(2)), but the second trust would be within the IHT relevant property regime.
[55] In each case (i.e. when A and B and the trustees) become absolutely entitled to settled property the trustees make a deemed disposal under TCGA 1992, s.71.
[56] *Lewin on Trusts: First Supplement to the Seventeenth Edition* (London, 2003) at p.84.
[57] [2002] W.T.L.R. 647.

the process of identifying the particular shares for which a beneficiary was entitled to apply and that, accordingly, the resolution did not amount to the exercise of the power to transfer part of the trust fund to or for the benefit of the claimant. It was not until the trustees acceded to a request and transferred the shares to the employee that the power to transfer the trust property was exercised.

However, it is not thought that *Cameron's* case necessarily supports the HMRC view. It (implicitly) confirms that a power to pay or apply may be exercised by resolution. Whereas in that case, the context indicated that "earmarking" was a stage preparatory to, and independent of, the power to transfer, in most cases where the trustees resolve to advance capital to a beneficiary there is nothing to suggest this two-stage process.

7.40 **Several beneficiaries becoming absolutely entitled:** difficulties can arise when several beneficiaries become absolutely entitled at the same time to a number of assets. Does each beneficiary become absolutely entitled to an aliquot share of each asset or can the trustees decide who gets what: e.g. where one beneficiary is non-UK resident the trustees may decide to appropriate the assets that show the least gain to him and the ones showing the most gain to the UK resident beneficiary where a hold-over claim is possible. Dicta in *Stephenson v Barclays Bank*[58] indicates that each beneficiary becomes entitled to an aliquot share but if there is a subsequent appropriation, HMRC do not in practice object if each beneficiary is treated as having become absolutely entitled to the actual assets appropriated to him.[59]

Crowe v Appleby problems

7.41 There are other problems arising where, for example, a beneficiary becomes entitled to a share in land but the remaining part of the land is still subject to the trusts of the settlement.[60] If a beneficiary is not treated as absolutely entitled for capital gains tax purposes, there will be no deemed disposal and this may affect the hold-over relief position.

EXAMPLE 7.14

> In 1996 Andrew set up a trust for his children Charlotte and Luke. They each become entitled to one half of the income and capital on reaching 25. (This is an "accumulation and maintenance trust" for IHT purposes). Charlotte becomes 25 in 2007 and Luke 25 in 2009. They do not take interests in possession until reaching 25. The only asset in the trust is a commercial property.
>
> When Charlotte reaches 25 in 2007 for capital gains tax purposes she does *not* become absolutely entitled to one-half of the land. Until the land is

---

[58] [1975] 1 All E.R. 625; [1997] S.T.C. 151.
[59] CG Manual para.37105.
[60] For a fuller discussion on absolute entitlement and HMRC's views on powers of appropriation see 5.09 *et seq.* and App. III A3.105 (Questions 34 and 35).

sold, Luke reaches 25 or dies under that age (when Charlotte will inherit his share), (whichever is the earlier) the trust continues and no disposal is made by the trustees. Hence only in 2009 on Luke's 25th birthday will the trustees make a deemed disposal of all the settled property. For inheritance tax the position is quite different. The trusts over Charlotte's share end on her 25th birthday so there is no IHT exit charge since she is within the transitional regime.[61] She is treated from 2007 as entitled to the half share in the property and if she died after that date it would form part of her estate for inheritance tax purposes and be taxable. Notice therefore that for IHT purposes the trust of this share has ended. This means that when Charlotte becomes absolutely entitled to her share for CGT purposes in 2009, CGT hold-over relief is not available under TCGA 1992, s.260 (in particular the relief available on the ending of an accumulation and maintenance trust given by s.260(2)(d) cannot apply since that trust ended—in respect of Charlotte's share—when she becomes 25).[62]

As a result of the IHT changes in the tax treatment of settlements the treatment of Luke's share when it vests in 2009 is not what was envisaged when the trust was set up.[63] From April 6, 2008 the privileged accumulation and maintenance treatment will be withdrawn with the result that when Luke becomes 25 an IHT exit charge will arise.[64] CGT hold-over relief will, however, be available under s.260 on that share.

Extending the CGT settlement: the trustees could make a settled advance[65] before Luke becomes 25 in 2009 so that he does not take outright (and hence Charlotte does not become absolutely entitled to the property for capital gains tax purposes). Instead the advance may provide that he is given an interest in possession with continuing trusts for his spouse and children. In these circumstances an IHT exit charge (at the date of the settled advance) will still arise and the trust will henceforth fall within the relevant property regime (with 10 year charges and exit charges) but a deemed disposal for capital gains tax purposes is avoided. The result of making the settled advance is as follows— **7.42**

(i) The trust continues for CGT purposes (i.e. *Crowe v Appleby* has in effect been extended!);

(ii) Charlotte's position is therefore improved in that there is no deemed disposal in 2009; the property remains settled for capital gains tax purposes;

---

[61] IHTA 1984, s.71(4)(a) and see Ch. 21.
[62] An interesting question would arise if Charlotte died before 2009. As stated above she is—for IHT purposes—the owner of 50% of the property (and is of course entitled to the income from that moiety). Does the CGT death uplift apply? TCGA 1992, s.72(1) deals with the death of a beneficiary entitled to an interest in possession in all or any part of the settled property but since Charlotte took her interest in possession after March 21, 2006 it is not a qualifying iip within s.72(1b), TCGA 1992. Therefore there is no deemed disposal for CGT purposes and no uplift: see App. III A3.105 (Question 35).
[63] The IHT changes in respect of accumulation and maintenance trusts are described in detail in Ch. 21.
[64] From April 6, 2008 the trust of Luke's share falls within IHTA 1984, s.71D (inserted by FA 2006).
[65] Assuming they have a widened power of advancement. Care would need to be taken to ensure that the exercise of the power did not create a new settlement for CGT purposes.

(iii) On Luke's share, however, IHT charges may arise under the relevant property regime and, were he to die, because his interest in possession is non-qualifying for IHT purposes, the value of his share will not be taxed as part of his estate but correspondingly there will be no CGT uplift. If the trust is then ended there will be a deemed disposal for capital gains tax purposes. There is no inheritance tax payable on Charlotte's share (because nothing has changed for inheritance tax purposes on her share since she is already treated as owning it) but no hold over relief is available. On Luke's share there will be an exit charge but CGT hold-over relief will be available.[66]

Use of trust losses

7.43 If a beneficiary became absolutely entitled to settled property prior to June 16, 1999 any allowable loss which had accrued to the trustees in respect of property which was, or was represented by, the property to which he had become entitled, was (assuming that the loss was not used by the trustees) treated as accruing to him.[67] This included losses resulting from the deemed disposal to the beneficiary as well as losses carried forward by the trustees from preceding tax years.

7.44 The position where a beneficiary became absolutely entitled to settled property on or after July 16, 1999 is, however, much more restrictive. This is discussed in further detail in chapter 12.[68]

7.45 Liability: if the trustees do not pay tax due on the deemed disposal within six months from the date when it became payable and the asset in respect of which the chargeable gain accrued is transferred to a person absolutely entitled to it as against the trustees, that person may be assessed and charged in the name of the trustees within two years from the time when the tax became payable.[69] The beneficiary cannot be assessed to tax on more than the chargeable gain and where only part of the asset is transferred he cannot be assessed for more than a proportional part of that amount.

EXAMPLE 7.15

In 2006/07 A becomes absolutely entitled as against the trustees to a piece of land. The trustees do not pay all the tax on the deemed disposal. A can be assessed for the tax. If A and B had become jointly absolutely entitled in equal shares each would be responsible for half the tax.

---

[66] However the trustees will continue to clock up taper relief on the asset even after Charlotte becomes entitled to the asset in 2007 for inheritance tax purposes so the rate of tax will reduce.
[67] s.71(2) as originally enacted
[68] Ch. 12 also considers the loss regime for trustees generally and see also s.79A, which prevents non-beneficiaries from using trust losses by purchasing interests in trusts.
[69] TCGA 1992, s.69(4).

Settlement ending on death of interest in possession beneficiary

If property ceases to be settled property on the death of a person with a **7.46**
qualifying interest in possession[70] a deemed disposal at market value by the
trustees takes place under s.71(1) but no chargeable gain accrues. There is
therefore an uplift in the value of the settled property but without any charge.
There is no loss relief if the deemed disposal results in a loss. This exemption
from charge does not apply to any part of the gain which represents an earlier
held over gain or if on the death of the life tenant the settled property reverts
to the settlor absolutely.[71]

This corresponds to the normal capital gains tax principle that on death
there is an uplift but no charge.[72]

EXAMPLE 7.16

> T was the life tenant of a pre-March 2006 interest in possession trust and
> an asset had been given to the trust by his mother in (say) 1986 with the
> benefit of hold-over relief. The gain held over was £20,000. On T's death,
> the held-over gain of £20,000 becomes chargeable and any additional
> gain is wiped out on T's death (see TCGA 1992, s.74). It will be possible
> to make another hold over claim to avoid paying tax on the £20,000 gain
> if T's death is a chargeable transfer, for IHT purposes (hold-over relief
> will then be available under TCGA 1992, s.260).
>
> Contrast the position if mother had given T the asset outright and hold-
> over relief had been claimed. In these circumstances there would be no
> clawback of the held-over gain on T's death.

EXAMPLE 7.17

> Property consisting of shares in Z Ltd is held on trust set up in 1996 for
> C for life, or until remarriage and thereafter to D absolutely.

---

[70] For the meaning of this term, see Ch. 17 and 15.19.
[71] See Ch. 27. If the death of the beneficiary causes the property to revert to the settlor absolutely (or to his widow or widower within two years of his death), the "reverter to disponer" exception applies. The death of the beneficiary in these circumstances does not lead to a charge to inheritance tax and, so, the normal uplift but no charge provisions of capital gains tax are modified to ensure that there is no double benefit. Therefore the death causes a deemed disposal and reacquisition, but for such a sum as ensures that neither gain nor loss accrues to the trustees (a no gain/no loss disposal): TCGA 1992, s.73(1)(b). On reverter to settlor trusts, see Ch. 27. For the triggering of the earlier held-over gain, see Ch. 9.
[72] TCGA 1992, s.73 as amended by FA 1996, Sch.39, para.6. Commonly the uplift in CGT value will be the same as the value taken for IHT purposes. Note, however, that there will be cases where the IHT value is not "ascertained" (i.e. agreed with HMRC Capital Taxes) and in this situation reliance cannot be placed on the figure submitted for IHT purposes when it becomes necessary to determine the uplifted CGT value: see TCGA 1992, s.274.

(1) If C dies there is a deemed disposal and reacquisition of the shares at the then value by the trustees, but capital gains tax is not charged. The settled property then belongs to D.

(2) By contrast if C had remarried, his life interest would then cease with the same consequences as in (1), save that capital gains tax may be chargeable on the ending of the trust.

7.47 If the life interest had subsisted in part only of the fund, the death of the beneficiary results in an uplift of the appropriate portion of each asset in the fund.[73]

7.48 **Termination of an interest on death when the settlement continues**[74]: the death of a beneficiary entitled to a qualifying interest in possession, in cases where the settlement continues afterwards, results in a deemed disposal and reacquisition of the settled property by the trustees at its then market value. Capital gains tax is not normally imposed, and the purpose of this provision is the familiar one of ensuring a tax-free uplift.[75]

The termination of an interest in a part of the fund, where the settlement continues afterwards, results in a proportionate uplift in the value of all the assets.[76]

EXAMPLE 7.18

Property is held in a trust set up in 2003 for A for life and then for his daughter D contingently on her attaining 25 years. A dies in 2007 when D is aged 20 and the income is being accumulated until she becomes 25.[77] The capital gains tax consequences are:

(1) Death of A. There is a deemed disposal of the property; there is a tax-free uplift. The settlement continues because D has not attained 25 and is, for IHT purposes, taxed as a relevant property settlement.

(2) D becomes 25. There is a further deemed disposal and capital gains tax may be charged on any increase in value of the assets since A's death. However because there is an IHT exit charge, CGT hold-over relief is available under TCGA 1992, s.260(2)(a).

---

[73] TCGA 1992, s.73(2) as amended (see fn 72, above).
[74] See TCGA 1992, s.72 as amended by FA 1996, Sch.39 para.5.
[75] TCGA 1992, s.72(1)(a).
[76] See TCGA 1992, s.72(1) as amended by FA 1996, Sch.39 para.5(2); note that similar rules apply if a beneficiary entitled to an interest in possession dies, albeit that the interest continues (e.g. an estate *pur autre vie*) and to certain annuity interests: TCGA 1992, s.72(3), (4) as amended. Until 1996, ss.72 and 73 were expressed in terms of life interests before being extended to include other interests in possession, e.g. an interest in possession terminable on a beneficiary attaining a certain age.
[77] If on the death of A the daughter was entitled to the income of the settlement (i.e. had an interest in possession) then for IHT purposes this would be a transitional serial interest given that A had died before April 6, 2008 so that D is treated as entitled to the capital of the trust fund (under IHTA 1984, s.49(1)) with the consequence that on attaining 25 no IHT charge arises and CGT hold-over relief is not available (unless the assets qualify as business assets under TCGA 1992, s.165).

Again, the full tax-free uplift on death does not apply to a gain held over on the creation of a settlement which therefore, becomes chargeable.[78] There is also a deemed disposal and base cost uplift where a beneficiary entitled to an interest in possession dies without that interest in possession coming to an end e.g. if his interest is an interest *pur autre vie* so that it passes under his will.[79]

7.49

Example 7.19

> Settled property is held on trust to pay the income to A for his life, subject thereto to B for life and subject thereto for C absolutely. A has an interest in possession and B has a future life interest not in possession. B's death during the lifetime of A will not have any capital gains tax consequences (no base cost uplift and no deemed disposal) and nor will it have any inheritance tax consequences.

Consider the position of surrenders and assignments of an interest in possession. Suppose a property is held on trust to pay the income to A for life and remainder to such of B, C and D as survive him and if more than one in equal shares. If A surrenders his life interest, it cannot be known which of B, C and D will become absolutely entitled to the settled property until A's death so their interests are not accelerated. The income arising prior to A's death will be distributable among such of them as are for the time being living. The property remains settled property and falls into the relevant property regime for inheritance tax purposes. When A dies B, C and D (if all living) take absolutely and there will be a deemed disposal under TCGA 1992, s.71(1). This does not result from the termination of an interest in possession on the *death* of the person entitled to it and so a chargeable gain could accrue (although, given the IHT exit charge which will occur, this may be held over).

7.50

What is the meaning of a qualifying interest in possession? Any interest in possession arising to an individual before March 22, 2008 is a qualifying interest in possession. With effect from March 22, 2006 TCGA 1992, ss.72 and 73 have been amended[80] so that if the interest in possession arises on or after March 22, 2006 there is no deemed disposal or base cost uplift to market value on the death of the life tenant (whether or not the property remains settled) unless:

7.51

(i) The interest is an immediate post death interest (IPDI); *or*

(ii) A transitional serial interest (TSI); *or*

(iii) A disabled person's interest within s.89B(1)(c) or (d) IHTA 1984; *or*

(iv) An 18–25 trust where the person dies under 18; *or*

---

[78] Unless another hold-over election is possible under the TCGA 1992, s.260: see Ch. 9.
[79] TCGA 1992, s.72(2).
[80] As a result of the IHT changes in the taxation of settlements and especially of the limitations on *qualifying* interests in possession. See 19.02.

(v) A bereaved minor trust.

7.52 The effects of all this can be summarised as follows:

EXAMPLE 7.20

Husband dies in 2007 leaving his assets on interest in possession trusts for his wife or a child with remainders over in his will. (Section 31 of the Trustee Act 1925 is excluded if the child is a minor so he will have an immediate entitlement to income.) In both cases this is an IPDI.[81] On the death of wife or child inheritance tax will be chargeable and capital gains tax base cost uplift is available.

If the wife or child's interest is terminated during her lifetime and the remainder beneficiaries take absolutely this is a PET and a disposal for capital gains tax purposes at market value.[82] No hold-over relief is available unless the settled property qualifies as business assets.

EXAMPLE 7.21

Husband has an interest in possession on a pre-March 22, 2006 Trust. He dies in 2009 and his wife then becomes entitled to an interest in possession. His wife's interest is a transitional serial interest (TSI)[83] under IHTA 1984, s.49B and the spouse exemption will prevent any IHT charge on the husband's death. On both husband and wife's deaths there is a base cost uplift for capital gains tax purposes. His wife's interest in possession will be subject to an IHT charge on her death.

EXAMPLE 7.22

Father dies leaving his estate on a bereaved minor trust for his two children, Amy and John. They are each given entitlement to income before they are 18 and Amy dies aged 17. There is no inheritance tax charge (s.71B(2)(b) of IHTA 1984) but a base cost uplift for capital gains tax purposes.[84] This is a better position than would have been the case under the old accumulation and maintenance regime where, if an infant child had become entitled to an interest in possession, the property would have been subject to inheritance tax on the child's death. Of course, it is likely to be fairly unusual for a minor to have been given an interest in possession.

---

[81] For the meaning of an IPDI, see Ch. 19.
[82] Under TCGA 1992, s.71.
[83] For the meaning of a TSI, see 18.14 *et seq.*
[84] TCGA 1992, s.72(1B).

EXAMPLE 7.23

Mother dies leaving her estate on trust for her only child Mary at 25. Mary is entitled to the income from the age of 16 and to capital at 25.[85] If she dies under the age of 18 then a base cost uplift for capital gains tax purposes is available under TCGA 1992, s.72(1A)(b) even if the property remains settled. There is no inheritance tax charge.[86] If Mary dies *after* reaching 18 *but before* 25 there is no base cost uplift for capital gains tax purposes but there is an inheritance tax exit charge on the ending of the s.71D trust.[87] A special charging regime is provided for in IHTA 1984, s.71F. CGT hold-over relief will be available if the trust ends at the time (under TCGA 1992, s.260).[88]

If the 18–25 trust is extended by the making of a settled advance so that Mary does not take outright at 25, there is then an inheritance tax charge at the top rate of 4.2 per cent unless the property qualifies for business property relief.[89] If she later dies after 25 with an interest in possession in the settled property there is no inheritance tax charge unless the trust then ends (in which case there is an exit charge at maximum 6 per cent) *but* there is no capital gains tax uplift since the property is within the relevant property regime. Hold-over relief will, however, be available.

EXAMPLE 7.24

Mother left her estate on trust for Mary at 30 with Mary being entitled to income at 18. She was aged 12 at the time of her mother's death. At 18 her interest in possession will not be qualifying (it is not an IPDI) and nor is the trust an 18–25 (s.71D) trust. It falls within the IHT relevant property regime. On Mary's death before or after 18 there is no inheritance tax payable unless the trust then ends (in which case there is an IHT exit charge) and no base cost uplift for capital gains tax purposes. If the trust does end on Mary's death there is a deemed disposal under TCGA 1992, s.71(1) but hold-over relief under TCGA 1992, s.260 would be available.

EXAMPLE 7.25

H sets up a trust during his lifetime giving his adult child an immediate interest in possession. Prior to March 22, 2006 the child had a qualifying interest in possession so that if he died there would be a base cost uplift on the settled property with no CGT charge. Unless the child is

---

[85] This is an 18–25 (s.71D) trust for IHT purposes: see Ch. 25.
[86] IHTA, s.71E(2)(b).
[87] IHTA, s.71F(2).
[88] See Ch. 9.
[89] For the calculation of the rate, see Ch. 25.

disabled this is no longer the case for trusts set up after March 21, 2006. Instead the settlement falls under the IHT relevant property regime and the child's interest in possession is not qualifying. Hence on the death of the child there is no base cost uplift for capital gains tax purposes. There is no inheritance tax charge unless the trust then ends in which case there is an exit charge under the relevant property rules and a deemed disposal for CGT purposes under TCGA 1992, s.71(1) with hold-over relief being available under s.260.

7.53 **Impact of deemed disposals:** when it is not possible to postpone payment of the tax (by a hold-over election), it may prove prohibitively expensive to end a settlement. In the case of a qualifying life interest settlement it may be preferable to wait for the death: in the case of discretionary trusts, because there is a chargeable transfer for inheritance tax purposes, hold-over relief under s.260 will be available. Consider whether it will be possible (and if so desirable) to postpone absolute vesting and therefore the s.71 deemed disposal.

EXAMPLE 7.26 (*POSTPONING THE DEEMED DISPOSAL*)

Fred sets up a pre-March 22, 2006 interest in possession trust for his son aged 18. His son is entitled to capital at 30 and is now aged 28. The trustees do not think it is wise for the son to take capital in two years' time and therefore in 2007 exercise their power of advancement to make a settled advance which has the effect of continuing the interest in possession trust for his son and then provides for an interest in possession trust for his wife remainder to his children absolutely. The trustees retain a power to advance capital to the son.

The result is that the interest taken by the son is a transitional serial interest[90] (provided that the trustees exercise their power before April 6, 2008). The interest taken by the son's spouse would not, however, be a transitional serial interest and so the continuing trust in favour of the son's wife will not qualify for spouse exemption and will be taxed according to the relevant property regime.

If the trustees wait until after April 6, 2008 before exercising their settled powers of advancement, any interest in possession taken by the son will not (it is thought) be qualifying and therefore the trust will become subject to the relevant property regime. There will be a transfer of value by the life tenant but no IHT charge even though the property becomes held on a relevant property trust).[91] There is no base cost uplift on his death because his life interest is not a qualifying interest in possession.

7.54 As can be seen from the above example considerable care needs to be exercised before extending the life of a settlement. Avoiding a CGT deemed disposal may now have unsatisfactory IHT consequences.

---

[90] On TSIs, see 18.14 and App. III A3.105 (Questions 5 and 6).
[91] Consider also whether the property will be taxed on his death for inheritance tax purposes because he has reserved a benefit: see FA 1986 s.102ZA (inserted by FA 2006).

Resettlements

When property passes into a new settlement (e.g. as a result of the exercise of a wide dispositive power by the trustees) a CGT charge may arise since, under TCGA 1992, s.71(1), there is a deemed disposal "on the occasion when a person becomes absolutely entitled to any settled property as against the trustee" which wording is capable of applying when new trustees (even the same trustees in a different capacity) become so entitled to the property.[92] *Exactly when a resettlement occurs remains a matter of some uncertainty.*[93]

7.55

In *Roome v Edwards*,[94] Lord Wilberforce stressed that the question should be approached "in a practical and common sense manner" and suggested that relevant indicia included separate and defined property, separate trusts and separate trustees, although he emphasised that such factors are helpful but not decisive and that the matter ultimately depends upon the particular facts of each case. He contrasted special powers of appointment which, when exercised, do not usually result in a resettlement of property, with wider powers (e.g. of advancement) which permit property to be wholly removed from the original settlement. A Statement of Practice[95] gives some guidance on when the exercise of a power of advancement or appointment is not treated as creating a new settlement.

7.56

EXAMPLE 7.27

> A family trust was created in discretionary form in 1965, since when 90 per cent of the assets have been irrevocably appointed on various interest in possession trusts, with the remaining 10 per cent being appointed on accumulation and maintenance trusts for beneficiaries who are all minors.[96] The various funds are administered by the original trustees of the 1965 discretionary trust. On these facts the property has remained comprised in the original settlement for capital gains tax purposes. Accordingly:
>
> (1) Even if separate trustees are appointed for, e.g., part of the assets held on interest in possession trusts, the trustees of the original 1965 trust remain liable for any capital gains tax attributable to that portion of the assets.
> (2) Only one trust annual exemption is available for gains realised in any part of the settled fund;
> (3) Losses realised in one part of the fund may reduce the chargeable gains realised in the other part. Whether the trust deed should

---

[92] See *Hoare Trustees v Gardner* [1979] Ch. 10: [1978] 1 All E.R. 791 and note especially that s.71(1) does not require a person to be "beneficially" absolutely entitled.
[93] See especially *Roome v Edwards* [1982] A.C. 279, [1981] 1 All E.R. 736, HL; *Bond v Pickford* [1983] S.T.C. 517, CA; and *Swires v Renton* [1991] S.T.C. 490.
[94] [1982] A.C. 279.
[95] See SP7/84 and 7.59.
[96] All these appointments occurred before the FA 2006 changes in the IHT taxation of settlements.

make any provision for "compensating" that part of the fund which produced the capital loss is a matter which should be considered by the trust draftsman.[97]

7.57 The *indicia* detailed by Lord Wilberforce were applied by the Court of Appeal in *Bond v Pickford*.[98] In this case the power which the trustees had exercised was a power to apply capital for the benefit of a beneficiary by allocating assets to him either absolutely or contingently. It was submitted by HMRC that the result of the exercise of the power of allocation was to create a new settlement, rendering the trustees of the new settlement absolutely entitled against themselves in their capacity as trustees of the original settlement and thereby giving rise to a deemed disposal of the allocated property for capital gains tax purposes. The Court of Appeal held that a new settlement had not been created. It emphasised the importance of considering each case on its own facts. They drew a distinction between powers in a *"wider form"* which authorised the trustees to remove assets altogether from the original settlement and powers in the narrower form which merely altered an existing trust. The exercise of the power in a narrower form could not create a new settlement. It was necessary to consider objectively both the nature of the trustees' powers and their intention in exercising them.

7.58 **A wider power exercised narrowly:** the Court of Appeal's approach in Bond v Pickford was followed by Hoffmann J. (as he then was) in Swires v Penton[99] where the intention of the trustees exercising their power, objectively assessed from the terms of the relevant deed rebutted the inference that a new settlement had been created even though the power was a power in a wider form which could have transferred property to a new settlement.

7.59 **SP 7/84** this emphasises the following matters:

1. each case must be considered on its own facts and by applying established legal doctrine in a practical and common-sense manner;

2. a deemed disposal cannot arise unless the power exercised by the trustees or the instrument conferring the power gives the trustees authority to remove assets from the original settlement by subjecting them to the trusts of a different settlement: i.e. it is a power in a "wider form";

3. even if such powers in a wider form exist, a deemed disposal will still not occur if the exercise is revocable, or the trusts declared of the advanced or appointed funds are not exhaustive, so that there exists a possibility at the time when the advancement or appointment is made that the funds covered by it will on the occasion of some event cease to be held upon such trusts, and once again become held on the original trusts of the settlement. HMRC also consider it unlikely that a deemed disposal will arise if duties in relation to the appointed assets still fall on the trustees of the original settlement in their capacity as trustees of that settlement. Although it may be appropriate to consider whether a separate settlement is established when there are separate trustees this factor in itself

---

[96] For the availability of a sub-fund election, see 7.72 *et seq*.
[97] [1983] S.T.C. 517.
[99] [1991] S.T.C. 490.

is by no means conclusive. It is not uncommon to have different trustees of different sub-funds which are still part of one settlement[1];

4. a power of advancement (e.g. a s.32 power) is a power in the wider form and can be exercised to effect a resettlement. So long as the new trust can be regarded as for the benefit of the advanced beneficiary he need not be the sole beneficiary of it[2];

5. in the case of a power of appointment, the question is whether it is a power in the wider or narrower form: i.e. do the trustees have power to take assets out of the settlement or do they only have power to declare new trusts on which the assets to be held which are treated as "read-back" into the existing settlement. Generally when exercising a special power, the trustee is merely (as it were) filling in a gap which the settlor left when establishing the settlement.[3]

Variations of settlements

Trusts may be varied by the agreement of all the beneficiaries who are sui juris and together entitled to the entirety of the beneficial interests. Trusts may also be varied where some beneficiaries are not sui juris (e.g. minors or unborns) by recourse to the Variation of Trusts Act 1958 which empowers the court to consent to variation on behalf of such beneficiaries (including any unborns). Where beneficiaries effect a variation without recourse to the court because they are all sui juris, it is thought that since they have power only to accept the settlement as it is or determine it altogether, they cannot vary the existing trusts except by creating new ones. Therefore the existing trustees become absolutely entitled as against themselves as trustees of the old settlement and this brings about a deemed disposal and reacquisition under TCGA 1992, s.71. 7.60

If, however, the variation requires the *consent* of the court under the Variation of Trusts Act 1958 what is the position? The House of Lords judgement in *IRC v Holmden*[4] provides strong support for the proposition[5] that so long as an arrangement under the Variation of Trusts Act 1958 is carefully drafted so as to make it clear that the intention is that the old settlement is to continue in existence, albeit in a varied form, the Order of the Court under the 1958 Act does not bring the existing settlement to an end but merely varies the settlement. HMRC are believed to accept that the question of whether there has been a revocation determining a trust or a mere variation of a trust which 7.61

---

[1] Section 37(1)(b) of the Trustee Act 1925 provides for the possibility of separate trustees being appointed over part of the trust property. See s.63(3), TCGA 1992 which provides that where part of the property comprised in the settlement is vested in one set of trustees and part in another they should be treated as together constituting a single body of trustees.
[2] See *Pilkington v IRC* [1964] A.C. 612; *Re Halstead's Will Trusts* [1937] 2 All E.R. 570; *Re Hampden Settlement Trusts* [1977] TR 177.
[3] See *Muir v Muir* [1943] A.C. 468. Of course this may be a matter of terminology since some practitioners would argue that if the power—albeit to appoint property—permits the transfer of assets into a separate trust then it is not a power of appointment *stricto sensu* but rather an advancement type power to transfer or apply assets.
[4] [1968] 1 All E.R. 148.
[5] Although the case was considering estate duty rather than capital gains tax.

continues to exist is one of construction.[6] Where a perpetuity period is extended (not uncommon in variations of old settlements) they may be more inclined to argue that a new settlement has been created.

The "anti flip-flop" legislation

7.62 These measures were introduced by FA 2000[7] and were primarily aimed at "flip-flop" arrangements widely used in offshore trusts to avoid triggering a s.86 charge.[8] The legislation is, however, widely drafted and capable of catching UK trusts despite the fact that, with the increase in the trust capital gains tax rate to 40 per cent,[9] there was no benefit to be obtained from a UK flip-flop scheme (and the courts also decided that it did not work!).

7.63 The scheme that Sch.4B was intended to counteract was known as the "flip-flop" scheme. It involved the following steps:

(i) in year 1 the trustees of Trust 1 borrowed money against the security of the trust assets and advanced the cash to a new settlement; the new settlement could benefit the settlor;

(ii) in the same tax year after the transfer of cash, the trustees of Trust 1 excluded the settlor and his spouse so it was no longer a settlor-interested trust (or in the case of an offshore settlement excluded the wider class necessary to make it non-settlor interested)[10]; *and*

(iii) in tax year 2, the trustees of Trust 1 realised gains by disposal of the assets in Trust 1. These were thought not to be chargeable on the settlor (who had been excluded from the trust) and prior to 2004 were taxed at only 25 per cent.

(iv) Distributions to the settlor were made from Trust 2 using the cash borrowed. The cash realised from the sale in Trust 1 was used to repay the borrowing.

7.64 In relation to UK-resident trusts the flip-flop scheme was eventually held not to have worked because of the definition of "derived property".[11]

7.65 The legislation applies if:

1. the trustees make a transfer of value on or after March 21, 2000, *and*

2. the transfer of value is linked with trustee borrowing. (It does not matter if the borrowing was taken out prior to that date); *and*

3. the trust is within s.77, s.86 or s.87, TCGA 1992, in the tax year.

Hence Sch.4B can apply not only to UK-resident trusts which are settlor-interested under s.77 but also to settlements which were previously non-UK

---

[6] See CG 37884 which indicates that the same principles apply to both variations by agreement and variations under the 1958 Act.
[7] See TCGA 1992, s.76B, Sch.4B as inserted by the FA 2000, s.92(1), (2), Sch.25. See Ch. 10.
[8] For the s.86 charge, see 00–00.
[9] With effect from April 6, 2004
[10] See Ch. 10.
[11] See *West v Trennery* [2005] S.T.C. 214, HL and Ch. 11 for further discussion.

resident but immigrated even if there is no brought-forward s.87 pool which has all previously been allocated to capital payments. See Sch.4B. para. 3(4).

If Sch.4B applies there is a deemed disposal with the result that the UK-resident trustees may pay capital gains tax on gains from such a disposal at 40 per cent: see 7.41. In theory a gain could also fall to be taxed on the beneficiaries because such gain goes into a Sch.4C pool and can be taxed on resident domiciled beneficiaries in receipt of capital payments from the settlement.

Transfer of value "linked" to trustee borrowing: by linked is meant that at the time of the transfer there is outstanding trust borrowing. Note that loans to the trust from underlying companies wholly owned by the trust, from beneficiaries or settlors are caught just as much as commercial loans. However, loans to companies owned by the trust are not trustee-borrowing although will be transfers of value if made by the trustees. Trust borrowing is outstanding until repaid. 7.66

Borrowing which is applied for normal trust purposes is disregarded. Normal trust purposes involve: 7.67

(i) expenditure such as a payment in respect of ordinary trust assets: e.g. buying shares or securities, tangible properties and payments in connection with a business carried on by the trustees.

(ii) discharging a pre-existing loan which has been applied for normal trust purposes;

(iii) bona fide expenses incurred by the trustees in administering the settlement or any of the settled properties.

Note that expenditure on intangibles such as insurance policies is not normal expenditure. In addition a simple debt such as a bank deposit is not covered so in theory trustees who borrow and then deposit the monies in a bank account are not making an application of the borrowings for normal trust purposes (*Tax Bulletin* 66 however commented that this is not a transfer of value.) There are other problems, e.g. when must the expenditure on ordinary trust assets occur: i.e. must it be as a direct application of the borrowing? What about repairs to property? This is not allowable expenditure within TCGA 1992, s.38 so in theory does not qualify. HMRC, however, stated that they would regard such expenditure as being for normal trust purposes under Sch.4B on the basis that it is reflected in the state or nature of the asset at the time it is incurred. 7.68

Particular care must be taken when trustees borrow and then lend to underlying companies. Such simple debts are not ordinary trust assets: accordingly the trustees need to subscribe for shares or securities in the company. The asset must be held by the trustees immediately after the transfer of value. HMRC have indicated that they would regard borrowing incurred to buy real property as continuing to satisfy the normal trust purposes test even if the property is subsequently let provided that it remains part of the trust fund. Bona fide current expenses include income and capital expenses and the payment of capital taxes but do not cover making a reserve in respect of future expenditure or borrowing taken out to pay off old unpaid debts or expenditure in administering any underlying holding company. This is because the 7.69

expenditure must be incurred in administering the *settlement* or on the *settled property*.

7.70   A transfer of value in this legislation is not the same as an IHT transfer of value. Trustees are treated as making a transfer of value if:

(i) they transfer an asset to any person *either* for no consideration *or* for a consideration which is less than market value; *or*

(ii) they lend money or any other asset to a person; *or*

(iii) they issue a security.[12]

7.71   **The effect of the legislation:** as noted above if the transfer of value is linked to trustee borrowing, there is a deemed disposal under Sch.4B. The disposal is deemed to occur at the date when the transfer of value is made and is of all the chargeable assets which are retained in the trust immediately after the material time. Even if there is only a small transfer of value linked to trustee borrowing there is still a deemed disposal but only of a proportion of each of the assets in the settlement. The deemed disposal is triggered even if the transfer of value is not actually funded or in any way related to the trustee borrowing; all that is necessary is that at the material time there is trustee borrowing which is outstanding. The base cost of the trust assets will be uplifted on the deemed disposal in the normal way.

Sub-fund elections

7.72   Trustees of a settlement may be able to make a sub-fund election under TCGA 1992, Sch.4ZA.[13] This depends on assets having been split into separate funds administered by a different group of trustees. In this case the trustees of the settlement are able to *elect* for that sub-fund to be treated as if it was a separate settlement for all income tax and capital gains tax purposes. As a result the CGT annual exempt amount[14] and the standard rate band will be split between the funds. The election can apply to both UK resident and non-resident trusts. The sub-fund settlement is then treated as a separate settlement. The sub-fund election triggers a deemed disposal of the settled property in the sub-fund so that capital gains tax may be payable by the trustees unless a hold-over claim can be made under the normal rules. As a result sub-fund elections are unlikely to be greatly used. In fact the legislation is likely to be useful only in those situations where trustees lack an express power to transfer assets to new settlements or do not want to do so given the IHT implications and are prepared to countenance a disposal for capital tax purposes (for instance if a chargeable gain will not result because the assets are cash).

Four conditions have to be satisfied in order to make the election:

(i) the principal settlement must not itself be a sub-fund settlement;

---

[12] See *Tax Bulletin* 66.
[13] Inserted by FA 2006, Sch.12, para.6.
[14] The annual exemption does not increase: the existing exemption is split equally: TCGA 1992, Sch.A1 inserted by FA 2006, Sch.12, para.44.

(ii) there must be some property left in the principal settlement which is not in the sub-fund;

(iii) there cannot be jointly-held assets between the principal settlement and sub-fund;

(iv) there is no person who is a beneficiary under both the principal settlement and the sub-fund (except in certain very limited circumstances).

7.73 The sub-fund election cannot be revoked once made. It cannot be made before April 6, 2006 nor after the second January 31 following the tax year to be affected by the election. In other words, if the election is to be deemed to have been made for 2006/7 it must be made by the time the enquiry period has ended on January 31, 2009.[15]

7.74 Condition 4 (set out above) that "no person will be a beneficiary under both the sub-fund settlement and the principal settlement" is the most onerous. However, a person is not to be regarded as a beneficiary under a settlement if property becomes payable to him by reason only of his marrying or entering into a civil partnership with a beneficiary under the settlement; the death of a beneficiary under the settlement; or the exercise by the trustees of the settlement of a power of advancement (but only a power of advancement in the statutory form or similar and not a power of advancement over the entire fund). Further, a person is not regarded as a beneficiary, if he can benefit only from the failure or determination of protective trusts.[16]

EXAMPLE 7.28

> The Frank Trust was set up in 2000 and gives an interest in possession to Frank (the settlor). He is divorcing and the trustees wish to transfer half the fund into a separate interest in possession settlement for Frank's wife (as part of the financial arrangements). However that new settlement will probably be regarded as a relevant property settlement for IHT purposes.[17] Instead therefore they vary the existing trust and appoint an interest in possession to the wife over half the existing trust property which will take effect as a TSI (provided done before April 6, 2008). However whilst the settlor can benefit from the settled property (even if he is excluded from the wife's part) he will continue to be taxed on all trust gains under TCGA 1992, s.77. If a sub-fund election is made, although there will be a deemed disposal of the property in the wife's fund, from that point onwards Frank will no longer suffer capital gains tax on gains in the wife's fund (assuming that his children were excluded

---

[15] The election procedure is in TCGA 1992, Sch.4ZA, paras 10–13. These provide that the election must be made by each trustee of the principal settlement (it would appear therefore that separate trustees of the sub-fund do not have to consent). The election must specify the date from which it is to take effect which must not be later than the date on which it is made: see para.2(1).

[16] TCGA 1992, Sch.4ZA, para.9(2).

[17] And hence subject to anniversary and exit charges: see Ch. 14. This assumes that a new interest in possession arising in a separate settlement cannot be a transitional serial interest. However, see 18.16, below for further discussion and App. III A3.105 (Question 6).

from that fund). It is likely that their children (assume they are adult) will benefit under both funds on the death of either parent. However, if the children can only benefit on the death of a parent and not by exercise of overriding powers of appointment then condition 4 is not broken and a sub-fund election can be made. Similarly, if the children can only benefit by exercise of the statutory power of advancement then the condition is not breached. See also Ch. 34.

CHAPTER 8

THE DISPOSAL OF A BENEFICIAL INTEREST

- The basic rule **(8.01)**
- Disposal of an interest in a non-resident settlement **(8.05)**
- Sale of an interest in a settlor-interested trust **(8.16)**

THE BASIC RULE

There is no charge to CGT when a beneficiary disposes of his interest.[1] The rationale is that there are rules taxing gains in the trust[2] so that to charge tax on the interest of a beneficiary would be a form of double taxation. There is, however, a growing list of exceptions, which is added to whenever tax avoidance schemes seek to exploit the basic exemption. **8.01**

Position of a purchaser: once a beneficial interest has been purchased for money or money's worth, a future disposal of that interest will be chargeable to CGT. The consideration does not have to be "full" or "adequate": i.e. any consideration however small will turn the interest into a chargeable asset. An exchange of interests by beneficiaries under a settlement is not treated as consideration so that a later disposal of either interest will not be chargeable.[3] **8.02**

EXAMPLE 8.1

> A is the remainderman under a settlement created by his mother. He sells his interest to his friend B for £350,000. No CGT is charged. If B resells the remainder interest to C for £410,000, B has made a chargeable gain of £60,000 (£410,000 – £350,000). Taper relief may be available. Note that the s.76 exemption is only excluded if there has been an acquisition

---

[1] TCGA 1992, s.76(1) as amended by FA 1998, s.128(1)(a): *cf.* the disposal of an interest in an unadministered estate (see 29.34).
[2] See Ch. 7.
[3] Compare the recent inheritance tax changes contained in FA 2006, s.157 amending s.48 of IHTA 1984 under which consideration for sales of interests in excluded property settlements can include exchanges of interests within a settlement. See 22.51.

of a beneficial interest for consideration. If A *gives* his interest to B, rather than selling it there is no chargeable gain on B later.

8.03 When a life interest has been sold, the wasting asset rules may apply on a subsequent disposal of that interest by the purchaser.

8.04 **Purchaser becoming absolutely entitled to any part of the settled property:** The termination of the settlement may result in the property passing to a purchaser of the remainder interest (of course, he may also become entitled to such property in other situations, for example if an advancement is made to or for his benefit). As a result, that purchaser will dispose of his purchased interest in return for receiving the property in the settlement.[4] The resultant charge that he suffers does not affect the deemed disposal by the trustees (and possible CGT charge on them).[5]

EXAMPLE 8.2

> Assume in *Example 8.1* above, that C becomes entitled to the settled fund which is worth £900,000. He has realised a chargeable gain of £490,000 (£900,000 − £410,000). In addition, the usual deemed disposal rules under s.71(1) operate to tax the trustees' gains (if any) on the disposal of the underlying assets.

DISPOSAL OF AN INTEREST IN A NON-RESIDENT SETTLEMENT

8.05 TCGA 1992, s.85(1) provides that the disposal of an interest in a non-resident settlement is chargeable: the basic exemption conferred by s.76(1) is excluded although it is provided that no charge arises under s.76(2) if the beneficiary becomes absolutely entitled to any part of the trust fund.

EXAMPLE 8.3

> A is life tenant of a non-UK resident trust.[6] A wishes to do some IHT planning and surrenders his life interest for nil consideration. He is deemed to make a disposal of that interest and is taxed on any gain— i.e. the difference between his base cost (likely to be nil given that he is the original beneficiary unless the trust had been exported after being set up[7] or he had the interest in March 1982) and the actuarial market value of his interest. Taper relief may be available to reduce the gain. His interest is likely to be a wasting asset.

---

[4] TCGA 1992, s.76(2).
[5] Under TCGA 1992, s.71(1).
[6] Or a UK resident trust that has received property from a non-UK resident trust.
[7] See 2.64 and 8.12.

8.06 **Involuntary termination:** what happens if the interest of a beneficiary in an offshore trust terminates not as a result of any voluntary action on his part (such as a sale or surrender), but by an act of the trustees: e.g. where a life interest is terminated by the trustees under a power reserved to them in the settlement? In this case it is thought that the termination will not amount to a disposal by the beneficiary since whilst it is true that under the capital gains tax legislation certain involuntary disposals (e.g. a sale under a compulsory purchase order) are subject to charge (so that a voluntary act on the part of the disponor is not always required) even in these cases there is a transfer of assets as opposed to a mere forfeiture of rights. In any event, if the interest of the beneficiary was revocable by the trustees at any time it would have little value so there would be no gain on a disposal.

If the trustees, therefore, exercise overriding powers of appointment in the case of a non-UK resident trust and terminate the life interest in favour (say) of trusts for children, there should be no CGT charge on the life tenant because he has made no disposal of his beneficial interest.

8.07 **Consents**: what is the position, however, if the trustees can exercise their overriding powers only with the consent of the life tenant? Is there any disposal by the beneficiary in these circumstances?[8] A classic example would be when the trustees exercise their power of advancement in favour of capital beneficiaries but the life tenant's consent is required under s.32 of the Trustee Act 1925. Does it make a difference if the beneficiary in question releases the requirement for his consent before any appointment or advancement by the trustees to some other person is in contemplation?

8.08 In the authors' view, the giving of consent or the release of such consent by a beneficiary is not a disposal of a beneficial interest under the settlement. Giving consent is not in itself a disposal of the beneficial interest under the settlement: it has merely enabled the trustees to exercise an overriding power which has had the effect of terminating the interest. In the past HMRC have indicated that if no consideration is given for the consent or any release of it there is no disposal of his interest by the beneficiary.[9]

8.09 However, is the *release* of a consent or the actual giving of consent a disposal of a separate personal *chose in action*?[10] If so, variations of any settlement whether UK resident or not, where the beneficiary has to consent

---

[8] This area is also discussed in the context of variations of trusts: see 7.60.
[9] An alternative view taken by some advisers is that if the life tenant releases his right to consent to the termination of (say) a life interest or does consent he has subjected his income interest to the exercise of an overriding power by the trustees. In these circumstances there is a resettlement of the beneficial interest for capital gains tax and income tax purposes and he is the settlor. However, see CG Manual paras 37881 and 37882 onwards which notes that where the trustees with the consent of the beneficiaries vary the terms of a trust if the property is held on the same trusts as before it is treated as a mere variation of the terms of the existing settlement and not a disposal for capital gains tax purposes. Even if the variation is such that there is a disposal, the assumption is that it is a disposal of the underlying assets not of the settled interest itself.
[10] The right might be an asset within s.21(1)(c) of the TCGA 1992 being "any form of property created by the person disposing of it or otherwise coming to be owned without being acquired." However, one would need a specific deeming provision to tax such right given that the term disposal does not cover a transaction in which an asset (here the right) is not acquired but merely extinguished. See *Welbeck Securities Ltd v Powlson* [1987] S.T.C. 468. See the following footnotes for discussion of whether any of the deeming provisions might apply.

might be problematic! If this asset is not settled property, there is a charge under other provisions of the capital gains tax legislation apart from ss.76 and 85 e.g. under ss.22, 24, 29 or 30? However, it would appear odd to create a new asset in connection with settled property given that the beneficiary already holds a separate beneficial interest under the trust in addition to the trust property, since that could lead to double or even triple charges. The short answer, it is suggested, is that even if the consent requirement is a form of proprietary right or interest on its own it would have a negligible value: without the interest which it "protects" it is of no use to anyone other than, possibly, the holder of the successive interests in whose favour the power of advancement could be exercised.[11] The position might be different if for example the life tenant was not merely giving up the right to consent to the exercise of a statutory power of advancement but was surrendering a power of appointment vested which allowed him to appoint the fund to any person.[12]

8.10 **Surrenders and the s.87 charge:** the effect of s.85 is that even if the settlor wants to be excluded from the non-resident trust (along with all defined persons) in order to avoid the s.86 charge, it may not be possible to do this easily without triggering a capital gains tax charge if the terms of the trust are such that the settlor can only be excluded if he surrenders his life interest.[13] It is clear that the surrender of an interest (as opposed to the consent to the disposal of such an interest) *will* be regarded as a disposal of the beneficial interest and so the settlor could be liable to CGT (since the life interest is likely to have a low or nil base cost).[14] The fact that the trust is now resident in the UK would not prevent a charge.[15]

---

[11] The position though remains unsatisfactory. Similar problems arose in the inheritance tax context in relation to a power of appointment where it was held in *Melville v IRC* [2001] S.T.C. 1271 that the power was a separate asset with value. In the inheritance tax context, the position was eventually dealt with by legislation: see s.47A, IHTA 1984 and 3.16.

[12] It is thought that the position is improved if the beneficiary releases his right to consent before any termination of his interest is in contemplation rather than consenting to an advancement which terminates his life interest. The consent right more obviously has a value as a separate piece of property if the giving of the consent directly results in the termination of his life interest (and the other concern that it is a disposal of the beneficial interest under the settlement itself is greater in these circumstances.) Sections 24 and 29(5) are the deeming sections which might be problematic if there is a concern that the right to consent or the release of that right is a separate chargeable asset although HMRC would still have to show that the asset has value. Section 24 deems a disposal to arise on the entire loss, destruction or extinction of an asset whether or not a capital sum is received. If the right to consent has been released or extinguished it is conceivable then that there might be a disposal but the problem (if there is one) could be avoided if the right is released only for a period of time. e.g. the life tenant releases his right to consent for one year. Section 29(5) provides that if an asset is subject to any description of right or restriction, the extinction or abrogation in whole or in part of the right or restriction by the person entitled to enforce it, shall be a disposal by him of the right or restriction. Here the better argument may be that the right has little value. This is assisted if the right is surrendered well before any appointment terminating the interest is exercised.

[13] For the s.86 charge and taxation of offshore trusts generally, see Ch. 10.

[14] Although note that the life interest may have a 1982 base cost (but still be a wasting asset) or have been uplifted to market value if the trust was exported. See s.85(3) and 8.12.

[15] See 8.14.

EXAMPLE 8.4

> The trustees of a pre-1991 offshore trust hold the property on interest in possession trusts for the settlor and subject thereto on interest in possession trusts for his children. The settlor wishes to carry out inheritance tax planning. The trustees have no power to terminate the settlor's life interest but instead in 2006/07 he surrenders his interest for no consideration. As a result the trusts for the children take effect and (assuming the surrender was done prior to April 2008) these would be transitional serial interests for inheritance tax purposes whilst the settlor has made a PET.[16] However, since the trust is offshore and the settlor has made a disposal of his beneficial interest this is subject to capital gains tax and he is charged on any gain. The life interest has a nil-base cost in his hands although he will be entitled to non-business assets taper relief. If he has held his life interest since before March 1998 he obtains nine years taper relief so (assuming that he is a higher rate tax payer) he is effectively taxed at a rate of 26%.

8.11 For this reason it is desirable to ensure that offshore trustees have wide overriding powers of appointment, exclusion etc. in order to enable the trustees to rearrange the beneficial interests without the consent or action of any beneficiary so that the beneficiary will not trigger unexpected charges under s.85.

8.12 **In-out schemes**: if the trust was originally UK resident, the appointment of non-resident trustees triggers an exit charge on the assets in the trust.[17] Some protection against a double charge is given if a beneficial interest is subsequently disposed of, see s.85(3):

> "For the purpose of calculating any chargeable gain accruing on the disposal of the interest, the person disposing of it shall be treated as having:
>
>> (a) disposed of it immediately before the relevant time, and
>> (b) immediately reacquired it,
>
> at its market value at that time."

The relevant time is the date of emigration.

The purpose of s.85(3) is to fix the acquisition cost of the disponor at the date when the trustees emigrated (i.e. the acquisition cost of his beneficial interest which might otherwise be nil is rebased to market value at that time).

EXAMPLE 8.5

> The X trust was set up in 1988 with J being entitled to the residue of the trust on the death of his sister, K who enjoys an interest in possession.

---

[16] For TSIs, see 18.14 *et seq.*
[17] See 2.47.

The trustees became non-UK resident on March 20, 1996 and J disposed of his remainder interest shortly afterwards (whether for consideration or otherwise). It was worth £150,000 at the date of disposal.

(1) J has made a chargeable disposal.[18]
(2) In order to compute his chargeable gain, if any, the market value of his remainder interest when the trust became non-resident on March 20 needs to be ascertained.

8.13 Section 85 was amended[19] to prevent what might be termed "the in-and-out scheme". Assume that a non-resident trust has stockpiled gains and is now a cash fund. UK trustees are appointed so that the trust becomes resident and subsequently it is exported (by the appointment of further non-resident trustees). On export, s.85(3) will operate to increase the base costs of all the beneficial interests but, given that the nature of the assets then in the trust, there will be no exit charge. Accordingly, a beneficiary could later sell his interest (effectively extracting stockpiled gains) tax free. From March 21, 2000[20] the disposal of a beneficial interest in a settlement which had stockpiled gains at "the material time" (i.e. when it ceased to be UK resident) cannot benefit from the uplift in value under s.85(3).

8.14 **Importing a non-resident trust:** disposals of beneficial interests in a trust which was at any time non-UK resident or non-UK resident under a double tax treaty (or which had received property from such a trust) were brought into charge in respect of disposals occurring on or after March 6, 1998.[21] This provision aimed to stop schemes intended to avoid a charge on gains which had accrued in foreign trusts by repatriating the trusts and the beneficiary then disposing of his interest.

EXAMPLE 8.6

In 1997, offshore trustees of a pre-1991 settlor-interested trust disposed of assets realising a gain which could not then be charged on the settlor under s.86[22] so that the gain was stockpiled. The settlor wanted to receive capital from the trust fund but could not sell his interest without triggering a s.85 CGT charge. The trust was therefore imported and then he was able to sell his beneficial interest under the settlement to a bank (by this time the settlement held cash) tax free. The bank was non-UK-resident and therefore did not care about the fact that there were s.87 gains in the settlement.

As amended, s.76(1A) now catches the disposal of *any* beneficial interest under a settlement if the trust has at any time been non-resident or if it has

---

[18] TCGA 1992, s.85(1).
[19] By FA 2000, s.95.
[20] The amendment to TCGA 1992, s.85 applies where the material time, within the meaning of TCGA 1992, s.85(10), falls on or after March 21, 2000: FA 2000, s.95(5).
[21] TCGA 1992, s.76(1A)(1B) and (3).
[22] See Ch. 10.

received property from a non-resident settlement. There is no charge if, or to the extent that, the beneficiary becomes absolutely entitled to the trust property (since this will trigger the charge on the stockpiled gain).

The provision is very wide-ranging. Consider the following: **8.15**

EXAMPLE 8.7

> A UK trust was set up to benefit children of the settlor in 1996. It has never been non-resident. Children of the settlor are life tenants entitled to capital at 30. One of the beneficiaries wishes to sell his interest to a purchaser in 1999. Just before he effects the sale the trustees receive £1,000 of property from an offshore settlement. The result is that the whole of the UK settlement is tainted and therefore a disposal of *any* of the interest by a beneficiary will be taxed.

SALE OF AN INTEREST IN A "SETTLOR-INTERESTED" TRUST[23]

The rules relating to the sale of an interest in a "settlor-interested" trust took effect from March 21, 2000 and when they apply *the trustees*, provided that they are UK resident, are treated as disposing and reacquiring trust assets at market value (i.e. there is a deemed disposal). Tax is then calculated at either the settlor rate (if the settlor is interested in the trust) or at the normal 40 per cent (if the trust is no longer settlor-interested but has been so in the previous two years) and in the latter case may be recovered by the trustees from the beneficiary who sold the interest. **8.16**

When is a settlor interested in his trust? The normal rules of the TCGA 1992, s.77(2) apply.[24] However, note that the trust must either be a settlor-interested trust when the interest is sold or must contain property derived from a trust which had been settlor-interested at any time in the previous two years. Notice that the disposal can be by *any* beneficiary: the legislation is not limited to disposals by the settlor. The settlor must, however, be either resident or ordinarily resident in the UK[25] or have been so in any of the previous five tax years. Years of UK residence before 1999/00 are disregarded. **8.17**

The mischief under attack: the intention was to prevent exploitation of the TCGA 1992, s.76(1) exemption by individuals who placed assets in trusts (instead of selling the assets) and retained an interest under the trust which they then sold. However, the scope of the legislation is not so limited and, as (2) below illustrates, can catch the wholly innocent. **8.18**

---

[23] TCGA 1992, Sch.4A as inserted by FA 2000, Sch.24. Note that with the extension of the definition of settlor interested trusts under s.77 post April 5, 2006 this provision is more wide-ranging than might be thought.
[24] So from April 6, 2006 if living dependent children are beneficiaries this would make a trust settlor-interested.
[25] The definition of a settlor-interested trust is considered in Ch. 11 and 6.04.

EXAMPLE 8.8

(1) In 1999 D settled unlisted shares and made a hold-over election under s.165 to avoid the payment of any CGT.[26] He became absolutely entitled to those assets on attaining 35 (which was, say, in four months' time). Before four months elapsed he sold this interest to E and F, trustees of a settlement with realised capital losses. As a result:

   (a) under general principles the sale by D of his interest did not attract a CGT charge[27];
   (b) when E and F become absolutely entitled a further hold-over election was available, and when they disposed of the assets they could reduce the resultant gain by their unused trust losses.

In these circumstances TCGA 1992, Sch.4A provides that when D sells his interest the trustees make a deemed disposal of the trust property and the tax charge (at D's rates) will be borne by him. The deemed disposal cannot qualify for holdover relief under either ss.165 or 260.

(2) The Z estate was settled in 1990 and X, the current life tenant, is the settlor. His son, Y, is the remainderman but is tired of waiting for his inheritance and so sells his interest. TCGA 1992, Sch.4A applies and the trust suffers a wholly undeserved CGT charge. Note that the tax charge is not on the value of the beneficial interest but on the underlying assets. There is no motive test. The disposal for consideration of *any* interest by *any* beneficiary in a UK resident settlor-interested settlement is sufficient to trigger a charge.

(3) A simple scheme which the legislation was intended to stop (as set out by HMRC in *CG 35101*) would have been something like this:

   - A owns a valuable holding of unlisted shares in a trading company which he wishes to sell to B.
   - He creates a settlement under which he has the life interest and his son C has the remainder.
   - He transfers the shares to the settlement, claiming hold-over relief under TCGA 1992, s.165.
   - He sells his life interest to B and C sells his remainder interest to D, B's son. The price would be based on the current market value of the shares, with some discount for potential future liability.
   - B and D are appointed trustees of the settlement.
   - B and D now have full control as beneficiaries and as trustees. They could get the shares out of the trust, using a TCGA 1992, s.165 hold-over claim to prevent CGT arising. But this would involve some liability under TCGA 1992, s.76. Alternatively they can simply leave the assets in the settlement.

---

[26] Such a claim will no longer be possible: since December 2003 hold-over relief is not available on transfers to settlor interested trusts: see Ch. 9 and 6.04. See also 12.06 and s.79A of TCGA 1992 which restricts use of trust losses where any person connected with the original transferor purchases an interest in a settlement.

[27] TCGA 1992, s.76(1) as amended by FA 1998, s.128(1)(a).

8.19 Consideration: consideration means actual consideration but excludes another interest in the same settlement save one previously disposed of for value. It does not include the incidental costs of a transaction.[28]

8.20 The charge: The deemed disposal is of all the trust assets even if the consideration is minimal unless one of two exceptions applies. First where the interest being sold is an interest in a specific fund in which case the deemed disposal is restricted to assets in that fund.[29] Second where the interest is in a specific fraction of the income or capital in which case the deemed disposal is of that fraction of the underlying assets.

8.21 Since the deemed disposal is made by the trustees of the settlement assets, liability for tax prima facie falls on trustees. If the settlement is within s.77 the settlor is liable but can recover tax from the trustees. Otherwise if the settlement has ceased to be settlor interested in the previous tax year the trustees are directly liable. However if the trustees bear the tax under Sch.4A they are entitled to recover it from the person who disposed of the beneficial interest. In *Example 8.8(2)*, X would recover his tax from the trustees who would in turn recover it from Y.[30]

8.22 Paragraph 13 has complicated provisions to deal with delayed completion. What happens if the beginning of the disposal of the beneficial interest and the effective completion of the disposal are in different tax years? The beginning of the disposal is when the contract is entered into or, if earlier, when any option is granted. Effective completion is when the buyer becomes unconditionally entitled to the beneficial interest. If they are in different tax years the disposal takes place in the year of effective completion and the residency test of the settlor and the trustees are applied by reference to both years. In addition, the rules as to whether the settlement is settlor-interested are applied for the year of completion.

8.23 It is curious that Sch.4A remains on the statute book. Since December 2003 hold-over relief has no longer been available on transfers to settlor-interested trusts and therefore the sort of scheme considered in *Example 8.8(1)* and *(3)* would no longer be possible. It is hard to see why HMRC would want to catch *Example 8.8(2)* anyway.

8.24 Planning: for settlor interested offshore trusts which contain large unrealised gains the disposal of a beneficial interest in a settlement may be taxed at a lower rate after taper relief and may therefore be more attractive than a sale of the trust assets.

EXAMPLE 8.9

> N is the life tenant and settlor of an offshore trust which was set up in 1995. N's son is the remainderman entitled to capital on N's death. The s.76 exemption will not apply so that if N sells his life interest this will be a chargeable disposal. The capital gain will be calculated under

---

[28] See *Tax Bulletin 66*, August 2003.
[29] Para.8(1).
[30] TCGA 1992, Sch.4A, para11.

normal principles (the life interest will normally be a wasting asset). If the sale of a life interest takes place during the 2006/07 tax year, N will have a qualifying holding period of eight years plus an additional year under TCGA 1992, s.2A(8)(b) for taper relief purposes. Assuming that N is a higher rate taxpayer he will therefore pay at an effective tax rate of 26% on any gain he makes on the disposal of his life interest.

8.25 **IHT link-up:** in these circumstances the inheritance tax implications of a disposal by an individual of his interest in possession needs careful consideration.[31] If N's qualifying interest in possession is worth £50,000 actuarially but the value of the property in which his interest subsists is £150,000 and he receives £50,000 for the sale of his life interest he will have made an IHT transfer of value of £100,000 (£150,000 − £50,000). He cannot rely on the no gratuitous intention exemption in s.10 because it only relieves dispositions that would otherwise have been transfers of value. The disposal of a life interest in a settlement is not itself a transfer of value (see s.51(1)(a)) but a deemed ending of the interest. If the sale of the life interest is to a company, such as a bank, this would be an immediately chargeable transfer. If the transferee is an individual it would be a PET (a TSI until April 6, 2008: thereafter the disposal will result in a chargeable transfer into a relevant property trust).[32]

Summary

8.26 Whether the disposal of a beneficial interest is taxable depends on:

1. Does it fall within the standard exemption under s.76?
2. If not is there actually a disposal at all? *or*
3. If there is a disposal does the interest being disposed of have no value? For example, where the trustees take away a particular beneficiary's right to capital and they do not need the consent of the person with the interest, that interest is of little market value.

---

[31] IHTA 1984, ss.51(1) and 52(1).
[32] See 17.11 for the IHT treatment of a termination of a qualifying interest in possession.

CHAPTER 9

CGT HOLD-OVER RELIEF

- Background **(9.01)**
- Gifts of business assets (s.165 relief) **(9.10)**
- Gifts subject to an immediate IHT charge (s.260 relief) **(9.33)**
- Resume **(9.39)**
- Disposals to a settlor-interested trust **(9.42)**
- Principal private residence relief and s.260 hold-over **(9.46)**
- Double charges: relief for IHT against CGT **(9.52)**

BACKGROUND

An overview of the law

Gifts and other non arms-length disposals are treated as taking place at market value. As a result a gain can accrue to a donor even though he has received nothing for the assets and has not generated any cash to pay the tax. In 1978 a form of hold-over relief was introduced for gifts of business assets (CGTA 1979, s.126). This was extended by FA 1980, s.79 which made it possible to postpone the payment of CGT on the majority of lifetime gifts, whatever the asset (including gifts into trust).[1] Provided that a joint election was made by donor and donee, the donor was treated as disposing of, and the donee as acquiring, the asset for its market value at the date of the gift minus the chargeable gain which was held over. This postponement of tax could continue until the asset was sold, because if the donee in turn made a gift of the asset, a further hold-over election was available. In the event that the donee died still owning the asset, the entire gain was wiped out by the death uplift in value. (There was an exception for gifts into trusts on which hold-over relief had been claimed.)[2] **9.01**

In his 1989 Budget speech, however, the then Chancellor of the Exchequer Nigel Lawson announced the repeal of general holdover relief for disposals **9.02**

---

[1] The relief given by FA 1980, s.79 (now repealed) was extended to include deemed disposals of settled property by s.82(1), FA 1982.
[2] See 7.46 and *Example 7.16*.

of property made on or after March 14 1989, citing as justification the fact that it:

> "was introduced . . . in 1980, when there was still capital transfer tax on lifetime gifts, in order to avoid a form of double taxation. But the tax on lifetime giving has since been abolished, and the relief is increasingly used as a simple form of tax avoidance."[3]

9.03 **Position after 1989:** after March 1989, the main occasions when hold-over relief has been available are—

(i) gifts of business assets;   "s.165 relief"

(ii) gifts of property qualifying for IHT agricultural property relief;

(iii) transfers into and out of trusts which are immediately chargeable for IHT purposes;   "s.260 relief"

(iv) transfers out of accumulation and maintenance trusts

9.04 **Settlor-interested trusts:** The opportunities of taking advantage of hold-over relief have been severely curtailed since December 10, 2003 in a bid to prevent the relief being used as part of a tax avoidance scheme (a "*Melville*"[4] scheme) and further on April 6, 2006 as part of the "modernisation" process. The changes involve hold-over relief not being available for gifts into settlor-interested trusts and the extension of the definition of settlor-interested trust after April 5, 2006.[5] These changes (and also the restrictions on the availability of principal private residence relief when a hold-over claim is made) are considered at 9.42 *et seq*.

9.05 **Priority of reliefs:** relief under s.260 takes priority to hold-over relief for gifts of business assets under s.165 in those cases where a disposal would meet the conditions of both reliefs. This may benefit the transferor if there would be some restriction of hold-over relief under s.165 (e.g. because the assets had not been used as business assets throughout the qualifying holding period).[6] Given that most disposals into trust after March 21, 2006 will be into relevant property settlements, s.260 is likely to be most relevant.

9.06 **Employee trusts:** In the case of gifts to employee trusts, TCGA 1992, s.239 affords relief from CGT by providing that the disposal is for such consideration as to ensure that there is neither a gain nor a loss. This section applies automatically where the conditions are met, in priority to hold-over relief. A claim is not required.

---

[3] As a reasoned statement this does not bear close scrutiny because there was (and is) still a potential inheritance tax charge on all lifetime gifts.

[4] As discussed at 3.16, a *Melville* scheme involved a chargeable transfer into a discretionary trust but by limiting the loss to the settlor's estate an immediate charge to IHT was avoided. The loss to the settlor's estate was limited by reserving to him a general power of appointment exercisable after (say) three months.

[5] Note that transfers *out* of settlor-interested trusts to individuals are not affected and can qualify for hold-over relief.

[6] See 9.15.

When is hold-over relief relevant to trustees? 9.07

(i) on the *inter vivos* creation of the trust which will involve a disposal of assets by the settlor by way of gift;

(ii) on the transfer of chargeable assets to a beneficiary: e.g. in the exercise of a trustee power of advancement;

(iii) on the deemed disposal under TCGA 1992, s.71 when a person becomes absolutely entitled to settled property against the trustees.[7] Not only will there be a deemed disposal on the ending of a trust (e.g. when a beneficiary becomes absolutely entitled to the trust fund) but also if there is a resettlement of the property.[8]

EXAMPLE 9.1

The trustees of the Scraggs Discretionary Trust No. 2 have wide powers of appointment and advancement.

(i) They appoint Blackacre on trusts under which Ronnie Scraggs—who is disabled—becomes entitled to an interest in possession.

- *For IHT purposes* Blackacre is now held on a qualifying interest in possession trust[9] and hence there is a charge on the ending of the relevant property regime;
- *For CGT purposes*, however, the settlement is continuing and there is no disposal of Blackacre;

(ii) They advance Whiteacre (which is farmland) to Reggie Scraggs who intends to farm it in hand.

- *For IHT purposes*: subject to the possible availability of agricultural property relief, an exit charge will arise when the property leaves the settlement;
- *For CGT purposes*: hold-over relief under s.260 will be available on a claim being made (note that this will take priority over any s.165 relief);

(iii) They transfer 2 Railway Cuttings to another family discretionary trust (the No. 1 Trust).

- *For IHT purposes*, s.80 of the IHTA 1984 prevents any charge and the property is treated as remaining comprised in the Scraggs Discretionary Trust No. 2.
- *For CGT purposes* the property has passed into a new settlement (i.e. the No. 1 Trust, the trustees of which have become absolutely entitled to it as against the No. 2 Trustees) but because there is no chargeable transfer for IHT purposes,

---

[7] For a consideration of the tax charge imposed by s.71 see 7.34 *et seq*.
[8] For a consideration of when a resettlement occurs for CGT purposes, see 7.55.
[9] See 19.02.

s.260 hold-over relief is not available. Of course this may not matter if (a) 2 Railway Cuttings is the main residence of a beneficiary entitled to occupy it under TCGA 1992, s.225 or (b) if it is a business asset so that hold-over relief is available under s.165.

9.08 If hold-over relief is claimed when the trust is set up the subsequent death of an interest in possession beneficiary in circumstances where there would normally be a tax free uplift does not wipe out the held-over gain which becomes chargeable.[10] However the payment of tax may be postponed if the conditions exist for a further hold-over election (as would be the case if IHT was charged on the ending of the interest in possession).

Claiming hold-over relief

9.09 Relief under ss.165 and 260 is not given automatically, it depends on the appropriate claim being submitted.[11] The claim must be made by the transferor and the person who acquires the asset ("the transferee") or, where the trustees are the transferor, by the transferor alone.[12] The time limit for making a claim is within five years of January 31 following the end of the year of assessment in which the gift was made. Where the gifted asset is not subject to any restrictions for partial non-business use under Sch.7[13] it is possible to make a hold-over relief claim without a formal determination of the market value of the asset or a computation of the gain.[14] HMRC are not bound by any valuations, however, and if this procedure is used it is not possible to revoke the hold-over claim. Otherwise revocation can be made within the normal time limits for amending a tax return. (For example, if a hold-over relief claim is made for a disposal in 2005/6 it can be revoked by the persons making the claim at any time before January 31, 2008.)[15] It may be useful to be able to revoke a claim particularly where the trust becomes settlor interested or the transferee emigrates.[16]

GIFTS OF BUSINESS ASSETS (S.165 RELIEF)

9.10 Availability of relief

Under TCGA 1992, s.165, hold-over relief is available (subject to the restrictions noted below) on a disposal of business assets.[17] There must be a disposal

---

[10] TCGA 1992, s.74 and see *Example 7.16*.
[11] TMA 1970, s.43. The claim must be on form IR295: *Relief for Gifts and Similar Transactions*.
[12] TCGA 1992, s.165(1)(b); s.260(1)(c).
[13] See 9.15.
[14] For the conditions to be satisfied, see SP 8/92 and *Tax Bulletin* April 1997.
[15] Note—queried this and waiting for relevant forms to check.
[16] See 9.44.
[17] Note that gifts to companies of freehold or leasehold land by a connected person are chargeable to SDLT on the basis of the market value of the land: FA 2003, s.53.

by an individual or trust and the disposal must be of a chargeable asset "otherwise than under a bargain at arm's length". Relief may therefore be available for both gifts and undervalue sales. The donee can be any UK resident "person", a term which includes individuals, trustees and companies.[18] A claim must be made: the relief is not automatic.

Definition of business assets

An asset is a business asset for the purposes of relief if[19]:   **9.11**

(a) It is, or is an interest in, an asset used for the purposes of a trade, profession or vocation carried on by:
- the transferor; or
- his personal company[20] (whether or not a trading company although it must carry on a trade in which the asset is used); or
- a member of a trading group of which the holding company is his personal company; or

(b) It consists of shares or securities of a trading company,[21] or of the holding company of a trading group, where:
- the shares or securities are neither listed on a recognised stock exchange, nor dealt in on the Alternative Investment Market; or
- the trading company or holding company is the transferor's personal company.

A mere disposal of assets suffices: it is not necessary for the disposal to be of part of a business.[22] An individual who transfers an asset used in a trade carried on by a partnership of which he is a member can claim relief.   **9.12**

Whether an asset is used for the purposes of a trade may sometimes be a moot point: for instance, would the relief be available on a gift of a valuable oil painting ("The Sick Corpse") which has adorned the offices of a funeral parlour for many years?   **9.13**

"*Trade*" has its normal meaning but is extended to include the commercial letting of furnished holiday accommodation and the occupation of woodlands managed on a commercial basis with a view to profit.   **9.14**

---

[18] However, note the restriction if the gifted property is shares or securities and the donee is a company: see 9.19.
[19] TCGA 1992, s.165(2) as amended by FA 1993, s.87, Sch.7 para.1(1) and by FA 2000, s.90(3).
[20] "Personal company" is defined in TCGA 1992, s.165(8)(a) (as substituted by FA 1998, s.140(4)) as "in relation to an individual, a company the voting rights in which are exercisable, as to not less than 5 per cent, by that individual".
[21] From April 6, 2003 the more restrictive taper relief definitions of trading company and trading group were extended to hold-over relief: FA 1998, s.140(4). For gifts before April 6, 2003, a trading company was a company whose business consisted wholly or mainly of the carrying on of a trade or trades. The wholly or mainly requirement is much less restrictive than the taper relief definition "a company carrying on trading activities which activities do not include to a substantial extent activities other than trading activities". "Substantial" is considered by HMRC to mean an 80 per cent rather than a more than 50 per cent test on trading activities.
[22] Contrast IHT business property relief.

Partial hold-over relief

9.15 Where an *asset* has not been used as a business asset throughout its period of ownership e.g. land has been used as to 50 per cent during ownership for the purposes of a trade and 50 per cent as let investment property, the held-over gain is reduced by reference to the period of ownership when it was not used as a business asset. *Note that any part of the period before March 31, 1982 is included in the computation.* Similar restrictions occur where the asset is a building or structure which is only partly used for a qualifying purpose during the period of ownership and in this case the restriction is in accordance with what is "just and reasonable".[23]

Hold-over relief on a transfer of *shares* is restricted where the company owns chargeable assets that are not business assets *but only* where *either* the transferor was able to exercise at least 25 per cent of the voting rights at any time in the 12 months before the transfer *or* the transferor is an individual and the company was his personal company at any time in the 12 months before the transfer.

When relief is restricted, the held-over gain is reduced by multiplying it by A/B where: A is the market value on the date of the transfer of the company's chargeable business assets and B is the value on the same date of all the company's chargeable assets. This can give rise to anomalies. For example, since the restrictions are by reference to the company's assets on the date of the transfer, if the transferor has control of the company, it could before making the gift dispose of any chargeable non-business assets that would otherwise restrict hold-over relief. The company would then be liable to corporation tax on the disposal but this would avoid a restriction on hold-over relief.

9.16 Since April 2003 a transferor has faced the more restrictive taper relief rules for determining whether company shares can qualify for hold-over relief in the first place *as well as* the pre-April 2003 provisions for restricting hold-over relief where a company owns non-business chargeable assets.

Example 9.2

> A uses Blackacre in his sole trade for three years. He then lets it for five years before bringing it back into business use. Hold-over relief on a gift into an interest in possession trust set up in 2004 is restricted to 3/8 of the gain.

Note that in the above example if A had used the land for farming purposes and then let it for agricultural use there would be no restriction of hold-over relief provided that the land qualified for IHT agricultural property relief at the date of disposal.[24]

---

[23] TCGA 1992, Sch.7, paras 5 and 6.
[24] See TCGA 1992, Sch.7, para.3.

Business assets hold-over relief for trustees[25]

9.17 The requirements for relief are modified when business assets are owned by trustees. Broadly, the relevant business asset must either be used for the purposes of a trade, profession or vocation carried on by the trustees or by a beneficiary with an interest in possession in the settled property. In the case of a disposal of shares in a trading company by trustees, either that company must not be listed on the Stock Exchange or, alternatively, at least 25 per cent of the voting rights at the company's general meeting must be exercisable by the trustees.[26]

It is not necessary for the beneficiary with an interest in possession to have a qualifying interest for IHT purposes.[27]

EXAMPLE 9.3

> A trust set up in May 2006 holds land which is used by Fred in his trade. Fred has an interest in possession in the land. Hold-over relief is available to the trustees on a disposal of the land. Note that it is only necessary for Fred to have the interest in possession *immediately before* the disposal. Curiously, the provisions restricting relief where the asset is not wholly used for business purposes throughout the period of ownership apply only if the trustees use it for their trade not if the interest in possession beneficiary uses it in his trade.[28]

9.18 The restrictions on the amount of hold-over relief in the case of a disposal of shares in unlisted companies are less onerous for trustees.

EXAMPLE 9.4

> The trustees hold a 20% share in an unlisted trading company. A beneficiary becomes absolutely entitled to the shares as against the trustees. The trustees claim hold-over relief. Even if the company owns some investments, there is no restriction on the claim (para.7(1)(b) only refers to individuals). Note, however, that if the trustees own 25% or

---

[25] TCGA 1992, Sch.7, paras 2–3.
[26] TCGA 1992, Sch.7, para.2 as amended by FA 2000, s.90(3) and by FA 2004, s.116, Sch.21, para.9.
[27] The meaning of a "qualifying" interest in possession is considered at 19.02.
[28] See Sch.7 para.(4)(2)(c) and para.5 which refer to the trustees being the transferor but do not discuss the position where the interest in possession beneficiary is using the land. Para.5 can never be satisfied by the interest in possession beneficiary because he is not the transferor; the restriction is imposed by para.5 on the transferor if the asset was not used for the purposes of the trade by the transferor throughout the period of its ownership. By definition this cannot occur if the asset qualifies for hold-over relief because the life tenant uses the asset in his trade. If para.5 needs to be satisfied, para.2(a)(ii) giving relief to an interest in possession beneficiary who uses the asset in his trade would be meaningless. Whether HMRC would argue that the interest in possession beneficiary is treated as the transferor in these circumstances and therefore has to use the asset for trading purposes throughout his period of ownership is not known.

more of the voting rights in the company there is a restriction (see para.7(1)(a)).

Suppose that the trustees owned 25% of the shares and that the business assets (goodwill, plant and machinery and a freehold interest in a property used for the company's business) are worth £1,295,000 and the chargeable non-business assets (let property and quoted shares) worth £1,105,000. Total chargeable assets are therefore worth £2,400,000. The chargeable gain is £150,000.

The held over gain is reduced from £150,000 to the following:

1295/2400 × £150,000 = £80,937.

The balance remains chargeable subject to any deduction for taper relief.

The restriction on hold-over relief could have been avoided if the trustees had disposed of 1% of their shares at least 12 months before the deemed disposal when the beneficiary became absolutely entitled.

Restrictions on gifts to companies

9.19 From November 9, 1999 it has not been possible to claim hold-over relief on the transfer of shares or securities to a company. The relief was withdrawn because it was being exploited in tax avoidance schemes. However, it is still possible to claim hold-over relief on transfers of *other assets* to a company.[29] HMRC confirmed in *Tax Bulletin 50*, December 2000 that disposals to a trust with a corporate trustee were not subject to the restriction:

> "under s.69(1) the trustees of a settlement are treated for capital gains tax purposes as being a single and continuing body of persons distinct from the persons who may from time to time be the trustees. The transfer is therefore treated for all purposes of capital gains tax as a transfer to trustees and not a transfer to a company."

A similar result applies when there is a transfer of shares to a company which is acting as trustee of a bare trust. The gift is regarded as a transfer to the beneficiaries.

Calculation of the held-over gain

9.20 It is the chargeable gain which is held-over. The chargeable gain is calculated by reference to market value of the asset at the date of the gift with an

---

[29] This provision restricting gifts of securities to companies was first introduced in FA 2000 and was inadvertently repealed for disposals on or after April 6, 2003. For a period of some four months between April and October people were happily giving shares to companies and claiming hold-over relief. The error was spotted and the provision was then re-enacted. The press release dated October 21, 2003 announced with effect from that date (not from December 5, 2003) that s.165 gifts relief is denied on the transfer of shares or securities to a company. A classic case of the tax system being so complicated that everyone lost the plot!

allowance for indexation where relevant. Taper relief, however, operates as a reduction in the rate of tax charged on a disposal. Hence the gain held over is the gain *before* taper relief. The transferees' qualifying holding period for taper relief purposes starts at the date the gift was made, with the result that the period of ownership of the transferor does not count.

EXAMPLE 9.5

Christopher gives shares in a unlisted trading company into an interest in possession trust for his children in July 2005. The shares were acquired by Christopher in January 1989 for £1,000 and in July 2005 were worth £51,500. The hold-over relief claim is made by Christopher alone.[30]

	£
Christopher's gain is	51,500
Less indexed base cost say	(1,500)
	£50,000

The effect of the hold-over relief claim is that Christopher has no CGT liability on the gift and the trustees' base cost of the shares is reduced to:

	£
Deemed consideration	51,500
Less held-over gain	50,000
	£1,500

Note that the trustees obtain all of Christopher's indexation allowance but none of his taper relief. HMRC do not require a formal valuation of the asset transferred *unless* there is a possibility that indexation will create a loss *or* where there is an interaction between hold-over relief and other reliefs such as retirement relief *or* where the transfer is a sale at an under value.[31] It is not, however, possible to make a partial claim for hold-over relief: e.g. to reduce the gain to the level of the transferor's annual exemption. However, the held-over amount could be restricted by making the transfer for an amount of consideration that produces the required gain or (depending on the type of asset involved) make gifts in separate tranches.

Sales at under value

Where the actual consideration for the transfer exceeds the expenditure on the asset that is allowable in calculating the gain, the held-over gain is reduced by that excess. Where the consideration does not exceed the allowable expenditure, the whole gain is held over.

9.21

---

[30] See 9.09 for who needs to make the claim.
[31] See 9.09 on claims generally.

Example 9.6

> In *Example 9.5*, if the trustees had paid Christopher £10,000 for the shares, hold-over relief would have been reduced by the excess of £10,000 (actual consideration) over £1,000 (the allowable cost before indexation)) namely £9,000. The gain held over would therefore be:
>
> | | £ |
> |---|---:|
> | Chargeable gain as calculated above | 50,000 |
> | Less reduction | 9,000 |
> | | £41,000 |
>
> Christopher would therefore have a chargeable gain of £9,000 and the trustees' base cost of the shares would be £51,500–£41,000 = £10,500, equivalent to the actual consideration paid plus the indexation allowance of £500 on Christopher's original base cost.

Non-residence of donee

9.22 No hold-over relief is available if the transferee is neither resident nor ordinarily resident in the UK or is regarded as resident elsewhere under a double taxation agreement.[32] Nor is hold-over relief available if the transferee is a dual resident trust[33] or the transferee is a company that is controlled by a person or persons who are neither resident nor ordinarily resident in the UK and connected with the transferor.[34] This can affect UK trustees where a beneficiary who becomes absolutely entitled is non-resident: in such cases, no hold-over relief claim is possible.

9.23 Subsequent emigration and claw-back: a held-over gain becomes chargeable if the transferee is an individual who becomes neither UK resident nor ordinarily resident within six years after the end of the year of assessment in which the disposal on which hold-over relief is claimed took place if the transferee still owns the asset at that time.[35] Again this can affect trustees who have made a hold-over claim when a UK resident beneficiary becomes absolutely entitled to the settled property and that beneficiary emigrates within six years. The trustees are chargeable on any clawed-back gain if the donee fails to pay the tax within 12 months of the tax becoming payable.[36]

9.24 If the transferee is a trust rather than an individual (e.g there is a transfer between settlements or a gift into trust) and the trust becomes non-resident on or after March 19 1991 there is no claw-back of the held over gain. This is because an exit charge is imposed anyway on emigration of a trust in respect of all the unrealised gains, not just the held over gain.[37]

---

[32] TCGA 1992, s.166.
[33] TCGA 1992, s.169.
[34] TCGA 1992, s.162.
[35] TCGA 1992, s.168(1).
[36] TCGA 1991, s.168(7) but note that no assessment shall be made under this provision more than 6 years after the end of the year of assessment when the relevant disposal was made: *ibid.* s.168(8).
[37] TCGA 1992, s.80: see 2.51.

Calculating the clawed-back gain: Where emigration of the individual transferee occurs, a chargeable gain equal to the hold-over relief is deemed to accrue to the transferee *immediately before* he becomes non-resident. The transferee is apparently not entitled to any taper relief on this gain because the gain does not arise on a disposal of assets.[38] The transferee is not charged tax on the transferor's gain *but is deemed to have a gain equal to the held-over gain and the held-over gain did not qualify for taper relief.* In other words neither the transferor nor the transferee benefits from taper relief. By contrast, trusts which emigrate under s.80 and suffer an exit charge are entitled to taper relief based on the trustees' period of ownership of the asset.[39] 9.25

As already noted, if the transferee does not pay the tax within 12 months of the due date of payment, the deemed gain can be assessed on the transferor in the name of the transferee within six years of the end of the year of assessment in which the disposal took place on which hold-over relief was claimed.[40] The transferor can, of course, recover any tax paid from a transferee but this might be difficult in practice if the transferee has left the UK. Hence trustees should ensure that they make some provision for the possibility of the beneficiary's emigration and bear in mind that they could end up with a higher tax liability than if no hold-over relief claim had been made because of the loss of accrued taper relief. One option for trustees would be to postpone making the hold-over relief claim until the last possible moment, namely five years after January 31, following the end of the year of assessment and only make the claim if the donee is still UK resident.[41] However, then the trustees would have had to pay the CGT on the gain which would only be repaid once the claim had been made. An alternative would be to retain sufficient trust assets to cover the tax at stake or to obtain security from the beneficiary. 9.26

EXAMPLE 9.7

> Sandra, an interest in possession beneficiary of a pre-March 2006 trust, becomes absolutely entitled to land qualifying for agricultural property relief[42] on attaining 30 in 2007. However she is UK resident and the trustees decide to make a hold relief claim. They do not take a charge over the property. She emigrates in March 2010 and sells the land free of CGT because she is non-resident. The gain held over is clawed back and CGT at 40% assessed on Sandra. If Sandra fails to pay the tax by January 2012, the trustees can be assessed for the tax. It would be attractive for the trustees to revoke the claim in these circumstances so that at least they can claim taper relief.[43]

There is no claw-back on emigration of the transferee if he goes abroad for full time employment, none of the duties of which are performed in the UK 9.27

---

[38] See TCGA 1992, s.2(A)(3).
[39] See 2.51.
[40] See fn.36 above.
[41] TCGA 1992, on claims for relief, see 9.09.
[42] On APR, see Ch. 32.
[43] The question of whether hold-over relief claims can be revoked is discussed at 9.09.

9.28 *and* the transferee again becomes resident or ordinarily resident in the UK within three years of his emigration and still holds the asset in question.[44]

It is questionable whether the claw-back charge on individuals (or indeed an exit charge on trusts) would be upheld by the European Court where the donee emigrates to a country within the EU. It may be argued that such a charge represents a restriction on freedom of establishment of nationals of a Member State in the territory of another Member State. (See Art.43 EC Treaty) *or* a restriction on freedom of movement of capital (whether or not between Member States). The UK Government specifically chose not to impose an exit charge on the emigration of individuals in 1998.[45] In *van Hilten – van der Heijden*[46] a Netherlands national emigrated to Switzerland. She died in Switzerland and her heirs were assessed to inheritance tax in the Netherlands on the basis that a Netherlands national who died within 10 years of having ceased to reside there should be deemed to have been resident there at the time of his death. The European Court held that national legislation which would discourage a national who wished to transfer his residence to another member state and thus hinder his freedom of movement could not for that reason alone constitute a restriction on the movement of capital within the meaning of Art.56 (formerly Art.73b). The taxpayer lost the argument but HMRC are aware that exit charges on the emigration of trusts and the claw-back of held-over gains on the emigration of an individual may be vulnerable if challenged by taxpayers. For this reason HMRC do not want to extend the hold-over relief provisions to other areas of the tax legislation.[47] The opportunities for avoidance might be too great if a hold-over claim was made, the transferee taxpayer then became non-UK resident and he was able to argue against a claw-back of the held-over gain.

9.29 A disposal by the transferee to his spouse is ignored for the purposes of determining whether the emigrating transferee has disposed of the asset. Hence there is still a claw-back if the transferee emigrates after a disposal to the spouse.[48] If the transferee does dispose of the asset after the claw-back charge has been made, no reduction to his base cost is made in respect of the hold-over gain otherwise there would be a double capital gains tax charge. See s.168(10).

9.30 The claw-back of the held-over gain on emigration is reduced by half if the donor acquired the asset before March 31, 1982; the gift took place between then and April 5, 1988 and the recipient emigrated on or after April 6, 1988.[49]

---

[44] TCGA 1992, s.168(5).

[45] See *de Lasteyrie du Saillant v Ministère* [2004] 6 I.T.E.L.R. 666. The taxpayer moved from France to Belgium with the result that he was taxed on the increase in value of certain securities. Despite the fact that the French tax code contained provisions permitting suspension of payment and would exonerate taxpayers entirely at the end of a 5 year period if they had still retained the assets, it was held that the exit charge was a disproportionate obstacle to freedom of establishment. The taxpayer was subject to disadvantageous treatment in comparison with the person who maintains his residence in France. (Contrast the *Hilten* case above where the taxpayer was not disadvantaged emigrating compared with staying in the Netherlands.) The Courts held in *Lasteyrie* that the transfer of a person's tax residence outside the territory of a member state does not in itself imply tax avoidance (stopping tax avoidance being regarded as a permitted exception to the article).

[46] [2006] W.T.L.R. 919.

[47] For example this was discussed in relation to sub-fund elections—see Ch. 7.

[48] TCGA 1992, s.168(3) but note that if there is a claw-back future disposals by the spouse shall be taken into account as if they had been made by the transferor with the base cost being calculated as if hold-over relief had not been given.

[49] Sch.4, para.4.

Agricultural Property

Land qualifying (or which would qualify on a chargeable transfer being made) for 100 per cent or 50 per cent IHT agricultural property relief is specifically included as a business asset for CGT purposes.[50] Hope value in the land also qualifies for hold-over relief even though the hope value does not itself qualify for agricultural property relief.[51]

9.31

EXAMPLE 9.8

> The facts are as in *Example 9.7* except that Sandra does not emigrate. The land is valued at £2m, with £1.5m hope value. Hold-over relief can still be claimed on the entire gain. Note that if Sandra had not been entitled to an interest in possession for at least two complete years immediately prior to the disposal, the land would not have been eligible for agricultural property relief and therefore no hold-over relief would have been available.[52]

Interaction with inheritance tax: This is discussed at 9.52

9.32

GIFTS SUBJECT TO AN IMMEDIATE IHT CHARGE (S.260 RELIEF)

Availability of relief[53]

Hold-over relief is available on a gift or undervalue sale if the relevant disposal "*is a chargeable transfer within the meaning of the Inheritance Tax Act 1984*", or would be such a transfer but for the availability of the annual exemption.[54]

9.33

Hence relief under s.260 is available on a gift to UK resident trustees which is not a potentially exempt transfer and on the transfer of property out of a settlement (typically the deemed disposal on its termination) which is not a potentially exempt transfer by a beneficiary. This category embraces the creation or termination of a relevant property settlement (i.e. almost all lifetime gifts to trusts after March 22, 2006 and, prior to that date, gifts to discretionary trusts).[55] However a gift to a settlor-interested trust cannot qualify for

---

[50] TCGA 1992, Sch.7 para.1. As to when agricultural property relief is available, see Ch. 32.
[51] It will often attract business property relief for IHT purposes.
[52] See Ch. 32.
[53] See TCGA 1992, s.260 as amended.
[54] The transfer of a business or of agricultural property qualifying for relief from inheritance tax is eligible for relief under TCGA 1992, s.260 because these reliefs reduce the *value* of the chargeable transfer. As to business and agricultural property relief, see Ch. 32 above.
[55] Assume that A becomes absolutely entitled to property held in a discretionary trust. For IHT purposes this is a chargeable occasion since the property ceases to be relevant property (see

relief.[56] A transfer out of a non-UK resident trust will qualify provided that it is a chargeable transfer *and* provided that the recipient is UK resident.[57]

Because s.260 specifies that to come within its terms the disposal must be to and by either an individual or the trustees of a settlement,[58] gifts to and by companies do not qualify[59] even though they may be chargeable transfers for IHT purposes.

9.34 It is not necessary for IHT to be *paid* for hold-over relief to be available.

EXAMPLE 9.9

Charlotte settles investment property on trust for her brother Luke in 2007.[60] The trust is not settlor-interested. The investment property is worth £280,000: i.e. is within her nil rate band. No IHT is payable but hold-over relief under s.260 is still available. Note that if Charlotte and her husband Alex own the property equally and settle their respective shares in a single trust, then this is treated as a gift by each of them.[61] If the property is worth (say) £570,000 the transfer each makes falls within their respective nil rate bands and no IHT is payable.

Note that there is no hold-over relief on the disposal of a property to a beneficiary within three months of the settlement being established (nor within three months of an IHT anniversary charge) because there is no IHT exit charge. If, in the above example, the trustees had transferred the property to Luke within three months of receiving it or within three months of a ten year anniversary, no hold-over relief would have been available.

9.35 Hold-over relief is also available in the following situations where the relevant transfer is exempt from any IHT charge[62]:

(i) gifts to political parties[63];

IHTA 1984, s.65(1)(a)). Although this is not a chargeable transfer as such "references in this Act to chargeable transfers shall be construed as including references occasions on which tax is chargeable under Chapter III Part III of this Act." (*ibid.*, s.2(3)). HMRC accept that CGT hold-over relief is available in such cases on the basis that the requirement for there to be an IHT chargeable transfer is met: see (1989) STI 844.

[56] TCGA 1992, s.169B-G inserted by FA 2004, s.116, Sch.21, paras 4, 10(4) with effect for disposals after December 9, 2003. The definition of a settlor-interested trust has been modified by FA 2006 from April 6, 2006. See Ch. 11.

[57] Hence a gift between two discretionary trusts will not qualify because it is not chargeable (see IHTA 1984, s.81: it is treated for IHT purposes as remaining comprised in the original settlement). Nor will a gift out of a discretionary trust within three months of being set up or within three months of a 10-year anniversary qualify for hold-over relief because there is no chargeable event.

[58] TCGA 1992, s.260(1) as amended by FA 2000, s.90(2) and by FA 2004, s.116, Sch.21 para.5(1), (2).

[59] Unless, of course, the gift to a company is of a business asset (other than shares and securities) when relief may be available under TCGA 1992, s.165 as amended: see 9.19, above. Note that a gift *by* a company can never qualify for hold-over relief.

[60] This will be a relevant property settlement.

[61] For IHT purposes this may be treated as creating two settlements: see IHTA 1984, s.44(2).

[62] See TCGA 1992, s.260(2) as amended by FA 1998, s.165, Sch.27 Pt IV.

[63] TCGA 1992, s.60(2)(b)(i).

(ii) gifts to maintenance funds for historic buildings and for disposals out of settlement to such funds;

(iii) gifts of designated property; and

(iv) gifts of works of art.

A+M trusts and trusts for children: s.260 relief is available for a disposal which, by virtue of IHTA 1984, s.71(4), "does not constitute an occasion on which IHT is chargeable".[64] This deals with the situation where an accumulation and maintenance trust comes to an end as a result of the property vesting in the beneficiary absolutely.[65] For instance, if the settlement had been set up in 1990 and provided for the property to be held on trust for B contingent on attaining the age of 18 then when he became 18 in 2005:

9.36

- there is no IHT charge as the result of s.71(4) *and*
- CGT hold-over relief is available.

In practice, the relief rarely applied since most accumulation and maintenance trusts became interest in possession (usually when the beneficiary attained 18) and so, when capital vested (usually when the beneficiary was 25), CGT hold-over relief under s.260 was not available because at the time when the disposal occurred *it was no longer an accumulation and maintenance trust*. When the beneficiary became entitled to income at 18, although the nature of the trust changed for IHT purposes, for CGT the same settlement was continuing, there was no disposal and so no occasion for s.260 to apply. This CGT problem on the ending of accumulation and maintenance trusts produced what was commonly called the "time bomb trust dilemma". Of course, since March 22, 2006 it has not been possible to set up new accumulation and maintenance trusts falling within IHTA 1984, s.71.[66] However, if someone is not yet entitled to the income of an existing accumulation and maintenance trust and they become entitled to the income e.g. at 18 it will no longer affect any later claim for hold-over relief when they become absolutely entitled to capital. The interest in possession is no longer a qualifying interest in possession and therefore hold-over relief is available under s.260(1) as a transfer out of a relevant property settlement.

FA 2006 partly replaced the old accumulation and maintenance trust with bereaved minor and s.71D (18–25) trusts but these are far more restrictive in scope, notably in that they can only be created by will and in favour of a child of the testator.[67] For such trusts, the availability of CGT hold-over relief is only significant when they come to an end and FA 2006 has amended s.260 to provide for relief to be available.[68]

9.37

---

[64] TCGA 1992, s.260(2)(d).
[65] For the meaning of a s.71 accumulation and maintenance trust, see Ch. 21.
[66] See 18.14 *et seq* and note the transitional rules that apply to existing trusts.
[67] Bereaved minor and s.71D trusts are considered in detail in Ch. 25.
[68] See TCGA 1992, s.260(2)(da)—trusts for bereaved minors and (db)—age 18–25 trusts—inserted by FA 2006, Sch.20 para.32.

EXAMPLE 9.10

>Jasper dies on April 23, 2006 and by his will leaves property to his son Conrad on attaining the age of 25.
>
>(i) Jasper has created a s.71D (18–25) trust for IHT purposes;
>(ii) Conrad will become entitled to income at 18 as a result of TA 1925, s.31;
>(iii) at 25 an IHT exit charge will arise (calculated by reference to the seven years from his eighteenth birthday) and CGT hold-over relief, under s.260(2)(a), will be available. Note that if Conrad became absolutely entitled to the assets before his eighteenth birthday hold-over relief would be available under s.2602)(db), TCGA 1992 with no IHT exit charge. If Conrad becomes absolutely entitled to the assets at any time between 18–25 there is a charge to IHT under s.71E and therefore hold-over relief is available under s.260(2)(a), TCGA 1992.[69]

Restrictions on relief under s.260

9.38 The same restrictions on UK residents and emigration of the donee[70] and the same computational aspects[71] as outlined above in relation to s.165 apply to relief under s.260. The same exclusion of taper relief in the computation of the held over gain applies.[72] Note also the problems that arise as a result of *Crowe v Appleby* when interests vest on attainment of a specified age but the beneficiary is not "absolutely entitled" for CGT purposes.[73]

RESUME

9.39 The operation of ss.165 and 260 can be illustrated by the following examples:

EXAMPLE 9.11

>A transfers two investment properties, which are commercially let, into a trust in June 2006. Even if the trust is interest in possession for his daughter, provided his daughter is adult and he and his wife and any living minor children are excluded from all benefit, hold-over relief is

---

[69] The fact that the tax charged is nil does not mean no hold-over relief is available. Compare the position on a transfer of assets out of the settlement within the first quarter of the commencement of a relevant property settlement or the first quarter after a 10-year anniversary of a relevant property settlement when there is no inheritance tax charge (see s.65(4), IHTA) and therefore no hold-over relief.
[70] See 9.25.
[71] See 9.20.
[72] *Ibid.*
[73] See 5.09 and 7.41 for discussion of *Crowe v Appleby* and see App. III A3.105 (Question 34 and 35)

available because A makes a chargeable transfer for IHT purposes. It does not matter that the transfer may fall within A's IHT nil rate band. If, however, A's daughter was a minor dependent child, hold-over relief would not be available unless the daughter was excluded from any benefit until she reached 18. If A wanted her to benefit while still a minor A would have to pay inheritance tax at 20% to the extent the value of the investment property exceeded his available nil rate and CGT on any gain. No deduction is given to A for one tax against the other. (See 9.52.)

EXAMPLE 9.12

The trustees of an offshore settlement (which is settlor-interested) own assets which show substantial unrealised gains. The trust is discretionary and the trustees resolve to advance all the assets to UK resident beneficiaries (including the settlor) and end the trust. The beneficiaries become absolutely entitled to the property previously held on discretionary trusts and hold-over relief is available. Note that if the trustees had previously realised capital gains (which are stockpiled gains under s.87) these gains will be charged on the beneficiaries since the trustees have made a capital payment.[74]

9.40 However hold-over relief may be a way round the s.86 charge if the trust is settlor-interested. In the above example if a hold-over relief claim was made no gains would be realised by the offshore trustees which could be taxed on the settlor.[75]

EXAMPLE 9.13

An accumulation and maintenance trust was set up in January 2004. Both the beneficiaries, A and B, are under the age of 25 and are not currently entitled to an interest in possession. The trustees decide to end the trust before April 6, 2008 in order to prevent it falling within the relevant property regime. They therefore advance the assets out to A and B and end the settlement. Hold-over relief is available.

9.41 Suppose in *Example 9.13* that the trustees merely converted the trust into an 18–25 (s.71D) trust before April 2008 so that no beneficiary becomes absolutely entitled. A and B will be entitled to the assets outright at 25. In those circumstances a hold-over relief claim will be available although an exit inheritance tax charge at a rate of 4.2 per cent will be levied. Note that even if the beneficiaries attained an interest in possession (i.e. entitlement to income) after March 21, 2006 this would not jeopardise the hold-over relief claim when they became absolutely entitled at 25. Such an interest in possession is not a qualifying interest for IHT purposes.[76]

---

[74] "Stockpiled gains" and the operation of s.87 is considered at 10.27 *et seq.*
[75] For the charge under s.86, see Ch. 10.
[76] See 19.02 for the IHT definition of a qualifying interest in possession.

DISPOSALS TO A SETTLOR-INTERESTED TRUST

9.42 From December 10, 2003 hold-over relief under ss.165 and 260 is not available if there is a disposal into any trust in which the settlor is interested.[77]

EXAMPLE 9.14

On December 10, 2003 X transfers shares in his family company into a life interest trust for himself with a view to restarting the taper relief clock (this in order to lose a "tainted" taper relief period). Hold-over relief under s.165 is not available so that the disposal may trigger a chargeable gain on the shares. (Note, however, that disposals *out of* settlor interested trusts remain eligible for hold-over relief if the transferee is not a settlor interested trust.) If X had made the disposal into trust on December 9, 2003 hold-over relief would have been available.

9.43 The main target of the change appeared to be so-called "*Melville*[78] schemes", which depended upon s.260 hold-over relief on a transfer into a settlor-interested discretionary trust although the change also struck at arrangements to restart the taper relief clock.[79] However, as the examples below show, the extension of the definition of settlor-interested trusts (from April 6, 2006) to include trusts for dependent children[80] suggests that HMRC are targeting also the use of children's annual capital gains tax exemptions and personal rate tax bands by use of hold-over relief into and out of trusts. The sums involved must surely be relatively small and it would have been simpler if HMRC had used the same mechanism as for income tax: i.e. a charge on the parent in respect of gains realised by the child personally or on gains distributed to the children by the trustees.[81] Curiously where gifts of business assets are made to minor children outright rather than into trust there is no restriction on hold-over relief.

Claw-back of hold-over relief

9.44 If a settlement is settlor-interested no hold-over relief is available under either s.165 or s.260. In addition, if the trust *becomes* settlor-interested within the relevant period (defined as six years after the end of the year of assessment in

---

[77] See FA 2004, s.116, Sch.21 which provides that relief to settlor interested trusts under TCGA 1992, ss.165 or 260 as amended is not to be available on certain transfers. This has effect in relation to disposals on or after December 10, 2003: see FA 2004, Sch.21, para.10.

[78] *Melville v IRC* [2001] EWCA Civ 1247; [2002] 1 W.L.R. 407; [2001] S.T.C. 1271, CA. See also 3.16

[79] In practice the tainted pre-2000 taper relief period had become increasingly less of a problem as periods of ownership lengthened.

[80] Defined as an unmarried (meaning also a child who has not entered into a civil partnership) minor child or step-child of the settlor. See also 6.04.

[81] See ITTOIA 2005, s.629, 4.38 above and Ch. 30.

which the disposal is made) there is a claw-back of any held-over gain. When the relief is clawed back the same problems regarding the availability of taper relief arise as discussed at 9.25. The gains and losses are determined on the basis that taper relief never applied.

EXAMPLE 9.15

> After April 5, 2006 A sets up a trust for his children. One of his children is under 18. If that child can benefit there is no hold-over relief and any future gains realised by the trustees will be subject to capital gains tax on the settlor (with a right of reimbursement). In the light of this, A ensures that his minor children are excluded from all benefit until they cease to be dependent.
>
> However, assume that three years later an adult child pays money into the trust. The trust becomes settlor-interested in relation to *the person* who has added property to the settlement because the child is a beneficiary. In those circumstances, even though the original settlor is not a beneficiary and the trust is not settlor-interested in relation *to him*, nevertheless there is a claw-back of hold-over relief.[82] A is subject to tax on the entire gain held over. If the trustees have disposed of trust assets already or do so in the future, their gains/losses are computed on the basis that there was no hold-over claim. If the trustees themselves claimed hold-over relief on a payment out, the claim made by the trustees is computed on the basis that there was no gain held-over on the original gift from the settlor.[83]
>
> The settlor, A, may therefore wish to obtain an indemnity from the trustees to cover any tax liability for which he may become liable if the trustees inadvertently accept property from a beneficiary.

Exceptions[84] The restrictions on hold-over relief into settlor-interested trusts in s.169B and s.169C do not apply in the following circumstances: **9.45**

(i) In the case of a gift to trustees of a maintenance fund for a historic building if they have elected under TA 1988, s.691(2) that income arising under the settlement or part of the settlement involved is not to be treated as income of the settlor for the tax year in which the disposal is made[85];

---

[82] See s.169C condition 1 which refers to "A settlor who has an interest in the settlement." It is enough for either condition 1 or condition 2 to be satisfied. There is no claw-back if the transferor who claimed hold-over relief has died in the claw-back period. TGCA 1992, s.169C(6).

[83] The Budget 2006 explanatory notes on this part of the legislation are misleading: "the second condition prevents the first condition being side-stepped by the use of a chain of transfers which interposes one or more intermediate settlements or individuals between an individual and a settlement of which he is a beneficiary and to which he wishes to transfer an asset and obtain the benefit of gifts relief." Subsequent questions raised by the Opposition in Committee did not suggest that the clause should be read in such a limited way.

[84] See TCGA 1992, s.169D.

[85] TCGA 1992, s.169D(1).

(ii) In the case of a gift into a trust for a disabled beneficiary (whether or not such person is the settlor).[86] Two conditions must be satisfied:

> First, *immediately* after the making of the disposal the settled property is held on trusts which secure that, during the lifetime of a disabled person, not less than half of the property which is applied, is applied for the benefit of the person concerned (the *capital* condition) and that person is entitled to not less than half of the income arising from the property or no such income may be applied for the benefit of any other person or no interest in possession subsists in the settled property (the *income* condition).[87]
>
> Second, if immediately after the making of the disposal, one or more settlors is "an interested settlor" or will or may acquire such an interest under subsisting arrangements, each such settlor is a disabled beneficiary.[88] For these purposes a settlor is an "interested settlor" only if he has an interest in the settlement or there are arrangements under which he will or may acquire such an interest.[89] In deciding whether the trust falls within the exception it is irrelevant that the settlor's spouse/civil partner or dependent children can benefit (or whether they are disabled).[90] The only requirements are that the trust must satisfy the requirements outlined above that it is for a disabled person and that, if he can benefit, the settlor is a disabled person.

EXAMPLE 9.16

(1) A sets up a settlement which is for the benefit of his disabled wife excluding himself from all benefit. Provided that the conditions relating to the use of income and capital in s.169D(3) are met this will be a qualifying trust with the result that CGT hold-over relief under s.165 or s.260 will be available provided that the normal conditions for that relief are met. The fact that his minor children may also benefit does not matter, even though they are not disabled.

(2) A sets up a settlement which is for the benefit of his disabled nephew which satisfies the conditions in s.169D(3). All of his wife and children who are not disabled can benefit. He is excluded. Provided that the normal conditions for relief are met then hold-over is available.

As a result of the IHT changes in the taxation of settlements[91] most new *inter vivos* trusts set up after March 21, 2006 will lead to an immediate IHT charge (since the relevant property regime will apply) and so s.260 hold-over

---

[86] For the definition of disability, see TCGA 1992, s.169D(7) and see 26.05.
[87] The requirements are the same as those laid down in FA 2005, s.34(2) which gives special CGT treatment to qualifying trusts for disabled persons.
[88] Note that this does not mean that the settlor has to be a beneficiary of the trust, merely that *if he is, he must be disabled*.
[89] See TCGA 1992, s.169D(5). Confusingly this provision is not therefore concerned with a "settlor-interested" trust!
[90] TCGA 1992, s.169D(5).
[91] See Ch. 14.

relief will be available. This treatment does not, however, apply if the trust establishes a "disabled person's interest" for *inheritance tax purposes*[92] because in that case the creation of the trust will be either a potentially exempt transfer by the settlor or, as in (1) of the above example is spouse exempt.[93] Accordingly, hold-over relief will then not be available under s.260 of TCGA 1992 but may be available under s.165 of TCGA 1992 provided that the assets settled are business assets. (It is hard to see how one could satisfy the conditions in s.169D(3) of TCGA 1992 without it also being a disabled person's interest and therefore a qualifying interest in possession for inheritance tax purposes. If it is a qualifying interest in possession for inheritance tax purposes then no hold-over relief under s.260 would be available.)[94]

PRINCIPAL PRIVATE RESIDENCE RELIEF AND S.260 HOLD-OVER

This change targeted a CGT saving scheme involving the "second home". **9.46**

EXAMPLE 9.17

> X owns a second home which has increased in value since he bought it. In due course he wants to sell but meanwhile his (unemployed) son has agreed to live in the property to obtain principal private residence (PPR) relief. X therefore puts the property into a discretionary trust claiming hold-over relief under s.260. It is envisaged that after the son (a beneficiary of the trust) has occupied the property as his PPR it will be sold and the entire gain (including the held-over gain) will be exempt from CGT. This arrangement will not be effective today:
>
> (1) If X or his spouse (or civil partner) or from April 6, 2006 dependent children (including stepchildren) are beneficiaries, the trust is "settlor-interested" and hold-over will not be available. This change affects disposals into trust on or after December 10, 2003.
> (2) If none of the above can benefit under the trust, the gain can be held-over but PPR relief will not be available on either the

---

[92] This term is defined in IHTA 1984, s.89B.
[93] For instance, if the trust is set up for a disabled child or grandchild, IHTA 1984, s.49(1A) applies s.49(1) so that the disabled person is treated as owning the trust capital and so the definition of a PET in s.3A(1A)(c)(i) or (ii) is met.
[94] Can one obtain hold-over relief under s.260 of TCGA 1992 if a gift of non-business assets is made into a trust that satisfies s.169D(3)? This is possible only if the trust that is established does not create a disabled persons interest for inheritance tax purposes and it is difficult to see how it could satisfy the conditions in s.169D(3) and not also be a disabled person's interest for inheritance tax purposes. If the disabled person is given an entitlement to income in only half the settled property and the capital condition in s.169D(3) is satisfied, it is possible that this does not satisfy s.89B(c) of IHTA which requires an interest in possession in the settled property—here the beneficiary has an interest in possession in only half the settled property. It would be odd if such a gift was treated as a PET as to half and hold-over relief is then available on the other half held on discretionary trusts. The drafting generally on disabled trusts is a mess!

held-over gain *or any gain accruing whilst the house is in the trust.*[95] Hence it is not possible to combine a hold-over claim with PPR relief on the property. There is a similar restriction if the house is taken out of the trust by a hold-over election.

EXAMPLE 9.18

Amy owns a house which is not her main residence. It shows a chargeable gain of £50,000 and is worth £250,000. In January 2007 she transfers it into a trust for her adult children from which she, her spouse and minor children are excluded. She makes a hold-over claim under s.260. One of her children occupies the property as his main residence. The trustees sell the property in December 2007 realising a gain of £75,000. The entire gain is taxable on the trustees including the £25,000 gain arising during the period of ownership of the trustees. If, however, Amy revokes[96] her hold-over relief claim then the trustees can claim principal private residence relief on a gain of £25,000 arising during their period of ownership but Amy will then pay CGT on her £50,000 gain (albeit with the benefit of taper relief).

9.47 There are transitional rules[97] to deal with the situation where the house had been put into trust before December 10, 2003 or taken out of the trust with a hold-over claim and principal private residence relief was available on such earlier periods of ownership. Broadly speaking it is important in such cases to trigger a disposal at the earliest available opportunity as the following examples show.

EXAMPLE 9.19

X set up a discretionary trust on March 10, 2003 into which he transferred his second home purchased for £100,000 in 2006. Its value was then £250,000; the gain held-over was £150,000. X is a beneficiary under the trust[98] and the property is occupied by X's son who moved in on June 1, 2003. Assume there is a disposal of the property on March 10, 2004, when it is worth £300,000.

	£	£
Disposal proceeds		300,000
Deduct: Acquisition cost	250,000	
Less: Held-over gain	150,000	
Base cost for the trustees		100,000
Gain		£200,000*

---
[95] Contrast s.74 of TCGA 1992 imposing a claw-back charge on the death of the life tenant only by reference to the hold-over gain of the gain subsequently accruing after the gift into the trust.
[96] For time limits on revocation, see 9.09.
[97] TCGA 1992, s.226A as inserted by FA 2004, s.117, Sch.22, para.6, with the transitional provisions in FA 2004, Sch.22, para.8.
[98] That did not matter in the case of disposals into trust before December 10, 2003.

Deduct: Main residence relief (including last 36 months)[99]	£200,000 × (275/365)	150,685
Chargeable	***£200,000 × (90/365)	49,315
Deduct: Annual exemption (say),		3,950
Taxable gain		45,365
Tax payable at 34%**		£15,424**

* *Less incidental costs of acquisition and disposal*
** *40% for disposals by trustees after April 5, 2004*
*** *Period from December 10 to date of disposal*

9.48 Paragraph 8 of Sch.22 to the FA 2004 introduced a "post commencement period" which is defined as the period beginning on December 10, 2003 and ending on the date of disposal. Main residence relief is restricted to that part of the gain referable, on a time basis, to the period of ownership up to December 10, 2003. The exemption given for the last 36 months of ownership is not available if any part of the period of ownership falls on or after December 10, 2003.

EXAMPLE 9.20

> The period of ownership is one year. Principal private residence relief is available up to December 10, (because looking back three years from the date of disposal this will cover all the period from March 2003) but not for the period from December 10, even though this period falls within the last three years of ownership. If the trustees had delayed selling the property until (say) March 2006 and the gain was still £200,000, main residence relief would only be available on 275/1095 of the gain (i.e. on £50,228) and the chargeable gain would be 820/1095 = £149,772.

9.49 Distributions to beneficiaries: note how the rules apply if the trustees have distributed the property to a beneficiary before or after December 10, 2003 and the beneficiary occupies as his main residence expecting to obtain principal private residence relief in due course.

EXAMPLE 9.21

> In December 1992 John settled cash into a discretionary trust for his children. The trustees purchased a house. In November 2001 the trustees advanced the property out to Harry, his son, who has been in occupation of the property as his main residence for most of the trustees' period of ownership. A hold-over claim was made because not all the gain realised by the trustees was covered by principal private residence relief. Harry continued to occupy the property as his main residence until he sold the house in January 2008. In these circumstances because Harry's allowable expenditure is reduced as a result of the trustees' hold-over relief claim he is not entitled to main residence

---

[99] TCGA 1992, s.223(2)(a).

relief on the entire gain. The transitional rule applies because the gift out of the trust on which a hold-over relief claim was made before December 2003. Effectively Harry will receive main residence relief from November 2001 up to December 10, 2003 but thereafter no relief. *The longer he owns the property after December 10, 2003, the less relief will be available.*[1]

In cases where the time limits have not expired the trustees might revoke the hold-over claim so that there is a small gain on the transfer out to Harry and then he can acquire the property at market value and claim main residence relief for the entire gain arising during his period of ownership.

9.50 Suppose in Example 9.21 that the trustees had advanced the property to Harry after December 9, 2003. In those circumstances if they claimed hold-over relief it would appear that no transitional relief is available to Harry because the relevant earlier disposal took place after December 9, 2003. Hence Harry loses the benefit of *any* principal private residence relief.

9.51 In general, when trustees transfer property to beneficiaries having made an earlier hold-over relief claim, whether before or after December 2003, the position needs to be reviewed where the beneficiary is in occupation of the property as his main residence.

DOUBLE CHARGES; RELIEF FOR INHERITANCE TAX AGAINST CAPITAL GAINS TAX

9.52 A settlor transferring assets into a settlor-interest trust faces potential double tax charges. He may pay inheritance tax on the gift into the settlement at 20 per cent (to the extent the value exceeds his unused nil rate band) as well as capital gains tax (at rates of up to 40 per cent depending on his taper relief position) on the chargeable gain. No relief for the inheritance tax payable is given when calculating the chargeable gain on the transferor's gift.

9.53 If, however, a hold-over claim is made (e.g. income where the trust is not settlor-interested), relief is given for the lesser of the inheritance tax attributable to the value of the asset and the amount of the held-over gain in calculating the chargeable gain subsequently realised when the transferee trustee disposes of the asset.[2] It does not appear to matter whether the transferor or transferee paid the inheritance tax on the transfer into trust.[3] The relief is the smaller of the inheritance tax attributable to the value of the asset and the amount that would be the transferee's chargeable gain on the disposal ignoring any relief for the inheritance tax due. Hence the relief cannot create a loss.

---

[1] Watch inheritance tax after March 21, 2006—previously he could have set up an interest in possession trust for himself with no inheritance tax consequences.

[2] See s.260(7) and s.165(10) of TGCA 1992 and see IHTA 1984, s.165 when the donee pays the CGT.

[3] The settlor may have paid the initial 20 per cent inheritance tax on a gift to relevant property settlement which will involve grossing up (see 00–00). However relief is only given on the value transferred excluding grossing up.

EXAMPLE 9.22

(1) In July 2006 X sets up a life interest trust for his wife. Although a chargeable transfer for IHT purposes, no hold-over relief is available because the trust is settlor interested. Assume that he pays IHT of £5,000 and CGT of £40,000. He cannot deduct one tax against the other. He dies in 2010 and further IHT is due of £5000. The trustees pay this. If the trustees sell the asset there is no relief for the IHT against the chargeable gain.

(2) If however, a hold-over relief claim could have been made on the initial gift into trust, the trustees can deduct the lesser of the IHT attributable to the value of the property settled and the chargeable gain held over against the gain on the sale.

(3) Assume in (1) that there is no sale. In 2011 the trustees—exercising a power to pay or apply capital—advanced the trust fund outright to Mrs X holding over the gain. On a subsequent disposal by Mrs X she can deduct the lesser of the inheritance tax payable on the termination of the trust (the "exit" charge) and the chargeable gain held over on a subsequent disposal of the asset by her. There is an uplift to market value for capital gains tax purposes on her death.

(4) As in (1) except that Mrs X dies in 2010 before the asset is sold whereupon the trusts end with the property being held for the couple's daughter absolutely. There is an IHT exit charge because of the ending of the trust but CGT hold-over relief is available on any gain accruing during the trustees' period of ownership. The position is better than in (3) above where both Mr and Mrs X could end up paying inheritance tax at 40% on the property. Care should be taken before breaking up relevant property trusts and placing the assets in the hands of elderly beneficiaries.

(5) On March 22, 2006 Mrs Y is entitled to a qualifying interest in possession which ends with her death in 2009 when the trust also ends. The value of the settled fund is taxed as part of Mrs Y's estate at 40% and there is a CGT uplift to market value. No hold-over claim is available and none is needed.

CONCLUSIONS

Limited tax planning (using hold-over elections) remains possible as follows: **9.54**

(a) Exits from relevant property trusts (whether or not settlor-interested) will still benefit from capital gains tax hold-over under s.260 of the 1992 Act. Hence *Melville* schemes already established on December 10, 2003 may be completed provided that the appointee is an individual rather than a new trust or the terms of the existing trust are merely varied.

(b) Use of a nil rate band relevant property trust for inheritance tax planning is still attractive.[4] The key is that the trust must not be "settlor-interested" within the wider definition post April 5, 2006.

EXAMPLE 9.23

X puts shares in his investment company into a discretionary trust for the benefit of his grandchildren. He can:
(1) limit the value transferred to his available nil rate band for inheritance tax;
(2) include his adult children; and minor children provided they cannot benefit until they reach 18;
(3) make an election for capital gains tax hold-over relief under s.260(2)(a) of the 1992 Act.

However, note that a gift within seven years of death can result in the worst of both worlds. The gift may be immediately chargeable to inheritance tax or become so if the PET fails but there is no tax free uplift for capital gains tax because the donor did not hold the asset at the date of death.

9.55 Note also that a claw-back of hold-over relief can result in a worse position because of the loss of taper relief.[5]

9.56 Before any hold-over relief claim is made consider whether the chargeable gain after the taper relief may be covered by annual exemptions or allowable losses. Bear in mind that if the donor sells the asset and passes on the proceeds the donor will be able to claim taper relief for his entire period of ownership. There is no point in giving the asset to the donee and making a hold-over claim if the donee then sells the asset shortly afterwards. Taper relief has been lost.

---

[4] As to nil rate band discretionary trusts see Ch. 20 and 28.04.
[5] See 9.25.

Chapter 10

OFFSHORE TRUSTS

- Settlor-interested trusts: UK domiciled and resident settlors **(10.08)**
- Taxing UK resident and domiciled beneficiaries **(10.24)**
- Anti "flip-flop" legislation **(10.41)**

The rules for the taxation of capital gains on offshore trusts are highly complex and have been subject to almost continuous legislative change. For foreign domiciliaries who live in the UK, establishing offshore trusts is still highly advantageous for capital gains tax purposes.[1] By contrast, for UK resident domiciliaries, the offshore trust regime can often result in penal tax charges and heavy compliance costs.[2] **10.01**

Of course offshore trusts are not the only offshore vehicles available: offshore companies, mutual funds and foreign life policies can also be used to mitigate UK tax.[3]

This chapter considers the following: **10.02**

(i) the tax treatment of non-UK resident trusts in cases where the settlor is UK resident and domiciled;

(ii) the tax treatment of non-UK resident trusts when the settlor is not resident in the UK (wherever domiciled).

(iii) the tax treatment of non-UK resident trusts when the settlor is not UK domiciled but is UK resident;

(iv) the taxation of beneficiaries of a non-UK resident trust whether UK domiciled or not.[4]

Overview: the CGT treatment of offshore trusts has undergone a number of radical changes of which the following is a brief summary. **10.03**

---

[1] Although a review was announced in 2003 for the taxation of foreign domiciliaries and the Government said in Budget 2006 that it was still considering the matter, no changes as a result of that review have emerged.
[2] See 10.08 *et seq*.
[3] The tax charge arising when a UK resident trust emigrates and the definition of a resident and non-resident trust are discussed in Ch. 2. Domicile and residence issues generally are also considered there along with the capital gains tax treatment for non-UK domiciled or non-UK resident individuals. See 2.10.
[4] For the rules determining the residence of trusts and FA 2006 changes, see 2.38.

10.04 **From 1965 to 1981:** FA 1965, s.42 imposed a charging system for non-UK resident trusts that led to major difficulties and was ultimately abandoned in 1981.

10.05 **From 1981 to 1991:** FA 1981, s.80 introduced a charging system based on capital distributions received by UK domiciled and resident beneficiaries provided that the trust had been established by a UK settlor. One consequence was that offshore trusts could be used to defer indefinitely the payment of CGT and, in addition, there was no exit charge when a UK trust migrated. Hence even if the trust was one that could benefit the settlor, no capital gains tax charge arose when gains were realised despite the settlor being UK resident and domiciled. It was only when capital payments were made to him that any tax was suffered. This meant that potentially there was an indefinite deferral of capital gains tax with no penalty paid for that deferral.

10.06 **From 1991 to 1998:** from March 19, 1991 the following changes were introduced:

(i) A penalty charge was imposed on UK resident and domiciled beneficiaries receiving capital payments if there was a delay in distributing gains. The intention was to impose a higher rate of tax on offshore trusts where gains were realised but were not immediately taxed. Despite the maximum penalty being an extra 24 per cent tax charge (so that taxpayers could end up paying at a rate of 64 per cent), this did not encourage the re-importation of trusts.

(ii) All new non-resident trusts set up after March 18, 1991 where the settlor, his spouse or children and their spouses could benefit were subject to an immediate CGT charge on the settlor if gains were made (these were known as "settlor-interested trusts"). Hence the deferral advantages were lost for new trusts.

(iii) However, trusts funded by foreign domiciled settlors were not affected by any of these changes even if all the beneficiaries were UK domiciled or resident: gains in these trusts were not subject to CGT even if capital payments were made to UK resident and domiciled beneficiaries. An income tax charge under TA 1988, s.740 might, however, be a problem in such cases.)

10.07 **From 1998 to the present:** The capital gains tax net was substantially widened as a result of FA 1998. First, the definition of settlor-interested trusts was extended to include all new trusts where grandchildren and their spouses (not just settlor, spouse, children and their spouses) were beneficiaries. An immediate capital gains tax charge was imposed on the UK resident and domiciled settlor when gains were realised by the trustees of such new trusts, whether or not such gains were paid out to the settlor. Second, any existing pre-1998 offshore trust whenever set up which could benefit settlor, spouse (including, since December 5, 2005 civil partners) and children/spouse was brought within the s.86 settlor charge. Third, even if the settlor was not UK domiciled, UK resident and domiciled beneficiaries could suffer a s.87 charge when they received capital or benefits from an offshore trust by reference to the level of "stockpiled trust gains."

SETTLOR INTERESTED TRUSTS—UK DOMICILED AND RESIDENT SETTLORS

The present legislation is contained in TCGA 1992, s.86 and Sch.5. It applies at any time in a tax year if two conditions are satisfied: **10.08**

(i) the settlor has an interest in the settlement *and* is resident and domiciled here; and

(ii) the settlement is a qualifying settlement.

The result

When both these conditions are satisfied, gains realised by the trustees, which would have attracted a UK CGT charge had they been resident, are taxed as gains of the settlor and form the top slice of his taxable gains for that year (although such gains can now be reduced by the "personal" losses of the settlor).[5] This charge is often called the "s.86 charge". If the settlor is not interested in the settlement (e.g. because all relevant defined persons have been excluded or he has died) then the fact that he is resident and domiciled in the UK will not result in any tax charge on him. As with UK resident trusts which are settlor-interested, the gains are not reduced by a trustee annual exemption whilst losses realised by the trustees (although available to set against future gains which they may make while the trust is non-UK resident) are not treated as losses of the settlor and cannot be set against his personal gains. **10.09**

EXAMPLE 10.1

(1) Fred set up and funded[6] an offshore trust in 1999. It is one from which he can benefit and he is UK domiciled and resident.[7] The trustees sell a picture realising a gain of £1m in 2006/07. The trustees do not pay any tax. Fred, however, is liable to pay the capital gains tax although he has a right of reimbursement against the trustees.[8]

If the trustees have losses of £500,000 realised in (say) 2005 these losses can be set against the gains and so reduce the tax charge on Fred. If the trustees had owned the picture on March 16, 1998, non-business assets

---

[5] See Ch. 12.
[6] A person is a settlor if the settled property consists of or includes property originating from him—Sch.5, para.6. The provision can be direct or indirect and reciprocal arrangements are countered. However some bounty must be involved (so commercial arrangements such as offshore employee benefit trusts set up to motivate staff are outside s.86). Moreover if there is one settlor X who settles £1m and Y adds say £100 to the trust, Y can only be taxed on the gains arising from the £100 not from the gains arising on £1m.
[7] If Fred was non-UK domiciled, s.86 does not apply. If he was non-resident then again it does not apply (although note the rules on temporary non-residence which can result in a charge if he returns to the UK within five years of ceasing to be resident: see 2.19).
[8] Such right of reimbursement is not treated as a capital payment under s.87 of TCGA 1992.

taper relief based on their period of ownership is available to reduce the gain charged on Fred. Hence the net gain after the losses will be £500,000 and after taper relief of 35% he will be taxed on a gain of £325,000. This is an effective rate of 26% on the net gains.

(2) Note that if the trust was imported to the UK in 2006/7 in the tax year after the losses had been realised such losses could not be set against the gains realised when the trust was UK resident. Those gains are now taxed on Fred under s.77 but the losses were realised when the trust was offshore and within the s.86 regime. If the losses had been realised when the trust was within the s.77 regime they could have reduced the gains realised within the s.77 regime.

(3) If Fred dies during 2006/07, no gains realised by the trustees can be attributed to him during his year of death.

When is a settlement "qualifying"?

It is not good news to be a qualifying settlement!

10.10 **Pre-1998 rules:** prior to March 17, 1998, a settlement was only qualifying if it was non-UK resident and made on or after March 19, 1991 or was made before that date but had been tainted on or after March 19, 1991. Tainting could arise if any one of four conditions was satisfied on or after March 19, 1991:

(i) Property or income was added to the trust (by anyone, unless the transaction was at arm's length).

(ii) The settlement was UK resident and became non-UK resident.

(iii) The terms of the settlement were varied so that a person within para.9(7) became for the first time a person who would *or* might benefit from the trust.

(iv) A person within para.9(7) who was not capable of benefiting from the trust before March 19, 1991 enjoyed a benefit for the first time.[9]

Old settlements were therefore generally outside the scope of the rules (and were known as "*golden trusts*") provided that tainting was avoided. The deferral advantages therefore remained. Only when benefits or capital were actually received by a UK resident and domiciled person from the trust was tax levied under s.87.[10]

EXAMPLE 10.2

Facts as in *Example 10.1* above except that Fred set up his trust in February 1991. The trustees sold the painting in 1997. He does not suffer capital gains tax under s.86 when the gain is realised.

---

[9] See SP 5/92 for examples of tainting.
[10] Under the capital payments code: 10.24 *et seq*.

EXAMPLE 10.3

> Facts as in *Example 10.1* above except that Fred added cash to his trust in May 1996. The trust has become "qualifying" and therefore all gains realised by the trustees in 1996/97 and subsequent years are taxed on Fred while he retains an interest in the trust or is UK resident.

Tainting: it was critical to avoid the tainting of a "golden" trust. **10.11**

EXAMPLE 10.4

(1) The Chamberlain Family UK Trust was set up in 1983. In 1997 the trustees become non-UK resident. Not only did that event trigger an exit charge[11] but, in addition, because the settlement was exported after March 18, 1991 it became a "qualifying settlement".

(2) Take the case of a Jersey settlement set up in 1989.

    (a) In 1994, a court order was obtained whereby the beneficial class was widened to include the settlor. This had the effect of turning the trust into "a qualifying settlement". By contrast, in settlements where the trustees have *always* had the power to add beneficiaries and exercised that power to add a "defined person" after March 1991 it was not thought that the terms of the trust had been varied so that it became a "qualifying settlement". (In SP 5/92 it is stated that "where the terms of the trust include a power to appoint anyone within a specified range to be a beneficiary, exercise of that power after March 19, 1991 will not be regarded as a variation of the settlement". When the trustees have a general power to add anyone the position remains unclear.); *or*

    (b) the trustees distributed funds to the settlor's spouse who was not a beneficiary. The effect of this breach of trust was to convert the trust into "a qualifying settlement" since she was now a person who had enjoyed a benefit (and was a "defined person") and she was not a person who might have been expected to have enjoyed such a benefit from the settlement after March 18, 1991; *or*

    (c) on April 1, 1992 the son of the settlor added property to his father's trust. Such an addition, whether by the settlor or another, had the effect of turning the trust into a "qualifying settlement" and the son would be taxable under s.86 in respect only of gains realised from property added by him. The father would be taxed on all other gains. This provision had to be watched carefully: it did not apply in cases where there was an accretion to settlement funds (e.g. where the trust received dividends or bonus shares from a company in which it had investments) nor if the settlor added property to discharge the administrative expenses of the *trust*

---

[11] For the exit charge, see 2.47 and 9.27.

(not the *company*) to the extent that such expenses could not be discharged out of trust income.[12]

The 1998 changes to the meaning of "qualifying settlements"[13]

10.12 As noted above, the 1991 changes did not persuade taxpayers to repatriate their *existing* trusts. Further, those trusts could still realise gains tax free and the beneficiaries might then emigrate before receiving capital. Although the 1991 changes reduced the number of *new* offshore trusts, the settlor could still set up an offshore trust for his grandchildren and obtain capital gains tax deferral advantages.

10.13 The FA 1998 changes introduced a more onerous regime for the emigration of individuals[14] and extended the settlor s.86 charge to *all* non-resident settlements, even those created before 1991 which were settlor interested. Consequently, any pre-1991 trust where the gains had not yet been realised lost all its capital gains tax advantages unless it was not settlor-interested. In addition the definition of "defined persons"[15] was extended to include "grandchildren" or their spouses if the trust was established or tainted after March 16, 1998.

When is a settlement settlor interested?

10.14 Prior to March 17, 1998 the settlor was only treated as having an interest in the settlement if the trust was set up on or after March 19, 1991 and any of the following "defined persons" could benefit[16]:

(i) Settlor or spouse;

(ii) Child or stepchild of the settlor or spouse of child or step-child (even if adults).

(iii) Any company controlled by any or all of the above and any company associated with such a company.

From March 17, 1998, if any of the above can benefit then the trust becomes settlor-interested and so gains are taxed on the settlor even if the trust was established prior to 1991. However, there were special provisions made for protected trusts and note that trusts set up or tainted on or after that date must also exclude grandchildren and their spouses (see 10.16, below).

Protected trusts

10.15 The s.86 settlor charge was avoided if during a transitional period (which lasted until April 6, 1999) all "defined persons" were excluded from benefit.

---

[12] On the meaning of "administrative expenses" and further details on tainting see SP 5/92 and especially para.26.
[13] FA 1998, s.132.
[14] See Ch. 2 and 2.19.
[15] For the significance of "defined persons", see 10.14.
[16] Sch.5, para.9.

Alternatively, the charge was avoided if the beneficiaries were before April 6, 1999 limited to infant children of the settlor; to grandchildren; to unborn persons, to future spouses etc., albeit that these persons would be within the class of "defined persons". Such a trust was known as a "protected settlement"[17][18]: see TGCA 1992, Sch.5 para.9(10A). A settlement cannot be made protected after April 6, 1999.

As a result for offshore trusts set up pre-March 17, 1998 all children (whether adult or minor) settlor and spouse and children's spouses[19] must be excluded if the settlement is not to be settlor-interested under TCGA 1992, s.86 (unless it was made protected before April 6, 1999). For trusts set up or tainted on or after March 17, 1998, grandchildren and their spouses must also be excluded. **10.16**

EXAMPLE 10.5

> Jonny set up an offshore trust for himself, his issue and his brothers and sisters and their issue in 1990. He is domiciled and resident in the UK. The trust has realised no gains since 1998. It has not been added to or tainted. In 2006/07 the trustees want to realise a substantial gain from the sale of a piece of land. Provided that Jonny, his spouse, children and their spouses and any company controlled by them are permanently excluded from any benefit in the tax year *before* the disposal (i.e. in 2005/06), then any gains realised by the trustees in the following tax year will not be taxed on Jonny. The only beneficiaries will then be his siblings, their issue and his grandchildren and remoter issue. None of these are defined persons in respect of settlements established *before* March 17, 1998. Note that the settlement is *not* a protected settlement and therefore the change in beneficiaries does not need to be done prior to April 1999 but can be done at any point provided the trust is not tainted after March 16, 1998. Grandchildren of the settlor can be retained within the class of beneficiaries. If no change to the class of beneficiaries is made in 2005/06, any gains realised in 2006/07 by the trustees will be taxed on Jonny under s.86 unless he dies in that year.

Contrast UK resident trusts: from April 6, 2006 such trusts (whenever established) are settlor-interested if the settlor, spouse or *minor* children are beneficiaries.[20]

Comments on the current position

The end result has been a relative freezing in the use of offshore trusts by UK domiciliaries. Further anti-avoidance measures affecting UK domiciliaries **10.17**

---

[17] See TGCA 1992, Sch.5, para.9 (10A): a settlement cannot be made protected after April 6, 1999.
[18] Contrast the position of UK resident trusts. From April 6, 2006 such trusts (whenever established) are settlor-interested if the settlor, spouse or *minor* children are beneficiaries: see Ch. 11 and 9.42.
[19] Spouses in each case include civil partners from December 5, 2005.
[20] See Ch. 11.

were passed in FA 2000, FA 2003 and F (No. 2) A 2005. Settlors have felt some resentment that disposals made now on business assets owned personally would qualify for business assets taper relief with an effective tax rate of 10 per cent. By contrast, those who settled such assets into offshore trusts where the trust made the disposal prior to 1998 are subject to a penalty charge if the gains are distributed to beneficiaries at rates of up to 64 per cent. Moreover some settlors have been excluded from all benefit but if the trust benefits their children or (if tainted or established after March 1998, their grandchildren) they still suffer a UK CGT charge. Note also the following:

(i) From March 17, 1998 to April 6, 1999 there was a "transitional period". During this time the trust could, for instance, become UK resident,[21] be wound up, or be converted into a "protected settlement" (considered above). However, if the trust remained offshore and was not converted into a protected settlement, gains realised during this period were also taxed on the settlor but they were deemed to *accrue* in the following tax year, i.e. on April 6, 1999.

(ii) A settlement which is currently qualifying because it benefits defined persons can be made non-qualifying at any time and the settlor will then escape the s.86 charge on future trust gains, provided the trust is non-qualifying for the entire tax year when the gain is made. The rules for making a settlement non-qualifying differ depending on whether the trust was set up pre or post March 17, 1998.

(iii) The s.86 charge does not apply in the year of the settlor's death. Hence if the trustees realise £1m gains in the tax year when the settlor dies (even before his death) there is no s.86 charge.

(iv) The s.86 charge only affects settlors who are UK resident *and* domiciled.

EXAMPLE 10.6

The Brown Jersey Trust was set up in 1988. The settlor, Neil, is life tenant with remainder to his infant children. With the introduction of the 1998 changes, the trustees in the exercise of powers under the settlement:

(1) Appointed half the fund to Neil absolutely. This was a deemed disposal by the trustees on which Neil was subject to CGT both on the gains realised by the trustees from the disposal and on stockpiled gains realised prior to March 1998 since he had received a capital payment.[22]

(2) The trustees then (and before April 6, 1999) excluded Neil from all future benefit in the trust with the result that, as the only beneficiaries were his infant children, the settlement became a "protected settlement". So long as it retains this status, future gains will not be taxed on Neil as the settlor.

---

[21] Advisable if settlor UK domiciled and trust could only benefit his issue if it becomes UK resident. It was not then settlor-interested, although note that from April 6, 2006 a UK resident trust will be settlor-interested if his dependant children can benefit.

[22] See 10.24.

(3) Protected settlement treatment is lost if the settlement is tainted. In addition, privileged treatment ceases in a year where the conditions are not satisfied: notably in the tax year following a beneficiary attaining 18 (the year after the first child of Neil becomes 18). At that point the children could be excluded altogether and the trust fund held only for his grandchildren (if appropriate).

Reimbursing the UK settlor on trust gains

The settlor is given a statutory right to recover any s.86 tax that he suffers from the trustees, but the extent to which this right may be enforced in a foreign jurisdiction is uncertain.[23] It is not, however, thought that a right of reimbursement is the same as the enforcement of foreign revenue laws: see Lord Mackay of Clashfern in *Williams & Humbert Ltd v W & H Trade Marks (Jersey) Ltd* (1986) where he commented that "the existence of (an) unsatisfied claim to the satisfaction of which the proceeds of the action will be applied appears to me to be an essential feature of the principle (that foreign revenue laws will not be enforced)". The proper law of the settlement may also be relevant: if it is English law, in practice reimbursement may be easier to enforce.[24]

10.18

Divorce

This can present problems under the CGT legislation and such problems have been exacerbated by the 2006 changes.

10.19

Example 10.7 (the charge under s.86)

On his divorce in 1990, Paul set up a Jersey trust for the benefit of his children under which he was prohibited from benefiting. He is estranged from his children. In 2000 the children become absolutely entitled to the trust fund leading to a gain of £2m. Paul is taxed on this gain with no prospect of recovering tax either from the trustees or his children.[25] If the trust has been made UK resident, future gains would not become taxable on Paul since it will no longer be a settlor-interested trust because all his children are adult. For many settlors trust immigration became the only option.[26]

---

[23] See CG 38321.
[24] See Trusts and Estates Law and Tax Journal, July/August 2004, p.5.
[25] See, however, the Jersey case of *re the T Settlement* (2002) 4 I.T.L.R. 820 where the settlor was expressly excluded from benefit but the Court nevertheless permitted a variation of the trust in order to allow the trustees to reimburse her the capital gains tax due under s.86. It was held that the variation would be for the benefit of unborn beneficiaries in that it included the discharge of certain moral obligations on their behalf.
[26] Consider though that trust immigration will mean the annual CGT exemption may be split among more trusts, and s.86 losses realised offshore cannot be carried forward.

EXAMPLE 10.8

John and Carolyn decide to divorce in 2007. They are both resident and domiciled in the UK. John's main asset is the offshore trust which he set up in 1991 and in which he has an interest in possession. It has £1m of stockpiled s.87 gains[27] and £0.5 m in unrealised gains. The trust is worth £4m. It is agreed that Carolyn should get half of this. However, if a payment of £2m is made to her or John outright, there will be s.87 gains attributed to the recipient of £1m since these are treated as coming out first plus the payment may trigger unrealised gains which are now taxed on John.

Accordingly, the parties decide to split the trust assets but to retain them in the trust structure. Pre-March 22, 2006 half the trust fund could have been advanced over to a UK resident interest in possession trust for the wife with the husband excluded, (assuming that the trustees had appropriate power to do this). Although this may have triggered s.86 gains on the settlor if the transfer itself realised gains (and posed certain s.87 risks for the wife if the transfer could be regarded as a capital payment to her) at least John would not be taxed on the future gains of the new trust.[28] £0.5m of the s.87 stockpiled gains would be transferred to the new trust under s.90. The two trusts could then operate independently.

However, if half the settled property of the 1991 trust is transferred to a separate interest in possession trust for Carolyn this cannot qualify as a TSI, but will instead fall within the relevant property regime. This is discussed further in Chapter 18. If the transfer to the new trust is a chargeable transfer, there is a 20% inheritance tax since IHTA 1984, s.10 does not apply to transfers out of trusts.[29] Hence it may be necessary to keep the funds within the existing trust and have one fund held on interest in possession trusts for Carolyn (which will qualify as a transitional serial interest if set up pre April 6, 2008)[30] and one fund retained on interest in possession trusts for John. However even though John is excluded from Carolyn's share, he still suffers capital gains tax on all future gains (and this is also the case even if the trust is brought back to the UK when s.77 would operate). The problem could be avoided if a sub-fund election was made under Sch.12 to the FA 2006, but the conditions necessary for sub-fund elections make this unlikely.[31] John will need to consider how he is to be reimbursed for capital gains tax arising on future disposals out of Carolyn's fund given that he is excluded from benefiting from that fund.[32]

---

[27] See 10.24.
[28] Once they are separated for the purpose of the s.86 charge it does not matter that his former spouse is benefiting.
[29] See 17.11 and fn. 31.
[30] On transitional serial interests see 18.14.
[31] On sub-fund elections, see 7.72.
[32] This problem is considered in more detail in chs 17 and 34.

Anti-flip flop legislation

10.20 TCGA 1992, s.76B and Sch.4B (inserted by FA 2000) were introduced to prevent the settlor charge under s.86 being avoided by a "flip-flop" arrangement. These provisions have been supplemented by further legislation in FA 2003 although these provisions do not increase the s.86 charge but affect the s.87 pool.[33]

EXAMPLE 10.9

> A simple flip-flop scheme worked as follows:
>> *Year 1*: Trustees of the A Trust, which has no stockpiled gains and only unrealised gains, borrow against the security of the trust assets and advance the cash to the B Trust (which includes the settlor as a beneficiary); they then exclude "defined persons" from the A Trust;
>> *Year 2*: A Trust disposes of assets to pay off the loan, whilst the cash is advanced out of B Trust to the settlor.
>
> Under this arrangement no gains were read through to the B Trust (because there were no stockpiled gains which had been realised before Year 2) so that the distribution (in Year 2) from B Trust was tax free. Further, the only disposal in the A Trust occurs at a time when the settlor charge does not apply.
>
> The amending legislation introduced by FA 2000 applies if three conditions are satisfied:
> (i) the trustees make a "transfer of value" (for instance, the transfer of moneys, to B Trust);
> (ii) in the year of transfer s.86 (the settlor charge), s.87 (the capital payments charge) or s.77 (UK trusts settlor charge) apply to the trust;
> (iii) that transfer of value is linked with trustee borrowing.
>
> If these conditions are satisfied and if a transfer of value occurs on or after March 21, 2000, the trustees are deemed to dispose of all the assets in A Trust and immediately reacquire them at market value. In a case where s.86 applies the resultant gain will be taxed on the settlor in the normal way. Otherwise the resulting gain passes into the Sch.4C pool.[34]

10.21 These provisions have created a number of problems: There is no motive test so perfectly innocent transactions which involved no tax avoidance and no diminution in the trust assets can be caught. For example, a trust that borrowed from one underlying company and lent funds to another wholly owned company to enable that company to make an investment is caught. The safest

---

[33] See 10.24.
[34] See further 10.41.

course for offshore trusts (and indeed UK resident trusts which had s.87 gains or were within s.77) is to avoid trustee borrowing at all, although curiously, companies wholly owned by trustees can borrow and are not caught by the legislation (see Tax Bulletin, issue 66 p.1048).

Losses and s.86/s.87

10.22　See Ch. 11 for a consideration of losses.

Non-UK resident or foreign domiciled settlors

10.23　Apart from the settlement needing to "qualify" and be settlor-interested, the legislation under which gains realised by offshore trusts are taxed on the settlor under s.86 only applies in years when the settlor is both domiciled *and* either resident or ordinarily resident in the UK. Gains realised in other years are not taxed as the settlor's and neither are gains realised in the tax year when the settlor dies.

EXAMPLE 10.10

Mr Smith (domicile of origin New Zealand) is the settlor and life tenant of an offshore trust that realises substantial gains. He is aged 90 and until now has successfully claimed he is not UK domiciled even though he has lived in the UK for many years. He does not pay tax on any gains realised by the trustees even if such gains are remitted to him or they have been realised on UK situated assets. In 2005–06, his domicile position changes because he now intends to remain in the UK permanently. He will be taxed under s.86 on all gains realised by the trustees after that date, whether or not they make capital payments to him.

Even if no changes are made to the law of domicile as such or Mr Smith's New Zealand domicile continues, it is relatively easy to envisage the Government changing s.87 so that gains realised by an offshore trust are taxable on a foreign domiciliary who is resident in the UK if they are remitted here or gains from UK situated assets realised by trusts are taxable on foreign domiciliaries who are settlors of such trusts.

TAXING UK RESIDENT AND DOMICILED BENEFICIARIES

10.24　TCGA 1992, ss.87 ff apply to non resident trusts in respect of gains made from 1981–82 onwards where the trustees are not resident nor ordinarily resident in the UK during the tax year. Note however that if s.86 (the settlor charge) applies, no s.87 gains arise.

Position pre-March 17, 1998

10.25 Prior to March 17, 1998, for the section to apply the settlor had to be domiciled and either resident or ordinarily resident in the UK at some time during the tax year or when the settlement was made. Hence, if the settlor was UK domiciled and resident at the date of the trust's creation the rules of s.87 always applied. By contrast, if the settlement was originally created by a non-domiciled settlor, who subsequently became a UK domiciliary, it was caught by these rules only for those years when the settlor was UK resident and ceased to be caught on his death. Trusts set up by non-resident but UK domiciled settlors were also not caught by s.87 until the settlor became UK resident.

EXAMPLE 10.11

> In 1995 P set up an offshore trust while domiciled in Hong Kong. Three beneficiaries are UK domiciled and resident but one is non UK domiciled. Until March 1998 none of the beneficiaries suffers CGT under a s.87 charge. There is no s.86 charge.

Position post March 16, 1998

10.26 In the case of gains realised by an offshore trust and capital payments received by UK resident and domiciled beneficiaries on or after March 17, 1998 the residence and domicile of the settlor became irrelevant. Section 87, therefore, now extends to all non-resident trusts irrespective of when set up and whether or not the avoidance of UK tax was one of the motives of the settlor.[35] However, it will only attribute trust gains realised post-March 16, 1998 and only if they are not already taxed under s.86.

"Settlement" and "settlor" are defined as for income tax and settlor includes the testator or intestate when the settlement arises under a will or intestacy.[36]

EXAMPLE 10.12

> (1) Facts as in *Example 10.11*. As a result of new rules introduced by FA 1998, capital payments (to P's UK resident and domiciled children) are within the CGT net. If no gains are realised in the trust, any s.87 tax charge will be postponed until gains are realised. The non-UK domiciled child is still outside s.87. Note that if Paul becomes resident and domiciled in the UK any gains realised by the trust after that time will

---

[35] Contrast the income tax provisions in TA 1988, ss.739–740 which are subject to a purposive defence.
[36] TCGA 1992, s.87 (9) and see 4.14.

be taxable on him under s.86. They cannot later be taxed on the children under s.87—they never go into the pool of stockpiled gains.

(2) J moved to Hong Kong in 1920 and when domiciled there settled his non-UK property on trust for his UK descendants who become absolutely entitled to the property in 2005 when the trust period ends. On this occasion a tax charge will arise and since the beneficiaries receive a capital payment on absolute entitlement it will be necessary for beneficiaries to include in their tax returns a calculation showing gains realised by the trust since March 17, 1998, including gains realised on the deemed disposal when they become absolutely entitled.

(3) The trustees of a non-UK settlement set up by Rudi, a Bulgarian finance dealer now deceased, hold the trust property for Rudi's four grandchildren; two of whom, Charlotte and Luke, are now resident and domiciled in the UK. Any capital payments made by the trustees to Charlotte and Luke prior to March 17, 1998 are not taxable on them even if gains are realised post March 17, 1998. Gains and losses accruing to the trustees before March 17, 1998 and capital payments received before March 17, 1998 are wholly ignored. However, if the trustees realise gains in 2003/04, any capital payments Charlotte and Luke have received after March 16, 1998 can be taxed on them. There may be some possibility of washing out gains by payments first to the non-UK domiciled beneficiaries if such payments are made in an earlier tax year *before* payments to UK-domiciled and resident beneficiaries although note the changes in FA 2003 which can limit this.

Operation of the s.87 charge

10.27 First the trust gains or ("stockpiled gains" or s.87 gains) must be calculated. A calculation is done for each tax year ("the amount on which the trustees would have been chargeable to tax . . . if they had been resident and ordinarily resident in the UK in the year"). Non-resident trustees are not entitled to the benefit of a CGT annual exemption, but the normal uplift in value in the settled assets will occur on the death of a life tenant in possession.[37] The principal private residence exemption may apply and taper relief is applied to reduce any trust gains. In computing this total,[38] gains made in offshore companies may be attributed to the trustees.[39] The anti "flip-flop" rules provide for a separate pool of stockpiled gains to be drawn on when the normal gains have been exhausted.[40]

Capital payments

10.28 The gains realised by the trustees are not taxable on beneficiaries when realised. They are only taxable when attributable to beneficiaries. Benefits

---
[37] See Ch. 12.
[38] Gains realised by trustees prior to March 17, 1998 are ignored if the settlor was not then UK domiciled.
[39] See TCGA 1992, s.13 (10).
[40] TCGA 1992, s.85A, Sch.4C and see 10.20 and 10.41.

and capital received by beneficiaries are subject to CGT being "capital payments" (unless otherwise taxed as income). A "capital payment" is widely defined[41] to include, inter alia, the situation where a beneficiary becomes absolutely entitled to the trust property as well as to "the conferring of any other benefit".

Benefits

Benefits can include, for example the rent-free occupation of houses owned by a trust; the use of pictures owned by a trust, as well as loans to beneficiaries. In *Billingham v Cooper; Edwards v Fisher*[42] it was decided that the provision of an interest-free loan which was repayable on demand conferred a benefit on the borrower (a beneficiary of the trust) every day for which the loan was left outstanding. That benefit was a "*payment*" within s.97(2) and a capital payment by virtue of s.97(1). The value of the benefit could be quantified retrospectively and the legislation would be applied year by year. Two other matters are worthy of note: **10.29**

(i) it was accepted that a fixed period loan (e.g. for 10 years) conferred a benefit once and for all at the date of the loan and that there was no subsequent conferment of a benefit;

(ii) the Court of Appeal rejected the argument that no benefit was received (or its value was nil) on the basis that if interest had been charged it would have gone to the beneficiary (who was life tenant of the settlement).[43] The following extract from the judgment of Lloyd J., at first instance, was expressly approved by the appeal court:

> "It seems to me that the legislation does not call for or permit a comparison of the position that the recipient might have been in if a different transaction had been undertaken by the trustees. There are too many different possible comparisons for that to be a tenable approach. The proper comparison is with the position of the recipient if the actual loan had not been made rather than if some other transaction had been entered into. The recipient of the actual loan, if it had not been made, would not have had the use of the money lent.
>
> It seems to me that this is particularly clear from the fact that the sections are directed to attributing gains not only to beneficiaries but also among beneficiaries in circumstances in which more than one beneficiary has received a capital payment, which of course is not true of either of these cases.
>
> I accept it is not sensible to suppose that the person entitled to income has a special status which exempts him from this treatment

---

[41] See TCGA 1992, s.97(1) and (2)
[42] [1999] S.T.C. (SCD) 176; [2000] S.T.C. 122; [2001] S.T.C. 1177, CA.
[43] It is questionable whether a life tenant of a *Archer-shee* trust (where he is treated as entitled to the income of the underlying assets rather than merely entitled to the income of the trust as a separate entity) could pay rent or interest to himself anyway.

or requires him to be treated more favourably than other beneficiaries."[44]

Settled advances

10.30 HMRC consider that a settled advance by the trustees in favour of a particular beneficiary can be a capital payment within s.97. Suppose the trustees of an old accumulation and maintenance offshore trust with a dead settlor decide that they wish to defer Jonny's absolute entitlement to a moiety of the capital at 25. (He would otherwise be subject to capital gains tax on the stockpiled gains.) Since he is the eldest child he will have the disadvantage of being taxed on all the stockpiled gains so far realised and effectively then "wash out" the gains to the benefit of the others. They have no overriding powers of appointment, but do have an enhanced power of advancement and exercise this power to make a settled advance for the benefit of Jonny[45] so that he does not become absolutely entitled. Is this a capital payment? Even if he has no right to demand the capital has he received a capital payment up to the value of the assets subject to the settled advance? Jonny may have been given only a revocable life interest: in these circumstances can he really be taxed on the whole capital value?

10.31 At best, there is a conflict between TCGA 1992, s.90 and 97. Section 90 provides that a proportion of outstanding trust gains are carried forward to the transferee settlement when a transfer of assets is made between settlements. However, s.97(2) provides that a payment includes the conferring of any benefit and s.97(5)(b) then states that a payment is received by the beneficiary if it is paid or "applied for *his benefit*".

The power of advancement can only be properly exercised if it is for the benefit of a beneficiary. HMRC apparently take the view that the precise terms of the settled advance is irrelevant and the value of the particular interest taken by the beneficiary is also immaterial because if the application is for his benefit it falls within s.97(5)(b). The alternative view is that s.97(5)(b) is concerned with payments made to a third party but where the *beneficiary still receives full value*. For example, payments made to a school in settlement of fees that are a parent's liability on behalf of a child could be classed as payments applied for the benefit of a parent.

In the above example the actual value of his settled interest may be far less than the value of the property applied on his benefit. If HMRC's view is right, a 64 per cent rate may apply and the beneficiary will have to find the tax out of his personal funds![46] In practice HMRC do not seem inclined to litigate this point! To the authors' knowledge, despite various HMRC statements, no case on the point has actually been taken even where full disclosure about the settled advance has been made on the tax return of the beneficiary in whose

---

[44] [2000] S.T.C. 122 at [135].
[45] Bearing in mind FA 2006, Sch.20 and the IHT implications: see 7.42 and 18.14.
[46] A classic settled advance will give the beneficiary a life interest with remainders over. Usually there will be a power to advance capital to him. It follows that in many cases the value of the interest that he is given will be nothing like the amount of the tax charge if the HMRC view is correct.

favour a settled advance has been made and the beneficiary has self-assessed on the basis that no charge under s.87 has arisen.

Method of attribution

Trust gains are attributed to all beneficiaries who receive capital payments as follows. The first beneficiary to receive a payment has (unless he is not UK resident or domiciled and the trust is caught by the FA 2003[47] changes) attributed to him all the gains then realised by the trustees to the extent of the benefit which he receives. This can produce unfair results: 10.32

EXAMPLE 10.13

> Bill and Ben become absolutely entitled to an overseas trust fund worth £200,000 in equal shares when they become 25. The trust fund has realised gains of £100,000 when Ben becomes 25 (Bill will become 25 in a later tax year). All the gains are attributed to Ben.

When more than one capital payment is made in a single tax year, gains are attributed to the payments pro rata.[48] (If a capital payment is made at a time when there are no trust gains, subsequent gains may be attributed to that beneficiary.)[49] If no capital payments are made, trust gains are carried forward indefinitely until such a payment occurs.[50] A non-UK domiciled or resident beneficiary can receive capital payments first in a tax year prior to a UK resident domiciliary to "wash out" the gains.

EXAMPLE 10.14

> A non-resident discretionary settlement has four beneficiaries, two of whom (A and B) are UK domiciled. Initially the fund had no income or gains. In 2003/4 the trustees pay A and B £100,000 each. No capital payments are made to the non-UK domiciled beneficiaries C and D. In 2005/06 the trustees realise gains of £50,000. A and B are each taxed in that year on £25,000 of the gains under s.87. In 2006/07 the trustees realise a further £150,000 gain and also make capital payments to C and D of £100,000 each. A and B are taxed on £150,000 between them. If C and D had received the payment in 2003/04 instead of A and B there would have been no tax payable.

The UK resident and domiciled beneficiary cannot deduct his personal losses from the gain attributed to him under s.87 (contrast the position of a settlor 10.33

---

[47] See 10.41.
[48] TCGA 1992, s.87(5).
[49] s.87(4).
[50] s.87(2).

beneficiary taxed under s.86)[51] but he may deduct his annual exemption and the balance will then attract tax at 10 per cent, 20 per cent or 40 per cent as appropriate. In calculating his liability, offshore gains will be treated as the lowest part of his total gains for the year (thereby enabling him to benefit from the beneficiary's annual exemption and, in appropriate cases, reducing any surcharge).[52]

Section 740 tie-in

10.34 A capital payment made by trustees may be treated as income in the hands of the recipient beneficiary under TA 1988, s.740. Such payments are charged to income tax up to the trust income for that year; income from previous years is included to the extent that such income has not already been charged to a beneficiary. It is only the *excess* that is treated as a capital payment for the purpose of the apportionment of trust gains. Section 740 takes priority over s.87.

The non-UK beneficiary

10.35 A beneficiary who receives a capital payment is subject to CGT on the attributed gains provided that he is UK domiciled *and* resident.[53] Accordingly, a non-UK resident or non-UK domiciliary may have trust gains attributed to him (subject to FA 2003) but will not suffer any tax on those gains.

Offshore losses

10.36 If non-resident trustees realise capital losses these will be set off against future gains made by those trustees in the normal way for the purposes of calculating s.87 gains attributable to a beneficiary.[54]

Deferring and avoiding the charge

10.37 A charge under s.87 can be deferred so long as the trustees avoid making capital payments. The charge can be avoided altogether if such payments are made to a non-UK resident or non-UK domiciled beneficiary or distributions are made to UK resident and domiciled beneficiaries which do not exceed their annual capital gains tax exemptions. Gains may, therefore, be washed out of the trust by the making of such payments in the tax year prior to distributions

---

[51] See Ch. 12.
[52] See CG 38321 in the context of the charge on the settlor.
[53] TCGA 1992, s.87(7).
[54] See Ch. 12.

to UK resident and domiciled beneficiaries.[55] Following the introduction of "temporary non-residents" by FA 1998, difficulties may arise if a settlor, who would otherwise be subject to the s.86 charge, ceases to be UK resident. As a result the capital payment rules in s.87 will apply, but if the settlor returns to the UK within five years of his departure gains during his absence will be attributed to him on his return.[56] To prevent a double charge, the gains taxed on the settlor will not include capital payments made to UK resident and domiciled beneficiaries (although note that no deduction is made for payments to non-resident beneficiaries: see TCGA 1992, s.86A).

The supplementary (interest) charge on s.87 gains

10.38 A "supplementary" charge may apply to beneficiaries who receive capital payments on or after April 6, 1992. This extra levy does not apply if the recipient beneficiary is non-resident or non-domiciled (TCGA 1992, ss.91–95). The charge operates as an interest charge on the delayed payment of CGT following a disposal of chargeable assets by non-resident trustees. It is, however, limited to a six year period and, therefore, the time covered by the charge begins on the later of (a) December 1 in the tax year following the year in which the disposal occurred, and (b) December 1 six years before December 1 in the year of assessment following that in which the capital payment was made. It ends in November of the year of assessment following that in which the capital payment is made. The rate of charge is 10 per cent per annum of the tax payable on the capital payment (this percentage may be amended by statutory instrument). The minimum period is two years so the minimum charge is 20 per cent (an additional 8 per cent charge for the 40 per cent taxpayer). For a higher rate taxpayer, the effective maximum rate of tax plus interest is 64 per cent.

EXAMPLE 10.15

The B Jersey Trust realises capital gains in the tax year 1998/99 and a capital payment is made to a UK domiciled and resident beneficiary on June 1, 2004.

(1) That beneficiary will be assessed to CGT on the capital payment received (at a rate of, say, 40%).
(2) The interest charge will apply for the period from December 1, 1999 to November 30, 2005 at 4% per annum so that the interest charge continues to run after the capital payment has been made. In all, six years will be subject to the additional charge (being 24 per cent) thereby giving a capital gains tax rate of 64 per cent. Note that if the beneficiary does not suffer a CGT charge—for instance

---

[55] Note, however, that if future gains are realised by the trustees such gains can be attributed to UK resident and domiciled beneficiaries who have received capital payments.
[56] See Ch. 2.

because he is able to set his annual exemption against the gains attributed to him—there is no interest charge.

10.39 The precise mechanics governing the supplementary charge are complex, with capital payments being matched first with total trust gains at April 6, 1991 and then on a first-in first-out basis. Trustees are given at least 12 months in which to distribute gains since the interest charge does not apply to gains realised in the same or immediately preceding year of assessment, to that in which the capital payment is made.

EXAMPLE 10.16

> In 1996/97 the B Offshore Settlement has accumulated trust gains of £100,000. Although the interest charge begins to run on December 1, 1997 no charge is levied on capital distributions made before April 6, 1998.

Impact of the 64 per cent rate

10.40 To what extent has the charge encouraged the break-up of existing offshore trusts? Much turns on the facts of individual cases but it should be remembered that one way of avoiding the s.87 charge—distributing to non-residents or non-UK domiciliaries—generally still remains available to "wash-out" all the potential tax including this interest charge provided the trust is not caught by the FA 2003 provisions.[57] For the wealthy family, who view their trust as a roll-up fund where they take the income rather than the capital, the deferral advantages are still highly advantageous because the fund is growing free of tax. At a later date some of the family may emigrate for five tax years and can receive capital tax free. Finally, remember that because income from offshore trusts may be taxed less heavily (at a maximum rate of 40 per cent) trustees should, in appropriate cases, ensure that income rather than capital is distributed.

ANTI "FLIP-FLOP" LEGISLATION

10.41 As noted earlier, FA 2000 attempted to stop flip-flop schemes by introducing Schs.4B and 4C. It applies to all settlor interested trusts and s.87 trusts.[58]

This prevented the use of old-style flip-flop schemes which had effectively worked by delaying the realisation of gains until a later year. The pre-2000 flip-flop schemes generally involved settlor-interested trusts where the intention was to avoid a s.86 charge on future gains. However, FA 2000 introduced a loophole that enabled trustees to reduce or eliminate stockpiled gains that could be attributed to beneficiaries on future capital payments under s.87.

[57] See 10.41.
[58] See 7.62 and 10.20.

10.42 This loophole was contained in TCGA 1992, s.90(5)(a) which prevented s.87 gains from being carried across to the transferee settlement (Trust B) to the extent that the transfer was (under Sch.4B) linked with trustee borrowing. The legislation that had aimed to stop s.86 avoidance thus opened up extensive opportunities for s.87 tax avoidance as illustrated in the following example:

EXAMPLE 10.17

> Offshore Trust A has £1m stockpiled gains and is worth £1m. It holds mostly cash or assets showing no gain. It borrows £1m and in 2002 appoints all the borrowed funds of £1m to Trust B. Since there was a transfer of value linked to trustee borrowing, s.90(5)(a) provided that the stockpiled gains of £1m did not pass across into Trust B. Trust B took £1m free of the stockpiled gains. There was a deemed disposal of the assets remaining in Trust A but since these showed no gains (or maybe the settlor was dead or not UK domiciled so that such gains would not be immediately taxable anyway) this did not matter. There was nothing to go into the Sch.4C pool.

10.43 Such "s.90" schemes were widely used in an attempt to get rid of the stockpiled gains which could not easily be washed out in cases where all the beneficiaries were UK resident. The Government response to the s.90 avoidance scheme was aggressive and "retroactive". FA 2003, s.163 amended Sch.4C. These changes are complex but the effects can be summarised as follows:

(i) The changes are relevant wherever trustees of a settlement have made a transfer of value linked to trustee borrowing after March 20, 2000 even if the original settlement (Trust A in the above example) has subsequently ceased to exist. Since, as noted above, a transfer of value linked to trustee borrowing can occur in a number of unexpected instances where there is no avoidance motive,[59] the position must be checked wherever trustees have borrowed.

(ii) The provisions do not affect beneficiaries who have received capital payments from Trust B prior to April 9, 2003. Thus in the above example if Trust B had distributed the entire £1m to the relevant beneficiaries before April 9, 2003, such beneficiaries are not caught by the FA 2003 legislation and the payments are tax free provided that the s.90 scheme works (it may fail for other reasons: eg if Trust B was a sham).

(iii) FA 2003 now provides that the Sch.4C pool comprises not only the Sch.4B gains realised on the deemed disposal *but also any outstanding s.87 gains* in the transferor settlement at the end of the tax year in which the transfer was made. Thus in the above example, Trust B no longer takes £1m cash free of the s.87 gains. All those s.87 gains fall into the Sch.4C pool (along with any deemed Sch.4B gains) and can be allocated to any future payments made to beneficiaries of either Trusts A or B.

---

[59] See 7.62 and 10.20.

(iv) The fact that (as in the above example) no gains may be realised on the deemed disposal under Sch.4B is irrelevant. If there is a transfer of value linked to trustee borrowing then the anti-avoidance legislation is triggered and a Sch.4C pool is formed comprising the Sch.4B trust gains plus the s.87 stockpiled gains.

(v) For the purposes of calculating the Sch.4C pool, the outstanding s.87 gains are calculated ignoring payments to non-resident or exempt beneficiaries in the tax year of the transfer of value (or subsequently) although payments to non-resident beneficiaries that took place prior to April 9, 2003 can reduce the s.87 stockpile.

(vi) The old s.87 stockpile in Trust A is reduced to nil. There is just one Sch.4C pool overhanging both trusts.

EXAMPLE 10.18

In 2003/04, Trust A borrows £2m and appoints the cash to Trust B in June 2003. There is a deemed disposal of all the assets in Trust A as at June 2003 (say shares in X Ltd worth £0.6 million with a base cost of £0.1 million) which disposal, therefore, realises a Sch.4B gain of £0.5 million (ignoring taper relief). The level of stockpiled s.87 gains in Trust A at the end of 2003/04 is £1m. The Sch.4C pool is therefore £1.5m and can be attributed to future capital payments made to beneficiaries out of either Trust.

Trust B then makes distributions of £1.5m to A and B, both not domiciled in the UK. and the following tax year Trust B distributes the balance of the fund, being £0.5m to C who is UK resident and domiciled. The distributions to A and B do not reduce the Sch.4C pool of gains (which remains at £1.5m) although A and B do not suffer a CGT charge. C pays tax on the entire £0.5m distributed to her. Similarly, if Trust A makes any distributions to A and B, such distributions will not reduce the Sch.4C pool and future capital payments to UK resident and domiciled beneficiaries such as C will be taxed.

(vii) Thus the risk of triggering a transfer of value is not only that one creates a deemed disposal of the remaining assets in the original settlement but also that one has also lost the opportunity to structure future capital payments tax efficiently—gains cannot be "washed out" by making distributions to non-chargeable beneficiaries.

(viii) The deemed disposal of the remaining assets in the original settlement means that those assets are rebased for all future purposes.

EXAMPLE 10.19

Facts as in *Example 10.18* except that Trust A actually sold the X Ltd shares 11 months later in May 2004 for £0.7m. The gain realised then would be £0.1m (which gain will not fall into the Sch.4C pool unless a further transfer of value is made). (The shares were rebased to £0.6 million as a result of the deemed disposal.)

(ix) In *Example 10.19* taper relief is available on the deemed disposal in June 2003 calculated on a period of ownership from the date of acquisition up to June 2003. However, no further taper relief is available on the actual disposal in May 2004 because the shares have not been held for 12 months. The actual gain of £0.1m realised on a later actual disposal of X Ltd shares is a s.87 gain which is not attributed to Trust B and can still be washed out on future payments by Trust A to non-resident or non-domiciled beneficiaries. It is only the Sch.4C gains that cannot be washed out.

(x) The interest charge can also apply to Sch.4C gains and to maximise the adverse effects, the legislation provides that Sch.4C gains of earlier years are attributed to beneficiaries before gains of later years.

(xi) When there are both s.87 and Sch.4C gains the earliest gains of either type are attributed to beneficiaries first. Where the s.87 and Sch.4C gains are of the same year, the Sch.4C gains are attributed first. This maximises the penalty charge.

(xii) There are wide anti-avoidance provisions catching further transfers to other trusts. Thus if in this example either Trust A, or B makes a further transfer of value creating a further Sch.4C pool then that pool can be visited on any of the beneficiaries who receive capital payments from Trusts A, B or C even if say, the beneficiaries are excluded from the Trust which made the further transfer of value.

EXAMPLE 10.20

The facts are as in the *Example 10.18* except that Trust B makes no distributions to A and B. Instead, Trust B transfers one-third of its fund to Trust C for the benefit of A and his issue and one-third to Trust D for the benefit of B and his issue and retains the remaining one-third for the benefit of C and her issue. A and B are excluded from Trust B; C and B are excluded from Trust C; and C and A are excluded from Trust D. Trust C realises further s.87 gains of say £1m in later tax years (which cannot at that point be attributed back to Trusts A, B or D) and in 2009/10 makes a further transfer of value linked to trustee borrowing. The Sch.4C pool that then arises is £1.2m. Since all the settlements remain relevant settlements for the purposes of Sch.4C as a result of the first transfer of value made in 2003/04, that £1.2m pool can now be attributed to any capital payments made to any of the beneficiaries of Trusts A to D. Each trust's original pool of Sch.4C gains has been retrospectively increased. In this case, the only person who would be concerned is C since the other beneficiaries are not UK domiciled, but she has no control over what Trust C does. There is also no obvious way in which she or indeed Trust B can require the trustees of Trust C to provide the necessary information to the trustees of Trust B regarding the calculation of the Sch.4C pool.

Thus once a transfer of value linked to trustee borrowing has been made, each transferor and transferee settlement will need to monitor any future transfers of value linked to trustee borrowing as well as the capital payments each trust makes and to whom, in order to establish whether the Sch.4C pool has been reduced. Trustees of transferee and transferor settlements should ensure that in these circumstances they make suitable provision in the documentation to require all trustees to provide the relevant information in the future.

Other matters[60]

10.44 FA 1994 widened the information provisions to catch all non-resident trusts, not just those in which a defined person retains an interest. Accordingly, they apply to additions to an existing trust; to the establishment by a UK resident and domiciled settlor of a foreign settlement and indeed to a foreign settlement created by a non-UK resident and domiciliary who subsequently becomes resident and domiciled and, finally, to the export of a UK trust. In all cases details of the date when the settlement was created; name and address of persons delivering the return and details of the trustees must be provided.[61]

10.45 For disposals of beneficial interests on offshore trusts, see chapter 8.

---

[60] TCGA 1992, s.98A, Sch.5A.
[61] The reporting duty is on the transferor or, on the export of a trust, the trustees.

CHAPTER 11

UK SETTLOR INTERESTED TRUSTS

- The importance of a trust being settlor-interested **(11.01)**
- What is a settlor-interested trust? **(11.03)**
- Definition of settlor **(11.10)**

This chapter discusses the capital gains tax position of UK resident trusts which are settlor-interested. The taxation of non-resident trusts which are settlor-interested is dealt with in Ch. 10.[1]

THE IMPORTANCE OF A TRUST BEING SETTLOR-INTERESTED

This is relevant for capital gains tax purposes for the following reasons: **11.01**

(i) For disposals from December 10, 2003 no hold-over relief is available on transfers into the settlement.[2]

(ii) Any gains arising within the trust will be treated as accruing to the settlor and be regarded as forming the highest part of the amount on which he is chargeable to capital gains tax and therefore taxed at his highest personal rate of tax. He has a right of reimbursement against the trustees.[3] The gains deemed to accrue to the settlor are reduced by allowable losses. Taper relief is then given in the normal way but the trust annual exemption is not available.[4]

(iii) Trusts which are settlor-interested are subject to a wider range of anti-avoidance legislation.[5]

---

[1] The definition of a settlor-interested UK resident trust is different from the definition of a settlor-interested non-UK resident trust. Compare 10.14 with 11.03.
[2] See Ch. 9.
[3] TCGA 1992, s.78: note the conditions that need to be satisfied to claim reimbursement. The capital gains tax must first be paid by the settlor who then receives a certificate from the Inspector before he can claim reimbursement.
[4] For computational aspects, see further 11.09 and 12.03.
[5] e.g. Sch.4A only applies to settlor-interested trusts or trusts which were settlor-interested in the last two years. Sch.4B applies to trusts within s.77.

(iv) Losses are relieved differently.[6]

It should be noted, however, that although trust gains are taxed on the settlor the trust is not fiscally transparent.[7] So, for example, disposals into the trust by the settlor and out of the trust back to the settlor will still be taxed as if they took place at market value. The death of a life tenant of a pre March 22, 2006 trust will result in a base cost uplift for capital gains tax purposes even if the settlor is not the life tenant[8]; and principal private residence relief can still be claimed even if the occupying beneficiary is not the settlor.

11.02 The definition of a settlor-interested trust differs for capital gains tax purposes according to whether the trust is UK resident or non-resident; a trust can be settlor-interested for capital gains tax purposes but not for income tax purposes[9]; a trust can be settlor-interested for capital gains tax purposes but there is no reservation of benefit for inheritance tax purposes.[10] Note also that a settlor who has any interest, however small in a settlement (even if he is excluded from some part of a designated fund), is at risk of being charged to tax in respect of capital gains accruing to the trustees *from the whole settlement* even from the disposal of assets in which he has no interest at all.[11]

EXAMPLE 11.1

In 1996 Henry sets up a trust in which he is the life tenant. In 2005 he decides to effect some inheritance tax planning and the trust is divided into two funds A and B. He retains an interest in possession in Fund A but Fund B is held on trust only for his grandchildren and he and all other defined persons are excluded from any possible benefit. Although for income tax purposes he will not be taxed on the income arising in Fund B nor for inheritance tax purposes treated as reserving a benefit in Fund B, for capital gains tax purposes he is taxed on gains realised within both Funds A and B.[12, 13]

---

[6] See Ch. 12.
[7] As might be the case on a US grantor trust. The idea of making a settlor-interested trust transparent for all tax purposes was discussed in the trusts modernisation consultation and might have been a significant move towards tax simplification and reduction in tax avoidance.
[8] Note the changes in FA 2006 in the IHT treatment of settlements. The uplift will generally only be available if the life interest is "qualifying": see 7.46.
[9] For example, the presence of minor living children as beneficiaries of a trust will not mean the income is taxed on the settlor unless paid out to the children while gains realised by such a trust will be taxed on the settlor.
[10] For example, a settlor might be excluded but his wife and children only can benefit. This would not involve a reservation of benefit for inheritance tax purposes. Similarly the trust could provide that the settlor could only benefit from capital in limited circumstances e.g. if all the earlier trusts failed. In these circumstances this would be a "carve out" for inheritance tax purposes (see Ch. 13) but generally such a trust would be settlor-interested for capital gains tax purposes.
[11] See *West v Trennery* [2005] S.T.C. 214 and comments of Lord Millett.
[12] Note the changes in FA 2006 in the IHT treatment of settlements, the uplift will generally only be available if the life interest is "qualifying": see 19.02.
[13] Consider whether a sub-fund election would be possible: see 7.72.

WHAT IS A SETTLOR-INTERESTED TRUST?

11.03 A settlor of a UK resident trust is treated as having an interest in the settlement in any tax year, if one of two conditions is met:

(i) Any property which may at any time be comprised in the settlement, or any derived property is, or will, or may become, payable to or applicable for the benefit of the settlor, his spouse, civil partner[14] or dependent children[15] in any circumstances whatsoever;[16] or

(ii) Any of the settlor, spouse, civil partner or dependent children enjoys a benefit deriving indirectly or directly from the property which is comprised in the settlement or from any derived property.

A dependent child is an unmarried child under the age of 18 years who does not have a civil partner. Child includes a stepchild.

Condition (i) above looks at the terms of the settlement and is focused on whether the trustees could benefit any of the above.

Condition (ii) focuses on actual rather than potential benefits received.

Exceptions

11.04 Even if condition (i) above is satisfied, the settlor is not treated as having an interest in the trust *if dependent living children are wholly excluded*, no actual benefit is enjoyed by any of him, or his spouse/civil partner or dependent child and either of the following conditions are met:

(a) None of the property or derived property can become payable or applicable for the benefit of settlor or spouse/civil partner except in the event of:

- the bankruptcy of an existing or future beneficiary;
- an assignment of or charge on the property being given by any beneficiary;
- in the case of a marriage settlement the death of both parties to, and of all the children of, the marriage; or
- the death of a child of the settlor who had become beneficially entitled to the property while aged not over 25;

or

(b) Some person is alive and under the age of 25 and during his life any property cannot become payable or applicable for the benefit of the

---

[14] With effect from December 5, 2005. Civil partners capable of receiving benefits or actually receiving benefits were brought into s.77 by the Civil Partnerships Regs 2005. The possibility of a future civil partner is ignored in determining whether UK resident settlements are settlor-interested. Future civil partners should be expressly excluded from non-UK resident settlements, since the possibility of future civil partners benefiting can mean that the trust is settlor-interested. HMRC have indicated in correspondence that they would not consider pre-December 2005 trusts to be settlor-interested merely because of the possibility that the settlor might contract a civil partnership if the general context showed no intention to benefit a civil partner.
[15] With effect from April 6, 2006: see s.77(2A).
[16] s.77(2)(A).

settlor or his spouse except in the event of that person becoming bankrupt or assigning or charging his interest in the property.

Note that the above let outs do not apply from April 6, 2006 if a dependent child can benefit.

EXAMPLE 11.2

(1) Peter settled assets into an interest in possession trust for his unmarried son aged eight in April 2000. He and his wife can only benefit if his child dies under 25 leaving no children. This has become a settlor-interested trust from April 6, 2006 because a dependent child can benefit.

(2) Facts as above except his son was 17 in April 2000. The trust is not settlor-interested from April 6, 2006 provided no other living dependent children of Peter can benefit from it. (This is because his son is no longer under 18 by April 2006).

Further conditions for the charge to arise

11.05 Even if the trust is settlor-interested within the above definition, gains are *not* treated as accruing to the settlor and the trust is *not* taxed as a settlor-interested trust if any of the following conditions exist:

(i) The only defined person who can benefit is his spouse/civil partner and the spouse/civil partner dies in the course of the tax year or the spouse/civil partner can only benefit after the death of the settlor.

(ii) In the course of the tax year, the only defined person who can benefit is his spouse or civil partner and the settlor and spouse/civil partner cease to be married/in a registered civil partnership or are separated during the course of the year (in circumstances where the separation is likely to be permanent).

(iii) The settlor dies during the tax year.

(iv) The settlor is not resident or ordinarily resident in the UK for a complete tax year. Note that the domicile of the settlor is irrelevant and that if the settlor is resident in the UK for any part of the tax year gains are taxed on him. Concession D2 does not apply.[17]

(v) The trustees are not resident or ordinarily resident in the UK during any part of the tax year[18] or,

(vi) The terms of the trust are such that although a spouse, civil partner or dependent child could benefit, the settlor is not married (or civil

---

[17] See Ch. 2.
[18] Generally then the trust would be taxed as a settlor-interested trust under s.86 if non-resident.

partnered) or does not have living dependent children. Hence no account is taken of future spouses, civil partners or dependent children.[19]

EXAMPLE 11.3

Harry set up a UK resident trust for his children, grandchildren and widow. All of his children are adult. The possibility of having children in the future is ignored until such time as he does have children. Similarly the fact that his wife can benefit after his death does not make the trust settlor-interested.

Contrast the following:

Harry set up a UK resident trust for his grandchildren. He can benefit from capital if all his grandchildren die before attaining 25 leaving no issue. The trust is settlor-interested for capital gains tax purposes since none of the above exceptions apply. (Harry would not be regarded as reserving a benefit for inheritance tax purposes given that his retained interest involves a carve out but he would be regarded as having an interest for pre-owned assets income tax purposes and indeed for income tax purposes generally.)[20]

If he was excluded from any further benefit in 2005/6 he would pay tax on trust gains realised in 2005/6 but not on gains realised in future tax years.

Derived property

The meaning of "derived property" (similar to that found in s.624 ITTOIA 2005 which refers to related property) was considered in *West v Trennery*[21] where the House of Lords held that property can be related or derived property even if it is no longer in the subject settlement.

11.06

Derived property was defined in s.77(8) as meaning:

> "income from that property or any other property directly or indirectly representing proceeds of, or of income from, that property or income therefrom."

Given the confusions this definition caused (discussed in *Trennery*) the definition was amended in FA 2006[22] and s.77(8) now reads:

> "derived property in relation to any property means—

---

[19] See s.77(5) and (3B) reversing the effect of *Unmarried Settlor v IRC* [2003] S.T.C. (SCD) 274.
[20] See Chs 4 and 13.
[21] [2005] S.T.C. 214.
[22] See Sch.12, para.13

(a) income from that property;
(b) property directly or indirectly representing
   (i) proceeds of that property; or
   (ii) proceeds of income from that property; or
(c) income from property which is derived property by virtue of paragraph (b) above."

The change is deemed always to have had effect. This amendment in FA 2006 was designed to put beyond doubt the definition of derived property, given that in *West v Trennery* the taxpayer had submitted that the definition meant only income from that property, or any other property.[23] Despite the fact that s.77(8) has been amended it is worth considering the facts of *West v Trennery* in some detail since the case raises other important issues. The taxpayer was successful at Special Commissioners,[24] lost in the High Court,[25] won at the Court of Appeal and lost in the House of Lords.

11.07 *West v Trennery* involved two UK resident trusts with almost identical terms. They were used to effect a flip-flop scheme[26] designed to reduce the rate of capital gains tax on a trustee disposal from 40 per cent to 25 per cent.[27] Each settlement created in April 1995, gave the settlor an initial interest in possession and so was settlor-interested. On April 4, 1995, the settlor transferred shares to Trust 1 and held-over the gain. On the same day those trustees borrowed 75 per cent of the value of the shares and transferred this sum to Trust 2. There was a mortgage over the shares. On April 5, 1995 the trustees of the first settlement excluded the settlor and all other defined persons as beneficiaries. The first trust remained interest in possession (with the intention that gains should only be taxed at 25 per cent not 40 per cent). In the following tax year the trustees of Trust 1 sold the shares and realised the gains. 75 per cent of the sale proceeds were used to repay the borrowings. The 25 per cent left over was used to pay the capital gains tax due. Nothing was left in Trust 1. All the value represented by the shares was in Trust 2.

Of course, if in fact the first trust was settlor-interested in the second tax year, gains would be taxable at 40 per cent on the settlor. HMRC therefore needed to show that in the tax year of sale (i.e. 1995/96), the settled property of Trust 1 or any derived property was payable or applicable for the benefit of the settlor in any circumstances whatsoever.

HMRC initially presented three arguments. Their first and primary argument was that the cash transferred to the second settlement remained derived property in relation to the first settlement and hence the first settlement remained settlor-interested. As a second argument they contended that the settlor retained a benefit because he had made the borrowing as one of the

---

[23] The Court of Appeal (see [2004] S.T.C. 170) had in any event rejected this interpretation.
[24] [2002] S.T.C. (S.C.D.) 370.
[25] [2003] EWHC 676 (Ch).
[26] Discussed in 7.62, 10.20 and 10.41.
[27] Given that all UK trusts now pay capital gains tax at 40 per cent the scheme ceased to have any relevance for UK trusts after April 5, 2004; i.e. from 2004/05 tax year. The anti-flip-flop legislation in FA 2000 (see Sch.4B, TCGA) could be repealed even if *West v Trennery* had been won by the taxpayer. In any event since *Trennery* was ultimately lost by the taxpayer it is hard to see any justification for Sch.4B applying to UK resident trusts which have never been non-resident or received property from a non-UK resident trust. Adverse inheritance tax consequences would also make this scheme a non-starter from March 22, 2006!

trustees; was personally liable for the borrowing and had a right of indemnity out of Trust 1. Their third argument was that on the construction of the documents the settlor had not been cut out of the first settlement because he could still benefit from Trust 1 through an advance to another settlement in which he was a potential beneficiary. The High Court decided in favour of HMRC on argument 1 but held that arguments 2 and 3 failed. Although the High Court decision in favour of HMRC on argument 1 was reversed by the Court of Appeal[28] the two secondary arguments decided in favour of the taxpayer in the High Court were not appealed by HMRC.

Peter Smith J. in the High Court held that the fact that as trustee the settlor had an implied right of indemnity did not mean he had a derived benefit. This was just

> "a normal right, which is an incident of trusteeship. The settlor has no personal benefit from that right of indemnity as it only vests in him in his capacity as trustee."[29]

He also held that the settlor does not have an interest in a settlement just because he could theoretically benefit if there was a transfer of the funds from Trust 1 to a transferee trust where he could be added as a beneficiary. He distinguished *IRC v Botnar*[30]: if the settlor could only benefit by the independent act of a third party, s.77 did not apply. His decision was presumably reached on the basis that the trustees and the settlor did not intend that the power to transfer funds to another settlement would be used to enable the money to be passed to the settlor. Ideally when excluding the settlor from the first trust the draftsman should have provided that the trustees could not exercise any of their dispositive powers (including any power to transfer to another settlement) in such a way as to benefit the settlor or his spouse. The decision is helpful in cases where this has not been done.

As already noted, the High Court decided that HMRC's first argument, namely that the property in Trust 2 was derived property from Trust 1, succeeded. Derived property included property outside the settlement and moneys raised by loan must be indirectly derived from the mortgage of the shares. However, the Court of Appeal held that property could only be derived property if it was settled property in the chargeable (first) settlement. If it had previously left the chargeable settlement it was not derived property. They rejected an argument that the benefits enjoyed by the settlor in Trust 2 were indirectly derived from Trust 1.

Like the Court of Appeal, the House of Lords rejected the taxpayer's first contention that s.77(8) applied only to income from the originally settled property and not capital.[31] However, they also rejected the taxpayer's other argument, that once the borrowed funds reached Trust 2 they were no longer derived property. They decided that the definition of derived property was not so limited. The mortgage of the shares meant that the money borrowed represented the proceeds of the shares. Section 77(8) referred to "the proceeds

---

[28] [2004] S.T.C. 170. The Court of Appeal decision was in turn reversed by the House of Lords.
[29] This may be relevant in the inheritance tax context, for example in the interpretation of s.103 FA 1986 where settlors may incur liabilities as trustees. See Ch. 23.
[30] [1999] S.T.C. 711.
[31] The amendment to s.77(8) in FA 2006 is designed to deal with this.

of the property" not the proceeds of sale of that property and therefore could include proceeds of a mortgage secured on the shares. Lord Millett attempted to put some limits on this and suggested that the cash appointed to the second trust ceased to be derived property once the first settlement sold the shares, for then the property which the borrowed money represented had gone. Lord Walker, however, did not impose any such limits and summarised the position as follows:

> "In my opinion the £770,000 started off as derived property (and was also, for a matter of hours or minutes, property comprised in the first settlement). It continued to be derived property after it was appointed out of the first settlement. The effect of the taxpayer's argument would be to cut off the operation of the derived property provision at the very moment when it started to have some work to do. The economic effect of the arrangements was to transfer about three quarters of the value of the shares to the second settlement, but without any disposal of the shares for CGT purposes . . . Section 77's requirement that the chargeable settlement should, in the year of assessment in question, contain some property to which the derived property can be linked provides some restriction on its scope but I would accept that it does not meet every possible hard case."

11.08 **Long term implications of the decision:**

(i) Great care is required if the intention is to ensure that a trust is no longer settlor-interested for capital gains tax purposes. If another trust has property derived from the first trust, that trust may well be settlor-interested.

(ii) Presumably the same wide reading of derived property applies for income tax purposes in relation to related property: see ss.625/626 of ITTOIA 2005.

(iii) It is not clear whether HMRC will attack flip-flop schemes carried out by offshore trusts on a similar basis. There is no definition of derived property in the offshore trust legislation but TCGA 1992, Sch.5 does refer to relevant property which can include property provided by the settlor "or property representing that property". The proceeds of a mortgage could still represent that property.[32]

Calculation of the tax charge

11.09 If a trust is settlor-interested the settlor is charged on trust gains after deduction of trust losses for that year and any trust losses brought forward. The settlor is prima facie charged on net trust gains after taper relief calculated in

---

[32] Offshore "flip-flops" are considered at 10.20.

accordance with the trustees' qualifying holding period. A settlor was initially prohibited from setting personal losses against trust gains but from 2003/04 this rule has been relaxed.[33]

The trustees should not include gains of a settlor-interested trust on their tax return because the gains are treated as accruing to the settlor. Since the gains are treated as forming the highest part of the amount on which the settlor is chargeable to tax, the annual exemption is not set first against trust gains although see Chapter 12 for the inter-relationship of the exemption and loss relief. HMRC gives the settlor a certificate stating the amount of gains on which the settlor has been charged and the tax he has paid and only then is he entitled to reimbursement from the trustees.

DEFINITION OF SETTLOR[34]

11.10 For the purposes of s.77 a person is a settlor if the settled property consists of or includes property originating from him.[35] Property is treated as originating from a person if he has provided it directly or indirectly or if another person has provided it pursuant to reciprocal arrangements.

However, as part of "trust modernisation" (!) TCGA 1992, s.68A now provides a definition of settlor which applies "for the purposes of this Act unless the context otherwise requires." Under this provision, "settlor" means a person who has made or entered into the settlement directly or indirectly or the settled property or derived property is or includes property of which he was competent to dispose immediately before his death and the settlement arose on his death. A person is treated as having made a settlement if he has provided or undertaken to provide property directly or indirectly for the purposes of the settlement or has entered into reciprocal arrangements. This seems a more long-winded definition of settlor than the one contained in s.79. It is not clear if it overrides or merely supplements s.79.

For s.77 purposes a person is only settlor in relation to that part of the trust property originating from him or property which represents such property, including accumulated income of the original property. If no such property is left in the settlement he ceases to be the settlor in relation to it.[36]

However, while a person is only taxed on gains in relation to that part of the trust property originating from him, if the trust becomes settlor-interested as to *any part of the property* comprised in a trust, a claw-back of any held-over gain can be triggered[37] even if the held-over gain relates to a disposal by a different settlor. The result is that additions by (say a) beneficiary can trigger a tax charge on the original settlor.[38] This may have been an accident of drafting (by a draftsperson drafting in "modern style" who did not understand trusts) but HMRC have been depressingly reluctant to agree that it is a mistake!

---

[33] See Ch. 12.
[34] See 5.16.
[35] s.79(1).
[36] See also TGCA 1992, s.68A(6).
[37] See 9.42 and 9.25.
[38] See s.169C(2).

Reform?

11.11 There is a good case for removing all the special rules that tax gains of settlor-interested trusts on the settlor unless such trusts are made entirely fiscally transparent. In 1988/89 fixed interest trust gains were taxed at 25 per cent and gains of individuals were taxed at 40 per cent. (Indeed in 1997/98 fixed interest trusts were taxed at 23 per cent). There was then a clear purpose to s.77. However, there is little point in s.77 now that trustees are taxed at 40 per cent anyway on all gains. Indeed there could be an advantage in engineering a settlor-interested trust where the settlor is taxed at a lower rate or has extensive personal losses!

Chapter 12

LOSS RELIEF

- Losses of settlor-interested trusts **(12.02)**
- Loss relief when beneficiary becomes absolutely entitled **(12.05)**
- Restriction on set-off of trust losses **(12.06)**
- Offshore trusts and losses **(12.08)**

Basic principles

Although capital losses are not themselves tapered, TCGA 1992, s.2A(1) states that losses must be deducted from gains before the application of taper relief. This is the case both for current year losses and for those brought forward from earlier years. **12.01**

A loss on a disposal to a connected person is deductible only from chargeable gains arising on other disposals to that same person while he is still connected.[1]

From 1991/92 onwards, trustees carrying on a trade are in certain circumstances entitled to set trading losses against capital gains. The applicable rules are the same as for individuals.[2] Losses realised on assets situated abroad by a foreign domiciliary are disallowed. See TCGA 1992, s.16(4) and chapter 2. Under self-assessment a loss is not allowable unless the taxpayer gives notice to HMRC in relation to the year of assessment in which the loss accrues.[3]

LOSSES OF SETTLOR-INTERESTED TRUSTS

The gains of settlor-interested trusts are attributed to settlors under TCGA 1992, ss.77 (if UK resident) and 86 (if non-UK resident).[4] The original rule was that, where there were attributed gains, taper relief would already have **12.02**

---

[1] See Ch. 6.
[2] FA 1991, s.72.
[3] TCGA 1992, s.16(2A).
[4] See Chs 10 and 11.

been taken into account in computing that gain; therefore, settlors could not deduct their personal (untapered) losses from the tapered trust gains attributed to them. Further trust losses were not attributed to settlors and so could not be deducted from personal gains.

An individual who had unrelieved personal capital losses and whose only chargeable assets were held in a settlor-interested trust could not, therefore, use those personal losses as and when his trust realised gains.

Fortunately this rather harsh position has been changed. FA 2002 provided that trust gains attributed to settlors for 2003/04 onwards (whether in respect of UK or non-UK settlor-interested settlements) will be the amount of the trust gains before the deduction of taper relief. If the settlor has personal capital losses, he must set them against his own chargeable gains first, but any surplus personal losses can then be deducted from the trust gains attributed to him under either TCGA 1992, s.77 or s.86. Taper relief by reference to the trustees' period of ownership is *then* applied. The settlor is assessed to tax on these tapered gains and is entitled to claim from the trustees of the settlement reimbursement of the tax paid.

There is no election procedure from 2003/04 and subsequent years. The relief is mandatory. The settlor cannot choose to set personal losses against attributed trust gains in priority to personal gains even if that gives a better taper relief position.

Although this regime did not come into force until April 6, 2003, a settlor could elect for these new arrangements to apply for the tax years 2000/01, 2001/02 and 2002/03. Elections could be made for one, two or all three of these years no later than January 31, 2005.[5]

It still remains the case that trust losses of settlor-interested trusts cannot be set against personal gains of the settlor.

12.03 Accordingly the tax position when trust gains are charged on the settlor is as follows:

(a) Calculate trust gains before taper relief but setting off trust losses against gains in the order specified by the taper relief rules so that the gains that would qualify for the highest percentage of taper relief are left in charge.

(b) Set off the settlor's personal losses against personal gains.

(c) Set off remaining personal losses against untapered trust gains in the order specified by the taper relief rules. Losses brought forward are only set off to the extent necessary to reduce the untapered gains to the level of the settlor's annual exemption.

(d) Reduce the remaining gains by the taper relief to which the trustees would have been entitled.

Note that if the settlor is chargeable on gains from more than one settlement the election for years 2000/01 to 2002/03 could be restricted to specified settlements.

The settlor's annual exemption is first set against settlor-interested trust gains and only the balance is set against personal net gains after taper relief.

---

[5] See s.2(5) of TCGA 1992, as amended by FA 2002, Sch.11; Sch.11 also added paras 6–8.

EXAMPLE 12.1

> The D settlement is a UK resident trust and realises trust gains after taper relief of £6,000 in 2003/04. These are charged on the settlor Richard. Richard also has personal gains of £11,000 before taper relief, personal losses in the year of £2,000 and personal losses brought forward of £14,000.
>
> The annual exemption of Richard for 2003/04 of £7,900 is first set against the trust gains of £6,000 leaving £1,900 exemption available.
>
> Richard's personal losses *of that year* of £2,000 are then set against personal gains of £11,000 leaving net personal gains of £9,000.
>
> Losses brought forward are then set against net gains of £9,000 to the extent needed to bring them down to the balance of the annual exemption. This requires the use of £7,100 of the losses (£9,000–1,900).
>
> The remaining losses brought forward (£14,000–£7,100 = £6,900) are available to carry forward.
>
> If in the above example the D settlement had realised £100,000 trust gains *before* taper relief and Richard had the same level of personal gains and personal losses, all the remaining brought forward losses of £6,900 would be set against the £100,000 trust gains. Richard would have then been taxed on the net trust gains of £93,100 but after deduction of taper relief. (Note that the personal losses brought forward and current year losses must first be deducted against the personal gains before being deducted against trust gains.)

Trust losses: trust losses cannot be set off against settlor gains.   **12.04**

EXAMPLE 12.2

> The D settlement (UK resident) has losses of £100,000 realised at a time when it was settlor-interested. Richard the settlor has personal gains of £50,000. He cannot set the trust losses against the personal gains. Fiscal transparency only works one way!

If a UK resident trust realises losses at a time when it is not settlor-interested and then realises gains during a period when it has become settlor-interested (e.g. because a dependent child is born who can now benefit) the losses realised in the earlier period cannot be set against the gains realised in the later period.[6]

---

[6] TCGA 1992, s.77 states that where *chargeable gains accrue to the trustees of a settlement* from the disposal of the settled property and after making any deduction provided for by s.2(2) of TCGA 1992, there remains an amount on which the trustees would be chargeable to tax, the trustees shall not be chargeable to tax in respect of those gains but chargeable gains "shall be treated as accruing to the settlor in that year." Section 2(2) provides that capital gains tax shall be charged on the "total amount of chargeable gains accruing to the person chargeable in the tax year after deducting losses accruing to that person in an earlier year." The difficulty is that the losses accrue to the trustees as the chargeable person when the trust is not settlor-interested while the gains are treated as accruing to the settlor. Hence the losses can only be set against gains realised when the trust ceases to be settlor-interested because it is only at that point

LOSS RELIEF WHEN A BENEFICIARY BECOMES ABSOLUTELY ENTITLED

12.05 When a beneficiary becomes absolutely entitled to the settled property, there is a deemed disposal of that property by the trustees at market value and the trustees are deemed immediately to reacquire it at the same value.[7] The deemed disposal ends the capital gains regime of the trust and even if the assets remain under the control of the trustees,[8] future gains or losses on that asset will be realised by the beneficiary. Any gains or losses arising on the deemed disposal are trust gains or losses whilst any subsequent gains or losses arising on the assets concerned will be those of the beneficiary. Where a person has become absolutely entitled to settled property as against the trustee, there is only a very restricted relief allowing trust losses *on the deemed disposal* to be set against future gains realised by the beneficiary. Any allowable loss which has accrued to the trustees in respect of the deemed disposal of the property to which the person has become entitled is transferred to the beneficiary in so far as it has not been used by the trustees against gains accruing to the trustees on that disposal or against earlier disposals in the same tax year.[9]

In summary, a trust loss will only be passed to the beneficiary when the following conditions are satisfied:

(i) the loss must accrue on the deemed disposal occasioned when the beneficiary became absolutely entitled;

(ii) the trustee must have no pre-entitlement gain against which to set the loss. A pre-entitlement gain is a gain realised on the deemed disposal or before the deemed disposal but in the same tax year. If there are such gains the trustee must set the deemed disposal loss against them before using any other trust losses (e.g. losses carried forward from earlier years);

(iii) the beneficiary must in the future realise a gain on the property which gave rise to the deemed disposal loss or, in the case of an estate or interest in land, on any derivative asset.

When all these conditions are met (!) the gain on the property sold by the beneficiary may be offset by the trustees' deemed disposal loss. The loss is deducted from the gain before any other loss relief that the beneficiary may have (which can then be carried forward).

EXAMPLE 12.3

In March 2004 Kate becomes absolutely entitled to one-half of the assets in her mother's trust. At that time the trustees have unused

---

the gains become chargeable on the trustees. From April 6, 2006 a trust becomes settlor-interested if a dependent child can benefit.

[7] TCGA 1992, s.71 and see 7.38.

[8] e.g. to satisfy liabilities or any other lien of the trustees. Subject to that the trustees hold the assets on a bare trust for the beneficiary.

[9] TCGA 1992, s.71(2), (2A).

brought forward capital losses of £50,000 and Asset A to which Kate becomes entitled is worth £40,000 less than when acquired by the trustees. She also receives Asset B which shows a loss of £20,000.

Note:

1. None of the realised losses of £50,000 will pass to Kate: they remain available for use by the trustees against future disposals of the remaining trust property.
2. The loss that occurs on the s.71 deemed disposal of the property to which she becomes entitled (£40,000 on asset A and £20,000 on B) passes to Kate but only to be set against future gains on a disposal of *that* property. If, however, the trustees could use all or part of the £60,000 losses either against gains realised earlier in the same tax year or against gains arising on the s.71 deemed disposal (e.g. if other assets showing a gain became vested in Kate) then to that extent the loss would not be passed to Kate.
3. Kate cannot set the loss on Asset A against a later gain on Asset B, only against a subsequent gain on Asset A, despite the fact that both assets were deemed to be disposed of on the same occasion.
4. The transfer of losses from the trustees to a beneficiary is mandatory if the trustees have no pre-entitlement gains. The trustees cannot set the losses off against their own gains realised in a later tax year.
5. Incidental costs incurred in making a deemed disposal may be allowable in calculating the deemed gain (loss) e.g. solicitors' and counsel's fees for advice.[10]

RESTRICTION ON SET-OFF OF TRUST LOSSES

12.06 Section 79A of TCGA 1992 was introduced by FA 2000 of s.93 and restricts loss relief for trustees. Prior to the change it had been possible for non beneficiaries to utilise unrelieved trust losses as illustrated in the following example.

EXAMPLE 12.4

The Jokey discretionary trust has unrelieved capital losses of £250,000. Sid adds assets to the settlement which have an unrealised gain of (say) £250,000. The trustees then appoint the property to beneficiary A

---

[10] See *IRC v Chubb's Trustee* (1971) 47 TC 353. Note that s.38(4) prevents *deemed* incidental costs from being deducted on a deemed disposal. In addition incidental expenses incurred in transferring the asset to the beneficiary are not allowed at that stage although can be deducted when the beneficiary subsequently disposes of the asset.

absolutely contingently on his being alive in seven days time. Sid purchases A's interest and therefore at the end of seven days becomes absolutely entitled to the trust property. The analysis was as follows—

(i) Sid would add the property but avoid any chargeable gain by making a hold over election[11];
(ii) On the deemed disposal under TCGA 1992, s.71(1), the gain realised by the trustees on Sid's added property would be wiped out by the carried forward trustee loss.

12.07 Section 79A prevents the trustees' losses from being set against the previously held-over gain. The basic requirements for the section to apply are that:

(i) Assets must be added to a settlement under a holdover relief election.

(ii) The transferor or a person connected with him must purchase an interest in the settlement. (Hence it appears not to catch additions by an existing beneficiary; although no hold-over relief would be available for such an addition,[12] the beneficiary could add assets that may appreciate in value later).

The aim of the legislation is to stop a trust with unused losses being exploited by someone holding assets outside the trust which are pregnant with gain but are passed into the trust at a low value using hold-over relief. With the restrictions on hold-over relief into settlor-interested trusts, it is thought that the scheme could not work now anyway and that s.79A is redundant.

This is a further addition to the armoury of anti-avoidance provisions on losses. The connected persons rule means that losses on disposals by the settlor to the trust can only be set against gains realised from disposals to the same trust. Section 71(2A) stops trust losses being passed out to beneficiaries except in very limited circumstances; s.79A prevents gains being brought in and used against trust losses.

OFFSHORE TRUSTS AND LOSSES

Section 87 gains and losses

12.08 The tax position in respect of trust gains attributed to UK resident and domiciled beneficiaries of offshore trusts following the receipt of a capital payment is completely different from UK trusts.[13] Personal losses of the beneficiary cannot be set against those stockpiled gains on which he is taxed under s.87, TCGA 1992. However, losses realised by the offshore trustees[14] can be deducted against future s.87 gains realised by them and thereby reduce the

---

[11] Note that this has not been effective since the introduction of the settlor-interested restriction on hold-over relief on December 5, 2003, given that Sid will acquire a beneficial interest.
[12] Since the trust is necessarily settlor-interested in relation to that beneficiary.
[13] See Ch. 10 for the capital gains tax treatment of offshore trusts.
[14] Assuming the trust is not within s.86 of TCGA 1992.

level of s.87 gains attributable to a beneficiary who receives a capital payment. This is the case even if the trust later becomes UK resident.

Example 12.5

> The Z Settlement is an offshore settlement primarily for the benefit of Angel and the settlor is dead. In 1998 it realises £100,000 gains. These are not taxed on the trustees or any beneficiary but go into the s.87 pool because no previous capital payments have been made.
>
> In 1999 the trust realises £40,000 losses.
>
> In 2000 the trust realises £30,000 gains. The 1999 losses are set against this gain thereby reducing it to zero. There are unrelieved losses of £10,000.
>
> In 2001 the trust makes a capital payment of £60,000 to Angel.
>
> The trust's s.87 pool at the end of 1999/2000 is £100,000 gains plus £10,000 losses brought forward which cannot be set against the £100,000 gains but can reduce future trust gains. The payment to Angel is treated as washing out £60,000 gains. (This is the case even if she is not UK domiciled or resident.) The trust pool of gains at the end of 2001/2 is therefore £40,000 gains (100–60) and the unrelieved losses of £10,000 can be used to reduce future gains.
>
> Gains attributed to a beneficiary under s.87 cannot be reduced by that beneficiary's personal losses. So even if Angel has £10,000 personal losses these cannot reduce the s.87 trust gains attributed to her.

Restrictions on s.87 losses

If losses have been realised in the trust prior to a period when it becomes a "qualifying" settlor-interested trust[15] and trust gains are realised after it became qualifying (e.g. in the case of a "pre-1991 trust"), the existing realised s.87 losses cannot be used to reduce future gains which are taxed on the settlor. Such gains may only be reduced by losses that are also realised during the period of the settlor charge. The existing losses from the period when the trust was non-qualifying may be used against future trust gains arising after the settlor charge has ceased to apply, e.g. when the settlor has died or the trust is imported and ceases to be settlor-interested. So in the above example, if the trust became settlor-interested in 2005[16] the trust losses of £10,000 could not be used to reduce any gains taxed on the settlor under s.86.

12.09

---

[15] i.e. the losses were realised at a time when s.87 rather than s.86 applied. The trust may later fall within s.86, e.g. if the settlor becomes domiciled here or as a result of the FA 1998 changes.
[16] e.g. the settlor was not dead but instead was non-resident until that tax year but then returned to the UK.

EXAMPLE 12.6

Chris (now dead) created a non-UK resident settlement in the mid-1980s. He was UK domiciled. Capital payments have not so far been made by the trustees and the gains (losses) of the settlement are as follows:

Tax year	Gain (loss)
1986/87	£2.5m
1987/88	(£1m)

Assume further that Chris' family now wish to import this trust and that there are some assets in the fund showing an unrealised gain and some showing an unrealised loss.

(1) The trust can be imported by the appointment of a majority of UK resident trustees.[17] Future gains will be taxed at 40 per cent with effect from the tax year of immigration. Note that the stockpiled gains realised in the past (£2.5m) will still remain on the clock until such time as capital payments are made to beneficiaries.
(2) The loss of £1m in 1987/88 may be offset against future trust gains including gains realised by UK resident trustees.
(3) If, however, the trust had become settlor-interested after 1991, e.g. Chris was alive and UK domiciled and resident and could benefit from the settlement, he would be subject to capital gains tax on trust gains under s.86 if the trust was non-UK resident or under s.77, TCGA 1992 if the trust was UK resident. Note that the loss realised in 1987/88 (which is a s.87 loss realised prior to when the trust become settlor-interested under s.86) cannot be used against gains realised by the trust when settlor-interested. The trustees would have to wait until the trust ceased to be settlor-interested before realising any gains to use up that loss.
(4) Note that if in the above examples Chris had not been domiciled here, all gains and losses of the settlement realised before March 17, 1998 would be ignored. If Chris was domiciled but not UK resident, trust gains and losses realised before April 6, 1981 are ignored.

Losses of offshore trusts within s.86

12.10 Losses which have arisen during a period of settlor charge under s.86 ("s.86 losses") cannot be used by the trustees against future gains that may otherwise be taxed under s.87 or against gains realised by the trust when it becomes UK resident, whether or not the trust remains settlor-interested.

---

[17] Or from April 6, 2007 by appointing just one UK resident trustee. Alternatively if the trust retains non-UK resident trustees it can still be imported for capital gains tax purposes *until April 6, 2007* merely by switching the general administration of the trust to the UK. After that date a UK resident trustee would need to be appointed. See 2.38.

EXAMPLE 12.7

> Charlotte is a UK domiciled and resident life tenant and settlor of a non-resident trust which realises losses of £100,000 in 2000. These are s.86 losses. The trust is then imported but otherwise the terms are not changed. The trust realises gains in 2003/4 of £50,000. The losses cannot be set against the gains even though the gains are realised by a settlor-interested trust within s.77. If the trust had remained non-resident or the trust had realised both losses and gains when UK resident the position would be different.[18] Hence there is a danger in importing a trust which has unused s.86 losses.

In the above example, if Charlotte died in 2003/4 the losses realised in 2000 will be unusable (wherever the trust is resident). Trust gains realised in the tax year of her death but before her death cannot be relieved against the s.86 losses because the trust is not in the s.86 regime in the tax year of her death. These gains would go into the s.87 trust pool but the losses are lost.

After Charlotte's death there will be no unrealised trust gains since her interest is a qualifying interest in possession for IHT purposes and hence there will be a base cost uplift to market value which would eradicate unrealised trust gains. Note though that unrealised gains within underlying companies and realised s.87 gains are not eradicated by Charlotte's death. So if the trust had realised s.87 gains of £10,000 in 1991 (before it became settlor-interested and which have not been distributed) and the trust ends on her death, UK resident and domiciled beneficiaries are treated as receiving capital payments and can be taxed on such s.87 gains. (This assumes that no capital payments have been made since 1991 and that the £10,000 gains are still in the s.87 pool).

Personal losses may be set off against gains of non-resident trusts attributed by virtue of s.10(A) to a settlor returning to the UK after a period of non-UK residence.[19]

Gains in an underlying offshore company

Under s.13, TCGA 1992, gains realised by a non-UK resident close company can be apportioned to UK participators. Losses resulting from a disposal by the company can be apportioned to the participators[20] but may not be set against the participator's general gains nor carried forward or back. Instead this s.13 loss may be set only against other gains apportioned to the participator under s.13 (whether in respect of that company or others) *in the same*

12.11

---

[18] s.86 and Sch.5 para.1(2) provide a specific mechanism for deducting losses against gains chargeable on the settlor under s.86 but this does not seem to carry over to allowing such losses to be deducted from gains realised by the trust when it becomes UK resident and the gains are chargeable on the settlor under s.77 TCGA 1992.
[19] However there is an exception where the amount to be attributed to the returning settlor in respect of the gains of a non-resident trust has been reduced because such gains have already been attributed to the beneficiaries of the trust under s.87: see Ch. 2.
[20] TCGA 1992, s.13(8).

tax year. The participator can set his personal losses against his s.13 gains insofar as the latter are not offset by s.13 losses.

If a UK resident trust owns an offshore investment company which realises gains on the disposal of its equities, such gains are attributed to and taxed on the UK resident trustees. If the trust is non-UK resident such gains are attributed to the trust and are included in the computation of s.87 gains or s.86 gains.

Section 13 gains cannot be set against any other losses realised by the trustees but only against losses realised by other s.13 companies owned by the trustees in the same tax year.

PART III: INHERITANCE TAX

The IHT treatment of settlements was radically altered by FA 2006. In this Part, Ch. 13 provides a general introduction to IHT, to the reservation of benefit rules and to pre-owned assets income tax whilst Ch. 14 gives an overview of the 2006 changes. The following chapters then consider the taxation of settlements in detail: Ch. 15 sets out the fundamental IHT definitions including the definition of an interest in possession. Chapter 16 deals with the IHT consequences of establishing a settlement and Ch. 17 with qualifying interest in possession trusts.

Prior to March 22, 2006 all interest in possession trusts set up by individuals were qualifying but from that date very few will qualify. The position of pre-March 22 interest in possession trusts and the transitional regime introduced by FA 2006 is considered in Ch. 18. Chapter 19 considers when qualifying interest in possession trusts can be created today. Chapter 20 deals with relevant property settlements: before the 2006 changes these comprised mainly discretionary trusts but the central object of the 2006 changes was to apply this tax treatment to all settlements with relatively few exceptions. Chapter 21 looks at the accumulation and maintenance trust primarily from the standpoint of what to do with existing trust given that new qualifying accumulation and maintenance trusts cannot be established. What this will mean in terms of making provision for minors and older children is considered in Ch. 25 which provides an in-depth treatment of bereaved minor and s.71D trusts. Chapter 22 considers the inheritance tax treatment of excluded property settlements and various IHT issues relevant to foreign domiciliaries. Chapter 23 discusses the deductibility of debts for IHT purposes. Chapter 24 looks at the reservation of benefit and POA rules in detail.

The special tax treatment of trusts for disabled beneficiaries is considered in Ch. 26. Chapter 27 deals with reverter to settler trusts and in particular considers the inheritance tax and pre-owned assets income tax position. Chapters 28 and Ch. 29 look at tax efficient will-drafting and post death variations, disclaimers and two year trusts.

CHAPTER 13

INHERITANCE TAX, RESERVATION OF BENEFIT AND PRE-OWNED ASSETS INCOME TAX—AN INTRODUCTION

- Potentially exempt transfers **(13.02)**
- The charge on death **(13.05)**
- Reservation of benefit **(13.07)**
- *Ingram* and *Eversden*—a summary **(13.14)**
- Avoiding the reservation of benefit rules **(13.27)**
- Impact of the pre-owned assets charge **(13.34)**

13.01 Inheritance tax can be charged on an individual who makes a transfer of value (typically a gift) during his lifetime and on his estate at death. Various exemptions and reliefs are available to prevent certain kinds of transactions from giving rise to a charge. For example, gifts between spouses are normally outside the scope of IHT,[1] as are certain family maintenance dispositions[2] and gifts of modest amounts.[3]

POTENTIALLY EXEMPT TRANSFERS ("PETS")

13.02 The majority of lifetime transfers became PETS in 1986. The name is something of a misnomer since such a transfer is treated as exempt *unless* the transferor dies within seven years of its making. Hence they might more properly have been called "potentially chargeable transfers". Initially the definition of a PET did not include transfers into an interest in possession trust nor the deemed transfer of value on the *inter vivos* termination of an interest in possession but that restriction was removed in 1987. From that date it was generally the case that all lifetime transfers of value were PETS with only limited exceptions, of which the most significant was for transfers into and out of discretionary trusts which remained immediately chargeable.

The changes in the IHT treatment of settlements have, however, had a significant impact on the PET definition. From March 22, 2006 whilst virtually

---

[1] IHTA 1984, s.18.
[2] IHTA 1984, s.11.
[3] IHTA 1984, s.19 (annual exemption); s.20 (small gifts) and s.21 (normal expenditure out of income). In the latter case the exemption can be used to make substantial IHT savings given that there is no prescribed ceiling on the payments: see *Bennett v IRC* [1995] S.T.C. 54.

all unsettled lifetime gifts remain PETS the majority of settled gifts will not qualify and instead will be immediately chargeable.

EXAMPLE 13.1

(1) S settles property on his son for life, remainder to the son's children. Prior to March 22, 2006 such a transfer would have been a PET by S. From that date, however, it is immediately chargeable.

(2) S settles property on trust for his minor grandchildren at 18. Prior to March 22, 2006 S would have made a PET (into an A+M trust). From that date, however, S's transfer is immediately chargeable.

(3) Under a settlement established in 2000 (i.e. a pre March 22, 2006 settlement) A is the current life tenant followed by a life interest for his eldest son. Prior to March 22, 2006 the termination of A's life interest during his lifetime (e.g. by a deed of surrender) would have been a PET with his son being treated as the owner of the settled property in accordance with the provisions of IHTA 1984, s.49(1). From that date, however, this result will only follow if the termination occurs during the transitional period (which runs until April 6, 2008). Thereafter any termination in favour of the son will result in A making an immediately chargeable transfer of value with the settled property falling into the relevant property charging regime.

(4) It was common for family settlements to provide for a life interest to (say) a child of the settlor with a successive life interest for that child's spouse. Often such trusts had started life as A+M settlements for the children of the settlor which had then been converted into interest in possession trusts for the children on or before they became 25.[4] Giving a successive life interest to the child's spouse was attractive for two reasons: *first* out of a wish to benefit the spouse but *second* because the transfer of value on the ending *of the son's* life interest would then be spouse exempt[5] but the spouse would not become absolutely entitled to the property.[6] The 2006 changes have restricted such planning in the future. It is still possible to provide for a surviving spouse through a trust set up in the Will of the deceased. However, for existing pre-Budget interest in possession trusts, future use of the spouse exemption will be restricted. Suppose that the son of the settlor had an interest in possession on March 22, 2006. Until April 6, 2008 spouse exemption is available if property passes on interest in possession trusts for the spouse of the son whether the son's interest ends *inter vivos* or on death.[7] After April 5, 2008 spouse exemption is only available on an inter vivos termination of the son's interest in possession if his spouse takes outright. However if the pre-Budget interest in possession ends on the son's

---

[4] The requirements for old style A+M trusts are considered in Ch. 21 including the requirement that income or capital must vest by age 25.
[5] Note that the spouse must be UK domiciled.
[6] Commonly the trustees would possess overriding powers to end the spouse's life interest which, if exercised, would result in that spouse making a PET.
[7] See 18.14.

death after April 5, 2008 and the spouse then takes on interest in possession trusts, spouse exemption is still available under the transitional rules.[8]

In addition, where the spouse has taken a transitional serial interest, the *inter vivos* termination of that spouse's life interest will now only be a PET if at the time when the interest ends the settlement also ceases. Hence property cannot be tied up in trust indefinitely without falling into the relevant property regime.

It will no longer be possible for a person to set up a new inter vivos settlement for the benefit of his spouse qualifying for the spouse exemption.[9]

13.03 These changes have resulted from amendments to the PET definition taking effect on March 22, 2006. From that day PETs are limited—

(i) To gifts to another individual[10];
(ii) To gifts into a disabled trust; or
(iii) To a gift into a bereaved minor's trust on the ending of an immediate post death interest (an "IPDI").[11]

Given the fact that no new qualifying *inter vivos* interest in possession settlement can be created from March 22, 2006 so that s.49(1) will not treat the trust fund as belonging to the interest in possession beneficiary, category (i) above has ceased to apply to gifts into an interest in possession trust and to the termination of an interest in possession in a new settlement (unless in the latter case the interest in possession is a qualifying interest in possession[12] and on *inter vivos* termination of such an interest in possession the settled property passes to an individual outright). Even in the context of existing settlements, new qualifying interests in possession can only arise under the transitional serial interest provisions.[13]

13.04 The disparity in the IHT treatment of settled and unsettled gifts is now striking and further restrictions on the scope of (or even the abolition of) PETS cannot be ruled out in the future.

THE CHARGE ON DEATH

13.05 IHT is chargeable on a person's death as if immediately before he died he made a transfer of value and the value transferred thereby was equal to the value of

---

[8] This assumes that the surviving spouse is UK domiciled or deemed domiciled: see s.18, IHTA 1984.
[9] See Ch. 14 and 18.14.
[10] In cases where an individual is entitled to a qualifying interest in possession, he is treated as entitled under IHTA 1984, s.49(1) to the property in the settlement. Accordingly the creation of such trusts fell within the PET definition being a gift to another individual.
[11] For IPDI's and bereaved minor trusts, see Ch. 19 and 25.
[12] e.g. an IPDI.
[13] See 18.14.

his estate at that time.[14] For this purpose a person's estate is the aggregate of all the property to which he is beneficially entitled, except that immediately before his death his estate does not include excluded property.[15] Since for IHT purposes a person entitled to a qualifying interest in possession in settled property is treated as beneficially entitled to the property in which his interest subsists, on the death of such a person the settled property will form part of his estate and be subject to IHT.[16]

Calculating the charge on death

13.06 This involves the following:

(i) Valuing all property in his estate immediately before his death (on the definition of "property" see IHTA 1984, s.272).

(ii) The estate may be swollen by trust property in which the deceased had enjoyed a qualifying interest in possession and by the value of property in which the deceased had reserved a benefit.

(iii) Excluded property is left out of account.[17]

(iv) The value of business and agricultural property may be reduced by either 100 per cent or 50 per cent: this is business property relief ("BPR") and agricultural property relief ("APR").

(v) Liabilities are deducted from the value of the property in the estate provided that such liabilities are incurred "for a consideration in money or money's worth" (IHTA 1984, s.5(5)).[18] IHT is calculated on the net value of the estate with the nil rate band applying up to £285,000[19] and thereafter tax being charged at a flat rate of 40 per cent.[20]

(vi) Property must be valued at "the price which the property might reasonably be expected to fetch if sold in the open market"[21] immediately before death. In this connection note the following:

---

[14] IHTA 1984, s.4(1). For an example of the valuation difficulties that can arise in valuing property *immediately before* death, see *Arkwright v IRC* [2004] S.T.C.(SCD) 392 (reversed [2004] S.T.C. 1323).

[15] IHTA 1984, s.5(1).

[16] IHTA 1984, s.49(1). Again this is subject to the excluded property rules. See Ch. 22. Primary responsibility for payment of the tax is on the trustees of the settlement. For the treatment of liabilities, see *St Barbe Green v IRC* [2005] S.T.C. 288 and Ch. 23. A major consequence of the 2006 legislation is to restrict severely the creation of new qualifying interest in possession trusts.

[17] IHTA 1984, s.5(1) and for the meaning of excluded property see *ibid* s.5 and s.48; Ch. 22.

[18] Note that special rules apply to artificial debts, see FA 1986, s.103. See Ch. 28. In general a liability secured on property will be deducted from the value of that property: see IHTA 1984, s.162(4) but for business property relief see *ibid* s.110.

[19] For 2006/07.

[20] If the deceased had made chargeable transfers or PETS within seven years of his death these may exhaust his IHT nil rate band since they are cumulated with his estate at death for the purpose of calculating the tax payable. In the event that tax is payable on lifetime transfers as a result of death within seven years primary responsibility for that tax rests with the donee: IHTA 1984, s.199(1)(b) and for the contingent liability of the deceased's personal representatives, see *ibid* s.199(2); 204(8) and for their right of recovery s.211(3).

[21] IHTA 1984, s.160.

(a) no discount is allowed for the fact that all the property is put onto the market at the same time;
(b) in certain cases a change in value of the assets resulting from the death may be taken into account (e.g. loss of goodwill in an owner-occupied business)[22];
(c) in general the IHT value will become the CGT acquisition cost of a legatee inheriting the assets of the deceased[23];
(d) it appears that if liabilities exceed the deceased's "free estate" they cannot be used to reduce the value of settled property in which he had an interest in possession.[24]

RESERVATION OF BENEFIT

Capital Transfer Tax had been a comprehensive cradle to grave tax whereby transfers both *inter vivos* and on death were taxable. With the introduction of the potentially exempt transfer in 1986, however, the majority of *inter vivos* transfers ceased to be immediately taxable and would escape tax altogether provided that the transferor survived the transfer by seven years. This raised the possibility of taxpayers giving away their assets and suffering no IHT charge on that gift but retaining the use of those assets until death. Such arrangements would have driven a coach and horses through the tax and it was to deal with them that the reservation of benefit rules were introduced in 1986.[25] In the event these rules proved inadequate to stop the avoidance of inheritance tax by "cake and eat it" arrangements and were bolstered by an income tax charge from April 6, 2005 (the pre-owned assets—or "POA"—charge).[26]

13.07

The fundamental provision in the reservation of benefit minicode which determines whether an individual has reserved a benefit is s.102(1) FA 1986, the essential part of which is as follows:

13.08

". . . this section applies where, on or after 18th March 1986, an individual disposes of any property by way of gift and either—

(a) possession and enjoyment of the property is not bona fide assumed by the donee at or before the beginning of the relevant period; or

---

[22] IHTA 1984, s.171.
[23] This will only be the case if the value has been "ascertained" for IHT purposes which will not be the case e.g. if the assets passed to the deceased spouse qualified for APR or BPR or if the deceased's estate fell within his IHT nil rate band: see TCGA 1992, s.274 and *Tax Bulletin* April 1995 p.209.
[24] This is the effect of *St Barbe Green v IRC* [2005] S.T.C. 288. Presumably liabilities on free estate will not be available to reduce the value of reservation of benefit property which is included in the free estate unless (possibly) the liability is charged on such reserved benefit property, see Ch. 23. It was accepted in this case that the value of trust property is the net value *after* deducting liabilities.
[25] It might be more accurate to say reintroduced since they had been in force at the time of estate duty and the 1986 legislation was very largely identical to its predecessor. See further Ch. 24.
[26] The change only applies if the arrangement is not caught by the reservation of benefit rules: see FA 2004, Sch.15 para.11(3)(5)(a) and generally the authors' "*Pre-Owned Assets and Tax Planning Strategies*" (2nd edn, 2005) and Ch. 24.

(b) at any time in the relevant period the property is not enjoyed to the entire exclusion, or virtually to the entire exclusion, of the donor and of any benefit to him by contract or otherwise;

and in this section 'the relevant period' means a period ending on the date of the donor's death and beginning seven years before that date, or, if it is later, on the date of the gift."

For this purpose, by FA 1986, Sch.20 para.6(1)(c), a benefit which a donor obtained by virtue of associated operations of which the disposal by way of gift is one, shall be treated as a benefit to him by contract or otherwise.

13.09 Notice two key points. First, that what activates the provisions is a *"gift"* made by an individual. There is no definition of gift which will presumably bear its normal meaning as a transfer of property with donative intent.[27] In any event, the use of "gift" as the triggering event distinguishes the reservation of benefit minicode from the rest of the IHT legislation where the key event is the making of a transfer of value. As a result, in certain circumstances there could be a transfer of value for IHT purposes which was not a gift and this dichotomy was exploited by taxpayers.[28]

Second, that what can trigger the rules once a gift has been made, is that the property is not enjoyed to the entire exclusion of the donor. This can mean de facto enjoyment. Notice that once a gift has been made it is never safe for the donor to enjoy benefits in the property (i.e. there is no seven-year period after which the slate is wiped clean).

Let-outs

13.10 The legislation provides that certain disposals by way of gift which would otherwise result in property being subject to the reservation of benefit provisions are taken outside the ambit of those provisions. For example, FA 1986, s.102(5) takes a disposal of property by way of gift which qualifies for the IHT spouse exemption outside the provisions.[29] Some of these let-outs are also effectively incorporated into the Pre-Owned Assets regime so that a transaction which qualifies for favoured treatment under the reservation of benefit provisions generally also does so for the purposes of the income tax charge.[30]

When the conditions in s.102(1) are satisfied, the property in question is prima facie "property subject to a reservation" and so caught by the reservation of benefit provisions. In certain cases, anti-avoidance legislation has the effect that property may be caught even though these requirements are

---

[27] See IHTM 14315.
[28] The main instance involved the termination of an interest in possession in circumstances where although the beneficiary made a transfer of value he did not make a gift so that if he continued to enjoy the use of the settled property the reservation of benefit rules were inapplicable. FA 2006 prevented this by extending the meaning of gift to cover the termination of a life interest: see FA 1986, s.102ZA inserted by FA 2006 and Ch. 24.
[29] It was this exemption which was exploited in the *Eversden* case: see 13.16. HMRC also take the view that there can be a gift without a transfer value, see IHTM 14315.
[30] A good example is "sharing arrangements" considered in detail at 31.57.

not satisfied. Conversely, there are various ameliorating provisions that mean that even if s.102(1) requirements are satisfied or the anti-avoidance provisions are prima facie infringed there is not necessarily a reservation of benefit problem.

Full consideration[31]

13.11 A key let-out is provided by FA 1986, Sch.20 para.6(1)(a) which provides that in the case of land and chattels the

> "retention or assumption by the donor of actual occupation of the land or actual enjoyment of an incorporeal right over the land or actual possession of the chattel shall be disregarded if it is for full consideration in money or money's worth".

EXAMPLE 13.2

(1) Jake gives his house "Marigold" to his daughter Sissie. He continues to occupy the property under an assured shorthold tenancy paying a full market rent. He is both outside the reservation of benefit provisions and not subject to the pre-owned asset charge.

(2) As in (1) above but Sissie and her family also occupy the property and Jake merely uses the converted loft space. If he now wishes to escape the reservation of benefit provisions by paying a full rent it is thought that this will be calculated by reference only to the loft space which he occupies (i.e. that he need not pay a rent for the whole property).

(3) Bill gave a 50 per cent share in his house to his brother Ben some years ago. Ben has now left and moved to Manila. Bill wishes to pay full consideration to avoid the reservation of benefit rules applying to the gifted half share but what is full consideration for the use of Ben's 50 per cent share in the property? No guidance is given in the legislation but to be "on the safe side" 50 per cent of a rent for the whole would undoubtedly suffice.

13.12 The following further points may be noted about the full consideration let-out:

(i) That the consideration must be full throughout the occupation of the property by the donor. If at any stage less than full consideration is paid, he will reserve a benefit. Hence normal commercial rent reviews should be incorporated into any tenancy agreement and should be observed!

---

[31] For the view of HMRC see IHTM 14341 where it is stated that "it is unlikely that any such arrangement could be overturned if that taxpayer can demonstrate that it resulted from a bargain negotiated at arm's length by parties who were independently advised and which followed the normal commercial criteria in force at the time it was negotiated". See also 31.101.

Ideally the parties should be able to show that the consideration has been negotiated between independent valuers.[32]

(ii) Whereas the pre-owned asset legislation sets out in some detail the terms of the lease on which the "rental value" of the property is arrived at,[33] FA 1986 gives no guidance on how "full consideration" is to be determined. It must, however, take into account all the terms of any letting so that if the donor takes over responsibility for repairing, insuring the property etc. this will reduce the amount to be paid in rent. This flexibility is not available under the POA legislation.

(iii) The full consideration let-out provides the basis for a widely used chattel scheme involving a gift and leaseback of the chattels. Its attraction is that the actual rent paid in such cases is relatively small.

(iv) Whilst full consideration will commonly involve the payment of rent the requirement may also be satisfied by the payment of a premium: for instance Jake in Example 13.2(1) does not want the uncertainties of a series of assured shorthold tenancies with the risk in the future of substantial rent increases which he might not be able to afford. Accordingly he negotiates a lease for his life with Sissie for which he pays a commercial premium.[34]

(v) The POA charge does not apply where this let-out applies to the GWR rules.[35] Note that if the donor ceases to pay full consideration but continues to use or enjoy the property he thereby falls within the GWR legislation *but remains outside the POA charge*.

The donor's spouse

13.13 One point should be noted in passing concerning the scope of the GWR provisions, namely that there is nothing in s.102(1) which makes property which the donor's spouse (but not the donor) is capable of enjoying or from which she benefits "property subject to a reservation" in relation to the donor.[36] On the contrary, the legislation confers favourable treatment on some gifts to spouses. This approach is also adopted (albeit with some significant differences) for the purposes of the POA charge.[37]

---

[32] Separate valuers negotiating on the rent that should be paid on a standard shorthold tenancy would be unusual but it is certainly advisable to have separate valuers acting for each party where full consideration arrangements relate to chattels or the arrangements over the land are unusual. E.g. a premium is payable on a lease for life. Any valuations should be in writing and retained by the taxpayer.
[33] Sch.15, paras 4, 5.
[34] For the taxation of rent and any premium paid on the grant of a lease, see ITTOIA 2005, Pt.3.
[35] Sch.15, para.11(3)(5(d).
[36] A benefit to the donor's spouse is, however, relevant under FA 1986, Sch.20, para.7. Also, the fact that the donor's spouse has a right may have adverse implications for the donor under FA 1986, s.102A.
[37] See FA 2004, Sch.15, para.10(1)(b)(c).

EXAMPLE 13.3

Silas establishes a discretionary trust of shares under which the beneficial class:

(i) includes Silas. He is therefore caught by the reservation of benefit rules.[38] If Silas is not a named beneficiary but the trustee has power to add any person (including Silas) as a beneficiary it is thought that the position is the same;

(ii) alternatively Silas is wholly excluded from benefit but his wife can benefit under the trust. Silas is not within the reservation of benefit rules nor does the POA charge apply since para.8 is only relevant if the settlor can benefit under the trust.

INGRAM AND EVERSDEN

Two IHT cases, *Ingram* and *Eversden*, are particularly important and will be reviewed briefly. **13.14**

The Ingram case[39]

Lady Ingram owned real property which she wished to give to her children and grandchildren subject to retaining the right to occupy the property during her life. To achieve this she transferred the property to her nominee. The next day, acting on her directions, he granted her a 20 year rent free lease and on the following day transferred the property, encumbered by the lease, to trustees who immediately executed declarations of trust whereby the property became held for the benefit of her children and grandchildren, to the exclusion of Lady Ingram. **13.15**

Following her death, HMRC issued a determination that, under the reservation of benefit rules, the property was deemed to be comprised in her estate immediately before she died. The House of Lords found unanimously for Lady Ingram's executors. The lease was valid, but even if it was not, the property given away was the encumbered reversion. Their Lordships stressed that it was important to identify precisely what property had been given away by the donor and what (if anything) he had retained. Continued enjoyment of the latter did not amount to a reservation in the former (arrangements of the type adopted in this case are known as "shearing" operations). Not long after the House of Lords' decision, anti-avoidance legislation, intended to nullify the

---

[38] See *IRC v Eversden* [2002] S.T.C. 1109 before Lightman J. where it was accepted by both parties that this was the case. The effect of settlor-interested trusts falling within the reservation of benefit rules is that the para.8 POA charge on settled intangible property will be inapplicable. Note that there is no reservation if (i) the settlor retains a life interest in his settlement or (ii) if he retains a remainder interest in circumstances where the "carve-out" principle applies.

[39] [1995] S.T.C. 564: on appeal [1997] 4 All E.R. 395, [1997] S.T.C. 1234, CA; reversed [1999] S.T.C. 37 (HL). For *Ingram* schemes see generally 31.34.

effect of the decision in relation to land, was introduced (now FA 1986, s.102A–C).[40]

The Eversden case[41]

13.16 In 1988 Mrs S settled the family home, which she then owned, upon trust to hold the same for herself as to 5 per cent absolutely and as to 95 per cent upon the trusts of a settlement under which her husband, Mr S, was the life tenant. After his death the trust fund was to be held upon discretionary trusts for a class of beneficiaries which included Mrs S.

During their joint lives Mr and Mrs S occupied the family home–Mr S under the terms of the settlement, and Mrs S by virtue of her retained interest as a tenant in common. After Mr S's death in 1992 Mrs S continued to occupy the family home. In 1993 the trustees sold the house and, out of the proceeds, including Mrs S's 5 per cent share, acquired a replacement property and an investment bond. Thereafter Mrs S had a 5 per cent interest in the replacement property and the bond. She died in 1998 having, in the interim, been in sole occupation of the replacement property, but having received no benefit from the bond.

HMRC argued that the entirety of the replacement property (and the bond) should, under the reservation of benefit provisions, be included in her estate immediately before she died by reason of her enjoyment of it.

The Court of Appeal unanimously rejected HMRC's appeal. The case was argued solely on the application of s.102(5) of the Finance Act 1986 which provided that a disposal of property which was a spouse exempt transfer was outside the scope of the reservation of benefit rules. HMRC sought to restrict the size of gift to which the spouse exemption applied by arguing there was a mismatch in the legislation between "gift" and "transfer of value". Although when Mrs S created the settlement she may have made a transfer of value to her husband of her 95 per cent interest, for the purpose of the reservation of benefit provisions she also made a series of gifts consisting of the equitable interests given to the various beneficiaries under the settlement and the exemption in s.102(5) was confined to the gift (of the life interest) which she made to her husband.

Carnwath L.J., with whom Brooke L.J. and Nelson J. agreed, rejected HMRC's argument. *Ingram* was concerned solely with the nature of the interest retained by the donor and was decided in a different context. The same applied to the *Perpetual Trustee*[42] case. Neither was concerned with and neither addressed the position of successive interests forming part of a gift

---

[40] Because this legislation was closely targeted to catch the *Ingram* scheme (a) it did not prevent similar arrangements involving chattels (although these are now caught by the POA legislation) and (b) it is not thought that it catches reversionary lease arrangements provided either that the donor had owned the property for at least seven years before entering into the scheme or had acquired it for full consideration. It appears from the POA guidance notes issued in May 2006 that HMRC do not agree this analysis and consider that such arrangements will since March 9, 1999 involve a reservation. See 31.52.

[41] *Essex (Executors) v IRC* [2002] S.T.C. (SCD) 30; affirmed *sub nom IRC v Eversden (Greenstock's Executors)* [2002] S.T.C. 1109 *affirmed* [2003] S.T.C. 822 (CA). See further 31.40.

[42] *Comr for Stamp Duties for New South Wales v Perpetual Trustee Co. Ltd* [1943] A.C. 425, PC.

into a settlement. Carnwath L.J. held that it was not possible to introduce conceptual subtleties into s.102(5) without distorting the language.

Given s.49(1),[43] Mrs S had clearly made a transfer of value of the whole of the settled property to her husband and to him alone. Section 102(5) applied to that transfer, and so Mrs S did not reserve a benefit. There was nothing in s.102 to modify the effect of s.49(1). If this caused problems then he concluded that they were for Parliament to correct.

Anti-Eversden legislation

HMRC heeded Carnwath L.J.'s comments and the FA 2003, s.185, duly introduced ss.102(5A)–(5C) into FA 1986 in order to reverse the Court of Appeal's decision. These provisions had effect in relation to disposals made on or after June 20, 2003. *Eversden* schemes set up before then were thus unaffected by the new provisions. **13.17**

Section 102(5A) provides that s.102(5)(a) (the spouse exemption) does not apply if or, as the case may be, to the extent that the four conditions are satisfied:

(1) the property becomes settled by virtue of the gift[44];
(2) by reason of the donor's spouse (who is referred to as "the relevant beneficiary") becoming beneficially entitled to an interest in possession in the settled property, the disposal is or, as the case may be, is to any extent within the spouse exemption because of s.49(1);
(3) sometime after the disposal during the donor's lifetime the relevant beneficiary's interest in possession comes to an end; and
(4) on the occasion when the interest in possession comes to an end, the relevant beneficiary does not become entitled to the settled property or to another interest in possession in the settled property.

For this purpose: (i) the disposal of an interest is treated as the termination of that interest; and (ii) references to any property or to an interest in any property include references to part of any property or interest.[45]

Section 102(5B) then provides that to the extent that s.102 applies by virtue of s.102(5A), s.102 has effect as if the disposal by way of gift had been made immediately after the relevant beneficiary's interest in possession came to an end. These anti-avoidance provisions were thus targeted directly at future *Eversden* schemes.

EXAMPLE 13.4

> H settles the house in which he lives on interest in possession trusts for his wife W in July 2003. The gift is spouse exempt. H does not reserve a benefit.

---

[43] To the effect that a qualifying interest in possession beneficiary is treated as beneficially entitled to the settled property: note that the scope of s.49(1) has now been severely limited by FA 2006. See 19.02.
[44] Note that if it already settled the anti-avoidance provision does not apply.
[45] FA 1986, s.102(5C).

In December 2003 the spousal interest is terminated by the trustees. He is still living in the house. H is then treated as reserving a benefit in the house. Note that if W's interest is terminated on or after March 22, 2006 (for example, in favour of the children) and both live in the house, both of them are treated as reserving a benefit in the house—H under s.102(5A) and W under s.102ZA! There is no POA charge in either case.

If, however, W's interest in possession had been terminated *before* June 20, 2003 so that H is *not* treated as reserving a benefit, he would then be subject to a POA charge unless on termination either H or W become absolutely entitled to the property.

Application of reservation of benefit provisions generally

13.18   When the GWR provisions apply, they have two consequences, namely a clawback on death under s.102(3) and a deemed PET under s.102(4).

Claw-back on death: s.102(3)

13.19   Section 102(3) provides that if, immediately before the death of the donor, there is any property which in relation to him is property subject to a reservation then, to the extent that the property would not otherwise form part of the donor's estate at that time, that property shall be treated as property to which he is beneficially entitled.[46] This is important in two ways.

Property comprised in the taxpayer's estate

13.20   That s.102(3) does not operate with respect to property which *already* forms part of the deceased's estate immediately before he dies is hardly surprising because the reservation of benefit provisions are designed to prevent individuals from enjoying property which has ceased to form part of their estate. If the property is still part of his estate, there is no reason to apply the reservation of benefit provisions to it. A benefit can be reserved in excluded property but because it is excluded it will not be taxed as part of the individual's estate on death.[47]

Excluded property

13.21   Section 102(3) is not itself a charging provision. It merely provides that the deceased was beneficially entitled to the property in question immediately

---

[46] It follows that property subject to a reservation in relation to an individual does not form part of his estate until immediately before his death (assuming that the reservation is then continuing). This view is not affected by s.102(4): see 13.24 below.

[47] Property will form part of the donor's estate if he owns it at the time of his death or then enjoys a qualifying interest in possession in it. See Ch. 22 for how the provisions operate in relation to excluded property.

before his death. The charge on death is then imposed on the property comprised in a person's estate, not on property to which he is beneficially entitled.[48] However, in many cases the point is not important, because the general rule is that a person's estate is the aggregate of all the property to which he is beneficially entitled.[49] That rule however, is subject to one important qualification, namely that, immediately before a person's death his estate does not include excluded property. So, where the property which is subject to a reservation is excluded property no charge will be imposed on a person's death in respect of it, notwithstanding that under s.102(3) he was treated as beneficially entitled to it immediately before he died.[50]

The position in respect of non-settled property is straightforward. Assume X, who is not domiciled in the UK for IHT purposes, dies having reserved a benefit in respect of a house in Florida. As non-UK situs property the house treated as owned by X, is excluded property and no problems arise. If on his death X had been domiciled or deemed domiciled in the United Kingdom when he died the property would not have been excluded property.

13.22 Change the facts and assume that the house was owned by a settlement which X had created when he was domiciled outside the UK. If he dies domiciled abroad the position will be exactly as it was in the first example. But what if X dies domiciled in the United Kingdom, e.g. under the IHT deemed domicile rules?[51] In that case the question which arises is which rules apply for determining whether or not the house is excluded property for the purposes of the reservation of benefit rules. If the fact that the house is settled property is ignored, the house will be prevented by X's domicile from being excluded property. If, on the other hand, account is taken of the fact that the house is settled property and the rules for determining whether or not settled property is excluded property are applied, the house will remain excluded property notwithstanding that X has become domiciled in the United Kingdom.[52]

Exemptions

13.23 The fact that s.102(3) operates to claw-back property into the deceased's estate does not necessarily mean that such property will be subject to IHT on the deceased's death.[53] Such a result will be avoided if the property qualifies for a relief such as business property relief.[54]

---

[48] IHTA 1984, s.4.
[49] IHTA 1984, s.5(1).
[50] Excluded property is defined in IHTA 1984, s.6 and, in the context of settlements and interests in settled property, see *ibid*. s.48.
[51] See IHTA 1984, s.267. For a consideration of the IHT domicile rules, see 22.02 *et seq*.
[52] IHTA 1984, s.48(3) provides that non-UK situs property comprised in a settlement is excluded property provided that the settlor was non-UK domiciled when he made the settlement. See Ch. 22 for further details. See *Private Client Business*, 2002, pp.3–4 "False Start in Change to Revenue IHT Excluded Property/Reservation of Benefit Practice" and 2003, pp.313–315 "Reservation of Benefit, *Eversden* Anti-avoidance, a Modest Proposal and a False Start". See also IHTM 14396 where the position seems thoroughly confused and commentary at 2.32.
[53] It may, for instance, fall within his IHT nil rate band.
[54] See Ch. 32.

Because property subject to a reservation is in the actual ownership of the donee it will not qualify for e.g. the spouse exemption on the donor's death because it will not then become comprised in that spouse's estate.[55]

Cessation of reservation: the deemed PET under s.102(4)

13.24 Section 102(4) provides that if, at any time before the end of the "relevant period"[56] any property ceases to be property subject to a reservation, the donor is treated as having at that time made a disposition of the property by a disposition which is a PET.[57]

Business relief and agricultural relief

13.25 In certain cases the rules governing the availability of business property relief and agricultural property relief are relaxed so that property which is subject to a reservation may qualify for relief on the basis that a notional transfer by the donee can include the donor's ownership and occupation periods in determining whether relief is due.[58]

A possible misunderstanding

13.26 The reservation of benefit rules sometimes give rise to a misunderstanding, the view being mistakenly taken that where an individual reserves a benefit he is (for IHT purposes) treated as though he had never given the property away. This is incorrect. The rules operate by clawing the property back into his estate immediately before he died, or by providing for a notional PET if he ceases to reserve a benefit but they do not operate by deeming the property never to have left his estate.

It accordingly follows that:

(i) As a matter of general law the property is comprised in the estate of the donee so that IHT will be payable on his death.

(ii) There is no CGT uplift on the death of the donor even though the reservation of benefit rules result in an IHT charge on the property.[59]

---

[55] For the spouse exemption, see IHTA 1984, s.18. For HMRC's views, see IHTM 14303: ". . . the GWR relief on fictitious treatments created only for the purposes of preventing IHT existence. They do not affect the actual devolution of the property in real life so the gifted property does not actually pass on death under the will or intestacy."

[56] The "relevant period" means a period ending on the date of the donor's death and beginning seven years before that date or, if it is later, on the date of the gift: FA 1986, s.102(1).

[57] Note that the property is not treated as forming part of the taxpayer's estate. HMRC accept that if the property becomes comprised in the donor's estate (for instance if the gift is unscrambled) this does not give rise to any charge on the deemed PET because there is no loss to the donor's estate.

[58] FA 1986, Sch.20 para.8. See Ch. 32.

[59] See Taxation of Chargeable Gains Act 1992, s.62 for the CGT rules on death.

(iii) It is the donee who is primarily liable to pay any IHT owing on the reservation property resulting from the death of the donor.[60]

(iv) The property is not treated as forming part of the donor's estate for IHT purposes while he is alive. This can sometimes be relevant for POA purposes, for example in relation to home loan schemes which are discussed below.

AVOIDING THE RESERVATION OF BENEFIT RULES

13.27 Inevitably taxpayers have sought to reduce their estates for IHT purposes by making PETs of property whilst at the same time wishing to retain benefits (e.g. use or income) from the property gifted. In some cases the taxpayer may be content simply to know that he will be able to obtain benefits from the gifted property if the need arises.

It is a testimony to the success of such arrangements that the Government felt it necessary to introduce the pre-owned assets charge. What therefore were the arrangements entered into by tax payers which have led to this new tax?

13.28 **The Home Loan (Double Trust) Scheme:** which was probably the single most important reason for the legislation.[61]

13.29 **The use of cash gifts:** an apparent weakness in the reservation of benefit legislation is that whilst there are tracing provisions which may apply if the original property given is switched into a new property, these rules do not appear to apply to an outright gift of cash. Hence if Albert were to give his son Sidney £400,000 which Sidney uses to purchase a house for occupation by Albert it is not considered that there is any reservation of benefit in the house. Not surprisingly, the POA regime therefore includes detailed provisions to catch cash contributions. They will still escape inheritance tax but instead suffer the POA charge if made after April 5, 1998 and the donor occupies the house or uses the chattel within seven years of the gift. (See Chapter 24 and 31.74.)

13.30 **Reversionary lease arrangements:** as noted above, it is widely thought that they were not caught by the anti-Ingram legislation provided that *either* the property had been owned more than seven years before the arrangement was entered into or that it had been purchased for full consideration at any time. Particularly difficult issues may arise in relation to self-assessment if the taxpayer is not certain whether he is within the POA Regime or not.[62]

---

[60] IHTA 1984, s.200(1)(c), 204(9), 211(3) and see Ch. 35.

[61] It is understood that HMRC will attack some of these arrangements on the basis that they fall within the reservation of benefit net because the debt is repayable on demand. This will not, however, prevent the POA charge from applying in respect of the property occupied because the property is still reduced by the excluded liability which is not treated as part of the donor's estate just because he has reserved a benefit in it: see HMRC guidance notes and 31.43 and 3.18 for details of home loan schemes.

[62] For example if he pays income tax now and then on his death it is found that there was a reservation of benefit so that he was never within the POA charge, does he get his income tax back? In fact the Guidance Notes are precise: pre-March 9, 1999 reversionary leases are not caught by the reservation of benefit rule and so are within the POA net whereas later schemes are within the reservation of benefit provisions as a result of the 1999 legislation so that no POA

13.31 **Chattel schemes:** these avoided the reservation rules either by a shearing arrangement or by satisfying the full consideration exemption. Whilst the former are within the POA charge, the latter—which rely on the full consideration let out[63]—are not.

13.32 **Ingram land schemes:** these have been caught by the reservation of benefit legislation since 1999 but pre-1999 arrangements are caught by the POA charge.

13.33 **Eversden schemes:** similar motivation. New schemes are within the 2003 legislation but "revenge" has been taken on past schemes via the POA charge.

IMPACT OF THE PRE-OWNED ASSETS CHARGE

13.34 The pre-owned assets charge is one of a number of measures designed to combat tax avoidance. Specifically it was announced that

> "action will be taken against avoidance of the Inheritance tax rules for gifts with reservation, where the former owner continues to enjoy the benefits of ownership of an asset".[64]

It was originally envisaged that the income tax charge would be freestanding and largely independent of the reservation of benefit provisions in FA 1986. Changes resulting from the consultation process, however, resulted in a close linkage of the charge with that legislation, for instance:

(a) the charge does not apply if the asset in question is caught by the reservation of benefit rules and so will form a part of the taxpayer's estate at death[65];

(b) the charge does not apply if the taxpayer "opts into" the reservation of benefit rules[66];

(c) a number of exemptions from the reservation of benefit legislation also apply to the income tax charge, e.g.:

- gifts to charities and political parties;
- gifts to housing associations and for national purposes;
- maintenance funds for historic buildings;
- employee trusts.[67]

income tax is payable. The taxpayer is entitled to self-assess differently if he considers that reservation of benefit does not apply. See further 31.52.

[63] See 31.99 for chattel arrangements.
[64] Pre-Budget Report 2003 "The strength to take the long-term decisions for Britain: Seizing the opportunities of the global recovery": December 10, 2003. A consultation paper was issued the following day.
[65] FA 2004, Sch.15 para.11(3), (5).
[66] FA 2004, Sch.15 paras 21–23. For instance a pre-1999 *Ingram* scheme did not fall within the reservation of benefit legislation but the taxpayer will be subject to the new income tax charge unless he makes this election or (more likely) ceases to occupy the property or pays a market rent. The election must be made on Form IHT 500 and in the case of "existing arrangements" caught by the charge on April 6, 2005, it must be made at the latest by January 31, 2007. See Ch. 24.
[67] FA 1986, s.102(5)(d)–(i) as amended by the FA 1989, s.171(5), (6).

(d) situations where the benefit is excluded from charge[68] (for example *de minimis* benefits; a benefit for which full consideration is provided and occupation of land by a donor at a time when he has become unable to maintain himself)[69];

(e) a transaction is excluded from the income tax charge if the property was transferred to the transferor's spouse or gifted into an interest in possession trust under which the spouse enjoyed an interest in possession.[70] This mirrors the spouse exemption in the inheritance tax legislation although note that for POA purposes (unlike inheritance tax) the spouse's domicile is irrelevant.[71] Even the qualification that the income tax rules may apply if the spouse's interest in possession ends otherwise than on death mirrors the qualification in the inheritance tax legislation which was introduced to reverse the *Eversden* decision.[72] Note, however, that if the spousal interest in possession ends on the *death* of the spouse reservation of benefit can still apply to the donor if the disposal into trust was made after June 19, 2003. POA would not apply.

(f) the charge does not apply if the disposal of property involved a redirection of a deceased's estate (for example by a deed of variation falling under the Inheritance Tax Act 1984, s.142)[73];

(g) the charge does not apply in cases where an interest in land is given away and both donor and donee occupy the property ("sharing arrangements").[74] Nor does it apply if the donor gives away cash and the donee uses that cash to buy a share in a new property with the donor;

(h) disposals of property before March 18, 1986 are ignored: this is in accordance with the reservation of benefit charge which was only introduced in respect of gifts made on or after that date.[75]

There are, however, significant differences. For example, there is no similar let out found in the POA legislation to that in s.102A where an *Ingram* scheme is carried out over seven years (i.e. at least seven years elapses between the creation of the lease and gift of the freehold). Most importantly POA can potentially apply to *any disposal* of land or chattels even if the disposal is a sale for full consideration i.e. even if there is no element of gift. Inheritance tax only applies where there is a transfer of value and the reservation of benefit rules depend on a gift. This can result in a POA charge where no inheritance tax saving was intended or indeed achieved at all. The obvious example is on a sale of part between connected parties.

---

[68] i.e. situations dealt with in FA 1986, Sch.20, para.6.
[69] FA 2004, Sch.15, para.11(5)(d).
[70] FA 2004, Sch.15, paras 10(1)(b)(c) and 10(2)(a)(b) but note that the income tax charge can apply if the spouse's interest in possession ends otherwise than on death.
[71] See FA 1986, s.102(5)(a) which incorporates the spouse exemption in IHTA 1984, s.18.
[72] See FA 1986, s.102(5A).
[73] FA 2004, Sch.15, para.16.
[74] FA 2004, Sch.15, para.11(5)(c) and see FA 1986, s.102B(4). See 31.57.
[75] FA 2004, Sch.15, paras 3(2)(a), 3(3), 6(2)(a), 6(3), and 8(2). Note that outright cash gifts made before April 6, 1998 are ignored in applying the contribution conditions: see para.10(2)(c). See 31.74.

The basics of the POA charge

13.35 The legislation provides separately for an income tax charge to apply to:

(a) land[76];

(b) chattels[77]; and

(c) intangible property comprised in a settlement in which the settlor retains an interest.[78]

13.36 As regards land the conditions for operation of the charge are as follows:

(a) an individual must occupy land (this is "the relevant land"); and

(b) either the "disposal condition" or the "contribution condition" is satisfied in respect of that land.

13.37 The "*disposal condition*" is that at any time after March 17, 1986 the individual owned an interest in the relevant land (or in other property which the relevant land replaced) and disposed of all or part of his interest. Certain disposals are ignored (they are "excluded transactions") namely Arm's length sales of whole or part of the interest in the land to an unconnected party or, if the sale is to a connected party, a sale of the whole interest in a "transaction such as might be expected to be made at arm's length between persons not connected with each other". Hence an arm's length sale to a relative is excluded[79] but note that the exclusion is not applicable to sales of part only of the property nor where the sale is at an undervalue.

13.38 The "*contribution condition*" is met where the individual directly or indirectly provides any of the consideration used to purchase an interest in the relevant land. In many ways this is the most significant condition, because the reservation of benefit rules rarely caught cash gifts. For instance, if G gives his daughter £100,000 in 1999 which she later uses to purchase a house which G occupies within seven years of the gift, the reservation of benefit rules are inapplicable but the income tax charge will apply to G in respect of his contribution.[80] The contribution condition not only catches only cash gifts but can apply where property is transferred and then later sold by the transferee and used to purchase a house or chattels which is then occupied or used by the original transferor.

13.39 The charge, in the case of land, is on the appropriate rental value for the land during the tax year. The tax charge suffered by G (on the benefit derived from his occupation) will be based on a market rent for the house. Accordingly, if the

---

[76] FA 2004, Sch.15, paras 3–5.
[77] FA 2004, Sch.15, paras 6, 7.
[78] FA 2004, Sch.15, paras 8, 9.
[79] FA 2004, Sch.15, para.10(1). Compare IHTA 1984, s.10 and note that an arm's length sale to a relative of the whole interest of the taxpayer in his main residence (other than any right expressly reserved by him) will lead to neither reservation of benefit nor income tax charges (some very limited forms of "equity release" within the family are hence permitted although sales of part at full value are not outside the POA charge post-March 8, 2005).
[80] The failure of the reservation of benefit rules to deal with this situation is because of the limited tracing rules in FA 1986, Sch.20.

house could be let for £2,000 per month the income tax charge on G for that year will be on a benefit of £24,000. (If G is a higher rate taxpayer he will therefore have to pay £9,600 in tax.[81]) There are two situations where part only of the full rent is taxed. First, if the taxpayer contributed part only of the purchase price and, second, if he disposed of part only of the interest in the relevant land.

13.40 The basic principles for *chattels* are the same: the key difference lies in valuing the benefit derived from the use of the chattels where it is to be calculated on the basis of the interest that would be payable at a prescribed rate (set at five per cent) on an amount equal to the value of the chattels. In practice the chattel charge catches *Ingram* chattel arrangements (where the taxpayer reserves a lien in the chattel and gives away the freehold interest). Given the exemptions set out in para.11(5)[82] it does not catch the more common arrangements in which the chattel is given away and then rented back for full consideration.

13.41 The third area of charge (*intangibles* held in a settlement) depends upon the settlor falling within ITTOIA 2005, s.624 in respect of income produced by the settlement: i.e. he has reserved an interest in the settlement (ignoring any interest reserved for his spouse). In such cases the charge is again calculated on the basis of an annual rate of interest (5 per cent) being applied to the property in the settled fund. The main settled property which may lead to the charge arising are stocks and shares and insurance policies: the charge will not apply to land or chattels held in a trust. Care will need to be taken in using "reverter to settlor" trusts.[83] This charge, catching capital assets that could be applied for the benefit of the settlor, is aimed at *Eversden* schemes under which intangible property, such as an insurance bond, was routed through the spouse (using the inheritance tax exemption) into a discretionary trust under which the settlor could benefit, but which was outside the reservation of benefit rules.[84]

An important limitation when the property is comprised in the taxpayer's estate

13.42 Assume that J continued to use property which had been settled under an *Eversden* arrangement[85] but which is then unscrambled so that the property is appointed back to J.

In such circumstances it is inappropriate for the income tax charge to apply on the basis of J's use or occupation of the property and it is accordingly excluded.[86] This exclusion from charge, along with that which applies when the arrangement is caught by the reservation of benefit rules, is crucial in limiting the width of the charging provisions. It ensures that the tax is closely focused

---

[81] The detailed provisions for calculating the chargeable amount are in FA 2004, Sch.15 paras 4, 5. See also the Charge to Income Tax by Reference to Enjoyment of Property Previously Owned Regulations 2005, SI 2005/724 fixing valuation dates.
[82] i.e. the exemptions in FA 2004, Sch.15 para.11(5)(d).
[83] For reverter to settlor trusts, see Ch. 27.
[84] See Ch. 24.
[85] As to *Eversden* arrangements see 13.16 and 31.40.
[86] FA 2004, Sch.15 para.11(1) but note that this exemption from charge is limited when the value of the person's estate is reduced by an excluded liability: see FA 2004, Sch.15 para.11(6)–(7). See also s.80, FA 2006 and Ch. 24.

and only operates in situations where the taxpayer has escaped from the inheritance tax net. It also means that innocent transactions will normally escape: for instance suppose to avoid the risk of future nursing home fees, M gifts her flat to her daughter.[87]

13.43 With the 2006 restrictions on creating qualifying interests in possession, the scope of this limitation has been limited. For instance, a further way of seeking to avoid the imposition of nursing home fees in the future has been for taxpayers to transfer property into a life interest trust for themselves. Before March 22, 2006 that would have been a nothing for IHT purposes (no reduction in the estate of the taxpayer) and for POA purposes, because the property was in the taxpayer's estate, the POA charge was inapplicable. From March 22, 2006, however, the trust created will be taxed as a relevant property settlement and the interest in possession as non-qualifying so that the property will not be treated as remaining comprised in the taxpayer's estate. The POA charge may still be avoided if the taxpayer has reserved a benefit in the settlement.[88]

---

[87] In this case the charge does not apply because M falls within the reservation of benefit rules. Note, however, that if M settled her flat on interest in possession trusts for herself and the flat was then sold and a new property purchased which M occupies, s.80 of FA 2006 would now impose a POA charge from December 5, 2005, although it is not thought that HMRC will take this point if M had an interest in possession throughout.

[88] On this question, see the *Eversden* case and 13.16 and 31.40 and Ch. 24 generally.

Chapter 14

THE NEW IHT RULES—AN OVERVIEW

- Historical background to the changes **(14.02)**
- The IHT treatment of settlements set up on and after March 22, 2006 **(14.08)**
- Exceptional cases: new settlements which are not taxed under the relevant property regime **(14.12)**
- Will drafting options **(14.19)**
- The position of existing settlements **(14.26)**
- Comments and conclusions **(14.32)**

The Budget on March 22, 2006 included proposals to "align the inheritance tax treatment for trusts".[1] These proposals, heavily amended in certain respects, were given statutory force by FA 2006, s.156 and Sch.20. The changes need to be taken into account by practitioners in drafting new trusts and will trusts and necessitate a review of existing settlements. This chapter provides an overview of what changed and the following chapters in this part will then consider the position in greater detail. **14.01**

BACKGROUND

The Capital Transfer Tax (and subsequently IHT) treatment of trusts was based upon a fundamental division into interest in possession trusts on the one hand and other settlements ("relevant property trusts") on the other. In the case of the former, the legislation provided for the interest in possession ("iip") beneficiary to be deemed to be the beneficial owner of the trust property.[2] Accordingly, on his death that property would be aggregated with his free estate and tax imposed on the total value.[3] This method of charging the iip beneficiary is of long standing dating back to the introduction of estate duty in 1894. It may be noted that its premise is fictional: in the real world the interest in possession beneficiary usually has no right to the **14.02**

---

[1] See Budget Note (BN) 25, reproduced in App. III at A3.01.
[2] IHTA 1984, s.49(1).
[3] Such aggregation could affect property values: for instance, if a taxpayer owned 25 per cent of the shares in X Ltd and a further 26 per cent were held in a trust in which he had an interest in possession the value of the combined shareholding would be arrived at on the basis of a controlling interest. It could also affect the availability of BPR: see IHTA 1984, s.105(1)(b) and Ch. 32.

capital of the settlement—the hallmark of his interest is a right to income (or to the use of trust property.[4])

14.03 Non-interest in possession trusts were subject to a wholly different regime. For convenience such trusts were commonly referred to as "discretionary trusts" but that oversimplifies the position since the taxing regime applied to *all* trusts *other than* qualifying iip settlements.[5] Especially in the light of the 2006 changes, it is important to use a different terminology to describe such trusts and in this book the term "relevant property settlement" is used.[6]

14.04 The taxation of such trusts has enjoyed a somewhat chequered history. In the days of estate duty, discretionary trusts were for many years untaxed (no property "passed" on the death of a beneficiary) and the belated attempt to impose a charge in 1969 (by attributing capital to beneficiaries who had received payments out of the trust) was a failure. A radical new system was therefore unveiled when Capital Transfer Tax was introduced in 1975 and which abandoned all attempts to attribute the trust property to a particular (or to a number of) beneficiaries. Instead, the trust itself was to be taxed as a separate entity. Initially the tax charge was penal (with a top rate of 75 per cent) and during a "transitional period" many discretionary trusts were converted into other—and more favourably taxed—types of settlement. In the main the favoured vehicle was the accumulation and maintenance trusts ("A+M Trust") which was a settlement without an interest in possession and which received privileged treatment.[7] Broadly speaking, provided that the relevant conditions were met the normal CTT/IHT charges were avoided so that the property could be held in such a trust and pass out of that trust without a charge arising. It is little wonder that such trusts became popular and, although intended to provide a vehicle to ensure that settled gifts to minor children would receive parity of treatment with gifts to adults, the generously drafted legislation meant that the privileged treatment could continue until a beneficiary attained 25 and because it was possible to pick and choose between beneficiaries, the trust could be drafted with a high degree of flexibility. Commonly, therefore the A+M Trust was used as *the* vehicle to hold the family wealth with the initial non-interest in possession trusts being replaced by iip trusts by the time the beneficiary became 25 and the trustees then being given wide overriding powers of appointment in favour of a wide class of beneficiaries.[8]

14.05 The 1975 treatment of relevant property settlements was overhauled in 1982 and the system then introduced continues in force. Such trusts are subject to charges every ten years (the "anniversary" charge) and, if property ceases to be held on such trusts, there is then an "exit" charge. In 1982 the top rate of charge was cut to 15 per cent; in 1984 that came down to 9 per cent and in 1986 to the present 6 per cent. Bearing in mind that the rate of charge on an iip trust is at a top rate of 40 per cent[9] this can hardly be described as penal.

---

[4] See for instance TLATA 1996, s.12.
[5] IHTA 1984, s.58(1) also provided that certain other settlements did not comprise relevant property. Qualifying iip is defined in *ibid* s.59. See 19.02.
[6] The charge under IHTA 1984, Ch. 3, Pt 3 is on settlements which contain "relevant property".
[7] IHTA 1984, s.71.
[8] The trust considered by the court in *Burrell v Burrell* [2005] S.T.C. 569 is typical of the highly flexible trusts that were employed.
[9] This will be the case if the iip beneficiary dies having used up his IHT nil rate sum. Of course, the 40 per cent rate was commonly avoided by ensuring that on the death of the iip beneficiary the trust fund was held for the benefit of his spouse (so that relief under IHTA 1984, s.18 was available if the

14.06 One other background point of great significance is that the lifetime establishment of iip and A+M trusts was generally a potentially exempt transfer (a PET) with the result that provided the settlor survived for seven years no tax was payable. By contrast the creation of a relevant property settlement was immediately chargeable.[10]

14.07 Diagrammatically the pre March 22, 2006 position can be represented as follows—

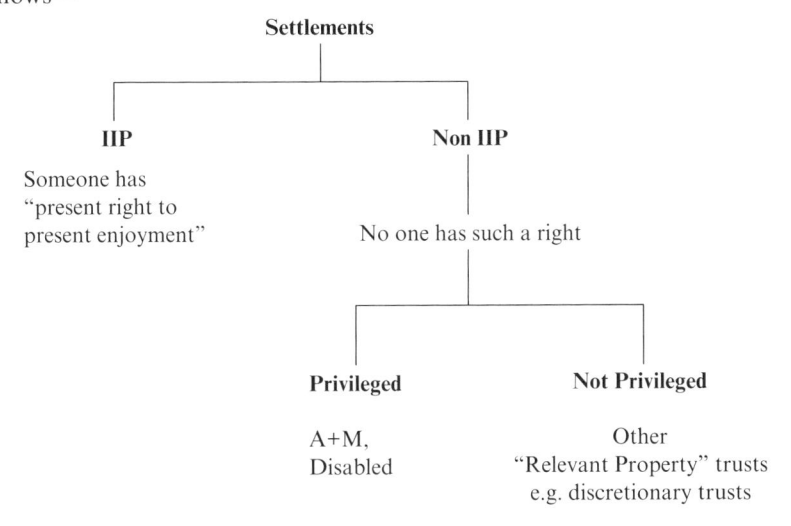

```
                        Settlements
                       /          \
                    IIP            Non IIP
            Someone has
            "present right to
            present enjoyment"    No one has such a right
                                   /              \
                              Privileged        Not Privileged
                              A+M,              Other
                              Disabled          "Relevant Property" trusts
                                                e.g. discretionary trusts
```

THE IHT TREATMENT OF SETTLEMENTS SET UP ON AND AFTER MARCH 22, 2006

14.08 With few exceptions,[11] "new" settlements are taxed as "relevant property" settlements under IHTA 1984, Pt III, Ch. III.[12] As a result:

(i) The lifetime creation of a settlement will generally be a chargeable transfer rather than—as had been the case—a PET;

---

recipient spouse was UK domiciled or neither spouse was UK domiciled) or by lifetime tax planning given that the inter vivos termination of the iip was commonly a potentially exempt transfer.

[10] PETs were introduced in 1986 but only in the following year were they extended to include the creation of an iip trust and the lifetime ending of an iip. The change was considered desirable to ensure a level playing field for settled and unsettled lifetime gifts. The justification for the separate treatment of discretionary trusts was that property was passing into a separate taxable structure: i.e. was ceasing to be comprised in the estate of any individual taxpayer. Further, the way in which the iip treatment worked meant that if A settled property on himself for life that was a "nothing" (since his estate was not reduced in value) whilst if on his death the settled property passed to his spouse for life that was a spouse exempt transfer. As limited compensation for the IHT charge on the creation of a relevant property settlement CGT hold-over relief was generally available under TCGA 1992, s.260 (although note the exclusion from December 10, 2003, of settlor-interested trusts from relief (and from s.165 relief) in order to stop "*Melville*" schemes). The definition of a settlor-interested trust for CGT purposes has been further widened from April 6, 2006. See Ch. 9 and 11.10.

[11] See 14.12 below.

[12] In the past it has been convenient to refer to these rules as taxing non-interest in possession (or discretionary) trusts. With the extension of the charge to include some settlements in which there is an interest in possession this practice has become misleading: better to say that the charge under these provisions is on "relevant property" as defined in IHTA 1984, s.58 (which has, of course, been amended).

(ii) The trust will be subject to IHT anniversary and exit charges.[13]

14.09 This major change in the IHT treatment of settlements is achieved by:

(i) the amendment of the definition of a qualifying interest in possession in IHTA 1984, s.59 (see new s.59(1)) and note that the Ch. III charge now applies to "certain settlements in which interests in possession ("iip") subsist";

(ii) the amendment of s.49(1) to exclude iips arising after March 21, 2006 with only three exceptions (this section provides for the iip beneficiary to be treated as beneficially entitled to the property in which the interest subsists);

(iii) the amendment of s.5 (definition of estate) to exclude the value of an interest in possession[14];

(iv) the amendment of the PET definition in s.3A: the old definition continues to apply to transfers of value made before March 22, 2006. The new definition—effective for transfers on and after that date—is in the new s.3A(1A). This preserves the status of the transfer which arises on the ending of an existing interest in possession *provided that* either the settlement then ends or the property becomes held on bereaved minor trusts which arise on the coming to an end of an immediate post death interest or the settled property is held on interest in possession trusts which qualify as transitional serial interests or a disabled person's trust.[15]

14.10 BN25 indicated that additions of property to an existing trust would be treated as a new settlement for these purposes but there is no specific provision to this effect in the Finance Act. Presumably therefore HMRC are relying on the wording of IHTA 1984, s.43(2)—the definition of "settlement"—to produce this result.[16]

Practical Advice

14.11 The main impact of the change is in the creation of settlements inter vivos since, unless the trust is one for a disabled person,[17] the settlor will make an immediately chargeable transfer for IHT purposes. The practical consequences of the changes are:

---

[13] BN 25 stated that the *inter vivos* creation of new trusts will automatically attract CGT hold-over relief given that it will involve a chargeable IHT transfer: this, however, is not the case since the exclusion of hold-over relief for disposals into a settlor-interested trust is to continue and, indeed, has been widened to include trusts under which a "dependent child" of the settlor can benefit (see the new TCGA 1992, s.169F (3A)). This is discussed further in Chs 6 and 9.
[14] The definition of a "reversionary interest" in IHTA 1984, s.47 has not been amended and hence does not include an interest in possession which is not therefore excluded property under IHTA 1984, s.48.
[15] See 18.14 for TSIs and Ch. 26 for disabled person's trusts.
[16] This issue is discussed further at 15.13 and in Ch. 22.
[17] See Ch. 26.

(i) that PETS are now generally limited to *outright gifts*. Settled gifts involve an immediately chargeable transfer[18];

(ii) lifetime trusts are likely in the future to be limited to:
- gifts up to the amount of the settlor's available IHT nil rate band (£285,000 for 2006–7). Bear in mind that both spouses (including civil partners) can establish nil rate band trusts and that gifts inter se (e.g. to enable both to set up such trusts) are spouse exempt[19];
- gifts into trust of property attracting 100 per cent relief so that no IHT is payable on the creation of the trust[20];
- a gift into a bare trust which will still take effect as a PET. (See Chapter 30.)

(iii) CGT problems remain—indeed have been exacerbated as a result of FA 2006. In general, the creation of a settlement will involve a disposal at market value for CGT purposes and hence a tax charge on the settlor if the asset transferred is chargeable and showing a gain. It might be thought that because lifetime settlements will now generally involve the making of a chargeable transfer for IHT purposes CGT hold-over relief will be available under TCGA 1992, s.260(2)(a). However, if the trust is settlor-interested, relief is denied and the scope of a settlor-interested trust has been extended from April 6, 2006 to include a settlement in which any property

"is or will or may become payable to or applicable for the benefit of a child of the (settlor) at a time when the child is a dependent child of his".

For these purposes a "dependent child" is a child of the settlor (including a stepchild) who is under the age of 18 and who is unmarried and does not have a civil partner.[21] This will not, of course, deny relief to grandchildren's settlements and does not apply if at the relevant time the settlor has no dependent children or dependent children are excluded while unmarried and under 18. So a settlement in favour of the children of the settlor at a time when he only has adult children will attract hold-over relief despite the fact that he might in the future have a further child. Note, however, the risk of a claw-back if a child is born in the period beginning with the making of the disposal and ending six years after the end of the year of assessment in which the disposal occurred and the child is not excluded while under 18.[22] To avoid this risk it may be desirable to limit the class of beneficiaries to the settlor's adult children or to provide that minor children can only benefit once the claw-back period has expired;

(iv) if a lifetime settlement is to be set up, the form of the settlement no longer affects its IHT treatment. Whether the trust gives someone an entitlement to income (which would be an interest in possession but not a qualifying interest in possession for inheritance tax purposes), is fully

---

[18] With the exception of a gift into a disabled persons trust. See Ch. 26.
[19] IHTA 1984, s.18.
[20] See IHTA 1984, Pt V, Chs I and II.
[21] TCGA 1992, s.169F (3A)(4A)(4B) inserted by FA 2006, Sch.12 para.4. See Ch. 11 on settlor-interested trusts and Ch. 9 on hold-over relief.
[22] TCGA 1992, s.169C and see 9.25 for further details of how the claw-back charge is calculated.

discretionary or gives trustees power to maintain and accumulate for infant beneficiaries it will be a relevant property settlement and hence subject to the usual anniversary and exit charges. In practice therefore the decision as to the form of the settlement may be—

(a) to select a discretionary trust for maximum flexibility; *or*
(b) to limit the beneficiaries e.g. to grandchildren with a view to the fund being used to pay school fees and to give the trustees powers to use the income and accumulate any surplus; *or*
(c) to provide a person with a right to income which may also be beneficial for income tax purposes.[23] There will, of course, be no CGT uplift on the death of that beneficiary (since he no longer has a qualifying interest in possession for IHT purposes) but nor will the assets of the trust be aggregated with his free estate on death unless the person with the right to income is the settlor and can also benefit from the capital.[24]

EXCEPTIONAL CASES: NEW SETTLEMENTS WHICH ARE NOT TAXED UNDER THE RELEVANT PROPERTY REGIME

14.12 The exceptional cases are—

- Disabled trusts[25]
- Bereaved minor trusts[26]
- Section 71D trusts[27]
- IPDI trusts[28]

14.13 *Disabled trusts* which fall under IHTA 1984, s.89 will have the same tax treatment as before the Budget (for instance, the *inter vivos* creation of the trust will be a PET). Further, the scope of a disabled beneficiary trust has been widened so that it includes:

(a) an old style IHTA 1984, s.89 trust;

(b) under new IHTA 1984, s.89A a self settlement made on or after March 22, 2006 by a person with a condition expected to lead to disability and which is taxed in the same way as s.89 trusts.[29]

---

[23] Notably in avoiding the charge under TA 1988, ss.686–7 and the penal levy on the distribution of dividend income: see 4.25.
[24] For the CGT rules on the death of a life tenant see 7.46. Whilst the uplift will continue to apply to interests in possession in existence on March 22, 2006 it will only apply to interests arising after that date in limited circumstances (i.e. to IPDI; TSI; bereaved minor interests and s.71D trusts if the beneficiary dies under 18 with an interest in possession and to a disabled person's interest trust under s.89B(1)(c) or (d)). See Ch. 24 and 16.02 for a consideration of the reservation of benefit position where the settlor is the life tenant of a trust made after March 21, 2006.
[25] Discussed further in Ch. 26.
[26] Discussed also in Ch. 25.
[27] Discussed also in Ch. 25.
[28] See Ch. 19.
[29] i.e. there is a deemed interest in possession so that the creation of the trust is a "nothing".

(c) In addition, s.89B defines a "disabled person's interest" widely so as to include an interest in possession trust for a disabled person set up after March 21, 2006 and an iip trust set up by a person whose condition makes it likely that he will become disabled (both involve *actual* rather than *deemed* iips). In all cases the disabled person is treated, under s.49(1), as the beneficial owner of the settled property and so the creation of such a settlement may be a PET.[30]

A trust for a "bereaved minor" ("BMT") is defined in new IHTA 1984, s.71A. **14.14** Such trusts can only be set up by will; must benefit a minor child of the testator and must provide for capital to vest at 18.[31] Statutory trusts for minors which arise on intestacy are also included. The tax treatment for these trusts is similar then to that which applied to accumulation and maintenance trusts: i.e. no anniversary or exit charges and nor is there a charge on the minor becoming absolutely entitled to the property nor when s.71A ceases to apply as a result of the death (under the age of 18) of the minor.[32] CGT hold-over relief is available on the ending of this trust.[33]

Section 71D Trusts

The Government responded to criticism that vesting capital at 18 was often **14.15** inappropriate by introducing, at Committee Stage, a new regime for age 18–25 trusts ("s.71D trusts").[34] Broadly speaking the same conditions have to be met as for BMT so that—

(a) the provisions only apply to trusts set up on the will of a deceased parent[35] (although note that existing A+M trusts can be converted before April 6, 2008 into s.71D trusts even if the trust was set up by someone other than the parent or the parent is still alive)[36];

(b) whereas BMT require absolute vesting at 18, s.71D trusts require capital and income to vest in the beneficiary (a bereaved child) not later than the attainment of age 25;

---

[30] IHTA s.49(1A)(b) and note that the CGT uplift is available on the death of the disabled person (which is not the case with s.89 and s.89A Trusts). See Ch. 26 for disabled trusts.
[31] It is tempting to see this as something akin to the accumulation and maintenance trust under IHTA 1984, s.71. However, the differences are striking: the new bereaved minor trust can only be set up by will; in favour of a minor child of the testator and must vest capital in him at 18. There is no flexibility to select amongst children. It does not matter that the minor has an interest in possession in the income before age 18.
[32] The existence of the s.32 power of advancement (including the usual widened power to allow 100 per cent of the presumptive share to be advanced and an equivalent express power) is specifically dealt with in s.71A(4) and s.71B(2)(c). Overriding powers of appointment will prevent the trust falling within s.71A.
[33] TCGA 1992, s.260(2)(da) and note that the death uplift is available on the death under 18 of the minor with an interest in possession (TCGA 1992, s.72(1A)).
[34] See IHTA 1984, s.71D–G.
[35] See Ch. 25.
[36] Or to trusts established under the Criminal Injuries Compensation Scheme or by virtue of a variation (under s.142(1)) of the will of the deceased parent dying after March 21, 2006. See also Ch. 21.

(c) as with BMT, the mere existence of the statutory power of advancement —even widened by the exclusion of the 50 per cent restriction in TA 1925, s.32(1)(a)—or of an express power "to the like effect" will not prevent the trust from satisfying the s.71D requirements.[37] Pending entitlement to capital the beneficiary must either be entitled to the income, or if it is accumulated, it must be accumulated for his benefit and there is no power to apply income for the benefit of any other person. The tax treatment of 71D trusts is as follows—

(A) while the beneficiary is under the age of 18, as for BMT (i.e. old style A+M treatment with no anniversary or exit charges);
(B) once the beneficiary attains 18 the special charging regime laid down in s.71F applies: in general up to age 18 there is no IHT charge but if the beneficiary dies after 18 but before 25 or the trust ends after the beneficiary reaches 18 or it becomes held on relevant property trusts there is a special exit charge. There are no ten year anniversary charges while the trust satisfies the conditions in s.71D.

For instance, if the parent died when his daughter A was aged six and under the terms of the will capital is to vest at 25, then a tax charge will arise calculated as follows:

(I) to age 18 no IHT;
(II) from 18–25 IHT is calculated in accordance with IHTA 1984, s.71F at a maximum rate of 4.2 per cent on the value of the property when the trusts cease to qualify as 18–25 trusts.[38] If A dies during this period there is an inheritance tax charge irrespective of whether the trust ends. There is no inheritance tax charge if a ten year anniversary arises during this period.[39]

IPDI trusts

14.16 An immediate post death interest in possession ("IPDI") trust will be taxed as an old style interest in possession: i.e. the property in the settlement will be treated as beneficially owned by the iip beneficiary.[40] An IPDI trust can only be established by a will[41] and the Finance (No. 2) Bill 2006 as originally published severely limited the scope for establishing such trusts. These restrictions were swept away as the result of a startling U turn performed by HM

---

[37] Overriding powers of appointment which might be exercised to divert the property away from the bereaved child mean that the trust will not fall within s.71D. For the certainty required by s.71A(3)(a) and s.71D(6)(a)—"will . . . become absolutely entitled"—compare s.71(1)(a) and see *Inglewood v IRC* [1981] S.T.C. 318 at 322. For the meaning of "powers to the like effect" see IHTA 1984, s.88, *Law Society Gazette*, March 3, 1976 and SPE7.

[38] s.71F(3) provides that the amount of tax shall be arrived at by multiplying the chargeable amount (the value of the property in the settlement to which the beneficiary becomes entitled: grossing up may apply if the entitlement is to part only of the fund) by the relevant fraction (30 per cent of the number of completed quarters (fortieths) from when the beneficiary became 18 to the vesting of the property) and multiplied by the settlement rate (a maximum of 20 per cent). Hold over relief under TCGA 1992, s.260 will be available on the ending of the s.71D trust.

[39] Contrast the position if the trust was a relevant property trust. If A died after 18 there would be no inheritance tax exit charge unless the trust ended but there could be a ten year anniversary charge.

[40] IHTA 1984, s.49(1A)(iii).

[41] Including a will varied by an instrument falling under IHTA 1984, s.142.

Paymaster General in Committee. Accordingly life interest trusts in a will (including, but not limited to, trusts of residue for a surviving spouse) will be IPDI's (provided that the beneficiary became entitled to the interest in possession on the death of the testator) irrespective of any overriding powers of appointment/ advancement vested in the trustees.[42]

14.17 Wills drafted to settle residue on trusts for the spouse for life will therefore not require amendment. However, care needs to be taken in administering such a trust since:

(a) any termination of the spouse's interest is—since March 22—treated as a gift by the spouse for the purposes of the reservation of benefit rules[43];

(b) in general the inter vivos termination of the interest will only be a PET if the settlement ends at that point (e.g. if the trusts are for A for life remainder to B absolutely and A's life interest is ended by an advancement to B. A is treated as making a PET). By contrast, if the settlement continues those continuing trusts will fall under the relevant property regime and so the spouse will be treated as making an immediately chargeable transfer. This would, for instance, be the case if after A's life interest the property was held on trust for her son for life. A surrender by A of her interest would therefore involve an immediately chargeable transfer (tax being charged at the lifetime rate of 0 per cent or 20 per cent with a supplemental charge if A were to die within seven years). The only exception (apart from the trust ending on termination of an IPDI) is if, on the termination of the life interest, the property is held on a bereaved minor's trust (in such a case A will make a PET).[44]

14.18 The new structure may be represented diagrammatically as follows:

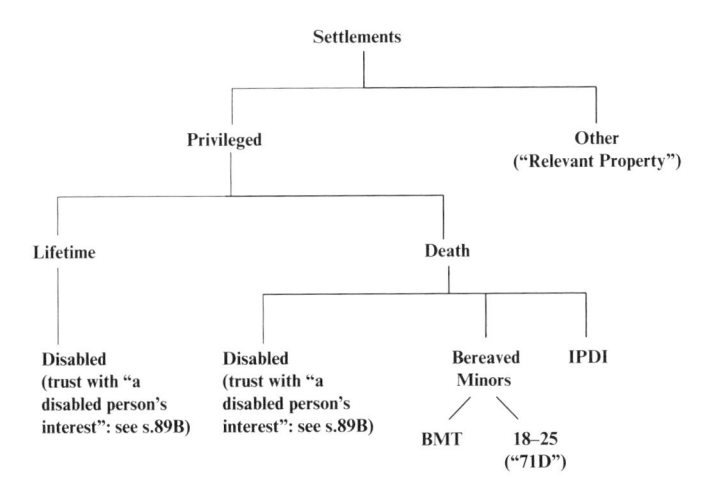

```
                        Settlements
                       /           \
                 Privileged         Other
                                ("Relevant Property")
              /          \
         Lifetime        Death
            |           /    |    \
        Disabled    Disabled  Bereaved  IPDI
     (trust with "a (trust with "a  Minors
     disabled person's disabled person's  /    \
     interest": see s.89B) interest": see s.89B) BMT  18–25
                                                ("71D")
```

---

[42] If the beneficiary is the testator's spouse the spouse exemption under IHTA 1984, s.18 will therefore be available if the spouse is UK domiciled see further Ch. 19.

[43] See FA 1986, s.102 ZA (inserted by FA 2006). As a result appointments revoking the interest in possession and establishing a nil rate band trust under which the spouse could benefit are now caught by the GWR legislation. Note, however, that the change was not retrospective so that terminations before March 22, 2006 are unaffected. See Ch. 24.

[44] IHTA 1984, s.3(1A)(c) (iii). For the question of whether an IPDI can be converted into a disabled person's trust, see Ch. 26.

WILL DRAFTING OPTIONS[45]

14.19 The exceptional cases are—with the exception of disabled trusts—concerned with will trusts. In IHT terms, the will draftsman has greater variety of trust at his disposal than the trust draftsman. The following matters are worthy of note—

14.20 It remains good IHT planning to make sure that the IHT nil rate band is used up on the death of the first spouse and a nil rate band discretionary trust remains the preferred vehicle. So far as residue is concerned this may be left to surviving spouse outright or on an IPDI trust: in both cases the spouse exemption will be available assuming the conditions in s.18 on domicile of the spouse are satisfied.

14.21 In terms of how to constitute the nil rate band discretionary trust it is likely that the debt/charge scheme will remain the preferred option. It does appear unlikely that in the future HMRC will be able to maintain that, for IHT purposes, the discretionary trust will be treated as an interest in possession trust for the surviving spouse (with a consequent tax charge on that spouse's death) given that it is not generally possible to create new interest in possession trusts after March 21, 2006. However, the position is not clear-cut given that an IPDI trust can arise within two years of death under IHTA 1984, s.144[46] so, conceivably, HMRC might argue that occupation during this period by the spouse has resulted in the creation of an IPDI. It is not thought that such arguments will necessarily succeed: indeed the trustees should take positive steps to ensure that no such interest has arisen.[47] However, even if the FA 2006 changes have improved the IHT position when the trust is set up with the share of the family home owned by the deceased, CGT uncertainties remain.[48] The risk of a ten year charge is also unwelcome. Practitioners are therefore likely to prefer to proceed by the debt/charge scheme, as before.[49]

14.22 So far as gifts of residue to the surviving spouse are concerned, an IPDI trust will be attractive:

(a) In cases where the testator wants to preserve the capital e.g. for children of an earlier marriage.

---

[45] See also Ch. 28.
[46] The section was amended by FA 2006 to enable IPDI; bereaved minor and s.71D trusts to be set up: see FA 2006, Sch.20 para.27. Note that for these purposes the *Frankland* trap (see Ch. 29) has been removed. It still remains, however, in the case of an outright appointment e.g. to a spouse or charity.
[47] This is discussed further in Ch. 28.
[48] Given that the death uplift will not be available—because the trust is discretionary—it will be important for the trustees to qualify for PPR relief under TCGA 1992, s.225 if the house is sold on the death of the surviving spouse at a gain. It is, however, uncertain whether that exemption applies when the trust is a sub trust owning an equitable interest in the property.
[49] Note also (i) that the SDLT considerations make it likely that the charge route will be the one adopted (ii) that the s.103 difficulty noted at Ch. 28 as arising if the house is sold and a further property is to be purchased by a loan from the trustees may now be solved by the trustees purchasing the property (or a share in it) and allowing the spouse to occupy. They could appoint an interest in possession to the spouse both to provide security and to assist in showing that CGT PPR relief is available on the share. Since March 21, 2006 it is no longer possible for them to create an IPDI once the two year period under s.144 has passed.

(b) In enabling the trustees to exercise overriding powers of appointment to cause PETS to be made by the spouse but note that from March 22, 2006 the spouse will only be treated as making a PET (rather than an immediately chargeable transfer) if the appointment is (1) to another beneficiary absolutely, (2) to a disabled person trust, or, (3) into a bereaved minor's trust.[50]

But the former advantage—that the spouse could continue to benefit from property that had been appointed away from her without falling into the IHT reservation of benefit rules or the pre-owed asset income tax charge—has been removed by FA 2006 in respect of appointments after March 21, 2006.[51] This reason for settling residue on flexible interest in possession trusts has therefore ceased to be valid.

In cases other than family wills for the first spouse to die (e.g. in the case of wills for the surviving spouse), if minor children of the testator are to benefit then the following trust options are now available— **14.23**

(1) a bereaved minor trust which has the attraction of A+M treatment once set up but which involves the vesting of capital at 18 with only limited flexibility permitted[52];

(2) a s.71D trust under which capital must vest no later than age 25. However, there may be an IHT charge after the child attains 18 if the trust has continued. Again there is only the same limited flexibility as with the bereaved minor trust,[53] but it would appear likely that testators will prefer to use the s.71D trust instead of the bereaved minor's trust. In will drafting it may be that the latter will therefore become something of a dead letter[54];

(3) set up an IPDI trust for the minor children. This will, for many testators, be the most attractive option since the interest in possession can be highly flexible: there can be overriding powers enabling the interest both to be enlarged and to be terminated. And, of course, it offers the prospect of the property remaining settled without IHT charges for longer periods than is permitted under either bereaved minor or s.71D trusts. Two other points to note—

---

[50] But not it appears into a s.71D trust (i.e. a trust for children of the deceased at an age no later than 25): see IHTA 1984, s.3A(1A)(c)(i)–(iii) inserted by FA 2006, Sch.20 para.9.
[51] See FA 1986, s.102 ZA and Sch.20 para.4A both inserted by FA 2006, Sch.20 para.33. See further Ch. 24.
[52] The flexibility comes in the form of a widened power of advancement which could be used—if the trustee considered such exercise to be for the "benefit" of the beneficiary—to make a settled advance and thereby postpone the vesting of capital beyond the age of 18: see IHTA 1984, s.71A(4); 71B(2)(c) both inserted by FA 2006, Sch.20 para.1. Once a settled advance has been made, the trusts that it creates will fall within the relevant property regime unless they provide for the vesting of capital at 25 and so come within s.71D.
[53] See fn. 44: a settled advance is possible to postpone vesting at 25. The resulting trust will be taxed according to the relevant property regime.
[54] Bear in mind that if a s.71D trust is ended by a transfer of assets to the beneficiary no later than the age of 18 there is no IHT liability. IHT will only arise if the trust continues beyond age 18. Hence in using a s.71D trust there is the ability to enjoy all the benefits of a bereaved minor trust if vesting capital at 18 becomes appropriate. However there is also the advantageous flexibility that the trust can be kept for a further seven years if this is desirable.

(a) TA 1925, s.31 must be excluded if the minor is to have the interest in possession which is necessary for an IPDI trust;[55]

(b) if the minor child were to die IHT would be payable on the termination of the IPDI;

(4) set up a relevant property trust for the minor: there is no attraction (unless the property falls within the testator's available IHT nil rate band or qualifies for 100 per cent relief) as compared to the options discussed above;

(5) leave the property to the minor on a bare trust. The property will form part of the minor's estate and he will be entitled to demand it from the trustees when he becomes 18.

14.24 So far as other beneficiaries are concerned (e.g. adult children/grandchildren) the option of using a bereaved minor or s.71D trust[56] is not available and so the options, if a trust is required, are narrowed to:

- an IPDI,
- a relevant property trust, or
- a bare trust.

14.25 Testators should remember that if an IPDI trust is set up for (say) a son that a subsequent interest in possession for the son's spouse will not qualify for the spouse exemption on the son's death. That successive life interest is not an IPDI: hence on the son's death the settled property does not become comprised in his spouse's estate and so the exemption under IHTA 1984, s.18 is not available.

---

[55] See Ch. 30 and App. III A3.137.
[56] This trust is, of course, available for a child of the testator who has not attained 25.

THE POSITION OF EXISTING SETTLEMENTS

General advice

As a rule of thumb it will be desirable to review all existing settlements given that the IHT treatment when set up will have changed. In some cases a review may need to be undertaken as a matter of urgency: e.g. in the case of an accumulation and maintenance trust in which a beneficiary is about to become entitled to an interest in possession. This section will consider the position of each of the main existing settlements likely to be encountered in practice. **14.26**

Discretionary Trusts

A trust which is discretionary in form on March 22, 2006 will be unaffected by the changes save that it will not be possible for an interest in possession falling within IHTA 1984, s.49 to arise in the future.[57] This means that— **14.27**

(i) the trustees of such trusts may consider appointing an interest in possession to a beneficiary so as to reduce the income tax charge on dividend income paid out to him;

(ii) such an appointment will not cause a new two year ownership period to arise in the cases of APR and BPR since the trustees are now treated as continuing to own the relevant business or agricultural property.[58]

A+M Trusts[59]

So far as existing A+M trusts are concerned, the current rules of s.71 will continue to apply until April 6, 2008 (in effect a two year transitional period) or until a beneficiary becomes entitled to income if earlier but will only apply thereafter if the terms of the trust provide for one or more beneficiaries to become entitled to the settled property (but not just an interest in possession) at 18. In the event that the terms of the trust do not so provide on or before April 6, 2008 the trust will then fall within the "relevant property" charging regime or, if capital will vest at 25 and the other conditions are met, within the **14.28**

---

[57] Consider what effect this will have on existing will trusts which were discretionary in form and own a share in the house occupied by the surviving spouse. Note, however, that appointments under discretionary will trusts falling within s.144 (as amended) will be read back into the will and may create an IPDI.

[58] See *Burrell v IRC* [2005] S.T.C. 569 where business property relief was not available because an accumulation and maintenance trust had ended with the beneficiary becoming entitled to an interest in possession and that beneficiary had not enjoyed the interest for the requisite two years when it was terminated by an appointment of the property onto discretionary trusts. See 32.24.

[59] See also Ch. 21.

s.71D trust regime. There is no IHT exit charge when the trust ceases to satisfy the amended s.71 requirements.[60]

Practical Advice for A+M trusts

There is no right or wrong answer to the question of how should an existing A+M trust be modified (if at all) to cope with the changed IHT treatment assuming, indeed, that suitable powers exist to enable the terms of the trust to be changed.[61] The following general matters should be borne in mind—

14.29 (i) first, make sure that the trust is still in A+M form: i.e. that the conditions of s.71 are met and that no beneficiary is entitled to an interest in possession in any part of the trust fund.[62] Ensure that the date when a beneficiary takes entitlement to income is diarised because after this date it will not be possible to convert the trust into a s.71D trust;

(ii) second, bear in mind that when a trust ceases to qualify as a s.71 A+M trust there is no exit charge and this includes ceasing to qualify as a result of the changes that come into force on April 6, 2008;

(iii) if the trust ceases to qualify for continued A+M treatment in 2008 and does not meet the conditions to be a s.71D trust by then, although it falls within the relevant property regime from that date, there is no immediate IHT charge and future charges will only accrue from the time when it becomes a relevant property trust (i.e. from April 6, 2008). For many this will represent a price worth paying to keep the property in a highly flexible settlement where the property does not become comprised in any beneficiary's estate for inheritance tax purposes;

(iv) converting the trust so that it falls within s.71D will mean that there can be no flexibility retained in respect of the shares to be taken by the beneficiaries. Instead each beneficiary must take an equal share. (Of course it may be possible to exclude beneficiaries who it is not intended to benefit before April 6, 2008)[63];

(v) the trust will benefit from CGT hold-over relief in all cases: viz if it remains a s.71 trust; if it satisfies the s.71D conditions (provided no distribution is made within three months of the beneficiary becoming 18) or it becomes a relevant property trust;

---

[60] FA 2006, Sch.20, para.3 and for the application of the s.71D regime, see IHTA 1984, s.71D(3)–(4). See also Ch. 21. Note that if during the transitional period a beneficiary becomes entitled to an interest in possession in the property then whilst there will be no IHT exit charge on the ending of the A+M trust the iip trust will then fall within the relevant property charging regime unless the conditions of a s.71D Trust are met *at the time when the beneficiary takes an interest in possession.*
[61] Otherwise an application to court will be necessary.
[62] If (say) beneficiary A is entitled to an interest in possession in 25 per cent of the trust then the A+M rules may apply to the remaining 75 per cent.
[63] Curiously if the trust is amended so that it continues to fall within s.71(viz capital is to vest at 18) the general flexibility in s.71(1)(a) ("one or more persons . . .") is preserved!

(vi) the change in the rules may result in unequal treatment of beneficiaries: for instance, if beneficiary A obtained an interest in possession in (say) one-quarter of the fund in 2005 there is no way that the other beneficiaries can be given an interest in possession after March 21, 2006 which will receive the same IHT treatment (unless they are disabled: see Ch. 31).

Interest in possession trusts

Finally, so far as an interest in possession trust is concerned the old tax treatment will continue (viz the settlement will not be relevant property) but on the ending of that interest the tax position will depend on whether or not the settlement then ends. If it does then the usual tax treatment applies: i.e. the interest is comprised in the beneficiary's estate and so he may, for instance, make a PET[64]; a spouse exempt transfer or a chargeable transfer. By contrast, if the trust does not end then the general principle is that he will make a transfer into a relevant property settlement.[65] This is, however, subject to an exception for "transitional serial interests" (TSI) which arise before April 6, 2008 and, as a result of Report Stage amendments, to a special rule for spouses when the iip ends on death.[66]

14.30

Under s.49C an interest in possession in existence at March 22, 2006 can be replaced—during the two year window—by one or more new iips which are then treated as falling within s.49. Assume, therefore, that under the terms of a settlement set up before March 22, 2006 A enjoys an iip and that thereafter his son will take an iip. If A were to surrender his interest during the transitional period thereby accelerating the interest of his son, then he will make a PET and his son will be treated as having an iip falling within s.49(1). By contrast, if nothing is done until 2009 when A surrenders his interest an IHT charge will arise since the continuing trust will fall within the relevant property regime.

The rules are modified in the case of spouses: the normal TSI window applies until 2008 so that if during this period a husband's iip is replaced by that of his spouse, the IHT spouse exemption will apply. After that date the spouse exemption will only be given if the husband's iip which arose pre-March 22, 2006 ends with his death.[67] The wife's interest is then a transitional serial interest falling within s.49(1).

Practical Advice for IIPs

1. Existing life interest trusts should be reviewed before the end of the transitional period (sooner rather than later!).

14.31

---

[64] See IHTA 1984(1A) read with s.3A(2).
[65] This is because no new iip can arise after March 21, 2006 within s.49 (except for IPDI, disabled trusts, and subject to the transitional relief for a "TSI").
[66] These are provided for in the (new) IHTA 1984, s.49 B–D. See 18.14.
[67] IHTA 1984, s.49D.

2. Until April 6, 2008 there is the opportunity to replace the current interest in possession by one or more replacement interests in possession. Note however that if A's interest is replaced by a similar interest for B and if B's interest were in turn to be replaced before 2008 by a similar interest for C then C's interest would not be a transitional serial interest (consequently on the termination of B's interest the trust would become subject to the relevant property regime and B would make a chargeable transfer of value). Contrast the position if A's existing interest in possession is ended before April 2008 and replaced by interests in possession for B and C both in half the trust fund. B and C both have transitional serial interests.[68]

3. Assume A is the life tenant and it is envisaged that his spouse will thereafter benefit from the property. The IHT spouse exemption will be available if—

   (i) on the ending of A's interest the trust ends with the property passing to Mrs A absolutely;
   (ii) A dies or surrenders his interest before April 6, 2008 (Mrs A takes an interest in possession in the trust fund: she has a transitional serial interest). (Note that if A surrendered his interest and the property passed back on interest in possession trusts to him on the death of Mrs A will not be a qualifying interest in possession and no spouse exemption is available on Mrs A's death);
   (iii) A dies on or after April 6, 2008 and Mrs A becomes entitled to an interest in possession in the trust fund.

   Relief is not therefore available if on or after April 6, 2008 A surrenders his interest and Mrs A becomes the interest in possession beneficiary. In this situation there will be a relevant property settlement and A will make a chargeable transfer.

4. In general, thought should be given to replacing an aged interest in possession beneficiary with one or more younger lives as interest in possession beneficiaries of a continuing trust. If this is accomplished in the transitional period, the existing beneficiary will make a PET and the replacement beneficiaries will be entitled to transitional serial interests.

5. The changes in the IHT rules can have an impact on standard divorce arrangements (see Chapter 34). The main problem in the case of existing trusts is illustrated by the following scenario.

A has been married for 20 years and has a life interest in a settlement set up by his father many years ago before his marriage. In June 2008 A separates from his wife and since the main family wealth is in the trust it is agreed that the trustees will appoint his spouse a life interest in part of the fund. In these circumstances IHTA 1984, s.10 provides no protection (A is taxed as if he had made a transfer of value but as he has not actually made a transfer of value s.10 cannot apply) and post April 2008 there is no TSI relief. It would be possible for the trustees to advance the property to the spouse absolutely but this may not be what A wants and it may trigger capital gains tax charges. In these

---

[68] See 18.14 *et seq*.

circumstances if they are only separated and not divorced spouse exemption applies.

Compare the position if A owns the property outright. In these circumstances a settlement by A for his wife is not subject to an immediate IHT charge because it is protected by IHTA 1984, s.10 although the new settlement will be taxed in accordance with the provisions of the relevant property regime.

Hence, every 10 years the trust suffers a 10-year charge plus an exit charge on final termination or earlier distributions of capital.

COMMENTS AND CONCLUSIONS

1. The changes radically alter the IHT treatment of lifetime giving: PETs are now, broadly speaking, limited to outright gifts. Ministers (and doubtless HMRC's) dislike of trusts is apparent and the "level playing field" treatment for outright gifts and gifts into trust has been abandoned. Looking to the future will the scope of PETs be further restricted or will they be abolished? **14.32**

2. Once property is in a "relevant property" settlement the current IHT rates are far from penal with a top rate of tax on 10 year anniversaries of 6 per cent.[69] However, there is no reason to believe that this rate will be retained: an increase to 10 per cent, for instance, would have the effect of producing an annual trust wealth tax of 1 per cent.

3. It is unlikely that much use will be made of bereaved minor trusts given the restrictions on their use and the unacceptably early outright vesting age. More likely that 18–25 trusts will be set up (which can be "extended" by the making of a settled advance before the beneficiary becomes 25). For those wishing to make lifetime gifts to minors (whether children or grandchildren) there may be attractions in using a bare trust albeit that income and capital will have to be paid out at 18. The creation of such a trust will be a PET (see Chapter 30).

4. Continuing use may be made of lifetime trusts falling within the settlor's IHT nil rate band or to hold 100 per cent relievable property.

5. Existing trusts should be reviewed: in the case of iip and A+M trusts the existence of the transitional period may afford something of a breathing space.[70]

6. With the demise of s.49, future iip trusts will not involve the aggregation of settled property with the free estate of the beneficiary.

---

[69] In 1975 the introduction of CTT resulted in a top rate on trusts of 75 per cent and the 1982 overhaul had a top rate of 15 per cent (reduced to 9 per cent in 1984 and to the present 6 per cent in 1986).

[70] Immediate decisions may of course need to be taken: e.g. if a beneficiary is about to become entitled to an iip in an A+M trust, should this be prevented if suitable overriding powers exist? A second example is the making of a settled advance to postpone the absolute vesting of property in the situation where the beneficiary currently enjoys an iip in the property. If effected before April 6, 2008 this appears to involve a TSI but thereafter may result in the creation of a relevant property settlement. See further 18.14 and App. III A3.105 (Questions 6–8).

CHAPTER 15

IHT DEFINITIONS AND CLASSIFICATION

- Meaning of "settlement" **(15.01)**
- Additions by the settlor **(15.13)**
- Classification of settlement **(15.17)**

This Chapter considers the definition of "settlement" for IHT purposes and what is meant by an interest in possession. Two preliminary points are worthy of note—

(i) that the 2006 changes were concerned with the IHT treatment of settlements and have had the result that there is now a striking difference between outright gifts and settled gifts.[1] Hence understanding the width of "settlement" for IHT purposes is vital;

(ii) that the vast majority of new settlements will now be subject to the "relevant property regime"[2] but the meaning of an "interest in possession" remains significant both in the context of old settlements and because of the limited situations in which new qualifying interest in possession trusts can be set up.

MEANING OF "SETTLEMENT"

15.01 "Settlement" is defined in s.43(2) as[3]:

"... any disposition or dispositions of property, whether effected by instrument, by parol or by operation of law, or partly in one way and partly in another, whereby the property is for the time being:

(a) held in trust for persons in succession or for any person subject to a contingency, or
(b) held by trustees on trust to accumulate the whole or part of any income of the property or with power to make payments

---

[1] See 16.01 *et seq*.
[2] Explained in Ch. 20.
[3] Commercial arrangements may be caught as there is no requirement that the settlor must have a donative intent (contrast the position for income tax: see *IRC v Plummer* [1980] A.C. 896, [1979] 3 All E.R. 775, HL).

out of that income at the discretion of the trustees or some other person, with or without power to accumulate surplus income, or

(c) charged or burdened (otherwise than for full consideration in money or money's worth paid for his own use or benefit to the person making the disposition) with the payment of any annuity or other periodical payment payable for a life or any other limited or terminable period, . . .

(3) A lease of property which is for life or lives, or for a period ascertainable only by reference to a death, or which is terminable on, or at a date ascertainable only by reference to, a death, shall be treated as a settlement and the property as settled property, unless the lease was granted for full consideration in money or money's worth; and where a lease not granted as a lease at a rack rent is at any time to become a lease at an increased rent it shall be treated as terminable at that time."

EXAMPLE 15.1

(1) Property is settled on A for life remainder to B and C absolutely in equal shares (this is a "fixed", interest in possession, trust). The property is "held in trust for persons in succession" within IHTA 1984, s.43(2)(a).

(2) Property is held on trust for "such of A, B, C, D, E and F as my trustees in their absolute discretion may select" (this is a discretionary trust and falls within IHTA 1984, s.43(2)(b)).

(3) Property is held on trust "for A (currently aged six) contingent on attaining 18 years" with a default gift over (a minor settlement). This settlement falls within IHTA 1984, s.43(2)(a).

(4) Property is held on trust by A and B as trustees for Z absolutely (a bare trust). For IHT purposes there is no settlement and the property is treated as belonging to Z.[4]

(5) A and B jointly purchase Blackacre. This gives rise to a statutory trust of land[5] with A and B holding the land on trust (as legal joint tenants) for themselves as either beneficial joint tenants or tenants in common. For IHT purposes there is no settlement and the property belongs to A and B equally.[6]

(6) A grants B a lease of Blackacre for B's life at a peppercorn rent. This is a settlement for inheritance tax purposes and A is the trustee of the property.[7] Under the Law of Property Act 1925, s.149(6) the lease is

---

[4] For the (similar) capital gains tax position, see Ch. 5 and, for bare trusts, Ch. 30.
[5] Law of Property Act 1925, ss.34, 36 as amended by the Trusts of Land and Appointment of Trustees Act 1996, s.5, Sch.2.
[6] For the (similar) capital gains tax position, see Ch. 5.
[7] IHTA 1984, s.45. As to the position where a lease is treated as a settlement, see 15.04 and 17.09. This situation does not produce a settlement for the purposes of other taxes.

treated as being for a term of 90 years which is determinable on the death of B.

When is property "held in trust for persons in succession"?

15.02   In *IRC v Lloyds Private Banking Ltd*[8] the relevant terms of the deceased's will were as follows:

> "(1) While my Husband Frederick Arthur Evans remains alive and desires to reside in the property and keeps the same in good repair and insured comprehensively to its full value with Insurers approved by my Trustee and pays and indemnifies my Trustee against all rates taxes and other outgoings in respect of the property my Trustee shall not make any objection to such residence and shall not disturb or restrict it in any way and shall not take any steps to enforce the trust for sale on which the property is held or to realise my share therein or obtain any rent or profit from the property.
> (2) On the death of my said Husband Frederick Arthur Evans I devise and bequeath the said property known as Hillcroft Muzzy Hill, Astwood Bank, near Redditch to my daughter Kathleen Roberts-Hindle absolutely."

The effect of this clause was that the deceased's husband was given a right of occupation in the property which was equivalent to an interest in possession[9] so that the property was settled within s.43(2)(a).[10] In practice, the issue has most commonly arisen when a will set up a "nil rate band discretionary trust" and, the property having been occupied by the surviving spouse, the question was whether an interest in possession had come into being.[11] This is discussed further at 15.30.

Section 43(2)(b) and bare trusts for minor beneficiaries

15.03   Consider the position when property is held in trust for a minor absolutely.[12] Because of his age the beneficiary is not entitled to demand either the income or the capital from the trustees who will (unless it has been excluded) have the standard power to apply income for the maintenance of the beneficiary and to accumulate any surplus under TA 1925, s.31. Does it follow that this arrange-

---

[8] [1998] S.T.C. 559.
[9] See further on rights of occupation, 15.25.
[10] See also *Woodhall (personal representatives of Woodhall) v IRC* [2000] S.T.C. (S.C.D.) 558; *Faulkner v IRC* [2001] S.T.C. (S.C.D.) 112; *IRC v Eversden* [2002] EWHC 1360, [2002] S.T.C. 1109 per Lightman J. at [27] (the issue of whether there was an interest in possession in the settled property was not considered on appeal); *Oakley (personal representatives of Jossaume Deceased) v IRC* [2005] S.T.C. (S.C.D.) 343.
[11] See also SP 10/79.
[12] In the light of the 2006 changes in the IHT treatment of trusts there may be attractions in setting up such bare trusts: see Ch. 30.

ment is a "settlement" within s.43(2)(b)? On the whole it is thought not, since the minor is, of course, entitled to all the income produced by the property: the fact that all or some is retained by the trustees does not mean that it is being accumulated in the sense envisaged by s.43(2)(b). In essence, the power is being used administratively by the trustees rather than dispositively. Hence, were the infant beneficiary to die before attaining 18 all the property (including accumulated income) held by the trustees for him would form part of his estate.[13] HMRC have not yet expressed a view.

Leases for Life

Section 43(3) includes four kinds of lease in the definition of a settlement: **15.04**

(i) a lease for life or lives;
(ii) a lease which is terminable on death (and note that if a lease is granted without any provision for the payment of a commercial rent but at any time will become a lease at an increased rent it is treated as terminable at that time: hence a provision for the payment of a commercial rent on the death of the tenant will result in the lease being treated as a lease for life);
(iii) a lease for a period ascertainable only by reference to a death; and
(iv) a lease terminable at a date ascertainable only by reference to a death.

The life in question need not be that of the tenant.[14]

Prior to March 22, 2006 the tenant would have been treated as enjoying **15.05** a qualifying interest in possession in the let property and the landlord as entitled to a reversionary interest (in the freehold or head lease which would not be excluded property given that he is treated as the settlor). From that date the inter vivos grant of a lease will involve the creation of a relevant property settlement by the landlord.

An important exclusion: a lease for life is not treated as a settlement if it is **15.06** granted for full consideration in money or money's worth. It is believed that HMRC accept that this exclusion will apply when the owner of property carves out a non-commercial lease for life and gives away the freehold or where property is transferred on the understanding that a lease for life at less than a commercial rent will be granted to him.[15]

When is there a disposition creating a settlement?

Difficulties have arisen in identifying, for CGT purposes, when property has **15.07** been resettled (i.e. when a new settlement has been created out of an existing

---

[13] See further *Capital Taxes*, 1984, at p.66 (N. Warren). See App. III A3.137 indicating that HMRC are taking advice on this matter.
[14] It is understood that a statutory tenancy is not regarded as a lease for life: see IHTM 16.91.
[15] See CTO Advanced Instruction Manual at E15 although the same statement does not appear in the revised version. See also Ch. 22 for treatment of reversions.

settlement).[16] Difficulties may also arise when it is necessary to determine whether the settlor has created one or more settlements.[17] Similar problems may arise for inheritance tax and the definition of "settlement" may not help to resolve these problems.[18]

Example 15.2

(1) Each year S creates a discretionary trust of £3,000 (thereby utilising his annual IHT exemption) and his wife does likewise. Accordingly, at the end of five years there are ten mini-discretionary trusts. As a matter of trust law, and assuming that each settlement is correctly documented and constituted, there is no reason why this series should be treated as one settlement. So far as the IHT legislation is concerned the settlements are not related settlements made on the same day[19]; the "associated operations" provisions would seem inapplicable[20]; and the principle in *WT Ramsay Ltd v IRC*[21] although of uncertain ambit, could only be applied with difficulty to a series of gifts. The trusts should be kept apart (there should be no pooling of property) and each settlement should be fully documented.[22]

(2) On June 1, 2006, A sets up an interest in possession trust for his son for life and the trustees are given wide powers to transfer all or part of the trust fund into another settlement—whenever established—under which the son can benefit. On December 1, 2006 the trustees transfer the assets into a protective life interest trust that had been established for A's son some years before.

The IHT position is as follows—

(i) by creating the settlement on June 1, 2006 A has made a chargeable transfer for IHT purposes. The settlement is subject to the relevant property regime;

---

[16] See 7.55.
[17] See 5.28, 5.35 and 7.08.
[18] See, for example, *Minden Trust (Cayman) Ltd v IRC* [1984] S.T.C. 434; affirmed [1985] S.T.C. 758, CA; and *Tax Bulletin*, Issue 27, February 1997, p.398. With the 2006 changes in the IHT taxation of settlements, because the majority of new settlements will fall within the relevant property regime IHTA 1984, s.81(1) will generally treat the property as remaining comprised in the first settlement.
[19] See IHTA 1984, s.62.
[20] See IHTA 1984, s.268, and see *Rysaffe Trustee Co (CI) Ltd v IRC* [2002] S.T.C. 872; affirmed [2003] EWCA Civ 356, [2003] S.T.C. 536, in which it was decided that for the purposes of the IHTA 1984, s.43 "disposition" had its ordinary meaning and was not extended to cover a disposition effected by associated operations. In general terms, therefore, provided that a trust lawyer would conclude that separate settlements had been established, albeit with identical property (in *Rysaffe*, private company shares), then the IHT legislation must be applied on that basis.
[21] *WT Ramsay Ltd v IRC* [1982] A.C. 300 HL.
[22] It is common for separate discretionary trusts to be created of substantial life insurance policies. Such trusts will normally be on identical terms, with the same trustees, but established on consecutive days. Each trust will contain a separate item of property (a particular insurance policy). It is understood that HMRC had taken the view that such a series of settlements fell within the IHTA 1984, s.268 (associated operations) and so could be treated as a single settlement. In the light of the *Rysaffe* case this argument is not thought to be tenable and the authors believe has been abandoned.

(ii) the transfer of assets on December 1, is ignored for IHT purposes and they are treated as remaining comprised in the original settlement.[23] It will therefore be necessary for the trustees to keep the transferred assets separate from the existing assets in that trust for the purposes of completing the appropriate IHT returns.[24]

The impact of IHTA 1984, s.81

15.08 For the purpose of the relevant property charge[25] when property ceases to be comprised in one settlement by becoming comprised in a separate settlement it is to be treated as remaining comprised in the first settlement.

EXAMPLE 15.3

Tom puts property into a life interest trust for his children in 2007 but the trustees have power to transfer all or any part of the trust fund into a qualifying settlement (defined as any settlement in which the children can benefit). In 2011 the trustees exercise this power to transfer the entire trust fund into a family discretionary trust which Tom had set up in 2000.

The property is treated—for IHT purposes—as remaining comprised in the 2007 settlement. Hence the first 10-year charge will be in 2017, etc. Note that there is no such rule for other taxes so that the transfer may give rise to a CGT charge[26] whilst as a matter of trust law the assets will merge with whatever property is already in the 2000 settlement.

The impact of IHTA 1984, s.80

15.09 Prior to March 22, 2006, s.80 provided that:

(i) if a settlement was established which conferred an immediate interest in possession on either the settlor or his spouse; *then*

(ii) for the purposes of the relevant property regime[27] *it was not to be treated as comprised in a settlement at that time*;

(iii) instead when the property is no longer held on trusts under which either of those persons is entitled to an interest in possession, the

---

[23] IHTA 1984, s.81(1).
[24] For CGT purposes the transfer will be a disposal and may result in charge under TCGA 1992, s.71 and note that hold-over relief will only be available if the assets are business assets within TCGA 1992, s.165. See 7.55.
[25] i.e. IHTA 1984, Pt III, Ch. III.
[26] See Chs 12 and 14. Hold-over relief will only be available if the property is a business asset within TCGA 1992, s.165. Hold-over relief is not available under s.260 because there is no inheritance tax payable—the property is treated as remaining in the first settlement for inheritance tax purposes.
[27] i.e. IHTA 1984, Pt II, Ch. III.

property is then to be treated as comprised in a separate settlement made by the settlor or spouse (as the case may be) who last ceased to be beneficially entitled to an interest in possession in it;

(iv) reference to spouse includes references to the settlor's widow or widower and registered civil partner;

(v) although the commencement of the relevant property settlement is deferred, 10 year anniversary charges run from the date when the settlement was initially created with the settlor/spouse interest in possession.[28]

EXAMPLE 15.4

X who died on March 20, 2006 provided in his will:
(a) for a nil rate band discretionary trust; and
(b) for the residue to be held on an interest in possession trust for his wife with remainder on a discretionary trust for his issue.

For IHT purposes—
(a) by virtue of s.80, for the purposes of the relevant property regime the trust of residue is treated as arising on the termination of the spouse's life interest. Note, however, that the anniversary charges will be dated by reference to March 20, 2006 when the trust was set up on his death;
(b) accordingly the trust of residue is not a "related settlement"[29] to be taken into account in taxing the nil rate band discretionary trust since (1) the settlor is not the same and nor (2) were the settlements created on the same day.

15.10 With the 2006 changes in the IHT treatment of settlements, s.80 was amended (from March 22, 2006) so that it will now only apply to new settlements which confer a "postponing interest" on either the settlor or his spouse.[30] A "postponing interest" is defined as either an IPDI[31] or disabled person's interest.[32] In Example 15.4 therefore the IHT consequences are unchanged since the trust of residue is an IPDI.[33]

Who is the settlor?

15.11 In the majority of cases it is not difficult to identify the settlor, because there is usually one settlor who has created a settlement by a "disposition" of property (which may include a series of associated operations).[34]

---

[28] IHTA 1984, s.61(2).
[29] For the definition of a "related settlement" see IHTA 1984, s.62.
[30] IHTA 1984, s.80(4)(a) inserted by FA 2006, Sch.20, para.23.
[31] "Immediate post death interest": See Ch. 19.
[32] IHTA 1980, s.80(4)(b) inserted by FA 2006, Sch.20 para.23. For a disabled person's interest, see IHTA 1984, s.89B and 26.
[33] For the offshore implications of s.80, see Ch. 22.
[34] IHTA 1984, s.272. See *Hatton v IRC* [1992] S.T.C. 140 and fn.30 above.

IHTA 1984, s.44(2) states:

> "Where more than one person is a settlor in relation to a settlement and the circumstances so require, this Part of this Act (except Section 48(4) to (6)) shall have effect in relation to it as if the settled property were comprised in separate settlements".

Thomas v IRC[35] indicates that this provision normally only applies where an identifiable capital fund has been provided by each settlor. The fund is then treated as two separate settlements in the case of relevant property trusts where both the incidence of the periodic charge and the amount of inheritance tax chargeable may be affected.[36] This can be relevant where, for example, husband and wife transfer a jointly owned property into a discretionary trust. For inheritance tax purposes this is two separate settlements and each trust has the benefit of the relevant settlor's unused nil rate band.

15.12 "Settlor" is defined (in terms similar to the income tax definition) as follows[37]:

> "In this Act 'settlor', in relation to a settlement, includes any person by whom the settlement was made directly or indirectly, and . . . includes any person who has provided funds directly or indirectly for the purpose of or in connection with the settlement or has made with any other person a reciprocal arrangement for that other person to make the settlement."[38]

ADDITIONS BY THE SETTLOR

15.13 Where there is only one settlor who adds property to his settlement: is this one settlement or two? The question is significant in relation to:

(i) discretionary trusts (especially with regard to timing and rate of the periodic and inter-periodic charges);

---

[35] *Thomas v IRC* [1981] S.T.C. 382.
[36] The existence of this section suggests that otherwise the addition of property to a settlement does not create a separate settlement.
[37] IHTA 1984, s.44(1).
[38] Compare the CGT definition of settlor, discussed at 5.16 and 11.10. In *Hatton v IRC* [1992] S.T.C. 140 Chadwick J. considered the impact of the associated operations provisions of the IHTA 1984, s.268 on the question of multiple settlors. He concluded in that case that the first settlement was made with a view to enabling or facilitating the making of the second (within the meaning of the IHTA 1984, s.268(1)(b)). Accordingly, there was a disposition by associated operations which was treated as a single disposition of property from the first settlor into the second settlement of which he therefore became a settlor. Given the nature of the property settled by these two settlors, the judge was then forced to conclude that both settlors had created a separate settlement of the entirety of the property in the second settlement. This approach (treating each settlor as having established a separate settlement of the entirety of the settled property) would, the judge suggested, also apply to reciprocal settlements.
   In a simple case A would settle property on X for a limited interest in possession remainder to A and as a quid pro quo B would settle property on Y for an initial interest in posession remainder to B. In both cases the reverter to settlor provisions would at first sight apply on the termination of X and Y's respective interests. Once it is accepted, however, that A is also a settlor of B's trust and vice versa (see IHTA 1984, s.44(1)) that analysis does not hold good. Instead, because B is a settlor of "A's settlement" on the termination of X's limited interest an inheritance tax charge may arise. The judge viewed the situation as one in which A and B were settlors of two separate settlements rather than accepting the view that B should be seen as "a dominant settlor" of A's trust.

(ii) where excluded property is comprised in a settlement[39]; and

(iii) when a settlor adds property to a pre March 22, 2006 settlement in which there existed on that date an interest in possession.

As a matter of trust law, there is a single settlement where funds are held and managed by one set of trustees for one set of beneficiaries, so that such additions do not lead to the creation of separate settlements. Hence, if it would be advantageous to have two settlements it is desirable that a separate settlement deed should be drawn up for the later property.

Approach of HMRC

15.14 The budget note that was issued by HMRC on March 22, 2006 stated that

"the new rules will apply . . . to new trusts, additions of new assets to existing trusts and to . . . other IHT relevant events in relation to existing trusts."

In effect, therefore, the addition is treated as creating a separate settlement which is in line with the views previously expressed in the context of excluded property trusts.[40] The view is thought to be based on the wording of s.43(2) which defines a settlement as "any disposition or dispositions of property . . ."[41] Presumably the HMRC view is that each disposition of property represents a separate settlement. However, the contrary could be argued from s.43: i.e. that several dispositions can create a single settlement.

Whilst it is the case that a settlement only arises when property is transferred to trustees it would be surprising to a property lawyer to be told that every time such a transfer is made a separate settlement is created. On such an analysis establishing a trust in pilot form (e.g. with a small sum of money) and then adding substantial assets subsequently would result in two separate settlements.

It is difficult to point to a specific provision in the IHT legislation which contradicts general trust law and, in particular, s.67 which deals with additions to relevant property settlements proceeds on the assumption that those additions are to be taxed as part of the settlement to which they were added.[42] If they were to be taxed as a separate settlement, there would have been no need for the

---

[39] See "Excluded Property Settlements by People Domiciled Overseas" *Tax Bulletin*, Issue 27, February 1997, p.398 and 22.20 for further comments on additions in the context of excluded property trusts.
[40] *ibid*. See also App. III A3.142.
[41] Consider also IHTA 1984, s.267(3)(a) which has a different tax regime depending on whether settled property "becomes comprised" in the settlement. However these words suggest that in the absence of any express provision in FA 2006 taxing property differently depending on when it "becomes comprised" in the settlement, additions to a pre-Budget interest in possession trust cannot be taxed as chargeable transfers simply on the basis that they are deemed to be separate settlements.
[42] Other provisions in Ch. III, Pt III are to the same effect: for instance IHTA 1984, s.81 is needed only because the assumption is that otherwise the added property would be comprised in the transferee settlement. It would be bizarre in the extreme if a different meaning were to be attributed to settlement for the purposes of Pt III—the s.43 definition is said to be for the purpose of "the Act".

section! Further, treating additions as comprised in a separate settlement was not a point taken by HMRC in the *Rysaffe* litigation.[43] HMRC point to ss.60 and 67 as suggestive that additions to interest in possession trusts are somehow different from additions to settlements taxed under Ch. III because the relevant property regime specifically deals with additions and clearly envisages one settled fund, while Ch. II dealing with interest in possession trusts contains no such provisions.[44] However, it is difficult to see any justification for the HMRC view that an addition to an existing settlement where property becomes comprised in the settlement is a new settlement "made" at that time. There is no provision in Ch. II that deems a new settlement to arise. FA 2006 should have referred to property "becoming comprised in a settlement" after March 21, 2006 if additions to a pre-March 22, 2006 interest in possession trust were to be taxed on the basis that they created a new settlement.

15.15 In the authors' view therefore the statement in BN 25 (and RI 166) is either wrong or at least inaccurate. Clearly though it is the intention of BN 25 that additions of property to an existing interest in possession trust should be taxed as the creation of a relevant property settlement. As discussed above, it is difficult to accept that this result follows on the basis that a separate settlement has been created. An alternative and perhaps better argument for HMRC would be to consider the definition of an interest in possession under s.49(1): specifically that section does not apply to an interest in possession to which a person becomes beneficially entitled after March 21, 2006 (with only relatively few exceptions): see s.49(1A). Although the Budget Notice does not so argue, it might be said that the interest in possession only arose in the new property when it was added. The taxpayer might have greater difficulty in arguing successfully that his interest in possession in "settled property" was an interest in possession which arose before Budget Day in respect of property added to the trust after March 21, 2006. Hence even if he can show an addition is not a new trust, this would not help him if the interest in possession in the settled property was treated as arising after March 21.

The above analysis covers additions of property to an interest in possession settlement. Different considerations arise where value rather than property is transferred to the trustees. This can arise where, for example, a settlor forgives a debt owed to him by the trustees or a beneficiary improves a house owned by the trustees. In this case it may be easier to maintain that the interest in possession in the settled property was indeed the interest in possession which arose before Budget Day and therefore no new settlement was created when value was added.

The legislation on transitional serial interests ("TSIs") and existing A+M trusts deals with the added property problem. A TSI can only be created in property *then* (i.e. immediately before March 22, 2006) comprised in the statement (see s.149C(2)(b)). In the case of A+M trusts the transitional rules may apply to the settled property immediately before March 22, 2006 (see s.71 (1A)(a)). No advantage can therefore be gained from adding to an A+M trust. Existing interests in possession are more problematic but it is clear that, even if the addition is taxed as a PET to the then beneficiary, his interest cannot be replaced by a TSI.

---

[43] And see fn. above.
[44] s.60 provides "in this chapter references to the commencement of a settlement are references to the time when property first becomes comprised in it".

Meaning of Trustee

15.16 The ordinary meaning is given to the term "a trustee", although it also includes any person in whom the settled property or its management is for the time being vested.[45] In cases where a lease for lives is treated as a settlement the landlord is the trustee.

CLASSIFICATION OF SETTLEMENTS

15.17 Settlements for IHT purposes are to be divided into three categories:

(i) *Category A*: a qualifying interest in possession settlement; for example where the property is held for a tenant for life under a pre-March 2006 trust who, by virtue of his interest, is entitled to the income and therefore has "an interest in possession".

(ii) *Category B*: a relevant property settlement; for example a trust where trustees are given a discretion over the distribution of the income or an interest in possession which is not qualifying. In the case of a discretionary trust, at most, beneficiaries have the right to be considered by the trustees, the right to ensure that the fund is properly administered, and the right to join with all the other beneficiaries to bring the settlement to an end.

(iii) *Category C*: this is a subcategory of Category B into which fall special or privileged trusts. They are not subject to the Category B regime. The main example was the old accumulation and maintenance trust and is now the bereaved minor trust.

To place a particular trust into its correct category is important for two reasons. First, because the inheritance tax treatment of each is totally different both as to incidence of tax and as to the amount of tax charged; and secondly, because a change from one category to another normally gives rise to an inheritance tax charge. For example, if a life interest ceases, whereupon the fund becomes held on discretionary trusts, the settlement moves from Category A to Category B, and a chargeable occasion (the ending of a life interest) has occurred.[46]

15.18 The 2006 changes have reduced the significance of this classification become virtually all new (i.e. post March 21, 2006) settlements will fall into Category B (i.e. they will be subject to the relevant property regime). However, it is still possible to create a qualifying interest in possession trust on death (an IPDI) whilst trusts which are set up to create a disabled person interest— whether inter vivos or on death—will similarly fall into Category A. Hence even if the glory days of the interest in possession trust are past, there are reasons in the future for understanding the borderline between Category A and Category B. And, of course, the tax treatment of old interest in possession trusts will to a large extent continue so that knowing what is meant by that term is important in the context of existing settlements.

---

[45] IHTA 1984, s.45.
[46] This event has never been a potentially exempt transfer: see the limitation in IHTA 1984, s.3A(1)(c) as inserted by FA 1986, s.101, Sch.19, para.1.

Meaning of an "interest in possession"

15.19 Normally trusts can easily be slotted into their correct category. Trusts falling within Category C are carefully defined so that any trust not specifically falling into one of those special cases must fall into Category B. Problems are principally caused by the borderline between Categories A and B where the division is drawn according to whether the settlement has an interest in possession or not. In the majority of cases no problems will arise: at one extreme stands the life interest settlement; at the other the discretionary trust. What, however, of a settlement which provides for the income to be paid to A, unless the trustees decide to pay it to B, or to accumulate it; or where the property in the trust property is enjoyed in specie by one beneficiary as a result of the exercise of a discretion (for example, a beneficiary living in a dwelling house which is comprised in the assets of a discretionary trust)? To resolve these difficulties, the phrase an "interest in possession" needs definition. The legislation does not assist; instead, its meaning must be gleaned from an HMRC press release[47] and the speeches of the House of Lords in *Pearson v IRC*[48] which largely endorsed the statements in that press release.

The view of HMRC

15.20 According to HMRC[49]:

> ". . . an interest in settled property exists where the person having the interest has the immediate entitlement (subject to any prior claim by the trustees for expenses or other outgoings properly payable out of income) to any income produced by that property as the income arises; but . . . a discretion or power, in whatever form, which can be exercised after income arises so as to withhold it from that person negatives the existence of an interest in possession. For this purpose a power to accumulate income is regarded as a power to withhold it, unless any accumulation must be held solely for the person having the interest or his personal representatives.
>
> On the other hand the existence of a mere power of revocation or appointment, the exercise of which would determine the interest wholly or in part (but which, so long as it remains unexercised, does not affect the beneficiary's immediate entitlement to income) does not . . . prevent the interest from being an interest in possession."

The first paragraph is concerned with the existence of discretions or powers which might affect the destination of the income after it has arisen and which prevent the existence of any interest in possession (for example a provision

---

[47] i.e. HMRC press release of February 12, 1976, the text of which can be found in HMRC booklet IHT1.
[48] *Pearson v IRC* [1981] A.C. 753; [1980] 2 All E.R. 479, HL. The term "interest in possession" is used in the Trusts of Land and Appointment of Trustees Act 1996 where it is assumed that it will bear the inheritance tax meaning and in the CGT legislation.
[49] See HMRC CG36321.

enabling the trustees to accumulate income or to divert it for the benefit of other beneficiaries). The second paragraph concerns overriding powers which, if exercised, would terminate the entire interest of the beneficiary, but which do not prevent the existence of an interest in possession (for example the statutory power of advancement). Administrative expenses charged on the income can be ignored in deciding whether there is an interest in possession, so long as such payments are for "outgoings properly payable out of income". A clause in the settlement providing for expenses of a capital nature to be so charged is, therefore, not covered and HMRC originally considered the mere presence of such a clause fatal to the existence of any interest in possession. This was held to be wrong in *Pearson v IRC* where a clause permitting the trustees to apply income in payment of administrative expenses of a capital nature did not preclude a beneficiary from having an interest in possession. HMRC now accept this.[50]

Pearson v IRC[51]

15.21   Both capital and income of the trust fund were held for the settlor's three adult daughters in equal shares subject to three overriding trustee powers:

(i) to appoint capital and income amongst the daughters, their spouses and issue;

(ii) to accumulate so much of the income as they should think fit; and

(iii) to apply any income towards the payment or discharge of any taxes, costs or other outgoings which would otherwise be payable out of capital.

The trustees had regularly exercised their powers to accumulate the income. What caused the disputed tax assessment was the irrevocable appointment of some £16,000 from the fund to one of the daughters. There was no doubt that, after the appointment, she enjoyed an interest in possession in the appointed sum; but did she already have an interest in possession in the fund? If so, no inheritance tax would be chargeable on the appointment[52]; if not, there would be a charge because the appointed sums had passed from a "no interest in possession" to an "interest in possession" settlement (Category B to Category A).

HMRC argued that the existence of the overriding power to accumulate and the provision enabling all expenses to be charged to income deprived the settlement of any interest in possession. It was common ground that whether such powers had been exercised or not was irrelevant in deciding the case. The overriding power of appointment over capital and income was not seen as endangering the existence of any interest in possession (see the second paragraph of the press notice).

For the bare majority in the House of Lords the presence of the overriding discretion to accumulate the income was fatal to the existence of an interest in possession. "A present right to present enjoyment" was how an interest in possession was defined and the beneficiaries did not have a present right.

---

[50] See ICAEW Guidance Note December 14, 1992.
[51] *Pearson v IRC* [1981] A.C. 753; [1980] 2 All E.R. 479, HL.
[52] As to advancements to a life tenant or absolute entitlement on the satisfaction of a contingency see 17.14.

Their enjoyment of any income from the trust fund depended on the trustees' decision as to accumulation of income. No distinction is to be drawn between a trust to pay income to a beneficiary (with an overriding power to accumulate), and a trust to accumulate (with a power to pay). Therefore, in the following examples there is no interest in possession:

- to A for life but the trustees may accumulate the income for the benefit of others; and
- the income shall be accumulated but the trustees may make payments to A.

Flexible interests in possession

In practice these have been extremely popular[53] and operate as follows: **15.22**

(i) the interest in possession may be terminated by the trustee exercising a wide overriding power of appointment. Normally the consent of the relevant beneficiary is not required although he will often be one of the trustees;

(ii) the trustees have power to advance capital to or for the benefit of the interest in possession beneficiary.

A high degree of flexibility is built into the structure: to some extent these trusts were a substitute for "full blown" discretionary trusts. A further (often the main) attraction was that they provided a vehicle to circumvent the GWR/POA legislation.[54] In simple terms if the interest in possession beneficiary suffered a termination of his interest he did not make a gift and therefore if he continued to use or benefit from the trust assets the GWR/POA legislation did not apply. FA 2006, by extending the concept of a "gift" to the transfer of value treated as happening on the termination of an interest in possession, has stopped this avoidance technique and, coupled with the changes in the IHT treatment of settlements will doubtless result in the eventual demise of flexible interest in possession trusts.

Problems remaining after Pearson v IRC[55]

The test laid down by the majority in the House of Lords provides some certainty in a difficult area of law and the borderline between trusts with and without an interest in possession is reasonably easy to draw. Where there is uncertainty about the entitlement of a beneficiary to income, it is likely that the settlement will fall into the "no-interest in possession" regime. In the light of the relatively favourable regime for taxing discretionary trusts introduced in 1982 that may be no bad thing for taxpayers. The following paragraphs consider some of the difficulties remaining after the case.   **15.23**

---

[53] See Ch. 18.
[54] This is considered at Ch. 24.
[55] *Pearson v IRC* [1981] A.C. 753; [1980] 2 All E.R. 479, HL.

(i) Dispositive and administrative powers

15.24 For there to be an interest in possession the beneficiary must be entitled to the income as it arises. Were this test to be applied strictly, however, even a trust with a life tenant receiving the income might fail to satisfy the requirement because trustees will always deduct management expenses from the gross income, so that few beneficiaries are entitled to all the income as it arises. This problem was commented on by Viscount Dilhorne in *Pearson v IRC*[56] as follows:

> "... Parliament distinguished between the administration of a trust and the dispositive powers of trustees ... A life tenant has an interest in possession but his interest only extends to the net income of the property, that is to say, after deduction from the gross income of expenses etc properly incurred in the management of the trust by the trustees in the exercise of their powers. A dispositive power is a power to dispose of the net income. Sometimes the line between an administrative and a dispositive power may be difficult to draw but that does not mean that there is not a valid distinction."

In *Pearson v IRC* the trustees had an overriding discretion to apply income towards the payment of any taxes, costs or other outgoings which would otherwise be payable out of capital and HMRC took the view that the existence of this overriding power was a further reason for the settlement lacking an interest in possession.[57] Was this power administrative (in which case its presence did not affect the existence of any interest in possession) or dispositive (fatal to the existence of such an interest)? Viscount Dilhorne decided that the power was administrative. Acceptable though this argument may be for management expenses, is it convincing when applied to other expenses and taxes (e.g. capital gains tax and inheritance tax) which would normally be payable out of the capital of the fund? In *Miller v IRC*[58] the Court of Session held that a power to employ income to make good depreciation in the capital value of assets in the fund was administrative. It must be stressed that the House of Lords did not have to decide whether HMRC's contention was correct or not and that Viscount Dilhorne's observations are obiter dicta.

(ii) Power to allow beneficiaries to occupy a dwelling house

Judge and other (representatives of Walden deceased) v HMRC[59]

15.25 The facts were that Mr Walden died on January 28, 2000 and in his will left his residuary estate on discretionary trusts for his wife and relatives. The

---

[56] *Pearson v IRC* [1981] A.C. 753 at 774, 775; [1980] 2 All E.R. 479 at 486, HL.
[57] HMRC accepts that a power to pay capital expenses out of income (which may be extremely useful given that it may be impractical to sell capital assets) if exercised will not prevent there being an interest in possession in the trust. Of course, the income will be "made good" when capital is realised. See further *Carver v Duncan* [1985] S.T.C. 356, 15.20 above and IHTM 16067.
[58] *Miller v IRC* [1987] S.T.C. 108, Ct of Sess.
[59] [2005] S.T.C. (S.C.D.) 863.

matrimonial home was separately dealt with by cl.3 of his will which was in the following terms—

> "I GIVE free of tax and of any monies secured thereon by way of legal charge or otherwise to my Trustees ALL THAT my interest in the property known as and situate at 30 Perrymead Street London SW6 OR the property in which I am at my death ordinarily resident or in which I have then last been ordinarily resident UPON TRUST with the consent in writing of my Wife during her lifetime to sell the same with full power to postpone sale for so long as they shall in their absolute discretion think fit and to hold the net proceeds of sale and other monies applicable as capital and the net rent and profits until upon the trusts and with and subject to the powers and provisions of my Residuary Fund (as hereinafter defined) as an accretion thereto AND I DECLARE my Trustees during the lifetime of my Wife to permit her to have the use and enjoyment of the said property for such period or periods as they shall in their absolute discretion think fit pending postponement of sale she paying the rates taxes and other outgoings and keeping the same in good repair and insured against fire to the full value thereof in some office of repute nominated by my Trustees in the names of my Trustees."

Mrs Walden had lived in the property for many years with her husband (although it appears that she had no beneficial interest in the property) and on his death his executors and trustees[60] wrote to her in the following terms:

> "I would confirm that under clause 3 of your late husband's will, 30 Perrymead Street is the sole asset of a Life Interest Trust and you will enjoy the occupancy of the property during your lifetime . . . you will be responsible for the actual payment of the premiums [for buildings insurance cover] as well as all the household bills etc. including council tax. . .
>
> Under Clause 4 of the will the residue of the estate is to be held on a discretionary trust for the benefit of yourself, your nephew and niece and also their children. As trustees we have the responsibility of exercising our discretionary powers under the terms of the will and also under trust law when considering making payment of capital and income to the discretionary beneficiaries. . . .
>
> This discretionary trust is slightly different in as much that you, as the surviving spouse, is not nominated as the 'primary beneficiary'. . . "

The letter was written on the basis that Mrs Walden had been given an interest in possession in the property (then worth £625,000) and the IHT return was completed on this basis with the result that no IHT was payable on his death.

Mrs Walden continued to live in the property until her own death on October 3, 2003. The Appellants took out letters of administration to her estate and in the IHT return her estate was valued at £392,344. They were advised that Mrs Walden had not enjoyed an interest in possession in the property under cl.3: instead it was comprised in a discretionary trust and so did not

---

[60] Commercial Union Trustees Ltd (subsequently Norwich Union).

fall to be aggregated[61] for the purpose of calculating the tax due on her free estate. HMRC thereupon issued a notice of determination because they were of the view that cl.3 had created an interest in possession. The matter came for decision before a Special Commissioner (Dr Brice).[62]

15.26 The Special Commissioner decided, in favour of the Appellants, that cl.3 did not give Mrs Walden an interest in possession in the property and nor had she at any later time acquired such an interest. The following points may be noted—

(i) for Mrs Walden to have an interest in possession it was necessary for her to have "a present right to the present enjoyment of" (the property)[63] and she would not have such a right if the trustees had a discretion as to whether or not she should occupy the property;

(ii) clause 3 was defectively drafted and posed serious problems of construction. The clause provided for the property to be held on a trust for sale (with any sale being dependant on Mrs Walden's consent) and pending any sale, rent and profits (if any) were to be held on the discretionary trusts of residue. In the final words of the clause dealing with occupation by Mrs Walden "for such period or periods as they [viz the Trustees] shall in their absolute discretion think fit" the Special Commissioner discerned the clear intention that the trustees retained a discretion to allow Mrs Walden "to reside in (the property) for no period or for any period".

15.27 Whilst the decision that no interest in possession existed, given the concluding words of cl.3 is understandable, the result, taking into account other factors, may be thought somewhat surprising. For instance:

(i) it meant that IHT was payable on Mr Walden's death and, even allowing for the ability to pay by instalments over 10 years, the result might have been to force a sale of the property. Mrs Walden was substantially younger than her husband and it might therefore have been thought that his intention would have been to defer the payment of tax until her death. It would be surprising if his overriding concern—as was suggested—was to avoid the value of the property being taxed on his wife's death;

(ii) the structure of the will might suggest, given that the residue established a discretionary trust, that the purpose of cl.3 was different and was

---

[61] Under IHTA 1984, s.49(1).
[62] The trustees of Mr Walden's will were not represented at the hearing. From the perspective of HMRC either tax on the property would fall due on Mrs Walden's death (as they contended before the Commissioner) or, failing that, the IHT return on Mr Walden's death was incorrect and instead of a spouse exempt gift, cl.3 by creating a discretionary trust would have resulted in a substantial liability to IHT at that time. That charge would fall on the executors and trustees of Mr Walden's estate who would not be protected even if in receipt of a certificate of discharge. Given the time delay interest would also be payable. Further if the house was sold after Mrs Walden's death—as seems likely—there would be no CGT uplift on her death and so the question of availability of CGT main residence relief would fall to be considered in the light of SP10/79 (which was not mentioned before the Special Commissioner).
[63] *Pearson v IRC* [1980] S.T.C. 318 at p.323 (Viscount Dilhorne) and for a right to occupy constituting an interest in possession see *IRC v Lloyds Private Banking* [1998] S.T.C. 559.

designed to confer rights—in excess of those enjoyed by a discretionary beneficiary—on Mrs Walden;

(iii) it was not argued on behalf of HMRC that the letter by the trustees to Mrs Walden (set out above) had the effect of giving her an interest in possession in the property: "rather the evidence supported the view that (the Trustees) thought that an interest in possession had been created by the Will."[64]

The wider significance of the case

Although widely reported in the national press it is difficult to accept that this case lays to rest the uncertainties that have arisen over when an interest in possession can arise when property is held in a discretionary trust.[65] Bear in mind that the case involved a severely deficient will and, of course, a trust which owned the entire house so that the trustees could—if they wished—have permitted a beneficiary to occupy. By contrast, in the "usual" case it is only a beneficial share of the property occupied by the surviving spouse which passes on the first spouse's death into a discretionary trust. The issues involved are then quite different: for instance, if all that the trustees own is an equitable share it would seem that they have no right to allow occupation. Instead as (usually) the sole surviving legal and beneficial owner of the other equitable share that right is with the surviving spouse. In these circumstances the trustees' acquiescence to the spouse's continued occupation may be seen as no more than an acceptance of the reality of the situation. The *Walden* decision is of some significance in confirming that mere usage (occupation) does not by itself prove that there is a right to occupy: this must be conferred by the trustees. **15.28**

---

[64] The issue here has a "*Hastings-Bass*" flavour: the trustees, presumably because they were acting under a misapprehension as to the legal effect of cl.3, did not validly exercise their discretion to confer a right of occupation on Mrs Walden. And yet even had they appreciated that the trust conferred a discretion on them, is it conceivable that they would have come to any other conclusion? The property had been Mrs Walden's home for many years and although it was accepted that she had no equitable interest therein she would surely have been entitled to at least the use the property if she had raised a claim under the 1975 Act. Although 15 years younger than her husband she in fact only survived him by three years: had she continued to live in the property for (say) a further 10 years would a court have concluded that she never had any right to occupy so that if the trustees discovered the true position she could have been evicted (or does she at some point obtain protection on the basis of a "legitimate expectation"?). The reference in the will to Mrs Walden being responsible for the payment of taxes, outgoings etc on the property must in the light of the decision be analysed as a fetter on the trustees' discretion: viz the trustees can only allow her to occupy on these terms. It might, however, also be viewed as laying down the terms on which she has the right to occupy with the consent to sale requirement being seen as protection for that right.

[65] It is uncertainties of this type which have led to the proliferation of debt/charge schemes in the will in an attempt to ensure that the deceased's IHT nil rate band will be utilised. On the question of CGT it is interesting to speculate on the position in *Walden* on sale of the property since it may be argued that Mrs Walden did indeed occupy under the terms of the trust so that the requirements of TCGA 1992, s.225 are met. By contrast, in the case of an equitable share only held in a trust which does not therefore carry a right to occupy it is more difficult to see how relief can be available. See 28.16 and 31.25.

Does it matter after March 21, 2006?

15.29 Because new *inter vivos* qualifying interest in possession trusts cannot be set up after March 21, 2006[66] it might be thought that the problem that arose in both *Lloyds Private Banking* and *Walden* will not arise in the future. Note, however,

(i) that wills can still create qualifying interest in possession trusts ("IPDI's") so that the *Lloyds Private Banking* decision remains of importance;

(ii) that if a will establishes a discretionary trust then if an interest in possession is created within two years of death that is read back as an IPDI. Hence in what circumstances an interest in possession can be considered to arise (as in *Walden*) remains an important issue.[67]

Discretionary Trust owning a house/share in a house

15.30 In recent years it has been suggested that HMRC take the view that if on the death of H his share of the matrimonial home is left by will on discretionary trusts (in practice a nil rate band discretionary trust) for a class of beneficiaries which includes Mrs H (who owns the other share in the property and, with the death of H, will usually be the sole legal owner) then if Mrs H continues to occupy the property exclusively after H's death she will be considered to enjoy an interest in possession in the share held under the trusts of H's will. No case has been taken to the Commissioners on this point and the *Walden* case offers no support for this supposed view of HMRC. The position is discussed further in Chapter 28 on Will drafting. Further the following matters are worthy of note—

(i) what the trustees own is a beneficial share in the property which does not give them any rights to sell/let the freehold interest;

(ii) Mrs H is in occupation by virtue of her equitable interest and it seems unlikely that the trustees would persuade a court to either order a sale of the property or to force the payment of a rent[68];

(iii) the Trustees may well take the view that, having been left this share in the property, their best course of action is to ensure that the property is being properly maintained and insured by Mrs H and, subject to that, to retain it as an appreciating asset.[69]

Recently HMRC appear to have agreed with this view at least where a share in the original property has been left on discretionary trusts and the authors'

---

[66] Save only in favour of disabled beneficiaries: see Ch. 26.
[67] See IHTA 1984, s.144 (3)–(6) as inserted by FA 2006, Sch.20, para.27. For HMRC's view, see App. III 3A.116.
[68] Consider the Trusts of Land and Appointment of Trustees Act, 1996 ss.12–15.
[69] A difficult question is then whether on sale of the property the trustees are entitled to claim the CGT principal private residence exemption in respect of their share in the property. Is Mrs A entitled to occupy it "under the terms of the trust" so that the requirement of TCGA 1992, s.225 are met. See further 28.16 and 31.25.

experience is that they have usually dropped arguments that an interest in possession has been conferred by the trustees.

In summary, a power to allow beneficiaries to occupy a dwelling house may exist both in settlements which otherwise have an interest in possession and in those without. The mere existence of such a power is to be ignored; problems may only arise if and when it is exercised.[70] HMRC's SP 10/79 indicates that if such a power is exercised to allow, for a definite or indefinite period, someone other than the life tenant to have exclusive or joint right of residence in a dwelling house as a permanent home, there may be an inheritance tax charge on the partial ending of that life interest. In the case of a fund otherwise lacking an interest in possession, the statement suggests that the exercise of the power will result in the creation of an interest in possession and therefore an inheritance tax charge would arise. **15.31**

Whether this view is correct is arguable; in *Swales v IRC*[71] for instance, the taxpayer's argument that the mandating of trust income to a beneficiary was equivalent to providing a residence for permanent occupation (and accordingly created an interest in possession) was rejected by the court. In practice, any challenge could prove costly to the taxpayer, and trustees who possess such powers should think carefully before exercising them.[72]

(iii) Interest-free loans to beneficiaries

It is thought that the view (once held by HMRC) that an interest-free loan to a beneficiary out of a discretionary trust created an interest in possession in the fund has now been abandoned.[73] As that beneficiary became a debtor (to the extent of the loan), one wonders in what assets his interest subsists; the money loaned would appear to belong to him absolutely. **15.32**

(iv) Position of the last surviving member of a discretionary class

If the class of beneficiaries has closed, the sole survivor must be entitled to the income as it arises so he enjoys an interest in possession. When the class has not closed, however, trustees have a reasonable time to decide how the accrued income is to be distributed and, if a further beneficiary could come into existence before that period has elapsed, the current beneficiary is not automatically entitled to the income as it arises so that there is no interest in possession.[74] Likewise, if the class has not closed and the trustees have a power to accumulate income. **15.33**

---

[70] See 15.29 above
[71] *Swales v IRC* [1984] 3 All E.R. 16.
[72] See also the Trusts of Land and Appointment of Trustees Act 1996, ss.12, 13.
[73] The problem can arise in relation to nil rate band discretionary will trusts where the debt scheme is implemented: see Ch. 28.
[74] *Re Trafford's Settlement: Moore v IRC* [1985] Ch. 32; [1984] 1 All E.R. 1108.

CHAPTER 16

CREATION OF SETTLEMENTS: INHERITANCE TAX POSITION FROM MARCH 22, 2006

- Charge to tax **(16.01)**
- Reservation of benefit on setting up a trust **(16.06)**
- Impact of the pre-owned assets charge **(16.10)**

CHARGE TO TAX[1]

16.01 If a settlement is created *inter vivos* there is no immediate IHT charge if the transfer is a potentially exempt transfer ("PET"). Before March 22, 2006 the transfer was a PET if the trust contained an interest in possession (when the settlor was treated as making a PET to the relevant beneficiary) or was to an accumulation and maintenance or disabled trust.[2] Nor did an inheritance tax charge arise in the circumstances set out in the following example.

EXAMPLE 16.1

(1) In 2005 S settled £500,000 on trust for himself for life with remainder to his children. As S, the life tenant, was deemed to own the property in the trust (and not simply a life interest in it) his estate had not fallen in value (a "nothing"). He does not reserve a benefit because the property is still comprised in his estate.

(2) In 2004 S settled £500,000 on trust for his wife for life, remainder to his children. S's wife was treated as owning the property in the trust so that S's transfer was an exempt transfer to a spouse.

An immediate charge at half rates was, however, imposed if a discretionary trust was created *inter vivos*.[3]

---

[1] For the CGT consequences of establishing a trust, see Ch. 6.
[2] IHTA 1984, s.3A(1)(c) as inserted by FA 1986, s.101, Sch.19, para.1.
[3] The fact that a gift of shares transferred into a discretionary trust was not a potentially exempt transfer and that IHT was immediately chargeable led to a successful professional negligence claim. The solicitor and counsel advising the settlor failed to point out the adverse IHT

Charge to tax in respect of settlements created on or after March 22, 2006

All inter vivos settlements set up on or after March 22, 2006 are within the charging regime for relevant property trusts with the exception only of a trust for a disabled beneficiary falling within the definition of "a disabled persons interest" in IHTA 1984, s.89B.[4] Accordingly, as had been the case in respect of discretionary trusts before March 22, 2006— **16.02**

(i) the creation of the trust will be an immediately chargeable transfer by the settlor and so tax will be payable if the value transferred exceeds the settlor's available IHT nil rate band[5];

(ii) CGT hold-over relief will be available unless the trust is settlor-interested.[6]

EXAMPLE 16.2

Taking the settlements considered in Example 16.1 and assuming that they were set up on or after March 22, 2006 the position is as follows:

(1) S establishes a relevant property trust and it is irrelevant that he has retained a life interest. IHT will therefore be payable (at 20 per cent) on the excess transferred above his available IHT nil rate band. The value of the interest retained is ignored in valuing S's estate so that the fall in value is £500,000 (plus, if appropriate, grossing up).[7] No longer is the property still comprised in his estate (because he does not enjoy a qualifying interest in possession within s.49(1)). Is S taxed on the settled property on his death?

The actuarial value of the life interest is not taxed on his death because it is now ignored when valuing his estate.[8] Could HMRC successfully argue that the retention of a life interest involves a reservation of benefit? It may be said that the retention of the life interest is a carve-out: i.e. that what he has given away is the remainder interest in which he has reserved no benefit.[9] He has not gifted the right to receive the income because he has always had it. Hence the value of the settled property is not taxed on his death under FA 1986, s.102(3).

This carve out argument would be fatally weakened if the trustees had a power to apply capital for his benefit which would be viewed as detracting from the gifted remainder interest. Further the carve out argument does not apply if the gifted property was an interest in land, given the wider provisions of s.102A FA, 1986.

---

consequences of creating a discretionary settlement when an interest in possession trust should have been considered. See *Estill v Cowling Swift and Kirchin* [2000] Lloyd's Rep PN 378.

[4] On trusts for a disabled beneficiary see Ch. 26.
[5] In general the charge is at half the IHT death rates: i.e. 0 per cent up to £285,000 and at 20 per cent on the excess. If tax is paid by the settlor grossing up will apply: see 16.04, below.
[6] See Ch. 19.
[7] See Ch. 20.
[8] See IHTA 1984, s.5(1)(a)(ii).
[9] See further 16.07, below.

If the arrangement is not caught by reservation of benefit the question of a pre-owned assets income tax charge becomes relevant. For example if the property which was settled comprised cash and S retains an entitlement to income, he would be subject to POA under FA 2004, Sch.15, para.8 since none of the let outs apply. It might be possible for S to circumvent this POA charge by settling cash if the trustees immediately invested it in let property (then the para.8 charge is inapplicable and because S is not in occupation the land charge under para.3 does not apply). Alternatively POA is avoided if S settles let chattels.

(2) The creation of this trust for the spouse will likewise be taxed as a relevant property settlement and no spouse exemption will be available. Assuming that the settlor has not himself reserved any benefit, the reservation of benefit provisions will not apply to him.

Will Trusts

16.03 The long standing rules continue to apply to the creation of will trusts: generally tax is charged unless e.g. the spouse exemption applies (as in para.(2) of Example 16.1).

Even after the 2006 changes it remains possible to create a qualifying interest in possession trust by will: known as an IPDI ("immediate post death interest"): see Chapter 19.

EXAMPLE 16.3

By his will Ferralty left a pecuniary legacy of £200,000 to her son Crysalis for life remainder to his child and the residue of her estate to her husband Alan for life remainder to the UFO society. She died in 2007: both Crysalis and Alan have IPDI's. Accordingly while the gift on trust for Crysalis is chargeable (but falls within Ferralty's nil rate band) the gift of residue is spouse exempt.

Liability to tax[10]

16.04 If any IHT payable on creation of the trust is paid by the trustees, the settlor does not as a result retain an interest in the settlement for income tax purposes.[11] If the IHT is paid by the settlor then he will suffer a greater fall in the value of his estate and this process is known as grossing-up.

---

[10] For the duty to deliver accounts and information see IHTA 1984, s.216 as amended and for the reporting requirements when non-resident trusts are established, see IHTA 1984, s.218. See also Ch. 35.

[11] SP 1/82. As to whether an agreement that the trustees should pay inheritance tax amounts to a reservation of benefit, see (1987) 84 L.S. Gaz. No. 14, 1041.

EXAMPLE 16.4

In June 2007, S transfers Blackacre worth £600,000 into a trust for his son. This is an immediately chargeable transfer by S and, assuming that he has a nil rate band of £300,000 available, the IHT position is as follows—

(i) *If S pays the tax* the transfer of value, ignoring S's annual exemption (s), will be grossed up as follows:

	£
total chargeable transfer of value	600,000
deduct nil rate amount	300,000
(a) amount chargeable	300,000

Gross up (a) by multiplying it by $^{100}/_{100} - R$
where R is the rate of IHT applicable. The calculation is—
(b) £300,000 × $^{100}/_{80}$ = £375,000.
Hence S's transfer of value is £675,000 and his tax liability £75,000.

(ii) *If the trustees pay the tax*, the chargeable transfer is limited to £300,000 and tax payable is *£60,000*. Note also that in this case the tax can be paid by instalments over 10 years.[12]

16.05 Primary liability for inheritance tax arising during the course of the settlement rests upon the trustees. Their liability is limited to the property which they have received or disposed of or become liable to account for to a beneficiary and such other property which they would have received but for their own neglect or default.

If trustees fail to pay, HMRC can collect IHT from any of the following[13]:

(i) Any person entitled to an interest in possession in the settled property. The liability of such person is limited to the value of the trust property, out of which he can claim an indemnity for the tax he has paid.
(ii) Any beneficiary under a discretionary trust up to the value of the property that he receives (after paying income tax on it) and with no right to an indemnity for the tax he is called upon to pay.
(iii) The settlor, where the trustees are resident outside the UK, because, if the trustees do not pay, HMRC cannot enforce payment abroad. A settlor who pays tax has a right to recover it from the trust.

RESERVATION OF BENEFIT ON SETTING UP A TRUST

16.06 The creation of *inter vivos* settlements can lead to problems in the reservation of benefit area or exceptionally to an income tax charge on the settlor under

---

[12] IHTA 1984, s.227.
[13] See IHTA 1984, s.201(1) and Ch. 35.

the pre-owned asset rules. The matters set out in the following paragraphs are especially worthy of note.

(i) Settlor appoints himself a trustee

16.07 If the settlor appoints himself a trustee of his settlement, that appointment does not by itself amount to a reserved benefit. A settlor may therefore retain control over the settled property. If the terms of the settlement provide for his remuneration as trustee, however, there may be a reservation in the settled property.[14] One way of overcoming this is for the settlor-trustee to be paid by an annuity, as such an arrangement will not constitute a reserved benefit and the ending of that annuity will not lead to any IHT charge.[15]

Particular difficulties are caused if the settlor-trustee is a director of a company whose shares are held in the trust fund. The general rule of equity is that a trustee may not profit from his position and this means that he will generally have to account for any director's fees that he may receive. It is standard practice, however, for the trust deed to provide that a trustee need not in such cases account for those fees. When the settlor-trustee is allowed to retain fees under the deed it is arguable that he has reserved a benefit in the trust assets. HMRC have however, indicated that they will not take this point so long as the director's remuneration "involves the continuance of reasonable commercial arrangements".[16]

(ii) Settlor reserves an interest for himself

16.08 If the settlor reserves an interest for himself under his settlement, whether he does so expressly or whether his interest arises by operation of law, there may be no reservation of benefit but instead he is treated as making a partial gift (this is a species of "carve-out").

EXAMPLE 16.5

> S created a settlement for his minor son, absolutely on attaining 21 years. No provision is made for what should happen if the son were to die before that age, and so there is a resulting trust to the settlor. The settlor has not reserved a benefit. Instead, he has made a partial gift; i.e. a gift of the settled property less the retained remainder interest in it.[17]

---

[14] *Oakes v Comr of Stamp Duties of New South Wales* [1954] A.C. 57, [1953] 2 All E.R. 1563, PC. It is understood that HMRC do not at present take this point: see IHTM 14334 provided "the fee is entirely reasonable."
[15] IHTA 1984, s.90. The retention of an annuity is seen as a "carve-out": i.e. property not given to the trustees.
[16] See HMRC letters of February 19, 1987, March 5, 1987, and May 18, 1987.
[17] *Stamp Duties Comr (New South Wales) v Perpetual Trustee Co Ltd* [1943] A.C. 425, [1943] 1 All E.R. 525, PC; see also *Cochrane v IRC* [1974] S.T.C. 335 where the settlor expressly reserved

If the settlor is one of the class of beneficiaries in a discretionary trust, he is not entirely excluded from the trust property. In view of the limited nature of a discretionary beneficiary's rights[18] he cannot be treated as making a partial gift. Hence, he will be treated as having reserved a benefit in the entire settled fund despite the fact that he may receive no benefit from it.[19] By contrast, the inclusion of the settlor's spouse as a discretionary beneficiary does not result in a reserved benefit. Were that spouse to receive property from the settlement, however, which was then shared with or used for the benefit of the settlor, HMRC may argue that he has reserved a benefit.

(iii) Gift to a spouse

The reservation of benefit rules did not apply to an exempt gift to a spouse. **16.09** Accordingly, it was possible to channel a benefit through a spouse.

EXAMPLE 16.6

> A settles property on his wife B for life and subject to this on discretionary trusts for a class of beneficiaries which includes A. B's life interest terminates after six months. A has not reserved any benefit since the gift is spouse exempt although he is one of the objects of the discretionary trust.[20]

This was prevented by the *anti-Eversden* legislation: see Chapter 31.

(iv) Cash gifts

As explained at 31.74 and in Chapter 24, outright cash gifts are not subject to the tracing provisions and are therefore a way of circumventing the reservation of benefit provisions.[21] However, cash gifts to a trust are not within para.2 at all but have their own tracing provisions in para.5. Hence if A gives cash to a trust which then purchases property in which he lives, he has reserved a benefit. Paragraph 5 does, however, contain inadequate tracing

---

surplus income. For a general consideration of so-called "shearing operations" see *Ingram (executors of Lady Ingram) v IRC* [2000] 1 A.C. 293; [1999] S.T.C. 37, HL and 13.14 and 31.34. The interest retained must be identified with some precision: classically it will be a reversionary interest. If this could be accelerated by the exercise of an overriding power of appointment, query whether a reservation of benefit then arises.
[18] See *Gartside v IRC* [1968] A.C. 553; [1968] 1 All E.R. 121, HL.
[19] See *IRC v Eversden* [2003] EWCA Civ 668, [2003] S.T.C. 822. It is thought that a similar result arises if the settlor, although not a discretionary beneficiary, is capable of becoming such a beneficiary (e.g. under a power to add to the class of beneficiaries).
[20] See *IRC v Eversden* [2003] EWCA Civ 668; [2003] S.T.C. 822 at [25].
[21] See Sch.20, para.2(b) of FA 1986.

provisions in respect of property coming out of the trust and these weaknesses are considered in Chapter 24.

IMPACT OF THE PRE-OWNED ASSETS CHARGE

16.10 The pre-owned assets charge is considered in Chapter 24.

CHAPTER 17

QUALIFYING INTEREST IN POSSESSION TRUSTS

- IHT treatment of a beneficiary entitled to a qualifying IIP **(17.03)**
- The nature of a non-qualifying IIP **(17.05)**
- Multiple IIP beneficiaries **(17.07)**
- Leases for life **(17.09)**
- Actual terminations **(17.11)**
- Deemed terminations **(17.12)**
- Purchase of reversionary interests **(17.15)**
- Depreciatory transactions **(17.16)**
- Exemptions and reliefs **(17.17)**
- Taxation of reversionary interests **(17.27)**

Scope of this Chapter

It is important to bear in mind that not all interest in possession trusts contain a "*qualifying*" interest in possession. As a result of changes effected by FA 2006, new *inter vivos* settlements will only be qualifying if the interest is a disabled person's interest within IHTA 1984, s.89B(1)(c) or (d).[1] A non-qualifying interest in possession settlement is taxed in accordance with the relevant property regime.[2] It remains possible to set up a qualifying interest in possession trust *by will* (this is an "IPDI")[3] and the definition of a qualifying interest in possession extends to an interest in possession to which an individual was entitled on March 22, 2006 and to a successive interest in possession in that settlement (a "transitional serial interest").[4]

17.01

EXAMPLE 17.1

(1) Under the Willie Wonker trust, which was set up in 1999, Willie is entitled to an interest in possession. On his death his son, Dilly, takes an

---
[1] This provision was inserted by FA 2006, Sch.20, para.6 in respect of trusts created on or after March 22, 2006. See 19.02 for the full definition, and Ch. 2.6.
[2] i.e. under IHTA 1984, Pt III Ch. III, see s.59(2) amended by FA 2006, Sch.20, para.20.
[3] "Immediate Post Death Interest": see IHTA 1984, s.49A inserted by FA 2006, Sch.20, para.5.
[4] IHTA 1984, s.49B–E inserted by FA 2006, Sch.20, para.5.

interest in possession with remainder over to a chocolate charity. Willie has a qualifying interest in possession. If his interest ends before April 6, 2008 Dilly will, in turn, become entitled to a qualifying interest in possession (a TSI). If, however, Willie's interest ends in 2009, Dilly's interest will not be qualifying and the trust will be taxed as a relevant property settlement.[5]

(2) Mindful of the attentions of his creditors, Nasty put his assets into a life interest trust for his wife in 2007. Mrs Nasty does not enjoy a qualifying interest in possession. The trust is taxed as a relevant property settlement.[6]

(3) By his will Theakston leaves his entire estate to his son for life then to his daughter in law for life with remainder to his grandchildren. On Theakston's death—whenever that occurs—the son enjoys a qualifying interest in possession (an IPDI if the death is after March 21, 2006 otherwise a qualifying iip under the old rules). The daughter in law's successive life interest will also be qualifying but only if Theakston dies before March 22, 2006 and her interest vests in possession either before April 6, 2008 or, if later, on the son's death (in these cases it will be a transitional serial interest).[7]

17.02 This Chapter is concerned with the IHT treatment of *qualifying* interests in possession. It is therefore important to bear in mind:

(i) That in considering whether the provisions discussed in this chapter apply the first stage is to consider whether the settlement creates an interest in possession[8]; and

(ii) If it does, whether that interest is qualifying.

IHT TREATMENT OF A BENEFICIARY ENTITLED TO A QUALIFYING INTEREST IN POSSESSION

17.03 The beneficiary entitled to income of a fund (usually the life tenant) is treated as owning that portion of the capital of the fund:

> "a person beneficially entitled to an interest in possession in settled property shall be treated for the purposes of the Act as beneficially entitled to the property in which the interest subsists."[9]

---

[5] Transitional Serial Interests are considered in detail at 18.14 *et seq*.
[6] Note that the spouse exemption is not available on creation of the trust: see Ch. 16.
[7] IPDIs are considered in detail in Ch. 19.
[8] Notice that the new tax treatment in FA 2006 has not affected the meaning of an interest in possession for IHT purposes—see 15.19 *et seq*. (Of course in the case of new *inter vivos* settlements the question will generally be irrelevant for inheritance tax purposes although whether someone has an interest in possession (even if not qualifying) can affect the availability of certain capital gains tax reliefs—for example taper relief and hold-over relief, and has income tax implications: see 4.25, 7.13 and Ch. 9). Some settlement deeds provide that the term "interest in possession" when used in the deed is to have its IHT meaning. It follows that such a definition does not present a problem post FA 2006 although this drafting practice is likely to end with the restriction of qualifying status in the case of new interest in possession settlements.
[9] IHTA 1984, s.49(1).

This rule is a fiction because in no real sense is the interest in possession beneficiary the owner of the capital in the fund. For IHT purposes, however, the capital forms part of his estate, so that on a chargeable occasion inheritance tax is charged on the trust fund at his rates. The settlement itself is not a separate taxable entity (contrast the rules for relevant property trusts),[10] although primary liability for any tax falls upon the trustees.[11]

The meaning of a reversionary interest

As the interest in possession beneficiary (typically a life tenant) is treated as owning all the capital in the trust, other beneficiaries with "reversionary interests" own nothing. "Reversionary interest" is defined in the legislation as: 17.04

> "a future interest under a settlement, whether it is vested or contingent (including an interest expectant on the termination of an interest in possession which, by virtue of section 50 . . ., is treated as subsisting in part of any property)".[12]

Generally, reversionary interests are excluded property and can be assigned without charge to IHT. It is not thought that the term catches the interests of discretionary beneficiaries because such rights as they possess (to compel due administration of the trust, to be considered and jointly to wind up the trust) are present rights. Their interests are neither in possession nor in reversion.

THE NATURE OF A NON-QUALIFYING INTEREST IN POSSESSION

The fictional entitlement posited by s.49(1) does not apply. However, a beneficiary who enjoys a non-qualifying interest in possession in a trust fund[13] may still have the benefit of a valuable *chose in action*. For IHT purposes: 17.05

(i) The interest is not a reversionary interest (i.e. it is not thereby made excluded property); *but*

(ii) IHTA 1984, s 5(1)(ii) and (1A)[14] provides that the estate of a person does not include a non-qualifying interest in possession.

---

[10] As to the treatment of relevant property trusts see Ch. 20.
[11] IHTA 1984, s.201.
[12] IHTA 1984, s.47. It follows that the assignment of a reversionary interest can have advantageous IHT consequences in terms of tax planning (for CGT purposes no chargeable gain will normally result on any assignment: see TCGA 1992, s.76(1) as amended by the FA 1998, s.128 and Ch. 8). For instance, A is entitled to a qualifying iip and is aged 80 and on his death the property passes to B, aged 79, absolutely. There is the prospect of two tax charges on the trust if A and B were to die in that order. Whilst a measure of quick succession relief might be available (see IHTA 1984, s.141) the IHT position would be improved if before A's death B assigned his reversionary interest, e.g. to his young grandson.
[13] i.e. one that arose post March 21, 2006 and is not a transitional serial interest.
[14] Inserted by FA 2006, Sch.20, paras 7 and 10.

Interestingly, therefore, a potentially valuable asset has been taken out of the IHT net.

EXAMPLE 17.2

(1) Jason sets up a settlement on June 1, 2006 giving his son, Fleece, then aged 30, an interest in possession. Sadly Fleece dies, wholly unexpectedly, shortly afterwards.

For IHT purposes the interest in possession is non-qualifying and Jason has created a relevant property settlement. On Fleece's death his estate does not include the interest in possession. Of course, if the settlement ends at that time the normal "exit" charge under the relevant property regime may apply.[15]

(2) Cunning's son enjoys a life interest in a family settlement the assets of which are worth £1m. The actuarial value of that life interest (taking into account the age of the son and income produced by the assets) is £100,000. Assuming that Cunning purchases the interest for £100,000, the IHT consequences are as follows—

   (i) Cunning's estate for IHT purposes is reduced by £100,000 (given that no value is to be included for the life interest);
   (ii) *but* provided that the arrangement is commercial the reduction in value does not give rise to an IHT charge: see IHTA 1984, s.10(1);
   (iii) the disposal of the life interest by the son will not normally give rise to a CGT charge[16];
   (iv) if the son's interest was a "qualifying" interest in possession its sale would have IHT consequences[17] but if it was non-qualifying then its disposal does not trigger the charging mechanism under the relevant property regime.

Consequences of the s.49(1) fiction

17.06 The value of the settled property is aggregated with the value of the estate of the interest in possession beneficiary. The consequences of this on the death of the beneficiary are illustrated in *Example 17.8* below. It would appear, however, that such aggregation does not apply for all purposes. If the beneficiary's free estate is insufficient to discharge his personal liabilities these cannot be deducted, for IHT purposes, against the value of settled property in which he had enjoyed an interest in possession.[18] In *St Barbe Green v IRC*[19] the deceased died with an insolvent estate and was the life tenant in certain

---

[15] See Ch. 20. At current rates the exit charge will be at something less than 6 per cent.
[16] See TCGA 1992, s.76(1) and Ch. 8.
[17] See IHTA 1984, s.51 and 17.12.
[18] It will be appreciated that as a matter of general law creditors of the deceased in such a case will have no right to claim against settled assets (save in exceptional cases, e.g. where the settlement had been set up by the deceased to put assets out of their reach).
[19] [2005] S.T.C. 288.

assets under three family settlements. Mann J. held that the net liabilities were not available to reduce the estate beyond the value of the free estate's assets that were available to meet them.[20]

MULTIPLE IIP BENEFICIARIES

17.07 The beneficiary entitled to a qualifying interest in possession is treated as being the beneficial owner of the trust property, or an appropriate part of that property. If there is more than one such beneficiary, it is necessary to apportion the settlement property between those beneficiaries.[21]

A beneficiary who has the right to the income of the fund for a period shorter than his lifetime (however short the period) is still treated for IHT purposes as owning the entire settled fund. (This assumes he has a qualifying interest in possession under s.49(1)). In cases where a beneficiary is not entitled to income but is entitled to use the capital assets in the fund, he is treated as owning those assets. If the entitlement to use is enjoyed by more than one beneficiary, the value of the fund is apportioned in accordance with the "annual value" of their respective interests.[22] Annual value is not defined.

EXAMPLE 17.3

> A and B, are jointly entitled to occupy property which is worth £750,000. That entitlement arose prior to March 22, 2006 and therefore they have qualifying iips. This capital value must be apportioned to A and B in proportion to the annual value of their respective interests. If their interests are equal the apportionment will be as to £350,000 each. If A dies, his half share (with no discount for joint ownership) is aggravated with his free estate and the value of his nil rate band opportioned *pro rata*. Note that if they were given an entitlement to occupy property under an *inter vivos* settlement established on or after March 22, 2006 such entitlement would not be a qualifying iip. The capital value would then not be apportioned to A and B.

---

[20] He was influenced by the decision in the estate duty case of *Re Barnes* [1938] 2 K.B. 684 of Lawrence J. who in the context of that legislation had commented that "I do not see how, in determining the value of an estate, allowance can be made for debts beyond the value of the assets out of which the debts are to be met". Mann J. concluded that, despite the different wording in IHTA 1984, s.5(3) which requires liabilities to be taken into account, Parliament would not have intended to change the estate duty position and allow a deduction in the situation where the property in question is not accountable for the payment of the debts. A similar result will occur in the case of property treated as part of a deceased's estate under the reservation of benefit rules: see Ch. 23.

[21] IHTA 1984, s.50(1).

[22] IHTA 1984, s.50(5). It is a moot point whether the decision by trustees of land under the Trusts of Land and Appointment of Trustees Act 1996, s.13 to exclude an interest in possession beneficiary from occupying trust property changes the IHT position: see "Trusts of land: new Act" 94 LS Gaz January 22, 1997 at p.30. On rights to occupy, see *Woodhall v IRC* [2000] S.T.C. (S.C.D.) 558.

Beneficiary entitled to a fixed income (including an annuitant)

17.08 Difficulties may arise where one beneficiary is entitled to a fixed amount of income each year (for example an annuity) and the remaining income is paid to another beneficiary. (This assumes that the annuity interest and remaining income give the beneficiaries qualifying iips under s.49(1).) If the amounts of income paid to the two were compared in the year when a chargeable event occurred, a tax saving could be engineered. Assume, for instance, that the annuity interest terminates so that IHT is charged on its value. The proportion of capital attributable to that interest and, therefore, the IHT would be reduced if the trustees invested in assets producing a high income in that year. As a result, a relatively small proportion of the total income would be payable to the annuitant who would be treated as owning an equivalently small portion of the capital. By contrast, when a chargeable event affects the interest in the residue of the income (for example, through termination) the trustees could switch the assets into low income producers, thereby achieving a similar reduction in inheritance tax.

IHTA 1984, s.50(3) is designed to counter such schemes by providing that the Treasury may prescribe higher and lower income yields which take effect as limits beyond which any fluctuations in the actual income of the fund are ignored.[23]

EXAMPLE 17.4

> The value of the assets settled in 2005 is £500,000; annual income £15,000. A is entitled to an annuity of £5,000 a year; B to the balance of the income. If there is a chargeable transfer affecting the annuity, A is not treated as owning £33,333 of the capital ($\frac{5,000}{15,000} \times £500,000$) but instead a proportion of the Treasury prescribed higher rate yield.
>
> Assume that the prescribed higher rate is 6% on the relevant date; the calculation is: Notional income = 6% of £500,000 = £30,000. A's annuity is £5,000; as a proportion of income it is £5,000/£30,000; A's share of the capital is, therefore, $\frac{6,000}{30,000} \times £500,000 = £100,000$.
>
> This calculation is used whenever the actual income yield exceeds the prescribed higher rate. The calculation cannot lead to a charge in excess of the total value of the fund.
>
> When a chargeable transfer affecting the interest in the balance of the income occurs, if the actual income produced falls below the prescribed lower rate, the calculation proceeds as if the fund yielded that rate. If both interests in the settlement are chargeable on the same occasion, the prescribed rates do not apply because the entire fund is chargeable.

---

[23] See the Capital Transfer Tax (Settled Property Income Yield) Order 1980, SI 1980/1000. See also App. III 3A.144.

Lease treated as a settlement

17.09 When a lease is treated as a settlement (for example a lease for life or lives not granted for full consideration), prior to March 22, 2006 the tenant was treated as owning the whole of the leased property save for any part treated as belonging to the landlord.[24] To calculate the landlord's portion it was necessary to compare what he received when the lease was granted with what would have been a full consideration for the lease at that time.[25]

EXAMPLE 17.5

(1) Land worth £100,000 is let to A for his life in 2005. The landlord receives no consideration so that A is treated as owning the whole of the leased property (i.e. £100,000). The granting of the lease is a transfer of value by the landlord of £100,000. This was a PET in 2005 (assuming A was not the landlord's spouse).

(2) As above, save that full consideration is furnished. The lease is not treated as a settlement.[26] No inheritance tax will be chargeable on its creation as the landlord's estate does not fall in value.

(3) Partial consideration (equivalent to 50% of a full consideration) is furnished so that the value of the landlord's interest is 50% of £100,000 = £50,000. The value of the tenant's interest is £50,000 and the granting of the lease is a transfer of value of £50,000.

(4) Assume the facts are as in (1) above except that the land is let to A for life in 2007. The landlord is treated as making a transfer of value of £100,000 but this is now a chargeable transfer not a PET. A is not treated as owning the whole of the leased property but the lease is held in a relevant property settlement.

When inheritance tax is charged

17.10 IHT may be charged whenever a qualifying interest in possession terminates. This may occur *inter vivos* or on death.[27] There are two types of terminations: actual and deemed. Actual terminations occur where the interest in possession of the beneficiary ceases (e.g. on his death or because the terms of the settlement provide it must end on the occurrence of a specific event such as remarriage) or it ends because the trustees exercise overriding powers which terminate the interest in possession.

---

[24] See 15.04.
[25] IHTA 1984, ss.50(6), 170.
[26] As to the meaning of "settlement" see 15.01.
[27] For the charge on lifetime terminations, see IHTA 1984, s.52 and note that the disposal of an interest (e.g. an assignment for value) is treated as the coming to an end of the interest: *ibid.*, s.51. The charge on death of the interest in possession beneficiary arises as a result of the combination of *ibid.*, s.49(1) and s.4(1).

Deemed terminations occur where the interest in possession continues but the person who was entitled to that interest ceases to own it. For example, a life tenant assigns his right to receive the income to another person.

ACTUAL TERMINATIONS

17.11 The IHT charge is calculated on the basis that the life tenant had made a transfer of value at that time and the value transferred had been equal to the value of the property in which his interest subsisted.[28]

EXAMPLE 17.6

£100,000 is held on qualifying iip trust for A for life or until remarriage and thereafter for B absolutely. If A remarries, his life interest terminates and he makes a transfer of value of £100,000. (The trustees should be aware of the IHT position and not hand the trust assets over to B without suitable protection.)

If A never remarried, but consented to an advancement of £50,000 to B, his interest ends in that portion of the fund and he makes a transfer of value of £50,000. Assume that three years later, A surrenders his life interest in the fund, now worth £120,000. This is another transfer of value.

Notice that in all cases of the *inter vivos* termination of the interest in possession, any tax charge is levied on a value transferred which is "equal to the value of the property in which his interest subsisted".[29] The principle of calculating loss to the donor's estate (as is normally the case for IHT purposes) does not apply in these cases.

EXAMPLE 17.7

Jackson has a qualifying interest in possession in a family trust which owns 20% of the shares in the family investment company. He owns a further 35% personally. Jackson surrenders his interest in possession and the shares in the trust pass to his daughter Lee. For the purpose of valuing Jackson's transfer of value only the property in the settlement is taken into account: i.e. the value of a minority 20% shareholding. Contrast the position if Jackson died when the aggregation of the trust shareholding with his personal shareholding would result in an IHT charge based on the value of a 55% shareholding.[30]

---

[28] IHTA 1984, s.52(1).
[29] IHTA 1984, s.52(1).
[30] HMRC formerly took the view that on lifetime terminations the settled shares were required to be valued as part of Jackson's whole estate so that the value transferred would be based on a 20 per cent disposal out of a majority shareholding. The practice was changed in March 1990.

Since on an actual termination of the qualifying iip the beneficiary is deemed to make a transfer of value under s.52(1) it would appear that the "no gratuitous intention, commercial transactions" exemption in s.10 is not available.[31]

DEEMED TERMINATIONS

17.12 If the beneficiary disposes of his beneficial interest in possession, that disposal "*is not a transfer of value, but shall be treated . . . as the coming to an end of his interest*".[32] The absence of gratuitous intent does not prevent an IHT charge on the termination of beneficial interests in possession. The value transferred is the value of the settled property in which the interest had subsisted less any consideration received for the disposal. Note that the beneficiary cannot rely on "the no gratuitous intention, commercial transactions" exemption in s.10 IHTA, 1984 because s.10 only relieves dispositions that would otherwise have been transfers of value. The disposal of a life interest in the settlement is not itself a transfer of value.

EXAMPLE 17.8

(1) A assigns by way of gift his life interest to C. For IHT purposes it is as if that life interest had terminated and A has made a transfer of value. C becomes a tenant *pur autre vie* and when A dies C's interest in possession terminates so raising the possibility of a further IHT charge.

(2) If, instead of gifting his interest, A sells it to C for £20,000 (actuarial value) at a time when the property in the trust fund was worth £100,000, A's interest is treated as terminating and is equal to the fall in his estate of £80,000 (£100,000–£20,000).[33]

Partition of the fund

17.13 A partition of the fund between life tenant and remainderman causes the interest in possession to terminate and the life tenant makes a transfer of

---

[31] Indeed even if he received consideration for consenting to that termination arguably this would not reduce the value transferred. Section 52(2) does not apply because the interest is not *being disposed of* by him but ended by the trustees.
  Suppose the life tenant agrees to consent to the advancement of half the settled property in which he has a qualifying iip so that it is held on iip trusts for his former spouse. The consent is given as part of the arrangements on a divorce settlement. Section 10 would not give protection. The iip for his spouse is not qualifying after April 6, 2008, hence there is a chargeable transfer with possibly 20 per cent IHT payable.

[32] IHTA 1984, s.51(1).

[33] IHTA 1984, s.52(2): note that if the consideration received by the iip beneficiary is a reversionary interest in the property or any other interest in the settlement, no deduction is allowed for the value of such an interest. Note also that s.52(2) applies only to an interest which "comes to an end *by being disposed of* by the person beneficially entitled thereto" and not to actual terminations of the qualifying iip either directly under s.52(1) or on death. In *Example 17.8(1)* C, the assignee, will in appropriate cases take a transitional serial interest (a "TSI"): see 18.14.

value equal to the value of that portion of the trust fund passing to the remainderman.

EXAMPLE 17.9

A (the life tenant) and B (the remainderman) partition a £100,000 fund in the proportions 40:60. A is treated as making transfer of value of £60,000 (£100,000–£40,000). Any tax payable will come out of the fund to be divided.[34]

Capital vesting in the interest in possession beneficiary

17.14 If all or part of the capital of the fund is paid to the interest in possession beneficiary (normally under an express power in the trust deed), or if he becomes absolutely entitled to the capital (for example on satisfying a contingency), his interest in possession determines *pro tanto*, but he does not make a transfer of value because there is no fall in the value of his estate.

EXAMPLE 17.10

Property is settled on an IPDI trust for D for life, capital at 30. (D is 18 at the date of the testator's death and therefore takes a qualifying iip since he is entitled to the income of the settlement.[35]) At age 30, that interest terminates, but, as he is now absolutely entitled to the capital, he does not make a transfer of value. There is a deemed disposal of the settled property for CGT purposes. See 7.38.

PURCHASE OF REVERSIONARY INTERESTS[36]

17.15 As the interest in possession beneficiary owns the fund for IHT purposes it follows that his potential tax bill could be reduced were he to purchase a reversionary interest in the settlement. To prevent this result, the reversionary interest is not valued as a part of the life tenant's estate at the time of its purchase (thereby ensuring that his estate has fallen in value); and the commercial bargain exemption[37] does not apply, thereby ensuring that the fall in value may be subject to charge even though there is no donative intent.

Assume, for instance, that B has £60,000 in his bank account and is the life

---

[34] Costs incurred by the testator may be deducted from the value transferred: see IHTM 16094.
[35] TA 1925, s.31 as amended by the Family Law Reform Act 1969, s.1(3), Sch.1 Pt I, TA 2000, s.40(1), Sch.2, para.25.
[36] See IHTA 1984, ss.10, 55(1) as amended by FA 1987, s.58, Sch.8, para.1 and 22.44.
[37] As to dispositions not intended to confer gratuitous benefit, see IHTA 1984, s.10 as amended.

tenant of a fund with a capital value of £100,000 (on his death the fund passes to C absolutely). For inheritance tax purposes, B is treated as owning £160,000. If B were to purchase the reversionary interest in the settlement from C, however, for its market value of £60,000, the result would be as follows:

(i) B's estate would not appear to have fallen in value. Originally it included £60,000; after the purchase it includes a reversionary interest worth £60,000 since it ceased to be excluded property once purchased by B.[38]
(ii) B's estate now consists of the settlement fund valued at £100,000 and has been depleted by the £60,000 paid for the reversionary interest so that a possible charge to inheritance tax on £60,000 has been avoided.

However, as the reversionary interest is not valued as part of B's estate, by paying £60,000 for it B has made a transfer of value of £60,000. This will be a chargeable transfer by B. C previously owned a reversionary interest worth £60,000 and now has cash of £60,000. The reversionary interest was part of his estate even though not taxed on his death (because it was excluded property) and therefore the £60,000 he receives has not increased his estate. So far as C is concerned the transaction is a "nothing".

DEPRECIATORY TRANSACTIONS

When the value of the trust fund is diminished by a depreciatory transaction entered into between the trustees and a beneficiary (or persons connected with him), tax is charged as if the fall in value were a partial termination of the interest in possession.[39] A commercial transaction lacking gratuitous intent is not caught by this provision. In *IRC v Macpherson*[40] the value of pictures held in a trust fund was diminished by an arrangement with a person connected with a beneficiary that, in return for taking over care, custody and insurance of the pictures, he was entitled to keep the pictures for some 14 years. Although this arrangement was a commercial transaction, lacking gratuitous intent when looked at in isolation, it was associated with a subsequent operation (the appointment of a protected life interest) which did confer a gratuitous benefit so that the exception for commercial transactions did not apply and the reduction in value of the fund was subject to charge.

17.16

EXAMPLE 17.11

> Trustees grant a 50 year lease of a property worth £100,000 at a peppercorn rent to the brother of a reversionary beneficiary. As a result the property left in the settlement is the freehold reversion worth only £20,000. The granting of the lease is a depreciatory transaction which

---

[38] IHTA, s.48(1)(a).
[39] IHTA 1984, s.52(3): contrast the differently worded provisions in IHTA 1984, Pt III Ch. III (relevant property) and in the bereaved minor trust and 18–25 (s.71D) trust legislation.
[40] *IRC v Macpherson* [1989] A.C. 159; [1988] 2 All E.R. 753, HL.

causes the value of the fund to fall by £80,000 and, as it is made with a person connected with a beneficiary, IHT may be levied as if the interest in possession in £80,000 had ended. (Contrast the position if the lease had been granted to the brother in return for a commercial rent.) Note that this deemed transfer of value cannot be a potentially exempt transfer: see IHTA 1984, s.3A(6).

EXEMPTIONS AND RELIEFS

(i) Reverter to settlor or spouse[41]

17.17 This exemption is considered in Chapter 27.

(ii) IHT exemptions

17.18 The spouse exemption may be available on the termination of the interest in possession if the person who then becomes entitled, is the beneficiary's spouse.[42]

Furthermore, the interest in possession beneficiary's annual exemption and the exemption for gifts in consideration of marriage may be available on the *inter vivos* termination of the interest if the beneficiary so elects.[43] Although there is no duty to report the making of a potentially exempt transfer, the life tenant should within six months give the appropriate notice to the trustees indicating that he wishes the transfer to be covered by his relevant exemption. If this procedure is carried out, the appropriate exemption will be available if needed.

(iii) Estate duty—surviving spouse exemption

17.19 The continuation of the estate duty relief available when property was left on death to a surviving spouse in such circumstances that the spouse was not competent to dispose of it (for example was given a life interest) is preserved by the Inheritance Tax Act 1984.[44] The first spouse must have died before November 13, 1974 and the relief ensures that tax is not charged on the termination of the surviving spouse's interest in the property (whether that occurs *inter vivos* or on death).[45]

---

[41] See IHTA 1984, s.53(3)–(5) for lifetime transfers and s.54(1), (2) for the exemption on death. For CGT position see TCGA 1992, s.73(1)(b) as amended by FA 1996, s.201, Sch.39, para.6(2), (4), (5).
[42] See IHTA 1984, s.18 and 18.02.
[43] See IHTA 1984, s.57.
[44] See IHTA 1984, s.273, Sch.6, para.2.
[45] Note that if the surviving spouse's interest is terminated during the spouse's lifetime there is no base cost uplift for capital gains tax purposes. In these circumstances it is generally preferable to let the surviving spouse retain the interest in possession until death in order to obtain the capital gains tax uplift.

(iv) Excluded property

17.20 If the settlement contains excluded property, inheritance tax is not charged on that portion of the fund.[46]

(v) Dispositions for maintenance of family

17.21 If the interest in possession is disposed of for the purpose of maintaining the beneficiary's child or supporting a dependent relative, IHT is not charged.[47] Section 51(2) provides that it shall not be treated as coming to an end.

EXAMPLE 17.12

> H is a life tenant under a settlement set up by his father in 1980. He assigns that life interest to his wife in 2009 as part of the arrangements made on their divorce. Assuming this is within s.11 as being for her maintenance, s.51(2) prevents this from being a transfer of value.[48]

(vi) Charities

17.22 Tax is not charged if on the termination of the interest in possession the property is held on trust for charitable purposes.[49]

(vii) Protective trusts

17.23 The forfeiture of a protected life interest is not chargeable.[50]

Variations and disclaimers

17.24 Dispositions of a deceased (made by will, on intestacy or otherwise) may be redirected after death by means of an instrument of variation or disclaimer without incurring a second IHT charge. Disclaimers are possible in the case both of settlements created by the deceased on his death[51] and for

---

[46] IHTA 1984, ss.5(1), 53(1).
[47] See IHTA 1984, s.11.
[48] See also Ch. 34. Contrast the position if the trustees terminated his interest and appointed the wife an iip: HMRC do not accept that a settlement of capital can be within the exemption.
[49] IHTA 1984, s.23.
[50] As to protective trusts see IHTA 1984, ss.73, 88 and 19.04.
[51] See IHTA 1984, s.142 as amended by the FA 1986, s.101(1), (3), Sch.19, para.24 and by the FA 2002, s.120(1).

pre-existing settlements in which the death has resulted in a person becoming entitled to an interest in the settled property.[52] Variations, on the other hand, are only permitted for settlements created on death by the deceased, not for settlements in which the deceased had been the beneficiary.

EXAMPLE 17.13

> If A by will leaves a life interest to his wife remainder to their daughter, Mrs A can accelerate the daughter's interest by a disclaimer of her life interest. Alternatively, if Mrs A has already received income from the interest (so that it is too late to disclaim), she may achieve the same result by a variation.[53]

Quick succession relief

17.25 This relief mirrors that for unsettled property. The first chargeable transfer may be either the creation of the settlement or any subsequent termination of an interest in possession (whether that termination occurs *inter vivos* or on death). Relief can therefore be engineered by the life tenant surrendering or assigning his interest (contrast unsettled property when it is only available on a death).[54]

Reliefs for business and agricultural property

17.26 In a settlement with a qualifying iip containing business property, that property is treated as belonging to the life tenant who as the transferor must fulfil the conditions for relief.[55] Similar principles operate for agricultural relief: i.e. the life tenant must satisfy the conditions of two years' occupation or seven years' ownership.[56]

TAXATION OF REVERSIONARY INTERESTS

17.27 As reversionary interests are generally excluded property[57] their disposition will not lead to an IHT charge. In the following cases, however, reversionary interests are not excluded property. (This is to prevent tax avoidance).[58]

---

[52] IHTA 1984, s.93.
[53] For variations and disclaimers, see Ch. 29 and note that the variation of a will involving the redirection of an interest in possession after the death of the beneficiary may not be possible under s.142.
[54] See IHTA Act 1984, s.141.
[55] As to business property relief, see IHTA 1984, ss.103–114.
[56] IHTA 1984, ss.115–124C. With the availability of relief at 100 per cent it is crucial to ensure wherever possible that the qualifying conditions are met. See Ch. 32.
[57] For the definition of a reversionary interest see 17.15 and 22.44.
[58] See IHTA 1984, s.48 as amended by the FA 1996, s.154(7), (9), Sch.28 para.8 and FA 2003, s.186.

(i) A sale of a reversionary interest to a beneficiary under the same trust, who is entitled to a prior interest[59];

(ii) A disposition of a reversionary interest which has at any time, and by any person, been acquired for a consideration in money or money's worth;

(iii) A disposition of a reversionary interest if it is one to which either the settlor or his spouse is, or has been, beneficially entitled;

(iv) The disposition of a reversionary interest where that interest is expectant upon the termination of a lease which is treated as a settlement. The result is that the landlord's reversion is treated in the same way as a reversionary interest purchased for money or money's worth so that on any disposition of it, IHT may be charged.

---

[59] As to the purchase of a reversionary interest by a life tenant, see 17.15.

CHAPTER 18

WHEN IHT IS CHARGED ON QUALIFYING INTEREST IN POSSESSION TRUSTS (INCLUDING TRANSITIONAL RELIEF)

- Background **(18.01)**
- How the rules operated before March 22, 2006 **(18.05)**
- The charging regime post March 21, 2006 **(18.13)**
- The meaning of a Transitional Serial Interest ("TSI") **(18.14)**

BACKGROUND

18.01 As discussed in Chapter 17:

(i) The interest in possession beneficiary is treated as the beneficial owner of the capital in the settlement.[1]

(ii) IHT may be payable on the termination of that interest which may occur during the lifetime of the beneficiary or on his death. There are circumstances where, for IHT purposes, the interest is deemed to terminate.

When tax is not payable on a termination

18.02 IHT will not be payable on the termination of a qualifying interest in possession if on that occasion the transfer is exempt from charge.

EXAMPLE 18.1

Property is held in trust for A for life with remainder to charity. On the termination of A's interest, whether that occurs *inter vivos* or on death IHT is not chargeable because of the exemption for gifts to charity.[2]

[1] IHTA 1984, s.49(1).
[2] IHTA 1984, s.23.

A similar result will occur if on the termination of A's life interest the property is held in trust for his spouse or civil partner absolutely. In this case the spouse exemption will prevent the charge from arising.[3]

When the termination is a potentially exempt transfer (a "PET")

FA 2006— 18.03

(i) severely restricts the scope for creating qualifying interests in possession; and

(ii) limits the PET definition so that (in general terms) a PET only applies to outright rather than settled gifts.

It follows that if on the inter vivos termination of a qualifying interest in possession the settlement continues the beneficiary will not make a PET[4] whereas if it ends at that time he will do so.[5] This contrasts strikingly with the rules that applied before March 22, 2006. At that time the termination of an interest in possession was generally treated as a PET—whether or not the settlement ended—unless there were continuing discretionary trusts. To deal with existing interest in possession trusts, FA 2006 provided for a measure of transitional relief which extends the PET definition (and qualifying interests in possession) to what the legislation terms "transitional serial interests" or "TSIs". (See 18.14 *et seq*.) 18.04

HOW THE RULES OPERATED BEFORE MARCH 22, 2006

FA 1986 originally restricted the definition of a PET[6] to exclude the creation of interest in possession settlements and chargeable occasions occurring during their continuance (e.g. the termination of the interest). This limitation, which cut across the principles of neutrality in the taxation of settlements and the fiction that the life tenant owned the fund, was imposed because of concern that the interest in possession trust would otherwise be used in schemes for IHT avoidance. It was feared that an interest in possession trust would be set up by a PET (thereby avoiding an immediate tax charge); terminated (thereby triggering an IHT charge but calculated according to the IHT rate of the chosen life tenant who would be a "man of straw"); and replaced by a discretionary trust. In this fashion the settlor would, in effect, create a discretionary trust by means of a potentially 18.05

---

[3] IHTA 1984, s.18. This assumes the spouse or civil partner is UK domiciled.
[4] Subject only to the rules for transitional serial interests discussed at 18.14.
[5] If there is an *inter vivos* termination of a non-qualifying interest in possession this is generally a non-event for inheritance tax purposes unless the settlement ends, in which case there could be an exit charge See IHTA 1984, s.52(2A).
[6] As to potentially exempt transfers see IHTA 1984, s.3A as inserted by the FA 1986, s.101, Sch.19 FA (No.2) para.1 and amended by ss.96(1)–(3), 104(4), Sch.9, Pt III. The definition has of course been further amended (restrictively) by FA 2006.

exempt transfer. In the event F(No 2)A 1987 extended the scope of the PET to interest in possession trusts, but continuing fears of abuse led to the introduction of complex anti-avoidance rules which are considered below.[7]

18.06 Accordingly, an actual or deemed termination of an interest in possession which occurred during the life of the relevant beneficiary was a potentially exempt transfer provided that the property was, after that event, held for one or more beneficiaries absolutely (so that the settlement was at an end), or for a further interest in possession or on accumulation and maintenance or disabled trusts. IHT was therefore only payable if the former interest in possession beneficiary died within seven years of the termination so that the PET failed. If the above requirements were not satisfied (for example where after the termination the fund was held on discretionary trusts) there was an immediate charge to tax on the termination of the interest in possession and the anti-avoidance rules could be triggered.[8]

EXAMPLE 18.2

(1) In 2003 S settled property on his daughter D for life, remainder to charity. The creation of the trust was a potentially exempt transfer and the anti-avoidance rules did not apply because the trust ended on D's death. At that time the charity exemption[9] will prevent a charge to tax from arising.

(2) In 2004 S settled property on a stranger, N, for life or until such time as the trustees determined his interest and thereafter the property was to be held on a discretionary trust for S's family and relatives. The creation of the trust was a potentially exempt transfer; a later termination of N's life interest was a chargeable transfer which could trigger the anti-avoidance rules if it occurred within seven years of the settlement (IHTA 1984, s.54(A)).

(3) In 2004 S settled property on D, his daughter, for life remainder to her twins at age 21 years. D surrendered her life interest in 2005 when the twins were (a) 17 years, or (b) 18 years, or (c) 21 years. The creation of the trust was a PET by S. If the life interest was surrendered at (a), the fund was then held on accumulation and maintenance trusts (a PET by D); if surrendered at (b), the transfer was to the twins as interest in possession beneficiaries (again a PET by D)); if surrendered at (c), the twins were absolutely entitled and so the settlement ended (a PET by D). Note that on the surrender of the life interest D has made a potentially exempt transfer. The anti-avoidance provisions do not apply to deem S to have made a further transfer of value in 2005, because no relevant property trusts arise.[10]

---

[7] As to the anti-avoidance provisions, see 18.08.
[8] *ibid*.
[9] IHTA 1984, s.23.
[10] See 18.08.

Charge on the death of the interest in possession beneficiary before March 22, 2006

As the assets in the settlement were treated as part of the estate of the deceased life tenant at the time of his death, IHT was charged on the settled fund at the estate rate appropriate to his estate. The tax attributable to the settled property was payable by the trustees. Notice that although the trustees pay this tax, the inclusion of the value of the fund in the deceased's estate could increase the estate rate, thereby causing a higher percentage charge on his free estate.

18.07

EXAMPLE 18.3

(1) A settlement consists of securities worth £500,000 and is held for A for life with remainder to A's son B for life. A dies on December 1, 2005 and the value of his free estate is £300,000; he had made a chargeable lifetime transfer of £75,000 six years before his death. The tax rate on transfers up to £275,000 is 0%, thereafter 40% (tax year 2005/06). Inheritance tax will be calculated as follows:

   (i) Chargeable death estate: £300,000 + £500,000 (the settlement) = £800,000.
   (ii) Join the inheritance tax table at £75,000 (point reached by lifetime transfers).
   (iii) Calculate death inheritance tax: £200,000 at 0% and £600,000 at 40% = £240,000.
   (iv) Convert to estate rate:

   $\frac{tax}{estate} \times 100$: i.e. $\frac{240,000}{800,000} \times 100 = 30\%$.

   (iv) Inheritance tax attributable to settled property is 30% of £500,000 = £150,000.

(2) If shortly before his death A had given away a further £200,000 by a PET that transfer is rendered chargeable because of his death within seven years. That transfer—along with the earlier £75,000 transfer—will exhaust his available IHT nil rate band. On his death the chargeable estate is therefore £600,000 which is taxed at 40% giving a liability of £240,000 which is now payable as to £200,000 by the trustees of the settled property.

(3) Since the nil rate band was allocated against the first transfer of value difficulties could arise if the life tenant's interest in possession was terminated *inter vivos*. For example, suppose H left his residuary estate worth £300,000 on interest in possession trusts for his second wife W. The trustees terminate W's interest in possession three years after H's death in favour of the children of the first marriage. This is a deemed PET by W of say £325,000 (assuming this is the value of the settled property then). Assume she made no earlier gifts.

W dies five years from the date of the termination. At her death the nil rate band is (say) £350,000. Her free estate passes to her own children. They find that £325,000 of the nil rate band has been used up on the transfer of value to H's children leaving only £25,000 available on the free estate which passes to them.

The Anti-avoidance rules

18.08 A non-interest in possession trust (typically a discretionary trust) could not be set up by a potentially exempt transfer, and this prohibition was reinforced by rules designed to prevent a settlor with a high cumulative total channelling property into such a trust via an initial short term interest in possession in favour of an individual with a nil or lower cumulative total.

(i) When the rules applied

18.09 The three prerequisites were that an interest in possession trust was set up by means of a PET[11]; it terminated either as a result of the life tenant dying or by his interest ceasing *inter vivos*; and at that time a non-interest in possession trust (other than an accumulation and maintenance settlement) came into being. If the termination occurred within seven years of the creation of the original interest in possession trust and at a time when the settlor was still alive, the anti-avoidance rules applied.[12]

(ii) Operation of the rules

18.10 The IHT charge on the property at the time when the interest in possession ended was the higher of two calculations. First, the IHT that would arise under normal charging principles: i.e. by taxing the fund as if the transfer had been made by the life tenant at the time of termination. The rates of charge were either half rates (where there was an *inter vivos* termination) or full death rates when termination occurred because of the death of the life tenant. By contrast, the second calculation deemed the settled property to have been transferred at the time of termination by a hypothetical transferor who in the preceding seven years had made chargeable transfers equal in value to those made by the settlor in the seven years before he created the settlement. For the purpose of this second calculation half rates were used.

---

[11] So one way of avoiding the provisions was to settle property on interest in possession trusts for the spouse so that the gift is spouse exempt. The spouse's interest in possession could then be terminated and discretionary trusts arise.

[12] See IHTA 1984, ss.54A, 54B as inserted by the FA (No. 2) 1987, s.96(1), (6), Sch.7, para.1.

EXAMPLE 18.4

Assume that in 2003 S settled £190,000 on trust for P for life or until remarriage and thereafter on discretionary trusts for S's relatives and friends. His cumulative total at that time of chargeable transfers was £140,000 and he had made PETs of £85,000. P remarried one year later at a time when she had made chargeable transfers of £50,000; PETs of £45,000; and when the settled property was worth £210,000.

(1) The anti-avoidance provisions are relevant because the conditions for their operation are satisfied.
(2) IHT would normally be calculated at P's rates: i.e. on a chargeable transfer from £50,000 to £260,000. Under the anti-avoidance rules, however, the tax may be calculated by taking a hypothetical transferor who has S's cumulative total at the time when he created the trust; therefore on this calculation the £210,000 will be taxed as a chargeable transfer at IHT rates from £140,000 to £350,000. The second calculation will be adopted because a greater charge to IHT results. This tax must be paid by the trustees.
(3) Assume that either S or P died after the termination of P's interest in possession. This may result in a recalculation of the IHT liability (the PETs made by that person in the seven years before death are chargeable). So far as the anti-avoidance rules are concerned, however, the basis on which the IHT calculation was made in the first place is not altered. As the greater tax was produced by taking the hypothetical transferor, the subsequent death of P is irrelevant since it cannot be used to switch the basis of computation to P's cumulative total. By contrast, the death of S may involve an additional IHT liability since his potentially exempt transfers of £85,000 may now become chargeable and therefore included in the hypothetical transferor's total when the settlement was created.

(iii) Escaping from the anti-avoidance rules

The following points should be noted: **18.11**

(a) If the interest in possession continued for seven years the anti-avoidance rules did not apply; nor did they apply if the settlor had died by the time the relevant interest in possession had come to an end;
(b) The anti-avoidance rules were not in point if the settlement had been created without an immediate interest in possession (for example if the settlor started with an accumulation and maintenance trust which subsequently turned into an interest in possession trust), or if the settlement was created by means of an exempt transfer (for example, if a life interest was given to the settlor's spouse and that interest was subsequently terminated in favour of a discretionary trust);
(c) Trustees could prevent the anti-avoidance rules from applying if, within six months of the ending of the interest in possession, they terminated

the discretionary trust either by an absolute appointment or by creating a further interest in possession; and

(d) It was always possible to channel property into a discretionary trust by a PET, if an outright gift was made by A to another individual B (a PET) who then settled the gifted property on the appropriate discretionary trusts. (The settlement was a chargeable transfer by B but taxed at B's rates so that, if he had made no previous chargeable gifts the rate was 0 per cent up to £285,000).[13]

18.12 **Effect of the FA 2006 changes:** so far as new trusts are concerned the anti-avoidance rules will largely be a dead letter since *inter vivos* settlements can generally no longer be set up by a potentially exempt transfer.[14] Settlements already in existence on March 22, 2006 may, of course, still be affected by the charge.

The position is as follows—

(a) on the termination of the current interest in possession—whether *inter vivos* or on death—s.54A will apply if there is then a chargeable transfer and there are continuing relevant property trusts. Obviously s.54A will be irrelevant if the trusts end at that point[15];

(b) in two situations the current interest in possession may end, *inter vivos*, in circumstances where although the settlement continues the beneficiary is treated as making a PET. These are if the replacement trusts involve (i) a transitional serial interest or (ii) a disabled person's interest. Section 54A is inapplicable at this stage (because there is no chargeable transfer) but may apply in the future on the inter vivos termination of that interest or on the death of the beneficiary *if* that TSI or disabled person's interest ends within seven years of the original PET by the settlor *and* the settlor is still alive at the date the relevant property trusts arise.

The amendment in s.54A(1A) is designed to ensure that the death charge is limited to these two situations when the beneficiary has an interest in possession which continues to be qualifying for IHT purposes.

THE CHARGING REGIME POST MARCH 21, 2006

18.13 The changes in the IHT treatment of settlements which took effect from March 22, 2006 has resulted in the following:

---

[13] HMRC might argue that A is the indirect settlor having directly or indirectly provided the funds. See *Hatton v IRC* 67 TC 759. However, even if A was treated as the settlor of the discretionary trust this would not mean HMRC could argue that A not B had made the chargeable transfer because A's estate is not diminished by the setting up of the trust—the gift has already been made to B. HMRC would have to show that the gift by A to B was a sham.

[14] The only exception is a disabled person's interest falling within IHTA 1984, s.89B(1)(c). In the other cases where a disabled interest can arise the terms of the trust will be such that s.54 can have no application.

[15] Curiously the reference is only to a termination on the *death* of the person entitled to the disabled person's interest or TSI: see s.54A(1A), IHTA 1984. But it is thought that s.54A can apply on inter vivos terminations of a disabled person's interest or TSI if the other conditions are satisfied.

(i) it is generally no longer possible to set up a lifetime settlement with a qualifying interest in possession[16];

(ii) the termination of a qualifying interest in possession can (subject to (iv) below) only be a PET if the settlement comes to an end at that time;

(iii) likewise exemptions from the tax (e.g. the spouse exemption) will only apply if on the termination the settlement ends;

(iv) there are, however, transitional rules which generally operate until April 6, 2008 whereby if an interest in possession which existed on March 22, 2006 is replaced during this period by a new interest in possession that is a transitional serial interest and the relevant beneficiary is treated under s.49(1) as beneficially entitled to the settled property.[17] In the case of spouses (including civil partners) there is a further extension of this relief after April 6, 2008 provided that the successive life interest arises on the death of the spouse who had enjoyed an interest in possession on March 22, 2006.

EXAMPLE 18.5 *(NEW TRUSTS)*

(1) In December 2006 Doris set up a life interest trust for her disabled son, Phil.[18] That transfer is a PET by Doris. Assume that Phil dies in 2009 whereupon the property passes to his siblings.

    (i) Phil had enjoyed a qualifying interest in possession;

    (ii) accordingly the value of the settled property was aggregated with his free estate and the IHT charge on his death calculated as in *Example 18.3* above;

    (iii) if the trustees had been given overriding powers of appointment which they exercised before Phil's death to terminate his life interest and appoint the property on continuing interest in possession trusts for his siblings the termination of Phil's life interest would be an immediately chargeable transfer by him since the continuing settlement is now a relevant property trust. Note that unlike a disabled person's trust within s.89, there are no restrictions on the application of capital during Phil's lifetime if an interest in possession trust is created for a disabled person: capital can be transferred to anyone on termination of his interest whether *inter vivos* or on death;

    (iv) note, however, that if Phil's life interest is terminated by his death and within seven years of the original settlement being made and the trust becomes a relevant property settlement, then s.54A can apply. In the above example Phil dies in 2009 and the settled property is then held on continuing trusts which are not qualifying interests in possession. In these circumstances the alternative

---

[16] As a result the anti-avoidance rules considered above are largely redundant since they are triggered by the termination of a qualifying interest in possession. However, they have some relevance in relation to TSIs and a disabled person's interest: see s.54A(1A), IHTA 1984.

[17] IHTA 1984, s.49(1A)(c); 49B–E inserted by FA 2006, Sch.20 para.5 with effect from March 22, 2006.

[18] Disabled trusts are considered at Ch. 26.

calculation outlined in *Example 18.4* has to be made unless the settlement is ended within six months of Phil's death and the beneficiaries take the settled property outright. Given that on the coming to an end of the disabled person's interest any continuing trusts will now always be subject to the relevant property regime, it will be desirable to take appropriate steps to prevent s.54A inadvertently applying.[19] (Prior to March 22, 2006 it was possible to avoid discretionary trusts by creating further interests in possession but these will no longer be qualifying.) Therefore ensure that if a disabled person's trust is set up within s.89(B)(c) the settlement ends automatically on the termination of the disabled person's interest on death unless there are good reasons for it to continue.

(2) By his will Reg (who died on Christmas Day 2006) left his estate on life interest trust to his second wife, Thelma with remainder over on life interest trusts for his three adult children. Twelve months after Reg's death the trustees terminate Thelma's life interest. *For IHT purposes*:

(i) on Reg's death the spouse exemption applies (the interest in possession for Thelma is an IPDI)[20];
(ii) on the termination of Thelma's interest in possession she makes an immediately chargeable transfer and the continuing trusts fall within the relevant property regime.[21]

EXAMPLE 18.6 *(EXISTING TRUSTS)*

(1) Jake becomes entitled to a life interest in his family settlement on January 1, 2000. He surrenders that life interest after March 22, 2006 as a result of which the trust property passes outright to his son, Jason. *Jake makes a PET.*

(2) As above but as a result of the surrender the trust fund becomes held on continuing interest in possession trusts for Jason. If the surrender occurs *before* April 6, 2008 Jake will make a PET and Jason will have a transitional serial interest. If it occurs *on or after* April 6, 2008 Jake will make an immediately chargeable transfer with the property becoming held on a relevant property settlement.

THE MEANING OF A TRANSITIONAL SERIAL INTEREST ("TSI")

18.14 IHTA 1984, s.49B–E[22] provide for TSIs. A TSI is a qualifying interest in possession so that the beneficiary is treated as owning the capital in the

---

[19] The trustees may not be aware of the problem until more than six months has elapsed from Phil's death. It is not possible then to prevent the s.54A provisions from applying.
[20] The meaning of an IPDI is considered in detail at Ch. 19.
[21] Under the pre March 22, 2006 regime this would have been a PET by Thelma. Note also that if Thelma continues to benefit from the settled property, the reservation of benefit rules will apply: see FA 1986, s.102 ZA and Ch. 24.
[22] Inserted by FA 2006, Sch.20, para.5

settlement.[23] It follows from this that when the TSI arises this can be as the result of a PET by the previous interest in possession beneficiary.

Four conditions must be satisfied.

1. *Condition 1*: the settlement commenced before March 22, 2006 and immediately before March 22, 2006 it contains an interest in possession.

2. *Condition 2*: that the pre-March 22 interest in possession ("the prior interest") ends on or after March 22, 2006 but before April 6, 2008.

3. *Condition 3*: on the termination of the prior interest someone immediately becomes entitled to an interest in possession in the settled property.

4. *Condition 4*: the person with the current interest does not have a disabled person's interest and nor does s.71A does not apply.

EXAMPLE 18.7

Under the Baggins trust, set up in 2001, Bilbo was entitled to an interest in possession on March 22, 2006. On January 1, 2007 he surrenders that interest as a result of which his cousin Frida becomes entitled to a life interest in the trust fund. The IHT position is as follows:

(i) Bilbo had been entitled to an qualifying interest in possession and Frida becomes entitled to a TSI;

(ii) Frida is therefore treated as owning the capital in the settlement and Bilbo makes a PET when his interest terminates.[24]

18.15 In general[25] a TSI must arise before April 6, 2008: Condition 2 in IHTA 1984, s.49C(3) provides that the prior interest (viz the interest in possession in existence on March 22, 2006) must come to an end "at a time on or after March 22, 2006 but before April 6, 2008" and the current interest (the TSI) must arise at that time. It follows that the prior interest in possession can be superseded only once. A second successive interest in possession arising during the transitional period will not be a TSI.

EXAMPLE 18.8

(1) Take the example of the Baggins trust (in *Example 18.7* above) and assume that after Bilbo has surrendered his interest Frida assigns her interest to her brother before April 6, 2008. This is treated as the termination of Frida's interest[26] and the brother is entitled to an interest in possession *pur autre vie*. Frida had been entitled to a TSI but the brother

---

[23] IHTA 1984, s.49(1A)(c) inserted by FA 2006, Sch.20 para.4.
[24] See the PET definition in IHTA 1984, s.3A(1A): the transfer constitutes a gift to another individual within (1A)(c)(i).
[25] But subject to the special rules for spouses: see 18.19.
[26] See *Example 18.7*, above.

is not: accordingly, the termination of Frida's interest is immediately chargeable and the trust is now subject to the relevant property regime.

(2) Suppose that the Baggins Trust had been set up in 2005 for Bilbo by Mr T who is still alive. Bilbo's interest is ended in 2007 and Frida takes a qualifying interest in possession (a transitional serial interest). Now suppose that Frida dies in 2009, i.e. within seven years of the settlement being established. If the trusts do not end on Frida's death (or within six months) then the settled property will be one in which no qualifying interest in possession subsists. In these circumstances s.54A can apply.[27] The calculation at 18.10 has to be made. Section 54A will also apply on inter vivos termination of Frida's TSI.[28]

18.16 There has been some confusion about the conditions to be satisfied for a TSI to arise. Clarification has been sought from HMRC on a number of points.[29] In particular:

(i) It has been suggested that the prior interest (in the above example Bilbo's interest) must wholly end during the transitional period. This is not the case: all that is necessary is for it to end at least in part of the settled property. The wording of s.49C(1) merely refers to B being entitled to an interest in possession in settled property in which a prior interest had existed. Condition 2 requires the prior interest to have come to an end but this is simply a timing provision to ensure that the prior interest must come to an end in *that part* of the settled property which is now comprised in the current (TSI) interest before April 6, 2008 ("the current interest"). The "current interest" is merely defined as an interest in possession in settled property and does not require *all* the settled property subject to the pre-March 22 to become current interest. Hence if A has a pre-March 22, 2006 life interest this can be ended as to half in favour of D before April 2008 and D takes a TSI. A is treated as making a PET of half the value of the settled property to D. If A's life interest is ended so that daughter and son each take a life interest in one-quarter of the settled funds and A retains half, both son and daughter have a TSI in their respective shares.[30]

(ii) A similar misconception is that the prior interest must have subsisted in the entire settled fund. Take the case where under an accumulation and maintenance trust A had become entitled at the age of 18 in 2005 to an interest in possession in (say) one-quarter of the trust. If that interest is replaced by a successive interest in possession before April 6, 2008 can that interest be a TSI? Again there is nothing in the wording of s.49C to

---

[27] On s.54A, see 18.08. See IHTA 1984, s.54A(2A) inserted by FA 2006, Sch.20, para.16.
[28] See IHTA, s.54A(1)(a).
[29] See CIOT/STEP letter to HMRC and replies in App. III A3.105 and especially A3.106–112.
[30] What if the trustees later appropriated assets between funds: e.g. suppose in the above example son and daughter each have a TSI in two houses of equal value. The trustees decide that son should take one house and the daughter the other house. Is this a further termination of the son/daughter's interest in possession which would therefore take the interests out of the TSI regime? It is not thought so: both were entitled to a TSI in 50 per cent of the settled property and an appropriation of specific assets to satisfy that entitlement does not change the position. This has been agreed by HMRC. See App. III A3.108.

prevent this: provided that there is an interest in possession in settled property on March 22, 2006 then the condition is met. Nowhere is it stated that the current or prior interest must subsist in the entire trust fund.

(iii) What if the prior life interest ends and the current interest arises under a different settlement? Consider the position if A was entitled on March 22, 2006 to a life interest and subject to that the settled property passes to B absolutely. In December 2005, B assigned his remainder interest into a trust giving his daughter C a life interest remainder to grandchildren. A dies in 2007 and the trust fund therefore passes on interest in possession trusts for C. Is C's interest in possession a TSI? No, even if both settlements commenced before March 22, 2006. The reference in Condition 1 to "the settlement" indicates that the prior and current interest must be comprised in a single settlement (see especially s.49c: HMRC have confirmed this view. See App. III A3.111). This may create problems where a life tenant is getting divorced when it is desirable to have the settled property which is transferred for the benefit of the other spouse held in a separate settlement.

(iv) If the person with the prior life interest (in the above example, A) assigns his life interest (the prior interest) to C, so C takes an interest *pur autre vie*, C's interest is a TSI. The original interest in possession held by A ("the prior interest") has come to an end by virtue of the assignment (see s.51(1)(b)) and so Condition 2 has been met.[31]

18.17 A TSI can arise even though that interest did not exist on March 22, 2006 and, indeed, the beneficiary might not even have been born at that date.

EXAMPLE 18.9

On March 22, 2006 Jim was entitled to an interest in possession subject to which the trust fund was held on discretionary trusts for his issue. On April 1, 2006 Jim's son Jake is born and on April 1, 2007 the trustees terminate Jim's interest and make an appointment in favour of Jake for life.[32] Jake has a TSI and Jim has made a PET.

18.18 Sometimes the question will arise as to whether the interest in possession in existence on March 22, 2006 has been replaced by a successive interest in possession. The legislation clearly assumes that the beneficiary of the prior interest can be the same person as the beneficiary of the current interest (the TSI: see s.49C(2)(b) which refers to "B or some other person"). Any such replacement during the transitional period will be a TSI but thereafter will result in a relevant property settlement coming into being.

---

[31] See App. III A3.112.
[32] It will be important to exclude TA 1925, s.31 otherwise Jake will not take a qualifying interest in possession because the trustees will have power to accumulate income and Jake will only be entitled to those accumulations if he survives till 18.

EXAMPLE 18.10

Property was settled on trust for Phileas at 30 absolutely. He was 25 on June 6, 2005 when he became entitled to the income.

(i) He therefore enjoyed an interest in possession on March 22, 2006 and will become entitled to capital on June 6, 2010. At that time there will be no IHT charge.[33] There may, however, be a capital gain tax charge[34] and, of course, it may be felt inappropriate for him to be entitled to all the trust capital at that date;

(ii) Commonly the trustees will possess an enhanced power of advancement which will enable them to apply all the capital of the trust fund for Phileas' benefit. They may choose to do this by making a settled advance which:

(a) will not create a new settlement for CGT purposes provided the power is exercised "in the narrower form"[35];
(b) but which will give Phileas only a life interest—albeit with a power for the trustees to advance him capital—with remainder over to his children.

It is thought that the interest in income that Phileas enjoyed (to income until age 30) on March 22, 2006 has been replaced by a life interest. Accordingly if the settled advance is made before April 6, 2008 this will be a TSI; if the settled advance is made on or after that date the new life interest is not a TSI and, although there is no entry charge (see IHTA 1984, s.53(2)), the settlement will then be taxed under the relevant property regime. The position is also important if Phileas dies and the settled property passes on life interest trusts for his spouse. The interest taken by the spouse cannot be a TSI and therefore if it has not already done so, the trust becomes a relevant property settlement. The spouse exemption is therefore not available.

Suppose in the above example Phileas is entitled to a qualifying pre-March 22, interest in possession but he is not entitled to capital although the trustees have a power to apply capital for his benefit. On his death the trust fund passes to his children. Phileas is ill and the trustees want to ensure that his wife takes an interest in possession. They therefore make a settled advance for the benefit of Phileas by appointing that (subject to his existing interest) on his death his wife takes an interest in possession. Provided that the advance is made subject to Phileas' existing life interest and does not alter that interest but makes provision for the position on his death, it is thought that the spousal interest in possession will qualify as a TSI. In general, care is needed when exercising powers of appointment and advancement to avoid disturbing pre-March 22, interests in possession unnecessarily.

---

[33] He is treated as owning the capital of the settlement under IHTA 1984, s.49(1) and hence there is no diminution in his estate when the trust ends.
[34] Under TCGA 1992, s.71: see 7.38.
[35] See 7.55 and 7.42.

18.19 The rules for spouses: there are special rules in the case of successive interests for spouses.[36] Until April 6, 2008 the normal TSI rules apply. Thereafter if on the death of an interest in possession beneficiary that person's spouse becomes entitled to an interest in possession it is a TSI. Note that this extension to the definition of a TSI does not apply if the earlier interest in possession ends during the lifetime of the beneficiary.

EXAMPLE 18.11

(1) On March 22, 2006 the Jenkins Family Trust is subject to a life interest for William then aged 28. In 2020 he marries Fiona and she is appointed a successive life interest in the settlement (subject to his existing life interest interest which remains undisturbed). On the death of William in 2021 the spouse exemption applies and Fiona enjoys a TSI.[37]

(2) On March 22, 2006 Ruth is entitled to a life interest in the family trust and has appointed her husband, David, a successive life interest. If Ruth surrenders her life interest before April 6, 2008 (a) the IHT spouse exemption will apply and (b) David will be entitled to a TSI.[38] If, however, she surrenders her interest on or after April 6, 2008 the spouse exemption will not apply. Instead she will make an immediately chargeable transfer and the family trust will become subject to the relevant property regime. In some circumstances it might be desirable to give the spouse a TSI while the existing life tenant is still alive: e.g. in the above example, David might be the better life and therefore it would be preferable if his interest is ended during his lifetime so that the PET is on his clock rather than on Ruth's. However, bear in mind that if David dies before Ruth and still owns the interest in possession, Ruth cannot take a qualifying interest in possession back on his death. There will therefore be an inheritance tax charge on David's death unless the property passes to Ruth absolutely. Care should therefore be taken before terminating any existing interest in possession in favour of a spouse. The spouses cannot change their minds and turn the clock back![39]

18.20 Contracts of life insurance: IHTA 1984, s.49E deals with settlements of life insurance policies in place on March 22, 2006.[40] The definition of a TSI is extended in such cases so that:

(i) until April 6, 2008 the normal rules for TSI apply *but thereafter*;

(ii) provided that successive interests in possession arise on the deaths of each of the previous interests in possession beneficiaries, each one is a TSI.

---

[36] Spouse includes a civil partner. The rules are found in IHTA 1984, s.49D.
[37] Under IHTA 1984, s.49D(4) which provides that a TSI arises provided that Fiona is married to William immediately before his death.
[38] Under IHTA 1984, s.49C.
[39] Note the reservation of benefit and POA position, discussed in Ch. 24, on terminations of spousal interests in possession.
[40] See also IHTA 1984, s.46A–B inserted by FA 2006, Sch.20, para.11.

This treatment will continue until the settlement ceases to comprise rights under the pre March 22, 2006 life insurance contract whereupon on the death of the then interest in possession beneficiary any subsequent interest in possession will not be a TSI.[41]

18.21 **Planning with TSIs:** the transitional period until April 6, 2008 offers scope for IHT planning. Assume, for instance, a family settlement under which on March 22, 2006 Alan, aged 65, is the life tenant. The trustees have wide powers of appointment in favour of his issue. These could be exercised during the transitional period with a view to triggering PETs by Alan and prolonging the life of the settlement. For instance TSIs could be created for his grandchildren. If they are minors it will be important to exclude TA 1925, s.31 but the trustees may reserve their wide overriding powers of appointment. In terms of overall strategy the result is:

(i) that the life of the settlement may then be prolonged;

(ii) however, were a grandchild to die, IHT would be payable on his "share";

(iii) in the future the overriding power could be exercised to trigger PETs by the interest in possession beneficiary.[42]

18.22 Consider the following:

EXAMPLE 18.12

Tad is entitled to an interest in possession on March 22, 2006. On April 1, 2007 the trustees (in exercise of overriding powers) terminate Tad's interest and appoint the property on trust for his twins, Leo and Oliver as joint life tenants with a provision that the survivor is to become sole life tenant. The consequences are:

(i) Tad has made a PET;
(ii) Leo and Oliver have TSIs;
(iii) assume that Leo dies so that Oliver becomes sole surviving life tenant. IHT will be payable on Leo's death in the normal way.[42]

But is a portion of the settlement (Leo's portion) now subject to the relevant property regime or does Oliver's life interest now encompass the entire fund? It is thought that although Leo and Oliver have a joint life interest, s.50(1) applies so each is treated as having a life interest in only half the settled property.[43] It is therefore thought that Oliver's TSI is limited to one-half of the trust fund. His interest in possession in Leo's part is not a TSI and that portion of the trust fund is subject to the relevant property regime.

---

[41] IHTA 1984, s.49E(4) and Ch. 33.
[42] The TSI must arise in the same trust (see 18.16) and age contingencies over the TSIs should not be included.
[43] See in particular s.50(5) of IHTA 1984.

CHAPTER 19

IMMEDIATE POST DEATH INTERESTS AND OTHER QUALIFYING INTERESTS IN POSSESSION AFTER FA 2006

- Meaning of a qualifying interest in possession after FA 2006 **(19.02)**
- Immediate post death interests (IPDIs) **(19.05)**
- Meaning of a transitional serial interest **(19.16)**

The hallmark of a qualifying interest in possession is that the relevant beneficiary is treated as beneficially entitled to the property in which the interest subsists (IHTA 1984, s.49(1)) and that the relevant property regime does not apply (IHTA 1984, s.58(1), 59). This chapter considers in detail one of the three qualifying iips that can arise after FA 2006, namely immediate post death interests. **19.01**

MEANING OF QUALIFYING INTEREST IN POSSESSION AFTER FA 2006

Section 49 now provides that the following are qualifying interests— **19.02**

(i) an interest to which an individual becomes entitled before March 22, 2006[1];

(ii) an interest to which a company is entitled if (1) the business of the company consists wholly or mainly in the acquisition of interests in settled property and (2) the company acquired the interest for full consideration in money or money's worth from an individual who was beneficially entitled to it.[2] From March 22, 2006 the interest purchased must be qualifying in accordance with the new rules;

(iii) if the individual becomes beneficially entitled to the interest on or after March 22, 2006 and it was:

- an immediate post death interest; *or*
- a disabled person's interest; *or*
- a transitional serial interest.

---

[1] IHTA 1984, s.59(1)(a)(i) inserted by FA 2006, Sch.20, para.20.
[2] IHTA 1984, s.59(2)–(4) and note that there are special rules (1) where the interest was acquired before March 14, 1975 and (2) where the company is an insurance company licensed to carry out contracts of long-term assurance.

19.03 Two special provisions in the legislation are worthy of note—

(i) when the interest in possession is owned by a close company the participators in the company are treated as beneficially entitled to it in accordance with their interests in the company[3];

(ii) a beneficiary who is entitled to the residue in an unadministered estate is treated as if residue had been administered: i.e. as if he had the interest from the death of the deceased. Although the section refers to an "interest in possession" it is thought to apply equally to an absolute entitlement to residue. No reduction in value is allowed for delay or costs of the administration.[4]

Protective Trusts

19.04 These trusts are subject to special rules. Essentially if the initial interest is forfeited (e.g. because of the bankruptcy of the beneficiary) with the result that a discretionary trust arises, for IHT purposes the interest in possession is deemed to continue.[5] For IIPs that arise from March 22, 2006 these rules only apply if the interest in possession is an immediate post death interest; a disabled person's interest or a transitional serial interest.[6] In line with the policy behind the changes it is no longer possible to create a qualifying protective trust *inter vivos* save for a disabled person. If the initial interest in possession arose before March 22, 2006 and is then forfeited after March 22, 2006 (e.g. because of the bankruptcy of the beneficiary) the beneficiary continues to be treated as beneficially entitled to a qualifying interest in possession.

EXAMPLE 19.1

(1) A is entitled to an interest in possession in a protective trust set up by his father in 2003. In 2007 he becomes bankrupt and the settled property as a result becomes held on discretionary trusts for A and his family. He is treated for inheritance tax purposes as if his interest continued and the trust therefore faces a tax charge on his death. There will be no capital gains tax uplift.[7]

(2) W becomes entitled to a protective life interest under the will of her late husband who died in 2007. This is an IPDI. W becomes bankrupt in 2008 and the interest in possession is forfeited and the fund held on discretionary trusts. W is treated for inheritance tax purposes as if her

---

[3] IHTA 1984, s.101(1).
[4] IHTA 1984, s.91, see App.III, A3.113.
[5] IHTA 1984, s.88 (pre 1978 protective trusts fell within the defectively drafted s.73).
[6] IHTA 1984, s.88(3)–(6) inserted by FA 2006, Sch.20, para.24.
[7] Because there is no equivalent provision in the CGT legislation which deems A to have an interest in possession.

qualifying interest in possession continued.[8] Again there will be no base cost uplift for capital gains tax purposes on the death of W.[9]

IMMEDIATE POST DEATH INTERESTS ("IPDIS")

IHTA 1984, s.49A states that where a person ("L") is beneficially entitled to an interest in possession in settled property it is an IPDI only if four conditions are met: **19.05**

(i) *Condition 1*—the settlement must be "effected by will or under the law relating to intestacy"[10];

(ii) *Condition 2*—the person entitled to the interest in possession ("L" in the legislation) must have become beneficially entitled to it "on the death of the testator or intestate";

(iii) *Condition 3*—s.71A (bereaved minor trust) does not apply to the property and nor is the interest a disabled persons interest[11];

(iv) *Condition 4*—Condition 3 must be satisfied at all times since the interest in possession arose at death.

BN 25 commented that the IPDI trust must be for **19.06**

"the benefit of one life tenant in order of time whose interest cannot be replaced (more than one such trust may be created on death so long as the trust capital vests absolutely when the life interest comes to an end)."

This statement of intent was reflected when the Finance Bill was published in a provision designed to limit the overriding powers possessed by the trustees to ensure that the trust must end when the interest in possession terminates. Various restrictions were inserted to prevent an interest in possession being ended without L's consent. It would have been difficult to satisfy the

---

[8] The same analysis would apply if W had a transitional serial interest or a disabled person's interest which was held on protective trusts.

[9] Is the capital gains tax position on the death of W any different in respect of post March 2006 protective trusts? In the above example, s.88(5) IHTA 1984 states that "this Act shall apply as if that interest in possession were a continuation of the immediate post death interest". So the immediate post death interest continues for inheritance tax purposes until W's death. Section 72(1B) TCGA 1992 states that there is a deemed disposal and reacquisition on the death of W if "the interest is an immediate post death interest within the meaning given by s.49A of IHTA 1984". Can one argue that W is *deemed* to have an immediate post death interest and therefore the capital gains tax uplift applies? It is thought not. A prior condition for s.72(1B) to apply at all is that an interest in possession terminates on the death of a person entitled to it (see ss.72(1) and (1A)). An interest in possession is given its normal meaning in this context and where the discretionary trusts were triggered prior to the death of the principal beneficiary, no interest in possession has terminated on the death.

[10] An IPDI will arise on intestacy when the deceased leaves a surviving spouse and issue. The spouse will be entitled to a life interest in one-half of the residue of the estate: see AEA 1925, s.46(1)(i).

[11] Bereaved minor trusts received a similar IHT treatment to that which applied to accumulation and maintenance trusts whilst disabled person's interests are qualifying interests in possession so that they do not need IPDI status.

conditions as drafted (for instance, a standard form power of advancement would have disqualified the trust from IPDI status!). Not surprisingly there was an outcry from the professional bodies given that the effect of the clause would also have been to deny spouse exemption in the majority of wills which had included a settled gift to the spouse. As a consequence the Government performed a somewhat ungracious U-turn with the result that all life interest trusts established on death will be IPDIs: the existence of overriding powers which could be exercised to terminate the IPDI (with or without the consent of the beneficiary) and extend the life of the trust are irrelevant.

19.07   It may be thought that the original BN 25 proposal was ill thought out. Government policy required two things—

(i) that flexible interest in possession trusts should not be used as a way of circumventing the reservation of benefit rules. However, this was separately dealt with in FA 2006[12] and did not require the definition of an IPDI to take this problem into account;

(ii) that trusts should not be a vehicle for avoiding the payment of IHT. Given that qualifying interest in possession trusts and the definition of a PET are dealt with elsewhere in FA 2006 it was again unnecessary to seek to define an IPDI restrictively so as to ensure that at its termination the settlement had to end. If the settlement does not end on the termination of the IPDI then in most cases it will simply fall into the relevant property regime at that point (with an entry charge of 20 per cent if this occurs during the lifetime of L).

EXAMPLE 19.2

In his will Jones leaves his entire estate on a flexible interest in possession trust for his wife Olive. He dies in December 2006 and the trustees then terminate Olive's interest in £285,000 which they appoint on discretionary trusts for a class of beneficiaries including Olive. The rest of the estate remains held on continuing trusts after the ending of Olive's interest in possession. The IHT position is that—

(i) Olive's interest in possession is an IPDI;
(ii) The termination of that interest in £285,000 takes effect as an immediately chargeable transfer by Olive[13] and because she is not excluded from benefiting under the discretionary trust she is treated as reserving a benefit in the appointed property which will therefore be taxed as part of her estate when she dies.[14]
(iii) On Olive's death the value of the settled property in which her interest in possession subsisted will be taxed along with her free estate. The continuing trusts will be taxed under the relevant property regime *unless* they satisfy the conditions of s.71A (bereaved minor trust) *or* s.71D (18–25 trust) *or* create a disabled person's interest (see s.89B).

[12] See s.102ZA of FA 1986.
[13] Note that the chargeable transfer is not made by Jones: see IHTA 1984, s.80 as amended.
[14] FA 1986, s.102 ZA inserted by FA 2006.

(iv) If Olive's interest in possession is terminated *inter vivos* whereupon the property is held on continuing trusts she will make an immediately chargeable transfer unless those trusts fall within s.71A (bereaved minor)[15] or constitute a disabled trust in which case Olive will make a PET.[16]

(v) Hence it is not possible to provide for qualifying interest in possession trusts for the grandchildren of the testator on termination of Olive's IPDI whether this occurs during her lifetime or on death. Any further interest in possession trusts will be non-qualifying and involve a chargeable transfer. One could provide for s.71D trusts to arise on Olive's death or during her lifetime if the testator's children were under 25. However, note that the creation of s.71D trusts on an *inter vivos* termination of Olive's interest is a chargeable transfer not a PET although such trusts are taxed according to the special regime in s.71F and so are not subject to ten year anniversary charges while the beneficiary is under 25.

Diagrammatically the position can be represented as follows: **19.08**

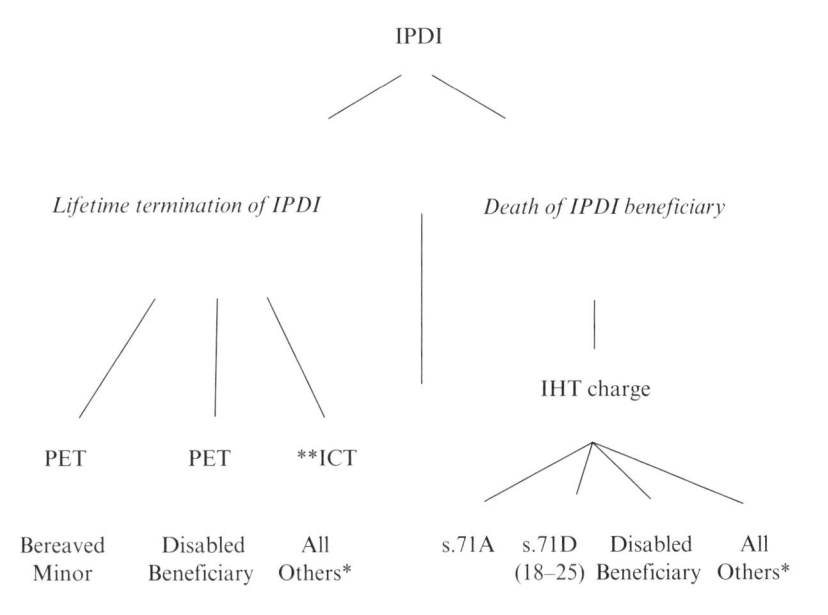

```
                                IPDI
                               /    \
              Lifetime termination of IPDI    Death of IPDI beneficiary
                  /     |     \                      |
                                                 IHT charge
                                                  /  |  \
                PET    PET    **ICT         s.71A  s.71D  Disabled   All
                                                   (18–25) Beneficiary Others*
             Bereaved  Disabled   All
              Minor   Beneficiary Others*
```

* Trusts taxed as relevant property settlements unless a s. 71D trust.
**Immediately chargeable transfer.

---

[15] See IHTA 1984, s.3A(1A)(c)(iii), (3B). It should be noted that if the ending of the IPDI results in property being held on trusts within s.71D (18–25 trusts) then the termination will not be a PET. It is difficult to see any justification for this different treatment.

[16] IHTA 1984, s.3A(1A) inserted by FA 2006, Sch.20, para.9. Note that (1A)(c)(ii) refers to a gift into a disabled trust, namely a trust to which s.89 applies (s.3A(1A)(3A)): in addition if an interest in possession trust for a disabled person is set up after March 21, 2006 because that will result in a qualifying interest in possession (see IHTA 1984, s.59(2)(c)) its establishment on the *inter vivos* termination of an IPDI will also be a PET since the transfer will fall within IHTA 1984, s.3A(1A)(c)(i) as a gift to another individual.

19.09 Condition 1

An IPDI can arise in the following circumstances—

(i) Established *by the will* of the deceased. Note that an IPDI can be created in favour of any person: it is not limited to an interest in possession trust for a spouse.[17]

(ii) Established on *intestacy*: for instance, the statutory trust of residue which will arise when the intestate is survived by spouse and children;

(iii) Established as the result of an instrument of *variation* falling within IHTA 1984, s.142(1)[18];

EXAMPLE 19.3

Alf's will leaves everything to his daughter when he dies in early 2007. Within two years of his death she enters into a variation within s.142(1) whereby Alf's estate (less £285,000) is settled on interest in possession trusts for Rosa, Alf's wife. The variation has established an IPDI.[19] Spouse exemption is available.

(iv) set up in accordance with the requirements of IHTA 1984, s.144 (*two year trusts*). In brief, if the will establishes a trust which is not an interest in possession and within two years of death an event occurs (e.g. a trustee appointment) which causes the property

> "to be held on trusts that would, if they had in fact been established by the testator's will, have resulted in (an IPDI) subsisting in the property."[20]

then the Act shall apply as if the will had set up an IPDI.

EXAMPLE 19.4

Thomas' will leaves his property on discretionary trusts. On January 1, 2007, within two years of Thomas' death, the trustees appoint:

(i) £285,000 on an interest in possession trust for Thomas' son, Gordon;

(ii) appoint the residue on an interest in possession trust for Thomas' surviving civil partner, Jonny.

By virtue of s.144 the appointments are "read back" into the will resulting in the creation of two IPDI's.

---

[17] IPDI's may be attractive vehicles for minor beneficiaries: see 28.40.
[18] See Ch.29.
[19] IHTA 1984, s.142(1) provides that for all purposes of the Act the variation shall be treated as having been effected by the Deceased. It is thought that this is sufficient to satisfy Conditions 1 and 2 in s.49A, see 29.15.
[20] IHTA 1984, s.144(3)–(6) inserted by FA 2006, Sch.20, para.27.

Condition 1: is somewhat ambiguous. Does it mean that the actual vehicle which contains the settled property has to be established by will or is it sufficient that the property which is subject to the interest in possession is settled as a result of the provisions of the will? The wording reads "the settlement was effected by will or intestacy" but this could mean "the settlement of the settled property in which L was entitled to an interest in possession was effected by will or intestacy". 19.10

EXAMPLE 19.5

> Carlo is a US citizen who is deemed UK domiciled. His wife Lottie is also a US citizen who is UK deemed domiciled. In order to avoid US probate duty Carlo's will leaves his residuary estate into a trust established in 1989 which is interest in possession for Lottie. Is this an IPDI? The settlement of the property was effected by the will albeit it passes into an existing settlement. Given HMRC's view that each addition to an existing settlement constitutes a new settlement for inheritance tax purposes, it should not matter that the property is added to an existing trust. The authors therefore consider that Condition 1 is satisfied. (This has been confirmed by HMRC: see App.III A3.120.)

Condition 2: the requirement that L became beneficially entitled to the interest in possession on the death of the testator/intestate means that an entitlement which arises subsequently, albeit as a result of a trust established in the will, does not suffice. 19.11

EXAMPLE 19.6

(1) Jim's will settles his chattels on life interest trusts for his son remainder to his grandchildren. After Jim's death in 2007 the trustees exercise their powers to terminate the son's interest and appoint the chattels on interest in possession trusts for Jim's grandson. Although the grandson enjoys an interest in possession in a trust set up by will it is not an IPDI. Hence on the termination of his interest the son makes an immediately chargeable transfer and the trust falls into the relevant property regime.

(2) On Jessie's death in 2007 her will provided for her assets to be held on discretionary trusts. After some three years the trustees appoint her husband a life interest. This is not an IPDI; the trusts continue to fall into the relevant property regime (for IHT purposes the appointment is a "nothing").[21]

Conditions 3 and 4: an interest in possession can subsist in a bereaved minor's trust and a disabled person's interest includes an interest in possession trust 19.12

---

[21] It is irrelevant that for general trust purposes the appointment is read back into the original settlement for perpetuity and accumulation purposes. If the appointment had occurred within two years of Jessie's death reading back under s.144 would have resulted in the husband having an IPDI: see 29.53.

established for that person. It is not intended that the IPDI regime shall apply in either case. In the case of bereaved minor trusts this is understandable since they are subject to a wholly different IHT charging regime. By contrast it is a little difficult to see why the disabled person's interest needs to be distinguished. The relevant trust must be one which gives an interest in possession to a disabled person within IHTA 1984, s.89B(1)(c) and this creates a qualifying interest in possession in the same way as an IPDI.

19.13 **Condition 4:** suggests that a will trust which creates an IPDI initially may subsequently cease to satisfy the requirements. For instance, if a minor child of the testator was given an immediate interest in possession on his parent's death and capital at 30 then his interest is an IPDI. If, however, the trustees exercised a power of appointment to vest capital in him at the age of 18 then the trust would now fall within s.71A as a bereaved minor's trust and so be outside the IPDI definition. The consequences of this happening are considered in Chapter 25.

A "DISABLED PERSON'S INTEREST"

19.14 The term is considered in detail in Chapter 26. It is defined in IHTA 1984, s.89B and comprises the following:

(i) an interest in possession which a disabled person is treated as enjoying under a trust falling within s.89. This covers the "*deemed*" interest in possession set up under an old style disabled trust[22];

(ii) an interest in possession which is deemed to arise under a self settlement made on or after March 22, 2006 by a person with a condition expected to lead to a disability. Again this is a *deemed* interest in possession[23];

(iii) an interest in possession in a settlement to which a disabled person becomes entitled on or after March 22, 2006. In this case the settlement contains an interest in possession (i.e. this is *not* a case of deemed interest) and note that the settlement can be established either by will or *inter vivos* by any person[24];

(iv) a self settlement (as in (ii) above) which gives an interest in possession to a disabled person. Again this is not a case of a *deemed* interest in possession.

19.15 The amendment to the PET definition[25] includes a transfer of value by an individual after March 22, 2006 which is a gift to a disabled trust (defined as a trust to which s.89 applies).[26] This means that the creation of a disabled trust within (i) can be by a PET. In the case of (ii) and (iv) above, because both are self

---

[22] See 26.29, *et seq*. In brief, although the settlement does not give the disabled person a right to income he is deemed to have an interest in possession.
[23] See IHTA 1984, s.89A inserted by FA 2006, Sch.20, para.6 and Ch. 26.
[24] IHTA 1984, s.89B(1)(c) inserted by FA 2006, Sch.20, para.6.
[25] IHTA 1984, s.3(A)(1A)(c)(ii) inserted by FA 2006, Sch.20, para.9.
[26] IHTA 1984, s.3A(1A)(3A) inserted by FA 2006, Sch.20, para.9.

settlements with the settlor retaining a qualifying interest in possession, there is no diminution in the settlor's estate (hence the creation of the settlement is a "nothing"). In the case of (iii) above the creation of the settlement may be a PET on the basis that it involves a gift to another individual within s.3A(1A)(c). In the event that an IPDI (or indeed a pre March 22, 2006 interest in possession trust) ends and the property thereupon becomes held upon trusts which create a disabled person's interest, the relevant beneficiary may make a PET.

MEANING OF A TRANSITIONAL SERIAL INTEREST

The meaning of this term is considered at **18.14**. **19.16**

CHAPTER 20

TAXATION OF RELEVANT PROPERTY SETTLEMENTS

- Creation of the settlement **(20.05)**
- Exit charges in the first 10 years **(20.07)**
- Charge on the first 10-year anniversary **(20.13)**
- Exit charges between anniversaries **(20.18)**
- Later periodic charges **(20.19)**
- Technical problems **(20.20)**
- Discretionary trusts created before March 27, 1974 **(20.29)**
- Exemptions and reliefs **(20.33)**

20.01 The method of charging settlements lacking a qualifying interest in possession is totally different from that for settlements with such an interest. Instead of attributing the fund to one or more of the beneficiaries, it is the settlement itself which is the taxable entity for inheritance tax. Like an individual, it must keep a record of chargeable transfers made, although, unlike the individual, it will never die and so will only be taxed at lifetime rates. With the major changes in the IHT taxation of settlements the relevant property settlement has become the norm[1]: the majority of new settlements will be taxed in accordance with the provisions in IHTA 1984, Pt III, Ch. III. Formerly such settlements were commonly referred to as "discretionary trusts". In fact this was always an oversimplification and the categories of settlements falling under this charging regime—even before the 2006 changes—were wider than mere discretionary trusts, catching for instance the type of settlement considered in *Pearson v* IRC[2] and trusts where the beneficiaries' interests were contingent but did not satisfy the requirements for an accumulation and maintenance trust. From March 22, 2006 the regime has been extended to catch "certain settlements in which interests in possession exist". Accordingly it is now wholly inappropriate to refer to Ch. III as the charging regime for discretionary trusts. The approach adopted in this book will be to describe it as the charge on relevant property settlements.[3]

---

[1] Hence the 2006 Budget Press Notice (BN 25) referred to the "alignment" of the IHT treatment of settlements.
[2] *Pearson v IRC* [1981] A.C. 753, [1980] 2 All E.R. 479, HL. See further 15.21, above.
[3] See IHTA 1984, s.58 defining "relevant property" as settled property in which no qualifying interest in possession subsists with the exceptions then enumerated and s.59 then defines a qualifying interest in possession. Both sections were heavily amended by FA 2006.

EXAMPLE 20.1

> The following are relevant property settlements:
>
> (1) £100,000 is held upon trust for such of A, B, C, D, E and F as the trustees may in their absolute discretion (which extends over both income and capital) appoint.
> (2) Dad settles property on trust for his son contingent on his attaining 30 years. The son is aged 21 years at the date of the settlement and the income is to be accumulated until his son attains 30 years.[4]
> (3) In 2006 A settles £300,000 on a life interest trust for himself.[5]
> (4) In the same year B settles a similar sum on a life interest trust for his spouse, Mrs B.[6]

20.02 Inheritance tax is charged on "relevant property"[7] defined as settled property (other than excluded property) in which there is no qualifying interest in possession, with the exception of property settled on accumulation and maintenance trusts and certain other special trusts considered below.[8] If within one settlement there exists a qualifying interest in possession in a part only of the settled property, the charge to inheritance tax under the relevant property provisions is on the portion which lacks such an interest.

Main features of the charge

20.03 The central feature in the taxation of relevant property trusts is the periodic or anniversary charge imposed at ten yearly intervals. The anniversary is calculated from the date on which the trust was created.[9]

EXAMPLE 20.2

> (1) S creates a discretionary trust on January 1, 1999. The first anniversary charge will fall on January 1, 2009; the next on January 1, 2019 and so on. If the trust had been created by will and the testator had died on December 31, 2005, that date marks the creation of the settlement.[10]

---

[4] Had the capital and income vested at 25 and the settlement been set up in Dad's will this would have fallen within s.71D: see Ch. 25.
[5] Before March 22, 2006 this settlement would have been a "nothing" for IHT purposes because A would have enjoyed a qualifying interest in possession as a result of which he would have been treated as owning the capital in the settlement under IHTA 1984, s.49(1) and hence his estate would not have been reduced.
[6] Before March 22, 2006 B would have made a spouse exempt transfer since Mrs B would have enjoyed a qualifying interest in possession and so under s.49(1) been treated as the owner of the capital. Hence the requirements for the s.18 spouse exemption were met.
[7] IHTA 1984, s.58.
[8] As to accumulation and maintenance trusts and trusts for minors see Chs. 21 and 25.
[9] IHTA 1984, s.61(1): note it is *not* calculated from the date when the settlement became a relevant property trust or from the date when property was added.
[10] IHTA 1984, s.83.

(2) On January 1, 2004 S created a flexible accumulation and maintenance trust.[11] On April 6, 2008 the trust ceases to qualify as accumulation and maintenance because of the amended s.71 requirements which came into force on that day.[12] It therefore became a relevant property settlement. The first anniversary charge will fall on January 1, 2014.[13]

20.04 Apart from the anniversary charge, IHT is also levied (the "exit charge") on the happening of certain events (the most important of which is the ending of the trust, e.g. by the outright appointment of capital to a beneficiary). In general, the tax then charged is a proportion of the last periodic charge. Special charging provisions operate for chargeable events which occur before the first 10-year anniversary when the first periodic charge is levied.

CREATION OF THE SETTLEMENT

20.05 The creation of the settlement will, generally, be a chargeable transfer of value by the settlor (it cannot be a potentially exempt transfer). The following matters should be noted:

(i) If the settlement is created *inter vivos*, grossing-up applies unless the inheritance tax is paid out of the settled property.

EXAMPLE 20.3

A who had made no previous chargeable transfers settles £295,000 on discretionary trusts in June 2006. A has already used her annual exemption.[14] The first £285,000 falls within her nil rate band and therefore inheritance tax is payable on the balance of £10,000 at 20 per cent. If A pays the inheritance tax on the gift, her estate falls in value by £295,000 plus the inheritance tax payable on the £10,000 i.e. A is charged on the cost of the gift by treating the £295,000 as a gift net of tax. Therefore the part of the gift on which inheritance tax is payable (£10,000) must be grossed up to reflect the amount of tax payable on the gift by using the formula:

100/100–R where R is the rate of inheritance tax applicable to the sum in question.

The calculation is £10,000 × 100/80 = £12,500 gross. (IHT is £2,500).

Hence, if A pays the tax the total cost of the gift for A is £295,000 + £2,500 = £297,500. The trust receives £295,000.

---

[11] For a consideration of A+M trusts and the transitional rules that apply, see Ch. 21.
[12] The trust was not amended to provide for vesting of capital and income at 18 nor so as to fall within s.71D: see 25.29.
[13] Note, however, that the charge will be calculated by reference to the period during which the trust qualified as a relevant property settlement: i.e. from April 6, 2008. See 20.22.
[14] Earlier gifts in the same tax year are given the annual exemption relief first. If A made an outright gift of £3,000 this would not be a PET but an exempt transfer in its own right. Therefore he cannot make a gift to a discretionary trust later in the tax year and claim the annual exemption.

If the trustees pay the tax the total cost of the gift for A is £295,000, the IHT liability is £2,000 (20% × £10,000) and the trust receives £293,000.

Note that once the transferor's cumulative total exceeds her nil rate band, tax is levied at 25% of the excess if the transferor pays the tax. So if in the above example A had already made chargeable transfers of £285,000 then a further chargeable transfer of £285,000 would attract tax of £71,250 on A.

(ii) The cumulative total of chargeable transfers made by the settlor is crucial because it forms part of the cumulative total of the settlement on all future chargeable occasions (i.e. the settlor's transfers do not drop out of the cumulative total after seven years when calculating 10 year and exit charges). Therefore, in order to calculate the correct IHT charge it is essential that the trustees know the settlor's cumulative total at the date when he created the trust.[15] This may not be easy if the settlor has made earlier lifetime gifts which were PETs because they are treated as exempt transfers unless and until the transferor dies within the following seven years and are therefore not cumulated in calculating inheritance tax on subsequent chargeable transfers. (See *Example 20.4*).

(iii) A "related settlement" is another settlement created by the same settlor on the same day as the discretionary trust (other than a charitable trust). Generally such settlements should be avoided.[16]

(iv) Additions of property by the original settlor to his settlement should be avoided unless the settlor has made no previous PETs or chargeable transfers and the additions are all within his unused nil rate band. If property is added by a person other than the original settlor, the addition is treated as a separate settlement for inheritance tax purposes.[17]

20.06 Particular problems may arise for the trustees if the settlor dies within seven years of creating the trust. If this happens, potentially exempt transfers made before the settlement was created and within seven years of his death become chargeable so that tax on creation of the settlement and the computation of any exit charge[18] made during this period may need to be recalculated. If extra tax

---

[15] If, as a result of the settlor's fraud, wilful default or neglect, there is an underpayment of inheritance tax, HM Revenue and Customs may recover that sum from the trustees outside the normal six year time limit. In such cases the time limit is six years from the date when the impropriety comes to the notice of HMRC.¹ Obviously a problem would arise for trustees if at the time when the underpayment came to light they held insufficient assets to discharge the extra inheritance tax because they could be made personally liable for the tax unpaid. HMRC have stated that where the trustees have acted in good faith and hold insufficient settlement assets they will not seek to recover any unpaid tax from them personally.

[16] As to the calculation of IHT on property in a related settlement see 20.08 post. Note that it is only the value of property comprised in the related settlement immediately after it commenced which is included so if two trusts of £10 were set up they would be related property settlements but subsequent additions would not be related. Charitable trusts are not related settlements. Settlements established in a will are related unless: IHTA 1984, s.80(4) applies (this provides that an IPDI or disabled person's interest for a surviving spouse (or surviving civil partner) is treated as only taking effect on the coming to an end of the "postponing interest": see 15.09.

[17] See s.44(2), IHTA 1984 and 20.26.

[18] As to exit charges see 20.07 below.

becomes payable, this is primarily the responsibility of the settlement trustees and their liability is not limited to settlement property in their hands at that time. Given this danger it is prudent for trustees who are distributing property from the discretionary trust within the first seven years to retain sufficient funds or take suitable indemnities to cover their contingent inheritance tax liability.[19]

EXAMPLE 20.4

Bird makes the following transfers of value:
(1) June 2002; £500,000 to his sister Cyd (a potentially exempt transfer).
(2) May 2006; £285,000 to a family discretionary trust.
(3) In May 2007 the trustees distribute the entire trust fund to the beneficiaries and in May 2008 Bird dies.

As a result of his death, the 2002 potentially exempt transfer is chargeable (the resultant IHT is primarily the responsibility of Cyd) and in addition tax on the creation of the settlement must be recalculated. When it was set up the potentially exempt transfer was ignored so that the transfer fell within Bird's nil rate band. With his death, however, inheritance tax must be calculated, at the rates in force in May 2006, on transfers from £500,000 to £785,000. In addition, no IHT will have been charged on the termination of the trust in May 2007 and therefore a recomputation is again necessary, with the trustees being primarily accountable for the resulting bill.

EXIT CHARGES BEFORE THE FIRST 10-YEAR ANNIVERSARY

20.07 An exit charge arises whenever property in the settlement ceases to be relevant property.[20] Therefore, if the trustees appoint property to a beneficiary absolutely or if (before March 22, 2006) an interest in possession arose in any part of the fund, there is an inheritance tax charge on the value of the property ceasing to be held on relevant property trusts. A charge is also imposed if the trustees make a disposition as a result of which the value of relevant property comprised in the settlement falls (a "depreciatory transaction"; notice that there is no requirement that the transaction be made with a beneficiary or with a person connected with him).[21]

If the resultant IHT is paid out of the property that is left in a continuing trust, grossing-up applies.

---

[19] Note also the PET trap. Where PETs are made within seven years following a chargeable transfer and the settlor survives seven years from the chargeable transfer but dies within seven years of the PET, more inheritance tax can be paid than if no PET had been made. In assessing the tax due on the failed PET the settlor's cumulative total at the time of the PET has to be calculated *taking into account* the chargeable transfer. This will affect the tax payable by the donee of the PET.

[20] IHT 1984, s.65(1).

[21] Contrast the position of interest in possession trusts, see 17–16.

The exit charge does not apply to a payment of costs or expenses (so long as fairly attributable to the relevant property), nor does it catch a payment which is income of any person for the purposes of income tax.[22]

Calculation of the settlement rate

The rate of inheritance tax to be charged is based upon half the full inheritance tax rates (sometimes called the lifetime rates) even if the trust was set up under the will of the settlor. The rate of tax actually payable is then 30 per cent of those rates applicable to a hypothetical chargeable transfer which is the sum of the following: **20.08**

(a) the value of the property in the settlement immediately after it commenced;

(b) the value (at the date of the addition) of any added property; and

(c) the value of property in a related settlement (valued immediately after it commenced).[23]

No account is taken of any rise or fall in the value of the settled fund and the value comprised in the settlement, and in any related settlement, can include property subject to a qualifying interest in possession.

Tax on this hypothetical transfer is calculated by joining the IHT table at the point reached by the cumulative total of previous chargeable transfers made by the settlor in the seven years before he created the settlement. Other chargeable transfers made on the same day as the settlement are ignored and, therefore, if the settlement is created on death, other gifts made in the will or on intestacy are ignored.[24] **20.09**

The resultant tax is converted to an average rate (the equivalent of an estate rate) and 30 per cent of that rate is then taken. The resultant rate (the "settlement rate") is used as the basis for calculating the exit charge. **20.10**

EXAMPLE 20.5

> Jasper settles £300,000 on discretionary trusts on April 1, 2003. His total chargeable transfers immediately before that date stood at £85,000. The trustees pay the inheritance tax. If an exit charge arises before the first 10-year anniversary of the fund (April 1, 2013) the settlement rate would be calculated as follows:
>
> (1) Calculate the hypothetical chargeable transfer. As there is no added property and no related settlement it comprises only the value of the property in the settlement immediately after its creation (i.e. £300,000).

---

[22] IHT 1984, s.65(5).
[23] IHTA, s.68(5).
[24] See the IHTA 1984, s.68(4)(b) as amended by the FA 1986, s.101(1), (3), Sch.19, para.18.

(2) Cumulate the £300,000 with the previous chargeable transfers of J (i.e. £85,000). Taking inheritance tax rates current at the time when the exit charge arises, tax on transfers between £85,000 and £385,000 is £20,000 (using tax year 2006/07 rates with a nil rate band of £285,000).
(3) The tax converted to a percentage rate is 6.66 per cent; (20,000/300,000). 30% of that rate produces a settlement rate of 1.99%.

Tax charge

20.11 The charge is on the fall in value of the property in the settlement.[25] To establish the rate of charge, a further proportion of the settlement rate must be calculated equal to one-fortieth of the settlement rate for each complete successive quarter that has elapsed from the creation of the settlement to the date of the exit charge. That proportion of the settlement rate is applied to the chargeable transfer (the "effective rate").

EXAMPLE 20.6

Assume in Example 20.5 that on March 25, 2007 there was an exit charge on £20,000 ceasing to be relevant property. The effective rate of inheritance tax is calculated as follows (using 2006/07 rates):

(1) Take completed quarters since the settlement was created, i.e. fifteen.
(2) Take 15/40ths of the "settlement rate" (1.99%) to discover the effective rate = 0.747%.
(3) The effective rate is applied to the fall in value of the relevant property. The inheritance tax is, therefore, £149.40 if the tax is borne by the beneficiary; or £150.52 if borne by the remaining fund (as a result of "grossing up").

20.12 There is no charge on events that occur in the first three months of the settlement[26] nor, where the trust was set up by the settlor on his death, on events occurring within two years of that death.[27] Note that if a beneficiary is appointed an interest in possession on or after March 22, 2006 the property remains relevant property (unless the beneficiary is disabled)[28] and no exit charge arises. Similarly if property is appointed to another settlement (other than a disabled trust) no exit charge will now arise even if the trust is an interest in possession trust. (It is not possible for a qualifying interest in possession to arise in a discretionary trust unless a disabled person's trust arises. Transitional serial interests cannot be created.)

---

[25] Hence if the trust had a 55 per cent shareholding in a company and the trustees appointed A a 15 per cent shareholding the loss of control would be taken into account.
[26] IHTA 1984, s.65(4).
[27] IHTA 1984, s.144(2).
[28] See IHTA 1984, s.89B.

The rate of tax is charged by reference to the initial value of the settled property. This has encouraged the creation of nil rate band discretionary trusts. Provided the settlor's cumulative total means that the rate of tax charged on the initial value is nil, any capital distributions before the tenth anniversary will be free of inheritance tax. Such planning can still work after March 21, 2006 but of course it will now be necessary for a beneficiary to take outright rather than just appointing the beneficiary an interest in possession. Note, however, that if the property originally settled was business or agricultural property qualifying for 50 per cent relief, tax will be paid if the value of what was originally settled *before* relief exceeded the nil rate band (see Chapter 32 and **20.28**).

CHARGE ON THE FIRST 10-YEAR ANNIVERSARY

20.13 The charge is levied on the value of the relevant property comprised in the settlement immediately before the anniversary[29] and at first sight no distinction appears to be drawn between income and capital in the fund. HMRC accept, however, that income only becomes relevant property, and therefore subject to charge, when it has been accumulated.[30] Pending accumulation the income is not subject to the anniversary charge and can, therefore, be distributed free from any exit charge. The crucial question is, therefore, at what moment is income accumulated? Obviously accumulation occurs once an irrevocable decision to that effect has been taken by trustees and it may also occur after a reasonable time for distribution has passed.[31] The legislation gives no guidance on what property is treated as being distributed first: i.e. if an appointment is made by the trustees out of property comprised in the settlement, does it come out of the original capital or out of accumulations of income? As a reduced charge may apply to property which has been added to the trust (such as accumulated income) this is an important omission.[32]

The assets in the trust fund are valued according to general principles and, if they include business or agricultural property, the reliefs appropriate to that

---

[29] See IHTA 1984, s.64.
[30] See HMRC SP 8/86 and see [1989] *Capital Taxes News* Vol 8, May 1989.
[31] But see *Re Locker's Settlement Trusts, Meachem v Sachs* [1978] 1 All E.R. 216; [1977] 1 W.L.R. 1323 where income which arose between 1965 and 1968 was still available for distribution in 1977 and it was accepted that it had not been accumulated. In that case a distinction was drawn between a trust where the trustees have a power to distribute and an obligation to accumulate in default of exercise of the power of distribution and a trust where there was an obligation to distribute but a mere power to accumulate. In the case of *Re Locker* there was a direction to distribute income: "the trustees *shall* pay, divide or apply the income of the trust fund to or for the beneficiaries" and the Court held that although in these circumstances it was the duty of the trustees to distribute the trust income within a reasonable time after it came into their hands they could still distribute some years later. The fact that they had failed in their duty earlier did not mean they could not carry it out now: "failure to exercise the permissive power within the proper limits of time left the default trusts standing. In the case of an obligatory power [to distribute] the failure to execute the trust promptly is an unfulfilled duty still in existence . . . the court can permit the existing trustees if willing and competent to do so to repair their own inaction." Cf. *Allen-Meyrick's Will Trusts* [1966] 1 W.L.R. where the power to distribute was discretionary.
[32] As to the reduction in the rate of the anniversary charge for property which has been added to the trust, see below.

property apply, subject to satisfaction of the relevant conditions. Any inheritance tax charged on such property is payable by instalments.[33]

Calculation of the rate of tax

20.14 Half rates are used in calculating the inheritance tax rate and, as with the exit charge,[34] the calculation depends upon a hypothetical chargeable transfer. The calculation is as follows:

Step 1 Calculate the hypothetical chargeable transfer which is made up of the sum of the following:

(i) the value of relevant property comprised in the settlement immediately before the anniversary;

(ii) the value, immediately after it was created, of property comprised in a related settlement; and

(iii) the value, at the date when the settlement was created, of any non-relevant property then in the settlement which has not subsequently become relevant property.

20.15 Normally the hypothetical chargeable transfer will be made up exclusively of property falling within paragraph (i) above. Property within paragraphs (ii) and (iii) above affects the rate of inheritance tax to be charged without itself being taxed. Related settlements are included because transfers made on the same day as the creation of the settlement are normally ignored and, therefore, an inheritance tax advantage could be achieved if the settlor were to set up a series of small funds rather than one large fund.[35] Non-relevant property in the settlement is included because the trustees could switch the values between the two portions of the fund.

20.16 *Step 2* Calculate tax at half rates on the hypothetical chargeable transfer by joining the inheritance tax table at the point reached by:

(i) the chargeable transfers of the settlor made in the seven years before he created the settlement; and

(ii) chargeable transfers made by the settlement in the first 10 years. Where a settlement was created after March 26, 1974 and before March 9, 1982, distribution payments (as defined by the capital transfer tax charging regime in force between those dates) must also be cumulated.[36]

Discretionary settlements therefore have their own total of chargeable transfers, with transfers over a 10 year period being cumulated (the seven-year period used for individuals is not employed for discretionary trusts). The unique feature of a settlement's cumulation lies in the inclusion (and they

---

[33] See IHTA 1984, ss.103–114, 115–124C, 227 as amended.
[34] As to exit charges before the first 10-year anniversary, see 20.07.
[35] This may still be possible if "pilot" trusts are used: see the *Rysaffe*.
[36] IHTA 1984, s.66(6).

never drop out) of chargeable transfers of the settlor in the seven years *before* the settlement is created.

Step 3 The inheritance tax is converted to a percentage and 30 per cent of that rate is then taken and charged upon the relevant property in the settlement. For the tax year 2006–07 the highest rate of inheritance tax is 20 per cent (half of 40 per cent). The highest effective rate (anniversary rate) is, therefore, 30 per cent of 20 per cent, i.e. 6 per cent.

20.17

EXAMPLE 20.7

Take the facts of *Example 20.5* (i.e., original fund £300,000, exit charge on £20,000; previous transfers of settlor £85,000). In addition, assume that Jasper had created a second settlement of £15,000 on April 1, 2003. The trust fund is worth £305,000 at the first 10-year anniversary.

(1) Relevant property to be taxed is £305,000.
(2) Calculate hypothetical chargeable transfer:

(a) Relevant property, as above	£305,000
(b) Property in related settlement	15,000
	£320,000

(3) Settlement's cumulative total:

	£
Settlor's earlier transfers	85,000
Chargeable transfers of trustees in the preceding 10 years	20,000
	£105,000

(4) Tax from the table (at half rates) on transfers from £105,000 to £425,000 (£320,000 + £105,000) = £28,000[37] (using 2006/07 rates) so that, as a percentage rate, inheritance tax is 9.18 per cent (28/305)

(5) The effective rate is 30 per cent of 9.18 per cent = 2.75 per cent.

Tax payable is £305,000 × 2.75% + £8,387.50.

EXIT CHARGES BETWEEN ANNIVERSARIES

The same events trigger an exit charge after the first 10-year anniversary as before it.[38] The inheritance tax charge is levied on the fall in value of the trust fund with grossing-up, if necessary. The rate of charge is a proportion of the effective rate charged at the first 10-year anniversary. That proportion is one-fortieth for each complete quarter from the date of the first anniversary charge to the date of the exit charge.[39]

20.18

---

[37] i.e. £320,000 is taxed at 0 per cent on the first £180,000 (£285,000 − £105,000) and 20 per cent on the balance.
[38] As to exit charges before the first 10-year anniversary see 20.07.
[39] See IHTA 1984, s.69.

EXAMPLE 20.8

Continuing *Example 20.7*, 15 months later the trustees appoint £25,000 to a beneficiary. The inheritance tax (assuming no grossing up) will be: £25,000 × 2.75% × 5/40 (five-quarters since the last 10-year anniversary) = £85.94.

If the rates of inheritance tax have been reduced (including the raising of the rate bands) between the anniversary and exit charges, the lower rates apply to the exit charge and, therefore, the rate of charge on the last anniversary has to be recalculated at those rates.[40] So long as the inheritance tax rate band remains linked to rises in the retail prices index,[41] recalculation is likely to be the norm.

LATER PERIODIC CHARGES

20.19 The principles that applied on the first 10-year anniversary operate on subsequent 10-year anniversaries.[42] So far as the hypothetical chargeable transfer is concerned the same items are included (so that the value of property in a related settlement and of non-relevant property in the settlement is always included. The value of the property in the related settlement is always the value immediately after the settlement commenced. Even if the related property trust has been ended, the value at commencement must still be included). The cumulative total of the fund includes, as before, the chargeable transfers of the settlor made in the seven years before he created the settlement and the transfers out of the settlement in the 10 years immediately preceding the anniversary (earlier transfers by the settlement fall out of the cumulative total). The remaining stages of the calculation are unaltered.

TECHNICAL PROBLEMS

20.20 The basic structure of the charging provisions is relatively straightforward. The charge to inheritance tax is built upon a series of periodic charges with interim charges (where appropriate) which are levied at a fraction of the full periodic charge. A number of technical matters should be noted as follows.

Reduction in the rate of the anniversary charge

20.21 If property has not been in the settlement for the entire preceding 10 years (as will be the case when income is accumulated during that period) there is a

---

[40] IHTA s.9, Sch.2, para.3 as amended.
[41] See IHTA 1984, s.8 as amended.
[42] As to the charge on the first 10-year anniversary, see 20.13.

proportionate reduction in the charge.[43] The reduction in the periodic rate is calculated by reference to the number of completed quarters which expired before the property became relevant property in the settlement. This proportionate reduction in the effective rate of the periodic charge does not affect the calculation of inheritance tax on events occurring after the anniversary, i.e. any exit charge is at the full effective rate.

There are no provisions which enable specific property to be identified. Therefore, the reduction mentioned above applies to the value of the relevant property in the trust at the 10-year anniversary "attributable" to property which was not relevant property throughout the preceding 10 years. Presumably, therefore, some sort of proportionate calculation is necessary where the value of the fund has shown an increase. Furthermore, if accumulated income is caught by the anniversary charge, a separate calculation has to be made with regard to each separate accumulation, as being property which has not been in the settlement for the whole of the previous decade.[44]

Conundrum

Charges on property converted by FA 2006 into relevant property—s.69(2): **20.22**

EXAMPLE 20.9

> On January 1, 1995 Yves created an accumulation and maintenance ("A+M") trust for his three children, each of whom is to attain an interest in possession on attaining 25. When Yves made the settlement he had a nil cumulative total and the property he settled was worth £200,000. On January 1, 2005, at the first ten year anniversary, the trust fund was worth £1m. Since the trust was still an A+M trust no periodic charge was imposed. All three children are now over 18 but none will have attained 25 by April 6, 2008 at which time the trust fund will become relevant property.[45]

What happens if there is an exit charge between April 6, 2008 and January 1, 2015 at a time when the trust fund is worth £3m?

Going back in time

There are provisions governing this, but they are far from easy to understand. **20.23**
The position appears to be as follows.

It is governed by IHTA 1984, s.69(2) which provides that the rate at which tax is charged is the appropriate fraction of the rate at which it would have

---

[43] IHTA 1984, s.66(2).
[44] See HMRC SP 8/86 and see 20.13 and fn.31.
[45] See 21.17 for the transitional rules for A+M trusts.

been charged at the previous 10-year anniversary if immediately before that anniversary ALL the property which has since become relevant property had then been relevant property. The effect of s.69(3) appears to be that for this purpose the value of the relevant property is the value of the property at the time of the exit charge, i.e. £3m.

If the property in respect of which the exit charge is imposed has not been relevant property throughout the period since the last ten year anniversary the appropriate fraction is reduced in the usual way, e.g. if the property on which the charge is imposed only became relevant property five years after the last 10-year anniversary it appears that the appropriate fraction will be 3/20ths; see s.69(4).

20.24 Two strange considerations emerge:

(1) It appears that the s.69(2) procedure has to be carried out each time there is an exit charge.

(2) Previous exit charges do not affect subsequent exit charges.

EXAMPLE 20.9 (CONTD)

Assume that on January 1, 2010 a part of the settled assets to a value of £750,000 was advanced to Adam just before his 25th birthday. The position is as follows:

(i) an IHT exit charge under IHTA, s.65(1)(a) applies. For CGT purposes, hold-over relief under TCGA 1992, s.260 is available;
(ii) to calculate the IHT exit charge go back to the last 10-year anniversary (January 1, 2005) and calculate what the charge would have been on the basis that relevant property in the settlement immediately before the anniversary was worth £3m. For these purposes[46]:

- There was no related settlement.
- When the settlement was created it contained non-relevant property which has all become relevant property (on April 6, 2008) and so is ignored.
- So far as the hypothetical chargeable transfers is concerned,[47] the settlor had made no chargeable transfer in the seven years before creating the settlement and nor had there been chargeable transfers out of the settlement in the previous 10 years,[48]

(iii) taking the 2007/8 rates, the nil rate band of £300,000 is deducted leaving £2.7m to be taxed at 20 per cent = £540,000 so that the rate of tax is 18 per cent (540,000 ÷ 3m) and 30 per cent of this produces a rate of tax of 5.4%.
(iv) normally the charge will be by reference to the number of complete successive quarters in the period from the last anniversary to the

---

[46] See *Example 20.17*.
[47] See 20.14.
[48] Of course there will often be cases when this is not true and the settlor will have followed the standard advice and created a discretionary trust to use his nil rate band (a chargeable transfer) before setting up the A+M trust (which he did by a PET). That earlier chargeable transfer will be taken into account if it occurred within seven years of setting up the A+M trust.

day before the occasion of charge.[49] However the settlement did not contain relevant property at that time and so[50] no quarter which expired before the day on which the property became relevant property is to be counted (unless that day—viz when the trust became relevant property—falls in the same quarter as that in which the exit charge arises when it is taken into account).

In this case there are exactly 20 complete quarters in the period from the last 10-year anniversary (January 1, 2005) to the exit occasion (January 1, 2010) and of these 13 are complete quarters before April 6, 2008 (when the property became relevant property). Hence there are only seven chargeable quarters so the tax rate becomes:

$$5.4 \times 7/40 = 0.945\%$$

Tax payable on the advance to Adam of £750,000 (ignoring grossing up) is £7,087.50.

Transfers between settlements

20.25 s.81 prevents a tax advantage from switching property between discretionary settlements by providing that such property remains comprised in the first settlement. Accordingly, property cannot be moved out of a discretionary trust to avoid an anniversary charge; property cannot be switched from a fund with a high cumulative total to one with a lower total; and the transfer of a property from one discretionary fund to another is not chargeable.[51]

Added property

20.26 Special rules operate if, after the settlement commenced (and after March 8, 1982), the settlor makes a chargeable transfer as a result of which the value of the property comprised in the settlement is increased.[52] Note that it is only additions by the settlor that trigger these provisions[53] and that it is the value of the fund which must have increased and not necessarily the amount of property in that fund. A transfer which has the effect of increasing the value of the fund is ignored if it was not primarily intended to have that effect and did not in fact increase the value by more than 5 per cent.

EXAMPLE 20.10

Sid, the settlor, creates in 2007 a trust of stocks and shares in S Ltd and the benefit of a life insurance policy on his life.

---

[49] IHTA 1984, s.69(4).
[50] IHTA 1984, s.69(4) applying s.68(3).
[51] IHTA 1984, s.81 and see (1989) *Capital Taxes News* Vol 8 p.219.
[52] IHTA 1984, s.67(1).
[53] Addition by another would be treated as creating a separate settlement.

(1) Each year Sid adds to the settlement property equal to his annual inheritance tax exemption.
(2) Sid continues to pay the premiums on the life policy each year.
(3) Sid transfers further shares in S Ltd to the trust.

The special rules for added property do not apply in either case (1) or (2), because S is not making a chargeable transfer; the first transfer is covered by his annual exemption and the second by the exemption for normal expenditure out of income. The transfer of further shares to the trust, however, is caught by the provisions relating to added property.[54]

20.27 If the added property provisions apply, the calculation of the periodic charge which next follows the addition is modified. For the purposes of the hypothetical chargeable transfer, the cumulative total of the settlor's chargeable transfers is the higher of the totals in the seven year period:

(i) immediately before creating the settlement plus transfers made by the trustees of the settlement before the addition; and

(ii) immediately before transferring the added property, deducting from this latter total the transfer made on creation of the settlement and a transfer to any related settlement.

In general, the settlor should avoid additions because they may cause more inheritance tax to be charged at the next anniversary. It will be preferable to create a separate settlement.

EXAMPLE 20.11

In 1987 X made an immediately chargeable transfer (a gift to a close company) of £70,000.

In 1992 on the same day X settled £100,000 on discretionary Trust A and £50,000 on discretionary Trust B.

In 1994 X made another chargeable transfer by giving £20,000 to the close company.

In 1999 X added £50,000 to Trust A and £30,000 to Trust B.

In 2002 the first 10-year anniversary charge of Trust A is calculated. The cumulative total used for working out the hypothetical chargeable transfer (see 20.16 above) is the greater of (i) £70,000 and (ii) £90,000 (£70k + £20k) so £90,000 will apply. If the chargeable transfer in 1994 had instead been made in 1998 i.e. more than 10 years after 1987 the figures would have been (i) £70,000 and (ii) £20,000 so (i) would have been taken.

The sum of £30,000 is ignored because it is a transfer made on the same day as value is added to A. The sum of £50,000 is ignored because it is

---

[54] IHTA 1984, s.67 as amended by FA 1986, s.101(1), (3), Sch.19 para.17.

taken into account in calculating the value used to find the effective rate.

The timing of the exit charge

Assume that a discretionary trust has been in existence for nearly 10 years and that the trustees now wish to distribute all or part of the trust property to the beneficiaries. Are they better off doing so just before the 10-year anniversary or should they wait until just after that anniversary? Generally it is advantageous to distribute before an anniversary because the inheritance tax payable is calculated at rates then in force but on historic values; i.e. on the value of the fund when it was settled or at the last 10-year anniversary. By contrast, if the trustees delay until after the anniversary, inheritance tax (still at current rates) is then assessed on the present value of the fund. To this general proposition, one major exception exists which may well be the result of defective drafting in the legislation. It relates to a fund which includes property qualifying for either business relief or agricultural relief when the fund was set up. In this situation, trustees should take care before breaking the fund before the first anniversary.

20.28

The rate of tax that applies when property ceases to be comprised in the trust is based upon "the value, immediately after the settlement commenced, of the property then comprised in it"[55] which makes no allowance for that property attracting business or agricultural property relief. Of course this will not matter if the property ceasing to be comprised in the settlement qualifies for 100 per cent BPR or APR since then the value transferred will be nil.

EXAMPLE 20.12

In 2006 Vince sets up a discretionary trust for his family into which he transfers:
  (i) stocks and shares worth £300,000;
  (ii) 25 per cent of the shares in the family trading company which are worth £1m but which attract 100% BPR.

In 2009 the trustees:
  (a) advance the stocks and shares (then worth £400,000) to beneficiary A, *or*
  (b) advance the family company shares (then worth £1.2m) to A.

The IHT consequences are as follows:
  (i) there is an "exit occasion" in 2009 and the tax rate will be calculated on the basis that the property put into the settlement by Vince was worth £1,300,000. If we assume that Vince had already used up his IHT nil rate band at the time when he set up the trust

[55] IHTA 1984, s.68(4); 69(5)(a).

(say he had given £500,000 to a close company two years earlier) the rate calculated under IHTA 1984, s.68(4)(5) will be 6%;
  (ii) if the distribution is of the stocks and shares ((a) above) that rate will be applied to the then value of £400,000 with a reduction based on the number of completed quarters that have elapsed from the creation of the settlement in 2006[56];
  (iii) if however the distribution is of the relevant business property—attracting relief at 100%—the tax charge is nil.

The problem does not arise with the calculation of the anniversary charge nor with exit occasions occurring thereafter (see further Example 32.4).

DISCRETIONARY TRUSTS CREATED BEFORE MARCH 27, 1974

20.29 **Discretionary settlements created before March 27, 1974:** are subject to special rules for the calculation of inheritance tax which generally result in less tax being charged.

Chargeable events occurring before first 10-year anniversary

20.30 As the settlement is treated as a separate taxable entity, only transfers made by the settlement are cumulated. Such chargeable transfers were either distribution payments (if made under the regime in force from 1974 to 1982) or are chargeable events.[57] Once the cumulative total is known, the rate of tax is calculated at half rates and the charge is at 30 per cent of that rate.[58]

First anniversary charge

20.31 No anniversary charge applied before April 1, 1983. Therefore, the first discretionary trust to suffer a charge was one created on April 1, 1973 (or 1963, 1953, 1943 and so on).

The amount subject to the charge is calculated in the normal way. In calculating the rate of charge, however, it is only chargeable transfers of the settlement in the preceding 10 years that are cumulated (as the settlement predates capital transfer tax/inheritance tax the settlor has no chargeable transfers to cumulate). Property in a related settlement and non-relevant property in the settlement are ignored. As before, the rate of charge is reduced if property has not been relevant property throughout the decade preceding the first anniversary.[59] The danger of increasing an inheritance tax bill by an addition of property

---

[56] IHTA 1984, s.68(2).
[57] See IHTA 1984, s.65.
[58] See IHTA 1984, s.68(6) as amended by FA 1986, s.101(1), (3), Sch.19, para.18
[59] As to such reduction in the rate of the anniversary charge see ante.

by the settlor[60] is even greater with these old trusts. If such an addition has been made, the settlor's chargeable transfers in the seven year period before the addition must be cumulated in calculating the rate of tax on the anniversary charge.[61] The effective rate of charge for the anniversary charge is (as for new trusts) 30 per cent of the rate calculated according to half the table rates.

Chargeable events after the first anniversary charge

The position is the same as for new trusts.[62] The charge is based upon the rate charged at the last anniversary. 20.32

EXEMPTIONS AND RELIEFS

Many of the exemptions from inheritance tax do not apply to property in relevant property trusts; for example the annual exemption, the marriage exemption, and the exemption for normal expenditure out of income. There is also no exemption if the settled fund reverts to either the settlor or his spouse (and note that if the settlor is a beneficiary the reservation of benefit provisions apply). Business and agricultural property relief may, however, be available, provided that the necessary conditions for the relief are met by the trustees.[63] There is no question of any aggregation with similar property owned by a discretionary beneficiary. 20.33

Exit charges are not levied in certain cases when property leaves the settlement, e.g.:

(i) Property ceasing to be relevant property within three months of the creation of the trust, or of an anniversary charge, or within two years of creation (if the trust was set up on death)[64] is not subject to an exit charge.

(ii) Property may pass, without attracting an exit charge, to such privileged trusts as employee trusts[65]; maintenance funds for historic buildings[66]; charities (with no time limits)[67]; political parties in accordance with the exemption in IHTA 1984, s.24[68]; national heritage bodies.[69]

If a discretionary fund contains non-relevant property, the periodic and exit charges do not apply to that portion of the fund.

---

[60] As to the addition of property by the settlor see ante.
[61] IHTA 1984, s.67(4) as amended by FA 1986, s.101(1), (3), Sch.19 para.17.
[62] As to exit charges after the first anniversary charge and between anniversaries see above. As to later periodic charges see 20.18.
[63] See Ch. 32.
[64] IHTA 1984, s.144 and see *Frankland v IRC* [1996] S.T.C. 735 discussed at 29.52.
[65] IHTA 1984, s.75.
[66] IHTA 1984, s.77, Sch.4.
[67] IHTA 1984, s.76(1)(a).
[68] IHTA 1984, s.76(1)(b).
[69] IHTA 1984, s.76(1)(c), Sch.3.

20.34 Under IHTA 1984, s.58 property is not relevant property if, although no qualifying interest in possession subsists in the settled property, the property is held on certain special trusts. These are as follows.

(a) Accumulation and maintenance trusts and trusts for bereaved children

For a detailed treatment of accumulation and maintenance trusts and trusts for bereaved children see Chapters 21 and 25.

(b) Charitable trusts

If trust property is held for charitable purposes only, whether or not for a limited time, there is no charge to inheritance tax and the fund is not "relevant property".[70] Transfers to charities are exempt, whether made by individuals or by trustees of relevant property trusts.[71] The IHTA 1984, s.70 is concerned with temporary charitable trusts which that section defines as "settled property held for charitable purposes only until the end of a period (whether defined by date or in some other way)"[72] and ensures that when the fund ceases to be held for such purposes an exit charge arises. That charge (which is calculated in the same way as for accumulation and maintenance trusts)[73] will never exceed a 30 per cent rate which is reached after 50 years.

(c) Trusts for the benefit of disabled persons

See Chapter 26.

(d) Pension funds

A registered pension scheme or s.615(3) scheme (defined as a superannuation fund to which s.615(3), TA 1988 applies) is not subject to the rules for relevant property trusts. It is common practice for the death benefit to be settled.[74] From April 6, 2006 the definition of approved pension schemes outside the relevant property regime has become more limited. Prior to that date s.151 covered any sponsored superannuation scheme as defined in s.624 TA 1988. The section provided that any property held for the purposes of a

---

[70] IHTA 1984, s.58(1)(a).
[71] IHTA 1984, s.76 as amended by FA 1998, ss.143(4)(a), 165, Sch.27 Pt IV.
[72] IHTA 1984, s.70(1).
[73] As to the calculation of such IHT see 21.15.
[74] As to the treatment of pension rights etc see IHTA 1984, s.151 as amended by the TA 1988, s.844, Sch.29 para.32, by the F(No 2)A 1987, s.98(4), and from April 6, 2006 by the FA 2004, ss.203(1), (4), 326, Sch.42.

scheme which satisfied the s.151 requirements was not relevant property and therefore 10-year and exit charges did not apply to it. Any scheme the purpose of which was to provide benefits on retirement death or disability where the employer met part or all of the cost of providing the benefits or of administering the scheme in a way which did not result in the employee paying income tax on the cost so met, satisfied s.624, TA 1988 and therefore fell within the sponsored superannuation scheme definition. Hence, provided the scheme was set up in such a way that some cost was funded by the employer and not taxed as an income benefit on the employee, there was no inheritance tax charged in the hands of the scheme trustees while the trust was continuing. Finance Act 2004, Sch.42 repealed s.624, TA 1988 and s.151, IHTA with effect from April 6, 2006. Policies which were (for example) excepted group life policies, cannot be employer financed retirement benefit schemes providing relevant benefits within s.393B, FA 2004 and are treated as providing excluded benefits. Excluded benefits also include benefits in respect of the death by accident of an employee during service.[75] If any of these benefits are settled on discretionary trusts they will now be relevant property settlements.

Schedule 36 para.56 provides that if no contributions are made after April 6, 2006 to existing trusts of such superannuation schemes, then the s.151 treatment continues to apply so there is no relevant property charge for inheritance tax purposes. If contributions are made after that date then the trust falls within the relevant property trust regime.

(e) Employee trusts

Broadly employee trusts are trusts for the benefit of employees in a particular trade or profession or employment by, or office with, a body carrying on a trade, profession or undertaking and those who are married to or dependent on them.[76]

(f) Compensation funds

Trusts set up by professional bodies and trade associations for the purpose of indemnifying clients and customers against loss incurred through the default of their members are exempt from the rules for non-interest in possession trusts.[77]

(g) Newspaper trusts

The provisions relating to employee trusts are extended to cover newspaper trusts.[78]

---

[75] See s.395 of FA 2004.
[76] See s.86(3) of IHTA 1984.
[77] IHTA 1984, ss.58–63.
[78] IHTA 1984, s.87.

(h) Maintenance funds for historic buildings

IHT exemptions are available for maintenance funds where property is settled and the Treasury gives a direction.[79] Once the trust ceases, for any reason, to carry out its specialised function, an exit charge occurs, calculated in the same way as for accumulation and maintenance trusts.[80]

(i) Protective trusts

The special treatment accorded to certain protective trusts is considered at 19.04.[81]

(j) Excluded property trusts

20.35 See Chapter 22.

---

[79] i.e. under IHTA 1984, Sch.4 para.1.
[80] IHTA 1984, s.77, Sch.4 para.8.
[81] See s.88 of IHTA 1984.

Chapter 21

ACCUMULATION AND MAINTENANCE ("A+M") TRUSTS

- Background **(21.01)**
- Tax treatment of A+M trusts prior to March 22, 2006 **(21.05)**
- Tax treatment of A+M trusts after March 21, 2006 **(21.16)**
- Summary of options **(21.22)**

BACKGROUND

The demise of accumulation and maintenance trusts

The so-called A+M trust was the creature of the capital transfer tax (later inheritance tax) legislation[1]: the only reason for establishing trusts of the complexity needed to fall within the statutory definition in that legislation was to take advantage of the inheritance tax benefits that were on offer.[2] A+M trusts were often considered under the title "trusts for infant beneficiaries". Of course they were that, but given the somewhat curious conditions that had to be satisfied (notably that it sufficed for income to vest in a beneficiary no later than the age of 25 years)[3] they could also be established for the benefit of children in the age bracket 18–25 years. The trust could also be drafted in the form of a highly flexible (i.e. discretionary) trust, which, because of the special IHT rules, did not give rise to the charges applicable to "pure" discretionary trusts.[4]

21.01

---

[1] See IHTA 1984, s.71 as amended by SI 2005/3229 and by FA 2006.
[2] It should be remembered that (by and large) it was only in the area of IHT that tax benefits were conferred. The income of the trust, for instance, was subject to the rate applicable to trusts or the Sch.F trust rate imposed by the Income and Corporation Taxes Act 1988 ss. 686, 687 as amended and if trust dividends were distributed to beneficiaries, a further burden resulted given that the tax credit on dividends could not be deducted from the tax at 40 per cent payable on distributions to beneficiaries.
[3] IHTA 1984, s.71(1)(a).
[4] It was a common mistake to assume that once a trust had been established in accumulation and maintenance form, it would continue to satisfy the requirements until it ceased to exist. In fact, the majority of accumulation and maintenance trusts underwent a process of metamorphosis into interest in possession trusts before finally terminating. A failure to appreciate this produced elementary errors, e.g.:

  (a) That there was no inheritance tax charge on the death of a beneficiary of an A+M trust. This was true provided that the trust was still in accumulation and maintenance form, but

21.02   The flexibility of these trusts combined with their tax advantages explains why the IHT legislation was changed in 2006 leading to the demise of the A+M vehicle. Speaking in the Standing Committee Debates on June 13, 2006, the Paymaster-General commented:

> "It was clear that A and M trusts have been routinely used to shelter large amounts of wealth from inheritance tax for long periods of time. We are talking about money going into trusts in excess of the IHT threshold. We are not talking about somebody's house, but about £285,000 going into a trust with specific objectives in mind about the tax consequences of the trust. . . .
>
> Trusts are set up ostensibly to provide for minor children, but that often happens in circumstances in which there is no particular need for a trust—the sums involved being grossly disproportionate to those required to provide for the child and most of the trust assets being destined ultimately for other beneficiaries. However, let us park the difference between sensible planning that allows children to have a nest egg—quite a large one in some cases—and cases in which there are other beneficiaries.
>
> I have repeatedly said that continued special provisions are justified when trusts for bereaved minor children constitute a way to protect children should they lose one or both parents, and that is precisely the situation with which the provisions of Sch 20 are designed to deal."[5]

if the beneficiary had obtained an interest in possession (e.g. at 18 years under the Trustee Act 1925, s.31 as amended by the Family Law Reform Act 1969, s.1(3), Sch. 1 Pt I, the Trustee Act 2000, s.40(1), Sch.2 para.25 and the Civil Partnership Act 2004, s.261(1), Sch.27 para.5) then his death resulted in the normal inheritance tax charge associated with the termination of an interest in possession.

(b) CGT hold-over relief was available on the termination of an accumulation and maintenance trust. This was true only if the trust was in accumulation and maintenance form at the time when it ceased to exist: Taxation of Chargeable Gains Act 1992, s.260(2)(d). If, however, the accumulation and maintenance trust had ended before March 22, 2006 as a result of an interest in possession coming into existence, then on that event there was no liability to capital gains tax (specifically, there was no deemed disposal under the TCGA 1992, s.71) and therefore no need for any hold-over election. If the trust subsequently ended as a result of the interest in possession beneficiary becoming entitled to the capital, hold-over relief under TCGA Act 1992, s.260(2)(d) was not available.

(c) That 25 years was the magic age for all purposes and therefore a settlement on N (aged two years) contingent on his attaining 50 years could not be a qualifying accumulation and maintenance trust. This was wrong; it would qualify provided that N became entitled to the income of the trust at no later than the age of 25 years.

Correctly identifying the form of the trust remains significant after the 2006 changes given that there are different transitional provisions dealing with accumulation and maintenance and interest in possession trusts in existence on March 22, 2006. Of course, if a trust is a qualifying accumulation and maintenance trust on that date but a beneficiary becomes entitled to an interest in possession during the transitional period (say on January 1, 2007) then the fund (or that portion of it if the interest in possession only arose in part) will, from that date, become held on a relevant property trust (unless it then satisfies the conditions to be an "age 18–25 trust" as set out in IHTA 1984, s.71D inserted by FA 2006)).

[5] Rt Hon. Dawn Primarolo, MP at col. 603.

From March 22, 2006 it has not been possible to set up new accumulation and maintenance trusts under IHTA 1984, s.71.[6] Existing trusts will, however, continue to receive the old IHT treatment during a transitional period which runs until April 6, 2008. On that date, however, the wording of s.71(1)(a) is changed so that instead of requiring that:

> "one or more persons . . . will, on or before attaining a specified age not exceeding twenty five become entitled to it or to an interest in possession in it",

18 is to replace the age of 25 and absolute vesting (not just entitlement to an interest in possession) is required. It is likely that the majority of existing settlements will then cease to qualify as accumulation and maintenance unless steps are taken before April 6, 2008 that provide for the conditions of the revised s.71(1)(a) to be met.

Establishing new trusts after FA 2006

The changes that came into effect from March 22, 2006 mean that— 21.03

(i) Any lifetime trust will—unless it falls within the definition of a trust which creates a "disabled person's interest"[7]—be immediately chargeable for IHT purposes. It does not matter that the trust is set up for the benefit of the settlor's children, grandchildren or other beneficiaries. There are no longer special rules for *inter vivos* trusts when beneficiaries take capital or income at a specified age.

(ii) There are special rules for certain will trusts but only if these are established by a testator for his own children. First, "bereaved minor trusts", which receive the same IHT treatment as s.71 accumulation and maintenance trusts (no anniversary or exit charges), but which require capital to vest no later than the age of 18. Secondly, "18–25 trusts" which, as the name suggests, enable the capital to vest at any time up until age 25 but which levy an IHT charge once the beneficiary has attained 18 (this may be seen as a "fine" for continuing to use the trust structure).[8]

Nothing will now be served by continuing to draft trusts in A+M form which are designed to satisfy the conditions in IHTA 1984, s.71 when no IHT advantages apply: old style accumulation and maintenance precedents can therefore be consigned to the dustbin of tax history.

This chapter is concerned with two matters— 21.04

---

[6] IHTA 1984, s.71(1A) inserted by FA 2006.
[7] As defined in IHTA 1984, s.89B inserted by FA 2006, Sch.20, para.6.
[8] The IHT charge does not arise on the beneficiary reaching 18. The exit charge is imposed if the trust ends at any time after the beneficiary reaches 18 with an increasing rate each year up to a maximum of 4.2 per cent if the beneficiary becomes entitled to capital at 25. If the trust does not end when the beneficiary reaches 25 but continues (e.g. because the trustees have made a settled advance: see 7.42 for CGT position) there is a 4.2 per cent charge then as the trust enters the relevant property regime. Thereafter 10 year charges and exit charges arise in the normal way. The main advantage of the s.71D trust is protection from 10 year charges until the beneficiary reaches 25.

(i) The definition of an A+M trust which remains important since—although new A+M trusts falling within the s.71 definition cannot be set up—the treatment of existing A+M trusts is changing. Practitioners will therefore need to review their existing trusts and will need to determine whether that trust satisfied the s.71 conditions on March 22, 2006.

(ii) How A+M trusts are now taxed following the changes which took effect on March 22, 2006.

TAX TREATMENT OF ACCUMULATION AND MAINTENANCE TRUSTS UNDER IHTA 1984, S.71 (TRUSTS SET UP BEFORE MARCH 22, 2006).

21.05 Before March 22, 2006, the *inter vivos* creation of an accumulation and maintenance trust was a potentially exempt transfer[9] and thereafter, so long as the property continued to be held on accumulation and maintenance trusts, the 10-year anniversary charge did not apply[10] and there was no proportionate exit charge when the property ceased to be held on qualifying accumulation and maintenance trusts.[11] As a result, for the purposes of IHT, the taxation of settled gifts to minors was treated in much the same way as outright gifts to adults.

The requirements for setting up an A+M trust before March 22, 2006

21.06 To qualify for the privileged IHT treatment, an A+M trust had to satisfy the three requirements considered below.[12] Failure to do so meant that the normal charging system for relevant property settlements applied. When the requirements ceased to be satisfied (e.g. because a beneficiary became entitled to the trust fund or to an interest in possession in it) IHT was not charged save in exceptional cases.[13]

Requirement 1

21.07 The first requirement was that one or more persons (beneficiaries) will, on or before attaining a specified age not exceeding 25 years, become beneficially entitled to, or to an interest in possession in, the settled property.[14] The age of 25 years was specified as a maximum age limit and this was a generously late age when one considers that the primary purpose of these rules was to deal with settlements for infant children.

---

[9] IHTA 1984, s.3A(1)(c) as inserted by FA 1986, s.101, Sch.19, para.1.
[10] See IHTA 1984, ss.58, 64 as amended by FA 2004, ss.203, 326, Sch. 42 Pt 3.
[11] IHTA 1984, s.71(4). For the unusual occasions when an exit charge arises see 21.15, below.
[12] IHTA 1984, s.71 as amended by SI 2005/3229.
[13] For the occasions when an exit charge will arise see 21.15.
[14] IHTA 1984, s.71(1)(a).

EXAMPLE 21.1

(1) In 2004 property was settled upon trust "for A absolutely, contingent on attaining the age of 18 years". A became entitled to both income and capital at 18 years so that Requirement 1 was satisfied.

(2) In 2005 property was settled upon trust "for B absolutely, contingent upon attaining the age of 30 years". B will not acquire the capital in the fund until after the age of 25 years but the requirement will be met if B acquires an interest in possession no later than age 25. B will do so, because TA 1925, s.31[15] (if not expressly or impliedly excluded) provides that when a beneficiary with a contingent interest attains 18 years, that beneficiary shall then be entitled to the income produced by the fund even though he has not yet satisfied the contingency.

21.08 The requirement that a beneficiary "will" become entitled required a degree of certainty. However, the possibility of death before attaining the specified age did not prevent the requirement from being satisfied while the beneficiary was still alive.[16] The word "will" caused particular problems when trustees possessed overriding powers of advancement and appointment (dispositive powers) which, if exercised, could result in entitlement being postponed beyond age 25. So long as the dispositive power could only be exercised amongst the existing beneficiaries and could not be used to postpone entitlement to an interest in possession beyond the age of 25 years, the trust would qualify for A+M status. Accordingly, a power to vary or determine the respective shares of members of the class, even to the extent of excluding some members altogether, was permissible so long as it was limited as indicated.[17]

EXAMPLE 21.2

Under a 2004 settlement, property was held on trust for the three children of A contingent upon their attaining the age of 25 years and if more than one, in equal shares. The trustees were given overriding powers of appointment, exercisable until the first beneficiary attains 25 years, to appoint the fund absolutely or for an interest in possession to one or more of the beneficiaries as they saw fit.

The property will vest absolutely in one or more of the beneficiaries no later than the age of 25 years. The existence of the overriding power of appointment cannot be exercised other than in favour of the class of beneficiaries and cannot be used to postpone the obtaining of an interest in possession until after a beneficiary has attained 25 years.

---

[15] i.e. TA 1925, s.31 as amended by the Family Law Reform Act, 1969 s.1(3), Sch.1 Pt I, TA 2000, s.40(1), Sch.2 para.25 and the Civil Partnership Act 2004, s.261(1), Sch.27 para.5.
[16] See *Lord Inglewood v IRC* [1981] S.T.C. 318; affd [1983] 1 W.L.R. 366; [1983] S.T.C. 133, CA. A similar requirement is included in the definition of a bereaved minor trust (see IHTA 1984, s.71A(3) inserted by FA 2006) and in the definition of an 18–25 trust (see IHTA 1984, s.71D(6) inserted by FA 2006).
[17] SP/E1 (June 11, 1975) and see the Law Society's Gazette, June 11, 1975.

21.09 The existence of a common form power of advancement did not prevent a settlement being A+M. However, such powers can be exercised so as to postpone a beneficiary's entitlement to income beyond the age stated in the trust document and so beyond the age of 25 years[18] and they can, in exceptional cases, result in property being paid to a non-beneficiary.[19] Obviously, if the power was so exercised the trust would cease to meet the s 71 requirements and a charge to IHT could result.[20]

EXAMPLE 21.3[21]

In 2002 property was settled "for the children of E contingent on their attaining 25 years". The trustees were given the following (alternative) overriding powers of appointment:

(1) *To appoint income and capital to E's sister F.* The mere existence of this power meant that the settlement did not qualify as an A+M trust. There was no certainty that the fund will pass to E's children because the power might have been exercised in favour of F.
(2) *To appoint income to E's brother G.* The same consequence followed because the mere existence of this power meant that the income could be used for the benefit of G.
(3) *To appoint capital and income to E's relatives so long as those relatives are no older than 25 years.* This power does not cause problems because whoever receives the settled fund, whether E's children or his relatives, will be no older than 25 years.

21.10 In *Lord Inglewood v IRC*, at first instance, Vinelott J. in considering the requirements of s.71(1)(a) distinguished between events provided for in the trust instrument and events wholly outside the settlor's control:

"... the terms of the settlement must be such that one or more of the beneficiaries, if they or one of them survive to the specified age, will be bound to take a vested interest on or before attaining that age ... Of course, a beneficiary may assign his interest or be deprived of it by an arrangement or by bankruptcy before he attains a vested interest. But he is not then deprived of it under the terms of the settlement, so these possible events, unlike the exercise of a power of revocation or appointment, must be disregarded."[22]

---

[18] See *Pilkington v IRC* [1964] A.C. 612; [1962] 3 All E.R. 622, HL.
[19] See *Re Hampden Settlement Trusts* [1977] TR 177.
[20] See [1975] BTR 437 (which became SP/E2 but in July 1994 was dropped as obsolete) in which HMRC confirmed that the "existence" of a "common form" power would not break the requirement; and see also *Lord Inglewood v IRC* above. The position was confirmed again in Revenue correspondence published in Taxation Practitioner Nov 1995.
[21] Taken from SP/E1 (June 11, 1975).
[22] *Lord Inglewood v IRC* [1981] S.T.C. 318 at 322; and see also [1983] 1 W.L.R. 366 at 372; [1983] S.T.C. 133 at 138, CA per Fox L.J. Note the unsatisfactory decision in *Crawford Settlement Trustees v RCC* [2005] S.T.C. (SCD) 457, which was compromised on appeal and is thought to be wrong.

Requirement 2

No interest in possession must subsist in the settled property and the income **21.11** from it must be accumulated so far as it is not applied for the maintenance, education or benefit of a beneficiary.[23] Accordingly, once an interest in possession arose, the settlement ceased to be an A+M trust.[24] If there must be no interest in possession in the income, what was to happen to it? Two possibilities were envisaged by Requirement 2: it could either be used for the benefit of a beneficiary (e.g. under a power of maintenance) or it could be accumulated. The official view was that a pure accumulation trust (without any power to maintain) was within IHTA 1984, s.71, as was an exhaustive trust for maintenance without any power of accumulation.[25]

Requirement 3

Either: **21.12**

(i) Not more than 25 years had elapsed since the commencement of the settlement or, if it was later, since the time (or latest time) when Requirements 1 and 2 became satisfied with respect to the property; or

(ii) All the persons who were, or had been, beneficiaries were, or had been, either:

- grandchildren of a common grandparent; or
- children, widows or widowers of such grandchildren who were themselves beneficiaries but died before the time when, had they survived, they would have become entitled as mentioned in Requirement 1.[26]

---

[23] IHTA 1984, s.71(1)(b).

[24] This remains the case for existing accumulation and maintenance trusts even though the interest in possession will not be "qualifying" if it arises after March 21, 2006. It can therefore result in the trust ceasing to fall within s.71 and becoming a relevant property settlement: see further 21.16 and 20.17 below.

[25] Care had to be taken in choosing the appropriate accumulation period if the intention was to accumulate income beyond the minorities of the beneficiaries. Various periods are permitted under LPA 1925, s.164 and 165 and under TA 1925, s.31,[26] but some of them (unless further restricted) would cause the trust to fall outside the definition of an accumulation and maintenance trust. In the case of an *inter vivos* trust, for instance, a direction to accumulate "during the lifetime of the settlor" would mean that an interest in possession might not arise until after the beneficiaries had attained the age of 25 years; likewise, a provision to accumulate for 21 years when some of the beneficiaries were already over the age of four at the commencement of the settlement would have been fatal.

[26] IHTA 1984, s.71(2) as amended by SI 2005/3229. Once more than 25 years passed since the creation of the accumulation and maintenance settlement and not all the beneficiaries were the grandchildren of a common grandparent, the settlement lost its privileged inheritance tax status. The earliest accumulation and maintenance settlement to lose its status in this way was one created on April 15, 1976, its status being lost on April 15, 2001. The settlement will become a relevant property settlement. Also, when that 25-year period expires, there is an inheritance tax charge at a rate of 21 per cent on the value of the trust assets: see 21.15 below.

Requirement 3 was first introduced in FA 1976 in an attempt to stop the A+M trust from being used to benefit more than one generation. There were two ways in which it could be satisfied. *Either* the trust must not last for more than 25 years from the date when the fund became settled on A+M trusts; *or* all the beneficiaries had to have a common grandparent.

Example 21.4

(1) In 2004 property was settled on an A+M trust for the children and grandchildren of the settlor. As there was no grandparent common to all the beneficiaries, the trust must not last for longer than 25 years if an exit charge to inheritance tax is to be avoided.

(2) In 2005 property was settled on A+M trust for the children of brothers A and B. As there is a common grandparent the duration of the accumulation and maintenance trust does not need to be limited to 25 years.

There was one case in which two generations could benefit: where the original beneficiaries had a common grandparent and one of those beneficiaries has died, substitution per stirpes was permitted.

In practice Requirement 3 did not succeed in curbing the use of trusts to benefit more than one generation. In simple terms an A+M trust would be set up for (say) children of the settlor who would be given interests in possession no later than age 25. The trustees, however, would have wide powers of appointment which could then be exercised to appoint onto fresh A+M trusts for the settlor's grandchildren. The children would make a PET (and survive seven years!).

Ending of A+M trusts

21.13 No IHT is charged when property from an A+M trust becomes subject to an interest in possession in favour of one or more of the beneficiaries, nor when any part of the fund is appointed absolutely to (or becomes held on trust for) such a beneficiary. In both cases, the event must occur on or before the beneficiary becomes 25. This exemption, together with the exclusion of the anniversary charge, meant that once the property was settled on these trusts there was no further inheritance tax liability (at least until after the beneficiary had obtained an interest in possession).

Example 21.5[27]

"... to A absolutely contingent on attaining 25 years". This straightforward trust satisfies the requirements of an A+M trust so long as A is a minor. Consider, however, the following possibilities:

[27] In this example it is assumed that A becomes entitled to the interest in possession before March 22, 2006: a later entitlement has very different consequences: see 21.16 onwards below.

(1) *A attains 18 years.* A is entitled to the income from the fund[1] and, therefore, Requirement 2 is broken. No IHT is charged on the ending of the A+M trust consequent upon the arising of A's interest in possession.
(2) *A attains 25 years.* Ordinary principles for interest in possession settlements apply; A's interest in possession comes to an end, but no inheritance tax is payable because A as the life tenant was already treated as being entitled to all the property.[28]
(3) *A dies aged 19 years.* Inheritance tax is charged on the termination of A's interest in possession.[29]

21.14 There was nothing to prevent an A+M trust from being created for an open class of beneficiaries, for example "for all my grandchildren both born and yet to be born". If such a trust was to be created it was desirable to ensure that the class of beneficiaries would close when the eldest obtained a vested interest in either the income or capital. Failure to do so would result in a partial divesting of any beneficiary with a vested interest when a further beneficiary was born, and this could sometimes lead to an inheritance tax charge. Class-closing rules could be implied at common law,[30] but it was safer to insert an express provision to that effect. IHTA 1984, s.71(4)(b) provides that tax shall not be charged on the death of a beneficiary before attaining the specified age. It follows that, if the entire class of beneficiaries is wiped out, an accumulation and maintenance trust ceases on the death of the final member, but, whoever then becomes entitled to the fund, no inheritance tax is payable. When it was necessary to wait and see if a further beneficiary is going to be born, however, this provision did not operate, because it was then not the death of the beneficiary which ended the accumulation and maintenance trust in such a case, but the failure of a further beneficiary to be born within the trust period.

Occasions when an exit charge arises

21.15 It was rare for property to leave an A+M trust otherwise than by appointment or advancement to a beneficiary and so long as this happened no inheritance tax is chargeable. Provision was, however, made for calculating an exit charge in the following circumstances:

(a) when a depreciatory transaction entered into by the trustees reduces the value of the fund[31];
(b) when the 25 year period provided for in Requirement 3 is exceeded and the beneficiaries do not have a common grandparent[32];
(c) when property is advanced to a non-beneficiary or resettled on trusts which do not comply with the requirements of an A+M trust[33]; and

---

[28] IHTA 1984, s.53(2).
[28] IHTA 1984, ss.4, 5, 49(1).
[30] *Andrews v Partington* (1790) 3 Bro CC 60, 401.
[31] IHTA 1984, s.71(3)(b).
[32] As to the third requirement of an A+M trust, see 21.12 above.
[33] As to requirements of an A+M trust, see 21.06 ante.

(d) if the trust ends some time after the final surviving beneficiary has died.

IHT is calculated in these cases on the value of the fund according to how long the property has been held on the accumulation and maintenance trusts.[34] The calculation is made as follows:

(i) 0.25 per cent for each of the first 40 complete successive quarters in the relevant period;

(ii) 0.20 per cent for each of the next 40 complete successive quarters;

(iii) 0.15 per cent for each of the next 40 complete successive quarters;

(iv) 0.10 per cent for each of the next 40 complete successive quarters; and

(v) 0.05 per cent for each of the next 40 complete successive quarters.

Therefore on expiry of the permitted 25 years, IHT at a rate of 21 per cent is payable on the fund. Subsequently, normal relevant property settlement rules apply, so that five years later there is an anniversary charge. These rules may still be relevant to trusts with young beneficiaries where by April 6, 2008 the trust is altered to require beneficiaries to take capital and income no later than 18. Such trusts remain A+M trusts.

TAX TREATMENT OF S.71 A+M TRUSTS AFTER MARCH 21, 2006

21.16 The section is concerned with the IHT treatment of A+M trusts set up before March 22, 2006 (from that date s.71 trusts cannot be set up).[35]

Of course, trusts may have been set up as A+M trusts but by March 22 one or more beneficiaries may have acquired interests in possession in all or part of the trust fund. In that event the trust will not be wholly accumulation and maintenance in form on March 22 and this section will only be relevant to any portion of the trust fund which is still held on trusts falling within s.71 on March 22, 2006. i.e. in respect of settled property where no beneficiary has an interest in possession.

The transitional period

21.17 Until April 6, 2008 the IHT treatment of a s.71 accumulation and maintenance trust will not change. This means that:

(i) anniversary and exit charges will not apply so that if the trust ends on the occasion when a beneficiary becomes absolutely entitled to the trust fund (or, indeed, if the trust ends because of the death under the vesting age of the beneficiary) there is no IHT exit charge;

---

[34] IHTA 1984, ss.70(6), 71(5).
[35] IHTA 1984, s.71.

(ii) during this period a beneficiary may become entitled to an interest in possession and this will have the following effects—

    (a) IHTA 1984, s.71 will cease to apply (requirement 2 is no longer satisfied) in respect of that part of the fund in which the interest in possession has arisen[36];

    (b) because "new" interest in possession trusts within s.49(1) cannot generally arise after March 21, 2006[37] the trust will be taxed as a relevant property settlement unless at the time when the interest in possession arises the conditions for an 18–25 trust are satisfied.[38]

What happens on April 6, 2008?

From April 6, 2008, Requirement 1 in the definition is amended to read   **21.18**

"one or more persons (beneficiaries) will, on or before attaining a specified age not exceeding 18 years become beneficially entitled to it"

(viz the settled property). As compared to the previous definition note that:

(i) The vesting age becomes 18 rather than 25;
(ii) At that age it is not sufficient for an entitlement to income to arise: the beneficiary must become entitled to capital in the settlement (which will therefore end).

It would however appear that the power of selection can remain since the words "one or more beneficiaries" are unaltered. This allows for greater flexibility than is available under s.71D.[39]

If the trust satisfies these amended requirements it will continue to be taxed under the s.71 provisions. In cases where the trust as presently drafted would not qualify the trustees may have sufficient powers under the terms of the settlement that will enable them to ensure that by April 6, 2008 these new requirements are met. Even if the trustees have sufficient powers, however, the question is whether it is appropriate that they be exercised in this fashion. Of course much will depend on the needs of the beneficiaries and the wishes of the family but a further factor for them to consider is what would be the IHT treatment if the trust falls outside the new s.71 requirements.

---

[36] There will be no IHT "exit" charge: see IHTA 1984, s.71(4)(a).
[37] IHTA 1984, s.49(1A) inserted by FA 2006.
[38] IHTA 1984, s.71D(3)–(4) inserted by FA 2006. In the case of flexible accumulation and maintenance trusts—the requirements in s.71(3) will not be met (e.g. because although the relevant beneficiary has become entitled to an interest in possession he will not become entitled to capital on or before attaining 25 as required by IHTA s.71D(6)). Accordingly it is important to review such trusts before the interest in possession arises since the conditions of s.71D(6) must be met *at the time* (in such flexible trusts it is likely that the trustees will have adequate powers which can be exercised to ensure that the s.71D(6) conditions are met).
[39] See 25.29.

The alternative treatment

21.19 No IHT charge will arise simply because on April 6, 2008 the trust ceases to qualify as an accumulation and maintenance trust under the revised requirements of s.71.[40] With that in mind the alternatives facing the trustees (assuming they wish the trust to continue) are—

21.20 The trustees could ensure that the provisions of the trust instrument satisfy the requirement for the trust to be an "18–25 Trust".[41] This will be the case if on April 6, 2008 the property is held on trust for the benefit of a person who has not yet attained the age of 25 and the conditions of s.71D(6) are met. In essence, the latter requires the capital to vest no later than age 25 and until that date income to either belong to the beneficiary (i.e. he may have an interest in possession) or be applied for the benefit of that beneficiary or accumulated for his benefit. Hence powers that would enable the trustees to vary the shares of beneficiaries or to postpone vesting beyond the age of 25 will generally mean that the conditions of s.71D are not met. Note, however, that the existence of a wide power of advancement is permitted so that it is possible for the trustees, if they feel it to be for the benefit of the beneficiary to postpone entitlement at 25 by making a "settled advance".[42]

21.21 If the conditions of s.71D are not met the trust will on April 6, 2008 become subject to the relevant property regime (i.e. to anniversary and exit charges).[43] Bear in mind:

(a) that the charge under this regime will start to accrue from the date when the settlement comprises "relevant property" (i.e. in this case from April 6, 2008);

(b) that the first anniversary charge will be on the 10th anniversary from the date when the trust was originally set up (*not* ten years from April 6, 2008 when it first comprised relevant property) but will only be levied by reference to the period when the trust was a relevant property settlement (i.e. the charge will be on the period from April 6, 2008).[44]

SUMMARY OF OPTIONS

21.22 There are three options available to trustees of an accumulation and maintenance trust. The first option is to retain existing A+M status by ensuring that the terms of the settlement are changed on or before April 5, 2008 to provide that the beneficiaries must become entitled to income and capital at 18.[45] The trust

---

[40] FA 2006, Sch.20, para.3(3).
[41] See IHTA 1984, s.71D–71G and notably s 71D(3)–(4) inserted by FA 2006, Sch.20 para.1(1). Note that *all* A+M trusts can be converted to fall within s.71D: they do *not*, for instance, have to have been set up in a will for the testator's children.
[42] IHTA 1984, s.71D(7).
[43] IHTA 1984, Pt III Ch. III.
[44] See further 20.03 Example 20.9 for the calculation of the charge in such cases.
[45] Of course it may be that the requirement is already met: e.g. a trust for beneficiaries contingent on attaining 18 and if more than one in equal shares suffices. Such a trust may be a bereaved minor trust provided it satisfies the conditions in s.71A see 25.13 and IHTA 1984, s.71(1B).

then retains existing A+M status even beyond April 2008. This option is worth considering if the trust has very young beneficiaries where the class has not yet closed and it is felt desirable to retain flexibility on how income and capital is distributed while they are under 18 since further beneficiaries may be born. The power of advancement could be retained so that if the trustees later felt the children should not take capital at 18 they could exercise that power and defer capital entitlement; the trust would then enter the relevant property regime. There would be no entry charge into the relevant property regime at that point but thereafter the existing trust would be subject to 10-year charges. It is not possible however, to convert an A+M trust which has continued beyond 2008 into a s.71D trust.

The second option is to convert the trusts into s.71D trusts before 2008. This will be worthwhile where beneficiaries are still some way off attaining 25 and the trustees want to avoid 10 year charges but are prepared to accept a small exit charge of 4.2 per cent when the beneficiary takes the capital at 25. (There may be some advantages in the way that the tax charge is calculated, see 25.34.) The main disadvantage of s.71D trusts is the loss of flexibility particularly where the class has not yet closed.

The third option is to end the trusts and advance the capital out to the beneficiaries. The fourth option is to do nothing. The trustees retain flexibility and the trust enters the relevant property regime in April 2008. If the trust was set up in say 1997 there will be no periodic charge until 2017 by which time the legislation may have changed! This option may be attractive for trusts holding valuable family property where it is not desirable for any beneficiary to take capital. If a beneficiary is nearly 25 in April 2008 there is little point in moving into the s.71 D regime and therefore the trustees may as well let the trusts fall into the relevant property regime.

EXAMPLE 21.6

> The trustees of an accumulation and maintenance trust set up in 2004 hold property on trust for such of the children of the settlor who reach 30 (with income entitlement at 25) and if more than one in equal shares. The class closes when the eldest child reaches 25. There are currently two children Charlotte and Luke aged eight and six but the settlor is likely to have other children whom he would want to benefit. If the trust is converted into a s.71D trust this would have to be done by 2008 and then Charlotte and Luke have to take fixed shares. The share each takes must be decided on the conversion. There is no ability for other children born later to come within the s.71D trust regime. Moreover there is no power to pay all the income of the trust fund to Charlotte one year and then to Luke in another while they are under 25.
>
> If the trust terms are altered to provide that Charlotte and Luke and any other child of the settlor born before the eldest child reaches 18 take capital at 18 this would remain an A+M trust beyond 2008. In these circumstances until the children reach 18 there is flexibility over income and capital—more can be paid to one beneficiary than another. Once Charlotte or Luke approach 18 however, the trust cannot be converted

into a s.71D trust because conversion to s.71D status is only permitted before April 6, 2008.[46]

Making the choice

21.23 For a wealthy family desirous of retaining the settlement, option 3—accepting the transition into the relevant property regime may be the preferred option especially as there is no immediate IHT charge when the property ceases to fall within s.71. The likely alternative is to accept vesting of capital at 25—so that the s.71D requirements are met—although the retention of a wide power of advancement would enable the trusts to be continued after 25 if thought desirable. Of course s.71D trusts are not free of IHT once the beneficiary is 18: from that date until 25 a charge accrues and may be levied at a top rate of 4.2 per cent when the beneficiary becomes entitled at 25.[47] In cases where the beneficiary is approaching 18 on April 6, 2008 there may be little advantage in seeking to amend the trusts so as to fall within s.71D if the long term goal is to keep the settlement in being for as long as possible and to retain flexibility. The only advantage of s.71D trusts is that the trust is not subject to the periodic charge so if a 10-year anniversary falls between the ages of 18 and 25 it may be worth considering this option. However, the disadvantage is that if a beneficiary of a s.71D trust dies after 18 but under 25 there is an inheritance tax exit charge even if the trust does not end. This would not be the case if the trust was subject to the relevant property regime rather than the s.71D regime on the death of a beneficiary and the trusts continued. Moreover while the beneficiary is under 25 on a s.71D trust there is no power of selection between beneficiaries—he must take a fixed share.[48]

If the class of beneficiaries is young or relatively small in number and future beneficiaries may be born then options 1 (conversion to 18) or 4 (do nothing) may be more attractive than a s.71D trust. Keeping the trust flexible allows for the possibility of selection and for other children to benefit. One other factor to bear in mind is that, whatever decision is taken by the trustees, CGT holdover relief will be available from April 6, 2008 because either the trust will be within s.71D or a relevant property settlement.

---

[46] IHTA 1984, s.71(D)(4).
[47] See IHTA 1984, s.71F for the calculation of this charge and see 25.32 for the advantages of this tax calculation.
[48] Before he reaches 25 the trustees could always defer his entitlement and convert into a relevant property settlement by exercising their power of advancement to make a settled advance at which point flexibility would be restored see fn. 44 above.

Chapter 22

EXCLUDED PROPERTY

- Basics **(22.01)**
- Exemptions for excluded property **(22.04)**
- IHTA 1984 ss.80–82 traps **(22.15)**
- Additions of property to an existing settlement **(22.20)**
- Reservation of benefit issues **(22.32)**
- Powers of appointment over settled property **(22.36)**
- Reversionary interests **(22.44)**
- Purchased interests in excluded property settlements **(22.51)**
- Pre-owned assets income tax: problems for foreign domiciliaries **(22.56)**

BASICS

Inheritance tax is not chargeable on excluded property.[1]
Unsettled property: this is excluded property if: **22.01**

(i) the owner of the property is not domiciled in the UK; and

(ii) the property is not situate in the UK.[2]

Deemed domicile: the general rules on domicile are discussed in Chapter 2. **22.02** Even if a person is domiciled outside the UK under general law he may be deemed domiciled in the UK for inheritance tax purposes if one of two conditions is satisfied.[3]

(a) If a person was domiciled in the UK on or after December 10, 1974 and was domiciled in the UK (under general law) within the three years immediately preceding the transfer in question. This catches the

---

[1] s.3(2) and 5(1). Note that s.3(2) states that no account shall be taken of the value of excluded property which ceases to form part of a person's estate. So a gift of excluded property is not a PET. Section 5 makes it clear, however, that excluded property is part of an individual's estate until the moment *before* his death. So, for example, in assessing the loss to his estate if they make a gift of non-excluded property the excluded property in their estate is taken into account.

[2] s.6 IHTA. Domicile is discussed in Ch. 2. There are certain exceptions where UK situated assets can be excluded property if held in a person's free estate. These exceptions are similar to those discussed for settled property, for example where an individual is non-resident and owns specified Government securities. Similarly authorised unit trusts or shares in an open-ended investment company will be excluded if owned by a non-domiciled individual.

[3] s.267 IHTA 1984.

taxpayer who was domiciled under general law and then emigrates. In this case for three years (but not three tax years) from the acquisition of a new domicile of choice he will retain a deemed domicile.

(b) if a person was resident for income tax purposes in the UK on or after December 10, 1974 and was UK resident for income tax purposes in not less than seventeen out of the twenty income tax years ending with the income tax year in which he made the relevant transfer. This catches the foreign domiciliary who has lived in the UK for a long time even though he retains his foreign domicile under general law. "Residence" is used in the income tax sense and does not require residence for a period of seventeen complete years only residence for a tax year.

EXAMPLE 22.1

(1) Kim who was domiciled in New Zealand comes to the UK on 1 April 2000. He is therefore UK resident for tax year 1999/2000. He will become UK deemed domiciled on April 6, 2015 even though he retains his NZ domicile. After that date any gifts he makes will be subject to inheritance tax if he dies within seven years and he can no longer set up excluded property settlements.

(2) Paul has lived in the UK all his life and has a UK domicile of origin. In March 2006 he emigrates to Portugal. In August 2010 he decides to remain in Portugal permanently. Although he will have been resident outside the UK for more than three tax years, until August 2013 he remains UK deemed domiciled because he had not lost his domicile under general law until 2010.

Until April 6, 2005 the concept of deemed domicile applied only for inheritance tax purposes. From that date someone who is UK deemed domiciled can also suffer an income tax charge under the pre-owned assets income tax regime. (This is discussed further at 25.56.) Hence foreign domiciliaries who are deemed domiciled and resident in the UK should consider not only their inheritance tax position but also whether they are subject to pre-owned assets income tax.

22.03 **Settled property:** this will only be excluded if both the following conditions are satisfied:

(i) the settlor was domiciled outside the UK at the time when he made the settlement: note that the position of the interest in possession beneficiary or the domicile of the settlor at the date of his death is irrelevant[4]; *and*

(ii) the settled property is not situated in the UK. It will not generally matter if UK situated property is held in an offshore company held by the trustees[5] as long as the settled property directly held by the trustees is not-UK situated.

---

[4] But see 22.15 for the effect of ss.80–82 and 22.32 concerning reservation of benefit problems.
[5] Although note the reservation of benefit problems outlined below where UK-situated property is added to a company and see 22.06 generally re. UK situated property.

As already noted, the domicile of the beneficiary is normally irrelevant (subject to the operation of ss.80–82 (see 22.15) and it does not matter whether the settlement is a fixed interest or discretionary trust. The residence of the trustees is also irrelevant for inheritance tax purposes although a non-domiciled person will normally want the assets to be held in a non-resident trust for capital gains tax purposes.[6] Even if the beneficiary is domiciled in the UK, there will be no charge to IHT on the termination of his interest in possession nor on any payment made by the trustees to him from a discretionary trust.

EXAMPLE 22.2

> A, domiciled in Portugal and now deceased, by his Will left shares in BVI companies on trust to pay the income to his nephew, B, for life. B is domiciled and resident in the UK. The property is excluded property, being property situated abroad settled by a settlor domiciled at that time outside the UK. There is no charge to inheritance tax on the death of A; there is no inheritance tax charge on the ending of B's life interest even though it is a qualifying interest in possession.[7] If A had settled those same BVI shares on discretionary trusts for his nephew and issue of B, all of whom were UK domiciled, the property would be, for the same reason, excluded property so that the normal discretionary trust charges would not apply.
> If, however, the trustees exchanged those shares for shares in UK companies, the property would no longer be excluded and there would be a charge to inheritance tax on the death of B (if he held a qualifying interest in possession), or the normal relevant property charges would apply if the trust were discretionary.
> (Note the adverse capital gains tax treatment for UK resident and domiciled beneficiaries receiving capital payments from non-resident excluded property settlements as a result of FA 1998 changes.)[8]

EXEMPTIONS FOR EXCLUDED PROPERTY

The basic exemptions are— 22.04

(a) The estate of a person immediately before his death does not include excluded property.[9]
(b) No account is taken of excluded property which leaves a person's estate in determining whether an *inter vivos* disposition is a transfer of value.[10]

---

[6] See: 10.24 and 2.10.
[7] B takes a qualifying interest in possession if A died before March 22, 2006 and a qualifying interest in possession if A died after March 21, 2006 because B's interest is an immediate post death interest.
[8] See 10.24.
[9] IHTA 1984, s.5(1).
[10] IHTA 1984, s.3(2).

(c) Relevant property (i.e. property in trust which is subject to ten-yearly anniversary and exit charges) does not include excluded property.[11]

(d) Excluded property which is held in a qualifying interest in possession trust is not subject to inheritance tax on the death of the beneficiary.

Situs

22.05 The "situs" of property is governed by common law rules and depends on the type of property involved, although it is important to remember that the rules can be subject to contrary provisions in double taxation treaties. The rules are briefly as follows:

(a) Any interest in land is situated where the land is physically located.

(b) Chattels are situated at the place where they are kept. It is therefore important that the foreign domiciliary avoids holding chattels in the UK at the date of his death.

(c) Registered shares and securities are situated where they are registered or, if transferable on more than one register, where they would normally be dealt with in the ordinary course of business.

(d) Bearer shares and securities transferable by delivery are situated where the certificate or other document of title is kept.[12]

(e) A bank account is situated at the branch which maintains the account although special rules apply to non-residents' foreign currency bank accounts.

UK situate assets

22.06 When the settlor is not UK domiciled at the time when he creates the trust it is important that trustees do not hold UK property directly. Consider the following:

EXAMPLE 22.3

> Eric, a foreign domiciliary, sets up a trust in 2003 with foreign currency in an account abroad. The trustees use the cash to invest in a UK property as supplied by Eric, who then dies before he becomes UK deemed domiciled.
> In these circumstances if the trust is interest in possession for Eric, the property is UK-situated and taxed on his death as it would be for any UK-domiciled beneficiary.

---

[11] IHTA 1984, s.58(4)(f).
[12] For the CGT position of bearer shares see CGT Manual 12452-3. See also TCGA 1992, s.275(1)(c) in relation to bearer debt securities to which the above rule does not apply.

If the trust is discretionary and Eric is a beneficiary then he has reserved a benefit with the result that there is again a tax charge on his death. Section 102(3) is not displaced by s.48(3).[13] In addition if the trust is discretionary and held UK property at any ten-year anniversary there would be an inheritance tax charge.

22.07 Foreign domiciliaries should take care where a foreign situate gifted asset is transferred into trust and subsequently brought to the UK. This can occur where non UK situated chattels are gifted into trust and then brought into the UK or where a UK house is gifted to an offshore company and then transferred to the trust. In these circumstances apart from a charge under the settlement rules, the gift with reservation rules may also result in a charge because the gifted property is not itself excluded property.[14] There are three occasions when it is particularly important to avoid having UK situated property in the trust:

(i) On settling assets into trust: if A transfers UK situated assets into a discretionary trust for himself and family, this is a chargeable transfer subject to immediate 20 per cent inheritance tax to the extent that the value exceeds his nil rate band.

(ii) On a 10-year anniversary: when a discretionary trust holds UK property at the time of a 10-year anniversary, the hypothetical transfer used in determining the rate is not just that of the UK property but also that of any non-UK property which is excluded property when put into the settlement. This is the case even if the non-UK property has remained so since then. Any property put into another settlement made by the same settlor and on the same day (a 'related settlement'). Hence even if the UK property is within the nil-rate band a charge may arise on a ten-year anniversary.[15]

(iii) On the death of the settlor. As noted in *Example 22.3* above, if Eric dies and at that time the settlement holds UK situated property and he has reserved a benefit in the trust assets, there is a reservation of benefit which cannot be avoided by saying that the property is excluded property.[16]

When UK situate property can be excluded property if held in trust

22.08 Despite the general principle that UK situate property is not excluded property, certain kinds of UK assets held in trust are deemed to be excluded property if various conditions are met. These are:

(i) UK Government securities or gilts;

(ii) interests in Authorised Unit Trusts ("AUTS") and Open Ended Investment Companies ("OEICS");

---

[13] See 22.32.
[14] See 22.30.
[15] IHTA 1984, s.67(4).
[16] See 22.32 below.

(iii) non-sterling UK bank accounts.

The rules are different in each case.

22.09 Gilts[17] which are held in an interest in possession settlement where the life tenant has a qualifying interest in possession[18] will be excluded property if the person entitled to the interest in possession is generally ordinarily resident[19] outside the UK.[20] Note that the domicile of the settlor is irrelevant. If the beneficiary is not domiciled in the UK but is UK resident then Government securities are not excluded property.

EXAMPLE 22.4

A is a non-resident interest in possession beneficiary of a will trust established when B died in 2004. A is UK deemed domiciled having only recently emigrated. The trustees decide to protect the inheritance tax position and invest entirely in exempt gilts where only non-UK residence is required. There is no inheritance tax charge on A's death because the gilts are excluded property. It does not matter that A is still UK resident nor that B the settlor was UK domiciled.

It will be much harder to come within this exemption now given that since FA 2006 a qualifying interest in possession arises only in limited circumstances.

22.10 If the trust is discretionary and holds UK gilts, none of the beneficiaries must be ordinarily resident (and if the gilt so requires domiciled) in the UK if the gilts are to be exempt from inheritance tax.[21] Note though that if a UK charity

---

[17] There are two classes of exempt gilts for IHT purposes, with different conditions attached:

(1) Gilts where the conditions require the individual to be domiciled and ordinarily resident outside the UK. These include:
  (a) 3½ per cent War Loan 1952 or after, issued under s.47 FA (No. 2) 1915.
  (b) Gilts issued under s.22 of FA (No. 2) 1931, where this was the condition set out in the prospectus.

(2) Gilts where the condition requires the beneficial owner to be ordinarily resident outside the UK but domicile is irrelevant. This applies to:
  (a) Gilts issued before April 6, 1998 without FOTRA conditions; these now have the benefit of "post-1996 Act conditions" under s.161 of FA 1998.
  (b) Gilts issued after 1996, where the prospectus sets out this condition. All gilts issued after April 29, 1996 contain this condition.

IHT Manual 27243 sets out a list of gilts where the requirement is that the beneficial owner is ordinarily resident outside the UK (domicile irrelevant). Para. 27244 sets out a list of the gilts where the requirement is that the beneficial owner is neither domiciled nor ordinarily resident in the UK. However, check the prospectus in each case.

[18] i.e. a pre-22 March 2006 interest in possession, a transitional serial interest or an immediate post death interest.

[19] Note that the conditions on domicile and residence for the IIP beneficiary are the same as for an individual. Generally non-UK residence is enough.

[20] See IHTA 1984 s.48(4).

[21] Note that if gilts are transferred from one settlement to another they will only be excluded property if the beneficiaries of both settlements are non-UK ordinarily resident. This prevents gilts

is a potential beneficiary then exemption is not denied.[22] Nor is exemption denied if there is a possibility that some currently unknown person such as an unborn child or future spouse of an existing beneficiary might become a beneficiary in the future and be UK resident.[23] Given that most trusts set up will now be relevant property settlements it will be harder to satisfy the conditions since it is more unlikely that all possible existing beneficiaries will be non-UK resident.

EXAMPLE 22.5

> A is a discretionary beneficiary of a trust established in 2004. He emigrates. Only if all known beneficiaries of the trust are non-resident (and in the case of some gilts also non-domiciled) can the trustees invest in exempt gilts and be sure that the property is excluded property. After March 21, 2006 it is not possible for the trustees to appoint a qualifying interest in possession to A and then purchase exempt gilts.

22.11 There is some debate about whether the gilts have to be registered in the name of the trustees or whether they can be held in the name of a nominee holder. In IHTM 04294 HMRC suggest that excluded property treatment is only available if the gilts are registered in the name of the individual trustees rather than nominees. It is difficult to discern any rational basis for this view. It is not thought that HMRC maintain this view when challenged.

22.12 **AUTS and OEICS:** the exception is different from the gilts exemption. AUTs and OEICS are excluded property if the settlor was domiciled in the UK at the time when the settlement was made.[24] The residence or domicile of any beneficiary is not relevant.

22.13 **Non-sterling UK bank accounts:** a UK bank account is excluded property if it is denominated in foreign currency and the settlor was not domiciled when he made the settlement, the trustees are non-resident and the settlement is subject to a qualifying interest in possession in favour of a person neither domiciled nor resident in the UK.[25] This exemption has limited value.

22.14 **Estate duty treaties:** a number of double tax treaties displace the deemed domicile rules in certain cases. These treaties are with France, Italy, India and Pakistan. While the treaties do not displace the deemed domicile rules on *inter vivos* transfers (so a PET would still become chargeable if the donor died within seven years) they are relevant on death.

> from being channelled from a discretionary trust where they were not excluded property to a new settlement. See *Minden Trust (Cayman) Ltd v* IRC [1984] S.T.C. 434. When a close company is a beneficiary of a trust any gilts owned by the trust will be excluded property only if all participators in the company are non-UK ordinarily resident, irrespective of the company's residence.

[22] See: IHTM 27249.
[23] See: IHTM 27248.
[24] See s.48(3A) inserted by FA 2003. The residence of the beneficiary is irrelevant. The rule has applied since October 16, 2002.
[25] s.157(4).

EXAMPLE 22.6

> In 1997 Cedric an Indian domiciliary set up a Jersey law interest in possession trust when he was deemed UK domiciled. The trust holds only non-UK situated assets (situs being determined under the treaty). He has a qualifying interest in possession. On his death, assuming he is domiciled in India under Indian law,[26] there will be no inheritance tax payable on the settled assets because they are non-UK situate and pass under foreign law. There is no Indian tax payable because India abolished estate duty in 1985. (Note that the treaty would not protect the making of the settlement from being a chargeable transfer if made after March 21, 2006; nor is the settlement protected from 10-year charges).

IHTA 1984, SS.80–82 TRAPS

22.15 If the settlor or his spouse is the initial qualifying interest in possession beneficiary of the settlement or they have successive qualifying interests in possession, the foreign situs settled property is only excluded property[27] if the settlor is not domiciled when the settlement is made and[28] he or his spouse is non-domiciled when the life interest or the successive life interest ends.[29] This rule applies only for the purposes of the relevant property regime. Prior to FA 2006 it had relatively little impact for foreign domiciliaries who could avoid the use of relevant property trusts.[30]

EXAMPLE 22.7

> (1) In 1997 Jason set up a trust when he was not UK domiciled. He took an interest in possession from the outset and there is a successive life interest for his spouse.[31] He died in 2004 UK deemed domiciled and his spouse later died in 2005 also UK deemed domiciled. There is no inheritance tax charge on the death of either Jason or his spouse because the settlement is an excluded property trust. Applying s.80, however, in the ending of the interest in possession of his spouse she was UK domiciled and hence the settled property will come within the relevant property regime at that point (unless his children take qualifying interests in possession or the property is held on a&m trusts.)[32] Hence ten year and exit charges will be payable. Prior to March 22, 2006 it was relatively easy to avoid this trap by ensuring that the trust funds never fell into the relevant property regime.

---

[26] Not merely domiciled in India under English law.
[27] 22.03.
[28] See Example 22.2 for the basic rules.
[29] ss.80/82 IHTA 1984.
[30] It is discussed in relation to UK domiciliaries at 15.09
[31] Note that if he took an interest in possession (say) six months after the funds were settled, ss.80/82 would not apply.
[32] The transitional period (during which a TSI can arise) ends on April 6, 2008; see 18.14.

(2) Assume facts as in (1) above except that his spouse died in 2007 As before, there is no inheritance tax charge on the death of Jason or his spouse. and the settled property will come within the relevant property regime at that point unless his children take qualifying interests in possession. As his wife had a pre-March 22 interest in possession and died in 2007, his children could take qualifying interests in possession (a transitional serial interest). However, once those interests end, the settlement will have to terminate in order to avoid the relevant property charges.

(3) As in (1) above except that his wife dies in May 2008. It is no longer possible for the children to take a qualifying interest in possession.[33] The settlement will have to end in order to avoid 10-year and exit charges. Note that if his wife died not domiciled here then the settlement could remain in place and would be excluded property for all inheritance tax purposes.

(4) Assume Jason dies in May 2008 UK domiciled having set up the trust in 1997. His wife's interest in possession is a transitional serial interest but on her death the trust must end if she dies UK domiciled in order to avoid charges under the relevant property regime.

If the settlement had been set up on or after March 22, 2006 and Jason had not been UK domiciled, then even if Jason had been given an initial interest in possession this would have been irrelevant as s.80 would have no application. The property is excluded property for all IHT purposes.

Foreign domiciliaries will need to review their trusts as a result of FA 2006 in the following circumstances: **22.16**

(a) if the trust was set up prior to March 22, 2006;
(b) if it was initially interest in possession for settlor or spouse; and
(c) if the last of the settlor/spouse to take an interest in possession dies deemed or actually UK domiciled.

In these circumstances the trusts must end on the last of the settlor and spouse to die after April 5, 2008 in order to avoid ten year and exit charges. This may be a particular issue for US individuals where it was common to avoid taking out a UK grant of probate by transferring property *inter vivos* into a grantor interest in possession trust for the settlor and then his spouse.

Transfers between settlements[34]

Where property is transferred between settlements, the relevant property trust regime provides that the property is treated as remaining comprised in the first settlement.[35] This applies whether or not the settlement comprises excluded property. However, IHTA 1984, s.82 also provides that in determining whether **22.17**

---

[33] Pre-March 22, 2006 it was possible to set up A+M trust falling under s.71 and all interests in possession owned by individuals were qualifying interests.
[34] IHTA 1984, s.82.
[35] s.81.

the settled property is excluded property, it is necessary to look both at the domicile of the settlor of the first settlement at the time it was *made* and at the domicile of the settlor of the second settlement at the time that the second trust was *made*. Only if both settlors had neither an actual nor deemed UK domicile at the time when each made their trust can the property be excluded property.

22.18 If the trustees transfer property from one trust to another, the settlor of the first settlement is also treated as the settlor of the second settlement to the extent that the property in the second settlement is derived from the first. In these circumstances the settlor of the first trust will need to be domiciled outside the UK when the original settlement was set up *and* at the date of the second settlement. Before the 2006 changes, s.82 had not been a major issue given that it only applied for the purposes of the relevant property regime. For instance, if property in the second settlement has been held on fixed interest or accumulation and maintenance trusts when a transfer to it was made while the settlor was alive and UK domiciled, then s.82 would not be relevant. With the restriction on the creation post March 21, 2006 of new qualifying interest in possession or A+M trusts this is no longer the case since trusts will generally fall within the relevant property regime. Hence resettlements after the settlor is UK deemed domiciled need to be considered carefully.

EXAMPLE 22.8

(1) Robert settled foreign shares into a discretionary settlement in 2000 when not UK domiciled. He then became UK domiciled in 2004. For income tax reasons the trustees decide that they wish to move the income producing assets into a separate UK resident trust. They transfer the assets to a new trust set up in May 2006 in which Robert is entitled to income. The new trust falls within the relevant property regime and was set up by a UK domiciled settlor. As a result of s.82 the property, transferred from the 2000 settlement ceases to be excluded. (There is no entry charge into the relevant property regime.) Ten-year charges arise even if the new trust holds non-UK property.

(2) If the transfer had been made in January 2006 then the new trust would have been a qualifying interest in possession for Robert and s.82 would not have applied.

Note also:

(a) Whether or not Trust 2 is established before or after March 22, 2006, Robert should not be excluded from it if he was a beneficiary of Trust 1 unless he is not UK domiciled at the date of the exclusion.[36]

(b) The residence of Trust 2 is irrelevant to the inheritance tax position.

(c) Provided Trust 2 does not hold UK situated property at Robert's death, even though he dies UK domiciled and has reserved a benefit in Trust 2 there should be no inheritance tax charge on his death under either (1)

---

[36] See 22.35 and note reservations of benefit issues.

or (2) above (since the reservation of benefit rules are displaced) unless the trust then ends, in which case under (1) above there will be an exit charge. The difference since March 22, 2006 is that if Trust 2 is established after 21 March it will be subject to inheritance tax charges every 10 years and exit charges whether or not Robert has an interest in possession because such an interest cannot be a "qualifying" interest in possession and so the relevant property regime applies.

22.19 What happens if both Trusts 1 and 2 were "made" at a time when the settlor was not UK domiciled but the actual transfer between settlements takes place at a time when the settlor is UK domiciled? HMRC have commented on the position where transfers between two settlements are effected <u>by the trustees</u>, both trusts were set up and funded at a time when the settlor was not domiciled here but the transfer was made by trustees at a time when one or more of the settlors was UK domiciled. Such a transfer is not caught by s.82. The position might be different if the settlor had a power of appointment and appointed the assets himself to a new trust.

EXAMPLE 22.9

> Robert set up two discretionary trusts in 2000 when not UK domiciled. He became deemed domiciled in 2006. In 2007 the trustees appoint property from one trust to another. The property remains excluded property provided no UK situated property is held directly by the trustees. The position would be different if Trust 2 was a *new* trust set up after he became deemed UK domiciled.

ADDITIONS OF PROPERTY TO AN EXISTING SETTLEMENT

22.20 A controversial issue relates to the question of additions of property.[37] What happens when the settlor adds property to his trust after a change of domicile? IHTM 27220 notes:

> "the legislation refers to the settlor's domicile at the time the settlement was made. You must proceed on the basis that, for any given item of property held in a settlement, the settlement was made when that property was put in the settlement. Consult TG or your Team Leader if this view is challenged."

EXAMPLE 22.10 (TAKEN FROM HMRC MANUAL)

> S, when domiciled abroad, creates a settlement of Spanish realty. Later he acquires a UK domicile and then adds some Australian property to

---

[37] This has also been discussed at 15.13.

the settlement. The Spanish property is excluded property because of S's overseas domicile when he settled that property. However the Australian property is not excluded property as S had a UK domicile when he added that property to the settlement.

22.21 The same view is repeated in RI 166. In other words, HMRC consider that every addition to an existing settlement constitutes the making of a new settlement in relation to that property. The example above makes it clear that adding property to an existing settlement which is excluded does not, in HMRC's view, jeopardise the exemption from inheritance tax on the original property provided that it has been kept segregated. It merely means that the new property does not qualify for protection. In RI 166 HMRC comment "if assets added at different times have become mixed, any dealings with the settled fund after the addition may also need to be considered." Hence the trustees will need to ensure that the original trust property is kept physically segregated from any subsequent additions where such additions are made when the settlor is UK domiciled. Otherwise the existing inheritance tax protection over the assets already settled could be jeopardised. "The trustees of a settlement should keep adequate records to enable any necessary attribution of the settled property to be made if . . . the settlor has added further assets to the settlement after it was made."

22.22 Are HMRC correct that an addition represents a new settlement? This has been discussed in Chapter 15 in the context of additions to pre-March 22, 2006 interest in possession trusts. Section 48(3) refers to the relevant time being the time "when the settlement was made" *not* "the time when the property was settled." It is true that property becomes comprised in the settlement at the time it is added but this is different from saying that a new settlement is "made" when the settlor adds property after he is deemed UK domiciled.

22.23 As a matter of trust law it is not correct to say that there are two separate settlements just because property is added.[38] Given the trust law position, HMRC would have to argue that where a person adds property to an existing settlement made by him, two separate settlements are *deemed* to be made. They can only argue this point if they are able to demonstrate that there is some provision in the inheritance tax legislation which enables them to deem that what as a matter of trust law and fact is one settlement should be treated as two trusts.[39] HMRC justify their position on the basis of the definitions of settled property and settlement in IHTA 1984, s.43. They argue that each gift to a settlement is a disposition and that each disposition represents a new and separate settlement. However s.43(2) defines settlement as meaning "any disposition or *dispositions* of property" which suggests this view is wrong. Section 43 envisages that two dispositions can be made to a single settlement.

22.24 HMRC may point out that IHTA 1984, s.60 states that *in relation to relevant property settlements* and other trusts charged under Chapter III,[40] references to

---

[38] See the *Rysaffe* case discussed at 15.13.
[39] See *Dymond* para 16.247: "in general it seems a reasonable inference from the above provisions as a whole that what would as a matter of everyday usage be regarded as a single settlement should only be split into separate settlements where there is a specific statutory direction to that effect or where there is more than one settlor." Such a direction was to be found in para.9 of Sch.5 of FA 1975 for its limited purposes but has not followed through into the inheritance tax legislation.
[40] So not qualifying interest in possession trusts.

the commencement of a settlement are *"references to when property first becomes comprised in it"*. Hence, in the absence of such an express provision for *interest in possession trusts*, a new trust is set up each time property is added. However, *s.60* does not apply to interest in possession trusts and so cannot be taken to mean that a new trust is created each time property is added. There is no need for such a provision in the interest in possession regime because the tax charge does not depend on when property enters a settlement. Indeed s.44 expressly refers to the possibility of two deemed settlements but only where more than one person is a settlor, not in relation to any other circumstances. It is noteworthy that in relation to capital gains tax HMRC accept that a new settlement is not generally made when property is added.[41]

22.25 The case of *Rysaffe v IRC*[42] is unhelpful for HMRC. The Court of Appeal expressly held at para 13:

> "section 43(2) supplies the definition of settlement to be applied in answering each of these questions [namely what is taken to be a settlement and what is referred to as property comprised in a settlement]. It should be noted that s.43 does not specifically address a numerical question: what is the number of relevant settlements existing in a particular inheritance tax situation. In the absence of specific statutory provisions the answer to the numerical question is to be found in the general law of trusts."

An attempt in that case by HMRC to treat five settlements as one (the reverse of what is being argued on additions) was rejected.

22.26 **Summary of position on additions:** although it is common sense to follow HMRC guidance where practical and never add to a settlement after a settlor has become deemed UK domiciled, in the light of the *Rysaffe* decision and the legislation there is a strong argument that additions to an excluded property trust made after the settlor is UK domiciled become excluded property because the property falls within the wording of s.48(3): the settlor was non-domiciled on the commencement date (notwithstanding that further property was added when the settlor was UK domiciled). One difficulty post-March 21, 2006, however, is that the addition will be a chargeable transfer, at least if made to an existing A & M or discretionary trust.[43] Conversion of a discretionary trust to a qualifying interest in possession trust for the settlor is not possible under the new regime.

Hence there may now be a significant chargeable transfer on additions of property to a discretionary trust even if the settlor successfully argues that the property falls outside the relevant property regime and the inheritance tax net after that addition.

22.27 If property is added to an existing pre-March 22, 2006 interest in possession trust for the settlor can one successfully argue that the addition is also held on qualifying interest in possession trusts and therefore that there is no transfer of value? This raises slightly different issues which are discussed at 15.13.

---

[41] See 5.35 and 7.08.
[42] S.T.C. 2003 536.
[43] And possibly if made to a pre-March 22, 2006 interest in possession trust—see 15.13.

EXAMPLE 22.11

(1) S settles assets into a discretionary trust in 2005 when not deemed UK domiciled. He becomes deemed domiciled in 2007. He adds further cash to the trust in 2008. That addition is a chargeable transfer even if it is within the protection of the excluded property regime thereafter.

(2) S settles assets onto a discretionary trust in 2005 which is converted to an interest in possession trust for S in January 2006. This is a qualifying interest in possession). S could add cash to such a trust and argue that there was no transfer of value because no loss to his estate. (ie that the new property settled in trust is also to the qualifying interest in possession). Otherwise the position is as in (1).

22.28 **Gifts to companies:** one way round this may be to add assets to a company owned by the trust: i.e. add value to the settlement. The trustees would establish a non UK company. Bearer shares should be avoided and the company should be incorporated and managed outside the UK. Assume that the company shares are already held on pre-March 22, 2006 qualifying interest in possession trusts for the settlor. The settlor then adds cash or other assets to the *company*. His qualifying interest in possession continues in the settled property, namely the shares. It is just that the asset value on the balance sheet of the trust has increased.

There are three issues to consider

22.29 First, a gift to a company is normally a chargeable transfer and hence the settlor would prima facie be subject to inheritance tax at 20 per cent on the value of the addition (assuming that he has used up his nil rate band). In order to avoid this problem the company shares need to be held already on pre-Budget qualifying interest in possession trusts. One would then argue that the value of his estate immediately after the disposition has not been diminished and therefore there is no transfer of value.[44] Commercially one might say that there has been some loss to the settlor's estate because the money is not his to deal with freely because it is now in the company. However, it is not believed that HMRC take this point.

22.30 Second, it is important to consider how the reservation of benefit rules operate. The cash or other asset is gifted to a company. The gifted property for the purposes of s.102(1) of the FA 1986 is the cash not the shares. Assuming that there is a reservation of benefit in the cash (because the settlor continues to be able to benefit from it), s.102(3) could apply at his death. It is disapplied on his death, however, if property in which he has reserved a benefit otherwise forms part of his estate on his death. But, it is the company shares which form part of his estate on his death not the cash or other assets which he has gifted because he has an interest in possession in the company shares not in cash.

---

[44] IHTA 1984, s.3(1) and see s.49(1): Treating the settlor who is beneficially entitled to an interest in possession as beneficially entitled to the company shares.

Hence although s.48(3) should protect the shares from an inheritance tax charge, the cash or other assets added would still be subject to a reservation of benefit. It seems preferable then that after the gift the trustees liquidate the company (not declare a dividend)[45] so that the cash or other assets is held directly by the trustees. The settlor may reserve a benefit in the assets but s.102(3) is then disapplied by s.49 (because of the settlor's interest in possession) and there is no charge under s.49 because of s.48(3). Note that it does not matter if the gifted property is non-UK situated. If he dies reserving a benefit and the gifted property is not held directly by the trustees there is a reservation of benefit problem if the settlor is UK domiciled at the date of death.

Third by giving cash to the company the settlor has significantly increased the value of the company shares. The result is that a large gain may be realised when the company is liquidated. This does not matter for the settlor who is not UK-domiciled under general law[46] but it does mean that a gain goes onto the clock of stockpiled s.87 gains which could be very disadvantageous for future beneficiaries after his death who are UK-resident and domiciled. (They could be chargeable on capital payments by reference to those gains at a rate of 64 per cent).[47]

22.31

RESERVATION OF BENEFIT ISSUES[49]

One analysis of the position is that if the settlor can benefit from the assets in his trust he has reserved a benefit; s.102(3) FA 1986 applies and prima facie he is taxed on his death if UK-domiciled because he is deemed to be beneficially entitled to the property. On this analysis the settled property rules are overridden by the reservation of benefit rules. However, this is contrary to s.48(3) which states that property is excluded if non-UK-situate and held in a settlement made when the settlor was not UK-domiciled.

22.32

How far should the deeming provisions in s.102(3) which treat the property as comprised in the settlor's free estate, override s.48(3) which specifically deals with settled property? Should the property be treated as "unsettled" for the purposes only of the reservation of benefit rules? If this is correct, then a settlor who holds property in an interest in possession trust could be in a better tax position than a settlor whose property is held in a discretionary trust. If the donor has a qualifying interest in possession in a trust and dies domiciled here, s.102(3) is displaced because the property forms part of his estate immediately before his death (because he has an interest in possession in it—s.49(1)). It can then obtain the protection of s.48(3) since there is nothing in s.49(1) to displace s.48(3).

HMRC confirmed in correspondence with the Law Society in 1986[49] that the settled property rules did override the reservation of benefit rules and that there was no tax to pay if the reserved benefit property was excluded property under s.48. This was confirmed in the *CTO Advanced Instruction Manual* at

22.33

---

[45] Which will be income of the settlor as life tenant.
[46] Given that the s.86 charge on the settlor will not apply: see 10.08.
[47] See 10.24.
[48] Reservation of benefit is discussed more generally in Chs 18 and 24.
[49] Law Soc Gaz 1986, p.3728.

D8 but the text was changed in October 2001 indicating that HMRC were reconsidering their position. The *IHT Manual* has been rewritten and is now in a complete muddle. It says:

> "Foreign property settled by a settlor with foreign domicile remains excluded property if the reservation of benefit continues *up to the settlor's death*, even though the domicile may have changed between those dates."[50]

That statement suggests that there is no tax problem for the settlor on the property if the reservation of benefit continues until his death. The following example is then given:

> "The donor, who is domiciled in Australia, puts foreign property into a discretionary trust under which he is a potential beneficiary. He dies five years later domiciled in the UK and without having released the reservation. The property is subject to a reservation of benefit and is therefore deemed to be part of the donor's death estate. Refer any cases where this is the situation to Litigation."

This is the opposite of the first statement, namely that there *is* a problem! But the Manual then goes on to consider what happens if he is excluded from benefit *during his lifetime* after he has attained a UK domicile and clearly distinguishes between the two situations where the reservation of benefit continues until his death and where the reservation of benefit ceases during his lifetime:

> "However,[51] had the donor ..attained UK domicile after the gift and then released the reservation during his lifetime, it is arguable that the release would have been a PET chargeable on his death within seven years" [under s.102(4)]

This suggests that HMRC still accept that there is no problem if the settlor reserves a benefit up until his death but that there is a deemed PET under s.102(4) of the FA 1986 if he is excluded from benefit during his lifetime when he is UK domiciled and that he would need to survive seven years to avoid an inheritance tax charge.

22.34 Subsequently, HMRC noted in correspondence with the authors:

> "So far as the application of s.102(3) *on death* is concerned HMRC remains bound in the absence of an announcement to the contrary to follow the view set out in . . . the LSG letter."

Of course where the reservation of benefit continues until death it would still be necessary to ensure that at the date of the settlor's death the trust holds non-UK-situated property. Otherwise s.48(3) affords no protection.

22.35 HMRC apparently *will* argue that the settlor makes a deemed PET under s.102(4) if he is excluded from any part of the discretionary part of the fund

---

[50] IHTM 14396.
[51] Suggesting that a different view is taken on lifetime terminations of a reservation of benefit.

while alive and deemed UK-domiciled and therefore in these circumstances it will be necessary for the settlor to survive seven years. This is more of a problem than might first be thought. If HMRC are right, it would mean that a deemed PET arises not only if the settlor is formally excluded from the trust but also if capital distributions are made to other beneficiaries, e.g. children, or property is appointed to a separate trust from which the settlor cannot benefit.

Where the settlor's reservation ends *inter vivos*, HMRC say a charge should be considered but only in circumstances where the settlor has acquired a UK domicile prior to the PET.[52] Are they correct? Unlike s.102(3), s.102(4) of the FA 1986 does not deem the property to be part of the donor's estate or treat it as property to which he is beneficially entitled. Section 102(4) simply deems the donor to have made a PET. A PET is a disposition which is a transfer of value. How does s.3(2) (which states that *"for the purposes of subsection (1) no account shall be taken of the value of excluded property which ceases to form part of a person's estate as a result of a disposition"*) interact with s.3(1) which defines the transfer of value?

If it is accepted that the settled property is excluded property, is the value transferred by the deemed PET nil because "no account" is taken of the value of excluded property for the purposes of assessing a transfer of value? Or does the fact that there is a deemed PET and transfer of value override s.3(2)? The difficulty with the latter argument (if HMRC are right that settled property is not excluded property when the reservation of benefit ceases during the settlor's lifetime), is that it is difficult to see why there should be any difference if the settlor is not domiciled here. In both cases a deemed PET is made and if HMRC are right s.3(2) is overridden. But HMRC have not argued that a settlor who is not UK domiciled makes a PET when a reservation of benefit ceases in non-UK situate property. The position therefore remains unsatisfactory but UK domiciled settlors are best advised to avoid the cessation of a reservation of benefit during their lifetimes.

POWERS OF APPOINTMENT IN RELATION TO EXCLUDED SETTLED PROPERTY

22.36 It is not uncommon for a foreign domiciled settlor to wish to retain wide powers of appointment or revocation over the settled property. This may be because the settlor is concerned that he has insufficient control over the trust assets or, in some cases, there are good tax reasons for a settlor or other beneficiary to retain a power of appointment or revocation. This is particularly true where the settlor or the beneficiaries are US citizens. In US trusts one often sees the power exercisable subject to the consent of a nominated person. This reflects the general nervousness from the UK perspective of giving the settlor (or other beneficiary) a power to appoint assets in favour of himself, on the basis that it may make the person a trustee; the trust a sham or that it will jeopardise the favourable inheritance tax treatment otherwise available on the death of the settlor.

---

[52] IHTM 14396.

Types of powers

22.37 It is not always easy to decide whether the power given is a special power, a general power or a hybrid power. A *general* power will give the donee[53] power to appoint in favour of anyone in the world including himself. A *special* power is a power which can be exercised only in favour of certain specified persons or classes, such as issue of the settlor. The donee of the power may himself be an object of the special power. A *hybrid* power is often described as an intermediate power which will give the donee power to appoint to all persons except a named or specified person or class, e.g. "to any person except the settlor or his estate". Of course, a donee who has a special power exercisable in favour of himself may not in tax terms be treated differently from a donee who has a general power exercisable in favour of anyone including himself.

Does inserting a requirement that the power is exercisable subject only to consent, affect the nature of the power or the tax treatment of the settled property? The case law on the first point is confusing. In *Re Dilke*[54] and *Re Phillips*[55] it was held that a power of appointment was a general power of appointment even though it could only be exercised with the consent of a third party. In both cases the power of appointment was subject to the consent of the trustees. By contrast in *Re Watts*[56] a power of revocation and reappointment was vested in the settlor. The power could only be exercised with the consent of the settlor's mother. It was held that this power was not a general power. It was suggested that there was a distinction between the situation where the consent was more in the nature of a veto (as in *Re Dilke* and *Re Phillips*) and the position where that third party was under a duty to consider the beneficial interests which the person exercising the power proposed to appoint, and the interests of those who would take in default of appointment (as in *Re Watts*).

In *Re Churston Settled Estates*[57] Roxburgh J. said that he could find no authority to support such a distinction. He held, following *Re Watts*, that a joint power of appointment exercisable with consent was not a general power. He also held that a joint power of appointment by itself was not a general power because it could only be exercised with the consent of the other donees of the power.

22.38 *Thomas on Powers* concludes that:

> "... a power to appoint to an unlimited class of objects, and which is subject to no restriction on the mode or manner of its exercise, may still not be a general power if it is exercisable only with the consent of another person (such a power often being referred to as a consent power)".[58]

---

[53] Often, but not always, the donee of the power is the settlor or the life tenant.
[54] [1921] 1 Ch. 34.
[55] [1931] 1 Ch. 347.
[56] [1931] 2 Ch. 302.
[57] [1954] Ch. 334.
[58] Sweet and Maxwell (1998) at para. 13–10.

For this proposition, he cites *Re Churston Settled Estates* and also *Re Earl of Coventry's Indentures*.[59] He does, however, note that:

> "It may be otherwise if consent is required as to the actual exercise of the power and not as to the selection of the appointee".[60]

In support of this caveat to the proposition, he cites *Re Dilke*,[61] *Re Phillips*,[62] *Re Watts*,[63] *Re Joicey*,[64] and *Re Triffitt's Settlement*.[65] Later, he states that:

> "A power which is exercisable only with the consent of trustees is a special and not a general power, unless the consent is required only to the actual exercise of the power and not to the selection or approval of the appointee".

Whether it is actually possible to separate consent to actual exercise from consent to the choice of appointment must be doubtful.[66] However, it appears that for tax purposes provided the power can be drafted in such a way as to ensure that the person whose consent is needed acts in a fiduciary capacity, the power, however wide the class of objects, will not be a general power or one which will in itself cause a tax problem.[67]

---

[59] [1974] Ch. 77.
[60] *Thomas*, para. 13–10, fn 26.
[61] *Re Dilke, Verey v Dilke* [1921] 1 Ch. 34.
[62] *Re Phillips, Lawrence v Huxtable* [1931] 1 Ch. 347.
[63] *Re Watts, Coffey v Watts* [1931] 2 Ch. 302.
[64] (1932) 76 Sol. Jo. 459.
[65] *Re Triffitt's Settlement, Hall v Hyde* [1958] Ch. 852.
[66] In *Re Earl of Coventry's Indentures*, Walton J. held that *Re Churston Settlement*, in following *Re Watts*, had overlooked that the latter turned on a question of construction of the terms of the power. He held that, in consequence, the decision in *Re Churston* could not bear the weight placed upon it and he felt compelled to re-examine the question afresh. .He considered the question in the context of the rule against perpetuities and observed:

> "Treating the matter as res integra, I fail for myself to see how a general power which is exercisable only with the consent of a third party can possibly be said to amount to an absolute vested interest in the subject matter of the power in the donee thereof. The plain fact of the matter is that such a person cannot appoint to whomsoever he chooses. He can only appoint in a manner approved by somebody else. The restriction on his ownership arises not from a restriction directly placed upon the possible field of selection by the terms of the power itself, but from the necessity of obtaining the specified consent. But in my judgment if a person can only pluck the fruit with the consent of somebody else it cannot in any meaningful sense be said to be vested in him".

His only reservation was:

> ". . . where in the case of a power exercisable with consent the person or persons whose consent was required upon being applied to said 'yes: exercise the power in any way you please, I (or we) don't care.' It appears to me that so long as such consent had been given and was not withdrawn (and of course unless the power to consent as a whole was capable of and had been duly released it could always be withdrawn) the donee of the power had an unfettered general power, and thus able to claim a fresh start for his appointment from the point of view of the rule against perpetuities."

[67] Except possibly in relation to reservation of benefit where the settlor has the power although this would not generally be an issue for excluded property settlements.

22.39 The inheritance tax consequences of a general power over settled property

Example 22.12

> A discretionary trust (T) is set up and funded with non-UK situs property at a time when the settlor (S) is not UK domiciled or deemed domiciled. S is given a power of revocation or general power of appointment over the settled property (for US tax reasons.) No consent is required. What is the correct tax treatment of the power?

The mere inclusion of a power of revocation or general power of appointment in an excluded property settlement should not in itself cause any inheritance tax problems assuming that it does not matter that S reserves a benefit in the settlement.[68] The result seems counter intuitive: while the donee of a general power is not technically the owner of the property which is the subject matter of the power, for the purposes of the rule against perpetuities the law looks to the substance rather than the form and that property is regarded as beneficially owned by the donee of the power.

However a power of revocation or general power of appointment which is vested in the settlor should not *in itself* result in the settled property in respect of which the power is exercisable being treated as property to which the settlor is beneficially entitled for inheritance tax purposes. This is because of the distinction drawn in the inheritance tax legislation between settled and non-settled property: in effect there is a special regime applicable to settled property and general powers.[69]

22.40 IHTA 1984, s.5(2) provides:

> "A person who has a general power which enables him, or would if he were sui juris enable him, to dispose of any property other than settled property, or to charge money on any property other than settled property, shall be treated as beneficially entitled to the property or money; and for this purpose "general power" means a power or authority enabling the person by whom it is exercisable to appoint or dispose of property as he thinks fit."

While the above makes it clear that the presence of the power cannot mean that the holder of the power is beneficially entitled to the *settled property*, *Melville*[70] disturbed this analysis by treating the *power itself* as a separate item of property. For foreign domiciled settlors this was a disaster if they died UK-domiciled because the power would be a valuable personal asset taxed on their death as part of their worldwide estate. The position was corrected in 2002

---

[68] S is probably a named beneficiary anyway so the insertion of a general power of appointment does not cause any additional reservation of benefit problems. If a beneficiary who is not the settlor has the power this would not in itself cause a reservation of benefit to arise in relation to that beneficiary because he has not gifted the assets.

[69] The position is slightly different for capital gains tax and income tax purposes but where the settlor is the person with the general power of appointment and he is not UK-domiciled, such a power does not usually cause additional income tax or capital gains tax problems.

[70] *IRC v Melville* 74 TC 372.

(and deemed always to have had effect) by the combined effect of the amended s.272 and s.47A of IHTA:

> Section 272: ". . . 'property' includes rights and interests of any description but does not include a settlement power;"
>
> Section 47A: "In this Act 'settlement power' means any power over, or exercisable (whether directly or indirectly) in relation to, settled property or a settlement."

22.41 There is one further problem: does the failure to exercise a power of revocation or power to appoint in favour of oneself constitute a an omission to exercise a right within s.3(3) IHTA 1984 which provides:

> "Where the value of a person's estate is diminished and that of another person's estate, or of settled property in which no interest in possession subsists, is increased by the first-mentioned person's omission to exercise a right, he shall be treated for the purposes of this section as having made a disposition at the time (or latest time) when he could have exercised the right, unless it is shown that the omission was not deliberate."

The better view is that s.3(3) has no effect because:

(i) the settlor's estate does not presently include the settled property (s.5(2)) or the settlement power (see s.47A). Therefore, the settlor's failure to exercise the power of revocation or of appointment in favour of himself cannot be said to have resulted in the value of his estate having been diminished;

(ii) even if this argument were to fail, the failure to exercise the power does not result in the value of another person's estate, or of settled property in which no interest in possession subsists, being increased. The value of the settled property remains the same.

The authors conclude therefore that the mere inclusion of a power of revocation or a general power of appointment in a settlement does not prevent the property being excluded settled property nor in itself cause an inheritance tax problem for the settlor of an excluded property settlement on his death.

22.42 It is not known if HMRC accept this analysis. It has been suggested that they might take a s.3(3) point but only if the settled property was not excluded property. (The exception for excluded property would be on the basis that s.3(2) directs that for the purposes of s.3(1) no account is taken of excluded property. If all of the property concerned is excluded property there cannot be a charge by reference to s.3.) Out of abundant caution, practitioners may prefer to make the exercise of the power of appointment or revocation subject to consent and provide that the consent is exercisable in a fiduciary capacity.

Exercise of a power of appointment

22.43 The above does not cover the inheritance tax consequences if the donee actually exercises a power of appointment or revocation. If the settlor revokes the settlement the assets fall into his free estate and if he is UK domiciled will be taxable on his death. Suppose instead the donee of a power (whether or not the settlor) exercises his general power of appointment to appoint the excluded settled property on different trusts or to another person outright? An outright appointment to someone else should not be a PET unless the settlor is the donee.[71] If the donee of a general power of appointment is settlor of the original trust and appoints on new trusts this might cause difficulties (a) if the settlor is excluded from any benefit or (b) if there is a resettlement of the assets and (c) in either case he is domiciled or deemed UK domiciled.

REVERSIONARY INTERESTS

22.44 Unlike the term "interest in possession", a reversionary interest is specifically defined in the legislation. Under s.47 it means "a future interest under a settlement whether it is vested or contingent (including an interest expectant on the termination of an interest in possession which, by virtue of s.50 below, is treated as subsisting in part of any property) . . ."

The term, therefore, includes an interest dependent on the termination of an interest in possession, whether that interest is vested or contingent. A contingent interest where the settlement does not have an interest in possession is also a reversionary interest for IHT purposes.

EXAMPLE 22.13

Property is settled on the following trusts:

(1) A for life, remainder to B for life, remainder to C. B and C both have reversionary interests for IHT purposes.

(2) To A absolutely contingent upon his attaining the age of 21. A is currently aged six and has a reversionary interest for IHT purposes.

The interest of a discretionary beneficiary is not, however a "reversionary interest", being in no sense a future interest. Such a beneficiary has certain rights, particularly the right to be considered by the trustees when they exercise their discretion and the right to compel due administration of the fund. The commercial value of such an interest is likely to be nil, however, since the beneficiary has no right to any of the income or capital of the settlement but has merely a hope.[72]

"Situs" of a reversionary interest

22.45 The courts have never clearly decided whether a reversionary interest is an interest in trust assets in specie (in which case it is situated where the trust

---

[71] In which case if the settlor is the donee HMRC will presumably argue there is a deemed PET under s.102(4) if he is deemed UK domiciled. See 22.35.

[72] As a result of the FA 2006 changes, an interest in possession created after March 21, 2006 is not included as an asset in the beneficiary's estate: see IHTA 1984, s.5(1)(a). On reversionary interests, see also 17.15 and 17.27.

assets are situated) or a "chose in action" (in which case it is situated where it is properly recoverable) but the better view in the case of a trust for sale is that it is a chose in action.[73] In other cases the position is unclear; but by analogy with estate duty principles it will be a chose in action if the settled assets are personalty; but an interest in the settled assets themselves if they are land. Since a chose in action is normally situated in the country in which it is recoverable,[74] in some cases the reversionary interest will not be situated in the same place as the settled assets but HMRC seem to take the view that a reversionary interest will normally be situated where the trustees of the property to which the interest relates reside.

The general exemption

A reversionary interest is excluded property for IHT[75] wherever situate and regardless of the domicile of the settlor or of the holder of the reversionary interest, subject only to three exceptions designed to counter tax avoidance: 22.46

EXAMPLE 22.14

(i) When it was purchased for money or money's worth:

Take a settlement on A for life, remainder to B. B sells his interest to X who gives it to his brother Y. X (a purchaser of the interest) has made a transfer of value (a PET) of a reversionary interest (which can be valued by taking into account the value of the settled fund and the life expectancy of A)

(ii) Where it is an interest to which the settlor or his spouse is beneficially entitled.

(iii) Where a lease for life or lives is granted for no or partial consideration, there is a settlement for IHT[76] and the lessor's interest is a reversionary interest.[77] Such a reversionary interest is only excluded property to the extent that the lessor did not receive full consideration on the grant.[78]

EXAMPLE 22.15

I grants a lease of property worth £30,000 to T for £10,000 for T's life. T is treated for IHT purposes, as having an interest in possession and, therefore, as absolute owner of the property (£30,000–£10,000). I is

---

[73] Re *Smyth, Leach v Leach* [1898] 1 Ch. 89.
[74] *New York Life Insurance Co v Public Trustee* [1924] 2 Ch. 101.
[75] IHTA 1984, s.48(1).
[76] IHTA 1984, s.43(3).
[77] IHTA 1984, s.46, see 17.09.
[78] IHTA 1984, s.48(1)(c).

treated as the owner of one-third of the property (because he received £10,000). Therefore, one-third of his reversionary interest is not excluded property.

The foreign element

22.47   As noted above, irrespective of where the settled property in which the reversionary interest subsists is situated, the general exemption in s.48(1) along with the three exceptions outlined above applies. Section 48(3) states:

> "where property comprised in a settlement is situated outside the UK
>
> > (a) the property (but not a reversionary interest in the property) is excluded property unless the settlor was domiciled in the UK at the time the settlement was made; and
> > (b) section 6(1) above applies to a reversionary interest in the property, but does not otherwise apply in relation to the property".

22.48   The proviso in (a) appears to exclude the operation of s.48(1) by saying that a reversionary interest in settled property situated abroad is only excluded property[79] if the interest is itself situated abroad and owned by a foreign domiciliary. That would mean that reversionary interests in settled property situated abroad were taxed adversely as compared to reversionary interests in settled property situated in the UK.

22.49   However, it is thought that s.48(3) only prevails over s.48(1) in cases of conflict and that there is no conflict here since the words *"but not a reversionary interest"* in s.48(3)(a) mean that whether a reversionary interest is excluded property depends first on the general rule in s.48(1) (so that where the settlor is domiciled here a reversionary interest in trust property situated outside the UK can still be excluded) and only if s.48(1) does not apply should one look at the rules in s.48(3).

So on that basis where the settled property in which the reversionary interest subsists is situated outside the UK, the interest can still be excluded property *even if one of the above exceptions* applies if the beneficial owner of the reversionary interest is a foreign domiciliary and the reversionary interest itself is situated outside the UK.[80]

22.50   However, where a person settles a reversionary interest (so that the interest itself becomes settled property as opposed to being merely an interest in settled property beneficially owned by someone) the position is more complicated. If the reversionary interest is itself settled property; is situated abroad and was settled by a foreign domiciliary then it will be excluded property under s.48(3)(a). If it is situated in the UK or is situated abroad and settled by a UK domiciliary it is thought that the settled reversionary interest can still be excluded property under s.48(1) provided that one of the three exceptions does not apply.[81]

---

[79] Under the general rule in s.6(1).
[80] s.6(1) and s.48(3)(b).
[81] Although some commentators consider that where a UK domiciliary settles his foreign situate reversionary interest, the settled reversionary interest can never be excluded property due to the s.48(3)(a) proviso.

PURCHASED INTERESTS IN EXCLUDED PROPERTY SETTLEMENTS

22.51 Prior to December 5, 2005, it was possible for a UK domiciliary to use excluded property trusts to mitigate his inheritance tax. The chargeable property was converted into excluded property.

EXAMPLE 22.16

> A is seriously ill and UK domiciled. He intends to leave all his estate worth £9m to his son. He is aware that 40 per cent inheritance tax will be payable. He therefore buys an interest in possession held by B in a settlement made by a foreign domiciliary. All the assets in the settlement are foreign situate and it is therefore an excluded property settlement. A pays B £9m for B's interest which is its commercial value. The settled interest is excluded property and there is no tax payable on the death of A. The chargeable cash has been converted into an interest under an excluded property settlement.

22.52 This example simplifies the scheme considerably. For example, if the settlement was established by a foreign domiciliary, B, specifically to sell an interest to A and the settlement was funded out of borrowed monies in anticipation of A buying the interest it is likely that HMRC could successfully contend that A was the settlor under s.44(1) on the basis that he provided property directly or indirectly for the purpose of the settlement.

There can be problems if the life interest purchased is terminable by exercise of overriding powers. A needed to be certain that his son acquired the remainder interests in the settlement otherwise on B's death the capital would pass to the remaindermen who are not A's family. If A pays more than the actuarial value of B's life interest then he is treated as making a transfer of value of the excess.[82]

22.53 With effect from December 5, 2005, s.157 of the FA 2006 has put an end to the scheme by amending s.48(3) and (3A) so that property in an excluded property settlement (including AUTS and OEICS) is not excluded property if

> "a person is or has been beneficially entitled to an interest in possession in the property at any time and the person is or was at that time an individual domiciled in the UK and the entitlement arose directly or indirectly as a result of a disposition made on or after 5th December 2005 for a consideration in money or money's worth."

Existing schemes are unaffected by the changes.

22.54 The section is in some ways wide ranging. Unlike TCGA 1992, s.76[83] there is no let out where the consideration consists of another interest in the settlement. Almost any type of consideration paid is enough to bring the section into play.

---

[82] IHTA 1984, s.49(1).
[83] See Ch. 8.

EXAMPLE 22.17

X who is domiciled in India sets up a settlement holding foreign situated land and shares for his children A and B. A takes a life interest in the trust and is UK domiciled. B is still non-UK domiciled.

It is eventually agreed that the trust fund should be split so that Fund A comprising foreign investments is held on trust for child A and Fund B comprising the land is held for child B. The trustees have insufficient powers to achieve this and therefore A and B agree this between them (or else there is an application to court).

In these circumstances has A acquired an interest in possession for consideration i.e. an interest in the investments? Even if the variation is done by court application, one beneficiary is still agreeing to give up his interest in return for receiving an entitlement to income in other types of assets.

Moreover what happens if in the above example A was not domiciled here at the date he acquired the interest for money's worth and then he later becomes domiciled in the UK still holding an interest in possession? In these circumstances he would appear to be caught if he is domiciled at any time when he holds the interest in possession.

22.55 Having said this, the section is in some ways narrowly drafted. It would appear that s.157 only operates on interests in possession not (for example) contingent interests over capital or the purchase of a reversionary interest in a settlement. It is not though necessary to purchase a *qualifying* interest in possession to be caught by s.158 so the rules will affect purchases beyond April 2008.

PRE-OWNED ASSETS INCOME TAX: PROBLEMS FOR FOREIGN DOMICILIARIES

22.56 Until December 5, 2005 foreign domiciliaries were in most cases protected from the effects of the pre-owned assets legislation. There are two specific mechanisms to protect foreign domicilairies—the let-outs given specifically in para.12, Sch.15 of FA 2004 and the para.11 exemptions available to taxpayers generally. Note also the basic territorial restriction of the POA charge which does not apply to any person for any tax year during which that person is not UK resident. This exclusion, in para.12(1), operates irrespective of the domicile of the taxpayer.

In summary, until recently relevant property contained in a settlement where the settlor retained a pre-Budget qualifying interest in possession wherever such property was situate and whether or not owned through a corporate structure was outside the POA Regime, due to either the para.12 or para.11 exemptions even if the settlor later became UK deemed domiciled. Similarly discretionary trusts set up by non-UK domiciliaries were thought to be outside the POA Regime even where the land or chattels were UK situs and owned through offshore companies and even where the foreign domiciliary became UK deemed domiciled. This was because the para.12 reliefs were available on the foreign sited property and the para.11(3) exemption would be applicable to relieve the UK property.

22.57 There are, however, three ways in which the POA can now be a serious problem for the foreign domiciliary living in the UK.

22.58 First, HMRC have now formally stated in the COP 10 letter to the professional bodies reproduced in Appendix III at A3.94, that where a trust or settlor has lent to a company which then holds a house, the company shares are worth less than the house and the loan does not derive its value from the house. This can mean a POA charge on the difference between the value of the company shares subject to the debt and the house even though company shares and loan may be in the settlor's estate.

22.59 Second, many foreign domiciliaries purchased UK homes using two interest in possession trusts—one holding the debt and the other holding the house subject to the debt. The idea was that although the debt was an excluded liability within para.11(7), it did not reduce the value of the settlor's estate for POA purposes because he had an interest in possession in the trust holding the debt (see para.11(6)). Nevertheless the debt did reduce the value of the house for inheritance tax purposes. Such structures already in existence may not be affected but cannot be done after March 21, 2006, since it is not possible to create an *inter vivos* debt trust with a qualifying interest in possession.

22.60 Third, and most seriously, s.80 of FA 2006 has an adverse effect on foreign domiciliaries where the trust is now a qualifying interest in possession trust or has been a qualifying interest in possession trust.[84] Unless s.80 is amended it could mean that the majority of foreign domiciliaries holding any UK situated assets in interest in possession trusts will be subject to POA from December 5, 2005.

22.61 **Reliefs relevant only to foreign domiciliaries:** these are contained in paras.12(2) and (3). They are briefly as follows:

22.62 **The basic relief under para.12(2):** where an individual is not domiciled or deemed domiciled in the United Kingdom for IHT purposes, the POA Regime does not apply to him unless the relevant property is situated in the United Kingdom.[85]

22.63 **The settled property relief—para.12(3):** in applying the POA Regime to a person who was at any time domiciled outside the United Kingdom for IHT purposes, no regard is had to foreign situs property which is excluded property by reason of being comprised in a settlement made by a settlor who was not domiciled in the United Kingdom when he made the settlement.[86]

22.64 **Exemptions relevant to all taxpayers—the paras.11(1) and (3) exemptions:** these apply regardless of the taxpayer's domicile and regardless of the situs of the property. They are briefly as follows:

22.65 **Ownership exemption under para.11(1)(a):** the POA Regime prima facie does not apply to an individual in respect of property which is included in his IHT estate. A person's estate for IHT purposes includes settled property in which

---

[84] This is discussed at 22.70.
[85] See Sch.15, para.12(2).
[86] See Sch.15, para.12(3).

the person concerned has a qualifying pre-March 22, 2006 interest in possession[87] as well as property he owns directly. It is important to realise that this exemption is wider than might at first sight appear because a person's estate may include excluded property albeit that such property will not be subject to IHT on that person's death. However, note the effect of s.80 of FA 2006 on this exemption—see 22.70 below.

EXAMPLE 22.18

> When domiciled in Norway Sam set up a Jersey settlement in 1997 which gives her a qualifying interest in possession. The Settlement was settled with cash and the trustees then formed a Jersey company which in turn purchased a UK property in which Sam now lives (she has recently become deemed domiciled in the UK). In considering the effect of the POA charge on Sam, the settled property (the shares) is, for IHT purposes, excluded property[88] and is not itself subject to POA (being within para 12(3)). The UK property was (at least until 5th December 2005) protected by para 11(1)—see next Example.

22.66 **Derived ownership exemption—para.11(1)(b):** the POA Regime also does not apply to an individual in respect of relevant property if that individual's estate includes property which derives its value from that relevant property (para.11(1)(b)). This is called the derived ownership exemption.

EXAMPLE 22.19

> Continuing with the example of Sam (see *Example 22.18* above) the excluded property (the shares) are treated as comprised in her estate[89] for the purposes of the ownership exemption and it may be that those shares derive their value from the UK property occupied by Sam. If this is the case then the POA regime—as a result of the derived ownership exemption—will not (at least until December 5, 2005) apply to the house occupied in the UK. If however, the value of the shares is "substantially less" than the value of the house then the POA regime will apply to the difference in value. This could arise if the trustees lend money to the company to buy the house. HMRC argue that the value of the house is more than the value of the company and the loan does not derive its value from the house.[90] This is discussed further below.

[87] IHTA 1984, s.49(1) or, rarely, a post Budget disabled person's interest under a trust set up after March 21, 2006.
[88] see IHTA 1984, s.48(3).
[89] See IHTA 1984, s.5(1) which provides that a person's estate is the aggregate of all the property to which he is beneficially entitled (as for instance settled property in which that person has a qualifying interest in possession) "except that the estate of a person *immediately before death* does not include excluded property". See also *ibid*. s.3(2) providing that the value of excluded property which ceases to form part of a person's estate as the result of a disposition shall not be a transfer of value.
[90] See COP 10 letter in Appendix III at A3.94.

In addition, section 80 FA 2006 could now mean that para 11(1) does not apply any longer to give protection because Sam has indirectly contributed to the purchase of a property she now occupies: instead Sam suffers a POA charge from 5th December 2005.

Reserved benefit exemption—paras 11(3)(a) and (5)(a): the POA Regime does not apply to an individual by reference to any property in which he has reserved a benefit. The "excluded liabilities" rules do not apply so if the reserved benefit property is subject to an excluded liability this will not matter.   **22.67**

EXAMPLE 22.20

> X dies deemed domiciled in the UK, having set up a discretionary trust comprising non UK *situs* property at a time when he was domiciled outside the UK. HMRC practice in such a case is not to impose a charge on the settled property on the basis that, as excluded property, it does not form part of X's estate immediately before he died. But this does not prevent the property from being property subject to a reservation and thereby (in terms of the POA charge) X obtaining the protection of para.11(5)(a).

Derivative reserved benefit exemption (para.11(3)(b)): The reservation of benefit exemption is extended by para.11(3)(b) to exempt property from the POA charge in which the donor reserves a benefit which **derives its value** from relevant property.   **22.68**

EXAMPLE 22.21

> Jude, non UK domiciled, set up a Jersey discretionary trust which incorporates a Jersey company to acquire a residential property in the UK. Some years later Jude becomes domiciled in the UK. Jude is a beneficiary of the trust and occupies the property. The IHT/POA analysis is as follows—
>
> (i) the settlement comprises excluded property (shares in the Jersey company) for IHT purposes;
>
> (ii) the property in the trust is not comprised (directly or indirectly) in Jude's estate (i.e. the ownership and derived ownership exemptions are not satisfied);
>
> (iii) Jude has however reserved a benefit in the property in the discretionary trust[91] (the shares) which derive their value from the UK property. Hence as a result of the derived reserved benefit exemption the POA charge is excluded. Note though that if the trust has lent to the company to enable it to purchase the house then HMRC

---

[91] See *IRC v Eversden* [2003] S.T.C. 822, CA.

will not accept at present that the loan and the shares together derive their value from the house and in that event there would be a POA charge on the different between the value of the house and the value of the company shares. It seems odd that HMRC consider the loan cannot be regarded as derived from the value of the house (rather than from the company's contractual undertakings) given that the loan could not be repaid if the company did not own the house. Foreign domiciliaries may want to self-assess making full disclosure of any loans if they differ from the stated HMRC view and/or capitalise the loan to the company.

22.69 **Hierarchy of let-outs and exemptions:** the legislation does not establish any hierarchy between the para.12 let-outs and the para.11 exemptions. In practice, it is simpler to apply the para.12 reliefs first because they are easier to apply conceptually than the para.11 exemptions and, unlike the para.11 exemptions, are not subject to any qualifications.[92] In particular s.80 of FA 2006 will not apply to property with para.12 protection.

22.70 **Section 80 FA 2006:** s.80[93] will only be a problem for those foreign domiciliaries with UK situated assets held in trusts. Where the assets are non UK situated and held in trust, the settlor can rely on the para.12 reliefs and will not need to depend on para. 11. Section 80 amends para.11(1) and can apply if one out of two conditions is satisfied.

(i) that the relevant property has ceased to be comprised in the person's estate for inheritance tax purposes **or**

(ii) that the person has directly or indirectly provided any consideration for the acquisition of the relevant property.

22.71 If at any subsequent time the relevant property or derived property is in his estate for the purposes of s.49 IHTA then the effect of s.80 is to provide that for POA purposes (but for no other) the settlor is not treated as having an interest in possession or having reserved a benefit in the property.

The difficulty is that s.80 (which was designed to target only reverter to settlor trusts) does not in fact distinguish between reverter to settlor trusts and *any* other trust set up after March 1986 but before March 22, 2006 where the settlor now has a qualifying interest in possession. Section 80 catches not only those transactions where, for example, land was given away and ceased to be comprised in the settlor's estate and then came back into his estate (condition (i) above). It also catches transactions where the settlor contributed directly or indirectly to the property held in the trust (condition (ii) above).

---

[92] There has been some question as to whether para.12(3) creates a problem by disapplying the Schedule in relation to excluded property of a former foreign domiciliary. "In the application of this Schedule to a person who was at any time domiciled outside the UK, no regard is to be had to any property which is . . . excluded property . . ." In these circumstances, can such a person rely on the para.11(1) exemption if the Schedule does not apply to excluded property— arguably the excluded property is not then part of the person's estate and therefore the underlying property cannot obtain the benefit of the derived ownership exemption. It is not thought this is the correct interpretation of para.12(3), which should be read more narrowly. HMRC confirmed this in their May 2006 guidance notes and in correspondence.

[93] See Ch. 27.

EXAMPLE 22.22

On the above wording the following cases would be caught by POA:

1. In 1987, A (foreign domiciliary) sets up an interest in possession trust for himself into which he gifted cash. The interest in possession is a qualifying iip within s.49. The trustees eventually use the cash either to purchase a house which is held direct or to fund a company which then purchases the house. Condition B is satisfied and therefore s.80 can apply.

2. Suppose the foreign domiciliary A settled one house—an Italian property—into an iip trust and the trustees eventually sell the house and purchase another property—a UK house. Unless the UK house was the original property settled and therefore has never left A's estate and he has not satisfied the contribution condition, there is now a POA charge by reference to his occupation of the UK house.

    Note that if A settled property into a trust post-March 21, 2006 s.80 cannot apply—he will not take an interest in possession that is qualifying.

    There is no indication from the explanatory notes or the press release that *all interest in possession trusts* where the settlor is the life tenant *were* intended targets under section 80 but this appears to be the effect.

    Even if A's interest in possession is now ended in favour of another person, this will not protect A from a POA charge unless he is entirely excluded because para.11(5) (the reservation of benefit protection) is specifically disapplied. It is thought that in practice HMRC will accept that (1) and (2) are not within s.80.

3. B is a foreign domiciliary who is UK resident and in 2004 he sets up a discretionary trust into which he transfers cash. He remains a beneficiary of the trust. The trust then funds a company which buys a house or possibly holds UK investments (and B will pay income tax under s.739 TA 1988 in respect of any UK income). The trust is later converted into an interest in possession trust for B. If there are any UK intangibles or UK property occupied by B which are held by the trustees within the interest in possession structure he is now subject to POA. Even if one reads "subsequent time" to mean that some time must elapse between the date when the gift is made and the date the property comes back into B's estate this would still not help B here because the trust was originally discretionary. If B had set up an interest in possession trust from the outset he is also caught by section 80. If B's pre-Budget interest in possession is now ended and discretionary trusts arise, s.80 is still a problem. (HMRC have indicated that s.80 is a problem and that B should elect.)

In summary, from the POA perspective an urgent review of trusts set up by foreign domiciliaries is required where: **22.72**

(i) the trust was established pre-March 22, 2006; and

(ii) the trust holds in its structure any UK situated property; and

(iii) the trust has at any time during its life been a qualifying interest in possession trust, particularly if it started off discretionary in form.

Foreign domiciliaries setting up trusts or converting discretionary in interest in possession trusts, on or after March 22, 2006 will not need to worry about s.80 because they cannot create a qualifying interest in possession as a result of the FA 2006 changes.

Accommodation arrangements

22.73 These are discussed in Ch. 31.

Chapter 23

LIABILITIES

- What liabilities are deductible? **(23.02)**
- Liabilities and excluded property **(23.06)**
- Liabilities and interest in possession trusts **(23.10)**
- The artificial debt rule in FA 1986 s.103 **(23.16)**
- Liabilities in the context of business and agricultural property **(23.23)**

The deduction of liabilities is dealt with in IHTA 1984, s.5 and in Chapters I and II of Pt VI: in particular s.162. Trustees need to consider four areas: **23.01**

(i) **Lending by trustees:** trustees often lend to a beneficiary or to the settlor when he is a beneficiary, and the beneficiary/settlor wishes to ensure that the debt is deductible in his estate at death. For example, the trustees of a nil rate band discretionary will trust set up by H may lend to the surviving spouse W. Is the debt deductible on W's death? Trustees frequently lend to settlors who may be the life tenant. In these circumstances is the transaction tax neutral (i.e. the debt is a deduction in the settlor's free estate but an asset of the trust) or is the debt non-deductible under s.103 FA 1986?[1]

(ii) **Trustees may incur liabilities to third parties or beneficiaries:** e.g. they borrow to purchase a house.[2] Is the debt incurred by the trustees deductible for the purposes of calculating the inheritance tax liability on the death of a life tenant?[3]

(iii) **Excluded property settlements:** trustees of an excluded property settlement may lend to a foreign domiciled settlor. Is the liability deductible by the settlor? Trustees may own both UK property and excluded property and need to know against what property the debt is deductible.[4]

(iv) **Agricultural and business property:** trustees may own business property or agricultural property. Against what property are trust liabilities deducted?[5]

---

[1] See 23.16.
[2] A typical illustration being the double trust/home loan scheme: see 3.18.
[3] See 23.10.
[4] See 23.06 and 23.08.
[5] See 23.23.

EXAMPLE 23.1

> Johnny is domiciled in China. At the date of his death he owns UK assets worth £1 million and has a Chinese estate worth over £4m. He owes £1m to a bank. If the debt is deductible against his UK estate there is no UK inheritance tax payable. His remaining property is excluded property. If the debt is deductible only against the Chinese property then tax is due on his UK estate. If the debt is deducted proportionately against the UK and Chinese property then four fifths of the UK estate remains chargeable to tax. IHTA 1984, s.162 lays down rules to determine the deductibility of debts in these circumstances but it is not entirely satisfactory.[6]

WHAT LIABILITIES ARE DEDUCTIBLE?

23.02 Section 5(3) lays out the general rule that in valuing a person's estate at any time his liabilities at that time are to be taken into account. The debt must be enforceable. No allowance can be made for liabilities which are not legally enforceable, except that a debt that is actually paid in the due course of administration of the estate will not be disallowed solely on the ground that it was statute-barred.[7] A specialty debt (i.e. a debt under deed), becomes statute-barred on the expiration of 12 years from the date on which the cause of action accrues.[8] The nil rate band debt scheme implemented on the first spouse's death[9] commonly involves a specialty debt. The cause of action accrues when the deed is executed. It is important therefore that the debtor (in this case the surviving spouse) acknowledges the trustees' claim in writing every 12 years. The 12-year period can then start running again from the date of acknowledgement.[10] Debts paid under a moral obligation are not enforceable.

23.03 Under s.5(5), liabilities incurred by a transferor (not being imposed by law) are taken into account only to the extent that they were incurred for consideration in money or money's worth.[11] Consideration in money or money's worth does not include marriage. A liability incurred for full consideration will be allowed in full, and one incurred for partial consideration will be allowed in part. Liabilities imposed by law are allowable, whether incurred for consideration or not: e.g. liabilities such as taxes, penalties and fines.

EXAMPLE 23.2

> A wishes to benefit his son B who is the principal beneficiary of a trust, The trust owns a property called Castle Mound worth £110,000. A

---

[6] See 23.06 *et seq.*
[7] *Norton v Frecker* (1737) 1 Atk. 524.
[8] Limitation Act 1980, s.8.
[9] See Ch. 28. In fact as consideration is furnished for the debt it can be by simple agreement.
[10] Limitation Act 1980, s.29(5) Note that IHTM 28384 states: "*a debtor may decide to pay the debt after the expiry of the time limits. Because of this you should allow a debt which is otherwise statute-barred if the personal representatives pay the debt and you receive evidence that the payment has been made.*"
[11] For the meaning of "money's worth", *see Secretan v Hart* [1969] 1 W.L.R. 1599 at 1603.

buys the property from the trustees for £200,000 leaving the purchase price outstanding as a debt owed to the trustees. On A's death, the debt of £200,000 is allowable only to the extent of £110,000, and so the value of A's estate is the same after the agreement as it was before. There is no transfer of value until he pays the money. If A were to pay the money then he would make a transfer of value of £90,000. If the money is paid to the trust after March 21, 2006 this would be a chargeable transfer by A.[12]

23.04 Under IHTA 1984, s.162(1) a liability in respect of which there is a right to reimbursement can be taken into account only to the extent that reimbursement cannot reasonably be expected to be obtained. This deals with guarantees. So a contingent liability under a guarantee would not be deductible if there was little risk of the guarantee being called in. This can be relevant where trustees guarantee a beneficiary's borrowings. Any deduction will be based on the facts existing at the death and will not necessarily correspond to the net amount, if any, eventually paid out of the trust.

A guarantee debt is normally incurred for consideration in money or money's worth, namely the creditor's granting (or continuing or extending) credit to the principal debtor. Where this is so, there may be a transfer of value when the guarantee is given. If the principal debtor is a person of substance, the liability incurred is likely to be largely offset by the right of reimbursement, and any value transferred will be small. On the other hand, guaranteeing the liability of an impecunious principal debtor will constitute a transfer of value at the point when the guarantee is given approximating to the full amount of the liability. If the guarantor is called upon to honour the guarantee, payments made by him to the creditor will not themselves be transfers of value.

EXAMPLE 23.3

(1) A pre-March 22, 2006 interest in possession trust owns £1m worth of assets. The life tenant, Sid, wishes to purchase a residential property and borrows from the bank. The bank is not prepared to lend unless the trustees guarantee the loan. Any transfer of value made by the trustees when giving the guarantee would be based on the likelihood of the guarantee being called in. If Sid's loan is secured on the home this may be seen as unlikely. In any event any transfer of value is passing to Sid the life tenant and so is not chargeable.[13] If Sid dies, the guarantee has to be considered when valuing the trust assets in which he has a qualifying interest in possession. A small deduction may be given for the contingent liability under the trust but this is unlikely given that Sid's estate is already reduced by the charge.

(2) Suppose Sid's interest in possession had arisen after March 21, 2006. The trustees enter into the same guarantee arrangement this time in respect of borrowings to fund Sid's business. The bank take no

---

[12] As a result of the FA 2006 changes in the IHT treatment of settlements.
[13] See IHTA 1984, s.52(3).

charge on Sid's assets and are relying on the guarantee. Sid has a history of failed businesses. In these circumstances, the trustees are making a depreciatory transfer out of a relevant property settlement at the point of giving the guarantee and there may be an exit charge.[14]

Future liabilities

23.05 IHTA 1984, s.162(2) provides that where a liability falls to be discharged after the time at which it is to be taken into account, it must be valued as at the time at which it is to be taken into account. In other words, debts payable at a future date without intermediate interest (or with interest at less than the market rate) are to be discounted.

LIABILITIES AND EXCLUDED PROPERTY

23.06 Section 162(4) and (5) set out the rules for determining which property is reduced by the liability but do not cover every situation. They are highly relevant in the case of excluded property setlements and foreign domiciliaires. Section 162(4) provides that a liability which is an incumbrance on any property must as far as possible be taken to reduce the value of that property. Accordingly, the entity to be valued is the property subject to the liability. In *Alexander* v *IRC*[15] the property could not in fact have been sold subject to the liability charged on it, but the Court of Appeal applied the principle of *IRC* v *Crossman*[16] and held that the property must be valued as if it remained subject to the charge in the hands of the purchaser.

EXAMPLE 23.4

A has a qualifying interest in possession in Fund A of a pre-March 22, 2006 trust. B has a qualifying interest in possession in Fund B of the same trust. A dies and Fund A comprises a house worth £1m subject to a charge of £300,000. The value of Fund A is £700,000. If B dies, the charge cannot be deducted against his fund.[17]

23.07 **Charging exempt property:** a debt charged on exempt property (e.g. a mortgage on a house left to the deceased's widow) cannot be deducted against chargeable property (e.g. the residuary estate left to children). Similarly a debt charged on instalment-option property cannot be deducted against non-instalment property.

---

[14] IHTA 1984, s.65(1)(b).
[15] [1991] S.T.C. 112.
[16] [1937] A.C. 26.
[17] See 23.10, below for a consideration of liabilities incurred by trustees.

Foreign liabilities: s.162(5) provides   **23.08**

> "where a liability taken into account is a liability to a person resident outside the UK which neither falls to be discharged in the UK nor is an incumbrance on property in the UK, it shall so far as possible, be taken to reduce the value of property outside the UK."

HMRC state[18] that if there are debts in more than one foreign country, the debts in any one country should be set against the assets in that country and any excess set proportionately against the assets in other foreign countries. There is no statutory basis for this view. HMRC appear to allow an unsecured debt due to a UK creditor (which can be discharged in or out of the UK) to be allowed in full against non-excluded property.[19] However, the position is unclear when the debt is secured on both UK and non-UK property or the liability is discharged in the UK but is secured on property outside the UK.[20] In these cases how do ss.162(4) and (5) interract? Section 162(4) prescribes a reduction in the value of the encumbered property outside the UK; s.162(5) requires the debt to be deducted against the UK property. This will generally only matter where there is excluded property or the property in the trust passes to different beneficiaries.

EXAMPLE 23.5

> A is not UK domiciled. He dies with a qualifying interest in possession in a trust owning UK land worth £1m and cash deposited in Jersey worth US $2m. The UK land is left to his son and the cash is left to his daughter. He owes £500,000 to a Jersey bank. In these circumstances it is thought the £500K will be deducted entirely from the US $2m with the result that inheritance tax is payable in full on £1m. His daughter receives $2m less £500K.
>
> If the debt is owed to a UK creditor and is discharged in the UK then the son pays inheritance tax on only £500,000. However, if the debt is secured on the foreign cash will the debt be allowed against the UK land for tax purposes albeit reduce the value passing to the daughter?[21]

---

[18] IHTM 28394.
[19] IHTM 28395.
[20] The place that is specified in the debt agreement is the place where the debt falls to be discharged. If none is specified the liability may fall to be discharged in the place of residence of the creditor.
[21] See also IHTM 28396:

> "If the deceased's estate includes both UK and foreign assets you should first deduct any UK debts against the UK assets and the deficiency if any against the foreign assets. Debts are UK debts if one of the following applies: they are owed to creditors resident solely in the UK; they are charged on property in the UK, or they are contracted to be paid in the UK. This practice should be applied notwithstanding the decision in Re Kloebe [1884] 28 Ch. D 175. This was that in the administration of the English estate of a deceased person domiciled abroad, foreign creditors are entitled to be paid along with those resident in the UK in shares proportionate to their respective claims."

HMRC take the view that s.162(4) takes priority over s.162(5) so if the debt is charged on excluded property it is deductible out of this property even if the debt is owed to a UK creditor.[22] This is probably right. The result is that the son pays tax on £1m and the daughter pays no inheritance tax but receives $2m less £500K.

23.09 In summary, trustees of excluded property settlements need to be careful that where possible liabilities are deductible against any UK property that they own. This can cause other problems. First, if the debt is charged against UK property but with the commercial borrowing coming from a foreign bank, HMRC may argue that interest payable on the debt is UK-source income. This raises questions about whether income tax should be deducted at source from the interest.

Second, if liabilities are incurred by borrowing from another excluded property settlement then it is important to ensure that the debt is not a UK-situate asset in the hands of the other trust.

EXAMPLE 23.6

A settles US $1m into Discretionary Trust 1. He is UK-resident but not UK-domiciled. Trust 1 lends the cash to Trust 2 also set up by A[23] which buys a UK house. Trust 1 wishes to take security for the loan and charges the house. The debt is a UK situate asset and Trust 1 faces 10-year and periodic charges as well as a liability under FA 1986, s.102(3) (reservation of benefit) on A's death if he dies deemed UK domiciled and Trust 1 still owns a UK-situate asset.[24]

If the debt is a specialty debt charged on UK land the question is whether the debt is situated where the land is located or where the deed is located.[25]

LIABILITIES AND INTEREST IN POSSESSION TRUSTS

23.10 When a trustee has incurred a liability as a trustee he has a lien over the trust fund for reimbursement. Problems can arise in relation to trusts in which the beneficiary has a qualifying interest in possession. Where the trustees have borrowed funds and the life tenant dies, inheritance tax is charged on the value of the estate of the individual which includes the property "in which the interest [in possession] subsists."[26] But in what property does his interest

---

[22] See IHTM 28395.
[23] Rather than to A personally to avoid FA 1986, s.103: see 23.16.
[24] See chapter 24 for discussion of reservation of benefit and for further discussion of the foreign domiciliary buying a house in the UK see Ch. 31.
[25] See *Dymond's* at Capital Taxes 30.350 for fuller discussion. *c.f. Commissioner of Stamp Duties v Hope* [1891] A.C. 476 with *Walsh v The Queen* [1894] A.C. 144 and see *Dicey's Conflict of Laws* 13th edition at 22.035. The original commentary on specialty debts at IHTM 27078 has been withdrawn and for some years there have been rumours of a case being taken on the point although nothing has so far emerged.
[26] IHTA 1984, s.49(1), see Ch. 15.

subsist—the gross or net value of the settled property? There is nothing in the legislation which specifically reduces the value of the settled property by the debt. Section 5(3) is of no assistance since it provides only that in determining the value of a person's estate his liabilities will be taken into account. In this case the liability is that of the trustees not the life tenant and the trustees do not have an estate as such, within the meaning of s.5, because they are not beneficially entitled to any property. Similar questions arise on the lifetime termination of an interest in possession where IHTA 1984, s.52 provides that the value transferred is equal to the value of the property in which the interest subsisted. Again one has to determine the value of the property in which the interest subsisted.

23.11 It would be unjust if the trustees were taxed on the gross value of the settled property in which the life tenant had an interest in possession without any account being taken of the debt and HMRC have always taken the view that trustees' liabilities can be taken into account for inheritance tax purposes.[27]

23.12 The correct analysis may be that the trustees' lien can be regarded as an incumbrance over the property and therefore s.162(4) can be relied upon to reduce the value of the settled property. In *Peter John St, Barbe Green and IRC*[28] the judge took a slightly different view and held that the value of the property in which the life tenant's interest subsisted was the settled property net of trust liabilities. In that case the deceased (the 12th Duke of Manchester) died in 2002 with almost nothing in his personal estate but owing around £48,000. He was tenant for life of three settlements worth in excess of £340,000. The trustees claimed to be able to deduct from the values of the settlements the amount of the deficit in the Duke's free estate. HMRC considered that a personal liability could not be deducted from the settled property. The taxpayers argued that under s.5(1) a person's free estate is aggregated with settled property in which he has an interest in possession so as to form one overall estate. Section 5(3) states that in determining the value of a person's estate at any time his liabilities at that time shall be taken into account and since a person's estate includes property in which he had an interest in possession the balance of the debt could be deducted against the settled property.

23.13 HMRC's argument was that in determining the value of the estate in the first place under s.5(1) one has to take into account the liabilities and the way one does this is to deduct them from the value of the property which is answerable to those liabilities. Since the trust assets were not available to pay the deceased's personal liabilities, those liabilities could not be offset for inheritance tax purposes.

Mann J. commented that despite this point, there was no inherent reason in the logical world created by the inheritance tax legislation under which an interest in possession in settled property was aggregated with free estate why liabilities in the free estate could not also be set off against the agggregated assets of the trust. Read literally, s.5(3) could be taken to mean that personal liabilities go to reduce the value of the whole estate—both trust and personal.

23.14 However, he held that under IHTA 1984, s.49(1) the deceased is beneficially entitled to the property in which the life interest subsists and "property" in this context means the property net of trust liabilities. Therefore the property of the deceased for the purposes of s.5(1) comprised the personal estate net of

---

[27] See old W56.
[28] [2005] EWHC 14(Ch).

liabilities and the settled property net of liabilities. Once the free estate is reduced to zero by those liabilities unrelieved liabilities have nothing against which they can be offset.

> "In other words it is at that stage [the stage of determining the value of the property for the purposes of s.5(1)] that the liabilities are dealt with. It is not necessary for s.5(3) to provide for a second time that the debts are to be deducted in arriving at the value for the deceased's property (or estate) and in my view it is not really doing that. It is in part confirmatory but in the main it is intended to provide a qualification . . . to the principle that debts are deductible—the meat of the subsection is in the closing words 'except as otherwise provided by this Act'."[29]

Incurring debts as a way of reducing the inheritance tax liability of an individual has been used extensively over the years. The home loan or double trust scheme is a classic example.[30]

23.15 **Foreign domiciliaries:** the question of whether debts are deducted against foreign or UK situated property has been discussed at 23.06. Many foreign domiciliaries have structured ownership of houses using a two trust structure. This relies on a foreign sited specialty debt to reduce the value of the UK home and is discussed further in Chapter 31.

Debts have been used in other contexts by foreign domiciliaries. For example, suppose that A is the life tenant of a trust set up by his father who was not UK domiciled. The trust owns a UK house worth £1m in which A lives. The property is not excluded property on A's death. If the trustees borrow £800,000 commercially charging that debt on the UK property and deposit that sum overseas, the value of the UK situated property is reduced by £800,000. (Note the problems outlined above where trustees borrow from other trusts or where the debt may be secured on foreign property but falls to be discharged in the UK.)

If the trust had been set up by a UK domiciled settlor but the life tenant was not UK domiciled, the trustees could not simply borrow because the cash borrowed would not be held in an excluded property settlement. However, they could advance the borrowings to the life tenant absolutely. The value of the life interest is reduced and the cash advanced is kept abroad by the non-UK domiciled life tenant and therefore not subject to inheritance tax. The capital gains tax implications of this transaction under TCGA 1992, Sch.4B would need to be considered carefully.[31]

THE ARTIFICIAL DEBT RULE IN FA 1986, s.103

23.16 Section 103 of FA 1986 restores the estate duty rule disallowing debts for which the consideration was property derived from the deceased or was given

---

[29] In the alternative Mann J. held that HMRC's construction of s.5(3) was supported by the estate duty case of *Re Barnes* [1938] *2 K.B. 684* and that it was correct that liabilities cannot be deducted from assets which are not liable to bear them. Note that a deficit on joint property that passes under the Will can be set against free assets.
[30] See 3.18.
[31] See 7.62 and 10.20.

by a person who had property derived from the deceased. The section is aimed mainly at cases where a donor, though not reserving any benefit from his gift, obtains a benefit by borrowing the property given (or sometimes other property) from the donee.

Sections 103 (1) and (6) forbids or restricts the deduction of debts or incumbrances incurred or created by the deceased after March 17, 1986, by making them 'subject to abatement' to the extent that the consideration consisted of:

(i) property derived from the deceased, ("Head A") or
(ii) other consideration given by any person who was at any time entitled to, or amongst whose resources there was at any time included, any property derived from the deceased ("Head B").

A simple example is as follows:

EXAMPLE 23.7

> A gives his son £50,000 in 1997. The son subsequently lends A £45,000. A dies before repaying the loan. The £45,000 cannot be deducted against A's estate. If A repays the loan before his death, that repayment is a PET.[32] The position might be different if the son wrote off the loan since no money or money's worth is being applied by A in reducing the debt as appears to be required by s.103(5). It would therefore be preferable for the son to release A from the loan rather than for A to repay it. Then the son makes a PET!

Section 103(4) restricts the definition of "property derived from the deceased" by excluding cases where there is no direct or indirect element of bounty, e.g. where the property was bought from the deceased for full value without any associated operations.

Head B: covers situations where the property itself is not lent back to A but the loan back is made by a person to whom A had given property earlier. In other words it applies where A makes a gift to B which enables B to make a loan out of property which B has owned all along.

23.17

EXAMPLE 23.8

> In 1999 H gives a picture to son worth £15,000. Son keeps picture but lends £16,000 to H. H dies in 2002—i.e. within seven years of the gift. £15,000 of the £16,000 is not deductible in H's estate unless it can be shown that the gift by H was not made with the aim of facilitating the loan by S. In addition the PET is chargeable. In these circumstances the IHT (Double Charges) Regulations 1987[33] may provide some relief.

---

[32] FA 1986, s.103(5).
[33] SI 1987/1130 see Reg.6.

EXAMPLE 23.9

> In 1985 H gives a share in his house (worth £250,000) to his wife, W. The gift is spouse exempt. The purpose of the gift was to ensure that his wife had sufficient property to use up her nil rate band. W dies in 1996 leaving property up to her IHT unused nil rate band on discretionary trusts and the trustees subsequently make a loan to H. There is a concern that the donor H has incurred a debt from W who was entitled to property derived from H. It does not matter that the gift was made prior to 1986.[34] In their guidance notes on POA[35] HMRC comment that in these circumstances s.103 could apply to disallow the deduction on H's death.[36]

The rule as it affects Head B property is relaxed by s.103(2) in two ways. The debt *can* be deducted to the extent that the value of the debt exceeded the property given by the deceased.

EXAMPLE 23.10[37]

> A gives his son B shares worth £20,000. B lends A out of his separate resources £25,000 at a time when the shares were worth £17,000. A dies and a deduction of £25,000 is claimed. The value in point is the realisable value of the shares at the time the debt was created. So the liability is reduced by £17,000 leaving £8,000 as a valid deduction. (Presumably if the shares were worth £25,000 then HMRC would argue that there is no deduction.)

Alternatively, if, in the last example, it can be shown that the gift by A to B was not made with the aim of facilitating the loan back to A then the debt may not be disallowed on A's death.[38] Take an example. In relation to Wills: if H gave W a share in the house for non-tax reasons (e.g. concern about creditors' claims) then this would not result in a disallowance of the debt incurred by H when the debt/charges scheme is implemented on W's death.[39]

---

[34] IHTM 28366.
[35] Issued in May 2006, see Appendix III A3.21.
[36] See Ch. 28.
[37] Set out in IHTM 28369.
[38] See s.103(2)(b).
[39] It is possible to give guidance only in very general terms as to the circumstances in which HMRC will in practice concede that a disposition by the deceased was not made "with reference to, or with a view to enabling or facilitating" the giving of the consideration for the debt. The word "shown" in subs.(2)(b), and also in subs.(4), puts the burden of proof on the taxpayer. In strictness, if there is no evidence either way there is no relief. If you can show that when the deceased made the disposition he never contemplated that it might be used to facilitate the creation of the debt, it is immaterial that at some later date it had such an effect or was consciously so used; but if the deceased kept his ideas to himself it may be difficult to establish this, though proof that the disposition was made for some *other* specific purpose will be helpful. If the disposition and the creation of the debt were contemporaneous, or nearly so, this difficulty may often prove insuperable, even if there was ostensibly another reason for the disposition. As to the death IOU scheme, see Ch. 28.

23.18 Trusts lending to settlors: Some care is needed where trusts lend to settlors. Suppose that A is the UK domiciled life tenant and settlor of a pre-March 22, 2006 trust. He is in need of funds and the trustees lend him cash.[40] In these circumstances, it would appear that he is caught by s.103 of the FA 1986. He has incurred a liability personally and the monies lent to him are derived from his earlier gifted property. Accordingly the concern is that the debt is non-deductible in the settlor's estate but the debt due to the trust is an asset in which he has an interest in possession and therefore taxable on his death. So there is double inheritance tax payable on the same asset! It is not clear whether HMRC take this view. It has been suggested that since the life tenant is deemed to own the money borrowed from the trustees under s.49(1) he cannot borrow from himself and therefore the borrowings are simply ignored for inheritance tax purposes. The same analysis would apply to all life tenants who borrow from a trust, whether or not they are the settlor. The borrowings would be ignored. The difficulty is that as a matter of law the life tenant does incur a personal liability owed to the trustees which has to be repaid and he is not the owner of the trust assets.

23.19 Section 103 can be circumvented if the debt is not incurred by the settlor personally.

EXAMPLE 23.11

> In 2003 Harry entered into a home loan (or double trust) scheme. He sold his residence to the trustees of an interest in possession trust for himself leaving the purchase price outstanding as a debt. The debt was given away to his son. On Harry's death the debt is not disallowed under s.103 even though the consideration was given by the trustees who had received property derived from Harry. This is because the debt was not incurred by Harry but by the trustees.

23.20 Foreign domiciled settlors: it is not uncommon for foreign domiciled settlors to settle assets and then receive loans back from the trustees.

EXAMPLE 23.12

> A settles foreign cash into a discretionary trust when not UK domiciled. The trust lends him some of the cash some years later under a specialty debt arrangement which is unsecured[41] and he dies owing the trust £1m when he is deemed UK-domiciled. Is the debt deductible against his free estate? Or does s.103 of the FA 1986 mean that the debt is not deductible because it represents consideration given by A to the trust?

---

[40] Loans to settlors are also common in the context of offshore trusts where UK domiciled settlors do not want to incur s.87 charges when they receive capital payments.
[41] To avoid the debt being sited in the UK and to avoid it being treated as an incumbrance.

It might be thought that even if s.103 could potentially apply, if A leaves all his free estate to an exempt person such as a charity or spouse[42] there is no problem anyway even if the debt turns out not to be deductible. The difficulty is that in these circumstances not all the property would then pass to the exempt person—at least part of it has to be repaid to the trust because of the debt. One cannot ignore the liability because it is legally enforceable. The result is that the debt is not deductible but charitable or spouse exemption is not available because the value attributable to the spouse or charity is only the net value. So in the above example, £1m of the estate would fail to qualify for exemption and therefore be taxable.

23.21 However, does s.103 apply at all to foreign domiciled settlors in these circumstances? Section 103(4) provides:

> "If the disposition first mentioned in (3) above [i.e. the original transfer into trust by the foreign domiciliary who is now deceased] was not a transfer of value and it is shown that the disposition was not part of associated operations which included:
>
> (a) a disposition by the deceased either alone or in concert or by arrangement with any other person otherwise than for full consideration in money or money's worth paid to the deceased for his own use or benefit or
> (b) a disposition by any other person operating to reduce the value of the property of the deceased
>
> the first mentioned disposition shall be left out of account for the purposes of subsections (1) and (3) above".

So if (4) can be satisfied then it does not matter whether the transaction comes within Head A or Head B above: the debt will not be disallowed. It is clear that the disposition first mentioned in (3) is not a transfer of value because the gift into the trust was a gift of excluded property.[43]

However, subs.(4) also requires that the disposition is not part of associated operations which included (a) or (b) above. The loan alone is clearly not an operation within (a) or (b)—it is incurred for full consideration because the foreign domiciliary receives the cash in exchange for the debt and the loan to him does not reduce the value of his estate because he receives cash of an equivalent amount. However, the disposition merely has to be part of an associated operation which *included* (a) or (b). So even if the loan back does not satisfy (a) or (b), one could argue that the gift of assets into the trust and the entry into the loan agreement are associated operations in relation to each other and clearly the gift of assets into the trust does satisfy (a).

So on that basis since the original gift is part of the overall associated operations and is itself within Head A or B, the subs.(4) let out cannot be satisfied. Section 103(4) is certainly not clear: in determining whether any associated operations include any dispositions such as are referred to in s.103(4)(a) or (b) does one disregard the original disposition into trust with which s.103(3) is

---

[42] Assuming that the spouse is deemed or actually UK domiciled.
[43] IHTA 1984, s.3(2).

concerned? However, if it is right that the transfer of assets to the trust itself falls within s.103(4)(a) the debt is not deductible unless one can show that the loan back to the settlor is not associated with the gift. This is awkward to argue despite *Reynaud v IRC*.[44]

23.22 If the debt is non-deductible what is a foreign domiciliary who has borrowed from a trust he funded to do? If he repays the debt that is a deemed PET although it is thought that HMRC would only take this point if he was UK-domiciled. If the loan is written off by the trustees in his favour has his estate been increased? If he has an interest in possession in the trust and the loan is written off, this does not affect the value of his estate since excluded property is part of his estate for inheritance tax purposes.

When the trust is discretionary he has reserved a benefit in the debt trust but the property is not part of his estate until death.[45] If the loan is written off his free estate is increased. However, in these circumstances there is nothing in s.103 that deems him to have made a PET. The trustees have reduced value but this should not matter since the trust fund comprises excluded property. It seems hard then to see how a write off of the debt could constitute a deemed PET under s.102(4) of the FA 1986. Accordingly, although the position is not entirely clear, it seems preferable that a foreign domiciliary should avoid incurring liabilities personally in respect of trusts which he has funded. Alternative options in relation to the family home are discussed in Ch. 31.

LIABILITIES IN THE CONTEXT OF AGRICULTURAL AND BUSINESS PROPERTY[46]

23.23 Note the general rules on liabilities in this context:

1. IHTA 1984, Part VI Chapter 1: dealing with liabilities generally provides, inter alia, that "a liability which is an incumbrance on any property shall, so far as possible, be taken to reduce the value of that property" (s.162(4)).
2. For the purpose of BPR "the value of a business . . . shall be its net value (and) net value . . . is the value of the assets used in the business . . . reduced by the aggregate amount of any liabilities incurred for the purposes of the business".[47]

But for APR there is no such qualification.

23.24 **Encumbrances on business property:** liabilities secured on assets which qualify for business relief reduce the value of *that property* for IHT purposes and so effectively reduce or eliminate the availability of the relief even if the liability was not incurred for the purposes of the business.

---

[44] [1999] S.T.C. (SCD) 185 and the *Rysaffe* case.
[45] FA 1986, s.102(3).
[46] See also Ch. 32.
[47] IHTA 1984, s.110.

EXAMPLE 23.13

> Trustees operate a factory which makes widgets. They also hold some UK equities. They wish to raise some funds to advance to a beneficiary and borrow on the security of the factory land. Even though this is not incurred for the purposes of the business it reduces the value of that business. If the borrowings had been secured on the UK equities, business property relief would be unaffected.

23.25 **Encumbrances on investments:** where, on the other hand, money has been borrowed on the security of a non business asset and used to purchase an asset which qualifies for business relief, the net effect is that value not qualifying for relief may be converted into value qualifying for relief.

Assume X borrows money on the security of his home and uses it to set up his internet business. The encumbrance will reduce the value of his home, and the business will qualify for business relief. It might be argued that s.110 should apply because the liability has been incurred for the purposes of the business. On that basis it would reduce the value of the internet business rather than the home. However, it is thought that s.162(4) is the governing provision. Contrast the position if the debts were unsecured when it might be expected that s.110 would require the debts to be set against the value of the business assets.[48]

23.26 **Agricultural property relief:** the position is different for agricultural property relief where liabilities are not deducted from the value of agricultural property unless they are charged on the property or (exceptionally) the debts charged on non-agricultural property exceed the value of the property on which they are charged.

EXAMPLE 23.14

> A farmer owns a let farm qualifying for 50% agricultural relief and worth £1m, subject to a mortgage of £500k taken out for the purposes of the business. His other main assets are investments worth £500K. Were he to die, the value of his estate on death would be £1m made up of the investments plus the farm after deducting the mortgage thereon. Agricultural relief at 50% would then be available on the *net* value of the farm (i.e. on £500k) which would reduce that to £250k leaving a chargeable death estate of £750k.
>
> Suppose, however, that before his death the farmer arranged with the appropriate creditor to switch the mortgage from the agricultural land to the investments. The result then would be that on death the value of his estate would, as above, be £1m made up of the value of the farm

---

[48] Is the loan incurred for the purpose of the business? It is thought so, but contrast the position if X had borrowed in order to purchase a business (e.g. from his retiring cousin). See also *Hardcastle (Vernede's Exors) v IRC* [2000] S.T.C. (SCD) 532.

(£1m) since the investments now, after deducting the mortgage, are valueless. Accordingly, agricultural relief would be available on the entire value of the farm and amounts to £500k leaving a chargeable death estate of £500k.

Chapter 24

GIFTS WITH RESERVATION AND THE PRE-OWNED ASSETS INCOME TAX REGIME

- Reservation of benefit **(24.03)**
- Pre-owned assets income tax **(24.18)**

Background

24.01 In Chapter 13, the reservation of benefit rules and pre-owned assets income tax (POA) rules were briefly summarised.[1] This chapter considers these provisions with particular reference to trusts. In considering whether an arrangement falls within either the GWR rules or the POA charge, consideration should first be given to the GWR position since if those rules are applicable then generally there is no scope for the POA charge.

24.02 At the end of May 2006, HMRC published revised guidance notes on POA and these are referred to in this chapter and can be found in Appendix III as can an exchange of correspondence (in the form of questions and answers) between STEP/CIOT and HMRC (called the "COP 10" letter).

RESERVATION OF BENEFIT

24.03 **When do the rules apply?** Under s.102(1) FA 1986 the rules apply where an individual disposes of any property by way of gift after March 17, 1986 and:

(a) possession and enjoyment of the property is not bona fide assumed by the donee at or before the beginning of "the relevant period", *or*

(b) at any time during "the relevant period" the property is not enjoyed to the entire exclusion, or virtually to the entire exclusion, of the donor and of any benefit to him by contract or otherwise.

---

[1] See 13.07 onwards for basic provisions on reservation of benefit, definition of gift, full consideration let out, spouse exemption, *Ingram* and *Eversden* schemes and the effect of reserving a benefit. See 13.34 onwards for the basic conditions of the POA charge.

"The relevant period" means a period ending at the donor's death and beginning seven years before the death or, if it is later, on the date of the gift. Under s.102(2) property within subs (1) (a) or (b) is referred to as "property subject to a reservation". Whether there is any such property has to be decided by looking back from the donor's death to the beginning of "the relevant period".

The meaning of "gift"

As noted previously,[2] rather surprisingly, neither s.102 nor Sch.20 contain any definition of the word "gift". The 1984 Act has a definition in s.42(1), but that is merely for the purposes of Chapter III of Part II of the Act (allocation of exemptions). In the context of s.102 one might expect "gift" to mean "transfer of value", and the word is used in that sense in subs.(5), which excludes various exempt gifts from the gifts-with-reservation rules. HMRC notes in the Manual that, in the context of reservation of benefit, "the word must be given its ordinary meaning".[3] 24.05

The relationship between a gift and transfer of value was considered in the *Eversden* appeal[4] where, in the context of s.102(5), Carnwath L.J. commented:

> "Rightly or wrongly (from the purist's point of view), the draftsmen clearly did find it possible to equate a disposal by way of gift with a transfer of value. That is the effect of posing, in the subsection, the question whether the disposal by way of gift 'is an exempt transfer', with specific reference to the provisions of Part II of the 1984 Act, all of which are references to 'transfers of value'."

These remarks should be read in context: at most they may be considered to imply that any gift will be a transfer of value. The converse (that all transfers of value are of necessity gifts) cannot be deduced from these comments.[5]

The fact that a transfer of value into an interest in possession trust was treated as a gift of the entire settled property to the settlor's spouse is not the same as arguing that (for example) the termination of a spousal life interest by the trustees must necessarily be a gift because it is a transfer of value.

Extension of "gift" to termination of an interest in possession: HMRC seem to have accepted the general principle that prior to March 22, 2006 a termination by the trustees of a life interest was not a gift by the life tenant unless (possibly) the life tenant consented[6] to such termination or (more likely) surrendered the interest himself. In other words, on the *inter vivos* termination of a life interest in settled property, the question whether the life tenant makes a gift (or, in the words of s.102(1), "disposes of property by way of gift") prior to the FA 2006 changes may depend on the way the interest was terminated. 24.06

---

[2] See 13.09, above.
[3] See IHTM 14315.
[4] For the *Eversden* case, see 13.16, above.
[5] For further discussion, see *Dymond's Capital Taxes* at 5A 204.
[6] Although it is difficult to see how the giving of consent could be treated as a disposition of property for the purposes of s.102(1); it is the subsequent advance by the trustees which is the effective disposition.

EXAMPLE 24.1

> Under the will of his father who died in 1999, A was life tenant of a house, but the trustees had power without A's consent to terminate his interest and transfer the house to his daughter. They did so in 1991, and A continued to live there until his death in 1999. It appears that HMRC accept this was not a gift with reservation.[7] If, however, A had assigned or surrendered his life interest (for instance because the trustees did not have any overriding powers to end his interest), HMRC consider that A has made a gift "in the real world" and that gift comprises the house.

24.07 In the latter situation, the question remains whether A has simply enabled a benefit to pass to his daughter or whether he has made a gift of his life interest (which has now ended so that he has not reserved a benefit in this) or a gift of the underlying settled property: i.e the house, in which case his continued occupation involves a reservation of benefit. In the real world A has only given up his life interest. He never owned the house so could not give it away. However, s.49(1) deems A to be beneficially entitled to the underlying property.[8] Does s.51 displace the real world gift and in conjunction with s.52 substitute the gift of the underlying capital as the relevant gift for reservation of benefit purposes? The Court of Appeal comments in *Eversden*, equating gifts with transfers of value, are obviously helpful to the approach of HMRC. However, s.51 says that the disposal of an interest in possession is not a transfer of value but is treated as the coming to an end of the interest and s.52 says that tax is charged "*as if* [A] had made a transfer of value and the value transferred had been equal to the value of the property in which his interest subsisted". Hence the legislation goes to considerable trouble to say that no *actual* transfer of value takes place. In this context it is hard to see how the reservation of benefit rules can apply even on a surrender of a life interest.

Could HMRC successfully argue that under the tracing provisions in para.2(4)(5) Sch.20 FA 1986 the life tenant continues to have an interest in possession in the settled property even though it has ceased to exist? It may be said that a simple surrender by the beneficiary does not involve a gift to anyone and that the interest of the remainderman was given to him when the settlement was created and so that is an end of the matter.

Changes in FA 2006

24.08 The "loophole" of a life tenant's interest being terminated by the trustees was used in a number of situations, including wills where the surviving spouse was left residue on interest in possession trusts and his interest was later terminated. The surviving spouse could continue to benefit from the settled assets but the property would not be taxed as part of his estate for inheritance tax purposes so that if he survived seven years the assets would pass onto the next generation tax free.[9]

---

[7] The position will be different if A's interest had terminated on or after March 22, 2006.
[8] From March 22, 2006 the scope for the operation of this fiction has been much reduced.
[9] See 28.34, below for how the strategy was used after the first spouse's death.

All this has changed following the amendments to s.102 FA 1986 inserted by FA 2006.[10] Termination of A's interest in possession post-March 21, 2006 in *Example 24.1* would now be treated as a gift by A under s.102ZA which provides:

> "For the purposes of section 102 and schedule 20 the individual shall be taken . . . to dispose on the coming to an end of the interest in possession of the no-longer-possessed-property by way of gift."

Hence the life tenant is deemed to make a gift for the purposes of the reservation of benefit rules. (Note that no attempt is made by the draftsman to change the reservation of benefit rules so that they are triggered by a transfer of value rather than by a gift.)

24.09

The change affects all pre-Budget 2006 qualifying interest in possession trusts where the life tenant's interest has not been ended by March 22, 2006 as well as post-Budget 2006 qualifying interests in possession. Hence it is important to remember to exclude the life tenant from future benefits under the settlement in order to avoid a future reservation of benefit problem unless the spouse or civil partner[11] of the life tenant is taking an interest in possession.[12]

EXAMPLE 24.2

> H set up an *Eversden* structure putting his house into an interest in possession trust for his wife in May 2003.[13] The trustees terminate her interest after March 21, 2006 whereupon the house is held on continuing trusts for the couple's children. Although H is protected from reservation of benefit by s.102(5) (since s.102(5A) does not affect transfers into trust before June 2003) the termination of Mrs H's interest in possession causes a pre-owned assets income tax ("POA") problem for H if he is in occupation of the house.[14]

If W continues to occupy the house after the termination of her interest she does not have a POA problem but she rather than H has a reservation of benefit problem because she is deemed to have made a gift for inheritance tax purposes even though she is not the settlor.

Note both of them must separately pay "rent" to the trustees—H to avoid a POA charge and W to avoid a reservation of benefit charge. HMRC consider that it is the full amount from each.[15]

The 2006 change has wider implications than might at first be thought.

24.10

---

[10] By s.156 and Sch.20, para.33(1)(2) and (4).
[11] Note that if the life tenant's interest is ended in favour of the spouse who takes a qualifying interest in possession, e.g. under the transitional serial interest rules, the reservation of benefit rules do not apply to the life tenant because of s.102(5). Section 102(5A) of FA 1986 (the anti-*Eversden* legislation) is not applicable because the property does not become settled by virtue of the gift—it is already settled. Of course, on a later termination of the spousal interest reservation of benefit could apply to the spouse.
[12] Or in situations when the reservation rules will not result in an IHT liability on the death of the former life tenant who has reserved a benefit or are considered a price worth paying for the creation of a TSI (*see Example 24.4*).
[13] See 13.16 for a discussion of the *Eversden* case.
[14] Since the transaction is no longer an excluded transaction.
[15] See question 38 of COP 10 : App III:A3.100.

EXAMPLE 24.3

> Mr B is the life tenant of a trust set up in 1979 by his father. He is now 65 and wishes to carry out some inheritance tax planning. Prior to March 22, 2006 the trustees could have terminated his life interest and appointed the settled property on interest in possession trusts for his son (assuming that they had the necessary powers). If they do so after March 21, 2006 but before April 6, 2008 the son takes a transitional serial interest (a qualifying interest in possession)[16] but Mr B has made a gift with reservation if he can still benefit from the trusts or continues to occupy the settled property. This is despite the fact that the property was originally settled prior to 1986 and Mr B was not the settlor.
>
> If the trustees terminate Mr B's life interest after April 5, 2008 and appoint the property on interest in possession trusts for his son Mr B then makes a chargeable transfer for inheritance tax purposes because the son does not take a qualifying interest in possession. The property is taxed as part of Mr B's estate on his death under the reservation of benefit rules. In addition it is subject to ten year anniversary charges even while Mr B is alive. There is no base cost uplift for capital gains tax purposes on Mr B's death.
>
> If Mr B's interest in possession was terminated *inter vivos* in favour of his spouse *before* April 6, 2008 this would be an exempt transfer (because the spouse[17] takes a transitional serial interest which is a qualifying interest in possession) and Mr B could continue to benefit from the use of the settled property. This option might be attractive if it was felt that tax planning could be done later and Mrs B was "a better life". In three or four years' time her life interest could be terminated in favour, for instance, of the children outright and she, not Mr B, would then be treated as making the PET. She along with Mr B would then need to be excluded from benefit.

24.11 In some cases a family will wish to retain the settled property in a trust structure for the long term but retain flexibility over inheritance tax planning. In these circumstances it might be worth appointing a younger person a transitional serial interest before April 2008 to keep the property out of the relevant property regime even though the original life tenant is not excluded.

---

[16] For "TSI", see 18.14.

[17] In simple terms s.102(5)(A)–(C) has effect if the following conditions are satisfied:

(i) property becomes settled property by virtue of the gift;

(ii) because the settlor's spouse has an interest in possession that disposal is spouse exempt;

(iii) at a later date during the settlor's life the interest in possession of the spouse ends without that spouse becoming absolutely entitled to the property or to another interest in possession.

If the above conditions are met s.102(5B) provides that s.102 is to be applied "as if the disposal by way of gift had been made immediately after the (spouse's) interest in possession came to an end". In this case the property does not become settled property by virtue of the gift by Mr B, it is already settled property.

EXAMPLE 24.4

Mr C, a widower, is the life tenant of a trust owning property settled by his now deceased father which had been set up in 1985. The trust is non-UK-resident and has realised substantial gains which are stockpiled.[18] All Mr C's children who will benefit on his death are UK resident and domiciled. If the trust ends on Mr C's death or on earlier termination of his interest, the s.87 gains will be taxed on the children who may suffer CGT at 64 per cent. However, if the trust continues after Mr C's death and he dies after April 5, 2008 the children's interests in possession are not qualifying and therefore the trust falls within the relevant property regime. One solution might be to appoint transitional serial interests to the children just before April 6, 2008. Even if Mr C continues to benefit, at least the interests taken by the children are not within the relevant property regime. If he dies still reserving a benefit then the property is taxed on his death but this would have been the case if he retained a life interest. The main downside is that there is no capital gains tax uplift on his death. However, at least going forward the trust is outside the relevant property regime and tax on the stockpiled gains has been postponed.

If Mr C wants to carry out inheritance tax planning before his death he can always cease to reserve a benefit: this will be a deemed PET even if this occurs after April 5, 2008.[19] Diagrammatically the position is as follows:

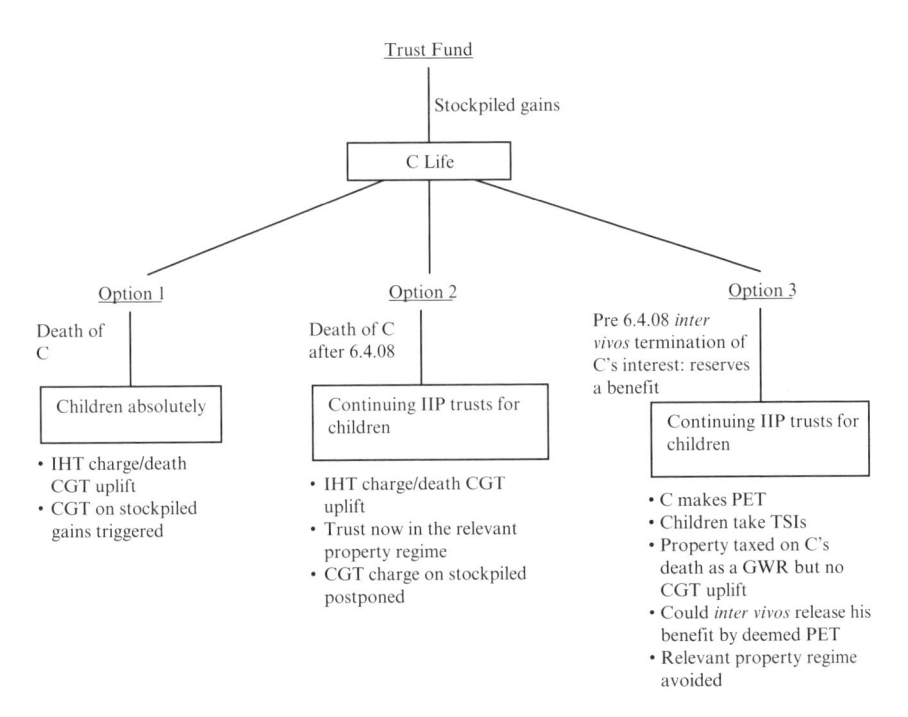

```
                        Trust Fund
                            |
                     Stockpiled gains
                            |
                         C Life
            _____|_____
           |                |                |
        Option 1         Option 2         Option 3
       Death of         Death of C      Pre 6.4.08 inter
         C              after 6.4.08    vivos termination of
                                        C's interest: reserves
                                        a benefit
       Children         Continuing IIP  Continuing IIP trusts for
       absolutely       trusts for      children
                        children
```

Option 1 (Death of C, Children absolutely):
- IHT charge/death CGT uplift
- CGT on stockpiled gains triggered

Option 2 (Death of C after 6.4.08, Continuing IIP trusts for children):
- IHT charge/death CGT uplift
- Trust now in the relevant property regime
- CGT charge on stockpiled postponed

Option 3 (Pre 6.4.08 inter vivos termination of C's interest: reserves a benefit, Continuing IIP trusts for children):
- C makes PET
- Children take TSIs
- Property taxed on C's death as a GWR but no CGT uplift
- Could inter vivos release his benefit by deemed PET
- Relevant property regime avoided

---

[18] See further 10.24.
[19] FA 1986, s.102(4): see 22.35.

Settled gifts—tracing provisions

24.12 Paragraph 2, Sch.20 of FA 1986 deals with the case where the gifted property is substituted. So if A gives B Whiteacre which is then sold by B who buys Blackacre for A to live in, there is a reservation of benefit in Blackacre under the tracing provisions. These tracing provisions in para.2 do not, however, apply if there is an outright gift of cash or if the property given becomes settled property by virtue of the gift.

24.13 Instead para.5 is a self-contained code for tracing where the property becomes settled property by virtue of the gift. The reservation of benefit rules apply as if the property comprised in the gift was the property in the settlement on "the material date" (i.e. the date of death or when the reservation of benefit ceased) except in so far as that property neither is, nor represents, nor is derived from, property originally comprised in the gift.

24.14 Under para.5(5), however, where there is a trust or power to accumulate, accumulations of income arising after the material date are not treated as derived from the gifted property. So, if the reservation is released, accumulations of income arising after the date of release escape tax.

24.15 Under para.5(2), if the settlement comes to an end at some time before the material date as respects all or any of the property which, if the donor had died immediately before that time, would have been treated as comprised in the gift, then:

> "the property in question, other than property to which the donor then becomes absolutely and beneficially entitled in possession, and
> any consideration (not consisting of rights under the settlement) given by the donor for any of the property to which he so becomes entitled",

must be treated as comprised in the gift (in addition to any other property so comprised). However, para.5 does not contain tracing provisions to deal with the position when the beneficiary of the settlement sells the property once he becomes absolutely entitled and uses the proceeds to buy further property in which the donor reserves a benefit.

EXAMPLE 24.5

> A settles shares on trust for, inter alia, his son. The trustees hold the shares for some years and then sell them and invest in pictures. The pictures are advanced to the son and the trust ended. If A derives some benefit from the pictures, e.g. they hang on his walls, then para.5(2) applies and he is treated as reserving a benefit. A would therefore need to pay full consideration for his use of the pictures in the normal way to avoid a reservation of benefit. However, if the son sells the pictures and then buys a house in which A lives (or buys more pictures), the reservation of benefit provisions do not apply. However, one would also need to consider the POA provisions which use the words "property directly or indirectly applied" so that the house which A now occupies would satisfy the condition in para.3 with the result that the POA charge

applies. The POA Regime arguably has better tracing provisions than reservation of benefit so far as settled property is concerned.

24.16 Under para.5(3), where property comprised in a gift is not settled by the gift but is settled by the donee before the material date, paras 5(1) and (2) apply in relation to the settled property as if the settlement had been made by the gift. For this purpose property settled by the donee's will or intestacy is treated as settled by him.

Under para.5(4), where property comprised in a gift becomes settled property either by virtue of the gift or as mentioned in para.5(3), any property which:

(a) on the material date is comprised in the settlement, and
(b) is derived, directly or indirectly, from a *loan* made by the donor to the trustees of the settlement,

must be treated for the purposes of para.5(1) as derived from property originally comprised in the gift.

24.17 Unlike the rest of para.5, para.5(4) had no counterpart in the estate duty legislation in FA 1957, s.38. In the debate on the 1986 Finance Bill, the Minister of State explained (*Official Report*, 10 June 1986, cols 423–424) that para.5(4):

> "is concerned with the type of avoidance scheme known as an inheritance trust. The scheme involves setting up a trust with a modest transfer of assets—the original gift—and then making a substantial interest-free loan to the trustees. The settlor retains a right to receive benefits from the trust, but the growth on the interest-free loan is just as much a gift from the settlor as the original gift itself and, as he has reserved rights to benefit from the growth, it is right that it should be subject to the gifts-with-reservation rules."

However, para.5(4) applies only where the inheritance trust involves an IHT settlement.[20] It does not touch the case where a donor makes a modest gift to a trustee for one or more beneficiaries absolutely (a bare trust) and then makes a substantial interest-free loan to that trustee.

PRE-OWNED ASSETS INCOME TAX

24.18 The Government introduced the pre-owned assets income tax charge in the teeth of widespread opposition albeit with substantial modifications to the original proposals contained in the Consultation Document of December 11, 2003. As a result it is now necessary to consider not only whether a proposed gift or transfer of value involves a reservation of benefit, but also whether, if it escapes these provisions, it will result in an income tax charge on the transferor. The legislation is found in FA 2004, s.84 and Sch.15 and all statutory

---

[20] See 15.01.

references are to Sch.15 unless otherwise stated. In addition, the primary legislation is supplemented by SI 2005/724 and SI 2005/3441 As announced in December 2005, s.80 of the Finance Act 2006 has been introduced to prevent reverter to settlor trusts being used to avoid the POA charge.[21]

The purpose of the POA charge

24.19 The main objective of the charge is to prevent the use of IHT avoidance schemes that fall outside the reservation-of-benefit rules: for instance, an unconditional cash gift by A to his son of £500,000 which is eventually used by the son to buy a flat into which A moves. Apart from preventing the future use of such arrangements, the legislation catches schemes carried out in the past and in this sense may be said to have a retrospective (or at least retroactive) effect. There are, however, two significant limitations on the application of the legislation:

(i) it does not apply to arrangements put in place before March 18, 1986 (this being the date on which potentially exempt transfers and the reservation of benefit rules were introduced: it marked the replacement of CTT by IHT);

(ii) it does not apply to outright cash gifts made before April 6, 1998 (this is the, probably unintended, effect of Sch.15, para.10(2)(c)).

24.20 Given that the object of the POA charge is to plug holes in the IHT legislation, the charge will not generally apply when the relevant property is comprised in the taxpayer's estate or when, in relation to him, it is property subject to a reservation. It should also follow that in cases where statute provides that the reservation-of-benefit charge does not apply despite the taxpayer having satisfied the basic charging conditions (for instance where he has given away land and continues to occupy it paying full consideration for his use[22]) then neither should the POA charge apply. Whilst this is generally the case[23] care needs to be exercised, however, since not all the reservation of benefit exclusions are carried over into the POA legislation. For instance, FA 1986, s.102A(5) provides that the grant of a right (e.g. a lease) is not significant if that grant occurred more than seven years before the date of the gift. Hence the reservation-of-benefit rules do not apply if having carved out a lease the taxpayer then waits at least seven years before giving away the encumbered freehold interest (see s.102A(5) of the FA 1986). This provision is not, however, carried over into the POA legislation which will therefore apply in such cases.

The charge in outline

24.21 The charge came into force on April 6, 2005: i.e. the first tax year of charge is 2005/06. The taxpayer is assessed on the "benefit" that he is deemed to receive

---

[21] See 24.33 and 22.70.
[22] See FA 1986, Sch.20 para.6(1)(a).
[23] See Sch.15 para.11(5)(b)–(d)5.

during the course of a tax year. In the case of land and chattels the benefit is arrived at on the basis of the occupation and use enjoyed (hence the tax charge will cease when the taxpayer ceases to occupy the relevant land or use the chattels). In the case of intangible property (i.e. all property other than land and chattels) held in a settlor-interested trust the charge applies because of the possibility of benefiting under the terms of the trust; hence it will cease only if the settlor ceases to be a beneficiary. In accordance with general income tax principles the benefit must be returned on the taxpayer's return and failure to do so may lead to interest and penalties. As part of the self-assessment system, the value of the benefit must be calculated by the taxpayer. Tax will then be charged with (at present) a top rate of 40 per cent. Trading losses may reduce the taxable benefit.

24.22 **Election:** the taxpayer can elect that income tax shall not apply to the benefit by opting into the reservation of benefit rules. Two points to note about the election are:

(i) that it must be made on prescribed form IHT 500 and should be submitted to the Capital Taxes division at Nottingham;

(ii) in the case of existing arrangements (caught in tax year 2005/06) the deadline for making the election is generally January 31, 2007 (the final date for the filing of tax returns for 2005/06). An election made on or before that date has the effect of preventing an income tax charge from applying with effect from April 6, 2005. The election is irrevocable once the 31 January deadline has passed. Only in exceptional circumstances will a late election be allowed.[24]

The effect of electing into the reservation of benefit rules is to bring s.102(3) (the charge on death) and s.102(4) (the deemed PET on lifetime cessation of benefit) into play. The conditions for the application of these charging provisions (such as the making of a gift after March 17, 1986) are considered to be satisfied by the making of the election. It is important to realise that the election does not result in an unscrambling of the arrangement: it merely affects the IHT position of the donor taxpayer and relieves him from an income tax charge.[25]

24.23 As noted at 13.35 the charging provisions in FA 2004, Sch.15 divide into three parts:

- Land (paras 3–5);
- Chattels (paras 6–7);
- Intangibles held in a settlor interested trust (paras 8–9).

This division reflects the fact that the computation of the benefit varies in each case: for instance, whereas the benefit of occupying land is relatively easily calculated on the basis of the market rent, the benefit of using chattels or the possibility of benefiting under a trust of intangibles is less apparent and involves different rules. The requirement for land and chattels may be met if either the disposal or the contribution condition is met.

---

[24] See generally the discussion in the HMRC Guidance Notes on this point App.III A3.21.
[25] See 24.40, above.

Exclusions

24.24 There are a number of excluded transactions in the case of disposals of land or chattels contained in para.10. Note that these exclusions do not apply to relieve a taxpayer from the para.8 intangibles charge. Some of these exclusions may better be described as "safe harbours" rather than exclusions since a transaction can start off as an excluded transaction but later become chargeable. Paragraph 10(1) provides for what is an excluded transaction in relation to the disposal condition; para.10(2) provides for what is an excluded transaction in relation to the contribution condition.

24.25 There are five exclusions in respect of the disposal condition:

(i) Full consideration: this requires either a disposal of the *whole* interest in the property (except for any right expressly reserved by the disponor over the property) either by a transaction made at arm's length with a person not connected with him or by a transaction such as might be expected to be made at arm's length between unconnected persons.

However, a sale of part of the property to an unconnected party (or to a connected party before March 7, 2005) is permitted as a result of SI 2005/724 reg. 5. Commercial arrangements in this area involve "equity-release schemes" and these are therefore outside the POA charge. By contrast, care needs to be exercised if equity release arrangements between members of the family are contemplated. The sale of part of a house to a child, albeit for full consideration, will lead to a POA charge unless exempted under the Regulations ("motive" is irrelevant[26]). Accordingly the only safe arrangement is as follows:

(a) Dad, who wishes to raise money on his property, carves out a lease for himself for (say) 20 years at a peppercorn rent;
(b) he then sells the freehold—encumbered by the lease—for full consideration.

Dad is protected by para.10 since he is selling his entire interest in the land save only for rights (the lease) which he has retained. There are attractions in this arrangement in terms of tax planning but note (i) that the children who purchase the freehold interest will be subject to SDLT on the price paid and (ii) that they will need to have sufficient money to pay full consideration for the freehold. It cannot be financed by a gift of cash from Dad unless the cash was given prior to April 1998.

(ii) Outright gifts or sales to a spouse or (where ordered by the court) a former spouse. It is not necessary that the spouse is UK domiciled so that this exclusion is wider than the inheritance tax spouse exemption. It does not matter that the spouse subsequently gives the property back to the donor or settles it in trust for him—this is a complete exclusion. From December 5, 2005 spouse includes a registered civil partner.

(iii) Gifts (not sales) into trust where the spouse (including civil partner as above) or former spouse takes a beneficial interest in possession. Note the exclusion only protects the settlor while the spousal interest in pos-

---

[26] It may be that the taxpayer's benefit falls within *de minimis*, see Sch.15, para.13.

session continues unless the spouse or former spouse dies (see para.10(3)). Thus *Eversden* schemes where the spousal interest has already been terminated are subject to the POA charge and consideration should be given to unravelling these arrangements. The section does not state that if the spouse takes an absolute interest in the property (so that her interest in possession is enlarged) then the exclusion still applies but HMRC take this view.

(iv) A disposal falling within s.11 of IHTA 1984 (disposition for maintenance of family).

(v) A disposal that is an outright gift to an individual and is wholly exempt from IHT by virtue of either IHTA 1984, s.19 (annual exemption) or s.20 (small gifts).

There are also five exclusions from the contribution condition as follows:

(i) If the consideration was provided for that person's spouse (or if ordered by the Court, former spouse).

24.26

(ii) If on its acquisition property acquired by means of the contribution became settled property in which the spouse (or former spouse) was beneficially entitled to an interest in possession. There is a similar limitation on this exclusion to that discussed above in relation to the disposal condition.

(iii) The provision of the consideration is a disposition within s.19 or s.20 of IHTA 1984.

(iv) The provision of the consideration is an outright gift within s.19 or s.20 of IHTA 1984.

The above mirrors the exclusions from the disposal condition. The fifth exclusion is, however, only relevant to the contribution condition:

(v) The provision of the consideration was an outright gift of money (sterling or any other currency) and was made *at least seven years before the earliest date* on which the chargeable person occupied the land or had possession or use of the chattels (as the case may be). Cash gifts made before April 6, 1998 are always outside the POA charge even if the seven year rate is not satisfied.

Gifts of intangibles (paras 8–9): para.8 applies to intangible property (excluding chattels, land or interest in those assets) held in trust. Hence the charge only applies to settled property. Two conditions must be satisfied if the charge is to apply:

24.27

(i) Any income arising under a trust would be treated as income of the settlor under s.624 of ITTOIA 2005 if there were such income, although if only the spouse of the settlor and not the settlor alone can benefit then para.8 does not apply.

(ii) The property in the settlement includes intangible property (including cash) which is or represents property which the individual "settled or added" to the trust after March 17, 1986.

24.28 Whether or not there is a para.9 income tax charge therefore depends on:

(a) the nature of the assets held in the trust—if land or chattels paras 8–9 cannot apply;

(b) the settlor retaining some sort of interest—note that if the settlor retains an interest the fact that his spouse may have an interest in possession in the settled property will not protect him; *and*

(c) the person adding or settling property. So if X only lent property to a trust and that loan was repayable on demand, then para.8 cannot apply.

EXAMPLE 24.6

In 2005 Dan transfers chattels into a trust in which he retains a remainder interest. Consider these alternatives:

(i) He does not use the chattels. HMRC accepts that he has not reserved a benefit (the remainder interest has never formed part of a gift); nor will a POA charge under para.6 apply (since he is not in possession/ using the chattels). Subsequently the trustees sell the chattels and keep the funds in cash. He is now subject to an income tax charge under para.9.

The trustees later purchase land which is let out. Dan is no longer subject to an income tax charge under para.9 although he will be subject to income tax on the rental income under s.624 of ITTOIA 2005.

(ii) Dan used the chattels but his spouse retained an interest in possession. There would be no POA charge due to the protection of para.10(1)(c) but on selling the chattels and retaining cash the trustees expose Dan to a POA charge even though the spousal interest in possession has not been terminated.

24.29 The chargeable amount under para.9 is arrived at on the basis of interest at the prescribed rate being applied to the value of the property comprised in a settlement.

In *Example 24.6* above, the chargeable amount on which Dan pays income tax under para.9 may result in an additional tax charge because s.624 tax is still payable as well (as POA tax) on actual income in the trust. There is no credit for the s.624 income tax, only a deduction against the chargeable amount.

EXAMPLE 24.7

In *Example 24.6* if the trust fund is wholly invested in stocks and shares and worth £1m and produces income of £40,000 gross, Dan pays income tax under s.624 on that income of (say) £16,000. He also pays para.9 POA tax on the chargeable amount being 5 per cent of £1m,

£50,000 less £16,000 = £34,000, so further income tax of £13,600 (40 per cent × £34,000) is due.

Paragraph 8 is principally aimed at insurance bonds and, in particular, *Eversden*-type arrangements. Note, however, that where the settlor merely retains a remainder interest in certain insurance schemes or has effected a loan-and-gift trust, HMRC have accepted that he will not generally be caught by Sch.15. This will not apply to reverter to settlor trusts holding other assets in which the settlor retains a remainder interest—these are within the para.8 charge.[27]

24.30

Exemptions (para.11)

24.31

The exemptions in para.11 apply to land, chattels and intangibles. The most important are:

(i) Property in person's estate—para.11(1) the ownership exemption:

The charge does not apply to a person at a time when his estate (for IHT purposes) includes the relevant property or property deriving its value from the relevant property (the latter being called here "the derived ownership exemption"). These exemptions mean that the charge will not apply if the property has been returned to the donor (i.e. if the original arrangement had been unscrambled) or if it is held in a trust under which the donor is entitled to a qualifying interest in possession or if he owns outright (or has a qualifying interest in possession in) shares in a company that owns the relevant property (e.g. land which he occupies). The changes in Finance Act 2006 have limited this exemption in two ways.

First, the only qualifying interest in possession capable of being established by lifetime transfer post-March 21, 2006 is a disabled interest or a transitional serial interest. In the case of other interests in possession s.49(1) does not apply and so the property does not form part of the person's estate.

24.32

EXAMPLE 24.8

B sells part of his house to his son for full value. The son then settles it on an interest in possession trust for B. If this settlement is made post-March 21, 2006 B does not take a qualifying interest in possession and therefore the property is not part of his estate for inheritance tax purposes. Hence he is not protected from a POA charge under para.11(1) and he is protected under the reservation of benefit provisions because the original disposal was a sale not a gift.

---

[27] See the COP 10 correspondence in App III at A3.61 *et seq*.

24.33 Second, s.80 amended para.11(1) Sch.15 with effect from December 5, 2005. New sub-para.11(12) applies where *at any time*:

(i) the relevant property has ceased to be comprised in a person (A's) estate for the purposes of IHTA 1984 (the first condition) or the person has directly or indirectly provided any consideration for the acquisition of the relevant property, (e.g. A sells half his house at an under value to son S (the second condition);

(ii) *and* at any subsequent time the relevant property or any derived property is comprised in A's estate for the purposes of IHTA 1984 as a result of s.49(1), e.g. the son settles the property on qualifying interest in possession trusts for A.

24.34 Note that such a trust would not be possible unless A was disabled if the son made the settlement after March 21, 2006 but the provision catches all trusts with qualifying interests in possession established after March 17, 1986 so A would be caught if the son had settled the property on interest in possession trusts prior to March 22, 2006.

In these circumstances the relevant property is not treated as comprised in A's estate for the purposes of paras 11(1) and (2) with the result that the POA charge applies.

Further POA problems?

24.35 The change in s.80 goes further than the December 2005 Press Release indicated. It does not just affect reverter to settlor trusts where, since there is no inheritance tax due on the death of A, it might be thought reasonable to impose a POA charge. Assume for instance, that in 1987 H set up a trust for himself to which he transferred his house Port Meadow. He may have done this for reasons that have nothing to do with IHT saving (e.g. he may have been motivated by asset protection considerations or, in the case of US persons, a desire to avoid the need for probate.) H is settlor and has an interest in possession. In 1998 the original Port Meadow property is sold. The trustees purchase a new property in which H lives. The second condition has been satisfied even though the relevant property has always been comprised in H's estate. H is within the POA charge from December 5, 2005. Accordingly the 2006 charge potentially affects all settlor-interested interest in possession trusts even though inheritance tax is payable on the death of the settlor. It has a particularly adverse affect on foreign domiciliaries, many of whom fund their excluded settlements with cash gifted to the trustees offshore and the trustees then purchase a UK property (possibly through an offshore company) in which the foreign domiciliary lives. That satisfies the second condition and so the foreign domiciliary is liable to POA (see further 22.70 *et seq*.).

24.36 Excluded liabilities: in cases where the value of a person's estate is reduced because of an "excluded liability" the relevant property is only treated as comprised in his estate and so exempt to the extent that its value exceeds the amount of the excluded liability. Note the following:

(i) a liability is an excluded liability if the creation of the liability and any transaction as a result of which the person's estate included the relevant property were "associated operations" (as defined in s.268 of IHTA 1984);

(ii) in cases where the value attributed in the person's estate is substantially less than the value of the relevant property the exemption does not apply but there is a deduction in the chargeable amount "by such proportion as is reasonable to take account of the inclusion of the property in his estate".[28]

The restriction when there is an excluded liability is intended to prevent double-trust/home-loan schemes from falling outside the income tax charge.

(ii) Property already subject to a reservation of benefit—para.11(3)(5)(a): **24.37**

If "the property or any other property which derives its value from the relevant property would fall to be treated . . . as property subject to a reservation of benefit" then the person is not subject to the POA charge. So in *Example 24.6* above, if the settlement had been discretionary with Dan as one of the beneficiaries, para.8 would not apply since the property would be subject to a reservation of benefit.[29]

(iii) Reservation of benefit let-out: **24.38**

There is an exemption if the gift would have been subject to the reservation-of-benefit provisions except for the s.102B(4) exemption.[30] Even if the original gift was cash and therefore the reservation-of-benefit provisions would not apply. nevertheless there is no POA charge (see para.11(3)). So, where mother gives cash to son and they then buy a house jointly, it is thought that there is no reservation of benefit (irrespective of s.102B) and in addition there is no POA charge (para.11(5)(c) and 11(8)).

Similarly, there is an exemption if the gifted property would have been subject to a reservation of benefit except for the let-outs in s.102C(3) and Sch.20 para.6 of FA 1986[31] The full-consideration let-out is the most important one. Despite rather obscure drafting HMRC accepts that *"and"* in para.11(5)(d) is disjunctive (otherwise the subsection cannot make sense) and therefore full-consideration arrangements involving both land and chattels are protected. The consequences for chattel schemes are discussed in Chapter 31.

---

[28] See para.11(2).
[29] It was accepted in the *Eversden* case that if a settlor could benefit under his discretionary trust he would reserve a benefit.
[30] Para.11(5)(c).
[31] Para.11(5)(d).

EXAMPLE 24.9

Father gifts chattels to his sons and pays full market rent for his continued use and enjoyment of them. He is not subject to the POA charge. Similarly if he gives away his house but pays full consideration for his continued occupation, there is no POA charge.

If the rent is less than market rent, there will be a reservation of benefit and therefore there is still no income tax charge due to the let-out in para.11(5)(a).

If father gives cash to son who then buys chattels which are used by the father and father pays rent there is no reservation of benefit so can exemption from the POA charge be claimed? Paragraph 11(8) deals with this situation and provides that the restriction on tracing through outright gifts of cash is to be ignored, so that the reservation rules are capable of applying and the exemption for full consideration is available.

Non-domiciliaries

24.39 The POA charge is limited to persons resident in the UK (see para.12(1)). Persons who are UK resident but non-domiciled (for these purposes the IHT definition incorporating "deemed domicile" applies[32]) are only taxed if the property in question is situated in the UK (see para.12(2)). However in the case of a person who was at any time non-UK domiciled, a POA charge is not imposed on excluded property within s.48(3)(a) IHTA 1984 (non-UK *situs* property in a settlement established at a time when the settlor was non-UK domiciled). These provisions are far from straightforward. In practice the foreign domiciliary should look first at para.12 exemptions before proceeding to see whether paras 11(1), (3) and (5) provide relief.

EXAMPLE 24.10

(1) Cyrus is resident but non-UK domiciled and occupies a flat in the Algarve which is owned by his trust. He is not subject to POA (para.12(2)).

(2) Betty (UK resident but non-domiciled) occupies a Knightsbridge flat which is owned by a Jersey company the shares of which are owned by a Jersey discretionary trust set up by Betty and under which she can benefit:

  (a) the trust is an excluded-property settlement in respect of the non-situs shares held by the trustees, and accordingly the para.8 charge will not apply. Paragraph 12(3) provides protection.
  (b) Betty is, however, occupying UK-situs property which is not excluded property. Paragraph 12 provides no protection in respect of

---

[32] See 22.02 for a detailed consideration of non-domiciliaries.

her occupation of the UK land and this is the case wherever she is now domiciled if she is resident in the UK. However, if the trust is discretionary she has reserved a benefit in property which derives its value from the land. Although on her death the excluded-property rules for settled property will override the reservation-of-benefit rules and there is no inheritance tax charge, para.11(3) nevertheless provides protection during her lifetime from a POA tax charge.

(c) Betty has an interest in possession in the trust which holds the UK land either directly or through a company, para.12 does not provide protection for the land wherever Betty is domiciled but para.11(1) will apply to exclude the POA charge. Such protection works through the ownership or derived ownership exemption.

In the case of (b) and (c) above, if the company holding the land was capitalised by a loan from the trustees rather than by share capital, HMRC consider[33] that the derived ownership or derived reservation of benefit exemption does not apply and there is a POA charge. They consider that the loan does not derive any of its value from the land. Even though the loan is part of the interest in possession trust or is property in which Betty has reserved a benefit this does not prevent a POA charge on the land.

Right of election 24.40

Paragraph 21 gives a right of election in respect of chattels and land; Para.22 in respect of intangibles. The effect of the election is that the donor is taxed as if he had reserved a benefit in the relevant property which will therefore be taxed as part of his estate for inheritance tax purposes on his death. The POA charge does not therefore apply.

The relief is limited; it does *not* put the individual who has undertaken tax planning in the same position as if the planning had never been done. For example, the property will not be uplifted to market value for capital gains tax purposes on his death; the donee may separately face capital gains tax charges on a disposal of the property (particularly in relation to *Ingram* schemes) and the property remains part of the donee's estate under general inheritance tax principles.

In addition in some cases (e.g. *Eversden* schemes) it may be that the property is taxed as part of the original donor's estate but someone else (in this case the spouse) will have made a PET. There is then the possibility of a double inheritance tax charge which is not relieved by the double charges regulations. (By contrast, if the donor has made the PET and reserved a benefit there is relief against a double charge.) Thus some thought must be given as to whether or not an election is the best option.

The donor is not required to notify the donee when making the election even though the donee will be primarily liable for the inheritance tax due on the donor's death. 24.41

The election must be made by January 31 following the end of the initial year (being the first year for which the POA charge applies to the individual in

---

[33] See the COP 10 letter in App. III at A3.61 *et seq*.

respect of the particular property etc.) and cannot be revoked after that date although the effect of the election will fall away if the use and enjoyment of the property ceases (the individual will then make a deemed PET under FA 1986, s.102(4)). The election is made on Form IHT 500 to HMRC Capital Taxes.

24.42 Taxpayers should consider carefully whether they are better off making an election. An election can prove problematic for married couples on the first death when the spouse exemption may not be available.[34]

If a person elects, but then pays full consideration for the use of land or chattels on or immediately *before* making the election, there is no deemed PET and the let out in para.6 Sch.20 applies. The effect is that as long as the person continues to pay full consideration while they use the land or chattel, the reservation of benefit rules are disapplied. Hence no PET arises from making the election and paying full consideration "so long as the taxpayer is paying full consideration at the point of election".[35]

In addition, HMRC consider that if someone elects and then the scheme is dismantled: e.g. the property is appointed back to the individual so it is part of his estate under general principles, there is no deemed PET under s.102(4) and the IHT effect of the election falls away.[36]

24.43 The Double Charges Regulations 2005 provide some relief from a double charge where a home loan scheme has been unscrambled with the debt being written off.[37]

EXAMPLE 24.11

A effected a home loan scheme in 2003. He sold his house to an interest in possession trust for himself and gave away the debt to an interest in possession trust for his children. As a result of the POA charge he wishes to unscramble the scheme and the children and trustees of the debt trust agree to write off the debt. The full value of his house is therefore subject to inheritance tax again. If he dies before 2010, however, he will suffer inheritance tax on the failed PET. Effectively inheritance tax will be charged on the same economic value twice. SI 2005/3441 gives relief in these circumstances. Inheritance tax is paid on the higher of the value of the house or the failed PET but not both. Note that A will pay the POA charge for the period from April 6, 2005 to the date the debt is released *unless* he makes an election. The children make PETs when the debt is written off if the house is held by A absolutely at the date of the write off. Where the house is still in the trust, the question is whether the addition of value by the children to an existing interest in possession trust for A constitutes a chargeable transfer post-March 21, 2006[38]. It is preferable that the house is removed from the trust before the debt is written off. SDLT charges may be avoided if care is used. If A makes the POA election no POA is payable (see especially App.III.3A.149).

---

[34] See COP 10 letter, Question 4, in App. III.A3.61.
[35] See COP 10 letter App. III.A3.61.
[36] See COP 10 in App. III.A3.61 and see App.III.A3.149.
[37] SI 2005/3441.
[38] See Sch.20 of FA 2006.

24.44 POA is a useful back up to Sch.20 for HMRC. Consider the following example:

EXAMPLE 24.12

> In 2007 Donald puts cash in a nil rate band trust under which he is given entitlement to income but is excluded from the capital which is left in trust for his grandchildren. Donald's transfer is a chargeable transfer but no IHT is payable because the value is less than his unused nil rate band. He has an income entitlement but this is not a qualifying interest in possession. Hence on Donald's death provided he is excluded from capital, there appears to be no reservation of benefit.[39] The life interest ceases on his death and so has no value. This might be thought the best of all worlds: Donald has the income but the capital is not taxed on his death. However, watch POA. Since Donald has an interest in the settlement, while it holds cash or other intangibles he is within the 5 per cent charge. If the trust moves into land or chattels there is a charge on Donald then only if he is in occupation and so the land should be let to avoid a POA charge.

---

[39] The arrangements may be seen as a carve out along the lines recognised by the House of Lords in the *Ingram* case, see 13.14 and 31.34.

PART IV: SPECIALIST TOPICS

This section looks at a number of specialist topics in some detail. Chapter 25 considers the taxation of trusts set up for minors and older children. It discusses the options open to parents and other relatives, such as grandparents, who want to make provision for minors and looks at the tax treatment of bereaved minor and 18–25 trusts. Chapter 26 considers the tax treatment (income tax, capital gains tax and inheritance tax) of trusts for disabled and other vulnerable beneficiaries. Chapter 27 looks at the capital gains, inheritance tax and pre-owned assets income tax treatment of reverter to settlor trusts and the impact of the changes that came into force on 5th December 2005. Chapter 28 looks at will drafting and Chapter 29 at deeds of variation and two year discretionary trusts. Chapter 30 considers bare trusts, their disadvantages and advantages. Chapter 31 covers the inheritance tax and capital gains tax treatment of the family home and chattels. This includes a discussion of main residence relief, the unwinding of house schemes, present options for minimising inheritance tax on the family home, and the position of foreign domiciliaries buying UK property. Chapter 32 covers business property relief and agricultural property relief and Chapter 33 life insurance products. Chapter 34 is concerned with trusts in the context of divorce and looks at nuptial settlements, trusts as a financial resource and the impact of Schedule 20 on trusts. Chapter 35 provides an overview of stamp duties and Chapter 36 of compliance and disclosure issues.

CHAPTER 25

TRUSTS FOR MINORS AND FOR OLDER CHILDREN

- Lifetime options **(25.03)**
- Provisions on death **(25.09)**
- Bereaved Minor Trusts (BMT) **(25.13)**
- 18–25 (s.71D) Trusts **(25.29)**
- Other death options **(25.46)**

Establishing new trusts after FA 2006

The IHT changes that came into effect from March 22, 2006 mean that— **25.01**

(i) any lifetime *trust* will—unless it contains a "disabled persons interest"[1]—be immediately chargeable for IHT purposes. It does not matter that the trust has been set up for the benefit of the settlor's children, grandchildren or other beneficiaries. There are no longer special rules for trusts for beneficiaries under a specified age.

(ii) there are special rules for two will *trusts* but only if these are established by a testator for his own children. First, "bereaved minor trusts", which receive the same IHT treatment as s.71 accumulation and maintenance trusts (no anniversary or exit charge), but which require capital to vest no later than the age of 18. Secondly, "18–25 trusts" which, as the name suggests, enable the capital to vest at any time up until age 25 but which levy an IHT charge if the beneficiary receives capital after 18 or the trusts continue after the beneficiary has reached 25. The maximum charge is 4.2 per cent. (This may be seen as a "fine" for continuing to use the trust structure).

Nothing will be served by continuing to draft trusts in a form which was **25.02** designed to satisfy the conditions in IHTA 1984, s.71 since the IHT advantages have now been withdrawn.[2] Instead the following options need to be considered by a would-be settlor or testator.

---

[1] See IHTA 1984, s.89B inserted by FA 2006, Sch.20, para.6.
[2] The position of existing s.71 accumulation and maintenance trusts is considered in Ch. 21.

LIFETIME OPTIONS

Discretionary trusts

25.03 In many cases a discretionary trust will be what the settlor really wants, but before March 22, 2006 he had been put off by the adverse tax consequences. In essence, these boil down to the inheritance tax charge at lifetime rates of 0 per cent and 20 per cent (for the tax year 2006–07) when the trust is established *inter vivos*, and thereafter to anniversary and exit charges.[3] If these charges either do not arise, or can be shown to be manageable, a discretionary trust should be used whenever the settlor wants his trustees to have the flexibility to "pick and choose" between an unlimited class of beneficiaries. Further, if the value of the property to be settled falls within the settlor's IHT nil rate band, or if it comprises property qualifying for 100 per cent business or agricultural property[4] relief, not only will the creation of the trust be free from an inheritance tax charge, but it may well be that subsequent ten-year anniversaries will pass without any charge to tax arising.[5] Even if IHT is payable during the continuance of the trust, the charges currently imposed on discretionary trusts are relatively light: the maximum anniversary charge is levied at only 6 per cent (tax year 2006–07), whilst exit charges attract tax at only a fraction of that rate.[6]

25.04 Relevant property trusts (including but not limited to discretionary trusts) possess a tax benefit in that CGT hold-over relief may be available both on creation and termination.[7] This is a major advantage of settled as opposed to unsettled gifts, because all too often in lifetime estate planning the attractions of the IHT potentially exempt transfer regime are offset by the CGT charge that would arise if a gift were made.[8] An important qualification needs to be

---

[3] As to the taxation of discretionary trusts see Ch. 20. The truly cautious (some might say wise) would also point out that a Labour government is in power for the foreseeable future, committed to rooting out tax avoidance. That party has, historically, shown a deep suspicion of all types of trust, but especially the type of flexible trust epitomised by the full blown discretionary trust. Indeed, the legislation introduced in 1975 for such "no interest in possession trusts" was widely seen as penal and a form of transitional relief was introduced to enable trustees (at a cut price rate) to switch into a more acceptable form. The current top rate of tax levied at ten yearly anniversaries is 6 per cent (being 30 per cent of the top lifetime IHT rate which is 20 per cent). This can hardly be described as penal. However, there are fears that the rate will increase in the future: for instance if 50 per cent of the lifetime rate were to be charged this would equate to a 10 per cent charge every 10 years or an annual wealth tax of 1 per cent.

[4] See Ch. 32.

[5] This will depend upon: (a) continuance of business and agricultural property reliefs at 100 per cent and the retention of qualifying property; (b) no reduction in the level of the nil-rate band; and (c) increases in the nil-rate band in line with increases in the value of the assets settled.

[6] When it is realised that, if the life tenant of an interest in possession trust established pre March 22, 2006 dies, tax may be charged at the 40 per cent rate, the relative generosity of the discretionary trust charges becomes apparent. Of course the charge on the ending of an interest in possession was frequently avoided, or at least postponed, by ensuring that the deceased's spouse enjoyed a successive life interest. Judicious use of overriding powers of appointment to terminate the interest in possession (triggering, usually, a potentially exempt transfer by that beneficiary) were also used to avoid the charge.

[7] TCGA 1992, s.260 as amended.

[8] Hold-over relief into a relevant property trust is available even in cases where IHT is not payable because of the availability of the settlor's nil-rate band provided that the trust is not settlor interested. Hence the attraction of "nil-rate band" discretionary trusts, see 28.04.

made, however, since if the trust is settlor interested CGT hold-over relief is not available on its creation. Prior to April 6, 2006 a trust was only settlor interested if:

(i) the settlor, or
(ii) the spouse (including, from December 5, 2005, a civil partner) of the settlor,

could benefit under its terms. From April 6, 2006, however, the concept of a "settlor-interested" trust has been extended to include a trust which is capable of benefiting a dependent child of the settlor.[9]

EXAMPLE 25.1

> Richard's first grandchild is born on January 1, 2007 and he determines to establish a trust for the benefit of that child and future grandchildren. He plans to settle (a) a cash sum and (b) investment properties showing a substantial gain. His alternatives prior to March 22, 2006 were:
>
> (a) an accumulation and maintenance trust. This was the most likely choice given the age of the one child, and would have been a PET by him for IHT purposes. The main advantages over options (b) and (c) were that it left open the possibility of other children being born later and benefiting and did not give the child an entitlement to income (or capital) at too early an age.
> (b) a bare trust for the child—this would have been a PET but it was an unlikely option unless Richard was happy for the child to take the properties outright at 18.
> (c) an interest in possession trust for the child—s.31 Trustee Act 1925 would need to be excluded. Again this would have been a PET by Richard.
> (d) a discretionary trust. This would have been a chargeable transfer for inheritance tax purposes but CGT hold-over relief would have been available on the investment properties which was not the case on the other three options.

Since March 22, 2006 Richard is presented with the following options—

> (i) if he wants a trust structure then he will make an immediately chargeable transfer for IHT purposes. Accordingly once the value transferred exceeds his available IHT nil rate band (£285,000 for 2006–7) tax at 20 per cent is charged on the excess whatever type of trust is used (apart from a bare trust). If he wishes to settle property worth more than his nil rate band he may still avoid an IHT

---

[9] TCGA 1992, s.169B; s.169F as amended by FA 2006. Note that the limitation on hold-over relief does not apply if the settlor does not have dependent children albeit that if he did they would benefit and nor does it prevent hold-over relief being available on the termination of a settlor-interested trust. Settlor-interested trusts are considered in detail in Ch. 11 and hold-over relief in Ch. 9.

charge by transferring assets to his wife who makes a similar settlement within her IHT nil rate band.[10] In that way either a single trust worth £570,000[11] or two nil rate band trusts can be set up;

(ii) so far as CGT is concerned any cash settled will not create problems and, provided that the trust that he establishes is not settlor-interested (or a bare trust) CGT hold-over relief will be available under TCGA 1992, s.260 in respect of the investment properties;

(iii) in terms of the *type of trust* to be set up, Richard is now freed from any possible constraints under s.71 (which had been necessary if an accumulation and maintenance trust was to be used) and, given,

- that he only has one grandchild, and
- that there is no guarantee that others will be born,

it will be important that he includes other beneficiaries than just grandchildren. It will, for instance, be sensible to include his children as beneficiaries albeit that his wish is to provide for the later generation.[12]

Richard's options are therefore more limited under the new regime. In one respect though the tax position is better. Previously if a child was given entitlement to income the settled property would be treated as part of his estate for inheritance tax purposes. Hence an *inter vivos* termination of that interest would generally constitute a PET. If Richard now settles assets on interest in possession trusts for his grandchild, this is a chargeable transfer for inheritance tax purposes but the settled property is not treated as part of the child's estate for inheritance tax purposes. The settled property remains within the relevant property regime. This gives the trustees flexibility to change who has entitlement to income without having to worry about any inheritance tax consequences. For example, the eldest grandchild could be given an initial interest in possession in the whole fund (which might be useful if the settled fund produced dividends rather than rental income).[13] If another grandchild is born later, the interest in possession of the first grandchild could be terminated by the trustees in whole or part. That would be a non-event for inheritance tax purposes. Richard can be a trustee and so have a decisive voice in who is to benefit. Income tax compliance is generally easier under an interest in possession trust and the income tax on dividend income is generally lower.

Of course if Richard does not want children to be given entitlement to income he may incline to a discretionary trust. Whatever type of trust is used, he can be a trustee and in case he were to die he can leave a non-binding letter of wishes which would doubtless be used by later trustees to determine the

---

[10] Inter-spouse transfers are taxed at no gain no loss: see TCGA 1992, s.58.
[11] Administratively a single trust has attractions: for IHT purposes, given joint settlors, tax will be charged on the basis that there are two separate trusts. For CGT purposes only a single trust annual exemption will be available, see 7.07.
[12] This will not give rise to CGT hold-over restrictions provided that *none of his children* is a minor: See 9–42.
[13] See Ch. 4 and especially 4.25.

future direction of the trust. In the future the class of beneficiaries could be limited to grandchildren and their issue. Interests in possession in the trust property for each of the grandchildren can be created or varied as the trustees determine.

As an alternative to using a trust structure, Richard might consider transferring the property to a bare trust for the grandchild. Whilst this would have the attraction of being a PET[14] and the grandchild would not, of course, be able to demand either income or capital from the property until he was 18 it is unlikely in this case that these factors will outweigh the disadvantages of—

- no CGT hold-over relief on investment properties;
- Richard is not creating a fund for grandchildren as a class but making a gift to a single grandchild;
- it is not possible to prevent the child taking capital and income at 18[15] so that there is a lack of flexibility.

Interest in possession trusts

Before March 22, 2006, interest in possession trusts were commonly drafted to incorporate a substantial element of flexibility; for example—   **25.05**

(a) the trustees were given power to advance capital to the interest in possession beneficiary;[16] and

(b) the trustees were given overriding powers of appointment which could be used to terminate the interest in possession in whole or in part.

Including provisions such as these explains why such trusts were seen as an alternative to the "pure" discretionary trust. Other factors that encouraged this use were:

(i) the creation of an interest in possession trust *inter vivos* was a potentially exempt transfer[17];

(ii) the trusts did not suffer IHT anniversary or exit charges[18];

(iii) there was no need to satisfy the onerous conditions for a qualifying accumulation and maintenance trust;

(iv) the termination of the interest in possession by the exercise of overriding powers vested in the trustees commonly resulted in the (former) beneficiary making a potentially exempt transfer and in the settlement continuing so that no liability to CGT arose; and

---

[14] For IHT purposes, a bare trust does not fall within the definition of a settlement and so the transfer would be treated as an outright gift to the minor beneficiary: see Ch. 30.
[15] See Ch. 30 for comments on the settled power of advancement.
[16] In some cases, the interest in possession beneficiary was given the right to call for all or a part of the capital which the trustees might have been obliged to pay or transfer to him, or which they could only refuse to do by a unanimous resolution.
[17] IHTA 1984, s.3A(2) as inserted by the Finance Act 1986, s.101, Sch.19, para.1 and amended by the Finance (No 2) Act 1987, ss.96(1), (2), 104, Sch.9, Pt III.
[18] Although note the charge that arose on the death of the life tenant: see IHTA 1984, s.49(1).

(v) a flexible interest in possession trust was used as a vehicle to protect a beneficiary against profligacy and the assets against third party claims against that person.[19]

25.06 However, it always had to be borne in mind that if an interest in possession trust was selected, the death of the beneficiary could result in a substantial IHT charge which was payable by the trustees.[20] It was common therefore for interest in possession trusts to be used for older children (typically over the age of 18) and under that age for the accumulation and maintenance trust to be used. In the situation where it was desired to give a minor beneficiary an interest in possession, it was important to exclude s.31 of the Trustee Act 1925 which has the effect of replacing the interest in possession with a power to pay income and to accumulate—during minority—any balance which would only be paid to the minor if he attained 18.[21]

25.07 As Example 25.1 illustrates however, the position was radically altered by the March 22 changes. From that date any *inter vivos* settlement established with an interest in possession is taxed as a relevant property settlement (unless it involves a disabled person's interest). Hence the decision about which type of trust should be used can be taken in the knowledge that the IHT charges on the trust *will be the same in all cases*.

For the taxpayer the question is therefore whether he wants to give a right to income to one or more of the beneficiaries and this he may wish to do. This may be appropriate if the trust is for his children who are in their twenties who may need the income, or if income is going to be paid out to a beneficiary anyway (e.g. to pay school fees), or the settled property produces dividend income where the rates of tax are generally higher when the trust falls within the TA 1988, s.686–7 regime.[22] There are settlors who prefer fixed trusts with the certainty that is provided to the flexibility of the discretionary trust. And, of course, a change in the trust (e.g. on the death of a life tenant or *inter vivos* termination of his interest in possession) will no longer be a chargeable occasion. IHT charges will only arise every 10 years and when the trust ends.

Bare trusts

25.08 Settlors are sometimes attracted to the idea of creating a trust for the absolute benefit of a minor and the attractions have undoubtedly increased as a result of the March 2006 changes in the IHT treatment of settlements. The creation of the trust is a PET because the beneficiary is treated as the owner of the property the settlement rules, and anniversary and exit charges, do not apply. The disadvantages of the arrangement are that:

(a) the beneficiary will become entitled to income and capital at age18; and

---

[19] On protective trusts, see 19.04.
[20] IHTA 1984, s.200(1)(b). In such cases, the life tenant (or trustees) might take out life insurance to cover the tax exposure.
[21] For a suitable exclusion clause, see App II A2.43.
[22] See 4.25.

(b) on his death inheritance tax will be attracted to the value of the settled property which will (whilst he remains a minor) pass on intestacy.[23]

PROVISIONS ON DEATH

Even after the March 2006 changes, testators have a range of possible trusts that can be established for young children and grandchildren in their wills. These comprise— **25.09**

(i) an interest in possession trust: (an IPDI)[24] in which the trust property is treated as belonging to the relevant beneficiary under IHTA 1984, s.49(1);

(ii) a bereaved minor trust: only suitable for minor *children* of the testator;

(iii) an 18–25 (s.71D trust): again only suitable for *children* of the testator;

(iv) a bare trust;

(v) a discretionary trust (a relevant property settlement).

As discussed in Chapter 28, the standard family will—taking into account IHT saving—will normally involve on the death of the first spouse: **25.10**

(i) use of the IHT nil rate band;

(ii) a spouse exempt gift of residue.

The nil rate band could, of course, be utilised by making a settled gift to children/grandchildren using one of the trusts listed above but in many cases the preferred option will be a nil rate band discretionary trust incorporating debt/charge clauses. It is therefore more likely that trusts for minors and older children will feature in the will of the surviving spouse.

In cases where the will of the first spouse to die leaves residue on an interest in possession trust for the surviving spouse (an IPDI), the will may provide for trusts over to take effect on the ending of that spouse's interest. Such trusts can qualify as bereaved minor trusts or s.71D (age 18–25) trusts but it is not possible to create successive IPDIs. Accordingly, were the will to provide for residue to be held on trust for the surviving spouse and then for the children of the testator on interest in possession trusts, the trusts for the children would be taxed under the relevant property regime and the surviving spouse would make a chargeable transfer if her interest was terminated or surrendered *inter vivos*. If the surviving spouse is keen that the children should take IPDIs on her death the trustees would need to advance the capital out to her and then she would set up IPDIs in her will for the children. **25.11**

---

[23] A bare trust is not, of course, a settlement for IHT purposes: see Ch. 30. A transfer into a bare trust will therefore be potentially exempt. The income of the trust will be taxed on the settlor if he is the parent of the beneficiary: see ITTOIA 2005, s.629(1)(b). However, the capital is treated as belonging to the minor and so his capital gains tax annual exemption will be available to set against trust gains: see TCGA 1992, s.60.

[24] These have been considered in detail in Ch. 19.

25.12 The options: a diagrammatic resumé

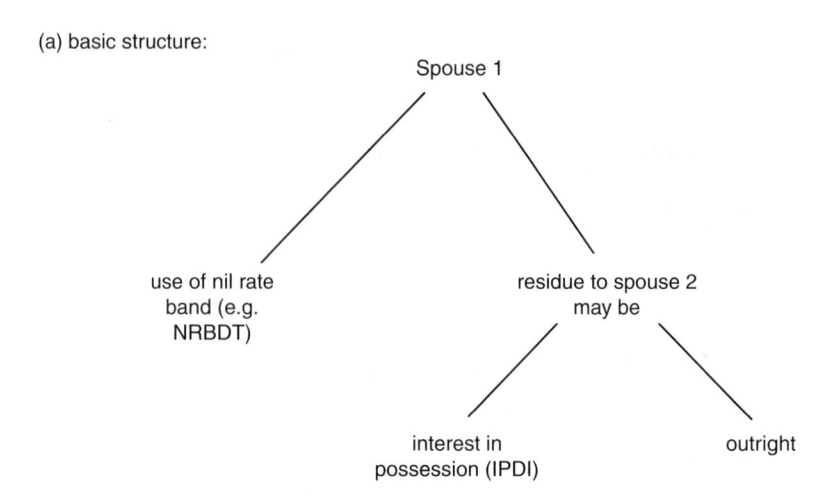

(a) basic structure:

```
                        Spouse 1
                       /        \
            use of nil rate    residue to spouse 2
            band (e.g.         may be
            NRBDT)             /        \
                    interest in         outright
                    possession (IPDI)
```

In both cases *s.18* spouse relief applies

(b) trusts of residue (spouse 1)

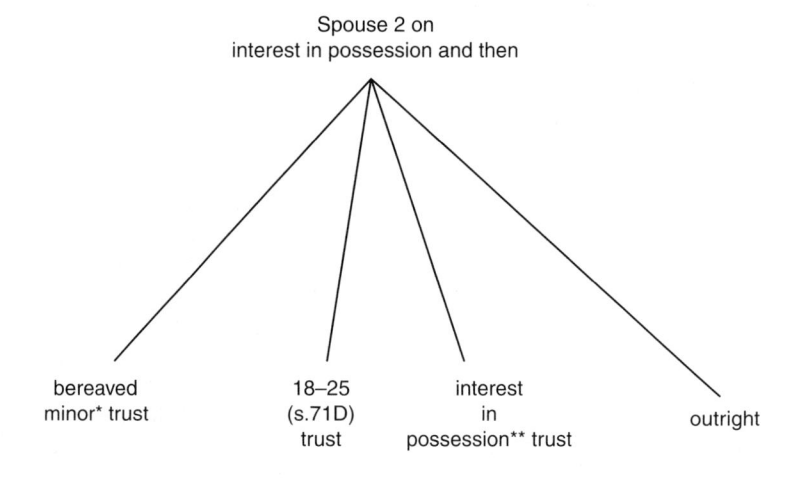

```
              Spouse 2 on
              interest in possession and then
             /      |      \      \
    bereaved    18–25    interest
    minor* trust (s.71D)  in          outright
                 trust    possession** trust
```

* If this trust takes effect on the lifetime ending of the spouse's interest in possession then the spouse is treated as making a PET (see IHTA 1984, s.3A(1A)(c)(iii) inserted by FA 2006). Note that in all other cases where there are continuing trusts (save for trusts creating a disabled person's interest) the spouse will make an immediately chargeable transfer.

** This will not be a qualifying interest in possession (it will not be an IPDI): hence the relevant property regime will apply.

(c) trusts in the will of the surviving spouse:

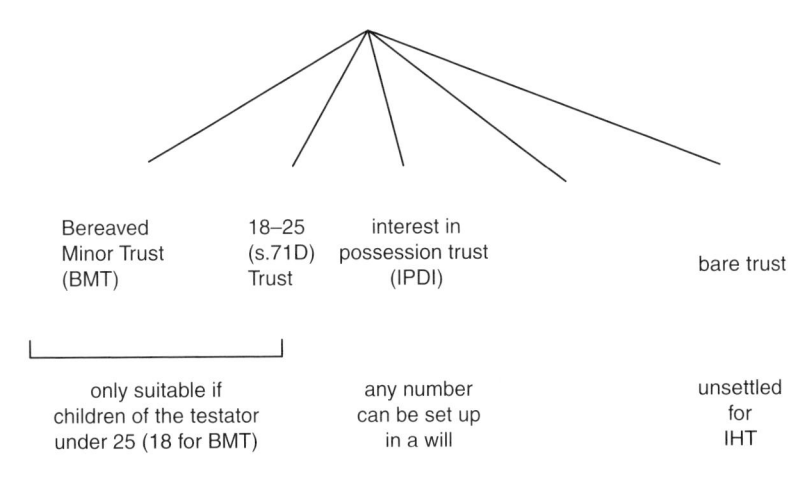

```
              Bereaved          18–25        interest in
              Minor Trust       (s.71D)      possession trust
              (BMT)             Trust        (IPDI)                bare trust

              |_____|
              only suitable if      any number          unsettled
              children of the testator   can be set up       for
              under 25 (18 for BMT)      in a will          IHT
```

BEREAVED MINOR TRUSTS

25.13 The requirements to be satisfied if such a trust is to be established are in IHTA 1984, s.71A and the tax treatment of such trusts is laid down in s.71B. The key limiting feature of these trusts is that they can only be set up in favour of a minor child of the testator (hence they cannot be set up for grandchildren) and the trusts must ensure that capital vests at 18. In response to widespread criticism of the latter requirement, the Government during the passage of FA 2006 through Parliament, introduced the 18–25 (s.71D) trust which enables the vesting of capital to be postponed until 25, albeit at an IHT cost. Practitioners should consider both options in advising clients on appropriate will trusts for their young children. It is likely that many will wish to use the s.71D trust which provides for some flexibility in the date of capital vesting and the possibility of a postponement even beyond the age of 25. It is unlikely that BMTs will be established under the terms of the will itself unless the testator has a particular wish that his children should take capital and income at 18. An IPDI or s.71D trust for the children is more likely. However, if he leaves residue on IPDI trusts for the surviving spouse and the surviving spouse wishes to make PETs for his children, either they must take outright or on BMTs on the *inter vivos* termination of her interest. It is not necessary that the terms of the BMT are set out in the will itself provided that the trustees exercise their powers of appointment (given to them in the will) to secure that on termination of the spousal IPDI the settled property is held on a BMT (see App.III A3.121). If the children are not financially responsible at 18 the trustees could always exercise their power of advancement to defer absolute entitlement at which point the trust will enter the relevant property regime but without an entry charge.[25]

---

[25] The trust could be converted into a s.71D trust at that point if it was felt preferable for the children to take at 25 not 18; then just before 25 their interests could be postponed again at which point the trust becomes a relevant property settlement!

Curiously while it would be possible to convert the trust into a s.71D trust on termination of the spousal IPDI this would not be a PET by the spouse but a chargeable transfer. However, the trust does not suffer anniversary charges until the beneficiary reaches 25.

Who is a bereaved minor?

25.14 A person who has not attained the age of 18 and at least one of whose parents has died.[26]

Qualifying trusts

25.15 The trusts for the bereaved minor must either arise under the will of the deceased parent; be established under the Criminal Injuries Compensation Scheme or be held on the statutory trusts for the benefit of a bereaved minor under s.46 and 47(1) of the Administration of Estates Act 1925 (i.e. in cases where the parent dies intestate).[27] In cases other than intestacy the trust must satisfy the further conditions in s.71A(3).[28] Only in the cases of intestacy is substitution permitted: this occurs when a child predeceases the intestate leaving issue living at the death of the intestate who stand in his shoes.

EXAMPLE 25.2

(1) By his will A leaves property to his son absolutely on attaining the age of 18, failing which it is to go to A's sister. When A dies his son is aged nine. This is a BMT. Although there is a substitutional provision in favour of the sister while the son is alive, capital and income can only be applied for his benefit and he takes absolutely at 18.

(2) B's will leaves property to his daughter at age 21 with remainders over. Until that age the trustees have power to use income for her maintenance and to accumulate any balance. He dies when she is nine. This is not a BMT but it will qualify as an 18–25 trust.[29]

---

[26] IHTA 1984, s.71C inserted by FA 2006, Sch.20, para.1. Given that the trust can only arise under the will of a parent it is a little odd to include the requirement for one of the parents to have died! The definition is modelled on trusts for vulnerable beneficiaries in FA 2005, s.39 which are considered at Ch. 26. A person's children are defined for the purposes of s.71 by s.71(8): there is no definition in s.71B. "*Parent*" is defined in s.71H and includes a step-parent.

[27] See IHTA 1984, s.71A(1)(2). The reference to s.47(1) of the AEA limits the qualifying trust in intestacy to one for the benefit of the children of the intestate at 18 (i.e. to cases where the deceased left a surviving spouse and issue when the residue is held as to one-half on the statutory trusts for the issue).

[28] I.e. that capital and income can only be applied for the benefit of the bereaved minor who must take at 18.

[29] See 25.29.

(3) C dies intestate survived by his three minor children. One, D, marries at 17 has a child but dies in childbirth still aged under 18. This is a BMT. D's one third share vested under the statutory trusts on marriage. Contrast the position if D had died before C leaving a surviving child. The trust still falls within the definition of a BMT and D's child stands in his shoes being contingently entitled to a one-third share.

(4) E's will mirrors the statutory trusts which arise on intestacy. Before E's death a child dies leaving issue: there are two surviving minor children. E's will establishes a BMT in respect of the surviving children: however the remaining one-third share for E's child does not qualify and is held on a relevant property trust.

(5) In 2005 (i.e. pre March 22, 2006) Jason died and left his young son, Rufus, then aged eight an immediate interest in possession (s.31, TA 1925 was excluded) with an entitlement to capital at 18. With the passage of FA 2006 the IHT position is as follows:

  (i) this is a BMT (see s.71A(1) which can apply to property settled *before* March 22, 2006);
  (ii) if Rufus were to die aged 17 no IHT would therefore be payable despite the fact that he had enjoyed an interest in possession (IHTA 1984, s.49(1B)). There is a capital gains tax uplift to market value on his death;
  (iii) if the trustees made a settled advance—along the lines of that considered in Example 25.3(4)—in 2014 then although Rufus' entitlement to capital at 18 is removed no tax is chargeable and this is irrespective of whether his interest in possession terminates (*ibid.* s.53(1A)). If the trustees defer his entitlement to capital until 25 (whether or not they still allow him to be entitled to the income) then the trust becomes an s.71D trust. Anniversary charges are avoided. There is an exit charge of up to 4.2 per cent if capital is advanced to Rufus or the trust becomes a relevant property settlement on or before he becomes 25. Curiously, although it is not possible to convert former A+M trusts into s.71D trusts when the beneficiary has become entitled to income after March 21, 2006, a BMT can be converted into a s.71D trust even though the beneficiary may already have an entitlement to income and indeed may retain it. What is odd about the above example is that if Jason had simply left his son an interest in possession in 2005 with no age of capital entitlement the interest would have been a pre March 22, 2006 qualifying interest in possession. The tax regime then is completely different: no age of capital entitlement is required and transitional serial interests can be created.

(6) Thomas died in 2005 leaving property on trust for his son Terry (then aged 16) giving him an immediate interest in possession and providing for capital to vest when Terry was 18. The trustees have a wide power of advancement which they exercise in 2007 by making a settled advance giving Terry a life interest with remainders over. The analysis is:

(i) the trust is a BMT even though Terry was entitled to a pre March 22, interest in possession (see *Example 25.2 (5)*):

(ii) the settled advance has caused the trust to fall outside s.71A (since capital will no longer vest in Terry at 18) but this will not give rise to an IHT exit charge[30];

(iii) as a result of the settled advance the property now falls within the relevant property charging regime. Terry's original life interest is not a pre March 22, 2006 qualifying interest in possession and the interest he takes subsequently after the settled advance is not a transitional serial interest.[31]

25.16 The requirement that the trust must be established *under the will* of a deceased parent can be satisfied—

(i) if the trusts arise as the result of an instrument of variation of the deceased's will which is read-back under IHTA 1984, s.142(1)[32];

(ii) if the trusts arise as the result of an event occurring within two years of death and falling under IHTA 1984, s.144[33];

(iii) unlike an IPDI,[34] it is not necessary that the property becomes immediately held on these trusts at death: a BMT can, for instance, be preceded by an IPDI.[35]

The amendments to s.144—which provide for reading back if the terms of a non interest in possession trust[36] are modified within two years of death so that the continuing trusts satisfy the requirements of s.71A—are of limited importance. If the conversion occurs within the permitted two year period, reading back ensures that the s.71A trust is effective from death so that there is no question of an exit charge when the existing relevant property settlement ends. But even after that period has passed, conversion into a s.71A trust out of a relevant property trust is possible albeit at the cost of an IHT exit charge. The trust thus created (typically by exercise of a power of appointment) will still be established under the will of the deceased parent.

---

[30] See IHTA 1984, s.71B(2)(c).

[31] IHTA 1984, s.49B(5)(a). Contrast the position if the property was held on trust on Thomas' death so that Terry takes an immediate entitlement to income but capital vests at 25. Whether or not the testator died before or after March 22, 2006 if Terry has an interest in possession it is not a s.71D trust (see s.71D(5)(c)). If however the testator died before or after March 22, 2006 giving Terry capital and income at 25 but no immediate entitlement to income this would be a s.71D trust. If after the conversion of a BMT the settled advance gave Terry capital at 25 but retained his income entitlement then this would be a s.71D trust!

[32] See Ch. 29.

[33] s.144 is considered at 29.49. Typically the will establishes a discretionary trust and within two years of death the trustees appoint all or part of the trust property on a bereaved minor trust: see IHTA 1984, s.144(4)(c)(ii); (5) and (6)(b). And see 00.00.

[34] See 25.12 and 25.13. An IPDI involves the beneficiary becoming entitled to the interest in possession on the death.

[35] If the IPDI ends during the lifetime of the interest in possession beneficiary he will make a PET into the BMT: IHTA 1984, s.3A(1A)(iii): contrast the position in the case of 18–25 (s.71D) trusts, see 25.13.

[36] A qualifying interest in possession is, of course, severely limited in its scope after March 22, 2006: see IHTA 1984, s.144(1A) inserted by FA 2006.

Vesting at 18

The child must, no later than the age of 18, become absolutely entitled to: **25.17**

(i) the settled property;
(ii) any income arising from it; and
(iii) income which has previously arisen from property held on trusts for his benefit and which has been accumulated.

The following matters are worthy of note—

(a) the terms of the trust must "secure" that this condition is met. There must therefore be no overriding powers of appointment which could be exercised to divert the property to other persons or to postpone vesting beyond the age of 18. This requirement resembles the provision in s.71 (dealing with accumulation and maintenance trusts) that beneficiaries "*will*" become entitled to property no later than the age of 25.[37] As in that case, it is clearly not possible for the terms of the trust to secure with absolute certainty that the property will vest at 18 since the beneficiary might die under that age. Rather the trust must provide for vesting at 18 and it must not contain any provisions which could prevent this from happening.

(b) that until the age of 18 if any of the settled property *is applied* for the benefit of a beneficiary it is applied for the benefit of the bereaved minor.[38] It is a little difficult to see that this adds greatly to the basic requirement that the trusts must secure vesting at 18;

(c) that until the age of 18 either the bereaved minor is entitled to the income or no such income can be applied for the benefit of any other person.[39] Notice therefore that the minor can enjoy an interest in possession before becoming entitled to capital at 18.[40] Not only must the application of income be for the benefit of the minor but if income is accumulated the accumulations must belong to the minor (see s.71A(3)(iii)). In general accumulated income passes with the share to a beneficiary who becomes absolutely entitled on attaining 18 (the position is different if the beneficiary then becomes entitled to a life interest).[41]

Powers of advancement

It is expressly provided in s.71A(4) that the existence of a common form power **25.18**
of advancement (even modified by the deletion of the 50 per cent ceiling on

---

[37] See Ch. 21.
[38] IHTA 1984, s.71A(3)(b).
[39] IHTA 1984, s.71A(3)(c).
[40] Contrast IHTA 1984, s.71(1)(b): the existence of an interest in possession prevented a trust from being an accumulation and maintenance settlement.
[41] See generally Snell's *Equity (31st edn)* at 12.46 and see *re Joel's WT* [1967] Ch. 14.

the sum advanced) or of an express power "*to the like effect*" to the statutory power or modified statutory power does not prevent the trust from being a BMT.[42] The words "to like effect" are found in IHTA 1984, s.88 which refers to trusts to the like effect to those found in TA 1925, s.33 (protective trusts). HMRC in SPE7 stated that they would interpret these words as applying to trusts "which are not materially different in their tax consequences".

The statement continued:

> "the Board would not wish to distinguish a trust by reason of a minor variation or additional administration duties or powers. The extension of the list of potential beneficiaries to, for example, brothers and sisters is not regarded as a minor variation."[43]

It is thought that the same approach will be applied to s.71A(4). This position expressly states that if the trustees' powers are subject to a less restrictive limit than one-half this will not mean the condition is breached. However, an express power which excluded the requirement for consent[44] is not thought to satisfy the BMT requirements.

25.19 Whilst the *existence* of powers of advancement does not prevent a trust from qualifying as a BMT, the *exercise* of such *powers* may, of course, cause the requirements to be broken. In such a case, however, this will not give rise to an IHT exit charge.[45]

EXAMPLE 25.3

> Adam's will leaves the residue of his estate to his son contingent on attaining 18 absolutely failing which it is to be divided amongst Adam's siblings. Sections 31 and 32 of the Trustee Act 1925 apply and in the latter case there is power to advance the entire presumptive share of a beneficiary. Adam's son is aged 10 at his death.
>
> > (1) The trust for the son is a BMT. Capital vests at 18; the existence of the modified statutory power of advancement is ignored and during the son's minority, s.31 ensures that income can only be

---

[42] In practice the existence of a common form power of advancement did not prevent a trust from qualifying as accumulation and maintenance under s.71: see 21.09. See also the similar provision in trusts for vulnerable beneficiaries in FA 2005, s.34(3).

[43] The reference to the trust being not materially different "in their tax consequences" is somewhat odd since this will depend on whether or not they are treated in the same way as a s.33 trust! Protective trusts are considered in at 19.04.

[44] This restriction requires the consent of beneficiaries whose prior interest is prejudiced by the proposed exercise of the power: see TA 1925, s.32(1)(c). When the trustees are exercising the power for the benefit of a beneficiary who would otherwise become entitled to capital at 18 and may already have an entitlement to income, his consent is not required because his interest is not being prejudiced. Hence the requirement for consent may not be a practical problem given that the powers of advancement have to be exercised for the benefit of the particular minor anyway. If the power of advancement was modified so as to allow the trustees to advance capital of a share held for a minor for the benefit of *any* beneficiary (including default beneficiaries) rather than for the benefit of the minor child concerned the condition would not be satisfied.

[45] See IHTA 1984, s.71B(2)(c).

used for his benefit and that he will become entitled to any accumulations at 18.

(2) On the attainment of 18, the BMT will end with the son becoming absolutely entitled to the trust property. There is no IHT exit charge[46] and CGT hold-over relief is available.[47]

(3) If the son dies under the age of 18, the BMT ends and again there is no exit charge[48] and CGT hold-over relief is available. Note that this is the position whoever takes the property under default trusts that will only apply if the minor does not survive until the age of 18.

(4) The trustees decide before the son attains 18 that it will be for his benefit that he does not become entitled to the trust property absolutely. Accordingly they exercise their power of advancement so that he becomes entitled to a life interest at 18 with the trustees reserving a power to advance capital to him in the future subject to which the trust fund is held for the benefit of his children.[49] His consent (or consent by his guardian on his behalf) is not required. This exercise of the power has the following results:

  (i) it brings the BMT to an end: however there is no IHT exit charge[50];
  (ii) provided that the power is exercised "in the narrower form" it will not create a new settlement for CGT purposes so that there will not be a deemed disposal of the property[51];
  (iii) the continuing trusts will be taxed under the relevant property regime for IHT purposes: the son's interest in possession is not "qualifying": specifically it is not an IPDI. There is no base cost uplift to market value on his death (see ss.72 and 73, TCGA 1992)[52] and the settled property is not treated as part of his estate for inheritance tax purposes under s.49(1), IHTA 1984.

(5) As in (4) above except that the trustees exercise their power to give the son an interest in possession at 18 and also provide for capital to vest in him at 25. The tax consequences are as in (4) above except that the trust now falls within s.71D (18–25 trusts).[53] This means that until the age of 25 the tax position is as set out in 25.29 below. The most material differences from (4) above are that (a) if the beneficiary dies between 18 and 25 there is an inheritance tax exit charge, (b) the trust is not subject to anniversary charges and (c) when the beneficiary reaches 25, or takes capital earlier, there is an exit charge at a *maximum* rate of 4.2 per cent.

---

[46] See IHTA 1984, s.71B(2)(a).
[47] TCGA 1992, s.260(2)(da) inserted by FA 2006, Sch.20, para.32.
[48] IHTA 1984, s.71B(2)(b); TCGA 1992, s.260(2)(da).
[49] Such an exercise of the power is commonly termed a "settled advance".
[50] IHTA 1984, s.71B(2)(c).
[51] See 7.42 and compare 7.55.
[52] See 7.46.
[53] See 25.29, fn.54.

The charge to tax

25.20 This is dealt with in s.71B which provides that IHT shall be payable when settled property ceases to be held on a bereaved minor trust and also when trustees make a disposition which has the result of reducing the value of the settled property (a "depreciatory transaction", as to which see 00–00).[54] However the charge on the cessation of the BMT does not apply in three situations—[55]

(i) if the bereaved minor becomes 18 or absolutely entitled under that age (hence there is no exit charge at 18: see *Example 25.3(2)*;

(ii) if the bereaved minor dies under the age of 18 (so that default trusts apply: see Example 25.3(3);

(iii) if the trustees pay or apply the settled property for the advancement or benefit of the bereaved minor (hence a settled advance is not subject to an IHT exit charge: see *Example 25.3(4)*.

25.21 Apart from depreciatory transactions, it is a little difficult to envisage situations where an IHT charge will arise since the exclusions from charge in s.71B(2) are otherwise going to deal with the common situations that are likely to arise. Any charge that may arise is calculated in the same way as the exit charge for existing accumulation and maintenance trusts.[56] There are provisions for aggregating the consecutive periods during which the property has previously been held on s.71 (accumulation and maintenance) or s.71D trusts.

A comparison with accumulation and maintenance trusts

25.22 It has been said that bereaved minor trusts are all that is left of the regime which applied to accumulation and maintenance trusts set up before March 22, 2006. That is true in respect of the basic charging regime: i.e. a bereaved minor trust is a privileged settlement and does not generally suffer an IHT exit charge.

25.23 The differences between the two are, however, striking and include the following:

(i) a BMT can only be established by will/intestacy. There is no equivalent to the *inter vivos* accumulation and maintenance trust;

(ii) a BMT can only be set up for the minor children of the testator. There is no special vehicle available for grandchildren;

---

[54] IHTA 1984, s.71B(1).
[55] *ibid.* s.71B(2).
[56] IHTA 1984, s.71B(3)(4) and compare *ibid.* s.71(5) and see 21.15 Although rare in practice the situations in which a charge was capable of arising under s.71 were more extensive. For further details see 21.15.

(iii) capital must vest at 18. Under the accumulation and maintenance regime it was sufficient for either income or capital to vest at or before the age of 25;

(iv) there is little flexibility in the BMT. By contrast, accumulation and maintenance trusts could be drafted in highly flexible form: all that was required was that one or more beneficiaries became entitled to income or capital not later than age 25 and that enabled the trustees to exercise powers of selection between their beneficiaries. It also meant that the A+M trust could end with beneficiary A being given an interest in possession in the settled property at 25 but that interest could be (and frequently was!) subject to wide overriding powers of appointment by which the property could, in effect, be resettled for other family members.

A right to income

25.24 A BMT can give the minor child an interest in possession yet still be a BMT: by contrast, once an interest in possession arose, an A+M trust came to an end (being replaced by an interest in possession trust). And CGT hold-over relief is available however a BMT ends: contrast the more restrictive relief that was available for A+M trusts.[57] There is an advantage in giving a minor an immediate interest in possession in a BMT in that:

(a) it does not affect the IHT treatment *BUT*

(b) for CGT purposes the death under the age of 18 of the minor will result in the death uplift.[58]

What is the position if the parents will gives the minor an immediate right to income (so that TA 1925, s.31 is excluded) with capital vesting at 18. Is that a BMT or an IPDI?[59] IHTA 1984, s.49A provides that if the conditions of s.71A are met the interest in possession is not an IPDI (i.e. the BMT rules take precedence—contrast the position of s.71D trusts: see *Example 25.2(5)(6)*).

25.25 The legislation also envisages the possibility of a trust beginning as an IPDI but then becoming a BMT.

EXAMPLE 25.4

> On Dad's death, property is settled on his son on terms which give the son an immediate right to income and vest capital when he becomes 25. At the date of Dad's death the son is aged two.

---
[57] See Ch. 9.
[58] TCGA 1992, s.72(1B)(b) inserted by FA 2006, Sch.20, para.30 note that the interest (which is not, of course, a qualifying interest in possession) only has to be in existence immediately before the minor's death. There is a similar amendment in TCGA 1992, s.73(2a)(a) dealing with the situation when the settlement ends with the death.
[59] For IPDIs, see Ch. 19.

(i) This is an IPDI since it cannot be a BMT and although capital vests at the requisite age for the purpose of the s.71D trust, IPDIs take precedence.[60]

(ii) Assume however that the trustees exercise their power to advance capital to the child by providing that he will become entitled to capital at 18. He continues to retain an interest in possession. This will satisfy the conditions in s.71A for a BMT and it would therefore appear that it ceases to be an IPDI trust, instead becoming a BMT. This follows from s.49A(5) which requires that "condition 3" (that s.71A does not apply to the property) "has been satisfied at all times since L became beneficially entitled to the interest in possession".

(iii) The IHT consequence if this were to happen is that the termination of the IPDI will be a PET by the child as a result of the revised PET definition in IHTA 1984, s.3A(1A)(iii)(3B). The curious result would then be that if the child were to die within seven years before having attained 18, although the ending of the BMT on death under 18 is not chargeable and he may well have continued to have an interest in possession, the PET will have failed and so IHT may be payable. Care should therefore be exercised before a trust is converted into a BMT.

Drafting a BMT

25.26 Whereas the drafting of an A+M trust was frequently a matter that required the equivalent of a higher degree in rocket science that is not the case with a BMT. There is so little room for manoeuver that the trusts will, of necessity, be straightforward. For instance:

> "I leave my residue on trust for my daughter Dolly contingently on attaining the age of 18 absolutely and subject thereto (insert default trusts)".

In the case of more than one child:

> "I leave my residue on trust for such of my children as (shall survive me and) attain the age of 18 and if more than one in equal shares absolutely and subject thereto (insert default trusts)."

If a child dies and the property passes to his siblings outright at 18 the share remains subject to the BMT not the relevant property regime.

25.27 Other types of substitutionary clauses are, however, problematic:

> "provided that if any child dies before me or before reaching the age of 18 leaving a child or children living at my death or born thereafter who reach the age of 21 then such child or children shall take by substitution and if more than one in equal shares the share of my residue which his her or their parent would have taken had such parent survived me and attained a vested interest".

---

[60] IHTA 1984, s.49A; 71D(5)(c)(ii) and see 25.40.

Clauses such as this are commonly used in order to preserve equality between the testator's children and their issue. However the definition of a BMT does not generally allow for substitutionary interests.[61] This has the following consequences:

1. If at the death of the testator all his children are minors and alive this is a bereaved minor trust. If subsequently a child dies in circumstances when the substitution rules apply and that deceased child's issue take then (a) there will be no IHT exit charge but (b) that portion of the fund will then be held on a relevant property trust.
2. If at the time of the death of the testator one of his children had died and the substitutionary rules apply so the child's issue take that share, the share for the issue of the deceased child will be held on a relevant property trust and the remaining shares of the minor children of the testator in a BMT.

In practice it is obviously fairly unlikely that a child will die under 18 leaving issue. However it is not uncommon for grandparents to want to benefit their grandchildren rather than adult children particularly if the adult children predecease. **25.28**

EXAMPLE 25.5

Andrew has three adult children X, Y and Z. They are all married with children. He leaves his property outright to his children with substitutional provisions for grandchildren at 18 if one of the children dies before him. X dies before Andrew leaving three young children who under Andrew's will take X's share in equal shares if they reach 18. Unless they are given immediate interests in possession (which would be IPDIs)[62] their shares will be held on relevant property trusts.

It will be sensible to include a widened power of advancement in all cases. Some of the potential difficulties posed by substitutionary clauses may then be solved as follows:

(i) the substitutionary trusts for the deceased's child's issue fall within the relevant property regime (as discussed above) and hence within IHTA 1984, s.144[63];
(ii) if desired, therefore, the trustees could exercise their power of advancement to *either* terminate the trusts (in which case if the beneficiaries were minor bare trusts would arise) *or* alternatively could create an IPDI interest for the beneficiaries with capital at (say) 18 or 21.[64] Although absolute parity of treatment would not

---

[61] See *Example 25.2(4)*.
[62] On IPDIs, see 25.29.
[63] See 29.49.
[64] For a precedent clause setting up an IPDI interest in possession for a minor, see App.II A2.43. To obtain reading-back under s.144 the interest must arise within two years of the testator's death.

then be obtained with the surviving children, the disparity of treatment that would result if a relevant property trust of the substituted share continued in being is avoided. *Note especially*:

(a) the great advantage of a BMT is the absence of IHT charges during and on the ending of the trust together with CGT hold-over relief;
(b) by contrast, an IPDI trust risks an IHT charge on the death of the beneficiary and although there is no IHT charge when the assets are advanced out to the beneficiary CGT hold-over relief will only be available if the trust property is business assets within TCGA 1992, s.165. However, there is a capital gains tax uplift on the death of a IPDI beneficiary;
(c) to leave the substituted share to be held on relevant property trusts means that IHT anniversary and exit charges will arise. Other settlements in the will (e.g. the BMT) will be aggregated (since they are related settlements) in order to work out the rate of charge. And, of course, there will be the administrative inconvenience of a part of the trust fund being subject to a different IHT regime with attendant compliance costs;
(d) it remains unsatisfactory that the position under wills is different from that which arises on intestacy.

A wide power of advancement would not, however, prevent relevant property trusts arising if a child died with an IPDI and the trust was established by the will of a grandparent.

Example 25.6

> Elizabeth died in 2007 leaving her property on an IPDI trust for her daughter Emma who is 45. Emma died unexpectedly in 2009 and the property became held on trust for her two minor children in equal shares contingently on reaching 18. Although Emma has died and hence the children are bereaved minors the trust is established under the will of the grandmother not the mother and therefore on the death of Emma the settled property held for her children is taxed under the relevant property regime. The power of advancement cannot be exercised to give the grandchildren IPDIs.

18–25 (s.71D) TRUSTS

25.29 These provisions were introduced into the 2006 Finance (No. 2) Bill by the Government in response to criticisms that the BMT was unsatisfactory in requiring capital to vest at 18.[65] Explaining the introduction of these

---

[65] See IHTA 1984, s.71D–G inserted by FA 2006, Sch.20, para.1. As with BMT, trusts created *before* March 22, 2006 can fall within s.71D.

provisions, the Paymaster General, the Rt. Hon. Dawn Primarolo, commented as follows:

> "The amendments tabled by the Government make sure that the legislation for trusts for bereaved minors operates in line with our intentions When a trust that is set up for a child in the event of the death of their parent is set to run on until the child is 18 and 25, the amendments provide that charges—as the hon. Member for Chipping Barnet acknowledged—will apply only after the child's 18th birthday. Amendment No. 384 makes it clear that the term 'parent', in the context of a new trust for bereaved minors, extends to step-parents. Taken together, the amendments mean that the rules will operate fairly, but of course if there is an absolute disagreement on whether the age should be 18 or 25, that cannot be resolved in this Committee; that is where the Government stand on the issue."[66]

25.30 The basic conditions to be satisfied are the same as for the BMT with the key difference that capital (together with income and accumulations of income) must vest in the beneficiary no later than the age of 25 (instead of 18). *Accordingly—*

(i) s.71D trusts can only be set up by will[67];

(ii) the trusts must *not* be A + M; BMT; IPDI trusts; interest in possession trusts in which the beneficiary became entitled to the interest before March 22, 2006; a TSI; or a disabled trust within IHTA 1984, s.89[68];

(iii) the testator must be the parent of the beneficiary;

(iv) until the beneficiary becomes entitled to the trust fund (which must not be later than age 25) any capital applied must be applied for his benefit and any income either paid out to him or accumulated for his benefit;

(v) as with BMT the trusts must "secure" that capital vests not later than the designated age and the existence of the statutory or an express power of advancement is permitted.[69]

EXAMPLE 25.7

> In his will Hugh made provision for his children Hattie and Henry (aged 21 and 15 respectively at the time of Hugh's death) by dividing his estate between them equally on the following trusts:

---

[66] Hansard Standing Committee Debate, June 14, 2006 Col. 604.
[67] Or under the Criminal Compensation Scheme: see generally IHTA 1984, s.71D(2). The statutory trusts for issue on intestacy will not qualify since they fall under s.71A (a BMT): see IHTA 1984, s.71D(5)(a). As with BMT, these trusts can also be set up by an instrument of variation and as a result of IHTA 1984, s.144 (in both cases "a reading-back" ensures that the trusts are set up on death).
[68] IHTA 1984, s.71D(5). Comprehensive though this list of exclusions would appear to be it is worth bearing in mind that a s.71D trust can arise before March 22, 2006 and that the list does not include a disabled person's interest trust under s.89B (which does not fall within s.89) so that there would appear to be a potential overlap.
[69] See 25.18.

(i) *in the case of Hattie's share*: to Hattie absolutely on her surviving to age 25: failing which the share is to be held on wide discretionary trusts;
(ii) *in the case of Henry's share*: to pay the income and capital to Henry at 25 but the trustees have an overriding power of appointment which they can exercise at any time in favour of a wide discretionary class including Hattie and Henry. The trustees are also enabled to release this power of appointment.

The IHT position is as follows:

(i) *Hattie's share*: because she is aged over 18 she will be entitled to the income from the share (see TA 1925, s.31 which vests income at 18 in this case). Although capital vests in her at 25 this is an IPDI not an 18.25 (s.71D) trust.[70,71] Accordingly capital of the share will be treated as part of Hattie's estate (under IHTA 1984, s.49(1)) and when she becomes 25 (so that the trust ends) there will be no IHT charge.[72] If Hattie dies before becoming 25, IHT will be charged on her share.[73]

Contrast the position if Hattie had been 17 when Hugh died: she does not have an IPDI: instead the trust falls within s.71D given that capital will vest in her at 25. Accordingly, there is no IHT charge when she becomes entitled to income at 18 but at 25 there will be the special IHT exit charge for 18–25 (s.71D) trusts[74] and CGT hold-over relief will be available.[75]

If Hattie (17 at Hugh's death) were to die before becoming entitled to the capital: there will be no IHT charge if this happens before she becomes 18 but thereafter there will be a charge under the special charging provisions on the ending of the s.71D trust.[76]

(ii) *Henry's share*: given his age Henry is not entitled to income from his share at the death of Hugh so does not enjoy an IPDI. Nor do the trusts fall within s.71D given the existence of the overriding power of appointment since they do not secure that he will become entitled to capital at 25. Accordingly this portion of the residue is held on a relevant property settlement. Were the

---

[70] IHTA 1984, s.71D(5)(a)(ii).
[71] If Hugh died before March 22, 2006 then the interest taken by Hattie would be a pre March 22, 2006 interest in possession and therefore transitional serial interests could arise before 2008. Hence Hattie's capital entitlement could be deferred indefinitely and her interest in possession extended if the trustees exercise a widened power of advancement by making a settled advance. The relevant property regime would not apply. By contrast, on the death of Hugh *after* March 21, 2006 if her capital entitlement is deferred beyond 25, the trust enters the relevant property regime with an entry charge when the power of advancement is exercised.
[72] IHTA 1984, s.53(2). CGT hold-over relief will not be available unless the assets are business property within TCGA 1992, s.165.
[73] IHTA 1984, s.49(1); s.4.
[74] See 25.31 below.
[75] Under TCGA 1992, s.260(2)(a): see 9.33.
[76] Query the position if on Hattie's death under the age of 25 the share was held in trust for Henry at 25. It would seem that there will be no charge on the ending of Hattie's s.71D trust because a new s.71D trust for Henry will arise.

trustees to release their power of appointment within two years of Hugh's death, reading back under s.144 results in the *s.71D conditions being met*.[77] If they released their power more than two years after Hugh's death the relevant property settlement would be replaced by a s.71D trust and there would be an IHT exit charge.[78]

Taxation of s.71D trusts

In crude terms there is a price to pay for retaining capital in trust beyond the age of 18. A special charging regime is provided for in IHTA 1984, s.71F–G and the following matters should be borne in mind in approaching these, at first sight, somewhat daunting provisions: **25.31**

(i) the basic charge in s.71E(1) occurs where settled property ceases to be property to which s.71D applies or where the trustees make a depreciatory disposition[79];

(ii) tax is *not*, however, charged

- if the bereaved miner becomes entitled to the capital and income of the trust fund on or before attaining 18[80];
- if the beneficiary dies under the age of 18[81];
- if the property becomes held on a BMT for the beneficiary before he is 18[82];
- if the property is paid or applied for the benefit of the beneficiary on or before he attains the age of 18.[83]

(iii) there are also some additional exclusions from charge which have no counterpart in the BMT provisions. These are:

- no tax is charged on a payment of costs or expenses; *or*
- on a payment or liability to make a payment which will be the income of any person for the purposes of income tax (or would be if he were UK resident)[84];
- in the case of a depreciatory disposition there is *no tax charge* if the disposition is such that—were the trustees beneficially entitled

---

[77] IHTA 1984, s.144.
[78] A s.71D trust must be established under the will of a deceased parent but they do not have to come into effect immediately on death (the position is the same for a bereaved minor trust: see 00.00): contrast IPDIs.
[79] Compare s.71B providing a similar structure for BMT.
[80] IHTA 1984, s.71E(2)(a). Here the trust is taxed in the same way as a BMT up to age 18.
[81] IHTA 1984, s.71E(2)(b). This again mirrors the BMT provisions.
[82] IHTA 1984, s.71E(2)(c). Accordingly if the testator exercises a power of advancement whereby capital is to vest in the beneficiary at 18 it appears that the trust has moved from being a s.71D trust to a s.71A BMT. It is a little difficult to see that this will have major practical implications save that if there is a prior IPDI the termination of that interest is only a PET if a BMT (not a s.71D trust) then arises.
[83] IHTA 1984, s.71E(2)(d) and compare s.71B(2)(c) in the case of BMT.
[84] IHTA 1984, s.71E(3) and see the similar exclusion in the case of relevant property settlements: IHTA 1984, s.65(5).

to the settled property—either IHTA 1984, s.10 or *ibid*. s.16 would prevent there being a transfer of value.[85]

(iv) the tax charge is levied either in accordance with the rules in s.71F or s.71G. Section 71F applies:

(a) on the beneficiary becoming absolutely entitled to the settled property on or before the age of 25;
(b) the death of the beneficiary after the age of 18;
(c) when property is paid or applied for the benefit of the beneficiary.

But remember in all cases that there is no charge if these events occur before the beneficiary is 18. The charge is therefore only levied on the period which has expired since the beneficiary's eighteenth birthday (or from when the trust arose if later).

All of which leaves s.71G as the residual charge: it applies when s.71F does not and is therefore concerned with depreciatory transactions.

EXAMPLE 25.8

The Wilton Trust established in the will of their father who died in 2007 provided for the twins Tim and Tom at 25 in equal shares. Assume that the value of the fund is £1m.

(i) When Tim is 24 the trustees make a settled advance of his 50 per cent share whereby he is given an interest in possession with remainder over to his wife and children.
(ii) Tom becomes 25 and takes the property absolutely.

The position is as follows:

(a) the Wilton Trust is a s.71D trust;
(b) the settled advance brings that trust to an end in respect of Tim's share (because Tim is no longer entitled to capital at 25) and triggers an exit charge under s.71F;
(c) the continuing trusts for Tim fall outside s.71D; he does not have a qualifying interest in possession and the relevant property rules apply;
(d) because Tim's trust continues there is no CGT disposal;
(e) so far as Tom is concerned his absolute entitlement brings the trust for him to an end; there is an IHT exit charge under s.71F and because this part of the settlement is ending a deemed disposal for CGT purposes on which hold-over relief is available.[86]

---

[85] There is a similar exclusion in the case of relevant property settlements, see IHTA 1984, s.65(6). S.10 is concerned with dispositions not intended to confer any gratuitous benefit and s.16 with grants of agricultural tenancies. On depreciatory transactions by trustees of interest in possession settlements, see IHTA 1984, s.52(3) and in the case of relevant property settlements, *ibid.* s.65(1)(b).

[86] Under TCGA 1992, s.260(2)(a).

Calculating the charge under s.71F

The charge closely resembles the relevant property charging regime but 25.32 because it is intended to tax the period between the beneficiary becoming 18 and the ending of the settlement (a period of at most seven years) it is inappropriate to impose an anniversary charge and instead the charge is in the form of a single *exit* charge. Take the case of Tim (in Example 25.8): his s.71D trust lasted from his eighteenth birthday until the settled advance was made just before his twenty-fourth birthday. Hence the charge is over a period of just under six years and is calculated as follows:

(i) calculate the value of the property ceasing to be comprised in the s.71D trust. Tim's share is worth £500,000[87];

(ii) calculate the number of complete quarters in the period beginning with the day on which he became 18 and ending with "the day before the occasion of charge".[88] In this case there are 23 complete quarters and so $^{23}/_{40}$ is the number in fortieths.[89] The "*relevant fraction*" is then $^{3}/_{10}$ multiplied by $^{23}/_{40}$;

(iii) the "*chargeable transfer*" is arrived at by aggregating (a) the value of the property in the settlement immediately after it commenced *plus* (b) the value, again immediately after it commenced, of property in a related settlement *plus* (c) the value of added property.[90] In this case there is no added property but Tom's settlement is related and hence it is necessary to know the value of the whole fund at the time when the twins' father died. Assume that this was £750,000. The chargeable transfer is of this amount treated as made by a hypothetical transferor who had cumulative transfers equal to the chargeable transfers made by the twins' father in the seven years before he died (disregarding any chargeable transfers made by his will). Assume that there were none;

(iv) the tax charge is on the basis of lifetime rates[91];

(v) the "*settlement rate*" can now be arrived at, being tax on the chargeable transfer (£750,000) made by a transfer—or with no cumulative chargeable transfers so that applying Sch.7 rates tax would be:

	£
chargeable transfer	750,000
less nil rate	(285,000)
balance	465,000
tax at 20% on balance equals	£93,000

this produces a settlement rate of **93,000/750,000 x 100 = *12.4%*.**

(vi) the amount of tax is given by:

---

[87] See IHTA 1984, s.71F(4): in this case the IHT will be paid out of Tim's share, not out of the property remaining in the settlement for Tom, and hence grossing-up does not apply.
[88] If the property only became comprised in the s.71D trust after the beneficiary had become 18, take this later time.
[89] IHTA 1984, s.71F(5) and compare *ibid.* s.68(2).
[90] IHTA 1984, s.71F(8).
[91] IHTA 1984, s.71F(8)(c).

chargeable amount (£500,000) × [relevant fraction (23/40) × (3/10) (0.2025) × settlement rate (12.4)]

Working through the bracketed calculations produces = *2.511%*.
So the tax is £500,000 × 2.511% = *£12.555*.

25.33 In the case of the s.71F charge, the top rate of charge is 4.2 per cent which would apply if:

(i) the property was held in trust until the beneficiary became 25 and the trust began not later than his eighteenth birthday. Hence the relevant fraction will be (28/40) × (3/10) = 0.21

(ii) the hypothetical transferor has exhausted his IHT nil rate band so that it is to be assumed that the rate applicable will be *20* per cent;

(iii) 0.21 × 20 = 4.2 per cent.

25.34 If the settled property had simply been treated as falling within the relevant property regime once the beneficiary attained 18 (ie if s.71D had not been introduced) the eventual IHT charge is likely to be similar. However, it might then be collected on the basis of an anniversary charge followed by a final exit charge. For instance, if in Example 25.8 the twins' father had died on October 1, 2008 and Tom had become 18 on October 1, 2017 and 25 in 2024 then there would have been an anniversary charge in 2018 followed by an exit charge in 2024: however, given that the anniversary charge would have made an allowance for the property only becoming relevant property in 2017 (when it ceased to enjoy the "up to 18" protection) the eventual result would have been much the same unless the property had increased in value significantly since death. There is, however, no doubt that the special regime in s.71F is simpler and easier administratively. It has the result that trustees can evaluate the IHT costs of keeping the settlement going with some precision. Taking the worst case scenario (a rate of 4.2 per cent at 25) the position is:

		rate (%)
(i)	distribute capital when Tom is 19	0.6
(ii)	distribute capital when Tom is 20	1.2
(iii)	distribute capital when Tom is 21	1.8
(iv)	distribute capital when Tom is 22	2.4
(v)	distribute capital when Tom is 23	3
(vi)	distribute capital when Tom is 24	3.6.

Calculating the charge under s.71G

25.35 As already stated, this charge is limited to depreciatory transactions and is levied on the basis of the charge under s.71B(3)[92] which in turn is modelled

---

[92] See 21.15.

on the exit charge for accumulation and maintenance trusts.[93] There are provisions to deal with the situation where, before becoming a s.71D trust, the settlement fell within s.71 when this charge is calculated by reference to the period during which the trust property was subject to both regimes.

EXAMPLE 25.9

The London A+M Trust was set up on April 1, 2000 for Emily and Emilia who were then aged 10 and 8 respectively. Before April 6, 2008 the terms of the trust are varied so as to provide for them to be absolutely entitled to capital at 25. If a charge to tax under s.71G arises in respect of a depreciatory disposition made by the trustees on April 1, 2014 the charge is calculated by reference to a 14 year period. The tax charge is as follows:

(i) first 10 years at 0.25 per cent for each quarter = 10 per cent +
(ii) final four years at 0.20 per cent for each quarter = 3.2 per cent
= *13.2 per cent*.[94]

Extending the life of a s.71D trust

As with s.71A/BMT the only permitted overriding power is one of advancement: see 25.31(ii) and Example 25.3(4). If that power is exercised in the case of a s.71D trust to postpone vesting beyond 25 then there will be an exit charge under s.71F and the continuing trusts will fall under the relevant property regime (see Example 25.8). Diagrammatically the charging regime for a s.71D trust can be represented as follows: 25.36

Vesting at 25	Settled advance postponing vesting
age of beneficiary	age of beneficiary
treated as BMT: no IHT charges	treated as BMT: no IHT charges
beneficiary aged 18	beneficiary aged 18
special charging regime top rate 4.2% at 25	special charging regime
beneficiary 25 (IHT charge at a top rate of 4.2%)	settled advance at 25 (IHT charge at a top rate of 4.2%)
	relevant property settlement (anniversary/ exit charges).

[93] IHTA 1984, s.71(5) incorporating the provisions of *ibid*. s.70(3)–(8) and (10). In the case of A+M trusts these provisions could provide for a charge at a top rate of 21 per cent.
[94] See IHTA, s.70(6).

Converting a s.71D trust into a BMT

25.37   It seems clear that such a conversion can occur: e.g. the trustees accelerate the vesting date of capital from 25 to 18 by use of their power of advancement. If this happens the trust ceases to be within the s.71D regime[95] but there is no exit charge.[96]

This leads to the question of whether it will ever be desirable to bring the s.71D trust into the BMT regime. In the following situation there will be an attraction in so doing.

EXAMPLE 25.11

Under a will, the residue of the estate is held on trust for the testator's surviving spouse for life (an IPDI)[97] remainder to his son Toby on attaining the age of 25. The trustees have a widened power of advancement. If the spouse is desirous of releasing her interest in possession the transfer of value that she makes is not a PET and will therefore be immediately chargeable. If, however, Toby's trust is modified (by exercise of the power of advancement) to vest capital in him when he gets to 18,[98] if the interest is then surrendered the spouse will make a PET.[99]

Converting a BMT into a s.71D trust

25.38   If trustees exercise a power of advancement to prevent vesting at 18 but do so in such a way that the conditions of s.71D are met then it is thought (a) that the trust ceases to be a BMT without an exit charge arising[1] and (b) becomes subject to the s.71D regime: see Example 25.3(5).[2]

An interest in possession trust?

25.39   Frequently trusts vesting capital at 25 will give the beneficiary a right to income before that age: e.g. as a result of TA 1925, s.31 or because the accumulation period expires before that age. The existence of such an interest:

(i) does not prevent the trust from satisfying the s.71D conditions;

---

[95] IHTA 1984, s.71D(5)(a).
[96] IHTA 1984, s.71E(1)(c).
[97] See Ch. 19; 25.12 and 25.13.
[98] It will, of course, be too late to perform this exercise if Toby is already over 18.
[99] See IHTA, 1984, s.3A(1A)(a)(iii); (3B).
[1] IHTA 1984, s.71B(2)(c).
[2] It is curious that the possibility of a trust moving from s.71A to 71D is not picked up in IHTA 1984, s.71G(3): presumably this is an occasion when Homer—in the guise of the legislative draftsman—has nodded.

(ii) is not a qualifying interest in possession for IHT purposes unless it is in existence when the testator dies (it will then be an IPDI);

(iii) but for CGT purposes will result in an uplifted value (but no charge) in the event that the beneficiary dies before the age of 18.[3] Note, however, that if he dies after that age there is no uplift (any CGT charge may be avoided by the making of a hold-over election under TCGA 1992 s.260(2)(a)). This distinction defies rational analysis!

Relationship with IPDIs

25.40 In effect IPDIs take precedence. Accordingly, if the will provides for the child to have an immediate right to income with capital vesting at 25 this is not a s.71D trust but instead gives the child a qualifying interest in possession.[4]

Relationship with s.144

25.41 Given that s.71A trusts must be established under the will of the deceased parent, rather than, as in the case of IPDIs having also to take effect from death, it follows that if they result from the conversion of a s.144 non interest in possession trust within two years of death they are read back to the date of death so that no exit charge on the ending of the earlier, relevant property settlement, will arise. By contrast, if the "conversion" of the s.144 trust occurs more than two years after the death, a s.71D trust will still come into being but only at that date and therefore with an IHT exit charge arising.[5]

The choice: BMT or s.71D?

25.42 The immediate reaction of many taxpayers is that they would prefer to postpone capital vesting until the child becomes 25 albeit that the trustees will be given a power to advance capital earlier. Further and at a slightly simplistic level, it might be thought that it will be sensible to draft wills with a s.71D trust on the basis that by advancing capital at 18 the trustees can, in effect, obtain BMT treatment. This is broadly correct but the following factors should be borne in mind.

(i) IHT will be chargeable once the trust continues after the beneficiary has attained 18 in accordance with the special charging regime in IHTA 1984, s.71F[6]; if the beneficiary dies there is an inheritance tax charge unless the property continues to be held on trust for other children of the deceased who are under the age of 25.

---

[3] TCGA 1992, s.72(1A)(b); s.73(2A)(b).
[4] Contrast the position with a BMT. IHTA, s.49A; s.71D(5)(c)(ii).
[5] This mirrors the position for s.71A BMT: see 25.24.
[6] See 25.32.

(ii) a PET will arise on the *inter vivos* ending of an IPDI but only if the continuing trust is a BMT: not if it is a s.71D trust.[7]

(iii) CGT death uplift is only available if the beneficiary enjoys an interest in possession and dies before the age of 18.[8] In fact the uplift is available whether the trust is a BMT or s.71D trust and the key features of the relief are (a) that the beneficiary must enjoy an interest in possession and (b) must die under the age of 18.

One further factor to bear in mind is that a BMT can always be extended by making a settled advance (assuming the trustees are given a widened power of advancement)[9] and become a s.71D trust[10] which may in turn be further extended.[11] The trust can then fall into the relevant property regime after the beneficiary reaches 25 and a wider class can potentially benefit.[12]

Drafting s.71D trusts

25.43   Similar comments to those made in connection with the drafting of BMT are appropriate: specifically, the legislation restricts any flexibility which the draftsmen might otherwise have sought to incorporate. The inclusion of an advancement type power is permitted as will be powers to give the beneficiary an interest in possession before e.g. the age of 18 when such an interest will commonly arise under TA 1925, s.31. However it is important not to include other powers which could be exercised so as to defeat the vesting requirements of IHTA 1984, s.71D(6)(a).[13]

s.71D link with existing accumulation and maintenance trusts

25.44   In general the object of s.71D is to regulate new will trusts for bereaved children of the testator. However, s.71D(3) and (4) are concerned with something quite different, namely trusts in existence on March 22, 2006 and which on that date satisfied the requirements for an accumulation and maintenance trust.[14] For such trusts there is a transitional period until April 6, 2008 after which the settlement will fall within the relevant property regime unless *either* (i) on that date the trusts provide for vesting of capital at 18 *or* (ii) as s.71D(3)

---

[7] See 25.11–13. It is sufficient if the s.71D trust has been converted into a BMT immediately before the interest in possession is terminated.
[8] It will be noted that the tope rate of charge is 4.2 per cent at age 25 which some will consider a fair price to pay for continuing the settlement. But, of course, rates may rise in the future.
[9] Specifically it will be desirable for the 50% restriction in TA 1925, s.32(1)(a) to be removed.
[10] See 25.38.
[11] See 25.36.
[12] Note that it may be hard to justify a settled advance as being for the benefit of a beneficiary under 25 if as a result of the advance a wider class can benefit. If the testator wants flexibility between siblings and their issue on distributions of income and capital it is preferable to fall within the relevant property regime from the outset.
[13] See App.II A2.26 for precedent s.71D trusts.
[14] Those requirements are in IHTA 1984, s.71 and are considered in Ch. 21.

provides, on that date the settled property is held on trusts for the benefit of a person who has not yet attained 25 and the normal conditions relating to the vesting of the property at 25[15] are met.[16] It is important to realise that in this situation the requirements of s.71D(1) and (2) *do not apply*. Hence it does not matter that the accumulation and maintenance settlement was not created by will nor that the beneficiaries were not the minor children of the testator nor that the settlor is still alive. The majority of accumulation and maintenance settlements were, of course, created *inter vivos* in favour of the settlor's grandchildren and they can benefit from this legislation.

s.71D link with pre-March 22, interest in possession trusts

The position is as follows: 25.45

(i) a s.71D trust can be set up before March 22, 2006;

(ii) however, if the beneficiary enjoyed an interest in possession in the property on March 22, 2006, s.49(1) will apply to treat him as beneficially entitled to the settled property[17]; and

(iii) s.71D does not apply.[18]

OTHER DEATH OPTIONS

Bereaved minor and s.71D trusts may well not fulfil the requirements of the testator. For instance: 25.46

(i) they only enable trusts to be set up for his children and he will often want to benefit grandchildren;

(ii) they require vesting at either 18 or 25 which he may consider to be unacceptable.[19] Specifically, he may wish to keep the property settled for the indefinite future or wish for flexibility on distributions of income and capital between beneficiaries while they are still young.

The main alternatives available to such testators are— 25.47

(i) in the case of *minor grandchildren*, consider the possible benefits of a bare trust[20]; and

(ii) where flexibility is felt desirable and where there is a wish to retain a long term settlement structure consider the merits of

---

[15] These are laid down in s.71D(6).
[16] Illustrations of the "conversion" of a s.71 trust into s.71D are given in *Example 21.6*.
[17] Note that IHTA 1984, s.49(1B) only excludes BMT from the operation of s.49(1): see 25.40.
[18] IHTA 1984, s.71D(5)(c)(i).
[19] Of course, the trusts may be extended by settled advances: see 25.18, *Example 25.3(4)* and *Example 25.8*.
[20] See Ch. 30.

(a) an IPDI, *or*
(b) a discretionary trust.

25.48 An IPDI can be set up giving an immediate interest in possession to a minor beneficiary: see Chapter 19 and, for a precedent clause, Appendix II at A2.43. No age of capital entitlement is required. Indeed it may be desirable not to insert an age when they take capital in order to avoid the interest in possession ceasing to be an IPDI if a settled advance is made.

25.49 The use of a "full blown" discretionary trust will involve an evaluation of the benefits derived from the continuing trust structure as against the periodic IHT charge. Unless the testator wishes the trustees to retain flexibility over who benefits, one option if he is a parent with young children may be to use the s.71D trust so that at least if he dies while the children are young there are no anniversary or other inheritance tax charges. The settled power of advancement can then be used to extend the trusts later—although it will, of course, have to be exercised for the benefit of that particular child and therefore there is only limited scope for trusts which benefit a wider class of beneficiaries.

Chapter 26

TRUSTS FOR VULNERABLE AND DISABLED BENEFICIARIES

- Income tax rules **(26.04)**
- CGT treatment **(26.14)**
- Inheritance tax before March 22, 2006 **(26.18)**
- Inheritance tax from March 22, 2006 **(26.23)**

26.01 It is often not desirable that the whole of the income arising in any tax year for the benefit of a disabled person or for the benefit of minors who have lost a parent should be paid out to those beneficiaries. With the increase in the income tax rate applicable to trusts to 40 per cent, FA 2005 introduced special income tax treatment for *qualifying trusts* for *vulnerable beneficiaries*, the effect of which was backdated to April 6, 2004.[1]

Qualifying trusts for *disabled persons* are differently defined in the IHT and CGT legislation and also qualify for certain reliefs from those taxes.[2] Since lifetime trusts set up after March 21, 2006 will generally be chargeable transfers for IHT purposes, trusts which create a disabled person's interest (which can still be established by a PET) have become of increased significance.[3]

A major difficulty is that the definition of a qualifying trust is different for each tax!

26.02 It is important to be clear about the aims of a particular trust in the context of the legislation. Is the primary purpose to obtain IHT advantages or is income tax saving the objective? Is a paramount objective to prevent loss of means testing benefits? If so, it may not be possible to obtain the tax reliefs as well. Often the tax reliefs require capital or income to be paid out to the disabled person who may then lose state benefits. Capital gains tax reliefs during the beneficialy's lifetime will rarely be a major issue unless hold-over relief is desired.[4] However, it may be important to secure the base cost uplift for capital gains tax purposes on the death of a beneficiary in which case an interest in possession trust will be required.

---

[1] FA 2005, Pt 2, Ch. 4 (ss.23–45).
[2] See IHTA 1984, s.89 and s.89A–B (inserted by FA 2006, Sch.20, para.6) and TCGA 1992, s.3, Sch.1, para.1 amended by FA 1993, s.83 and by SI 1996/2975.
[3] See 14.08 *et seq*.
[4] See Ch. 9.

Who should be treated as disabled or vulnerable for these purposes?

26.03 Calls in the 2006 Finance Bill Standing Committee to adopt the Disability Discrimination Act 1995 definition of a disabled person for inheritance tax purposes as:

> "a person who has a physical or mental impairment which has a substantial and long term adverse effect on his ability to carry out normal day to day activities"

were rejected by the Government.[5] The current definition of mental incapacity based on the Mental Health Act 1983 is "incapable of managing his property or administering his affairs." As one Opposition MP said:

> "Many of those whom we think of as vulnerable are neither disabled nor lacking in mental capacity. It is a class of people that includes the naïve and impressionable as well as the dissolute and insatiable."

The 1983 definition does not cater for persons with partial or fluctuating mental capacity or those with a progressive illness which would in time lead to loss of capacity.[6] The Opposition called for the definition in the Mental Capacity Act 2005 (due to come into force in 2007) to be adopted, on the basis that at least it would cater for those with partial capacity rather than the all or nothing test of the MHA 1983.[7]

INCOME TAX RULES

26.04 To obtain special income tax treatment the trust must be a *qualifying* trust for *vulnerable beneficiaries*. Vulnerable beneficiaries fall into two groups:

---

[5] See *Taxation* July 27, 2006 article by Robin Williamson of Low Incomes Tax Reform Group for trenchant criticism of the inheritance tax legislation.

[6] Alzheimer's, Parkinson's and HIV are examples of a progressive illness which may be dealt with by a self-settlement but not otherwise until the illness is sufficiently far advanced for the beneficiary to be classified as disabled within the s.89(4) meaning.

[7] It seems odd that the Government resisted attempts to adopt the more modern definition of mental incapacity that it has introduced elsewhere—presumably more people might qualify and therefore it would cost the Treasury more! The MCA 2005 definition that was requested by the various lobby groups does not cater for those with a progressive illness but does cater for partial or fluctuating capacity:

"For the purposes of this Act a person lacks capacity in relation *to a matter* if at the material time he is unable to make a decision for himself . . . because of an impairment of, or a disturbance in the functioning of, the mind or brain . . . It does not matter whether the impairment or disturbance is permanent or temporary."

The Government did in the end allow self-settlements where there was a progressive illness.

Disabled persons

A "disabled person" is a person who is incapable by reason of mental disorder **26.05**
of administering his property or managing his affairs[8]; or who is in receipt of an
attendance allowance under the Social Security Contributions and Benefits Act
1992 s.64; or in receipt of a disability living allowance under the Social Security
Contributions and Benefits Act 1992 s.71 by virtue of entitlement to the care
component at the highest or middle rate.[9] A person may be treated as being in
receipt of an attendance allowance or disability living allowance provided that
they would be entitled to receive the relevant allowances if they were to meet the
necessary residence requirements.[10] Note that people resident in the UK who
claim other disability benefits or who do not claim benefits at all, are excluded.

Relevant minors

These are persons under the age of 18 who have lost at least one parent.[11] **26.06**

What are qualifying trusts for income tax purposes?

Trusts for *disabled persons* will be qualifying provided that, during the disabled **26.07**
person's lifetime or until the earlier termination of the trusts, any settled

---

[8] Mental disorder is defined in MHA as "mental illness, arrested or incomplete development of mind, psychopathic disorder and any other disorder or disability of mind which results in abnormally aggressive or seriously irresponsible conduct."
[9] FA 2005, s.38(1). To qualify for the *middle rate* disability living allowance you must be so severely disabled physically or mentally that you require:
  frequent attention from another person throughout the day in connection with your bodily functions; or
  continual supervision throughout the day in order to avoid substantial danger to yourself or others; or
  prolonged or repeated attention at night in connection with your bodily functions; or
  another person to be awake at night for a prolonged period or at frequent intervals to watch over you in order to avoid substantial danger to yourself or others.
(i.e. you must have either daytime or nightime supervision needs).
  To qualify for the *highest rate* disability living allowance you must be so severely disabled physically or mentally that you require:
  frequent attention throughout the day in connection with your bodily functions, or continual supervision throughout the day in order to avoid substantial danger to yourself or others; *and*
  prolonged or repeated attention at night in connection with your bodily functions; or in order to avoid substantial danger to yourself or others you require another person to be awake at night for a prolonged period or af frequent intervals to watch over you; or
  you are terminally ill.
(i.e. you must have both daytime and nightime supervision needs or be terminally ill.)
  To qualify for *attendance allowance* you must be aged 65+ and either terminally ill or if you were under 65 you would satisfy the conditions for disability living allowance care component at the highest or middle rate and have done so throughout a period of six months in the two years before the award begins.
[10] FA 2005, s.38(2).
[11] FA 2005, s.39. Note that it does not matter that the minor is married or has entered into a civil partnership: contrast the definition of a dependent child in the context of settlor-interested trusts: TCGA 1992, s.77(3A) inserted by FA 2006, Sch.20, para.3 and Ch. 9.

property (i.e. *capital*) applied for the benefit of a beneficiary must be applied for the benefit of the disabled person[12] and either the disabled person is entitled to all the *income* (if there is any)[13] or the income may not be applied for the benefit of any other person.[14]

This seems to envisage that if the trusts end while the disabled person is alive, capital can be applied for the benefit of another, non-disabled person. So, for example, suppose that A left property in his will to his children on interest in possession trusts in equal shares with the trusts terminating after five years and it was provided that all capital advancements in respect of each share must be made to the relevant child having the interest in possession during that five year period. If one child is disabled, the trust is qualifying in respect of that share even though at the end of the five year period the capital might pass to someone different.

26.08 Trusts for *relevant minors* will qualify only if they were established under the will of a deceased parent of the minor[15] or under the Criminal Injuries Compensation Scheme or as a result of the statutory trusts arising under the Administration of the Estates Act 1925 for a minor whose parent or parents have died intestate.[16]

26.09 Additional conditions are laid down in the case of trusts for relevant minors. These are:

(a) that the minor will, on reaching 18, become absolutely entitled to the property, any income arising from it and any income accumulated for his or her benefit before that time;

(b) until that time any of the property that is applied during the minor's lifetime must be applied for his or her benefit; and

(c) until that time and while the minor is alive, either the minor must be entitled to all of the income (if any) from the property or no such income may be applied for the benefit of any other person.[17]

Special income tax treatment

26.10 The aim is to ensure that the amount of income tax charged on income and gains arising to the trustees is *no more than it would have been had the income arisen directly to the vulnerable person*. This apparently simple objective is obscured by some impenetrable drafting. The amount of the relief is the difference between the total tax paid by the trustees and the vulnerable

---

[12] This does not *require* the distribution of capital but merely imposes restrictions on who can benefit if it is distributed.
[13] Hence the trust can give the disabled person an interest in possession.
[14] FA 2005, s.34: property is to be distinguished from income and is confined to the capital of the trust fund. Note that the capital condition in the IHT and CGT provisions (described below) only requires that during the lifetime of a disabled person not less than half the settled property must be applied for his benefit. The income tax requirement is that if *any* of the capital is applied for the benefit of a beneficiary it is *all* applied for the benefit of the vulnerable person.
[15] Hence grandparent trusts set up by will are not covered.
[16] FA 2005, s.35. Compare the definition of a bereaved minor trust for IHT purposes: see 25.13.
[17] FA 2005, s.35(3)–(4).

beneficiary *without special treatment* and the amount that would be paid if the trust income was deemed to be that of the vulnerable beneficiary. Hence account will be taken of the beneficiary's personal allowances and the starting and basic rate bands.[18]

Example 26.1

> Chris died in 2003 leaving his property in his will to Daisy contingently on her attaining the age of 18 with remainders over. Daisy is currently aged 10. During the tax year 2006/7 the trustees received rental income of £10,000 and dividend income of £25,000 (including the tax credit). They decided to accumulate this for Daisy's benefit. Daisy is a relevant minor and the trust is a qualifying trust. The special income tax treatment is arrived at as follows.
>
> Calculate first the trustees' liability and Daisy's tax liability under the general income tax rules. Compare this with the amount of income tax that would be paid if the trust income of £35,000 was deemed to be that of Daisy. Then reduce trustees' liability to income tax accordingly. Distributions to Daisy from the trust are ignored in calculating her liability.[19]

The Election

In order for the special income tax (and capital gains tax treatment[20]) to apply, the trustees and the vulnerable person (or if a minor, his parent or guardian) must jointly make an election.[21] Once made, the election is irrevocable. It can be made at any time up to 12 months after the filing date for the trustees' tax return: i.e. 12 months after January 31, following the end of the tax year in question. The earliest tax year to which an election can apply is 2004/5 with the time limit for making an election for that year being January 31, 2007. **26.11**

The notice of election must include a statement that the trusts are qualifying trusts; a declaration that all the information included is correct and a declaration by the beneficiary that he authorises the trustees to make the election. Although irrevocable the election is only effective until either the beneficiary ceases to be a vulnerable person or the trusts cease to be qualifying trusts or are terminated. Once made an election applies for both income tax and capital gains tax purposes.[22]

An election can be made where a trust has a mixture of vulnerable and non-vulnerable beneficiaries provided that the property for vulnerable beneficiaries is ring-fenced. If there is more than one vulnerable beneficiary of the same trust, a **26.12**

---

[18] FA 2005, ss.25–29. The reduction is given by reference to the formula TQTI–VQTI, the terms of which are defined in these sections.
[19] FA 2005, s.28(5).
[20] See 26.15
[21] FA 2005, s.37.
[22] On capital gains tax, see 26.15 *et seq*.

separate election is required for each beneficiary for whom the trustees wish to claim the special tax treatment. An election will not be effective in the tax year the vulnerable beneficiary dies. Note that no election is effective for income tax or capital gains tax purposes if the trust is settlor-interested although if the trust is settlor-interested for capital gains tax purposes *solely* because it can benefit a dependent child of the settlor then this is ignored and an election can be made. [23]

EXAMPLE 26.2

> Barbara is the settlor of a trust which she set up for her disabled minor child in June 2006. She and her spouse/civil partner and all other minor children of Barbara's are excluded. The trust is settlor-interested for capital gains tax purposes[24] but s.30(1A) allows a vulnerable beneficiary election to be made.

Personal injury payments

26.13 If a trust for a disabled beneficiary is set up as part of a personal injury claim, ITTOIA 2005, Pt 6, Ch. 8 provides that periodical payments are not subject to income tax. Section 733 limits this to cases where payments are made to the person entitled to the damages, a person who receives the payments on behalf of that person and a trustee who receives the payments on trust for the benefit of the vulnerable beneficiary. The terms of the trust must provide that the disabled person is, while alive, the only person who may benefit.[25]

CGT TREATMENT

There are two separate CGT relieving provisions, *which cannot be combined in a single trust*.

Annual exemption

26.14 Trustees are entitled to the same annual exempt amount as an individual if the trusts secure that:

> (a) not less than one-half of the property which is applied during the lifetime of the disabled person while the trust continues is applied for the benefit of a disabled beneficiary (the *capital condition*);

---

[23] s.30(1A).
[24] See Ch. 11.
[25] While this will satisfy the requirements for income tax vulnerable beneficiary treatment it will not satisfy the requirements of IHTA 1984, s.89: see 26.18 *et seq*.

(b) that a disabled beneficiary is entitled to not less than half of the income arising from the property, or no such income may be applied for the benefit of any other person (the *income condition*).[26]

The presence of powers of advancement will not as such disqualify the trust from relief and requirements that income be applied for qualifying purposes during the lifetime of a person are deemed satisfied if income is applied for such purposes during a period when it is held for that person on disabled trusts. The definition of disabled person is the same as that adopted for income tax purposes.[27] Note also that this definition of qualifying trust (rather than the definition in 26.15 below) applies for determining whether a gift to a settlor-interested trust for a disabled person is capable of qualifying for hold-over relief.[28]

Vulnerable beneficiaries

26.15 In addition, there is a separate capital gains tax relief for trusts for vulnerable beneficiaries which was introduced in FA 2005 if the trust is qualifying and an election is made.[29] In order to be qualifying the same conditions must be satisfied as in the income tax provisions (i.e. the trust must be for a relevant minor held on the same conditions as set out in 26.08 or be for a disabled beneficiary held subject to the same conditions as in 26.07). The most notable difference from the capital gains tax definition of disabled trust for the purposes of the annual exemption and hold over relief is that FA 2005, ss.23–37 require that if *any of the capital* is applied for the benefit of a beneficiary it must be applied for the benefit of a disabled person and that the disabled person is either entitled to all of the income arising from any of the property or no such income may be applied for the benefit of any other person.

The following capital gains tax relief is given:

(1) If the vulnerable person is *UK resident*, CGT is charged as if he were a settlor in relation to the settlement. Hence CGT is charged on the vulnerable beneficiary with a right of reimbursement and therefore the beneficiary benefits from his annual exemption and lower rates of tax. Note however that if the trust is settlor-interested (unless it is settlor-interested solely because the child is a dependent child of the settlor), then the election is not effective for capital gains tax purposes.[30]

(2) If the vulnerable person is *not UK resident* the trustees remain liable to CGT but their liability will be reduced by an amount equal to TQTG—VQTG where TQTG is the amount of CGT to which the trustees would, if not for the new rules, be liable in the tax year in respect of the qualifying trust gains, and VQTG is calculated using the formula TLVA-TLVB.

---

[26] TCGA 1992, Sch.1 para.1(1).
[27] TCGA 1992, Sch.1 para.1(1)(6). In 2006/7 the annual exemption for disabled trusts is £8,800.
[28] See Ch. 9 and s.169D of TCGA 1992. See 9.45.
[29] The trustees must be resident or ordinarily resident in the UK and the trust not settlor-interested so that the trustees are chargeable in respect of trust gains.
[30] See FA 2005, s.30.

TLVB = the total amount of income tax and capital gains tax to which the vulnerable person would be liable for the tax year if his income for the tax year were equal to the sum of his "acutal income" and the "trustees specially taxed income" and his taxable amount for capital gains tax purposes for the tax year were equal to his "deemed capital gains tax taxable amount".

TLVA is what TLVB would be if his taxable amount for capital gains tax purposes included his "notional s.77" gains for the tax year.

For this purpose the vulnerable person's *actual income* for a tax year is the income which would be assessable to income tax for the year on the assumption that he was resident and domiciled in the UK throughout the year. The *trustees' specially taxed income* for a tax year is the income of the trustees for the year from property held on qualifying trusts for the benefit of the vulnerable person in connection with which special income tax treatment applies by virtue of a claim under these provisions.

The *deemed capital gains tax taxable amount* for a tax year is the total of his taxable amount for the year calculated by reference only to actual gains and actual losses and his taxable amount calculated only by reference to *assumed gains* and *assumed losses*. *Assumed gains* are any chargeable gains other than actual gains in respect of which the vulnerable person would be charegable to capital gains tax on the assumption that he is resident and domiciled in the UK throughout the tax year and he has given a notice to HMRC quantifying the amount of any losses accruing in the tax year. *Notional s.77 gains* are the chargeable gains that would be treated as accruing to him under s.77 if he was a UK resident beneficiary of a vulnerable trust subject to an election. (It is hard to see why any non-UK resident beneficiary would be interested in becoming subject to these provisions anyway!)

Election for capital gains tax purposes

26.16 See 26.11 above: the election cannot be made separately from the income tax election.

26.17 This almost incomprehensible legislation, drafted in so-called plain English, cannot be regarded as a serious attempt to help vulnerable beneficiaries. A more useful course of action if the Government was serious about improving the situation of disabled persons would have been to ensure that the rules governing trusts for disabled beneficiaries were aligned between income tax, CGT and IHT.

INHERITANCE TAX BEFORE MARCH 22, 2006

26.18 IHTA 1984, s.89 provides that a trust which meets the s.89 conditions is not subject to the relevant property 10-year exit and set-up charges as the disabled person is deemed to have a qualifying interest in possession. Hence, a gift to the trust is a PET *or* if the disabled beneficiary himself set it up it is not a transfer of value.[31]

26.19 The s.89 conditions (which have not been materially changed in FA 2006 but have rather been extended to include other types of disabled trusts) are that the settled property must be held on trusts which provide that:

(a) during the lifetime of the disabled person, there is no entitlement to income (*the income condition*), *and*

(b) not less than half of the settled property which is applied during the lifetime of the disabled beneficiary must be applied for his benefit (the *capital condition*). (It does not actually have to be applied for the beneficiary so long as during the lifetime of the beneficiary not less than one-half cannot be applied for the benefit of anyone else.) There is no restriction on how the settled property passes after his death: i.e. it does not have to pass to anyone outright. The trusts can continue or end.

26.20 A "*disabled person*" is defined as:

(a) a person incapable by reason of mental disorder from managing his affairs or administering his property, *or*

(b) in receipt of an attendance allowance or in receipt of a disability living allowance at the highest or middle rate.

Favoured treatment is not lost if the person recovers after the settlement is made.

26.21 If the disabled person is the settlor of the trust then income can be accumulated during his lifetime. Therefore it is possible to provide that the income is either paid to the disabled person (or another) or accumulated. The settlor has no entitlement to income and yet income can be paid for his benefit.[32] This will ensure the disabled person does not lose means tested benefits.

If the disabled person is not the settlor, it is still possible to satisfy s.89 conditions after the accumulation period has expired and allow the trust to remain discretionary since the reference to "settled property" is to the capital of the trust fund and so a trust under which some or all the income can be applied for the benefit of a person other than the disabled person will still qualify for favoured treatment. Indeed there is no actual requirement that the disabled person should even be a member of the class of income beneficiaries. However, such a trust would not qualify for the CGT[33] full annual exemption nor as a trust for a vulnerable beneficiary. In the latter case the requirement is that all income must be paid or payable for the disabled person's benefit.

26.22 Assets in a s.89 trust do not qualify for the CGT uplift on the death of the disabled beneficiary because the disabled person only has a *deemed* interest in

---

[31] Until 1981 different provisions regulated disabled trusts: see IHTA 1984, s.74.
[32] See LPA 1925, s.164(1)(a) for the power to accumulate during the life of the settlor. Commonly accumulation is permitted for a period of 21 years from the creation of the settlement and during minorities.
[33] As noted above, to qualify for the full capital gains tax annual exemption, the disabled person must be *entitled* to not less than half the income arising from the trust or no such income may be applied for the benefit of any other person. (The capital requirement is the same as for s.89: the terms of the trust must provide that during the life of the beneficiary not less than half of the settled property which is applied during his lifetime is applied for his benefit.)

possession. Nevertheless the assets will be subject to inheritance tax on his death. The main advantage of such a trust was that because the disabled person had no *right* to income there was no loss of means tested benefits.[34]

If trustees advanced property to a beneficiary other than the disabled person during his lifetime this would be treated as a transfer of value by the disabled person.[35]

If the s.89 trust was not acceptable then a straightforward interest in possession trust could have been set up which gave the disabled person a life interest. This was simply taxed under s.49(1) in the normal way. The following Example illustrates the options available before the change in the IHT treatment of settlements on March 22, 2006.

EXAMPLE 26.3

(1) A is a disabled beneficiary who has inherited valuable property. Under the Court of Protection his guardian sets up a discretionary trust under which income can be accumulated during his lifetime but if distributed during his lifetime must be paid for his benefit. The terms of the trust also provide that if capital distributions are made, not less than half the trust capital must be applied for his benefit. The trust qualifies under s.89, IHTA 1984 as a disabled trust. No PET is made by A because he is deemed to have an interest in possession. There is no transfer of value for IHT purposes.

The trust will also qualify for the full annual capital gains tax exemption even though income can be accumulated during the life of the disabled person because it is not payable to anyone else during his lifetime. On the disabled person's death there will be no CGT base cost uplift but inheritance tax will be payable.

It is not possible to make a vulnerable beneficiary election. Even if the tax provisions were amended so that all the capital could be applied for A's benefit, he is the settlor and therefore an election is not possible.

(2) If before March 22, 2006 A settled funds on interest in possession trusts for himself there would be no difference from (1) above for inheritance tax purposes because there is no transfer of value. He is deemed to own the underlying property because he has a qualifying interest in possession. The main differences are that on his death there will be a base cost uplift to market value for capital gains tax purposes and, of course, his entitlement to income may mean that he loses means tested benefits.

EXAMPLE 26.4

In 2005 S decides to settle property on trust for his daughter T who is severely disabled. He is concerned about the possibility of T losing

---

[34] If the intention had been simply to make a PET then this could easily have been done by using an interest in possession trust prior to March 22, 2006.
[35] See s.52(1), IHTA.

means tested benefits. He faces the following choices:

(i) He can settle the funds on interest in possession trusts for T. This will be a PET by S. T will receive all the income and this may jeopardise means tested benefits. If the trust provides that any capital distributions made during her lifetime *must* be made to T or applied for her benefit then a vulnerable beneficiary's election can be made and gains and income will effectively be taxed at her rates. If no election is made, the trust would qualify for a full capital gains tax exemption. There is a CGT base cost uplift to market value on the settled property when T dies.

Alternatively

(ii) He can settle the funds on discretionary trusts for T and provide that any capital distributions must be applied as to at least half for T during her lifetime. This will be a PET for inheritance tax purposes because the trust falls under s.89. There are no exit or periodic charges. A vulnerable beneficiary election is not possible. There is no base cost uplift for capital gains tax purposes on the death of T. The full annual capital gains tax exemption is not available.

INHERITANCE TAX FROM MARCH 22, 2006

26.23 With the new rules for the IHT treatment of settlements introduced from March 22, 2006 the preservation of the s.89 special rules for disabled trusts is significant in that they are now (apart from other types of disabled trusts in s.89B) the only example of a qualifying interest in possession trust that can be established *inter vivos* by a PET. Initially F(No. 2)B 2006 made only minor amendments to the regime for disabled trusts. Subsequently more extensive changes were announced.[36] Apart from a limited change to the definition of disabled to bring it into line with the definition used for vulnerable beneficiaries, the legislation introduced two changes. *First*, to cover self-settlements where the settlor may reasonably expect to become disabled and *second*, an interest in possession in settled property to which a disabled person becomes entitled on or after March 22, 2006 will qualify as a disabled person's interest and is therefore outside the relevant property regime.

---

[36] Note that the definition of disabled person was extended to include non-residents who would otherwise qualify but otherwise has not changed. The House of Lords Economic Affairs Committee at para.201 criticised the lack of consultation between HMRC and the various bodies working in the field and felt that there should be greater alignment of the definitions and that it might be appropriate to include people who do not meet the conditions simply because they do not claim benefits to which they are entitled. For example, the new regime will not necessarily apply to trusts which are ordered to be set up by the courts as part of a personal damages award. In these cases it is not uncommon for the injured party to be in receipt of the lower care component of the disability living allowance.

Self-Settlements

26.24 Section 89A[37] introduced new rules for settlements set up by persons on or after March 22, 2006 if they have a condition expected to lead to a disability within the meaning of s.89(4) (if the settlor was already disabled then he can rely on the provisions in s.89 for disabled trusts generally). These provisions only apply if the person with the likely disability sets up the trust (a "*self-settlement*").

EXAMPLE 26.5

(1) A has just been diagnosed with Alzheimers. She has not yet lost mental capacity. She settles all her property into trust for herself on trusts which satisfy the requirements of s.89A (see below). This is not a transfer of value for inheritance tax purposes because she is treated as having a qualifying life interest. It is a "nothing". The property is taxed on her death but with no CGT base cost uplift unless she has an interest in possession in the settled property.

(2) As above, except that a contribution to the settlement is also made by A's child for her benefit. The contribution is a chargeable transfer by the child and is treated as being comprised in a separate settlement for IHT purposes which is taxed under the relevant property regime. If though, A had *already* lost mental capacity the addition by her daughter would be a PET assuming the trust qualifies under s.89.

(3) B is a young person who is not "financially acute" but not mentally disabled, nor likely to become so. She is "encouraged" to self-settle her inheritance from her aunt who died three years ago. The trust that she creates is not a disabled person's trust and is within the relevant property regime.[38] B makes a transfer of value when creating the trust.

26.25 The special conditions for s.89A to apply are as follows:

(i) A must satisfy HMRC that it was reasonable to expect that at the date of transfer into the trust he had a condition that would lead to him becoming disabled within the s.89 defintion.[39] Subsequent improvements in his condition will not affect the tax treatment of the settlement.

(ii) He is beneficially entitled to the property being settled immediately before it is transferred to the trust.[40] It is not clear whether he has to be entitled absolutely to the property or whether if he has a qualifying interest in possession in the property this is sufficient.

---

[37] Inserted by FA 2006, Sch.206(1) and (3).
[38] A could have entered into a deed of variation if he had acted within two years of his aunt's death and then he could have set up an IPDI for himself which would have been a qualifying interest in possession.
[39] IHTA 1984, s.89A(1)(b).
[40] IHTA 1984, s.89A(1)(a).

(iii) During the life of A no interest in possession subsists in the settled property.[41]

(iv) The provisions of the trust "secure" that if any of the settled property is applied during A's lifetime for the benefit of a beneficiary it is applied for the benefit of A (Condition 1) *and* also ensure that any power to bring the trust to an end during A's lifetime is such that in the event of the power being exercised either A or another person will then be absolutely entitled to the settled property or a disabled person's interest within either s.89B(1)(a) and (c)[42] will arise. (Condition 2).

26.26 It is far from easy to reconcile Conditions 1 and 2. The reference to settled property in Condition 1 is to "the capital of" the settlement. It would appear that whilst Condition 1 is concerned with an advancement type power (to pay or apply capital), Condition 2 is concerned with a power of appointment and the restriction is intended to ensure that if such a power is exercised during the disabled person's life it must either end the trust (i.e. make an outright appointment) or appoint into trusts creating a disabled person's interest (falling within s.89B(1)(a)—a s.89 trust—or s.89 (1)(c)—an interest in possession trust. This requirement makes little sense:

(i) if the trusts are terminated with the disabled person receiving the settled property this is a "nothing" for IHT purposes;
(ii) if another person becomes absolutely entitled he will make a PET;
(iii) if the property becomes held in the disabled trust indicated he will likewise make a PET.

In all other cases the disabled person would have made a chargeable transfer when the trusts continued but would that have mattered? It seems to be accepted that property in a s.89A trust can be appointed away from the disabled person so why make it a condition of obtaining s.89A status that, in general, the appointment must be absolute. The likely explanation is that it reflects the desire of HMRC to curtail the use of settlements whenever possible (see Appendix III A3.141).

EXAMPLE 26.6

Sissy, diagnosed with a condition that will lead to disability within the legislation, settles her property on trusts under which:

(i) during her lifetime the trustees have a discretion to pay income to a class of beneficaries including Sissy and her siblings with power to accumulate any surplus (this satisfies the requirements in s.89A(1)(c)(i): "during the life of [Sissy] no interest in possession in the settled property subsists");
(ii) the trust has a power to pay or apply capital for the benefit of any beneficiary but is limited by a proviso that during Sissy's lifetime it can only be exercised in her favour (this satisfies Condition 1);

---
[41] IHTA 1984, s.89A(1)(C).
[42] See 26.29.

(iii) the trustees also have a wide power of appointment in favour of any of the beneficiaries but again limited so that during Sissy's life the power can only be exercised *either* to make an outright appointment or to create trusts for a disabled person falling within IHA 1984, s.89 or which give the disabled beneficiary an interest in possession.

26.27 It is rather odd to refer to the trust being brought to an end if a disabled interest then arises. The reference is presumably to the existing s.89 A trust ending when either a person must become absolutely entitled or a qualifying disabled interest arises.

26.28 If the conditions in s.89A are satisfied A is treated as beneficially entitled to an interest in possession in the settled property (a "deemed" interest). Hence there is no transfer of value on setting up the trust since A's estate is not diminished. The tax consequences are therefore the same once the trust has been set up as for a s.89 trust.

"Disabled person's interest"

26.29 Section 89B inserts a new definition, "a disabled person's interest". Four different types of trust can qualify as a disabled person's interest.

Type (i) A s.89 trust for a disabled person ⎫
⎬ a *"deemed"* interest in possession
Type (ii) A s.89A self-settlement ⎭

Type (iii) An interest in possession trust for a disabled person—there are no capital conditions.   an *"actual"* interest in possession

Type (iv) An interest in possession trust created by a self-settlement where the s.89A conditions apart from Condition 2 in 26.25 above are met.

26.30 The significance of the concept of a "disabled person's interest" is that IHTA 1984, s.49(1A) provides that it is taxed in accordance with the rules in s.49(1): i.e. the beneficiary with the interest in possession (the disabled person) is treated as beneficially entitled to the property in which the interest subsists. As a result the *inter vivos* creation of the trust:

(i) will be a PET if made by a person other than the disabled person;

(ii) if made by the disabled person will be a "nothing".

26.31 Trusts which create a disabled person's interest are:

(i) a disabled trust falling within s.89: in this case the beneficiary has a "deemed" interest in possession;

(ii) a self-settlement within s.89A, a "deemed iip";

(iii) a self-settlement in which the disabled settlor is given an interest in possession. Note that as with s.89A settlements, the property must have been settled on or after March 22, 2006. Unlike s.89A the only restriction is that the trusts secure that if any of the settled property is applied during the disabled person's life it is applied for his benefit. This corresponds to Condition 1 in the s.89A legislation. Condition 2 from that legislation has not been incorporated.

EXAMPLE 26.7

> Sissy in Example 26.6 above decided instead of creating a settlement to comply with the s.89A requirements to settle property on an interest in possession trust for herself with remainders on continuing trusts for her children. The trustees are given a power to pay or apply capital which during Sissy's life can only be exercised in her favour. They also have a wide overriding power of appointment which would enable them to terminate Sissy's interest and to appoint the property on continuing trusts or outright for any person in the wide beneficial class. It would appear that this trust satisfies the requirements of s.89B(1)(a) and creates a "disabled person's interest" for Sissy.

(iv) "an interest in possession in settled property (other than one within s.89 or s.89A) to which a disabled person becomes entitled on or after March 22, 2006." Note that:

   (a) the settlement may have been set up before March 22, 2006 but the disabled interest must arise after March 21;
   (b) there are no restrictions on power to pay or apply capital or to terminate the settlement.

EXAMPLE 26.8

> The Rotham Family Trust was set up in 2000. Jenny has been entitled to an interest in possession but in 2007 this is terminated by the trustees who appoint Rowley, a disabled person, an interest in possession in the settled property. The position is that:
>
> (i) Rowley's interest is a "disabled person's interest" within s.89B(1)(c);
> (ii) Rowley's interest cannot be a transitional serial interest and so it does not matter when Jenny's interest is terminated (it could be after April 6, 2008);
> (iii) the termination of Jenny's interest involves the making of a PET by her;
> (iv) it does not matter that the trustees retain overriding powers of advancement/appointment which could be exercised to terminate Rowley's interest.

EXAMPLE 26.9

(1) A plans to settles property on trust for his disabled child—the trust can be interest in possession or discretionary. If it is interest in possession it is not necessary that capital can only be applied for the benefit of the disabled child. Hence A has more flexibility and can provide that the capital passes to someone else before or after the child death. An *inter vivos* transfer by A will be a PET.

(2) *Alternatively*, if A is a person who can satisfy HMRC that he will become a disabled person, he sets up an interest in possession trust for himself. In this case the terms of the trust must provide that if any capital is applied during A's lifetime it is applied for the benefit of A. On A's death the trusts can continue (in which case they will fall within the relevant property regime) or end but in either case there will be a 40 per cent tax charge (unless either the spouse or charity exemption applies).

26.32 The main differences between the various types of trust as listed above can be summarised as follows:

(i) Type (i) and Type (ii) trusts cannot qualify for the capital gains tax uplift on the death of the disabled beneficiary. Type (iii) and (iv) trusts can.[43]

(ii) Type (i) and (ii) trusts must give no entitlement to income: they are drafted as discretionary trusts. Type (iii) and (iv) trusts must give the disabled person or person who may become disabled actual entitlement to income as it arises. In Type (i) and (ii) trusts it is not even necessary that the disabled person receives the income or is an income benefiicary.

(iii) Type (i) trusts require that at least half the capital if applied during the disabled person's lifetime is applied for his benefit. Type (ii) and (iv) trusts require that if any of the capital is applied for a beneficiary during the settlor's life it is applied for his benefit. Type (iii) trusts do not impose any capital requirements.

(iv) Types (i), (iii) and (iv) trusts do not impose requirements on what is to happen in the event of the trust ending during the disabled person's lifetime. Type (ii) trusts do.

(v) A Type (ii) or (iv) trust must qualify as a disabled person's interest from the outset (by self-settlement). By contrast the other types can arise out of existing settlements.[44]

EXAMPLE 26.9

Vincent dies in August 2006 leaving his property on IPDI trusts for Chrissy with power to advance her capital and then to her children.

---

[43] See 7.46 *et seq.* and s.72(1B) of TCGA 1992.
[44] s.89A(1): This section applies to *property transferred* by a person A into settlement on or after March 22, 2006 if A was beneficially entitled to the property immediately before transferring it into settlement.

Chrissy is aware that she is likely soon to become mentally incapable. She decides that it is preferable she does not have entitlement to income. At her wish the trust is ended by a transfer of the settled property to her. She then sets up a s.89A trust which is discretionary. This is not a transfer of value by her. However, unlike the IPDI there can be no discretion for the trustees to be able to pay all the capital to someone other than Chrissy while she is alive.

The trustees cannot convert the existing IPDI into a s.89A trust. It is questionable whether if they transfer the property to a new (pilot) s.89A trust set up by her that will count as a s.89A trust. (Arguably Chrissy is beneficially entitled to the property before transfer since she has an IPDI in it, and therefore she will be treated as making the transfer into a new self-settlement.)

If however, Chrissy is *already* disabled or becomes disabled then the trustees could, assuming that they have appropriate powers and when she is disabled convert the IPDI into a s.89 (Type (i)) trust and this would be treated as a non-event for inheritance tax purposes because she is already deemed to be beneficially entitled to the property.

EXAMPLE 26.10

Assume the above facts i.e. that Vincent leaves property on IPDI trusts for his wife Chrissy, who is not disabled. However, some years later Chrissy's adult child Jane becomes severely disabled and Chrissy wants to make some provision for her. Can the IPDI trust now be converted into a s.89 disabled trust for Jane (whether discretionary within s.89 or interest in possession within s.89B(c)) such that it remains outside the relevant property regime? If so, is the conversion a PET by Chrissy or a chargeable transfer?

Section 3A(1A)(iii) refers to a "gift into a bereaved minor's trust" on the coming to an end of an IPDI but says nothing about a gift into a disabled trust. Section 3A(3B) has detailed provisions for dealing with conversions of IPDIs into BMIs but not for conversions of IPDI into disabled trusts. However, it appears unnecessary to have such provisions since the person with the IPDI is treated as beneficially entitled to the settled property and therefore if their interest is terminated they make a transfer of value. If that transfer of value constitutes a gift to a disabled trust then the gift can take effect as a PET under s.3A(1A)(c)(ii).

CHAPTER 27

REVERTER TO SETTLOR TRUSTS

- Tax treatment prior to December 5, 2005 **(27.02)**
- The IHT position prior to March 22, 2006 **(27.03)**
- The IHT position from March 22, 2006 **(27.19)**
- The POA position from December 5, 2005 **(27.28)**

27.01 Prior to December 5, 2005, reverter to settlor trusts had become increasingly popular for both IHT and CGT planning purposes and as a way of sorting out pre-owned assets income tax problems. However, the pre-Budget statement on December 5, 2005 made it clear that the latter use was to be stopped although the actual legislation was not published until Finance (No. 2) Bill 2006 in April 2006. The new IHT rules taxing settlements, apart from largely stopping the creation of new trusts benefiting from reverter to settlor relief, have also rendered the IHT position of existing reverter to settlor trusts problematic, particularly after the end of the transitional period on April 6, 2008.

This chapter first outlines the tax treatment of reverter to settlor trusts prior to December 5, 2005 and then considers the tax treatment of such trusts from that date.

TAX TREATMENT OF A REVERTER TO SETTLOR TRUST PRIOR TO DECEMBER 5, 2005

27.02 A trust which attracted IHT reverter to settlor relief involved the following ingredients—

(i) the trust fund was held on an interest in possession trust (note that property held in a discretionary trust could not benefit from reverter to settlor relief although, before March 22, 2006, it was of course possible to convert such a trust into a qualifying interest in possession trust)[1];

(ii) on the termination of the interest in possession (whether during the lifetime of the beneficiary or on his death) the trust fund had to revert to either—

(a) the settlor; *or to*

---

[1] The trust did not have to start off as interest in possession in order to qualify for reverter to settlor relief.

(b) the settlor's spouse or registered civil partner[2] during his lifetime provided they were UK domiciled; *or to*
(c) the settlor's widow or widower or surviving civil partner provided that this occurred within two years of the settlor's death and that person was UK domiciled;

(iii) the reverter could be absolutely or on interest in possession trusts.

It was not necessary for the settlor to be UK domiciled for relief to be available although in practice it was unlikely that a non-UK domiciled settlor would use such arrangements, because he could rely on the excluded property provisions.

INHERITANCE TAX POSITION PRIOR TO MARCH 22, 2006[3]

27.03 IHTA 1984 ss.53(3) and 54(1) provided that IHT was not chargeable on the termination of an interest in possession (whether on the death of the life tenant or otherwise) if, when the interest came to an end, the property in which the interest subsisted reverted to the living settlor.[4] Additionally, reverter to settlor relief applied where the settled property reverted to the spouse or civil partner of the settlor while the settlor was alive *or* to the widow/widower or surviving civil partner of the settlor within two years of his death.[5]

27.04 The result, if these conditions were satisfied, was that:

(i) IHT was not chargeable if the interest in possession ended during the lifetime of the beneficiary[6]; and
(ii) on the death of the beneficiary the value of the settled property was left out of account in determining the value of his estate immediately before his death.[7]

EXAMPLE 27.1

Angela set up a trust in 2000 for her father Fred for life reverter to Angela absolutely on the death of Fred or on earlier termination of Fred's interest. The trust owned the house in which Fred lived as his main residence. Fred died and the property passed back to Angela.

(i) the creation of the trust was a PET by Angela;
(ii) there was no IHT on the death of Fred as the property then reverted to Angela;

---

[2] From December 5, 2005.
[3] For HMRC guidance, see IHTM 04351-3; IHTM 16121–23.
[4] As already noted the reversion in these cases could be absolute or on interest in possession trusts for the settlor.
[5] See IHTA 1984, s.53(4) and s.54(2).
[6] Hence the ending of the interest in possession was not a potentially exempt transfer: see IHTA 1984, s.53(3); 53(4).
[7] This is discussed at 27.07.

(iii) if, instead, the property had reverted to Angela's spouse while Angela was alive or to her widower within two years of her death, there would still be no IHT payable on the ending of Fred's interest;

(iv) however, if Angela died while Fred was still alive, the trust fund had to revert to Angela's widower within two years of her death in order to secure the relief.[8]

27.05 The exemption was often used (as in the above example) when children wanted to provide for their parents or for other elderly relatives. In the above example, CGT principal private residence relief was available to the trustees if the house was sold during Fred's lifetime. This would not have been possible if the house had been owned by Angela and she simply allowed Fred to live there under licence. The reverter to settlor relief could also be useful where a settlor wanted to make provision for a minor child but wished to ensure that if the child died before becoming absolutely entitled, the funds would revert to him.[9] Additionally, the trust was sometimes used in a matrimonial context where one spouse was providing for another but wished to retain a long term interest in the assets being transferred. Finally, the exemption was sometimes used in the context of "s.102B sharing arrangements" to deal with the problems that arose if the donee moved out.[10]

27.06 The exemption was only applicable at the point when the settled property reverted to the settlor. Thus if property was settled on trust for A for life, then to B for life with a reverter to the settlor, C, there was no IHT on the death of B when the property reverted to C but there will have been IHT (subject to the availability of any other reliefs, such as the spouse exemption) on the death of A when it passed in trust for B.

Restrictions

27.07 The IHT relief was not available if—

(i) the settlor (or spouse/widow/widower etc as the case may be) had acquired a reversionary interest in the property for a consideration in money or money's worth. This restriction was extended to catch the situation where the settlor acquired the reversion as a result of transactions "which include a disposition for such consideration (whether to him or another) of that interest or of other property",[11]

(ii) the relief depended upon a reversionary interest having been transferred into a settlement on or after March 10, 1981.[12]

---

[8] This was an important practical point: whilst children may assume that parents die first it does not always happen. Deaths in the wrong order could result in multiple IHT charges.
[9] As discussed below, for relief to be available, the trust for the child had to be interest in possession: it could not, for instance, be in the form of an accumulation and maintenance trust.
[10] See 31.68.
[11] IHTA 1984, s.53(6); 54(3).
[12] IHTA 1984, s.53(5) and see s.54(3).

The first qualification was designed to prevent tax being avoided in the following way.

EXAMPLE 27.2

> Assume that Sol settled property on trust for Bill for life some time ago remainder to Bruce. Bill is elderly. The property settled is worth £500,000 and Bruce's reversion is worth £200,000. But for the above qualification the tax that would otherwise have been payable on Bill's death could have been avoided by the settlor Sol purchasing Bruce's reversion for £200,000 with the result that on Bill's death no charge would have arisen (thanks to the reverter to settlor relief) and the £200,000 would have reached Bruce free of tax.
>
> The second qualification was designed to counteract the sort of planning that proved successful in *IRC v Fitzwilliam*.[13]

EXAMPLE 27.3

> Many years ago Adam (now deceased) settled property on trust for Bertram for life remainder to Claude. Bertram is now elderly. On the death of Bertram an IHT charge would arise on the ending of his interest in possession. Bertram and Claude might have sought to avoid this charge by:
>
> (i) Claude settling his remainder interest on trusts for Bertram for life with remainder to himself. This would not involve any IHT charge (Claude's remainder interest was excluded property) nor any CGT charge (see TCGA 1992, s.76(1));
> (ii) Bertram then surrendered his life interest under the original settlement: no IHT was payable as he remained entitled to a qualifying interest in possession in the trust fund (see IHTA 1984, s.53(2)). (Query whether for CGT purposes there could be a charge on a deemed disposal under TCGA 1992, s.71 on the basis of the property passing into a new settlement);
> (iii) when Bertram subsequently died the property reverted to Claude.
>
> Due to the second qualification reverter to settlor relief is not available on Bertram's death since it depends on the transfer of a reversionary trust into a settlement. (Of course the scheme cannot generally be done after March 21, 2006 since the new settlement set up by Claude would not give Bertram a qualifying interest in possession unless he was disabled).

27.08 HMRC consider that the relief is only available if the property which reverts is the underlying property in which the interest in possession subsists. This

---

[13] [1993] S.T.C. 502

prevents arrangements which involve a settlement *of the interest in possession* (not within the statutory restriction considered above which is concerned with reversionary interests).

EXAMPLE 27.4

> Whiteacre was settled by Cynthia on trust for Robin for life remainder to Sarah. Assume that Robin settled his life interest on trust for Jane for her life remainder to Robin. The position was:
> (i) Robin's settlement involved a termination of his life interest under IHTA 1984, s.51 and was a PET;
> (ii) Jane was entitled to an interest in possession in Whiteacre but on her death there was no reverter to settlor relief on that property since what was reverting to Robin was the life interest which he settled and not Whiteacre.

Reservation of benefit and reverter to settlor trusts

27.09 By retaining a reversionary interest did the settlor reserve a benefit? In general the answer was no: the interest retained was not a reservation of benefit but a carve-out. The settlor retained his interest in reversion and merely gave away the immediate enjoyment of the settled property (viz the interest in possession).[14]

If, however, the trustees had power to appoint the settled funds back to the settlor at any time (i.e. to bring the interest in possession to an end), then the carve out argument was less persuasive —see the statements of Lightman J. in the *Eversden* case confirming that a settlor reserved a benefit when he was an object of his discretionary trust.[15]

The remainder interest would anyway have had some value in the settlor's estate because it was not excluded property.[16] However, if the interest could be defeated by the exercise of overriding powers of appointment its value was likely to be nominal. In any event, the planning was obviously done on the basis that the settlor would survive the life tenant. The Finance Act 2006 did not change the reservation of benefit rules in so far as they may affect the settlor of a reverter to settlor trust.

27.10 From the perspective of the life tenant the position was slightly different. Suppose he had previously owned the property but given it to X who then later settled it on trust for that life tenant reverter to X. In these circumstances the life tenant reserves a benefit in the property originally given away. However, it was not taxed under the reservation of benefit rules provided the interest in

---

[14] This was confirmed in an HMRC letter to the Law Society dated May 18, 1987. See also *Re Cochrane* [1906] 2 I.R. 200.
[15] The whole concept of a carve-out in reverter to settlor trusts is difficult to reconcile with the decision of the Court of Appeal in *Eversden* (see 31.40) that there is only a single gift to the interest in possession beneficiary.
[16] See IHTA 1984, s.48(1)(b).

possession continued until his death.[17] The *property* was in his estate but the *value* was ignored. As a result reverter to settlor trusts were sometimes seen as a way of preserving a sharing arrangement when the donee had ceased to occupy the property.

EXAMPLE 27.5

> Cynthia lived in Blueberry Villas with her daughter Jane. She gave Jane a 50% share in Villas relying on s.102B(4) of FA 1986 to avoid a reservation of benefit (this is a "sharing arrangement").[18] However, Jane unexpectedly married at age 45 and moved out. Cynthia was no longer protected from reservation of benefit. But if Jane settled her 50% share on reverter to settlor trusts giving Cynthia a life interest, then Cynthia reserved a benefit in the gifted share but it was not taxable on her death.[19]
>
> It might be thought that the distinction between property being comprised in the estate of the deceased life tenant but its value not being taxed is wafer thin but it is a distinction carefully drawn in a number of places in the IHT legislation: for instance, in relation to a business attracting 100 per cent relief (the business assets are in the estate but are untaxed) and in the context of the estate duty exemption for the surviving spouse which is carried over into IHT by IHTA 1984, Sch.6, para.2

Failed PET

If the settlor died within seven years of making the settlement, he had made a failed PET. In calculating the transfer of value, the value (if any) of his reversionary interest was taken into consideration.

27.11

EXAMPLE 27.6

> In February 1990 Alan settled property worth £100,000 on interest in possession trusts for his mother Mischa, remainder to him. His mother had a life expectancy of 10 years. Alan died two years after the settlement was made. At the date of the settlement Alan's reversionary interest was worth £20,000 and therefore the loss to his estate in making the transfer into trust was £80,000. By the time A died, however, his

---

[17] FA 1986, s.102(3).
[18] See further 31.57.
[19] See FA 1986, s.102(3) which taxes reservation of benefit property on the death of the donor unless the property forms part of his estate immediately before his death. Because of his life interest it does form part of his estate but because of the reverter to settlor relief the value is untaxed. The position would be different on an *inter vivos* termination of the life interest since s.102(4) does not deem the property to be part of the person's estate immediately before termination but simply deems a PET to arise.

reversionary interest was worth £40,000. He will have been taxed on his death on the value of the reversionary interest (£40,000) and the failed PET of £80,000 will be taxable.

A settlor-interested trust

27.12 The settlor retained an interest in the settlement for the purposes of income tax (see ITOIA 2005, s.624) and capital gains tax (see TCGA 1992, s.77), and therefore he (rather than the trustees or life tenant) would be subject to tax on any settlement income and chargeable gains. Reverter to settlor trusts were therefore commonly used to hold property which produced neither income nor chargeable gains, e.g. a family home which was occupied by the life tenant or an insurance bond.[20]

Capital gains tax before March 22, 2006

27.13 On the life tenant's death, if the trust then ended, the property was deemed to be disposed of at no gain no loss and the normal death uplift did *not* apply. The settlor would therefore receive back the trust assets without a CGT charge but (broadly speaking) at a base cost equal to the market value of the assets when he first put them into trust.[21]

For this reason it was normally preferable to ensure that on the death of the life tenant the settlor became entitled to an interest in possession with the trustees having power to advance him capital. This still secured the IHT reverter to settlor relief but meant that the death uplift was available for CGT purposes when the life tenant died.[22] (It is this aspect that is now a problem for existing reverter to settlor trusts which continue after April 6, 2008.)[23]

EXAMPLE 27.7

> In 1999 Kindly purchased a pleasant riverside flat for his mother which he settled on trusts under which she had an interest in possession and subject thereto on the following (alternative) trusts:
>
> > (i) *for Kindly absolutely*: when Mother dies and the property reverts to Kindly, IHT is avoided but there is no uplift in the CGT base cost of the flat so that if it has increased in value and is now sold by Kindly the gain will be taxable (see TCGA 1992, s.73(1)(b));

---

[20] Insurance products are considered generally in Ch. 33. Many employ a carve-out principle using a settlor interested trust.
[21] TCGA 1992, s.73(1)(b) which applies if the settlement ends on the death of the interest in possession beneficiary.
[22] TCGA 1992, s.72: there is no logic in the different CGT treatment of a continuing trust which is thought to result from a legislative oversight.
[23] See 27.20.

(ii) *for Kindly on interest in possession trusts*: IHT relief is available (as above) and there is nothing to prevent the normal CGT uplift from applying (see TCGA 1992, s.72 which does not contain a restriction similar to that in s.73). Some doubt had been expressed as to whether reverter to settlor relief was available where the property reverted to the settlor on interest in possession trusts rather than absolutely but the HMRC Manual confirmed at IHTM 16121 that relief was available.[24]

(iii) *for Kindly's wife either absolutely or on interest in possession trusts*: provided that Kindly is alive when the interest in possession of his mother ends, IHT relief was available in both cases. For CGT purposes the death uplift will be available in *both* cases (TCGA 1992, (s.73(1)(b) only excludes this if the property reverts to the *disponer*);

(iv) the same results as in (iii) follow if the property passes to Kindly's widow (either absolutely or on interest in possession trusts) *within two years of his death*. For CGT purposes the death uplift will be available.

Note that if the property is sold during Mother's life the trustees will be entitled to principal private residence relief under TCGA 1992, s.225. It does not matter, for this purpose, what trusts are to take effect after the mother's interest in possession.

Putting a house in the trust

A reverter to settlor trust was therefore often used to obtain principal private residence relief on what was effectively a second home of the settlor.

27.14

Example 27.8

Eric wanted to purchase a property for the use of his mother. In 2005 he settled cash on interest in possession trusts for his mother, reverter to himself. The trustees purchased the property. On the death of the mother in February 2006 there was no charge to IHT as a result of the reverter to settlor exemption.[25]

If the house had been sold during the mother's lifetime (while she was in occupation or within three years of her ceasing to occupy it) principal private residence relief under s.225 of the TCGA 1992 would have been available to the trustees, and no chargeable gains would arise to be assessed on the settlor, Eric, under TCGA 1992, s.77. This was advantageous since if Eric had bought the property personally then unless he was also in occupation, no principal private residence relief would have been available on the sale.[26]

---

[24] This will no longer be the case if the reverter to Kindly occurs after April 5, 2008: see 27.23.
[25] See IHTA 1984, s.53(3).
[26] Relief for dependent relatives was abolished in 1988: TGCA 1992 s.226.

POA regime prior to December 5, 2005

27.15 The POA Regime impacted on reverter to settlor trusts in two ways. *First*, HMRC consider that the POA charge can apply to the settlor if the trust fund includes intangibles.[27] *Second*, reverter to settlor trusts were used as a way of avoiding the POA charge.

27.16 Dealing with the first point, in the case of Eric and his mother (see Example 27.8 above), there was no charge on Eric under the POA Regime. Eric was not in occupation of the property and so the land charge had no application[28] despite the fact that he had either satisfied the disposal condition (if he settled the house) or the contribution condition (if he provided the trust with funds to purchase the house). If Eric later moved into the property with his mother, then para.3 might have proved a problem.[29]

Assume, however that Eric's mother moves into a nursing home and the trustees sell the house. At that point the trust holds intangibles (cash) and all the other conditions for the para.8 charge to apply are satisfied.[30] If Eric wished to keep the trust going to provide income for his mother (although he derives no income tax benefit from this since it is taxed on him) the trustees should invest in assets *other than* intangibles so that he is not subject to POA.

Once the trust property comprises land or chattels (which are not occupied or used by Eric), there is no POA charge.

EXAMPLE 27.9

If the cash from the sale of the house is (say) £1m, the chargeable amount for POA purposes for the whole year at 5% is £50,000. Assume the cash is held by the trustees for one month before being reinvested in land. The chargeable amount for the taxable period of one month is £4,166. This falls within the de minimis exemption and therefore Eric pays no tax. If, however, the cash sum was more and the taxable benefit was (say) £6,000, then tax is charged on Eric as follows. Assume also that the cash produces income (e.g. £1,000 in the relevant month), and that Eric is a 40% taxpayer.

Trust income

£400 income tax under ITTOI A 2005, s.624

POA Regime charge

Chargeable amount is

£6,000 less £400 = £5,600 × 40% = £2,240.

Total income tax liability is £2,640 (£2,240 + £400)

---

[27] See FA 2004, Sch.15, para.8.
[28] Under FA 2004, Sch.15, para.3.
[29] The remainder interest has value in his estate and will provide a partial exemption from the POA Regime within para.11(1). However, if, in addition to his reversionary interest, Eric is a beneficiary of the trust (e.g. he is an object of the trustees' overriding powers he will reserve a benefit and no POA is payable anyway. (See FA 2004, Sch.15, para.11(3)).
[30] FA 2004, Sch.15, para.8.

In these circumstances there is no benefit to Eric in keeping the trust going and it is preferable to appoint him an interest in possession to take effect immediately on the sale of the house. If an interest in possession is appointed to Eric before April 2008 it will be a transitional serial interest. After April 5, 2008 the trust would need to be ended in favour of Eric or his wife to obtain reverter to settlor relief.[31]

Reverter to settlor trusts were also used to avoid the POA charge. **27.17**

EXAMPLE 27.10

> Emma carried out an *Ingram* scheme in 1998 giving the freehold reversion to her daughter Rose.[32] Rose might decide to settle the freehold reversion in 2005 on interest in possession trusts for her mother Emma with reverter to Rose. In these circumstances the entire property (freehold and lease) formed part of Emma's estate under FA 2004, Sch.15 para.11(1) so that there was no POA charge. Provided that on Emma's death the settled property (the freehold interest) reverted to Rose, relief was available from inheritance tax on Emma's death.[33] This position changed from December 5, 2005 (see 27.29, below).
>
> However, the analysis was different if Emma's interest in possession was ended during her lifetime. In these circumstances there was a deemed PET because her reservation of benefit ceased and s.102(4) FA 1986 was not displaced. Hence Emma's interest in possession had to continue until her death if IHT protection was sought.

Other uses of reverter to settlor trusts pre December 5, 2005

Apart from their use in providing for aged relatives and to circumvent the POA charge reverter to settlor trusts were used in the following situations: **27.18**

(i) As part of a property purchase arrangement: assume that Dad retained a lease and sold the encumbered freehold of his main residence for full market value. This was outside the POA charge as the result of para.10(1).[34] Funds for its purchase were settled by the children on a reverter to settlor trust for Dad remainder to them. Provided that the trust was appropriately drafted, the CGT death uplift would apply on Dad's death. (Of course, the entire property could have been bought by such a trust if the children had sufficient funds.)

(ii) As part of post-death planning: on Dad's death his half share in the family home was left in his will to his daughter Clara. She settled that interest on

---

[31] For transitional serial interests, see 18.14.
[32] For *Ingram* schemes, see 13.14 and 31.34.
[33] The fact that there is no inheritance tax payable on Emma's death does not prevent the property from being part of her estate while she is alive or displacing s.102(3), FA 1986 (gifts with reservation) on her death. See earlier.
[34] See FA 2004, Sch.15, para.10(1) provides that this will be an excluded transaction given that Dad is disposing of his whole interest in the property apart from the rights reserved under the lease.

reverter to settlor trusts for her Mum (the other beneficial owner, who is in occupation of the property). Main residence relief or death uplift (as appropriate) would then be available on the share held in trust.[35]

(iii) As part of a marketed IHT avoidance scheme: Jim gave his house to his son reserving a shorthold tenancy (on commercial terms) to permit his continued occupation. At the end of that tenancy the son settled the property on a reverter to settlor trust giving Jim an interest in possession. This type of arrangement involved exploiting the distinction between *property* and *value* in order to circumvent the POA/GWR rules.

THE IHT POSITION FROM MARCH 22, 2006[36]

The IHT relieving sections

27.19 (Sections 53(3) and (4) and 54(1) and (2)) are not themselves directly amended by FA 2006. However, the revised IHT legislation on settlements affects reverter to settlor trusts in two ways.

Existing trusts

27.20 In order to obtain reverter to settlor relief for existing trusts the property must revert to the settlor or his spouse either absolutely or on interest in possession trusts so that they become "beneficially entitled". The interest in possession must be a "qualifying" interest and in the case of interests arising after March 21, 2006 means that the interest in possession must either be an IPDI; a disabled person's interest; or a TSI.[37] The only qualifying interest in possession which is of relevance is the TSI.

27.21 Hence if the settlor is to obtain reverter to settlor relief on existing trusts it is necessary to satisfy one of two conditions:

(i) either the settlor (or his spouse/civil partner if the settlor is still alive or had died two years previously) must take *absolutely* on the ending of the interest in possession; *or*

(ii) the settlor/(or spouse/civil partner if settlor alive or died two years previously) must take on an interest in possession which is a TSI.

EXAMPLE 27.11

Eric settles a house on interest in possession trusts for his mother in February 2005. The intention behind the trust was CGT

---

[35] Although there were potential problems: see Ch. 31.
[36] For the changes in the IHT treatment of settlements generally, see 16.02 *et seq.*
[37] IHTA 1984, s.49(1A).

planning.[38] His mother is still alive but in poor health in July 2006. The settlement was drafted so that on mother's death the property would revert to Eric on interest in possession trusts so as to obtain the base cost uplift for CGT purposes.[39] For reverter to settlor relief now to apply, Eric's interest in possession must arise before April 6, 2008. It will then be a TSI. After that date there will be an IHT charge on mother's death when the continuing trusts will be subject to the relevant property regime. If the trusts had provided for Eric to take absolutely on the termination of his mother's interest (or if they are so amended) then the relief will be available whenever the mother's interest ended. Of course, the CGT uplift will then be lost.

The definition of a TSI can present problems

27.22 In the above example, if mother died and the trust property passed to her widower on interest in possession trusts the spouse exemption would be available. The widower takes a transitional serial interest.[40] However, on the death of the widower, unless the property reverts to Eric or his spouse absolutely (if Eric has died already then it needs to revert to Eric's widow within two years of his death) there is an IHT charge. Note even if the widower dies before April 6, 2008 and Eric takes an interest in possession, Eric's interest cannot qualify as a transitional serial interest (so no reverter to settlor relief is available on widower's death) because it is not the *first* interest that arose after the termination of mother's interest. For the same reason, if mother's interest had been replaced before April 6, 2008 during her lifetime (e.g. by an interest in favour of her spouse) so that Eric did not take outright or on interest in possession trusts at the point mother's interest ends, Eric will have to take absolutely on the death of the second life tenant. Otherwise there is no reverter to settlor relief.[41]

Conclusions

27.23 All existing reverter to settlor trusts should be reviewed. From April 6, 2008 the settlor (or his spouse/civil partner) must take *absolutely* on the death of the life tenant or on *inter vivos* termination of his interest if reverter to settlor relief is to be available. If, however, the life interest terminates before that date the settlor/spouse/civil partner can take on interest in possession trusts (that interest will be a TSI).

27.24 There is no change to the reservation of benefit rules. Hence in Example 27.11, even if mother had originally given the property to Eric there is no reservation of benefit if her life interest ends on her death although there

---

[38] Either to secure principal private residence relief on a sale of the property during the lifetime of mother or death uplift.
[39] See 27.13. The trustees would have power to transfer the settled property to Eric and thereby the trust could be ended.
[40] Even if mother died after April 5, 2008: see 18.14 *et seq*.
[41] For a consideration of transitional serial interests, see 18.14 *et seq*.

would be a deemed PET under FA 1986, s.102(4) if her interest ended during her lifetime.[42]

The position for new trusts

27.25 New trusts which will qualify for reverter to settlor relief cannot be established on or after March 22, 2006 except in very limited circumstances because few new trusts can be set up in which the life tenant enjoys a qualifying interest in possession.[43]

27.26 Reverter to settlor relief may be available in the following circumstances:

(i) If B (the person who takes the interest in possession in settled property) is entitled to a disabled person's interest[44]; *or*

(ii) If B has a transitional serial interest (not strictly a new settlement but the variation of an existing trust) *or*

(iii) If B becomes entitled on or after March 22, 2006 to an immediate post death interest (an IPDI). In these circumstances the settlor was the testator (who gave B the IPDI by his will) and so reverter relief can only be available if the settlor's surviving spouse or civil partner becomes absolutely entitled to the property within two years of the testator's death.

EXAMPLE 27.12

Andrew died in 2007 leaving his house to his son Paul on an immediate post death interest in possession with remainder to Andrew's spouse, Emma absolutely who is UK domiciled. Paul dies in 2008 and the trusts end. In these circumstances reverter to settlor relief is available and the house is not taxed on Paul's death.

27.27 It is obviously fairly unlikely that Andrew would leave his house to his son Paul rather than Emma in these circumstances but it may occur if, say, Paul had a special need falling short of being disabled.

THE POA POSITION FROM DECEMBER 5, 2005

27.28 As discussed above,[45] reverter to settlor relief was seen as a way round the POA provisions: see, for instance, *Example 27.10*.

---

[42] See 27.10 above. As a result of s.102ZA of FA 1986 (as inserted by FA 2006) even if mother had not given the property to Eric for him to settle, if her life interest is terminated on or after March 22, 2006 there is a potential reservation of benefit problem since mother is deemed to have made a gift and must be excluded from any ongoing benefit.

[43] See IHTA 1984, s.54(2A).

[44] See Ch. 26 for conditions on disabled trusts.

[45] See 27.17 *et seq.*

27.29 Such arrangements now need reviewing. FA 2006, s.80 amended the POA legislation with effect from December 5, 2005 so that the interest in possession of Emma in that example is ignored and the property is not treated as part of her estate for the purposes of the POA legislation. Accordingly, from December 5 she falls within the pre-owned income tax charge. As expected, the inheritance tax protection for Emma has not been directly attacked but a POA charge imposed.

27.30 The amending legislation inserts new sub-paras 11(11) and (12) into para.11 of FA 2004, Sch.15 as follows:

> "(11) Sub-paragraph (12) applies where at any time –
>
>> (a) the relevant property has ceased to be comprised in a person's estate for the purposes of IHTA 1984, or
>> (b) he has directly or indirectly provided any consideration for the acquisition of the relevant property,
>
> and at any subsequent time the relevant property or any derived property is comprised in his estate for the purposes of IHTA 1984 as a result of section 49(1) of that Act (treatment of interests in possession).
>
> (12) Where this sub-paragraph applies, the relevant property and any derived property –
>
>> (a) are not to be treated for the purposes of sub-paragraphs (1) and (2) as comprised in his estate at that subsequent time, and
>> (b) are not to be treated as falling within sub-paragraph (5) in relation to him at that subsequent time.
>
> (13) For the purposes of sub-paragraphs (11) and (12) references, in relation to the relevant property, to any derived property are to other property –
>
>> (a) which derives its value from the relevant property, and
>> (b) whose value, so far as attributable to the relevant property, is not substantially less than the value of the relevant property.".

27.31 This goes much further than the change indicated in the pre-Budget Press Release issued in December 2005. It does not affect just reverter to settlor trusts but can affect *any trust* set up at any time on or after March 18, 1986 even where the settlor is entitled to an interest in possession in the settled property so that reverter to settlor relief is not relevant.

EXAMPLE 27.14

> In 1987 H set up an interest in possession trust for his wife W into which he put a beneficial interest in his house. He may have done this for tax reasons or for marriage settlement reasons. This was a spouse exempt transfer for inheritance tax purposes and is protected from any POA charge while W's interest continues.[46]

---

[46] FA 2004, Sch.15 para.10(1)(c).

Assume that W's interest is terminated on January 1, 2007 (so the transaction ceases to be excluded from the POA charge) and the property reverts to H on an interest in possession trust (a TSI and so qualifying for IHT purposes). The property is comprised in his estate for inheritance tax purposes (see IHTA 1984, s.49(1)). but POA is payable by H from January 1, 2007 as a result of the amended legislation.

Notice in this case that the reverter to settlor relief is wholly irrelevant to the taxation of H. The property is in his estate as the result of a spouse exempt transfer under a settlement which H created! The key point is that although the property will be taxed as part of his estate (as a result of IHTA 1984, s.49(1)) his former protection against a pre-owned assets charge has been removed. Of course, the problem would not arise if H became absolutely entitled (rather than taking an interest in possession) but this could present CGT problems in some cases.[47]

Suppose W had died rather than her interest being terminated by the trustees. In these circumstances the transaction would remain excluded from a POA charge on H under para.10 unless the trust then owned intangibles in which case there would be a charge on a benefit equal to 5% of the capital value of the intangibles. Again this charge would not apply if he became absolutely entitled.

27.32 Problems can also arise on divorce where one spouse may have given assets to the other and receives them back as part of a divorce settlement. It is important that the original donor receives them back *outright* rather than on interest in possession trusts.

27.33 Although the legislation goes further than the terms of the press release, the Paymaster General indicated that these points were "obscure" when they were raised in Standing Committee debates. Note that FA 2006, s.80 potentially affects all reverter to settlor trusts whenever set up although the income tax charge only applies from December 5, 2005 onwards.

Conclusions

27.34 Reverter to settlor relief has been severely curtailed. The sort of arrangement discussed at 27.18 where Dad leaves his house in his will to his only daughter who then settles it on trust for Mum will not attract reverter to settlor relief. Such a trust is now a chargeable transfer for IHT purposes and Mum does not have a qualifying interest in possession. However, it may be that reverter to settlor relief is not necessary in these circumstances. It is likely that Dad's share in the house is within his nil rate band. Accordingly, if the daughter then settles that share on an *inter vivos* trust for her mother, giving her an entitlement to occupy the property, that is a chargeable transfer but no inheritance tax is payable (assuming the daughter has made no other chargeable transfers).

On the death of the mother, there is still no inheritance tax payable if the trust continues because her entitlement to occupy the property or enjoy its

---

[47] There are other problems caused by s.80 which are discussed at 22.70 and 24.33.

income is ignored for inheritance tax purposes.[48] Further, it may still be possible for the trustees to benefit from principal private residence relief so the trust might still be thought worthwhile.

EXAMPLE 27.15

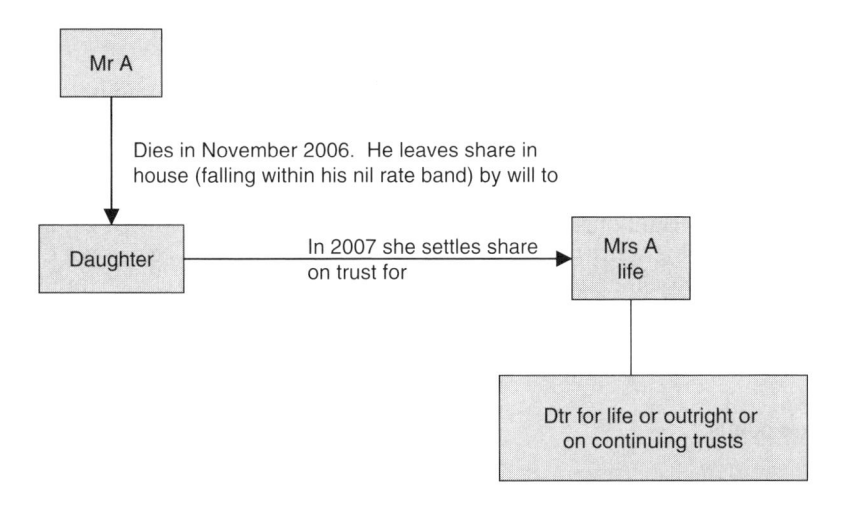

```
Mr A
  │
  │ Dies in November 2006. He leaves share in
  │ house (falling within his nil rate band) by will to
  ▼
Daughter ── In 2007 she settles share ──▶ Mrs A
             on trust for                  life
                                             │
                                             ▼
                                    Dtr for life or outright or
                                    on continuing trusts
```

Notes

1. The gift by daughter of her interest in the land is a chargeable transfer as opposed to a PET. Since the gift is within her nil rate band this generally makes little odds.
2. If the house is worth more than the nil rate band at the 10 year anniversary then inheritance tax will be payable but only on the excess above the nil rate band and at a maximum rate of 6 per cent. If Mrs A dies within the first 10 years and the trust is ended, then there is no inheritance tax charge even if the house is worth more than the nil rate band at that point.
3. Principal private residence relief for capital gains tax purposes may be available if Mrs A is in occupation of the property as her main residence: see TCGA 1992, s.225.[49]
4. It does not matter if the daughter or her spouse does not survive Mrs A in terms of the IHT position on Mrs A's death. On Mrs A's death there is no inheritance tax charge because her life interest is ignored for inheritance tax purposes (it is not qualifying).
5. On Mrs A's death there is no base cost uplift for capital gains tax purposes. She does not have a qualifying interest in possession. On disposal

---

[48] The relevant property regime applies and tax may be charged if the trust ends at that time (an exit charge) although the value of the settled property means that this is unlikely since it will be covered by the IHT nil rate band.
[49] See further 31.19.

of the house by the trustees, however, (whether on a deemed disposal if the trust ends and the daughter takes the house outright or on an actual disposal if the house is sold by the trustees) they are entitled to principal private residence relief and taper relief. Hence capital gains tax may not be a problem.

6. If the daughter dies then she may be treated as having reserved a benefit in the property[50] so that inheritance tax is payable but this is no different from the position before March 22, 2006.

7. There is no POA charge unless the daughter occupies the house or the trust fund comprises intangibles and even then only if the daughter does not reserve a benefit. The position is the same as before the 2006 changes.

8. Does it matter if Mrs A previously gave the interest in the house to Mr A which is now left to the daughter and which before March 22, 2006 the daughter settled for Mrs A? Is Mrs A subject to POA because of s.80? No, because the transaction between Mr and Mrs A is excluded for POA purposes.[51] In any event Mrs A's interest in possession is not a qualifying interest in possession so would not be caught by s.80.

Other points:

27.35 (i) For pre March 22, 2006 reverter to settlor trusts, review the principal private residence relief. Does the life tenant have a right to occupy under the terms of the settlement? Consider the position particularly carefully where the life tenant also owns a half share of the same property in her own right (as is the case in *Example 27.15* above and see 31.25 below).

(ii) For pre March 22, reverter to settlor trusts the POA position must be reviewed for both the settlor and the life tenant. The settlor is not caught if not in occupation of the house or chattels and provided that the trust does not own intangibles. However, s.80 may cause problems for the life tenants of such trusts.[52]

(iii) Review pre March 22, reverter to settlor trusts where the settlor does not take outright on the death of the life tenant to ensure that transitional serial interest protection will be available. Consider changing the terms of all existing trusts so that either the settlor takes outright on the termination of the life tenant's interest in possession or (to avoid capital gains tax problems) the settlor's spouse or civil partner takes outright since then the base cost uplift is available.

---

[50] See Ch. 24.
[51] FA 2004, Sch.15, para.10(1)(b).
[52] See FA 2004, sch.15, para.10(1)(b).

Chapter 28

TAX EFFICIENT WILL DRAFTING

- Use of IHT nil rate band (**28.02**)
- Dealing with residue (**28.32**)

This chapter is concerned with drafting IHT efficient wills. In recent years the availability of a range of lifetime planning opportunities meant that wills had become of diminished significance. All that has now changed and for many married couples the will is now a principal tool in the battle to save inheritance tax.[1] **28.01**

This chapter will concentrate on the traditional family will and to simplify the discussion will consider what would be an appropriate will for Ted who is married to Violet with two adult children and minor grandchildren. Further, it will be assumed that it is Ted who will die first and that Ted and Violet's combined estate is such that IHT is an issue.

USE OF IHT NIL RATE BAND

Ted's will should make use of his IHT nil rate band: in tax year 2006/07 that is worth £114,000 (£285,000 x 40 per cent).[2] This may be utilised: **28.02**

(i) by making gifts to chargeable persons (children/grandchildren). But if it is felt that Violet (the survivor) may need the use of all the assets in Ted's estate then

(ii) by establishing a discretionary trust (the classic nil rate band discretionary trust) under which Violet, as one of the beneficiaries, is entitled

---

[1] Unmarried tax payers will not find the will an especially attractive tax planning vehicle. Same-sex couples may enjoy the advantages of a married couple from December 5, 2005 by registering under the Civil Partnership Act 2004. Recently two sisters living together took a case to the European Court arguing that the spouse exemption should be extended to them given that they were living together and in the same economic position as civil partners. The decision has not yet been given.

[2] In the situation where assets are unequally split between spouses so that Ted does not have sufficient assets to cover his nil rate band it will be desirable for Violet to transfer assets to him. This is sometimes referred to as "equalising estates". If the IOU route is to be implemented then some care is needed in connection with the artificial debt rule in s.103, FA 1986 if the estates have been equalised at the time of drafting the wills. See 23.16 and 28.24.

to benefit. She can, for instance, be paid at the trustees' discretion all the income of the trust if considered appropriate.

There will be cases where leaving all or the bulk of the estate on a discretionary trust with a view to taking advantage of IHTA 1984, s.144 is attractive and this option is considered in Ch. 29.

Outright gifts to children[3]

28.03 If Ted's estate is sufficiently large this will be the easiest way to utilise his nil rate band. In cases where the main value of the estate is represented by the deceased's share in the matrimonial home consider gifting his share in the property outright to his children.[4] Say, for instance, that Ted's beneficial share as a tenant in common was worth £285,000 and that it is left outright to the children.

Violet's position is that with Ted's death she will normally become the sole legal owner of the property.[5] She owns beneficially a 50 per cent share in the property and on her death this share will attract IHT. The other share owned by the children will not be taxed: there is no reason to impute the ownership of this share to Violet. The arrangement will not, however, be appropriate in many cases. Violet may, for instance, be uneasy at the children having rights in the house (especially if the children are from Ted's first marriage!).[6]

Further, a major downside is that the children's share will not qualify for CGT principal private residence relief: hence if sold after Violet's death a chargeable gain may result. Prior to March 22, 2006 this difficulty could have been overcome by the children settling their share on a reverter to settlor trust giving Violet an interest in possession. Provided that the share reverted to the children on continuing interest in possession trusts this not only secured reverter to settlor relief from inheritance tax but the death uplift for capital gains tax purposes. Although this arrangement has been stopped by the FA 2006 changes in the IHT treatment of trusts (which largely prevent the creation of new *inter vivos* qualifying interest in possession trusts) this may not matter. The children could still settle their respective shares in the house on *inter vivos* interest in possession trusts for Violet.[7] The share will be within each child's nil rate band so although a chargeable transfer no inheritance tax

---

[3] Or, indeed, to other chargeable persons—for instance, grandchildren or issue of a first marriage.
[4] For problems involved in valuing shares in land in the light of the *Arkwright* decision, see fn.12, below.
[5] See LPA 1925, ss.34,35.
[6] It seems unlikely in this situation that the children would succeed in persuading the court to order a sale of the property or to force Violet to pay them a "rent": note the wide powers of the court under the Trusts of Land and Appointment of Trustees Act 1996, ss.14–15. Of course, the children could sell their beneficial share but the price received is likely to be heavily discounted. If a child was to become bankrupt the normal factors considered by the court on application from an order for sale do not apply. Instead the trustee in bankruptcy will apply to the court having jurisdiction in the bankruptcy where regard will be had to the interests of the bankrupt's creditors as well as to all the circumstances of the case. However, 12 months after the bankrupt's assets first vested in the trustee the interest of the creditors outweighs all other considerations unless the circumstance of the case are exceptional. At this point it is therefore likely that an order for sale will be made: see IA 1986, s.335A.
[7] See *Example 27.15*.

is actually payable. *Whether or not the property reverts to them on Violet's death*, her interest in possession is not a qualifying interest in possession and therefore it is not taxable on her death. Although there is no capital gains tax uplift on her death, if the trustees dispose of the property (whether on termination of the trust or on sale of the property) principal private residence relief should be available.[8]

The nil rate band discretionary trust[9]

If Ted prefers to leave £285,000 worth of assets into a discretionary trust rather than outright to the children then some thought is needed. The discretionary beneficiaries of the trust will normally include Violet as well as the children and in many cases it is envisaged that Violet will be the principal beneficiary and will be paid any income that arises. It is important that nothing is done which would result in Violet becoming entitled to an interest in possession in the trust fund within two years of Ted's death since were that to occur she would become entitled to an IPDI and the value of the trust fund would be taxed on her death[10] with the result that Ted's nil rate band will have been wasted. **28.04**

A practical problem is to select appropriate assets to go into the trust. At first blush, stocks and shares would seem to be ideal but the income tax treatment of dividends distributed as income to beneficiaries of discretionary trusts produces an unacceptably high income tax rate.[11] However, one benevolent effect of the FA 2006 changes in the IHT treatment of settlements in that once two years have elapsed from the date of death an interest in possession can be appointed to the surviving spouse which—although of no effect for IHT purposes—will result in the dividend income belonging to the spouse and so the extra income tax charge being avoided. **28.05**

If a (two year) discretionary trust over residue is used, then one should not at the same time create a nil rate band discretionary trust. Instead a cash sum equal to the Deceased's unused nil rate band can be paid out to a child or children by the trustees or kept in trust for them. **28.06**

The Matrimonial home

Of course, in many estates the reason for the IHT problem is that the couple own a house which has soared in value. Apart from the house, a few investments and pensions the couple will have no other assets. In this case, the question of what assets should be put into the discretionary trust can be reduced to the choice between putting Ted's share of the house into the trust (or at least a portion of it up to the value of the IHT nil rate band) or using what is popularly known as the "debt scheme". **28.07**

---

[8] See s.225 of TCGA 1992 and Ch. 31.
[9] For a precedent nil rate band discretionary trust, see App.II A2.27.
[10] See IHTA 1984, s.144: after the two year time limit it will not matter since the appointment of an interest in possession after March 21, 2006 is a "nothing": see 29.62.
[11] See 4.25.

28.08 Assume that the decision is taken to put Ted's 50 per cent share of the matrimonial home into the discretionary trust given that its value[12] equates with his available IHT nil band and there are no other assets in his estate.[13] Assume that Violet survives for a further six years during which time she continues to occupy the property as her main residence. Given that she is entitled to a 50 per cent share in the equity (as well as being the sole legal owner/trustee) it may be thought that when she dies all that will be taxed is her 50 per cent beneficial share with an appropriate discount. Concerns have been expressed, however, that in a case like this, HMRC may argue successfully that by virtue of her sole occupation of the property Violet enjoys an interest in possession in the share of the property held in the discretionary trust.[14]

28.09 HMRC's argument might be strengthened if the original house was sold and a replacement bought, again for Violet's sole use within the two years of death. Instead of the argument relying to some extent of trustees' inertia, it might now be said that the trustees have exercised their powers to purchase a property for Violet's use and have therefore given her a right to immediate possession, the hallmark of an interest in possession.[15]

HMRC's argument analysed

28.10 HMRC's argument appears to centre on the idea that the

> "continuation of the deceased's sole occupation of his home . . . arises from a conscious decision of the trustees not to disturb that enjoyment to the exclusion of the others".

---

[12] For the value of joint property owned by husband and wife, see *IRC v Arkwright* [2004] EWHC 1720 (Ch). A half share of a jointly owned house where the house is worth £570,000 will not necessarily be half this i.e. £285,000. *Arkwright* suggests that a discount should be applied, so that in the above case Ted's share would not fully satisfy the amount due to the discretionary trustees under the terms of his will. They are entitled to receive £285,000 but have received a half share worth less than this. This point is also relevant if the IOU scheme is adopted. The executors cannot charge a half share of the house with a debt for more than the half share is worth. Additional assets would need to be appropriated to the trustees to make up the difference (or made subject to the charge) unless the trustees decide that any additional amount due to them is appointed to the wife outright within two years of Ted's death (then reading back is obtained under s.144). Bear in mind that when the charge is imposed the share may have risen in value: that increased value may be enough to cover the sum charged.

[13] It is important that the decision to appropriate the property share into the trust is minuted and desirable for the trustees to protect their interest by having a restriction put on the property at the Land Registry. The general principle is that property must be appropriated on the basis of its value at the date of appropriation (and not therefore on the basis of its probate value, if different). It may therefore be that whilst the value of the property share equates with the available IHT nil rate band of the deceased at the time of his death, it has subsequently increased in value so that the personal representatives discover that only a part of the share can be put into the trust (e.g., if the value of the share had increased to £300,000 when the available nil rate band was £275,000, 91.66 per cent (only) can be appropriated to the trust).

[14] The authors are not convinced by such arguments and believe that, if raised, they should be fiercely resisted. Since the FA 2006 changes, the task of HMRC has been made even more difficult since they will be forced to argue that any interest in possession arose within two years of the deceased's death in order for a qualifying interest in possession to arise (an IPDI created as a result of IHTA 1984, s.144): otherwise even if an express interest in possession is appointed to the surviving spouse it is a "nothing".

[15] See Lightman J. in *IRC v Eversden* [2002] S.T.C. 1109. Again this must happen within two years of the deceased's death.

HMRC consider that the trustees must have taken some positive decision to allow the spouse to stay there in sole occupation otherwise they would have been in breach of trust and *Billingham v Cooper*[16] indicates that trustees must be assumed not to have acted in breach of trust. But this assumes that the trustees actually had some power to prevent her rent free occupation in the first place and that by failing to exercise such power they must thereby have conferred occupation rights on her.[17]

The difficulty for HMRC is that while s.12 Trusts of Land and Appointment of Trustees Act 1996 does give the spouse rights of occupation to the property, such rights are derived from her own share not that of the Trustees.

28.11 In the authors' view the trustees have no power to prevent the surviving spouse continuing to occupy the property. If the trustees ask her to agree a sale of the property or to pay rent for her occupation the surviving spouse can refuse. If the trustees go to court then the court will look to the provisions of s.12 which emphasise that interest in possession beneficiaries under trusts of land have rights of occupation in the land. There are no other beneficiaries who have interests in possession (in particular, the trustees have no right to occupy) and who are being excluded and no competing interests which require compensation to be paid. It would therefore be reasonable for the trustees to take the view that a court would be extremely unlikely to order a sale of the property under s.14. The trustees' failure to go to court to obtain an order for sale or seek payment of rent therefore cannot be taken to imply that the trustees had positively conferred on the spouse exclusive occupation or an interest in possession.[18]

28.12 SP10/79[19] makes it clear that for an interest in possession to arise, any power exercisable by the trustees granting the spouse rights over the home has to be expressly drawn and exercised in terms wide enough to confer an exclusive right of residence. For the reasons noted above, there is generally no evidence that the trustees have exercised their powers in such a way as regards the original home. In general, the courts are reluctant to imply that decisions or acts have been taken by the trustees where there is no evidence that these have been taken (a point emphasised in the *Walden* case).[20]

Section 12 (subject to the limitations set out in that section) confers rights of occupation on an interest in possession beneficiary: it does not say that someone in occupation must have an interest in possession in the entire property. Further there is no need for them to have an interest in possession in the whole property to have rights of occupation.[21]

28.13 This analysis is to some extent borne out by the judgment of Lightman J. in the *Eversden* case where it appears to be accepted that the trustees only exercised their discretions and conferred rights of occupation in respect of the replacement property because they took the positive decision to use the sale proceeds to buy a property for occupation by the beneficiary. Even then

---

[16] [2000] S.T.C. 122 aff'd [2001] 177, CA.
[17] See the *Walden* case discussed at 15.25 indicating the need for positive action on the part of the discretionary trustees if an interest in possession is to arise.
[18] Normally trustees of a discretionary trust will only create interests in possession by the exercise (usually by deed) of a power of appointment.
[19] Which was not considered in the *Walden* case.
[20] See 15.25 for further discussion of the *Walden* case.
[21] See *Woodhall v IRC* [2000] S.T.C. (SCD) 558: a person can have an interest in possession in land even though he chooses not to exercise any rights of occupation.

Lightman J. drew back from stating explicitly that the settlor had an interest in possession in the trust assets. It appears that in relation to the original property the trustees had not exercised any powers to confer any rights of occupation and the settlor's continued sole occupation did not mean that the trusts ceased to be discretionary trusts.[22]

Advice to trustees

28.14 If properly advised, trustees will not simply sit back and do nothing. It is thought that any body of trustees faced with the situation where the trust fund comprises a beneficial share in a residence occupied by the deceased's spouse's will:

(i) obtain advice as to what their rights are viz à viz the property. It is unlikely that the spouse will be willing to sell and to give the trustees a 50 per cent share of the proceeds and any attempt to persuade the court to order a sale (under the Trusts of Land and Appointment of Trustees Act 1996 ss.14–15) as noted above is unlikely to succeed given the purpose for which the property was bought. Similarly any attempt to force the wife to pay a commercial rent (what would that be given that she owns a beneficial 50 per cent share in the property?) will be resisted again and as noted above there are no competing interests in possession. In many cases the wife will be unable to afford to pay a rent;

(ii) the trustees will be concerned to ensure that the property is insured and is being kept in a proper state of repair. Doubtless these are matters that the spouse is attending to but the trustees should take steps to ensure that their investment is protected. Were there to be a problem this is a matter to bring to the court's attention in an application for sale[23];

(iii) the trustees should register a restriction at the Land Registry to protect their position in the event that the spouse decides to sell the property;

(iv) the trustees may consider selling the beneficial 50 per cent share but there will be difficulties in finding anyone to buy and any purchaser would obtain a very substantial discount to reflect the spouse's continued non-rent paying occupation;

(v) the trustees should consider the range of beneficiaries: are any of them in dire need of either income or capital? In most family arrangements of this type the answer is no but were there to be a problem then it would be a factor to bring to the court's attention in an application to have the property sold.

28.15 In the light of the foregoing, the trustees may feel that they are left with no real alternative but to retain the property: this is likely to be in the best interest of the beneficiaries especially if the property is rising in value. The above

---

[22] See [2002] S.T.C. 1109.
[23] Under s.13(3) the trustees of land may impose reasonable conditions in respect of any beneficiary's occupation of the land.

process should be evidenced in writing so that the trustees' train of thought is documented. In cases where the original property is sold and a replacement property is to be purchased it may be:

(a) that trust monies will not be needed; *or*
(b) that the trustees could loan the spouse a sum repayable on demand and take security in the form of a legal charge on the new property. Alternatively, once two years have elapsed from death, the trustees may safely convert the trust into an interest in possession settlement and acquire a share in the new property, which will have no adverse IHT implications, since FA 2006 should ensure that the trustees' share will attract CGT principal private residence relief.

On any sale of the original property it is important that the trustees receive their share of the proceeds and then consider whether they wish to reinvest the cash in a replacement property. The cash should not automatically be put into a new property at the behest of the surviving spouse. The appropriate exercise of the trustees' discretion should be carried out and documented.

CGT downside

A further point to bear in mind is the future CGT position if, after Violet's death, the property is sold. Given that she did not enjoy an interest in possession in the moiety held in trust, there will be no CGT death uplift and the availability of CGT principal private residence relief will depend on whether she is entitled to occupy the property under the terms of the settlement.[24] The FA 2006 changes in the IHT treatment of trusts mean that after two years the trustees can appoint the spouse an interest in possession without there being a qualifying IPDI interest. Will that assist in securing principal private residence relief? It may be argued that the conditions for relief are as follows: **28.16**

(i) that the beneficiary actually occupies (which she does); and
(ii) that she is entitled to occupy under the terms of the settlement.

Even whilst the trust is discretionary the terms of the trust will commonly permit any beneficiary to occupy trust property: in *Sansom v Peay*[25] it was considered sufficient that the beneficiary was actually in occupation (by a licence from the trustees) and as a beneficiary of the trust was entitled to occupy by virtue of a power in the trustees. Giving the beneficiary an interest in possession might make the position clearer but the principle should not be different.

However, the question (discussed in chapter 31) is whether even if the trustees have a power under the will to permit beneficiaries to occupy trust property, principal private residence relief can be available under s.225, TCGA

---

[24] See TCGA 1992, s.225; *Sansom v Peay* [1976] 3 All E.R. 375 and SP10/79. It is a difficult balancing exercise to obtain the best of both worlds: i.e. no IHT charge but CGT relief: see also 31.25.
[25] [1976] S.T.C. 494: the case concerned a trust of the entire property.

1992 if the trustees do not or cannot exercise such discretions because they have no power to prevent the surviving spouse from occupying the house anyway (as a result of the limited interest that they have been left under the deceased's will). On one reading of s.225, difficulties will arise only if the will does not enable the trustees to permit beneficiaries to occupy the property. The fact that the spouse occupies in another capacity should not matter.

Loan schemes

28.17 These have become popular in recent years and spawned a voluminous literature.[26] In brief, the discretionary trust is constituted by *either* a debt owed to the trustees by Violet who receives all the assets of Ted's estate *or* by a charge being placed over the assets in Ted's estate (and typically his share in the house) which are then assented to Violet. For many couples the practical results of this arrangement are ideal since Violet will enjoy the benefit of all the couple's assets whilst Ted has used up his IHT nil rate band on death. However, a number of issues need to be addressed before opting for the loan trust, such as:

28.18 Will the trust be vulnerable to attack as a "sham" or as one in which Violet enjoys an interest in possession?[27]

28.19 What are the terms of Violet's debt or of the charge? The standard precedents provide for it to be re-payable on demand but should it carry interest (rolled up and so only payable with the principal on her death) or be index-linked? In principle, it will be attractive for IHT purposes to ensure that the value of the debt is maintained but the matter is not clear cut and the following points may be noted:—

(a) the trustees will have power to lend money—on whatever terms they consider appropriate—to beneficiaries including Violet. They could decide not to charge interest/index-link the debt. It is, however, important that the question is considered and the decision of the trustees minuted;

(b) interest which is rolled up and paid when the principal is paid will only attract an income tax charge in the hands of the trustees when it is received[28];

(c) there will be no attraction in providing for either interest or index-linking unless Violet's estate is reduced by the rolled up interest/indexed sum on her death. This will, of course, be the case provided that the

---

[26] See for instance, the *Encyclopaedia of Forms and Precedents*, vol.42(1), [2003 Reissue], Ch. 11 and for appropriate documentation see App.II A2.31 *et seq.*

[27] See *Taxation* April 29, 2004, p.116. In practice it is not thought that this will create a problem provided that the trustees act in a trustee-like manner. They should, for instance, ensure that the debt is secured and that they hold (once a year?) minuted meetings in which they review the operation of the trust (should they amend the interest charged etc bearing in mind then the debt will be repayable on demand?) and the needs of their beneficiaries. Of course a qualifying interest can only arise if an IPDI comes into existence within two years of death.

[28] For the taxation of interest, see ITTOIA 2005, s.370 and for the meaning of "arising" see *Parkside Leasing v Smith* (1984) 58 TC 282 and *Dunmore v McGowan* (1978) 52 TC 307.

liability has been incurred "for a consideration in money or money's worth"[29];

(d) there may be an element of "swings and roundabouts" since the interest while deductible in the spouse's estate (thereby saving IHT at 40 per cent) is subject to income tax in the hands of the trustees when paid at 40 per cent. All or part of this income tax may, however, be repaid if the trustees distribute the interest to a non taxpaying beneficiary or one whose rate of income tax is less than 40 per cent[30];

(e) so far as index-linking is concerned—whether by reference to the RPI or to (say) a property index—the tax treatment of the indexed sum in the hands of the trustees needs consideration. It is not thought that the relevant discounted securities provisions in FA 1996, Sch.13 (now ITTOIA 2005, Pt 4, Ch. 8) will apply to an on demand loan.[31] Under general principles capital gains tax will not apply,[32] which means that unless the sum can be classified as "interest" (and so subject to income tax) it will be free from tax. "Interest" is generally considered to catch any payment compensating the lender for the use of his money: however, the uncertainty over whether indexation will produce a return for the lender may indicate that it is in the nature of a gamble and a tax free windfall.

28.20 If Ted's estate includes an interest in land, will SDLT be in point on the basis that Violet acquires that interest?[33] The current approach of HMRC is set out in the statement "Stamp Duty Land Tax and nil rate band Discretionary Trusts" which was issued November 12, 2004.[34] From this statement it appears:

(a) that a simple debt arrangement may attract a charge to SDLT on the basis that the surviving spouse is acquiring an interest in land;

(b) that the charge route whereby the executors charge the deceased's property with payment of the nil rate legacy and then assent the property—burdened by the charge—to the surviving spouse will not give rise to an

---

[29] IHTA 1984, s.5(3)–(5) but note FA 1986, s.103 which disallows the deduction of "artificial debts": see 43.00.
[30] Bold spirits have suggested that on the death of Violet the rolled up interest should be deducted as a liability in Violet's IHT return but that the nil rate band trustees may subsequently take the decision to waive payment. It is thought that this will avoid any income tax charge (since those trustees never receive the interest) and that, given the beneficiaries under Violet's will are likely to be the same persons who benefit under this trust they will be acting properly in so doing. It is common for Capital Taxes to raise a query as to when the interest has been/is to be paid and, if not, will seek to disallow it as a deduction in Violet's estate.
[31] Given that the debt is repayable on demand it is not thought that there is a sum payable on redemption.
[32] See TCGA 1992, s.251(1).
[33] In the case where the only asset in Ted's estate is his share in the matrimonial home it may be argued that any debt entered into by Violet must be in consideration for acquiring Ted's interest (and, of course, to obtain the IHT deduction on Violet's death the debt must have been incurred for a consideration in money or money's worth). What, however, if Ted owns personalty which could be appropriated to satisfy the nil rate legacy? In this case there is no obvious reason why SDLT should be payable on the whole value of the land: either an apportionment may be in point or by first appropriating the land to Violet the trustees could show that insofar as the debt was consideration it was for the acquisition of personalty.
[34] This is set out in App.III A3.16.

SDLT liability *provided that* the spouse does not become personally liable for payment of the legacy and that there is no change in the rights or liabilities of any person in relation to the debt secured by the charge[35];

(c) if the arrangement is the result of a deed of variation which has established the trust then any debt or charge that may be created is not a land transaction for SDLT purposes.

28.21 It has been argued that HMRC's statement, insofar as it relates to simple debt arrangements, is misconceived[36] but most practitioners will settle for the charge route on the basis that it is accepted that it will avoid any SDLT charge arising. It may also be the preferred route in order to circumvent possible s.103 problems.[37]

28.22 Is FA 1986, s.103, capable of operating to disallow the debt on Violet's death? It will be appreciated that the inheritance tax attractiveness of the loan trust lies in the debt being fully deducted from the estate of the surviving spouse on death. If, for some reason, the debt is not deductible, the tax saving will not materialise and the tax saving arrangement will have failed.

FA 1986, s.103(1) may apply in two situations:

(i) if on death of the surviving spouse there is an outstanding liability arising from a debt incurred by that deceased surviving spouse; *or*

(ii) if the outstanding liability arises from an encumbrance created by a disposition made by that spouse.

Note, therefore that s.103 is not capable of applying if the surviving spouse neither incurred the debt nor made the disposition which created the encumbrance.

28.23 What activates s.103 is if all or part of the consideration for the liability has been derived from property originating with the surviving spouse (whether directly or indirectly). Consider, for instance, the following example:

- In 2004 H transfers half the matrimonial home (of which he is the absolute beneficial owner) to W. The value of that share is £500,000.

- W dies in 2005 and the standard loan arrangement is implemented, that is, H accepts an indebtedness of £275,000 to the nil rate band trustees.

- Having given W £500,000 it may then be said that H has furnished consideration for the loan. Loosely, he is buying back his own property leaving the price outstanding. Hence the debt of £275,000 is non-deductible on H's death.

Section 103 does not prescribe when the debtor furnished the consideration. The gift from H in the above example may have occurred at any time. Can s.103 apply in the circumstances of the loan trust? In their revised guidance

---

[35] In effect any charge must be non-recourse. Note therefore that the executors cannot charge the share in the property for a sum greater than the share is worth. See earlier fn.12 and *Arkwright*.

[36] See, for instance, Kessler *"Drafting Trusts and Will Trusts"* (7th edn, 2004, app.4) (replaced 19/12/2004).

[37] See App.II A2.48 for an instrument of equitable charge over the share in the family home owned by the deceased.

notes on the POA charge, HMRC indicate that in their view it is capable of applying.

Practical advice on s.103

Always check whether substantial inter spouse gifts have been made (these may have been necessary to "equalise the estates").[38] This check should be done both at the time when the wills are made and again after the death of the first spouse. The problem will only arise if it is the donor spouse who survives.

28.24

How can one avoid being caught by s.103? Provided that the spouse does not incur the debt or create the encumbrance, s.103 cannot apply. The best way of dealing with the problem is for the executors to impose a charge not just over property passing to the surviving spouse under the residue clause, but also over property which would but for the charging clause pass to that spouse.[39] The executors will normally have power to charge the nil rate sum on any property passing to the surviving spouse and can then be protected from claims by the nil rate band trustees if they do so. They may then assent the charged property to the surviving spouse who is not personally liable for the debt. If this procedure is followed then although there is an encumbrance (a secured debt) it was not imposed by a disposition made by the spouse; and the surviving spouse has never personally incurred a debt. Accordingly, there is no room for the application of s.103. A note of warning is needed here: because the surviving spouse must not on a strict reading of s.103 be a party to the disposition creating the encumbrance, he or she should not be one of the executors of the estate (or if appointed in the will should not take out a grant). If this problem only materialises after a grant has been taken out then it may be avoided if the charge is created after the administration of the estate has been completed and at a time when the executors have become bare trustees for the beneficiaries entitled under the will. Before the charge is created the surviving spouse can resign as a trustee so that he or she is not involved in imposing the charge (it is, of course, important to ensure that the conditions for retirement of a trustee are met).

The one problem which remains arises if the charged property is sold, whereupon the debt falls to be repaid to the trustees. Provided that the surviving spouse does not need the use of the repaid money, no problems arise, but if he or she requires any part to be loaned back then the loan will fall foul of s.103 because at that point the surviving spouse incurs a debt personally. It is at this point that the FA 2006 changes are helpful since if the trustees were to purchase a share in the replacement property with the spouse, at the same time appointing her an interest in possession, then—

28.25

(i) for IHT purposes that appointment is a "nothing"[40];

(ii) s.103 issues do not arise;

---

[38] i.e. to ensure that both spouses have sufficient assets to use up their IHT nil rate band.
[39] See App.II A2.31 *et seq.* and especially A2.36.
[40] Provided not done within two years of death: see IHTA 1984, s.144 and 29.62.

(iii) CGT main residence relief should be secured on the share owned by the trustees.[41]

Conclusions on the house

28.26 It has been suggested that since FA 2006 there are fewer risks of any interest in possession arising if the first spouse leaves his or her share of the house on nil rate band discretionary trusts with the surviving spouse in occupation. The authors' conclusion is that it is still preferable to satisfy the nil rate band by use of the IOU scheme rather than a share of the house for the following reasons:

(i) if the surviving spouse takes an interest in possession within two years of death, this is read back under s.144 and will be an IPDI and therefore a qualifying interest in possession. The purpose of the planning to use the deceased's nil rate band has been defeated. The arguments on whether the trustees have conferred an interest in possession on the spouse therefore remain much as before. The authors do not think that merely allowing the spouse to continue in occupation of the original property could be regarded as conferring an interest in possession whether this occurs before or after March 22, 2006 but difficulties could arise if the original property was sold and a replacement property purchased within two years of the death of the first spouse—not an uncommon situation.

(ii) capital gains tax main residence relief remains in question although the authors think it is at least arguable that it should be available even on the original property.[42]

(iii) perhaps the biggest argument against putting the share of the house into the discretionary trust is that given the substantial increase in property values it may well mean that on the ten year anniversary there is an inheritance tax bill to pay.[43] Of course, it may be possible to avoid this by advancing the share in the house outright to a beneficiary such as a child just before the ten year anniversary[44] but this may not always be practical. One can no longer avoid the ten year charge by appointing a qualifying interest in possession to the child.

On the other hand the loan route undoubtedly has disadvantages:

(i) it can be complicated to set up and explaining it to a client is not always easy;

---

[41] It is clear in the case of a replacement property that the trustees do have discretions and do *exercise* them to allow a beneficiary into occupation. This differs from the position on the original property where the trustees may have the necessary powers under the will but cannot exercise them.
[42] See 28.16 and 31.25.
[43] At a maximum rate of 6 per cent on the excess above the then nil rate band.
[44] Since the house was within the nil rate band when it went into the trust there is no exit charge if the trust is ended before the ten year anniversary.

(ii) there are s.103 traps that have to be watched;

(iii) The IOU route has the vulnerability of any inheritance tax scheme which is that the rules could be altered before the relevant death. HMRC do not like inheritance tax planning involving debts and it is not inconceivable that the legislation may be changed in the future. Such changes could be "retroactive" so that such debts are not deductible on the death of the surviving spouse where that spouse has not yet died. Putting a share of the house into a discretionary trust is arguably less vulnerable to legislative change.

Business and agricultural property

28.27 If Ted's estate includes property which attracts IHT relief at 100 per cent, then simply leaving that property to Violet may be considered to be a "waste" in that the spouse exemption will result in the business relief being redundant. The difficulty for the adviser in drafting the will is that it may not be certain that the relevant property attracts relief at 100 per cent; for instance, it may be a farming business which has diversified.[45] And, of course, the test is not whether the business attracts relief when the will is made but whether it does so *at the time of death*.[46] Bear in mind also that HMRC will not normally consider the eligibility of property for relief *unless tax is at stake*. So leaving the property to Violet and envisaging a deed of variation to redirect it to the children if the property attracts 100 per cent relief will not work when there is doubt as to the availability of relief, since the availability of relief will not be considered by HMRC. Likewise leaving the property to (say) the son "if it attracts 100 per cent relief" and if not, to Violet, will be problematic since, again, the availability of relief will not be considered by HMRC. For these reasons putting the business into a discretionary trust has advantages which will be considered below at 28.30.

BPR/APR and nil rate gifts

28.28 A "standard" will establishing a nil rate band discretionary trust and leaving residue to the surviving spouse will, in a case where the deceased owned property attracting 100 per cent relief, operate so that part of the benefit of the business or agricultural property relief will accrue to the nil rate trust (i.e., the trustees will receive more than £285,000 but not the whole value of the business property) and the remainder of the relief will be attributed to property passing to the spouse and so will be wasted.[47] The position may be illustrated by the following example.

---

[45] As for instance, in *Farmer (Exors of Farmer dec'd) v IRC* [1999] S.T.C. (SCD) 321.
[46] There can be no guarantee that relief in its present form will continue in the future.
[47] See IHTA 1984, s.39A.

EXAMPLE 28.1

Consider an estate of £1m where the deceased left a nil rate band legacy in the form set out below to his daughter and the residue to his spouse. The estate includes property eligible for relief worth £500,000. The deceased made no lifetime transfers.

> "I give to my daughter such sum as at my death equals the maximum amount which could be given by this will without inheritance tax becoming payable on my estate."

Will the daughter take £285,000?

No, the IHT value of the legacy will be reduced by multiplying it by reduced value of estate (after deducting any specific gifts qualifying for relief) ("R") divided by the unreduced value of the estate (after deducting any specific gifts qualifying for relief) ("U"). A legacy with an IHT value of £285,000 will actually be twice that amount.

Accordingly the daughter will take £570,000, the IHT value of which will be reduced to £285,000 thereby being covered by the deceased's nil rate band as follows—

$$\frac{£5700,000 \times £500,000(R)}{£1,000,000 \ (U)} = £285,000$$

28.29 This may be good news as more assets are passed to the daughter tax free. If, however, the testator is concerned that the spouse may be left with too little, it is possible to include a cap on the amount to pass under the legacy. However, to obtain the full benefit of the 100 per cent relief ensure that a specific gift of the qualifying assets is made.

"Two bites at the cherry" relief

28.30 Assume that Ted owns a farm qualifying for 100 per cent APR and worth £1m. It is envisaged that Violet will take over the business after his death but if he leaves her the farm the relief will be wasted. Consider therefore the following—

(i) the farm is left to his daughter. IHT is not payable because of the relief;

(ii) after his death the farm is sold to Violet with the daughter receiving £1m in cash;

(iii) once Violet has owned the farm for two years, relief may be available on her death;

(iv) in addition the daughter can be given a cash legacy of the nil rate band.

STEP 1

```
           T
         /   \
Daughter      Mrs T
£285,000      residue
business (value £1m)   (value (say) £1.5m)
```

STEP 2

Daughter ⎯⎯⎯⎯⎯⎯⎯⎯⎯⎯⎯⎯⎯⎯→ Mrs T
Sale of business for £1 m

So that the end result is:

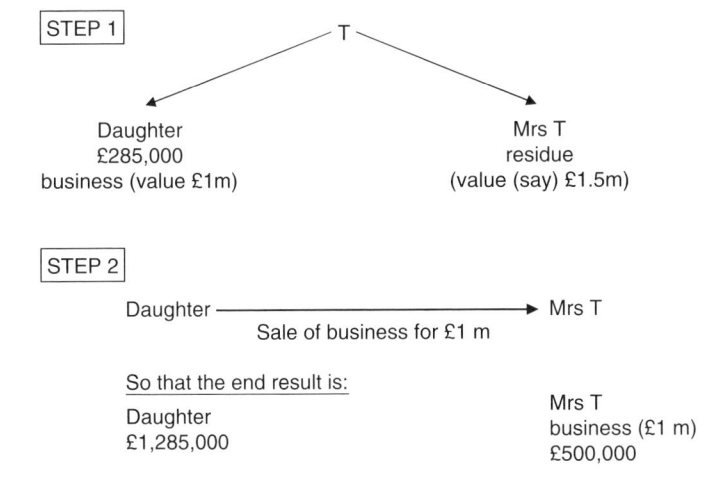

Daughter
£1,285,000

Mrs T
business (£1 m)
£500,000

Note in connection with the above—

(i) that SDLT will be payable by Violet on the acquisition of an interest in land;
(ii) that there is no clawback of APR or BPR if the property is sold (however soon!) after the death;
(iii) that if it is desired to protect Violet's position she could be given an option to purchase the farm in the will;
(iv) consider, if Violet has insufficient money to purchase the farm, leaving all or part of the purchase price outstanding as an interest free loan from the daughter.

Leaving the business into a discretionary trust

28.31 If put into a discretionary trust the availability of the IHT relief must now be considered by HMRC since IHT is at stake. When the position is known (provided that this occurs within two years of the deceased's death) then the trustees—

(i) if the property attracts 100 per cent relief may leave it on discretionary or other trusts for the children or appoint it outright to them;
(ii) if HMRC consider that relief is not available the trustees may appoint it to the deceased's surviving spouse so that the spouse exemption will prevent IHT from arising.[48]

[48] This is the effect of "reading back" under IHTA 1984, s.144 as to which see 29.49 *et seq*. This assumes, however, that HMRC give a determination either way on the availability of relief before the expiry of the two year period. Disputes on business property relief or agricultural property relief may drag on beyond the two year period and reading back cannot be obtained if an appointment is made after the two year period. Where the estate is left on discretionary trusts and the trustees are worried that if HMRC may refuse business property relief or

DEALING WITH RESIDUE

28.32 Having used up his nil rate band (and in appropriate cases made sure that 100 per cent relievable property has been satisfactorily dealt with), the residue of Ted's estate should be left to Violet in order to take advantage of the spouse exemption.[49] It is important to realise that this exemption is available whether the residue is given absolutely to Violet or on flexible life interest trusts (which will be an IPDI).[50]

IHT planning for Violet

28.33 Before the 2006 changes in the IHT treatment of trusts and in the reservation of benefit rules, flexible life interest trusts were widely used as follows. The key was that the trustees were given overriding powers of appointment which could be exercised to bring Violet's interest to an end:

- in whole or in part; and
- in relation to specific property

and the trustees could exercise the power to establish continuing trusts (including discretionary trusts) or to make outright appointments of property: e.g. to children. If the overriding power was exercised (e.g. to appoint assets absolutely to the children) then Violet made a PET.

Link up with reservation of benefit and the pre-owned assets regime before March 22, 2006

28.34 Assume that the trustees exercised their power of appointment to create a small (value £275,000) discretionary trust under which the family (including Violet) could benefit. What was the tax analysis prior to March 22, 2006?

(i) the termination of Violet's life interest was a chargeable transfer but given that she had not used up her nil rate band no IHT was payable (notice that although Violet is not the settlor, it is her nil rate band which is relevant given that she makes the transfer of value: see IHTA 1984, s.80(1)); and

(ii) whilst the IHT legislation provides that Violet makes a "deemed" transfer of value[51], prior to the changes in FA 2006, it was not considered that she made a "gift" as required if the reservation of benefit rules were to

---

agricultural property relief then they appoint the property to the surviving spouse. However, it is worth submitting the probate papers as soon as possible after the death to obtain a view from HMRC.

[49] See IHTA 1984, s.18. Even if Violet does not need this property it should not be left to the children on Ted's death given that it will attract a 40 per cent IHT charge. Better to leave it to Violet and for her to make lifetime gifts (PETs) to the children.

[50] IPDI's are considered in detail in Ch. 19.

[51] See IHTA 1984, s.52(1).

apply nor was it thought that she made a disposal of property or settled property for the purposes of the pre-owned asset legislation.[52]

The upshot was that the discretionary trust so established would be used, at the trustees' discretion, as a vehicle to benefit Violet during her life without the trust being subject to IHT on her death (it was exactly comparable to the nil rate band discretionary trust set up in Ted's will). Violet therefore had the comfort of knowing that assets to a value of over half a million pounds were available for her use but would not attract an IHT charge on death.

Diagrams showing Ted's estate held on two separate discretionary trusts with the remaining residue on flexible life interest trusts for Violet   28.35

STEP 1 (Ted's will)

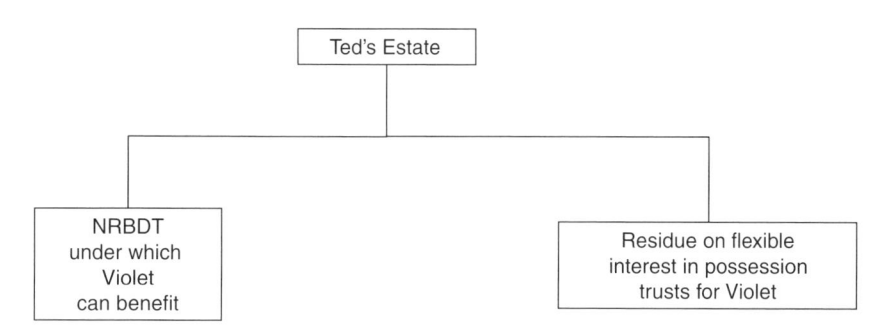

```
                    Ted's Estate
                   /            \
        NRBDT                    Residue on flexible
        under which              interest in possession
        Violet                   trusts for Violet
        can benefit
```

STEP 2 (trustees exercise dispositive powers)   28.36

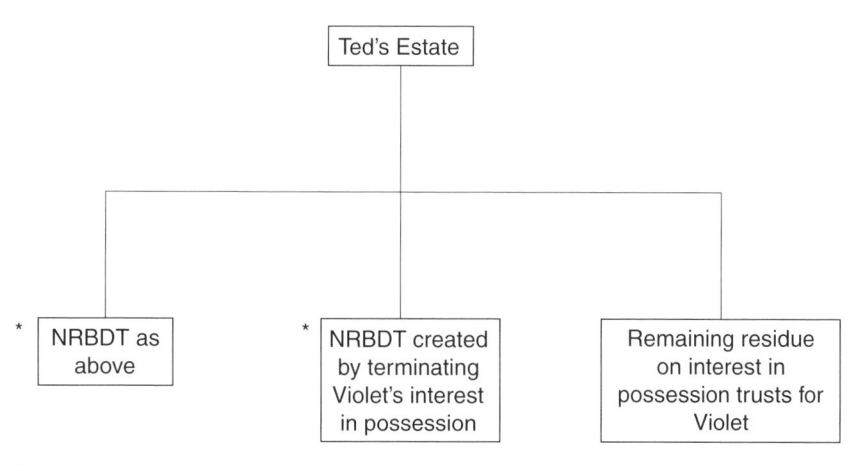

```
                    Ted's Estate
             /           |            \
   * NRBDT as    * NRBDT created    Remaining residue
     above         by terminating   on interest in
                   Violet's interest possession trusts for
                   in possession    Violet
```

*Not taxed on Violet's death even though she benefits from both

---

[52] The position was less clear cut if she had to consent to the exercise of the power whilst if she surrendered her interest it was thought that she had made a gift. See 13.09 and 24.05.

Impact of FA 2006

28.37 This strategy has been nullified from March 22, 2006 as a result of an amendment to the reservation of benefit rules. This provides that if:

(i) an individual became entitled to an interest in possession in settled property before March 22, 2006; *or*

(ii) on or after that date becomes entitled to such an interest if it was qualifying (i.e. an IPDI; disabled person's interest or a TSI); *and*

(iii) that interest comes to an end during the individual's life,

then the individual is to be taken to dispose of the settled property in which the interest had subsisted *by way of gift* for the purpose of the reservation of benefit rules.[53] As a result, if the trustees exercised their power of appointment to terminate Violet's interest in possession on or after March 22, 2006 then she will be treated as making a gift for GWR purposes so that, if she continues to benefit under a discretionary trust created by the appointment, the property will be taxed as part of her estate on her death.[54]

28.38 This amendment only applies in respect of the termination of interests in possession on or after March 22, 2006. Accordingly if Violet's interest had been terminated before that date the GWR rules would not apply.[55]

Should the surviving spouse be left residue absolutely or on interest in possession trusts?

28.39 In considering whether to leave a surviving spouse residue absolutely or on an interest in possession trust the following points should be borne in mind:

(i) in some cases the testator will wish to give his spouse a life interest (usually supplemented by a power in the trustees to pay capital to the spouse) in order to preserve the capital for e.g. children of an earlier marriage. A surviving spouse who is merely left a life interest with no right to capital is likely to have a claim to capital under The Inheritance (Provision for Family and Dependants) Act 1975 anyway so this may not protect the capital unless the surviving spouse is prepared to accept such limited provision. A life interest can be useful in ring-fencing assets if the surviving spouse (in the example Violet) remarries. Any new spouse of Violet is less likely to be able to claim the capital if it is left on trust for Violet by Ted if Violet dies or divorces[56];

---

[53] FA 1986, s.102 ZA; Sch.20 para.4A inserted by FA 2006, Sch.20 Pt 5. See also Ch. 24, reservation of benefit and see 24.08.
[54] FA 1986, s.102(3): for a general consideration of the GWR legislation, see Ch. 24.
[55] FA 2006, Sch.20 para.33(4). The position might, however, be different if Violet had been required to consent to the appointment or if she had surrendered her interest in possession. In both cases she might be considered to have made a gift. See 24.08 *et seq.*
[56] See further Ch. 34.

(ii) if property is given to the spouse outright the spouse can make gifts which will be PETs;

(iii) if the residue is settled, the *inter vivos* termination of the spouse's interest in possession will only be a PET by the spouse if:
  (a) the settlement thereupon ends, *or*
  (b) the property then becomes settled on a bereaved minor's trust,[57] *or*
  (c) it becomes held on trusts under which there is a disabled person's interest;

(iv) if residue is given to the spouse outright the spouse can only make gifts if s/he has mental capacity or an application is made to the Court of Protection. If the house is left on trust the trustees can take the decision as to whether the spousal interest should be terminated in whole or part and PETs made;

(v) if the surviving spouse is left the residuary estate outright, that surviving spouse can establish IPDIs for the children in his or her will. If, however, the first spouse leaves residue on IPDI trust for the surviving spouse, no further IPDIs can be created thereafter;

EXAMPLE 28.2

Ted dies leaving the residue of his estate outright to Violet, his wife. They have three children one of whom—Chris—is a spendthrift. At the age of 30 he has spent all the inheritance left to him by his aunt and is now in debt. If Violet dies she can leave the property on IPDI trusts for her children and so protect the capital so that Chris does not have access to it except at the discretion of the trustees. If however Ted leaves residue on IPDI trusts for Violet, on her death the trusts must end and the children take outright otherwise the property will fall into the relevant property regime.

(vi) there may be capital gains tax advantages in transferring the property into trust for Violet. Future disposals that might trigger gains can be minimised;

EXAMPLE 28.3

Ted dies leaving residue outright to Violet. One of the assets is an investment property. Five years later Violet decides to settle it on trust for her children. It shows a large gain. She can transfer the property into an *inter vivos* trust; this is a chargeable transfer for inheritance tax purposes but provided she, any spouse and any dependent children are excluded from benefit the gain can be held over under TCGA 1992, s.260. However a new taper relief period is started. This would be disadvantageous if the trustees sold the property in the next ten years. If instead Ted left the

---

[57] Note that if the property becomes held on s.71D (age 18–25) trust this is not a PET. The continuing trusts must provide for capital to vest at 18 (i.e. fall within s.71A). See 25.11 and 25.13

investment property on interest in possession trusts for Violet, the trustees could terminate her interest at a later date and appoint the property on continuing trust for the children. Although the inheritance tax treatment is the same—this is a chargeable transfer by Violet—for capital gains tax purposes provided the appointment is merely a variation of the existing settlement there is no disposal by the trustees. Hence no hold-over relief claim is needed and there is no interruption in the period of ownership for taper relief purposes. Moreover some of the traps that can arise if a hold over relief claim has been made are avoided[58];

(vii) if property is left outright to the spouse, s/he cannot make lifetime gifts on trust for the children which take effect as PETs.[59] They will be chargeable transfers. By contrast if the spouse is given an IPDI in the will which is then terminated so that the property becomes held on bereaved minor trusts during her lifetime this will be a PET. Given the restricted scope of bereaved minor trusts,[60] however, it is not thought that this difference in treatment between settled and unsettled gifts of residue is likely to be significant in encouraging the widespread use of an IPDI trust for the surviving spouse.

Dealing with residue if there is no surviving spouse[61]

28.40 In broad terms the options are:

(i) outright gifts (e.g. "to my children equally");

(ii) IPDI trusts. It is important to bear in mind that although the main use of the IPDI is likely to be in a trust for a surviving spouse *any interest in possession trust set up in a will is an IPDI*.[62] This is the only option for a grandparent who wishes to leave assets on trust for his grandchildren but avoid the relevant property regime. Note that no age contingency should be inserted. Section 31, Trustee Act 1925 should be excluded if the intended beneficiaries are minors.

---

[58] In particular the claw-back charge; see 9.25.
[59] Save only for trusts which create a disabled person's interest under IHTA 1984, s.89B.
[60] Considered in detail at 25.13 onwards.
[61] See also 19.23 for practical advice on how to draft a will and what sort of trusts to use where there is no surviving spouse or where the testator desires to make provision for others apart from his children.
[62] Combining a nil rate band discretionary trust (see 28.04 *et seq.*) with an IPDI trust of residue for the surviving spouse will not lead to a problem of "related settlements". In general for the purpose of calculating the rate of IHT charge on a relevant property trust (such as the nil rate band discretionary trust) the value of property in a settlement set up by the same settlor on the same day must be taken into account: see IHTA 1984, s.62 (definition of a related settlement); s.83 (will trusts are treated as commencing on the date of death); s.66(4)(c), s.68(5)(b). When the IPDI trust is for the benefit of the surviving spouse the property is—for the purpose of the Ch. III relevant property charge—*not* treated as having become comprised in the settlement at the date of death but only on the termination of that interest in possession (see IHTA 1984, s.80(4) inserted by FA 2006, Sch.20, para.23). Hence the related settlement rules will not apply. This protection is not, however, available in other cases where an IPDI trust is set up and therefore it is important to avoid the combination of a nil rate band discretionary will trust with an IPDI for any person other than the surviving spouse.

EXAMPLE 28.4

> Donald, a lonely widower, wishes to make provision for his grandchildren Charlotte and Luke but he is anxious they do not receive capital at too early an age. (His children are already well provided for.) He therefore leaves his residuary estate in equal shares to his grandchildren on interest in possession trusts with capital vesting at 30. When he dies they are still minors. Section 31, Trustee Act 1925 has been excluded. The trusts are IPDIs and the grandchildren receive the income equally. The trusts are not taxed under the relevant property regime. However, just before Charlotte reaches 30, in 2020 the trustees decide to defer her capital entitlement in order to avoid a large capital gains tax charge on her share of the assets. They exercise the widened power of advancement included in the settlement. HMRC consider that when they extend her interest in possession they take the trust outside the IPDI regime since her interest in possession is a "new" one which is now within the relevant property regime. The result is that capital gains tax is deferred but her share is henceforth subject to exit charges and anniversary charges. She has made a chargeable transfer and inheritance tax is payable at 20 per cent on the excess over her nil rate band. Moreover since Charlotte was the life tenant and has not been excluded from the settled property, after termination of her qualifying interest in possession the reservation of benefit rules apply since she is deemed to have made a gift. The property therefore remains subject to inheritance tax on her death. Even if the settled property passes to her spouse outright on her death there is no spouse exemption.
>
> In addition her interest in possession is no longer a qualifying interest so there is no capital gains tax uplift on her death.[63] A tax disaster!
>
> By contrast, if Donald had not inserted any age contingency the trustees would not have needed to defer her capital entitlement and Charlotte would continue to have held a qualifying interest in possession until her death or earlier termination of her interest. The settled property would be taxed only on her death (with spouse exemption if the settled property then passed to her spouse outright) and with capital gains tax uplift. There are no exit or anniversary charges before her death and no chargeable transfer has been made by Charlotte.

(iii) a relevant property settlement: such a trust will fall within IHTA 1984, s.144 and so provide up to two years worth of flexibility.[64]

(iv) a bare trust: this may be attractive, e.g. for minor grandchildren of the testator[65];

(v) a bereaved minor or s.71D (18–25) trust: may be used when the testator wishes to leave assets to his children who are aged under 25. These trusts are considered in detail in Chapter 25 (Trusts for Minors and Older Children). They are not available to grandparents. There is no reason

---

[63] See ss.72,73, TCGA 1992 and 7.46.
[64] s.144 is considered in detail at 29.49 *et seq*.
[65] See further Ch. 30.

why the BMT or s.71D trust has to be set up in the will itself. If the estate is left on discretionary trusts the trustees can exercise their powers at any time and alter the terms of the trust to secure that the BMT or s.71D conditions are met.[66] Hence it is probably better to leave residue on discretionary trusts and then take a view at the time as to whether it is worthwhile to set up BMTs or s.71D trusts. Much will depend on the ages and circumstances of the children at the date of death.

EXAMPLE 28.5

John a young widower, leaves his residuary estate on discretionary trusts for his only son Ben. When the Will was drafted Ben was only four. If John dies when Ben is aged say seven, it may well be sensible to convert the trust into a BMT within two years of his death so that anniversary and exit charges are avoided over the next 11 years. Just before Ben is 18 the trustees could:

(a) let Ben take the capital; the trusts end and there is no exit charge; *or*
(b) make a settled advance deferring his capital entitlement until 25. The trust is thereby converted into a s.71D trust without any exit charge and anniversary charges are avoided until he is 25. Just before Ben is 25 the trustees can consider whether they wish to defer his capital entitlement again. Whether he takes outright or the trusts continue there is a 4.2% exit charge at 25. If the trusts continue the relevant property regime applies from that date; *or*
(c) make a settled advance so Ben does not take capital at any specified age. The settled property falls into the relevant property regime when he is 18.

If however John dies when Ben is 21 the trustees may consider it is more appropriate to give Ben the property outright or create an IPDI. In either case they should exercise their powers within two years of death so that reading back under s.144 is obtained.[67] Unlike a BMT or a s.71D trust, an IPDI cannot be created out of a discretionary will trust more than two years after the testator's death.

---

[66] See 25.24 and 25.41 for further comments on this. If the trust is altered more than two years after death, s.71D or BMT treatment can be secured from that date but there is no reading back to the date of death so until the point of conversion the settled property is within the relevant property regime and may suffer an exit charge.
[67] See Ch. 25 generally for a detailed review of BMTs and s.71D trusts.

CHAPTER 29

PLANNING AFTER DEATH—VARIATIONS, DISCLAIMERS AND S.144 ARRANGEMENTS

- Variations: inheritance tax treatment: **(29.03)**
- Variations: CGT treatment: **(29.31)**
- Variations: income tax: **(29.38)**
- Variations: impact of the POA regime: **(29.41)**
- Variations: Stamp duty and SDLT: **(29.42)**
- Disclaimers: **(29.44)**
- Section 144: discretionary will trusts: **(29.49)**

This chapter is concerned with post death tax saving arrangements, namely: **29.01**

(i) *Instruments of variation* (dealing with their inheritance tax, capital gains tax and income tax, treatment);

(ii) *Disclaimers*;

(iii) *Section 144* (two year discretionary trusts).

As will be seen, instruments of variation remain a valuable planning tool in the taxpayer's armoury conferring the three advantages, namely:

(1) that the relevant beneficiary does not make any transfer of value;

(2) that the reservation of benefit rules will not apply even if he continues to use or enjoy the redirected property; and

(3) that they are outside the pre-owned assets charge.

Moreover they enable a person who wishes to effect lifetime planning for his children to set up a trust by way of variation by creating qualifying interest in possession trusts (IPDIs) not falling within the relevant property regime.

It is worth bearing in mind that in the "real world": **29.02**

(i) it is not possible to vary a deceased's will; and

(ii) that any variation is accordingly a gift by the person who is redirecting the property.

Section 142, however, creates a fictional world which extends as far as enabling beneficial joint tenancies to be, in effect, severed after the death of one of the joint tenants.[1]

VARIATIONS: INHERITANCE TAX TREATMENT

29.03 If a beneficiary varies the dispositions of property comprised in a deceased's estate in accordance with the conditions laid down in IHTA 1984, s.142(1), then "this Act shall apply as if the variation had been effected by the deceased." It is commonly said that the terms of the variation are "read back" into the deceased's will.[2]

Requirements under s.142, IHTA 1984:

29.04 **(i) Statement for reading back:** FA 2002 removed the need to send an election to HMRC whenever beneficiaries of a deceased's estate vary their entitlements with the aim of such variation being treated for IHT purposes as if it had been made by the deceased. For variations made from August 1, 2002, no formal election is required. The variation will be read back to death if the instrument of variation itself contains a statement that this is intended.[3] Only if more IHT becomes payable as a result of the variation does it have to be sent to HMRC within six months[4] and the personal representatives must then be parties to the instrument as well as the person effecting the variation.[5]

The requirement to include the reading back statement in the deed of variation itself has removed some flexibility. Under the old regime it was possible to wait for up to six months before making an election. Now a decision either way has to be taken when the instrument is made.[6]

29.05 **(ii) The property must be comprised in the deceased's estate:** s.142 can only apply to property comprised in a person's estate immediately before his death. Excluded property is within this definition[7] but not settled property in which the deceased had a life interest (see s.142(5)). It will also include jointly owned

---

[1] The extent of the "deeming" that is required by s.142 was considered in the context of multiple variations of the same property in *Russell v IRC* [1988] S.T.C. 195.
[2] Of course, it should be remembered that variations are not confined to the situation where the deceased left a will but also apply to alter dispositions of property occurring under the intestacy rules and to property passing by survivorship under a beneficial joint tenancy.
[3] Typical wording is "the provisions of IHTA 1984, s.142(1) and of TCGA 1992, s.62(6) shall apply to the variation effected by this instrument." Of course it may be desirable to opt for reading back for one tax but not the other.
[4] IHTA 1984, s.218A inserted by FA 2002, s.120(2); (4).
[5] IHTA 1984, s.142(2A) substituted by FA 2002, s.120(1)(7). Note that personal representatives can only decline to make a reading-back statement "if no, or no sufficient, assets are held by them in that capacity for discharging the additional tax".
[6] A statement of intent is not required for a disclaimer: if one is not included it precludes the instrument from being treated as a variation in the event that the conditions for a disclaimer are not met: IHTM 35058.
[7] For the meaning of excluded property, see Ch. 22.

property[8] but not gift with reservation property.[9] Although HMRC have confirmed that a deceased's joint tenant's interest passing by survivorship can be redirected by deed of variation, it is not thought that as a matter of law a surviving joint tenant can make an effective disclaimer. (For a precedent variation incorporating a severance, see Appendix II A2.51). Variations are possible even if the beneficiary has only been given a life interest by the will but the beneficiary in question can, of course, only vary what he has—in this case the life interest.

(iii) Requirement for writing: whether a variation or a disclaimer, the instrument must be in writing. This does not necessarily mean that a deed is required, but it is thought that a variation can only receive the favourable tax treatment if effective in property terms, which means that the variation has to be binding and enforceable.[10] To obtain the tax advantages there must be no extraneous consideration and therefore a deed is invariably used.   **29.06**

(iv) Parties: the variation or disclaimer must be made by the persons who benefit under the dispositions: i.e. all parties who are prejudiced by the deed of variation must agree it. Unlike the old deeds of family arrangement, anyone can benefit—not necessarily members of the family—including limited companies.[11]   **29.07**

(v) Parties who vary must be sui juris: a minor cannot be a party to a deed of variation without the court's consent on his behalf, although obviously he can benefit under someone else's deed of variation. Provided that the minor's interest under the will or intestacy is not adversely affected, a variation can go ahead without his consent. For example, if the will creates a trust in which the remainder interest is left to a minor, there is no objection to any prior interest being the subject of a deed of variation. However, a deed of variation cannot be used to take away an interest of the minor beneficiary and replace it with a different interest even if the minor will benefit overall. Such a variation can only go ahead with the approval of the court.   **29.08**

The Inheritance Tax Manual states that:

---

[8] Whether the jointly held property is realty or personalty such as bank accounts. See the words "or otherwise" in s.142(1). Note that if the property is beneficially owned by three joint tenants, one dies and only one of the surviving joint tenants wishes to vary the jointly held property he can do so by "severing" the joint tenancy: for s.142 purposes it is only his share which is treated as passing to whoever he designates. The other surviving joint tenant's interest is unaffected.

[9] Although note that a disclaimer of settled property can be made under s.93: see 29.47. On the disclaimer of a life interest, see 29.45.

[10] But see IHTM 35022: "you can accept a letter or note from the beneficiary redirecting their inheritance as a valid variation so long as the document conforms to the guidelines and otherwise meets the conditions in s.142".

[11] It will not be necessary to include the personal representative as parties (only if extra tax is payable: see fn. 5 above) but as a matter of practice this is commonly done and is obviously important if the estate has not been fully administered. It is also common practice to include the person benefiting from the variation: again this is not strictly necessary but it does mean that he has signified his acceptance of the gift. If the variation establishes trusts the designated trustees will normally be joined to indicate their consent to act. Assume that by will S leaves property to his wife for life and on her death to her daughter if she is then living or, if dead, to her children and the daughter is aged over 55 with one adult child. HMRC accept that a variation can be made by the wife, daughter and adult child and that as a result of *re Pettifor's Will Trusts, Roberts v Roberts* [1966] Ch. 257 the daughter is presumed to be past the age of child bearing so that there is no question of adversely affecting the interests of unborn children: see IHTM 35048.

"an IoV which adversely affects the interests of minor or unborn beneficiaries can achieve total validity only by obtaining the approval of the Court (on an application under the Variation of Trusts Act or under the Court's inherent jurisdiction). A parent's signature on behalf of a minor is not sufficient."[12]

29.09 Personal representatives can stand in the shoes of a deceased beneficiary, if the beneficiary died after the testator, for the purposes of effecting a deed of variation or making a disclaimer. This is often referred to as a double death variation.

EXAMPLE 29.1

Husband dies leaving everything to his wife who then dies six months later. The wife leaves all the property to the children. The combined estates of the husband and wife exceed the nil rate band of the wife and the husband's nil rate band has been wasted.

Even if the beneficiaries benefiting under the variation are those who would have taken under the wife's will in any event, so that there is no movement overall in the beneficial interests, it does not appear that HMRC will object to wife's executors varying husband's will so that the nil rate band is used on his death.[13] Note that if husband leaves everything to his wife who has lost capacity by the time of his death her attorneys (even if acting under an enduring power of attorney) cannot vary her interest. They would have to obtain the consent of the Court of Protection. If she dies within the two-year period, however, her personal representatives can make the deed of variation even though she did not have capacity.

29.10 **(vi) No consideration payable[14]:** s.142(1) does not apply to a variation or disclaimer which is made for any consideration in money or money's worth other than consideration consisting of the making of a variation or disclaimer in respect of another of the dispositions made under the will. The donor to the deed of variation should pay the legal costs, not the personal representatives or donee, and there must be no understanding that the beneficiary will give the property back to the donor at any later date.[15]

---

[12] IHTM 35045.
[13] HMRC consider that it must be shown that the personal representatives were acting with the consent of the persons who would take under the deceased's will. Commonly this consent is stated in a recital to the variation, see *Tax Bulletin* February 1995, p.194.
[14] See IHTM 35100.
[15] However, IHTM 35094 states that where the deceased is domiciled abroad, then if the facts are as in the Example below "you should refer [such] cases immediately to the TA Team Leader without making any preliminary enquiries."

EXAMPLE

T dies domiciled in Switzerland. He has a London house worth £1m (non-excluded property) which he leaves to his son and excluded property (such as gilts and foreign property) worth the same amount left to his spouse or charities. A variation is made such that the son now gets the excluded property and the spouse or charities get the London flat.

It should be noted that where there is a deed of variation or disclaimer in favour of the deceased's surviving spouse, so that less IHT becomes payable as a result of the spouse exemption, HMRC are likely to raise questions designed to elicit whether lifetime gifts are contemplated by the spouse in favour of the varying beneficiaries: i.e whether there is some consideration or the variation is a sham.

(vii) Two year time limit: the variation or disclaimer must be made "within two years after a person's death". Hence if the deceased died on January 1, 2006 the last day for making the variation is generally assumed to be December 31, 2007.[16]

29.11

Link-up with Reservation of Benefit

HMRC accept that "*this Act*" in s.142(1) includes all the IHT legislation which therefore encompasses the reservation of benefit legislation in FA 1986. Hence a redirection of property will not be caught by these rules even if the beneficiary continues to derive a benefit from it.

29.12

EXAMPLE 29.2

> On her husband's death in June 2006, Joyce is left his entire estate including the couple's seaside cottage ("Fishnets") worth £285,000. By deed of variation falling within s.142(1), she transfers this property to her son Barney. Joyce continues to use the property on a regular basis.

Tax analysis

> (a) The variation is read back into her husband's will and falls within his hitherto unused IHT nil rate band.

If T was domiciled here such rearrangement would appear to be uncontroversial because although there is consideration it is a rearrangement within the terms of the Will. However HMRC appear to object to the above and in these circumstances it may be advisable to ensure that the assets being varied are not equal in value.

[16] It might be argued that the two-year period commenced from the day "after a person's death" and hence the last day might be January 1, 2008. The question is whether the day of death is included or excluded in calculating the two-year period or whether the two-year period runs from the instant of death in which case it would expire on January 1, 2008 at 10 am if the deceased had died on January 1, 2006 at 10 am! The statutory rule of interpretation is that fractions of a day will normally be disregarded when the occurrence of a particular event starts or stops the period running and hence the period begins not at the instant the relevant event (here the death) occurs but either at the commencement or the termination of the day during which the death occurs. There is no known case on the point but HMRC are believed to consider that the day of death is included in calculating the two-year period.

(b) Joyce should also consider whether to make a statement for reading back for CGT purposes: this will be desirable if the property has increased in value since her husband's death by more than Joyce's annual exemption.[17] Otherwise she will be treated as making a disposal of the house at market value and she will be taxed on any gain.

(c) Although Joyce continues to derive a benefit from the use of the property she is not within the reservation of benefit rules given that, because of read-back, she has never made a gift of the property. Likewise she is not caught by the income tax pre-owned assets charge.[18]

29.13 The FA 2006 changes in the IHT taxation of settlements do not affect Joyce because no trust is involved in the above transaction. However, the property passing under the will or intestacy can be varied *into* a trust. From March 22, 2006 it is preferable for the variation itself to set out the trusts. For instance, if Joyce varied the property into a discretionary trust from which she could benefit, this is not treated as a gift by her for IHT purposes and hence the reservation of benefit rules do not apply. The new trust would, of course, be a relevant property settlement. Suppose she varied her interest into a trust (set out in the deed of variation) under which she took an immediate interest in possession and opted for reading back for IHT purposes? Her interest in possession will be an IPDI[19] and therefore no IHT saving would be achieved: the interest in possession is treated as set up by her husband and is spouse exempt. She will be taxed on her death as if she owned the property beneficially since she has a qualifying interest in possession under IHTA, s.49A.

IHT position post-FA 2006 when the variation establishes a settlement

29.14 When considering the IHT regime for variations made on or after March 22, 2006 there are six possibilities to consider.

(i) Testator dies after March 21, 2006 and variation is made with reading back for IHT purposes.

(ii) Testator dies after March 21, 2006 and a variation is made with no reading back for inheritance tax purposes.

(iii) Testator dies before March 22, 2006 and a variation is made with reading back before March 22, 2006.

(iv) Testator dies before March 22, 2006 and a variation is made pre March 22, 2006 but with no reading back.

(v) Testator dies before March 22, 2006 and a variation is made after March 21, 2006 but with reading back.

---

[17] The CGT provisions are in TCGA 1992, s.62(6)–(10). The "reading back" is more limited in its effect under the CGT legislation: see 29.31.
[18] See 29.41.
[19] For the meaning of an IPDI, see 19.05.

(vi) Testator dies before March 22, 2006 and a variation is made after March 21, 2006 with no reading back.

Each of these possibilities will be looked at in turn.

Testator dies after March 21, 2006 and variation is effected with reading back for inheritance tax purposes. **29.15**

EXAMPLE 29.3

> Maurice leaves the matrimonial home (wholly owned by him at his death) on trust for his widow for life then to his children for life with remainders over. He dies in 2007. She surrenders her life interest so that her children take immediate interests in possession and she makes a reading back statement. The children's interests qualify as IPDI's. IHT may be payable on Maurice's death but the widow can continue to live in the home without a reservation of benefit problem.[20]

Instruments of variation can still be used to take advantage of a deceased's foreign domicile.

EXAMPLE 29.4

> Joyce inherits non-UK situs property from her uncle who died in 2007 domiciled in Monaco. She enters into a deed of variation (with reading back) so that the property becomes held on interest in possession trusts for herself with the trustees having power to advance her capital. The trustees are UK resident but the trust holds only non-UK situs assets.
>
> The trust is treated as having been set up by the uncle in his will for Joyce giving her an IPDI interest in possession within s.49A and is an excluded property settlement.
>
> It does not matter that the trust is UK resident nor that the interest in possession beneficiary is UK domiciled. The important determinant of the IHT liability is where the assets are situated at the date of Joyce's death[21] and the domicile of the settlor (the uncle for IHT purposes). Even if the trustees hold UK situated assets directly during Joyce's lifetime the trust is not within the relevant property regime because it is an IPDI. (Of course, in such a case there would be a risk of Joyce dying

---

[20] Note that unless she retains some interest in the home under the trust or the children live in it no principal private residence relief will be available on the eventual sale of the property: see 31.25 and s.225 TCGA 1992. Contrast the position if the trustees had terminated her interest in possession (or if the widow did not opt to read back) when the reservation of benefit rules are now in point: see 24.08.

[21] Since it is an IPDI if the trust holds UK situated assets at the date of Joyce's death she has a qualifying interest in possession and therefore there would be inheritance tax payable.

while the trustees held UK assets and IHT being payable.) The trust is an excluded property settlement only while (or to the extent that) it holds non-UK situated assets.[22]

For CGT purposes, Joyce will be treated as the settlor (see 00.00). Joyce has a qualifying interest in possession and so for capital gains tax purposes there will be a base cost uplift to market value on her death.[23]

Even if there were ongoing trusts after Joyce's death, provided that the trustees do not hold UK situated assets the trust property remains excluded for IHT purposes. If the trustees did hold UK situated assets directly then they would need to consider 10-year charges because after Joyce's death the trust will fall within the relevant property regime even if her children take interests in possession.

Testator dies after March 21, 2006 and a variation is effected with no reading back for IHT purposes

29.16 If in Example 29.3 the widow of Maurice did not make a reading back statement, then spouse exemption continues to be available on Maurice's death but she is treated as making a chargeable transfer because the interests of her children cannot be IPDIs; the settlement falls within the relevant property regime. On the death of the children their interests do not form part of their estates for inheritance tax purposes. The widow could not continue to benefit from the trust e.g. live in the house rent free otherwise she will be treated as having reserved a benefit.[24]

29.17 *Testator dies before March 22, 2006 and a variation is completed (with reading back) before March 22, 2006.*

EXAMPLE 29.5

Maurice left the matrimonial home (wholly owned by him) on trust for his widow for life remainder to his children for life. He died in 2005. The widow surrenders her life interest in February 2006 and opts for reading back. In these circumstances there is a chargeable transfer from Maurice to the children which takes place on his death (which may fall within his IHT nil rate band) and the children take qualifying interests in possession which arise under the pre Budget regime. The wife can continue to benefit from the settled property (by living in the house) without any reservation of benefit since she has opted for reading back under s.142 and so the gift is treated as made by Maurice for all IHT purposes.[25]

---

[22] Excluded property settlements are considered in detail in Ch. 22.
[23] See TCGA 1992, s.72 and 7.46.
[24] See FA 1986, s.102ZA inserted by FA 2006, and see 24.08.
[25] See 29.12, above.

Testator dies before March 22, 2006 and a variation is completed before **29.18**
March 22, 2006 with no reading back.

EXAMPLE 29.6

> Facts as in *Example 29.5* except that the widow does *not* opt for reading back. The children take life interests which are qualifying interests in possession (since they arise under the pre March 2006 regime). This surrender is a PET by the widow. However, because her life interest was surrendered rather than terminated by *action of the trustees prior to March 22*, then it is thought that if she benefits from any ongoing trusts she will be treated as making a gift (not merely a transfer of value) and so is caught by the reservation of benefit rules.[26]
>
> Suppose however that the widow's interest was terminated *by the trustees* before March 22, 2006. In these circumstances the reservation of benefit rules do not apply.[27] The spouse exemption is available on her husband's death and she needs to survive her PET by seven years to avoid an IHT charge. If she retains (say) a 5% interest in possession, the trustees will be able to claim principal private residence relief on the eventual sale of the property.

Testator dies before March 22, 2006 and a variation is made with reading back **29.19**
on or after March 22, 2006

EXAMPLE 29.7

> Maurice leaves the matrimonial home (wholly owned by him) on trust for his widow for life remainder to his children for life. He dies in 2005 and the widow carries out a variation after March 21, 2006 so that her children take immediate interests in possession. She opts for reading back. In these circumstances there is a chargeable transfer from Maurice to the children which takes place on his death (which may fall within his IHT nil rate band) and the children take qualifying interests in possession which arise under the old pre-Budget regime *even though the variation was completed after March 21, 2006*. The IHT legislation applies "as if the variation had been effected by the deceased" and at the date of the deceased's death it was still possible to set up old-style interests in possession. The wife can continue to benefit from the property (e.g. by living in the house) since the gift is treated as made by Maurice for IHT purposes.
>
> Note that since the children have pre March 22, 2006 interests in possession in both *Example 29.5* and *Example 29.7* it is possible for further

---

[26] See 24.08 *et seq*.
[27] She has not made any gift. The position was changed for terminations after March 21, 2006 by FA 2006, Sch.20 Pt 5 inserting new s.102ZA into FA 2006.

interests in possession to be set up before April 6, 2008 and for those interests in possession to be transitional serial interests.[28]

Suppose in Example 29.7 that the widow (or child) had been given the property outright by the deceased who had died before March 22, 2006. Even if the variation is completed on or after March 22, 2006, if the taxpayer opts for reading back old style accumulation and maintenance ("A+M") trusts can be established.[29]

EXAMPLE 29.8

Maurice dies in 2005 leaving all his property to his wife. In 2007 she varies his will leaving his unused nil rate band on A+M trusts for his children who take income at 25 and capital at 30. This is an A+M trust falling within IHTA 1984, s.71. After April 6, 2008 the trust will fall into the relevant property regime unless its terms are altered to either vest capital at 18 or to make it an 18–25 trust (i.e. its terms provide that the beneficiaries will be entitled to capital no later than age 25).

There is a limited advantage in setting up old style A+M trusts where the variation is being made in respect of a pre March 22, 2006 estate since until April 6, 2008 there is no need to fix the interests of each child under 25. Under an 18–25 trust flexibility is lost: the trustees cannot pay out more income to one child under 25 than another in the course of a tax year: the shares each take must be predetermined.[30]

Testator dies before March 22, 2006 and a variation is effected (with no reading back) on or after March 22, 2006

29.20 In these circumstances any ongoing trusts set up by the person making the variation will be within the relevant property regime. So in Example 29.7 there would be a chargeable transfer by the widow and the trusts in favour of the children would not be qualifying interests in possession but within the relevant property regime. Moreover in the future the widow must be excluded from any benefit because her life interest has been terminated.[31]

Multiple variations

29.21 It is not possible to have more than one variation falling within s.142(1) in respect of the same property[32] (so if father varies in favour of son and reads

---

[28] For what is meant by a TSI, see 18.14.
[29] Although the requirements for continued A+M status under IHTA 1984, s.71 are changed from April 6, 2008: see Ch. 21.
[30] For the requirements for an 18–25 Trust, see 25.34.
[31] FA 1986, s.102ZA inserted by FA 2006, Sch.20 Pt 5.
[32] *Russell & Anor v IRC* [1988] S.T.C. 195.

back any further variation by the son of the same property will not fall under s.142). However, there can be a number of variations made at different times within the two year period in relation to the same estate, provided that each variation deals with separate property.[33]

Rectification

29.22 If a deed of variation is made and contains an error (for example, a gift is stated to be free of tax instead of subject to tax), rectification may be possible but a court application is required for it to be accepted by HMRC even if the parties are in agreement that an error has been made.[34]

Appointments and advancements followed by variations

29.23 If an appointment is made out of a discretionary will trust within two years of death, and given effect to under s.144 of IHTA 1984, a deed of variation may subsequently (but still within two years of the death) be made by the beneficiary who has been appointed the property. Section 142 of IHTA 1984 will apply if a statement for reading back is made.

Similarly HMRC accept that the following is effective:

EXAMPLE 29.9

> A is left property in a Will on trust for life with capital contingent on her attaining 25. There is a wide power of advancement. The trustees exercise this power so that A becomes absolutely entitled to the property.
>
> A then redirects that property to her son and opts for reading back under s.142(1). Assuming that the two year time limit is met, HMRC accept that this is an effective variation and the gift to the son is made by the deceased not A even though A had not been absolutely entitled to the property at the date of death.

Typical uses of variations

29.24 (i) Variations are often employed to use the otherwise wasted nil rate band of the deceased person. For example, where the will leaves everything

---

[33] It is also possible to combine variations with two year discretionary trusts under IHTA 1984, s.144: see 29.23 below.
[34] Be careful that you limit any nil rate band trust set up in a deed of variation to the value of the NRB *in force at the date of death*: *Martin v Nicholson* [2005] W.T.L.R. 175. In this case the variation created a legacy of £200,000. This was the figure for the NRB at the time when the variation was executed but the NRB at the date of death was only £154,000 so prima facie £46,000 was chargeable to IHT. Fortunately the court rectified the instrument.

outright to the surviving spouse, he may execute a deed of variation varying up to the unused nil rate band in favour of children or on discretionary trusts. Variations can also be used to maximise reliefs such as BPR and APR.[35]

(ii) The estate of a beneficiary alive at the date of the deceased's death can be increased by a subsequent variation made after that beneficiary's death. For instance, if H dies leaving his entire estate to his daughter and W (H's wife) dies shortly afterward without sufficient assets to use up her IHT nil rate band, the daughter can vary H's will in favour of W.[36]

(iii) A variation may be used to redirect a posthumous increase in the value of an estate without any IHT charge. Assume that the death estate was worth £200,000 but increased in value shortly after death so that it became worth £1m. The will had left everything to the widow. She could by instrument of variation provide for a legacy of £200,000 to herself with residue passing to her children. Under IHTA 1984, ss.36–42 the value of the death estate (£200,000) will be wholly attributed to the spouse exempt legacy.

Variations and short lived trusts[37]

29.25 Watch s.142(4) which imposes special rules where a "variation . . . results in property being held on trust for a person for a period which ends not more than two years after the death." The disposition taking effect at the end of this period will be treated as if it had taken effect on death.

EXAMPLE 29.10

Daughter is left property by her father on his death in 2007. By a read-back deed of variation she sets up an interest in possession trust (an IPDI) in favour of her stepmother (to whom her father was married at death) which will end automatically one year after the father's death whereupon the property will revert to the daughter. There will be no spouse exemption; instead as a result of s.142(4) the father's estate will be treated as if it had been left direct to daughter.

Suppose the variation gives the stepmother a life interest and she dies within two years of the father's death. Now it is the death not the variation that results in the trust ending within two years of death and HMRC accept that s.142(4) does not apply. (They will collect IHT on the death of the stepmother!)

What happens if the variation creates a terminable life interest and the trustees terminate the interest within two years of the deceased's death?

---

[35] On will drafting generally, see Ch. 28.
[36] See *Tax Bulletin*, February 1995, p.94.
[37] See IHTM 35133.

Is it the variation which results in the termination of the trust (on the basis that it creates the terms allowing the termination) or is it the act of the trustees? The position is unclear. To avoid arguments a terminable life interest created by variation for a surviving spouse should last for at least two years from the deceased's death.[38]

Varying life interests where the life tenant has died. 29.26

EXAMPLE 29.11

A dies leaving by will a life interest to B, remainder to charity and B dies within two years of A's death. In these circumstances there would have been IHT payable on the death of A. However, if the property can be treated as passing direct from A to the charity there is no IHT payable. Can A's Will be varied so that the life interest in favour of B is effectively deleted? This can be done while B is alive by surrender of his life interest. Can it be done by the personal representatives of B after B's death?

In the December 2001 issue of the *IHT Newsletter*, HMRC stated:

"It is a pre-requisite if the provisions are to have any impact that a real life disposition or transfer took place so that the transferor can decide whether or not to make an election in order to trigger the deeming provisions."[39]

HMRC's argument was that the deceased cannot be deemed to bring about effects which the beneficiaries cannot or do not bring about in the real world. Since the life interest of B in the above example has already ended, his personal representatives cannot effect a variation of it.

In *Soutter's Executry v IRC*[40] the deceased, Miss Soutter, left a "free life- 29.27 rent and useful occupation of the house at Drevaburn as long as Miss Greenlees wishes to reside there." Miss Soutter died in November 1999 and her estate was under the inheritance tax threshold. Miss Greenlees lived in the house until she became ill. She died in November 2000 and her estate was substantially over the inheritance tax threshold. The executors and beneficiaries of both estates executed a deed of variation purporting to remove the liferent provision in Miss Soutter's will.

The Special Commissioner decided that in order for a right to be assigned or renounced it must belong to the assignor at the date of the assignment. There can be no assignment of something that does not exist. The executors of Miss Greenlees never held the liferent and had nothing to assign because it had ceased on her death. He decided that although a deed of variation is deemed to be made by the deceased that is only a deeming for tax purposes. It

---

[38] The terminable life interest does not need to last two years from the creation of the trust by variation.
[39] And see IHTM 35042.
[40] [2002] S.T.C. (SCD) 385.

29.28 cannot affect the law of property nor the question of whether those making the deed of variation had any right to do so.

The decision has been heavily criticised, rightly so the authors believe. An alternative view is that the sense of s.142 is to deem the deed of variation to take effect at Miss Soutter's death and therefore the fact that the liferent did not exist at Miss Greenlees' death is irrelevant. What is varied is the disposition of property made by Miss Soutter and this could be done by removing the liferent and the assignability of that interest at the time of the variation is irrelevant.

The executors pointed out that the position was no more unusual than a beneficiary spending a cash legacy (so that he no longer had the property) and then varying the disposition of the will conferring the legacy. HMRC accepts that in these circumstances a variation is effective. Similarly where property such as a house has been sold after death, HMRC accept that the beneficiary can execute a deed of variation in respect of the gift of the house.

Some commentators have argued that *Soutter* does not apply in England, particularly where the life interest is in income producing property and income arises between the two deaths which falls to be apportioned. And, of course, it is possible for the life tenant of a Will trust to vary his life interest *while alive* within two years of the death of the testator. Thus if Miss Greenlees had executed a variation the day before her death this would have been effective.

Example 29.12

> H leaves his estate of £280,000 to W (his wife) on IPDI trusts for life, remainder to his son, Sam. W dies 12 months later with a free estate of £280,000 which she leaves her estate to Sam.
>
> If W's PRs vary H's will to delete the life interest, there is a substantial tax saving as the estate of each spouse will pass to the son within their respective nil rate bands. HMRC do not accept this is possible. However her personal representatives may disclaim her life interest if she had not accepted it.[41]

29.29 In summary, HMRC accept that:

(i) a life tenant can vary before death;

(ii) a life tenant's PRs can disclaim the benefit of a life interest if it had not been accepted.[42]

Varying settled property

29.30 Section 142 does not apply to property in which the deceased had a qualifying interest in possession.[43]

---

[41] On disclaimers, see 29.44.
[42] But see 29.45.
[43] IHTA 1984, s.142(5).

Example 29.13

> A dies in 2007 leaving his free estate to his child B outright. A was the life tenant of a pre March 2006 trust set up by his mother which now passes to child B for life (this will be a TSI[44]) remainder to B's children living at A's death. B can vary the free estate (e.g. by passing it to A's spouse so as to obtain the spouse exemption) but cannot vary A's life interest nor vary the life interest which he now enjoys under s.142.
>
> However, B could *disclaim* his life interest under IHTA 1984, s.93[45] so that the settled property was treated as passing directly from A to B's children. A disclaimer would be more difficult if B's children were only contingently entitled (e.g. on surviving B). It might have been preferable if B had assigned his life interest to the desired beneficiary before A's death. This would not have been a transfer of value by B because it was of excluded property (a reversionary interest).[46]

VARIATIONS: CGT TREATMENT

29.31 Subject to conditions, which are the same as for IHT, any variation of the deceased's will or of the intestacy rules, or any disclaimer, made within two years of the deceased's death may be treated:

(1) as if it were not a disposal: TCGA 1992, s.62(6)(a); *and*
(2) "this section shall apply"[47] as if it had been effected by the deceased or, in the case of a disclaimer, as if the disclaimed benefit had never been conferred *ibid.* s.62(6)(b).

29.32 As with IHT, the instrument must be in writing made within two years of the death and the variation (or disclaimer) must not be made for consideration in money or money's worth other than consideration consisting of the making of a variation or disclaimer in respect of another of the dispositions: see Example 29.14 below. The variation can be made regardless of whether the administration of the estate is complete or whether the property has already been distributed in accordance with the original disposition. The same property cannot be subject to more than one variation.

Example 29.14

> A dies leaving a house Blackacre to B and a house Whiteacre to C. B would rather have Whiteacre and C would rather have Blackacre. They

---

[44] See 18.14.
[45] s.93 is considered at 29.47.
[46] For the definition of a "reversionary interest", see 17.15 and 22.44.
[47] The difference in wording to s.142(1)—"this section" as opposed to "this Act"—is significant: see 29.12.

enter into a deed of variation so that A is deemed to have left Whiteacre to B and Blackacre to C. Although each enters into the variation in consideration of the other also varying his interest, this does not prevent reading back for both CGT and IHT purposes. Accordingly B will take Whiteacre and C Blackacre at probate value.

EXAMPLE 29.15

Andrew is entitled under his mother's will to a picture worth £100,000. Within two years of his mother's death Andrew varies the will so that the picture (now worth £150,000) passes to his brother Robert. Provided that the appropriate statement for reading back is made this will be treated as if his mother's will had provided for the picture to pass to Robert. Accordingly, Robert acquires the asset at its market value at death (£100,000) as legatee.[48]

"Reading back" (TCGA 1992, s.62(7) as amended)

29.33 Prior to August 1, 2002, reading back did not apply to a variation unless the person or persons making the instrument so elected within six months of the instrument (or such longer period as the Board might allow). From that date, as with IHT, the requirement for a separate election was abolished: if "reading back" is desired the instrument of variation itself must now so provide.[49]

In many cases, it will be desirable that the variation is read back for both CGT and IHT purposes. This is not necessary, however, since the decisions can be taken independently of each other with the result that a taxpayer may decide to read back for IHT purposes without doing so for CGT and vice versa. Careful thought should be given to this problem. Consider the following:

EXAMPLE 29.16

(1) A's will leaves quoted shares worth £100,000 to his daughter. By instrument of variation, she transfers the shares within two years to her mother (the testator's surviving spouse). The shares are then worth £106,000.

For IHT reading back will be desirable as the result will be to reduce the testator's chargeable estate at death by £100,000 since the shares are now an exempt transfer to a surviving spouse.

For CGT if the daughter makes a chargeable disposal, her gain will be £106,000 − £100,000 = £6,000 which will be covered by her annual CGT

---

[48] If the picture had increased in value since the mother's death by no more than Andrew's CGT annual exemption then Andrew should not opt to read back since the gain is then exempt and Robert will acquire the assets at its market value at the date of the variation: see *Example 29.16*.
[49] See 29.04.

exemption. Her mother will then acquire the shares at the higher base cost of £106,000. Hence she should not make the reading back statement.

(2) A will leaves quoted shares worth £100,000 to the testator's surviving spouse. After they have risen in value to £140,000 she decides (within the permitted time limit) to vary the will in favour of her daughter.

For IHT it is debatable whether the disposition should be read back. If it is, £100,000 will constitute a chargeable death transfer so that, assuming that the nil rate band has already been exhausted, tax will be charged at 40 per cent. If it is not, the widow will make a lifetime gift (a PET) of £140,000 that, if she survives by seven years, will be free of all tax. On the other hand, if it is likely that she will only survive her husband by a few weeks, then it will be necessary to consider whether it is better for £100,000 to be taxed as part of her dead husband's estate or for £140,000 to be taxed on her death.

For CGT the disposal should be read back into the will since otherwise there will be a chargeable gain of £140,000 − £100,000 = £40,000. Generally reading back is desirable for capital gains tax purposes when the administration of the estate is not completed in order to avoid any "chose in action" problems.[50]

Who is the settlor? *Marshall v Kerr*[51]

29.34 This case raised the question of who was the settlor of a trust for CGT purposes when a deed of variation with election for reading back was made. The testator died in 1977 domiciled in Jersey and Mrs Kerr (UK resident and domiciled) became entitled to one-half of the residuary estate. By a deed of family arrangement executed in January 1978 made before the administration of the estate had been completed, her half share was to be retained by the PRs (a Jersey resident company) as trustees for, inter alia, Mrs Kerr. In due course gains were realised by those trustees and capital advanced to Mrs Kerr. If Mrs Kerr was the settlor then TCGA 1992, s.87 applied and capital payments made to her attracted a CGT charge.[52] Given that she had transferred property to trustees, on general principles she would be treated as the settlor of that trust: but was this conclusion displaced by the deeming provisions in s.62(6) whereby if a variation is made within two years of death—provided that the appropriate election is made—it takes effect "as if the variation had been effected by the deceased"?

HMRC succeeded in the House of Lords by taking a point not argued in the lower courts. While accepting that s.87 took effect subject to the various deeming provisions contained in s.62, the argument presented before the Lords was that there was nothing in the latter section to prevent Mrs Kerr

---

[50] See HMRC Capital Gains Manual 31900 onwards for a somewhat puzzling interpretation of the position.
[51] [1994] S.T.C. 638, HL. The case did not affect the IHT treatment of instruments of variation and disclaimer: see RI 101 (February 1995).
[52] s.87 is discussed at 10.24.

from being treated as a settlor. Lord Browne-Wilkinson analysed matters as follows:

(1) Two assumptions were made in the lower courts, neither of which was correct: *first*, that the variation constituted a settlement of assets comprised in the testator's estate and, *secondly*, that those were assets of which the testator was competent to dispose and so were acquired by the PRs under s.62(1).

(2) When the variation was made the estate was unadministered and hence Mrs Kerr did not dispose of specific assets but of a *chose in action*: namely her right to have the estate properly administered. Although an asset for CGT purposes, this was not an asset owned by the deceased, and so was not an asset of which the deceased had been competent to dispose.

(3) The disposal of the *chose* was not itself subject to charge because of s.62(6)(a).

(4) Under s.62(6)(b) the interest of the "new" beneficiary is deemed to arise under the will of the deceased with the result that:

> "an asset of which the deceased was competent to dispose at the death which is not sold in the course of the administration but is vested in the varied beneficiaries is deemed to have been acquired by the varied beneficiary as legatee under the Will."

The "new" beneficiary is therefore only deemed to acquire qua legatee if two conditions are satisfied. First, the asset must be one of which the deceased was competent to dispose and, secondly, that asset must be vested in the varied beneficiary as legatee. The process of administering the estate cannot be ignored: assets acquired by the PRs during administration are treated as if that acquisition were by the legatee who is not treated as acquiring those assets at death.

(5) Given that Mrs Kerr settled a *chose in action*, it followed that the trustees could not trace their ownership of the settled property to the PRs and thence back to the date of death. There was therefore nothing to displace the general proposition that Mrs Kerr was the settlor of the property. It would appear from the judgment of Lord Browne-Wilkinson that a similar conclusion would be arrived at even if the estate had been fully administered.[53]

Statutory provisions

29.35 The position has now been put on a statutory footing. FA 2006, Sch.12 introduced provisions on the identification of the settlor for CGT purposes where there is a variation of a will or intestacy which sets up new trusts.[54]

If property becomes settled property as a result of the variation, the person making the variation is treated as the settlor. However, if property was *already*

---

[53] And see CG 37888 but note the criticism of the case in *Taxation*, May 3, 2002, p.105.
[54] TCGA 1992 s.68C inserted by FA 2006.

settled under the will or intestacy and then becomes comprised in another trust as a result of the variation, the deceased person and not the person making the variation is treated as the settlor for CGT purposes. This is presumably because if several persons act to vary their entitlements under a will trust and re-settle the assets in a new trust, it would be difficult to establish who is the settlor.

29.36 The position is unclear where a variation merely amends or varies a will trust rather than transferring the property to a new settlement or where the person making the variation (e.g. the life tenant) simply varies their own interest under the settlement. Does the settled property then become comprised in a new trust? Is the life tenant the settlor of the new trust? It is thought not. Hence, suppose the life tenant assigns her interest to a discretionary trust under which income is rolled up. If the trustees then make gains, it would appear that she is not taxed on those gains even though she may be a beneficiary under the trust.

EXAMPLE 29.17

> Frederick dies leaving his foreign property absolutely to his son. Frederick is not UK domiciled. His son is. His son therefore executes a deed of variation under which the property he inherits is settled on trust for himself and his children. Reading back for inheritance tax purposes Frederick is treated as a settlor of an excluded property settlement. For CGT purposes, however, the son is treated as the settlor.

Contrast the position where a variation alters the trust set up under the will. In this case the deceased is treated as the settlor.

EXAMPLE 29.18

> Frederick dies leaving his property on life interest trusts for his spouse and then to his children outright. Spouse and children execute a deed of variation setting up a new trust for grandchildren. In these circumstances the settlor is the deceased.

Extension of "settlor interested trust" definition

29.37 The definition of settlor-interested trust was extended for all UK trusts after April 5, 2006 (whenever established) with the result that parents who have entered into a variation setting up a trust in favour of their dependent minor children will find themselves taxed on the gains realised by the trust under (amended) TCGA 1992, s.77.[55]

---

[55] The concept of a settlor interested trust is significant in the CGT context for two reasons: (i) because trust gains will be taxed on the settlor and (ii) because hold-over relief under TCGA 1992, s.165 and s.260 will not be available. See Ch. 11.

EXAMPLE 29.19

> Barry, domiciled in Portugal, leaves his Portuguese villa and moneys in his Swiss bank account to his son Chris who is UK resident and domiciled. By a variation of the terms of his will made within two years of Barry's death, the property is settled on discretionary trusts with the trustees resident in Jersey for the benefit of Chris, his spouse and his issue, who include two minor children.
>
> For IHT purposes, reading back ensures that the settlement is of excluded property. Hence the trust is not subject to IHT and there is no ten year anniversary or exit charge provided that no UK situs assets are part of the trust property on those occasions.
>
> For CGT purposes, the settlement has been created by Chris, a UK resident domiciliary, so that the charging provisions in TCGA 1992, s.86 ff will apply given that he can benefit from the trust. Even if the trust is brought onshore with UK resident trustees and Chris and his spouse (and any possible civil partner) are excluded from any benefit, as his minor children are still beneficiaries he is taxed on all gains arising in the trust. If, however, his children were excluded from benefit until they were 18 then he would not be caught. In fact, since the rates of tax are the same (40 per cent) given that Chris is a higher rate taxpayer, and since he has a right of reimbursement from the trustees it will usually not make much difference if his minor children are excluded or not.[56]
>
> For income tax purposes, the settlement has been created by Chris and as he and his wife can benefit, all trust income will be taxed on him wherever the trustees are resident or the assets are sited.[57]

VARIATIONS: INCOME TAX

29.38 The income tax legislation contains no provisions similar to those in the IHT and CGT legislation. The original beneficiary under the will or intestacy used to be taxed in respect of any relevant income arising between the date of death and the date of execution of any deed of variation affecting the property. Thus any income due to the beneficiary (whether received or not) up to the date of the variation would be his income for tax purposes.

However, from April 6, 1995 residuary beneficiaries have only been taxed on a receipts basis. Accordingly, if, prior to the deed of variation, income has not yet been distributed to the original beneficiary under the will, all income will be assessed on the new beneficiary assuming that it is all paid to him.

29.39 There are new statutory provisions in TA 1988, s.685D which identify the settlor for income tax purposes when a deed of variation is made. The rules

---

[56] There would be some flexibility in the use of losses if the trust was settlor-interested. For example, if Chris had unused personal losses these could be set against trust gains if the trust was settlor interested: see Ch. 11. Note that it does not matter when the trust was set up.
[57] On income tax, see 29.38.

are the same as those for CGT[58]: where the variation creates a settlement that would *not otherwise have existed*, the person making the variation, not the deceased, is treated as the settlor for income tax and CGT purposes. Where a variation alters an existing will trust set up under the will and sets up a new one, the deceased is treated as the settlor.

29.40 Since there are no provisions for reading back in the income tax legislation, if a beneficiary varies his share of the estate on trusts in favour of his minor unmarried children he will be regarded as the settlor. He is not taxed on the income if he and spouse are excluded from benefit but if income is paid out to the children while minor then it is taxed as the parent's income.[59]

VARIATIONS: IMPACT OF THE PRE-OWNED ASSETS REGIME

29.41 It is expressly provided[60] that a disposition is disregarded for the purposes of the POA charge if, by virtue of s.17 of IHTA 1984, it is not treated as a transfer of value by the chargeable person. That section provides that a variation to which s.142 applies is not a transfer of value, and hence the person making the deed of variation will not be caught by the pre-owned asset charge. So in Example 29.2 Joyce can continue to benefit from the assets without a pre-owned assets income tax problem.[61]

In cases where the residue of a deceased's estate was left to the surviving spouse absolutely, there were attractions before Budget 2006 in effecting a variation to create flexible life interest trusts.[62] In that event, whilst the variation would fall within s.142(1)—since it involved a redirection of property—it would not involve any transfer of value by the surviving spouse. Hence s.17 would be irrelevant. It has, however, been confirmed by HMRC (despite the somewhat unfortunate wording in para.16) that such a variation is not caught by the POA charge.

VARIATIONS: STAMP DUTY AND SDLT

29.42 Before the introduction of SDLT on December 1, 2003 an instrument of variation attracted £5 fixed duty unless certified under the Stamp Duty (Exempt Instruments) regulations 1987. Most post-death variations were certified under category L as being a disposition for which no consideration was given. However, certification under category M was required where there was consideration e.g. Beneficiary A gave up the London flat left to him in the will in consideration of Beneficiary B giving up the house in the country left to him in the will.

29.43 The current position is as follows:

---

[58] See 29.35.
[59] ITTOIA 2005, s.629. See Ch. 4.
[60] In FA 2004, Sch.15, para.16 ("Change in distribution of deceased's estate").
[61] IHTA 1984 s.17 performs something of a "belt and braces" function in that it says that Joyce does not make a transfer whilst s.142 deems the disposition to have been made by the deceased. Had s.142 stood alone, it might have been argued that Joyce had still made a transfer of value.
[62] The advantages of such trusts are considered at 00.00 et seq.

1. There is no SDLT on the variation of a disposition of land[63];
2. Stamp duty is limited to instruments affecting the transfer of shares or securities. HMRC accept that instruments of variation are not subject to Stamp Duty and do not need to include any certification.[64]

DISCLAIMERS

29.44 A beneficiary's right to disclaim is a matter of property law. HMRC adopt the following principles:

(1) the beneficiary must not have accepted any benefit from the property he purports to disclaim;

(2) the disclaimer must not be conditional;

(3) the only disclaimer that can be made by joint tenants is a disclaimer made by them all[65];

(4) the disclaimer must be of the whole of the benefit from the gift: e.g. a legatee cannot disclaim part of a legacy. However, some authority to the contrary may be found in *Guthrie v Walrond*,[66] where Fry J. took the view that it depended on the testator's intention, and *Dewar v IRC*,[67] where Maugham L.J. said:

> "I conceive that there is no doubt that in the case of pecuniary legacies the legatee is entitled to disclaim part of the legacy if he likes".

HMRC accept that a partial disclaimer of residue is possible under Scots law[68] or where specifically permitted in the will.[69]

HMRC accept that if a beneficiary is given two gifts by will, for instance, a pecuniary legacy and a share of residue, he may accept one and disclaim the other. Generally a disclaimer should be made by deed since it is not being made for consideration.

29.45 A disclaimer may be a way round HMRC's view that deeds of variation are not possible in the case of a life interest once the life tenant has died.[70]

EXAMPLE 29.20

Mr Smith dies in 2007 leaving his wife a life interest (an IPDI) with remainder to children alive on his death. His wife dies six months after

---

[63] FA 2003, Sch.3 para.4.
[64] See *IHT Newsletter* April 2004 Vol. 3 pt 5.
[65] Re *Schär, Midland Bank Executor & Trustee Co Ltd v Damer* [1951] Ch. 280.
[66] (1883) 22 Ch. D 573.
[67] [1935] 2 K.B. 351.
[68] Statement of Practice E18.
[69] Partial disclaimer was the subject of correspondence in *Capital Taxes News & Reports*, July 1989, pp. 246–248.
[70] See 00.00: a precedent is at App.II A2.62.

him. Can a disclaimer of her life interest be effected? Given that she has not accepted the interest (e.g. received no income benefit from it) the answer is thought to be yes. Is there a problem if the IPDI trust owned a share in a house in which wife lived. (Assume that she owned the other share.) Would HMRC argue that wife had accepted the life interest because she had continued to live in the house so that she cannot disclaim? It is not thought that such an argument would succeed because she was living in the house by virtue of her half share and neither the trustees nor she did anything which could constitute an act of acceptance.

HMRC accept that disclaimers of a life interest after death are *in principle* possible:

> "if the situation had been that it was possible for the life tenant's executors to disclaim his life interest as a matter of general law, then that should fall within the protection of section 142."[71]

HMRC consider that in order to disclaim a life interest of a deceased life tenant under general law there must be some property to give up: i.e. some undistributed income. However, is this correct? Whilst a variation is a disposition or gift of property made by the beneficiary, a disclaimer is a refusal to accept something, which is altogether different. It is arguable that executors can refuse to accept something on behalf of the deceased life tenant (accrued or undistributed income or the right to receive the same or even an interest of no value which would however increase the IHT burden on the deceased's free estate) even if they cannot give away something that has ceased to exist.

29.46 The quicker a disclaimer is made the better. *Dymond's Death Duties* (15th edn) says in relation to death duties at p. 227:

> "if the life tenant disclaimed his interest before he has received any benefit and the interests subject thereto are accelerated, it is considered that the disclaimed interest does not take effect in possession so is outside the terms of section 2(1)(b); and this is in practice treated as so where he has died within a short time of succeeding to his interest and the interests have been effectively disclaimed by his personal representatives."

In the IHT Manual it is stated disclaimers of a life interest are allowed where owing to ill health, ignorance or lack of time the deceased was never in a position to accept or disclaim.

29.47 **Disclaiming under IHTA 1984, s.93:** this deals with the situation where a person becomes entitled to an interest in settled property but disclaims that interest. The Act shall apply as if he had not become entitled to the interest. Note:

(i) the disclaimer must not be for a consideration in money or money's worth (and there is no saving for another interest under the settlement);

---

[71] See IHTM 35042: note though *Re Smith* [2001] 3 All E.R. 552.

(ii) although no time limit is specified, the requirement that the interest must not have been accepted and no benefit been obtained from it will normally impose its own time restriction.

29.48 Because s.142 does not apply to settled property in which the deceased had enjoyed a life interest, s.93 may sometimes assist in enabling the beneficiary who then becomes entitled to disclaim that entitlement.[72]

SECTION 144—DISCRETIONARY WILL TRUSTS

29.49 Section 144(1) deals with

- property comprised in a person's estate immediately before his death which is settled by his will (this excludes the case where property is given by will for immediate absolute distribution at the discretion of executors or others)[73]; *and*
- within two years of that person's death, *and*
- *before* any interest in possession has subsisted in the property[74]
- an event occurs which would normally lead to an IHT charge (e.g. property is appointed onto new trusts outside the relevant property regime or passes to a beneficiary outright).[75]

In these circumstances, provided that the further conditions set out below are met, there is no charge on the ending of the discretionary trust and IHT is applied as if the will had provided that on the testator's death the property should be held as it is, in fact, held after the event.

This means that any exemption appropriate to the beneficiary who receives the property is available. So, assuming that the above conditions are met, if the trustees distribute property within the prescribed period to the testator's surviving spouse, that property benefits from the spouse exemption, being treated as having been left by the testator to his spouse. The relevant property trust is in effect ignored. Similarly if the trustees distribute the property to a charity within two years, the charitable exemption again relates back to the death.

The 2006 changes

29.50 The section was amended three times in the course of the 2006 Finance Bill's progress through Parliament in order to accommodate the new regime for the

---

[72] See Example 29.13 and IHTM 35164.
[73] A s.144 trust can however, be established by an instrument of variation: see 29.23.
[74] The meaning of "interest in possession" has changed for these purposes as a result of the FA 2006 alterations to the IHT treatment of settlements: see IHTA 1984, s.144(1A).
[75] This condition had to be modified to deal (especially) with IPDIs: see 29.50. It resulted in the "*Frankland Trap*": see 29.52.

IHT treatment of settlements. The result is a drafting mess and a trap for the unwary. As amended (the changes are highlighted below) s.144 now reads as follows:

"*144 Distribution etc from property settled by will*

(1) Subsection (2) below applies where property comprised in a person's estate immediately before his death is settled by his will and, within the period of two years after his death and before any interest in possession has subsisted in the property, there occurs:

(a) an event on which tax would (apart from subsection (2) below) be chargeable under any provision, other than section 64 or 79, of Chapter III of Part III of this Act, or
(b) an event on which tax would be so chargeable but for section 75 or 76 above or paragraph 16(1) of Schedule 4 to this Act.

(1A) Where the testator dies on or after 22nd March 2006, subsection (1) above shall have effect as if the reference to any interest in possession were a reference to any interest in possession that is

(a) an immediate post-death interest, or
(b) a disabled person's interest.

(2) Where this subsection applies by virtue of an event within paragraph (a) of subsection (1) above, tax shall not be charged under the provision in question on that event; and in every case in which this subsection applies in relation to an event, this Act shall have effect as if the will had provided that on the testator's death the property should be held as it is held after the event.

(3) Subsection (4) below applies where—

(a) a person dies on or after 22nd March 2006,
(b) property comprised in the person's estate immediately before his death is settled by his will, and
(c) within the period of two years after his death, but before an immediate post-death interest or a disabled person's interest has subsisted in the property, there occurs an event that involves causing the property to be held on trusts that would, if they had in fact been established by the testator's will, have resulted in—

(i) an immediate post-death interest subsisting in the property, or
(ii) section 71A or 71D above applying to the property.

(4) Where this subsection applies by virtue of an event—

(a) this Act shall have effect as if the will had provided that on the testator's death the property should be held as it is held after the event, but

(b) tax shall not be charged on that event under any provision of Chapter 3 of Part 3 of this Act.

(5) Subsection (4) above also applies where—

(a) a person dies before 22nd March 2006,

(b) property comprised in the person's estate immediately before his death is settled by his will,
an event occurs—

   (i) on or after 22nd March 2006, and

   (ii) within the period of two years after the testator's death, that involves causing the property to be held on trusts within subsection (6) below,

(d) no immediate post-death interest, and no disabled person's interest, subsisted in the property at any time in the period beginning with the testator's death and ending immediately before the event, and

(e) no other interest in possession subsisted in the property at any time in the period beginning with the testator's death and ending immediately before 22nd March 2006.

(6) Trusts are within this subsection if they would, had they in fact been established by the testator's will and had the testator died at the time of the event mentioned in subsection (5)(c) above, have resulted in—

(a) an immediate post-death interest subsisting in the property, or

(b) section 71A or 71D above applying to the property."

It can be seen from the above that s.144 deals with three different scenarios:

29.51 **Settlement ending**: s.144(1) and (2) deal with the straightforward case of testator leaving assets on discretionary trusts and outright appointments being made to spouse or other beneficiaries (or the settlement automatically ending, e.g. after 23 months).

EXAMPLE 29.21

Ron dies in 2007 and leaves all his property on discretionary trusts for his spouse, children and remoter issue. The Executors pay inheritance tax on the entire estate. A year after his death, the trustees appoint the house to his spouse outright. That is read back to Ron's death, i.e. it is treated as a gift by Ron to his spouse and will qualify for the spouse exemption. A tax repayment can be claimed.

29.52 Note the trap in *Frankland v IRC*[76] and avoid making any outright appointments within three months of death if reading back is desired. In *Frankland* the trustees of a discretionary will trust appointed an interest in possession to the deceased's spouse within three months of the death. They hoped to obtain relief under s.144(1)(a) and s.18; but because of s.65(4) there was no exit charge under s.65 and so no event which would bring s.144 into play (this is because "reading back" is only available if there occurs an event "on which taxed would be chargeable" and there is no such event if the trust ends within three months of its creation[77]). The estate could not be treated as if it had been given to the spouse by the deceased, and consequently the benefit of the spouse exemption was lost. That was a pre-Budget case and it was necessary to wait three months when appointing any interest in possession or outright interest to obtain reading back. Now (as will be discussed below[78]) it is not necessary to wait three months before appointing an IPDI *but the trap remains for outright appointments.*

29.53 **Appointments on continuing IPDI or s.71A or 71D trusts**: s.144(3) and (4) deal with the position where the testator dies on or after March 22, 2006 and the trustees wish to appoint the property on continuing interest in possession trusts for the deceased's spouse or other beneficairies (i.e. an IPDI trust) or on bereaved minor trusts or s.71D trusts. It was necessary to amend s.144 by adding the new sections because giving a beneficiary an interest in possession is not "an event on which tax would (apart from s.144) be chargeable"[79] so there would have been no reading back. If there was no reading back the relevant property trust would continue and there would be no IPDI.[80]

29.54 It might have been easier to take out the words "an event on which tax would be chargeable" in subs.144(1)(b) but, initially, to get out of this catch 22 situation the Government amended s.144 to allow reading back on appointments out of discretionary trusts to an IPDI, s.71A or s.71D trust but, initially, only if the death occurred after March 21, 2006.

EXAMPLE 29.22

> Donald dies in 2007 leaving his estate on discretionary trusts. The trustees appoint his wife Elizabeth a life interest within two years of Donald's death. This is an IPDI and reading back operates so that spouse exemption is obtained even if the appointment is made within three months of death. Note that it is not possible to appoint a disabled person's interest and obtain reading back.

---

[76] [1997] S.T.C. 1450, CA.
[77] See IHTA 1984, s.68(2).
[78] 29.53.
[79] Because it is ignored for IHT purposes.
[80] This is because an IPDI must take effect on the death (see IHTA 1984, s.49A(3)) so that reading back is imperative. The position of s.71A and s.71D trusts is different since they merely have to be "established under the will": hence all that reading back does is to avoid the exit charge when the relevant property settlement ends.

Deaths pre March 22, 2006

29.55 The above change did not cover the taxpayer who died before March 22, 2006 leaving property on two year discretionary trusts where the trustees had not exercised their powers of appointment on March 22, 2006. In such a case they could not bring themselves within s.144 unless the appointment was outright to the spouse or children. Appointing on continuing trusts had no effect for IHT purposes (because of s.144(3)(a)) and the relevant property regime would continue. The fact that the death occurred before Budget Day did not enable the appointment to be read back and treated as taking place before Budget Day.

29.56 This was corrected at Report Stage with the insertion of s.144(5) and (6). The result is that if in *Example 29.22* Donald had died in January 2006 (i.e. before Budget Day) and the trustees only exercised their powers of appointment to appoint on continuing trusts on July 1, 2006, there is reading back if those trusts are IPDI or s.71A or 71D. Again disabled trusts are not included.

Uses of s.144

29.57 Section 144 enables the executors to maximise the reliefs available on the testator's death taking into account the legislation at that time. It is, of course, always desirable for the testator to leave a non-binding letter of wishes to act as guidance for the trustees in these circumstances.

As noted above, provided the trustees exercise their powers of appointment within two years there is reading back for IHT purposes. However, there is no need to draft the will so that the trust ends automatically within two years unless the testator particularly wants to ensure that certain default trusts come into effect. The discretionary trust can continue for the full perpetuity period if thought desirable although s.144 will not apply to appointments made after the two year period has elapsed. The ten year charge and any exit charge arising after two years will be calculated from the date of death in the usual way.

When can powers of appointment be exercised?

29.58 At one time HMRC took the view that the trustees of a discretionary trust created by will could not exercise their powers until assets had been vested in them by the executors. This meant either at completion of the administration of the estate or by an express assent of the property by the executors. This might lead to unnecessary cash flow problems where there was a surviving spouse since probate had to be obtained and IHT paid before any appointment could be made in favour of a spouse.

It is now accepted by HMRC[81] that there is no requirement that residue must be ascertained and assented to will trustees before the powers granted by

---

[81] See *Capital Taxes News* July 1998 p.98. It is common to permit expressly the trustees to make an appointment even though the administration of the estate is not complete and assets have not been assented to them. See also *Fitzwilliam v IRC* [1993] 3 All E.R. 184.

a will can be exercised. In each case the time at which a valid exercise of those powers may be made is a question of construction of the particular will concerned. If the will defines "my trustees" as the executors and trustees of the will for the time being and the Trust Period begins from the date of death with "my trustees" having the power of appointment, HMRC accept that the trust is validly constituted at the date of the testator's death and that the executors in their capacity of trustees can exercise their powers during the administration.

Appointing to existing trusts

Can s.144 be used to appoint to existing trusts? Consider the following. **29.59**

EXAMPLE 29.23

(1) A dies in 2007 leaving his property on discretionary trusts. In 2005 he had set up the *inter vivos* Binns Life Interest Trust for his wife prior to his death which holds £100. The trustees of the discretionary trust appoint the residuary estate within two years of death onto the Binns Life Interest Trust. Is this an IPDI? The settlement of the property is effected by the will and, although the trust itself was not set up by will, the authors consider that an IPDI trust has been established.[82]

(2) Assume that A had created six pilot settlements all on different days before his death. The will then adds assets to those trusts. In this situation:

   (a) it is thought that each trust may benefit from a full nil rate band[83];
   (b) but the trustees have two years flexibility under s.144 to make amendments to their trusts which are read back into A's will.

CGT problems

There is a potential capital gains tax danger in s.144 trusts. If an appointment **29.60** is made out of a discretionary trust within two years from the date of death, such an appointment is automatically read back under s.144 for IHT purposes and there is then no capital gains tax hold-over relief available under TCGA 1992, s.260 (because the appointment does not generate a chargeable transfer). There is no equivalent to s.144 which provides reading back for capital gains tax (or income tax) purposes. In practice, however, if the estate is not fully

---

[82] In this case the Binns Life Interest trust is a "pilot" settlement. It might, however, have been set up with substantial assets and then added to by the discretionary trustees. This would raise the question of whether additions of property to a pre March 22, 2006 interest in possession trust are to be taxed as new settlements, as to which see Ch. 20. For a discussion of IPDIs generally see Ch. 19.
[83] See the *Rysaffe* case: 15.07; 15.14 and 20.15.

administered at the date of the appointment, HMRC accept that the beneficiaries take *qua* legatees at probate value.

Using s.144 to solve the "Budget problem"

29.61 Suppose a will has created an accumulation and maintenance trust for grandchildren who take income at 25 and capital at 30 (assume the testator died after March 21, 2006 and the trustees have not yet exercised their powers) and the trustees wish to prevent it being treated as a relevant property trust. They can appoint in such a way that the trust is now IPDI for each of the grandchildren or a s.71A or s.71D trust. Reading back is obtained provided the normal two year requirement is met.

The two year trap and nil rate band discretionary will trusts

29.62 It has been suggested that the deceased's share in the matrimonial home should be settled on nil rate band discretionary trusts and then the testator's spouse could be appointed an interest in possession which will not make the house part of her estate because it is not qualifying IPDI. However because of s.144 such an appointment would take effect as an IPDI for the spouse (even if done within three months of death) and the whole property would therefore be taxed on her death. So do *not* appoint an interest in possession to someone within two years of death if the intention is that the property should remain within the relevant property regime. Reading back is not optional under s.144.[84]

---

[84] The topic of nil rate band discretionary will trusts and the matrimonial home is discussed in App.III A3.116 (see question 14 and HMRC answer)

Chapter 30

BARE TRUSTS

- Uses **(30.03)**
- Tax position of a bare trust **(30.04)**

A bare trust is commonly one in which a single beneficiary has an immediate and absolute title to both income and capital.[1] The beneficiary is entitled to the entire equitable interest in the trust fund and his entitlement is not subject to any contingency. It is sometimes said that the trustee has no discretion in respect of the trust property other than the stewardship of that property on behalf of the beneficiary. However, it is thought that the bare trustee is still a fiduciary so that, for example, the rule against self-dealing and the rule against making secret profits, will apply.[2] Further, a trust for a minor or an incapacitated person who is absolutely entitled to the property gives the trustees active duties to perform: for instance in respect of the management and investment of the trust fund. **30.01**

A bare trust falls within the definition of a trust of land in s.1(2)(a) of the Trusts of Land and Appointment of Trustees Act 1996. The trustees are entitled to deal with the property held under the trust as though its absolute owner.[3] It is also clear that at least parts of the Trustee Act 1925 and Trustee Act 2000 apply to bare trustees.[4] **30.02**

USES

Sometimes a bare trust is used where a donor wishes to transfer the property immediately but there are formalities which will delay the passing of legal title, such as obtaining a consent or giving notice to a third party. This may happen in the case of shares in a private company which commonly cannot be transferred without obtaining the consent of other shareholders or giving other shareholders the option to purchase them. An effective transfer of the beneficial ownership can, however, still take place under a declaration of trust (*if* the articles do not prohibit this). A bare trust can therefore be used to transfer the **30.03**

---

[1] This will not always be the case: there will be a bare trust if at the conclusion of the administration of an estate property is held for A and B who are jointly absolutely entitled.
[2] See Thomas & Hudson, *Law of Trusts*, OUP 2004 at 1.52 and PCB, 2005 at 226 and 336.
[3] S.6(1) of TLATA 1996.
[4] See *X v A* [2000] 1 All E.R. 490.

beneficial interest immediately with legal title to follow later. If the property is registered land the beneficiary's interest may be protected on the land register by entry of the trustee restriction.

"Blind trusts" are usually bare trusts. They are used where an individual puts assets into a trust for himself on terms which allow the trustees to buy and sell trust assets as they see fit without informing him. Such a trust is often used by a politician who will then not declare an interest in any of the assets in the trust given that s/he does not know at any time what assets are owned by the trust. A transfer into the bare trust is not a disposal for capital gains tax purposes if the disponer is the absolutely entitled beneficiary so does not trigger chargeable gains (it is a nothing). Nor will it be a transfer of value for inheritance tax purposes.

TAX POSITION OF A BARE TRUST

30.04 In general, the beneficiary of a bare trust should return the income and gains on his personal tax returns and the trustees are not required to make a tax return. Although the trustees may pay the tax due to HMRC on behalf of a beneficiary, it is the beneficiary who is chargeable to tax.[5]

Income tax

30.05 Prior to the FA 1999 changes (which came into force on March 9, 1999), bare trusts enabled a parent to avoid paying income tax on the child's income derived from property which he settled on his minor child. During minority income was neither paid to or for the child's benefit nor accumulated in the formal trust sense[6] but was retained by the trustees until the child reached 18.[7] The child's personal allowance and lower rate bands could be set against the income. The income was not paid out to the child until 18 because he could not give a receipt, although it could be applied for his benefit. However, provided the income was not so used while the child was under 18, the provisions in s.660B of TA 1988 (now s.629 of ITTOIA 2005) which tax a settlor on his minor child's income from the settlement were not triggered. Bare trusts created on or after March 9, 1999[8] no longer have these income tax advantages. From that date, if a parent settles property on a bare trust for a minor unmarried child then the income in excess of £100 per annum is taxed on the settlor (parent) as it arises.[9] Bare trusts already in existence at that date are

---

[5] Subject to the parental settlement provisions: see ITTOIA 2005, s.629 and 30.05.
[6] Even if s.31 of TA 1925 is not excluded, for income tax purposes if the beneficiary has an indefeasibly vested interest in the trust income and capital and the trustees have discretion over the use of income for the benefit of the minor and must accumulate the balance. It may still be a bare trust rather than a settled property. However, see App. III A3.138 (Question 3) where HMRC have not resolved the matter.
[7] Or earlier marriage (entering into a civil partnership): TA 1925, s.31(2)(i).
[8] See FA 1999, s.64.
[9] See ITTOIA 2005, s.629, previously TA 1988, s.660B(1)(b) which refers to income which during the life of the settlor is paid to or for the benefit of an unmarried child of the settlor or "would otherwise be treated ..as income of an unmarried minor child of the settlor". See Ch. 4.

unaffected although no property should be added. If property is added then an apportionment of income is made on a just and reasonable basis. The income assessed on the settlor is taxed at his highest marginal rate but he is entitled to recover from the trustee the amount of tax so paid (although it has to be paid by him to HMRC first before he has a statutory right to reimbursement). "Child" is widely defined to include a step-child, an illegitimate child and an adopted child.

Capital gains tax

Despite the loss of income tax advantages on parental bare trusts, these trusts are still used by parents or grandparents in order to utilise the capital gains tax annual allowance of minors. This is particularly useful when a parent has a number of children. Because the property is held on trust "for any person who would be [absolutely] entitled but for being an infant or other person under a disability" it is not settled for CGT purposes.[10] Gains are therefore taxed as the child's gains with the benefit of a full individual capital gains tax exemption.   **30.06**

A disposal of assets into a bare trust is treated as a disposal to the beneficiary (unless the beneficiary of the bare trust is also the disponer, as in the case of blind trusts). Accordingly, if the trust assets are being held on trust for a beneficiary under a disability (e.g. a minor), there is no disposal when he reaches 18 and he can claim the assets because he is treated as having owned the asset throughout.   **30.07**

Hold over relief is available on a gift of a business asset into a bare trust. The restrictions[11] on hold over relief for trusts for dependent children are only relevant if the property is settled and therefore do not apply to a bare trust arrangement.   **30.08**

In summary, if a parent sets up a bare trust for his minor child the trustee should not invest in high income-producing assets (since the income is taxed on the parent). But it is desirable to generate sufficient gains each year to use up the child's capital gains tax annual exemption.   **30.09**

EXAMPLE 30.1

> Trustees hold property on trust for Charlotte absolutely (she is aged 8). Because of her age, Charlotte cannot demand the property from the trustees until she is 18 but for CGT purposes she is treated as owning the assets in the trust fund. Compare the position if the trust deed provided for the property to be held on trust for Charlotte contingent upon her attaining the age of 18. In these circumstances, Charlotte is not treated as absolutely entitled to the property which is therefore settled property for capital gains tax purposes.[12]

---

[10] See TCGA 1992, s.60 and Ch. 5.
[11] See Ch. 9.
[12] See Ch. 5.

Inheritance tax

30.10 Is a bare trust for an infant beneficiary a settlement for inheritance tax purposes? If it is then post- March 21, 2006 its creation will be a chargeable transfer.

> EXAMPLE 30.2
>
> S declares that he holds a house on trust for his infant daughter D. Nothing is said about s.31 of the Trustee Act 1925. If this creates a settlement for inheritance tax purposes, S has made a chargeable transfer and the trust is within the relevant property regime with ten year and exit charges. By contrast, if the gift is treated as a gift to D absolutely (despite the trustees' discretion to withhold income under s.31 Trustee Act 1925) then S's transfer is a PET, being an unsettled gift to an individual and there is no relevant property settlement.

Under s.43(2)(a) of IHTA 1984, "settlement" is defined to include property held in trust for persons in succession or contingently. If s.31 of TA 1925 has not been excluded this might be sufficient to make the property settled on the basis that the trustees can withhold income or distribute it at their discretion. However, it is thought that since the accumulations belong to the infant's estate, HMRC do not regard a bare trust as a settlement: i.e. accumulation under s.31 TA of 1925 in the case of a minor absolutely entitled is not regarded as accumulation for s.43 purposes because the accumulation is more in the nature of an administrative power. Assuming that is right, even if s.31 TA 1925 is not excluded, a gift of property to "my infant son absolutely" will be a PET being an outright gift.

30.11 On the death of the beneficiary, the trust property is treated as the beneficiary's so that if the child dies (whether before or after 18) the funds form part of his estate for inheritance tax purposes. This will not lead to a charge if the value of his estate is below the inheritance tax threshold.

Other points

30.12 If the child dies before the age of 18 the property will pass under the intestacy rules and therefore normally back to the child's parents. After the age of 18 the fund will pass according to the will of the child (or his intestacy if there is no will).

At 18[13] the child can call for the trust property to be transferred to him. If the child is handicapped, the effect of any bare trust on means-tested state benefits should be considered.

---

[13] 16 in Scotland.

Entitlement at 18

Bare trusts will no doubt be popular following the FA 2006 changes in the inheritance tax treatment of settlements.[14] Donors need to bear in mind that the beneficiary is absolutely entitled and on reaching 18 can call for the trust property. However, there would appear to be no reason why the trustees of a bare trust cannot exercise a power of advancement just before a child reaches 18 to make a settled advance postponing vesting of the capital.[15] It might be desirable for the declaration of trust to contain an express power of advancement, otherwise the trustees will be relying on the statutory power of advancement under s.32 of the Trustee Act 1925 and therefore be limited to one half of the beneficiary's entitlement. If the power of advancement is exercised in this way it will constitute a disposal (for capital gains tax purposes) by the child (since the property now becomes settled) and a chargeable transfer by him for inheritance tax purposes since the trust will be taxed under the relevant property regime.[16]

30.13

---

[14] See precedent in Appendix II at A2.01.
[15] It is thought that the statutory power in TA 1925, s.32 will be implied and that an express power—permitting the advancement of 100 per cent of the child's interest—may be included in the trust document.
[16] Unless it creates a disabled person's interest within IHTA 1984, s.89B.

CHAPTER 31

THE FAMILY HOME AND CHATTELS

- The family home **(31.01)**
- Inheritance tax planning for the family home—summary of options **(31.29)**
- The fate of past schemes **(31.33)**
- Future arrangements on the family home **(31.52)**
- Co-ownership/sharing arrangements **(31.57)**
- Cash gifts **(31.74)**
- Selling the family home **(31.84)**
- Foreign domiciliaries, and the family home **(31.92)**
- Chattel arrangements **(31.99)**

THE FAMILY HOME

CAPITAL GAINS TAX: Principal private residence relief

31.01 The capital gains tax exemption is available on any gain arising on the disposal by gift or sale by a taxpayer of:

(i) his only or main residence, or

(ii) land held for occupation and enjoyment with that residence as its garden and grounds up to the permitted area. The permitted area is up to half an hectare or such larger area as is required for the reasonable enjoyment of the dwelling-house.[1]

This excludes from capital gains tax what for the majority of people is their most substantial asset. The exemption is extended in certain circumstances to include dwellings which are settled property and lived in by one or more beneficiaries.[2] The conditions for principal private residence relief are briefly considered with particular reference to issues such as permitted area and outbuildings, which may be relevant to settled property.

31.02 *Meaning of dwelling house and residence:* the term dwelling-house is not defined in the legislation but its dictionary definition, "*a house occupied as a*

[1] TCGA 1992, ss.222–224.
[2] s.225 TCGA 1992: see 31.19.

place of residence", has been approved by the Court of Appeal.³ The term includes flats as well as houses and can include caravans with the necessary degree of permanence.⁴

A distinction has to be drawn between a residence and temporary accommodation. It appears that there must be some continuity of occupation intended for the house to qualify for relief: the question is one of fact and degree.⁵

Two or more units

A single dwelling-house may comprise several units. For example, large country houses may have separate staff quarters, garages or stables. There is now a substantial body of conflicting case law on when the relief is available and the question may be particularly relevant to trustees since large properties are often held within a trust. 31.03

The entity test: in *Batey v Wakefield*⁶ a separate bungalow within the grounds of the taxpayer's house used by a caretaker to enable him to perform the duties of his employment with the taxpayer was considered by the Court of Appeal to be exempt from capital gains tax on its sale. 31.04

> "A dwelling-house or a residence, can comprise several dwellings which are not physically joined at all."

The fact that the bungalow was physically separate from the main dwelling house was considered to be irrelevant.

This was followed in *Williams v Merrylees*⁷ where it was noted by Vinelott J. that:

> "*what one is looking for is an entity which can be sensibly described as being a dwelling house though split into different buildings performing different functions.*" (This came to be called "the entity test".)

The curtilage test: however, in *Markey v Sanders*⁸ Walton J ignored the entity test and suggested two alternative tests: either the buildings must be closely adjacent and occupation of the secondary building had to increase the taxpayer's enjoyment of the main house or, looking at the group of buildings as a whole, it must be possible to regard them as a single dwelling-house. In this case a staff bungalow 130 metres away from the main residence and standing in its own grounds was not closely adjacent and so could not be treated as part of a single residence. 31.05

---

³ *Lewis v Lady Rook* [1992] STC 171, 177.
⁴ *Makins v Elson* [1977] S.T.C. 46 where the taxpayer bought some land intending to build a house on it. In the meantime he lived there in a caravan. He never built the house and later sold both land and caravan at a profit. The caravan was held to be a dwelling house—it was connected to mains services etc. Compare *Moore v Thomson* [1986] S.T.C. where the courts held that since there was no supply of water or electricity the caravn in question was not a dwelling house.
⁵ See *Goodwin v Curtis* [1998] S.T.C. 475 CA where the taxpayer contracted to buy a farmhouse in 1983 but in March 1985 instructed agents to sell it. On April 1, 1985 he left his wife, completed the purchase and moved in. On April 3, 1985 the taxpayer completed the purchase of another property and on May 3, 1985 he sold the farmhouse and moved in the other property. The General Commissioners held that one month's residence did not mean he was entitled to the exemption. The nature, quality, length and circumstances of the taxpayer's residence did not establish the expectation of continuity. The Court of Appeal held that this finding was open to them on the facts. His occupation was a stop gap measure. The taxpayer made a gain of over £100,000!
⁶ [1982] 1 All ER 61.
⁷ [1987] S.T.C. 445.
⁸ [1987] S.T.C. 256.

31.06   *The curtilage test:* the Court of Appeal reviewed these decisions in *Lewis v Rook*[9]. A cottage which had been occupied by the taxpayer's gardener some 200 yards from the main house was sold. The cottage was visible from the house so that the taxpayer could signal to the cottage if she wanted assistance. The Court of Appeal reversed the High Court decision and concluded that no building could form part of a dwelling house that included the main house unless the building was "*appurtenant to and within the cartilage of the main house.*" This was called "the curtilage test". Hence, the main residence relief was not available on the cottage. The entity test was rejected (even though it had previously been adopted by the Court of Appeal in *Batey*).

In *Honour v Norris* the judge rejected as "an affront to common sense" the suggestion that a number of separate flats in a square could constitute a single dwelling house. HMRC then set out their thinking in RI 75 August 1994 and unsurprisingly noted that they apply the curtilage test in *Lewis v Rook*. The statement emphasises the smallness of acceptable curtilage that will qualify for relief. A wall, fence or road separating two buildings normally prevents them being in the same curtilage.

31.07   However, this view that curtilage must necessarily mean a small area, may not be correct. *Secretary of State for the Environment Transport and the Regions v Skerritts of Nottingham Ltd*[10] was an appeal against a listed building enforcement notice where the statute defined a listed building as including "*an object or structure within the curtilage of the building which forms part of the land.*" The issue was whether a stable block was part of the curtilage of the main house. Robert Walker LJ noted:

> "in my respectful view this court went further than it was necessary to go [in a right to buy case Dyer v Dorset Country Council[11]] in expressing the view that the curtilage of a building must always be small or that the notion of smallness is inherent in the expression. No piece of land can ever be within the curtilage of more than one building, and if houses are built to a density of twenty or more to an acre the curtilage of each will obviously be extremely restricted. But Nourse LJ [in Dorset] recognised that in the case of what the now moribund Settled Land Act 1925 refers to as a principal mansion house . . . the stables and other outbuildings are likely to be included within its curtilage. I also respectfully doubt whether the expression curtilage can usefully be called a term of art. It is . . . a question of fact and degree."

It can be dangerous to use a judicial interpretation of one statute in support of another. Nevertheless, these comments are suggestive that smallness is not a necessary characteristic in determining curtilage and that everything depends on the nature of the properties in question.

More than one residence

31.08   Where the taxpayer has two residences, only the residence which is his main residence can qualify for relief. The taxpayer can, however, elect for one to be

[9] [1992] S.T.C. 171.
[10] [2001] Q.B. 59 [2000] 3 W.L.R. 511.
[11] [1988] 3 W.L.R. 21.

treated as his main residence[12] but note that an election cannot be made on a property that is not being used by him as a residence: eg. let property. The election must be made within two years of the acquisition of a second or subsequent residence[13] although it can be backdated by two years. In the absence of an election the question of which one is the main residence is a question of fact.

Determining which is factually the main residence can sometimes be difficult, particularly as the taxpayer now has to self assess the position. No hard and fast rules can be laid down. In some cases the taxpayer may spend more nights in one house than the other (e.g. a flat in London occupied while the taxpayer is at work) but still regard his country house as his main home. CG Manual 64552 lists various criteria which it suggests are useful in deciding which is the main residence. Some of these are open to question. For example, it is suggested that the place to which the tax return or other third party correspondence is sent might be the main residence but often such correspondence will go to an office address and not a home address so sending it to one of two homes cannot be regarded as particularly noteworthy! HMRC suggest the location of the individual's place of work is relevant but a second home may be bought precisely to ease a long commute.

Other factors listed in the Manual would appear more relevant, such as where the taxpayer keeps valuable items; where the family of a married person is based; where the taxpayer is registered to vote. One should look at where the taxpayer intends to return to on a regular basis or which property he would base himself in were it not for the demands of work or other commitments.

If a taxpayer owns one property and occupies the other under a tenancy (rather than a licence) an election that the owned property is to be the main residence should be made to avoid any possible difficulties. Similarly, if trustees own property occupied by a beneficiary who also owns or rents other property, an election should be made to avoid doubt. It can always be switched to the other property for a short time in order to secure the last 3 years' exemption[14] on a sale!

31.09

EXAMPLE 31.1

> Trustees own a large mansion house occupied by the beneficiary and his family under the terms of the settlement. The beneficiary also owns personally a *pied à terre* in London. Factually the mansion house is the main residence but the beneficiary is likely to sell the London flat first. If an election is made by trustees and beneficiary on the mansion house it can be switched later to the flat. Even if the election on the flat is only for a period of 6 months, the last 3 years of ownership on the flat will be exempt. So the mansion house loses 6 months of exemption but overall there is likely to be a tax saving for the beneficiary. The beneficiary may decide that since the mansion house is never likely to be sold it is better to elect on the *pied à terre* for the entire period of ownership.

---

[12] s.222(5) of TCGA 1992.
[13] *Griffin v Craig-Harvey* [1994] S.T.C. 54.
[14] See 31.11.

Calculating the gain

31.10 No part of the gain accruing on the disposal of a dwelling house is chargeable if it has been the taxpayer's only or main residence throughout the his period of ownership. If it has not been his only or main residence throughout that time only a fraction of the gain is exempt. In calculating the gain, an individual's period of ownership cannot start before March 31, 1982.

Where the individual has acquired different interests in his residence at different times, his period of ownership is treated as starting with the first acquisition which would be taken into account in computing his allowable expenditure even if that interest did not in itself entitle him to live in the property.

31.11 The last three years of ownership is exempt in any event (even if the individual is living elsewhere) if the property has been his main residence at any time during the period of ownership and in this case even if the actual residence occurred only before March 31, 1982 disposals after April 5, 1988 will still qualify for the last 36 months exemption.[15]

31.12 Certain periods of non-residence are disregarded:

(i) an individual who intends in due course to occupy a dwelling as his only or main residence may be treated as occupying it as a residence for such time as he is living in job-related accommodation;[16]

(ii) if the dwelling house was the individual's only or main residence at some time (but not necessarily immediately) before *and* after the period of absence and during the period of absence he had no other house eligible for relief, then certain periods of absence can be treated as periods when the residence was the only or main residence even if the residence is let. These are:

(a) any period of three years. In practice, HMRC allow relief for three years even if there is a longer period of absence;
(b) any period, however long, during which the individual works in an employment or office entirely outside the UK; *or*
(c) any period, not exceeding in total four years, during which by virtue of a reasonable condition imposed by his employer, he cannot live in his own house.

31.13 *Business use:* if part of a dwelling house is used *exclusively* for the purposes of a trade or business the gain must be apportioned and no principal private residence relief is due on that part of the gain. Unfortunately such gain does not then qualify for full business assets taper relief and therefore the rate of tax is not 10 per cent as might be expected. This is because TCGA 1992, Sch.A1, para.9 provides that where the asset is used for both business and non-business purposes the chargeable gain must be apportioned on a *pro rata* basis into a business and non-business gain prior to the application of taper relief.

---

[15] The restriction of the period of ownership to the period since March 31, 1982 applies only to s.223, the section determining the amount of the relief, and not to s.222, the section which governs whether relief is available.

[16] s.222(8) of TCGA 1992.

EXAMPLE 31.2

A works as a lawyer from his home which is owned in an interest in possession trust for him. One quarter of the rooms are used exclusively for the purposes of his business. On sale in 2006 (after owning the home for seven years) the trustees make a gain of £100,000. Given that the gain arises wholly in respect of business use, they might expect that the computation will be as below:

	£
Gain	100,000
Exempt as main residence	75,000
Chargeable gain before taper	25,000
Less Business taper relief 75%	(18,750)
Chargeable	£6,250

In fact, this is wrong in principle: the computation must reflect the fact that the whole of the chargeable gain arises on a single asset which has been used as to only one-quarter for business purposes. The correct computation is as follows:

	£
Gain	100,000
Exempt as main residence	75,000
Chargeable gain before taper	25,000
Business taper relief (at 75%) on 25% of gain	(4,687)
Non-business taper relief (at 25%) on 75% of gain	(4,687)
Chargeable	£15,625

Garden and grounds

31.14 Land of up to half an hectare is exempt only if it is being used for the taxpayer's own occupation and for the enjoyment of his residence. Larger grounds can obtain relief if "*required for the reasonable enjoyment of the house, having regard to its size or character.*"[17] Otherwise an apportionment of the gain must take place on the excess land which will mean agreeing values.

31.15 There is no definition of grounds but HMRC stated in *Tax Bulletin*, August 1995 that land surrounding the residence and in the same ownership is accepted as the grounds of the residence unless it is used for some other purpose such as agriculture or business. Land which has previously been used for business purposes can still obtain relief if it constitutes garden or grounds at the time of disposal but note that it has to be for enjoyment *with the house*. Hence there is no relief on the sale of a part of a garden *after* the disposal of the house.[18]

---

[17] s.222(2) of TCGA 1992. The issue is one of fact, what is required for the reasonable enjoyment of the house as a residence. It is an objective test requiring one to look at the size and character of the dwelling house. The leading case is *Longson v Baker* [2001] S.T.C. 6 where the judge rejected a claim that paddocks could qualify on the grounds that objectively horses are not required to enjoy a house as a residence. In *Green v IRC* [1982] S.T.C. 485 HMRC accepted that grounds of 15 acres were required for the reasonable enjoyment of a mansion of 23,374 square feet.
[18] *Varty v Lynes* [1976] S.T.C. 508 and *Tax Bulletin* August 1994, Issue 12.

EXAMPLE 31.3

> Trustees own a house with 1 acre of garden. The house is occupied by an elderly life tenant. The bottom half of the garden has been fenced off for development for some years and is overgrown. It will not qualify for relief even though within the permitted area. If, however, the trustees take down the fence and bring the land back into the garden (say) a year before the sale then on a disposal (whether of that land or of the house and garden) relief is available on all the gain, not just one year's worth. (See *Henke* discussed further below.)

31.16 In some cases trustees or individuals will own garden in excess of the permitted area. In the *Tax Bulletin* for February 1992 HMRC note that in general land is treated as garden or grounds qualifying for relief if it is "*enclosed land...*for ornamental recreation, surrounding or attached to a dwelling house or other building".

A number of factual questions should be asked when considering relief on land of over half a hectare: is the excess acreage let? Is it being sold off and the house retained? How big is the house? What is the period, style and locality of house. Are there comparables? What is the historical association of the land with the house—has it been recently acquired? Has there ever been a time when the grounds were not part of the house? How much would appear to be garden to the ordinary observer? Contemporaneous evidence is important and the owner should take photographs prior to the sale. It can be difficult to prove to HMRC that all the extensive grounds are part of the house if an enquiry is made into the tax return over two years after the disposal has been made and no evidence of the position is available. Access back to the house may be denied by the new owners or it may have been radically altered.

31.17 The word "*grounds*" is presumably intended to extend the concept beyond land which is specially cultivated or regularly tended to paddocks and meadowland but this can be difficult if the land is in agricultural use. Are there obvious physical boundaries on the property or the beginnings of a wild area, eg. by ditches or an abrupt change in ground level? Views of the garden from the house are important: do principal rooms face the gardens? What would a reasonable man require for his reasonable enjoyment?

31.18 The question of what land is comprised in the permitted area is seen as an objective test.[19] In *Newhill* the judge said:

> "'required does not mean merely that the occupiers of the house would like to have it or that they would miss it if they lost it ... required means that without it there will be such a substantial deprivation of amenities or convenience that a real injury would be done to the property owner.'"

In *Henke and another v HMRC*[20] the definition of permitted area was considered. Mr and Mrs Henke had jointly purchased a freehold plot of land comprising 2.66 acres. They subsequently built a house on the land which became their main residence in June 1993. In July 1995 they obtained planning

---

[19] *Re Newhill Compulsory Purchase Order* [1938] ALL E.R. 163.
[20] SpC 550 reported at [2006] S.T.C. Issue 28.

permission for two houses to be built in front of their house and sold plots 1 and 2 in 1999 with the planning permission. The houses were built on both plots. It was held that the costs of building the original house could not be deducted in computing the gain on the sale of the plots unless reflected in those plots. The permitted area test was to be applied by reference to what was required in the circumstances prevailing at the time of the disposal and was an objective test. There were two distinct tests for a house and a garden. In relation to a house, the test for principal private residence relief was "at any time". For land the test was whether it was a garden or ground at the time of disposal. The Special Commissioner held that in this case the permitted area was 2.03 acres and the apportionment of the sale proceeds of the plots should be on the basis of the respective areas of the non-exempt and the exempt areas. A further apportionment was required because the house was built on the land after the land had been acquired and therefore the property had not been occupied as the principal private residence throughout the period of ownership.

Trustees

31.19 Section 225 extends the exemption to a residence which is settled property provided the trustees satisfy the conditions as to ownership. The relief requires a claim by the trustees and is available if and to the extent that the conditions as to residence are satisfied by one or more beneficiaries who are entitled to occupy the house under the terms of the settlement. Any notice of election between two or more residences has to be signed jointly by the trustees and the beneficiary.

It is not necessary that the beneficiary has an interest in possession in the whole of the settled property for the trustees to claim relief on the entire gain.

EXAMPLE 31.4

> An interest in possession trust owns a property occupied by Ruth, one of three life tenants. Her two brothers also have interests in possession but live in other properties. Principal private residence relief is available on the whole gain realised by the trust even though Ruth only has an interest in possession in one third of the settled property.

31.20 *Meaning of entitled to occupy under the terms of the settlement:* in *Sansom v Peay*[21] it was accepted that when a beneficiary of the trust occupies trust property under powers given to the trustees, relief under section 225 can be due. Before *Sansom* was decided in 1976 HMRC took the view that an individual was only entitled to occupy a dwelling house under the terms of the settlement if the settlement specifically gave that individual *a right* to occupy the property.

31.21 In *Sansom,* the trustees had a discretionary power to permit any beneficiary to occupy upon such terms as the trustees in their discretion thought fit HMRC argued that the beneficiaries were occupying by licence of the trustees not under the terms of the settlement. However it was held that:

---

[21] [1976] S.T.C. 494.

"the beneficiaries were in occupation pursuant to the exercise by the trustees of a power expressly conferred by the settlement to permit those beneficiaries to go into occupation and remain in occupation. The trustees exercised that power, and the beneficiaries thereupon became entitled to go into occupation and to continue in occupation until the permission was withdrawn. The trustees never did withdraw permission until they required vacant possession in order to complete the exchange. Therefore looking at the matter at the date of the disposal, the beneficiaries were persons who, in the events which have happened were entitled to occupy the house and did occupy it under the terms of the settlement."

In other words the trustees can exercise their discretion and the beneficiary's entitlement to occupy arose from exercise of that discretion.

31.22 It is also accepted by HMRC that a beneficiary can pay rent to the trustees to occupy a dwelling house and that this will not prevent relief. For instance, trustees may charge rent to one beneficiary who occupies the house in order to compensate others who do not occupy. (Contrast this with the exercise of the trustees' managerial powers).[22]

EXAMPLE 31.5

Three brothers jointly own three cottages and each brother lives in one property as his main residence. The cottages are of unequal value. Each brother could put his share of each property into a trust[23] for the benefit of all three and obtain s.225 relief.

31.23 There is no restriction of relief under s.225 where the trust is settlor interested but the settlor himself is not in occupation.[24] The trustees could charge the relevant beneficiary rent as compensation to the others for being excluded.

31.24 For restrictions on principal private residence relief for trustees and individuals where there has been a previous hold-over relief claim, see 9.46.

Nil rate band discretionary trusts and principal private residence relief

31.25 At 28.16, capital gains tax problems if the deceased died leaving a half share of the house on discretionary trusts in a case where his surviving spouse owned the other share beneficially, were mentioned. HMRC may raise a number of points:

(i) If there is no express power in the will for trustees to allow a beneficiary to occupy the house, the conditions of s.225 are not satisfied because he is not occupying "under the terms of the settlement". It might be argued,

---

[22] See CG 65448.
[23] Note there is no hold over relief because the trust is settlor interested.
[24] Hence the reason why reverter to settlor trusts became popular—the settlor could settle a house on trust for the occupying person and principal private residence relief would be available on a later sale. See Ch. 27.

however, that where discretionary trustees acquire a half share in property by way of gift not purchase they have power as a matter of general trust law to retain such property for occupation by a beneficiary if they so choose and therefore that the beneficiary is entitled to occupy under the terms of the settlement even if there is no express power in the will.[25]

(ii) The provisions of The Trusts of Land and Appointment of Trustees Act 1996 need to be considered. In this case normally the trustee of the legal estate is not the trustees of the discretionary trust but the surviving co-owner and the discretionary trustees are merely trustees of an equitable interest in the land (a sub-trust). Section 12 of TLATA 1996 does not give them rights of occupation nor does it explicitly give the discretionary beneficiaries of the sub-trust any rights of occupation.[26] HMRC may therefore argue that the trustees of a sub-fund over land have no ability to allow any beneficiary to occupy the trust property while the spouse is beneficial co-owner and in occupation and so no beneficiary can occupy under the terms of their settlement.

(iii) The surviving spouse occupies by virtue of his personal share and not as a result of his or her position as a beneficiary under the settlement.[27]

31.26 One response to these arguments might be that if the trustees have express power under the Will to allow a beneficiary to occupy the property then the fact that the relevant beneficiary also occupies for some other reason (e.g. personal ownership), makes no difference: relief is still due. The words in section 225 are *"has been the ..main residence of a person entitled to occupy it under the terms of the settlement"*. A restrictive reading would suggest that the person actually has to be entitled as a matter of fact to occupy the house *by virtue* of being a beneficiary and the trustees must have the necessary powers on the particular facts to allow him into occupation. A nil rate band discretionary trust holding only a share in land left by will would not therefore qualify for relief. However, these words could be read more widely so that provided the terms of the settlement permit a beneficiary to occupy the property, the fact that beneficiary occupies by virtue of some other interest does not matter and similarly the fact that the trustees have no power on these facts to allow a beneficiary into occupation of the original property left in the will is irrelevant.

Principal private residence relief for personal representatives

31.27 Where personal representatives dispose of a private dwelling house which, both before and after the testator's death, was occupied by a person who is

---

[25] Cf *Re Power's Will Trusts* [1951] Ch. 1074.
[26] Rights of occupation are only given to a beneficiary with an interest in possession under TLATA 1996, s.12.
[27] Where the trustees have sold the half share and a replacement property has been purchased, albeit that a half share is also held by the surviving spouse, it is easier to argue that the trustees have positively exercised their discretions to confer benefits on the spouse and allow that spouse to occupy *qua* beneficiary; conversely it might be more likely then that HMRC argue she has been given a qualifying interest in possession although this risk falls away if the new property is purchased more than two years after the death. See s.144 of IHTA 1984.

entitled on death to the whole or substantially the whole, of the proceeds of sale from the house, either absolutely or for life, personal representatives were by concession given the benefit of the principal private residence relief exemption (ESC D5). The concession addressed the sort of situation where a house-owner died and his widow was left the house in the will and continued to occupy the house. "Substantially the whole" meant 75 per cent of the proceeds. The concession did not cover disposals of part of the house or an interest in the house or grounds. Nor did it help the person who moved into the house on the death of the testator.

Schedule 22 of FA 2004[28] gave statutory force to ESC D5 and provided that relief is available if the person or persons who occupied the house immediately before and after the death are together entitled to at least 75 per cent of the net proceeds of disposal. The test is applied on the assumption that none of the net proceeds are required to meet inheritance tax liabilities. Disposals of part are covered but this will still not help the situation where a daughter moves into the house on the death of the mother.

EXAMPLE 31.6

> Charlotte and her brother Luke live in Charlotte's house. On her death Charlotte leaves the house to Luke who goes on living in it. The property has to be sold by the personal representatives to pay Charlotte's credit card bills. Any gain will be exempt.

31.28 In some cases, where sales are in contemplation but the exemption for personal representatives is not available, it will be worth transferring the house to a trust.

EXAMPLE 31.7

> Bill dies leaving his house on IPDI trusts for his children Charlotte and Luke in equal shares.[29] Charlotte moves into the house on his death but it is not intended to retain the house. If the executors sell the house, no principal private residence relief is due. Charlotte did not occupy the house before death and even if she had, she is not entitled to substantially the whole sale proceeds. However, if the house is assented to the trustees and they sell the house, principal private residence relief will be due on the entire gain even though Charlotte alone is in occupation.[30]
>
> If Bill had left the house to his children outright and the personal representatives had vested the property in Charlotte and Luke rather than selling it there is no capital gains tax due because Charlotte and Luke, as the legatees, are deemed to acquire it at the time of death and at the probate value.[31] Charlotte but not Luke will obtain principal private residence relief on any later sale.

[28] Inserting s.225A into TCGA 1992.
[29] An IPDI trust confers an interest in possession. See 19.05.
[30] See *Example 31.4*.
[31] s.62(4) of TCGA 1992.

INHERITANCE TAX PLANNING FOR THE FAMILY HOME: SUMMARY OF THE TAX PLANNING OPTIONS

In retrospect the tax planning opportunities available for family homes pre-December 10, 2003, resemble a "golden age": by contrast the current climate makes planning with the family home much tougher. **31.29**

The major change was the announcement in the Chancellor's Autumn Statement, delivered (rather late) on December 10, 2003, of the introduction of a pre-owned assets income tax.[32] This not only affected future schemes but also past schemes going back to 1986. The climate that now exists is hostile to *"unacceptable inheritance tax planning"* and was encapsulated in the Finance Committee debates in July 2005 when the Shadow Chief Secretary to the Treasury suggested that relief should be given for the potential double inheritance tax charge when in the case of home loan schemes, the debt is released.[33] The Paymaster General responded:

> "Call me a cynic, but I have a horrible feeling that the sudden desire to unwind is prompted by the discovery of a way to replan. I also think that election is a good and fair answer for all taxpayers."

For many the family home is *the* major asset and one on which they particularly resent paying inheritance tax. Hence the keen demand for schemes that enable the taxpayer to continue to live in the home but inheritance tax is saved if he survives 7 years. **31.30**

However, any professional adviser should exercise extreme caution before advising his client to carry out any inheritance tax planning with the family home. It is suggested that as far as possible advantage should be taken of statutory exemptions since these are less likely to be attacked or changed. More aggressive tax planning may well (when discovered) provoke the wrath of an easily enraged Exchequer. It is relatively easy for any Government to change the POA legislation so that income tax can be imposed on an *'unacceptable'* tax scheme.[34]

Safe inheritance tax planning: before undertaking any planning with the family home it is worth checking that the basic IHT exemptions and reliefs (annual exemption; small gifts, and PETs) have been used. Making larger gifts is still possible provided that the donor retains no benefit or interest in the gift and that the gift is (generally) outright rather than into a trust. More interesting is the normal expenditure out of income exemption which, the courts have decided, has a wider application than had originally been thought to be the case. For a taxpayer in his 50s with substantial surplus earnings it is to be recommended as a way of controlling the growth in value of his estate.[35] **31.31**

---

[32] See Ch. 3 for an overview of the changes in FA 2004/FA 2006 generally and Ch. 36 for the introduction of the disclosure regime.

[33] Although note that the Paymaster General was, in the end, persuaded of the need for double charges relief! Home Loan Schemes are considered at 31.43.

[34] The Conservatives have not indicated that they would repeal either Schedule 15 FA 2004 or Schedule 20 FA 2006!

[35] See IHTA 1984, s.21 and see *Bennett v IRC* [1995] S.T.C. 54 and *McDowell v IRC* [2004] S.T.C. (SCD) 362. However, gifts made under the normal expenditure out of income exemption are potentially within the POA Regime. Note though that such gifts can avoid an entry charge if settled on trust. See 36.02.

Business property (as defined) and farming can attract IHT relief at 100 per cent irrespective of the value of the enterprise. This is a crucial valuation relief and should be safeguarded at all costs. For instance, it is important not to depress the value of business property by raising mortgages against it[36] nor to rush into *inter vivos* tax planning given that full relief will be available on death.[37] A well-drafted Will may provide a reasonable solution for the married couple.[38] The authors feel that the following arrangements—some of which are considered in detail below—can be considered "*safe*":

(i) sharing arrangements for the family home;

(ii) cash gifts taking advantage of the seven-year "window";

(iii) tax planning via deeds of variation;[39]

(iv) commercial sales (equity releases); and

(v) flexible Will planning.[40]

31.32 **The Family debt scheme:** more aggressive planning might be the following arrangement—a variant of the home loan scheme—between spouses.

EXAMPLE 31.8

Tobias owns commercial properties which show a large unrealised capital gain. He can no longer carry out a *Melville* scheme[41] but wishes to give the properties to his grandchildren.

He decides to sell the properties at market value to his wife Ruth. The purchase price for the properties is left outstanding as a debt owed by Ruth which is repayable on the last of them to die. The debt is given by Tobias to his grandchildren.

The tax consequences are as follows:

(i) SDLT is payable on the consideration payable for the purchase of the commercial properties;

(ii) there is no capital gains tax payable by Tobias on the disposal of the properties because under s 58 of TCGA 1992 the sale is treated as taking place at no gain no loss;

(iii) the POA Regime will not apply because the transfer is to a spouse;

(iv) for inheritance tax purposes, the properties are part of Ruth's estate but subject to a debt in favour of the grandchildren.[42] On Ruth's

---

[36] See IHTA 1984, s.162(4).
[37] A good example is a gift by a farmer of his farmland and retention of the farmhouse. On his death, because the house is no longer be a farmhouse, relief will not be available: see *Rosser v IRC* [2003] S.T.C. (SCD) 311.
[38] See Ch.32 and 23.06.
[39] Ch. 29.
[40] Ch. 28.
[41] For *Melville* schemes, see 3.16.
[42] It is of course critical that the debt is deductible (eg. on Ruth's death) and hence FA 1986, s.103 needs to be born in mind: see 23.16 and 28.23.

death the properties can pass to Tobias if he is still alive subject to the debt. On the last of Tobias and Ruth to die, the debt is repayable. Tobias has made a PET of the debt; provided that he survives seven years there is no inheritance tax. There is no reservation of benefit provided the debt is not made repayable on demand;[43]

(v) there may be capital gains tax or income tax repercussions on the eventual repayment of the debt, depending on how it is structured.

(vi) the income arising from the commercial properties is paid to Ruth but may be taxed as Tobias' under the settlement provisions.[44]

A variant of this scheme involves a sale of the family home between spouses. Although the property continues to be occupied by Tobias, the transfer to his wife is an excluded transaction (see para.10(1)(b)). Hence POA is avoided.

Since the 2006 legislation the debt must be given outright to the children or grandchildren and not on trust in order to avoid an immediately chargeable transfer.

THE FATE OF PAST SCHEMES

31.33 The main schemes involving the family home were—*Ingram*[45]; *Eversden*; home loan; and reversionary lease schemes. Although each could take a number of different forms, most are now caught by POA so are likely to be used only in limited circumstances now even if they still work for IHT purposes.[46]

Ingram schemes

31.34 These have been discussed briefly in Chapter 13. Land was divided into different interests and the individual might, for instance, retain an interest (such as a lease) which gave him a continued right of occupation and then give away the encumbered freehold interest in the land (this process is usually referred to as a "*shearing operation*").

31.35 Divisions of land could be horizontal (as in *Ingram* schemes when a single property is being carved into different slices) or vertical. In *Ingram*, Lord Hoffmann referred to the history of the legislation and noted that the decided cases showed that although its provisions prevent a donor from "having his cake and eating it", there is nothing to stop him from "carefully dividing up the cake, eating part and having the rest". He decided the appeal on the assumption that the lease granted by the nominee came into existence only at the time when the freehold was acquired by the trustees.[47] He held that the

---

[43] See HMRC guidance notes, App. III A3.54 (and see COP 10 letter).
[44] See 4.33 and 4.14.
[45] *Ingram v IRC* [1995] 4 All E.R. 334; on appeal [1997] 4 All E.R. 395 (CA), revs'd [1999] S.T.C. 37, HL. See 3.14.
[46] For example, home loan schemes have not been stopped in the inheritance tax legislation.
[47] The consequences of such a "contemporaneous carve-out" involved a consideration of the estate duty case of *Nichols v IRC* [1975] S.T.C. 278 CA which had concerned a gift by Sir Philip

31.36 trustees never acquired the land free of Lady Ingram's leasehold interest. He also noted that a nominee lease was valid as a matter of English law for reasons given by Millet L.J. in the Court of Appeal.

Amending legislation followed in FA 1999 which stopped *Ingram* schemes. Section 102A of FA 1986 extended the reservation of benefit provisions and the following points should be noted:

(i) There must be a *gift* of an interest in land. Hence gifts of chattels are not caught by anti-*Ingram* legislation nor are sales of a freehold interest subject to a lease.

(ii) The donor must retain "a significant right or interest to the land" or be party to a significant arrangement in relation to the land.[48]

31.37 A number of *Ingram* schemes were carried out before March 9, 1999. Although accepted as effective for inheritance tax purposes, when the donor dies the following problems may arise:

(i) what value is to be attributed to the retained lease? Specifically did it give security of tenure/a right to enfranchise? A lease for more than 21 years gives the donor rights of enfranchisement or possession on expiry of the term which will increase the value of that lease. Even if there is no right to enfranchise, the fact that the lease may be non assignable does not mean it has no value. What has to be valued is what the hypothetical purchaser would pay to have rent free occupation for the remaining term subject to the same covenants against alienation and the same covenants as to repair. (Section 160 of IHTA 1984 provides that the value is the price which the property might reasonably be expected to fetch in a hypothetical sale if sold on the open market at that time.) HMRC usually raise two arguments: that there is a special purchaser and that the lease has some marriage value. The donee of the freehold has an interest in purchasing the property and to that extent can be counted as a special purchaser. However, he may have no resources to fund that purchase. HMRC have also argued that a proportion of the vacant possession premium or marriage value should be allocated to the lease.

Nichols of his country house and estate to his son, Francis, subject to Francis granting him an immediate leaseback. Goff J., giving the judgment of the Court of Appeal, concluded that such an arrangement involved a reservation of benefit by Sir Philip:

"... we think that a grant of the fee simple, subject to and with the benefit of a lease-back, where such a grant is made by a person who owns the whole of the freehold free from any lease, is a grant of the whole fee simple with something reserved out of it, and not a gift of a partial interest leaving something in the hands of the grantor which he has not given. It is not like a reservation or remainder expectant on a prior interest. It gives an immediate right to the rent, together with a right to distrain for it, and, if there be a proviso for re-entry, a right to forfeit the lease."

In the event the *Nichols* case fell to be decided on the basis of the covenants given by the son in the lease in which he assumed the burden of repairs and the payment of tithe redemption duty, and which amounted to a reservation. The wider statement of Goff J. quoted above to the effect that a leaseback must *by itself* involve a reservation constituted the main authority relied upon by HMRC in Ingram (and the comment that the *Munro* case involved a "prior independent transaction" had subsequently been widely debated).

[48] See further the analysis of reversionary lease scheme, 31.52.

(ii) The CGT uplift will only apply to the leasehold interest. The encumbered freehold is likely to have a low base cost and will not benefit from the CGT main residence relief. It will benefit from non-business assets taper relief which means that after April 2007 (assuming the freehold reversion was owned by the donee prior to 17 March 1998) the maximum rate of CGT will be 24 per cent. Otherwise it is a ten-year ownership period.

31.38 In addition, since April 6, 2005, the para.3, Sch.15 pre-owned assets income tax charge will apply given that:

(i) the donor is in occupation of land; *and*

(ii) the disposal condition is met in respect of that land.

EXAMPLE 31.9

In 1998, A retained a 20-year, rent free lease in Blackacre and gave the encumbered freehold to his daughter. Assume that on the "**valuation date**" the value of the interest disposed of (the freehold) is £750,000 and the value of the "**relevant land**" (on the basis of a freehold with vacant possession) is £1.5m. Assume further that the rental value (calculated in accordance with the provisions of FA 2004, Sch.15, para.5) is £15,000 p.a.

Applying the formula:
R = £15,000
DV = £750,000
V = £1,500,000

A's benefit is therefore £7,500 so that if he is a higher rate taxpayer he will suffer income tax of £3,000.

The benefit is taxed each year whilst A continues to occupy the land. "The valuation date" is April 6, 2005 and so a revaluation will not be required until April 6, 2010.

31.39 **Practical advice on Ingram schemes in the light of Sch.15 of FA 2004:** There are limited options open to the taxpayer who has effected an *Ingram* scheme:

Option 1—*Pay the income tax charge:* this will in effect be 40 per cent (for most individuals) of a full rent for the property but with a discount which aims to reflect the value of the retained lease. In fact, the DV/V valuation method may not truly reflect the value of the lease in the taxpayer's estate. In those cases where seven years have elapsed so that the PET of the freehold is outside the IHT net and the taxpayer (or his family) can afford to pay the income tax this may be the most attractive option. Bear in mind the following when ascertaining the taxable benefit and therefore the income tax due:

(a) The rental value as at April 6, 2005 is arrived at on the assumption that the letting is with vacant possession. However, the house may be in need of modernisation and not easy to let. In these circumstances the rental value will be significantly reduced. In arriving at the rent the valuer shall assume that the donor pays all those expenses normally paid by the tenant and the donee bears the costs of repairs and buildings insurance. (The fact that this is not actually the case does not matter: it is a hypothetical valuation.)

(b) The freehold reversion must be valued at April 6, 2005 but this will not take into account marriage value. Any valuation should consider the terms of the lease: i.e. that the lessee is able to live in the property rent free. A typical Ingram scheme was for 15 years, and so if the lease was granted in 1999 it will expire in 2014. The donor will have no right to occupy beyond that date. In these circumstances it may be that the freehold reversion will only be discounted from the vacant possession value by something in the region of 25–35 per cent (but, of course, each case will depend on its own facts). The owner of the freehold reversion is not generally required under the terms of the lease to carry out any repairs which will increase the value of his interest and therefore the DV element.

If the taxpayer is in poor health, paying the tax may be the most sensible option.

Option 2—*the donor ceases to occupy the property:* if it is desired to retain the IHT advantage but not pay income tax this affords one way out. Of course alternative accommodation will need to be found! Before surrendering the lease consider carefully the tax implications: *e.g.* if the freehold gift is accelerated will this amount to an associated operation? If the fag end of the lease is assigned to the freeholder (or surrendered) there is a concern that there has been a disposition of the unencumbered freehold by associated operations at the point of surrender which might be disastrous in IHT terms. A slightly less radical alternative would be for the donor to occupy part only of the property: e.g. a cottage on the estate. In these circumstances HMRC accept that the income tax charge is limited to the property that the donor actually occupies rather than the property originally gifted.

Option 3—*donor pays rent or equivalent:* there are two options. The first is for the donor (say Mrs X) to assign or surrender her lease. The donor would then no longer have any rights of occupation. To avoid a reservation of benefit the donor would then need to pay full consideration for her continued occupation of the property.[49] Such arrangements might not involve paying the same rent as would be due under a commercial assured shorthold tenancy. Instead, the donor could take on responsibility for repairs etc under a tenants repairing lease and in that way reduce the rent payable. Independent valuations should be obtained by both parties.

This arrangement is also exempt from the POA Regime.[50] There is no need for the donor to self-assess nor to obtain valuations of the DV/V figure. One simply needs to ascertain what is full consideration for the donor's continued occupation. The value of the freehold reversion is irrelevant. Any payments made to the donee will be taxable as income in his hands but he could deduct the usual landlord's expenses.

---

[49] See FA 1986, Sch.20, para.6.
[50] Para.11(5)(d) of FA 2004.

The alternative option is for the donor to bring herself within para. 4(1), Sch.15 and to make payments to the donees "*in pursuance of a legal obligation . . .in respect of the occupation of the land.*" The section does not refer to the payments being rent. Under the terms of the lease the donor is under no legal obligation to pay for her continued occupation; she has a right to occupy rent free. However, she could *put herself* under a legal obligation by covenanting with the donees that for as long as she occupies the property she will make payments to them by deed of covenant. Such payments will reduce her POA charge. So if the appropriate rental value (ascertained as if it were an assured shorthold tenancy) is, say, £32,500 and she paid £30,500 under the deed of covenant, she would only be chargeable to POA income tax on £2,000.

Entering into a deed of covenant is a gift by the donor because she has no need to do this, having a right to occupy under the lease. Such payments may fall within the normal expenditure out of income exemption or will be PETs if the donee is not a trust. The payments that she makes under the deed of covenant are not taxable income in the hands of the donees: they are annual payments and outside the income tax net.[51] Nor are the payments "rent" because no letting business is being run. The donees should self-assess on this basis. This option depends on the donor being prepared to pay much larger sums to the donees. Instead of paying 40 per cent of the rental value to *HMRC* she is paying the rental value itself over to the *children*. One difficulty with this arrangement is if the freehold is held in a trust. Payments under the deed of covenant to the trustees might be regarded as additions to a settlement and, after March 21, 2006, as chargeable transfers unless they can be financed out of surplus income.

Option 4—*Election opt into the reservation of benefit rules:* for the individual wishing to remain in occupation of the property and unable/unwilling to pay the income tax charge, making the election is an option. The person who will eventually end up suffering the IHT is the donee. All the IHT savings are lost!

Option 5—*Reverter to settlor relief:* prior to December 5, 2005 the donees could give their freehold reversion to an interest in possession trust for the donor and retain the remainder interest. There was no SDLT payable although capital gains tax on the disposal of freehold interest was likely. The carve out done by the donor ceased and the donor (Mrs X) was treated as owning the freehold reversion by virtue of her interest in possession. She also reserved a benefit in the property (the reversion) which she had gifted. As noted in chapter 24, the wording of s.102(3) FA 1986 results in the reservation of benefit rules being disapplied.

Such a course would (prior to December 5, 2005) also avoid the POA charge because of the exemption under para 11(1); while Mrs X has an interest in possession in the freehold and owns the leasehold interest she is exempt from POA. From December 5, 2005, however, Mrs X (the original donor) is subject to POA.[52] In addition, *inter vivos* settlements of freehold interests will lead to the creation of a relevant property trust after March 21, 2006. Mrs X cannot take a qualifying interest in

---

[51] ITTOIA 2005, s.727.
[52] See chapter 24.

possession unless disabled and would therefore reserve a benefit in the gifted property without being able to rely on s.102(3) to displace those rules. Hence this option is now a non-starter.

Option 6—*Buying back the freehold:* if the donor Mrs X has sufficient resources she could buy back the freehold reversion at market value. Then the entire relevant property (the land) becomes part of her estate again and there is no POA charge. The inheritance tax savings are preserved except that the donees now hold cash rather than the freehold interest.

If this course of action is followed the donor would have to pay SDLT on the purchase of the freehold reversion. There will also be capital gains tax for the donees to pay on the sale of the freehold interest (assuming it shows a gain) and, of course, it will not be possible to effect the transaction by leaving the purchase price outstanding as a debt because the debt will be disallowed under FA 1986, s.103.[53]

Eversden arrangements

31.40 These were outlined at 13.16. A typical scheme was as follows:

EXAMPLE 31.10

In May 2003, John settled his house worth £800,000 on flexible interest in possession trusts for his wife Emma. After six months, Emma's interest in possession in the house was terminated (without her consent being required) say as to 95%—with her children then taking revocable interests in possession which conferred rights of occupation (albeit they might choose not to exercise such rights). John and Emma continue to occupy the property.

Diagrammatically the position can be illustrated as follows:

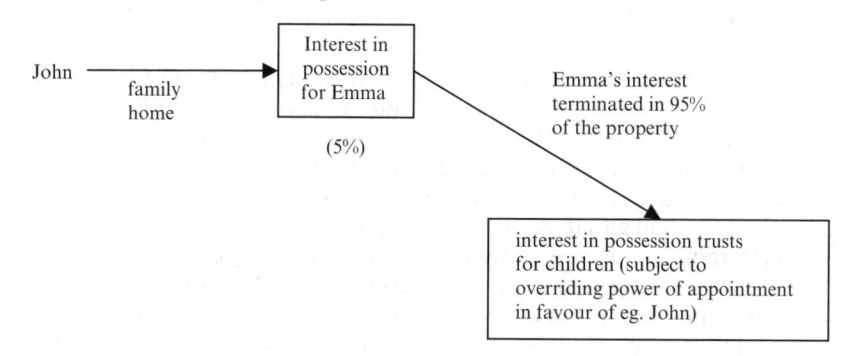

```
                        ┌──────────────┐
                        │  Interest in │
     John  ──────────▶  │  possession  │          Emma's interest
          family        │  for Emma    │          terminated in 95%
          home          └──────────────┘          of the property
                             (5%)       ╲
                                         ╲
                                          ▼
                                  ┌─────────────────────────────┐
                                  │ interest in possession trusts│
                                  │ for children (subject to     │
                                  │ overriding power of appointment│
                                  │ in favour of eg. John)       │
                                  └─────────────────────────────┘
```

31.41 Tax effects: on a sale of the house during the parents' lifetimes, any gain would qualify for principal private residence relief under s.225, TCGA 1992 because of the occupation of the property by a beneficiary of the trust.[54]

---

[53] See 23.16.
[54] See 31.19.

The reservation of benefit rules were displaced on John's gift to Emma by s.102(5) of FA 1986 (exempt gifts to spouses).[55] Once Emma's interest in possession was terminated she made a transfer of value under s.52 IHTA 1984 which was a PET if the children took outright or on interest in possession trusts. She therefore needed to survive seven years for the full IHT savings to be secured. It was not, however, considered that she made a gift (so that the reservation of benefit provisions were not in point even though she continued to benefit from the settled property).[56] Of course if Emma's interest was terminated on or after 22 March 2006 she would be deemed to make a gift and hence be caught by the reservation of benefit rules.

Eversden schemes were for all practical purposes stopped from June 20, 2003, but any arrangements already completed before that date have been caught by the POA Regime.

Options to avoid the pre-owned assets income tax charge on Eversden schemes: 31.42
Option 1—avoid termination of the spousal interest in possession; end trust: if the spouse interest (in the above example, Emma's interest) has not yet been terminated it may be sensible to leave the structure in place and do nothing to end it. If the property is advanced back to the settlor or to the spouse, HMRC accept that in both cases POA ceases to apply.[57] There is little point in retaining the structure now since FA 2006 means that a termination of Emma's interest in favour of the children will lead to a reservation of benefit arising at that point. Alternatively, if Emma's interest has already been ended it may be preferable therefore to transfer the property back to Emma as life tenant rather than John as settlor in order to maximise double charges relief if Emma dies within seven years of the original PET.

Option 2—pay the income tax charge: if John (the settlor) is ill it may be worth preserving the IHT advantages and, if necessary, paying the income tax charge until his death. In these circumstances how much tax will John pay? Assume the value of the house is £800,000 and its rental value is £25,000. John is charged on:

$$25,000 \times \frac{DV}{V(£800,000)}$$

The unknown figure is DV—what is the value of the interest disposed of by John? Following the decision in *Arkwright*,[58] it appears that HMRC have conceded the principle that IHTA 1984, s.161(4) has no application and that the value of a half share in a house owned by spouses is not necessarily a **mathematical one half of the vacant possession value of the property**. In any event, there is nothing comparable to s.161 in Sch.15 and so the general principles of valuing a share (which may result in a discount) will apply.

If, say, the value of John's interest (DV) is discounted to £340,000 the chargeable amount on which he would pay income tax is £10,625, giving rise to a tax liability (for a 40 per cent tax payer) of £4,250 pa. In the circumstances this might be thought an acceptable price to pay to preserve the IHT advantage. However, the settlor cannot change his mind after January 31, 2007 and opt into the reservation of benefit rules.

---

[55] See Ch.24 and FA 1986, s.102(5).
[56] See 13.09, 24.05 and 24.08 and s.102ZA FA 1986 which, from March 22, 2006, treat such terminations as a gift by Emma.
[57] See COP 10 letter—App. III A3.61.
[58] [2004] EWHC 1720 (Ch); [2004] S.T.C. 1323.

Option 3—making the election: should John make an election under FA 2004, Sch.15, para.21? (It is the settlor not the spouse who needs to make the election because he is the one liable to the POA charge.) Generally no, because there are three disadvantages:

(i) The property remains part of the children's estate for IHT purposes. Remember that an election does not alter the property law consequences of what has happened;

(ii) There is an IHT charge on the property on the death of the settlor before the spouse. This could pose cash flow difficulties for the spouse. No spouse exemption is available;

(iii) If the settlor elects there could be double charges if the spouse then dies within seven years of the original gift: once on her failed PET and again on the death of the settlor.

Home loan schemes

31.43 The home loan (or as it is sometimes called the "double trust") scheme was a prime target of the POA Regime. The schemes are described in detail at 3.18. HMRC are inclined to challenge those home loan schemes where the debt is made repayable on demand even if it is interest bearing with interest rolled up and compounded. This is on the basis that by failing to call in the loan before the death of the donor he has reserved a benefit in the debt by associated operations. The result (if this argument is correct) is that the debt is taxed as part of the settlor's estate on his death and any inheritance tax savings nullified.

31.44 Excluded liability: it is thought that, on balance, the pre-owned assets income tax applies to home loan schemes.[59] Although the property is part of the settlor's estate for inheritance tax purposes it is subject to an excluded liability, namely the debt.[60] This provision is intended to operate in the following way: assume that the value of the house is now £500,000 and the debt remains £450,000.

(i) To the extent that the value of the property exceeds the amount of the excluded liability (£500,000–£450,000) the exemption in Sch.15 para.11(1) operates. This is consistent with the general scheme of the legislation since £50,000 is included in the settlor's estate for IHT purposes; and

(ii) as to the amount of the excluded liability (£450,000), the POA Regime applies (in percentage terms to 90 per cent of the value of the house).

---

[59] For detailed analysis see "Pre-Owned Assets Tax Planning Strategies" (2nd edn) Ch. 17.
[60] See FA 2004 Sch.15 para. 11(7). "a liability is an excluded liability if
   (a) the creation of the liability, and
   (b) any transaction by virtue of which the person's estate came to include the relevant property or property which derives its value from the relevant property or by virtue of which the value of property in his estate came to be derived from the relevant property were associated operations, as defined by s.268 of IHTA 1984."

Note that the value of the excluded liability is the face value of the debt plus rolled up interest as at April 6, 2005.[61]:

Options to avoid the POA charge on home loan schemes

31.45 Much will depend on the particular scheme adopted by the taxpayer but the following general points should be noted.

(i) *Pay the income tax and/or consider repaying (part of) the loan.*

The taxpayer should calculate the POA income tax charge that will be payable This means obtaining a market value for the house as at 6th April 2005; identifying the face value of the liability outstanding then plus interest and obtaining a rental value of the house at the same date. There is no need to carry out any further valuations until April 6, 2010.

EXAMPLE 31.11

> A, a higher rate taxpayer, effected a home loan scheme in 2003. On April 6, 2005 the house is worth £1m with a rental value of £40,000. The loan's face value is £800,000 but its commercial value, given that it is not repayable until A's death, is £400,000. No interest is payable.
>
> A's income tax charge for the year 2005/06 (and thereafter until the tax year 2010/11) will be on a benefit of £40,000 reduced by the amount of property still in his estate. The amount of excluded liability is £800,000 which means that 80% of the market rent is the deemed benefit: i.e. £32,000 = income tax of £12,800.
>
> One point to bear in mind is that if the annual rental value of the property is less than £5,000 (£10,000 for a married couple) the *de minimis* exemption excluded the POA charge.

31.46 One option is to negotiate repayment of the loan when the house is sold if the taxpayer moves to a smaller house. The two sets of trustees could agree an early repayment of the loan (which will be heavily discounted commercially). An actuarial valuation of the loan should be obtained and arm's length negotiations carried out between the two sets of trustees. So for example a debt with a face value of £1m carrying no interest and repayable only on the death of the taxpayers might be discounted by as much as 50 per cent if the settlors were a married couple in their 50s. Once any new house is free of debt the POA charge ceases to apply.[62]

31.47 **Unscrambling the scheme:** there are a variety of ways in which the scheme could be unscrambled. Much will depend on how the debt was structured.

> (a) *Unscrambling scheme if loan note not an RDS:*[63] it may be possible to unscramble the entire arrangement. The benefit of the debt could be

---

[61] See COP 10 letter question—Appendix III A3.61.
[62] If a small debt is left it may be that the "benefit" will fall within *de minimis*. Cash should not be added to the settlement after March 21, 2006 since it will involve a chargeable transfer.
[63] RDS = relevant discounted security.

assigned to the settlor (or settlors if a married couple effected the scheme) and Double Charges Relief will then be available in the event that one of them dies within seven years of the original gift of the debt.

Stage 1: If the benefit of the debt is transferred to the children who assign it to the settlor(s) each child will make a PET. To avoid this, the Trustees of Trust 2 (the children's trust) appoint the benefit of the debt to the children contingent on their being alive in (say) twenty one days. During the twenty one day period the children assign their benefits under that appointment to the settlor(s). (Note that the children retain their existing interests in possession which will terminate only when the contingency is met after 21 days.) So far as the children are concerned this assignment will not have adverse tax consequences since

(i) for IHT the assignment is of a reversionary interest (viz a future interest under the settlement) which is excluded property.[64] It is assigned outright to the parents not in trust so is not caught by schedule 20;

(ii) for CGT purposes the disposal is of an interest under a settlement on which, as a result of TCGA 1992, s.76(1), no chargeable gain accrues.

The making of the appointment by the trustees will not have any tax consequences.

Stage 2: at the end of 21 days the settlor(s) becomes absolutely entitled to the debt. The Children's Trust (Trust 2) has ended as a result of the appointment. The debt is not at this point written off. If the settlor were to die within seven years of having entered into the scheme the position (after *Stage 1* and *Stage 2* have been effected) is as follows:

(i) the taxpayer is taxed on the value of the house in Trust 1 less the value of the debt. Hence any tax charge will be limited to the growth in value of the property above the amount of the debt;

(ii) in addition the benefit of the debt is in his free estate and accordingly taxed. However, reg.4 of the 1987 Double Charges Regulations will prevent there being a charge on both the failed PET of the debt and on the debt itself.[65]

The end result is that the scheme has been unscrambled and whilst the settlor has obtained no IHT advantage he will not suffer any IHT double charge.

The tax consequences of *Stage 2* are as follows—

(i) the children's interests in possession in Trust 2 have ended with the absolute vesting of the trust property in the settlor. This does not involve the children making a PET because of the availability of reverter to settlor relief (unaffected by FA 2006, Sch.20 as the settlor takes outright).[66]

---

[64] For the definition of excluded property, see IHTA 1984, s.48(1).
[65] The taxpayer will need to make a chargeable transfer equal to the value of the failed PET for the relief to be of benefit to him.
[66] See Ch. 27.

(ii) on the ending of the debt trust no CGT charge will arise provided that the debt falls within TCGA 1992. s.251(1) (which provides that no chargeable gain arises on its disposal).[67]

Diagrammatically the unscrambling arrangement is as follows—

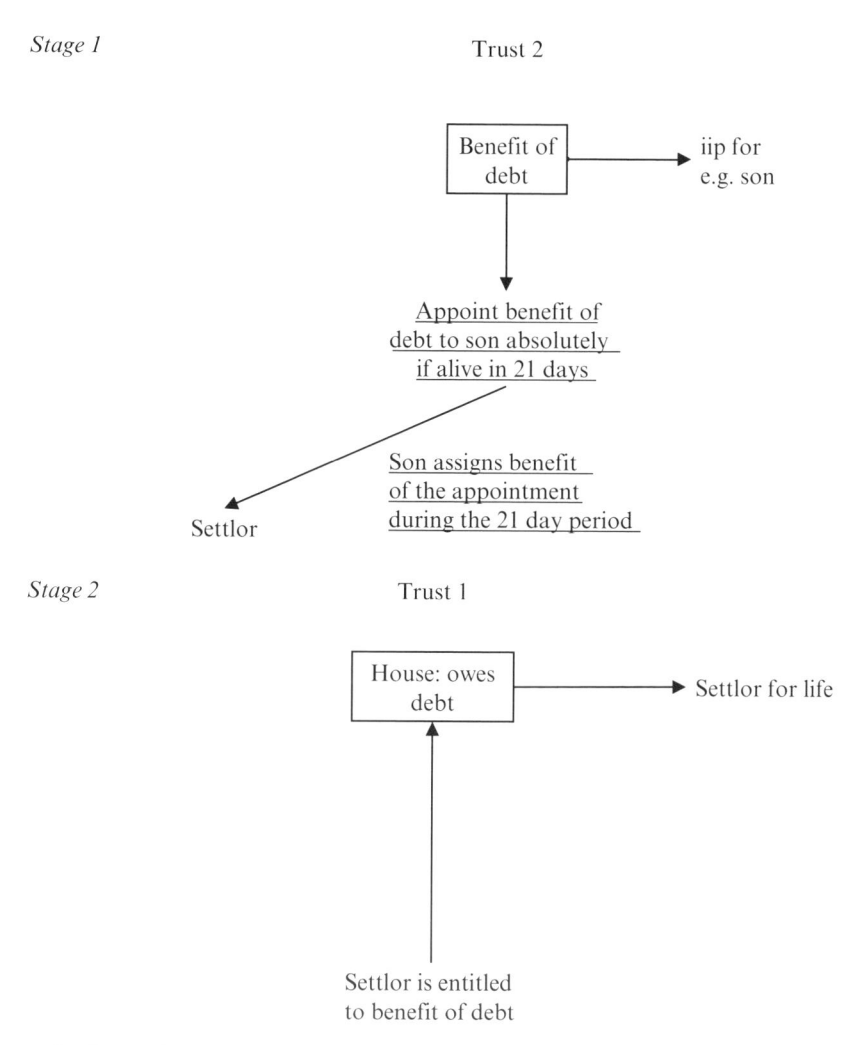

Stage 1

Trust 2

```
                    ┌──────────┐
                    │Benefit of│ ──────▶  iip for
                    │  debt    │          e.g. son
                    └──────────┘
                         │
                         ▼
                 Appoint benefit of
                 debt to son absolutely
                 if alive in 21 days
                        ╱
                       ╱
                      ╱  Son assigns benefit
                     ╱   of the appointment
                    ╱    during the 21 day period
                   ▼
              Settlor
```

Stage 2

Trust 1

```
                    ┌──────────┐
                    │House: owes│ ──────▶  Settlor for life
                    │   debt   │
                    └──────────┘
                         ▲
                         │
                 Settlor is entitled
                 to benefit of debt
```

So far as the POA charge is concerned once the debt is back in the settlor's estate the excluded liability (viz the debt which affects the house) does not reduce the value of the settlor's estate so that the POA charge will not apply from that date whether or not the debt is then written off.[68] If the debt were to

---

[67] This is where the various schemes differ: if the debt had been assigned to the trustees of Trust 2, for instance, so that they are not the original creditors then any gain may be chargeable. If the debt is a relevant discount security, its transfer may trigger an income tax charge.

[68] Sch.15, para.11(6) and see COP 10 letter: App. III A3.61. It is thought that for these purposes the settlor's estate must be looked at "in the round": viz as the aggregate of the settled property and his free estate (contrast the approach adopted in *St Barbe Green v IRC* [2005] S.T.C. 288).

be written off it is not thought that this will involve an addition of property to the settlement so as to lead to a chargeable transfer by the settlor (see 15.13) but if this was felt to be a concern then the property could be charged with the debt on a non-recourse basis, then transferred to the settlor (in order to avoid any SDLT charge) and only then released. Double charges relief will be available if the property is back in the settlor's estate.[69]

(b) *Unscrambling scheme if loan note is an RDS:* if the loan note is an RDS then the above method of unscrambling may involve income tax charges for the Debt Trustees if the RDS shows a profit on assignment. (In some cases it has been structured in such a way as to avoid a profit arising.) Accordingly unscrambling is likely to involve the following steps:

(i) vary the Debt Trust so that only adults are beneficiaries;
(ii) the two sets agree to secure the debt over the house by a non recourse charge;
(iii) appoint equitable interest in house out of Property Trust back to the settlors with them taking on no personal liability to repay the charge;
(iv) the trustees of the debt trust, with the concurrence of the beneficiaries, release the RDS.

The tax analysis of these steps is as follows:

(i) although a breach of trust, the release is voidable rather than void and thus unable to be upset as the beneficiaries have all concurred in it. It is possible that minor beneficiaries who have been excluded may bring proceedings later;
(ii) the release avoids an income tax charge on the RDS;
(iii) the release of the RDS means that there is no liability affecting the property with the result that Sch.15 no longer applies (para.11(1));
(iv) the POA charge between April 6, 2005 and the date of release may be avoided by the £5,000 *de minimis* exemption (Sch.15, para.13) if the release is effected before the notional rent exceeds £10,000 (when husband and wife have jointly entered into the scheme so that two £5,000 exemptions are available). Alternatively the settlor could elect into the reservation of benefit rules before January 31, 2007. If the house is back in his estate free of debt the effect of the election is nullified;[70]
(v) the property will be fully eligible for the spouse exemption on the death of the settlor and any other "normal" inheritance tax saving measures;
(vi) the children have made a PET resulting in the termination of their interests in possession equal to the value of their share in the debt;
(vii) SDLT can be avoided if the transfer of the house subject to the debt back to the parents is structured with a non recourse charge;
(viii) double charges relief is available if the entire debt is written off and the settlor parents die within seven years;

---

[69] See SI 1987/1130.
[70] See HMRC correspondence, App. III A3.149.

(ix) note that writing off the debt while the house is still in the property trust *might* be taxed as a chargeable transfer rather than a PET[71]. Hence ideally the house should be extracted from the trust first (subject to a charge) before the debt is written off.

Election: this is the route that the Government has offered as a way of avoiding the POA income tax charge. It may well be an attractive option if the scheme is also being wound up, since it avoids the income tax charge from 6th April 2005.[72]   31.48

Pay rent under a legal obligation by setting up a deed of covenant: the taxpayer uses the let out in Sch.15, para.4(1) and makes payments under a legal obligation equal to the appropriate rental value in respect of his occupation. Note that the legislation does not require the payment of *rent* as such. The taxpayer could therefore enter into a deed of covenant and agree to pay to the Property Trustees a sum equal to the market rent of the property for so long as he remains in occupation. The sums paid do not suffer income tax in the hands of the recipient trustees. Otherwise the structure remains unchanged. In connection with this arrangement note—   31.49

(i) it is thought that payments under the deed are not rent: they are voluntary payments outside the income tax net.[73]
(ii) prior to March 22, 2006, because the payments were to the property trust in which the payer has a life interest there was no transfer of value for IHT purposes. Now they may be chargeable transfers as additions to a property settlement.[74]
(iii) CGT principal private residence relief will not be affected.

Reverter to Settlor Trust: this involved reorganising the Property Trust to preserve the inheritance tax savings whilst avoiding the income tax charge by transferring the house into a reverter to settler trust. This is now a non-starter given s.80 of FA 2006 which stops any POA advantages and Sch.20 of FA 2006 which imposes an inheritance tax charge on the creation of the trust.[75]   31.50

Home loan schemes today: old style home loan schemes in respect of the taxpayer's *dwelling house* will not be entered into today: *first*, because of the   31.51

---

[71] See 15.13 for discussion on additions.
[72] See 00.00. Note that the election may have slightly unexpected effects in the case of home loan schemes. There are some who consider that the election does not prevent a home loan scheme working. See Ch. 17 of "Pre-Owned Assets Income Tax Strategies" by Chamberlain and Whitehouse (2nd edn) for further discussion.
[73] See ITTOIA 2005, s.727.
[74] The payments may fall within the normal expenditure exemption or within the taxpayer's IHT nil rate band.
[75] See Ch. 27. The restructuring essentially involved the following:

1. The settlor surrendered his life interest in the Property Trust to his children so they became entitled to interests in possession. He was excluded as a beneficiary of the Property Trust; he paid a market rent for his continued occupation.
2. The Children's Trustees then appointed the benefit of the debt (owed to it by the Property Trust) to the Property Trust which now had the same beneficiaries. Alternatively the Children's Trustees wrote off the debt.
3. Subsequently, the Property Trust appointed the house to the children absolutely.
4. The children then resettled the property on a new trust, being a reverter to settlor trust for the settlor (Third Trust).

pre-owned assets charge, *secondly*, because of the SDLT charge (rates up to 4 per cent) and *third* because of Schedule 20 and the inheritance tax charges on *inter vivos* gifts into trusts. Even home loan schemes on let property using the double trust scheme are no longer feasible given that setting up such trusts will involve immediately chargeable transfers for inheritance tax purposes. Hence home loan schemes are likely to be limited to transfers between spouses.[76]

FUTURE ARRANGEMENTS ON THE FAMILY HOME

Reversionary lease schemes

31.52 The development of reversionary lease arrangements was closely linked to *Ingram* schemes. In particular:

(i) like *Ingram* schemes reversionary leases involve a shearing operation;

(ii) similar CGT problems arise in the event of a sale of the property. Hence they were ideal in cases where it was envisaged that the property would never be sold but would be retained within the family.

Whereas in *Ingram* arrangements, it was necessary <u>first</u> to carve out a lease and <u>then</u> to gift an encumbered freehold reversion, reversionary leases were a single stage transaction involving merely the grant of a lease.

EXAMPLE 31.12

A owns Manor Farm which he wishes to pass on to his eldest son, B. He wishes to occupy the Manor for the rest of his life. It is inconceivable that the property will be sold outside the family. The "scheme" operates as follows:

(i) A grants B a long lease over the property (say 125 years) to take effect in 20 years time.[77] Because the lease does not give B occupation rights immediately it is called a deferred or reversionary lease. The terms of the lease do not involve the payment of any rent nor do they impose onerous conditions on B;

(ii) A can continue to occupy the property for the next 20 years because he remains the freeholder;

(iii) The gift of the lease is a PET by A and so free from IHT provided that he survives by seven years;

---

[76] See 31.32.
[77] Could the period of deferral exceed 21 years? This might be desirable if A were (say) in his mid 60s so that he could easily live for another 25 years. This involves the construction of s.149(3) of the Law of Property Act 1925 which provides "a term [i.e. lease] at a rent or granted in consideration of a fine, limited to take effect more than 21 years from the date of the instrument purporting to create it, shall be void." It is thought that a lease which does not involve the payment of any rent (or fine) is outside these provisions.

(iv) The freehold interest (of diminishing value) remains in A's estate and will be taxed accordingly on his death.[78]

(v) If A is still alive at the end of 20 years and wishes to continue to occupy the property he will need to pay B a market rent: otherwise he will have reserved a benefit in the lease gifted to B.

Reservation of benefit analysis: A continues to occupy by virtue of his retained freehold property: he does not retain a benefit in the gifted property which is the reversionary lease. Like *Ingram* the arrangement is a horizontal carve-out. This analysis has been accepted by HMRC in respect of reversionary lease arrangements set up before March 9, 1999. 31.53

HMRC consider, however, that the legislation introduced in 1999 to stop *Ingram* arrangements also applied to reversionary leases. This view is not shared by most practitioners and, on its face, the 1999 legislation appears to be carefully targeted at *Ingram* schemes (there was no mention in the accompanying Press Release of other similar arrangements being caught).

The argument that reversionary leases are *not* caught is as follows[79]: 31.54

(i) the basic conditions in the legislation that have to be satisfied are, first, that the taxpayer disposes of an interest in land by way of gift (this A undoubtedly does when he grants B the deferred lease). Second he must retain "a significant right or interest or (be) party to a significant arrangement in relation to the land." Of course A retains his freehold interest—does that satisfy the second requirement?

(ii) the short answer is that it all depends on the facts! By s.102A(5), "a right or interest is not significant if it was granted or acquired before the period of seven years ending with the date of the gift." In the vast majority of cases, persons wishing to enter into reversionary lease arrangements will do so in respect to property which they have owned for at least seven years. In such cases it is considered that the s.102A(5) let-out applies and the gifted lease is not property subject to a reservation.

(iii) An alternative argument is based on s.102A(3) which excludes a right, interest or arrangement which enables the donor to occupy the land "for full consideration in money or money's worth." If A had originally purchased his freehold interest (whether or not within seven years of the date of the gift) for full consideration then this let out should apply so that again the arrangement remains outside reservation of benefit. Of course, a reversionary lease granted within seven years of A inheriting the property would be caught because neither of the let-outs would then be available.

The Guidance Notes on POA issued by HMRC in March 2005 and then reissued in May 2006 do not accept that reversionary lease schemes post March 8, 1999 are outside the reservation of benefit provisions. HMRC comment that: 31.55

---

[78] Could the lease be made to vest in possession on the earlier of 21 years from the date of grant and the death of A (the freeholder)? If so, this would have an obvious attraction in reducing the value of the freehold interest in A's estate. Some concern has been felt that this could convert the reversionary lease into a lease for life under IHTA 1984, s.43(3).

[79] The legislation is in App. I.

> "the occupation[of the donor] is considered to be a significant right in respect of the relevant land and it is thought therefore that a reservation of benefit for inheritance tax will arise. As such, the property will not be subject to the income tax charge."

Presumably, this statement is on the basis that the donor is party to a significant arrangement. Section 102A(5) refers to a significant right or interest but not to arrangements. It would seem that even if the settlor is party to the arrangement when he enters the scheme this does not as such enable him to go on living in the property. It is the freehold interest that enables him to live there and this he has obtained outside the arrangement.

31.56 **Impact of the POA Regime:** it is considered that taxpayers such as A in *Example 31.12* who have entered into reversionary lease arrangements on property originally owned personally will be subject to an income tax charge under the POA Regime from April 6, 2005. The analysis is much the same as for *Ingram* schemes.[80] The practical advice and options available will therefore be much the same.

As with those schemes an apportionment of the appropriate rental value will be necessary under Sch.15, para.4. The property gifted (the leasehold interest: DV in the formula) is likely to show a year-on-year increase in much the same way as the freehold reversion in *Ingram* schemes. Once again the fact that one only has to revalue every five years will generally be advantageous for the taxpayer.[81]

Despite this, reversionary lease schemes may have a place in future tax planning.

EXAMPLE 31.13

> A is the elderly life tenant of a trust set up by his father in 1985. A is not the settlor of the trust and all the assets were settled pre-1986. A now wishes to carry out inheritance tax planning. The trust owns a large country mansion worth £3m.
>
> The trustees grant a reversionary lease to a nominee to take effect in, say, 17 years time. In 2007 the reversionary lease is then appointed (by exercise of their overriding powers) on interest in possession trusts for A's son. Given s.102ZA FA 1986, the life tenant is deemed to have made a gift of the underlying settled property (even though the life tenant is not the settlor and the trust is pre-1986).[82] This creates a transitional serial interest for son and involves a PET by A. A retains the freehold and continues to occupy the property. A has had a life interest for at least seven years so should be within the protection of s.102A(3). He is not a party to any arrangement given that it was the trustees who took away his interest.

---

[80] See 31.34.
[81] It is not clear what should happen where a taxpayer disagrees with HMRC that reversionary lease schemes effected post-March 8, 1999 are caught. HMRC say they are caught by reservation of benefit and not subject to income tax. Many disagree.
[82] See 24.08 for a consideration of the scope of s.102ZA.

Any POA charge should be minimal. Even if A has made a disposal of an interest in land (which must be doubted) the value of what he has given away as life tenant has a small value being the right to receive rent in 17 years' time for the rest of his life.

CO-OWNERSHIP/SHARING ARRANGEMENTS

31.57 During the consultation period on the POA Regime, it became apparent that the Government was anxious not to disturb "genuine" house sharing arrangements, which have always qualified for protection from the reservation of benefit rules provided that certain conditions are satisfied. Since co-ownership arrangements have statutory protection, in appropriate circumstances they offer a valuable IHT planning tool.

31.58 **Inheritance tax position:** the IHT treatment of co-ownership arrangements is not entirely straightforward. Prior to March 9, 1999, the following Ministerial statement ("*the Hansard Statement*") governed the position:

> "It may be that my Hon Friend's intention concerns the common case where someone gives away an individual share in land, typically a house, which is then occupied by all the joint owners including the donor. For example, elderly parents may make unconditional gifts of undivided shares in their house to their children and the parents and the children occupy the property as their family home, each owner bearing his or her share of the running costs. In those circumstances, the parents' occupation or enjoyment of the part of the house that they have given away is in return for similar enjoyment of the children of the other part of the property. Thus the donors' occupation is for full consideration.
>
> Accordingly, I assure my Hon Friend that the gift with reservation rules will not be applied to an unconditional gift of an undivided share in land merely because the property is occupied by all the joint owners or tenants in common, including the donor".[83]

31.59 This is a somewhat puzzling statement. The parents' occupation is surely by virtue of their owning a share in the property: the children are not "allowing" them to live there. The statement also implies that the house is divided into discrete parts so that the parents' use of the children's part is in return for the parents letting the children use their part. In reality, the parents have the right to occupy the entire property as the owners of an undivided share.

Presumably the "full consideration" referred to in the above statement is intended to be that "I will let you use my 50 per cent of the house in consideration for you allowing me to use your 50 per cent". This is the basis of the supposed 50 per cent ceiling in the size of the gift.

However, it is arguable that this arrangement is more in the nature of a carve out—the parents' right to occupy the entire property is derived from the interest they have retained and does not amount to a reservation in the gifted share.

---

[83] Statement of Mr Peter Brooke, Minister of State, Treasury Standing Committee G; Hansard, June 10, 1986, col.425.

This carve out argument was considered in the *Eversden* case (of course the taxpayer was not in joint occupation and therefore could not rely on the full consideration argument or on the *Hansard* statement). The Special Commissioner and Lightman J. appeared to accept it, at least in relation to the original property, although the latter did not agree there was a carve out in relation to the replacement property.[84]

If the carve out argument is right, then the full consideration and therefore the precise interest retained is irrelevant under pre-1999 arrangements since even a 5 per cent retained share would confer the right to occupy the property in its entirety. In correspondence between the Law Society and HMRC in 1987, the latter accepted that an arrangement would not necessarily be jeopardised simply because it involved a gift of an unequal share in the home. However, that statement made it clear that the owners had to remain in joint occupation and that the donee should not pay the donor's share of running costs. It was also seen as important that the donee occupied the property as his family home. The position was substantially altered by the "anti-*Ingram*" legislation in 1999.

31.60 Position post-March 8, 1999: for gifts of undivided shares in land from March 9, 1999, the position is regulated by s.102B FA 1986. In general, the gift of an undivided share in land will involve a reservation of benefit in cases where the donor continues in occupation (see s.102B(2)). Subsection 102B(4), however, provides that there shall not be a reserved benefit in the following circumstances:

1. the donor disposes by way of gift, on or after March 9, 1999, of an undivided share of an interest in land;
2. the donor and the donee occupy the land; and
3. the donor does not receive any benefit, other than a negligible one, which is provided by or at the expense of the donee for some reason connected with the gift.

31.61 Occupation: note that, post-*Hansard,* there is no longer any requirement for occupation by the donor and donee as *the family home*. Further, there is no reference to full consideration as the basis for the exemption, so it is thought that the donor is able to give away more than a 50 per cent interest.

EXAMPLE 31.14

(1) Judith now widowed lives in the family home at Sandbanks. Her married daughter lives in south London and comes to stay with Judith with her two young children most weekends and holidays. Judith gives the daughter a 50 per cent share in the house.
  (i) It is thought that s.102B(4) will apply given that both occupy the property. The daughter comes and goes as she pleases; leaves possessions in the property; has her own bedrooms etc. From her point of view it is like owning a second home.
  (ii) Consider the daughter's CGT position assuming that she owns a house in south London. Which is to qualify as her principal private

---

[84] For the facts of the case, see 13.16 and 31.40.

residence (consider the use of the election under TCGA 1992 s.222(5))?

(2) Some years ago Ben gave a one-third share in his home to his daughter Sheila who lives at home and looks after him. He now gifts a further one-third share to his son, an airline pilot who spends most of his time in New York but who stays with Ben ("treats the place like home") when he is in the UK (on average 6 weeks a year). It is thought that both gifts are protected by s.102B(4).

31.62 HMRC give a wide meaning to "*occupation*" for the purpose of the para 3 charge in the POA Guidance Notes.[85] Hence if storage or a right to use the property combined with minimal actual usage constitute occupation by the donor for the purpose of the para 3 charge, presumably the same will constitute occupation by the donee for the purposes of s.102B(4)!

31.63 **Expenses:** HMRC are known to dislike arrangements where the donor gives away (say) 90 per cent and retains 10 per cent, and are likely to investigate carefully the third condition set out above—*i.e.* has the donor received any connected benefits from the donee? That in turn will involve scrutinising how expenses have been split between them.

Under both *Hansard* and s.102B there has been some misunderstanding of precisely how the running costs should be split. A cursory reading of the *Hansard* statement might suggest that running expenses should be split in proportion to the *beneficial* interests that each has in the property. However, "*his share of the running costs*", as HMRC subsequently confirmed in 1987, is referring to the donor and donee's *actual* expenses incurred. Thus if there is a 90/10 beneficial split in the property, the donee arguably should not pay 90 per cent of the expenses but instead pay no more than the expenses he has actually incurred; when donor and donee live together full-time, this will generally mean a 50 per cent split.

For instance, HMRC's view is that just because a person owns 90 per cent of a property, it does not mean that he uses 90 per cent of the gas, electricity and water, and if the donee agrees to pay 90 per cent of those expenses he is therefore conferring a benefit on the donor. The focus is on what collateral benefits, if any, are being provided by the donee in connection with the gift. HMRC do not appear to distinguish between capital and living expenses although it may be argued that repair bills should be split in proportion to ownership of the property. The concern is the potential width of "benefit" to the donor. Assume, for instance, that Bob has always occupied his house with his unmarried son, Bill, and has paid all the property expenses. He now gives Bill a share in the property (say 60 per cent) and Bill takes over 60 per cent of the property bills. Nothing else changes in their relationship, Bob continues living in the property (as before) but is now relieved of the worry of paying 60 per cent of the property bills.

(i) Bob must not receive a benefit (however small?) from Bill which is in some way connected with the gift;
(ii) there is nothing in the IHT legislation or in common sense to suggest that if Bill does not pay a share of expenses the gift of the 60 per cent is in any sense a "sham"; **accordingly**

---

[85] See also COP 10 letter and App. III A3.61.

(iii) it will be sensible to err on the side of caution—better for Bob to overpay (or even pay all expenses!) than for there to be a risk that he is in receipt of a benefit. Quite often Bob will be content to do this: it was, after all the arrangement prior to the gift, and children are increasingly happy to be financially dependent on their parents! It may also represent sensible IHT planning for Bob to deplete his estate in this way.

EXAMPLE 31.15

In 2000, Barry gave 50 per cent of his house to his son, David, who lives in a flat in town during the week but spends most weekends at the property. On these facts, are the donor and donee both "occupying" the land? This is a question of fact and degree but a person may be in occupation of more than one property. If David pays 50 per cent of the outgoings but is using the property less than Barry, arguably a benefit is being conferred in connection with the gift and s.102B(4) is not satisfied so that the gift is caught by the reservation of benefit rules.

The correct course is for Barry (as donor) to pay at least the share of the outgoings reflecting his *actual* use. So as he is there more often than David, one would expect him to pay a significantly greater share of the running costs. Indeed to be safe, he may want to consider paying almost all the outgoings, including capital expenditure on the property.

31.64 **Position under the POA Regime:** prima facie, the POA Regime can apply to co-ownership arrangements because there has been a disposal of an interest in land and the donor continues to occupy the property. Thus, the basic disposal and occupation conditions in para.3 of Sch.15 are satisfied.

However, para.11(5)(c) provides a rather tortuous exemption. If property "would fall to be treated as property which is subject to a reservation of benefit" *but for* s.102B(4), such a disposal is protected from a POA charge. Since s.102B(4) can only apply to, and therefore protect, post-March 8, 1999 arrangements, the legislation also provides that a disposal made before March 9, 1999 will not be subject to the POA Regime if one assumes that had it been made on or after that date it would then have qualified for s.102B(4) protection.

Thus, if in *Example 31.15* we assume that the gift had been made in 1997, then Barry would not be subject to a charge in respect of the gift made in 1997, whilst David continues in occupation because para.11(5)(c) gives protection. What is slightly odd about this is that if this particular gift had been made in 1997 it might not have had *Hansard* protection given that the donee was not occupying as his family home, albeit it would qualify for s.102(B)(4) protection if made now. The POA Regime does not distinguish between the different conditions required under *Hansard* as opposed to s.102(B)(4) and it may be that HMRC does not in practice require occupation as a *family home* in relation to pre-March 1999 arrangements, even in the inheritance tax context. Of course, if the pre-1999 gift was *not* protected under *Hansard* or on the basis of the carve-out argument then there would have been a reservation of benefit so that the POA Regime will not apply anyway (see Sch.15, para.11(5)(a)).

Sales of part: it is somewhat odd that gifts of part falling within s.102B(4) are protected from the POA charge but that sales of part at full value are not so protected (albeit that such transactions are not gifts and therefore are not subject to the gifts with reservation rules). This is discussed further below.[86] It is assumed[87], that sales of part at an undervalue are gifts as to the undervalue and may still qualify for protection from the reservation of benefit rules under s.102B(4) and therefore exemption from charge under the POA Regime, at least as to the undervalue.

31.65

Cash gifts: what happens if in *Example 31.15* Barry does not give an undivided interest in the land to his son but instead gives him cash? For example, suppose Barry gives cash of £100,000 to David and together they buy a house worth £200,000, owning it in equal shares and both living there. Section 102B(4) is not satisfied because Barry has not satisfied the first condition—he has not made a gift of an undivided share in land. He has, however, not made a gift which is caught by the reservation of benefit rules unless the cash gift was conditional on David using it to purchase the property (and then it may be analysed as a gift of a share in the property rather than cash so that s.102B(4) can apply) Does Barry then have a problem under the POA Regime? He has satisfied the contribution and the occupation conditions and therefore prima facie is caught by para.3. He is not directly protected under the para.11(5)(c) exemption as he does not have s.102B(4) protection. However, para.11(8) provides that in determining whether any property falls within para.11(5)(c) in a case where the contribution condition is met, para.2(2)(b) of FA 1986, Sch.20 (exclusion of gifts of money from the tracing rules) is to be disregarded. The consequences of this deeming appear to be as follows:

31.66

(i) FA 1986, Sch.20, para.2(2)(b) is disapplied;
(ii) accordingly a gift of cash falls within the general "tracing" rule in *ibid.* para.2(1): viz if the donee ceases to have possession and enjoyment of the gifted property (the cash) then any property which that donee received in substitution for the cash (the share in the purchased property) *shall be treated as having been comprised in the original gift instead of the cash*;
(iii) it follows that if the original gift had been of an undivided share in land then s 102B(4) protection will be available if the relevant conditions are met.

In this situation if the donee ceases to occupy the property so that the POA protection of para.11(5)(c) is lost, the gift is not caught by the reservation of benefit rules and so the POA charge *will* apply.

Donee dies or moves out[88]: in considering whether a sharing arrangement is appropriate for a particular taxpayer it should be remembered that if either of the requirements of s.102B(4) is broken then the basic charge under s.102B(2) will

31.67

---

[86] See 31.84.
[87] And see COP 10 letter in App. III A3.6.
[88] Although s.102B(4) refers to the need for both donor and donee to occupy the property it is not thought that IHT problems will arise if it is the donor who ceases to occupy (e.g. he may move into a nursing home). In this situation because the donor is not in occupation of the gifted property there is no reservation of benefit: see FA 1986, s.102B(3)(a).

operate. From the date of the breach there is a reservation of benefit (one way of looking at the position is to say that although the donor has reserved a benefit in the gifted share, the reservation of benefit rules will not apply to him whilst the donee occupies the property and he receive no benefit from that donee).

EXAMPLE 31.16

Sally gives a 50% share in her Reading house to her daughter Shula who is aged 18 and studying at university. After obtaining her degree in media studies, Shula moves out to take up a well paid job in London.

The IHT/POA consequences are as follows:—

(i) Sally no longer has the protection of s.102B(4) because sub-section (a) is no longer satisfied;
(ii) Accordingly the gifted share is not property subject to a reservation and the usual charging provisions in FA 1986, s.102(3) and s.102(4) apply.
(iii) Because Sally is caught by the reservation of benefit rules the POA charge does not apply (para.111(5)(a)).

As the above example shows, it is important that a gift is only made when it is likely that the joint occupation of the property is going to be long term. Otherwise the position can end up in a mess. It is not, for instance, true to say that Sally is back where she started as a result of falling foul of the reservation of benefit rules: all that these do is to bring the gift back into her estate for IHT purposes either to be taxed at death or to form the subject matter of a lifetime PET. Accordingly should she wish to sell the property in a few years then not only would Shula be entitled to 50 per cent of the proceeds but full CGT main residence relief will not be available on that share.

31.68 **Reorganising the arrangement:** in cases where the donee intends to cease to occupy so that the spectre of a reservation of benefit is looming consider the following restructuring options—

Donor pays a "full consideration" for his occupation of the whole property:

In these circumstances he will not be subject to the reservation of benefit rules because he is protected by FA 1986, Sch.20, para.6; nor will he be subject to the POA Regime which gives protection under para.11(5)(d). There are, of course, difficulties in determining what would be full consideration for these purposes given that the donor is already entitled to occupy the property as a co-owner. Does he pay the rent that a lodger would have to pay to share with him or does he have to pay 50 per cent of the full market rent payable if the property were let with vacant possession? The former is likely to be much lower than the latter!

It is noteworthy that under the POA Regime the rental value is the full market rent if the property were let with vacant possession; the only unknown factor to determine is the DV—the value of what has been given away. By contrast, in the case of FA 1986, Sch.20, para.6 arrangements, full consideration is not defined. In practice it is understood that HMRC consider that full consideration in this situation is the appropriate percentage (based on the size of the share given away) of the rent for the whole property.

Donee settles gifted share on a reverter to settlor trust

An alternative strategy prior to March 22, 2006 would have been for the donee to settle the gifted share in the property on a reverter to settlor trust for the donor for life.[89] This is no longer attractive for inheritance tax purposes post March 21, 2006 unless the original donor is disabled. If Shula in *Example 31.16* settles her share back on interest in possession (iip) trusts for Sally who is now disabled this will be a qualifying iip and a PET. Moreover, on Sally's death reverter to settler relief is available and s.102(3) FA 1986 is disapplied. However, Sally as the original donor is subject to a POA charge from December 5, 2005.[90]

Practical issues: there are a number of practical issues that should always be considered before entering into this sort of arrangement. For example, what happens if the donee marries someone whom the donor does not like? The spouse may then move in with donee. Or suppose that the donor wishes to sell and move somewhere smaller, does he have sufficient funds from his retained share to rehouse himself? Bear in mind that if the donee dies not only is there inheritance tax potentially payable on his share but the donor will then have to pay full consideration for continued occupation to avoid a reservation of benefit.

31.69

EXAMPLE 31.17

Sebastian's one substantial asset is Flyte Hall, an Edwardian property worth £1m. His son, recently divorced, lives with him and as the arrangement is likely to be permanent Sebastian gives him a 90 per cent share in the property. Unfortunately the son dies in a motor accident shortly afterwards leaving Sebastian devastated. The son dies intestate and his share in the property passes to his young children who live in London with their mother. Sebastian dies shortly afterwards.

(i) **death of the son**: IHT will be charged on 90 per cent of Flyte Hall. One of the problems that Sebastian was struggling with when he died was how to raise the money to pay the tax either in whole or on the instalment basis. It is always important in entering into a sharing arrangement to consider not just the IHT position of donor but also of donee.

(ii) **death of Sebastian**: because he has continued to live in the Hall after the son's death the reservation of benefit rules will result in the entire property being taxed on his death. Double charges relief may be available if he died within seven years of his original gift.

---

[89] See Ch. 27.
[90]

31.70 A further concern is whether the gift of a share to one child will disadvantage another child. Assume that Barry has given a share in his house outright to his youngest son David, and that share was worth £295,000. That is in excess of his nil rate band but more or less covered by two years' annual inheritance tax exemptions. However, if Barry dies within seven years of the gift, although David suffers no extra inheritance tax as donee, John, Barry's other son, who has been left the rest of Barry's estate will find that he ends up footing the entire IHT bill—the benefit of the nil rate band has been allocated entirely against David's gift and John suffers 40 per cent inheritance tax on the estate.

Other problems can arise if the house increases in value faster than the rest of the estate or the remaining estate has to be used to pay nursing home fees. Suppose Barry gives David a 90 per cent interest in the house and retains 10 per cent. The 90 per cent share is worth £285,000 and the 10 per cent share £31,000. Barry's other investments such as cash and equities are worth around £300,000 at the time of the gift. He leaves all these to John by will. Unfortunately within three years of the gift Barry becomes ill and has to move into a nursing home. (Although s.102B(4) will thereupon cease to be satisfied, Barry will not fall within the reservation of benefit rules given that he no longer occupies the property.) David remains in the property but all Barry's liquid assets are used to pay the nursing home fees. Three years later Barry dies and his remaining investments are by then worth only £150,000. In addition, John has to pay tax at 40 per cent. He has received significantly less than David.

31.71 Who is the donee? an outright gift of an undivided share is the most common situation but assume, for instance, that Barry would prefer to settle an interest in the property for the benefit of David (perhaps because David is a disabled child in receipt of state benefit or because it is hoped that the trustees can later equalise any disparities between the children). A gift into a flexible life interest trust for David was considered to fall within the protection of s.102B(4) on the basis that, as life tenant, David is treated as owning the property in the settlement (by virtue of IHTA 1984, s.49(1)) and hence is the donee. This remains the position even post FA 2006 because David as the disabled person can take a qualifying interest in possession and so Barry has made a PET.[91]

However, if David is not disabled he does not take a qualifying interest in possession and is therefore not treated as owning the property. The trustees own the property and they do not occupy it and so the protection of s.102B(4) is not available to Barry. Some flexibility in the scheme has therefore been lost as a result of Sch.20.

However, it may well be possible to reorganise existing trusts where the property is already held on pre-March 22 interest in possession trusts and occupied by the life tenant. For example, suppose the life tenant is the father and both father and son occupy. The son could be given a transitional serial interest in part of the settled property. He is deemed to be the donee for these purposes. Hence father and son might have equal interests in possession; father is deemed to make a gift (s.102ZA FA 1986) to son (if the partial termination of father's interest in possession takes place before 6th April 2008) and the provisions of s.102B would seem to be satisfied.

---

[91] See Ch. 26.

Second homes: in cases where it is desired to gift a share in a second home not attracting principal private residence relief, which it is considered will be protected by s.102B(4) provided that both donor and donee occupy the property, a problem which frequently arises is the CGT charge on the disposal of the share in the property. To deal with that the gifted share may be put into a trust (in order to obtain the benefit of CGT holdover relief under TCGA 1992, s.260(2)(a)) and subsequently appointed out to the intended donee, (again with the benefit of holdover relief). The difficulty with this arrangement is reconciling it with the wording of s.102B(4) since the occupying person will not be the original donee of the gift. That will be the trustees and hence it is thought that s.102B(4) will not afford protection so that the share settled by the donor will be caught by the reservation of benefit rules. The problem cannot be corrected later: the original donee has to be the person in occupation. Can this be made to work to the taxpayer's advantage?   **31.72**

EXAMPLE 31.18

> A gives a large share in his house to his son B and occupies it with B. B subsequently gives part of that share to his adult children who are not in occupation.
>
> In these circumstances is A still protected from reservation of benefit under s.102B(4)? Both donor and original donee still occupy the land so the basic conditions in s.102B(4) are satisfied.

Conclusions: co-ownership arrangements may be regarded as one of the safer lifetime IHT planning options provided that the donee continues to occupy the property and the various family and practical issues mentioned above are resolved. The donor can avoid both the reservation of benefit rules and the POA Regime. These exemptions under both the IHT legislation and the POA Regime are unlikely to be removed Bear in mind that the relief is for shared occupation *and shared ownership*: it is crucial that the donor retains an interest in the property. Give away a 90 per cent share and GWR/POA problems may be avoided: give away a 100 per cent share and the reservation of benefit rules will catch the donor. Similarly a gift of cash used to purchase a 100 per cent interest in the home occupied by the donor results in a POA charge. By contrast if the donor also purchases a *share* and there is *joint* occupation, then there is no POA charge!   **31.73**

CASH GIFTS

Cash gifts have been a fruitful area for IHT planning because of the curiously limited tracing rules, in FA 1986, Sch.20.   **31.74**

EXAMPLE 31.19

> Jason has lived abroad for many years and plans to return home. In 2000 he gives his daughter, Ruth, £250,000 which she uses later to purchase a

Suffolk property ("the Crow's Nest"). On his return to England in 2002, Jason occupies the property with Ruth. Jason acquires no interest in the property.

31.75 Jason has made a gift to his daughter and now occupies the property purchased: is he caught by the reservation of benefit rules in FA 1986? The relevant provisions are as follows:

(i) Section 102(1) of the FA 1986 provides that there is a gift with reservation if an individual disposes of any property (here the cash) by way of gift and either: (a) possession and enjoyment of the property is not *bona fide* assumed by the donee, or (b) at any time in the seven years prior to the donor's death the property is not enjoyed to the entire exclusion or virtually the entire exclusion of the donor and of any benefit to him by contract or otherwise.

(ii) Paragraph 6(1)(c) of Sch.20 to the FA 1986 is also relevant. This provides that in determining whether any property which is disposed of by way of gift is enjoyed to the entire exclusion of the donor and of any benefit to him by contract or otherwise, a benefit which the donor obtained by virtue of any associated operations of which the disposal by way of gift is one shall be treated as a benefit to him by contract or otherwise.

(iii) Associated operations are defined by s.268 IHTA 1984 to mean any two or more operations of any kind being: (a) operations which affect the same property or one of which affects some property and the other or others of which affect property representing that property or (b) any two operations of which one is effected with reference to the other or with a view to enabling the other to be effected or facilitating its being effected.

(iv) Finally Sch.20, para.2 ("substitutions and accretions") deals with substitutions but the paragraph does not apply if the property is a gift of cash.[92]

31.76 Has Jason reserved a benefit in the cash gifted?: *prima facie* it does not appear that there is any reservation of benefit in the cash itself because the cash has gone and Sch.20 provides no tracing provisions for outright gifts of cash. There is no direct link between the benefit received (donor living in the property) and the gift of cash. The benefit to Jason of occupying the house does not arise from the gift of cash unless that gift was in some way made conditional on being used to purchase a property.

The property gifted (*i.e.* the cash) has been enjoyed to the entire exclusion of Jason provided that the gift had not been made *conditional* on being used to purchase the property: otherwise there is a risk that the gift is in fact of an interest in land or alternatively (and more likely here) that Jason is treated as receiving a benefit in the cash gifted because it was made on the basis and on

---

[92] Paragraph 2(2)(b). Note also that different rules apply if the original property disposed of by the gift is not cash or is cash which "becomes settled property by virtue of the gift": ibid., para.2(2)(a). The rules affecting settled gifts are in para.5 which treats the gift as being of property comprised in the trust fund from time to time. There is therefore no exemption for settled cash gifts.

the understanding that he should be allowed to continue in occupation. (The benefit does not need to come from the gifted asset as such if it arises out of the gift). So, HMRC might consider that Ruth is estopped from denying Jason's occupation once the gift has been made, because he had made the gift under an agreement that she would use the funds to purchase the property and so she is estopped from changing her mind later.

In this case, however, it seems difficult to argue that the gift of cash was in reality a gift of the Crow's Nest. On the basis of estate duty cases such as *Sneddon v Lord Advocate*[93] (gift of cash used to purchase shares three days later) and *Potter v Inland Revenue*[94] (gift from donor of cash expressed to be to enable the donee to purchase shares), the subject matter of the gift was nevertheless the cash not the property purchased, and this is important in the context of reservation of benefit. The fact that the money was given for a particular purpose does not mean that the gift was subject to a legally enforceable condition.

Effect of the associated operations rule: it is not thought that the associated operations rule will affect the conclusion: either the arrangement involves a reservation in the gifted property or the reservation of benefit provisions are inapplicable. It might be argued that the gift of cash and the purchase of the freehold are associated transactions in that the gift of cash was made at least with reference to the subsequent purchase and questions of estoppel and conditional gifts are not relevant. But is para.6(1)(c) of Sch.20 wide enough to deem the benefit from the associated operation (the purchase) to be a benefit to the donor in the property disposed of (the gift of cash)? If, as is thought, the benefit enjoyed from the associated operation must entrench in some way upon the possession of the actual gifted property in order for there to be a reservation of benefit, then associated operations do not cause an additional reservation of benefit problem. The benefit enjoyed (*i.e.* the occupation of the house) does not in itself entrench on the gift of the cash. Put another way, the point is that HMRC may be able to establish that Jason has received a benefit from the associated operation made by his daughter (namely the purchase of the property) but they also have to show that the gifted property (*i.e.* the cash) is not enjoyed to the entire exclusion of any benefit to Jason. Unless the cash gift was conditional or Ruth was estopped from using the cash in any other way, Jason does not enjoy a benefit from the cash as such. The purchase of a property by Ruth combined with her allowing him to live there benefits him but this is still not a benefit from the cash itself which has been spent. 31.77

Approach of HMRC: in the Manual[95] HMRC accept that the tracing rules do not apply to an absolute gift of a sum of money. This is qualified in two ways: 31.78

(i) if the absolute cash gift is itself subject to a reservation then the sum of money will be taxable; and

(ii) "a gift which initially seems to be of cash may in reality be a GWR, by associated operations, of other property". The example given involves A giving £100,000 cash to B which B uses to buy A's residence (worth

---

[93] [1954] A.C. 257.
[94] [1958] S.L.T. 198.
[95] See IHTM14372.

£100,000) in which A continues to reside. HMRC comment that "this is a GWR, by associated operations, of the residence."

As already noted, it is difficult to see how the associated operations rules can be used to re-characterise a gift as being of property rather than of cash. Of course, the specific example involves a circular arrangement in which the actual cash may never have changed hands. The weakness of the argument appears underlined by the subsequent comments (under the heading "What to do").

> "You will not normally raise any enquiries to see if a gift which appears to be of cash may be a gift, by associated operations, of other property. Only ask questions if there is a positive reason for doing so, e.g. where:
> the gift is of an odd amount, such as £49,563.15, which suggests it may be related to a purchase by the donee, or
> there is specific information that the gift was related to the acquisition by the donee of property, especially if the acquisition is from the donor."

Despite the example cited in the Manual, HMRC appear to take a more circumspect position in the POA Guidance Notes: "where an absolute gift of cash may later be used by the recipient to purchase property occupied or enjoyed by the donor, for example, the application of the reservation of benefit rules to this property is precluded unless the transaction can be shown to be a gift with reservation of benefit by associated operations, of the purchased property."

31.79 In conclusion, it does not follow that all benefits referable to a gift will come within s.102. It is not sufficient to take the situation as a whole and find that the donor has continued to enjoy substantial advantages which have *some relation* to the gifted property. Each advantage must be considered separately to determine whether it is a benefit within the statute.[96] In the authors' view outright cash gifts to an individual will rarely be caught by the reservation of benefit rules.

31.80 **Impact of the pre-owned asset regime:** given that Jason's gift is not caught by the reservation of benefit rules, it will fall within the POA Regime so that he will suffer an income tax charge from April 6, 2005. The following points may be noted:

(i) Paragraph 3 applies given that Jason is in occupation of the property and that the contribution condition is met.

(ii) If Ruth had provided some of the purchase price for the "Crow's Nest", para.4(2) will require an apportionment of DV to determine such part of the value of the relevant land as may be attributed to the consideration provided by Jason.

(iii) Although Jason is not in sole occupation, no allowance appears to be made for this in fixing the rental value of "Crow's Nest".

---

[96] *Oakes v Stamp Duties Commissioner of New South Wales* [1954] A.C. 57 at 72 and see *St Aubyn v AG* [1952] A.C. 15.

(iv) Note that if Jason acquired a 5 per cent interest in the new property he would be protected from POA while they are both in joint occupation.[97]

The seven-year defence: if the facts are varied so that Jason made the gift to his daughter in March 2000 and only returns to England in April 2007 when he occupies the property for the *first* time, then as a result of FA 2004, Sch.15, para.10(2)(c),[98] the pre-owned asset charge will not apply. **31.81**

Only outright cash gifts after April 5, 1998 are caught by the POA Regime even if occupation of the property purchased with the gifted money took place soon after. Accordingly if Jason had made the cash gift in March 1998 and then in 2002 took up occupation no POA charge is due even though he occupied the property within seven years of the cash gift.[99]

Curiously para.10(2)(c) refers to outright cash gifts "to the other person" and hence could include gifts of cash into settlement.[1] As noted above, such gifts are generally caught by the reservation of benefit provisions anyway because the tracing provisions apply but there may be circumstances in which a cash gift into settlement is exempt from the reservation of benefit provisions and also from the POA charge. **31.82**

EXAMPLE 31.20

In 2002 Perseus settles cash on interest in possession trusts for his spouse under which he can benefit. As noted previously such a transaction cannot be excluded because para.8 transactions can never be excluded transactions within para.10.

In 2003 the trustees then purchase a house with the cash and terminate the spousal interest in possession. The property is rented out but then in 2010 Perseus occupies the house.

The POA analysis is that the transaction is not excluded under para. 10(2)(b) because of the proviso in para.10(3) but it could be excluded under para.10(2)(c) as an outright gift of money to a person. Hence provided Perseus does not occupy the property within seven years he is protected from a charge under the POA Regime.[2]

Options for taxpayers: what are the options for Jason in *Example 31.19* if he is caught by the POA charge, e.g. because the cash gift was made *on or after 6th April 1998* and he occupies the purchased property within seven years? **31.83**

(i) Election: Jason could elect for the reservation of benefit rules to apply[3] in order to avoid the income tax charge.

---

[97] See 31.83(ii)—cash gifts and co-ownership.
[98] The arrangement is an excluded transaction.
[99] See POA Guidance Notes in App. III A3.321.
[1] Contrast the wording in para.10(2)(e) which refers expressly to a gift to an individual. The Independent Manual comments that "a gift is not an outright gift if it is subject to conditions or if it could revert to the donor in any circumstances whatsoever".
[2] Note that from March 22, 2006 Perseus will make an immediately chargeable transfer when he sets up the trust.
[3] See Ch. 24 (especially 24.22 and 24.44).

(ii) shared occupation: Suppose Jason gives Ruth cash to purchase a house. Ruth and Jason eventually pool resources and *jointly* buy a house for their joint occupation. In these circumstances there is no POA charge (see para.11(8) and 31.42, above). The conclusion is that if people are going to live together it is preferable that each party has an undivided share in the land. In these circumstances there will be no charge under the POA Regime and no reservation of benefit.

(iii) Improvement: if Jason gave cash away which was used only to *improve* rather than *acquire* an interest in a house in which he lives then there is no POA charge or reservation of benefit.

SELLING THE FAMILY HOME

31.84 One of the curious features about the POA Regime is the approach taken to sales of land and chattels. Unlike the reservation of benefit legislation, the POA Regime can apply even when no gift has been made. Any disposal of land which the disponer continues to occupy can, in principle, be caught by the POA Regime unless it comes within a specific exemption.

Example 31.21

Rose and Emily, two sisters, have lived together for some years. Rose alone owns the house worth £800,000. She decides to sell for full consideration a half share in the property to Emily. (She may want the cash to supplement her lifestyle or may wish to give it away, to Emily or to other relatives.) Emily pays £400,000 for a 50 per cent share in the property.

(i) Despite the fact that Rose has not made Emily a gift nor made a transfer of value for inheritance tax purposes, she is prima facie caught by the POA Regime. A disposal of the property has been made and Rose continues in occupation. By contrast, if Rose had *given* away a half share to Emily, she would have no POA charge as a result of the protection of para.11(5)(c) (incorporating the "sharing arrangements" in FA 1986, s.102B(4));

(ii) The fact that Emily has paid full consideration for her share does not help Rose: the sale is not protected under para.10(1)(a) because it is not a sale of the whole interest in the land;

(iii) the pre-owned assets charge cannot be reduced under the non-exempt sale provisions because these require a transfer of the *whole* interest in land.

31.85 In the March 2005 Regulations[4], reg.5 provides for certain exemptions from POA where there are sales of part at full value, namely

---

[4] SI 2005/724.

a) an exemption for commercial sales of part (see reg.5(1)(a)); and

b) other sales before March 7, 2005.

EXAMPLE 31.22

> Mary needs to raise cash on her home. After taking financial advice she enters into an equity release scheme with Rest Assurance Inc to whom she sells a 40% share of the property. Under the general terms and conditions Mary is entitled to go on living in the property for the rest of her life. Mary is exempted from any POA charge by reg.5.
>
> There is also an exemption for connected person disposals provided that (a) it was such as might be expected to have been made at arm's length between persons not connected with each other and **either** the disposal was for a consideration not in money or in the form of readily convertible assets **or** the disposal was made before the date of the Ministerial Statement (March 7, 2005).

31.86 The upshot is that unless the sale to a connected person occurred before March 7, 2005 Rose in *Example 31.21* is caught by the POA charge. Accordingly, she will pay income tax on any interest generated by the cash of £400,000 plus a POA charge on the appropriate rental value. The cash of £400,000 is also part of Rose's estate for IHT purposes and similarly a half share in the property is part of Emily's estate. In calculating the POA charge on Rose, allowance will be made for the 50 per cent interest in the land which she retains.

31.87 **Sales of whole for full consideration:** it is curious that what are arguably more controversial arrangements do not appear to be caught by the POA Regime. The starting point for any planning depends on using the exclusion given in para.10(1)(a). This provides a complete protection from the POA charge if the disposal is:

> "of his whole interest in the property except for any right expressly reserved by him over the property either by a transaction made at arm's length with a person not connected with him or by a transaction such as might be expected to be made at arm's length between persons not connected with each other."

The disposal need not be for cash: it can be an arm's length exchange of property.

One option that has been used in the past (and is still available) is for the *whole* house to be sold by the individual to a member of his family for full market value. The purchaser can then allow the vendor to live there free of charge. There is no gift so the reservation of benefit provisions do not apply. The cash is part of the vendor's estate for inheritance tax purposes and he can, if he wishes, give it away in due course. This apparently simple transaction does, however, pose a number of problems. Whilst acceptable for IHT purposes, there are difficulties if the purchaser does not have sufficient cash to pay the purchase price. If the purchaser borrows from a Bank and the vendor then gives cash to the purchaser to pay off the mortgage then the contribution condition is satisfied and a POA charge arises. In those circumstances, he might want the vendor to agree to leave the purchase price outstanding as a long-term loan (in which case any subsequent gift of the debt by the vendor would be more problematic for IHT purposes).

In order to ensure that the para.10(1)(a) exclusion applies, the terms of the loan must be the same as those offered by any bank or building society, *i.e.* it should be on normal terms, interest bearing with interest being paid not rolled up, secured and with the usual deposit paid. One has to demonstrate that the whole arrangement is a transaction *"such as might be expected to be made at arm's length between persons not connected with each other."*

SDLT will be payable by the purchaser and another problem is that the purchaser may end up suffering capital gains tax on eventual sale of the property because the donor who occupies the property does not own it. In the past the problem could be solved by the donee settling the house on reverter to settlor trusts but this is no longer feasible.[5]

31.88 **Sale of freehold reversion subject to leases:** given the difficulties involved in finding sufficient cash to pay for the purchase of the whole property an alternative arrangement involves the taxpayer first carving out a lease for himself for a fixed term (or possibly for life) at a nil or nominal rent, and then selling the freehold interest (subject to that lease) for full market value. There is no gift by the vendor, and therefore the disposal is not caught by s.102A FA 1986. However, he has devalued the freehold reversion by carving out the lease in his own favour. Accordingly, the purchaser has to pay far less for the freehold reversion: in the case of a 15-year lease one might expect the freehold value to be devalued by as much as one half.

Such an arrangement is acceptable for IHT purposes, although it is important to ensure that the proper price is paid so that there is no element of bounty. The valuations are difficult, not least because the transaction is not a common one. One problem is that there is almost certainly a loss of marriage value; the value of the freehold subject to the lease and the value of the lease are together unlikely to be equal to the vacant possession value. Should the children pay for the marriage value as well as for the freehold reversion? If so, that would cause a problem under the POA Regime since it is not the sort of transaction that would be made between parties at arms length: see para.10(1)(a)(ii).

If, instead, the vendor sells the reversion for a price equal to the value it has in the hands of the children and they pay nothing for loss of marriage value, the vendor's estate has been diminished for IHT purposes. However, such a transaction will not be a transfer of value if there was no intention to confer a gratuitous benefit on the children.[6] Even if the vendor has made a transfer of value, he has not made a gift within the meaning of FA 1986, s.102(1) or s.102A(1). The question that remains is whether such a transaction can qualify for para.10(1)(a)(ii) protection from the POA charge. In a commercial transaction between unconnected parties (such as an equity release scheme) it would be common for the vendor to receive no payment for the loss of marriage value.

---

[5] As a result of the 2006 changes in the IHT treatment of settlements.
[6] IHTA 1984, s.10.

31.89 It is important to ensure that when fixing the price for the encumbered freehold interest, account is taken of the terms of the lease to be retained (i.e. the lease should already be in existence and its terms considered by the valuers). Whilst there is some debate as to whether a lease for life or a lease for a term of years should be granted, the better view is that a lease for life should be avoided because of s.43(3) of the IHTA 1984: it is hard to argue that such a lease has been acquired for full consideration (although this seems to be accepted by HMRC in the IHT Manual).

The capital gains tax problems mentioned above are still an issue. If the property is sold, the vendor will obtain principal private residence relief in respect of the lease but the purchaser will find that the freehold reversion is an appreciating asset in his estate which will not qualify for relief.

31.90 **Funding the purchase price:** despite the reduced purchase price, difficulties can remain: suppose the purchasing child has insufficient cash to fund the purchase? Perhaps he cannot borrow from the bank and security on the property itself is of limited value because the child only owns the reversion and receives no rent. Can the vendor safely give cash to his child to enable the child to fund the purchase? The reservation of benefit substituted property rules do not apply to non-settled cash (Sch.20, para.2(2)(b)), assuming that the gift of cash was not made conditional on the purchase of the freehold reversion by the child. This would, however, cause pre-owned asset problems. The contribution condition has been satisfied because consideration, namely cash, has been paid by the purchaser for the acquisition of an interest in the land that the vendor occupies and that consideration has been directly or indirectly provided by the vendor.[7]

31.91 **Conclusions:** IHT planning involving sales of the house (or chattels) to members of the family is still possible even under the POA Regime but considerable care is needed to ensure that the more stringent conditions in Sch.15, para.10(1)(a) are satisfied. It is unlikely that HMRC will accept that sales of freehold reversions subject to a retained lease are within the protection of para.10(1)(a) without some clear valuation evidence, and great care must be taken if the cash is given away. SDLT will increase the costs and CGT issues remain a problem if the vendor wishes to move.

FOREIGN DOMICILIARIES AND THE FAMILY HOME

31.92 For many years a foreign domiciliary who wished to own, *e.g.* a house in London, was advised to establish a trust which owned all the shares in an offshore company which in turn owned the house. The thinking was that the relevant asset for IHT purposes would be the shares in the company which would be held in an excluded property settlement. There then arose a protracted

---

[7] Of course, the normal limitations on the scope of the contribution conditions apply: for instance, if there had been an outright gift of cash before April 6, 1998 the POA charge will not apply.

controversy concerning the possible exposure of the foreign domiciliary to a charge to income tax under what was then Sch.E (now ITEPA 2003, ss.97–113) by reason of the benefit of the occupation conferred upon him if he was an actual or a shadow director of the company. The *Dimsey*,[8] *Allen*[9] and *Deverell*[10] cases exacerbated this problem and accordingly new structures were developed.

31.93 **Offshore "home loan" arrangements:** often these involved two trusts. In essence, the foreign domiciliary created two trusts. He funded the first trust, which was often discretionary, which in turn funded a company wholly owned by that trust. The company lent the funds to the second trust, under which the foreign domiciliary had an interest in possession and which used the funds to purchase the house. The loan, which was secured on the house, was left outstanding interest-free and repayable on demand.

Diagrammatically the position was as follows—

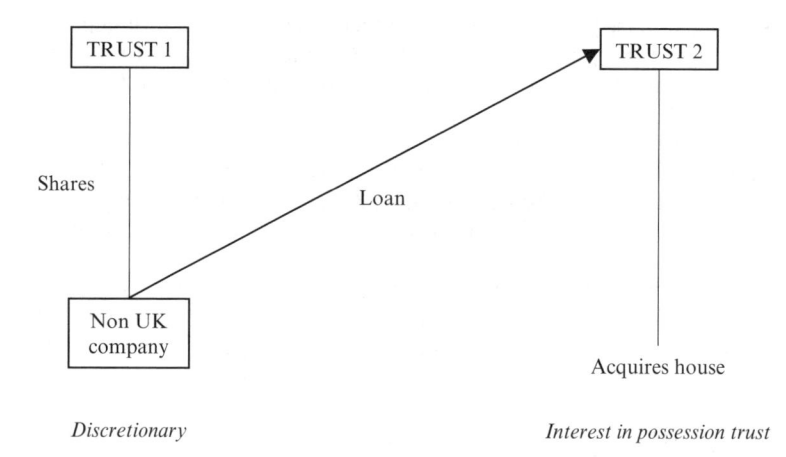

```
    TRUST 1                                    TRUST 2
       |                                          |
   Shares                                         |
       |          Loan                            |
       |    ──────────────────►                   |
    Non UK                                        |
    company                                       |
                                             Acquires house

  Discretionary                          Interest in possession trust
```

31.94 It will be noted that the house is no longer owned by a company so that the shadow director problem no longer applies. An alternative structure was for the discretionary trust to lend the cash by way of a specialty debt to the interest in possession trust with no charge taken over the house. This was thought to make the loan non-UK situated (and in any event both debtor and creditor are non-UK resident) but in order to ensure the IHT deductibility of the debt by the interest in possession trustees, the interest in possession trust held no other property.[11]

Assume that the company (or discretionary trust) lent to the interest in possession trust £1,500,000 all of which the trust used to purchase the house and that ten years later, when the foreign domiciliary died, the house was worth £2,000,000. For IHT purposes the value of the property would be reduced by the debt owed to the company and so worth only £500,000. The debt was a non-United Kingdom *situs* asset so excluded property in the hands of the discretionary trustees. The net result was to take the amount of the debt outside

---

[8] *R v Dimsey* [2001] S.T.C. 1520.
[9] *R v Allen* [2001] S.T.C. 1537.
[10] *Secretary of State for Trade & Industry v Deverell* [2001] Ch. 340.
[11] See s.162 IHTA 1984 and Ch. 23.

the scope of IHT. In many cases the foreign domiciliary and his spouse had successive life interests in the property, so that if the foreign domiciliary's spouse survived him any charge on the excess value of the property on his death was deferred until the death of his spouse. Alternatively any exposure to UK tax was covered by insurance arrangements.

31.95 The POA Regime adversely affected the tax effectiveness of some of these arrangements. Although both the para.12(2) basic relief and the settled property para.12(3) relief will operate in respect of the shares in the company (or the debt if held directly by the trustees and non-UK *situs*), neither of these reliefs is available in respect of the house, because it is situated in the United Kingdom and is not excluded property. If the foreign domiciliary has a qualifying interest in possession in the house, the para.11(1) ownership exemption will *prima facie* be available in respect of the house but only to the extent that the value of the house exceeds the "excluded liability" of, returning to the above example, £1,500,000. The effect (given that it seems clear that the debt is indeed an excluded liability) is that the first £1,500,000 of the house will be within the POA Regime and be subject to annual income tax charges.

31.96 However, Sch.15 para.11(6) provides that there is a POA charge on the debt only "where the value of someone's estate for the purposes of IHT is reduced by an excluded liability affecting any property". Accordingly, if the discretionary trust holding the debt was converted into a qualifying interest in possession trust, the effect was that the debt was now part of the foreign domiciliary's estate for IHT purposes so that the value of his estate was not reduced. Although the debt is excluded property and so outside the inheritance tax net at death, nevertheless the POA income tax charge does not apply to the debt as an excluded liability because the condition in para.11(6) is not satisfied: the foreign domiciliary's estate is not reduced by the debt. Accordingly, foreign domiciliaries amended their double trust structure by converting the discretionary trust into an interest in possession trust.[12]

31.97 Since March 22, 2006 it will no longer be possible to convert the discretionary trust into a qualifying interest in possession trust[13] and therefore the trust holding the debt will not be treated as part of the donor's estate and para. 11(6) is satisfied—the foreign domiciliary's estate is reduced by the debt even though he reserves a benefit in the debt of the discretionary trust. Reserved benefit property is not treated as part of a person's estate: it is merely taxable on death. Hence a debt in which the foreign domiciliary reserves a benefit *is* one that reduces his estate and the POA charge can apply.

31.98 What are the alternatives now? Direct ownership is simple. The risk of IHT may be mitigated by taking out term assurance which is written in trust or taken out offshore. The tax payer may rely on having sufficient warning of his death to transfer the house into an offshore company moments before death (albeit with an SDLT charge).

---

[12] Note that the value of the house in the property trust is still reduced by the debt and so that property in the taxpayer's estate is reduced in value. However, the reduction is then comprised in his estate by virtue of the interest in possession in the debt trust. Overall therefore there is no reduction in value of his total estate because of the debt. It is not considered appropriate in this case to consider the two trusts in isolation (contrast the approach of Mann J in St Barbe Green v IRC [2005] S.T.C. 288).

[13] See generally Ch. 20.

CHATTEL ARRANGEMENTS

31.99 For some taxpayers, chattel collections (or even the ownership of individual items) raise the spectre of a substantial IHT liability on death. Hence there has been a demand for an arrangement under which the chattels can be given away (whether outright or into trust for children and issue) whilst at the same time leaving the taxpayer able to continue to use and enjoy them. In recent years two main "schemes" have been employed to meet these requirements.

31.100 **Ingram schemes:** in simple terms the arrangement blessed by the House of Lords in the *Ingram* case is applied to the chattels: viz the taxpayer retains a lease which enables him to continue to possess the chattels and gifts the "freehold" interest. Doubt was originally expressed in some quarters as to whether a land shearing operation was capable of applying to chattels but HMRC have accepted that such arrangements are possible.[14] Of course the "*Ingram* scheme" was reversed by legislation in FA 1999 but that legislation was expressly limited to land and interests in land.[15]

31.101 **Gifts and commercial leaseback:** this arrangement has been widely used. The designated chattels are gifted to donee and then leased back to the donor who pays full consideration for his continued use: hence the reservation of benefit rules are inapplicable.[16] In the case of land (to which a similar exemption applies), the commercial rent will frequently be beyond the means of the taxpayer. In the case of chattels, however, there is no ready market in rentals and no standard type of agreement. In practice, experts are engaged by both donor and donee to negotiate a full value for the enjoyment of the chattels. Arrangements are entered into under which there is payment of a relatively small rent (perhaps 0.75 per cent of the value of the chattels each year) provided that the donor/lessee is made responsible for insuring and maintaining the item in question (which will often include the provision of a suitable

---

[14] See *Taxation*, October 16, 2003 (Nicholas Brown). In the particular case the chattels in question were individually valued at under £6,000 but collectively had a value of £750,000. A lease for 17 years was retained and on the death of the taxpayers there was seven years left to run on the lease: the PET of the assets (subject to that lease) occurred more than seven years before the deaths and so was an exempt transfer. The value of the remainder of the lease was then worth £13,000 and the collection of chattels £1,380,000. HMRC initially argued that unlike land it was not possible to create different interests in chattels with the result that there had been a gift of the entire interest in the chattels with a contractual arrangement (not involving the payment of full consideration) permitting their use and which amounted to a reserved benefit. See now IHTM 14314.

[15] In the Press Release of March 1999 announcing the blocking of Ingram arrangements, it was stated that

> "if no action were taken, the [*Ingram*] decision would jeopardise a large part of the tax base. As the decision affects only gifts involving land, the changes to the gifts with reservation rules are limited to such gifts. However, the operation of these rules will be closely monitored and the Government will not hesitate to act to prevent any tax avoidance through other gifts."

[16] See FA 1986, Sch.20, para.6(1)(a): actual enjoyment of a chattel "if it is for full consideration in money or money's worth" is disregarded in applying the reservation of benefit rules.

security system). Similar negotiations are necessary to agree the terms of any rent reviews.[17] The agreement is often made non-assignable by the donor. Some agreements contain price adjuster clauses.[18]

HMRC attach importance to the parties having the benefit of independent advice: see comments in their letter to the Law Society dated 18th May 1987 in relation to land:

> "whether an arrangement is for full consideration will of course depend on the precise facts. But among the attributes of an acceptable arrangement would be the existence of a bargain negotiated at arm's length by parties who were independently advised and which followed the normal commercial criteria in force at the time it was negotiated."

HMRC commented in the same letter in relation to chattels:

> "it would be difficult to overturn an arm's length commercial arrangement entered into by parties who were independently advised."

The CGT dimension: in both arrangements it was important to bear in mind the CGT consequences of disposing of the chattel (or an interest in it). There is a general exemption for chattels which are individually worth £6,000 or less,[19] whilst if the item is a wasting asset then gains are exempt without limit. A wasting asset is one with a predictable useful life of 50 years or less and includes yachts, caravans, animals and all plant and machinery, the latter term to include, in HMRC's view, such assets as antique clocks and watches, certain vintage cars and (generally) shotguns.[20]   **31.102**

Impact of the POA Regime: the December 2003 consultation paper made it clear that a main target of the new charge was to be chattel schemes: it referred to tax being charged at a specified percentage of capital value in cases where there was no market evidence of an appropriate rent as in the case of "art or antiques". As introduced, the charge under para.6[21] will apply to *Ingram* arrangements (in essence the analysis is much the same as in the case of *Ingram* arrangements affecting the land: see 31.34). Hence the options open to the taxpayer are much the same.   **31.103**

---

[17] See generally *Christie's Bulletin for Professional Advisers*, Autumn 1995 (Manisty) and Autumn 1998 (McCall).
[18] An alternative approach suggested by Christopher McCall QC in his article in *Christie's Bulletin* in Autumn 1998 vol.3 no.3 was for the donor to warrant for himself and his estate that the fee he pays is full consideration for the purposes of Sch.20, para.6 and to covenant that at the end of the term if so required he will make good any shortfall which the donee is able to establish by reference to the warranty. The covenant is made under deed.
[19] TCGA 1992, s.262(1): note that there are special rules for sets: ibid., s.262(4). In the case of more valuable chattels the gift could be into a discretionary trust taking advantage of holdover relief under *ibid.*, s.260(2)(a) provided that the value was limited to the donor's available IHT nil rate band (so as to avoid an immediate IHT charge).
[20] *Tax Bulletin*, October 1994 and February 2000: TCGA 1992, s.44.
[21] Note that para.6(2)(b) refers to a disposal of all or part of his interest in the chattel and para.6(4) treats the creation of a new interest out of an existing interest as the disposal of part of the existing interest. The authors are not aware of reversionary leases being used for chattels.

EXAMPLE 31.23

In 2003 Andrew effected an *Ingram* scheme over chattels under which the "freehold" interest in chattels was gifted to an interest in possession trust for his daughter Charlotte. He is now caught by the POA Regime.

If he surrenders his leasehold interest, this may be an associated operation with the result that a large transfer of value, equal to the full market value of the chattels (less the earlier transfer), is now made. What happens if instead Andrew assigns his leasehold interest to another member of the family? At that point he would need to pay full consideration for his continued use of the chattels in order to avoid a reservation of benefit. However, as noted above, full consideration can often be relatively cheap for example, 1% of the value of the asset. Does this then protect Andrew from a POA charge by virtue of para. 11(5)(d)?

31.104 A concern is that "the relevant property" for the purposes of para.11(3) is the property disposed of: i.e. both the leasehold and freehold interests. He does not reserve a benefit in respect of the freehold interest merely because he has assigned his lease. To be sure of the para.11(5)(d) protection he would need to surrender the lease and as noted above this may cause IHT problems. Hence paying full consideration does not appear to let him off the POA charge. Could Andrew instead make a payment in pursuance of a legal obligation to the owner of the chattel for his use and possession of the chattel? If he does not assign or surrender the lease the only way he can put himself under a legal obligation is to enter into a deed of covenant. The amounts involved may be substantial.

EXAMPLE 31.24

The freehold value of the chattels is now £1m. The market value without the lease is £1.5m. The appropriate amount is 5% x £1.5m = £75,000. £75,000 x 1/1.5 = £50,000. Tax on £50,000 (at 40%) = £20,000 pa

Andrew enters into a deed of covenant with the trustees of Charlotte's trust under which he agrees to pay £50,000 being "the appropriate amount". Arguably such amount is not taxable in the hands of the recipient trustees.[22] However, he has made an addition to a trust which is a chargeable transfer.

Another option is to enter into a full consideration arrangement and then immediately elect into reservation of benefit. In these circumstances HMRC accept that there is no deemed PET.[23] He would first need to give away his

---

[22] See 31.49 for a consideration of the use of deeds of covenant.
[23] See App. III A3.61.

lease of the chattels which should be by an outright gift rather than a gift into trust.

Gift and leaseback arrangements: the POA Regime does not apply to full consideration arrangements: see para 11(5).[24]   **31.105**

A number of gift and leaseback schemes were under consideration by the IR Capital Taxes Division which was concerned to ascertain whether full value has been paid in "rent". Bear in mind that if it can be shown that there is *any* element of undervalue the protection of Sch.20, para.6(1)(c) will be lost and the taxpayer will have reserved a benefit in the chattels. HMRC queried some gift and commercial lease back arrangements on the basis that if there was no real market in letting country house chattels they do not have to accept a rate agreed by expert valuers. Instead in the absence of a "real world market" HMRC suggested that a Canadian Court of Appeal case[25] provides useful guidance on what constitutes full consideration and argued that full consideration was in reality the return that the donee would obtain if he invested an amount equivalent to the cash value of the chattels on deposit or in government securities. This would obviously equate much more to the fixed rate return of 5 per cent set out in para.7 of Sch.15.

However, *Youngman* was concerned not with full consideration but with benefits to the taxpayer. The shareholder was living in a house built by his company and was paying full market rent for his occupation. The market rent was below the rate of return the company could have obtained from investing the cash. The judge held that in determining the value of the benefit to the taxpayer one should take the *cost* of providing that benefit to the company into account. Hence free market rent was not in all circumstances the sole indicator of real value. By contrast, in the case of chattel arrangements one is concerned not with benefits as such to the donor but with whether he has paid full consideration which is a very different test. Furthermore, in the Canadian case the company had used its own cash to build a unique residential property for the taxpayer while in chattel arrangements the donee is simply being given an existing asset which he is likely to want to retain within the family. It is thought that HMRC have not pursued these arguments and that full consideration arrangements have been accepted as not involving any reservation of benefit.

Alternatives: FA 2004, Sch.15, para.10(a) provides that the sale of chattels is an excluded transaction if it is a sale of the taxpayer's whole interest in the property at market value except for any right expressly reserved by him over the property.   **31.106**

EXAMPLE 31.25

> Edward owns a valuable picture which shows little gain. He carves out a lease for himself and then sells (rather than gives) the chattel subject to this lease to his son at full market value. The transaction is not a gift and

---

[24] FA 2004, Sch.15, Para.11(5).
[25] *Youngman v The Queen* [1991] 90 DTC 6322.

so will not be caught by the reservation of benefit rules and will be excluded from the POA charge under para.10(1)(a). Note that if there is any undervalue element one moves into the problems posed by non-exempt sales. There is no stamp duty payable (contrast the position with land).

Edward does not need to worry about what constitutes full consideration, he pays no rent and is not caught by the POA income tax charge. However, he must not have given the cash to his son in order to enable the son to purchase the chattel from him, otherwise he falls foul of the contribution condition.

31.107 An alternative option is to use para.10(2)(c).

EXAMPLE 31.26

Edward gives cash to his son in 1997. Son uses the cash to buy a picture which Edward hangs on his wall. He pays no rent. Edward is not caught by reservation of benefit nor does he suffer the POA charge because the gift was made prior to 6th April 1998. Alternatively, Edward could give cash to the son and then wait seven years before using any chattels purchased with it.

31.108 A further option is to consider the *shared* use and possession of the chattels.

EXAMPLE 31.27

Luke and Charlotte jointly use a holiday home which contains chattels owned by Luke. He gives a half share in those chattels to Charlotte. For IHT purposes there is no similar relief from the reservation provisions as that contained in section 102B(4) for land. Accordingly Luke's use of the chattels might be seen as in consideration of allowing Charlotte the same level of use. In these circumstances it would probably be unwise for Luke to give Charlotte more than 50 per cent. The alternative analysis is that the gift of a part share in chattels is more in the nature of a carve out and that the donor has retained the right to continue using them. POA would be applicable in this case.

31.109 In fact, a part owner of a chattel does not have the same rights as a part owner of land/property or a part shareholder of a company. The only relevant legislation is section 188(1) of LPA 1925 which states:

"Where any chattels belong to persons in undivided shares, the persons interested in a moiety or upwards may apply to the court for an order for the division of the chattels or any of them, according to a valuation or otherwise, and the court may make such an order and give any consequential direction as it thinks fit."

No cases have been decided under s.188 but it is thought that this justifies a discount in the valuation of a half share[26]. There is no reason to think that the co-owner of chattels has the same rights of use and possession as a co-owner of land and accordingly that discount may be substantial.

---

[26] See *Christies' Bulletin*, Summer issue 2005.

CHAPTER 32

BUSINESSES AND FARMS (BPR AND APR)

- Background **(32.01)**
- How the reliefs work for settled property **(32.19)**
- Application of the reservation of benefit rules **(32.27)**
- Impact of the pre-owned assets charge **(32.32)**

BACKGROUND

32.01 This is an area of considerable importance and some difficulty. The importance derives from the value frequently attributed to the business or farm and, in many cases, to the availability of 100 per cent relief from IHT.[1] The difficulty arises from the relatively complex structures that are often employed: a business may operate as a sole trade; partnership, limited liability partnership or as an incorporated entity and may be held in a family trust.

Many businesses are family run and frequently adjustments are made to the ownership and running of the business, classically with parents handing over control and ownership to their children. When the business is held in a trust it may be managed by the life tenant or by the trustees.

Relationship between APR/BPR

32.02 Although the two reliefs are similar and overlap, the following distinctions are worthy of note:

(1) APR is given in priority to BPR (IHTA 1984, s.114(1)).

(2) Differences exist in the treatment of woodlands, crops, livestock, deadstock, plant and machinery, and farmhouses etc. When APR does not apply, consider whether BPR is available (it can apply to any part of the value transferred not relieved under APR: e.g. the hope value of agricultural land);

---

[1] See IHTA 1984, Pt V, Ch. 1 (business property) and Ch. 2 (agricultural property). Agricultural property relief takes precedence over business relief: see IHTA 1984, s.114(1).

(3) APR is only available on property situated in the UK, Channel Islands and Isle of Man whereas BPR is not so restricted.

(4) In the *Tax Bulletin*, 1994, p.182, HMRC commented that:

> "Where agricultural property which is a farming business is replaced by a non-agricultural business property, the period of ownership of the original property will be relevant for applying the minimum ownership condition to the replacement property. Business property relief will be available on the replacement if all the conditions for that relief were satisfied. Where non-agricultural business property is replaced by a farming business and the latter is not eligible for agricultural property relief, s.114(1) does not exclude business property relief if the conditions for that relief are satisfied.
>
> Where the donee of the PET of a farming business sells the business and replaces it with a non-agricultural business the effect of s.124A(1) is to deny agricultural property relief on the value transferred by the PET. Consequently s.114(1) does not exclude business property relief if the conditions for that relief are satisfied: and, in the reverse situation, the farming business acquired by the donee can be 'relevant business property' for the purposes of s.113B(3)(c)".

A major restriction on BPR

Although "business" is a word of wide import (e.g. it covers a landlord letting with a view to profit), the relief is not available **32.03**

> "if the business . . . consists wholly or mainly of one or more of the following, that is to say, dealing in securities, stocks or shares, land or buildings, or making or holding investments" (IHTA 1984, s.105(3)).[2]

The IHT legislation does not define an investment business but some guidance may be obtained from *Cook v Medway Housing Society Ltd*[3] in which Lightman J. defined "investment" as "the laying out of moneys in anticipation of profitable capital or income return" and further commented:

> "In determining what is the business of a company . . . it is necessary to have regard to the quality, purpose and nature of the company and its activities, and this includes the full circumstances in which the relevant assets are acquired and retained, including the objects clause in the memorandum of association of the taxpayer and the objects of a society . . . as revealed in its rules. It is relevant to have regard to the actual activities carried on by the taxpayer at the relevant date, but if these are viewed without regard to the taxpayer's past history or future

---

[2] Note the "mixed business" cases especially: *Farmer v IRC* [1999] S.T.C. (S.C.D.) 321; *IRC v George (Exors of Stedman)* [2003] S.T.C. 468, CA.
[3] [1997] S.T.C. 90.

plans they may give only a partial or incomplete picture. The critical question is whether the holding of assets to produce a profitable return is merely incidental to the carrying on of some other business or is the very business carried on by the taxpayer."

A business which is carried on otherwise than with a view to making a profit does not qualify for relief.[4]

The Phillips case[5]

32.04 Mr Phillips owned shares in eight related family companies, including P Ltd and an estate agency company, which he had established or acquired and which had shareholders and/or directors in common. P Ltd was established in 1958 and its principal object as stated in its articles of association, was to acquire land and buildings for the purposes of investment only and with a view to receiving income. By April 1989 P Ltd held at least 18 investment properties. However, the estate agency company was struggling financially. In late 1989, Mr Phillips sold 14 investment properties to the estate agency company for £450,000, which was raised by a £300,000 loan from the bank, which had a first charge on the properties, and a £150,000 loan from P Ltd.

At the time of the transfer the properties were let to protected tenants and so the values were reduced. The arrangement was that, as and when each property became available with vacant possession, the estate agency company would sell the property on the open market and repay first the bank loan and then P Ltd's loan. At the same time Mr Phillips decided that P Ltd would not invest in any other property but would only make loans to other related companies. Those loans financed the purchase by the related companies of investment property, were repayable on demand and were informal in character.

The Special Commissioner (Dr Nuala Brice) decided that looking at all the facts in the round, the business carried on by P Ltd at the date of Mr Phillips' death did not consist wholly or mainly of making or holding investments. If one started with the definition in IHTA 1984, s.105(3), and asked whether on its ordinary meaning the business of the company fell within it, the answer was no. P Ltd did not make or hold investments; it made informal loans to its related companies and money lending was not normally regarded as investment. The criteria for making each loan were whether the value of the purchased property was commensurate with the amount of the loan. Despite the stated objects of P Ltd being to acquire land and buildings for the purposes of investment for some years it had lent money to its related companies. All the loans were repayable on demand with no security which also indicated that the loans were not in the nature of investments. *P Ltd was in the business of making loans and not in the business of investment in loans.* The loans were not assets acquired or held by the company for the purpose of making profits for division among the shareholders but were rather made for the purpose of providing a benefit to the other companies. P Ltd did not

---

[4] *Grimwood Taylor v IRC* [2006] S.T.C. (S.C.D.) 39.
[5] *Phillips and Others (Exors of Phillips Deceased) v IRC* [2006] S.T.C. (S.C.D.) 639.

acquire any interest in the shares of the borrowing companies, or in the acquired properties, or any rights in the increased value of the purchased properties. All it was entitled to was the interest payable to it by the borrowing companies.

Turning to HMRC's submissions, she considered that the first loan was made to the estate agency company which was accepted by HMRC to be a trading company. In addition, if a loan was not an investment, it could not become an investment by the fact that the company to whom the loan was made was in common ownership and control or was controlled by the deceased and her family. P Ltd did not itself own any shares in the related companies. The fact that a loan was made to an investment company did not result in the making of the loan being an investment. Lastly the purpose of the loans was to enable the borrowing companies to invest in real properties and the criteria for each loan were whether the borrowing company could afford to make interest payments and whether the value of the purchased property was commensurate with the amount of the loan. Whilst P Ltd took no security, (which differed markedly from any loan made by a third party), that did not convert the business of making loans into the making or holding of investments.

32.05 The decision is surprising and it will be interesting to see if an appeal by HMRC is lodged. It suggests that if an investment business is funded by a money-box company, shares in the latter may attract BPR. By contrast a direct investment in the investment business would not!

32.06 The "wholly or mainly" test in s.105(3)[6] was also considered in the Special Commissioner case of *Clark and Another v IRC*[7] but there have been a number of earlier cases on "mixed businesses" particularly in relation to caravan parks.[8] In *Clark*, the deceased died owning shares in T. Clark & Son Ltd ("the company"). HMRC refused business property relief considering that the company was carrying on the business mainly of making or holding investments and was therefore disqualified from relief under s.105(3), IHTA 1984.

The company had originally been involved in building houses (in the 1920s) which they then sold but over time they had bought back these houses and gradually let them out. This was its first and primary activity. The properties required a great deal of maintenance which the company did itself. Ninety-two houses, four shops, four offices, two industrial units and twenty lock-up garages were let. Whilst the company retained some building land, its activities were in respect of the rental properties. Its second activity consisted of the management of 141 dwellings owned by other members of the Clark family for which it charged a management fee of 7.5 per cent of the rent. The Special Commissioner agreed that the company was mainly an investment company. The property management side represented a relatively small activity with turnover of about £40,000 compared with rental income of approximately £480,000. It was difficult to see how the *management* of the rental side could represent the main business of the company.

The executors had argued first, that the view that rented property was invariably an investment activity was outmoded given its "active" (as opposed

---

[6] See 32.03, above.
[7] [2005] S.T.C. (S.C.D.) 823.
[8] See, for example, *Hall (Executors of Hall) v IRC* [1997] S.T.C. (S.C.D.) 126 where it was held that the receipt of commissions on the sale of caravans was ancillary to the main business of receiving rents from owners of caravans and lessees of chalets and contrast *Furness v IRC* [1999] S.T.C. (S.C.D.) 232 where the reverse was found.

to "passive") management and, second, that there should not be a differentiation between income received from managing properties owned by the family (non-investment) and income received from managing properties owned by the company as investments. The Special Commissioner rejected the active/passive distinction and followed the decision in *IRC v George and Another (the Executors of Stedman deceased)*[9] that the exploitation of a proprietary interest in land for profit was an investment activity. The element of services provided by the Company was not sufficient to make it mainly a trading business. Unlike *George* the Company's maintenance activity was not the separate provision of services but inherent in the property ownership. Even if the management of the Company's own properties was treated as a trading activity (classified as bringing in approximately 7.5 per cent of the rent) the business was still mainly one of holding investments.

The case once again reaffirms the distinction between property investment and trading activities (however actively managed the property investment) and approved the tests laid down in *Farmer v IRC*[10] and *George*.

32.07 "Wholly or mainly" is not defined in the legislation but it is accepted by HMRC that a sole trader, partnership or company may conduct within a single business, two activities. The question is whether looked at in the round, that business is "mainly" (more than 50 per cent) trading or "mainly" investment.

EXAMPLE 32.1

> A company owns a portfolio of investment properties and also carries on a trade of selling mobile phones. The trading profits exceed the rental income; turnover on the mobile phone side is greater than turnover on the investment properties and most of the employees are engaged in running the mobile phone business; the asset value of the trading part taking into account goodwill is greater than the net asset value of the investment side. The result is that business property relief is available on the company shares in respect of the entire value of the company, not just the trading part. Provided the company is "mainly" trading, the fact that it also has investment activities does not mean there is no relief on the value represented by that part.
>
> By contrast, if the company's trading activities comprise only 40% of the total, no business property relief is available at all, even on the trading part.

32.08 The test can prove particularly problematic where a company or business changes in nature over time. For example in *Farmer* there was a single composite business comprising farming and letting. The let buildings were mainly former farm buildings but there were some were buildings that had never been used in the farm. It was decided by the Special Commissioner that in applying the wholly or mainly test by taking the business in the round and looked at over

---

[9] [2004] S.T.C. 147, CA.
[10] [1999] S.T.C. (S.C.D.) 321.

a period of time it still comprised mainly farming. Hence the whole business qualified for business property relief. The property in question was a landed estate with most of the land used for farming; lettings were subsidiary to the farming business and were of short duration. Of capital employed, two-thirds was appropriated to farming; farm turnover exceeded letting turnover in six out of eight years; employees spent more time on the farming side than the lettings; but in every year the net profit of the lettings exceeded the net profit of the farm. Despite the latter factor, the character of the business *as a whole* was still farming. *Farmer* has subsequently been approved by the Court of Appeal in *George* and the various factors identified above are of key importance.

Note also that in the case of an unincorporated business, BPR is only available if the transfer is of the business or "an interest in a business."[11] Unlike APR it is not available on a mere transfer of assets. **32.09**

EXAMPLE 32.2

Jackie runs a family business comprising some 150 acres of arable land, Recently, six acres of land have been zoned for development and accordingly now have substantial "hope" value. What is the IHT position (a) in the event of Jackie's death, (b) if she were to give away the six acres by transferring them into a family trust so that any future growth in value will take place outside her estate?

(a) position on Jackie's death: APR will be available (assuming that the two year ownership condition is met[12]) on the agricultural value of agricultural property used in the business. This will include the five acres but will not give relief on their "hope" value. BPR—also at 100 per cent—will, however, provide relief since the death transfer is of Jackie's business.

(b) position if a lifetime gift: the six acres will attract APR on the agricultural value but BPR will not be available on the "hope" value unless it can be said that she is transferring an interest in the business rather than merely an asset used in the business. If the nature of the business is unchanged it is difficult to see how BPR can be available.[13]

The scope of APR 32.10

"'Agricultural property' means agricultural land or pasture *(part 1)* and includes woodland and any building used in connection with the intensive rearing of livestock or fish if the woodland or building is occupied

---

[11] IHTA 1984, s.105(1)(a).
[12] IHTA 1984, s.117: there is a similar requirement for BPR: see *ibid.*, s.106.
[13] A similar test had applied for CGT retirement relief and there are a number of cases exploring the border between a gift of assets as opposed to a share in the business. In general, it is dangerous to say that if APR does not apply, BPR will: in truth it may but only if the conditions for its application are met.

with agricultural land or pasture and the occupation is ancillary to that of the agricultural land or pasture *(part 2)*; and also includes such cottages, farm buildings and farmhouses, together with the land occupied with them, as are of a character appropriate to the property *(part 3)*."

The division into parts is adopted from the *Starke* and *Rosser* cases and is intended to identify the three separate sections of the definition.

The Starke and Rosser cases

32.11 *Starke v IRC*[14] concerned the transfer of a 2.5 acre site containing within it a substantial six-bedroomed farmhouse and an assortment of outbuildings together with several small areas of enclosed land which was used as part of a medium-sized farm carrying on mixed farming. The court concluded that the relevant property did not constitute "agricultural land" within the above definition of "agricultural property". The decision is hardly surprising but it does point to the dangers of a farmer giving away the bulk of his farm retaining only the farmhouse and a relatively small area of land. Such retained property will rarely qualify for relief as was emphasised in *Rosser v IRC*,[15] where the deceased having given away 39 acres of land was left owning only a house, barn and two acres of land when she died. Two acres and (significantly) the barn attracted relief but not the house.

32.12 The farmhouse must be of a character appropriate to "the property" What is meant in this context by "the property"? In *Rosser* the Special Commissioner had no doubt about the required nexus commenting:

> "The nexus between the farm buildings and the property in section 115(2) is that the farm buildings and the property must be in the estate of the person at the time of making the deemed disposition under section 4(1) of the 1984 Act. The alternative view that the farm buildings are in the estate but the property to which they refer is not is untenable. This view would seriously undermine the structure for inheritance tax and create considerable uncertainty about when tax is chargeable and the amount of the value transferred. I would add, however, that estate is defined in the 1984 Act as the aggregate of all property to which the person is beneficially entitled. Property is widely defined in the 1984 Act to include rights and interests of any description. It will therefore cover not only tangible property but also equitable rights, debts and other choses in action, and indeed any right capable of being reduced to money value. Thus, under the situation covered in section 115(2) if the person making the deemed disposition at death legally owned the farm buildings and had a legal interest such as a right of profit in the property to which the character of the farm buildings is appropriate then the farm buildings and the property would be part of the estate."[16]

---

[14] [1994] S.T.C. 295.
[15] [2003] S.T.C. (S.C.D.) 311.
[16] See also *McDougall* in 2004 PCB p.135: the character appropriate test when the land is owned and farmed by a partnership.

Case law on the farmhouse and character appropriate test

The cases (all decided by the Special Commissioners) may be summarised as follows: **32.13**

> In *Dixon v IRC*[17] the property comprised a cottage, garden and orchard totalling 0.6 acres. Although surplus fruit was sold it was decided that the property was not agricultural land or pasture: rather there was a residential cottage with land.
>
> In *Lloyds TSB (PRs of Antrobus Deceased) v IRC*[18] it was agreed that Cookhill Priory (a listed six-bed country house) was a farmhouse[19] and that the surrounding 125 acres (pus 6.54 acres of tenanted land and buildings including a chapel) were agricultural property. The Special Commissioner decided that the character appropriate test was also satisfied.[20]
>
> In *Higginson's Exors v IRC*[21] Ballywood Lodge, formerly a nineteenth-century hunting lodge of six beds with 63 acres of agricultural land; three acres of formal gardens and 68 acres of woodland and wetland around Ballywood Lake, was considered not to be a farmhouse ("not the style of house in which a typical farmer would live").
>
> Of the three, the most important decision in terms of laying down a guiding principle is the *Antrobus* case in which the Commissioner summed up the factors to be taken into account in applying the character appropriate test as follows:
>
>> "Thus the principles which have been established for deciding whether a farmhouse is of a character appropriate to the property may be summarised as: first, one should consider whether the house is appropriate by reference to its size, content and layout, with the farm buildings and the particular area of farmland being farmed (*Korner*); one should consider whether the house is proportionate in size and nature to the requirements of the farming activities conducted on the agricultural land or pasture in question (*Starke*); thirdly, that although one cannot describe a farmhouse which satisfies the 'character appropriate' test one knows one when one sees it (*Dixon*); fourthly, one should ask whether the educated rural layman would regard the property as a house with land or a farm (*Dixon*); and, finally, one should consider the historical dimension and ask how long the house in question has been associated with the agricultural property and whether there was a history of agricultural production (*Dixon*)."[22]

---

[17] [2002] S.T.C. (S.C.D.) 53.
[18] [2002] S.T.C. (S.C.D.) 468.
[19] It may be noted that this was agreed by HMRC on the basis that Miss Antrobus was a full time-working farmer.
[20] See further 32.15 for a consideration of *Antrobus ll*.
[21] [2002] S.T.C. (S.C.D.) 483.
[22] Note the additional factor that the same Special Commissioner considered relevant in *McKenna*. See 32.16A.

"Agricultural value"[23]

32.14 It is the "agricultural value" of such property which is subject to the relief: defined as the value which the property would have if subject to a perpetual covenant prohibiting its use otherwise than as agricultural property. Enhancement value attributable to development potential is not subject to the relief. BPR may apply to this excess value in the case of farmland although not in the case of the farmhouse: in practice the agricultural value is often considered to be around two-thirds of open market value, although in current market conditions a much smaller discount may be appropriate. This point was made by the Special Commissioner in the *Higginson* case when he commented:

> "A property may command a high price in the open market value because of potential for development; and subsection (3) clearly caters for that situation. But it seems to me that the notional restrictive covenant would have much less of a deprecatory effect in a case where the property has a value greater than ordinary not because of development potential but rather because of what I might call 'vanity value' on account of its site, style or the like. In the light of my decision the point is academic".

32.15 As noted above, in *Lloyds TSB (PRs of Antrobus Deceased) v IRC*[24]:

(i) HMRC conceded that Cookhill Priory was a farmhouse and

(ii) the Special Commissioner decided that it was of a character appropriate to the property so that it constituted agricultural property and qualified for APR.

The amount of relief due on the farmland was then considered by the Lands Tribunal. It was agreed that the market value of Cookhill Priory was £608,475 but HMRC contended that the agricultural value was only £425,932.50 (i.e. a discount of some 30 per cent on the market value). The taxpayer considered that there was no discount on market value. Finding in favour of HMRC the Lands Tribunal decided[25]:

(1) That the covenant under s.115(3) prohibited the use of the property otherwise than as "agricultural property".

(2) Under the s.115(2), the definition of "agricultural property" includes a farmhouse and Cookhill Priory would only qualify if it was a farmhouse. This has been conceded by HMRC "but only in the particular circumstances of Miss Antrobus' occupation of the house and land" and in particular her active farming of the 123 acres of freehold agricultural land and the 6.54 acres of leased land.

---

[23] IHTA 1984, s.115(3).
[24] [2002] S.T.C. (S.C.D.) 468
[25] See in the matter of a notice of reference between *Lloyds TSB Banking Plc (as PRs of Antrobus Deceased) and Peter Twiddy (IR Capital Taxes)* decision dated October 10, 2005.

(3) The taxpayers argued that the property would remain a farmhouse if purchased by someone who carried on a farming business on the land even though he might spend little time in the business.²⁶ Thus they would have been unaffected by the s.115(3) covenant since they would have complied with it and as they will be the highest bidders in the market the agricultural value would therefore be equal to the amount which the highest bidder would pay.²⁷ This was rejected by the Tribunal in the following terms:

> "A farmhouse is the chief dwelling-house attached to a farm, the house in which the farmer of the land lives. There is no dispute about the definition when it is expressed in this way. The question is: who is the farmer of the land for the purpose of the definition in section 115(2)? In our view it is the person who lives in the farmhouse in order to farm the land comprised in the farm and who farms the land on a day to day basis. It is likely, although it may not necessarily always be the case that his principal occupation will consist of farming the land comprised in the farm. We do not think that a house occupied with a farm is a farmhouse simply because the person living there is in overall control of the agricultural business conducted on the land; and in particular we think that the lifestyle farmer, the person whose bid for the land is treated by the appellant as establishing the agricultural value of the land, is not the farmer for the purpose of the provisions."

It was considered that the following factors supported this conclusion— **32.16**

   (i) the "character appropriate" test which supports the idea of the farmhouse being "the dwelling of a working farmer who requires a suitable *house to support his working* life";

  (ii) the deletion of "mansion house" from the definition of agricultural property in 1975;

 (iii) the other elements of the definition "cottages and farm buildings" support the idea of a working farm.

(4) HMRC were "not wrong" in treating the s.115(3) covenant in relation to farmhouses as equivalent to the standard planning AOC for the purposes of establishing values.²⁸

---

²⁶ The so-called "lifestyle farmer". Giving expert evidence for the taxpayers Mr Clive Beer commented that:
"There were at least three ways in which a lifestyle buyer could carry on a farming business without prior experience and without spending much time at the farm. Firstly, the land could be farmed with the assistance of one or more employees, for example a farm manager, or through a contract farming arrangement. Secondly, the land could be farmed in partnership with an active local farmer. Thirdly, the new owner could come to a share-farming arrangement, whereby the landowner would grow grass or other crops for sale to a local livestock farmer, whose cattle or sheep would eat down the crop which he had bough in situ. Whichever of these methods was adopted by the lifestyle farmer, the farmhouse would continue to be occupied by him and used as agricultural property".

²⁷ Mr Beer accepted that the open market value would fail to be discounted for any actual or potential non-agricultural uses of the property to which additional value might be attributable (e.g. any value attributable to sporting rights; development potential or mineral rights). It appears that there were no such factors present in this case.

²⁸ The "agricultural occupancy condition" (AOC) in a planning permission provides that "the occupation of the dwelling shall be limited to a person solely or mainly working, or last

(5) The conclusion that a farmhouse for s.115(2) purposes was limited to a property occupied by a full-time working farmer meant that the agricultural value under s.115(3) had to be decided on the basis that the covenant would not be satisfied by a "lifestyle" farmer. Accordingly the Tribunal accepted that the 30 per cent deduction in value proposed by HMRC was appropriate.[29]

(6) At the end of its decision the Tribunal considered the value which the property would have

> "on the assumption that our interpretation of the legal position is incorrect and that the demand from the lifestyle farmer may be taken into account in calculating its agricultural value".

On this basis it concluded that the relevant discount would be only 15 per cent thereby giving an agricultural value for the property of £517,203.75.[30]

The McKenna case

32.16A Mr McKenna died on January 29, 2003 and his wife, Lady Cecilia, on June 16, 2003. Since 1997 they had been the joint owners of the Rosteague Estate. This comprised a substantial Grade II* house (Rosteague House); some 187 acres (of which around 52 were foreshore and 110 were agricultural land); various farm outbuildings and a cottage, stable flat and lodge. The estate had originally been purchased by Mr McKenna in 1945 as a second home and only occupied as the main home on his retirement in 1984. Initially the land was tenanted but in 1984 the tenancy was surrendered and thereafter it was contract farmed under a succession of agreements with different contractors. A land agent, acting for the McKennas, was responsible for the management of the land, the farming activities and dealing with the contractors. He purchased a property on the estate and hence was on the spot to supervise and manage the farming operation. At the date of death, Mr McKenna was aged 91 and had suffered from ill health since 1997. After his death Lady Cecilia, who was aged 92 and who had been weak since a heart seizure in 1998, entered a nursing home.

32.16B The Special Commissioner decided —

1. *that Rosteague House was not a farmhouse;*[31].

---

working, in the locality in agriculture or in forestry, or a widow or widower of such a person and to any resident dependants" (see *DoE Circular No 11/95*, para.45). The Tribunal considered that in some respects the terms of the AOC were less restrictive than those of the s.115(3) covenant.

[29] There was a dearth of comparable evidence. Three AOC properties were of no assistance and the only comparable used comprised a farm in which there had been an agreement as to agricultural value (a 33.4 per cent discount). It involved a seven bed house with 217.9 acres of land.

[30] The Tribunal considered that there would still be a discount over the open market value of the property since (i) the lifestyle farmer would be buying the property together with all the land whereas (ii) a higher price would be obtained by someone who bought the house and part only of the land and who was not subject to the s.115(3) covenant.

[31] The sale particulars (the estate was sold for in excess of £3m after the McKennas' deaths) described the house as follows —

"long hall, dining room, library, study, drawing room, flower room, main foyer and stairs, cloakroom, rear hall, kitchen, staff sitting room, back kitchen, seven bedrooms, three

She made the following general comments on the meaning of "farmhouse" in IHTA 1984, s.115(2):

(i) that the wording of the legislation makes it clear that the agricultural land is paramount: other things must be either ancillary or of a character appropriate to the land;
(ii) there is nothing to suggest that every farm must have a farmhouse: the reference in s.115(2) is to farmhouses generally;
(iii) she adopted the definition given in the *Rosser* case[32] as "a dwelling for the farmer from which the farm is managed" and accepted that the Land Tribunal conclusion in *Antrobus II* that "the farmer of the land is the person who farms it on a day to day basis rather than the person who is in overall control of the agricultural business conducted on the land" was a "helpful principle";
(iv) the status of the occupier of the property is not the test: rather it is the purpose of the occupation which is relevant;
(v) whether a building is a farmhouse is a matter of fact to be decided on the circumstances of each case and according to ordinary ideas of what is appropriate in terms of size, content and layout in the context of the particular farm buildings and the area of land farmed.

On the particular facts of the case, she concluded that it was the land agent who was responsible for the management of the farming operation (albeit as agent for the McKennas). Hence "the purpose of Mr McKenna's occupation of Rosteague House was not to undertake the day to day farming activities. In any event . . . Rosteague House was larger, grander, more elaborate and more expensive than was required for the reduced farming purposes for which it was in fact used. Its size, content and layout, taken in conjunction with the farm buildings and the particular area of farm being farmed points to the conclusion that it was primarily a rich man's residence rather than a farmhouse".[33] **32.16C**

2. *on the basis that, if it was a farmhouse, was it of a character appropriate?* **32.16D** Again the Special Commissioner decided that the requirements for relief were not met. Following the criteria that she had identified in *Antrobus*[34] she added a further factor: the relationship between the value of the land and the profitability of the land.[35] She concluded that the return from agriculture (a profit of £6,820 in 1998 falling to a loss of £7,975 in 1994) "would not provide a living income for a person who paid over £3 million for the whole estate and so would not attract demand from a commercial farmer."[36]

---

bathrooms, sewing room, laundry room, staff flat, detached lodge, cottage, music room, garage, gardens, range of outbuildings".

There was no mention of it being a farmhouse!

[32] [2002] S.T.C. (SCD) 311 at para.53: see 32.12, above.
[33] At para.92.
[34] See 32.13.
[35] From the evidence of comparables it was clear that Rosteague was at the "top end" of the size of a Cornish farmhouse and that a house of that size would generally have more land. It only came into use as a farmhouse in 1984 (so the historical association is weak) whilst lack of repair went, she considered, to value rather than character.
[36] At para.113.

32.16E 3. *was the property occupied for the purposes of agriculture throughout the period of two years ending with the death of the owners?*[37] Whilst this issue did not have to be decided given the Special Commissioner's decision in (i) and (ii), she concluded that "it is clear that neither Mr McKenna nor Lady Cecilia were able to engage in farming matters throughout the period of two years ending with the relevant dates of death."[38]

32.16F Whilst the case will undoubtedly make it difficult for a "lifestyle" farmer to obtain relief on the house which he occupies, the following matters should be borne in mind:

(a) The relationship between farming income and the value of the property has not been fully explored. Is the test that a house can only be a farmhouse if it is capable of being maintained out of the farming profit? (This, of course, begs the question— maintained to what standard?) Or is it that the house will only qualify if "required" by the actual farming operation carried on?[39]

(b) The position of the land agent is also in need of further consideration. Once it is accepted that the land can be farmed by employees, including a farm manager, answerable to the owner, then drawing the line between that situation and the facts in *McKenna* is difficult. If Mr McKenna had dealt directly with the contractor would that have made a difference? Arguably yes, since there is nothing in the decision to suggest that contract farming per se will prevent APR being available.

32.17 The value of agricultural property may be artificially enhanced for the purposes of the relief by charging the costs of acquiring the agricultural property against non-qualifying property, IHTA 1984, ss.5(2), 162(4) and *cf.* BPR. Further, it is not necessary to transfer a farming business or part thereof in order to obtain relief which can be given on a mere transfer of assets.[40]

Will drafting and 100 per cent relief

32.18 This important topic is considered at 28.27 *et seq.*

HOW THE RELIEFS WORK FOR SETTLED PROPERTY

32.19 Both BPR and APR are valuation reliefs: i.e. they operate by reducing the value transferred by a transfer of value. Thus IHTA 1984, s.104(1) provides:

---

[37] See IHTA 1984, s.117(a).
[38] At para.119.
[39] It might be thought that if the purpose of relief is to prevent farms having to be sold to pay IHT then, provided that the occupier of the property is the farmer, a precise link should not be made between farming income and property values. Bear in mind that the same test will be applied even if the property is not sold and so may deny relief when it is retained within the family. Note the similar issue in CGT main residence relief concerning what area of land is required for each owner of the property.
[40] See Ch. 23.

"When the whole or part of the value transferred by a transfer of value is attributable to the value of any relevant business property, the whole or part of the value transferred shall be treated as reduced . . ."[41]

32.20 In the case of settlements with a qualifying interest in possession, any transfer of value will be made by the relevant beneficiary.[42] Hence, in general, he will need to satisfy the conditions for the relief.

32.21 In the case of relevant property settlements, however, the position is different. IHTA 1984, s.103(1) provides that:

"references to a transfer of value include references to an occasion on which tax is chargeable under Chapter III of Part III of this Act".[43]

Two further provisions are needed to ensure that the reliefs apply to property which is settled:

(i) references to the value transferred by a chargeable transfer include references to the amount on which tax is then chargeable; *and*

(ii) references to a "transfer" include reference to the trustees of the settlement *"concerned"*.[44]

32.22 The level of relief for trustees is the same as for individuals: i.e.

(i) 100 per cent relief for all unquoted shares and for businesses belonging to the trust (and for a partnership share in such a business owned by the trust)[45];

(ii) 50 per cent relief for controlling shareholdings in listed companies owned by the trust[46];

(iii) 50 per cent relief for land or buildings, plant or machinery owned by the trust but which are used in a business carried on by the interest in possession beneficiary.[47]

(iv) 100 per cent relief on the agricultural value of agricultural property falling within IHTA 1984, s.116(2)(a)(b) and 50 per cent relief on let agricultural land.

32.23 *Fetherstonehaugh v IRC*[48] concerned the availability of relief when land held under a strict settlement was used by the life tenant as part of his farming

---

[41] And see the similar wording in s.116(1) in the case of agricultural property. The reduction, in both cases, is either 100 per cent or 50 per cent.
[42] See IHTA 1984, s.49(1); s.52(1); s.4(1).
[43] i.e. anniversary and exit charge.
[44] IHTA 1984, s.103(1)(a)(b) and, for APR, see s.115.
[45] IHTA 1984, s.105(1)(e).
[46] IHTA 1984, s.105(1)(a); (1)(b). "Listed" means listed on a recognised stock exchange or dealt in on the Unlisted Securities Market. In general securities on AIM are not listed and hence can attract BPR under (i) unquoted shares. But beware of dual listing on overseas recognised stock exchanges and check whether AIM companies have excessive cash reserves; undertake non-qualifying activities, risks of takeover, acquisition, flotation, insolvency, etc.
[47] IHTA 1984, s.105(1)(cc). It may be noted that this part of the legislation has not been amended to reflect the FA 2006 changes in the definition of a qualifying interest in possession. The reference in s.105 is to any interest in possession whether or not qualifying.
[48] [1984] S.T.C. 261, CA.

business (he was a sole trader absolutely entitled to the other business assets). The Court of Appeal held that 100 per cent (then 50 per cent) relief was available under s.105(1)(a) on the land in the settlement with the result that the subsequent introduction of 50 per cent (at that time 30 per cent) relief (see iii) is apparently redundant in such cases. HMRC accepts that in cases similar to *Fetherstonehaugh* the maximum 100 per cent relief will be available since the land will be treated as an "asset used in the business" and, as its value is included in the transfer of value, the land will be taxed on the basis that the deceased was the absolute owner of it. (Of course, if the interest in possession was not qualifying: e.g. if it was set up after March 21, 2006 this reasoning would not hold good. Relief under (iii) above would, however, still be available).

32.24 BPR depends upon ownership for a two-year period[49] which has given rise to problems when the terms of a trust have changed so that instead of the trust either being accumulation and maintenance or discretionary a beneficiary has become entitled to a qualifying interest in possession.

EXAMPLE 32.3

> The Jenkins' accumulation and maintenance trust was set up in 1997 and owns the family wine importing business. In 2004 Jason Jenkins became entitled to an interest in possession on becoming 21. In 2005 the trustees determined that interest by exercising an overriding power of appointment and appointed the property on discretionary trusts for the family. The IHT position is as follows:
>
> (i) In 2004 the accumulation and maintenance trust ended, being replaced by a qualifying interest in possession trust. There is no IHT charge at that time.[50]
> (ii) From 1997–2004 the trustees were the owners of the business but in 2004 Jason is treated as the owner for the purposes of IHT business property relief.[51] Accordingly, to qualify for relief he must own the property for a period of two years.
> (iii) The termination of his interest in 2004, however, results in his making a chargeable transfer[52] which does not attract BPR. To benefit from the relief the trustees should have waited until his interest in possession had been in existence for two years.[53]
> (iv) The changes in FA 2006 to the IHT treatment of settlements mean that after March 21, 2006 new qualifying interests in possession will rarely arise. For instance, if Jason's interest had only arisen after that date (so that the trust had continued in accumulation and maintenance form until then) it would not have been a qualifying interest. The trust would have become a relevant

---

[49] IHTA 1984, s.106: note, however, that there are special rules for replacement property (*ibid.*, s.107) and for successions (*ibid.*, s.108).
[50] IHTA 1984, s.71(4).
[51] See IHTA 1984, s.49(1): Jason is treated as beneficially entitled to the property (i.e. the business) in the settlement.
[52] IHTA 1984, s.52.
[53] See *Burrell v IRC* [2005] S.T.C.

property settlement[54] and so the trustees would have continued to be the owners of the business for IHT purposes. And, of course, they would have been entitled to the relief since they satisfied the two year ownership requirement.

The relevant property charge

In general the relief will apply in the normal way but note two wrinkles: **32.25**

(i) in the case of exit charges arising before the first 10 year anniversary, the rate of charge is calculated by reference to

"the value, immediately after the settlement commenced, of the property then comprised in it"[55]

which does not permit any reduction to the value for either BPR or APR;

(ii) if business or agricultural property is comprised in a settlement on the occasion of a 10 year charge, relief is available, in the usual way, and if that property is then sold there is no adjustment in the calculation of the rate of the exit charge during the next 10 year period.

EXAMPLE 32.4

The Benji Discretionary Trust was set up on August 1, 2000. On August 1, 2010 it contained shares in Benji Blow-Out Ltd, the family trading company, valued at £1m and which qualified for relief[56–57] at 100%. They were subsequently sold for £1.2m and on July 31, 2020 the trustees appointed the moneys out to the Benji Brothers thereby ending the trust. The tax position is as follows:—

(i) at the time of the 10-year charge in 2010 the value of the property in the settlement was £1m but this will benefit from 100% relief so that the amount on which tax is charged will be reduced to nil.
(ii) the sale of the shares will give rise to a CGT charge but taper relief will reduce the effective rate of tax to 10%
(iii) the calculation of the exit charge in July 2020 will depend on the rate charged at the time of the last anniversary: i.e. nil.[58]

"Control"

This is relevant, for instance, in the case of relief for listed securities and for assets held outside a company.[59] This test is applied at the time when the **32.26**

---

[54] It might have satisfied the requirement for an 18–25 trust but the result would be the same in terms of the trustees continuing to own the property for the purposes of BPR.
[55] IHTA 1984, s.68(5)(a) and for a consideration of the implications of this provision see 20.28.
[56–57] Under IHTA 1984, s.105(1)(bb)
[58] IHTA 1984, s.69(1) and see App. IV at A4.06.
[59] See IHTA 1984, s.105(1)(b); (1)(cc); (1)(a).

transfer occurs: it is not necessary for the transferor to have had control of the company during the preceding two years. In applying the control test, IHTA 1984, s.269(3) provides that when shares or securities are held in a settlement the voting powers given to the trustees

> "shall be deemed to be given to the person beneficially entitled in possession to the shares".

Notice that there is no requirement that the interest in possession shall be "qualifying".

EXAMPLE 32.5

> Jasper Rougley owns 25% of the ordinary shares in Rougley Make-Up, a successful fashion company. A further 30% are held in a discretionary trust established by his father. Jasper owns land as a warehouse by the company which is currently worth £1m and he is minded to give it to his daughter:—
>
> (i) BPR will only be available on the land if the conditions of s.105(1)(d) are met: i.e. Jasper at the time of transfer has control of the company.
> (ii) if the trustees were to appoint him an interest in possession in the 30% shareholding and he was then to transfer the land, relief at 50% would be available. The trustees could then, if they wished, revoke Jasper's interest.
> (iii) if Jasper was not a beneficiary of the trust but his wife was and the trustees appointed her an interest in possession, then although under s.269(2) related property (e.g. shares in the estate of a spouse) must be included, because the interest in possession is not qualifying the shares will not be in his spouse's estate and so will not enable Jasper to obtain relief.

APPLICATION OF THE RESERVATION OF BENEFIT RULES

32.27 These are as capable of applying to gifts of business and agricultural assets as to gifts of any other assets. However, the following may be noted.

Full consideration let out

32.28 Take the case where father farms land and decides to take the son into partnership, giving him (say) a 50 per cent interest in the land and an accompanying 50 per cent share of all profits. In such a case, there may be no element of gift (it may be a commercial bargain) or the full consideration let out in FA 1986, Sch.20, para.6[60] may apply so that there is no reservation of benefit in that gift.

---

[60] The legislation is in App. I at A1.23.

It involves looking at the matter in the round and saying that the benefits in the form of profits should be consistent with the contributions that father and son make in the form of capital and labour. With this in mind the sharing arrangements should stack up commercially.[61]

Illustrations

IHIM provide a number of useful examples of the operation of the reservation of benefit ("GWR") rules in the area of businesses and companies including the following:

EXAMPLE 32.6[62]

> Father and son have been in partnership together since 1980 sharing profits equally. The land is owned by the father and occupied by the partnership rent free without any formal tenancy agreement. In 1989 the father gives the land to the son but the partnership continues to occupy it on the same basis. At the same time the profit sharing ratio is adjusted in favour of the son.
>
> Provided the increase in the son's share of profits represented full consideration in money or money's worth for occupation of the land, FA 1986, Sch.20, para.6(1)(a) will apply and this will not be a GWR.
>
> The father is in effect occupying the land through the partnership and this prima facie constitutes a reservation. However, HMRC accept that the let-out in para.6(1)(a) may be satisfied by an appropriate upward adjustment (in lieu of rent) reflected in the donee's share of the partnership profits. The circumstances of the case must determine what is "appropriate" having regard to what might be agreed under an arm's length deal between unconnected persons.

EXAMPLE 32.7[63]

> A, who is a partner, withdraws capital from his partnership capital account and gives it to B. B then lends the partnership an equivalent cash sum.
>
> This is a reservation. Though the partnership may pay B a commercial rate of interest for the loan, this payment will not prevent the loan being a reservation. (This is a rare example of a benefit being reserved in a cash gift).

---

[61] See also *Dymond's Capital Taxes* at 9.300 and *AG v Boden* [1912] 1 K.B. 539.
[62] See IHTM 14341.
[63] See IHTM 14336.

EXAMPLE 32.8[64]

A, a farmer, retires and gives his farmhouse, lands and farming assets to his son, but A continued to live in the farmhouse rent free until his death.

The donor's continued residence in the farmhouse constitutes a reservation so far as that particular property is concerned, but the reservation does not extend to the remainder of the gifted lands and farming assets.

EXAMPLE 32.9[65]

A gives all the shares in his family company to B, it being part of the agreement that B would appoint A to the Board of Directors, a salaried position entitling him to a company car and other fringe benefits.

This would be regarded as the reservation of a benefit to the donor "by contract or otherwise".

EXAMPLE 32.10[66]

A husband and wife each own 50% of the issued capital of a limited company. The company owns the freehold property in which they live. The spouses transfer their shares into an accumulation and maintenance settlement for their grandchildren. They continue to live in the house rent-free until the husband's death.

This is not a GWR. The continued occupation of the property is not referable to the gift (consider, however, POAT issues).

EXAMPLE 32.11[67]

A farmer, on taking his son into partnership, makes a gift to him of a share of all the partnership assets including the land. They then share the profits and losses in the same proportion as they own the partnership assets at commencement. The farmer dies ten years later.

This is not a GWR. The son has taken possession and enjoyment of the partnership share gifted to him in the form of his share of profits. The father's share of profits is referable to his own partnership share, not the share gifted. (Note that the analysis is not that full consideration is

---

[64] See IHTM 14334.
[65] See IHTM 14334.
[66] See IHTM 14334.
[67] See IHTM 14332.

being paid to prevent the GWR provisions from applying but that there was no reservation in the first place. This may have implications for the POA charge although if the gift is analysed as of a partnership share (a chose in action) rather than of each and every asset (including land) it should not give rise to problems in practice).

Shared occupation

Broadly speaking if Dad gives Son a share in his land which they both occupy and Dad receives no benefit, other than a negligible one, from Son, which is for some reason connected with the gift, then there is no reservation in the gifted property.[68] **32.29**

Application of relief if there is a reservation

Business (and agricultural) property which is caught by the reservation of benefit rules is treated as comprised in the donor's estate for IHT purposes at his death if the reservation is continuing. Alternatively, if the reservation ceases *inter vivos* he makes a PET.[69] In both cases, relief may be available to reduce the value of the property subject to charge.[70] The requirements are complex but two sets of conditions need to be satisfied: **32.30**

(i) *at the time of the gift* the property has to qualify for relief either as relevant business property or as agricultural property[71]; and

(ii) *at the time of the tax charge* the property has to satisfy a number of conditions, the basis of which is the concept of a *notional transfer by the donee*.[72]

In deciding whether the business property relief ownership condition is met,[73] ownership by the donor prior to the gift is treated as ownership by the donee[74] and if the donee dies before the donor (or before the reservation of benefit ceases), his personal representatives or his beneficiaries under his will or intestacy are treated as if they were the donee.[75]

In general, if the conditions are met the rate of relief is then decided by reference to the notional transfer by the donee. This is, however, subject to the qualification that whether certain stocks and shares are relevant business property is to be decided on the basis that they remained owned by the donor.[76] (This has the effect of preventing aggregation with other property of

---

[68] See FA 1986, s.102B(4). See Ch. 31 for a detailed consideration of this exemption.
[69] This is the effect of FA 1986, s.102(3) and s.102(4).
[70] See FA 1986, Sch.20, para.8 and see IHTM 25381 *et seq*.
[71] *ibid.*, para.8(1).
[72] *ibid.*, para.8(1A)(b).
[73] See IHTA 1984, s.106.
[74] See FA 1986, Sch.20, para.8(2)(a).
[75] *ibid.*, para.8(5).
[76] *ibid.*, para.8(1A)(a).

the donee: however, the restriction is of reduced importance given the availability of 100 per cent for minority shareholdings). Similar rules apply in the case of agricultural property relief: for instance, ownership and occupation by the donor before the gift is treated as that of the donee and in the case of the occupation condition, occupation by the donor *after* the gift is also treated as that of the donee.[77]

Take the example of Dan who gives his farm (which he has owned and farmed for many years) to his son Phil. Dan continues in occupation until his death 18 months later. The analysis is as follows:

(i) Dan has made a gift which is caught by the reservation of benefit rules and which will be subject to IHT on his death.

(ii) At the time of the gift the property qualified for agricultural property relief.

(iii) At the time of Dan's death, Phil is treated as making a notional transfer of value and has satisfied the ownership/occupation requirement for agricultural property relief to be available.

Reasonable remuneration

32.31 A question that frequently arises in the context of a gift of shares in the family business is whether the donor can safely continue to be remunerated for working in the business or whether such payment gives rise to a reservation of benefit. The views of HMRC were published in letters dated February 19, 1987 and May 18, 1987. They make the key point that

> "the continuation of reasonable commercial arrangements in the form of remuneration and other benefits for the donor's services to the business entered into prior to the gift would not, by itself, amount to a reservation provided that the benefits were in no way linked to or affected by the gift."[78]

IHTM 14395 gives the following illustration:

EXAMPLE 32.12

> The donor transfers shares in an unquoted company into a settlement of which she is trustee (but not a beneficiary). She is entitled to retain remuneration for her services as director of that company.
>
> The continuation of reasonable commercial arrangements governing the remuneration of any other benefits for the donor's services in the

---

[77] *ibid.*, para.8(2).
[78] The problems posed by this statement are many: what for instance is "reasonable" in the context of remuneration? Why must the arrangements pre-date the gift if the rationale for the statement lies in the commerciality of the services? Note that FA 1986, Sch.20, para.6(1)(a) is limited to land and chattels but does the donor receive a benefit within FA 1986, s.102(1)(b) if the consideration represents no more than a fair commercial payment for his services?

company entered into before the gift would not, by itself, amount to a reservation, provided the benefits were in no way linked to or affected by the gift.

On the other hand, if, as part of the overall transaction, including the gift, new remuneration arrangements are made, consider whether the new package amounts to a reservation "by contract or otherwise".

IMPACT OF THE PRE-OWNED ASSETS CHARGE

32.32 There are no provisions in FA 2004, Sch.15 that deal specifically with businesses and farms. Accordingly, the application of the POA regime depends on general principles.

In considering the application of the regime it will be important to identify the property gifted. For instance:

(i) a gift of shares will only be a problem if the para.8 charge is in point (i.e. because the shares become held in a settlor interested trust); and

(ii) a gift of a partnership share, as for instance when father gives part of his capital account to his son, in a case where land is a partnership asset is a gift of the share (chose in action) and not of an interest in land. Again, therefore, there will only be a problem if the para.8 charge could apply.[79]

In cases where the full consideration let out prevents the reservation of benefit rules from applying to land and chattels, the pre-owned assets charge is equally inapplicable.[80]

Default election

32.33 If the regime would otherwise apply, the election is available to the taxpayer to opt into reservation of benefit.[81] As a result:

(a) no income tax will be payable, *and*

(b) the asset may attract business or agricultural property relief on the death of the taxpayer or earlier cessation of the reservation.

---

[79] Para.8 will not apply if the gifted property is not held in trust.
[80] See Sch.15, para.11(5)(d). See further Ch. 24.
[81] See Ch. 24 for a consideration of the election.

CHAPTER 33

INSURANCE-BASED ARRANGEMENTS

- Existing trusts (**33.03**)
- New trusts (**33.09**)

33.01 There are a wide variety of arrangements involving insurance policies held in a trust of which the following are the most common:

(i) Family protection policies: typically term assurance policies and second death whole of life policies aimed at providing for the payment of inheritance tax or the provision of a tax free lump sum in case the main earner dies; these will generally be written on trust so that the proceeds pass to the persons whom the life assured wants to benefit after his death.

(ii) Trusts of single premium bonds: a non income producing investment with a 5 per cent tax deferred withdrawal facility.

(iii) Loan trusts: based on a loan being made to trustees.

(iv) Discounted gift trusts: based upon the settlor retaining certain rights in the investment.

33.02 Prior to the FA 2006 changes, many of the above were based on flexible interest in possession trusts.[1] Given that (save for a disabled person's interest[2]) it is no longer possible to create new qualifying interest in possession *inter vivos* trusts it follows that thought needs to be given as to how best to accommodate such arrangements. Consideration also needs to be given to the treatment of existing trusts. HMRC have taken a greater interest in life policies recently. In particular the revised form of IHT200 account introduced in May 2000 incorporated the form D9 in respect of life policies which asked for considerably more information.

EXISTING TRUSTS

33.03 Assume that a life policy is held in a trust created before March 22, 2006. The transitional rules that apply are as follows:

---

[1] Note though the differences between Scotland vs England/Wales and Northern Ireland. See IHTM 20154 and 20155.
[2] IHTA 1984, s.89B.

(i) if the trust is accumulation and maintenance: there are no special provisions and accordingly the normal transitional period until April 6, 2008 ensures that A+M treatment will continue until that time but that thereafter the relevant property regime may apply;[3]

(ii) if the trust is interest in possession: in principle, the tax treatment of the trust will not be affected so long as the policy remains in trust. This result is achieved as follows.

The TSI regime: the flexible interest in possession trust envisages a succession of such interests with the settlement continuing to hold the policy until such time as it is encashed. The usual transitional period until April 6, 2008, which allows the existing interest in possession to be replaced by a transitional serial interest, applies.[4] As discussed below, however, the period has been extended for existing life insurance trusts.[5] 33.04

BN 25 indicated that the addition of property to an existing settlement would involve the creation of a new settlement.[6] Concern was expressed that if premiums were paid in respect of existing policies held in trust this could result in the creation of a new relevant property settlement. To provide reassurance the 2006 Finance Bill was amended in Standing Committee by the introduction of: 33.05

(i) s.46A (into IHTA 1984) to deal with policies held in interest in possession trusts on March 22, 2006;

(ii) s.46B to deal with policies held in accumulation and maintenance trust on March 22, 2006.

In both cases if a "premium payable under the contract is paid, or an allowed variation is made to the contract, at a particular time on or after (March 22, 2006)" then any rights under the contract which, as a result of the payment of the premium or the variation, are comprised in the settlement shall be deemed to have become so comprised (and so that the relevant interest shall be treated as subsisting in them) before March 22, 2006.[7] Note that any variation must "take place by operation of, or as a result of rights conferred by, provisions forming part of the contract immediately before March 22, 2006". So for example cashing in the existing policy and taking out a new one would not be protected by these provisions although of course premium payments on any new life policy may well be exempt under the normal expenditure out of income rules anyway.

It is also provided that if the payment of a premium in such cases involved a transfer of value that transfer is a potentially exempt transfer.[8] It appears the premium must actually be paid. So if the settlor pays the life company direct then that would be within the scope of ss.46A or B. If the settlor added funds 33.06

---

[3] For a consideration of the treatment of A+M trusts, see Ch. 21.
[4] On TSIs, see 18.14.
[5] S.49E of IHTA 1984.
[6] For BN 25, see App. III A3.01 for a criticism of this statement, see 15.13. It was thought that the payment of any premium merely maintained rather than increased the policy benefits so that it was in any event debatable whether it involved an addition of property.
[7] IHTA 1984, s.49A(2) and see s.49B(2) providing that such rights shall be treated as falling within a qualifying A+M settlement.
[8] IHTA 1984, s.49A(4); s.49B(5).

33.07 to the trust to enable the trustees to pay the premium, strictly that would not be within the scope of these sections although it is not thought that HMRC would take the point. Note that the relief only applies to a pre-Budget policy held in a pre-Budget interest in possession or A+M trust.

Also at Committee stage and, somewhat surprisingly, the Government allowed for an extended transitional period in respect of the pre-Budget policy held subject to a trust not just the payment of the premiums on such a policy. These provisions are now in IHTA 1984, s.49E and were explained by the Paymaster General as follows[9]:

> "The first condition is that the policy was already held in the settlement on Budget day and was subject to an interest in possession at that date. The second condition is that the current interest in possession either arose on the death of the person who held the interest on Budget day, arose on the death of someone holding a transitional serial interest in succession to them, or on the death of someone holding a transitional serial interest by virtue of a previous application of section 49(E). That means that where a person has the interest in possession in a pre-Budget trust holding a life insurance policy, but dies before the person whose life is insured, they can be replaced as the person without an impact and the transitional treatment will continue.[10]
>
> The third condition is that the life policy has been held in trust in question throughout the period from Budget day to the start of the current interest in possession. The fourth condition will mean that transitional serial interest treatment is only due where the interest in question would not also qualify as a trust for a bereaved minor or as a disabled person's interest. That is because it is clear that such trusts are eligible for the same IHT treatment as a transitional serial interest."

33.08 It is far from clear what justification there can be for the extension of transitional serial interest treatment in the case where the trust fund is comprised of a pre-March 22, 2006 settled life insurance policy. Note that if the pre-Budget life policy is encashed or lapses and a new one taken out then the new one will not fall within the transitional serial interest relief provisions.

EXAMPLE 33.1

On March 22, 2006 a life insurance policy is held on flexible interest in possession trusts for A.

(i) On April 1, 2007 the trustees determine A's interest in possession and appoint an interest in possession for his son, B. B is entitled to a transitional serial interest and A makes a PET.

(ii) On April 1, 2009, B unexpectedly dies and the policy becomes held on interest in possession trusts for his sister, C. She obtains a transitional

---

[9] The Standing Committee Debates, January 15, 2006 at Vol. 682.
[10] Note that post-April 5, 2008 the replacement must occur on death. Cp the extended treatment under s.49D on death of spouse or civil partner: see 18.14 *et seq*.

serial interest under IHTA 1984 s.49E. There is a chargeable transfer on B's death.

(iii) On August 1, 2010 the trustees receive cash on the death of the life insured. C dies soon afterwards and the cash fund becomes held in trust for her two children on flexible interest in possession trusts. There is a chargeable transfer on the death of C and her children do *not* enjoy transitional serial interests so that the property is now held on relevant property trusts.

Note:

(a) s.49E only extends TSI treatment (1) whilst the pre-March 22, 2006 policy is in the trusts and (2) if the interest arises on death. Hence if B had surrendered his interest (rather than dying) in 2009, C would not have obtained a TSI. Instead the continuing trust would fall within the relevant property regime and B would make an immediately chargeable transfer;

(b) it is not entirely clear how the special rules for life insurance settlements link-in with the s.49D provision under which a spouse can obtain a transitional serial interest after April 5, 2008. Presumably condition 2(a) of s.49E is met in such cases (In this example if on B's death his wife had become entitled to an interest in possession and on her death C had taken an interest in possession it is thought—given that the policy is still held in trust—that C obtains a TSI.)

NEW TRUSTS

Family Protection Policies

After March 21, 2006 any trust set up to hold the policy will be a relevant property settlement. In fact in many cases before that date discretionary trusts (viz relevant property settlements) had been used. In general therefore the position is unchanged and the following matters may be noted: **33.09**

(i) the annual premiums that will normally be payable will usually be exempt from IHT as a result of the normal expenditure out of income exemption;[11]

(ii) the settlement will be subject to anniversary and exit charges. The value of the policy at the relevant time will determine whether tax is payable. Whole of life and term policies whilst providing for a substantial sum assured will have a low surrender value until the death of the life insured or that person becoming seriously ill[12];

(iii) of course when the life insured dies and the trustees receive cash at the occasion of a ten year anniversary the charge will be calculated on that

---

[11] IHTA 1984, s.21.
[12] See IHTA 1984, s.167 which in certain circumstances substitutes for market value a premiums paid basis of valuation: it does not apply to the classic IHT term assurance.

value. When substantial insurance is being taken out it is normal to take out a number of policies to cover the desired amount and to employ a number of trusts (ensuring that they are not related settlements).

EXAMPLE 33.2

S wishes to take out life insurance to a value of £2.5m. To guard against the risk of a substantial IHT charge if the policy is held in a single relevant property settlement:

(i) S creates 10 separate settlements on consecutive days (in each case settling a nominal sum on the trusts);
(ii) 10 life policies are taken out and on the same day are assigned to the 10 settlements (one to each).

Given that the settlements are not "related settlements" (since they were not created on the same day)[13] each will benefit from a full IHT nil rate band when calculating charges during the life of each settlement.[14] The entry charge is not reduced but in practice the value of the life policies at the date of settlement is unlikely to exceed the settlor's nil rate band. Provided that the addition is made on the same day to all the settlements, in calculating the charge on any one settlement the additions to the others will be ignored.[15] It is, of course, important that the settlements are treated as discrete settlements and not administered as a single fund (e.g. separate returns need to be made and assets separately invested).

33.10 It is not thought that the continued payments of premiums by the settlor will give rise to problems since:

(i) if paid directly to the insurance company they will not fall within the s.67 provision dealing with additions to the settlement (value has been added but not property);
(ii) in addition they will not normally involve a chargeable transfer by the settlor since they will either qualify for the normal expenditure out of income or annual exemption.

Trusts of single premium bonds

33.11 These may be held in a trust from which the settlor is wholly excluded. From the perspective of trustees the bond is non-income producing and the 5 per cent

---

[13] IHTA 1984, s.62.
[14] Assuming that the settlor has not already used this up. The nominal sum settled into trusts 1–9 are of course transfers of value made by the settlor in the seven years before the creation of trust 10 but the amounts may fall within his IHT annual exemption or within the normal expenditure out of income exemption.
[15] IHTA 1984, s.67(3)(b)(i) (added property) and see *Rysaffe Trustees v IRC* [2003] S.T.C. 536 which is considered at 15.07 and 15.14.

withdrawal facility means that cash can be extracted from the investment without an immediate tax charge.

The Loan Trust

This is normally structured as in the following example. 33.12

EXAMPLE 33.3

S establishes a trust for his family from which he and his spouse (including civil partner) are wholly excluded.[16] The form of the trust (whether it is flexible life interest, discretionary, or accumulation and maintenance) is now irrelevant for IHT purposes since it will be taxed as a relevant property settlement. The initial trust fund comprises a nominal sum but S then lends the trustee £1m on terms that are interest free and repayable on demand. The trustees invest in a single premium bond and use the 5 per cent withdrawal facility to make partial repayments of the loan to the settlor each year. The tax position is as follows:

(i) because the loan is repayable on demand it is not thought that S makes an immediate transfer of value although he may make a gift;
(ii) the 5 per cent withdrawal payments to the settlor are free from tax;
(iii) any growth in value of the bond takes effect outside the settlor's estate (the arrangement is sometimes referred to as "*asset freezing*");
(iv) the trust may benefit from a nil rate band, and ten year charges will be on the amount by which the value of the bond exceeds the then outstanding debt.

It will be appreciated that this type of trust can be established to invest in any asset: the attraction of a bond lies in the 5 per cent withdrawal facility.

The discounted gift arrangement[17]: the loan trust affords no immediate IHT 33.13
advantage to the settlor: the benefit comes with the future growth (if any!) in the value of the bond. By contrast, the discounted gift arrangement can confer immediate benefits. The essence of a discounted gift plan is that the settlor makes a gift into settlement but with certain rights in the settled property being retained. Typically the rights retained may be in a series of single premium policies maturing on successive anniversaries of the creation of the settlement or to future capital payments if the settlor is alive at the prospective payment date.

---

[16] If the settlor is not wholly excluded then para.5(4)(b), Sch.20 provides that any property directly or indirectly derived from a loan made by the settlor (but not his spouse) to the trust is treated as property in which he has reserved a benefit.

[17] See IHTM 20423 for a list of the companies running discounted gift schemes.

Diagrammatically the position is as follows:

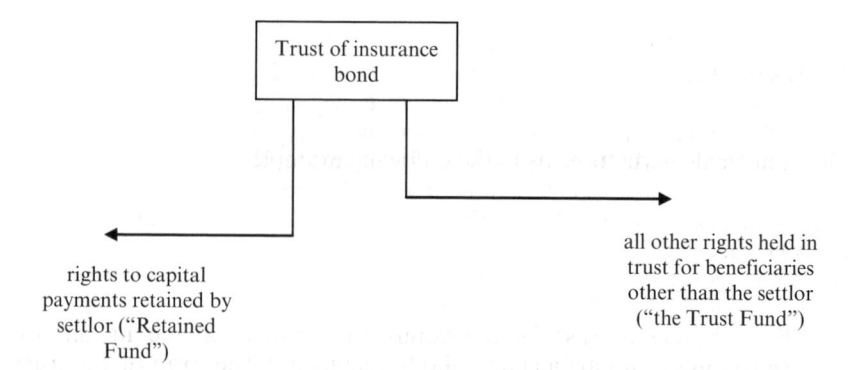

```
                    ┌──────────────────┐
                    │ Trust of insurance│
                    │       bond        │
                    └──────────────────┘
                    ↙                  ↘
   rights to capital               all other rights held in
   payments retained by            trust for beneficiaries
   settlor ("Retained              other than the settlor
   Fund")                          ("the Trust Fund")
```

33.14   **IHT analysis:** the arrangement is viewed as a "carve-out" or a "shearing arrangement" so that provided that the rights retained by the settlor are sufficiently clearly defined and that he is excluded from all benefit in the Trust Fund there is no reservation of benefit.[18]

33.15   One of the attractions of the discounted gift plan lies in the "discount". The transfer of value made by the settlor when establishing his trust is the fall in value of his estate and in calculating this it is necessary to arrive at a value for the rights that he retains in the retained fund (e.g. to 5 per cent capital payments out of the trust each year for as long as he lives). This will depend on such factors as age, health and sex and on the size of the capital payments that he will receive. The question therefore is what is the value of the trust fund taking into account the existence of the retained fund. For instance, if A, a healthy 70 year old, put £500,000 into a discounted gift plan reserving a right to 5 per cent annual withdrawals of capital over the next 20 years[19] (if he is then alive) a substantial discount will be in order. If it is of (say) 40 per cent then the transfer of value made by A is reduced to £300,000. If, however, A had been uninsurable when the scheme was effected then the retained rights would be worthless and therefore the transfer of value much larger.

33.16   **Taxing the retained fund:** when A dies the right to payments under the terms of the retained fund ceases. Does this mean that there is no IHT charge (in effect that the discounted amount is wholly free from charge)? It is believed that HMRC's current practice is to treat the retained fund as valueless but it is far from clear that this is correct. The issue is whether the valuation exercise is to be performed *immediately before death* taking into account only factors known at that time or with the benefit of hindsight (i.e. with knowledge of the deceased's imminent demise). If the former method were to be adopted (which seems to the authors to be the correct approach) then a reduction in value as

---

[18] The arrangement involves a *chose in action* (viz rights under an insurance bond) which are not capable of separate transfer: i.e. unlike land where a settlor can retain a leasehold interest and transfer only the encumbered freehold, in this case the entire bond must be held in trust but with the rights under it split into a retained fund (for the settlor) and a settled fund (from which he is excluded). On the need for precision in defining the gifted property, see the speech of Lord Hoffman in the *Ingram* case which is discussed at 13.14 and 31.34.

[19] To avoid an income tax charge on the excess—see *Sugden v Kent* [2001] S.T.C. 158.

a result of the death under IHTA 1984, s.171 would not seem appropriate given that what is coming to an end on death is "any interest".[20]

The POA dimension: the introduction of the POA income tax charge in FA 2004 (with effect from April 6, 2005) led to concerns that discounted gift trusts were settlor interested trusts which, because they contained intangible property, fell within the para.8 charge.[21] Surprisingly, however, the position was not viewed in this light by HMRC who developed further the analysis adopted for reservation of benefit by concluding that the retained fund had not only been carved out and retained by the settlor but that the rights in it were held on bare trust for the settlor. Hence the para.8 charge did not apply to this fund[22] and nor did it apply to the trust fund given that the settlor could not benefit under it.[23] It is thought that this argument is flawed since there is no separate property in the retained fund: rather a single asset is held in trust and the settlor is entitled to certain benefits from that asset. Needless to say, many discounted gift arrangements have been established in reliance on this HMRC statement. 33.17

Impact of the 2006 legislation: more recently the future of these plans has been thrown into doubt as a result of the changes in the IHT treatment of settlements. The preferred trusts of the Trust Fund had been flexible interest in possession so that the creation of the trust was a PET. From March 22, 2006 it is no longer possible to create qualifying interests in possession[24] so that the trust created will involve an immediately chargeable transfer by the settlor. Accordingly, if the (discounted) value transferred exceeds the settlor's available IHT nil rate band tax at 20 per cent will be payable on the excess. Further, the settlement so created will be subject to anniversary and exit charges and concern was raised that for this purpose the value to be taxed would include the rights in the retained fund. Such fears appear to be ill founded, however, since correspondence with the HMRC indicates: 33.18

(i) that the same approach to that adopted for POA will be followed: i.e. the retained fund will be treated as a bare trust and so as a separate settlement and not therefore aggregated with the trust fund;

(ii) for the purpose of imposing the 10-year charge it will be necessary to value the insurance bond on the basis of what would a purchaser pay for it given that certain rights have been reserved to the settlor (in the form of the retained fund). Hence the normal discount will apply.

---

[20] The correct valuation procedure was recently considered in *Arkwright (PR of Williams Deceased) v IRC* [2004] S.T.C. (SCD) 89. See further *McCutcheon on Inheritance Tax*, 4th edn at 13.50 *et seq*. Oliver L.J. in *Fetherstonhaugh v IRC* [1984] S.T.C. 261 at 268 commented (in an *obiter dicta*) that:

"*The occasion of the deemed transfer of value is, it is true, related to the moment before the death of the deceased but there is nothing in the statute to suggest that the valuation is to be conducted on the basis that the impending demise of the deceased is a known factor which the hypothetical valuer is to take into account*".

[21] For the para.8 charge, see Ch. 24.
[22] Because it is not *a settlement* for IHT purposes.
[23] The analysis may be found in the POA Guidance Notes, see App. III A3.21 *et seq*.
[24] There are only restricted exceptions which are not relevant in this context.

33.19 The main impact of the 2006 legislation is in limiting the value of the discounted gift to £285,000 (or relevant nil rate band) which is necessary if an immediate IHT charge is to be avoided. For the majority of taxpayers who purchase discounted gift plans that ceiling will not be a problem. For those wishing to invest more there is the possibility of the Trust Fund being held on a bare trust for one or more individuals. This would mean that the transfer of value would then be a PET and so the nil rate band restriction overcome.[25]

[25] See Ch. 30 on bare trusts.

Chapter 34

TRUSTS AND DIVORCE

- Claiming trust assets on divorce **(34.02)**
- Tax position **(34.12)**

Introduction

Given that approximately two in five marriages end in divorce it is understandable that those who have accumulated or inherited wealth wish to keep that wealth within the family and ensure that the "family property" is not lost on a divorce. Parents set up trusts to ensure some continuing control over assets while starting the clock running for inheritance tax purposes. How effective or useful are trusts in protecting assets in the event of their child's divorce? Trusts are sometimes set up *as part* of a divorce settlement. A spouse may be more inclined to give assets to the other spouse if s/he knows that they are held in trust for that ex-spouse's benefit rather than given outright. Hence trusts can facilitate the reaching of a matrimonial settlement. Finally, existing trusts may need to be divided up in a divorce settlement so that both spouses' needs can be satisfied. 34.01

The changes to the inheritance tax regime in FA 2006 have made the position more difficult for divorcing couples who might otherwise have used or varied trusts to settle matrimonial claims.

CLAIMING TRUST ASSETS ON A DIVORCE

If a beneficiary under a trust is getting divorced, will the assets of the trust be counted as part of his property? There are three possibilities: the Family Courts may regard the trust as a financial resource of the beneficiary or the trust as a nuptial settlement capable of variation by the Courts. In cases where the beneficiary has a fixed interest under the trust with no power for the trustees to revoke it, the Courts may order the beneficiary to assign such interest to the divorcing spouse. 34.02

EXAMPLE 34.1

> A is a beneficiary of a trust set up by his father when A was a baby. A has a life interest, is aged 40 and is getting divorced. The settlement should not be regarded as a nuptial settlement (see post) but it is possible (although unlikely) that A could be ordered to assign his life interest to his wife so she takes an interest *pur autre vie*.[1] The right to receive the income is a financial resource. How much that resource would be taken into account by a court is discussed further below.

When is a trust a nuptial settlement?

34.03 The Court has jurisdiction under s.24 of the Matrimonial Causes Act 1973 to make:

> "an Order varying for the benefit of the parties of the marriage and of the children of the family or either of them any ante-nuptial or post-nuptial settlement . . . made on the parties to the marriage."

This is much wider than merely taking a trust into consideration as a financial resource because the interests of other beneficiaries who are not even parties or children of the marriage can be adversely affected.[2]

An ante-nuptial or post-nuptial settlement is not defined but may specifically include one made by will or codicil.[3] The terminology, "nuptial settlement", originates from the Matrimonial Causes Act 1859 and is generally regarded as a settlement that provides some benefit for either one or both spouses by reference to their married state. The classic definition of a post nuptial settlement is found in *Prinsep v Prinsep*[4] where it was stated:

> "it is upon the husband in the character of husband or upon the wife in the character of wife, or upon both in the character of husband and wife. It should provide for the financial benefit of one or other or both of the spouses as spouses and with reference to their married state."

There is an important difference between Jersey and the UK in that the Jersey Courts may only interfere with a settlement if it has been entered into *between* the parties to the marriage, whereas UK legislation confers

---

[1] Since A's wife would lose all right to receive the income on A's death such a result might be regarded as unsatisfactory for her. The tax position of interests *pur autre vie* is not straightforward and after April 2008 could have adverse inheritance tax consequences. If A's interest could be ended at any time, without the need for his consent by the trustees, it is obviously not satisfactory to make A assign his interest to his wife.
[2] In *Brooks v Brooks* [1996] 3 All E.R. 257, HL. Lord Nicholls expressly stated that the court's power is not confined to varying the interests of the parties to the marriage under the settlement.
[3] Although it is presumably less likely that a settlement in a will by a deceased person for his child could be regarded as a nuptial settlement.
[4] [1929] P. 225.

jurisdiction over settlements made *by anyone* provided that it is *on* the parties to the marriage.[5]

In *Brooks v Brooks*[6] it was considered that the term nuptial settlement should be given a wide meaning and that s.24 is concerned **34.04**

> "with a settlement made on the parties to the marriage. So, broadly stated, the disposition must be one which makes some form of continuing provision for both or either of the parties to a marriage with or without provision for their children."

A settlement can be in respect of a particular marriage and therefore be a nuptial settlement in relation to that marriage even though the spouse of a subsequent marriage might be the person who eventually takes. (However, curiously, the settlement will only be nuptial in relation to the first marriage because the second marriage will not usually be in contemplation at the time of the first!)

The Court is entitled to take into account the substance of the transaction but the motive in entering into a settlement is irrelevant.[7]

The Court has no power to vary a settlement made by either spouse which was not made after or in contemplation with the marriage but merely gave the settlor power to appoint an interest to any future spouse.[8] A declaration that the settlement is not a marriage settlement does not prevent it from being a marriage settlement and a settlement with a foreign governing law may be a marriage settlement.

It is not clear whether the question of whether a settlement is a marriage settlement is determined only at the time the settlement is made or whether subsequent variations or appointments over the settlement can turn a nuptial settlement into a non-nuptial settlement and vice versa. In *Example 34.1* above the settlement for A is clearly not a nuptial settlement since it was not made on A in the character of husband with reference to his married state. However, if after A's marriage, the trustees varied the trust so as to include the spouse does it become a marriage settlement? It is thought that it could do so.

In *Charalambous v Charalambous*[9] the husband argued that the removal of himself and his wife from the class of beneficiaries[10] rendered it no longer a settlement capable of variation under s.24(1)(c) of MCA 1973. The High Court rejected this argument stating that the removal of any "nuptial elements" could not deprive the Court of jurisdiction but in any event there were a number of factors which continued to make the trust nuptial. Although husband and wife were removed as beneficiaries they remained joint protectors over the settlement which gave them extensive powers of control; their children remained as beneficiaries and the husband financially benefited from the settlement after he ceased to be a beneficiary. The Court of Appeal upheld **34.05**

---

[5] See for example *J v M* [2002] J.L.R. 330 where the trust was not varied in the Jersey Courts and contrast *E v E (financial provision)* [1989] F.C.R. where a discretionary settlement set up by the husband's father of which H and W were beneficiaries, was varied.
[6] [1996] 3 All E.R. 257.
[7] *Prescott v Fellowes* [1958] 3 All E.R. 55, CA where the deed described itself as a settlement on marriage but was nevertheless held not to be a marriage settlement.
[8] *Hargreaves v Hargreaves* [1926] P. 42.
[9] [2004] EWCA Civ 1030.
[10] They were removed in January 2001 and the marriage broke down in 2002. The husband had benefited subsequently by substantial loans from the trust to his businesses.

the decision but did hold that the removal of the nuptial elements could in some cases deprive the court of jurisdiction, albeit that this had not occurred in the present case. Presumably the reverse could also occur: a non-nuptial settlement could become nuptial if subsequently varied. It is assumed that a settlement for the children of the marriage from which the parents are permanently excluded is not a marriage settlement.

The husband also argued in *Charalambous* that since the settlement was governed by Jersey law, only the Jersey Courts had jurisdiction to entertain the wife's claim for an order for variation of the settlement. In the alternative the husband argued that if the English Courts did have jurisdiction only the law of Jersey should be applied (which would have prevented a variation because the trust was on the parties to the marriage but not made by the parties to the marriage). Both the High Court and the Court of Appeal rejected this argument holding that while Art.6 of the Hague Convention required that a trust be governed by the law chosen by the settlor, this did not prevent the English court from having jurisdiction in a divorce by virtue of Art.15 of the Convention which provided an exception for the "the personal and proprietary effects of marriage . . .".

Avoiding a nuptial settlement

34.06 It is therefore sensible for settlors to make provision for their children well before any marriage is in contemplation. In *Hargreaves v Hargreaves* it was held that the settlement was not made in anticipation of marriage even though it was made less than a month before the marriage was agreed. However it is wise to make provision well before this! Where children are already married, rather than making separate settlements for each married child and his family, the settlor will do better to create one trust for both children and issue and exclude spouses or widows/widowers. If desired the settlor can insert a power to add beneficiaries.

34.07 The trustees are entitled to be heard in opposition to any proposed variation of their settlement and they can be joined as a third party. The Family Division can remove trustees and will do so in appropriate circumstances.[11] The court has to consider whether any proposed variation might adversely affect a minor child of the marriage in which case the child should have the protection of separate representation.[12] Section 24(1)(d) empowers the court to extinguish or reduce the interest of either party under a marriage settlement other than one in the form of a pension arrangement. Powers of appointment by a party over his own fund can be extinguished although the court will not usually remove the power of appointing new trustees if the relevant party still has an interest in the fund.

Financial resource

34.08 It is not enough to ensure that a trust is not a nuptial settlement. An interest under a trust (even a discretionary interest or a flexible life interest) can be a

---

[11] See *E v E (financial provision)* [1990] 2 F.L.R. 233.
[12] See *E v E* above and *White v White and King* (1972) 116 Sol. Jo. 219 CA.

financial resource which the court is entitled to take into account when determining financial provision.[13] The courts look at the "reality of the situation".[14] They ignore fine points of trust law. The fact that the beneficiary can be excluded or his interest determined does not mean the courts will ignore the trust if the beneficiary may reasonably expect to receive benefits from it. If there has been a history of capital or income distributions then the trust can be regarded as a financial resource and the beneficiary may face a greater lump sum order or higher maintenance payments than would have been the case if the trust had not existed. If the beneficiary is excluded from capital but is entitled to income the financial resource may be limited to taking the income into account. Even if the trustees refuse to pay out to fund the beneficiary's liabilities arising from the divorce order the ultimate sanction is that the court can commit the spouse to prison for non-payment.[15] However, where a spouse receives income from assets over which he genuinely has no control the court should not take such income into account other than on the basis of actual receipt. The court should not put improper pressure on the trustees to exercise their discretions for the benefit of the spouse whilst at the same time the court should not be misled by appearances.[16] The position is different where the spouse has effective control over the trust, e.g. is a protector with power to appoint and remove trustees or to consent to distributions of capital.[17]

So while the courts may not be able to vary a settlement because it is not nuptial, the trust may well be a financial resource that has to be taken into account.

34.09 As noted above, the Courts have taken what can only be called a robust approach when looking at trusts in divorce cases. In the recent case of *Charman v Charman*[18] the position of a discretionary offshore trust set up by the husband in 1987 was considered. The trust was worth £67m. The beneficiaries included the settlor husband and his issue. The trustees made distributions out of income to Mr Charman until 1997 but not out of capital nor out of capital gains. Mr Charman failed in his argument that the trust assets should be left entirely out of account because they were part of a long term plan to found a "dynastic trust" for the benefit of a yet unborn members of the family. The judge rejected the settlor's contention that this was his true intention:

> "the failure to indicate any such dynastic plan on the face of any of the letters of wishes . . . is quite frankly incredible".

---

[13] In two recent high profile big money cases *Miller v Miller* and *McFarlane v McFarlane* [2006] UKHL 24 no trusts were involved.
[14] *Thomas v Thomas* [1996] 2 F.C.R. 544.
[15] See the extreme case of *Browne v Browne* [1989] 1 F.L.R. 291, CA. Assets were held in a foreign discretionary trust set up by the wife and all previous requests by the wife for sums to be advanced to her had been granted.
[16] See *Thomas v Thomas*, cited above "if on the balance of probability the evidence shows that if trustees exercised their discretion to release more capital or income to a husband, the interests of the trust or of other beneficiaries would not be appreciably damaged, the court can assume that a genuine request for the exercise of such discretion would probably be met by a favourable response. In that situation if the court decides that it would be reasonable for a husband to seek to persuade trustees to release more capital or income to him to enable him to make proper financial provision for his children and his former wife, the court would not in so deciding be putting improper pressure on the trustees."
[17] See *Howard v Howard* [1945] 1 All E.R. 91, CA and compare *Browne v Browne* above and *B v B* [1982] 3 F.L.R. 298, CA *Minwalla v Minwalla* [2004] EWML 2823, [2005] 1 F.L.R. 771.
[18] [2006] EWHC 1879 (Fam).

Even if that had been Mr Charman's true intention the Judge doubted that it would have made much difference. The assets in the Trust had been generated during the course of a long marriage and even if the wife had agreed to the husband's plan this would not have assisted Mr Charman's position.

> "At the end of a marriage of this length for a spouse to be excluded from benefit by such an informal arrangement even if consensual and created at a time when the marriage was sound would be grotesquely unfair."[19]

34.10 Where, however, the trust was not set up by the divorcing spouse and the assets were settled some time prior to any marriage and for a range of beneficiaries, trusts may provide some protection on a divorce.[20] The court may depart from the yardstick of equality where the claimant's financial needs can be met out

---

[19] In this case it is noteworthy that the Bermudan Trustee (Codan) chose not to participate in the proceedings and refused to produce any information on communications between Codan and Mr Charman on the basis that they did not "consider it in the interests of the trust to participate in a discovery procedure in the English Courts." The UK courts may draw its own adverse conclusions about arrangements even if an order for discovery against a third party may not be enforceable in the overseas court.

[20] See *Miller* and *McFarlane* above. The court looks first at needs with a cross test to the yardstick of equality. The overriding requirement is to produce a fair outcome and essentially "to give each party an equal start on the road to independent living." That does not necessarily mean an equal split of assets. In assessing fairness, one has to look at need, compensation and sharing. *Compensation* is to re-address actual or prospective significant economic disparity between the parties arising from the way they conducted their marriage. For example where one party has sacrificed their own career or income/capital earning for the benefit of the other spouse. What Baroness Hale described as compensation for "relationship generated disadvantage". The third strand is *sharing*. This is based on "the concept of equality permeating marriage as understood today" and Lord Nicholls described a husband and wife being now for all practical purposes equal partners in marriage. They commit themselves to sharing their lives, to living and working together and so when the partnership ends each is entitled to an equal share of the assets of the partnership unless there is good reason to the contrary. "The yardstick of equality is to be applied as an aid not a rule". Baroness Hale referred to it as sharing the fruits of the matrimonial partnership. In *Miller* several categories of property were distinguished. Lord Nicholls broke these down as follows:

(a) Property acquired during the marriage otherwise than by inheritance or gift. This is termed the financial product of the parties' common endeavour. Such matrimonial property includes property acquired during periods of pre-marital cohabitation and engagement. Lord Nicholls did not distinguish between matrimonial "family" assets and matrimonial "business and investment" assets. The entitlement of each party to a share of these matrimonial assets was the same however long or short the marriage may have been. In other words the matrimonial property of a short marriage is to be shared—this was the rationale in *Miller*.

(b) The family home is normally regarded as matrimonial property even if brought into the marriage by only one of them. In addition, family assets such as bank accounts will generally be regarded as matrimonial property.

(c) For non-matrimonial property, the length of the marriage is of relevance. In the case of a short marriage, fairness may require that the claimant is not entitled to a share of the non-matrimonial property and in these circumstances there may be a good reason for departing from equality. Hence inheritances and gifts and other property that each party brings to the marriage (apart from the matrimonial home) are less likely to be subject to a claim or division on a short marriage. Baroness Hale seemed to endorse this part of the approach in that she noted that if the assets are not family assets or not generated by the joint efforts of the parties then the duration of the marriage, (i.e. its shortness) may justify a departure from the yardstick of equality (see [153]).

In the case of *Miller* the wife obtained an Order for £5m against personal assets of approximately £20m after a three year marriage so the percentage was about 25 per cent.

of other property if there are pre-acquired or inherited assets. Trusts make the existence of the "pre-marital" assets held by each party prior to the marriage rather clearer because they are necessarily segregated from the personal assets.

Pre-nuptial agreements

Where one of the parties is the beneficiary of numerous trusts then it may be desirable to have a pre-nuptial agreement ("PNA") prior to the marriage. The English Courts do not ignore a PNA. While they are not obliged to obey its terms (and maintain strongly that their jurisdiction under MCA 1973 cannot be excluded) they can nevertheless take the terms of the PNA into account as a relevant factor when deciding how to exercise their discretions. If the parties can show that they have reached a reasonable agreement before marriage on how the assets should be divided a Court will generally consider such an agreement carefully, particularly on a relatively short marriage. It is hard then for one party to argue that they had different expectations. Obviously if circumstances change during the course of a marriage, e.g. one party becomes disabled or the marriage is a very long one or the assets earned by them personally during the course of the marriage increase substantially, the extent to which such an agreement is taken into account decreases. 34.11

The key is to demonstrate that each party has signed the document willingly and in full knowledge. So complete disclosure would have to be made of all trusts where a party is a potential or actual beneficiary along with details of that trust and whether benefits have been received.

TAX POSITION

Capital gains tax

The main problem for divorcing couples prior to March 22, 2006 was capital gains tax rather than inheritance tax. Whilst spouses are living together any transfer of assets between them takes place on a no gain no loss basis.[21] This treatment continues for inter-spousal transfers made in the tax year of separation. However, if assets are transferred after the tax year of separation, s.58 no longer applies and such disposals are treated as taking place at market value.[22] 34.12

EXAMPLE 34.2

> H and W separate in May 2006. Provided that any transfers take place between them before April 6, 2007 they are treated as taking place on

---

[21] TCGA 1992, s.58.
[22] Husband and wife remain connected persons until decree absolute. See s.286 of TCGA 1992.

a no gain no loss basis. After April 5, 2007 the transfers are treated as taking place at market value.

Inheritance tax

34.13 By contrast, assets can be transferred between husband and wife without attracting an inheritance tax charge up to decree absolute, whether or not they are separated.[23] After decree absolute the exemption in s.18 does not apply but two statutory exemptions may still provide relief. First, s.10 of IHTA 1984 which provides that a transfer of assets not intended to confer any gratuitous benefit will not be a transfer of value. This exemption will cover transfers of property pursuant to court orders.[24] It can include transfers into trust but not variations of existing interests under trust.[25] Section 10 is considered in more detail below.

34.14 The second exemption is in s.11 of IHTA 1994 which provides that a disposition will not be a transfer of value if it is made by one party to the marriage (or civil partnership) in favour of the other party or to a child of either party to the marriage or former marriage and is:

> for the maintenance of the other party; or
>
> for the maintenance, education or training of the child for a period ending not later than the year ending April 5, in which the child attains 18, or if later, finishes full time education.

In view of the definition of marriage and civil partnership in s.11(6), s.11 can apply to dispositions for the maintenance of a divorced spouse or civil partner made on the occasion of the dissolution or annulment of a marriage/civil partnership and the variation of a disposition so made, e.g. on the remarriage of the other party.

In most cases dispositions made on divorce or on termination of a civil partnership are made following arms length negotiations or under the terms of a Court Order and so are not treated as transfers of value because they come within s.10. "Maintenance" is given a wide meaning and will cover transfers of property as well as ordinary maintenance agreements. However, it will not cover gifts by way of settlement if the child can receive benefits under the settlement after reaching 18 and ceasing full time education or training. See also 17.21.

Use of trusts and FA 2006, Sch.20

34.15 In many "big money" cases, it will be seen as desirable that some of the property transferred to the spouse (usually the wife) is retained in trust for her, rather than given to her outright. The other spouse (usually the husband) then

---

[23] IHTA 1984, s.18. The Law Society has in the past made representations that the capital gains tax treatment should be similarly extended beyond the year of separation.
[24] See Statement of Practice E12.
[25] See 17.11 and 10.08.

feels that there is some guarantee that the assets will eventually pass to the children of the marriage rather than to a future partner of the ex-spouse.

Before FA 2006, a husband would have settled the assets on interest in possession trusts for the spouse. Spouse exemption would have been available if the transfer took place before decree absolute and the trust would be outside the relevant property regime. The spouse could enjoy the income and use of the assets with control by the trustees and the assets could then pass on to the children on the spouse's death.

Since March 22, 2006 all *inter vivos* transfers into trusts, whether or not interest in possession for the spouse, will be chargeable transfers unless the spouse is disabled.[26] The trust property will fall within the relevant property regime. So a transfer of £500,000 into an interest in possession trust for the spouse will prima facie attract a lifetime 20 per cent inheritance tax charge on the excess above the £285,000 threshold and the trust will be subject to ten year anniversary charges and exit charges. Despite strong representations from the professional bodies, the Government resisted attempts to change this.

Transfers into trust for a spouse which are made as part of arm's length negotiations or pursuant to a court order are likely to be protected by the s.10 exemption (no gratuitous intention). Hence in the above example there should be no immediate inheritance tax to pay on setting up the trust. However, the settled property will be subject to 10-year and exit charges. On the other hand there is no inheritance tax payable on the death of the spouse who has the interest in possession since it is not a qualifying interest in possession.[27]

EXAMPLE 34.3

> As directed by court order in matrimonial proceedings, Mr A settles £10m million on life interest trusts for his wife in June 2006. This creates a relevant property settlement but there should be no inheritance tax charge since the transfer is protected under s.10.
>
> Every 10 years the trust will suffer a 10-year charge and there is an exit charge on final termination.

---

[26] See Ch. 26.

[27] HMRC generally accept that s.10 applies where each party to the divorce is independently advised such that there is strong evidence of negotiation between the parties. Until recently HMRC argued that this also meant that any transfer by one spouse to the other of assets as part of a divorce settlement was for money or money's worth because the assets were transferred in return for the surrender by the transferee of rights over other property which he would otherwise have been able to exercise. Hence no hold-over relief was available even if the transfer was made pursuant to a court order under MCA 1973 on the grounds that the recipient spouse gave actual consideration in the form of surrendered rights which he could otherwise have exercised to obtain alternative financial provision. However, since July 31, 2002 as a result of *G v G* [2002] EWML 1339; [2002] 2 F.L.R. 1143, hold-over relief should be available on transfers of business assets made under Court Order. In *G v G* the court held that neither party was giving up assets or rights as a quid pro quo: the court was exercising the statutory powers vested in it by law. Hence neither party was giving money or money's worth for capital gains tax purposes. HMRC will still not give hold-over relief where there is no recourse to the courts. Does *G v G* undermine the case for s.10 inheritance tax exemption: if hold-over relief is available on transfers pursuant to a court order does the transaction fall within s.10? Is there any transaction made by the parties at all when the disposition is made by Court Order? It does not appear that HMRC take this point.

Matrimonial home

34.16 For many divorcing couples the matrimonial home will be their most significant asset. As part of the divorce settlement, it is usual for the matrimonial home to be sold and the proceeds split or for one spouse to transfer his or her interest in it to the other. The sale of the home might be immediate following the divorce or it might be deferred under what is commonly known as a *Mesher* order.[28]

HMRC took the view that a *Mesher* order created a settlement[29] and the transfer of the home from either or both spouses to themselves as trustees to hold on trust for sale was a disposal for capital gains tax purposes deemed to take place at market value. In practice, principal private residence relief is likely to protect both spouses from any capital gains tax charge assuming the transfer into trust takes place within three years of either spouse having vacated the property.[30] When the *Mesher* order terminates, upon the children reaching the specified age, the trust ends and there is a deemed disposal back to the spouses (alternatively the order may provide that the house is to be sold by the trustees within a stated time after a child reaches 18). However, the trustees are entitled to principal private residence relief on the entire gain because one spouse, as a beneficiary, had occupied the house throughout the period of the settlement.[31,32]

EXAMPLE 34.4

H and W separate and the house is the main asset. It is agreed that when the children are 18 it should be sold and the proceeds divided between H and W equally. If H and W remain joint owners then on sale more than three years after H ceases to occupy the property, H will suffer a capital gains tax charge. Before March 22, 2006 the house could instead have been put into an interest in possession trust for wife so that s.225 relief applied to relieve the whole gain, even though part of the proceeds was eventually distributed to H.[33] This is no longer possible without considering the

---

[28] Called after the case *Mesher v Mesher and Hall* [1980] 1 All E.R. 126 in which the Court ordered that a house which was jointly owned should be held in trust for both spouses in equal shares and should not be sold until the youngest child reached 17. The wife was at liberty to live in the house rent-free subject to paying all outgoings.
[29] See CGTM 65367.
[30] In other cases ESC D6 may apply and prevent a charge.
[31] TCGA 1992, s.225.
[32] The other common arrangement—deferred charge—has become less popular although remains unaffected by Sch.20. With a deferred charge, one spouse has 100 per cent of the matrimonial home vested in them whilst the other spouse takes a charge, either for a fixed or variable amount. The order will specify when the charge can be realised, for example, when the other spouse dies or remarries or when the children attain a specified age or finish full time education. The tax treatment of a deferred charge is less favourable than a *Mesher* order since when the charge is realised HMRC's view is that the charge is an asset when it is over a percentage of the sale proceeds rather than a fixed amount and the capital gain is calculated on the difference between the amount received and the value of the charge when it was created. If the charge is for a fixed amount the spouse has probably disposed of his entire interest in the house in return for the charge and this charge represents a debt falling within s.251(1) of TCGA 1992.
[33] Reverter to settlor relief (see Ch. 27) would have applied.

inheritance tax implications. The transfer by both of them is a chargeable transfer and the trust is within the relevant property regime.

Trust assets

Divorce settlements may not simply involve one spouse transferring assets outright to the other or even settling assets owned outright on trust for the other. The principal financial resource of the family may in fact be the assets contained in a settlement where one spouse has a life interest and it is desired that the trust should be varied to allow the other spouse to receive benefits. The trustees may not have power to advance capital to either spouse and in any event may be reluctant to do so if the settlor was, say the father, who wanted capital to pass to grandchildren. The trust assets may not be readily realisable or the trust may have been offshore and contain significant stockpiled gains which will make an outright distribution of capital to the spouse expensive. In these circumstances, how can the trust assets best be rearranged? **34.17**

EXAMPLE 34.5

(1) A has been married for 20 years and has a life interest in a settlement set up by his father some years before the marriage. In June 2006, A separates from his wife and since the main family wealth is in the trust it is agreed that A will assign part of his life interest to his wife so she takes an interest *pur autre vie*. In these circumstances s.10 provides no protection even if the disposition takes place as part of arms' length negotiations because it only relieves dispositions that would otherwise have been transfers of value. The disposal of a life interest under s.51 IHTA is taxed as if he had made a transfer of value but A has not actually made a transfer of value[34]: his interest is merely treated as coming to an end.

Until April 2008 an assignment of part of his life interest to his wife will result in her obtaining a transitional serial interest.[35] A will make a PET if they are divorced: otherwise the transfer is spouse exempt. After April 5, 2008 the assignment of A's interest in possession will not be a TSI and so not spouse exempt or a PET. A will make an immediately chargeable transfer of value.

(2) Contrast the position if A did not assign his life interest but the trustees instead terminated that interest in part and appointed an interest in possession to A's spouse by exercise of their overriding powers. If this occurred before April 6, 2008 then the interest in possession taken by A's wife is a TSI and A has made a PET or spouse exempt transfer (depending on whether decree absolute has been granted). If, however, A's

---

[34] IHTA 1984, s.51(1)(a).
[35] See TSIs, see 18.14.

divorce occurs after April 2008 and A is anxious to avoid a chargeable transfer on the termination of his interest in possession, can s.10 apply?

A's interest has actually come to an end so s.52 applies. Under s.52(1), tax is charged as if A had made a transfer of value. In this case can A rely on the s.10 exemption? It is thought not. Although A is deemed to have made a transfer of value the disposition has been made by the trustees. No disposition is made by A of his interest. It is difficult to argue that a disposition by the trustees is not intended to confer a benefit on anyone.[36]

34.18 In the above example if the couple are still married it would be possible to obtain spouse exemption if the trustees terminate A's interest in part and advance the property to the spouse *absolutely* even if this occurs after April 5, 2008. Otherwise if the divorce occurs after April 2008 the couple will need to consider the potential inheritance tax charges arising both on varying an existing trust to give an interest in possession for A's spouse and in terms of ten year anniversary charges.

Hence after April 2008 variations of existing settlements will be more problematic. It may be possible to argue that a variation of a settlement which gives the spouse a life interest is exempt under s.11 of IHTA. HMRC comment in IHTM 4173:

> "if a settlement is made on divorce or termination of a civil partnership or is a variation of an existing settlement, in so far as it is made in satisfaction of a claim for maintenance of a former spouse or civil partner it is within s 11(1)(a) IHTA."

34.19 **Consider**: A is entitled to an interest in possession in a trust where he is the settlor and it is agreed in divorce proceedings that a life interest should be given to his wife in part of the trust assets. Although A may be excluded from the fund for his wife, he is still taxed on all the gains arising (although not the income of her fund). In these circumstances it may be appropriate to make a sub-fund election under Sch.12 FA 2006.[37]

Would it be preferable to appoint the spouse an interest in possession in a separate settlement? TSI relief will not be available even if this is done before April 6, 2008 and the resettlement will trigger CGT if the assets transferred to the new trust for wife show a gain.[38]

If no new trust is created and the existing trust is simply varied to give A's wife an interest in possession, does A need to be excluded from all benefit in that fund? For income tax purposes if A is the settlor and not excluded from his wife's fund he will be taxed on the income of that fund. If A is the settlor he is taxed on all gains in wife's fund whether or not he can benefit.

Although a transfer on interest in possession trusts for A's spouse before 2008 will be spouse exempt[39] and A's interest has terminated, the reservation of benefit rules should not apply to A,[40] so that he can continue to be a potential beneficiary in the event of his wife's death. However, the POA

---

[36] See fn.31 in Ch. 17; see 17.12.
[37] See 7.72.
[38] See 7.55.
[39] TCGA 1992, s.72(1) (being a TSI).
[40] See s.102(5) and Ch. 24.

regime could apply to A if the wife's part of the trust holds intangibles and A is the settlor. Hence it is desirable that A is excluded from the wife's fund if he is the settlor although he will want to retain a right to reimbursement for any capital gains tax payable by him on gains realised from his wife's fund.

Chapter 35

STAMP DUTY LAND TAX AND STAMP DUTY

- Stamp Duty Land Tax **(35.01)**
- Stamp Duty **(35.06)**

STAMP DUTY LAND TAX

35.01 From December 1, 2003 stamp duty has no longer applied to any contract, conveyance, transfer, grant, lease, surrender, assignment, release or variation of any interest in land[1]. Instead the purchaser (which broadly means the person deriving the benefit of the transaction such as a tenant or a buyer) of an interest in or right over land may be liable for stamp duty land tax ('SDLT') on the chargeable consideration paid[2]. Under SDLT there is no need for any documentation for the tax to be imposed. It is a transaction based tax.

The person acquiring the interest in land is the person liable for SDLT provided that he is a party to the transaction or has given consideration for it. Where the purchaser comprises two or more persons who are jointly entitled to the interest acquired, the liability to pay the tax is joint and several although any of them may in fact discharge it.[3]

The stamp duty legislation did not impose an obligation to stamp an instrument; it merely imposed certain sanctions if the instrument were not stamped. It was therefore viewed as a voluntary tax. SDLT, however, is not voluntary. There is a mandatory requirement on the purchaser in every SDLT transaction to pay the tax due and to account to HMRC for that tax on a self-assessment basis. Payment of SDLT is made by sending to HMRC a land transaction return[4] within 30 days of the effective date of the transaction, together with the tax due (as calculated by the purchaser).

35.02 On delivery of the return and payment of the SDLT, HMRC will issue the taxpayer with a certificate[5] confirming that the return has been delivered.

---

[1] As to the meaning of consideration see post.
[2] See post. As to trusts and powers in relation to stamp duty land tax, see further FA 2003, Sch.16.
[3] For the position of trustees, see 35.02 and 35.04.
[4] The prescribed form is HMRC Land Transaction Return Form SDLT1. No longer are the documents produced to HMRC to have stamps impressed on them recording the duty which has been paid; nor is there any need for a particulars delivered ("PD") form.
[5] HMRC Land Transaction Return Certificate Form SDLT4.

Certain transactions, ones where no SDLT is payable, are not notifiable to HMRC. Instead, the purchaser must complete a self-certificate that no land transaction return is required in respect of the transaction.[6] Without a certificate the Land Registry cannot accept the taxpayer's application for registration of his title.[7] Trustees are personally liable for any SDLT or interest on SDLT though not penalties. SDLT due can be recovered by HMRC from any one of the "responsible trustees" defined in FA 2003, Sch.16, para.5(3) as the persons who are trustees at the effective date of the transaction and any subsequent trustee. The trustee will have rights of recovery from the trust fund or from the other trustees under trust law.

Meaning of consideration

Many land transactions involving trustees and beneficiaries will be outside the SDLT provisions because of the absence of consideration. Note however, that the following may amount to consideration: **35.03**

(i) the assumption of liability for an outstanding debt by the purchaser[8]; note the SDLT thresholds. Even if within the £120,000 threshold for residential property (unless less than £1,000) or £150,000 for non-residential property, an SDLT 1 form must be submitted.

(ii) an exchange of interests in land which is treated as two separate transactions[9];

(iii) the giving of an indemnity by the purchaser to the vendor. Note, however, FA 2003. Sch.4, para.16A (inserted by Regulation) that an indemnity for CGT or IHT given to the trustees is not treated as chargeable consideration[10]; and

(iv) a partition of land when equality money is paid: the SDLT charge being limited to that equality money[11].

Typical trust transactions

In relation to transactions involving land passing into and out of a trust or settlement, the position is as follows: **35.04**

(i) If the settlor transfers land into a settlement, SDLT will not be payable because a land transaction is exempt from charge if there is no

---

[6] As to self-certification, see FA 2003, s.79(3)(b), Sch.11.
[7] FA 2003, s.79(1).
[8] FA 2003, s.50, Sch.4, para.8 as amended by the FA 2004, s.301. In relation to assents and appropriations under wills see the FA 2003, s.49, Sch.3 para.3A(2)–(4) as inserted by the FA 2004, s.300(1). This largely replicates the position that had obtained under the previous stamp duty legislation.
[9] FA 2003, s.47 as amended by the FA 2004, s.326, Sch.42 Pt 4(2) and by SI 2004/1069.
[10] SI 2006/875.
[11] FA 2003, s.50, Sch.4, para.6.

chargeable consideration for the transaction.[12] The trustees will need to self-certify that a land transaction return is not required in respect of the transaction.[13]

(ii) Trustees who buy and sell land are in the same position, so far as SDLT is concerned, as any other vendor or purchaser.[14]

(iii) If land is appointed out to a beneficiary or, at the end of the trust, vested in a beneficiary and is transferred to him, this will normally be an exempt transaction because of the absence of any consideration. The beneficiary will need to self-certify that a land transaction return is not required in respect of the transaction.[15]

(iv) If a power of appointment is exercised over a chargeable interest in land and the person in whose favour it is exercised provides chargeable consideration, SDLT will be charged in the usual way.[16] Such situations will be rare.

(v) If land is switched between the funds of a single settlement (for example land in Fund A is moved to Fund B with securities of equivalent value moving in the opposite direction) then in most cases, it is not considered that there is a land transaction, so that SDLT is not relevant. This is on the assumption that the SDLT definition of settlement carries the capital gains tax meaning. Hence the appropriation as between funds would not constitute a land transaction because there is no acquisition of an interest in land. At one time HMRC were convinced that SDLT would arise on such a transaction. For instance, if Fund A holds land on accumulation and maintenance trusts and Fund B holds assets on interest in possession trusts and those assets are re-appropriated between the funds then has the life tenant of Fund B acquired an interest in land by (in effect) giving up his life interest over the other assets? Is the life tenant a purchaser? Alternatively, if land were to be exchanged between Fund A and Fund B then could the life tenant be taken to have furnished consideration calculated under the normal rules for exchanges: viz on the basis of the value of his life interest in the land acquired?

Initially HMRC accepted that the possibility of a charge in these cases only arose when there was a transfer of land into an interest in possession trust: in the case of other trusts it was impossible to say that any beneficiary had acquired an interest in land. It was widely felt that any attempt to impose SDLT even in the case of an interest in possession trust was misconceived. It was difficult to see how a beneficiary can fairly be said to acquire an interest in land when he is not a party to the swap

---

[12] As to what constitutes chargeable consideration see FA 2003, s.49, Sch.3, para.1, Sch.4, para.1(1).
[13] FA 2003 s.79, Sch.11. As to completion of a self-certificate by trustees, see 35.02 above.
[14] FA 2003, Sch.16, para.4. Reference in the FA 2003 Part 4 to "purchaser" and "vendor" in relation to a land transaction are to the persons acquiring and the person disposing of the subject matter of the transaction: FA 2003, s.43 (4). The trustees are treated as purchasers of the whole of the interest acquired, including the beneficial interest. Hence although the interest in possession beneficiary becomes entitled to an interest in the land he is not a purchaser for SDLT purposes.
[15] FA 2003, Sch.11. An area of doubt used to surround the position if the beneficiary agreed to indemnify the trustees, eg, against future inheritance tax charges. See now SI 2006/875 providing that IHT and CGT indemnity given to trustees do not count as consideration.
[16] FA 2003, Sch.16, para.7

transaction and, indeed, may be unaware of it. Even under the interest in possession trust the life tenant does not acquire any right to the capital, only to the income. Often his life interest would be valueless anyway given that the trustees might have power to terminate it. The uncertainty has now been resolved by FA 2006, s.165 which inserts a new para.8 in FA 2003, Sch.16 and provides that the mere giving of consent by a beneficiary to his acquisition of property under a settlement and his ceasing to have an interest in other trust property vested in trustees shall not amount to chargeable consideration. It is effective for any acquisition of an interest of which the effective date is on or after Royal Assent—July 19, 2006. Note that it only applies to an exchange within two funds of one trust. An exchange of land between two family trusts (with or without payment of any equality money) or the acquisition of land for cash by one trust from another will attract SDLT in the ordinary way.

(vi) If a beneficiary gives up his interest in a trust which holds land (for example a life tenant surrenders his interest) it is considered that there is no SDLT liability.

(vii) In relation to a trust of land, if the life tenant and remaindermen agree to partition the land, for example on an actuarial basis where the life tenant receives 30 per cent and the remaindermen 70 per cent, it is thought that no SDLT is payable.[17] Where there is a partition for consideration the rule in Sch.4, para.6 is that only any equality money or other value counts as chargeable consideration.

(viii) The acquisition of a chargeable interest in land by a bare trustee is treated as an acquisition by the beneficial owner of the land.[18] The grant of a lease to a bare trustee is, however, treated as a grant to the trustee, not to the beneficiary.[19]

(ix) Trustees are treated as a single and continuing body so that a change of trustees of a trust fund which includes land, where the new trustees take on existing trust borrowings or agree to indemnify the retiring trustees in respect of claims against them (that is, where the new trustees acquire an interest in land for valuable consideration), will not lead to any liability to tax.[20]

(x) If a settlor settles land on an interest in possession trust for his wife under which that interest ends after seven days, subject to which the

---

[17] See FA 2003, s.50, Sch.4, para.6 (partition or division of a chargeable interest to which persons are jointly entitled). It is understood that HMRC interpret "jointly entitled" as covering the case where persons are entitled in succession as well as concurrently: *c.f.* the capital gains tax position, for which see *Kidson (Inspector of Taxes) v Macdonald* [1974] Ch. 339, [1974] 1 All ER 849, [1974] S.T.C. 54.

[18] FA 2003, Sch.16, para.3(1) as substituted by the F(No 2)A 2005 s 49, Sch.10, paras 1, 11 in relation to leases granted after May 19, 2005.

[19] FA 2003, Sch.16, para.3(3).

[20] See in relation to CGT: TCGA 1992, s.69(1) and see *Stamp Duty Land Tax Manual SDLTM31750: Application: Trusts and powers* (changes in trustees of a pension fund) and revised SDLT manual at 31745. This is despite the fact that the new trustees are taking on liabilities and therefore might be regarded as giving consideration and therefore outside the para.1 Sch.3 exemption. See Sch.4, para.8(1A) and (1B). "A change in the composition of trustees is not a land transaction –this means in particular that there is no charge on such an occasion where trust property is secured by a mortgage or other borrowing."

property is held for the settlor absolutely, then, if during the seven day period the settlor sells his remainder interest to a purchaser, it is thought that SDLT will be payable. This SDLT avoidance device will arguably not work because the purchaser will acquire (in the form of a remainder interest) a significant interest in land on which SDLT is payable.

(xi) In relation to nil rate band discretionary will trusts[21] a stamp duty land tax liability may arise in certain cases, for example on the transfer of the matrimonial home or other land to the surviving spouse if the beneficiary is deemed to have given chargeable consideration. For example, where trustees accept a promise to pay in satisfaction of the pecuniary legacy and in consideration of that promise land is transferred to the surviving spouse or where land is transferred to the surviving spouse and the spouse charges the property with payment of the amount of the pecuniary legacy. In the latter case the charge is money's worth and so is chargeable consideration for SDLT purposes. However, where the personal representatives charge land with the payment of the pecuniary legacy and the trustees have no right to enforce payment of the amount of the legacy personally against the owner of the land for the time being and the property is assented to the surviving spouse subject to the charge, there is no chargeable consideration for SDLT purposes provided that the assent doesn't result in change in the rights or liabilities of any person in relation to the debt secured by the charge.[22]

35.05 When a pension scheme merges with another pension scheme or there are other transfers of assets between such schemes, to the extent that the assets comprise interests in land and the consideration for the transfer of the transferring pension scheme's assets comprises only the assumption by the receiving scheme of the obligation to pay pension benefits (and any other approved benefits permitted by HMRC to be provided by approved pension schemes) to the former members of the transferring scheme, no SDLT charge will arise.[23]

For the SDLT position on deeds of variations, See 29.42.

STAMP DUTY

Instruments relating to stock and marketable securities

35.06 The stamp duty regime, with its exemptions, continues to apply to stock and marketable securities.[24] Trustees purchasing shares will accordingly suffer stamp duty at 0.5 per cent. As a result of the introduction of SDLT, FA 2003

---

[21] See Ch. 28.
[22] See *Stamp duty land tax and "nil-rate band discretionary trusts"* reproduced in App. III A3.16.
[23] See further *Pension Schemes—Stamp Duty, SDRT and SDLT* (June 6, 2005) available from HMRC.
[24] FA 2003, s.125 as amended by the FA 2003, s.296, Sch.39.

limits stamp duty to "*instruments relating to stock and marketable securities*". "Relating to" is "somewhat vague but the position is thought to be as follows:

(i) the usual 0.5 per cent duty will be payable on all purchases of stock and marketable securities;

(ii) when stock is transferred for no consideration (as for instance when it is settled and transferred into the names of the trustees) duty is not payable and the usual certificate (viz that the transfer falls under Category L in the Schedule to the Stamp Duty (Exempt Instruments) Regulations 1987) should be included in the stock transfer form;

(iii) declarations of trust—which formerly attracted a £5 fixed duty stamp—are no longer stampable unless they "relate to stock and marketable securities". This will be the case if the settlor declares himself a trustee over shares which he owns when the fixed stamp duty will still be appropriate.

When a pension scheme merges with another pension scheme or there are other transfers of assets between such schemes, if the consideration for the transfer of assets comprises only the assumption by the receiving scheme of the obligation to pay pension benefits (and any other approved benefits permitted by HMRC to be provided by approved pension schemes) to the former members of the transferring scheme, no SDRT charge will arise nor will any ad valorem stamp duty arise. However, where the assets comprise stock or marketable securities, each stock transfer form will be subject to fixed rate duty of £5.[25] **35.07**

---

[25] See further *Pension Schemes—Stamp Duty, SDRT and SDLT* (June 6, 2005) available from HMRC.

CHAPTER 36

COMPLIANCE AND DISCLOSURE

- Delivery of inheritance tax accounts **(36.02)**
- Information powers **(36.10)**
- Disclosure rules for tax avoidance schemes **(36.13)**

36.01 This chapter considers briefly when an IHT account needs to be submitted to HMRC and by whom and then looks at the tax disclosure rules.[1] Accounts detailing the relevant transfer are required only from the personal representatives of a deceased person and in the case of lifetime transfers from limited categories of other persons who are liable for tax—see s.216 of IHTA 1984. Very exceptionally, an account may be required from a person who is not liable.

DELIVERY OF INHERITANCE TAX ACCOUNTS

36.02 There is no need to notify exempt transfers or PETs (which are assumed to be exempt when made unless and until the donor dies within seven years) to HMRC or send in an account. An account is only required of a PET if the transferor dies within seven years. HMRC need not be notified of a transfer of excluded property.

Transfers which are exempt as normal expenditure out of income need not be reported even if they are to an *inter vivos* trust although the transferor should keep annual records demonstrating the basis of the claim that the transfer is made out of income. See Appendix III A3.143.

EXAMPLE 30.1

(1) H is a city trader with an annual salary of £4m. He decides to give £100,000 into trust for his nieces every year for the foreseeable future. Such transfer is made out of his surplus income and is exempt from IHT even though into a trust.[2] However, the trust will still face the 10-year

[1] POA is an income tax and therefore subject to the disclosure rules.
[2] IHTA 1984, s.21.

anniversary and exit charges calculated in the normal way, even though the original transfer was exempt.[3]

(2) F is a foreign domiciliary who sets up a discretionary trust containing non-UK situs property worth £10m. Although the gift is into a settlement it is an excluded property trust and does not need to be reported. There are no 10-year or exit charges provided the trust owns no UK-situated property at those dates.

Notification of lifetime transfers: the following must be notified as set out below and an IHT100 account submitted to HMRC. The person primarily liable for inheritance tax and notification on a chargeable lifetime transfer is the transferor.[4] **36.03**

1. Every person who is liable as transferor for tax on *a chargeable transfer* is liable to submit an account even if the transfer is within his nil rate band.[5] So an individual setting up a nil rate band *inter vivos* trust *of any sort* on or after March 21, 2006 must now submit an IHT100 unless the trust is for a disabled person or the transfer falls under the normal expenditure example. This is subject to the excepted regulations outlined below.

2. Every trustee liable for tax on a notional transfer of value (e.g. a life tenant whose life interest has ceased *inter vivos* in favour of relevant property trusts (a chargeable transfer) or who has died) must submit an account.[6] In theory, the obligation on the trustees is to submit an account whether or not the transfer of value made by the life tenant is chargeable or exempt. However, HMRC do not in practice require this in relation to PETs unless the PET has become chargeable because the life tenant has died within seven years. If it is intended to use the interest in possession beneficiary's annual exemption against the transfer made on termination of his interest in part or whole, notification must be given by the interest in possession beneficiary to the trustees of the availability of the annual exemption and the notice submitted to HMRC within six months of the transfer.[7]

3. The donee of *a failed PET* must deliver an account to HMRC within 12 months of the end of the month of the donor's death. Personal representatives must also report such transfers. Tax on the failed PET (if any) is payable six months after the end of the month of death.

4. *Failed deemed PETs.* (e.g. where a person ceases to reserve a benefit[8] or repays a non-allowable debt[9]). The person whose estate has been

---

[3] Note that the calculations will be complicated by the fact that each payment will be an addition of property: see 20.05 and 20.27.
[4] IHTA 1984, s.199 although note certain cases where spouse can be held liable as a transferor to prevent him divesting himself of property to his spouse so that he is unable to meet the tax bill—s.203 of the IHTA 1984. The transferee can be made liable if the transferor does not pay it, e.g. discretionary trustees.
[5] s.216.
[6] s.216(1)(b). The trustees need not submit an account if the personal representatives have submitted an account.
[7] IHTA 1984, s.57.
[8] FA 1986, s.103(4).
[9] FA 1986, s.103.

increased must submit an account if the transferor dies within seven years of either event.

5. *Reservation of benefit.* Where property is clawed back into a person's estate on his death under the reservation of benefit provisions, any person in whom the property is vested at any time after the death should submit an account.

6. *Exit and periodic charges.* Every trustee liable for tax on an exit or periodic charge or who would be liable if tax were chargeable must submit an account.[10] This is subject to the excepted regulations considered below.

36.04 **Excepted lifetime chargeable transfers:** Regulations[11] eliminate the need to submit accounts in respect of certain small lifetime chargeable transfers. It is expected that the limits will be increased now that most lifetime transfers into trust will be chargeable.

No account need be submitted in respect of an excepted transfer which is an actual disposition by an *individual* where:

(i) the value transferred by that chargeable transfer and any other chargeable transfers made by the transferor in the same year ending with April 5 does not exceed £10,000 and

(ii) the aggregate value transferred by that and all previous chargeable transfers within 10 years does not exceed £40,000.[12]

36.05 This does not relieve trustees of relevant property trusts from having to submit accounts on very small values at a 10-year anniversary. In response to representations on the burden that this requirement imposed in relation to pilot trusts and trusts holding life term assurance policies of minimal value, SI 2002/1732 dispensed with the need to deliver an account of the property comprised in an excepted settlement, i.e. where no qualifying interest in possession subsists on the occasion of a chargeable event under ss.64 or 65 of IHTA 1984 on or after April 6, 2002 and where:

(a) the settled funds consist only of cash;

(b) after making the settlement, the settlor added no further property to the settlement;

(c) the trustees have been resident in the United Kingdom throughout the existence of the settlement;

(d) the gross value of the settled property at the time of the chargeable event does not exceed £1,000 and

(e) there are no related settlements as defined in s.62 of IHTA 1984.

---

[10] s.216(1)(c).
[11] Inheritance Tax (Delivery of Accounts) (Excepted Transfers and Excepted Terminations) Regulations 2002 (SI 2002/1731).
[12] There are also limited let outs for "excepted terminations" where there is a lifetime termination of an interest in possession.

Accounts in the case of transfers on death: s.216(1) requires the personal representatives of a deceased person to deliver an account (IHT200) specifying all the property which formed part of the deceased's estate immediately before his death including property in which the deceased was beneficially entitled to an interest in possession and property over which he had a general power. However, there have been a series of regulations for "excepted estates" when there is no need for an account to be presented. **36.06**

An excepted estate[13] is defined as an estate where the total gross value of the estate immediately before death does not exceed a specified amount, currently £285,000 for deaths on or after April 6, 2006 where an application for a grant is made on or after August 6, 2006. **36.07**

Conditions: apart from the gross value, other conditions are:

- any trust assets in which the deceased had an interest in possession were held in a single trust and do not exceed £150,000 in value (increased from £100,000);
- non-UK property does not exceed £100,000 in value (increased from £75,000);
- any chargeable lifetime gifts made within seven years before death were only of cash, quoted shares or securities or land and buildings (and contents given at the same time) which did not exceed £150,000 (increased from £100,000) in total; and
- the deceased had not at any time made a gift subject to a reservation of benefit.

Where the deceased died non-UK domiciled (and had never been domiciled or treated as domiciled in the United Kingdom), the estate will be excepted if the value of UK assets does not in total exceed £150,000 (increased from £100,000) and consists only of cash or quoted shares or securities. **36.08**

Any estate where a charge arises on an alternatively secured pension fund under IHTA 1984, s.151A–C is excluded from qualifying as an excepted estate.

Miscellaneous points on the payment of tax: note the following: **36.09**

(i) in certain circumstances IHT can be paid by instalments: see IHTA 1984, ss.227–229;

(ii) the liability of trustees to pay tax (e.g. on the death of the life tenant) means that they need to exercise caution in distributing the trust fund;

(iii) in three situations personal representatives may incur a liability if the person primarily accountable for the tax fails to pay within 12 months after the end of the month of death. These occasions are:

- when a chargeable lifetime transfer is subject to additional IHT because of the death of the settlor within seven years (e.g. a settlement where the trustees are primarily liable);
- a failed PET. In this case the donee is primarily liable for the tax. A difficulty for PRs is that such transfers may turn up years after

---

[13] See SI 2002/1733, amended by SI 2003/1658.

the death, long after they have distributed the estate. In these circumstances limited comfort is provided by a letter dated February 11, 1991 and sent by HMRC to the Law Society;
- if the estate includes property subject to a reservation of benefit. The primary liability is on the owner of the property (the donee) and in this case the PR are given a statutory right to recover any tax which they pay against that person.[14]

INFORMATION POWERS

36.10 Under IHTA 1984, s.218(1) and (2) where any person, in the course of a trade or profession (other than that of a barrister) carried on by him, has been concerned with making a settlement (otherwise than by will) and knows or has reason to believe

(i) that the settlor was domiciled in the United Kingdom; *and*

(ii) that the trustees are not or will not be resident in the United Kingdom,

he must, within three months of the making of the settlement, make a return to the Board stating the names and addresses of the settlor and the trustees.[15]

When are trustees regarded as UK resident for the purposes of s.218? General administration must be carried on in the United Kingdom and a majority of trustees be UK resident.

36.11 The precise scope of this reporting duty has been somewhat unclear: foreign lawyers working in the UK have, for instance, sometimes taken the view that they are not obliged to make a return. It now appears that HMRC take a wide view of the scope of this provision to include non-resident advisers:

> "Capital transfer tax was and inheritance tax is eligible against persons domiciled in the UK on their property worldwide. Settled property, where the settlor was domiciled in the UK, is similarly so chargeable. You should bear in mind that for inheritance tax purposes the term 'domiciled in the UK' includes persons so domiciled under general law and also those deemed to be domiciled in the UK by section 267 of the Act.... It was established in *IDC v Stype Investments (Jersey) Ltd Re Clore (deceased)* (1982) S.T.C. 625 by the Court of Appeal that the English courts have jurisdiction over causes of action which arise in England against that Jersey company ... We consider that the obligations imposed by s.218 IHTA 1984 in connection with UK domiciled settlors have extra-territorial effect for the same reasons ... that leading counsel has advised at least one non-resident trustee company that that is indeed his opinion ... section 218 places the duty upon any 'person' rather than upon an 'individual'...The words in the course of a trade or profession are deliberately widely drawn and do not necessarily require that a payment or fee be made for the activity involved in the making of a set-

---

[14] IHTA 1984, s.211(3). In other cases any recovery is more problematic, see PCB, 1998 at p.58.
[15] See also the general information powers contained in IHTA 1984, s.219 and s.219A.

tlement. The phrase 'concerned with' is sufficiently broad to include persons through whom funds are transmitted. The persons or firms typically obliged to make the return include the solicitors accountants IFAs banks assurance companies or trustee companies or other professionals in any way involved in or concerned with the making of the settlement. The term 'settlement' embraces a broad variety of trusts beyond the obvious settlements and includes for example employee benefit trusts, pension schemes and insurance policies written in trust. . .On a strict reading of the section it is not a requirement that the making of the settlement involves a chargeable transfer. A settlement made by A on himself for an interest in possession which may be defeasible by the action of trustees where those trustees are not UK resident is quite common and would not give rise to a chargeable transfer. The creation of such a settlement is nonetheless within the ambit of section 218.

Given that there are certain inheritance tax advantages attached to employee benefit trusts, there is no reason in principle why the notification requirements of section 218 should not apply to these where the trustees are outside of the UK. Although the concept of a company having a domicile does not feature widely in the world of taxation, attention being more commonly directed towards central management and control, when we turn to inheritance tax we are mainly concerned with issues of domicile and situs but not those of management and control. The person domiciled in the UK referred to in section 218 could therefore be a company.

The terms 'settlement' and 'settlor' are defined in sections 43 and 44 of the Act. Your attention is particularly drawn to the latter—'settlor' in relation to a settlement, includes any person by whom the settlement was made directly or indirectly and in particular . . . includes any person who has provided funds directly or indirectly for the purposes of or in connection with the settlement or has made with any person a reciprocal arrangement for that other person to make the settlement. So, for example, where a non-UK trust company makes a declaration of trust to which pre-existing settlement a UK domiciled person causes property to be added, then that person becomes a settlor and the settlement, is to that extent than made by him. Any person involved with the transmission of property in those circumstances could be 'concerned with the making of a settlement' for the purposes of section 218.

There is no prescribed form for making returns: they are normally simply made by letter referring to section 218 which states the date and name of the settlement or trust, together with the names and addresses specified by section 218(1). Returns should be made to IR Capital Taxes Ferrers House Nottingham."

36.12 The penalties for failure to make a return under s.218 are contained in s.245A as added by s.198 of FA 1999. Persons in default are liable to a penalty not exceeding £300 and to a further penalty not exceeding £60 per day if the failure continues after it has been declared by a court or the Special Commissioners.

It should be remembered that just because a settlement is offshore does not mean that the usual inheritance tax rules do not apply. Hence, an offshore trust which is discretionary will still be a chargeable transfer if made by a UK domiciled settlor and the transferor must deliver an account unless the chargeable transfer does not exceed £10,000 and the aggregate value transferred by that and all previous chargeable transfers within 10 years does not exceed £40,000.[16]

DISCLOSURE RULES FOR TAX AVOIDANCE SCHEMES

36.13 In his 2004 Budget, the Chancellor announced his intention to introduce a regime under which promoters of tax-avoidance schemes would be required to disclose such schemes to the Inland Revenue soon after they were first promoted. So far a general anti-avoidance regime rule has not been introduced. Presumably if the Government feels that the disclosure regime fails to put a stop to artificial avoidance a general anti-avoidance rule will follow.

There are separate disclosure regimes for direct and indirect taxes. This chapter briefly summarises the rules applicable for direct taxes as amended in the FA 2006. The intention of the disclosure rules is to give HMRC early warning of tax-avoidance schemes so that they can then decide whether the law needs to be changed. Whilst "standard" tax planning is not intended to be within the disclosure regime it has proved difficult to define exactly where the boundaries lie between the sort of planning that ministers wish to stop and the sort of planning which is regarded as legitimate. Hence the difficulties in defining what needs to be disclosed.

36.14 The primary legislation for direct taxes is found in FA 2004, ss.306–319. However the meat of the provisions is found in various regulations. There is also extensive HMRC guidance on the operation of the regime.[17]

It is important to understand that the disclosure regime is not restricted to packaged tax-avoidance products but can cover bespoke planning. The disclosure requirements cover arrangements involving income tax, corporation tax and capital gains tax avoidance but notably exclude inheritance tax and national insurance. (SDLT and VAT have separate disclosure regimes not discussed here.)

36.15 **Basic rules regarding the way in which the disclosure regime operates:** from August 1, 2004 a promoter of a tax scheme is required to disclose that scheme to HMRC if certain conditions are satisfied. In certain circumstances the obligation falls instead on the user of the scheme rather than the promoter. From August 1, 2006 disclosure of a wider range of schemes is required.

Where disclosure is required a report has to be made to HMRC at the Anti-Avoidance Intelligence Group (Intelligence) AIG on a specified form. It is not necessary to disclose details of the client when the disclosure is made but disclosure must include a description of the scheme including information about each element involved, the accepted tax consequences and the statutory provisions relied upon.

---

[16] See IHTA 1984, s.216 and SI 2002/1731.
[17] See the Tax Avoidance Schemes (Promoters and Prescribed Circumstances) Regs 2004 (SI 2004/1065); SI 2004/1865 as amended by the Tax Avoidance Schemes (Information) Regs 2004 (SI 2004/2613) and the Tax Avoidance Schemes (Promoters, Prescribed Circumstances and Information) (Amendment) Regs 2004. The Tax Avoidance Schemes (Prescribed Descriptions of Arrangements) Regs 2004 (SI 2004/1863); the Tax Avoidance Schemes (Prescribed Descriptions of Arrangements) (Amendment) Regs 2004 (SI 2004/2429); SI 2004/2613—SI 2006/1543.

Once the scheme has been reported it does not have to be reported again by the same promoter whether it is used by the same or other clients. HMRC issue a reference number for the scheme within 30 days of receipt of the disclosure notice. The promoter is required then to issue all clients who use the scheme with that reference number within 30 days of the date on which he first becomes aware that the client has taken the first step to implement the scheme. The client is then required to disclose the reference number on his tax return. No other specific disclosure about the scheme has to be made on his return and the normal date for the submission of the return is not affected. If a client fails to include a number on their tax return when they have used a scheme that has been disclosed there is a penalty imposed of £100 initially increasing to £1,000 for three or more failures.

A penalty is imposed of £5,000 on a promoter for each failure to disclose with the possibility of £600 per day for persistent failure.

The taxpayer will be required to disclose if it is an in-house scheme or the scheme was provided by a foreign promoter who has not registered with HMRC in which case the taxpayer will himself be required to disclose the details of the scheme on his tax return. The promoter must disclose the scheme within five days of the date on which the scheme is made available for implementation. This is defined as the date the scheme was first marketed to a client or, if earlier, when implementation actually started.

36.16 *Definition of promoter:* there are two types of promoters: those who design schemes and those who make them available for implementation by others. A promoter is defined as somebody who in the course of a relevant business is responsible for the design, organisation and management of the proposed or actual arrangements to any extent or makes a notifiable proposal available for implementation by others. The relevant business is any business involving taxation services or carried on by a bank or securities house. Lawyers, accountants and tax consultants will clearly be promoters but other types of professional such as valuers who also give tax advice may be within the scope of this definition.

Difficulties can arise where an adviser merely comments on a scheme that someone else has designed in terms of advising whether it works—has he designed it himself? If a firm just provides trust administration services in relation to a scheme which it has not designed or marketed then it will not be a promoter provided that it is not connected with a person who is responsible for the design of the scheme. A company which provides tax services to other members of the same group of companies is not a promoter because it is subject to its own in-house disclosure regime which is separate.

An employee of a firm which is a promoter will not be a promoter in his own right.

It may be the case that there is more than one promoter because more than one firm of advisers is involved in the design or implementation of the scheme. Where this occurs s.308(4) provides that compliance by any of the promoters discharges the duty to disclose of the others. Of course there may be difficulties in establishing whether a promoter has actually disclosed or how a particular scheme is disclosed.

If there is an overseas promoter the client must notify HMRC of the scheme within five days of entering into the scheme if the offshore promoter has not done so.

Legal professional privilege: While s.314 of FA 2004 expressly preserved legal professional privilege, initially HMRC maintained that LPP was not in itself jeopardised by disclosure because the rules give details of the product rather than the client. The Law Society advised that advice to clients on tax measures is protected by LPP and did not have to be disclosed. Accountants then objected that lawyers had a commercial advantage because their schemes would not be subject to disclosure. The result was amended rules which require clients to make disclosure in place of the promoter where the promoter believes the scheme is protected by LPP.

36.17 **What schemes need to be disclosed?** Initially it was intended that the disclosure requirements would apply to schemes involving employment or financial products where capital gains tax, income tax or corporation tax was being avoided. Financial product was widely defined and included any loan or share where the tax advantage arose "to a significant degree" from the inclusion of the financial product in the arrangements. Hence, even where the overall aim was to save inheritance tax, a scheme might still be disclosable if part of its structure related to the inclusion of a financial product which gave rise to a capital gains tax, income tax or corporation tax advantage and the tax advantage was the main benefit or one of the main benefits that might be expected to arise under the scheme.[18]

EXAMPLE 36.3

> X wishes to give land to his children with a view to saving inheritance tax on his death. The land shows a significant gain. He enters into a scheme under which capital gains tax is avoided; the scheme involves a loan. Despite the fact that the aim is to save inheritance tax, it may still be disclosable given that a loan is a financial product.

36.18 Originally there were certain "filters" or exclusions to ensure that routine tax planning was excluded. If the arrangements passed the premium fee test, the confidentiality test **and** the off-market terms test, they did not have to be disclosed.

Under the new regulations in force from August 1, 2006, however, the requirement to disclose is extended to cover all arrangements involving an income tax, corporation tax or capital gains tax advantage with the restriction to financial or employment products being removed. The filters have been removed. Instead disclosure is required if one of a series of "hallmarks" applies. Arrangements are required to be disclosed where:

1. Any element of the arrangements giving rise to the tax advantage would be exepcted to be kept confidential from any competing promoter or HMRC.

2. They are likely to command the payment of a fee, the amount of which is contingent on or attributable to a tax saving by a client with experience of purchasing sophisticated tax services.

---

[18] Tax-advantage is defined as: relief or increased relief from or a repayment or increased repayment of tax or the avoidance or reduction of a charge to tax or of an assessment to that tax or the avoidance of a possible assessment to that tax or deferral of any payment of tax or advancement of any repayment of tax or avoidance of any obligation.

3. The promoter of the scheme is also a party to it (such as a bank) and the product is not offered on similar terms to those that can be obtained in the open market for a product that is the same or broadly similar;
4. They are mass-marketed tax products historically associated with unacceptable tax avoidance. Certain schemes are exempted, e.g. SAYE option schemes; EMIs; pension schemes; ISAs.
5. They are loss-making schemes used by high-wealth individuals to reduce their income tax or capital gains tax liability, or
6. They are leasing arrangements containing features associated with avoidance.

APPENDICES

APPENDIX I

LEGISLATION
Inheritance Act 1984	**A1.01**
Finance Act 1986	**A1.23**
Taxation of Chargeable Gains Act 1992	**A1.31**

APPENDIX II

PRECEDENTS
Bare trust	**A2.01**
Disabled person's trust	**A2.09**
Bereaved minor trust	**A2.25**
18–25 trust	**A2.26**
Specimen Will clauses	**A2.27**
IPDI Trust of Residue for (Minor) Children	**A2.43**
Debt/Charge Documents	**A2.47**
Deed of Variation	**A2.51**
Disclaimer of a Life Interest	**A2.62**
Appointment of IPDI Trust	**A2.64**

APPENDIX III

MISCELLANEOUS MATERIAL
BN 25	**A3.01**
SDLT and NRBDT: HMRC statement	**A3.16**
POA Guidance Notes	**A3.21**
POA COP 10 Letter	**A3.61**
Schedule 20: Questions and Answers	**A3.105**
Tax Bulletin 83: HMRC Statement on *Hastings-Bass*	**A3.148**
POA correspondence with HMRC on elections	**A3.149**

APPENDIX IV

Examples of the IHT charging provisions for relevant property trusts	**A4.01**

APPENDIX I

LEGISLATION

IHTA 1984 .... **A1.01**
    s.3A (PET definition):
    s.5 (meaning of estate);
    s.49–49E (interests in possession; IPDIs and TSIs);
    s.71 (A&M trusts)
    s.71 A–C (BMT)
    s.71D–G (18–25 trusts)
    s.142 (variations);
    s.144 (two year will trusts)

FA 1986: ss.102–3; Sch.20 para.4A, 5 (reservation of benefit) **A1.23**

TCGA 1992: ss.71–74 (settled property: deemed disposals) **A1.31**

INHERITANCE TAX ACT 1984

A1.01   **s.3A Potentially exempt transfers**

(1) Any reference in this Act to a potentially exempt transfer is a reference to a transfer of value—

- (a) which is made by an individual on or after 18th March 1986 but before 22nd March 2006; and
- (b) which, apart from this section, would be a chargeable transfer (or to the extent to which, apart from this section, it would be such a transfer); and
- (c) to the extent that it constitutes either a gift to another individual or a gift into an accumulation and maintenance trust or a disabled trust.

(1A) Any reference in this Act to a potentially exempt transfer is also a reference to a transfer of value—

- (a) which is made by an individual on or after 22nd March 2006,
- (b) which, apart from this section, would be a chargeable transfer (or to the extent to which, apart from this section, it would be such a transfer), and
- (c) to the extent that it constitutes—
    - (i) a gift to another individual,
    - (ii) a gift into a disabled trust, or
    - (iii) a gift into a bereaved minor's trust on the coming to an end of an immediate post-death interest.

(1B) Subsections (1) and (1A) above have effect subject to any provision of this Act which provides that a disposition (or transfer of value) of a particular description is not a potentially exempt transfer.

(2) Subject to subsection (6) below, a transfer of value falls within subsection (1)(c) or (1A)(c)(i) above, as a gift to another individual,—

- (a) to the extent that the value transferred is attributable to property which, by virtue of the transfer, becomes comprised in the estate of that other individual, or
- (b) so far as that value is not attributable to property which becomes comprised in the estate of another person, to the extent that, by virtue of the transfer, the estate of that other individual is increased.

(3) Subject to subsection (6) below, a transfer of value falls within subsection (1)(c) above, as a gift into an accumulation and maintenance trust or a disabled trust, to the

extent that the value transferred is attributable to property which, by virtue of the transfer, becomes settled property to which section 71 or 89 of this Act applies.

(3A) Subject to subsection (6) below, a transfer of value falls within subsection (1A)(c)(ii) above to the extent that the value transferred is attributable to property which, by virtue of the transfer, becomes settled property to which section 89 below applies.

(3B) A transfer of value falls within subsection (1A)(c)(iii) above to the extent that the value transferred is attributable to settled property (whenever settled) that becomes property to which section 71A below applies in the following circumstances—

(a) under the settlement, a person ("L") is beneficially entitled to an interest in possession in the settled property,

(b) the interest in possession is an immediate post-death interest,

(c) on or after 22nd March 2006, but during L's life, the interest in possession comes to an end,

(d) L is beneficially entitled to the interest in possession immediately before it comes to an end, and

(e) on the interest in possession coming to an end, the property—

    (i) continues to be held on the trusts of the settlement, and
    (ii) becomes property to which section 71A below applies.

(4) A potentially exempt transfer which is made seven years or more before the death of the transferor is an exempt transfer and any other potentially exempt transfer is a chargeable transfer.

(5) During the period beginning on the date of a potentially exempt transfer and ending immediately before—

(a) the seventh anniversary of that date, or

(b) if it is earlier, the death of the transferor,

it shall be assumed for the purposes of this Act that the transfer will prove to be an exempt transfer.

(6) Where, under any provision of this Act other than section 52 tax is in any circumstances to be charged as if a transfer of value had been made, that transfer shall be taken to be a transfer which is not a potentially exempt transfer.

(7) In the application of this section to an event on the happening of which tax is chargeable under section 52 below, the reference in [subsection (1)(a) or (1A)(a)][1] above to the individual by whom the transfer of value is made is a reference to the person who, by virtue of section 3(4) above, is treated as the transferor.

s.5 Meaning of estate   A1.02

(1) For the purposes of this Act a person's estate is the aggregate of all the property to which he is beneficially entitled, except that—

(a) the estate of a person—

    (i) does not include an interest in possession in settled property to which section 71A or 71D below applies, and
    (ii) does not include an interest in possession that falls within subsection (1A) below, and

---

[1] Words inserted by Finance Act (2006 c.25), Sch.20(3), para.9(6).

(b) the estate of a person immediately before his death does not include excluded property.

(1A) An interest in possession falls within this subsection if—

(a) it is an interest in possession in settled property,

(b) the settled property is not property to which section 71A or 71D below applies,

(c) the person is beneficially entitled to the interest in possession,

(d) the person became beneficially entitled to the interest in possession on or after 22nd March 2006, and

(e) the interest in possession is—

    (i) not an immediate post-death interest,
    (ii) not a disabled person's interest, and
    (iii) not a transitional serial interest.[2]

(2) A person who has a general power which enables him, or would if he were sui juris enable him, to dispose of any property other than settled property, or to charge money on any property other than settled property, shall be treated as beneficially entitled to the property or money; and for this purpose "general power" means a power or authority enabling the person by whom it is exercisable to appoint or dispose of property as he thinks fit.

(3) In determining the value of a person's estate at any time his liabilities at that time shall be taken into account, except as otherwise provided by this Act.

(4) The liabilities to be taken into account in determining the value of a transferor's estate immediately after a transfer of value include his liability for inheritance tax[3] on the value transferred but not his liability (if any) for any other tax or duty resulting from the transfer.

(5) Except in the case of a liability imposed by law, a liability incurred by a transferor shall be taken into account only to the extent that it was incurred for a consideration in money or money's worth.

A1.03   s.49 Treatment of interest in possession

(1) A person beneficially entitled to an interest in possession in settled property shall be treated for the purposes of this Act as beneficially entitled to the property in which the interest subsists.

(1A) Where the interest in possession mentioned in subsection (1) above is one to which the person becomes beneficially entitled on or after 22nd March 2006, subsection (1) above applies in relation to that interest only if, and for so long as, it is—

(a) an immediate post-death interest,

(b) a disabled person's interest, or

(c) a transitional serial interest.

(1B) Where the interest in possession mentioned in subsection (1) above is one to which the person became beneficially entitled before 22nd March subsection (1) above does not apply in relation to that interest at any time when section 71A below applies to the property in which the interest subsists.[4]

---

[2] Added by Finance Act (2006 c.25), Sch.20(3) para.10(3).
[3] See Finance Act 1986, s.100(1) and (2)—for any liability to tax arising on and after 25 July 1986 any reference in the legislation to capital transfer tax has effect as a reference to inheritance tax.
[4] Added by Finance Act (2006 c.25), Sch.20(2) para.4(1).

(2) Where a person becomes entitled to an interest in possession in settled property as a result of a disposition for a consideration in money or money's worth, any question whether and to what extent the giving of the consideration is a transfer of value or chargeable transfer shall be determined without regard to subsection (1) above.

s.49A Immediate post-death interest

A1.04

(1) Where a person ("L") is beneficially entitled to an interest in possession in settled property, for the purposes of this Chapter that interest is an "immediate post-death interest" only if the following conditions are satisfied.
(2) Condition 1 is that the settlement was effected by will or under the law relating to intestacy.
(3) Condition 2 is that L became beneficially entitled to the interest in possession on the death of the testator or intestate.
(4) Condition 3 is that—

- (a) section 71A below does not apply to the property in which the interest subsists, and
- (b) the interest is not a disabled person's interest.

(5) Condition 4 is that Condition 3 has been satisfied at all times since L became beneficially entitled to the interest in possession.[5]

s.49B Transitional serial interests

A1.05

Where a person is beneficially entitled to an interest in possession in settled property, for the purposes of this Chapter that interest is a "transitional serial interest" only—

- (a) if section 49C or 49D below so provides, or
- (b) if, and to the extent that, section 49E below so provides.[6]

Notes:
By Finance Act 1986, section 100(1), on and after 25 July 1986 the Capital Transfer Tax Act 1984 may be cited as the Inheritance Tax Act 1984.

s.49C Transitional serial interest: interest to which person becomes entitled during period 22nd March 2006 to 5th April 2008

A1.06

(1) Where a person ("B") is beneficially entitled to an interest in possession in settled property ("the current interest"), that interest is a transitional serial interest for the purposes of this Chapter if the following conditions are met.
(2) Condition 1 is that—

- (a) the settlement commenced before 22nd March 2006, and
- (b) immediately before 22nd March 2006, the property then comprised in the settlement was property in which B, or some other person, was beneficially entitled to an interest in possession ("the prior interest").

---

[5] Added by Finance Act (2006 c.25), Sch.20(2) para.5(1).
[6] Added by Finance Act (2006 c.25), Sch.20(2) para.5(1).

(3) Condition 2 is that the prior interest came to an end at a time on or after 22nd March 2006 but before 6th April 2008.

(4) Condition 3 is that B became beneficially entitled to the current interest at that time.

(5) Condition 4 is that—

  (a) section 71A below does not apply to the property in which the interest subsists, and

  (b) the interest is not a disabled person's interest.[7]

Notes:
By Finance Act 1986, section 100(1), on and after 25 July 1986 the Capital Transfer Tax Act 1984 may be cited as the Inheritance Tax Act 1984.

A1.07 **s.49D Transitional serial interest: interest to which person becomes entitled on death of spouse or civil partner on or after 6th April 2008**

(1) Where a person ("E") is beneficially entitled to an interest in possession in settled property ("the successor interest"), that interest is a transitional serial interest for the purposes of this Chapter if the following conditions are met.

(2) Condition 1 is that—

  (a) the settlement commenced before 22nd March 2006, and

  (b) immediately before 22nd March 2006, the property then comprised in the settlement was property in which a person other than E was beneficially entitled to an interest in possession ("the previous interest").

(3) Condition 2 is that the previous interest came to an end on or after 6th April 2008 on the death of that other person ("F").

(4) Condition 3 is that, immediately before F died, F was the spouse or civil partner of E.

(5) Condition 4 is that E became beneficially entitled to the successor interest on F's death.

(6) Condition 5 is that—

  (a) section 71A below does not apply to the property in which the successor interest subsists, and

  (b) the successor interest is not a disabled person's interest.[8]

A1.08 **s.49E Transitional serial interest: contracts of life insurance**

(1) Where—

  (a) a person ("C") is beneficially entitled to an interest in possession in settled property ("the present interest"), and

  (b) on C's becoming beneficially entitled to the present interest, the settled property consisted of, or included, rights under a contract of life insurance entered into before 22nd March 2006,

the present interest so far as subsisting in rights under the contract, or in property comprised in the settlement that directly or indirectly represents rights under the contract,

---

[7] Added by Finance Act (2006 c.25), Sch.20(2) para.5(1).
[8] Added by Finance Act (2006 c.25), Sch.20(2) para.5(1).

is a "transitional serial interest" for the purposes of this Chapter if the following conditions are met.

(2) Condition 1 is that—

(a) the settlement commenced before 22nd March 2006, and
(b) immediately before 22nd March 2006—
   (i) the property then comprised in the settlement consisted of, or included, rights under the contract, and
   (ii) those rights were property in which C, or some other person, was beneficially entitled to an interest in possession ("the earlier interest").

(3) Condition 2 is that—

(a) the earlier interest came to an end at a time on or after 6th April 2008 ("the earlier-interest end-time") on the death of the person beneficially entitled to it and C became beneficially entitled to the present interest—
   (i) at the earlier-interest end-time, or
   (ii) on the coming to an end, on the death of the person beneficially entitled to it, of an interest in possession to which that person became beneficially entitled at the earlier-interest end-time, or
   (iii) on the coming to an end of the second or last in an unbroken sequence of two or more consecutive interests in possession to the first of which a person became beneficially entitled at the earlier-interest end-time and each of which ended on the death of the person beneficially entitled to it, or
(b) C became beneficially entitled to the present interest—
   (i) on the coming to an end, on the death of the person entitled to it, of an interest in possession that is a transitional serial interest under section 49C above, or
   (ii) on the coming to an end of the second or last in an unbroken sequence of two or more consecutive interests in possession the first of which was a transitional serial interest under section 49C above and each of which ended on the death of the person beneficially entitled to it.

(4) Condition 3 is that rights under the contract were comprised in the settlement throughout the period beginning with 22nd March 2006 and ending with C's becoming beneficially entitled to the present interest.

(5) Condition 4 is that—

(a) section 71A below does not apply to the property in which the present interest subsists, and
(b) the present interest is not a disabled person's interest.[9]

s.71 Accumulation and maintenance trusts   A1.09

(1) Subject to subsection (2) below, this section applies to settled property if—

(a) one or more persons (in this section referred to as beneficiaries) will, on or before attaining a specified age not exceeding twenty-five, become beneficially entitled to it or to an interest in possession in it, and[10]

---

[9] Added by Finance Act (2006 c.25), Sch.20(2) para.5(1).
[10] From 6th April 2008 "eighteen" replaced "twenty-five" in s.71(1)(a) and the words "or to an interest in possession in it" are omitted. And see FA 2006, Sch.20 para.3(3), no IHT charge on a trust falling outside s.71 as a result of these changes taking effect.

(b) no interest in possession subsists in it and the income from it is to be accumulated so far as not applied for the maintenance, education or benefit of a beneficiary.

(1A) This section does not apply to settled property at any particular time on or after 22nd March 2006 unless this section—

(a) applied to the settled property immediately before 22nd March 2006, and

(b) has applied to the settled property at all subsequent times up to the particular time.

(1B) This section does not apply to settled property at any particular time on or after 22nd March 2006 if, at that time, section 71A below applies to the settled property.[11]

(2) This section does not apply to settled property unless either—

(a) not more than twenty-five years have elapsed since the commencement of the settlement or, if it was later, since the time (or latest time) when the conditions stated in paragraphs (a) and (b) of subsections (1A) to (1) above became satisfied with respect to the property, or

(b) all the persons who are or have been beneficiaries are or were either—

   (i) grandchildren of a common grandparent, or
   (ii) children, widows or widowers or surviving civil partners of such grandchildren who were themselves beneficiaries but died before the time when, had they survived, they would have become entitled as mentioned in subsection (1)(a) above.

(3) Subject to subsections (4) and (5) below, there shall be a charge to tax under this section—

(a) where settled property ceases to be property to which this section applies, and

(b) in a case in which paragraph (a) above does not apply, where the trustees make a disposition as a result of which the value of settled property to which this section applies is less than it would be but for the disposition.

(4) Tax shall not be charged under this section—

(a) on a beneficiary's becoming beneficially entitled to, or to an interest in possession in, settled property on or before attaining the specified age, or

(b) on the death of a beneficiary before attaining the specified age.

(5) Subsections (3) to (8) and (10) of section 70 above shall apply for the purposes of this section as they apply for the purposes of that section (with the substitution of a reference to subsection (3)(b) above for the reference in section 70(4) to section 70(2)(b)).

(6) Where the conditions stated in paragraphs (a) and (b) of subsection (1) above were satisfied on 15th April 1976 with respect to property comprised in a settlement which commenced before that day, subsection (2)(a) above shall have effect with the substitution of a reference to that day for the reference to the commencement of the settlement, and the condition stated in subsection (2)(b) above shall be treated as satisfied if—

---

[11] Added by Finance Act (2006 c.25), Sch.20(1) para.2(3).

(a) it is satisfied in respect of the period beginning with 15th April 1976, or
(b) it is satisfied in respect of the period beginning with 1st April 1977 and either there was no beneficiary living on 15th April 1976 or the beneficiaries on 1st April 1977 included a living beneficiary, or
(c) there is no power under the terms of the settlement whereby it could have become satisfied in respect of the period beginning with 1st April 1977, and the trusts of the settlement have not been varied at any time after 15th April 1976.

(7) In subsection (1) above "persons" includes unborn persons; but the conditions stated in that subsection shall be treated as not satisfied unless there is or has been a living beneficiary.

(8) For the purposes of this section a person's children shall be taken to include his illegitimate children, his adopted children and his stepchildren.

s.71A Trusts for bereaved minors　　　　　　　　　　　　　　　　　　　　　　A1.10

(1) This section applies to settled property (including property settled before 22nd March 2006) if—

(a) it is held on statutory trusts for the benefit of a bereaved minor under sections 46 and 47(1) of the Administration of Estates Act 1925 (succession on intestacy and statutory trusts in favour of issue of intestate), or
(b) it is held on trusts for the benefit of a bereaved minor and subsection (2) below applies to the trusts,

but this section does not apply to property in which a disabled person's interest subsists.

(2) This subsection applies to trusts—

(a) established under the will of a deceased parent of the bereaved minor, or
(b) established under the Criminal Injuries Compensation Scheme,

which secure that the conditions in subsection (3) below are met.

(3) Those conditions are—

(a) that the bereaved minor, if he has not done so before attaining the age of 18, will on attaining that age become absolutely entitled to—
　(i) the settled property,
　(ii) any income arising from it, and
　(iii) any income that has arisen from the property held on the trusts for his benefit and been accumulated before that time,
(b) that, for so long as the bereaved minor is living and under the age of 18, if any of the settled property is applied for the benefit of a beneficiary, it is applied for the benefit of the bereaved minor, and
(c) that, for so long as the bereaved minor is living and under the age of 18, either—
　(i) the bereaved minor is entitled to all of the income (if there is any) arising from any of the settled property, or
　(ii) no such income may be applied for the benefit of any other person.

(4) Trusts such as are mentioned in paragraph (a) or (b) of subsection (2) above are not to be treated as failing to secure that the conditions in subsection (3) above are met by reason only of—

(a) the trustees' having the powers conferred by section 32 of the Trustee Act 1925 (powers of advancement),

(b) the trustees' having those powers but free from, or subject to a less restrictive limitation than, the limitation imposed by proviso (a) of subsection (1) of that section,

(c) the trustees' having the powers conferred by section 33 of the Trustee Act (Northern Ireland) 1958 (corresponding provision for Northern Ireland),

(d) the trustees' having those powers but free from, or subject to a less restrictive limitation than, the limitation imposed by subsection (1)(a) of that section, or

(e) the trustees' having powers to the like effect as the powers mentioned in any of paragraphs (a) to (d) above.

(5) In this section "the Criminal Injuries Compensation Scheme" means—

(a) the schemes established by arrangements made under the Criminal Injuries Compensation Act 1995,

(b) arrangements made by the Secretary of State for compensation for criminal injuries in operation before the commencement of those schemes, and

(c) the scheme established under the Criminal Injuries Compensation (Northern Ireland) Order 2002.

(6) The preceding provisions of this section apply in relation to Scotland as if, in subsection (2) above, before "which" there were inserted "the purposes of".[12]

A1.11   **s.71B Charge to tax on property to which section 71A applies**

(1) Subject to subsections (2) and (3) below, there shall be a charge to tax under this section—

(a) where settled property ceases to be property to which section 71A above applies, and

(b) in a case where paragraph (a) above does not apply, where the trustees make a disposition as a result of which the value of settled property to which section 71A above applies is less than it would be but for the disposition.

(2) Tax is not charged under this section where settled property ceases to be property to which section 71A applies as a result of—

(a) the bereaved minor attaining the age of 18 or becoming, under that age, absolutely entitled as mentioned in section 71A(3)(a) above, or

(b) the death under that age of the bereaved minor, or

(c) being paid or applied for the advancement or benefit of the bereaved minor.

(3) Subsections (3) to (8) and (10) of section 70 above apply for the purposes of this section as they apply for the purposes of that section, but—

(a) with the substitution of a reference to subsection (1)(b) above for the reference in subsection (4) of section 70 above to subsection (2)(b) of that section,

---

[12] Added by Finance Act (2006 c.25), Sch.20(1) para.1(1).

(b) with the substitution of a reference to property to which section 71A above applies for each of the references in subsections (3), (5) and (8) of section 70 above to property to which that section applies,

(c) as if, for the purposes of section 70(8) above as applied by this subsection, property—
  (i) which is property to which section 71A above applies,
  (ii) which, immediately before it became property to which section 71A above applies, was property to which section 71 above applied, and
  (iii) which, by the operation of section 71(1B) above, ceased on that occasion to be property to which section 71 above applied,

had become property to which section 71A above applies not on that occasion but on the occasion (or last occasion) before then when it became property to which section 71 above applied, and

(d) as if, for the purposes of section 70(8) above as applied by this subsection, property—
  (i) which is property to which section 71A above applies,
  (ii) which, immediately before it became property to which section 71A above applies, was property to which section 71D below applied, and
  (iii) which, by the operation of section 71D(5)(a) below, ceased on that occasion ("the 71D-to-71A-occasion") to be property to which section 71D below applied,

had become property to which section 71A above applies not on the 71D-to-71A occasion but on the relevant earlier occasion.

(4) In subsection (3)(d) above—

(a) "the relevant earlier occasion" means the occasion (or last occasion) before the 71D-to-71A occasion when the property became property to which section 71D below applied, but

(b) if the property, when it became property to which section 71D below applied, ceased at the same time to be property to which section 71 above applied without ceasing to be settled property, "the relevant earlier occasion" means the occasion (or last occasion) when the property became property to which section 71 above applied.[13]

s.71C Sections 71A and 71B: meaning of "bereaved minor" — A1.12

In sections 71A and 71B above "bereaved minor" means a person—

(a) who has not yet attained the age of 18, and
(b) at least one of whose parents has died.[14]

Notes:
By Finance Act 1986, section 100(1), on and after 25 July 1986 the Capital Transfer Tax Act 1984 may be cited as the Inheritance Tax Act 1984.

---

[13] Added by Finance Act (2006 c.25), Sch.20(1) para.1(1).
[14] Added by Finance Act (2006 c.25), Sch.20(1) para.1(1).

A1.13 s.71D Age 18-to-25 trusts

(1) This section applies to settled property (including property settled before 22nd March 2006), but subject to subsection (5) below, if—

(a) the property is held on trusts for the benefit of a person who has not yet attained the age of 25,

(b) at least one of the person's parents has died, and

(c) subsection (2) below applies to the trusts.

(2) This subsection applies to trusts—

(a) established under the will of a deceased parent of the person mentioned in subsection (1)(a) above, or

(b) established under the Criminal Injuries Compensation Scheme,

which secure that the conditions in subsection (6) below are met.

(3) Subsection (4) has effect where–

(a) at any time on or after 22nd March 2006 but before 6th April 2008, or on the coming into force of paragraph 3(1) of Schedule 20 to the Finance Act 2006, any property ceases to be property to which section 71 above applies without ceasing to be settled property, and

(b) immediately after the property ceases to be property to which section 71 above applies—

  (i) it is held on trusts for the benefit of a person who has not yet attained the age of 25, and
  (ii) the trusts secure that the conditions in subsection (6) below are met.

(4) From the time when the property ceases to be property to which section 71 above applies, but subject to subsection (5) below, this section applies to the property (if it would not apply to the property by virtue of subsection (1) above) for so long as—

(a) the property continues to be settled property held on trusts such as are mentioned in subsection (3)(b)(i) above, and

(b) the trusts continue to secure that the conditions in subsection (6) below are met.

(5) This section does not apply—

(a) to property to which section 71A above applies,

(b) to property to which section 71 above, or section 89 below, applies, or

(c) to settled property if a person is beneficially entitled to an interest in possession in the settled property and—

  (i) the person became beneficially entitled to the interest in possession before 22nd March 2006, or
  (ii) the interest in possession is an immediate post-death interest, or a transitional serial interest, and the person became beneficially entitled to it on or after 22nd March 2006.

(6) Those conditions are—

(a) that the person mentioned in subsection (1)(a) or (3)(b)(i) above ("B"), if he has not done so before attaining the age of 25, will on attaining that age become absolutely entitled to—
   (i) the settled property,
   (ii) any income arising from it, and
   (iii) any income that has arisen from the property held on the trusts for his benefit and been accumulated before that time,
(b) that, for so long as B is living and under the age of 25, if any of the settled property is applied for the benefit of a beneficiary, it is applied for the benefit of B, and
(c) that, for so long as B is living and under the age of 25, either—
   (i) B is entitled to all of the income (if there is any) arising from any of the settled property, or
   (ii) no such income may be applied for the benefit of any other person.

(7) For the purposes of this section, trusts are not to be treated as failing to secure that the conditions in subsection (6) above are met by reason only of—

(a) the trustees' having the powers conferred by section 32 of the Trustee Act 1925 (powers of advancement),
(b) the trustees' having those powers but free from, or subject to a less restrictive limitation than, the limitation imposed by proviso (a) of subsection (1) of that section,
(c) the trustees' having the powers conferred by section 33 of the Trustee Act (Northern Ireland) 1958 (corresponding provision for Northern Ireland),
(d) the trustees' having those powers but free from, or subject to a less restrictive limitation than, the limitation imposed by subsection (1)(a) of that section, or
(e) the trustees' having powers to the like effect as the powers mentioned in any of paragraphs (a) to (d) above.

(8) In this section "the Criminal Injuries Compensation Scheme" means—

(a) the schemes established by arrangements made under the Criminal Injuries Compensation Act 1995,
(b) arrangements made by the Secretary of State for compensation for criminal injuries in operation before the commencement of those schemes, and
(c) the scheme established under the Criminal Injuries Compensation (Northern Ireland) Order 2002.

(9) The preceding provisions of this section apply in relation to Scotland—

(a) as if, in subsection (2) above, before "which" there were inserted "the purposes of", and
(b) as if, in subsections (3)(b)(ii) and (4)(b) above, before "trusts" there were inserted "purposes of the".[15]

---

[15] Added by Finance Act (2006 c.25), Sch.20(1) para.1(1).

A1.14 s.71E Charge to tax on property to which section 71D applies

(1) Subject to subsections (2) to (4) below, there shall be a charge to tax under this section—

  (a) where settled property ceases to be property to which section 71D above applies, or
  (b) in a case where paragraph (a) above does not apply, where the trustees make a disposition as a result of which the value of the settled property to which section 71D above applies is less than it would be but for the disposition.

(2) Tax is not charged under this section where settled property ceases to be property to which section 71D above applies as a result of—

  (a) B becoming, at or under the age of 18, absolutely entitled as mentioned in section 71D(6)(a) above,
  (b) the death, under the age of 18, of B,
  (c) becoming, at a time when B is living and under the age of 18, property to which section 71A above applies, or
  (d) being paid or applied for the advancement or benefit of B—
      (i) at a time when B is living and under the age of 18, or
      (ii) on B's attaining the age of 18.

(3) Tax is not charged under this section in respect of—

  (a) a payment of costs or expenses (so far as they are fairly attributable to property to which section 71D above applies), or
  (b) a payment which is (or will be) income of any person for any of the purposes of income tax or would for any of those purposes be income of a person not resident in the United Kingdom if he were so resident,

or in respect of a liability to make such a payment.

(4) Tax is not charged under this section by virtue of subsection (1)(b) above if the disposition is such that, were the trustees beneficially entitled to the settled property, section 10 or section 16 above would prevent the disposition from being a transfer of value.

(5) For the purposes of this section the trustees shall be treated as making a disposition if they omit to exercise a right (unless it is shown that the omission was not deliberate) and the disposition shall be treated as made at the time or latest time when they could have exercised the right.[16]

A1.15 s.71F Calculation of tax charged under section 71E in certain cases

(1) Where—

  (a) tax is charged under section 71E above by reason of the happening of an event within subsection (2) below, and
  (b) that event happens after B has attained the age of 18,

the tax is calculated in accordance with this section.

---

[16] Added by Finance Act (2006 c.25), Sch.20(1) para.1(1).

(2) Those events are—

(a) B becoming absolutely entitled as mentioned in section 71D(6)(a) above,

(b) the death of B, and

(c) property being paid or applied for the advancement or benefit of B.

(3) The amount of the tax is given by—

(4) For the purposes of subsection (3) above, the "Chargeable amount" is—

(a) the amount by which the value of property which is comprised in the settlement and to which section 71D above applies is less immediately after the event giving rise to the charge than it would be but for the event, or

(b) where the tax is payable out of settled property to which section 71D above applies immediately after the event, the amount which, after deducting the tax, is equal to the amount on which tax would be charged by virtue of paragraph (a) above.

(5) For the purposes of subsection (3) above, the "Relevant fraction" is three tenths multiplied by so many fortieths as there are complete successive quarters in the period—

(a) beginning with the day on which B attained the age of 18 or, if later, the day on which the property became property to which section 71D above applies, and

(b) ending with the day before the occasion of the charge.

(6) Where the whole or part of the Chargeable amount is attributable to property that was excluded property at any time during the period mentioned in subsection (5) above then, in determining the "Relevant fraction" in relation to that amount or part, no quarter throughout which that property was excluded property shall be counted.

(7) For the purposes of subsection (3) above, the "Settlement rate" is the effective rate (that is to say, the rate found by expressing the tax chargeable as a percentage of the amount on which it is charged) at which tax would be charged on the value transferred by a chargeable transfer of the description specified in subsection (8) below.

(8) The chargeable transfer postulated in subsection (7) above is one—

(a) the value transferred by which is equal to an amount determined in accordance with subsection (9) below,

(b) which is made at the time of the charge to tax under section 71E above by a transferor who has in the period of seven years ending with the day of the occasion of the charge made chargeable transfers having an aggregate value equal to that of any chargeable transfers made by the settlor in the period of seven years ending with the day on which the settlement commenced, disregarding transfers made on that day, and

(c) on which tax is charged in accordance with section 7(2) above.

(9) The amount referred to in subsection (8)(a) above is equal to the aggregate of—

(a) the value, immediately after the settlement commenced, of the property then comprised in it,

(b) the value, immediately afer a related settlement commenced, of the property then comprised in it, and

(c) the value, immediately after it became comprised in the settlement, of any property which became so comprised after the settlement commenced and before the occasion of the charge under section 71E above (whether or not it has remained so comprised).[17]

Notes:
By Finance Act 1986, section 100(1), on and after 25 July 1986 the Capital Transfer Tax Act 1984 may be cited as the Inheritance Tax Act 1984.

A1.16   **s.71G Calculation of tax charged under section 71E in all other cases**

(1) Where—

(a) tax is charged under section 71E above, and

(b) the tax does not fall to be calculated in accordance with section 71F above,

the tax is calculated in accordance with this section.
(2) The amount on which the tax is charged is—

(a) the amount by which the value of property which is comprised in the settlement and to which section 71D above applies is less immediately after the event giving rise to the charge than it would be but for the event, or

(b) where the tax is payable out of settled property to which section 71D above applies immediately after the event, the amount which, after deducting the tax, is equal to the amount on which tax would be charged by virtue of paragraph (a) above.

(3) The rate at which the tax is charged is the rate that would be given by subsections (6) to (8) of section 70 above—

(a) if the reference to section 70 above in subsection (8)(a) of that section were a reference to section 71D above,

(b) if the other references in those subsections to section 70 above were references to section 71E above, and

(c) if, for the purposes of section 70(8) above, property—

  (i) which is property to which section 71D above applies,
  (ii) which, immediately before it became property to which section 71D above applies, was property to which section 71 applied, and
  (iii) which ceased on that occasion to be property to which section 71 above applied without ceasing to be settled property,

had become property to which section 71D above applies not on that occasion but on the occasion (or last occasion) before then when it became property to which section 71 above applied.[18]

---

[17] Added by Finance Act (2006 c.25), Sch.20(1), para.1(1).
[18] Added by Finance Act (2006 c.25), Sch.20(1) para.1(1).

s.71H Sections 71A to 71G: meaning of "parent" A1.17

(1) In sections 71A to 71G above "parent" includes step-parent.

(2) For the purposes of sections 71A to 71G above, a deceased individual ("D") shall be taken to have been a parent of another individual ("Y") if, immediately before D died, D had—

(a) parental responsibility for Y under the law of England and Wales,

(b) parental responsibilities in relation to Y under the law of Scotland, or

(c) parental responsibility for Y under the law of Northern Ireland.

(3) In subsection (2)(a) above "parental responsibility" has the same meaning as in the Children Act 1989.

(4) In subsection (2)(b) above "parental responsibilities" has the meaning given by section 1(3) of the Children (Scotland) Act 1995.

(5) In subsection (2)(c) above "parental responsibility" has the same meaning as in the Children (Northern Ireland) Order 1995.[19]

s.89 Trusts for disabled persons A1.18

(1) This section applies to settled property transferred into settlement after 9th March 1981 and held on trusts—

(a) under which, during the life of a disabled person, no interest in possession in the settled property subsists, and

(b) which secure that not less than half of the settled property which is applied during his life is applied for his benefit.

(2) For the purposes of this Act the person mentioned in subsection (1) above shall be treated as beneficially entitled to an interest in possession in the settled property.

(3) The trusts on which settled property is held shall not be treated as falling outside subsection (1) above by reason only of the powers conferred on the trustees by section 32 of the Trustee Act 1925 or section 33 of the Trustee Act (Northern Ireland) 1958 (powers of advancement).

(4) The reference in subsection (1) above to a disabled person is, in relation to any settled property, a reference to a person who, when the property was transferred into settlement, was—

(a) incapable, by reason of mental disorder within the meaning of the Mental Health Act 1983, of administering his property or managing his affairs, or

(b) in receipt of an attendance allowance under section 64 of the Social Security Contributions and Benefits Act 1992 or section 64 of the Social Security Contributions and Benefits (Northern Ireland) Act 1992, or

(c) in receipt of a disability living allowance under section 71 of the Social Security Contributions and Benefits Act 1992 by virtue of entitlement to the care component at the highest or middle rate.

(5) The reference in subsection (1) above to a disabled person includes, in relation to any settled property, a reference to a person who, when the property was transferred into settlement—

---

[19] Added by Finance Act (2006 c.25), Sch.20(1), para.1(1).

(a) would have been in receipt of attendance allowance under section 64 of either of the Acts mentioned in subsection (4)(b) above had provision made by regulations under section 67(1) or (2) of that Act (non-satisfaction of conditions for attendance allowance where person is undergoing treatment for renal failure in a hospital or is provided with certain accommodation) been ignored, or

(b) would have been in receipt of disability living allowance by virtue of entitlement to the care component at the highest or middle rate had provision made by regulations under section 72(8) of either of the Acts mentioned in subsection (4)(c) above (no payment of disability living allowance for persons for whom certain accommodation is provided) been ignored.

(6) The reference in subsection (1) above to a disabled person also includes, in relation to any settled property, a reference to a person who satisfies the Commissioners for Her Majesty's Revenue and Customs—

(a) that he would, when the property was transferred into settlement, have been in receipt of attendance allowance under section 64 of either of the Acts mentioned in subsection (4)(b) above—

(i) had he met the conditions as to residence under section 64(1) of that Act, and
(ii) had provision made by regulations under section 67(1) or (2) of that Act been ignored, or

(b) that he would, when the property was transferred into settlement, have been in receipt of a disability living allowance by virtue of entitlement to the care component at the highest or middle rate—

(i) had he met the prescribed conditions as to residence under section 71(6) of either of the Acts mentioned in subsection (4)(c) above, and
(ii) had provision made by regulations under section 72(8) of that Act been ignored.[20]

A1.19 **s.89A Self-settlement by person with condition expected to lead to disability**

(1) This section applies to property transferred by a person ("A") into settlement on or after 22nd March 2006 if—

(a) A was beneficially entitled to the property immediately before transferring it into settlement,

(b) A satisfies the Commissioners for Her Majesty's Revenue and Customs that, when the property was transferred into settlement, A had a condition that it was at that time reasonable to expect would have such effects on A as to lead to A becoming—

(i) a person falling within section 89(4)(a) above,
(ii) in receipt of an attendance allowance mentioned in section 89(4)(b) above, or
(iii) in receipt of a disability living allowance mentioned in section 89(4)(c) above by virtue of entitlement to the care component at the highest or middle rate, and

(c) the property is held on trusts—

(i) under which, during the life of A, no interest in possession in the settled property subsists, and
(ii) which secure that Conditions 1 and 2 are met.

---

[20] Added by Finance Act (2006 c.25), Sch.20(2), para.6(2).

(2) Condition 1 is that if any of the settled property is applied during A's life for the benefit of a beneficiary, it is applied for the benefit of A.

(3) Condition 2 is that any power to bring the trusts mentioned in subsection (1)(c) above to an end during A's life is such that, in the event of the power being exercised during A's life, either—

(a) A or another person will, on the trusts being brought to an end, be absolutely entitled to the settled property, or
(b) on the trusts being brought to an end, a disabled person's interest within section 89B(1)(a) or
(c) below will subsist in the settled property.

(4) If this section applies to settled property transferred into settlement by a person, the person shall be treated as beneficially entitled to an interest in possession in the settled property.

(5) For the purposes of subsection (1)(b)(ii) above, assume—

(a) that A will meet the conditions as to residence under section 64(1) of whichever of the 1992 Acts is applicable, and
(b) that there will be no provision made by regulations under section 67(1) and (2) of that Act.

(6) For the purposes of subsection (1)(b)(iii) above, assume—

(a) that A will meet the prescribed conditions as to residence under section 71(6) of whichever of the 1992 Acts is applicable, and
(b) that there will be no provision made by regulations under section 72(8) of that Act.

(7) For the purposes of subsection (3) above, ignore—

(a) power to give directions as to the settled property that is exercisable jointly by the persons who between them are entitled to the entire beneficial interest in the property, and
(b) anything that could occur as a result of exercise of any such power.

(8) In this section "the 1992 Acts" means—
the Social Security Contributions and Benefits Act 1992, and
the Social Security Contributions and Benefits (Northern Ireland) Act 1992.[21]

s.89B Meaning of "disabled person's interest" — A1.20

(1) In this Act "disabled person's interest" means—

(a) an interest in possession to which a person is under section 89(2) above treated as beneficially entitled,
(b) an interest in possession to which a person is under section 89A(4) above treated as beneficially entitled,
(c) an interest in possession in settled property (other than an interest within paragraph (a) or (b) above) to which a disabled person becomes beneficially entitled on or after 22nd March 2006, or

---

[21] Added by Finance Act (2006 c.25), Sch.20(2), para.6(1).

(d) an interest in possession in settled property (other than an interest within paragraph (a) or (b) above) to which a person ("A") is beneficially entitled if—

    (i) A is the settlor,
    (ii) A was beneficially entitled to the property immediately before transferring it into settlement,
    (iii) A satisfies Her Majesty's Commissioners for Revenue and Customs as mentioned in section 89A(1)(b) above,
    (iv) the settled property was transferred into settlement on or after 22nd March 2006, and
    (v) the trusts on which the settled property is held secure that, if any of the settled property is applied during A's life for the benefit of a beneficiary, it is applied for the benefit of A.

(2) Subsections (4) to (6) of section 89 above (meaning of "disabled person" in subsection (1) of that section) have effect for the purposes of subsection (1)(c) above as they have effect for the purposes of subsection (1) of that section.

(3) Section 71D above does not apply to property in which there subsists a disabled person's interest within subsection (1)(c) above (but see also section 71D(5) above).[22]

A1.21   s.142 Alteration of dispositions taking effect on death

(1) Where within the period of two years after a person's death—

(a) any of the dispositions (whether effected by will, under the law relating to intestacy or otherwise) of the property comprised in his estate immediately before his death are varied, or

(b) the benefit conferred by any of those dispositions is disclaimed, by an instrument in writing made by the persons or any of the persons who benefit or would benefit under the dispositions, this Act shall apply as if the variation had been effected by the deceased or, as the case may be, the disclaimed benefit had never been conferred.

(2) Subsection (1) above shall not apply to a variation unless the instrument contains a statement, made by all the relevant persons, to the effect that they intend the subsection to apply to the variation

(2A) For the purposes of subsection (2) above the relevant persons are—

(a) the person or persons making the instrument, and

(b) where the variation results in additional tax being payable, the personal representatives.

Personal representatives may decline to make a statement under subsection (2) above only if no, or no sufficient, assets are held by them in that capacity for discharging the additional tax.[23]

(3) Subsection (1) above shall not apply to a variation or disclaimer made for any consideration in money or money's worth other than consideration consisting of the making; in respect of another of the dispositions, of a variation or disclaimer to which that subsection applies.

(4) Where a variation to which subsection (1) above applies results in property being held in trust for a person for a period which ends not more than two years after the death, this Act shall apply as if the disposition of the property that takes effect at the

---

[22] Added by Finance Act (2006 c.25), Sch.20(2), para.6(1).
[23] s.142(2) and (2A) substituted for s.142(2) by Finance Act (2002 c.23), Pt 5, s.120(1).

end of the period had had effect from the beginning of the period; but this subsection shall not affect the application of this Act in relation to any distribution or application of property occurring before that disposition takes effect.

(5) For the purposes of subsection (1) above the property comprised in a person's estate includes any excluded property but not any property to which he is treated as entitled by virtue of section 49(1) above or section 102 of the Finance Act 1986.

(6) Subsection (1) above applies whether or not the administration of the estate is complete or the property concerned has been distributed in accordance with the original dispositions.

(7) In the application of subsection (4) above to Scotland, property which is subject to a proper liferent shall be deemed to be held in trust for the liferenter.

s.144 Distribution etc. from property settled by will

(1) Subsection (2) below applies where property comprised in a person's estate immediately before his death is settled by his will and, within the period of two years after his death and before any interest in possession has subsisted in the property, there occurs—

- (a) an event on which tax would (apart from subsection (2) below) be chargeable under any provision, other than section 64 or 79, of Chapter III of Part III of this Act, or
- (b) an event on which tax would be so chargeable but for section 75 or 76 above or paragraph 16(1) of Schedule 4 to this Act.

(1A) Where the testator dies on or after 22nd March 2006, subsection (1) above shall have effect as if the reference to any interest in possession were a reference to any interest in possession that is—

- (a) an immediate post-death interest, or
- (b) a disabled person's interest.

(2) Where this subsection applies by virtue of an event within paragraph (a) of subsection (1) above, tax shall not be charged under the provision in question on that event; and in every case in which this subsection applies in relation to an event, this Act shall have effect as if the will had provided that on the testator's death the property should be held as it is held after the event.

(3) Subsection (4) below applies where—

- (a) a person dies on or after 22nd March 2006,
- (b) property comprised in the person's estate immediately before his death is settled by his will, and
- (c) within the period of two years after his death, but before an immediate post-death interest or a disabled person's interest has subsisted in the property, there occurs an event that involves causing the property to be held on trusts that would, if they had in fact been established by the testator's will, have resulted in-
    - (i) an immediate post-death interest subsisting in the property, or
    - (ii) section 71A or 71D above applying to the property.

(4) Where this subsection applies by virtue of an event—

- (a) this Act shall have effect as if the will had provided that on the testator's death the property should be held as it is held after the event, but
- (b) tax shall not be charged on that event under any provision of Chapter 3 of Part 3 of this Act.

(5) Subsection (4) above also applies where—

(a) a person dies before 22nd March 2006,

(b) property comprised in the person's estate immediately before his death is settled by his will,

(c) an event occurs—

(i) on or after 22nd March 2006, and
(ii) within the period of two years after the testator's death,

that involves causing the property to be held on trusts within subsection (6) below,

(d) no immediate post-death interest, and no disabled person's interest, subsisted in the property at any time in the period beginning with the testator's death and ending immediately before the event, and

(e) no other interest in possession subsisted in the property at any time in the period beginning with the testator's death and ending immediately before 22nd March 2006.

(6) Trusts are within this subsection if they would, had they in fact been established by the testator's will and had the testator died at the time of the event mentioned in subsection (5)(c) above, have resulted in—

(a) an immediate post-death interest subsisting in the property, or

(b) section 71A or 71D above applying to the property.[24]

FINANCE ACT 1986

Sections 102–3; Sch.20 para.4A, 5

A1.23 **s.102 Gifts with reservation**

(1) Subject to subsections (5) and (6) below, this section applies where, on or after 18th March 1986, an individual disposes of any property by way of gift and either—

(a) possession and enjoyment of the property is not bona fide assumed by the donee at or before the beginning of the relevant period; or

(b) at any time in the relevant period the property is not enjoyed to the entire exclusion, or virtually to the entire exclusion, of the donor and of any benefit to him by contract or otherwise;

and in this section "the relevant period" means a period ending on the date of the donor's death and beginning seven years before that date or, if it is later, on the date of the gift.

(2) If and so long as—

(a) possession and enjoyment of any property is not bona fide assumed as mentioned in subsection (1)(a) above, or

---

[24] Added by Finance Act (2006 c.25), Sch.20(3) para.27(5).

(b) any property is not enjoyed as mentioned in subsection (1)(b) above,

the property is referred to (in relation to the gift and the donor) as property subject to a reservation.

(3) If, immediately before the death of the donor, there is any property which, in relation to him, is property subject to a reservation then, to the extent that the property would not, apart from this section, form part of the donor's estate immediately before his death, that property shall be treated for the purposes of the 1984 Act as property to which he was beneficially entitled immediately before his death.

(4) If, at a time before the end of the relevant period, any property ceases to be property subject to a reservation, the donor shall be treated for the purposes of the 1984 Act as having at that time made a disposition of the property by a disposition which is a potentially exempt transfer.

(5) This section does not apply if or, as the case may be, to the extent that the disposal of property by way of gift is an exempt transfer by virtue of any of the following provisions of Part II of the 1984 Act,—

(a) section 18 (transfers between spouses or civil partners), except as provided by subsections (5A) and (5B) below;

(b) section 20 (small gifts);

(c) section 22 (gifts in consideration of marriage or civil partnership);

(d) section 23 (gifts to charities);

(e) section 24 (gifts to political parties);

(ee) section 24A (gifts to housing associations);

(f) section 25 (gifts for national purposes, etc.);

(h) section 27 (maintenance funds for historic buildings); and

(i) section 28 (employee trusts).

(5A) Subsection (5)(a) above does not prevent this section from applying if or, as the case may be, to the extent that—

(a) the property becomes settled property by virtue of the gift,

(b) by reason of the donor's spouse [or civil partner][25] ("the relevant beneficiary") becoming beneficially entitled to an interest in possession in the settled property, the disposal is or, as the case may be, is to any extent an exempt transfer by virtue of section 18 of the 1984 Act in consequence of the operation of section 49 of that Act (treatment of interests in possession),

(c) at some time after the disposal, but before the death of the donor, the relevant beneficiary's interest in possession comes to an end, and

(d) on the occasion on which that interest comes to an end, the relevant beneficiary does not become beneficially entitled to the settled property or to another interest in possession in the settled property.

(5B) If or, as the case may be, to the extent that this section applies by virtue of subsection (5A) above, it has effect as if the disposal by way of gift had been made immediately after the relevant beneficiary's interest in possession came to an end.

---

[25] Words inserted by SI 2005/3229 (Tax and Civil Partnership Regulations), reg.44(3).

(5C) For the purposes of subsections (5A) and (5B) above—

(a) section 51(1)(b) of the 1984 Act (disposal of interest in possession treated as coming to end of interest) applies as it applies for the purposes of Chapter 2 of Part 3 of that Act; and

(b) references to any property or to an interest in any property include references to part of any property or interest.

(6) This section does not apply if the disposal of property by way of gift is made under the terms of a policy issued in respect of an insurance made before 18th March 1986 unless the policy is varied on or after that date so as to increase the benefits secured or to extend the term of the insurance; and, for this purpose, any change in the terms of the policy which is made in pursuance of an option or other power conferred by the policy shall be deemed to be a variation of the policy.

(7) If a policy issued as mentioned in subsection (6) above confers an option or other power under which benefits and premiums may be increased to take account of increases in the retail price index (as defined in section 8(3) of the 1984 Act) or any similar index specified in the policy, then, to the extent that the right to exercise that option or power would have been lost if it had not been exercised on or before 1st August 1986, the exercise of that option or power before that date shall be disregarded for the purposes of subsection (6) above.

(8) Schedule 20 to this Act has effect for supplementing this section.

A1.24 **s.102ZA Gifts with reservation: termination of interests in possession**

(1) Subsection (2) below applies where—

(a) an individual is beneficially entitled to an interest in possession in settled property,

(b) either—

    (i) the individual became beneficially entitled to the interest in possession before 22nd March 2006, or

    (ii) the individual became beneficially entitled to the interest in possession on or after 22nd March 2006 and the interest is an immediate post-death interest, a disabled person's interest or a transitional serial interest, and

(c) the interest in possession comes to an end during the individual's life.

(2) For the purposes of—

(a) section 102 above, and

(b) Schedule 20 to this Act,

the individual shall be taken (if, or so far as, he would not otherwise be) to dispose, on the coming to an end of the interest in possession, of the no-longer-possessed property by way of gift.

(3) In subsection (2) above "the no-longer-possessed property" means the property in which the interest in possession subsisted immediately before it came to an end, other than any of it to which the individual becomes absolutely and beneficially entitled in possession on the coming to an end of the interest in possession.[26]

---

[26] Added by Finance Act (2006 c.25), Sch.20(5), para.33(2).

s.102A Gifts with reservation: interest in land   A1.25

(1) This section applies where an individual disposes of an interest in land by way of gift on or after 9th March 1999.

(2) At any time in the relevant period when the donor or his spouse [or civil partner][27] enjoys a significant right or interest, or is party to a significant arrangement, in relation to the land—

- (a) the interest disposed of is referred to (in relation to the gift and the donor) as property subject to a reservation; and
- (b) section 102(3) and (4) above shall apply.

(3) Subject to subsections (4) and (5) below, a right, interest or arrangement in relation to land is significant for the purposes of subsection (2) above if (and only if) it entitles or enables the donor to occupy all or part of the land, or to enjoy some right in relation to all or part of the land, otherwise than for full consideration in money or money's worth.

(4) A right, interest or arrangement is not significant for the purposes of subsection (2) above if—

- (a) it does not and cannot prevent the enjoyment of the land to the entire exclusion, or virtually to the entire exclusion, of the donor; or
- (b) it does not entitle or enable the donor to occupy all or part of the land immediately after the disposal, but would do so were it not for the interest disposed of.

(5) A right or interest is not significant for the purposes of subsection (2) above if it was granted or acquired before the period of seven years ending with the date of the gift.

(6) Where an individual disposes of more than one interest in land by way of gift, whether or not at the same time or to the same donee, this section shall apply separately in relation to each interest.

s.102B Gifts with reservation: share of interest in land   A1.26

(1) This section applies where an individual disposes, by way of gift on or after 9th March 1999, of an undivided share of an interest in land.

(2) At any time in the relevant period, except when subsection (3) or (4) below applies—

- (a) the share disposed of is referred to (in relation to the gift and the donor) as property subject to a reservation; and
- (b) section 102(3) and (4) above shall apply.

(3) This subsection applies when the donor—

- (a) does not occupy the land; or
- (b) occupies the land to the exclusion of the donee for full consideration in money or money's worth.

---

[27] Words inserted by SI 2005/3229 (Tax and Civil Partnership Regulations), reg.45.

(4) This subsection applies when—

(a) the donor and the donee occupy the land; and

(b) the donor does not receive any benefit, other than a negligible one, which is provided by or at the expense of the donee for some reason connected with the gift.][28]

A1.27   s.102C Sections 102A and 102B: supplemental

(1) In sections 102A and 102B above "the relevant period" has the same meaning as in section 102 above.

(2) An interest or share disposed of is not property subject to a reservation under section 102A(2) or 102B(2) above if or, as the case may be, to the extent that the disposal is an exempt transfer by virtue of any of the provisions listed in section 102(5) above.

(3) In applying sections 102A and 102B above no account shall be taken of—

(a) occupation of land by a donor, or

(b) an arrangement which enables land to be occupied by a donor,

in circumstances where the occupation, or occupation pursuant to the arrangement, would be disregarded in accordance with paragraph 6(1)(b) of Schedule 20 to this Act.

(4) The provisions of Schedule 20 to this Act, apart from paragraph 6, shall have effect for the purposes of sections 102A and 102B above as they have effect for the purposes of section 102 above; and any question which falls to be answered under section 102A or 102B above in relation to an interest in land shall be determined by reference to the interest which is at that time treated as property comprised in the gift.

(5) Where property other than an interest in land is treated by virtue of paragraph 2 of that Schedule as property comprised in a gift, the provisions of section 102 above shall apply to determine whether or not that property is property subject to a reservation.

(6) Sections 102 and 102A above shall not apply to a case to which section 102B above applies.

(7) Section 102A above shall not apply to a case to which section 102 above applies.[29]

A1.28   s.103 Treatment of certain debts and incumbrances

(1) Subject to subsection (2) below, if, in determining the value of a person's estate immediately before his death, account would be taken, apart from this subsection, of a liability consisting of a debt incurred by him or an incumbrance created by a disposition made by him, that liability shall be subject to abatement to an extent proportionate to the value of any of the consideration given for the debt or incumbrance which consisted of—

(a) property derived from the deceased; or

(b) consideration (not being property derived from the deceased) given by any person who was at any time entitled to, or amongst whose resources there was at any time included, any property derived from the deceased.

---

[28] Added by Finance Act (1999 c.16), Pt V, s.104.
[29] Added by Finance Act (1999 c.16), Pt V, s.104.

(2) If, in a case where the whole or a part of the consideration given for a debt or incumbrance consisted of such consideration as is mentioned in subsection (1)(b) above, it is shown that the value of the consideration given, or of that part thereof, as the case may be, exceeded that which could have been rendered available by application of all the property derived from the deceased, other than such (if any) of that property—

(a) as is included in the consideration given, or

(b) as to which it is shown that the disposition of which it, or the property which it represented, was the subject matter was not made with reference to, or with a view to enabling or facilitating, the giving of the consideration or the recoupment in any manner of the cost thereof,

no abatement shall be made under subsection (1) above in respect of the excess.

(3) In subsections (1) and (2) above "property derived from the deceased" means, subject to subsection (4) below, any property which was the subject matter of a disposition made by the deceased, either by himself alone or in concert or by arrangement with any other person or which represented any of the subject matter of such a disposition, whether directly or indirectly, and whether by virtue of one or more intermediate dispositions.

(4) If the disposition first-mentioned in subsection (3) above was not a transfer of value and it is shown that the disposition was not part of associated operations which included—

(a) a disposition by the deceased, either alone or in concert or by arrangement with any other person, otherwise than for full consideration in money or money's worth paid to the deceased for his own use or benefit; or

(b) a disposition by any other person operating to reduce the value of the property of the deceased,

that first-mentioned disposition shall be left out of account for the purposes of subsections (1) to (3) above.

(5) If, before a person's death but on or after 18th March 1986, money or money's worth is paid or applied by him—

(a) in or towards the satisfaction or discharge of a debt or incumbrance in the case of which subsection (1) above would have effect on his death if the debt or incumbrance had not been satisfied or discharged, or

(b) in reduction of a debt or incumbrance in the case of which that subsection has effect on his death,

the 1984 Act shall have effect as if, at the time of the payment or application, the person concerned had made a transfer of value equal to the money or money's worth and that transfer were a potentially exempt transfer.

(6) Any reference in this section to a debt incurred is a reference to a debt incurred on or after 18th March 1986 and any reference to an incumbrance created by a disposition is a reference to an incumbrance created by a disposition made on or after that date; and in this section "subject matter" includes, in relation to any disposition, any annual or periodical payment made or payable under or by virtue of the disposition.

(7) In determining the value of a person's estate immediately before his death, no account shall be taken (by virtue of section 5 of the 1984 Act) of any liability arising under or in connection with a policy of life insurance issued in respect of an insurance made on or after July 1, 1986 unless the whole of the sums assured under that policy form part of that person's estate immediately before his death.

SCHEDULE 20

A1.29   **4A**

(1) This paragraph applies where—

    (a) under section 102ZA of this Act, an individual ("D") is taken to dispose of property by way of gift, and

    (b) the property continues to be settled property immediately after the disposal.

(2) Paragraphs 2 to 4 above shall not apply but, subject to the following provisions of this paragraph, the principal section and the following provisions of this Schedule shall apply as if the property comprised in the gift consisted of the property comprised in the settlement on the material date, except in so far as that property neither is, nor represents, nor is derived from, property originally comprised in the gift.

(3) Any property which—

    (a) on the material date is comprised in the settlement, and

    (b) is derived, directly or indirectly, from a loan made by D to the trustees of the settlement,

shall be treated for the purposes of sub-paragraph (2) above as derived from property originally comprised in the gift.

(4) If the settlement comes to an end at some time before the material date as respects all or any of the property which, if D had died immediately before that time, would be treated as comprised in the gift,—

    (a) the property in question, other than property to which D then becomes absolutely and beneficially entitled in possession, and

    (b) any consideration (not consisting of rights under the settlement) given by D for any of the property to which D so becomes entitled,

shall be treated as comprised in the gift (in addition to any other property so comprised).

(5) Where, under any trust or power relating to settled property, income arising from that property after the material date is accumulated, the accumulations shall not be treated for the purposes of sub-paragraph (2) above as derived from that property.[30]

SETTLED GIFTS

A1.30   **5**

(1) Where there is a disposal by way of gift and the property comprised in the gift becomes settled property by virtue of the gift, paragraphs 2 to 4 above shall not apply but, subject to the following provisions of this paragraph, the principal section and the following provisions of this Schedule shall apply as if the property comprised in the gift consisted of the property comprised in the settlement on the material date, except in so far as that property neither is, nor represents, nor is derived from, property originally comprised in the gift.

(2) If the settlement comes to an end at some time before the material date as

---

[30] Added by Finance Act (2006 c.25), Sch.20(5), para.33(3).

respects all or any of the property which, if the donor had died immediately before that time, would be treated as comprised in the gift,—

(a) the property in question, other than property to which the donor then becomes absolutely and beneficially entitled in possession, and

(b) any consideration (not consisting of rights under the settlement) given by the donor for any of the property to which he so becomes entitled,

shall be treated as comprised in the gift (in addition to any other property so comprised).

(3) Where property comprised in a gift does not become settled property by virtue of the gift, but is before the material date settled by the donee, sub-paragraphs (1) and (2) above shall apply in relation to property comprised in the settlement as if the settlement had been made by the gift; and for this purpose property which becomes settled property under any testamentary disposition of the donee or on his intestacy (or partial intestacy) shall be treated as settled by him.

(4) Where property comprised in a gift becomes settled property either by virtue of the gift or as mentioned in sub-paragraph (3) above, any property which—

(a) on the material date is comprised in the settlement, and

(b) is derived, directly or indirectly, from a loan made by the donor to the trustees of the settlement;

shall be treated for the purposes of sub-paragraph (1) above as derived from property originally comprised in the gift.

(5) Where, under any trust or power relating to settled property, income arising from that property after the material date is accumulated, the accumulations shall not be treated for the purposes of subparagraph (1) above as derived from that property.

TAXATION OF CHARGEABLE GAINS ACT 1992

s.71 Person becoming absolutely entitled to settled property A1.31

(1) On the occasion when a person becomes absolutely entitled to any settled property as against the trustee all the assets forming part of the settled property to which he becomes so entitled shall be deemed to have been disposed of by the trustee, and immediately reacquired by him in his capacity as a trustee within section 60(1), for a consideration equal to their market value.

(2) Where, in any case in which a person ("the beneficiary") becomes absolutely entitled to any settled property as against the trustee, an allowable loss would (apart from this subsection) have accrued to the trustee on the deemed disposal under subsection (1) above of an asset comprised in that property—

(a) that loss shall be treated, to the extent only that it cannot be deducted from pre-entitlement gains of the trustee, as an allowable loss accruing to the beneficiary (instead of to the trustee); but

(b) any allowable loss treated as accruing to the beneficiary under this subsection shall be deductible under this Act from chargeable gains accruing to the beneficiary to the extent only that it can be deducted from gains accruing to the beneficiary on the disposal by him of—

(i) the asset on the deemed disposal of which the loss accrued; or

(ii) where that asset is an estate, interest or right in or over land, that asset or any asset deriving from that asset.

(2A) In subsection (2) above "pre-entitlement gain", in relation to an allowable loss accruing to a trustee on the deemed disposal of any asset comprised in any settled property, means a chargeable gain accruing to that trustee on—

(a) a disposal which, on the occasion on which the beneficiary becomes absolutely entitled as against the trustee to that property, is deemed under subsection (1) above to have taken place; or

(b) any other disposal taking place before that occasion but in the same year of assessment.

(2B) For the purposes of subsection (2)(b)(ii) above an asset ("the relevant asset") derives from another if, in a case where—

(a) assets have merged,

(b) an asset has divided or otherwise changed its nature, or

(c) different rights or interests in or over any asset have been created or extinguished at different times,

the value of the relevant asset is wholly or partly derived (through one or more successive events falling within paragraphs (a) to (c) above but not otherwise) from the other asset.

(2C) The rules set out in subsection (2D) below shall apply (notwithstanding any other rules contained in this Act or in section 113(2) of the Finance Act 1995 (order of deduction))—

(a) for determining for the purposes of this section whether an allowable loss accruing to the trustee, or treated as accruing to the beneficiary, can be deducted from particular chargeable gains for any year of assessment; and

(b) for the making of deductions of allowable losses from chargeable gains in cases where it has been determined that such an allowable loss can be deducted from particular chargeable gains.

(2D) Those rules are as follows—

(a) allowable losses accruing to the trustee on a deemed disposal under subsection (1) above shall be deducted before any deduction is made in respect of any other allowable losses accruing to the trustee in that year;

(b) allowable losses treated as accruing to the beneficiary under this section, so far as they cannot be deducted in a year of assessment as mentioned in subsection (2)(b) above, may be carried forward from year to year until they can be so deducted; and

(c) allowable losses treated as accruing to the beneficiary for any year of assessment under this section, and allowable losses carried forward to any year of assessment under paragraph (b) above—

(i) shall be deducted before any deduction is made in respect of any allowable losses accruing to the beneficiary in that year otherwise than by virtue of this section; and

(ii) in the case of losses carried forward to any year, shall be deductible as if they were losses actually accruing in that year.[31]

---

[31] s.71(2)–(2D) substituted for s.71(2) by Finance Act (1999 c.16), Pt III, s.75(1).

(3) References in this section to the case where a person becomes absolutely entitled to settled property as against the trustee shall be taken to include references to the case where a person would become so entitled but for being an infant or other person under disability.

s.72 Termination of life interest on death of person entitled

A1.32

(1) On the termination, on the death of the person entitled to it, of an interest in possession in all or any part of settled property—

(a) the whole or a corresponding part of each of the assets forming part of the settled property and not ceasing at that time to be settled property shall be deemed for the purposes of this Act at that time to be disposed of and immediately reacquired by the trustee for a consideration equal to the whole or a corresponding part of the market value of the asset; but

(b) no chargeable gain shall accrue on that disposal.

For the purposes of this subsection an interest which is a right to part of the income of settled property shall be treated as an interest in a corresponding part of the settled property.

(1A) where the interest in possession mentioned in subsection (1) above is one to which the person becomes entitled on or after 22nd March 2006, the first sentence of that subsection applies in relation to that interest only if—

(a) immediately before the person's death, the interest falls within subsection (1B) below, or

(b) the person dies under the age of 18 years and, immediately before the person's death, section 71D of the Inheritance Tax Act 1984 (age 18-to-25 trusts) applies to the property in which the interest subsists.

(1B) an interest falls within this subsection if—

(a) the interest is—
   (i) an immediate post-death interest, within the meaning given by section 49A of the Inheritance Tax Act 1984,
   (ii) a transitional serial interest, within the meaning given by section 49B of that Act, or
   (iii) a disabled person's interest within section 89B(1)(c) or (d) of that Act, or

(b) section 71A of that Act (trusts for bereaved minors) applies to the property in which the interest subsists.

(1C) Subsection (1A) above does not have effect in relation to the operation of subsection (1) above as applied by subsection (2) below (but see subsection (2A) below).

(2) Subsection (1) above shall apply where the person entitled to an interest in possession in all or any part of settled property dies (although the interest does not then terminate) as it applies on the termination of such an interest.

[(2A) Where the interest in possession mentioned in subsection (2) above is one to which the person becomes entitled on or after 22nd March 2006—

(a) subsection (2) above, and

(b) the first sentence of subsection (1) above as applied by subsection (2) above, apply in relation to that interest only if, immediately before the person's death, the interest falls within subsection (1B)(a) above.]³²

(3) This section shall apply on the death of the person entitled to any annuity payable out of, or charged on, settled property or the income of settled property as it applies on the death of a person whose interest in possession in the whole or any part of settled property terminates on his death.

(4) Where, in the case of any entitlement to an annuity created by a settlement some of the settled property is appropriated by the trustees as a fund out of which the annuity is payable, and there is no right of recourse to, or to the income of, settled property not so appropriated, then without prejudice to subsection (5) below, the settled property so appropriated shall, while the annuity is payable, and on the occasion of the death of the person entitled to the annuity, be treated for the purposes of this section as being settled property under a separate settlement.

(5) If there is an interest in a part of the settled property and, where that is an interest in income, there is no right of recourse to, or to the income of, the remainder of the settled property, the part of the settled property in which the interest subsists shall while it subsists be treated for the purposes of this section as being settled property under a separate settlement.

A1.33   s.73 Death of life tenant: exclusion of chargeable gain

(1) Where, by virtue of section 71(1), the assets forming part of any settled property are deemed to be disposed of and reacquired by the trustee on the occasion when a person becomes (or would but for a disability become) absolutely entitled thereto as against the trustee, then, if that occasion is the death of a person entitled to an interest in possession in the settled property—

    (a) no chargeable gain shall accrue on the disposal, and

    (b) if on the death the property reverts to the disponer, the disposal and reacquisition under that subsection shall be deemed to be for such consideration as to secure that neither a gain nor a loss accrues to the trustee, and shall, if the trustee had first acquired the property at a date earlier than 6th April 1965, be deemed to be at that earlier date.

[(1A) Subsection (1)(b) above shall be treated as having effect in relation to a sub-fund settlement if the property does not revert to the trustees of the principal settlement in relation to that sub-fund settlement by reason only that—

    (a) a sub-fund election is or has been made in respect of another sub-fund of the principal settlement, and

    (b) the property becomes comprised in that other sub-fund settlement on the death of the person entitled to the interest in possession.³³

(2) Where the interest referred to in subsection (1) above is an interest in part only of the settled property to which section 71 applies, subsection (1)(a) above shall not apply but any chargeable gain accruing on the disposal shall be reduced by a proportion corresponding to that represented by the part.

(2A) Where the interest in possession referred to in subsection (1) above is one to which the person becomes entitled on or after 22nd March 2006, subsections (1) and (2) above apply in relation to that interest only if—

³² Added by Finance Act (2006 c.25), Sch.20(4), para.30(3).
³³ Added by Finance Act (2006 c.25), Sch.12(3), para.42.

(a) immediately before the person's death, the interest falls within section 71B, or

(b) the person dies under the age of 18 years and, immediately before the person's death, section 71D of the Inheritance Tax Act 1984 (age 18-to-25 trusts) applies to the property in which the interest subsists.

(3) The last sentence of subsection (1) of section 72 and subsection (3) to (5) of that section shall apply for the purposes of this section as they apply for the purposes of section 72(1).

s.74 Effect on sections 72 and 73 of relief under section 165 or 260   A1.34

(1) This section applies where—

(a) a claim for relief was made under section 165 or 260 in respect of the disposal of an asset to a trustee, and

(b) the trustee is deemed to have disposed of the asset, or part of it, by virtue of section 71(1) or 72(1)(a).

(2) section 72(1)(b) and 73(1)(a) shall not apply to the disposal of the asset or part by the trustee, but any chargeable gain accruing to the trustee on the disposal shall be restricted to the amount of the held-over gain (or a corresponding part of it) on the disposal of the asset to him.

(3) Subsection (2) above shall not have effect in a case within section 73(2) but in such a case the reduction provided for by section 73(2) shall be diminished by an amount equal to the proportion there mentioned of the held-over gain.

(4) In this section "held-over gain" has the same meaning as in section 165 or, as the case may be, 260.

APPENDIX II

PRECEDENTS

Bare trust	**A2.01**
Disabled person's trust	**A2.09**
Bereaved minor trust	**A2.25**
18–25 trust	**A2.26**
Specimen Will clauses	**A2.27**
IPDI trust of residue for (minor) children of the testator with substitution in the case of a pre-deceasing child leaving issue	**A2.43**
Debt/Charge documentation	**A2.47**
Deed of Variation (a) severing beneficial joint tenancy and (b) creating a nil rate band discretionary trust with debt/charge provisions	**A2.51**
Disclaimer of a life interest where life tenant has died within two years of the deceased who established the trust	**A2.62**
Appointment of IPDI trust out of a two-year discretionary trust	**A2.64**

BARE TRUST[1]

A2.01 THIS DECLARATION OF TRUST is made the .... day of .... 200............. by .... of .... ('the Donor')

WHEREAS:

(A) The Donor is the legal and beneficial owner of the property described in the Second Schedule ("the Property").

(B) The Donor wishes to make provision by way of gift for [insert details of beneficiary] who is under 18 years of age ("the Beneficiary") by declaring himself trustee of the Property.

A2.02 NOW THIS DEED IRREVOCABLY WITNESSES as follows:

1. DEFINITIONS

In this Deed where the context so admits:

1.1 "the Trust Fund" shall mean the property described in the Second Schedule and any additions to the Trust Fund by way of further declaration or otherwise and the assets from time to time representing the said property and additions or any part or parts thereof.

1.2 "the Trustees" shall mean the Donor or other the trustees or trustee for the time being of this Declaration.

2. DECLARATION OF TRUST

A2.03 The Donor declares that from the date of this Declaration he holds the Trust Fund and any income thereof upon the following trusts and subject to the following provisions.

3. BENEFICIAL INTEREST

A2.04 The Trustees shall hold the Trust Fund and the income thereof upon trust for the Beneficiary absolutely.

4. POWER OF APPOINTMENT OF TRUSTEES

A2.05 The power of appointing a new or additional trustee or trustees of this Declaration shall be vested in the Donor during his lifetime and thereafter the statutory power of appointment shall apply.

---

[1] See Ch. 30.

5. ADMINISTRATIVE POWERS

Until the Beneficiary attains the age of 18 years the powers and provisions contained in the First Schedule shall apply to the Trust Fund and the income of it.

A2.06

6. POWER OF MAINTENANCE

S. 31 of the Trustee Act 1925 shall not apply to this Declaration to the intent that the Beneficiary shall have the immediate right to the income of the Trust Fund notwithstanding his minority.

A2.07

7. EXTENDED POWER OF ADVANCEMENT[2]

S. 32 of the Trustee Act 1925 shall be deemed to apply as if the words "one half of" were omitted from proviso (a) of subsection (1).

A2.08

THE FIRST SCHEDULE

(insert administration provisions)

THE SECOND SCHEDULE

[Insert details of property settled]

In witness etc.

DISABLED PERSON'S TRUST[3]

THIS DECLARATION OF TRUST[4] is made the .... day of .... Two thousand and .... BY *insert names of trustees* (together "the Trustees" which expression shall where the context so admits include the trustees or trustee for the time being hereof).

A2.09

WHEREAS:

(A) The Criminal Injuries Compensation Authority ("the Authority") administers the Criminal Injuries Compensation Scheme.

(B) An award has been made under the terms of the said Scheme in favour of .... ("**the Settlor**") and it has been determined pursuant to the powers

---

[2] See 30.13.
[3] This trust envisages a disabled settlor (i.e. someone who is already disabled rather than about to become disabled) making the trust. Suitable adjustments can be made where the disabled person is not the settlor but the settlor is making provision for the disabled person: e.g. in the definition of Excluded Person. The Accumulation Period would not then be the settlor's life but the 21 years from the date of the settlement.
[4] See Ch. 26. This form has been drafted to satisfy the requirements of IHTA 1984, s.89.

thereby conferred to settle the sum of £ .... ("the Specified Sum") on the trusts hereinafter declared.[5]

(C) For the purpose aforesaid the Authority has caused the Specified Sum to be paid to the Trustees to be held on the trusts hereby declared.

(D) This Settlement is to be known as "**The** .... **Disabled Person's Trust** "

A2.10 **NOW THIS DEED IRREVOCABLY WITNESSES** as follows:

DEFINITIONS

1. In this Deed the following expressions have the following meanings namely:

(a) the expressions **"the Authority" "the Settlor" "the Trustees"** and **"the Specified Sum"** have the meanings hereinbefore respectively assigned to them

(b) **"the Trust Fund"** includes:
   (i) the Specified Sum and
   (ii) all other capital accepted by the Trustees as an addition to the Trust Fund and all accumulations (if any) of income directed to be held as an accretion to capital
   (iii) the money investments and property from time to time representing the same.

(c) The expression **"Excluded Person"** or **"Excluded Persons"** means [*insert details. This will be the settlor and usually spouse/other minor children of the settlor if the settlor is not the disabled person and wishes to avoid a reservation of benefit (in which case he must be excluded) or the trust being treated as settlor interested (in which case spouse and dependent children apart from the disabled person must be excluded.)*]

(d) **"the Trust Period"** means the period ending on the last day of the period of eighty years commencing from the date hereof which period (and no other) shall be the applicable perpetuity period.

(e) **"the Principal Beneficiary"** means .... born on .... (who is the Settlor)

(f) **"the Beneficiaries"** shall mean such of the following as are alive now or born during the Trust Period:
   (i) the Principal Beneficiary and his issue;
   (ii) the Principal Beneficiary's spouse or widow if any
   (iii) .... (**"the Secondary Beneficiaries"**)[6]

(g) **"Charity"** means any corporation association society or other institution or trust being charitable according to the laws of England and Wales

(h) the **"Accumulation Period"** means the period of 21 years immediately following the execution of this Deed or until the earlier death of the Settlor (being the Principal Beneficiary)[7]

(i) (i) the singular number shall include the plural number and vice versa

---

[5] Note that this deed envisages a payment by the Criminal Injuries Board but it could be a number of other bodies making the payment for the disabled person. The disabled person is regarded as the settlor when being paid compensation for injuries etc.

[6] The disabled person may not be able to have children: hence is sensible to have a wide class or at least power to add other persons (other than Excluded Persons).

[7] This will need to be modified if the Settlor is not the Principal Beneficiary so that the words "or until etc" to the end of the sentence are deleted.

(ii) the masculine gender shall include the feminine and neuter genders and vice versa

(iii) words importing persons shall include firms and corporations

TRUST FOR INVESTMENT

2. The Trustees shall hold the Trust Fund UPON TRUST to invest the same in investments of any nature hereby authorised with full power to vary or transpose such investments into others of a like nature.

TRUSTS WHILE PRINCIPAL BENEFICIARY IS ALIVE

3. (1) The Trustees shall hold the Trust Fund during the life of the Principal Beneficiary UPON TRUST to pay or apply the income thereof to or for the maintenance support or benefit of the Principal Beneficiary in such manner as they think fit[8] PROVIDED that:

(a) the Trustees may during the Accumulation Period accumulate the whole or any part or parts of the income of the Trust Fund by investing the same and the resulting income thereof in investments of any nature hereby authorised and so that all accumulations so made shall form part of the capital of the Trust Fund for all purposes

(b) the Trustees may during the life of the Principal Beneficiary if they consider it to be for the benefit of the Principal Beneficiary distribute or apply the whole or such part as they think fit of the income of the Trust Fund to or for the benefit of all or any one or more of the Beneficiaries for the time being living in such manner and if more than one in such shares as they think fit

(c) the exercise of the above powers is subject always to the restrictions contained in clause 10 (exclusion of Excluded Persons from any benefit).

(2) Notwithstanding the foregoing trusts and powers the Trustees may at any time or times and from time to time during the life of the Principal Beneficiary pay transfer or apply the whole or any part or parts of the capital of the Trust Fund to or for the advancement or benefit of the Principal Beneficiary in such manner as they think fit and may if they consider it to be for the benefit of the Principal Beneficiary[9] (subject to clauses 10 hereof) distribute or apply the whole or such part or parts as they think fit of the capital of the Trust Fund to or for the benefit of all or any one or more of the Beneficiaries for the time being living in such manner and if more than one in such shares as they think fit.

(3) The exercise of the above powers is subject always to the restrictions contained in clause 14 (compliance with s.89 Inheritance Tax Act 1984).

TRUSTS AFTER THE DEATH OF THE PRINCIPAL BENEFICIARY

4. Upon the death of the Principal Beneficiary the Trustees shall hold the Trust Fund and the income thereof upon trust:

A2.11

A2.12

A2.13

---

[8] This form envisages that the income can be paid to Principal Beneficiary as well as other Beneficiaries but in fact all the income could be paid to others. It is not a requirement in IHTA 1984, s.89 that the Principal Beneficiary (being the disabled person) should receive a minimum amount of income from the trust.

[9] This envisages no distributions of capital to anyone else during the lifetime of the Principal Beneficiary unless such distributions are for his benefit: e.g. to reimburse someone who is looking after him. The inheritance tax legislation is in fact more flexible: it does permit payments to others even if this does not benefit the Principal Beneficiary provided that the payments to others do not exceed one half during the lifetime of the Principal Beneficiary.

(1) to pay such funeral expenses (including the cost of a memorial) as they consider appropriate for the Principal Beneficiary and subject thereto
(2) for such person or persons (other than any Excluded Persons) or charitable purposes as the Principal Beneficiary may by deed or deeds revocable during his lifetime (but not by any deed made irrevocable during his lifetime) or by will or codicil (including any statutory will or codicil executed pursuant to Part VII Mental Health Act 1983) appoint and subject thereto
(3) upon trust for such of the Principal Beneficiary's child or children as shall [either attain the age of 21 years][10] before the end of the Trust Period or shall be living and under that age at the end of the Trust Period and if more than one in equal shares absolutely PROVIDED always that if any such child shall die under the age of 21 years before the end of the Trust Period leaving a child or children who shall either attain the age of 18 years before the end of the Trust Period or shall be living and under that age at the end of the Trust Period then such child or children of that deceased child shall take (and if more than one in equal shares absolutely) the share of the Trust Fund and the income from it to which such deceased child would have been entitled if he or she had attained a vested interest;
(4) Notwithstanding the above trusts the Trustees shall after the death of the Principal Beneficiary have power at any time or times during the Trust Period to appoint the whole or any part of the capital and/or income of the Trust Fund to or for the absolute benefit of any Beneficiary or upon trust for or for the benefit of such of the Beneficiaries, at such ages or times, in such shares, upon such trusts (which may include interest in possession, discretionary or protective trusts) and in such manner generally as the Trustees shall in their absolute discretion by deed revocable or irrevocable during the Trust Period appoint. Any such appointment may include such powers and provisions for the maintenance, education or other benefit of the Beneficiaries or for the accumulation of income, and such administrative powers and provisions, as the Trustees think fit.
(5) Subject thereto the Trustees shall from time to time during the Trust Period pay or apply the income and may pay or apply the whole or any part or parts of the capital of the Trust Fund upon such charitable trusts or for such charitable purposes under the laws of England and Wales as they shall from time to time in their absolute discretion determine.
(6) Subject to and in default of such determination or appointment under sub-clause 4(5) above the Trust Fund and the income thereof shall at the end of the Trust Period be held in equal shares for the following charities:

[*Name charities connected with disability*]

Provided that if any of the above organisations shall be found not to exist at the end of the Trust Period or to have amalgamated with another organisation or shall no longer be charitable under the laws of England and Wales, the share in the Trust Fund otherwise passing to that organisation shall be given to such organisation or organisations having the same or similar exclusively charitable objects under the laws of England and Wales as the Trustees may in their absolute discretion select and determine such selection and determination to be made on or before the end of the Trust Period.

ADMINISTRATIVE POWERS

A2.14   5. The Trustees shall in addition and without prejudice to all statutory powers have the powers and immunities set out in the Schedule hereto provided that the

---

[10] Alter as appropriate.

Trustees shall not exercise any of their powers so as to conflict with the beneficial provisions of this Settlement or clauses 10 and 14.

EXTENDED POWER OF MAINTENANCE

6. S.31 of the Trustee Act 1925 shall be deemed to apply as if the words "may in all circumstances be reasonable" had been omitted from paragraph (i) of sub-section (1) and in substitution there had been inserted the words "the Trustees may think fit" and as if the proviso at the end of sub-section (1) had been omitted   A2.15

EXTENDED POWER OF ADVANCEMENT

7. S.32 of the Trustee Act 1925 shall be deemed to apply as if the proviso (a) of sub-section (1) had been omitted.   A2.16

TRUSTEE CHARGING CLAUSE

8. (1) Any trustee being a trust corporation or company authorised to undertake trust business shall be entitled in addition to reimbursement of its proper expenses to remuneration for its services in accordance with its published terms and conditions for trust business from time to time and in the absence of any such published terms and conditions in accordance with such terms and conditions as may from time to time be agreed by the Trustees   A2.17

   (2) Any trustee who shall be an individual engaged in any profession or business either alone or in partnership shall be entitled to charge and be paid and to retain all professional or other proper charges for any business done or time spent or services rendered by him or his firm in connection with the trusts powers and provisions of this settlement or of any assurance of immovable property and the proceeds of sale thereof to be held on the trusts of this Settlement and shall also be entitled to retain any share of brokerage or commission paid to him or his firm by any broker agent or insurance office in connection with any acquisition of or dealing with any investments or property or the effecting or payment of any premium on any policy of insurance subject or intended to become subject to the trusts of this settlement or any such assurance

   (3) No trustee holding any directorship or other office or employment or retainer in relation to any company all or any of whose shares stock or securities shall at any time be subject to any trusts of this Settlement shall be accountable for any remuneration received in connection with such directorship office employment or retainer.

APPOINTMENT OF NEW TRUSTEES

9. (1) Subject as hereinafter provided the statutory power of appointing trustees shall apply hereto and shall be vested in the Trustees provided that: A2.18

   (a) if the Trustees shall refuse or be incapable of acting or if there shall at any time be no Trustee hereof the said power shall be vested in the Authority which shall be entitled to act for this purpose by its duly appointed agent

   (b) in no circumstances shall any Excluded Person or the Principal Beneficiary be appointed a Trustee hereof

   (2) At all times there must be at least two Trustees hereof of whom at least one must be a solicitor accountant registered medical practitioner or other suitably qualified professional person

(3) In the event that the number of Trustees falls below two or there is at any time no professional person no power or discretion vested in the Trustees shall be exercisable other than the power to appoint new or additional trustees

EXCLUSION OF EXCLUDED PERSONS

A2.19 10. (1) No discretion or power by this Settlement or by law conferred on the Trustees or any other person shall be exercised and no provision of this Settlement shall operate directly or indirectly so as to cause or permit any part of the capital or income of the Trust Fund to become in any way or at any time payable to lent to or applicable for the benefit of the Excluded Persons and the Trust Fund and income thereof shall at all times be held and enjoyed to the entire exclusion of the Excluded Person or of any benefit to the Excluded Persons by contract or otherwise.

(2) The prohibition in this clause shall apply notwithstanding anything else contained or implied in this Settlement.

CLAUSE HEADINGS

A2.20 11. Clause headings are included for reference only and do not affect the interpretation of this Settlement.

PROPER LAW FORUM AND PLACE OF ADMINISTRATION

A2.21 12. (1) The proper law of this Settlement shall be that of England and Wales and all rights under this Settlement and its construction and effects shall be subject to the jurisdiction of and construed according to the laws of England and Wales

(2) The Courts of England and Wales shall be the forum for the administration of these trusts.

TRUSTS OF LAND

A2.22 13. The provisions of S.11(1) of the Trusts of Land and Appointment of Trustees Act 1996 ("the Act") shall not apply to any land situated in England and Wales which or the proceeds of sale of which may at any time be subject to the trusts of this settlement or any trusts appointed or arising under it or to any assurance of immovable property situated in England and Wales such that the property or the net proceeds of sale of it are held on the trust of this settlement.

RESTRICTIONS ON POWERS

A2.23 14. In exercising any of their powers under this deed (whether fiduciary or administrative) the Trustees must ensure that not less than one half of the value of the settled property which is applied during the lifetime of the Principal Beneficiary is applied for his benefit and shall not do anything to prevent s.89 of the Inheritance Tax Act 1984 applying to the Trust Fund during the lifetime of the Principal Beneficiary.

PROTECTION OF TRUSTEES

A2.24 15. In the professed execution of the trusts and powers of this Settlement none of the Trustees (being an individual) shall be liable for any loss arising by reason of any improper investment made in good faith or the retention of any improper investment or any failure to see to the insurance of or preservation of any chattels or the making or revising of any inventory of them or for the negligence or fraud of any agent employed by him or by any other of the Trustees (although the employment of such agent was not strictly necessary or expedient) or by reason of any other matter or thing whatever except wilful and individual fraud or wrongdoing on the part of that one of the Trustees who is sought to be made liable or (in the case of a professional Trustee entitled to charge for his services as trustee and who does so charge) except for the negligence of such Trustee.

IN WITNESS whereof the parties hereto have hereunto set their hands and seals the day and year first above written.

THE SCHEDULE

[Administrative Powers]

BEREAVED MINOR TRUST

(i) *a single child:*   A2.25

"I leave the sum of (insert e.g. IHT nil rate band) to my daughter Daisy absolutely contingently on her attaining the age of 18 and subject thereto to my sister Phoebe absolutely".[11]

(ii) *Consider adding a widened power of advancement:*

"Section 32 of the Trustee Act 1925 shall apply but with the deletion of the words 'one half of' in Section 32(1)(a)."[12]

(iii) *more than one child:*

"I leave the sum of [*insert amount*] to such of my children as survive me".[13]

---

[11] For bereaved minor trusts, see 25.13 *et seq*. If desired Daisy could be given an immediate right to income (s.31 of the TA 1925 would need to be excluded: see A2.44). It would still be a BMT (not an IPDI) and the CGT death uplift would be available in the event of Daisy dying before the age of 18.
[12] For the advantage of including this widened power, see 25.8.
[13] This excludes the substitution provided for in Wills Act 1837 s.33: see *re Horton* (1979) 88 DLR (3d) 264 (Brit. Columbia). Consider, however, whether substitution is desirable (See 25.27). Also consider adding a widened power of advancement. For HMRC's views see App. III A3.123 *et seq.*

18–25 TRUST

A2.26 "I leave the residue of my estate to such of my children as shall survive me and attain the age of 25 and if more than one in equal shares absolutely".

Notes:

1. It is recommended that a widened power of advancement be included which could be used (a) to accelerate vesting so that a child could become absolutely entitled at 18 and thereby avoid an IHT charge[14] or (b) to postpone vesting beyond 25 (a "settled advance").[15]
2. If the will gives the children immediate interests in possession the trust will be an IPDI and not fall within the s.71D regime.[16]
3. If the trustees subsequently exercise a widened power of advancement to give a minor child an immediate right to income this will not prevent s.71D from continuing to apply.[17]
4. If a minor child dies under the age of 18 there is no IHT charge and, if he had enjoyed an interest in possession at the date of death, a CGT uplift.[18]
5. Assume that a child dies under the age of 25 and that his share accrues to his siblings; the IHT position is that if the siblings are under the age of 25 so that their shares are held on 18–25 trusts there is no IHT charge. When the siblings are over 25, if the deceased child is over 18 the normal s.71D exit charge will apply to his share.[19]

SPECIMEN WILL CLAUSES

(i) Definitions

A2.27 6. (1) In clause 7 of this Will where the context so permits the following expressions shall have the following meanings:

(i) "**the Discretionary Beneficiaries**" shall mean subject to the provisions of clause 6(2) below:

(aa) my said husband/wife

(bb) my children and remoter issue

(cc) the spouses widows and widowers of the persons mentioned in (bb)

and "**discretionary beneficiary**" shall have a corresponding meaning.

---

[14] See HTA 1984, s.71E(2)(a).
[15] See 25.36.
[16] See HTA 1984, s.49A.
[17] So long as the power is not exercised within two years of death otherwise an IPDI will be read back under IHTA 1984, s.144(3)–(5).
[18] See 25.39.
[19] See HTA 1984, s.71F(2)(b).

(ii) "**the Trust Period**" shall mean the period commencing with the date of my death and ending Eighty years thereafter and such period of Eighty years shall be the perpetuity period applicable to the dispositions made by my Will PROVIDED THAT my Legacy Fund Trustees may declare by irrevocable deed that the Trust Period (but not the said perpetuity period) shall terminate on such date as they may specify therein (such date of termination to be earlier than the end of the said period of Eighty years but the same as or later than the date of such deed)

(iii) "**the accumulation period**" shall mean the period commencing with the date of my death and ending Twenty-one years thereafter or on the earlier termination of the Trust Period

(iv) "the Legacy Fund Trustees" shall mean (*insert details*) or other the trustee or trustees for the time being of the Legacy Fund.

A2.28

(2) (i) SUBJECT to sub-clause (b) below:

A2.29

(a) My Legacy Fund Trustees (being not less than two in number or a trust corporation) shall have power by any deed or deeds revocable (during the Trust Period) or irrevocable executed during the Trust Period to declare that any individual or individuals whether or not then born or ascertained or any Charity or Charities (other than any individual then a trustee of the Legacy Fund and other than any individual or Charity previously excluded under the power set out in (b) below) shall from such time and (subject to any future exercise of the power set out in clause 2(i)(b) below) either permanently or for such period or periods as shall be specified in any such deed or deeds be included in the class of Discretionary Beneficiaries defined in Clause 6(1)(i) above and

(b) The Legacy Fund Trustees (being not less than two in number or a trust corporation) shall also have power by any deed or deeds revocable (during the Trust Period) or irrevocable executed during the Trust Period to declare that any individual or individuals whether or not born or ascertained or any Charity or Charities who or which is or are a member or members (or eligible to be added as a member or members) of the class of Discretionary Beneficiaries immediately prior to the execution of such deed or deeds shall from such time and either permanently or for such period or periods as shall be specified in any such deed or deeds cease to be a member or members (or eligible to become a member or members) of such class.

(ii) PROVIDED always that no such deed made in exercise of either of the powers conferred by sub-clause (i) shall affect the validity or effect of:

A2.30

(a) any distribution previously made to or for the benefit of any beneficiary under or pursuant to any power or discretion

(b) any transmissible interest (whether vested or contingent) previously conferred on any beneficiary

(c) any future distribution to any beneficiary consequent on the absolute vesting in possession of any such interest as is mentioned in sub-clause (ii)(b) and

(d) the Legacy Fund Trustees (being not less than two in number or a trust corporation) may at any time or times during the Trust Period by deed or deeds extinguish (or restrict the future exercise of) both or either of the powers (but not any of the restrictions applicable to them) conferred by sub-clause (i) above.

(ii) **Legacy Fund—Nil rate band discretionary trust (with loan/charge provisions)**

A2.31

7. (1) THIS clause shall not take effect unless the gift made to my [husband/wife] by Clause [*insert number*] of my Will takes effect (or but for this Clause would do so).

(2) IN this Clause "**the Nil-Rate Sum**" means the largest sum of cash which could be given on the trusts of this Clause without any inheritance tax becoming due in respect of the transfer of the value of my estate which I am deemed to make immediately before my death.

(3) I GIVE the Nil-Rate Sum to my Legacy Fund Trustees on trust to invest it in exercise of the powers of investment given them by my Will and by law and to hold it and the property which currently represents it ("**the Legacy Fund**") on the trusts and with and subject to the powers and provisions set out in this clause.

A2.32 (4) DURING the Trust Period my Legacy Fund Trustees (being at least two in number or a trust corporation) may at any time or times:

    (i) by deed or deeds revocable (during the Trust Period) or irrevocable appoint that all or any part or parts of the income or capital of the Legacy Fund shall be held on such trusts (including discretionary and protective ones) in favour or for the benefit of all or any one or more of the Discretionary Beneficiaries and with and subject to such powers (including dispositive and administrative ones exercisable by my Legacy Fund Trustees or any other person) and other provisions as my Legacy Fund Trustees think fit and

    (ii) transfer all or any part or parts of the income or capital of the Legacy Fund to the trustees of any Settlement wherever established (whose receipt shall be good discharge to them) to be held free from the trusts of my Will and on the trusts and with and subject to the powers and provisions of that Settlement but only if those trusts powers and provisions are such that (at the time of the transfer) they could themselves have created them under (i) above.

A2.33 (5) IN default of and subject to any exercise of the powers given them by the preceding provisions:

    (i) during the Trust Period my Legacy Fund Trustees shall pay or apply the income of the Legacy Fund to or for the maintenance education support or otherwise for the benefit of such one or more of the Discretionary Beneficiaries as my Legacy Fund Trustees may in their absolute discretion think fit but with power (during the period of 21 years from my death) to accumulate such income or any part or parts of it (with power to apply the accumulations of past years as if they were income of the current year) and with power (during the Trust Period) to resolve to hold the whole or any part or parts of such income as income on trust for any of the Beneficiaries absolutely and

    (ii) on the expiry of the Trust Period my Legacy Fund Trustees shall hold the Legacy Fund as to both capital and income on trust absolutely for such of my issue as are then living and if more than one in equal shares through all degrees according to their stocks and so that no issue shall take whose parent is alive and so capable of taking.

A2.34 (6) MY Legacy Fund Trustees (being at least two in number) may by deed or deeds (and so as to bind their successors) wholly or partially release or restrict the powers given them by this clause.

A2.35 (7) ANY other non-residuary gifts made by my Will or any Codicil to it shall have priority to this one.

A2.36 (8) INSTEAD of satisfying the legacy wholly by the payment of cash (or by the appropriation of property) to the Legacy Fund Trustees my Trustees may:

    (i) require the Legacy Fund Trustees to accept in place of all or any part of the Nil-Rate Sum a binding promise of payment made by my Trustees as trustees of any residuary property given by this Will or any Codicil hereto on trusts under which my [husband/wife] has an interest in possession for the purposes of Inheritance Tax which debt shall be repayable on demand*

      (ii) charge all or any part of the Nil Rate Sum on any property which is (or but for this clause would be) given by this Will or any Codicil to it on trusts under which my [husband/wife] has an interest in possession for the purposes of Inheritance Tax.*

(9) THE Legacy Fund Trustees may lend money currently held by them to my spouse.   A2.37

(10) IN amplification of the foregoing provisions   A2.38

     (i) if my Trustees exercise their powers under (8)(i) above they shall be under no further liability to see that the Legacy Fund Trustees receive the sum promised and if they exercise their powers under (8)(ii) they shall (to the extent of the value at my death of the property charged) be under no further liability to see that the Legacy Fund Trustees receive the sum secured

     (ii) if my Trustees exercise their powers under (8)(ii) above they may give an assent of the property subject to the charge and no one in whose favour the assent is made shall become personally liable for the sum secured

     (iii) the Legacy Fund Trustees may require security to be given for any debt to be created by a promise within (8)(i) above or by a loan within (9) and in relation both to such debts (whether or not secured) and to any debt to be secured by a charge within (8)(ii) (all of which shall be debts payable on demand) they

        (1) may (subject to the foregoing provisions) impose such terms (if any) as they think fit including terms as to interest and the personal liability of the borrower and terms linking the debt to the Index of Retail Prices or otherwise providing for its amount to vary with the passage of time according to a formula and

        (2) may subsequently leave the debt outstanding for as long as they think fit and refrain from exercising their rights in relation to it and waive the payment of all or any part of it or of any interest due in respect of it

and they shall not be liable if my Trustees are or become unable to pay the debt or a security is or becomes inadequate or for any other loss which may occur through their exercising or choosing not to exercise any power given by this sub-clause

     (iv) the powers given by this clause are without prejudice to any other powers given by this Will or any Codicil to it or by the general law and are exercisable even though my Trustees and the Legacy Fund Trustees may be the same persons and my spouse may be among them (but they are not exercisable while my spouse is the sole Legacy Fund Trustee) and any of the Legacy Fund Trustees may exercise or concur in existing all powers and discretions given to him by this clause or by law notwithstanding that he has a direct or other personal interest in the mode or result of any such exercise.   A2.39

(iii) IPDI Trust of Residue   A2.40

8. I GIVE DEVISE AND BEQUEATH all my property both movable and immovable of whatever nature and wheresoever situated except property otherwise disposed of by this Will or by any Codicil hereto unto my Trustees UPON TRUST to sell call in and convert the same into money (so far as not already consisting of money) with power to postpone the sale calling in and

---

* amend if residue given outright to spouse.

conversion thereof (even as regards property of a terminable hazardous or wasting nature) in the absolute and uncontrolled discretion of my Trustees without being liable for loss and to hold the net proceeds and my ready money upon the following trusts:

(1) UPON TRUST to pay thereout (in exoneration of any property which would otherwise be liable for payment of the same) all my funeral and testamentary expenses and debts and any general legacies given by this Will or any Codicil hereto and any tax or duty arising in respect of my death (even if not a testamentary expense) on all gifts in this Will and any Codicil hereto given free of such tax or duty

(2) UPON TRUST if necessary to invest the remainder after such payment in or upon any investments hereinafter authorised for the investment of trust funds with power to vary and transpose the same

(3) UPON TRUST to stand possessed of such investments and such of my estate as remains for the time being unsold and my ready money and all property from time to time respectively representing the same (hereinafter together called "**my Residuary Trust Fund**") and the income thereof upon the following trusts.

A2.41   **9. Trusts for the surviving spouse**[20]

9.1 THE income of my Residuary Trust Fund shall be paid to my [Husband/Wife] during [his/her] lifetime.

9.2 THE Trustees may, at any time during the Trust Period, pay or apply the whole or any part of the Trust Fund in which my [Husband/Wife] is then entitled to an interest in possession to [him/her] or for [his/her] advancement or otherwise for [his/her] benefit in such manner as the Trustees shall in their discretion think fit. In exercising the powers conferred by this sub-clause, the Trustees shall be entitled to have regard solely to the interests of my [Husband/Wife] and to disregard all other interests or potential interests under my Will.

A2.42   **10.   Remainder Trusts**

The provisions of this clause shall apply subject to the provisions of sub-clause 9.1 and to any exercise of the power conferred by sub-clause 9.2.

10.1 The Trustees shall hold the capital and income of my Residuary Trust Fund for such of my children as shall survive me and attain the age of 18 years before the end of the Trust Period, or shall be living and under that age at the end of the Trust Period, and, if more than one, in equal shares absolutely.

[10.2 If any child of mine shall die in my lifetime or before attaining a vested interest leaving issue who shall attain the age of 18 years before the end of the Trust Period or be under that age and living at the end of the Trust Period, then such issue shall take the share of the Trust Fund which such child would otherwise have taken. If there shall be more than one of such issue they shall take in equal shares per stirpes, so that no one shall take a share if any of his ascendants is alive and takes a share.]

10.3 Subject as above, the Trustees shall hold the capital and income of the Trust Fund upon trust for [   ] absolutely.

---

[20] If desired flexible trusts may be adopted: e.g. the trustees may be given a power of appointment in favour of the Discretionary Beneficiaries (as defined above) which could be exercised to terminate the interest in possession of the surviving spouse. The existence of such a power will not prevent there being an IPDI.

IPDI TRUST OF RESIDUE FOR (MINOR) CHILDREN OF THE TESTATOR WITH SUBSTITUTION IN THE CASE OF A PRE-DECEASING CHILD LEAVING ISSUE

Residuary estate A2.43

8. **I GIVE** all my property not otherwise disposed of by this Will or any Codicil to my Trustees:—

   (1) With power at their discretion to sell all or any of such property when they think fit and to invest the proceeds in any investments hereby authorised and with power from time to time to vary investments for others of an authorised nature.

   (2) To pay all debts funeral and executorship expenses legacies and tax.

   (3) To hold the remainder and the income thereof ("my Residuary Estate") for such of my children as survive me ("my Children") and if ore than one in equal shares but if any of them dies before me leaving a child or children [*who attain the age of [twenty one]*] such child or children shall take the share of my Residuary Estate which my deceased child would otherwise have taken and if more than one in equal shares absolutely and **PROVIDED ALWAYS** that the share in my Residuary Estate of any child of mine ("My Child") shall not vest in him absolutely but shall be retained and invested by my Trustees and held upon the following trusts.

   (4) The provisions of sub-clauses (5) to (7) shall apply to the share of the Trust Fund held upon trust for My Child under sub-clause (32). In these provisions, such share is called "**Share**" and that one of My Children who is primarily interest in the Share is called the "**Life Tenant**". A2.44

   (5) The income of the Share shall be paid to the Life Tenant during his lifetime. If and so long as the Life Tenant is under the age of 18, the Trustees may pay or apply any income of the Share to him or for his maintenance or education or otherwise for his benefit as they shall in their discretion think fit. Any balance of the income shall be retained by the Trustees upon trust for the Life Tenant absolutely. Any such retained income may, at any time, be paid or applied as if it was income arising in the then current year. Section 31 of the Trustee Act 1925 shall not apply to the Share so long as the Life Tenant is under the age of 18.

   (6) The Trustees may, at any time or times, during the Trust Period, pay or apply the whole or any part of the Share in which the Life Tenant is then entitled to an interest in possession to him or for his advancement or otherwise for his benefit in such manner as the Trustees shall in their discretion think fit. In exercising the powers conferred by this sub-clause the Trustees shall be entitled to have regard solely to the interests of the Life Tenant and to disregard all other interests or potential interests under this Deed. A2.45

   (7) The Life Tenant shall have power to appoint his spouse a life or lesser interest (including an interest terminable by the Trustees at any time) in the income of all or any part of the Share. The Life Tenant may make the commencement of such interest dependent upon conditions as to survivorship or otherwise as he shall in his absolute discretion determine [*and he may confer on the Trustees the same power for the benefit of his spouse as they have under sub-clause (6) for his benefit*]. No such appointment shall be valid unless, at the date if takes effect, the Life Tenant is entitled to an interest in possession in the Trust Fund or the part of the Trust Fund to which the appointment relates.[21]

---

[21] Note that for deaths on or after March 22, 2006 the IHT spouse exemption will not be available in respect of this subsequent interest in possession on the death of the Life Tenant. Instead this share will be subject to the relevant property regime.

A2.46 (8) Subject as above, the capital and income of the Share shall be held upon trust for such of the children of the Life Tenant as attain the age of 25 before the end of the Trust Period or are living and are under that age at the end of the Trust Period; and if more than one, in equal shares absolutely.

(9) Subject as above, the Share, together with any accrual to it, shall accrue to the other Shares the trusts of which shall not previously have failed or determined (otherwise than by absolute vesting) and if more than one, equally between them. Each such accrual shall be held upon, with and subject to the same trusts, powers and provisions as the Share to which it accrues.

DEBT/CHARGE DOCUMENTS[22]

DEBT SCHEME – DOCUMENTATION AFTER DEATH

A2.47 **1. Draft Letter from the Executors to the Trustees of the Legacy Fund (when a charge being imposed by the Executors)**

This letter records the agreement that has been reached between us as to the way in which the Legacy Fund is to be constituted.
   Under the Will of [   ] Deceased he provided that the Legacy Fund should have a value equal to the unused portion of his nil rate band and gave the executors power to require the trustees of that fund to accept in place of either cash or other property either a binding promise of payment by the surviving spouse or a charge over any property passing to that surviving spouse. At the same time the Trustees may, *inter alia*, impose terms as to the payment of interest or linking the sum outstanding to an appropriate index.
   It has now been agreed that you as Trustees will be entitled to the nil rate sum (£285,000) which will be charged over property which will pass to his surviving spouse. In line with the provisions in the Will we as executors will have no further liability to ensure that you receive this amount and when the assets comprised in the residue are transferred to the surviving spouse he/she will likewise will have no personal responsibility to ensure that you receive the relevant property. Your only recourse therefore is against the charged property.
   It is also confirmed that the sum outstanding is repayable on a written demand being made by yourselves either to the executors or, once the assets have been transferred to the surviving spouse to that spouse. [You have further agreed that the debt shall not carry interest nor be linked to an index.]

A2.48 **2. Equitable Charge**

THIS CHARGE is made the [. . . . . .] day of [. . . . .] 200 [. . .] between [. . . . .] ("the Executors") of the one part and [   ] ("the Trustee") of the other part.
SUPPLEMENTAL to the Will ("the Will") of [   ] Deceased ("the Testator")

WHEREAS

(1) The Testator died on [   ] and the Will was proved by the Executors in the [   ].

---
[22] For a consideration of the debt/charge scheme, see 28.17 *et seq.*

(2) The Legacy Fund and the 'Nil Rate Sum' has the same meaning as in the Will and the Nil Rate Sum amounts to £285,000.

(3) The Trustees were appointed trustees of the Legacy Fund by clause [ ] of the Will.

(4) The Executors hold the property described in the Schedule ("the property").

(5) In exercise of the powers given to them by clause [ ] of the Will the Executors have required the trustees to accept in place of the Nil Rate Sum a debt to be secured by a charge over the property [and the Trustees have required this sum to be indexed linked by reference to the RPI at the date of the Testator's death].

NOW THIS DEED WITNESSES as follows:

1. In this Deed "**the Sum Owing**" shall mean the Nil Rate Sum multiplied by the index figure in the Retail Prices Index for the month in which the Sum Owing is being calculated and divided by the index figure in the Retail Prices Index for the month in which this Deed is executed.

2. The Executors hereby charge the property with the payment to the trustees of the Sum Owing and the Executors are under no further liability to ensure that the same is paid to the Trustees who accept that their only recourse in respect of the Sum Owing is against the charged property.

3. It is confirmed that in the event that the Executors vest the property in the residuary beneficiary ("the Beneficiary") of the Testator's estate
    (a) they will serve notice in writing on the Trustees and
    (b) the Beneficiary shall not be under any personal liability to ensure that the sum owing is paid to the Trustees.

4. if the Retail Prices Index shall have been replaced by another official index and/or if there shall be any change in the manner in which the Retail Prices Index operates the Trustees shall have power in their absolute discretion to determine the amount of the Sum Owing in accordance with such formula as seems to them to be just and reasonable in the circumstances.

IN WITNESS whereof the parties have executed these presents as a Deed the date and year first before written

SCHEDULE

(the Property)

Signed etc

Note: The charge will be over property in the Deceased's estate. In many cases the main asset will be a beneficial interest in the main residence. The charge will accordingly be over this asset and will, of necessity, be equitable. In cases where the Deceased had been sole legal and equitable owner of the house a standard legal charge may be employed.

DEED OF VARIATION (A) SEVERING BENEFICIAL JOINT TENANCY AND (B) CREATING A NIL RATE BAND DISCRETIONARY TRUST WITH DEBT/CHARGE PROVISIONS[23]

A2.51 **THIS DEED OF VARIATION** is made the [   ] day of [   ] by [   ] of [   ] ("the Widower")

SUPPLEMENTAL TO the will of [   ] ("the Deceased") dated [   ] ("the Will")

WHEREAS

1. The Deceased died on [   ] and probate of the Will was granted to the Widower out of the District Registry at [   ] on [   ];

2. At the date of her death the Deceased and the Widower owned as beneficial joint tenants (1) two accounts with the [   ] Bank numbers [   ] ("the Accounts") and (2) [   ][24] ("the Property") all of which assets passed to the Widower by survivorship.

3. In the events which have happened the Widower is the sole residuary beneficiary of the Deceased's estate and is now desirous of varying the dispositions of assets comprised in the Deceased's estate in accordance with the provisions set out in this Deed.

A2.52 **NOW THIS DEED WITNESSES**

1. That it shall be deemed that the Widower had immediately prior to the death of the Deceased severed their beneficial joint tenancy in the Accounts and in the Property so that at the date of her death her beneficial half share in the said Accounts and Property formed part of her free estate.

2. That the Will shall be varied as if there were inserted immediately before clause [   ] the following pecuniary legacy.[25]

A2.53 [ ] (A) **Definitions**[26]
In this clause:

  (i) "**the Nil-Rate Sum**" means the largest sum of cash which could be given on the trusts of this clause without any inheritance tax becoming due in respect of the transfer of the value of my estate which I am deemed to make immediately before my death

  (ii) "the Trust Period" means the period starting with my death and ending 80 years afterwards (and that period is the perpetuity period applicable to this clause)

  (iii) "the Beneficiaries" means my Husband and[27]

---

[23] For instruments of variation, see Chapter 29.
[24] This will normally be the matrimonial home.
[25] Some draftsmen may prefer to set out the trust in a Schedule to the Deed.
[26] These clauses will be incorporated in a will which leaves the residue to the surviving spouse absolutely. The draftsman will doubtless wish to make the operation of the clauses dependent upon the surviving spouse surviving to take the residue. It is not considered that this creates problems even if the entitlement of the surviving spouse depends upon the satisfaction of a survivorship period since though IHTA 1984, s.92 will not apply to the trust the tax treatment will not alter i.e. there will be a chargeable transfer whether or not the clauses take effect.
[27] If desired further flexibility could be given by permitting the Legacy Fund trustees to add further persons as beneficiaries.

(1) any issue of mine who are alive at the start of or born during the Trust Period and

(2) anyone who is at any time during the Trust Period the spouse or (whether or not remarried) the widow or widower of any such issue or of any issue of mine who are already dead or die before me

and "Beneficiary" shall have a corresponding meaning

(iv) "my Legacy Fund Trustees" shall mean [   ] or such other trustees or trustee for time being of this Legacy Fund.[28]

(B) Declaration of Trust   A2.54

I GIVE the Nil-Rate Sum to my Legacy Fund Trustees ON TRUST to invest it in exercise of the powers of investment given them by this Will or by law and to hold it and the property which currently represents it ("the Legacy Fund") on the trusts and with and subject to the powers and provisions set out in this clause.

(C) Powers of Appointment   A2.55

DURING the Trust Period my Legacy Fund Trustees (being at least two in number or a trust corporation) may at any time or times

(i) by deed or deeds revocable or irrevocable appoint that all or any part or parts of the income or capital of the Legacy Fund shall be held on such trusts (including discretionary and protective ones) in favour or for the benefit of all or any one or more of the Beneficiaries and with and subject to such powers (including dispositive and administrative powers exercisable by my Legacy Fund Trustees or any other person) and other provisions as my Legacy Fund Trustees think fit and

(ii) transfer all or any part or parts of the income or capital of the Legacy Fund to the trustees of any Settlement wherever established (whose receipt shall be a good discharge to them) to be held free from the trusts of this Will and on the trusts and with and subject to the powers and provisions of that Settlement but only if those trusts powers and provisions are such that (at the time of the transfer) they could themselves have created them under (i) above

(D) Default Trusts   A2.56

IN DEFAULT of and subject to any exercise of the clause (c) power of appointment

(i) during the Trust Period my Legacy Fund Trustees shall pay or apply the income of the Legacy Fund to or for the maintenance education support or otherwise for the benefit of such one or more of the Beneficiaries as my Legacy Fund Trustees may in their absolute discretion think fit BUT with power (during the period of 21 years from my death) to accumulate and add to capital such income or any part or parts of it (and to apply the accumulations of past years as income of the current year) AND with power (during the Trust Period) to resolve to hold the whole or any part or parts of such income as income on trust for any of the Beneficiaries absolutely and

(ii) on the expiry of the Trust Period my Legacy Fund Trustees shall hold the Legacy Fund as to both capital and income ON TRUST for such of my issue as are then living and if more than one in equal shares although through all degrees accord-

---

[28] There are attractions in selecting persons other than the Executors to be trustees of the Legacy Fund although in practice it is common for the same persons to act in both capacities. See further clause E(v).

ing to their stocks and so that no issue shall take whose parent is alive and so capable of taking.

(E) Constitution of Trust by Debt or Charge

A2.57 INSTEAD of satisfying that legacy wholly by the payment of cash (or by the appropriation of property) to the Legacy Fund Trustees my Executors[29] may:

    (i) require the Legacy Fund Trustees to accept in place of all or any part of the Nil-Rate Sum a binding promise of payment made by my[husband[30]

    (ii) charge all or any part of the Nil Rate Sum on any property which is (or but for this clause would be) given by this will or any codicil to it to my husband absolutely[31]

(F) Loans to Beneficiaries

A2.58 THE Legacy Fund Trustees may lend any money to a Beneficiary or Beneficiaries

(G) Position of my Executors

A2.59 (i) if my Executors exercise their powers under (E)(i) above they shall be under no further liability to see that the Legacy Fund Trustees receive the sum promised and if they exercise their power under (E)(ii) they shall (to the extent of the value at my death of the property charged) by under no further liability to see that the Legacy Fund Trustees receive the sum secured

    (ii) if my Executors exercise their power under (E)(ii) above they may give an assent of the charged property subject to the charge and no one in whose favour the assent is made shall become personally liable for the sum secured.[32]

(H) Powers and Protection of the Legacy Fund Trustees

A2.60 THE Legacy Fund Trustees may require security to be given for any debt to be created by a promise within (E)(i) above[33] or by a loan within (F) and in relation both to such debts (whether or not secured) and to any debt to be secured by a charge within (E)(ii) (all of which shall be debts payable on demand) they

    (i) may (subject to the foregoing provisions) impose such terms (if any) as they think fit including terms as to interest and the personal liability of the borrower

---

[29] Ensure this definition fits in with the will.

[30] This is the "simple" debt arrangement. Note also clauses (G)(i); (iii).

[31] This is the "charge route" which may be employed to avoid s.103 and SDLT problems. The clause enables the executors to impose the charge not just over property passing to the surviving spouse under the residue clause but also over property which would **but for this clause** pass to that spouse. Take the following example: the value of the Testator's estate is £290,000 of which £285,000 is left on the nil rate band trust leaving only £5,000 in residue. If the trust is to be established by a charge then it is important that the full value of the estate is subject to the charge and not just the £5,000 which passes under the residue clause.

[32] It is important that no liability is imposed on the recipient of the charged property since (a) this could lead to the disallowance of the debt under s.103 and (b) if liability to discharge the debt is assumed Stamp Duty Land Tax will be payable (if land is involved).

[33] The Legacy Fund Trustees should give serious consideration to requesting security from the surviving spouse who will (in the majority of cases) have become absolutely entitled to the family home (so that the giving of such security should not pose problems).

and terms linking the debt to the Index of Retail Prices or otherwise providing for its amount to vary with the passage of time according to a formula and[34]

(ii) may subsequently leave the debt outstanding for as long as they think fit and refrain from exercising their rights in relation to it and waive the payment of all or any part of it or of any interest due in respect of it and they shall not be liable if my [husband/wife] is or becomes unable to pay the debt or a security is or becomes inadequate or for any other loss which my occur through their exercising or choosing not to exercise any power given by this clause

(iii) the powers given by this clause are without prejudice to any other powers given by this Will or any Codicil to it or by the general law and are exercisable even though my Executors and the Legacy Fund Trustees may be the same persons and my husband may be among them (but they are not exercisable while my husband is the sole Legacy Fund Trustee) and any of the Legacy Fund Trustees may exercise or concur in existing all powers and discretions given to him by this clause or by law notwithstanding that he has a direct or other personal interest in the mode or result of any such exercise.[35]

A2.61

3. The provisions of the Inheritance Tax Act 1984, s.142(1) and of the Taxation of Chargeable Gains Act 1992 s 62(6) shall apply to the dispositions of property effected by this deed.[36]

DISCLAIMER OF A LIFE INTEREST WHERE LIFE TENANT HAS DIED WITHIN TWO YEARS OF THE DECEASED WHO ESTABLISHED THE TRUST[37]

THIS DEED OF DISCLAIMER is made the [　　　　] day of [　　　　] 200[　　] BY A and B of [　　　　] ("the Executors") acting in their capacity as personal representatives of [　　　　][38] ("the Deceased Life Tenant") who died on [　　　　].

A2.62

WHEREAS:

(A) [　　　　] ("the Testatrix") died on [　　　　]

(B) Under clause - of the Will of the Testatrix dated ————- ("the Will") the residuary estate as therein defined (which property is set out in the Schedule hereto and is called in this deed "the Trust Assets") was left upon trust to pay the income therefrom to the Deceased Life Tenant (her husband) during his lifetime or until his remarriage and thereafter to hold the same as to capital and income for her children [　　　　] in equal shares absolutely.

---

[34] It is unlikely that the surviving spouse will wish (or often be in a position) to pay interest on the outstanding debt. Given the power to lend money to a beneficiary, the trustees will often be content to leave the debt interest free but doubtless repayable on demand.
[35] Frequently the surviving spouse is both executor and legacy fund trustee but it remains important that he/she is not the sole executor or legacy fund trustee and there may be cases where he/she should not act as executor.
[36] For reading-back and the "election", see 29.04
[37] See 29.44.
[38] Insert name of deceased life tenant.

(C) In the events that have happened the Deceased Life Tenant died after the Testatrix on [   ] but within two years of the death of the Testatrix and the said children of the Testatrix survived her and therefore take the Trust Assets in equal shares absolutely.

(D) The Deceased Life Tenant had not done any act or thing which could constitute an acceptance of any part of the Trust Assets. The Executors hereby wish to disclaim on his behalf his interest in the Trust Assets.

NOW THIS DEED WITNESSES as follows:

A2.63

1. **THE** Executors hereby irrevocably disclaim and renounce all the rights, interest and entitlement of the Deceased Life Tenant in the Trust Assets and all other rights, interest and entitlement (if any) that he may have arising under clauses [   ] of the Will and disclaim and renounce all and any benefit therefrom.

2. **THE** Executors confirm that the Deceased Life Tenant did not accept his interest in the Trust Assets and received no benefit from the same.

IN WITNESS whereof the parties have hereunto executed this document as their deed the day and year first before written

THE SCHEDULE

hereinbefore referred to

[insert all details of Residuary Estate disclaimed]

APPOINTMENT OF IPDI TRUST OUT OF A TWO-YEAR DISCRETIONARY TRUST[39]

A2.64 **THIS DEED OF APPOINTMENT** is made the [   ] day of [   ] 200[ ] by [   ] and [   ] of [   ] (together called "the Appointors") and is **SUPPLEMENTAL TO:**

(A) A will dated [   ] ("the Will") made by [   ] ("the Deceased") and

(B) An assent dated [   ] ("the Assent") under which certain freehold land known as [   ] as more particularly described therein ("the Property") was assented to the Appointors as trustees to hold on the discretionary trusts set out in clause [   ] of the Will.

WHEREAS:

A2.65

1. The Deceased died on [   ] and the Will was proven on [   ] at [   ] District Probate Registry.

---

[39] For a consideration of IHTA 1984, s.144 and "reading-back", see 29.49 *et seq.*

2. The Appointors are the present trustees of the residuary estate of the Deceased.

3. Under clause [   ] of the Will the residuary estate of the Deceased (therein called "the Trust Fund") is held on such trusts in favour or for the benefit of all or any one or more of the Discretionary Beneficiaries and in such shares or proportions and with and subject to such powers and provisions for their respective maintenance education or other benefit as the Appointors [being at least two in number] by any deed or deeds revocable during the Discretionary Period (which period is defined in the Will as $80/2^{40}$ years from the date of the Deceased's death) or irrevocable and executed during the Discretionary Period shall appoint.

4. The Discretionary Beneficiaries include the children of the Deceased namely A and B and their respective spouses widows widowers children and remoter issue.

5. The Appointors have not yet exercised their aforesaid powers of appointment but are now desirous of exercising their powers under the WIll revocably and as hereinafter set out.

NOW THIS DEED WITNESSES as follows:

1. **EXPRESSIONS** used in this deed shall where the context so admits have the same meanings as set out in the Will but in this deed "the Appointed Fund" means the Property (as described in the Assent) the net sale proceeds thereof and the assets from time to time representing the same. A2.66

2. **IN** exercise of their powers contained in the Will under clause [   ] and of every other power them enabling the Appointors hereby revocably appoint and declare that the Appointed Fund and the income thereof shall from the date of this Deed be held upon trust to divide the same into two equal parts of which the first such equal part and the assets from time to time representing the same ("A's Fund") shall be held upon the trusts declared in clause 3 below and of which the second such equal part and the assets from time to time representing the same ("B's Fund") shall be held upon the trusts declared in clause 5 below.

3. **THE** Trustees shall until the end of the Discretionary Period hold A's Fund and the income thereof upon the following trusts and subject to the following powers and provisions: A2.67

    (a) The Trustees shall pay the income of A's Fund to A during the life of A.[41]
    (b) Subject thereto[42] The Trustees may, at any time or times pay, transfer or apply to or for the advancement or benefit (whether absolutely or in trust) of A the whole or any part of A's Fund to which A is then entitled to an interest in possession. In exercising the powers conferred by this sub-clause, the Trustees shall be entitled to have regard solely to the interests of A and to disregard all other interests or potential interests in A's Fund.

4. **IF** the trusts of A's Fund shall fail the Trustees shall hold A's Fund as an accretion to B's Fund and upon the trusts appertaining thereto (including absolute beneficial interests therein) the trusts of which have not failed and as one fund therewith.

5. **THE** Trustees shall hold B's Fund and the income thereof upon the trusts contained in clauses 3 and 4 above with the substitution wherever the same appears:

---

[40] Sometimes the discretionary period ends automatically on expiry of two years from death.
[41] This takes effect as an IPDI for A. No age of capital entitlement needs to be specified.
[42] Set out continuing trusts after A's death or on earlier termination of interest. BMT would be possible on A's death or on earlier termination of interest but only if the bereaved minors are children of the deceased. Otherwise all ongoing trusts e.g. for A's spouse will be relevant property trusts.

(a) For A's Fund of B's Fund
(b) For A of B
(c) For B's Fund of A' Fund
(d) For B of A.

A2.68

6. **THE** administrative and other provisions contained in the Will shall continue to apply to the Appointed Fund in so far as those powers and provisions are consistent with the provisions declared by this Deed.

7. **THE** Trustees shall have power at any time or times before the end of the Discretionary Period[43] by deed or deeds wholly or partly to revoke or vary all or any of the trusts powers and provisions which apply to the Appointed Fund by virtue of this deed and if thought fit by the same or similar deed or deeds to make such fresh appointment in exercise of their said powers of appointment conferred by the Will as they may in their absolute discretion think fit provided that no exercise of their powers of revocation shall invalidate any prior payment or application of all or any part or parts of the capital or income or deprive a beneficiary of income or capital to which he has already become entitled.

8. **THE** Trustees may by deed release or restrict the future exercise of their powers of revocation hereunder either wholly or to the extent specified in the relevant deed.

IN WITNESS whereof etc.

---

[43] Or trust period if defined differently.

APPENDIX III

MISCELLANEOUS MATERIAL

BN 25 Budget 2006 .... **A3.01**
SDLT and NRBDT (HMRC Statement) **A3.16**
POA Guidance Notes May 2006 .... **A3.21**
POA COP 10 Letter **A3.61**
Schedule 20: Questions and Answers **A3.105**
Tax Bulletin 83: HMRC statement on *Hastings-Bass* **A3.148**
POA correspondence with HMRC on elections **A3.149**

BN 25 (BUDGET 2006)

ALIGNING THE INHERITANCE TEX TREATMENT FOR TRUSTS

Who is likely to be affected?

A3.01 1. People who have set up, or have an interest in, "accumulation & maintenance" trusts (A+Ms) and/or "interest in possession" trusts (IIPs) that do not meet new inheritance tax (IHT) rules about their terms and the circumstances in which they are created.

General description of the measure

A3.02 2. This measure refines the current IHT rules for A&Ms and IIPs. Trusts of this type that currently receive special treatment but do not qualify under the new rules will come within the mainstream IHT regime for "relevant property" trusts. This change will apply also to existing A&Ms and IIPs, subject to the transitional rules described below.

Operative date

A3.03 3. The new rules will apply on and after March 22, 2006 to new trusts, additions of new assets to existing trusts and, subject to transitional provisions, to other IHT-relevant events in relation to existing trusts. Transitional rules will provide for a period of adjustment for certain existing trusts up to 6 April 2008, and for continuing exclusion from the "relevant property" charges if they satisfy conditions for ongoing protection

Current law and proposed revisions

A3.04 4. Part III, Chapter III Inheritance Tax Act 1984 (IHTA) provides a specific regime for "relevant property" trusts—broadly, those trusts in which no person has an interest in possession. It combines:

- an immediate "entry" tax charge of 20% on lifetime transfers that exceed the IHT threshold into "relevant property" trusts;
- a "periodic" tax charge of 6% on the value of trust assets over the IHT threshold once every ten years, and
- an "exit" charge proportionate to the periodic charge when funds are taken out of a trust between ten-year anniversaries.

5. There are special rules for A&M trusts (section 71 IHTA) and IIP trusts (Part III, Chapter II IHTA) Lifetime transfers into these trusts are exempt from IHT if the settlor survives seven years, and the trusts are not subject to the periodic or exit charges.　　**A3.05**

6. Legislation in the Finance Bill will limit these special rules to trusts that:　　**A3.06**

- are created on death by a parent for a minor child who will be fully entitled to the assets in the trust at age 18; or
- are created on death for the benefit of one life tenant in order of time whose interest cannot be replaced (more than one such trust may be created on death as long as the trust capital vests absolutely when the life interest comes to an end); or
- are created either in the settlor's lifetime or on death for a disabled person (see section 89(4) IHTA).

Any other trusts will fall into the mainstream IHT rules for "relevant property" trusts.

New trusts

7. In the case of trusts created on and after 22 March 2006, this means that lifetime transfers into trusts are no longer eligible for special treatment unless they are set up for a disabled person. All other transfers will be immediately chargeable. Trusts that do not qualify for special treatment—whether they are created in life or on death—will be liable to the periodic and exit charges applying to "relevant property" trusts.　　**A3.07**

Existing A&M trusts

8. Where existing A&M trusts provide that the assets in trust will go to a beneficiary absolutely at 18—or where the terms on which they are held are modified before 6 April 2008 to provide this—their current IHT treatment will continue.　　**A3.08**

9. Where they do not, the trust assets will become "relevant property" from 6 April 2008 and the periodic and exit charges will apply. Ten-yearly anniversaries will arise by reference to the original date of settlement. For the first ten years after 6 April 2008, the rate of charge will reflect the fact that the property has not been "relevant property" throughout a full ten- year period. For example, if the first ten-yearly anniversary falls in November 2008, it will be one twentieth of the normal charge.　　**A3.09**

Existing IIP trusts

10. The current rules for existing IIP trusts will run on until the interest in the trust property at 22 March 2006 comes to an end. If someone then takes absolute ownership, this will be a transfer by the person with the interest in the property—either a transfer on death or a "potentially exempt transfer" if they are still living—and will receive the same IHT treatment as now. The trust will have no further IHT consequences.　　**A3.10**

11. If the interest comes to an end so that the property remains on trust, this will be treated as the creation of new settled property;　　**A3.11**

- if it comes to an end during the lifetime of the person beneficially entitled to it, this will be a transfer creating "relevant property" (unless the new trusts are for charitable purposes) and will therefore be immediately chargeable; and

- if the interest comes to an end on death, it will form part of the person's IHT estate as now and the settled property will then become "relevant property" (unless the charity exemption applies). In both cases, the periodic and exit charges will apply.

A3.12 12. However, any new IIP that arises when an IIP created before 22 March 2006 comes to an end before 6 April 2008—whether on death or otherwise—will be treated as an IIP that was in place on 22 March 2006.

Gifts with reservation

A3.13 13. Where an individual is beneficially entitled to an interest in settled property, and continues to be treated for IHT purposes as owning the property, a termination of the interest in the individual's lifetime on or after 22 March 2006 will be treated as a gift for purposes of the IHT "gift with reservation" rules. So if they retain the use of the settled property after their interest in it ends, it will remain chargeable in their hands in the same way as if they had formerly owned it outright.

Capital gains tax consequentials

A3.14 14. Changes to the IHT treatment of trusts will have a number of implications for CGT:

- transfers into and out of trusts that will now come within the "relevant property" rules will automatically be eligible for hold-over relief under Section 260(2)(a) Taxation of Chargeable Gains Act 1992 (TCGA)[1];
- hold-over relief under Section 260(2)(d) TCGA will be restricted to trusts that meet the new IHT rules for trusts for minor children;
- the special rules in Section 72 and Section 73 TCGA relating to the death of a person entitled to an IIP will be restricted to assets that are subject to an IIP which meets the new IHT rules.

Further advice

A3.15 15. If you have any questions about the changes, please contact the Probate/IHT Helpline on 0845 3020 900. Information about Budget measures is available on the HM Revenue & Customs website at www.hmrc.gov.uk.

SDLT AND NRBDT (HMRC STATEMENT)

STAMP DUTY LAND TAX AND 'NIL-RATE BAND DISCRETIONARY TRUSTS'

A3.16 1. We have received a number of enquiries about the interaction between Stamp Duty Land Tax and 'nil-rate band discretionary trusts' ('NRB Trusts'). This note should enable taxpayers and their advisers to decide on the Stamp Duty Land Tax consequences of transactions with NRB Trusts. This note does not cover any taxes other than Stamp Duty Land Tax. Neither does it cover the powers or fiduciary responsibilities of

---

[11] This statement is severely misleading, see 9.33.

trustees of NRB Trusts, or of personal representatives, under general law. Trustees and personal representatives may wish to take independent legal advice on those aspects.

2. An NRB Trust is commonly established under the Will of a deceased person. The typical form is a pecuniary legacy, not exceeding the nil-rate band for inheritance tax, to be held by the trustees of the NRB Trust ('the NRB trustees') on discretionary trusts for a specified class of beneficiaries. The residue of the estate, often including the matrimonial home, commonly passes to the surviving spouse, although it may pass to residuary trustees. A3.17

3. Where the personal representatives discharge the pecuniary legacy by payment of the specified sum to the trustees no Stamp Duty Land Tax issue arises. However in many cases the personal representatives satisfy the legacy otherwise than by payment of the specified sum. It is in these cases that a Stamp Duty Land Tax liability may arise on the transfer of the matrimonial home or other land to the surviving spouse or residuary trustees. A3.18

4. The transfer of an interest in land, whether to a residuary beneficiary or to any other person, and whether in satisfaction of an entitlement under a Will or not, is a land transaction for Stamp Duty Land Tax purposes. The question is whether the transferee gives any chargeable consideration for the transfer. Very often a beneficiary gives no chargeable consideration for the transfer of land under a Will. However transactions in connection with NRB Trusts may result in the beneficiary giving chargeable consideration. A3.19

5. The commonest examples of such transactions, and their Stamp Duty Land Tax consequences, are as follows: A3.20

- The NRB trustees accept the surviving spouse's promise to pay in satisfaction of the pecuniary legacy and in consideration of that promise land is transferred to the surviving spouse. The promise to pay is chargeable consideration for Stamp Duty Land Tax purposes.

- The NRB trustees accept the personal representatives' promise to pay in satisfaction of the pecuniary legacy and land is transferred to the surviving spouse in consideration of the spouse accepting liability for the promise. The acceptance of liability for the promise is chargeable consideration for Stamp Duty Land Tax purposes. The amount of chargeable consideration is the amount promised (not exceeding the market value of the land transferred).

- Land is transferred to the surviving spouse and the spouse charges the property with payment of the amount of the pecuniary legacy. The NRB trustees accept this charge in satisfaction of the pecuniary legacy. The charge is money's worth and so is chargeable consideration for Stamp Duty Land Tax purposes.

- The personal representatives charge land with the payment of the pecuniary legacy. The personal representatives and NRB trustees also agree that the trustees have no right to enforce payment of the amount of the legacy personally against the owner of the land for the time being . The NRB trustees accept this charge in satisfaction of the legacy. The property is transferred to the surviving spouse subject to the charge. There is no chargeable consideration for Stamp Duty Land Tax purpose provided that there is no change in the rights or liabilities of any person in relation to the debt secured by the charge.

We have also been asked about the consequences for Stamp Duty Land Tax purposes of a Deed of Variation made by beneficiaries after the death of the deceased person. A Deed of Variation may effect a land transaction if it alters the beneficial interests in land, for example by settling land in trust. However, placing a charge on land is not in itself a land transaction. In addition paragraph 4 of Schedule 3 FA 2003 provides that under certain conditions a land transaction effected by a Deed of Variation is exempt from charge.

(November 2004)

HMRC POA GUIDANCE NOTES MAY 2006

INCOME TAX AND PRE-OWNED ASSETS GUIDANCE: SECTION 1

Contents

- 1. Outline of the charge to income tax
- 1.1 The circumstances in which the charge applies
- 1.2 What property is affected?
- 1.2.1 Land and chattels
- 1.2.2 Intangible property
- 1.3 When the charge does not apply
- 1.3.1 Excluded transactions
- 1.3.2 Exemptions from the charge
- 1.3.3 Residence or domicile outside the United Kingdom
- 1.3.4 De minimis exemption
- 1.3.5 Changes in the distribution of a deceased's estate
- 1.3.6 Guarantees

1. Outline of the charge to income tax

1.1 The circumstances in which the charge applies

A3.21 Section 84 of the Finance Act 2004 gave effect to the provisions of Schedule 15 of that Act. The schedule provides for a charge to income tax on benefits received by a former owner of property. Broadly it applies to individuals (the chargeable person) who continue to receive benefits from certain types of property they once owned after 17 March 1986 but have since disposed of. The schedule has effect for the tax year 2005–06 and subsequent years.

The property within the scope of the charge can be grouped into three headings:

- Land
- Chattels
- Intangible property

If the chargeable person has either disposed of any property within these headings by way of gift or, in some circumstances, sale, or contributed towards the purchase of the property in question and they continue to receive some benefit from the property they are potentially liable to the charge. The benefit may be occupation of the land, use of the chattel or the ability to receive income or capital from a settlement holding intangible property.

The preceding paragraph may suggest that every instance where an individual may have disposed of, or made a contribution to the purchase of, the relevant property will come within the scope of the charge. However, there are several types of transactions relating to land and chattels that are excluded from the scope of the charge. There are also provisions exempting the relevant property from the charge where the property is subject to a charge to inheritance tax or where specific protection from inheritance tax is given by legislation.

If the income tax charge applies the Schedule contains provisions enabling the taxable benefit to be calculated. In the case of the occupation or use of land and chattels the calculation of the taxable benefit will be determined to a large extent by the proportion which the value of the chargeable person's original interest in, or contribution to the purchase, bears to the current value of the property.

The following sections provide more detail on the conditions required for the charge to arise, where the transaction may be excluded or where the property is exempted, and how the benefit is calculated. All references to 'this Schedule' refer to Schedule 15 unless otherwise specified. References to 'the charge' refer to the charge to income tax arising under Schedule 15.

1.2 What property is affected?

The conditions required for the charge to apply are virtually identical where the property in question is land or chattels but they differ slightly in respect of intangible property.

A3.22

1.2.1 Land and chattels

The charge applies where the chargeable person occupies any land or uses or possesses any chattels, either alone or with other persons, and either the 'disposal condition' or the 'contribution condition' is met. Paragraphs 3 and 6 of this Schedule define the conditions.

The disposal condition

The disposal condition will apply if the chargeable person, at any time after 17 March 1986, owned relevant land or chattels, or other property whose disposal proceeds were directly or indirectly applied by another person towards the acquisition of the relevant land or chattels, and then disposed of all or part of their interest in the relevant land or chattels (or other property). If the disposal was an excluded transaction (see 1.3.1) the disposal condition will not apply.

Note that the disposal condition will apply to the chargeable person's occupation or use of property even if that property was never actually owned by them. If they gave away other property (apart from cash) to another person who sold such property and used these proceeds to purchase the relevant land or chattel the disposal condition is satisfied, unless it qualifies as an excluded transaction.

A disposition that creates a new interest in land or in a chattel out of an existing interest is taken to be a disposal of part of the existing interest.

The contribution condition

The contribution condition will apply if the chargeable person, at any time after 17 March 1986, provided any of the consideration given by another person for the acquisition of an interest in the relevant land or chattel, or for the acquisition of any other property the proceeds of the disposal of which were directly or indirectly applied by another person towards an acquisition of an interest in the relevant land or chattel. As with the disposal condition, if the provision of the consideration qualifies as an excluded transaction, this condition will not apply.

It can be seen that the contribution condition can apply not only where the contribution provided by the chargeable person is directly used to purchase the relevant land or chattel but where the contribution is indirect too. If they provided all or part of the consideration (eg. a cash gift) for the purchase of property by another person, who then sold the property and used the proceeds to purchase the land occupied, or the chattel used, by the chargeable person, the contribution condition is satisfied, unless it qualifies as an excluded transaction (see 1.3.1).

HMRC do not regard the contribution condition set out in Schedule 15, para 3(3) as being met where a lender resides in property purchased by another with money loaned to him by the lender. Our view is that since the outstanding debt will form part of his estate for IHT purposes, it would not be reasonable to consider that the loan falls within the contribution condition [and therefore not reasonably attributable to the consideration (Sch 15, para 4(2)(c)], even where the loan was interest free. It follows that the 'lender', in such an arrangement, would not be caught by a charge under Schedule 15.

1.2.2 Intangible property

In contrast to the provisions relating to land and chattels there is only one condition to be met for the charge to apply. Paragraph 8 of this Schedule defines the condition.

The charge applies where the chargeable person settles intangible property or adds intangible property to a settlement after 17 March 1986 on terms that any income arising from the settled property would be treated under section 624 ITTOIA 2005 (income arising under a settlement where the settlor retains an interest) as income of the chargeable person as settlor and any such income would be so treated even if subsection (2) of that section did not include any reference to the spouse of the settlor. In other words, a charge under paragraph 8 is not triggered where section 624 applies only because the settlor's spouse rather than the settlor has retained an interest. The settlor in this case is, of course, the chargeable person. For example if A sets up a trust for his wife on marriage and he is excluded from all benefit there is no possibility of paragraph 8 applying. However, if he sets up a trust where his wife receives the income but he can benefit if she dies then para 8 could potentially apply subject to any relevant exemptions.

In this context 'settlement' has the same meaning as it does for inheritance tax purposes. The definition of 'settlement' can be found in section 43(2) Inheritance Tax Act 1984. The fact that there is no element of bounty does not matter.

Intangible property means assets such as stocks and securities, insurance policies and bank and building society accounts. The provisions of this paragraph do not apply to land and chattels included in a settlement.

1.3 When the charge does not apply

A3.23   There are a number of situations where a charge to tax under Schedule 15 will not arise. Certain transactions are excluded from the charge and there are also exemptions from the charge where certain conditions are met.

1.3.1 Excluded transactions (Sch. 15, para. 10)

The concept of excluded transactions has no application to intangible property. They only serve to exclude from the income tax charge certain transactions relating to land and chattels.

For the purposes of the disposal conditions relating to land and chattels, the disposal of any property is an excluded transaction in relation to the chargeable person if

- It was a disposal of their whole interest in the property, except for any right expressly reserved by them over the property, either i. y a transaction made at arm's length with a person not connected with them, or ii. y a transaction such as might be expected to be made at arm's length between persons not connected with each other.

The exclusion clearly only applies to sales of the entire interest in the property at full market value although the words "except for any right expressly reserved" would envisage the sale of a freehold reversion subject to a lease but only if it was on arms length terms.

Concern was expressed that sales of a part share of property to commercial providers of equity release schemes would not qualify as an excluded transaction and an individual would be subject to the charge if he remained in occupation of the land. This concern was recognised in the Regulations to the charge which specifically exempted from the charge disposals of part of an interest in any property by a transaction made at arm's length with a person not connected with the chargeable person. Furthermore, the exemption is extended to disposals of a part share to anyone provided that they were made on arm's length terms and either took place before 7 March 2005, or took place on or after that date for a consideration not in the form of money or assets readily convertible into money.

- The property was transferred to their spouse or civil partner, or former spouse or civil partner where the transfer has been ordered by a court.
- The disposal was by way of gift (or in accordance with a court order for the benefit of a former spouse or civil partner) by virtue of which the property became settled property in which his spouse or civil parter or former spouse or civil partner is beneficially entitled to an interest in possession. The spouse or civil partner must take an interest in possession from the outset. It is **not** an excluded transaction, however, if the interest in possession of the spouse or civil partner or former spouse or civil partner has come to an end other than on their death unless the spouse or civil partner or former spouse or civil partner has become absolutely entitled to the property in which case we would accept that the benefit of the exclusion is not lost.
- The disposal was a disposition falling within section 11 Inheritance Tax Act 1984 (disposition for maintenance of family).
- The disposal is an outright gift to an individual and is for the purposes of the Inheritance Tax Act 1984 a transfer of value that is wholly exempt by virtue of section 19 (annual exemption) or section 20 (small gifts).

For the purposes of the contribution conditions relating to land and chattels, the provision by the chargeable person of consideration for another's acquisition of any property is an excluded transaction in relation to the chargeable person if

- The other person was their spouse or civil partner, or former spouse or civil partner where the transfer has been ordered by a court.
- On its acquisition the property became settled property in which their spouse or civil partner or former spouse or civil partner is beneficially entitled to an interest in possession. The spouse or civil partner must take an interest in possession from the outset. It is **not** an excluded transaction, however, if the interest in possession of the spouse or civil partner or former spouse or civil partner has come to an end otherwise than on their death unless the spouse or civil partner or former spouse or civil partner has become absolutely entitled to the property.
- The provision of the consideration constituted an outright gift of cash by the chargeable person to the other person (in this context the "other person" means the person referred to in paragraphs 3(3) and 6(3)) and was made at least 7 years before the earliest date on which the chargeable person occupied the land or had possession or use of the chattel As the earliest date the conditions can be met is 6 April 2005, any provision of consideration by way of an outright gift of cash made before 6 April 1998 will be an excluded transaction.
- The provision of the consideration is a disposition falling within section 11 of the Inheritance Tax Act 1984.

- The provision of the consideration is an outright gift to an individual and is for the purposes of the Inheritance Tax Act 1984 a transfer of value that is wholly exempt by virtue of section 19 or section 20.

1.3.2 Exemptions from the charge (Sch. 15, para. 11)

Property in the estate (para 11(1)) exemption

The charging provisions in schedule 15 relating to land, chattels and intangible property do not apply to a person at a time when their estate for the purposes of the Inheritance Tax Act 1984 includes the relevant property, or other property which

- derives its value from the relevant property, and
- whose value so far as attributable to the relevant property, is not substantially less than the value of the relevant property.

Where their estate includes property which derives its value from the relevant property and whose value, so far as attributable to the relevant property, is substantially less than the value of the relevant property

- the appropriate rental value of the relevant land, or
- the appropriate amount in respect of the chattel, or
- the chargeable amount in relation to the relevant intangible property must be reduced by such proportion as is reasonable to take account of the inclusion of the property in their estate.

For example if Mr B transfers his house to a company wholly owned by him, then provided there are no loans to the company one can say that the value attributable to the company is not less than the value of the house. But if Mr B gave the house to a company which was owned 25% by his wife then the value of the 75% shares he holds would be substantially less than the value of the house. If he has lent money to the company and the company holds the house we take the view that the company's value is less than the house unless (possibly) the loan is charged on the house.

Gifts with reservation Para 11(3) exemption

The charging provisions also do not apply to a person at a time when, for IHT purposes, the relevant property or property deriving its value from relevant property falls within the Gifts with Reservation provisions set out in Finance Act 1986.

The provisions of Schedule 15 are also disapplied if the property

- would fall to be treated as subject to a reservation but for any of sections 102(5)(d) to (i) of the Finance Act 1986 (certain cases where disposal by way of gift is an exempt transfer for purposes of inheritance tax). But where s.102(5)(h) is in point, Schedule 15 is disapplied only when the property remains subject to trusts complying with the requirements of Schedule 4, para 3(1) Inheritance Tax Act 1984 (maintenance funds),
- would fall to be treated as subject to a reservation but for subsection (4) of section 102B of the Finance Act 1986 (gifts with reservation: share of interest in land), or would have fallen to be so treated if the disposal by way of gift of an undivided share of an interest in land had been made on or after 9 March 1999. This refers to situations where the chargeable person transfers a share (usually 50%)

of their property to the donee and both the donee and the chargeable person continue to occupy the property, paying their share of household expenses, or
- would fall to be treated as subject to a reservation but for section 102C(3) of, and paragraph 6 of Schedule 20 to, the Finance Act 1986 (exclusion of benefit). This refers to situations where the chargeable person continues to use or occupy the property but pays full consideration in money or money's worth, or where they leave the property but have to move back at a later date due to an unforeseen change in their circumstances and are unable to look after themselves because of age or infirmity.

Where the contribution condition relating to land or chattels applies, paragraph 2(2)(b) of Schedule 20 (which excludes gifts of money from the provisions that apply where property is substituted for the original gift) should be disregarded. For example, if A gives cash to his son and they buy a home jointly and live together then while they live together, the POAT charge will not apply.

Schedule 15 also contains provisions for the chargeable person to elect that the relevant property that would otherwise be subject to the charge be treated as property subject to a reservation for the purposes of the Inheritance Tax Act 1984. If the election is made no charge under the Schedule will apply. Full details of these provisions are given in part 3 of these notes.

Excluded liability

Where at any time the value of a person's estate for the purposes of the Inheritance Tax Act 1984 is reduced by an 'excluded liability' affecting any property, only the excess of the value of the property over the amount of the excluded liability can be treated as comprised in their estate for the purposes of this schedule.

A liability is an excluded liability if

- the creation of the liability, and
- any transaction by virtue of which the person's estate came to include the relevant property or property which derives its value from the relevant property or by virtue of which the value of the property in their estate came to be derived from the relevant property, were associated operations, as defined by section 268 of the Inheritance Tax Act 1984.

The "amount" of the excluded liability will be the face value of the debt, including any rolled up interest or accrued indexation where this has been allowed for under the terms of the agreement. For the purposes of computing the charge under this schedule, it will be sufficient for the debt to be revalued taking into account outstanding interest, or accrued indexation, at the 5 yearly valuation dates. Any reduction of the debt resulting from a repayment can be taken into account as it occurred, and may be reflected in a revised computation of the tax in the relevant year and subsequently.

1.3.3 Residence or domicile outside the United Kingdom (Sch 15 para 12)

No charge to tax under this Schedule can arise in relation to any person for any year of assessment during which they are not resident in the United Kingdom.

If a person is resident in but domiciled outside the United Kingdom in any year of assessment, the provisions of this Schedule will only apply to land, chattels or intangible property situated in the United Kingdom.

In applying this Schedule to a person who was at any time domiciled outside the United Kingdom, no regard should be had to any property which is for the purposes of the Inheritance Tax Act 1984 excluded property in relation to them by virtue of section 48(3)(a) of that Act.

A person is to be treated as domiciled in the United Kingdom at any time if they would be so treated for the purposes of the Inheritance Tax Act 1984. Hence the deemed domicile rules will apply for the purposes of this income tax charge.

1.3.4 De minimis exemption (Sch 15 para 13)

An exemption from charge under this Schedule applies where in relation to any person in a year of assessment (example 1), the aggregate of the amounts specified below in respect of that year do not exceed £5,000 (example 2). Those amounts are

- in relation to any land to which paragraph 3 applies, the appropriate rental value as determined under paragraph 4(2)—see 2.1 below,
- in relation to any chattel to which paragraph 6 applies, the appropriate amount as determined under paragraph 7(2)—see 2.2 below, and
- in relation to any intangible property to which paragraph 8 applies, the chargeable amount determined under paragraph 9—see 2.3 below.

Example 1:

> The £5,000 is based on the chargeable amount for the year. So if a person is chargeable throughout the whole tax year and the annual benefit is calculated at £5,000 or less they do not have to declare the benefit on their income tax return. If a person is chargeable for only part of the year, say they only become chargeable for the last six months of the year where the full annual benefit would be £8,000, their exposure for the last six months is half that and the benefit of £4,000 would be covered by the de minimis. Where two people are equally chargeable for the whole year in respect of the same property, for example a property with an annual rental value of £8,000, their benefit would be £4,000 each and would be covered by the de minimis. (On the death of one, you should consider former ownership of the property, and the terms of occupation, in deciding whether the whole or a half of the rental value is chargeable on the survivor.)

Example 2:

> a person is chargeable under Para 3 for a benefit from land with an annual value of £4,000 and under Para 6 for a benefit from a chattel with an annual value of £3,000. The aggregate benefit is £7,000 and therefore not de minimis. If, in this example, an annual rental of £4,000 is paid to obtain the aggregate benefit, although the net benefit is £3,000 it is not de minimis because the annual open market rental value exceeds £5,000 and therefore the amount of the benefit (£3,000) would need to be declared. A person cannot avoid the tax charge by paying an annual rent to bring himself below £5000.

The de minimis is set against the annual benefit for intangible property after deduction of any tax paid under the headings of Para 9(1) of Schedule 15.

Example:

> A person benefits from a settlor interested trust where the benefit is calculated to £7,000 (N). The fund generates income on which tax of £3,000 (T) is payable. The net amount of the benefit (N-T) is £4,000 and is de minimis. The amount of

£5,000 does not represent a nil-rate band, therefore where the aggregate chargeable value exceeds £5,000 it is subject to the charge in full. When a taxpayer is chargeable for only part of a year, the £5,000 exemption is not pro-rated.

Where the de minimis exemption under paragraph 13 is not exceeded the transferor cannot make an election because he is not chargeable to income tax under Schedule 15.

1.3.5 Changes in the distribution of a deceased's estate (Sch. 15, para. 16)

Any disposition made by the chargeable person in relation to an interest in the estate of a deceased person is disregarded for the purposes of this Schedule if under section 17 Inheritance Tax Act 1984 the disposition is not a transfer of value by the chargeable person for IHT purposes. All dispositions covered by section 17, including disclaimers and variations where the provisions of section 142(1) Inheritance Tax Act 1984 apply, will be exempted from the charge by paragraph 16 of this schedule. [see Appendix 1 example]

For the purposes of this paragraph 'estate' has the same meaning as it has for the purposes of the Inheritance Tax Act 1984.

1.3.6 Guarantees (Sch. 15, para. 17)

Where a person ("A") acts as a guarantor in respect of a loan made to another person ("B") by a third party in connection with B's acquisition of any property, the mere giving of the guarantee is not regarded as the provision by A of consideration for B's acquisition of the property.

INCOME TAX AND PRE-OWNED ASSETS GUIDANCE: SECTION 2

Contents

- 2. How to calculate the benefit subject to the charge
- 2.1 Land
- 2.2 Chattels
- 2.3 Intangible property
- 2.4 Avoidance of double charge to income tax

2. How to calculate the benefit subject to the charge

Where the provisions of paragraphs 3 (land), 6 (chattels) and/or 8 (intangible property) apply to a person in respect of the whole or part of a year of assessment, an amount equal to the chargeable amount specified by the Schedule is treated as income of theirs chargeable to income tax.

A3.24

Unless stated otherwise, the approach to valuing property for the purposes of Schedule 15 follows the rule for Inheritance Tax set out in section 160 IHTA 1984. In other words, it is the price that the property might reasonably be expected to fetch if sold in the open market at that time, without any scope for a reduction on the ground that the whole property is to be placed on the market at one and the same time (see paragraph 15 of this Schedule).

The valuation date for property subject to the charge is 6 April in the relevant year of assessment or, if later, the first day of the taxable period.

When valuing relevant land or a chattel it is not necessary to make an annual revaluation of the property. The property should rather be valued on a 5-year cycle. Before the first 5-year anniversary the valuation of the property will be that set at the first valuation date. Thereafter the valuation at the latest 5-year anniversary will apply.

The "relevant land" for the purposes of paragraph 4(5) is the land currently occupied by the chargeable person. Therefore, where a valuation has been carried out in respect of a charge arising under Schedule 15, and within the 5-year cycle the subject property is sold and a smaller less valuable property is purchased for occupation by the chargeable person, then a new valuation will need to be carried out which will be used for the remainder of that 5-year cycle.

The 5-year anniversary is the fifth anniversary of 6 April in the first year of assessment in which the provisions of this Schedule relating to land or chattels apply to the chargeable person. The first valuation date is the date on which the provisions of this Schedule relating to land or chattels first applied to the chargeable person. If there is an interruption in the person's use or occupation of the property and the year of a 5-year anniversary is not a taxable period, the year in which the provisions of this Schedule are applied again will be treated as the next 5-year anniversary.

Example

> A is first chargeable to Schedule 15 on 6th April 2005. A valuation is obtained then. He becomes non-UK resident for three years from 6th April 2006 to 6th April 2009. The charge does not apply during this period. He returns to the UK on 7th April 2009. A new valuation is made then and this is the start of the next five year anniversary.

2.1 Land (Sch. 15, paras. 4 & 5)

A3.25   The chargeable amount in relation to the relevant land is the appropriate rental value, less the amount of any payments which the chargeable person is legally obliged to make during the period to the owner of the relevant land in respect of their occupation.

The appropriate rental value is

$$R \times \frac{DV}{V}$$

R is the rental value of the relevant land for the taxable period.
DV is

- Where the chargeable person owned an interest in the relevant land, the value as at the valuation date of the interest in the relevant land that was disposed of by the chargeable person or, where the disposal was a non-exempt sale, the "appropriate portion" (see final paragraphs of this section below) of that value,

- Where the chargeable person owned an interest in other property, the proceeds of which were used to acquire an interest in relevant land, such part of the value of the relevant land at the valuation date as can reasonably be attributed to the property originally disposed of by the chargeable person or, where the original disposal was a non-exempt sale, to the appropriate portion of that property,

- If the contribution condition applies, such part of the value of the relevant land at the valuation date as can reasonably be attributed to the consideration provided by the chargeable person.

V is the value of the relevant land at the valuation date.

The 'rental value' of the land for the taxable period is the rent which would have been payable for the period if the property had been let to the chargeable person at an annual rent equal to the annual value. The annual value is the rent that might reasonably be expected to be obtained on a letting from year to year if

- The tenant undertook to pay all taxes, rates and charges usually paid by a tenant, and
- The landlord undertook to bear the costs of the repairs and insurance and the other expenses, if any, necessary for maintaining the property in a state to command that rent.

The rent is calculated on the basis that the only amounts that may be deducted in respect of the services provided by the landlord are amounts in respect of the cost to the landlord of providing any relevant services. Relevant service means a service other than the repair, insurance or maintenance of the premises. In other words, if the landlord provides other relevant services, for example the maintenance of the common parts in a block of flats, that are reflected in the rent then the cost of providing those services may be deducted from the rent.

The regulations do not specify the sources from which the required valuations should be obtained. However we would expect the chargeable person to take all reasonable steps to ascertain the valuations, as they would do if, for example, they were looking to let a property on the open market.

Paragraph 4(4) introduces the concept of a 'non-exempt sale' for a disposal which is a sale of the chargeable person's whole interest in the property for cash, but which is not an excluded transaction as defined in paragraph 10. The 'appropriate proportion", which is relevant for ascertaining the "appropriate rental value in paragraph 4(2), can be determined using the formula

$$\frac{MV - 9}{MV}$$

Where MV is the value of the interest in land at the time of the sale and P is the amount paid.

Example

> A sells his house to his daughter for £100,000. It is worth £300,000. He lives in the house. In these circumstances we would say that only two thirds of the value of the house is potentially within the charge to POAT. However, since he made a gift of that two thirds we would accept that he is protected under para 11(5)(1) reservation of benefit from a charge on that two thirds. Note that if he sold part of his house to his daughter at an undervalue then the non-exempt sale provisions would not apply. So in the above example if he sold half his house to his daughter for £100,000 and that half share was in fact worth £300,000, although he would have reserved a benefit in two thirds of that half share, the £100,000 cash would be subject to POAT.

2.2 Chattels (Sch. 15, para. 7)

The chargeable amount in relation to any chattel is the appropriate amount, less the amount of any payments that the chargeable person is legally obliged to make during the period to the owner of the chattel for the possession or use of the chattel by the chargeable person.

The appropriate amount is

$$N \times \frac{DV}{V}$$

N is the amount of the interest that would be payable for the taxable period if interest were payable at the prescribed rate on an amount equal to the value of the chattel at the valuation date. The prescribed rate is the official rate of interest at the valuation date. The official rate has the meaning given in section 181 of the Income Tax (Earnings and Pensions) Act 2003.

Example

In 2005/6 A was caught by schedule 15 in respect of an earlier disposal of chattels. The chattels were worth £1,000,000 at the relevant valuation date on 6th April 2005. He will be treated as receiving a taxable benefit of 5% (current official rate of interest in 2005/6) × £1m = £50,000.

Note that the charge is computed differently from land and while any rental payments made to the owner will reduce the amount on which he is chargeable, the fact that he pays a market rent for their use does not prevent an income tax charge arising. Hence if he pays £10,000 rent he will still be taxable on a £40,000 benefit. Tax is due on 31 January 2007 unless A elects.

The provisions for ascertaining DV, V and defining a "non-exempt sale" and the "appropriate proportion" in relation to chattels that are similar to the provisions relating to land (see 2.1 above).

2.3 Intangible property (Sch 15 para 9)

The chargeable amount in relation to the relevant property is N minus T.

N is the amount of the interest that would be payable for the taxable period if interest were payable at the prescribed rate on an amount equal to the value of the relevant property at the valuation date. The prescribed rate is the official rate of interest at the valuation date. The official rate has the meaning given in section 181 of the Income Tax (Earnings and Pensions) Act 2003.

T is the amount of any income tax or capital gains tax payable by the chargeable person in respect of the taxable period by virtue of any of the following provisions

- Sections 547, 660A (now s.624 of the Income Tax (Trading and Other Income) Act 2005) or 739 of the Income and Corporation Taxes Act 1988,
- Sections 77 or 86 of the Taxation of Chargeable Gains Act 1992

so far as the tax is attributable to the relevant property.

Example

Mr A is the UK resident and domiciled settlor of a non-resident settlor interested settlement. (You should assume that Mr A has not reserved a benefit in the settled property nor has an interest in possession in the trust and is therefore subject to the POAT charge).

The settlement comprises 'intangible' property of cash and shares with a value of £1,500,000 at the valuation date. In the tax year 2005/06 the trustees receive income of £60,000 which is chargeable to income tax on Mr A under s.624. A further £150,000 Capital Gains are realised which are deemed to be Mr A's gains by virtue of s.86 TCGA '92. In these circumstances £24,000 Income Tax is payable on the £60,000 and £60,000 in CGT on the £150,000. The tax allowance (T) against the potential Schedule 15 charge is therefore £84,000. The chargeable amount (N) under Schedule 15 is 5% of £1,500,000 = £75,000. Since the tax allowance is greater than the chargeable amount, a charge under Schedule 15 will not arise.

2.4 Avoidance of double charge to Income Tax

The Schedule contains two provisions to avoid a double charge to income tax arising if the provisions of this Schedule apply. **A3.28**

- If the chargeable person is subject to the charge under more than one provision of this Schedule, i.e. if they were chargeable under paragraph 3 in respect of land they occupied and also under paragraph 8 (intangible property) if the land was owned by a company whose shares had been owned by them and had been settled on trusts of which they were a potential beneficiary, the charge will only apply to the provision that produces the higher amount of tax. If this amount does not exceed the de minimis limit no tax will be payable—the lower amount is disregarded completely.
- If the chargeable person occupies land or possesses or uses a chattel and is chargeable to income tax under the provisions of this Schedule and under the benefits code of Part 3 of the Income Tax (Earnings and Pensions) Act 2003, the provisions of Part 3 have priority. Tax will only be chargeable under this Schedule on any amount that exceeds the amount treated as earnings under Part 3.

INCOME TAX AND PRE-OWNED ASSETS GUIDANCE: SECTION 3

Contents

- 3   The election into Inheritance Tax
- 3.1   The effect of the election
- 3.1.1 Land and chattels
- 3.1.2 Intangible property
- 3.1.3 Withdrawal of election
- 3.2   How to elect
- 3.3   When to elect
- 3.4   Circumstances in which a late election will be accepted

3. The election into Inheritance Tax

3.1 The effect of the election

Paragraphs 21 and 22 give the chargeable person the option of electing that any relevant property that would otherwise be subject to the charge be treated as subject to a reservation for the purposes of Part 5 of the Finance Act 1986. If an election is made the property will not be subject to the charge under this Schedule but will instead be subject to a charge to inheritance tax on their death. The charge to inheritance tax will be incurred unless the occupation or use (of property otherwise within this Schedule) ceases permanently (and is not recommenced) at least 7 years before their death or (in **A3.29** the case of land or chattels) the chargeable person pays full consideration for use of the relevant property. If the person is already paying full consideration for use of the land or chattels before making an election and then elects we accept that there is no deemed PET at that point. However, if the person ceases to pay full consideration in the 7 years prior to death and is still in occupation of the property the effect of the election is that they will be subject to an inheritance tax charge on their death.

In the case of a couple who are married or in a civil partnership who jointly owned a property and who are both caught by the provisions of this Schedule, if they both wish to have it treated as property subject to a reservation, they must both make an election. An election by one cannot affect the other. Hence one of them may instead choose to pay the income tax charge in respect of their share, whilst the other may elect for a GWR under paragraph 21.

3.1.1 Land and chattels (Sch. 15, para. 21)

This paragraph applies where the chargeable person is potentially chargeable for any year of assessment by reference to their enjoyment of any land or chattels for the first time. Enjoyment refers to occupation of the land and possession or use of the chattel in question.

The chargeable person may elect that the relevant property, or property substituted for it, shall not be subject to the charge but so long as they continue to enjoy it, the chargeable proportion of the property will be treated as property subject to a reservation and sections 102(3) and (4) Finance Act 1986 will apply.

The 'chargeable proportion' means

$$\frac{DV}{V}$$

where DV and V are the values detailed in sections 1.4.1 and 1.4.2 of these guidance notes. The valuation dates to be used in these circumstances are

- in the case of property falling section 102(3) Finance Act 1986, the date of death of the chargeable person, and
- in the case of property falling within section 102(4) Finance Act 1986, the date on which the property ceases to be treated as property subject to a reservation.

When calculating DV the transactions to be taken into account should include transactions after the time when the election takes effect as well as before that time.

3.1.2 Intangible property (Sch. 15, para. 22)

This paragraph applies where the chargeable person is potentially chargeable for any year of assessment by reference to any relevant intangible property for the first time.

The chargeable person may elect that the relevant property, or property which it represents or is derived from, shall not be subject to the charge but, provided certain conditions are met, it will be treated as property subject to a reservation and sections 102(3) and (4) Finance Act 1986 will apply. The conditions are

- that the relevant property, or property which it represents or is derived from, remains comprised in the settlement, and
- that any income arising under the settlement would be treated by virtue of section 624 ITTOIA (formerly 660A of the Taxes Act 1988) as income of the chargeable person.

3.1.3 Withdrawal of election

Whether it relates to land, chattels or intangible property the election may be withdrawn or amended during the life of the chargeable person at any time on or before the relevant filing date (see 3.3). If the election is withdrawn the property will be subject to the charge from the tax year 2005–06 or the year on which they would have first become chargeable under this Schedule.

3.2 How to elect

The election must be made on form IHT 500. Guidance on how to complete the form, together with the form itself, can be found elsewhere on this website.

A3.30

3.3 When to elect

The election must be made on or before 'the relevant filing date'. If the chargeable person was subject to income tax from the initial year of the charge the relevant filing date is 31 January 2007. If they become subject to the charge in a later year of assessment the relevant filing date is 31 January in the year of assessment immediately following, i.e. if they first became subject to the charge during the year 2007–08, the election must be made by 31 January 2009. An extension may only be granted if the chargeable person can show a reasonable excuse for the failure to make the election by that date.

A3.31

The election takes effect for inheritance tax purposes from the initial year of the charge (2005–06) or, if later, the date on which the chargeable person would have first become chargeable under this Schedule but for the election.

3.4 Circumstances in which a late election will be accepted

Where the chargeable person can show reasonable excuse for the failure to make the election on or before the relevant filing date, the election must be made on or before such later date as may be prescribed.

A3.32

The term 'reasonable excuse' is not defined and each case is judged on its own merits. We do take the view generally, however, that an excuse is only reasonable if some event beyond the control of the taxpayer prevented them from sending us the election by the relevant filing date. If the chargeable person is able to manage the rest of their private or business affairs during the period which is claimed to be covered by the reasonable excuse we are unlikely to accept that they were otherwise prevented from delivering the election on time.

Examples of what we may agree as a reasonable excuse are:—

The election lost or delayed in the post

We expect the chargeable person to allow sufficient time for the election to reach us by the relevant filing date. But where an election is posted in good time, we accept as a reasonable excuse any unforeseen event that disrupted the normal postal service and led to the loss or delay of the election. This might include

- a fire or flood at the Post Office where the election was handled, or
- prolonged industrial action within the Post Office.

Loss of the chargeable person's financial records or other relevant papers

The loss of records through fire, flood or theft is a reasonable excuse. But we may need evidence of the circumstances. We also need to be satisfied that information necessary for the completion of the election could not be replaced in time for it to be completed by the relevant filing date.

Serious illness

For an illness to be treated as a reasonable excuse it must generally be so serious that it prevented the chargeable person from dealing with the election before the relevant filing date and from that date to the time the completed election is sent in. Examples of such illnesses include

- coma
- major heart attack
- stroke
- any serious mental or life-threatening illness.

If an illness involves a lengthy stay in hospital or convalescence the chargeable person is expected to have made arrangements for completing and sending in the election on time. But there may be reasons why this is not possible and we may accept it as a reasonable excuse.

If the excuse is the serious illness of a close relative or partner, we agree this only if

- the situation took up a great deal of the chargeable person's time and attention during the period from the relevant filing date to the date the completed election was sent in, and
- steps had already been taken to have the election ready on time.

Bereavement

We agree the death of a close relative or partner shortly before the relevant filing date is a reasonable excuse as long as the necessary steps had already been taken to have the election ready on time.

INCOME TAX AND PRE-OWNED ASSETS GUIDANCE: SECTION 4

Contents

- 4. HMRC's approach to certain issues
- 4.1 Domicile/residence issues
- 4.2 Tracing and contributions
- 4.2.1 House sharing
- 4.3 Reasonable attribution
- 4.4 Full or part consideration
- 4.5 Sales at undervalue
- 4.6 Occupation/Possession
- 4.7 "Substantially less"
- 4.8 Double charges
- 4.9 Insurance policies
- 4.10 Valuation

4. HMRC's approach to certain issues

This section of the guidance looks at the HMRC's approach to certain practical issues regarding the pre-owned assets charge under this Schedule.   A3.33

Examples of how we view particular situations can be found in Appendix 1 to the guidance material.

4.1 Domicile/residence issues

Schedule 15 does not apply to a person who is not resident for Income Tax in the United Kingdom in the year of assessment. To be regarded as resident in the UK you must normally be physically present in the country at some time in the tax year. You will always be resident if you are here for 183 days or more in the tax year. If you are here for less than 183 days, you may still be regarded as resident for the year under other tests. If you consider that residency is an issue for you, and one that has not been previously agreed with HMRC, you may wish to consult leaflet IR20, which discusses the position in more detail. The person's domicile in this case is immaterial.   A3.34

A person's domicile becomes material if that person is resident for Income Tax purposes in the United Kingdom for any year of assessment. If the person is resident in, but domiciled outside, the United Kingdom, only relevant property situated in the United Kingdom will be subject to the charge. As the treatment of domicile for the charge is the same as that for Inheritance Tax, a person's domicile under section 267 Inheritance Tax Act 1984 as well as that under general law is relevant.

A person is deemed domiciled in the United Kingdom under this section if

- they were domiciled on or after 10 December 1974 in the United Kingdom and within the three years immediately preceding the relevant time, or
- they were resident for income tax purposes in the United Kingdom in not less than seventeen of the twenty years of assessment ending with the year of assessment in which the relevant time falls.

The relevant time for the purposes of the charge will be the first day of the year of assessment in question.

Paragraph 12(3) of the schedule provides that if any property situated outside the United Kingdom became comprised in a settlement when the person settling the property was domiciled outside the United Kingdom it will not be subject to the charge. Even if that person becomes domiciled in the United Kingdom at a later date this property will remain excluded from the charge.

Paragraph 12(3) provides that a charge under this Schedule shall not arise in relation to property regarded as excluded by virtue of section 48(3) IHTA'84. We do not regard this provision as having an impact on paragraph 11 in determining whether there is derived property in the taxpayer's estate, or GWR property in relation to him (see foreign domiciliary example in appendix).

If the person adds property, wherever situated, to the settlement after they became domiciled in the United Kingdom the additional property would be subject to the charge if it falls within the provisions of paragraphs 3, 6 or 8 of the schedule. If applicable the general exclusions and exemptions would still be available, as they would be for any United Kingdom situated property where the person is domiciled outside the United Kingdom.

4.2 Tracing and contributions

An absolute gift of cash is not subject to the inheritance tax reservation of benefit provisions unless the donor retains a benefit in the cash itself. For example, A, who is a   A3.35

partner in a business, withdraws capital from his capital account and gifts this to B, who then lends the partnership an equivalent cash sum. That sum is still on loan to the partnership when A dies. The cash sum is treated as a gift with reservation under section 102(3) Finance Act 1986. But the provisions in paragraph 2 Schedule 20 FA 1986 that enable the reservation of benefit provisions to apply to property that is substituted for the original gift do not apply where the original gift is of cash (para 2(2)(b)).

Thus, where an absolute gift of cash may later be used by the recipient to purchase property occupied or enjoyed by the donor for example, the application of the reservation of benefit rules to this property is precluded, unless the transaction can be shown to be a gift with reservation of benefit, by associated operations, of the purchased property.

These 'tracing' rules do not apply to the application of the income tax charge under this schedule. The arrangement referred to above would satisfy the contribution condition of paragraph 3(3) of this schedule if the contribution was made on or after 18 March 1986. The income tax charge would then apply unless the provision of consideration was an excluded transaction (paragraph 10(3)(2)) or it fell within one of the exemptions from the charge in paragraph 11. For the purposes of the latter paragraph and more particularly sub-paragraphs 11(5)(b), (c) and (d) the restriction on the tracing of cash gifts normally imposed for inheritance tax purposes does not apply when considering whether there is an exemption from the income tax charge (paragraph 11(8) Sch 15).

4.2.1 House sharing

Where people enter into an arrangement whereby they contribute to a shared property (land & buildings) owning venture and whereby they intend to and do in fact share the occupation of and the expenses arising from the occupation of the property **broadly equally**, it is not the intention of Sch 15 FA 2004 to levy an income tax charge on any part of that arrangement. Such circumstances are generally covered by section 102 B (4) FA 1986, which is made applicable to Sch15 by para.11(5)(c). However, if the situation is that the contribution made by each person is not commensurate with their respective enjoyment of the property and / or the expenses were shared unequally, the circumstances may fall to be scrutinised in the context of Sch 15 FA 2004. In such circumstances, a charge to income tax may well result.

4.3 Reasonable attribution

A3.36   Paragraphs 3(2)(a)(ii) and 3(3) relating to land and 6(2)(a)(ii) and 6(3) relating to chattels apply where the chargeable person has either disposed of property and the proceeds of this disposal were used to acquire the relevant property, or where the chargeable person has contributed any of the consideration (directly or indirectly) to acquire the relevant property. Where these provisions apply it is necessary to calculate the proportion of the value of the relevant property that can be reasonably attributed to the property originally disposed of or to the consideration provided. How should this proportion be calculated?

Each case will turn on its own facts and the value of the land disposed of and its ultimate sale price, the consideration provided and the independent financial resources of the recipient will all have to be taken into account when making a reasoned judgement as to the value reasonably attributable.

For example, the disposal condition in paragraph 3(2)(a)(ii) would be met if the chargeable person transferred land to another ("X"), who later sold the land and used the proceeds to purchase a second property which the chargeable person occupies. If the land was valued at £100,000 at the date of transfer, sold for £300,000 and the new property purchased for £150,000, we would consider it reasonable to treat the whole value of the new property to be attributable to the property originally disposed of. If the value of the new property exceeds the proceeds received from the sale of the original property the proportion of the value reasonably attributable to the original property will be reduced. The value reasonably attributable to the new property cannot exceed the final value of the property originally disposed of.

If in the above example X used the sale proceeds to buy another property (Blackacre) which the chargeable person did not occupy but also used his own resources to buy a house (Whiteacre) which the chargeable person did occupy then we will not treat the value of Whiteacre as attributable to the property originally disposed of unless X had borrowed on the security of Blackacre.

If X purchases Whiteacre for £200,000 and half the purchase price (say £100,000) comes from the sale proceeds of the original land given to him and half comes from his own resources we would argue that half the value of Whiteacre was attributable to the property originally disposed of. Note that the reasonable attribution is not limited to the £100,000 originally put into Whiteacre but is half the value of Whiteacre at the relevant valuation date.

4.4 Full or part consideration

If the chargeable person's occupation of the relevant land, or enjoyment of the relevant chattel, is for full consideration in money or money's worth, i.e. a full market rent is paid by them for their continued occupation/enjoyment, their occupation/enjoyment is not a reservation of benefit for inheritance tax purposes (para 6(1)(a) Sch 20 Finance Act 1986). This treatment is extended to the income tax charge under this schedule by virtue of paragraph 11(5)(d). Any arrangement or transaction entered into on or after 18 March 1986 where the chargeable person pays full consideration for their enjoyment or occupation of the relevant asset will not be subject to the income tax charge.

A3.37

If the consideration paid by the chargeable person is less than full consideration, or if they initially pay a full consideration but, over time, this falls below market rates, the asset in question will be treated as subject to a reservation of benefit from the date the chargeable person ceased to pay full consideration. There will be no income tax charge under this schedule provided that the provisions of paragraph 11(5)(a) apply.

4.5 Sales at undervalue

The application of paragraph 4(4) in respect of land to which the disposal conditions of paragraph 3(2) applies by virtue of a 'non-exempt sale' is restricted to sales of the whole interest in the property. If there is a sale of part only of the chargeable person's interest in the relevant land, no account can be taken of the consideration actually paid by the purchaser. (for an example see 2.1 above)

A3.38

As the consideration must be paid in sterling or another currency this sub-paragraph will not apply if the consideration took another form, i.e. if one item of land was exchanged for another. Example: X exchanges his house valued at £800,000, for Y's property valued at £200,000 (Y's property in this example could be taken to mean land, a business, a right, in fact any property other than cash). X continues to live in his former property. Under the provisions of paragraph 4(4) the value of Y's property is not regarded as consideration to be taken into account, and X will be subject to a POA charge on £200,000. On X's death there will be a GWR in respect of a ¼ share of his former property, and his estate for IHT purposes will include the £200,000 from Y.

4.6 Occupation/Possession

Land

A3.39   Paragraph 3 of the schedule applies where the chargeable person occupies any land that they had either both previously owned and disposed of, or contributed to its acquisition. In this context 'occupation' is construed quite widely. For example, the chargeable person would be regarded as in occupation not only if they were resident in the relevant property but also if they used it for storage or had sole possession of the means of access and used the property from time to time (see Appendix 1) . The chargeable person would not be regarded as occupying a property from which they receive rental payments from the person(s) actually in occupation.

If the person's occupation or use of the property is only very limited in its nature or duration it may not come within the provisions of paragraph 3. Each case will ultimately be decided on the facts and circumstances relating to it. However, in line with the HMRC's Interpretation of inheritance tax and gifts with reservation—RI 55 (November 1993)—some examples can be given of limited occupation that will not bring the chargeable person within paragraph 3. These include

- a house which is the owner's residence but where the chargeable person subsequently stays with the other person for less than one month each year or, in their absence, stays for not more than two weeks each year,
- social visits, excluding overnight stays by the chargeable person as a guest of the owner. The extent of the social visits should be no greater than the visits that may be otherwise be expected if the chargeable person had never previously owned the property, or made a contribution to its acquisition,
- temporary stay for some short term purpose, for example, while the chargeable person convalesces after medical treatment, or they look after the owner while they are convalescing, or while the chargeable person's own home is being redecorated,
- visits to a house for domestic reasons, for example baby-sitting by the chargeable person for the owner's children,
- a house together with a library of books which the chargeable person visits less than five times in any year to consult or borrow a book,
- land which the chargeable person uses to walk their dogs or for horse riding provided this does not restrict the owner's use of the land.

More significant use of the property may bring the chargeable person within the scope of paragraph 3. Examples are

- a house in which the chargeable person stays most weekends or for more than a month each year,
- a second home or holiday home which the chargeable person and the owner both then use on an occasional basis,
- a house with a library in which the chargeable person continues to keep their own books, or which they use on a regular basis, for example because it is necessary for their work.

Chattels

Similar considerations apply to the possession or use of previously owned chattels when the application of paragraph 6 is contemplated. Very limited or occasional use of the chattel in question will not incur an income tax charge under this schedule.

For example, a car used to give occasional lifts (i.e. less than three times a month) to the chargeable person will not be liable to the charge. But if the chargeable person is taken to work every day in the car it is likely an income tax charge will be incurred.

4.7 "substantially less"

Where any relevant property is included in the chargeable person's estate for inheritance tax purposes, or is subject to the inheritance tax reservation of benefit provisions, the value of that property is exempt from the charge (see 1.3.2). If other property that derives its value from the relevant property is included in the estate or is subject to a reservation of benefit the charge will not apply either. However, if the value of that derived property that can be reasonably attributed to the relevant property is "substantially less" than the value of the relevant property, only that proportion of the value of the relevant property that can be reasonably said to be included in the estate is exempted from the charge.

A3.40

The term "substantially less" is not defined by the legislation but by analogy with the Capital Gains Tax taper relief rules we would regard a reduction of value of less than 20% as not substantially less for the purposes of this Schedule. If the circumstances of a particular case suggest that the "substantially less" provision should be triggered by a reduction of more or less than 20%, it will be judged on its individual merits.

Where the value of the property in the estate is substantially less than the value of the relevant property the appropriate rental value of any land, and the appropriate chargeable amounts relating to chattels or intangible property, for the purposes of this Schedule will be reduced by a reasonable proportion to take into account the property in the estate.

4.8 Double charges

The regulations relating to the income tax charge (SI 2005 No. 724) include provisions to avoid a double charge to inheritance tax where the chargeable person elects that the gift with reservation provisions apply to the relevant property. A double charge may arise where the chargeable person makes a gift of property that is a potentially exempt transfer for inheritance tax. If that property is then liable to the income tax charge they may decide to make an election that the property is subject to the inheritance tax reservation of benefit provisions. If they then die within 7 years of the original gift a double charge to inheritance tax will arise—firstly on the original transfer that must now be aggregated with the death estate and secondly on the property subject to the reservation.

A3.41

The provisions to avoid double charges effectively retain the charge on the transfer that produces the higher overall amount of inheritance tax and reduce the other transfer to nil. The application of these provisions may best be illustrated using an example.

Mr G entered into a lifetime loan scheme (or double trust scheme as it may be known) in June 2003. He sold his house to a trust fund of which he is the life tenant for £500,000. The trustees do not pay the purchase price but give Mr G an IOU instead. Mr G then makes a gift of the IOU (the outstanding purchase price) to a second trust for the benefit of his children. He remains in occupation of the property and, as the outstanding debt reduces the value of the house for inheritance tax purposes to nil (see 1.5.2 and 'excluded liability'), he is liable to the income tax charge from 6 April 2005. To avoid paying the charge he makes an election under paragraph 21 of Schedule 15 that the house is subject to the gift with reservation provisions. Mr G dies in July 2007 and the house is valued at £750,000 at that date.

As the death occurred less than 7 years after the original gift of the IOU it must be aggregated with Mr G's estate when calculating the inheritance tax liability. But the house is also chargeable on the death as a gift with reservation following the election.

A double charge to inheritance tax would arise but for the double charges provisions which apply in this instance, as the gifted property (the IOU) represents the proceeds of the disposal of the relevant property (the house). The two potential charges should be considered in isolation. In these examples Mr G's estate is valued at £500,000 and the inheritance tax threshold at the time of writing of £285,000 is used.

Charge to tax using original gift

Gift now taxable		£500,000
Estate		£500,000
Aggregate chargeable transfer		£1,000,000

Taxable gift	£500,000	
Less nil-rate band	−£285,000	
Excess	£215,000	
Tax @ 40%	£86,000	
Taper relief due @ 40%	(£34,400)	
Tax payable		£51,600

Taxable estate	£500,000	
Nil-rate band used against gift	£0	
Tax @ 40%		£200,000

Total inheritance tax payable		£251,600

Charge to tax using gift with reservation

Estate	£500,000
Gift with reservation	£750,000
Aggregate chargeable transfer	£1,250,000
Less nil-rate band	−£285,000
Excess	£965,000
Total inheritance tax payable @ 40%	£386,000

(apportioned between estate and gift with reservation)

In this scenario the charge to tax using the gift with reservation will be used and the charge using the original gift will be reduced to nil by the double charges provisions and disregarded.

Further regulations were made SI 2005 No.3441 (PDF 24K) to deal with the double charges that may arise where the taxpayer decides to dismantle a "double trust scheme" and return to the position they were in prior to that arrangement.

Example:

Mrs X sells her house to a trust in which she has an interest in possession in exchange for an IOU from the trustees, which she then gifts to a second trust for the benefit of her children. The gift of the IOU is a potentially exempt transfer for IHT purposes and its value will be chargeable if the taxpayer dies within seven years of making it. The "double trust" arrangement is then dismantled e.g. by the cancellation of the IOU, so that the full value of the house will return to her estate and also be subject to IHT on her death. There is therefore the potential for a double charge.

Statutory Instrument 2005, No. 3441, therefore extended the previous regulations by introducing The Inheritance Tax (Double Charges) Regulations 2005, to provide relief from the double charge that would otherwise arise in the above example. As in the previous example, tax is calculated on the basis of the failed PET, and again with the house as an asset of the death estate. Inheritance Tax is then charged on whichever transfer produces the greater tax, and the other transfer is reduced to nil.

It should be noted that the double charges provisions will not always apply when a perceived double charge arises. In particular, if an election is made in respect of property subject to an 'Eversden' type arrangement with the result that the life tenant has made a potentially exempt transfer and the settlor's estate includes property subject to a reservation, both charges to tax are unaffected by the double charges provisions. The provisions only apply where there is a double charge in respect of the same individual.

4.9 Insurance policies

There may be certain instances where schemes involving insurance policies fall within the scope of paragraph 8 of the schedule. However, the majority of the more common schemes should not be affected. Examples of those that might be caught can be found in Appendix 1. A3.42

Where a charge to tax under this Schedule arises, paragraph 15 of this Schedule requires that the open market value of the policy at the relevant time should be used in establishing the chargeable amount determined under paragraph 9 (see 4.10 below).

4.10 Valuation

Paragraph 15 of this Schedule is taken from the wording of section 160 Inheritance Tax Act 1984. This provides that "Except as otherwise provided by this Schedule, the value of any property shall for the purposes of this Schedule be the price which the property might reasonably be expected to fetch if sold in the open market at that time; but that price shall not be assumed to be reduced on the ground that the whole property is to be placed on the market at one and the same time". A3.43

INCOME TAX AND PRE-OWNED ASSETS GUIDANCE: SECTION 5

Contents

- Land—straightforward gift or sale of whole
- Land—straightforward gift or sale of part share
- Land—equitable interests
- Partnership interests
- Land—lease carve out (Ingram scheme)
- Chattels—lease carve out
- Land—settlement on interest in possession trust (Eversden scheme)

- Intangible property—Eversden scheme
- Land—reversionary lease scheme
- Land—death scheme involving a loan
- Land—lifetime scheme involving a loan (double trust scheme)
- Insurance policies
- Land—Occupation
- Post-death variations of an estate
- Foreign domiciliaries—excluded property
- Reverter-to-settlor trusts.

Land—straightforward gift or sale of whole

A3.44   As previously mentioned at 1.3.1 of this guidance, a disposal of property is an excluded transaction "if it was a disposal of his whole interest in property", coming within the provisions of paragraph 10. As this wording makes clear, "his whole interest" is precisely that, and can for example be a half share, or a quarter share of the whole land if that share is all that he owns.

In 2000 Mr A conveyed his house to his daughter Miss B. He continues to live there.

- While Mr A remains in occupation the property is subject to a gift with reservation for inheritance tax, whether or not Miss B also lives there. The income tax charge will not apply by virtue of paragraph 11(5)(a) of this schedule.
- If Mr A pays a full market rent to Miss B for his occupation the property will not be subject to a reservation by virtue of paragraph 6(1)(a) Schedule 20 Finance Act 1986 and the income tax charge will not apply by virtue of paragraph 11(5)(d) of this schedule.
- If the conveyance to Miss B was not a gift but a sale at full market value there will be no transfer of value for inheritance tax. The transaction is a disposal for the purposes of paragraph 3(2) of this schedule but it is an excluded transaction by virtue of paragraph 10(1)(a). An income tax charge will not arise under this schedule.
- If Mr A had carved out a lease of his property for himself, and sold the freehold reversion to Miss B, that disposal will be an excluded transaction by virtue of paragraph 10(1)(a), provided that the sale was a transaction such as might be expected to be made at arms length between persons not connected with each other. If this provision has been met an income tax charge under this Schedule will not arise. The reversion is regarded as a distinct item of property, and the sale was of the entire interest in it. Mr A continued to occupy the house by virtue of his leasehold interest, which is a separate item of property. There is of course a "marriage" value for the two interests and a truly arms length transaction must take account of this along with any other factors.

Land—straightforward gift or sale of part share

A3.45   In 2001 Mr A conveyed his house into the joint names of himself and his daughter Miss B. He continues to live there.

- If Miss B does not occupy the property the half-share gifted by Mr A is subject to a gift with reservation for inheritance tax. The income tax charge will not apply by virtue of paragraph 11(5)(a) of this schedule.
- If Miss B does not occupy the property but Mr A pays Miss B a full market rent for his occupation of her half-share, the half-share will not be subject to a reservation by virtue of paragraph 6(1)(a) Schedule 20 Finance Act 1986 and

the income tax charge will not apply by virtue of paragraph 11(5)(d) of this schedule.

- If Miss B does occupy the property with Mr A and they share the running costs of the property in the same proportion, the half-share will not be subject to a reservation by virtue of section 102B(4) Finance Act 1986 and the income tax charge will not apply by virtue of paragraph 11(5)(c) of this schedule.

- If the conveyance to Miss B was not a gift but a sale at full market value there will be no transfer of value for inheritance tax. The transaction is, though, a disposal for the purposes of paragraph 3(2) of this schedule. Furthermore, the transaction is not an excluded transaction under paragraph 10(1). However, the Regulations (PDF 29K) provide that, as the sale took place before 7 March 2005, the income tax charge under this schedule will not apply. If the sale had taken place on or after 7 March 2005 Mr A's occupation of the half-share would be subject to an income tax charge if the appropriate rental value exceeds the de minimis limit in paragraph 13. There is a further exception that may apply if the sale was for a consideration not in the form of money or an asset readily convertible into money (see following examples).

- If the sale of a part share had been to a commercial provider of equity release schemes the income tax charge will not apply. This is so whether or not such a sale takes place on or after 7 March 2005.

Land—equitable interests

If Miss B acquired her interest in the property by way of an equitable arrangement rather than for cash—for example, she had given up work to care for Mr A on the understanding that she would receive a share of the property in return—the income tax charge will not apply. Regulation 5 (PDF 29K)   **A3.46**

In considering whether the conditions were satisfied, we would need information about how the essential elements of the transaction had been arrived at. We do recognise that there is a substantial body of case law dealing with the circumstances in which an interest in a house is acquired in consequence of a person acting to his detriment. The Ministerial Statement had these sorts of situations in mind and we would interpret Regulation 5 accordingly. In particular, we accept that the requirement that "the disposal was by a transaction such as might be expected to be made at arm's length between persons not connected with each other" would be interpreted with such cases in mind. Where the parties had sought separate advice and acted upon it or had obtained a court order confirming the property entitlement, that would reinforce the claim that the conditions were satisfied. But we would not expect parties to such an arrangement to have done this. We recognise that detriment that the acquirer can demonstrate he has suffered can provide consideration for the acquisition of the interest and prevent the transaction from being gratuitous.

Partnership interests

The treatment of a share of a partnership interest for Schedule 15 purposes follows that applied for IHT purposes. In other words, we do not regard the partnership interest as transparent, and the disposal of a share is unlikely to give rise to a Schedule 15 charge in any circumstances.   **A3.47**

Land—lease carve out (Ingram scheme)

A3.48 Mr R transfers title to his property to a nominee who then grants Mr R a 20-year lease of the property at a peppercorn rent. The encumbered freehold reversion is then gifted to his son. Mr R continues to occupy the property.

If the transfer was effected on or after 9 March 1999 the property will be subject to a reservation of benefit for inheritance tax by virtue of section 102A Finance Act 1986. No charge to income tax will then arise under this schedule.

If the transfer was effected before 9 March 1999 the arrangement is not caught by section 102A Finance Act 1986 and will be subject to the income tax charge under paragraph 3(2) of this schedule. The value subject to the charge will be the value attributable to the property actually disposed of, calculated in accordance with the formula in paragraph 4(2).

Chattels—lease carve out

A3.49 The provisions of section 102A Finance Act 1986 only apply to interests in land. If the subject matter of the scheme referred to above is chattels rather than land, therefore, the provisions of this section do not bite. The property will not be subject to a reservation for inheritance tax regardless of when the scheme was actually effected.

It does, however, represent a disposal by the chargeable person who will be subject to an income tax charge under paragraph 6(2) of this schedule. The value subject to the charge will be the value attributable to the property actually disposed of, calculated in accordance with the formula in paragraph 7(2).

Land—settlement on interest in possession trust (Eversden scheme)

A3.50 Mrs T transfers 95% of her property to a settlement for the benefit of her husband for his life. On his death the property passes to a discretionary trust, of which she is one of the potential beneficiaries. She remains in occupation of the property.

If the transfer was effected on or after 20 June 2003 the property will be subject to a reservation of benefit by Mrs T for inheritance tax by virtue of section 102(5A) Finance Act 1986 and the income tax charge will not apply.

If the transfer was effected before 20 June 2003 the property will not be subject to a reservation of benefit. If the interest in possession of Mrs T's husband continued until his death the property will not be subject to the income tax charge because, although the disposal condition in paragraph 3(2) is met, the transaction is an excluded transaction by virtue of paragraph 10(1)(c).

However if her husband's interest in possession ended during his lifetime the transaction will not be excluded because of paragraph 10(3) and the property disposed of will be subject to the income tax charge. The value of the property will be determined by the formula in paragraph 4(2).

Intangible property—Eversden scheme

A3.51 Intangible property may also be settled on Eversden-type scheme, i.e. the chargeable person settles cash on interest in possession trusts for their spouse or civil partner, which the trustees then invest in a bond. If the terms of the settlement fall within the definition in paragraph 8 of this schedule similar results to the scheme involving land referred to above apply.

For example, if the spouse or civil partner's interest in possession ends during their lifetime and the property is now held on discretionary trusts of which the settlor is one of the potential beneficiaries, the income tax charge will apply under paragraph 8 if the settlement was effected before 20 June 2003. The charge will be calculated with reference to paragraph 9 of this schedule.

It should be noted that the excluded transaction provisions have no application with regard to intangible property so paragraph 10(1)(c), which may have a bearing in respect of certain Eversden-type schemes involving land, has no relevance here.

If the settlement was effected on or after 20 June 2003 the property is subject to a reservation of benefit for inheritance tax by virtue of section 102(5A) Finance Act 1986 and the income tax charge will not apply.

Land—reversionary lease scheme

Mr V has owned his house since 1990. In 2002 he grants a 999-year lease to his daughter but this is not to take effect until 2022. He continues to occupy the property. A3.52

In view of the provisions of section 102A Finance Act 1986, Mr V's occupation of the property is considered to be a significant right in respect of the relevant land and it is thought, therefore, that a reservation of benefit for inheritance tax will arise. As such the property will not be subject to the income tax charge.

Section 102A only applies to transfers on or after 9 March 1999. If, in the example above, Mr V granted the lease in 1998 to commence on 2018, it will not be treated as a reservation of benefit. It will, though, be regarded as a disposal of an interest in the relevant land under paragraph 3(2) of this schedule. The charge to income tax will apply, calculated in accordance with the formula in paragraph 4(2), unless Mr V elects into the reservation of benefit provisions.

Land—death scheme involving a loan

Mr and Mrs S own a house in equal shares as tenants in common. Under the Will of Mr S, assets not exceeding the 'nil-rate band' for inheritance tax pass into a discretionary trust, of which Mrs S is one of the potential beneficiaries. The remainder of his estate passes to Mrs S. Following the death of Mr S in June 2005 his executors transferred his half share of the property to Mrs S and, in return, she executed a loan agreement equivalent to the value of the half-share. No inheritance tax is payable. A3.53

The income tax charge under this schedule will not apply here. As Mrs S did not own her husband's share at the relevant time and did not dispose of it the disposal conditions in paragraph 3(2) do not apply. If she did not provide Mr S with any of the consideration given by him for the purchase of his half share the contribution condition in paragraph 3(3) will not apply either. Even if she had provided him with some or all of the consideration the condition will still not apply as it would have been an excluded transaction under paragraph 10(2)(a). In the final scenario, however, the debt would not be allowable for inheritance tax on the death of Mrs S by virtue of section 103 Finance Act 1986.

Land—lifetime scheme involving a loan (double trust or home loan scheme)

There are a number of variants of this scheme—one of the more straightforward types is referred to in the Double Charges section of this guidance (see 4.8)—and the income tax charge under this Schedule will apply. (Guidance on whether the loan may be chargeable under the IHT reservation of benefit provisions is given at the end of this section). A3.54

As the chargeable person is usually still occupying the house as the life tenant of an interest in possession trust the exemption in paragraph 11(1) of this Schedule would appear to prevent the charge from applying. However, the value of the property in the estate will be reduced by the debt now owned by the trustees of the second trust in the scheme. For example if the house is valued at £500,000 and the debt is valued at £400,000, only the net value of £100,000 is chargeable to inheritance tax. In this scenario the concept of excluded liabilities will apply—paragraphs 11(6) and 11(7) of this Schedule (see 1.3.2). The exemption in paragraph 11(1) is restricted to the value of the relevant property that exceeds the amount of the excluded liability—in this example £100,000. The remaining part of the house will be subject to the charge—in this example four-fifths of the appropriate rental value. If, in the above example, the debt is expressed as a percentage of the value of the house, the income tax charge would be payable on the same percentage of the rental value.

Reservation of benefit in the loan—HMRC's view

A3.55   The essence of many of these schemes involves the chargeable person(s) (the vendors) selling their home for full value to a newly formed trust (trust 1) with the sale proceeds left outstanding on loan. An IOU for the loan is gifted to a second trust (trust 2) for the benefit of the vendor's family. The vendor(s) continue to occupy the property under the terms of trust 1, and the loan is repayable to trust 2 on demand. HMRC's view on this is that since the loan was repayable on demand, there will be a GWR in respect of it, until such time as the trustees call in the loan. The reason for this is that if trust 2 had called in the loan, trust 1 would have been forced either to sell the home to repay the debt, or to seek finance from elsewhere. If the house were sold, then the vendor(s) would have been unable to occupy it under the terms of trust 1. In order to avoid the need for a sale, trust 1 would have had to find a third party willing to lend 100% of the value of the property on the basis of a covenant by the trustees, and security over the house. Even if such borrowing could be obtained, which must be extremely doubtful, it would be prohibitively expensive. Trust 1 could only justify taking on such borrowing if they were financed by the vendor(s) (the life tenants) who would be benefiting from the property by residing in it. On the foregoing basis it is considered that the trustees of trust 2, in not calling in the loan, have enabled the vendor(s) to retain a significant benefit in it, and therefore that the debt was not enjoyed to the entire exclusion of any benefit to the vendor(s) by contract or otherwise.

A variant of the scheme described above is where the terms of the loan provide that the debt is only repayable at a time after the death of the life tenant. Since, unlike the position with loans repayable on demand, the loan can not be called in by the loan trustees, it is generally thought that these schemes will not be caught as gifts with reservation.

If the loan is subject to a reservation of benefit this does not mean the vendor can avoid paying income tax. The reservation of benefit is in the loan not the house and he has still made a relevant disposal of the house which is subject to an excluded liability and which therefore reduces his estate. Reserved benefit property does not form part of someone's estate while he is alive. (see ss 102(3)(4) FA 1986). In these circumstances if A does not wish to pay the income tax charge the debt should either be appointed back to him or written off (in which case the excluded liability ceases to reduce the value of his estate and there is no income tax charge from the date the debt is written off or appointed back to him) or he should elect (in which case there is no income tax charge at all).

Insurance policies

A3.56   • The settlor effects a discounted gift scheme comprising a gift into settlement with certain "rights" being retained by them. The retained rights may, for instance, be a series of single premium policies maturing (usually) on successive anniversaries of the initial investment or on survival, reverting to the settlor, if they are alive on the maturity date, or the settlor carves out the right to receive future capital payments if they are alive at each prospective payment date. The gift with reservation provisions do not apply.

In the straightforward case where the settlor has retained a right to an annual income or to a reversion under arrangements, that right is not property within paragraph 8 as the trustees hold it on bare trust for the settlor. A bare trust is not a settlement for inheritance tax purposes. The settlor is excluded from other benefits under the policy and so this schedule does not apply.

There may be more complex cases where the settlor's retained rights or interests are themselves held on trust. But that would normally be construed as being a separate trust of those benefits in which the settlor had an interest in possession, and no charge to tax will arise under this schedule by virtue of paragraph 11(1).

Even if, in less common cases, the paragraph 11 provisions did not apply so as to exempt the case from charge completely, any charge under this schedule would apply by reference to the value of the rights held on trust for the settlor, not by reference to the value of the underlying life policy.

- The settlor effects a policy and settles it on trust for the benefit of others. He then makes a substantial interest free loan to the trustees, repayable on demand. The trustees use the loan to purchase more policies, and make partial surrenders each year to pay off part of the loan.

This arrangement is not a gift with reservation for inheritance tax. The settlor is not a beneficiary of the trust itself and the making of the loan does not constitute a settlement for the purposes of inheritance tax. No charge to tax will arise under this schedule.

Pension Policies

Pension policies may typically provide pension and lifetime benefits for the scheme member, and other benefits that are payable on death at the discretion of the scheme trustees. It is considered that the pension and other lifetime benefits would either represent unsettled property or a trust separate from that on which the death benefits are held. In the arrangement described, both parts can be treated as mutually exclusive and therefore provided the scheme member could not benefit from the trusts governing the death benefits, a charge under this schedule will not arise.

A charge under Schedule 15 will not arise in relation to approved pension arrangements or, from 6 April 2006, pension arrangements under registered schemes. Neither are such arrangements caught as GWR's, as HMRC's statement of practice 10/86 makes clear. Non-registered schemes do not fall within the statement of practice, and so may well come within Finance Act 1986, in which event, the same dispositions would not come within Schedule 15.

Business trusts (or partnership policies)

In some cases, policies are taken out on each partner's life solely for the purposes of providing funds to enable their fellow partners to purchase his/her share from the partner's beneficiaries on their death. The partner is not a potential beneficiary of his/her "own" policy. In such circumstances, a charge to tax under paragraph 8 of this schedule will not arise.

However, in many cases, the partner retains a benefit for themselves, for example they can cash in the policy during their lifetime for their own benefit. In such cases, even if the arrangement is on commercial terms so that it is not a gift with reservation for inheritance tax, the trust is a settlement for inheritance tax purposes and a charge to tax under paragraph 8 will arise.

The valuation of a partner's, or settlor's, interest in a policy for the purposes of paragraph 8 of Schedule 15 should be his share of its open market value as at 6 April each year. That valuation will be relevant for determining the amount of charge for that year of assessment.

Where the policies are term assurances, in the vast majority of cases the policyholder will be in normal health, and therefore it is likely that the chargeable amount, as calculated under paragraph 9 of Schedule 15, will have little marketable value and will fall below the de minimis exemption in paragraph 13. Therefore, a policyholder in normal health at the valuation date may assume that he will survive beyond the term of the assurance, and complete his tax return accordingly. However, in circumstances where the policyholder has been advised that their state of health is such that it casts doubt on their survival to the end of the term of assurance (i.e. there becomes a realistic prospect of the policy paying out and therefore having a material market value), then consideration should be given to obtaining actuarial advice about the value of the policy.

Pre-18 March 1986 Policies settled on trusts

A charge under Schedule 15 does not arise where, before 18th March 1986, a life policy has been contracted and settled on trusts from which the settlor can benefit, even where premiums are paid after this date.

Land—Occupation

A3.57 Example 1: Mr A gives his house to his daughter in 1987. The disposal condition of paragraph 3(2) has been met. He occupies the property along with his daughter, and later when she moves out, on his own. This was 'relevant land' at all times since 1987, for the purposes of paragraph 3(1), of Schedule 15. It is protected from POAT throughout because it is subject to a reservation of benefit.

Example 2: Mr A sells his house and makes a cash gift to his daughter, who uses the money towards the purchase of a house of her own also using some of her own money. The contribution condition of paragraph 3(3) is met. Within 7 years of this gift he moves in with his daughter and occupies a self-contained part of the house, and has the means of access to the remainder of the property, and actually uses it from time to time. E.g. storing furniture there. In these circumstances, the whole property is considered to be "relevant land" for the purposes of paragraph 3(1). However, while he occupies with his daughter there is no POAT charge due to para 11(8). Had Mr A moved into occupation more than 7 years after the cash gift, the provision of that consideration will be an excluded transaction, coming within paragraph 10(2)(c) of Schedule 15.

Example 3: The scenario is that of example 2, however Mr A does not have means of access to the rest of the house, and his access to the self-contained part is via an external door. He visits the rest of the house only when invited e.g. for Sunday lunch. He stores no furniture there. In this example, only the self-contained part is "relevant land" for the purposes of paragraph 3(1).

Post-death variations of an estate

A3.58 Mrs W is bequeathed a house, which she occupies, under her husband's Will. She completes a deed of variation within two years of her husband's death altering the terms of the Will so that the house passes to her son instead. The deed of variation is effective for inheritance tax purposes as the provisions of section 142(1) Inheritance Tax Act 1984 apply. Although she continues to occupy the house the income tax charge will not apply by virtue of paragraph 16 of this Schedule.

The provisions of paragraph 16 will also apply if the deed of variation referred to above had merely changed Mrs W's absolute interest in the property to a life interest in possession, with her son as remainderman. If her life interest is terminated during her lifetime (but more than two years after her husband's death) and she continues to occupy the property the income tax charge will not apply provided that the deed of variation satisfied the provisions of section 142(1) Inheritance Tax Act 1984. In any event, if her life interest was terminated after 21 March 2006 and she continues to occupy the property the reservation of benefit provisions will apply. (S102ZA FA 1986 as amended by Finance Bill 2006.)

Foreign Domiciliaries—excluded property

An arrangement that is not uncommon is where a foreign domiciliary settles a trust which owns a UK house through a foreign registered company. The shares in this company (and any loan made to it) are excluded property, coming within the provisions of section 48(3) IHTA '84. Paragraph 12(3) provides that Schedule 15 will have no application to such assets. However in considering the application of paragraph 11 in respect of the house he occupies, the operation of paragraph 12(3) does not mean that the shares (or any loan made to the company) are automatically disregarded in determining whether, for the purposes of paragraph 11, there is derived property which is in the taxpayer's estate or GWR property in relation to him. In these circumstances we would accept that the exemptions in paragraph 11 can apply to the foreign domiciliary.

A3.59

Reverter-to-settlor trusts

Legislation introduced in the 2006 Finance Bill will, from the 5th December 2005, prevent property gifted by the donor but still enjoyed by him as a beneficiary of a reverter-to-settlor trust from escaping an income tax charge under Schedule 15.

Previously the donor could gift property that would then be settled back on him on trusts which allowed him to continue to enjoy the property, but which on his death would revert back to the settlor (the original donee). The property was (for trusts established pre Budget 2006) treated as part of the donor's estate for IHT purposes, but on his death was excluded from a charge to IHT under sections 53 and 54 IHTA'84, as it reverted back to the settlor (the original donee). A charge under Schedule 15 would also not arise because the property was still regarded as part of the donor's estate for IHT purposes.

The new legislation will allow a Schedule 15 charge to apply in situations where the former owner of an asset (or a person who contributed to its acquisition) enjoys the asset under the terms of a trust, and the trust property reverts to the settlor—or to the spouse or civil partner, widow, widower or surviving civil partner of the settlor.

A3.60

POA COP 10 LETTER[2]

SUMMARY OF QUESTIONS

Valuation issues

1. Moving properties
2. Calculation of POAT on home loan schemes
3. Reduction of debt on home loan scheme
4. Calculation of POAT charge where mix of intangibles/house on home loan schemes
5. Discounts on DV
6. Commercial group life policies
7. Partnership life policies
8. Pension life policies
9. Pre-1986 life policies
10. Scope of Reg.6: election and home loan schemes/double charges

Home Loan Schemes

11. Assigning debt back to settlor
12. Valuing the excluded liability
13. Commercial borrowing by trust
14. Reservation of benefit on loan. Does POA apply?
15. Which home loan schemes work?

Election

16. Election by one spouse only
17. Effect of election on home loan schemes and s.102(4)
18. Spouse exemption and home loan schemes
19. New elections on change of property
20. Life interest settlor interested trusts and para.8
21. Elections on home loan schemes—whole house or only on debt part
22. Elections where only part of gifted property caught
23. Late elections
24. Wrong payment of income tax

Equity release

25. Regulation 5 and part disposals. Promissory estoppel
26. Definition of RCAs
27. Sales of whole
28. Carving out a lease

Reversionary leases

29. Paying rent under legal obligation
30. HMRC policy on reversionary leases

Miscellaneous

31. Disposal and contribution conditions
32. Meaning of "provision" and loans. The contribution condition
33. Occupation of house owned by company funded by loan

---

[2] The questions were submitted on behalf of STEP, CIOT and LITRG on July 14, 2005. HMRC's replies have been incorporated.

34. Overdrawn discounts
35. "Outright gift to another person"—para.10(2)(c)
36. Partnerships and POAT
37. Annual exemption
38. Interaction of ROB/POAT and full consideration
39. Para.10(3). Spousal interest in possession. Spouse becomes absolutely entitled
40. Meaning of occupation
41. Non-exempt sales

Foreign domiciliaries

42. Interaction of paras 12(3) and 11

Para.8 charge

43. Reverter to settlor trusts holding intangibles
44. Intangibles and the election

1. Valuation issues

1.1 Regulation 4 provides that in relation to land and chattels the valuation is by reference to the first valuation date and this valuation is used for a period of 5 tax years. This is favourable to taxpayers where the gifted land increases in value. For instance, in relation to existing *Ingram* and reversionary lease schemes, one takes the value of the gifted propery as at 6th April 2005 even though the gifted interest (the DV) is likely to increase in value over the next 5 years.

However, the position is unclear where the property is sold and the taxpayer moves to a smaller house.

Example 1

> A Gave £300,000 to his son in April 2000. Son later uses all the cash to purchase a house and contributes none of his own funds. A goes into occupation of house in April 2002. He falls within the contribution condition and is subject to the POA charge from 6th April 2005. The house is worth £1 million on 6th April 2005. He pays income tax in 2005/6 by reference to the rental value of the house.
>
> In 2007 Son sells house and buys a new one for £500,000 into which A moves. In these circumstances there seems to be no mechanism for assessing A to income tax on the rental value of the new house.
>
> Does A continue to pay income tax on a hypothetical rental value of the original £1 million house until 2010?
>
> Similar problems can arise if A moves into a discrete part of the house and only occupies that part, letting the remainder. If he has not done this by 6 April 2005 it would appear that his charge is not reduced for the next 5 years.

Question 1

Do HMRC interpret the legislation in this restrictive way or do they take the view that the relevant land for the purposes of para 4(5) is the land that the taxpayer actually occupies and therefore a new valuation is done when the taxpayer first occupies the smaller property or the smaller part? This is on the basis that a new taxable period then starts in which that property or part is the relevant property. The Regulations would then apply on the basis that the first day of such occupation is the first day of the taxable period.

A3.61

HMRC answer to question 1

The "relevant land" for the purposes of paragraph 4(5) is the land currently occupied by the chargeable person. A new valuation should be done when the occupation of that property starts, and we would intend that the new valuation should then be used for the remainder of that 5-year cycle.

A3.62   1.2 Particular valuation problems arise in relation to the double trust or home loan schemes.

Example 2

B sells his house to a trust in which he retains an interest in possession ("the property trust") and the purchase price of £900,000 is left outstanding as a debt. B gives away the debt. Assume that B is caught by POA and that the debt is an excluded liability. The house is worth £1 million on 6th April 2005 and the debt is £900,000. Based on HMRC's example in the Appendix of the Guidance Notes, B pays income tax on 9/10 of the rental value attributable to the house.

Question 2

Can HMRC confirm that this is the view taken? i.e. that where the debt is only a percentage of the value of the house the taxpayer pays income tax on the same percentage of the rental value?

There seems no express provision in para 11 to allow for a percentage reduction in the charge in the event that the property is subject to a debt but has some excess value. We assume from the example in the Appendix that HMRC interpret the interaction of paras 11(6) and (1) and in particular the words "to the extent that" to mean that if the value of the property exceeds the excluded liability by 10% there is a 10% reduction in the charge under para 4.

HMRC answer to question 2

We confirm that, where, as in Example 2, the debt is only a percentage of the value of the chargeable property, income tax is payable on the same percentage of the rental value. As you suggest, this follows from the interaction of paras. 11(6) and (1). As far as subsequent valuation cycles are concerned, we would adjust the proportion of the rental value charged to reflect any adjustment to the value of the chargeable property.

A3.63   1.3 If the debt was reduced to £500,000 (by partial repayment or by writing off) then it would appear that B would pay income tax from that date on half the rental value of the property and that Regulation 4 does not prevent a reduction in the income tax charge on repayment of the debt even if this is done half way through the five year period. Half the value of the property is now deemed to be comprised in the person's estate under para 11(1) and there is no charge on this part.

Question 3

Can HMRC confirm that if the debt "affecting" the property is reduced for any reason the income tax charge reduces by the same proportion even if this reduction occurs during the five year period?

Suppose in the above example the home loan scheme had been effected by a married couple H and W but only H later added the £500,000 to the property trust to enable the property trustees to repay part of the loan. Are we correct to assume that the loan is pro rated so that the excluded liability is reduced for H and W by £250,000 each rather than the repayment just reducing H's share of the excluded liability?

HMRC answer to question 3

We confirm that the income tax charge would be reduced by the same proportion by which the debt affecting the property was reduced. In view of the reference in paragraph 11(6) to "at any time", we confirm that the charge would be reduced even if the reduction of the debt occurred during the 5-year period.

Where the scheme had been effected by a married couple, H & W, we assume that the answer would depend on the precise terms of the property trust. But, assuming that the property is held by H & W equally, the addition by H of £500,000 to the trust would diminish his estate by £250,000 (an exempt transfer to W). On that basis, we would agree that the excluded liability for H & W would be reduced by £250,000 each.

1.4 Suppose that the house is sold by the property trust and the trustees then purchase a smaller property for say £600,000. The debt of £900,000 is not repaid but left outstanding and the spare cash of £400,000 is invested in intangibles to produce an income for B. On a literal reading of Regulation 4 it would appear that B still pays income tax on the market rental of the original property as at the April 2005 valuation (reduced by one tenth).

A3.64

Question 4

We assume that HMRC consider that once a smaller property is purchased during the five year period, what is valued for the purposes of the POA charge under para 4 is indeed that smaller property. Please confirm.

HMRC answer to question 4

Assuming that the intangibles are held on the original trusts and that the debt of £900,000 is left outstanding, we agree that the smaller property would be within the charge under paragraph 4 and that the intangibles would come within paragraph 8.

In line with the answer to Q1, we would suggest that the paragraph 4 computation should be based on the value of the newer, smaller property with the intangible property being charged under paragraph 8. The parts chargeable under paragraphs 3 (as quantified in accordance with paragraph 4) and 8 should then be arrived at by apportioning the loan rateably between the two components. However if the loan was originally secured specifically on the land, one would calculate the paragraph 3 charge simply by reference to the value of the new, smaller property with the balance of the loan being charged under paragraph 8.

1.5 Suppose husband has given away his 50% share in the home originally owned jointly with his wife. The gift was into an Eversden settlement and is now caught by POA. In these circumstances, professional surveyors consider that the 50% share should be discounted and hence "the DV" figure be reduced.

A3.65

Questions of valuation are not specifically addressed in the Guidance Notes but we assume that HMRC accept that, if professionally so advised, a discount for joint ownership would be appropriate for the DV figure.

Question 5

Can a standard percentage discount be agreed with HMRC in relation to jointly held interests?

HMRC answer to question 5

We agree that the 50% share of the house chargeable under POA should be valued on normal open market principles for the purposes of ascertaining DV. This would imply a discount, but not sure that we can agree a standard discount in advance, any more than we would do for "normal" IHT purposes.

A3.66 1.6 There are difficulties in valuing settled insurance policies caught by para 8. For example, in their Guidance Notes HMRC take the view that life policies settled on a commercial basis by partners or shareholders for each other will be caught under POA if the settlor retains an interest. The settlor will often retain such an interest since there is usually a provision that the life policy will revert to the business owner if he leaves the business before death.

Question 6

(a) In these circumstances how does one value the intangible property?

(b) Would it be based on the surrender value of the life policy?

HMRC answer to question 6

Our current view is that a group policy taken out for the partners or shareholders is within the scope of the paragraph 8 charge, because each partner, as settlor, is not excluded from benefit. This appears to be the case whether or not each partner can benefit on leaving the partnership and whether or not the only benefits that can accrue to a partner are those arising on the death of a partner. As far as valuation is concerned, we would expect the value of the policy to be its open market value at the relevant time, not its surrender value.

A3.67 1.7 The comments on life policies taken out by partnerships and other businesses contained at the end of the revised Guidance Notes seem to go directly against Government policy which is to encourage such arrangements (as illustrated by the relieving legislation introduced in FA 2003 s 539A for income tax purposes).

Question 7

Are HMRC considering an extra statutory concession to relieve such arrangements from the POA charge?

This would appear to be appropriate given that such arrangements are commercial with no donative intent and therefore outside the reservation of benefit provisions.

If the only interest of the settlor in the trust is that the life policy reverts to the settlor if he leaves the business before his death, do HMRC agree that the settlor's interest under such arrangement can be regarded as similar to his interest under discounted gift schemes and therefore outside the POA charge—see 8.1?

HMRC answer to question 7

An Extra Statutory Concession is not in view, as far as we are aware, and we do not think it is for us to comment on whether one would be appropriate. As far as the settlor's interest in the policy is concerned, We are doubtful that there is an exact analogy with Discounted Gift Schemes as you suggest. While this would depend on the terms of the policy concerned, it is not clear to us that the value of the settlor's contingent interest and the value of the interests of the surviving partners can be sufficiently distinguished in the way that we have agreed they can be for Discounted Gifts.

A3.68 1.8 We should be grateful for some clarification of HMRC policy in respect of pension policies (whether retirement annuity or personal pension policies and whether approved or unapproved). Typically such policies provide that retirement benefits and other lifetime benefits such as a payment on demutualization are held for the absolute benefit of the individual member with death benefits being held on discretionary trusts.

Question 8

HMRC take the view that the analysis on such policies is similar to discounted gift schemes and that the retirement benefits represent separate unsettled property? See 8.1. Can HMRC confirm that the POA Regime does not apply to such pension arrangements? Does their view change if the individual member can benefit from the discretionary trust over the death benefits?

HMRC answer to question 8

(a) As a general rule, the pension and other lifetime benefits for the scheme member and the benefits paid on death are mutually exclusive. On this basis, we would agree that an analogy can be drawn with discounted gift schemes so that the pension benefits would either represent unsettled property or a trust separate from that on which the death benefits are held.

(b) On the basis of the above, we would agree that the POA regime would generally not apply to pension arrangements, where the individual scheme member was not able to benefit from the discretionary trust governing the death benefits.

1.9 Valuation problems arise where a settlor takes out a life policy and writes it on trust pre-18 March 1986. The reservation of benefit rules did not apply then and so he is often a potential beneficiary. Suppose that for the last 20 years he has been paying the premiums on such policy. Section 102(6) FA 1986 provides an exemption from reservation of benefit in respect of premiums paid post 17 March 1986 where the policy was taken out before 18 March and the premiums increase at a pre-arranged rate. However, there has been concern that premiums paid post 17 March 1986 would appear to be within the POA Regime.

A3.69

Question 9

(a) Do HMRC consider that such policies are caught? We would suggest that premiums paid since 17 March 1986 are not themselves additions to the settled property if paid direct to the insurance company but merely maintain the value of the settled property and therefore are not strictly within the wording of para 8.

(b) We understand from correspondence in Taxation that HMRC believe POA does apply and apportion the premiums between pre 18 and post 17 March 1986.

(c) In the light of the comment in (a) above will HMRC reconsider their views in respect of payments on such policies?

HMRC answer to question 9

In our view, it is correct to regard premiums paid after 17 March 1986 in respect of settled policies as additions to the settled property and so within paragraph 8 if the settlor is a potential beneficiary. As you suggest, the proportion of the settled property chargeable under paragraph 8 is arrived at by apportioning the premiums between those paid pre -18 and post -17 March 1986.

2. Home Loan or Double Trust Schemes

We have a number of specific queries on home loan schemes and would welcome clarification with regard to the following points.

A3.70

A3.71   2.1 We welcome the provision for the avoidance of a double charge in the event of the GWR election being made. However, as discussed below, the election still has a number of uncertainties. Furthermore Regulation 6 is defective in a number of respects.

Firstly, it should not be limited to gifts into settlements (see Regulation 6(a)(ii)) since in some cases the gift of the debt was outright to a child rather than into trust.

A3.72   2.2 Secondly, Regulation 6 should not be limited to a gift of property representing "the proceeds of the disposal of relevant property".

Many schemes proceeded on the basis of taxpayers lending money to the trustees by a loan agreement and the trustees then using that money to buy the house. The loan does not represent the proceeds of the house. There should be relief in these circumstances.

Question 10

Will HMRC in practice apply Regulation 6 to relieve all home loan schemes from a potential double charge where the donor has died having made an election or is Regulation 6 being amended to cover the above points?

HMRC answer to question 10

We note your view that Regulation 6 of SI 2005/724 is not wide enough to cover all cases where a double charge may arise after the taxpayer has elected. At this stage, we cannot give an assurance that we will apply the regulation more widely than its terms indicate, but we will pass on your views on this point.

A3.73   2.3 One of the ways that taxpayers are unravelling home loan schemes is to appoint the debt to the children who then assign it back to the settlor thus losing all inheritance tax benefits but at least ensuring (provided that the children took interests in possession under the original trust) that if the settlor dies within 7 years of the original PET, there is relief under the Double Charges Regulations. (This course is often preferable unless double charges relief is to be given for the release of a debt.)

Although there is still an excluded liability in existence, the excluded liability does not appear to be relevant any longer in that it does not reduce the value of the parents' estates under paragraph 11(6) albeit it affects the value of the house. The wording in para 11(6) refers "to the value of the person's estate" and we assume that this means the value of someone's total estate for inheritance tax purposes.

Therefore the fact that the loan continues to reduce the value of the house does not mean that the loan is caught under para 11(6).

Question 11

Is the analysis in 2.4 correct (a) in stating that there is relief under the Double Charges Regulations if the children assign the debt back to the settlor and the settlor dies within 7 years of the original gift of the debt and (b) that para 11(6) is no longer in point once the assignment has been effected back to them because the debt no longer reduces the value of their estates?

HMRC answer to question 11

We agree with your analysis in paragraph 2.4(a): the circumstances you have in mind seem to be covered by Regulation 4 of SI 1987/1130. As far as paragraph 2.4(b) is concerned, we agree that paragraph 11(6) would no longer be in point.

A3.74   2.4 Para 11(6) refers to "the amount of the excluded liability". We seek clarification as to whether this is the face value of the debt (including any rolled up interest or accrued indexation) or the commercial value of the debt.

Example 3

C entered into a home loan scheme. The house is worth £2 million and the debt is repayable on C's death, is linked to the RPI and has a face value of £1.9 million. Its commercial value is discounted due to the fact that it is not repayable until C's death. Allowing for the fact that the debt is linked to the RPI, its market value would be, say, £1.2 million but increasing.

In these circumstances the question is, whether the excess value which is treated as part of C's estate and therefore protected from the POA charge under para 11(1) is:

(i) £100,000
(ii) £800,000 or
(iii) some other figure such as £100,000 less accrued indexation?

Question 12

What is HMRC's view regarding the amount of the excluded liability in the above scenario?

It would appear that the correct view is to take the commercial value of the debt as reducing the person's estate because in reality the property is "affected" by this amount of debt. Obviously the POA charge would become higher as the commercial value of the debt increased towards the end of the donor's lifetime and hence less property exceeded the value of the debt.

HMRC answer to question 12

In our view, the fact that paragraph 11(6) refers to the "amount" of the excluded liability indicates that it is the face value of the debt, including any rolled-up interest or accrued indexation, that is relevant. In practice, we would only seek to adjust the value of the debt to take account of interest and indexation at the 5-yearly valuation dates, though we would be prepared to allow any reduction of the debt resulting from any repayment be taken account as it occurred and to be reflected in a revised computation of tax in the relevant year and subsequently.

2.5 A common scenario (both for foreign and UK domiciliaries) is where cash is settled into an interest in possession trust for the donor life tenant. The trustees then buy a house for the donor to live in using the gifted cash plus third party borrowings. Although not a home loan scheme, the legislation appears to affect such arrangements.

Example 4

E settles cash of £200,000 into an interest in possession trust for himself in 2003. The trustees purchase a property worth £500,000, borrowing £300,000 from a bank. There are other assets in the trust which can fund the interest but the borrowing is secured on the house which E then occupies.

In these circumstances, one would not expect a POA charge. There is no inheritance tax scheme since the property is part of E's estate and the borrowing is not internal. One would argue that E's estate still includes the house and therefore protection is available under para 11(1). The difficulty is that on one view the loan is an excluded liability within para 11(7) reducing E's estate, albeit it is a loan on commercial terms with a bank.

We would argue that the relevant property for the purposes of para 11 is simply the value of the property net of the commercial borrowing. As this is part of E's estate there is no POA charge.

A3.75

Question 13

Is the above analysis correct?

HMRC answer to question 13

A3.76　We agree with your analysis in paragraph 2.6.
2.6 In those home loan schemes where HMRC consider that there is a reservation of benefit in the debt, it would appear that the taxpayer can still face a POA charge—because he has made a disposal of land which is subject to an excluded liability. The fact that he has reserved a benefit in the debt does not make the debt part of his estate such that the excluded liability can be ignored.

Question 14

Where there is a reservation of benefit in respect of the loan can HMRC confirm that they would not expect the taxpayer to pay both POA and IHT and that the inheritance tax charge would take priority?

HMRC answer to question 14

We agree with the analysis at 2.6. (Even if there is a reservation of benefit in the loan for IHT purposes, it is the land, not the loan, which is the relevant property for POA purposes and para.11, Sch.15 in particular. And although the loan may be property subject to a reservation for IHT purposes, it remains an excluded liability within paras.11(6) and (7), Sch.15 for the purposes of the POA charge.) As matters currently stand, there is no provision to disapply the charge that may arise under Sch.15.

Question 15

Will any statement be issued by HMRC as to which home loan schemes of the various types seen they consider do not work for inheritance tax purposes?
Otherwise taxpayers may self-assess and pay the income tax charge, thinking to preserve the inheritance tax savings but be unaware of HMRC's view.

HMRC answer to question 15

We will shortly be issuing updated technical guidance that will include material to identify the circumstances in which we consider a reservation of benefit in the loan exists. Hopefully, this will give some indication to providers of schemes affected whether or not we consider their scheme to be one where a reservation of benefit in the loan exists. This in turn may make it easier for providers to help any clients (or ex-clients) who seek their assistance over completion of their tax return.

3. The Effect of the Election

A3.77　3.1 In the case of a married couple who have sold their jointly owned house to the property trust and given the debt to a second trust, it is assumed that one of them can elect to come within the gift with reservation rules and one can choose not to elect: i.e. it is not necessary for both to make the election.

Question 16

Will HMRC please confirm this point?

HMRC answer to question 16

As far as we can see, it is possible for one spouse and not the other to elect under paragraph 21.

3.2 There is some uncertainty about the effect of the election because para 21 does not as such deem there to be a gift for inheritance tax purposes but simply states that the property is treated as property subject to a reservation.

Furthermore in para 21(2)(b)(ii) it is stated that only sections 102(3) and (4) are to apply and not specifically section 102(8) which brings in Schedule 20.

We assume that the wording in para 21(2)(b)(i) referring to the property being treated as property subject to a reservation of benefit for the purposes of the 1986 Act does not limit the scope of the reservation of benefit provisions so that only sections 102(3) and (4) apply.

Example 5

> D effected a home loan scheme. He elects into reservation of benefit and then in April 2010 starts to pay full consideration for the use of his house. Has he made a deemed PET at that point (under s 102(4)) and is he protected from a reservation of benefit charge provided he continues to pay a market rent? We assume that HMRC take the view that para 21(2)(b)(ii) does not narrow the effect of 21(2)(b)(i) and the let-outs in para 6 Schedule 20 apply.

Question 17

(i) Please confirm that on making an election there is a reservation of benefit in the house and not the debt in respect of the home loan scheme and that, once an election is made, all the provisions relating to reservation of benefit in FA 1986 and in particular Schedule 20 apply?

Please also confirm the position on deemed PETs in the example above where the person who elects is already paying full consideration.

(ii) Suppose A elects into GWR in respect of his home. The house is then appointed back to him absolutely (i.e. the arrangement eg. a home loan scheme, is unscrambled). In these circumstances the reservation of benefit has ceased but the house is back in their estates anyway. Is there a deemed PET under s.102(4)? FA 1986.

HMRC answer to question 17

(i) We confirm that on making an election under paragraph 21, there would be a reservation of benefit in the house, not the debt in respect of the home loan scheme. In our view, the reference to section 102(4) Finance Act 1986 in paragraph 21(2)(b)(ii) envisages circumstances in which the property ceases to be subject to a reservation and there is nothing to suggest that these would not include circumstances in which the provisions of paragraph 6, Schedule 20 Finance Act 1986 would be in point.

(ii) By analogy with the view we have taken for "actual" gifts with reservation, we believe that the tax treatment for the purposes of Sch.15 would depend on whether or not the taxpayer starts to pay full consideration for the continued use of the house or chattel immediately on making an election or after a period of time. We think it would only be in the latter case that there would be a deemed PET under section 102(4) FA 1986.

(iii) In our view, the provisions of s.102(4) do, in terms, apply, by virtue of para.21(2)(b)(ii), when the taxable property is appointed back to the chargeable person. But the value of A's estate would not be decreased by this deemed PET.

On that basis we do not regard the deemed PET by A has having any practical consequences for A, because it would have no value.

A3.79 3.3 We seek clarification of the position on home loan schemes when both spouses elect and one then dies.

Example 6

H and W have effected a home loan scheme. They both elect. On H's death his share in the house is worth £400,000 but is perhaps entirely subject to debt. His share passes to W but the value of her estate is not increased because H's share is subject to the debt. Hence the concern is that the effect of the election is to make H's share taxable immediately on his death by virtue of s 102(3) as to £400,000.

In our view it would appear that the spouse exemption is available on the first death since the deceased's share in the house passes to the surviving spouse under the terms of the property trust or otherwise becomes comprised in the survivor's estate as IHTA 1984 requires. This is so even if the value of the debt equals or exceeds that of the house.

Question 18

(a) Do HMRC agree with this interpretation? (See also Statement of Practice E13.)
(b) Is HMRC's view that:
  1. full spouse exemption is available even if the debt equals the value of the house; or
  2. full spouse exemption is available provided the spouse's estate is increased by even a small amount; or
  3. spouse exemption is only available to the extent the value of the house exceeds the debt?

HMRC answer to question 18

In the circumstances outlined in Example 6, the starting point is the disposals of property that H & W have each made in order to effect a home loan scheme. If then they elect under paragraph 21 and H then dies, we think the effect would indeed be to bring £400,000 into H's estate immediately before his death for IHT purposes by virtue of section 102(3) Finance Act 1986. As far as we can see, there is no scope for spouse exemption as regards this chargeable item as the property disposed of by H in setting up the home loan scheme did not become comprised in the estate of W. Nor, having regard to paragraph 21(3) can we see any scope for reducing the amount charged under section 102(3) FA 1986 by the amount of the debt. Of course, H's estate for IHT purposes will also include his interest in possession in the property trust. We imagine this would consist of his share in the house, subject to the debt. Undoubtedly spouse exemption would be available, but only to the extent that the value of H's share in the house exceeded the debt.

A3.80 3.4 As noted in 1.5 above there are technical difficulties if the property is sold after an election. Assume that a smaller replacement property is acquired by the trustees but the debt is not repaid. Accepting that the replacement property will be within the para 3 land charge, what of the surplus cash which has been invested in intangibles?

Example 7

Suppose the taxpayer moves out of the home and has made an election. He purchases a smaller replacement house a week later. The balance of the proceeds are invested and he enjoys the income as life tenant.

Question 19

(a) Does a new election need to be made at that point under para 22 in relation to the intangibles part and/or under para 21 in relation to the smaller home?

(b) What happens if the time limits for making the election on the original property have passed?

HMRC answer to question 19

Para 21(2)(a) states that when an election has been made the income tax charge won't apply to the taxpayer's enjoyment of the relevant property "or of any property which has been substituted for the relevant property". From the "any property" we take that to include not only property in the form of land and chattels but also intangible property even though that is subject to a separate paragraph for the election. The equivalent measure in Para 22(2)(a) uses the phrase "or any property which represents or is derived from the relevant property". We think this difference is necessary as it may not be possible to "substitute" intangible property for other intangible property.

But we assume you can convert intangible property into something different and we think an election under Para 22 would similarly cover cases where intangible property is converted into land or chattels and would otherwise be subject to an election under Para 21. So as the paragraphs cover substitutions/derivations, we do not think we require a fresh election when the underlying property changes. In any event, if the taxpayer apparently has an interest in possession in the intangible property, would not paragraph 11(1) be in point assuming a home loan scheme was not involved? As we would not be looking for a fresh election, we assume part (b) of the question is not relevant.

3.5 It may be said that the deeming provision in section 660A(1) TA 1988 (now s 624 ITTOIA 2005) is irrelevant to interest in possession trusts where the settlor is life tenant given that there is no question of the income being taxed as that of any other person as envisaged in that provision. **A3.81**

Question 20

Does the para 8 charge apply to cash held in such a trust on the basis that this is a settlor interested trust to which section 660A TA 1988 (now s.624 ITTOIA 2005) is therefore applicable or does the fact that the settlor is the life tenant of this trust preclude the application of section 660A? This would obviously affect the election mechanism. This is relevant to home loan trusts now holding intangibles.

HMRC answer to question 20

We are not sure that we can see how the application of section 624 ITTOIA 2005, and therefore paragraph 8 is explicitly precluded per se.

Question 21

3.6 When an election is made on a double trust scheme, is this election in respect of the entire land or just the part subject to the debt? Can HMRC confirm the former is correct given that in para 21(3) the DV/V formulation would mean that the entire value of the land equals DV? **A3.82**

HMRC answer to question 21

It seems to us that the relevant property in terms of Schedule 15 generally and specifically for the purposes of the election would be the land in its entirety.

A3.83   3.7 The election mechanism does not satisfactorily deal with the position where part of the original gifted property is not within the Regime and part is.

Example 8

Andrew gives his house on interest in possession trusts for spouse Emma in 2000. Her interest in possession is terminated in all but 20% of the fund. Hence the gift ceases to be an excluded disposal in relation to 80%.

Andrew decides to make an election rather than to pay the income tax charge. In these circumstances is the chargeable proportion 100% (being the DV/V figure) or 80%?

It is assumed the latter on the basis that Andrew is chargeable only by reference to his enjoyment of the 80% not by reference to his enjoyment of 100% (see wording in para 21(1)(a)). Hence "the relevant property" on which he can elect is only 80%.

Question 22

Do HMRC agree with this analysis?

HMRC answer to question 22

A3.84   We would agree that, in the circumstances set out in Example 8, the "relevant property" would be 80% of it. The use of the formula DV/V, as ordained in paragraph 21(3), would simply mean that all of the 80% would be treated as the chargeable proportion.

3.8 Where a taxpayer is doubtful as to whether he is caught by the Regime in the first place he can put full details of his arguments on the additional information pages of the return and presumably would then be treated as having made full disclosure and be protected from a discovery assessment. Of course, even if a taxpayer does obtain finality in one tax year, this will not prevent HMRC raising an enquiry in later years if the taxpayer continued to self assess on the basis that the Regime does not apply to him.

Suppose HMRC do not enquire into the taxpayer's return for 2005/6. In 2006/7 he continues to self assess on the basis that he is outside the Regime; HMRC make an enquiry and it is established that the taxpayer was wrong to self assess on the basis that no income tax was due under the Regime. Possibly a court case clarifies the position or there is a change in legislation which is deemed to have always had effect.

In these circumstances the taxpayer will have missed the deadline for making the election (he first became chargeable under the Regime in 2005 and therefore needed to elect by January 31, 2007) and will have to pay income tax going forward or else try to unravel the arrangement.

Question 23

Will the taxpayer be able to make a late election in these circumstances?

HMRC answer to question 23

Whether the taxpayer is protected from a discovery assessment in the circumstances described will depend on whether the argument he presents is tenable and if not whether he could then be considered negligent in submitting an insufficient self assessment. Tenability would need to be judged against the practice generally prevailing at the time the return was made. We would consider that the taxpayer was bound by the time limit for that year of assessment for making an election regardless of whether HMRC made an enquiry relating to that year or a later year. It would be for the taxpayer to demonstrate that he had a reasonable excuse for failing to make an election in time.

In a situation where a court decision overturns the previous practice or legislation makes changes which is deemed to have always had effect, then the taxpayer would be protected for earlier years and he would be chargeable only from the time the change in practice or legislation was made. It would not be unreasonable to assume he would then have until the deadline for that year of assessment to make an election.

3.9 Another difficulty arises if the taxpayer wrongly pays income tax on the basis that he was within the Regime when in fact he was not. This is particularly pertinent in relation to home loan schemes where HMRC appear to accept that some work and some do not.

A3.85

Question 24

What position will be taken by HMRC in these circumstances? Will the taxpayer (or his personal representatives) be able to make a claim for repayment of the tax paid under a mistake of law for 6 years from the date of overpayment?

HMRC answer to question 24

Providers of certain home loan or double trust schemes are already aware that HMRC takes the view that the gifts with reservation of benefit legislation applies to them. We will include in our guidance information about the circumstances in which we consider the GWR legislation applies.

If the taxpayer has made an excessive self assessment by virtue of error or mistake in his return then he can claim relief under section 33 of the Taxes Management Act 1970. The time limit for doing so is 5 years from the 31 January following the year of assessment to which the erroneous return relates.

4. Regulation 5 and Para.10(1)(a)—Equity Release Schemes

4.1 The relief given in Regulation 5 seems unnecessarily restrictive as a matter of principle and we do not fully understand the Ministerial Statement or the Guidance Notes on this. It is suggested that where a child moves into the house to care for an aged parent and acquires an equitable interest in the shared home in consideration for providing caring services, the parent is protected from a POA charge under Regulation 5(b). However, such a disposal does not seem to be by way of a transaction at arm's length between persons not connected with each other. These are not normal commercial arrangements. It is difficult to put a value in advance or even retrospectively on what the services to be provided will actually be worth in terms of a share in the house.

A3.86

Question 25

What evidence is required to satisfy Regulation 5(b)? It will be difficult to establish what would be regarded as an arms length transaction without a court hearing which would generally only occur in the event of a dispute.

HMRC answer to question 25

In considering whether regulation 5(b) was satisfied, we would need information about how the essential elements of the transaction had been arrived at. We do recognise that there is a substantial body of case law dealing with the circumstances in which an interest in a house is acquired in consequence of a person acting to his detriment. The Ministerial Statement had these sorts of situations in mind and we would interpret Regulation 5 accordingly. In particular, we accept that the requirement that "the disposal was by a transaction such as might be expected to be made at arm's length between persons not connected with each other" would be interpreted with such cases in mind. We would not therefore expect the parties to have sought separate advice and acted upon it or to have obtained a court order confirming the property entitlement. We recognise that detriment that the acquirer can demonstrate he has suffered can provide consideration for the acquisition of the interest and prevent the transaction from being gratuitous.

A3.87 4.2 Suppose that something that had not been a readily convertible asset and was therefore protected under para 5(1)(b) subsequently became a RCA under ITEPA. We are concerned that a transaction that was previously protected could now lose such protection.

Question 26

What happens if the definition of readily convertible asset in ITEPA 2003 changes?

HMRC answer to question 26

If the definition of "readily convertible asset" in ITEPA 2003 were to change, I think we would need to review the appropriateness of Regulation 5(2). We are not aware that any such alteration is in prospect, however.

A3.88 4.3 There are difficulties where land is held under one title but is physically discrete—for example, two fields. Suppose father sells one of the two fields to his son for full value and continues to farm in partnership over that field. Does father have a pre-owned assets problem.

Question 27

Is the father protected under para 10(1)(a)? Can it be treated as a sale of whole if son becomes beneficially and legally entitled to the entire field even though father is selling only one of the fields?

HMRC answer to question 27

The first issue is what constitutes "the property" for the purposes of paragraph 10(1)(a). We think it would be possible to regard each of the two discrete fields as "the property", so the disposal of one of them would be a disposal of the whole interest in that asset. As far as your example is concerned, a sale by father to son would be within paragraph 10(1)(a)(ii) on the basis that father receives a full open market price for his land.

A3.89 4.4 It is not uncommon for taxpayers to enter into transactions whereby they carve out a lease for themselves and sell the freehold reversion at full market value. Indeed some commercial equity release schemes are structured along these lines. In earlier informal discussions HMRC appeared to agree that the wording in para 10(1)(a) did cover such arrangements but the Guidance Notes suggest there has to be a disposal of the taxpayer's entire interest without any reservation of a lease. The provisions on non-exempt sales of course use a different wording.

Question 28

Can HMRC confirm that a disposal of a taxpayer's whole interest in the property "except for any right expressly reserved by him over the property" as set out in para 10(1)(a) is intended to cover a transaction where F has carved out a lease for himself and sold the encumbered freehold reversion for full market value to his son? If so, will the Guidance Notes be amended to confirm this?

HMRC answer to question 28

In our view, paragraph 10(1)(a) does cover the scenario you envisage in 4.4. We will amend the Guidance Notes.

5. Reversionary Lease Arrangements

5.1 In the case of reversionary lease arrangements, the taxpayer retains the freehold interest giving away a long lease which vests in possession in (say) 20 years time. Assuming that he is within para 3 i.e. that the arrangement does not involve a reservation of benefit, the taxpayer may wish to pay a full rent for his use of the land so as to avoid a POA charge: see Schedule 15 para 4(1). The difficulty is that the owner of the relevant land in this case appears to be himself and he cannot pay rent to himself.

Question 29

Does this mean that in the context of reversionary leases this part of the legislation is meaningless? To obtain relief under para 4, will the taxpayer have to transfer his freehold to an interest in possession trust for himself and pay rent to the trustees?

HMRC answer to question 29

We agree that it would be difficult for the taxpayer to pay rent to himself in order to avoid a charge under Schedule 15. But, as you suggest, it would be possible to overcome the difficulty.

5.2 The Guidance Notes state that reversionary lease arrangements effected post 8 March 1999 are not caught because they are subject to a reservation of benefit. You will be aware that many advisers do not agree with this view. On the basis of HMRC's current advice there is no requirement for a taxpayer to self assess and pay the pre-owned asset income tax charge. If, however, it turns out that HMRC are wrong in their view that post 8 March 1999 reversionary lease schemes are caught by the reservation of benefit rules, pre-owned assets income tax would have been due.

Question 30

(a) If HMRC's views are successfully challenged in the courts will the taxpayer be subject to back tax, interest and penalties?

(b) We would hope that HMRC would not in these circumstances seek to collect income tax (and interest) in respect of past years but only in respect of future years.

(c) Will it be a requirement for all taxpayers who have done a reversionary lease scheme post March 1999 to put this on their tax return in the white space and explain why they are not paying income tax?

HMRC answer to question 30

Our view on the IHT treatment of reversionary leases and, in particular, the application of section 102A Finance Act 1986 to them is under review at the moment. We will be issuing guidance as soon as we can.

6. Miscellaneous Problems

6.1 There are difficulties in determining whether both contribution and disposal conditions have been met in a single transaction and this can be relevant when applying the exclusions in para 10 and the exemptions in para 11.

Para 3(2) provides that the disposal condition is met if the chargeable person owned an interest in the relevant land or "in other property the proceeds of the disposal of which were directly or indirectly applied by another person towards the acquisition of an interest in the relevant land."

Para 3(3) refers to the contribution condition being met where the chargeable person "has directly or indirectly provided, otherwise than by an excluded transaction, any of the consideration given by another person for the acquisition of an interest in the relevant land or an interest in any other property the proceeds of the disposal of which were directly or indirectly applied by another person towards the acquisition of an interest in the relevant land."

Question 31

Is the correct analysis of the interaction between the disposal condition and the contribution condition as follows?

1. If the transferred property is itself the relevant land (i.e. is occupied by the donor) only the disposal condition is met.
2. If the transferred property is cash and that cash is used by the donee to buy the relevant land occupied by the donor, only the contribution condition is met. If HMRC agree with this can the Guidance Notes be amended at 1.2.1 which suggest (we think wrongly) that the disposal not the contribution condition is breached if cash is given to the donee who then purchases a property for occupation by the donor.
3. If the transferred property is an asset other than cash, and the donee then sells that asset and uses the proceeds to buy the relevant land, both the disposal and the contribution conditions are met.
4. In such a case Sch 15 para 11(9)(a)(ii) means the relevant land is the relevant property for the purposes of para 11, so that the para 11 exemptions can apply if the other conditions in para 11 are met.

HMRC answer to question 31

Taking your four questions in turn:

- If the property disposed of by the chargeable person is the relevant land, we agree that only the disposal condition in paragraph 3(2) is in point.
- If the chargeable person transfers cash, which is then used by the donee to acquire relevant land, we agree that it is the contribution condition in paragraph 3(3) that is in point, not the disposal condition. As you suggest, our guidance at paragraph 1.2.1 needs revising on this point.
- We agree that the contribution condition contemplates circumstances in which a chargeable person has indirectly provided consideration by way of a disposal of assets other than cash. Such a disposal might also meet the disposal condition, as you suggest.
- Paragraph 3 makes it clear that, for the purposes of either the disposal or the contribution conditions, the "relevant land" is the land occupied by the chargeable person. In a case where the contribution condition (paragraphs 3(3) or 6(3), as appropriate) is in point, the "relevant property" for the purposes of the exemptions in paragraph 11 is the "property representing the consideration directly or indirectly provided": We think this must mean provided by the chargeable person. Whether this is the "relevant land must, we think, depend on whether paragraph 3(3)(a) or 3(3)(b) apply.

A3.93   6.2 The meaning of the "provision" of "consideration" in the context of the contribution condition needs to be clarified. On the basis of the case law the word provided suggests some element of bounty.

On this basis our view is that if there is a transfer of Whiteacre by A (or another asset) to his son at full market value which is then sold by son and the sale proceeds used to purchase Blackacre for A to occupy this is a breach of the disposal but not the contribution condition because it lacks the necessary element of bounty.

Similarly the provision of a loan on commercial terms by A to his son to enable son to purchase a house which A then occupies in our view does not fall within the contribution condition.

Question 32

Do HMRC agree with this analysis?

HMRC answer to question 32

Now confirmed that loans are not caught by the contribution condition.

6.3 Clarification is requested on the position where a house is owned by a company but the company is funded by way of loan. The concern is over paras 11(1)(b) and 11(3)(b).   **A3.94**

Example 9

> B owns 100 £1 shares in X Limited and otherwise funds it by shareholder loan. (Or the house is owned by a company held within an interest in possession trust for B and again the funding for the purchase comes by way of loan from trustees to company.) X Limited buys the house in which B lives. B prima facie falls within the para 3 charge. It would appear that para 11(1) protects him. The shares are not themselves property which derive much value from the house because they are worth substantially less than the house (see para 11(1)(b)(ii)) but the shares and the loan together are comprised in B's estate and between them indirectly derive their value from the house. On that basis para 11(1) does offer full protection.

Question 33

Do HMRC agree with this analysis or do they consider that the loan derives its value from the contractual undertakings that oblige the borrowing company to repay?

It would be odd if there is a POA problem when the company is funded by way of loan but not if it is funded by way of share capital.

HMRC answer to question 33

In our view, the loan, albeit an asset of B's estate, is not property that derives its value from the relevant property. However, our response to Q32 above would no doubt be applicable here in appropriate circumstances.

6.4 How is the charge computed under para 9 when the settled property comprises say a deposit account but also an overdrawn current account at 6th April in the relevant year? Is the POA tax charge based simply on the value of the deposit account without deducting the overdraft?   **A3.95**

The definition of relevant property is property which is or represents property which the chargeable person settled. If A settles cash into trust retaining a remainder interest and then the trust invests that cash unwisely e.g. in a hedge fund incurring losses which require the trustees to borrow to settle, is it the net or gross value of the trust fund that is taken in computing the POA charge?

Question 34

Can HMRC clarify the above?

HMRC answer to question 34

In our view, it is the net value of the trust fund as at 6 April in the relevant year that should form the basis of the computation under paragraph 9.

A3.96   6.5 The excluded transaction provision in para 10(2)(c) refers to an outright gift "to the other person" whereas the wording in para 10(2)(e) refers expressly to an outright gift to an individual. The word person must include trusts and companies. In our view para 10(2)(c) applies to settled gifts and gifts to individuals although of course cash gifts into trust will be caught by the tracing rules in schedule 20 and are therefore generally gifts with reservation if the donor can benefit from the trust and protected anyway under para 11(3).

Question 35

Do HMRC agree with this analysis?

HMRC answer to question 35

We think the "other person" referred to in paragraph 10(2)(c) must be the person referred to in paragraphs 3(3) and 6(3) as acquiring an interest in the relevant land etc. We agree that such a person need not necessarily be an individual. But we are more doubtful that an "outright" gift of money could include a gift to be held on trusts.

6.6 Partnership issues

A3.97   The Guidance Notes suggest that a partnership is transparent for inheritance tax purposes. While this is true for capital gains tax purposes, as a matter of law a gift of a partnership interest is not a gift of the underlying assets within the partnership.

We therefore do not understand the example given in Appendix 1 which refers to C who gives his son D an interest in the partnership in return for D taking on the day to day running. In these circumstances why is there a disposal of land or chattels at all? There is a fundamental distinction between a firm's capital on the one hand and its individual assets on the other. C's proportionate interest in the capital may be equal to the value of the land or chattels but it is not an interest in the land or chattels itself and therefore he cannot dispose of that land (or the chattels) when he makes the gift of the partnership interest. See Lindley on Partnerships 17th Edn.

Question 36

Are HMRC treating partnerships as transparent for POA income tax purposes?

HMRC answer to question 36

A3.98   We do not intend to treat partnerships as transparent for the purposes of Schedule 15. We will amend the example in Appendix 1 of the Guidance that you refer to.
   6.7 Certain questions arise in relation to the annual exemption.

Example 10

> X carried out a home loan scheme. In June 2005 he dismantles the scheme. The benefit enjoyed for POA purposes from April to June is £4,000.

Question 37

Will HMRC confirm that :

(a) where the de minimis exemption under para 13 is not exceeded it is not possible for the transferor to make an election because he is not "chargeable to income tax"?

(b) the £5,000 exemption is not pro-rated when a taxpayer is chargeable for only part of the year?

HMRC answer to question 37

We confirm both (a) and (b) are correct.

6.8 In a number of circumstances it is possible for (say) the husband to be caught by POA charge because he has made a disposal but not a gift and the wife to be caught potentially by gift with reservation.

In these circumstances do they each have to pay full consideration to escape their respective charges?

A3.99

Example 11

In 1998 H transfers some properties into a company he wholly owns in consideration of the issue of shares. He has breached the disposal condition. He gives the shares to his wife. In 2003 W gives the company shares to her sons and later both of them occupy one of the properties owned by the company. H and W are not directors of the company.

In these circumstances H might wish to pay rent under paragraph 4 and W might want to pay full consideration under para 6 Schedule 20 in order respectively to avoid a pre-owned assets tax charge and a reservation of benefit situation.

Question 38

(a) Is it sufficient that they pay such rent under an assured shorthold tenancy from their joint account and are jointly and severally liable for the rent?

(b) Or does each person have to pay the full consideration separately?

HMRC answer to question 38

It seems to us that Example 11 is dealing with concurrent charges under two separate regimes: Schedule 15, and section 102 Finance Act 1986. In our view, it is arguable that H and W each has to pay full consideration separately in order to meet the separate requirements of paragraph 4(1) Schedule 15 and paragraph 6 Schedule 20 Finance Act 1986.

6.9 In 1.3.1 of the Guidance Notes under the bullet points relating to the spouse having to take an interest in possession from the outset it is not clear whether, if the interest in possession of the spouse or former spouse has come to an end other than on their death, the transaction is not an excluded transaction from the outset or whether it becomes so from the time the interest in possession terminates. It must surely cease to be an excluded transaction only from the time the interest in possession terminates.

A3.100

Question 39

Will HMRC please clarify this point and confirm that the transaction only ceases to be an excluded transaction from the date the spousal interest terminates and therefore it is only from that point onwards there is a POA charge. Furthermore para 10(3) states that a disposal is not an excluded transaction if the interest in possession of the spouse comes to an end otherwise than on death of the spouse. Suppose a spouse becomes beneficially entitled to the property absolutely e.g. if the trustees advance the property outright to her so she becomes absolutely entitled. In these circumstances does the excluded transaction protection end? Her interest in possession has ended but only because she has become absolutely entitled to the property.

HMRC answer to question 39

In view of the way in which paragraph 10(3) is drafted, it is clear that the transaction ceases to be an excluded transaction only from the time that the interest in possession comes to an end otherwise than on the death of the (former) spouse.

As far as para.10(3) is concerned, we can see how it might be said that, where a spouse becomes absolutely entitled, the protection afforded by paras.10(1)(c) or 10(2)(b) is no longer available, particularly as the property in question would no longer be settled property. That would be a less than satisfactory result in our view, particularly bearing in mind the related provisions in paras.10(1)(b) and (2)(a). A more satisfactory approach might be to regard the interest in possession, which is not limited in terms to settled property as far as the reference in para.10(3) is concerned, as not coming to an end in these circumstances.

A3.101 6.10 4.6 of the Guidance Notes give some examples of what HMRC consider constitutes occupation and the helpful letter from Mr McNicol dated 22 April 2005 gives further explanation. However, we do not fully understand HMRC's comments in this area. Please could the following common scenarios be clarified so that the taxpayer can self-assess appropriately. This is particularly relevant in relation to holiday homes.

Question 40

(a) If there is a right to use a property throughout the year but it is not in fact used by the chargeable person, is it correct that there is no POA charge?

(b) If there is a right to use a property throughout the year and the chargeable person uses the property but it falls within the de minimis limits set out in the guidance notes, is it correct that there is no POA charge?

(c) If there is a right to use a property throughout the year and the chargeable person uses the property for say 3 months of the year there is a POA charge based on the whole year, even though others may have the right to use the property during that period (we are thinking particularly here of holiday homes)?

(d) If there is a right to or actual storage of items in the relevant property but the chargeable person never lives there and the property is occupied by someone else, is it correct that there is no occupation of land within schedule 15?

(e) Would the position of HMRC differ in (d) above if the property remained empty?

HMRC answer to question 40

Before dealing with your individual questions, we think it is worth reminding you of our view that occupation and use should be construed widely and are not confined to physical occupation.

(a) If there is a right to use, but no occupation or use (in the wider sense) by the chargeable person in the year, it is unlikely that there would be a Schedule 15 charge.

(b) We are not sure we can confirm that no Schedule 15 charge would arise in these circumstances. The examples of de minimis use given in paragraph 4.6 of the

Guidance Notes do not contemplate (or, at least, do not assume) a right to use in the hands of the chargeable person for the rest of the year. If there is a right to use the property with even a small amount of use, the issue of how in fact the property was used for the rest of the year would need to be considered and whether this use also constituted use by the chargeable person.

(c) We would agree that a Schedule 15 charge based on the whole year would arise.

(d) We think it is difficult to give an assurance that there is no occupation of land under Schedule 15 by the chargeable person, if he is actually storing assets in the property. Particularly if he might have a right of access to these items, the circumstances might suggest that both the chargeable person and the person living in the property were using it.

(e) By saying that the property remains empty, we assume you are envisaging that no-one is living in it. On that basis, if the chargeable person is storing items there, it seems clear that he is using the property for the purposes of Schedule 15.

6.11 The position on non-exempt sales is unclear. It is our view that there is no POA charge because the cash element paid is excluded under the computation in para 4 and the undervalue element is a reservation of benefit anyway and therefore exempted from POA under para 11(3).   **A3.102**

If there is a part exchange at an undervalue with a cash adjustment, i.e. Y transfers Whiteacre worth £800,000 to X in exchange for Greenacre worth £200,000 and X also pays Y cash of £500,000, if at 6/4/05 Whiteacre is worth £800,000 (i.e. total consideration is paid by X of £700,000) we assume that POA is payable only on £200,000. The cash element is excluded under para 4 and the undervalue element is excluded under the reservation of benefit provisions.

Question 41

Is the above analysis correct?

HMRC answer to question 41

We broadly agree with this analysis. (We have assumed that, in order for this question to arise at all, Y continues to occupy Whiteacre after the transfer.)

In more detail, we would regard Y's disposition as one partly by way of gift (as to £100,000) and partly by way of sale (as to the remaining £700,000). In the circumstances envisaged, the proportion of the value of Whiteacre disposed of by way of gift would be treated as property subject to a reservation, thus remaining in Y's estate for IHT purposes and so, by virtue of paragraph 11(3), disapplying paragraph 3 to that extent. And, again in the circumstances envisaged, the disposition by way of sale would not be an excluded transaction and thus would be a non-exempt sale for the purposes of paragraphs 4(2) and (4).

We then need to apply this analysis to the provisions of paragraph 4 that determine how the chargeable amount is to be calculated and, in particular the R x DV/V formula in paragraph 4(2). First, we assume that, in this example, the relevant land would consist of 7/8ths of Whiteacre and, for any taxable period, V, in paragraph 4(2), would be the value of 7/8ths of Whiteacre at the appropriate valuation date. Looking at DV, we agree that, in applying the formula at paragraph 4(4) to arrive at the "appropriate proportion", P would be limited to the cash element of the consideration. Thus, in your example, (MV—P)/MV would be (£700,000–£500,000) / £700,000, or 2/7.

In order to calculate the chargeable amount for a taxable period, let us assume that at the valuation date 7/8 of Whiteacre is worth £875,000 (the whole being worth £1,000,000) and the rental value (R) is £38,500. The appropriate rental value, as prescribed in para.4(4) would therefore be £38,500 x (2/7 x £875,000) / £875,000: in other words, £11,000.

(More simply, the calculation is £38,500 x 2/7.)

7. Foreign Domiciliaries

A3.103 7.1 Paragraph 12(3) states that no regard is to be had to excluded property. In a case where a trust settled by a foreign domiciliary) owns a UK house through a foreign registered company the shares in the company (and any loan to the company) are excluded property. Concern has been expressed that since para 12(3) says that no regard is to be had to these assets, this in turn means that the shares and loan have to be ignored in applying para 11 and in particular cannot be taken into account in determining whether there is derived property which is in the taxpayer's estate or GWR property in relation to him (which the shares and loans otherwise are). We think that this argument is misconceived but it has been advanced.

Question 42

Can HMRC confirm that they agree para 12(3) does not operate in this way and that para 11 can still work to protect the UK house or underlying assets owned by the offshore company in these circumstances?

HMRC answer to question 42

We agree with what you say in paragraph 7.1 about the interaction between paragraphs 12(3) and 11.

8. Scope of the Para. 8 Charge

A3.104 8.1 In addition to the points raised on valuation, we note that on insurance schemes involving for example quantitative carve outs (for example where the settlor taxpayer is the remainderman in the settlement as in a reverter to settlor trust) the settlor is treated as being outside the POA charge. This is on the basis that his interest in the trust property is either held on bare trust or on a separate trust.

Question 43

Will HMRC confirm that reverter to settlor trusts holding other assets are also outside the para 8 charge?

HMRC answer to question 43

If you are suggesting that reverter to settlor trusts are outside the scope of sections 624 and 625 ITTOIA 2005, we would be interested to see the reasoning put forward in support of this proposition. In the insurance schemes you mention, which we have agreed do not fall within the said sections 624 and 625 and therefore are outside the scope of paragraph 8, the interests held on trust for the settlor are, as you suggest, carved out of the gift and retained by him. In our view, such schemes are not analogous with reverter to settlor trusts.

Question 44

There is a potential problem about the wording in para 22(3): if income is treated as income of the chargeable person by virtue of section 660A then due to paragraph

22(3)(b) it shall be treated as property subject to a reservation. Income could be taxed under s 660A (now s 624 ITTOIA) if only a spouse could benefit and that would not normally bring para 8 into play in the first place although this exclusion is not carried forward once an election is made.

So if someone elects on intangibles and then he but not his wife is excluded from benefiting under the settlement does this mean that the conditions in para 22(3) are satisfied and hence that he is still treated as having a reservation of benefit? Or does paragraph 22(2)(b)(ii) (which says sections 102(3) and (4) shall apply) mean that if he ceases to reserve a benefit in the property himself the effect of the election falls away so that there is a deemed PET then, even if the conditions in para 22(3) are prima facie satisfied because his wife can still benefit?

HMRC answer to question 44

We lean towards your first interpretation of the effect of para.22(3)(b). If someone is in a position to make an election under para.22(2), he or she must be someone who is (or would be) chargeable under para.8 for that year of assessment. Clearly, the condition in para.22(3)(b) would also be met at that time. It does seem that this condition would continue to be met until such time that both the chargeable person and his or her spouse (or civil partner) were excluded from benefit. At that point, a PET would be deemed to have arisen by virtue of para.22(2)(b)(ii).

SCHEDULE 20 QUESTIONS AND ANSWERS

Index of questions and answers A3.105

Section A. Questions 1–10:   transitional serial interests
Section B. Questions 11–13: administration of estates
Section C. Questions 14–18: immediate post death interests
Section D. Questions 19–32: bereaved minors trusts; 18–25 trusts, section 71A trusts
Section E. Questions 33–35: absolute interests, bare trusts, *Crowe v Appleby*
Section F. Question 36:   disabled trusts
Section G. Questions 37–39: general points – additions and annuities
Section H. Questions 40–42: deeds of variation

The questions were submitted to HMRC on September 7, 2006 and replies received on November 3, 2006. The questions appeared in a slightly revised version on the STEP/CIOT websites.

A. Transitional serial interests (TSI)

1. Condition 1 contains the requirement that "immediately before March 22, 2006, the property then comprised in the settlement was property in which B, or some other person, was beneficially entitled to an interest in possession ("the prior interest")". A3.106

2. Can it be confirmed that this requirement will be satisfied where B, or some other person, has a beneficial interest in possession in some of the property then comprised in the settlement but not all the property so comprised. A3.107

Example 1

> Under a trust there are two funds. In Fund A, Mr Smith has an interest in possession. In Fund B, Mr Jones has an interest in possession.

Question 1

Will Condition 1 be satisfied separately in relation to Fund A and/or Fund B?

HMRC answer

We can confirm that condition 1 can be satisfied separately in relation to both funds.

The new s.49C starts from the point of the view of the "current interest" – a beneficial interest in settled property. Given the wide definition of that term in s.43 IHTA, it seems that the beneficial IIP referred to in s.49C(1) can quite easily be in a fund or in property that was previously part of a larger disposition or settlement – and there is nothing to suggest that there must have been a single beneficiary.

Moreover, there is no requirement that the settlement must have been wholly IIP in nature (question 2 below) or that it must have come to an end in its entirety (question 3).

If one can then accept that the property referred to in s.49C(1) is also the property referred to in s.49C(2), and in which the "prior interest" (s.49C(2) & (3)) existed, the concerns raised in questions 1 to 4 fall away.

Question 2

Can it be confirmed that Condition 1 will be satisfied in relation to Fund A where Fund B is held not on trusts giving Mr Jones an interest in possession but on discretionary trusts? There is nothing in the wording of s.49C to suggest that the pre-Budget interest in possession must subsist in the entire fund.

HMRC answer

We agree.

A3.108 3. Section 49C(3) provides that Condition 2 requires the prior interest to come to an end at a time on or after March 22, 2006 but before April 6, 2008.

Question 3

Will Condition 2 be satisfied where the prior interest comes to an end in that period in part only of the settled property in which that interest subsists?

HMRC answer

Yes – see the response to question 1 above.

Example 2

> In the example given above, if Mr Smith's interest in possession in Fund A comes to an end in 60% of Fund A and is replaced by an interest in possession in favour of Mr Smith's daughter, but Mr Smith's interest in possession continues in relation to the remaining 40% of Fund A, can it be confirmed that the interest in possession in favour of the daughter will be a transitional serial interest?

HMRC answer

We can confirm this – for the reasons given immediately below.

While it has been suggested that Condition 2 requires that the prior interest comes to an end in all the property in which the interest subsists, Condition 2 does not state this and given the definition of current interest it appears that Condition 2 must be construed as referring to the prior interest coming to an end in the settled property concerned in which B takes a current interest but not necessarily in all the settled property of a particular settlement. The "current interest" is merely defined as an interest in possession in settled property and does not in any way require all the settled property comprised in the settlement to be a current interest.

Question 4

Please also confirm that the remaining 40 per cent of Fund A continues to satisfy Condition 1 so that a transitional serial interest could be created in that 40 per cent prior to April 6, 2008.

HMRC answer

We can confirm this.

Question 5(1)

Please also confirm that in the above example if 40 per cent of Mr Smith's pre-Budget interest in possession is ended as to half for his daughter and half for his son, both son and daughter take transitional serial interests in their respective shares.

HMRC answer

We can confirm this.

Question 5(2)

If later the trustees wished to appropriate assets between the two funds for son and daughter and the assets were of the same value as the assets previously contained in each fund, do HMRC accept that such appropriation does not represent the termination of any qualifying interest in possession and therefore does not result in an inheritance tax charge?

HMRC answer

We agree.

4. We would be grateful for your views on the circumstances in which the prior interest would be considered to have come to an end and have been replaced by a current interest. This is relevant because if a prior interest is considered to have come to an end and have been replaced by a current interest (in favour of the same beneficiary) there will be no possibility of the interest being replaced by a transitional serial interest later and the point is particularly important in relation to spousal relief because spouse exemption will not be available if a spouse of a life tenant who already has a transitional serial interest takes an interest in possession on the death of that life tenant.

A3.109

Example 3

> Under a pre-Budget 2006 trust a beneficiary A is entitled to the capital contingently on attaining the age of 30 years. A was 21 on March 22, 2006 and had been entitled to an interest in possession under section 31 of the Trustee Act 1925 from the age of 18. The interest is therefore an interest in possession which subsisted on March 22, 2006. Before 2008 the trustees exercise their [enlarged] powers of advancement under s.32 of the Trustee Act 1925 to defer the vesting of the capital from the age of 30 to the age of 45 and A's interest in possession in the fund will therefore continue until age 45. Clearly A reaches 30 after 2008 in the above example.

Question 6

There are two possible interpretations of the above and we should be grateful if HMRC could confirm which view they take.

Option 1: The exercise of the trustees' powers in this way creates a new interest in possession for A immediately on exercise of the power of advancement which therefore takes effect as the "current interest" or "transitional serial interest". Any successive interest in possession after A's interest in possession has ended cannot then be a transitional serial interest. The property will be taxed as part of A's estate on his death if he dies with the transitional serial interest. He continues to have a transitional serial interest until termination at 45 or earlier death.

Option 2: A's new interest only arises when A attains the age of 30. Until then he has a pre-Budget qualifying interest in possession.

The new interest cannot take effect as a transitional serial interest at all since on the above facts it will arise after April 2008. Until 30 A will have a pre-Budget interest in possession on the basis that nothing has changed until he reaches 30. Only from 30 will he take a new non-qualifying interest so the settled property will then become relevant property. There will not be an entry charge for A at 30 of 20 per cent due to s.53(2) IHTA.

If A dies before reaching 30, then on this analysis his pre-Budget interest will not previously have ended and therefore if his spouse takes an interest in possession this is a transitional serial interest or if his children take interests in possession before 2008 these will be transitional serial interests.

Does the answer to whether option 1 or option 2 applies depend on whether the advancement is drafted in such a way that it extends the interest in possession from 30 without restating A's existing interest in possession until then? Or would any variation of A's interest in possession be regarded as a transitional serial interest from the date of the variation even if the variation only took effect in the future.

HMRC answer

We consider that A's original IIP (until 30) will have "come to an end" when the trustees exercised their power of advancement and been replaced by a new IIP (until 45), which will therefore qualify as a TSI. A's interest is expressed as an entitlement to capital contingent on his attaining 30. It seems reasonable to regard the exercise of the s.32 Trustee Act power as immediately bringing this interest to an end and replacing it with a new one.

A3.110   5. An interest in possession might also subsist as follows:

Example 4

> Under a trust A has a life interest with remainder to his children. The trustees have a power of advancement and exercise such a power to provide that subject

to A's existing life interest A's spouse takes a life interest on A's death with remainder to the children at the age of 25. A's interest in possession is not in any way altered.

Question 7

Can HMRC please confirm that the exercise of a power of advancement to create an interest in possession for the spouse, which is expressly made subject to A's existing life interest and does not in any way alter that interest but merely comes into effect on his death, will be a transitional serial interest. Similarly, if spouse predeceases A and the advancement on interest in possession trusts for A's children is made subject to A's interest and takes effect before 2008 (e.g. A surrenders his interest) presumably these trusts could also be transitional serial interests.

HMRC answer

Assuming that A's IIP existed before 22 March 2006, we can confirm that the spouse's IIP – if it arises before 6 April 2008 – will qualify as a TSI. The same would apply to any IIP taken by A's children instead of the spouse before 6 April 2008.

If, however, A's interest was in any way amended (e.g. the trustees exercised powers of revocation and reappointment restating A's interest in possession albeit in the same terms and then declaring interests in possession for A's spouse or for children if she has predeceased, presumably the interests for spouse and children could never be transitional serial interests?

HMRC answer

We agree.

6. Can it be confirmed that an interest in possession can be a transitional serial interest where the interest arises under a different settlement to that in which the original interest subsisted?

Example 5

> Under Trust A Mr Smith has an interest in possession and subject to that, the capital passes to Mr Jones absolutely. Mr Jones on December 30, 2006 assigns his reversionary interest into Trust B set up in December 2006 under which his children have interests in possession. Mr Smith's interest in possession then comes to an end on November 30, 2007 at which time the interests in possession of Mr Jones's children in Trust B fall into possession.

Question 8

Will the interest in possession that Mr Jones' children have following the termination of Mr Smith's interest in possession qualify as a transitional serial interest bearing in mind that the interests arise in relation to the same settled property even though not under the trusts of the original settlement? A similar situation could arise where there is technically a different settlement under which the successive life interest arises due to the exercise of the trustees' powers of appointment in the wider form (as referred to in *Bond v Pickford* [1983] (STC 517)).

HMRC answer

Taken with question 9 below.

A3.111

Question 9

If the difficulty is that Condition 1 is not satisfied because the second settlement is "made" post Budget does it make any difference if the second settlement was made pre-Budget and the interests in the first settlement fall into the second settlement before 2008 to be held on interest in possession trusts. This is a very common situation where there are "trusts over" and there appears nothing in the conditions to prevent this.

HMRC answer

We do not consider that the IIPs of Mr Jones's children will qualify as TSIs whether the second settlement was made before or after Budget 2006.

As we said earlier, s.49C begins from the point of view of the "current interest". Condition 1 requires that "the settlement" in which that interest subsists "commenced" before 22 March 2006.

It goes on to require that, immediately before that date, the property "then comprised" in the settlement – i.e. the same settlement – was subject to the "prior interest".

The IIPs of Mr Jones's children arise under a different settlement (albeit one which happens to hold, following Mr Smith's death, the property that comprised the earlier one) and will not, therefore, qualify as TSIs – and it will make no difference when the settlement was made.

For the same reasons, the exercise of powers of appointment in such a way that assets are removed from one settlement and subjected to the trusts of another will not give rise to TSIs.

Question 10

A3.112 7. What is the position if the beneficiary holding the pre-Budget interest in possession assigns that interest in possession to another person? Does the assignee's interest qualify as a transitional serial interest? The concern here is that the original interest in possession is not "terminated" by virtue of the assignment, and so the precise terms of the legislation do not appear to have been met.

HMRC answer

We consider that the assignee's interest can be a TSI in this case because the assignor's IIP will have "come to an end" for the purposes of s.49C(3). (The interest will be in the original settlement, so the problem outlined in our response to question 9 will not be an issue).

B Administration of estates

Question 11

A3.113 8. Can it be confirmed that where a will provides that a beneficiary has an interest in possession in residue, that interest in possession will be treated as commencing on the date of death of the deceased and not only when the administration of the estate is completed. This appears to be the case by virtue of s.91 of the IHTA 1984.

HMRC answer

We can confirm this.

Question 12

9. Can it be confirmed that the position will be the same as in *Question 11* above where the interest in possession is in a settled legacy of specific assets not forming part of residue. It seems that this should be the case: *IRC v Hawley* [1929] 1 KB 578.

A3.114

HMRC answer

We agree.

This is important for two reasons:

- in order for an interest in possession to satisfy Condition 2 in section 49A for an Immediate Post-Death Interest (IPDI), L must have become beneficially entitled to the interest on the death of the testator or intestate;
- in determining whether an interest in possession is one which subsisted prior to March 22, 2006 where the deceased died before March 22, 2006 but the completion of the administration of the estate was on or after March 22, 2006 there would be difficulties if the pre-Budget interest in possession was not regarded as commencing on the death of the deceased.

Question 13

10. Many wills include a provision which provides that a beneficiary will only take if he survives the testator by a period of time. Please confirm that such a provision would not by itself prevent an IPDI arising.

A3.115

HMRC answer

We can confirm this. We consider that s.92 IHTA removes any doubt here.

C IPDIs generally

Question 14

11. Can it be confirmed that if on the death of X a discretionary trust set up in his Will (e.g. a nil rate band legacy trust) is funded by a share in property, and the trustees allow the surviving spouse L to occupy it on an exclusive basis albeit at their discretion along the lines that occurred in *Judge & Anor (Representatives of Walden Deceased)* Sp. C 506, this will not automatically be an IPDI but it will depend on the terms on which she occupies.

A3.116

HMRC answer

We agree.

There is a 3 month requirement for reading back under s.144 in respect of appointments of absolute interests but this does not apply to appointments of IPDIs. Therefore if the trustees immediately on the death of X or subsequently, conferred exclusive rights of occupation on L this could indeed be an IPDI.

HMRC answer

We agree.

It appears to us unlikely that mere exclusivity of occupation could in itself be a problem because as Judge confirms a person can occupy exclusively but not have rights which constitute an interest in possession. Indeed if the surviving spouse merely continued in occupation on the same terms as before X's death without the trustees' doing anything positive either way to affect her occupation it would appear they have not exercised their powers so as to give her any IPDI anyway.

HMRC answer

We agree.

(Indeed it is doubtful that they have any ability under the Trusts of Land and Appointment of Trustees Act 1996 to disturb her occupation if she already owns a half share in the property personally and therefore the trustees have not exercised any power to confer her a present right to present enjoyment which could constitute an immediate post death interest.)

It would be helpful (given how common this situation is) if HMRC could give some guidance on the various scenarios in which they would or would not regard the surviving spouse as taking an IPDI in a property left on nil rate band discretionary trusts in the will if she is already in occupation.

HMRC answer

This will depend on the precise terms of the testator's will or any deed of appointment exercised by the trustees after the testator's death, and we will continue to examine each case on its particular facts.

Question 15

A3.117 12. Can it be confirmed that where a settlement (including a settlement created by will) includes a general power of appointment and that power is exercised by will giving an immediate interest in possession, the interest created over the trust property will qualify as an IPDI?

HMRC answer

We can confirm this.

Question 16

A3.118 13. Can it be confirmed that HMRC takes the view that if an individual (I) leaves by will a gift to a person's estate, when the assets in the estate are held on trusts which qualify as trusts for bereaved minors or age 18–25 trusts, the property added pursuant to I's will would also be treated as being held on trusts which qualify as trusts for bereaved minors or 18–25 trusts.

HMRC answer

We have assumed that the scenario envisaged here is: I dies leaving a legacy in their will to P; P dies after I but before the legacy has been paid; P's estate is held on trusts that meet s.71A or s.71D. We agree that, in those circumstances, the legacy from I's estate would qualify under those provisions, also.

Example 6

I leaves his estate to his widow for life with remainder to his son S if alive at I's death. S survives I but predeceases the widow leaving a Will under which his estate passes to his children on trusts which qualify as trusts for bereaved minors. The widow dies when the children are aged 10 and 12, so that I's estate falls to be held on the trusts of S's Will. Will the property in I's estate benefit from trusts for bereaved minors status? I is the grandparent but the property is passing according to S's Will.

HMRC answer

We consider that the property added pursuant to I's will in this example would also fall within s.71A.

Question 17

14. If a property is left outright to someone by a will and they disclaim within two years of the deceased's death such that an interest in possession trust takes effect, can HMRC confirm that the trust will qualify as an IPDI? A3.119

HMRC answer

We can confirm this.

Question 18

15. Can it be confirmed whether, when a will leaves property to an existing settlement (whether funded or unfunded) and under that settlement a beneficiary takes an immediate interest in possession, that interest will qualify as an IPDI. Such arrangements are common for US and other foreign domicilaries in order to avoid complex probate issues. It might be argued that the interest in possession in the existing settlement does not arise under the will of the deceased. However, there are two arguments against this. A3.120

First, HMRC's own analysis is that additions by individuals to existing settlements should be treated as new settlements. Hence the addition by will to an existing settlement is a new settlement set up by virtue of the will.

Second, the wording in s.49A, Condition 1 refers to "the settlement was effected by will or under the law of intestacy". The question though is what "the settlement" refers to. It would seem that it refers not as such to "the settlement" in the sense of a document but rather to the settlement into trust of the settled property which certainly is effected by will. The same wording is used on deeds of variation under s.142 of IHTA and HMRC have always accepted that where property is added by will to a pre-existing settlement there is no reason why the beneficiary of that settlement cannot vary his entitlement.

HMRC answer

We can confirm that the IIP in this scenario would qualify as an IPDI. We agree that "settlement" in this context relates to the contribution of property into the settlement rather than the document under which it will become held.

D Trusts for bereaved minors, 18–25 trusts and modified s.71 trusts: s.71A and s.71D

Question 19

16. Can it be confirmed that trusts otherwise satisfying the requirements of s.71A or s.71D will be regarded as satisfying those conditions where the trusts were appointed under powers contained in the will and were not provided in the will itself at the outset. A3.121

HMRC answer

We can confirm this – where the trusts are set up as a result of the exercise of a special power of appointment. We consider the position is different with general powers, on the basis, broadly speaking, that having a general power of appointment is tantamount to owning the property.

Example 7

> H dies in 2007. His Will leaves an IPDI for his surviving spouse and subject thereto on discretionary trusts for issue of H. The trustees exercise their overriding powers of appointment to create s.71A trusts for the children of H. It would appear that the s.71A provisions do not need to be incorporated within the Will Trust from the start to qualify for relief but it would be helpful to have this confirmed. Presumably the presence of overriding powers of appointment over capital in favour of surviving spouse would not be treated as breaching the s.71A conditions while the s.71A interest was a remainder interest.

HMRC answer

We agree (subject to our comments at question 19).

Question 20

A3.122   17. Can it be further confirmed that the analysis in 16 above will apply both where the prior interest in possession is an IPDI and also where there is an interest in possession arising under the will of a person who died prior to March 22, 2006 where the interests will, by definition, not be an IPDI although in all other respects identical to an IPDI.

HMRC answer

We can confirm this.

Question 21

A3.123   18. Can it be confirmed that, where a will contains a gift "to such of my children as reach 18 and if more than one in equal shares" or "to such of my children as reach 25 and if more than one in equal shares" all the interests will qualify as trusts for bereaved minors (or as age 18–25 trusts) even though one or more of the children might die after the testator but before the capital vests (so that their shares are divided between their siblings).

HMRC answer

We can confirm this. We consider that each child while alive and under 18/25 has a presumptive share that is held for his or her benefit, and one can apply s.71A or s.71D child by child and presumptive share by presumptive share.

Question 22

A3.124   19. Can it be confirmed that the answer to *Question 21* is not affected by a gift over provision that substitutes the children (if any) of a deceased child who attain a certain age, so that the increase of the siblings' shares is dependent upon whether the child dies childless.

HMRC answer

We can confirm this: the siblings' presumptive shares simply increase (or not) when one of their number dies, depending on whether or not the deceased child had any children of their own.

Question 23

20. Can it be confirmed that agricultural property relief (apr) and business property relief (bpr) will apply to charges arising under s.71E. It would appear that these reliefs should be applicable as the charges under s.71D (by reference to s.71E) are charges under Ch. III or Pt III of the IHTA and the reliefs are expressly extended to events of charge under this Chapter (s.103(1) of the IHTA in relation to bpr and s.115(1) in relation to apr). Further, the formula for calculating the charge under s.71F is similar, in principle, to the charges as calculated under s.65 and s.68 of the IHTA in relation to exit charges for relevant property generally. Can HMRC confirm this analysis is agreed?

HMRC answer

We agree – for the reasons given.

Question 24

21. Section 71E(4) provides that there will be no event of charge where a transaction is entered into by trustees as a result of which the assets held subject to the 18–25 trusts are diminished in value, where the disposition by the trustees would not have been a transfer of value under s.10 or s.16 of the IHTA if they had been beneficially entitled to the trust assets. There is a further exemption in s.71E(3). There are no similar provisions in relation to actions by trustees concerning assets which are held on trusts qualifying under s.71A. Can it be confirmed that in practice HMRC would apply similar principles in relation to events of charge under s.71B for s.71A trusts?

HMRC answer

The provisions in s.71E that the question refers to are not reproduced in s.71B because the charge there arises under s.70 – and s.70 already includes identical provisions at subsections (3) and (4). S.71B(3) says:
"Subsections (3) to (8) and (10) of section 70 apply for the purposes of this section as they apply for the purposes of that section..."

Question 25

22. Can HMRC confirm that trusts which are held for beneficiaries as a class (e.g. on trust for such of my children as attain the age of 25 and if more than one in equal shares) will qualify as age 18–25 trusts under s.71D(3) and (4) notwithstanding that the class could be diminished by reason of the death of members of the class under the age of 25. While it might be said that the class gift does not fall within the strict wording of s.71D(6)(a) it might be said that nonetheless the assets are held on trust, for the time being, for each child being under the age of 25. HMRC are requested to confirm their view in relation to the continued application of s.71D to class gifts where a beneficiary (B) dies before reaching 25 and the assets pass to the other beneficiaries under 25 on s.71D trusts. (This is a separate point from the situation where in relation to existing *inter vivos* A&M trusts the class increases as a result of future beneficiaries being born before the eldest reaches 25.)

HMRC answer

We can confirm this.

Question 26

A3.128   23. HMRC is asked to confirm that s.71A and s.71D will apply to trusts for a class of children whether or not the assets have been appropriated to each child's share.

HMRC answer

We can confirm this.

Question 27

A3.129   24. There will be a number of circumstances where different sets of beneficiaries under one accumulation and maintenance settlement may require to be treated differently (for example, a settlement for grandchildren where they differ widely in age). Can HMRC please confirm that trusts will qualify as 18–25 trusts or modified s.71 trusts (capital vesting at age 18) if those trusts exist in only part of the settled property. Thus, a settlement might be divided into two sub-funds, one for A's children who are approaching adulthood and for whom an 18–25 trust is appropriate and another for B's children who are very young and where the trustees value retaining flexibility so that that sub-fund will be allowed to fall within the relevant property regime with effect from April 6, 2008 (or be converted into an 18 trust).

HMRC answer

We can confirm this.

Question 28

A3.130   25. There has been some confusion about the interaction of s.71D(3) and (4) with s.71D(1) and (2). Please confirm that existing A&M trusts set up before the Budget where the settlor may still be alive (and the beneficiary's parent has not died) can qualify for 18–25 status if converted before April 2008 if this occurs immediately after the funds cease to qualify under s.71.

HMRC answer

We can confirm that s.71D can apply to existing A&M trusts if the conversions occurs *before* the funds cease to qualify under s.71 – for the reasons set out in example 8 below.

Further that there is no inheritance tax charge on conversion of an existing accumulation and maintenance trust to a s.71D trust. i.e. that sch.20 para.3(3) protects all pre-Budget accumulation and maintenance trusts so that there is no inheritance tax entry charge either under s.71 or otherwise, at the point the trust starts to qualify for s.71D status (or indeed enters the relevant property regime).

HMRC answer

We can confirm this.

Example 8

> U sets up an accumulation and maintenance trust for his two nieces S and T in 1999. On March 22, 2006 neither has an interest in possession. Currently the

nieces take capital at 30 and income at 21. S becomes 21 in January 2007. T becomes 21 in January 2011.

The trustees exercise their powers to ensure that the trusts qualify for 18–25 status in February 2007, i.e. after S has attained entitlement to income (albeit this is not a qualifying interest in possession post Budget). They provide that each child takes capital outright at 25 in a fixed half share. In these circumstances it would appear that S's share cannot qualify for 18–25 status because immediately after the property ceased to be subject to s 71 it did not then fall within s 71D. T's interest could however qualify under s 71D. There is no inheritance tax charge in February 2007 on S's part although there would be a ten year charge in 2009 on her share because this share is now within the relevant property regime and there would be an exit charge when she reaches 25. There are no ten year or entry or exit charges on T's interest until she reaches 25 at which point her share is subject to tax at 4.2%. (This assumes that she does not die before reaching 25).

It would be helpful if this could be spelt out in the guidance notes because trustees need to be aware of the requirement to act swiftly if beneficiaries are about to take entitlement to income. It would also be helpful if examples could be given as to how 18–25 trusts work in practice and their main advantages i.e. to avoid the ten year anniversary charge.

HMRC answer

We agree with the consequences set out in the example and will incorporate them in guidance.

Question 29

26. It would appear that on the death of a child before 18 on a bereaved minor trust or on an 18–25 trust there is no inheritance tax charge even if they are entitled to income (albeit there is a base cost capital gains tax uplift if they are entitled to income).   A3.131

HMRC answer

We agree – by virtue of s.71B(2)(b) or s.71E(2)(b) and new s.5(1)(a)(i).

It would appear that after a child reaches 18 there is an exit charge on an 18–25 trust if the property ceases to be held on 18–25 trusts but no base cost uplift for capital gains tax purposes whether or not the child has a right to income. Please confirm.

HMRC answer

We can confirm this.

Question 30

27. It would appear that, if a child reaches 18 and on his death his share of the trust fund remains on 18–25 trusts for his siblings under cross-accruer provisions, there will be no exit charge at that time. Please confirm.   A3.132

HMRC answer

We can confirm this.

Question 31

28. In the HMRC Customer Guide to Inheritance Tax recently published HMRC state under the heading of "What is an age 18 to 25 trust?"   A3.133

"If the terms of the trust are not rewritten before 6 April 2008 and the trust has not come to an end then existing accumulation and maintenance trusts will automatically become relevant property trusts on the 18th birthday of the beneficiary."

What is the statutory justification for this view. First it is surely the case that an existing A&M trust can become subject to the relevant property regime before April 6, 2008 if a beneficiary takes a post-Budget interest in possession.

HMRC answer

We agree and will amend the Customer Guide.
Second our understanding is that such trusts will become relevant property trusts on the April 6, 2008 or the beneficiary becoming entitled to an interest in possession before that date unless the trust meets the requirements of a s.71D trust. If nothing has been done by April 2008 and a beneficiary is not entitled to an interest in possession then the trust falls within the relevant property regime from that date whether or not the beneficiary is a minor. This point needs to be clarified urgently and the information amended.

HMRC answer

We agree. S.71D(5)(b) provides that s.71D does not apply to property to which s.71 applies. A&M treatment will therefore continue up to an including 5 April 2008 if the trusts of the settlement meet s.71, and will fall away on 6 April 2008. If the trusts provide for absolute entitlement at 18 or 25, the settlement will then fall within s.71A or s.71D as appropriate; if they do not, the settlement will be "relevant property" from that date.

Question 32

A3.134   29. Please also confirm whether or not hold over relief will be available if assets are distributed within 3 months of a beneficiary's 18th birthday under an 18–25 trust. There will be no inheritance tax charge as there will be no complete quarters since the 18th birthday. In these circumstances is hold over relief denied?

HMRC answer

No. The distribution is still an occasion on which IHT is chargeable – it is just that the charge will be nil. There is no provision in s.71F along the lines of s.65(4).

E Absolute interests, bare trusts, *Crowe v Appleby*

A3.135   30. Where assets are held by a person on bare trusts for minor children s.31 of the Trustee Act is implied in most cases without express reference and will apply unless expressly excluded.

A3.136   31. It might be said that the application of the section will cause the property concerned to be settled property within s.43(2)(b) in view of the provisions for the accumulation of income under s.31(2) of the Trustee Act. However, the contrary argument is that the accumulations of income are held for the absolute benefit for the minor concerned and would pass to his estate if he died under 18 (the minor not being able to give a good receipt) and the assets are therefore not held in any real sense subject to any contingency or provision for the diversion of income from the minor. This latter view seems to be in line with the analysis in the IHT Manual which contemplates that s.43(2)(b) deals with the position where there is relevant property held on discretionary trusts (para.4602). The statement in the Inland Revenue letter of February 12, 1976 where, in the last sentence of the second paragraph, it is stated that a provision to accumulate income will not prevent there being an interest in possession if the accumulations are held for the absolute benefit of the beneficiary, supports the view that s.31 of the Trustee Act will not in these circumstances cause the relevant property regime to apply.

Question 33

32. Can HMRC confirm that the application of s.31 of the Trustee Act 1925 to assets held on a bare trust for a minor will not result in the assets being settled property within the meaning of s.43 of the IHTA? **A3.137**

HMRC answer

We are seeking advice from our solicitors on this point.

33. There appear to be new and unforeseen capital gains tax problems now where *Crowe v Appleby* [1975] (S.T.C. 502) applies to settled property. The position is complex albeit common and can best be illustrated by example. **A3.138**

Example 9

In February 2006 Andrew set up a trust for his children Charlotte and Luke. They each become entitled to one half of the income and capital on reaching 25. Charlotte becomes 25 in 2007 and Luke becomes 25 in 2009. They do not take interests in possession until reaching 25. The trust only holds one piece of land.

When Charlotte reaches 25 in 2007 she becomes absolutely entitled for inheritance tax purposes since *Crowe v Appleby* has no application for IHT purposes. The trusts over her share end for inheritance tax purposes before April 6, 2008 so there is no exit charge since she is within the transitional regime. She is treated from 2007 as entitled to the half share in the property and if she died after that date it would form part of her estate for inheritance tax purposes and hence be potentially taxable.

There is a further problem. For capital gains tax purposes Charlotte does not become absolutely entitled to one half of the land. Until the land is sold or Luke reaches 25 and becomes absolutely entitled (whichever is the earlier) there is no disposal made by the trustees.

There is no inheritance tax change on April 6, 2008 but from that date Luke's share is no longer within A&M trust protection but is taxed as an 18–25 trust. There is no ten year anniversary charge before Luke reaches 25 but if he dies before then there is an inheritance tax charge (likely to be less than 4.2%). As noted above, there is no base cost uplift for capital gains tax purposes.

On Luke reaching 25 in 2009 there is an exit charge on Luke's share of 4.2%.

HMRC answer

(Note: we do not consider this is quite right. We assume that the 4.2 per cent is referred to on the basis of 7/10ths × 6 per cent. However, the charge will not be based on the 7 years from Luke's 18th birthday. S.71F(5)(a) provides that the starting date for calculating the relevant fraction is his 18th birthday "or, if later, the day on which the property became property to which section 71D above applies" – in this case, 6 April 2008).

If the land has not yet been sold there will at that point be a disposal of all the land by the trustees for capital gains tax purposes because both beneficiaries become absolutely entitled. Hold over relief is available on Luke's part under s.260 of the TCGA 1992, but not on Charlotte's part since there is no exit charge. In summary, the trustees will have to pay capital gains tax on any gain on Charlotte's share in 2009 and cannot hold over the gain on that share.

Question 34

A3.139   Prior to the Finance Act 2006, Charlotte would have been treated as having a qualifying interest in possession in her share of the trust assets. If she died before Luke reached 25, there would have been a charge to inheritance tax on her death but because she had a qualifying interest in possession, for capital gains tax purposes, there would be an uplift in base cost on her share of the land under s.72(1) of the TCGA 1992.

Post the Finance Act 2006, if Charlotte dies before Luke reaches 25 there will be a charge to inheritance tax but s.72(1) of the TCGA 1992 does not seem to be applicable because Charlotte does not appear to have a qualifying interest in possession which qualifies her for the uplift. Hence she is subject to inheritance tax on her death with no uplift for capital gains tax.

Will HMRC regard her as having a qualifying interest in possession within s.72 for these purposes?

HMRC answer

No – with the result, as stated, that there would be no CGT uplift under s.72(1) TCGA.

Question 35

A3.140   If Charlotte attained 25 in say June 2015 and Luke only reached 25 in 2017 there would be an exit charge on both Luke and Charlotte's shares when each becomes 25 (rate = 4.2 per cent) but hold over relief is only available on Luke's share when the disposal of the land takes place for capital gains tax purposes.

Prior to the Finance Act 2006 there would have been no exit charge when Charlotte reached 25. However, the effect of the new rules is that on reaching 25 Charlotte will now suffer an exit charge but without any entitlement to hold-over the gain which arises when the land is distributed to her when Luke reaches 25. Will HMRC in these circumstances allow hold over relief on both shares?

HMRC answer

No – hold-over relief will be due on Luke's share only.

F Disabled trusts

A3.141   33. Section 89A(2) appears to conflict with s 89A(3). Condition 1 states that if any of the settled property is applied for A it is applied for the benefit of A but Condition 2 envisages that capital could be paid to A or another person on the termination of A's interest during his life provided that the other person became absolutely entitled.

Question 36

Is HMRC's view that capital can be appointed to someone else on the termination of the trust only if it can be demonstrated that it is for the benefit of A?

HMRC answer

No – we do not consider that that condition is in point.

Otherwise why does s.89A(3), Condition 2 refer to other persons at all?

HMRC answer

We do not agree with the proposition that there is a conflict between s.89A(2) and (3). Condition 1 refers to the application of "settled property" – i.e. to property that is held on the trusts referred to in s.89A(1)(c). Condition 2, however, is applying conditions that are effective in the event of such trusts being brought to an end.

G General points

Question 37(1)

34. New ss.46A(4) and 46B(5) provide that additions (by way of payment of further premiums) to a pre-Budget interest in possession or A&M trust which holds an insurance policy would not result either in a chargeable transfer or in any part of the trust falling within the relevant property regime.

A3.142

It is understood that HMRC believe that additions of cash or other property to existing pre-Budget interest in possession settlements are subject to the new rules in Sch.20.

There are other payments which are often made by settlors or beneficiaries on behalf of a trust. For example, buildings insurance premiums and general maintenance costs, payments to cover trust, administration and taxation expenses.

It is noted that for the purposes of TCGA 1992, Sch.5 para.9(3) the payment of expenses relating to administration and taxation of a trust are not be treated as the addition of property to the trust. In SP 5/92 the costs of acquiring, enhancing and disposing of a trust asset are not regarded as expenses relating to administration but other property expenses appear to fall within the definition and therefore are not treated as the addition of property to the trust. Would HMRC maintain that the addition of cash or other property to a settlement which may be used either to enhance trust property (e.g. payment of costs relating to the building of an extension to property) or to purchase other property will be treated as additions but accept that the payment of other trustee expenses (e.g. trustee fees, buildings insurance premiums and general maintenance costs) will not be treated as chargeable additions?

HMRC answer

Schedule 5 TCGA is a statutory provision relating to certain, specific circumstances. There is no legal basis on which payments of "other trustee expenses" should not be treated as chargeable additions for IHT purposes.

Question 37(2)

If any of the additions do bring the trust within the new rules, what property within the trust will be caught and how will it be valued? For example, if an addition of cash was made which was then spent by the trustees and HMRC regard this addition as within the relevant property regime (e.g. an addition to pay expenses or improve properties), how would the proportion of the settled property subject to the new rules be calculated? Would a valuation be needed of the property before and after the improvement? In HMRC's view, do all subsequent post Budget additions need to be kept physically segregated?

HMRC answer

If a payment of cash was made and then spent immediately on, say, a tax liability or another administration expense, then that short period will be the extent of its time as

"relevant property" and there will be no question of having to consider what proportion of the existing settled property represents it going forward.

If a payment was made towards the improvement of a property, then this would appear to require "with" and "without" valuations when there is a chargeable event.

It is clearly up to trustees to decide whether to keep post-Budget additions separate from the rest of the trust fund. We think that it may be sensible to do so – or, at least, to keep good records of additions. (The trustees of discretionary trusts already need to do this, of course, in order for the 10-year anniversary value of each addition to be identified correctly in light of the relief in s.66(2) IHTA for property that has not been "relevant property" for a full 10-year period).

Question 38

A3.143   35. It is understood that additions to a trust which fall within the normal expenditure out of income exemption will not need to be reported as and when they are made as, following the normal rules, it is not necessary to report exempt transactions? Please confirm.

HMRC answer

We can confirm this.

Question 39

A3.144   36. It is not unknown for wills to include a gift of an annuity. Some wills give the executors sufficient powers to enable them to choose how best to satisfy the annuity. In such a case there are typically four methods which executors may use to deal with an annuity.

- Pay the annuity out of residue. In such a case the executors delay the completion of the administration of the estate until the annuitant dies.
- Create an appropriated annuity fund. In such a case the executors appropriate a capital fund of sufficient size to pay the annuity.
- Purchase an annuity. The executors purchase an annuity from an insurance office or life company.
- Commute the annuity. The executors pay the annuitant a cash sum sufficient to allow him to purchase the annuity personally.

The first two options create settled property. Will HMRC confirm that a provision in a will conferring the payment of an annuity upon a person (e.g. to make a gift of an annuity of £x for life) which the executors satisfy by one of the first two options outlined above will be treated as the creation of an IPDI in favour of the annuitant?

HMRC answer

We can confirm this.

Under s 50(2), where a person is entitled to a specified amount (such as an annuity) for any period his interest is taken to subsist in that part of the property that produces that amount in that period. The property in which his interest subsists may therefore vary over time.

Example 10

Say A is entitled to an annuity of £1,000 and the executors set aside a fund of £40,000 to pay this annuity. In year 1 the income from the £40,000 is £2,000 and half is paid to the annuitant. In year 2 the income from the £40,000 is £1,000 and all the income is paid to A. In year 3 (the year in which the annuitant dies) the income from the £40,000 is £4,000 and a quarter is paid to A. Please could HMRC confirm what property would fall within A's estate on his death (assuming he is treated as having an IPDI) and the basis upon which this has been calculated?

HMRC answer

We would follow the existing principles set out in s.50(2) to s.50(5) IHTA at the date of A's death. (As Dymond, at 16.611, points out, s.50(2) does not give any guidance as to the period over which the income of the settled property should be computed. But the learned authors suggest that looking at the income in the year immediately before the chargeable occasion would normally be a reasonable approach and we would agree.)

H Deeds of variation

Questions have arisen as to the effect of deeds of variation post-Budget.　　　A3.145

Example 11

> 37. Testator dies pre-Budget leaving everything outright to X. His will is varied by X and an election made under s.142 to treat the variation as made by the will.

Question 40

Any trust established by the variation will be treated as having been established pre-Budget whether or not the variation is actually made pre- or post-Budget. If an interest in possession trust is established under such a variation by X, we assume it will be a qualifying interest in possession given it is deemed to be set up prior to the Budget by the deceased and not by X for inheritance tax purposes and further that it will be possible to create a transitional serial interest in relation to this trust before April 2008. Please confirm.

HMRC answer

We can confirm this.

Example 12

> 38. Testator dies post-Budget leaving everything outright to Y. His will is varied　　A3.146
> to establish ongoing trusts and an election made under s.142 to read the variation back into the will.

Question 41

Assuming that the terms of the trusts are appropriate, it is possible to establish IPDIs, 18–25 trusts and BMTs by way of such a variation made by Y. Please confirm. As in *Question 40* it is assumed that for inheritance tax purposes the settlor is the deceased rather than Y.

HMRC answer

We can confirm this.

Example 13

A3.147 39. The testator is not domiciled in the UK at his death leaving everything outright to Z. His will dealing with property outside the UK is varied to establish trusts and an election made under s.142 to read the variation back into the will.

Question 42

Any trusts established by the variation holding non-UK property will be excluded property trusts whatever the domicile status of Z (the beneficiary making the variation) and whatever the terms of the new trusts. This will be the case whether or not the testator died pre- or post-Budget. Please confirm.

HMRC answer

We can confirm this.

TAX BULLETIN 83—HMRC STATEMENT ON HASTINGS-BASS

RI INTERPRETATION—TAX BULLETIN 83: HMRC AND THE HASTINGS-BASS PRINCIPLE

A3.148 The purpose of this article is to give an indication of HMRC's current views on some aspects of the so-called "Hastings-Bass" principle. The principle has been applied in the context of trusts where a trustee is given a discretion as to some matter, on which he acts, but where the purported exercise of his discretion has unintended consequences.

Traditionally the courts have been reluctant to interfere in the exercise of a trustee's discretion but there is now a growing line of authority revealing the emergence of a principle whereby a court, in certain circumstances, will or may intervene. It is a principle that has been developed by the courts in England & Wales, and has been applied by the Royal Court in Jersey, although it seems that there is no equivalent principle in Scotland.

The name of the principle comes from the case of *Re Hastings-Bass deceased* [1975] Ch 25 ("*Hastings Bass*"). In that case the Court of Appeal upheld the validity of an exercise by trustees of the statutory power of advancement, save to the extent that it was necessarily void for perpetuity, on the basis that the court should not interfere where a trustee is given a discretion as to some matter in which he acts in good faith, notwithstanding that his action does not have the full effect which he intended, unless it is clear that he would not have acted as he did

- had he not taken into account considerations which he should not have taken into account or
- had he not failed to take into account considerations which he ought to have taken into account.

The second limb of the principle was purportedly reformulated into a more readily understood, positive version by Warner J. in *Mettoy Pension Trustees Ltd v Evans and ors* [1990] 1 W.L.R. 1587 ("*Mettoy*") at 1621A-H as follows:

"Where a trustee acts under a discretion given to him under the terms of the trust, the court will interfere with his action if it is clear that he would not have acted as he did had he not failed to take into account considerations which he ought to have taken into account."

This reformulation in fact involved a substantial leap from the original formulation of the principle in Hastings-Bass itself, for two reasons. First, the word "will" apparently denotes an obligation on the court to intervene whenever the stated conditions are satisfied.

Second, the negative proposition that the court should not interfere unless certain conditions are fulfilled is not logically equivalent to the much wider positive proposition that the court should, or even may, interfere if those conditions are fulfilled.

Nevertheless, after reviewing a number of authorities Warner J. concluded in Mettoy that there was a principle in the positive form stated above which was separate both from the equitable remedy of rectification and from the jurisdiction of the court to set aside a written instrument for mistake. Over the past few years there has been an increase of interest in and reliance on the principle, which has resulted in a number of decided cases at first instance, including *Abacus Trust Company Ltd v NSPCC* [2001] S.T.C. 1344 ("*Abacus v NSPCC*"), *Breadner v Granville-Grossman* [2001] Ch. 523, *Abacus Trust Company Ltd v Barr* [2003] Ch 409 ("*Abacus v Barr*"), *Burrell v Burrell* [2005] S.T.C. 569 and *Sieff v Fox* [2005] 1 W.L.R. 3811 ("*Sieff v Fox*") which contains a detailed and valuable review of the case law by Lloyd L.J. Apart from case law, the emerging principle has also generated a great deal of discussion and commentary by academics and practitioners alike.

An interesting, but perhaps not surprising, feature of the majority of these cases is that the unintended consequence of the mistake by the trustees was a liability to tax. For this reason HMRC have been interested in this area of the law, as it develops and is shaped by the courts. In recent years it has been the usual practice of HMRC to decline invitations to be joined as a party in cases where the court is being asked to set aside a transaction in reliance on the principle. However, in *Sieff v Fox* Lloyd L.J. observed in para.83 that the court's task might be easier in some cases if HMRC did not always decline the invitation to take part in cases of this kind. In the light of that observation, and our increasing concern (which is shared by many commentators) that the principle as currently formulated is too wide in its scope, HMRC will now give active consideration to participating in future cases where large amounts of tax are at stake and/or where it is felt that we could make a useful contribution to the elucidation and development of the principle.

We will be particularly ready to intervene in cases where there would otherwise be no party in whose interest it would be to argue against the application of the principle.

It would be beyond the scope of this article to discuss the issues which arise in any depth, and HMRC must in any event reserve the right to advance whatever arguments appear to us appropriate in the circumstances of any given case. Subject to that caveat, however, we would make the following points in order to give an indication of our present thinking on some of the main questions which arise.

(1) In the first place, it should be noted that the principle in its present form has little or nothing to do with the type of situation which was considered by the Court of Appeal in *Hastings Bass* itself, and that it owes its origin to the logically flawed positive reformulation of the principle in Mettoy. We consider that any positive formulation of the principle should state merely that the court "may" interfere with the trustee's action, not that it "will" do so.

(2) Second, and allied to point (1) above, we consider that the effect of the principle, if it applies at all, should be to make the relevant decision by the trustee voidable and not void, or at the very least should permit the court to take into account the same sort of equitable considerations that apply when it is deciding whether to grant other forms of equitable relief.

(3) Third, we would tentatively suggest that the principle, as it develops, should as far as possible be assimilated with the general principles of law by reference to which (a) the exercise of a discretion by trustees may be impugned (as to which see the decision of the Court of Appeal in *Edge v Pensions Ombudsman* [2000] Ch. 602, especially at 627–30 and 633), and (b) the courts will set aside voluntary transactions or written instruments for mistake. It may be the case that, properly understood, there is no room or need for a separate Hastings-Bass principle at all.

(4) Fourth, in cases where the trustee acts under a discretion and is not obliged to act, we would agree with the view expressed by Lloyd LJ in Sieff v Fox, that the relevant test is whether the trustee "would" have acted differently if the correct considerations had been taken into account, not whether the trustee "might" have acted differently.

(5) Fifth, while accepting that fiscal consequences are generally amongst the matters which a trustee should take into account when deciding how to act, we consider that a distinction needs to be drawn between cases where the trustee fails to take relevant fiscal considerations into account at all, and cases where the trustee takes steps to obtain fiscal advice but that advice turns out (for whatever reason) to be wrong. While there may be scope for the principle to apply in cases of the former type, it is felt that in cases of the latter type (which include *Sieff v Fox*) the principle should not apply. Similarly, in cases where the trustee obtains advice about the tax consequences of a proposed transaction, but then fails to implement the transaction in accordance with that advice (as in *Abacus v NSPCC*), it is also felt that the principle should not apply. A common feature of cases like *Sieff v Fox* and *Abacus v NSPCC* is that the trustee has sought appropriate tax advice, and in reliance on it has deliberately taken certain steps which in trust terms achieve precisely the effect which they were intended to achieve. Why then should the trustee be entitled to have the transaction set aside, in a way that would not be open to an individual taxpayer, merely because the advice which he obtained was incorrect, or because he negligently failed to follow the advice correctly? In such cases, it is suggested, the court should not interfere, tax should be paid on the basis of the transaction actually carried out, and the trust should be left to pursue whatever remedies it may have against the trustee and/or the trustee's professional advisers.

(6) Finally, despite what was said by Lightman J. in *Abacus v Barr*, we are inclined to agree with Lloyd LJ in *Sieff v Fox* that a breach of duty by the trustee or the trustee's agent or advisers is not in itself a separate requirement that has to be satisfied if the principle is to apply.

In the remainder of this article, some brief comments will be made on various practical issues which have arisen from time to time.

In some instances HMRC have been asked to consent to a reversal of the tax consequences of a particular trustee decision without an order of the court, on the basis that the principle in Hastings-Bass applies, to save the parties the trouble and expense of going to court.

We have generally maintained that we require an order of the court before we will review the tax consequences of a decision on the basis of the Hastings-Bass principle, and this remains the basic position. The nature and parameters of the Hastings-Bass principle are still unclear in many respects and although this is something that we will consider in the context of each case as it arises, it is felt that we would not generally be entitled to agree to unwind a decision, even if we were minded to do so. Crucially, it remains to be clarified by a higher court whether the effect of an application of the principle is to make a decision void or voidable. If the decision is voidable, the question of whether it should be avoided is one for the court and cannot be resolved by consent between the parties. At other times we have been asked to determine the tax consequences of obtaining an order, while parties consider whether or not to apply to the court. We have generally declined to do this, on the basis that the court may have a wide discretion as to the terms upon which it makes any order. Facts and circumstances in cases susceptible to consideration under the principle vary considerably and these variations may well affect the approach of the court and, in consequence, the tax treatment.

Finally, in a number of cases we have been invited to join the proceedings themselves. Some parties have complained of hardship where we have insisted on a court order before we will review the tax consequences, particularly where the parties are themselves agreed that the decision should be set aside. However, we do not consider that our insistence on a court order leads necessarily to the conclusion that we ought to be joined as parties to those proceedings, although as we have said above it is now likely that there will be cases in the future where HMRC would wish to be joined or to intervene in order to resist an application of the principle in a particular case, or to seek to influence the development of the principle in a particular direction.

This article sets out HMRC's current position on the principle in *Hastings Bass* and seeks to give an indication of the type of stance we might take should we become involved in a case in the future. We are not, however, limiting ourselves to these arguments. Clearly this is a developing area of the law, certain aspects of which will require clarification by the higher courts in due course. As things evolve we will keep the principle, and our policies, under review but it is hoped that this article will assist taxpayers and practitioners in the meantime.

October 13, 2006

POA CORRESPONDENCE WITH HMRC ON ELECTIONS (OCTOBER 2006)

There is some uncertainty about the actual effect of the election because para 21 does not as such deem there to be a gift for Inheritance Tax purposes but simply states that the property is treated as property subject to a reservation. Schedule 15 provides for what happens if the person ceases to benefit from the elected property but does not provide for what happens if the property actually comes back into a person's estate.

In the COP 10 letter we asked (at question 17) what happens if A makes the election in respect of his home on a home loan scheme (or indeed any other type of Inheritance Tax Scheme). The house is then appointed back to him absolutely i.e. the arrangements are unscrambled. The reservation of benefit has ceased because the house is back in his estate and you confirmed that even if there was a deemed PET under Section 102 (4) FA 1986, appointing the property back to A would have no immediate practical inheritance tax consequences because it is back in his estate anyway. This accords with how the reservation of benefit rules on actual gifts work. (See answer to question 17.)

As you will be aware, many people are unravelling schemes but also wish to make the election in order to avoid an income tax charge from 6th April 2005. If once the property is back in their estates the effect of the election ceases to apply for all inheritance tax purposes (in the same way that a reservation of benefit on gifted property would cease if it was transferred back to the donor) then spouse (and charities) exemption is available. If the election is made and the scheme is not unravelled, spouse exemption is not available.

I am therefore requesting confirmation that HMRC apply the Schedule 15 of FA 2004 legislation on elections in the same way as the reservation of benefit legislation on an actual gift. So even though HMRC would produce the election on any death, on being shown evidence that the property had been appointed back and the scheme

A3.149

entirely unravelled, the election would then be ignored for inheritance tax purposes. Spouse exemption is then available. If that approach is indeed the one HMRC adopt, does it matter if the election is made before or after the scheme is unravelled?

A3.150 *Response from HMRC Capital Taxes Nottingham*

20th October

Pre-owned assets and elections

Thank you for your letter of 13th October

I can confirm that we do believe that the Schedule 15 FA 2004 legislation on elections should be applied in the same way as the reservation of benefit legislation on an actual gift. As I suggested when you originally raised this question with me on the phone, section 102(3) Finance Act 1986 only has practical force in relation to property that is subject to a reservation immediately before death and only to the extent that it would not form part of the estate in any event.

On that basis, if evidence is produced that property, in respect of which an election under the Schedule 15 legislation had been made, has been appointed back to the estate, we would ignore the existence of the election for the purpose of determining the IHT estate on death.

On your supplementary question, we do not consider the timing of the election to be material. Even if it were made after the unscrambling, the chargeable person would still have been chargeable for the period up to the unscrambling, thus enabling the requirements of paragraphs 21(1) or 22(1), as appropriate, to be met.

APPENDIX IV

EXAMPLES OF THE IHT CHARGING PROVISIONS FOR RELEVANT PROPERTY TRUSTS[1]

Set out below are eight illustrations of the various IHT charges which can hit relevant property trusts.

ILLUSTRATION 1

A4.01

On August 31, 2003, Nelson set up a discretionary trust for the benefit of his brother and his brother's family. The trust assets comprised cash and quoted shares totalling £320,000.

Nelson had a cumulative total for IHT purposes of £81,000 as a result of a chargeable transfer made some five years earlier. He had made no other gifts.

The IHT payable in connection with the creation of Nelson's discretionary trust (assumed to be payable by the trustees) was:

	£	Gross £	IHT £
b/f		81,000	—
31.8.03			
Discretionary trust	320,000		
Less: Annual exemptions	6,000		
		314,000	28,000
		£395,000	£28,000

This calculation, using 2003/04 lifetime rates, runs as follows:

	£
On 81,000 − 255,000 = 174,000 @ 0%	—
On 255,000 − 395,000 = 140,000 @ 20%	28,000
	£28,000

If Nelson had paid the tax, grossing up would be involved.

---

[1] Supplied by Robert Jamieson MA FCA CTA (Fellow), tax partner in Mercer & Hole and former President of the Chartered Institute of Taxation.

Unfortunately, on December 31, 2006, Nelson was killed in an accident. As a result, death rate tax is due in respect of the chargeable transfer on August 31, 2003. This is calculated (using 2006/07 rates) as follows:

	£
On 81,000 – 285,000 = 204,000 @ 0%	–
On 285,000 – 395,000 = 110,000 @ 40%	44,000
	44,000
Less: Taper relief (20%)	8,800
	35,200
Less: Tax on lifetime transfer	28,000
ADDITIONAL IHT PAYABLE BY TRUSTEES	£7,200

A4.02 Illustration 1 demonstrated how IHT is computed when a discretionary trust is set up. It is now the turn of the exit charge calculation. On the assumption that we are looking at an exit charge *before* the discretionary trust has suffered its first 10-year charge, there are several factors which have to be taken into account:

(a) the settlor's cumulative total of chargeable transfers at the time when the settlement commenced (s.68(4)(b) of IHTA 1984);
(b) the "initial value" of the discretionary trust—this is the actual value of the property which started off within the discretionary trust regime (s.68(5)(a) of IHTA 1984);
(c) the length of time for which the property has been in the discretionary trust (s.68(2) of IHTA 1984); and
(d) the value of the property for IHT purposes which is leaving the discretionary trust (s.65(2) of IHTA 1984).

A4.03 ILLUSTRATION 2

Darin created a discretionary trust on December 20, 1998. His cumulative total of chargeable transfers immediately prior to this settlement was £242,000.

The property which he transferred to the trust was some let farmland which he had owned for many years and which was worth £450,000. Agricultural property relief (APR) of 50 per cent was available (assume that the market value and the agricultural value of the farmland were the same).

Darin had not used his 1998/99 annual exemption. The IHT due was paid by the trustees under the instalment option out of the rental income derived from the let farmland. Thus:

		Gross	IHT
	£	£	£
b/f		242,000	3,800
20.12.98			
Discretionary trust	450,000		
Less: APR (50%)	225,000		
	225,000		
Less: Annual exemption	3,000		
		222,000	44,400
		£464,000	£48,200

On May 14, 2006, the trustees appointed the farmland (now valued at £800,000) to one of the discretionary beneficiaries absolutely. It still qualified for relief at 50 per cent.[2] The exit charge is calculated as follows (this assumes that the beneficiary paid the relevant IHT):

	£	IHT £
b/f	242,000	–
Initial value (450,000 − 44,400)	405,600	72,520
	£647,600	£72,520

Note: The initial value is not, for these purposes, reduced by the 50% relief.

The IHT at 2006/07 lifetime rates on the initial value is £72,520. This gives an initial rate of:

$72,520/405,600 \times 100 = 17.8797\%$

The rate of tax actually payable is:

$17.8797\% \times 30\% \times 29/40 = 3.8888\%$

Note: The initial rate is multiplied by 30 per cent and then by the number of complete successive quarters which have elapsed since the start of the trust divided by 40 (see s.68(2) of IHTA 1984).

The taxable value of the exit charge is:

	£
Let farmland	800,000
Less: APR (50%)	400,000
	£400,000

The IHT paid by the beneficiary amounts to $3.8888\% \times £400,000 = £15,555$.

The calculation of a 10-year anniversary charge is somewhat different. This is shown in Illustration 3 below, along with the regime for computing IHT on an exit *after* a 10-year anniversary.

ILLUSTRATION 3   A4.04

Holly set up a discretionary trust on February 3, 1997 at a time when his cumulative total of chargeable transfers was £123,400.

In the 10 years since then, the trustees have made capital appointments of trust property amounting to £130,600.

The first 10-year anniversary charge for Holly's discretionary settlement falls on February 3, 2007 and the quoted shares, cash and other assets still in the settlement on that date are worth a total of £411,000. The IHT due in respect of this 10-year anniversary is computed as follows:

---

[2] Because the trustees have owned it for more than seven years.

	£
Holly's chargeable transfers prior to trust	123,400
Add: Exit charges	130,600
	254,000
Add: Value of discretionary trust property	411,000
	£665,000

IHT at 2006/07 lifetime rates on the value of this discretionary trust property is:

	£
On 254,000 − 285,000 = 31,000 @ 0%	–
On 285,000 − 665,000 = 380,000 @ 20%	76,000
	£76,000

Thus:

76,000/411,000 × 100 = 18.4915%

The rate actually charged is:

18.4915% × 30% = 5.5475%

Therefore, the trustees must settle an IHT liability of 5.5475% × £411,000 = £22,800.

The relevant legislation for computing a 10-year anniversary charge is found in s.66 of IHTA 1984. Typically, this will involve an aggregation of:

(a) the settlor's cumulative total of chargeable transfers made in the seven years prior to the commencement of the settlement (s.66(5)(a) of IHTA 1984);

(b) the total of all exit charges imposed in the 10 (*not* seven) years prior to the anniversary in question (s.66(5)(b) of IHTA 1984); and

(c) the value of the discretionary trust property still in the settlement on the anniversary date (s.66(4)(a) of IHTA 1984).

Tax is charged at current lifetime rates on the value of the discretionary trust property (see (c) above), taking into account what IHTA 1984 calls a "postulated" prior chargeable transfer equal to the sum of (a) and (b) above (s.66(3) of IHTA 1984). The purpose of including (b) above is to render ineffective any transfer out of the trust of property just before the 10-year anniversary in order to reduce the value of the trust property subject to the charge.

A4.05 If, in this illustration, the trustees subsequently made a capital appointment of quoted shares worth £80,000 to Holly's cousin, Valens, who was one of the discretionary beneficiaries, on May 13, 2008, the IHT calculation would proceed as follows by virtue of s.69 of IHTA 1984:

(a) the 10-year anniversary charge is recomputed using 2008/09 lifetime rates;

(b) the resulting tax figure is expressed as a percentage of the value of the discretionary trust property on February 3, 2007;

(c) this percentage is multiplied by 30 per cent and then by the number of complete successive quarters which have elapsed since the 10-year anniversary charge divided by 40; and finally

(d) the scaled down percentage is applied to the value of the capital appointment on May 13, 2008 (grossed up, if the trustees, rather than Valens, are to bear the tax).

Thus:

	£
Holly's chargeable transfers prior to trust	123,400
Add: Exit charges	130,600
	254,000
Add: Value of discretionary trust property	411,000
	£665,000

IHT at 2008/09 lifetime rates on the value of the discretionary trust property is:

	£
On 254,000 − 312,000 = 58,000 @ 0%	–
On 312,000 − 665,000 = 353,000 @ 20%	70,600
	£70,600

This produces:

$70,600/411,000 \times 100\% = 17.1776\%$

The rate of IHT ascribed to this transaction is:

$17.1776\% \times 30\% \times 5/40 = 0.6442\%$

Thus the tax on the appointment which is to be paid by the trustees so that grossing-up applies is:

$$\frac{0.6442}{100 - 0.6442} \times 80,000 = £519$$

Note: The gross amount of the exit charge is £80,519 and $0.6442\% \times £80,519 = £519$.

The next illustration shows the effect of an exit charge after a 10-year anniversary charge where:

(a) the trust property was wholly eligible for 100 per cent business property relief (BPR) at the 10-year anniversary date; and

(b) the property has since been sold so that it is cash which is appointed out.

ILLUSTRATION 4   A4.06

The Pitney Discretionary settlement was established by Mr Pitney on April 5, 1997 with a 40 per cent holding of shares in Tulsa Enterprises Ltd (an unquoted trading company). The beneficiaries comprised Mr Pitney's children and grandchildren.

On April 5, 2007, the only assets in the trust were:

(a) shares in Tulsa Enterprises Ltd worth £800,000; and
(b) undistributed cash of £13,600.

Mr Pitney's cumulative total of chargeable transfers prior to April 5, 1997 was nil and there have been no distributions of capital from the trust since it was set up.

The IHT due in respect of the trust's 10-year anniversary on April 5, 2007 is computed as follows:

	£	£
Mr Pitney's chargeable transfer prior to trust		–
Add: Exit charges in 10 years to April 5, 2007		–
		–
Add: Value of discretionary trust property on April 5, 2007:		
Shares in Tulsa Enterprises Ltd	800,000	
Less: BPR (100%)	800,000	
	–	
Cash	13,600	
		13,600
		£13,600

IHT at 2006/07 lifetime rates on the value of the discretionary trust property is nil.

On February 17, 2009, Tulsa Enterprises Ltd was taken over by a large plc and the trustees received a cash payment of £1,000,000 for their shares. After settling their CGT liability of £80,000 on January 31, 2010, the trustees made a capital distribution of £920,000 to the beneficiaries on February 14, 2010 and the trust came to an end. Any undistributed income had already been paid out.

Because the rate of tax on the previous 10-year anniversary, using 2009/10 lifetime rates, was 0 per cent, the exit charge on February 14, 2010 is IHT-free. This can be a useful advantage whenever trust property which attracts relief at 100 per cent is sold and cash is then appointed out.

Another problem which comes up from time to time is where a settlor has added further property to an existing discretionary trust. Illustration 5 examines the complications where there is an exit charge from such a settlement.

ILLUSTRATION 5

A4.07   Presley set up a discretionary trust on August 16, 1997 with cash of £750,000. He had a cumulative total for IHT purposes of £125,000 as a result of a chargeable transfer made in 1993.

On the assumption that no annual exemption was available, the IHT payable in connection with the creation of Presley's discretionary trust (assumed to be payable by the trustees) was:

		Gross	*IHT*
		£	£
	b/f	125,000	–
16.8.97			
Discretionary trust		750,000	132,000
		£875,000	£132,000

This calculation, using 1997/98 lifetime rates, runs as follows:

	£
On 125,000 − 215,000 = 90,000 @ 0%	–
On 215,000 − 875,000 = 660,000 @ 20%	132,000
	£132,000

The remaining cash was then invested in a portfolio of quoted stocks and shares.

On January 8, 2005, when the settled property included 12,000 ordinary shares in Aaron plc, Presley added a further 120,000 ordinary shares in Aaron plc to the trust and paid the IHT himself. The IHT value for these quoted shares was then 300p per share.

The IHT payable in connection with this addition was (again no annual exemption was available):

	Gross	IHT	Net
	£	£	£
b/f	–	–	–
8.1.05			
Discretionary trust (120,000 × 300p)			360,000
Grossed up	384,250	24,250	
	£384,250	£24,250	£360,000

Note: Presley's earlier chargeable transfers have dropped out under the seven-year rule. His cumulative net transfer of £360,000 exceeds the 2004/05 nil rate band of £263,000 by £97,000, the gross equivalent of which is £97,000 × 100/80 = £121,250. The tax payable is therefore £121,250 − £97,000 = £24,250 and the gross chargeable transfer is £360,000 + £24,250 = £384,250.

On February 1, 2007, the trustees appointed 66,000 ordinary shares in Aaron Plc (now valued at 360p per share) to Priscilla absolutely. She was one of the discretionary beneficiaries and she agreed to pay any tax due.

The initial value of the property originally settled is £750,000 − £132,000 = £618,000. The initial value of the addition (which must also be taken into account when calculating the exit charge—see s.68(5)(c) of IHTA 1984) is £360,000. The exit charge tax is computed as follows:

	£	£	IHT £
b/f		125,000	–
Initial value of settlement	618,000		
Initial value of addition	360,000		
		978,000	163,600
		£1,103,000	£163,600

The IHT at 2006/07 lifetime rates on the combined initial values is £163,600. This gives an initial rate of:

163,600/978,000 × 100 = 16.728%

To the extent that the exit charge comes out of the property originally settled, the initial rate is multiplied by 30% and then by the number of complete successive quarters which have elapsed since the start of the trust—this comes to 37—divided by 40.

However, to the extent that the exit charge comes out of the addition, the number of quarters taken is 37 less the number of complete successive quarters prior to the addition—this comes to 29—and so the fraction becomes 8/40ths.

The IHT payable on the distribution of 66,000 ordinary shares in Aaron Plc (valued at 66,000 × 360p = £237,600) to Priscilla is:

Out of property originally settled

	£
16.728% × 30% × 37/40 × 237,600 × 12,000/132,000	1,003
Out of addition	
16.728% × 30% × 8/40 × 237,600 × 120,000/132,000	2,168
	£3,171

Note: The capital appointment to Pricilla is deemed to come pro rata from the property originally settled on August 16, 1997 and from the addition on January 8, 2005.[3]

The creation of most interest in possession trusts made on or after March 22, 2006 will bring the relevant property regime into play. Illustration 6 below compares the incidence of IHT under the new regime with what a similar trust would have suffered had the pre-March 22, 2006 rules still been around.

A4.08 ILLUSTRATION 6

Cochran set up a life interest trust for his wife, Sharon, on June 1, 2006. Cochran's chargeable transfers prior to the creation of this trust totalled £200,000 and the value of the assets going into the trust was £506,000.

Following Cochran's death in a car accident on April 17, 2017, Sharon remarried on October 3, 2020 and, under the terms of the trust, her life interest terminated. The trust capital went to their three children absolutely.

On the assumptions that the trust property had the following values:

(a) £760,000 on June 1, 2016; and
(b) £890,000 on October 3, 2020

and that 2009/10 tax rates apply to all transactions after the initial setting up of the trust, the IHT payable in respect of this trust is as follows:

Creation of trust on June 1, 2006

		£	Gross £	IHT £
	b/f		200,000	—
1.6.06				
Sharon's trust		506,000		
Less: Annual exemptions		6,000		
			500,000	83,000
			£700,000	£83,000

---

[3] The special rule in IHTA 1984, s.67 dealing with additions of property is not relevant for an exit charge on February 1, 2007.

Thus £83,000 was payable by the trustees out of the assets settled. Under the pre-March 22, 2006 rules, this would have been an exempt transfer.

10-year anniversary charge on June 1, 2016

	£
Cochran's chargeable transfers prior to trust	200,000
Add: Value of trust property	760,000
	£960,000

IHT at 2009/10 lifetime rates on the value of this trust property is:

	£
On 200,000 – 325,000 = 125,000 @ 0%	–
On 325,000 – 960,000 = 635,000 @ 20%	127,000
	£127,000

Thus:

$127,000/760,000 \times 100\% = 16.7105\%$

The rate of IHT actually charged is:

$16.7105\% \times 30\% = 5.0132\%$

Therefore, the trustees must settle an IHT liability of $5.0132\% \times £760,000 = £38,100$. Under the pre-March 22, 2006 rules, there would have been no 10-year anniversary charge.

Termination of trust on October 3, 2020

The value of the property leaving the interest in possession trust on October 3, 2020 following Sharon's remarriage is £890,000. This will be taxed as an exit charge under s.69 IHTA of 1984.

The rate of IHT ascribable to this transaction is:

$5.0132\% \times 17/40 = 2.1306\%$

If the tax on this appointment is paid by the three children, the liability will be:

$2.1306\% \times 890,000 = £18,962$

Under the pre-March 22, 2006 rules, this appointment would have been treated as a potentially exempt transfer made by Sharon and so IHT would only have been due if she had died within seven years of October 3, 2020.

IHT summary

	New rules	Old rules
	£	£
June 1, 2006	83,000	–
June 1, 2016	38,100	–
October 3, 2020	18,962	–
	£140,062	£Nil

The next illustration looks at the position of an accumulation and maintenance trust when the terms of the trust are not modified prior to April 6, 2008, with the result that the trust assets become relevant property on April 6, 2008. The particular point of this example is the calculation of the 10-year anniversary charge.

A4.09 ILLUSTRATION 7

On December 1, 1998, Faith, whose chargeable transfers totalled £180,000, set up an accumulation and maintenance trust for the benefit of his young nephews and nieces, each of whom was to come into a share of income at the age of 18 and capital at the age of 30.

Despite learning of the Chancellor's plans for accumulation and maintenance trusts in FA 2006, Faith refused to lower the vesting age on the ground that, as he put it, "18 is too young for someone to be given a substantial amount of capital".

Accordingly, on April 6, 2008, Faith's trust effectively became a discretionary settlement and the first 10-year anniversary charge arose on December 1, 2008, at which date the trust property was worth £772,000. However, because the assets in the trust had not been relevant property throughout the 10-year period, s.66(2) of IHTA 1984 allows the rate at which the tax is charged to be scaled down by 1/40th for each complete successive quarter which had elapsed before the trust assets became relevant property. In this case, 37 quarters expired between December 1, 1998 and April 6, 2008, leaving a fraction of 3/40ths to be applied to the IHT rate. The computation proceeds as follows:

	£
Faith's chargeable transfers prior to trust	180,000
Add: Value of trust property	772,000
	£952,000

IHT at 2008/09 lifetime rates on the value of this trust property is:

	£
On 180,000 − 312,000 = 132,000 @ 0%	–
On 312,000 − 952,000 = 640,000 @ 20%	128,000
	£128,000

Thus:

128,000/772,000 × 100% = 16.5803%

The rate actually charged is:

16.5803% × 30% × 3/40 = 0.3731%

Therefore, the trustees must settle an IHT liability of 0.3731% × £772,000 = £2,880.[4]

The final illustration demonstrates the calculation of the tax charge under s.71D of IHTA 1984 where capital vests on an appointment to an age 18–25 trust beneficiary.

---

[4] For the position if the trust had been set up more than 10 years before April 6, 2008, so that a 10-year anniversary had passed, and there was an exit charge before the next 10-year anniversary, see 20.22.

ILLUSTRATION 8   A4.10

Holliday died on October 29, 2003 and, in his will, he left part of his estate on trust for his only son, Michael, who had been born on November 26, 1994. The terms of the trust were that income was to be accumulated to the extent that it was not paid out for Michael's maintenance, education or benefit. The trust capital (and any accumulated income) vested absolutely in Michael on his 25th birthday.

This trust was originally an accumulation and maintenance settlement, but, because Michael's vesting age was not amended prior to April 6, 2008, it then became an age 18-to-25 trust. In other words, following Michael's 18th birthday (November 26, 2012), the trust assets were subject to the special charging regime in s 71 E-G. Accordingly, seven years later, when the trust assets vested on November 26, 2019, there is an exit charge under s.71E of IHTA 1984.

On the assumptions:

(a) that the trust assets were worth £520,000 on November 26, 2019;
(b) that the initial value of the trust on Holliday's death (i.e. October 29, 2003) was £268,000;
(c) that Holliday's cumulative total for IHT purposes immediately prior to his death was £149,000; and
(d) that 2009/10 tax rates apply,

the calculation of the IHT on Michael's 25th birthday proceeds as follows by virtue of s.71F of IHTA 1984:

	£	IHT £
b/f	149,000	–
Initial value[5]	268,000	18,400
	£417,000	£18,400

The IHT at 2009/10 lifetime rates on the initial value is £18,400. This gives an initial rate of:

$18,400/268,000 \times 100 = \underline{6.8657\%}$

The rate of tax actually payable is:

$6.8657\% \times 30\% \times 28/40 = \underline{1.4418\%}$

Note: 28 quarters have elapsed since Michael's 18th birthday.

The IHT paid by Michael on the vesting of the trust property is 1.4418% × £520,000 = £7,497.

---

[5] Note that the "initial value" may be significantly less than the value of the property in the trust when it ends. The trust may, for instance, have been set up over 20 years ago. Discovering the value of the property at that time may present problems (its original creation may well have been a PET so no IHT value will have been agreed) and it will also be necessary to discover the chargeable transfers of the Settlor in the previous seven years. Bear in mind that standard advice was that if a taxpayer wished to make a chargeable transfer (e.g. create a discretionary trust) he should do so before making a PET.

INDEX

Absolute entitlement of beneficiary
  loss relief, 12.05
  settled property, 5.07–5.15, 7.38
Accrued income schemes, 4.07
Accumulation and maintenance trusts
  after March 2006, 14.29–14.30, 14.33
  background, 21.01–21.02
  bereaved minor trusts compared, 25.22–25.25
  discretionary will trusts, 29.61
  link with s.71D trusts, 25.44
  Old rules—exit charge, 21.15
  New rules—exit charge, 20.22
  relevant property settlements, 20.34
  summary of options, 21.22
  tax treatment after March 2006, 21.16–21.21
  tax treatment before March 2006, 21.05–21.15
  Transitional rules, 21.17
Actual disposals
  annual exemptions, 7.07
  date made, 7.08
  death exemption, 7.46
  deferral relief, 7.11
  general principles, 7.02
  main residence exemption, 7.06
  overview, 7.01
  rates of tax, 7.03
  roll-over relief, 7.10
  settlor interested trusts, 7.04
  taper relief, 7.13–7.32
  vulnerable beneficiaries, 7.12
Additions to settlements
  addition defined inheritance tax issues, 15.13–15.15
  after changes of domicile, 22.20–22.35
  single or multiple settlements for capital gains tax, 5.35, 7.08
    additions to companies, 22.28
    additions to discretionary settlements—problems, 20.05, 20.27
Advancement
  bereaved minor trusts, 25.18–25.19
  income tax liability of beneficiaries, 4.26–4.29

Advancement—*contd*
  offshore trusts, 10.30
  overview, 1.11–1.12
  settled advances, 7.42
  variation of wills or intestacy, 29.23
Agricultural property relief
  'agricultural value' defined, 32.14–32.17
  business asset hold-over, 9.31
  deduction of liabilities for IHT
    areas for consideration, 23.01
    general rule, 23.26
  discretionary will trusts, 28.27–28.30
  impact of POA regime, 32.32–32.33
  importance, 32.01
  qualifying IIPs, 17.26
  relationship with BPR, 32.02
  reservation of benefit, 13.25, 32.27–32.31
  scope, 32.10–32.13
  settled property, 32.18–32.26
Annuities, 17.08
Annual exemptions
  actual disposals, 7.07
  multiple settlements, 5.32
Anti-avoidance
  artificial debts, 23.16–23.22
  disclosure rules
    basic rules, 36.15
    legal professional privilege, 36.16
    overview, 36.13–36.14
    'promoter' defined, 36.16
    scope, 36.17–36.18
  flip-flop schemes
    deemed disposals, 7.62–7.65
    legislative measures, 10.41–10.44
    settlor interested trusts, 10.20
  income tax
    capital payments to settlor, 4.41–4.43
    settlor interested trusts, 4.30–4.37
    unmarried minor children, 4.38–4.40
  Melville schemes, 3.17
  non-interest in possession trusts, 18.08–18.12
  offshore settlor interested trusts, 10.17
  overview, 3.24–3.31
  reservation of benefit, 13.17, 13.27–13.33

819

Anti-avoidance—*contd*
  retrospective legislation, 3.04–3.07
Appointments
  discretionary will trusts, 29.58–29.59
  offshore trusts, 8.11
  precedent, A.2.64
  property excluded from IHT, 22.36–22.43, 22.43
  settlor defined, 5.25
  single or multiple settlements, 5.34
  stamp duty land tax, 35.04
  variation of wills or intestacy, 29.23
Appropriations of settled property, 5.09
Artificial debts, 23.16–23.22
Authorised Unit Trusts (AUTS), 22.08, 22.12

Bare trusts
  capital gains tax, 30.06–30.09
  death of child before 18, 30.12
  entitlement at 18, 30.13
  income tax, 30.05
  inheritance tax, 30.10–30.11
  meaning and scope, 30.01–30.02
  minor beneficiaries, 15.03, 25.08, 25.09–25.12, 25.47
  precedent, A.2.01
  settled property, 5.04
  stamp duty land tax, 35.04
  tax returns, 30.04
  trustee liability for income tax, 4.03
  uses, 30.03
  will drafting, 28.40
Beneficial interests
  consents, 8.07
  disposals
    basic rule, 8.01–8.-04
    non-resident settlements, 8.05–8.15
    settlor interested trusts, 8.16–8.26
  exporting trusts, 2.64
  sale of beneficial interests, 8.16
  treatment of qualifying IIPs, 17.03
Beneficiaries
  absolute entitlement
    loss relief, 12.05
    settled property, 5.07–5.15
  defined, 1.05
  death of,
    actual disposals exempt, 7.09
    deemed disposals for CGT, 7.46–7.52
  income tax liability
    advancement of capital, 4.26–4.29
    annuitants, 4.23
    discretionary beneficiaries, 4.24
    dividends, 4.25
    general principles, 4.21–4.22
    joint beneficiaries of settled property, 5.06
Bereaved minors trusts
  A & M trusts compared, 25.22–25.25
  advancement, 25.18–25.19
  'bereaved minor' defined, 25.14
  charge to tax, 25.20–25.21
  drafting considerations, 25.26–25.28

Bereaved minors trusts—*contd*
  key limiting features, 25.13
  older children (s.71D trusts)
    comparisons with, 25.42
    conversion to, 25.38
  overview of new rules, 14.14, 14.33
  precedent, A.2.25
  qualifying trusts, 25.15–25.17
  will drafting, 28.40
Blind trusts, 30.03/07
Budget Note BN 25(2006), A.3.01
Business property relief
  deduction of liabilities for IHT
    areas for consideration, 23.01
    general rules, 23.23–23.25
  discretionary will trusts, 28.31
  hold-over
    agricultural property, 9.31
    availability, 9.10
    calculation of gain, 9.20
    defined, 9.11–9.14
    gifts to companies, 9.19
    non-resident donees, 9.22–9.30
    partial relief, 9.15–9.16
    for trustees, 9.17–9.18
    undervalue sales, 9.21
  impact of POA regime, 32.32–32.33
  importance, 32.01
  qualifying IIPs, 17.26
  relationship with APR, 32.02
  reservation of benefit, 13.25, 32.27–32.31
  restrictions on availability, 32.03–32.09
  settled property, 32.18–32.26
  taper relief, 7.15, 7.25–7.30, 7.32
    business property relief and agricultural property relief in Wills, 28.27 onwards—example 28.1 drafting issue

Calculation of tax charge
  capital gains tax
    hold-over relief, 9.20
    principal private residence relief, 31.11–31.12
    settlor interested trusts, 11.09
  inheritance tax, 13.06
Capital gains tax
  actual disposals
    annual exemptions, 7.07
    date made, 7.08
    death exemption, 7.09
    deferral relief, 7.11
    general principles, 7.02
    main residence exemption, 7.06
    overview, 7.01
    rates of tax, 7.03
    roll-over relief, 7.10
    settlor interested trusts, 7.04
    taper relief, 7.13–7.32
    vulnerable beneficiaries, 7.12
  bare trusts, 30.06–30.09
  changes since 1997
    Finance Act 1998, 3.09

Capital gains tax—*contd*
  changes since 1997—*contd*
    Finance Act 1999, 3.10
    Finance Act 2000, 3.11
    Finance Act 2003, 3.12
    Finance Acts 2004 and 2006, 3.13
  claiming trust assets on divorce, 34.12
  creation of settlements
    disposals to connected parties, 6.01–6.05
    double charges, 6.08
    holdover relief, 6.05–6.06
    instalment option, 6.07
    rates of tax, 6.09
  deemed disposals
    beneficiary becoming absolutely entitled, 7.34–7.45
    death of beneficiary where settlement continues, 7.48–7.52
    death of interest in possession beneficiary, 7.46–7.47
    flip-flop schemes, 7.62–7.65
    overview, 7.01
    postponement of impact, 7.53–7.54
    relevant circumstances, 7.33
    resettlements, 7.55–7.59
    sub-fund elections, 7.72–7.74
    transfers linked to borrowing, 7.66–7.71
    variations of settlements, 7.60–7.61
  definitions
    disposals, 5.39–5.40
    settled property, 5.02–5.15
    settlor, 5.16–5.27
    single or multiple settlements, 5.28–5.35
    trustees, 5.36–5.38
  disabled trusts, 26.14–26.17
  discretionary will trusts, 29.60
  disposal of beneficial interests
    basic rule, 8.01–8.-04
    non-resident settlements, 8.05–8.15
    settlor interested trusts, 8.16–8.26
  domicile and capital gains tax, 2.10
  emigration of trusts
    bed and breakfasting, 2.57, 2.60
    beneficial interests, 2.64
    capital payments, 2.63
    disposals in year of migration, 2.62
    double taxation relief, 2.58–2.59
    EU uncertainty, 2.61
    export charges, 2.51–2.56
    feasibility, 2.47–2.50
    inadvertent emigrations, 2.66–2.67
    trustee borrowing, 2.65
  hold-over relief
    business assets, 9.10–9.32
    double charge relief for IHT and CGT, 9.46–9.51
    interaction with main residence exemption, 9.46–9.51
    overview, 9.01–9.09
  loss relief
    absolute entitlement of beneficiary, 12.05
    basic principles, 12.01

Capital gains tax—*contd*
  loss relief—*contd*
    multiple settlements, 5.32
    no offset of gains, 12.04
    non-residents, 2.13
    offshore trusts, 10.36, 12.08–12.11
    restriction on set-off, 12.06–12.07
    settlor interested trusts, 12.02–12.03
  minor beneficiaries, 25.04
  non-residents
    changes post-2007, 2.43–2.45
    double taxation relief, 2.22–2.24
    general rule, 2.10
    loss relief, 2.13
    professional trustees, 2.38–2.41
    remittance of gains, 2.12–2.16
    split-year treatment, 2.24–2.26
    temporary non-residence, 2.17–2.21
    UK traders, 2.11
  offshore trusts
    flip-flop schemes, 10.41–10.44
    overview, 10.01–10.07, 10.01–10.07
    settlor interested trusts, 10.08–10.23
    UK resident and domiciled beneficiaries, 10.24–10.40
  principal private residence relief
    applicability, 31, 31.01–31.10
    business use, 31.13
    calculation of gain, 31.11–31.12
    garden and grounds, 31.14–31.18
    nil rate discretionary trusts, 31.25–31.26
    personal representatives, 31.27–31.28
    settled property, 31.19–31.24
  residents, 2.09
  reverter to settlor trusts, 27.13
  settlor interested trusts
    calculation of tax charge, 11.09
    importance, 11.01–11.02
    meaning, 11.03–11.08
    reform proposals, 11.11
    settlor defined, 11.10
  variation of wills or intestacy, 29.31–29.37
  vulnerable beneficiaries, 26.14–26.17
Cash gifts
  IHT planning, 31.73–31.82
  in lieu of co-ownership, 31.65
Charitable relief
  qualifying interest in possession trusts, 17.22
  relevant property settlements, 20.34
Chartered Institute of Taxation (CIOT)
  request for Sch.20 guidance, A.3.105
Chattels
  chattels generally, 31.99
  co-ownership of chattels, 31.108
  pre-owned assets, 13.40, 24.23
  reservation of benefit, 13.31
Children
  see also **Minors**
  older children (s.71D trusts)
    basic conditions, 25.30
    BMT compared, 25.42

Children—*contd*
  older children (s.71D trusts)—*contd*
    calculating the charge, 25.32–25.35
    charge to tax, 25.31
    converting to bereaved minors trust, 25.37
    drafting considerations, 25.43
    extending life of trust, 25.36
    interest in possession trusts, 25.39
    link with A & M trusts, 25.44
    link with IIP trusts, 25.45
    overview of new rules, 14.15
    precedent, A.2.26
    purpose, 25.29
    relationship with IPDIs, 25.40
  residuary gifts, 28.40
  use of nil rate band, 28.03
Clawback
  holdover relief
    business assets, 6.05–6.06, 9.23–9.30
    settlor interested trusts, 9.44
  reservation of benefit, 13.19–13.23
Co-ownership of family home
  cash gifts in lieu, 31.65
  donee moves out or dies, 31.66
  generally, 31.57 and 27.10
  practical issues, 31.68–31.72
  position after March 1999, 31.59–31.62
  position before March 1999, 31.56–31.58
  pre-owned assets regime, 31.63
  re-organisation of arrangement, 31.67
  reverter to settlor trusts, 31.67
  sales of part, 31.64
Compensation funds, 20.34
Consents, 8.07
Creation of settlements
  accumulation and maintenance trusts after 2006, 21.03
  co-ownership generally, 31.57 and 27.10
  disposals to connected parties, 6.01–6.05
  double charges, 6.08
  holdover relief, 6.05–6.06
  instalment option, 6.07
  minor beneficiaries, 25.01–25.02
  rates of tax, 6.09
  relevant property settlements, 20.05–20.06
Criminal Injuries Compensation Scheme, 25.15

Day—definition of day on variations, 29.11
Death of beneficiaries
  actual disposals exempt, 7.09
  Crowe v Appleby 5.09 and 7.41
  deemed disposals for CGT
    death of beneficiary where settlement continues, 7.48–7.52
    death of interest in possession beneficiary, 7.46–7.47
Debts—see below
Deduction of liabilities
  areas for consideration, 23.01
  artificial debts, 23.16–23.22
  business assets, 23.23–23.25

Deduction of liabilities—*contd*
  excluded property, 23.0609
  general rules, 23.02–23.05
  interest in possession trusts, 23.10–23.15
Deeds of variation. *see* **Variation of wills or intestacy**
Deemed disposals
  beneficiary becoming absolutely entitled, 7.34–7.45
  death of beneficiary where settlement continues, 7.48–7.52
  death of interest in possession beneficiary, 7.46–7.47
  flip-flop schemes, 7.62–7.65
  overview, 7.01
  postponement of impact, 7.53–7.54
  relevant circumstances, 7.33
  resettlements, 7.55–7.59
  sub-fund elections, 7.72–7.74
  variations of settlements, 7.60–7.61
Deferral relief
  actual disposals, 7.11
  offshore trusts, 10.37
Deemed domicile, 22.02
Deed of covenant, 31.49 and 31.104
Depreciatory transactions, 17.16
Derived property, 11.06
Disabled persons trusts
  Disabled persons interest 9.14 and 26.29
  Definition, 26.05
  Hold over and disabled, 9.45
  PETs and disabled trusts, 26.30
  Transfers from other trusts, 26.32
Disabled trusts and IPDI, 19.07
  see also **Vulnerable beneficiaries**
  capital gains tax, 26.14–26.17
  discretionary will trusts, 29.50
  income tax, 26.04–26.13
  inheritance tax
    after FA 2006, 26.23–26.32
    before FA 2006, 26.18–26.22
  overview, 26.01–26.3
  overview of new rules, 14.13
  precedent, A.2.09
  qualifying IIPs after FA 2006, 19.14–19.15
  settled property, 5.05
Disclaimers
  general principles, 29.44–29.48
  precedent, A.2.62
  qualifying interest in possession trusts, 17.24
  varying life interests, 29.26
Disclosure rules on tax schemes
  basic rules, 36.15
  legal professional privilege, 36.16
  overview, 36.13–36.14
  'promoter' defined, 36.16
  scope, 36.17–36.18
  Section 216, 36.11
Discounted gift plans, 33.01–33.02, 33.13–33.19

Discretionary trusts
  agricultural property relief and business property belief clawbacks on discretionary trusts, 20.28 and see Example 32.4
  calculation of tax on related trusts, 20.08 and 20.17
  duty to accumulate income, 20.13
  exit charge, 20.22
  exit charge prior to 10 year anniversary, 20.08
  first ten year anniversary charge, 20.13
  grossing up on gift to discretionary trust, Example 16.4
  hypothetical chargeable total, 20.16
  interests in possession
    flexible interest in possession trusts, 15.22–15.29
    interest-free loans, 15.32
    last surviving beneficiary, 15.33
    occupation of matrimonial home, 15.30–15.31
  Melville schemes, 3.16–3.17
  minor beneficiaries, 25.03–25.04, 25.09–25.12, 25.49
  nil rate band
    agricultural property, 28.27–28.30
    business assets, 28.31
    general principles, 28.04–28.06
    HMRC Statement, A.3.16
    loan schemes, 28.17–28.25
    matrimonial homes, 28.07–28.16, 28.26
    precedent, A.2.31
    principal private residence relief, 31.25–31.26
    stamp duty land tax, 35.04
    variation of will, A.2.51
  position under new rules, 14.28
  precedents, A.2.64
  relevant property settlements created before March 1974, 20.29–20.32
  taxation of beneficiaries, 4.24
  will trusts
    accumulation and maintenance trusts, 29.61
    appointments, 29.58–29.59
    CGT problems, 29.60
    changes after March 2006, 29.50–29.54
    deaths before March 2006, 29.55–29.56
    nil rate band, 29.62
    statutory provisions, 29.49
    uses, 29.57

Discretionary will trusts
  accumulation and maintenance trusts, 29.61
  appointments, 29.58–29.59
  CGT problems, 29.60
  changes after March 2006, 29.50–29.54
  deaths before March 2006, 29.55–29.56
  nil rate band, 29.62, A.2.31
  statutory provisions, 29.49
  uses, 29.57

Disposals
  actual disposals
    annual exemptions, 7.07
    date made, 7.08
    death exemption, 7.09
    deferral relief, 7.11
    general principles, 7.02
    main residence exemption, 7.06
    overview, 7.01
    rates of tax, 7.03
    roll-over relief, 7.10
    settlor interested trusts, 7.04
    taper relief, 7.13–7.32
    vulnerable beneficiaries, 7.12
  bare trusts, 30.07
  beneficial interests
    basic rule, 8.01–8.-04
    non-resident settlements, 8.05–8.15
    settlor interested trusts, 8.16–8.26
  creation of settlements, 6.01–6.05
  Crowe v Appleby, 5.09 and 7.41
  deemed disposals
    beneficiary becoming absolutely entitled, 7.34–7.45
    death of beneficiary where settlement continues, 7.48–7.52
    death of interest in possession beneficiary, 7.46–7.47
    flip-flop schemes, 7.62–7.65
    overview, 7.01
    postponement of impact, 7.53–7.54
    relevant circumstances, 7.33
    resettlements, 7.55–7.59
    sub-fund elections, 7.72–7.74
    transfers linked to borrowing, 7.66–7.71
    variations of settlements, 7.60–7.61
  defined, 5.39–5.40
  pre-owned assets condition, 13.37

Dividends
  family companies (*Arctic Systems* case), 4.44–4.53
  taxation of beneficiaries, 4.25
  taxation of trustees, 4.20

Divorce
  claiming trust assets
    capital gains tax, 34.12
    inheritance tax, 34.13–34.19
    overview, 34.01
    possible approaches, 34.02–34.11
  offshore settlor interested trusts, 10.19
  reverter to settlor trusts, 27.32
  splitting of two funds, 10.8, 35.10 and 17.11

Domicile
  choice, 2.29–2.32
  deduction of liabilities for IHT, 23.20–23.22
  deemed domicile, 22.02
  dependence, 2.33–2.34
  excluded property
    exemptions and reliefs, 22.61–22.63
    pre-owned assets, 22.56–22.73

823

Domicile—*contd*
excluded property—*contd*
purchased interests, 22.51–22.55
HMRC rulings, 2.35–2.37
inheritance tax/capital gains tax, 9.52
origin, 2.28
overview, 2.26–2.27
POA income tax, 24.39
property excluded from IHT
additional property, 22.20–22.35
basic exemptions, 22.06–22.07
overview, 22.02
powers of appointment, 22.36–22.43
requirement to inform HMRC, 36.10–36.12
Double charges, 6.08
Double taxation relief
capital gains tax, 2.22–2.24
export charges, 2.58–2.59
importation of trusts, 8.14–8.15
POA income tax, 24.40–24.43
property excluded from IHT, 22.14
Double trust schemes, 3.18–3.21, 31.43–31.50

Elections
agricultural property relief, 32.33
business property relief, 32.33
Emigration of trusts 9.25 and 2.47 and in and out schems, 8.12
HMRC Guidance, A.3.147
POA income tax, 24.22, 24.40
sub-fund elections, 7.72–7.74
vulnerable beneficiaries
capital gains tax, 26.16
income tax, 26.11
Employee trusts
exempt from relevant property settlement rules, 20.34
hold-over relief, 9.06
pre-owned assets, 13.34
***Eversden* schemes**, 13.16–13.17, 13.33, 31.40–31.42
Excluded property
basic exemptions, 22.04–22.14
deduction of liabilities
areas for consideration, 23.01
general rules, 23.06–23.09
overview, 22.01–22.03
powers of appointment, 22.36–22.43
pre-owned assets income tax, 22.56–22.73
purchased interests, 22.51–22.55
ss 80-82 traps
additional property, 22.20–22.35
foreign domiciliaries, 22.16
qualifying IIPs, 22.15
transfers between settlements, 22.17–22.19
Exemptions and reliefs
see also **Specific headings**
claiming trust assets on divorce, 34.13–34.19
excluded property, 22.61–22.71
management expenses, 4.15–4.18

Exemptions and reliefs—*contd*
nil rate band
discretionary trusts, 28.04–28.31
drafting options, 28.02
outright gifts to children, 28.03
pre-owned assets, 24.24–24.26
qualifying interest in possession trusts, 17.17–17.26
relevant property settlements, 20.33–20.34
Exit charges
accumulation and maintenance trusts, 21.15
bereaved minor trusts
advancement, 25.18–25.19
charge to tax, 25.20–25.21
relevant property settlements
between anniversaries, 20.18
exemptions and reliefs, 20.33
in first ten years, 20.07–20.12
timing, 20.28
Exporting trusts
bed and breakfasting, 2.57, 2.60
beneficial interests, 2.64
capital payments, 2.63
disposals in year of migration, 2.62
double taxation relief, 2.58–2.59
EU uncertainty, 2.61
export charges, 2.51–2.56
feasibility, 2.47–2.50

Family home
co-ownership
cash gifts in lieu, 31.65
donee moves out or dies, 31.66
practical issues, 31.68–31.72
position after March 1999, 31.59–31.62
position before March 1999, 31.56–31.58
pre-owned assets regime, 31.63
re-organisation of arrangement, 31.67
reverter to settlor trusts, 31.67
sales of part, 31.64
double trust scheme, 3.18–3.21, 13.28, 31.43–31.50
IHT planning
cash gifts, 31.73–31.82
past schemes, 31.33–31.50
reversionary lease schemes, 31.51–31.55
summary of options, 31.29–31.32
principal private residence relief
actual disposals, 7.06
applicability, 31.01–31.10
business use, 31.13
calculation of gain, 31.11–31.12
discretionary will trusts, 28.07–28.16, 28.26
garden and grounds, 31.14–31.18
interaction with hold-over relief, 9.46–9.51
nil rate discretionary trusts, 31.25–31.26
personal representatives, 31.27–31.28
reverter to settlor trusts, 27.14
settled property, 31.19–31.24

Family protection policies, 33.01, 33.09–33.10
Finance Act 1986, A.1.23
Flip-flop schemes
 anti-avoidance measures, 10.41–10.44
 deemed disposals, 7.62–7.65
 settlor interested trusts, 10.20
Foreign domiciliaries
 family home, 31.97
 full consideration arrangements, 31.101
Foreign domiciliaries—Family home, 31.97
 POA, 22.56
 Reservation of benefit, 22.32

Gifts with reservation (GWR). *see* **Reservation of benefit**
 added to companies, 22.28
 and section 102ZA, 24.08
 definition for inheritance tax, 13.09, 24.05
 for inheritance tax purposes and hold over relief, chapter 9
 inheritance tax and capital gains tax interaction, 9.33
 of business assets, 9.10
 UK situate excluded property, 22.08
Gilts, 22.08–22.1

Hastings Bass rule
 HMRC Statement, A.3.146
 overview of taxation, 1.17–1.21
 pre-owned assets, 3.23
Historic buildings, 20.34
Hold-over relief
 bare trusts, 30.08
 business assets
  agricultural property, 9.31
  availability, 9.10
  calculation of gain, 9.20
  defined, 9.11–9.14
  gifts to companies, 9.19
  non-resident donees, 9.22–9.30
  partial relief, 9.15–9.16
  for trustees, 9.17–9.18
  undervalue sales, 9.21
 claims, 9.09
 clawback, 9.25
 death, 7.46
 disabled and hold over relief, 9.45
 divorce foonote 37, chpater 34
 double charge relief for IHT and CGT, 9.52–9.-53
 inheritance tax
  availability, 9.33–9.37
  restrictions, 9.38
  resume, 9.39–9.41
 interaction with main residence exemption, 9.46–9.51
 overview, 9.01–9.09
 planning limitations, 9.54–9.56
 settlor interested trusts, 6.05–6.06, 9.42–9.45

Home loan (double trust) scheme, 3.18–3.21, 13.28, 31.43–31.50
 hypothetical chargeable total, 20.16
 release and election, 24.43

Immediate post death interest in possession trusts (IPDI)
 Age contingencies, 28.4, 18.18, Example 18.10
 bereaved minor trusts, 25.25
 condition 1, 19.09–19.10
 condition 2, 19.11
 conditions 3, 19.12
 conditions 4, 19.13
 conditions to be met, 19.05–19.6
 definition of IPDI, 19.05
 diagrammatic representation, 19.08
 government policy, 19.07
 IPDIs and PETS, 25.13 and 25.11
 IPDI and s.71D—what takes precedence, 25.40
 minor beneficiaries, 25.47–25.48
 older children (s.71D trusts), 25.37, 25.40
 overview of new rules, 14.16
 precedents
  appointment, A.2.64
  minor children, A.2.43
  surviving spouse, A.2.40
 problems for US persons and IPDI, 19.10
 provision for minors, 25.11
 will drafting, 28.40
Importation of trusts, 8.14–8.15
In-out schemes, 8.12–8.13
Income tax
 anti-avoidance
  capital payments to settlor, 4.41–4.43
  settlor interested trusts, 4.30–4.37
  unmarried minor children, 4.38–4.40
 bare trusts, 30.05
 disabled trusts, 26.04–26.13
 family companies (*Arctic Systems* case), 4.44–4.53
 liability of trustees
  accrued income schemes, 4.07
  bare trusts, 4.03
  capital receipts, 4.06
  distributions, 4.19
  dividends, 4.20
  general principles, 4.01
  income taxed as of settlor, 4.14
  management expenses, 4.15–4.18
  non-residents, 4.0910
  rates of tax, 4.04–4.05
  returns, 4.02
  stock dividends, 4.07–4.08
  trusts affected, 4.11–4.13
 non-residents, 2.08, 2.42–2.45
 pre-owned assets
  introduction, 3.22–3.23
  pre-owned assets and reservation of benefit background, 24.01–24.02

825

Income tax—*contd*
  pre-owned assets and reservation of benefit—*contd*
    property excluded from IHT, 22.56–22.73
    purpose and application of POA charge, 24.18–24.44
    reservation of benefit defined, 24.03–24.17
  residents, 2.07
  reverter to settlor trusts, 27.12
  taxation of beneficiaries
    advancement of capital, 4.26–4.29
    annuitants, 4.23
    discretionary beneficiaries, 4.24
    dividends, 4.25
    general principles, 4.21–4.22
  variation of wills or intestacy
    general principles, 29.38–29.40
    impact of POA regime, 29.41
  vulnerable beneficiaries, 26.04–26.13

***Ingram* land schemes**, 13.14–13.15, 13.32, 31.34–31.39

Inheritance Act 1984, A.1.01

Inheritance tax
  accumulation and maintenance trusts
    background, 21.01–21.02
    creation after FA 2006, 21.03
    summary of options, 21.22
    tax treatment after March 2006, 14.29–14.30, 14.33, 21.16–21.21
    tax treatment before March 2006, 21.05–21.15
  bare trusts, 30.10–30.11
  bereaved minor trusts, 25.20–25.21
  charging regime for qualifying IIPs
    background, 18.01–18.04
    operation of rules after March 2006, 18.13–18.22
    operation of rules before March 2006, 18.05–18.12
  claiming trust assets on divorce, 34.13–34.19
  deduction of liabilities
    areas for consideration, 23.01
    artificial debts, 23.16–23.22
    business assets, 23.23–23.25
    excluded property, 23.0609
    general rules, 23.02–23.05
    interest in possession trusts, 23.10–23.15
  delivery of accounts
    excepted lifetime transfers, 36.04
    general principles, 36.02
    lifetime transfers, 36.03
    miscellaneous points, 36.09
    non-residents, 36.08
    relevant property settlements, 36.05
    transfers on death, 36.06–36.07
  disabled trusts
    after FA 2006, 26.23–26.32
    before FA 2006, 26.18–26.22
  discounted gift plans, 33.14–33.16

Inheritance tax—*contd*
  double charges, 6.08
  excluded property
    basic exemptions, 22.04–22.14
    overview, 22.01–22.03
    powers of appointment, 22.36–22.43
    pre-owned assets, 22.56–22.73
    purchased interests, 22.51–22.55
    reversionary interests, 22.44–22.50
    ss 80-82 traps, 22.15–22.35
  family home
    cash gifts, 31.73–31.82
    co-ownership and sharing, 31.56–31.72
    past schemes, 31.33–31.50
    reversionary lease schemes, 31.51–31.55
    summary of planning options, 31.29–31.32
  hold-over relief
    availability, 9.33–9.37
    double charge relief for IHT and CGT, 9.46–9.51
    restrictions, 9.38
    resume, 9.39–9.41
  IHT treatment
    multiple variations, 29.21
  minor beneficiaries
    bare trusts, 25.08
    creation of settlements, 25.01–25.02
    discretionary trusts, 25.03–25.04
    interest in possession trusts, 25.05–25.07
    provision on death, 25.09–25.12
  older children (s.71D trusts)
    calculating the charge, 25.32–25.35
    charge to tax, 25.31
    extending life of trust, 25.36
  overview
    charge on death, 13.05–13.06
    home loan schemes, 3.18–3.21
    legislative background, 3.14–3.15
    Melville schemes, 3.16–3.17
    potentially exempt transfers, 13.02–13.04
    pre-owned assets, 3.22–3.23
  pre-owned assets
    anti-avoidance measures, 13.27–13.33
    background, 24.01–24.02
    basics of charge, 13.35–13.36
    chattels, 13.31
    contribution condition, 13.38–13.43
    disposal condition, 13.37
    impact of charge, 13.34
    purpose and application of POA charge, 24.18–24.44
    reservation of benefit defined, 24.03–24.17
  qualifying IIPs after FA 2006
    disabled trusts, 19.14–19.15
    immediate post death interests (IPDIs), 19.05–19.13
    meaning and scope, 19.01–19.04
  relevant property settlements
    charge on first ten-year anniversary, 20.13–20.17

Inheritance tax—contd
  relevant property settlements—contd
    creation of settlement, 20.05–20.06
    discretionary trusts before March 1974, 20.29–20.32
    exemptions and reliefs, 20.33–20.34
    exit charges between anniversaries, 20.18
    exit charges in first ten years, 20.07–20.12
    illustrations of charging provisions, A.4.01–A.4.10
    later periodic charges, 20.19
    meaning and scope, 20.01–20.04
    technical problems, 20.20–20.28
  reservation of benefit
    anti-avoidance, 13.27–13.33
    background, 24.01–24.02
    business and agricultural relief, 13.25
    cessation of reservation, 13.24
    clawback on death, 13.19–13.23
    defined, 24.03–24.17
    full-consideration let-out, 13.11–13.13
    key points, 13.07–13.09
    operation of rules, 13.26
    purpose and application of POA charge, 24.18–24.44
    replacement property and bond (*Eversden* case), 13.16–13.17
    'shearing' operations (*Ingram* case), 13.14–13.15
  reverter to settlor trusts
    treatment after March 2006, 27.19–27.35
    treatment prior to December 2005, 27.01–27.02
    treatment prior to March 2006, 27.03–27.18
  settlements
    classification, 15.17–15.33
    creation of new settlements, 16.01–16.10
    definitions, 15.01–15.16
    overview of new rules, 1401–25
  single or multiple settlements, 5.31
  treatment of qualifying IIPs
    actual and deemed terminations, 17.10–17.14
    consequences of entitlement, 17.01–17.04
    depreciatory transactions, 17.16
    exemptions and reliefs, 17.17–17.26
    leases, 17.09
    multiple beneficiaries, 17.07–17.08
    nature of non-qualifying interests, 17.05–17.06
    reversionary interests, 17.15, 17.27
  variation of wills or intestacy
    after FA 2006 where settlement established, 29.14–29.20
    appointments and advancements, 29.23
    deceased life tenants, 29.26–29.29
    rectification, 29.22
    requirements of s.142 IHTA 1984, 29.03–29.13
    settled property, 29.30

Inheritance tax—contd
  variation of wills or intestacy—contd
    short lived trusts, 29.25
    typical uses, 29.24
  vulnerable beneficiaries
    after FA 2006, 26.23–26.32
    before FA 2006, 26.18–26.22
Insurance based arrangements
  discounted gift plans, 33.13–33.19
  family protection policies, 33.09–33.10
  life policies, 33.02–33.10
  loan schemes, 33.12
  loan trust, 33.12
  premium bonds—single premium bonds, 33.11
  premium payments, 33.10
  scope, 33.01
  transitional serial interests (TSI), 18.20
Intangibles, 13.41, 24.23, 24.27
Interest in possession trusts
  see also **Immediate post death interest in possession trusts (IPDI)**
  charging regime for qualifying IIPs
    background, 18.01–18.04
    operation of rules after March 2006, 18.13–18.22
    operation of rules before March 2006, 18.05–18.12
  classification, 15.17–15.21
  deduction of liabilities, 23.10–23.15
  flexible interests in possession, 15.22–15.29
  interest-free loans, 15.32
  last surviving beneficiary, 15.33
  minor beneficiaries
    lifetime options, 25.05–25.07
    provision on death, 25.09–25.12
  occupation of matrimonial home, 15.30–15.31
  older children (s.71D trusts), 25.39, 25.45
  position under new rules, 14.31–14.32
  qualifying IIPs after FA 2006
    disabled trusts, 19.14–19.15
    immediate post death interests (IPDIs), 19.05–19.13
    meaning and scope, 19.01–19.04
  section 54A problems 18.08, *et seq.*
  stamp duty land tax, 35.04
  treatment of qualifying IIPs
    actual and deemed terminations, 17.10–17.14
    consequences of entitlement, 17.01–17.04
    depreciatory transactions, 17.16
    exemptions and reliefs, 17.17–17.26
    leases, 17.09
    multiple beneficiaries, 17.07–17.08
    nature of non-qualifying interests, 17.05–17.06
    reversionary interests, 17.15, 17.27

Judicial attitudes to tax avoidance, 3.26

Leases
    for life, 15.04
    reservation of benefit, 13.14–13.15
    reversion for landlord, 22.46
    reversionary lease schemes, 31.51–31.55
    treatment of qualifying IIPs, 17.09
Legal professional privilege, 36.16
Lending
    artificial debts, 23.16–23.22
    deduction of liabilities for IHT, 23.01
Liabilities. *see* **Deduction of liabilities**
Life interest trusts, 3.18–3.21
Life policies
    insurance based arrangements, 33.02–33.10
    transitional serial interests (TSI), 18.20
Loan schemes
    discretionary trusts, 28.17–28.25
    double trust schemes, 3.18–3.21, 13.28, 31.43–31.50
    insurance based arrangements, 33.01, 33.12
    life interest trusts, 3.18–3.21
    precedent, A.2.47
Loss relief
    absolute entitlement of beneficiary, 12.05
    basic principles, 12.01
    multiple settlements, 5.32
    no offset of gains, 12.04
    non-residents, 2.13
    offshore trusts, 10.36, 10.33
        losses within s.86, 12.10
        restriction on losses, 12.09
        s.87 gains and losses, 12.08
        underlying companies, 12.11
    reform proposals, 11.11
    restriction on set-off, 12.06–12.07
    settlor interested trusts, 12.02–12.03

Maintenance for family, 17.21, 34.14, 34.18
Main residence relief
    actual disposals, 7.06
    applicability, 31.01–31.10
    business use, 31.13
    calculation of gain, 31.11–31.12
    discretionary will trusts, 28.07–28.16, 28.26
    garden and grounds, 31.14–31.18
    interaction with hold-over relief, 9.46–9.51
    nil rate discretionary trusts, 31.25–31.26
    personal representatives, 31.27–31.28
    reverter to settlor trusts, 27.14
    settled property, 31.19–31.24
Management expenses, 4.15–4.18
Married women, 2.33
Melville schemes, 3.16–3.17, 9.43
Minors
    see also **Bereaved minors trusts**; **Children**; **Vulnerable beneficiaries**
    domicile of dependence, 2.34
    lifetime options
        bare trusts, 25.08
        creation of settlements, 25.01–25.02
        discretionary trusts, 25.03–25.04
        interest in possession trusts, 25.05–25.07

Minors—*contd*
    provision on death
        bare trusts, 25.47
        bereaved minor trusts, 25.13–25.45
        immediate post death interest in possession trusts (IPDI), 25.47–25.48
        possible trusts, 25.09–25.12
        settled property, 5.05
        will drafting, 28.40
Multiple settlements, 5.28–5.35
    when trust made for capital gains tax purposes, 5.35, 7.08 *see also* additions
    Melville schemes, 3.16

Newspaper trusts, 20.34
Nil rate band
    discounted gift plans, 33.19
    discretionary trusts
        agricultural property, 28.27–28.30
        business assets, 28.31
        general principles, 28.04–28.06
        HMRC Statement, A.3.16
        loan schemes, 28.17–28.25
        matrimonial homes, 28.07–28.16, 28.26
        principal private residence relief, 31.25–31.26
        stamp duty land tax, 35.04
    discretionary will trusts, 29.62, A.2.31
    drafting options, 28.02
    Judge/Walden case, 15.25
    outright gifts to children, 28.03
    Putting house in NRB trust—conclusions, 28.28
    variation of wills or intestacy, 29.24
Nominees, 5.04
Non-residents
    see also **Exporting trusts**
    business asset hold-over relief, 9.22–9.30
    capital gains tax
        changes post-2007, 2.43–2.45
        double taxation relief, 2.22–2.24
        general rule, 2.10
        loss relief, 2.13
        professional trustees, 2.38–2.41
        remittance of gains, 2.12–2.16
        split-year treatment, 2.24–2.26
        temporary non-residence, 2.17–2.21
        UK traders, 2.11
    delivery of accounts, 36.08
    exporting trusts
        feasibility, 2.47–2.50
    income tax, 2.08, 2.42–2.45
    mobile workers, 2.05, 2.06
    requirement to inform HMRC, 36.10–36.12
    trustee liability for income tax, 4.0910
Non-sterling bank accounts, 22.08, 22.13
Normal expenditure out of income exemption, 36.02

Offshore trusts
  capital gains tax
    flip-flop schemes, 10.41–10.44
    overview, 10.01–10.07
    settlor interested trusts, 10.08–10.23
    UK resident and domiciled beneficiaries, 10.24–10.40
  disposal of beneficial interests, 8.05–8.15
  loss relief
    losses within s.86, 12.10
    restriction on losses, 12.09
    s.87 gains and losses, 12.08
    underlying companies, 12.11
  migration of trusts
    bed and breakfasting, 2.57
    double taxation relief, 2.58–2.59
    export charges, 2.51–2.56
    feasibility, 2.47–2.50
    inadvertent emigrations, 2.66–2.67
    requirement to inform HMRC, 36.10–36.12
    single or multiple settlements, 5.30
    taper relief, 7.31
Open Ended Investment Companies (OEICS), 22.08, 22.12
Ordinary residence, 2.04

Pension schemes
  exempt from relevant property settlement rules, 20.34
  stamp duty, 35.07
  stamp duty land tax, 35.04
Personal injury payments, 26.13
Pooling arrangements, 5.06
Post-death arrangements
  see also **Variation of wills or intestacy**
  disclaimers, 29.44–29.48
  discretionary will trusts, 29.50–29.62
  variation of wills or intestacy, 29.01–29.43
Potentially exempt transfers
  bare trusts, 30.10
  delivery of accounts
    general principles, 36.02
    lifetime transfers, 36.03
  disabled trusts, 19.15
  overview, 13.02–13.04
  reverter to settlor trusts, 27.11
Powers of appointment. *see* **Appointments**
Pre-owned assets regime
  see also **Reservation of benefit**
  agricultural property relief, 32.32–32.33
  basics of charge, 13.35–13.36
  business property relief, 32.32–32.33
  cash gifts, 31.79
  co-ownership of family home, 31.63
  discounted gift plans, 33.17–33.19
  foreign domiciliaries, 22.56
    release, 24.43
    election, 24.22 and 24.44
  HMRC Guidance Notes May 2006
    approach to specific issues, A.3.33
    calculation of benefit, A.3.24
    election into IHT, A.3.29

Pre-owned assets regime—*contd*
  HMRC Guidance Notes May 2006—*contd*
    land, A.3.44
    outline of IT charge, A.3.21
    subsequent clarification, A.3.147
  home loan (double trust) scheme, 31.43–31.50
  impact of charge, 13.34
  introduction, 3.22–3.23
  POA and release and home loans, 24.43
  POA generally, 24.18
    section 80, 22.15, 22.70, 24.33
  POA as a back up to schedule 20, 24.44
  reservation of benefit
    income tax regime, 24.01–24.44
    property excluded from IHT, 22.56–22.73
  variation of wills or intestacy, 29.41
Powers of appointment, excluded property
  general powers, 22.36
  exercise of powers of appointment, 22.43
Premium payments, 33.01, 33.10
Principal private residence relief
  and taper relief, Example 31.2
  applicability, 31.01–31.10
  business use, 31.13
  calculation of gain, 31.11–31.12
  cartilage test, 310.5, 310.6
  discretionary will trusts, 28.07–28.16, 28.26
  entity test, 31.04
  garden and grounds, 31.14–31.18
  hold over relief, 9.46
  nil rate discretionary trusts, 31.25–31.26
  personal representatives, 31.27–31.28
  reverter to settlor trusts, 27.14
  settled property, 31.19–31.24
  two residences election, 31.08
Professional trustees, 2.38–2.41
Protected settlements, 10.15
Protective trusts
  qualifying IIPs after FA 2006, 19.04
  qualifying interest in possession trusts, 17.23
Protectors, 1.07, 2.46
Purchased interests, 22.51–22.55
Purchased interests in excluded property settlements
  section 157 FA 2006, 22.51

Qualifying interest in possession trusts
  charging regime
    background, 18.01–18.04
    operation of rules after March 2006, 18.13–18.22
    operation of rules before March 2006, 18.05–18.12
  effects of FA 2006
    disabled trusts, 19.14–19.15
    immediate post death interests (IPDIs), 19.05–19.13
    meaning and scope, 19.01–19.04

Qualifying interest in possession trusts—contd
  IHT treatment
    actual and deemed terminations,
      17.10–17.14
    consequences of entitlement, 17.01–17.04
    depreciatory transactions, 17.16
    exemptions and reliefs, 17.17–17.26
    leases, 17.09
    multiple beneficiaries, 17.07–17.08
    nature of non-qualifying interests,
      17.05–17.06
    reversionary interests, 17.15, 17.27
Qualifying offshore trusts, 10.10
Quick succession relief, 17.25

Ramsay doctrine, 3.24–3.31
Rates of tax
  capital gains tax
    actual disposals, 7.03
    creation of settlements, 6.09
  income tax, 4.04–4.05
Remuneration, 16.07, 32.31
Reservation of benefit
  see also **Pre-owned assets regime**
  agricultural property relief, 32.27–32.31
  anti-avoidance, 13.27–13.33
  business and agricultural relief, 13.25
  business property relief, 32.27–32.31
  carve outs, 16.02
  cash gifts, 31.73–31.82
  cessation of reservation, 13.24
  clawback on death, 13.19–13.23
  companies, 22.30
  disabled and PETs, 26.30
  example on carve out, 16.2, 24.11
  foreign domiciliaries, 22.32
  full-consideration let-out, 13.11–13.13
  generally, 13.06
  inter vivos settlements, 16.06–16.09
  key points, 13.07–13.09
  operation of rules, 13.26
  pre-owned assets
    income tax regime, 24.01–24.44
    property excluded from IHT,
      22.56–22.73
  remuneration, 16.07, 32.31
  replacement property and bond (*Eversden*
    case), 13.16–13.17
  reservation of benefit and deemed PETs,
    22.35
  reservation of benefit and TSIs—
    preserving TSIs, 24.11
  reservation of benefit on setting up a trust,
    16.06
  reverter to settlor trusts, 27.09–27.10
  'shearing' operations (*Ingram* case),
    13.14–13.15
  tracing rules, 24.12
  variation of wills or intestacy, 29.12–29.13
Resettlements
  deemed disposals, 7.55–7.59
  settlor defined, 5.22

Residence
  see also **Non-residents**
  essential requirements, 2.03
  importance, 2.02
  mobile workers, 2.06
  non-residents, 2.05
  ordinary residence, 2.04
Residents
  see also **Non-residents**
  capital gains tax treatment, 2.09
  income tax treatment, 2.07
Residuary gifts
  no surviving spouse, 28.40
  spouse exemption, 28.32–28.39
Retrospective legislation, 3.04–3.07
Returns
  bare trusts, 30.04
  stamp duty land tax, 35.02
  trustee liability for income tax, 4.02
Reversionary interests
  property excluded from IHT,
    22.44–22.50
  treatment of qualifying IIPs
    meaning, 17.04
    section 10 transactions, 17.11–17.15
    taxation, 17.27
    termination by purchase, 17.15
Reversionary lease schemes, 31.51–31.55
Reverter to settlor trusts
  and principal private residence relief,
    27.14
  co-ownership of family home, 31.67
  treatment after March 2006,
    27.19–27.35
  treatment prior to December 2005,
    27.01–27.02
  treatment prior to March 2006,
    27.03–27.18
Roll-over relief, 7.10

Sales of part/whole
  family home, 31.81
Section 71D trusts
  calculation, 25.34
  conversion of A+M trust to s.71D,
    Example 21.6
  definition, 25.29
  settled advance and s.71D, example 25.8
  which takes precedence—IPDI or s.71D,
    25.40
Settled advance, 7.42
Settled property
  see also **Excluded property**
  agricultural property relief, 32.18–32.26
  business property relief, 32.18–32.26
  defined, 5.02–5.15
  principal private residence relief,
    31.19–31.24
  property excluded from IHT, 22.03
  variation of wills or intestacy, 29.30
Settlements
  bare trusts, 30.10

Settlements—*contd*
  creation
    disposals to connected parties, 6.01–6.05
    double charges, 6.08
    holdover relief, 6.05–6.06
    instalment option, 6.07
    rates of CGT, 6.09
  definitions
    disposals, 5.39–5.40
    settled property, 5.02–5.15
    settlor, 5.16–5.27
    single or multiple settlements, 5.28–5.35
    trustees, 5.36–5.38
  disposal of beneficial interests
    basic rule, 8.01–8.-04
    non-resident settlements, 8.05–8.15
    settlor interested trusts, 8.16–8.26
  family companies (*Arctic Systems* case), 4.44–4.53
  income tax anti-avoidance
    capital payments to settlor, 4.41–4.43
    settlor interested trusts, 4.30–4.37
    unmarried minor children, 4.38–4.40
  inheritance tax
    classification, 15.17–15.33
    definitions, 15.01–15.16
    overview of new rules, 1401–25
  relevant property settlements
    charge on first ten-year anniversary, 20.13–20.17
    creation of settlement, 20.05–20.06
    delivery of accounts, 36.05
    discretionary trusts before March 1974, 20.29–20.32
    exemptions and reliefs, 20.33–20.34
    exit charges between anniversaries, 20.18
    exit charges in first ten years, 20.07–20.12
    illustrations of charging provisions, A.4.01–A.4.10
    later periodic charges, 20.19
    meaning and scope, 20.01–20.04
    technical problems, 20.20–20.28
    will drafting, 28.40
  stamp duty land tax, 35.04
  variations after FA 2006, 29.14–29.20
Settlor interested trusts
  actual disposals, 7.04
  calculation of tax charge, 11.09
  clawback of holdover relief, 6.05–6.06
  disposal of beneficial interests, 8.16–8.26
  hold-over relief, 9.04, 9.42–9.45
  importance, 11.01–11.02
  income tax anti-avoidance, 4.30–4.37
  inheritance tax, 15.11
  loss relief, 12.02–12.03
  meaning, 11.03–11.08
  offshore trusts, 10.08–10.23
  reform proposals, 11.11
  settlor and hold over relief, 9.42
  settlor defined, 5.16, 11.10

Settlor interested trusts—*contd*
  settlor interested capital gains tax, 6.04
  settlor interested—income tax, 4.14
Settlors
  artificial debts, 23.18
  defined
    capital gains tax, 5.16–5.27, 11.10
    inheritance tax, 15.11–15.12
  powers
    'wide' and 'narrow' forms distinguished, 1.13
  trustee liability for income tax, 4.14
Sharing arrangements inheritance tax, 31.57
  see co-ownership
'Shearing' operations (*Ingram* case), 13.14–13.15, 13.32
Society of Trust and Estate Practioners (STEP)
  request for Sch.20 guidance, A.3.105
Split-year treatment, 2.24–2.26
Spouse exemptions
  gifts to spouse in will—outright or on iip trusts, 28.39
  qualifying interest in possession trusts, 17.18
  transitional serial interests (TSI), 18.19
  will trusts, 28.32–28.39
Stamp duty
  abolition, 35.01
  pension schemes, 35.07
  stocks and shares, 35.06
  variation of wills or intestacy, 29.42–29.43
Stamp duty land tax
  applicable trust transactions, 35.04
  'consideration', 35.03
  general principles, 35.01
  HMRC Statement, A.3.16
  returns, 35.02
  variation of wills or intestacy, 29.42–29.43
Statutory trusts for sale, 5.06
Stock dividends, 4.07–4.08
Stockpiled gains, s.87, 10.24
Sub-fund elections, 7.72–7.74
Surviving spouse exemption, 17.19

Taper relief, 7.13–7.32
Taxation of Chargeable Gains Act 1992, A.1.31
Temporary non-residence, 2.17–2.21
Transfers between settlements, 20.25, 22.17, 22.25
Transitional serial interests (TSI)
  age contingencies, 18.18, example 18.10
  conditions to be satisfied, 18.16
  interests arising after March 2006, 18.17–18.18
  insurance, 18.20, 33.04
  life policies, 18.20, 33.04
  meaning, 18.14
  new trusts, 18.16

831

Transitional serial interests (TSI)—*contd*
  planning, 18.21
  reservation of benefit and transitional serial interest, 24.11
  reverter to settlor trusts, 27.19–27.23
  second successive interests, 18.15
  spouses, 18.19
Treaty relief. *see* **Double taxation relief**
Trustees
  borrowing
    deemed disposals, 7.66–7.71
    export charges, 2.65
  business asset hold-over relief, 9.17–9.18
  defined
    capital gains tax, 5.36–5.38
    generally, 1.04
    inheritance tax, 15.16
  lending
    artificial debts, 23.16–23.22
    deduction of liabilities for IHT, 23.01
  liability for income tax
    accrued income schemes, 4.07
    bare trusts, 4.03
    capital receipts
    distributions, 4.19
    dividends, 4.20
    general principles, 4.01
    income taxed as of settlor, 4.14
    management expenses, 4.15–4.18
    non-residents, 4.0910
    rates of tax, 4.04–4.05
    returns, 4.02
    stock dividends, 4.07–4.08
    trusts affected, 4.11–4.13
  overview, 1.14
  powers
    advancement, 1.11
    classification, 1.09
    dispositive, 1.10
    example, 1.11
    express limitations, 1.12
    flexible interest in possession trusts, 15.22–15.29
    Hastings Bass rule, 1.17–1.21
  residence for CGT, 2.38–2.41
  stamp duty land tax, 35.04
Trusts
  see also **Settlements**
  essential ingredients, 1.01–1.06
  example, 1.06
  flexibility, 1.08
  management expenses, 4.15–4.18
  overview of taxation, 1.15–1.16
    anti-avoidance, 3.24–3.31
    capital gains tax, 3.09–3.13
    inheritance tax, 3.14–3.23
    policy change, 3.01–3.03
    retrospection and retroaction, 3.04–3.07

Undervalue sales, 9.21
Unit trusts, 22.08

US persons and IPDI, 19.10

Variation of wills or intestacy
  capital gains tax, 29.31
  CGT treatment, 29.31–29.37
  deeds of variations and appointments together, 29.33
  definition of day, 29.11
  IHT treatment
    after FA 2006 where settlement established, 29.14–29.20
    appointments and advancements, 29.23
    deceased life tenants, 29.26–29.29
    multiple variations, 29.21
    rectification, 29.22
    requirements of s.142 IHTA 1984, 29.03–29.13
    settled property, 29.30
    short lived trusts, 29.25
    typical uses, 29.24
  inheritance tax, 29.03
  IT treatment
    general principles, 29.38–29.40
    impact of POA regime, 29.41
  nil rate discretionary trusts, A.2.51
  POA, 29.41
  scope, 29.01–29.02
  settlor defined, 5.26
  shortlived trusts, 29.25
  stamp duty, 29.42
  stamp duty and SDLT, 29.42–29.43
Variations of settlements
  deemed disposals, 7.60–7.61
  qualifying interest in possession trusts, 17.24
Vulnerable beneficiaries
  actual disposals, 7.12
  capital gains tax, 26.14–26.17
  income tax, 26.04–26.13
  inheritance tax
    after FA 2006, 26.23–26.32
    before FA 2006, 26.18–26.22
  overview, 26.01–26.3

Will trusts
  BMTs and s.71D trusts in will itself, 25.24, 25.41, Example 28.5
  discretionary will trusts
    accumulation and maintenance trusts, 29.61
    appointments, 29.58–29.59
    CGT problems, 29.60
    changes after March 2006, 29.50–29.54
    deaths before March 2006, 29.55–29.56
    nil rate band, 29.62
    statutory provisions, 29.49
    uses, 29.57
  drafting, 14.19–14.25
  Frankland problems, 29.52
  general IHT principles, 16.03

Will trusts—*contd*
  nil rate band
    discretionary trusts, 28.04–28.31
    drafting options, 28.02
    outright gifts to children, 28.03
  overview, 28.01
  precedents
    definitions, A.2.27
    legacy fund, A.2.31
    residual IPDI trust, A.2.40

Will trusts—*contd*
  precedents—*contd*
    variation, A.2.51
  residuary gifts
    no surviving spouse, 28.40
    spouse exemption, 28.32–28.39
  section 144 generally, 29.49
  two year traps, 29.62, A3.116
  when can executors exercise s.144 powers, 29.58